# CONCISE EDITION
# SPANISH–ENGLISH
# ENGLISH–SPANISH
# DICTIONARY

# GEDDES & GROSSET

# List of Abbreviations

The following abbreviations are used throughout the dictionary.

| | Abbreviation | Abreviaturas |
|---|---|---|
| *abbrev* | abbreviation | abreviatura |
| *adj* | adjective | adjectivo |
| *adv* | adverb | adverbio |
| *art* | article | artículo |
| *auto* | automobile | automóvil |
| *aux* | auxiliary | auxiliar |
| *bot* | botany | botánica |
| *chem* | chemistry | química |
| *col* | colloquial term | lengua familiar |
| *com* | commerce | comercio |
| *compd* | in compounds | usada en palabras compuestas |
| *comput* | computers | informática |
| *conj* | conjunction | conjunctión |
| *excl* | exclamation | exclamación |
| *f* | feminine noun | sustantrivo femenino |
| *fig* | figurative use | uso figurado |
| *gr* | grammar | gramática |
| *imp* | impersonal | impersonal |
| *interj* | interjection | interjección |
| *invar* | invariable | invariable |
| *law* | law term | jurisprudencia |
| *m* | masculine noun | sustantivo masculino |
| *math* | mathematics | matemáticas |
| *med* | medicine | medicina |
| *mil* | military term | lo militar |
| *mus* | music | música |
| *n* | noun | sustantivo |
| *pej* | pejorative | peyorativo |
| *pl* | plural | plural |
| *pn* | pronoun | pronombre |
| *poet* | poetical term | vocablo poético |
| *pref* | prefix | prefijo |
| *prep* | preposition | preposición |
| *rad* | radio | radio |
| *rail* | railway | ferrocarilero |
| *theat* | theatre | teatro |
| *tec* | technology | téchnica, tecnologia |
| *TV* | television | televisión |
| *vi* | intransitive verb | verbo intransitivo |
| *vr* | reflexive verb | verbo reflexivo |
| *vt* | transitive verb | verbo transitivo |

Published 2010 by Geddes & Grosset,
144 Port Dundas Road, Glasgow, G4 0HZ, Scotland

© 2002 Geddes & Grosset

First published 2002, reprinted 2002, 2003, 2005, 2006, 2007, 2008, 2009, 2010

ISBN 978 1 84205 217 4

Printed and bound in the UK

# Spanish–English Dictionary

## A

**a** *prep* to; in; at; according to; on; by; for; of.

**abacería** *f* grocery.

**abacero** *m* grocer.

**ábaco** *m* abacus.

**abad** *m* abbot.

**abadejo** *m* cod.

**abadesa** *f* abbess.

**abadía** *f* abbey.

**abajo** *adv* under; underneath; below; ~ **de** *prep* under, below.

**abalanzarse** *vr* to rush forward.

**abalorio** *m* glass bead.

**abanderado** *m* (*mil*) ensign; standard bearer.

**abandonado/da** *adj* derelict; abandoned; neglected.

**abandonar** *vt* to abandon; to leave; ~**se** *vr* ~ **a** to give oneself up to.

**abandono** *m* desertion; neglect; retirement.

**abanicar** *vt* to fan.

**abanico** *m* fan.

**abaratar** *vt* to lower the price of.

**abarca** *f* sandal.

**abarcar** *vt* to include.

**abarrancarse** *vr* to get into difficulties.

**abarrotado/da** *adj* packed.

**abarrotar** *vt* to tie down.

**abastecedor/ra** *m/f* supplier, purveyor.

**abastecer** *vt* to supply, provide.

**abastecimiento** *m* supplying; provisions.

**abasto** *m* supply of provisions.

**abate** *m* abbé, French abbot.

**abatido/da** *adj* dejected, low-spirited.

**abatimiento** *m* low spirits *pl*; depression.

**abatir** *vt* to knock down; to humble.

**abdicación** *f* abdication.

**abdicar** *vt* to abdicate.

**abdomen** *m* abdomen.

**abdominal** *adj* abdominal.

**abecé** *m* alphabet.

**abecedario** *m* alphabet; spelling book, primer.

**abedul** *m* birch tree.

**abeja** *f* bee; ~ **reina** queen bee.

**abejar** *m* beehive.

**abejarrón** *m* bumblebee.

**abejón** *m* drone; hornet.

**abejorro** *m* bumblebee.

**aberración** *f* aberration.

**abertura** *f* aperture, chink, opening.

**abeto** *m* fir tree.

**abetunado/da** *adj* dark-skinned.

**abierto/ta** *adj* open; sincere; frank.

**abigarrado/da** *adj* multicoloured.

**ab intestato** *adj* intestate.

**abismal** *adj* abysmal.

**abismo** *m* abyss; gulf; hell.

**abjuración** *f* abjuration.

**abjurar** *vt* to abjure, to recant; *vi*: ~ **de** to abjure, to recant.

**ablandamiento** *m* softening.

**ablandar** *vt*, *vi* to soften.

**ablativo** *m* (*gr*) ablative.

**ablución** *f* ablution.

**abnegación** *f* self-denial.

**abnegado/da** *adj* selfless.

**abnegar** *vt* to renounce.

**abobado/da** *adj* silly.

**abobamiento** *m* stupefaction.

**abobar** *vt* to stupefy.

**abocado/da** *adj* light (wine).

**abocar** *vt* to seize with the mouth; ~**se** *vr* to meet by agreement.

**abochornar** *vt* to swelter; ~**se** *vr* to shame.

**abofetear** *vt* to slap.

**abogacía** *f* legal profession.

**abogado/a** *m/f* lawyer; barrister.

**abogar** *vi* to intercede; ~ **por** to advocate.

**abolengo** *m* ancestry; inheritance from ancestors.

**abolición** *f* abolition, abrogation.

**abolir** *vt* to abolish.

**abolladura** *f* dent.

**abollar** *vt* to dent.

**abominable** *adj* abominable, cursed.

**abominación** *f* abomination.

**abominar** *vt* to detest.

**abonado/da** *adj* ready; prepared; * *m/f* subscriber; season ticket holder.

**abonar** *vt* to settle; to fertilize; to endorse; ~**se** *vr* to subscribe; * *vi* to clear up.

**abono** *m* payment; subscription; dung, manure.

**abordaje** *m* boarding.

**abordar** *vt* (*mar*) to board; to broach.

**aborigen** *m* aborigine.

**aborrecer** *vt* to hate, to abhor.

**aborrecible** *adj* hateful, detestable.

**aborrecimiento** *m* abhorrence, hatred.

**abortar** *vi* to miscarry; to have an abortion.

**abortivo/va** *adj* abortive.

**aborto** *m* abortion; monster.

**abortón** *m* abortion.

**abotagado/da** *adj* swollen.

**abotinado/da** *adj* tied up.

**abotonar** *vt* to button.

**abovedado/da** *adj* vaulted.

**abrasar** *vt* to burn; to parch; ~**se** *vr* to burn oneself.

**abrazadera** *f* bracket; clasp.

**abrazar** *vt* to embrace; to surround.

**abrazo** *m* embrace.

**abrebotellas** *m invar* bottle opener.

**abrecartas** *m invar* letter opener.

**abrelatas** *m invar* can opener.

**abrevadero** *m* watering place.

**abrevar** *vt* to water (cattle).

**abreviación** *f* abbreviation, abridgement; shortening.

**abreviar** *vt* to abridge, to cut short.

**abreviatura** *f* abbreviation.

**abridor** *m* opener.

**abrigar** *vt* to shelter; to protect; ~**se** *vr* to take shelter.

**abrigo** *m* coat; shelter; protection; aid.

**abril** *m* April.

**abrillantar** *vt* to polish.

**abrir** *vt* to open; to unlock; ~**se** *vr* to open up; to clear the way; to be open.

**abrochador** *m* buttonhook.

**abrochar** *vt* to button; to do up.

**abrogar** *vt* to abrogate.

**abrumador/ra** *adj* overwhelming; annoying.

**abrumar** *vt* to overwhelm.

**abrupto/ta** *adj* abrupt; steep.

**absceso** *m* abscess.

**absentismo** *m* absenteeism.

**absolución** *f* forgiveness, absolution.

**absoluto/ta** *adj* absolute.

**absolutorio/a** *adj* absolutory.

**absolver** *vt* to absolve.

**absorbente** *adj* absorbent.

**absorber** *vt* to absorb.

**absorción** *f* absorption; takeover.

**absorto** *adj* engrossed.

**abstemio** *adj* teetotal.

**abstención** *f* abstention.

**abstenerse** *vr* to abstain.

**abstinencia** *f* abstinence.

**abstinente** *adj* abstinent, abstemious.

**abstracción** *f* abstraction.

**abstracto/ta** *adj* abstract.

**abstraer** *vt* to abstract; ~**se** *vr* to be absorbed.

**abstraído** *adj* absent-minded.

**absuelto/ta** *adj* absolved.

**absurdidad** *f*, **absurdo** *m* absurdity.

**absurdo** *adj* absurd.

**abuela** *f* grandmother.

**abuelo** *m* grandfather.

**abulia** *f* lethargy.

**abultado/da** *adj* bulky, large, massive.

**abultar** *vt* to increase, to enlarge; * *vi* to be bulky.

**abundancia** *f* abundance.

**abundante** *adj* abundant, copious.

**abundar** *vi* to abound.

**aburrido/da** *adj* boring, dull.

**aburrimiento** *m* boredom.

**aburrir** *vt* to bore.

**abusar** *vt* to abuse.

**abusivo/va** *adj* abusive.

**abuso** *m* abuse.

**abyección** *f* abjectness.

**abyecto/ta** *adj* abject, wretched.

**acá** *adv* here.

**acabado/da** *adj* perfect, accomplished.

**acabar** *vt* to finish, to complete; to achieve; ~**se** *vr* to finish; to be over; to run out; * *vi* to finish; to die, to expire.

**acabose** *m*: **el** ~ the last straw.

**acacia** *f* acacia.

**academia** *f* academy.

**académico/ca** *m/f* academician; * *adj* academic.

**acaecer** *vi* to happen.

**acallar** *vt* to quiet, to hush; to soften, to appease.

**acalorado/da** *adj* heated.

**acalorarse** *vr* to become heated.

**acampar** *vt* to camp.

**acanalado/da** *adj* grooved; fluted.

**acanalar** *vt* to corrugate.

**acanto** *m* acanthus.

**acantonamiento** *m* cantonment.

**acantonar** *vt* to billet.

**acaparar** *vt* to monopolize; to hoard.

**acariciar** *vt* to fondle, to caress.

**acarrear** *vt* to transport; to occasion.

**acarreo** *m* carriage, transportation.

**acaso** *m* chance; * *adv* perhaps.

**acatarrarse** *vr* to catch (a) cold.
**acaudalado/da** *adj* rich, wealthy.
**acaudalar** *vt* to hoard.
**acaudillar** *vt* to command.
**acceder** *vi* to agree; ~ **a** to have access to.
**accesible** *adj* attainable; accessible.
**acceso** *m* access; fit.
**accesorio/ria** *adj, m* accessory.
**accidentado/da** *adj* uneven; hilly; eventful.
**accidental** *adj* accidental; casual.
**accidentarse** *vr* to have an accident.
**accidente** *m* accident.
**acción** *f* action, operation; share.
**accionar** *vt* to work.
**accionista** *m* shareholder.
**acebo** *m* holly tree.
**acebuche** *m* wild olive tree.
**acechador/ra** *m/f* spy, observer.
**acechar** *vt* to lie in wait for; to spy on, observe.
**acecho** *m* spying, watching; ambush.
**aceitar** *vt* to oil.
**aceite** *m* oil.
**aceitera** *f* oilcan.
**aceitoso/sa** *adj* oily.
**aceituna** *f* olive.
**aceitunado/da** *adj* olive-green.
**aceitunero** *m* olive seller.
**aceituno** *m* olive tree.
**aceleración** *f* acceleration.
**aceleradamente** *adv* swiftly, hastily.
**acelerador** *m* accelerator.
**acelerar** *vt* to accelerate; to hurry.
**acelga** *f* (*bot*) chard (a variety of beet).
**acento** *m* accent.
**acentuación** *f* accentuation.
**acentuar** *vt* to accentuate.
**aceña** *f* water mill.
**acepción** *f* acceptation.
**aceptable** *adj* acceptable.
**aceptación** *f* acceptance; approval.
**aceptar** *vt* to accept, to admit.
**acequia** *f* canal, channel; drain.
**acera** *f* pavement.
**acerado/da** *adj* steel *compd*, made of steel; sharp; steely.
**acerbo/ba** *adj* rigorous, harsh; cruel.
**acerca** *prep* about, relating to.
**acercar** *vt* to move nearer; ~**se** *vr* ~ **a** to approach.
**acerico** *m* pincushion.
**acero** *m* steel.
**acérrimo/ma** *adj* staunch; bitter.
**acertado/da** *adj* correct, proper; prudent.

**acertar** *vt* to hit; to guess right; * *vi* to get it right; to turn out true.
**acertijo** *m* riddle.
**acervo** *m* heap, pile.
**acetato** *m* (*chem*) acetate.
**achacar** *vt* to impute.
**achacoso/sa** *adj* sickly, unhealthy.
**achantar** *vt* (*col*) to scare; ~**se** *vr* to back down.
**achaparrado/da** *adj* stunted; stocky.
**achaque** *m* ailment; excuse; subject, matter.
**achicar** *vt* to diminish; to humiliate; to bale (out).
**achicharrar** *vt* to scorch; to overheat.
**achicoria** *f* (*bot*) chicory.
**achisparse** *vr* to get tipsy.
**aciago/ga** *adj* unlucky; ominous.
**acíbar** *m* aloes; (*fig*) bitterness; displeasure.
**acicalar** *vt* to polish; ~**se** *vr* to dress in style.
**acicate** *m* spur.
**acidez** *f* acidity.
**ácido** *m* acid; * ~**/da** *adj* acid, sour.
**acierto** *m* success; solution; dexterity.
**aclamación** *f* acclamation.
**aclamar** *vt* to applaud, to acclaim.
**aclaración** *f* clarification.
**aclarar** *vt* to clear; to brighten; to explain; to clarify; ~**se** *vr* to understand; * *vi* to clear up.
**aclimatar** *vt* to acclimatize; ~**se** *vr* to become acclimatized.
**acne** *m* acne.
**acobardar** *vt* to intimidate.
**acodarse** *vr* to lean.
**acogedor/ra** *adj* welcoming.
**acoger** *vt* to receive; to welcome; to harbour; ~**se** *vr* to take refuge.
**acogida** *f* reception; asylum.
**acolchar** *vt* to quilt; to cushion.
**acólito** *m* acolyte; assistant.
**acometer** *vt* to attack; to undertake.
**acometida** *f* attack, assault.
**acomodadizo** *adj* accommodating.
**acomodado/da** *adj* suitable, convenient, fit; wealthy.
**acomodador/ra** *m/f* usher, usherette.
**acomodar** *vt* to accommodate, to arrange; ~**se** *vr* to comply.
**acomodaticio/cia** *adj* accomodating; pliable.
**acompañamiento** *m* (*mus*) accompaniment.
**acompañar** *vt* to accompany; to join; (*mus*) to accompany.

**acompasado/da** *adj* measured; well proportioned.

**acondicionado/da** *adj* conditioned.

**acondicionar** *vt* to arrange; to condition.

**acongojar** *vt* to distress.

**aconsejable** *adj* advisable.

**aconsejar** *vt* to advise; ~**se** *vr* to take advice.

**acontecer** *vi* to happen.

**acontecimiento** *m* event, incident.

**acopio** *m* gathering, storing.

**acopiar** *vt* to gather, to store up.

**acoplamiento** *m* coupling.

**acoplar** *vt* to couple; to fit; to connect.

**acorazado/da** *adj* armoured; * *m* battleship.

**acordado/da** *adj* agreed.

**acordar** *vt* to agree; to remind; ~**se** *vr* to agree; to remember.

**acorde** *adj* harmonious; * *m* chord.

**acordeón** *m* accordion.

**acordonado/da** *adj* cordoned-off.

**acordonar** *vt* to tie up; to cordon off.

**acorralar** *vt* to round up, corral; corner.

**acortar** *vt* to abridge, to shorten; ~**se** *vr* to become shorter.

**acosar** *vt* to pursue closely; to pester.

**acostado/da** *adj* in bed; lying down.

**acostar** *vt* to put to bed; to lay down; ~**se** *vr* to go to bed; to lie down.

**acostumbrado/da** *adj* usual.

**acostumbrar** *vi* to be used to; ~**se** *vr* ~ **a** to get used to; * *vt* to accustom.

**acotación** *f* boundary mark; quotation in the margin; stage direction.

**acotar** *vt* to set bounds to; to annotate.

**ácrata** *m/f* anarchist.

**acre** *adj* acid; sharp; * *m* acre.

**acrecentamiento** *m* increase.

**acrecentar** *vt* to increase, to augment.

**acreditar** *vt* to guarantee; to assure, to affirm; to authorize; to credit; ~**se** *vr* to become famous.

**acreedor** *m* creditor.

**acribillar** *vt* to riddle with bullets; to molest, to torment.

**acriminar** *vt* to incriminate; to accuse.

**acrimonia** *f* acrimony.

**acrisolar** *vt* to refine, to purify.

**acritud** *f* acrimony.

**acróbata** *m/f* acrobat.

**acta** *f* act; ~**s** *fpl* records *pl*.

**actitud** *f* attitude; posture.

**activar** *vt* to activate; to speed up.

**actividad** *f* activity; liveliness.

**activo/va** *adj* active; diligent.

**acto** *m* act, action; act of a play; ceremony.

**actor** *m* actor; plaintiff.

**actriz** *f* actress.

**actuación** *f* action; behaviour; proceedings *pl*.

**actual** *adj* actual, present.

**actualidad** *f* present time; ~**es** *fpl* current events *pl*.

**actualizar** *vt* to update.

**actualmente** *adv* at present.

**actuar** *vt* to work; to operate; * *vi* to work; to act.

**acuarela** *f* watercolour.

**acuario** *m* tank.

**Acuario** *m* Aquarius (sign of the zodiac).

**acuartelamiento** *m* quartering of troops.

**acuartelar** *vt* (*mil*) to quarter (troops).

**acuático/ca** *adj* aquatic.

**acuchillar** *vt* to cut; to plane.

**acuciar** *vt* to urge on.

**acuclillarse** *vr* to crouch.

**acudir** *vi* to go to; to attend; to assist.

**acueducto** *m* aqueduct.

**acuerdo** *m* agreement; **de ~** (*col*) OK, all right.

**acumular** *vt* to accumulate, to collect.

**acuñación** *f* coining.

**acuñar** *vt* to coin, to mint; to wedge in.

**acuoso/sa** *adj* watery.

**acupuntura** *f* acupuncture.

**acurrucarse** *vr* to squat; to huddle up.

**acusación** *f* accusation.

**acusador/ra** *m/f* accuser; * *adj* accusing.

**acusar** *vt* to accuse; to reveal; to denounce; ~**se** *vr* to confess.

**acusativo** *m* (*gr*) accusative.

**acuse** *m*: ~ **de recibo** acknowledgement of receipt.

**acústica** *f* acoustics *pl*.

**acústico/ca** *adj* acoustic.

**adagio** *m* adage, proverb; (*mus*) adagio.

**adalid** *m* chief, commander.

**adamascado/da** *adj* damask.

**adaptable** *adj* adaptable.

**adaptación** *f* adaptation.

**adaptador** *m* adapter.

**adaptar** *vt* to adapt.

**adecuado/da** *adj* adequate, fit; appropriate.

**adecuar** *vt* to fit/to accommodate/to proportion.

**adefesio** *m* folly/nonsense.

**adelantado/da** *adj* advanced; fast.

**adelantamiento** *m* progress/improvement/advancement; overtaking.

**adelantar** *vt, vi* to advance, to accelerate; to pass; to ameliorate, to improve; ~**se** *vr* to advance; to outdo.

**adelante** *adv* forward(s); **de hoy en ~** from now on; **más ~** later on; further on; * *excl* come in!

**adelanto** *m* advance; progress; improvement.

**adelfa** *f* (*bot*) rosebay.

**adelgazar** *vt* to make thin/slender; * *vi* to lose weight.

**ademán** *m* gesture; attitude.

**además** *adv* moreover, besides; **~ de** besides.

**adentrarse** *vr* to get inside; to penetrate.

**adentro** *adv* in; inside.

**adepto/ta** *m/f* supporter.

**aderezar** *vt* to dress, to adorn; to prepare; to season.

**aderezo** *m* adorning; seasoning; arrangement.

**adeudado** *adj* in debt.

**adeudar** *vt* to owe; **~se** *vr* to run into debt.

**adherencia** *f* adhesion, cohesion; alliance.

**adherente** *adj* adhering to, cohesive.

**adherir** *vi*: **~ a** to adhere to; to espouse.

**adhesión** *f* adhesion; cohesion.

**adición** *f* addition.

**adicionar** *vt* to add.

**adicto/ta** *adj*: **~ a** addicted to; devoted to; * *m* supporter; addict.

**adiestrar** *vt* to guide; to teach, to instruct; **~se** *vr* to practise.

**adinerado/da** *adj* wealthy, rich.

**adiós** *excl* goodbye; hello.

**aditivo** *m* additive.

**adivinanza** *f* enigma; riddle.

**adivinar** *vt* to foretell; to guess.

**adivino/na** *m/f* fortune-teller.

**adjetivo** *m* adjective.

**adjudicación** *f* adjudication.

**adjudicar** *vt* to adjudge; **~se** *vr* to appropriate.

**adjuntar** *vt* to endorse.

**adjunto/ta** *adj* united, joined, annexed; * *m/f* assistant.

**administración** *f* administration.

**administrador/a** *m/f* administrator.

**administrar** *vt* to administer.

**administrativo/va** *adj* administrative.

**admirable** *adj* admirable, marvellous.

**admiración** *f* admiration; wonder; (*gr*) exclamation mark.

**admirar** *vt* to admire; to surprise; **~se** *vr* to be surprised.

**admisible** *adj* admissible.

**admisión** *f* admission, acceptance.

**admitir** *vt* to admit; to let in; to concede; to permit.

**admonición** *f* warning.

**adobado** *m* pickled pork.

**adobar** *vt* to dress; to season.

**adobe** *m* adobe, sun-dried brick.

**adobo** *m* dressing; pickle sauce.

**adoctrinar** *vt* to indoctrinate; to teach.

**adolecer** *vi* to suffer from.

**adolescencia** *f* adolescence.

**adolescente** *adj, m/f* adolescent.

**adonde** *adv* (to) where.

**adónde** *adv* where.

**adopción** *f* adoption.

**adoptar** *vt* to adopt.

**adoptivo/va** *adj* adoptive; adopted.

**adoquín** *m* paving stone.

**adoración** *f* adoration, worship.

**adorar** *vt* to adore; to love.

**adormecer** *vt* to put to sleep; **~se** *vr* to fall asleep.

**adormidera** *f* (*bot*) poppy.

**adornar** *vt* to embellish, to adorn.

**adorno** *m* adornment; ornament, decoration.

**adosado/da** *adj* semidetached.

**adquirir** *vt* to acquire.

**adquisición** *f* acquisition.

**adrede** *adv* on purpose.

**adscribir** *vt* to appoint.

**aduana** *f* customs *pl*.

**aduanero** *m* customs officer; **~/ra** *adj* customs *compd*.

**aducir** *vt* to adduce.

**adueñarse** *vr*: **~ de** to take possession of.

**adulación** *f* adulation.

**adulador/ra** *m/f* flatterer.

**adular** *vt* to flatter.

**adulterar** *vt* to adulterate; * *vi* to commit adultery.

**adulterio** *m* adultery.

**adúltero/ra** *m/f* adulterer, adulteress.

**adulto/ta** *adj, m/f* adult, grown-up.

**adusto/ta** *adj* gloomy; stern.

**advenedizo** *m* upstart.

**advenimiento** *m* arrival; accession.

**adverbio** *m* adverb.

**adversario** *m* adversary; antagonist.

**adversidad** *f* adversity; setback.

**adverso/sa** *adj* adverse.

**advertencia** *f* warning, foreword.

**advertido/da** *adj* sharp.

**advertir** *vt* to notice; to warn.

**Adviento** *m* Advent.

**adyacente** *adj* adjacent.

**aéreo/rea** *adj* aerial.

**aerobic** *m* aerobics *pl*.

**aerodeslizador** *m* hovercraft.
**aerodeslizante** *m* hovercraft.
**aerogenerador** *m* wind turbine.
**aeromozo/za** *m/f* air steward/ess.
**aeronauta** *m* aeronaut.
**aeronáutica** *f* aeronautics.
**aeronave** *f* spaceship.
**aeroplano** *m* aeroplane.
**aeropuerto** *m* airport.
**aerosol** *m* aerosol.
**aerostática** *f* aerostatics.
**afabilidad** *f* affability.
**afable** *adj* affable.
**afán** *m* hard work; desire.
**afanar** *vt* to harass; (*col*) to pinch; **~se** *vr* to strive.
**afanoso/sa** *adj* hard, industrious.
**afear** *vt* to deform, to misshape.
**afección** *f* affection; fondness, attachment; disease.
**afectación** *f* affectation.
**afectadamente** *adv* affectedly.
**afectado/da** *adj* affected.
**afectar** *vt* to affect, to feign.
**afectísimo/ma** *adj* affectionate; **~ suyo** yours truly.
**afectivo/va** *adj* fond, tender.
**afecto** *m* affection; passion; **~/ta** *adj* affectionate; disposed; reserved.
**afectuoso/sa** *adj* affectionate; moving; tender.
**afeitar** *vt*, **~se** *vr* to shave.
**afeite** *m* make-up, rouge.
**afeminado/da** *adj* effeminate.
**afeminar** *vt* to make effeminate.
**aferrado/da** *adj* stubborn.
**aferrar** *vt* to grapple, to grasp, to seize.
**afianzamiento** *m* strengthening.
**afianzar** *vt* to strengthen; to prop up; **~se** *vr* to become established.
**afiche** *m* poster.
**afición** *f* affection; hobby; fans *pl*.
**aficionado/da** *adj* keen; * *m/f* lover, fan; amateur.
**aficionar** *vt* to inspire affection; **~se** *vr* **~ a** to grow fond of.
**afiladera** *f* grindstone.
**afilado** *adj* sharp.
**afilar** *vt* to sharpen, to grind.
**afín** *m* related; similar.
**afinar** *vt* to tune; to refine.
**afincarse** *vr* to settle.
**afinidad** *f* affinity; analogy; relationship.
**afirmación** *f* affirmation.
**afirmado** *m* road surface.

**afirmar** *vt* to secure, to fasten; to affirm, to assure.
**afirmativo/va** *adj* affirmative.
**aflicción** *f* affliction, grief.
**aflictivo/va** *adj* distressing.
**afligir** *vt* to afflict, to torment.
**aflojar** *vt* to loosen, to slacken, to relax; * *vi* to grow weak; to abate; to relent; **~se** *vr* to relax.
**aflorar** *vi* to emerge.
**afluente** *adj* flowing; * *m* tributary.
**afluir** *vi* to flow.
**afónico/ca** *adj* hoarse; voiceless.
**aforismo** *m* aphorism.
**afortunado/da** *adj* fortunate, lucky.
**afrancesado/da** *adj* Frenchified.
**afrenta** *f* outrage; insult.
**afrentar** *vt* to affront; to insult.
**afrontar** *vt* to confront; to bring face to face.
**afuera** *adv* out, outside.
**afueras** *fpl* outskirts *pl*.
**agacharse** *vr* to stoop, to squat.
**agalla** *f* gill; **~s** *pl* pluck, guts; tonsils *pl*; tonsillitis.
**agarradero** *m* handle.
**agarrado/da** *adj* miserly, stingy.
**agarrar** *vt* to grasp, to seize; **~se** *vr* to hold on tightly.
**agarrotar** *vt* to tie down; to squeeze tightly; to garrotte.
**agasajar** *vt* to receive and treat kindly; to regale.
**agasajo** *m* graceful reception; kindness.
**ágata** *f* agate.
**agazaparse** *vr* to crouch.
**agencia** *f* agency.
**agenciarse** *vr* to obtain.
**agenda** *f* diary.
**agente** *m* agent; policeman.
**ágil** *adj* agile.
**agilidad** *f* agility, nimbleness.
**agitación** *f* shaking; stirring; agitation.
**agitanado/da** *adj* Gypsy-like.
**agitar** *vt* to wave; to move; **~se** *vr* to become excited; to become worried.
**aglomeración** *f* crowd; **~ de tráfico** traffic jam.
**aglomerar** *vt*, **~se** *vr* to crowd together.
**agnóstico/ca** *adj*, *m/f* agnostic.
**agobiar** *vt* to weigh down; to oppress; to burden.
**agolparse** *vr* to assemble in crowds.
**agonía** *f* death throes *pl*.
**agonizante** *adj* dying.
**agonizar** *vi* to be dying.

**agorar** *vt* to predict.

**agostar** *vt* to parch.

**agosto** *m* August.

**agotado/da** *adj* exhausted; finished; sold out.

**agotador/ra** *adj* exhausting.

**agotamiento** *m* exhaustion.

**agotar** *vt* to exhaust; to drain; to misspend.

**agraciado/da** *adj* attractive; lucky.

**agraciar** *vt* to pardon; to reward.

**agradable** *adj* pleasant; lovely.

**agradar** *vt* to please, to gratify.

**agradecer** *vt* to be grateful for; to thank.

**agradecido/da** *adj* thankful.

**agradecimiento** *m* gratitude, gratefulness, thanks *pl*.

**agrado** *m* agreeableness, courteousness; will, pleasure; liking.

**agrandar** *vt* to enlarge; to exaggerate; to aggrandize; ~se *vr* to get bigger.

**agrario/ria** *adj* agrarian; agricultural.

**agravante** *f* further difficulty.

**agravar** *vt* to oppress; to aggrieve; to aggravate; to exaggerate; ~se *vr* to get worse.

**agraviar** *vt* to wrong; to offend; ~se *vr* to be aggrieved; to be piqued.

**agravio** *m* offence; grievance.

**agredir** *vt* to attack.

**agregado** *m* aggregate; attaché.

**agregar** *vt* to aggregate, to heap together; to collate; to appoint.

**agresión** *f* aggression, attack.

**agresivo/va** *adj* aggressive.

**agresor** *m* aggressor, assaulter.

**agreste** *adj* rustic, rural.

**agriar** *vt* to sour; to exasperate.

**agrícola** *adj* farming *compd*.

**agricultor/ra** *m/f* farmer.

**agricultura** *f* agriculture; ~ biológica organic farming.

**agridulce** *adj* sweet and sour.

**agrietarse** *vr* to crack.

**agrimensor** *m* surveyor.

**agrimensura** *f* surveying.

**agrio** *adj* sour, acrid; rough, sharp, rude, unpleasant.

**agronomía** *f* agronomy.

**agropecuario/ria** *adj* farming *compd*.

**agrupación** *f* group(ing).

**agrupar** *vt* to group, to cluster; to crowd.

**agua** *f* water; slope of a roof; ~ fuerte etching; ~ bendita holy water; ~s *pl* waters *pl*.

**aguacate** *m* avocado pear.

**aguacero** *m* short, heavy shower of rain.

**aguachirle** *f* slops *pl*.

**aguado/da** *adj* watery.

**aguador** *m* water carrier.

**aguafuerte** *m* etching.

**aguamarina** *f* aquamarine (precious stone).

**aguanieve** *f* sleet.

**aguantar** *vt* to bear, to suffer; to hold up.

**aguante** *m* firmness; patience.

**aguar** *vt* to water down.

**aguardar** *vt* to wait for.

**aguardiente** *m* brandy.

**aguarrás** *f* turpentine.

**agudeza** *f* keenness, sharpness; acuteness; acidity; smartness.

**agudizar** *vt* to make worse; ~se *vr* to get worse.

**agudo/da** *adj* sharp; keen-edged; smart; fine; acute; witty; brisk.

**aguero** *m*: **buen/mal** ~ good/bad omen.

**aguijar** *vt* to prick, to spur, to goad; to stimulate.

**aguijón** *m* sting of a bee, wasp etc; stimulation.

**aguijonear** *vt* to prick; to spur; to stimulate.

**águila** *f* eagle; genius.

**aguileño/ña** *adj* aquiline; sharp-featured.

**aguilucho** *m* eaglet.

**aguinaldo** *m* Christmas box.

**aguja** *f* needle; spire; hand; magnetic needle; (*rail*) points *pl*.

**agujerear** *vt* to pierce, to bore.

**agujero** *m* hole.

**agujetas** *fpl* stitch; stiffness; pains *pl* from fatigue.

**agustino** *m* monk of the order of St Augustine.

**aguzar** *vt* to whet, to sharpen; to stimulate.

**ahí** *adv* there.

**ahijada** *f* goddaughter.

**ahijado** *m* godson.

**ahijar** *vt* to adopt (as one's own child).

**ahínco** *m* earnestness; eagerness.

**ahogar** *vt* to smother; to drown; to suffocate; to oppress; to quench; ~se *vr* to drown; to suffocate.

**ahogo** *m* breathlessness; financial difficulty.

**ahondar** *vt* to deepen; to study deeply; * *vi*: ~ en to penetrate into.

**ahora** *adv* now, at present; just now.

**ahorcar** *vt* to hang; ~se *vr* to hang oneself.

**ahorrar** *vt* to save; to avoid.

**ahorrativo/va** *adj* thrifty, careful with money.

**ahorro** *m* saving; thrift.

**ahuecar** *vt* to hollow, to scoop out; ~se *vr* to get pig-headed.

**ahumar** *vt* to smoke, to cure (in smoke); **~se** *vr* to fill with smoke.

**ahuyentar** *vt* to drive off; to dispel.

**airado/da** *adj* angry.

**airarse** *vr* to get angry.

**airbag** *m* airbag.

**aire** *m* air; wind; aspect; musical composition.

**airearse** *vr* to take the air.

**airoso/sa** *adj* airy; windy; graceful; successful.

**aislado/da** *adj* insulated; isolated.

**aislar** *vt* to insulate; to isolate.

**ajar** *vt* to spoil; to abuse.

**ajardinado/da** *adj* landscaped.

**ajedrez** *m* chess.

**ajedrezado/da** *adj* chequered.

**ajenjo** *m* wormwood, absinth.

**ajeno/na** *adj* someone else's; foreign; ignorant; improper.

**ajetrearse** *vr* to exert oneself; to bustle; to toil; to fidget.

**ajetreo** *m* activity; bustling.

**ají** *m* red pepper.

**ajo** *m* garlic.

**ajorca** *f* bracelet.

**ajuar** *m* household furniture; trousseau.

**ajustado/da** *adj* tight; right; close.

**ajustar** *vt* to regulate, to adjust; to settle (a balance); to fit; to agree on; * *vi* to fit.

**ajuste** *m* agreement; accommodation; settlement; fitting.

**ajusticiar** *vt* to execute.

**al = a el.**

**ala** *f* wing; aisle; row, file; brim; winger.

**alabanza** *f* praise; applause.

**alabar** *vt* to praise; to applaud.

**alabastro** *m* alabaster.

**alacena** *f* cupboard, closet.

**alacrán** *m* scorpion.

**alado/da** *adj* winged.

**alambique** *m* still.

**alambrada** *f* wire fence; wire netting.

**alambrado** *m* wire fence; wire netting.

**alambre** *m* wire.

**alambrista** *m/f* tightrope walker.

**alameda** *f* avenue; poplar grove.

**álamo** *m* poplar.

**alano** *m* mastiff.

**alarde** *m* show.

**alargador** *m* extension lead.

**alargar** *vt* to lengthen; to extend; to hasten; to stretch out; to spin out; **~se** *vr* to get longer; to drag on.

**alarido** *m* outcry, shout; **dar ~s** to howl.

**alarma** *f* alarm.

**alarmante** *adj* alarming.

**alarmar** *vt* to alarm.

**alarmista** *m* alarmist.

**alazán** *m* sorrel.

**alba** *f* dawn.

**albacea** *m* executor.

**albahaca** *f* (*bot*) basil.

**albañil** *m* bricklayer.

**albañilería** *f* bricklaying.

**albarán** *m* invoice.

**albarda** *f* saddle.

**albaricoque** *m* apricot.

**albedrío** *m* free will.

**alberca** *f* reservoir; swimming pool.

**albergar** *vt* to lodge, to harbour; **~se** to shelter.

**albergue** *m* shelter; **~ de juventud** youth hostel.

**albóndiga** *f* meatball.

**albor** *m* dawn; whiteness.

**alborada** *f* dawn; reveille.

**alborear** *vi* to dawn.

**albornoz** *m* bath robe.

**alborotado/da** *adj* restless, turbulent.

**alborotar** *vi* to make a row; * *vt* to stir up; **~se** to get excited; to get rough.

**alboroto** *m* noise; disturbance, riot.

**alborozar** *vt* to exhilarate; **~se** *vr* to rejoice.

**alborozo** *m* joy.

**albricias** *fpl* good news *pl*.

**albufera** *f* lagoon.

**álbum** *m* album.

**albumen** *m* egg white.

**alcachofa** *f* artichoke.

**alcahuete/ta** *m/f* pimp, bawd.

**alcalde** *m* mayor.

**alcaldesa** *f* mayoress.

**alcaldía** *f* office and jurisdiction of a mayor; mayor's office.

**alcalino/na** *adj* alkaline.

**alcance** *m* reach; bad balance.

**alcancía** *f* money box.

**alcanfor** *m* camphor.

**alcantarilla** *m* sewer; gutter.

**alcanzar** *vt* to reach; to get, to obtain; to hit; * *vi* to suffice; to reach.

**alcaparra** *f* caper.

**alcatraz** *m* gannet.

**alcayata** *f* hook.

**alcázar** *m* castle, fortress.

**alcoba** *f* bedroom.

**alcohol** *m* alcohol.

**alcohólico/ca** *adj, m/f* alcoholic.

**alcoholismo** *m* alcoholism.
**alcornoque** *m* cork tree.
**aldaba** *f* knocker.
**aldea** *f* village.
**aldeano/na** *m/f* villager; * *adj* rustic.
**ale** *excl* come on!
**aleación** *f* alloy.
**aleatorio/ria** *adj* random.
**aleccionar** *vt* to instruct; to train.
**alegación** *f* allegation.
**alegar** *vt* to allege; to quote.
**alegato** *m* allegation; argument.
**alegoria** *f* allegory.
**alegórico/ca** *adj* allegorical.
**alegrar** *vt* to cheer; to poke; to liven up;
~**se** *vr* to get merry.
**alegre** *adj* happy; merry, joyful; content.
**alegría** *f* happiness; merriment.
**alegrón** *m* sudden joy; flicker.
**alejamiento** *m* remoteness; removal.
**alejar** *vt* to remove; to estrange; ~**se** *vr* to
go away.
**aleluya** *f* hallelujah.
**alemán/ana** *adj*, *m/f* German; * *m* German
language.
**alentador/ra** *adj* encouraging.
**alentar** *vt* to encourage.
**alergia** *f* allergy.
**alero** *m* gable-end; eaves *pl*.
**alerta** *adj*, *f* alert.
**alertar** *vt* to alert.
**aleta** *f* fin; wing; flipper; fender.
**aletargarse** *vr* to get drowsy.
**aletazo** *m* flap.
**aletear** *vi* to flutter.
**aleteo** *m* fluttering.
**alevosía** *f* treachery.
**alevoso/sa** *adj* treacherous.
**alfabéticamente** *adv* alphabetically.
**alfabético/ca** *adj* alphabetical.
**alfabeto** *m* alphabet.
**alfalfa** *f* (*bot*) lucerne.
**alfarería** *f* pottery.
**alfarero** *m* potter.
**alféizar** *m* window sill.
**alférez** *m* second lieutenant; (US navy)
ensign.
**alfil** *m* bishop (at chess).
**alfiler** *m* pin; clip; clothes peg.
**alfiletero** *m* pincushion.
**alfombra** *f* carpet; rug.
**alfombrar** *vt* to carpet.
**alfombrilla** *f* mouse mat.
**alforja** *f* saddlebag; knapsack.
**alga** *f* (*bot*) seaweed.

**algarabia** *f* gabble, gibberish.
**algarroba** *f* (*bot*) carob.
**algarrobo** *m* (*bot*) carob tree.
**algazara** *f* din.
**álgebra** *f* algebra.
**álgido/da** *adj* chilly; crucial.
**algo** *pn* something; anything; * *adv* somewhat.
**algodón** *m* cotton; cotton plant; cotton
wool.
**algodón azucarado** *m* candyfloss.
**algodonero** *m* cotton plant; dealer in cotton.
**alguacil** *m* bailiff; mounted official.
**alguien** *pn* someone, somebody; anyone,
anybody.
**alguno/na** *adj* some; any; no; * *pn* someone, somebody.
**alhaja** *f* jewel.
**alhelí** *m* wallflower.
**aliado/da** *adj* allied.
**alianza** *f* alliance, league; wedding ring.
**aliar** *vt* to ally; ~**se** *vr* to form an alliance.
**alias** *adv* alias.
**alicaído/da** *adj* weak; downcast.
**alicates** *mpl* pincers *pl*, nippers *pl*.
**aliciente** *m* attraction; incitement.
**alienación** *f* alienation.
**aliento** *m* breath; respiration.
**aligerar** *vt* to lighten; to alleviate; to hasten; to ease.
**alijo** *m* lightening of a ship; alleviation;
cache.
**alimaña** *f* pest.
**alimentación** *f* nourishment; food; grocery.
**alimentar** *vt* to feed, to nourish; ~**se** *vr* to
feed.
**alimenticio/cia** *adj* food *compd*; nutritious.
**alimento** *m* food; ~**s** *mpl* alimony.
**alineación** *m* alignment; line-up.
**alinear** *vt* to arrange in line; ~**se** *vr* to line up.
**aliñar** *vt* to adorn; to season.
**aliño** *m* dressing; ornament, decoration.
**alisar** *vt* to plane; to polish; to smooth.
**alistarse** *vr* to enlist, to enrol.
**aliviar** *vt* to lighten; to ease; to relieve, to
mollify.
**alivio** *m* alleviation; mitigation; relief; comfort.
**aljibe** *m* cistern.
**allá** *adv* there; over there; then.
**allanamiento** *m*: ~ **de morada** burglary.
**allanar** *vt* to level, to flatten; to overcome
difficulties; to pacify; to subdue; to burgle;
~**se** *vr* to submit; to tumble down.

**allegado/da** *adj* near; * *m/f* follower.

**allí** *adv* there, in that place.

**alma** *f* soul; human being.

**almacén** *m* warehouse, store; magazine.

**almacenaje** *m* storage.

**almacenar** *vt* to store (up).

**almanaque** *m* almanac.

**almeja** *f* clam.

**almena** *f* battlement.

**almendra** *f* almond.

**almendrado/da** *adj* almond-shaped; * *m* macaroon.

**almendro** *m* almond tree.

**almiar** *m* haystack.

**almíbar** *m* syrup.

**almidón** *m* starch.

**almidonado/da** *adj* starched; affected; spruce.

**almidonar** *vt* to starch.

**almirantazgo** *m* admiralty.

**almirante** *m* admiral.

**almirez** *m* mortar.

**almizcle** *m* musk.

**almohada** *f* pillow; cushion.

**almohadilla** *f* small pillow; pad; pincushion.

**almohadón** *m* large cushion.

**almorranas** *fpl* haemorrhoids *pl*.

**almorzar** *vt* to have for lunch; * *vi* to have lunch.

**almuerzo** *m* lunch.

**alocado/da** *adj* crazy; foolish; inconsiderate.

**alocución** *f* allocution.

**áloe** *m* (*bot*) aloes.

**alojamiento** *m* lodging; housing.

**alojar** *vt* to lodge; ~**se** *vr* to stay.

**alondra** *f* lark.

**alpargata** *f* rope-soled shoe.

**alpinismo** *m* mountaineering.

**alpinista** *m/f* mountaineer.

**alpiste** *m* canary seed.

**alquería** *f* farmhouse.

**alquilar** *vt* to let, to rent; to hire.

**alquiler** *m* renting, letting; hiring; rent; hire.

**alquimia** *f* alchemy.

**alquimista** *m* alchemist.

**alquitrán** *m* tar, liquid pitch.

**alquitranado/da** *adj* tarred.

**alrededor** *adv* around.

**alrededores** *mpl* surroundings *pl*.

**alta** *f* discharge from hospital.

**altanería** *f* haughtiness.

**altanero/ra** *adj* haughty, arrogant, vain, proud.

**altar** *m* altar; ~ **mayor** high altar.

**altavoz** *m* loudspeaker.

**alterable** *adj* changeable.

**alteración** *f* alteration; disturbance, tumult.

**alterar** *vt* to alter, to change; to disturb; ~**se** *vr* to get upset.

**altercado** *m* altercation, controversy; quarrel.

**alternar** *vt, vi* to alternate.

**alternativa** *f* alternative.

**alternativo/va** *adj* alternate.

**alterno/na** *adj* alternate; alternating.

**Alteza** *f* Highness (title).

**altibajos** *mpl* ups and downs *pl*.

**altillo** *m* hillock.

**altiplanicie** *f* high plateau.

**altísimo/ma** *adj* extremely high, most high; * *m* **el A~** the Most High, God.

**altisonante, altísono/na** *adj* high-sounding, pompous.

**altitud** *f* height; altitude.

**altivez** *f* haughtiness.

**altivo/va** *adj* haughty, proud, high-flown.

**alto/ta** *adj* high; elevated; tall; sharp; arduous, difficult; eminent; enormous; * *m* height; story; highland; (*mil*) halt; (*mus*) alto; **¡~!, ¡~ ahí!** *interj* stop!

**altramuz** *m* (*bot*) lupin.

**altura** *f* height; depth; mountain summit; altitude; ~**s** *pl*: **las ~s** the heavens.

**alubia** *f* bean.

**alucinación** *f* hallucination.

**alucinar** *vt* to blind, to deceive; * *vi* to hallucinate; ~**se** *vr* to deceive oneself, to labour under a delusion.

**aludir** *vi* to allude.

**alumbrado** *m* lighting; illumination.

**alumbramiento** *m* lighting; illumination; childbirth.

**alumbrar** *vt* to light; * *vi* to give birth.

**aluminio** *m* aluminium.

**alumno/na** *m/f* student, pupil.

**alunizar** *vi* to land on the moon.

**alusión** *f* allusion; hint.

**alusivo/va** *adj* allusive.

**aluvión** *m* alluvium; flood.

**alvéolo** *m* socket; cell of a honeycomb.

**alza** *f* rise; sight.

**alzacuello** *m* dog collar.

**alzada** *f* height; appeal.

**alzamiento** *m* rise; elevation; higher bid; uprising.

**alzar** *vt* to raise, to lift up; to construct, to build; to gather (in); ~**se** *vr* to get up; to rise in rebellion; ~**se con algo** *vr* to make off with something.

**ama** f mistress, owner; housewife; foster mother; ~ **de llaves** housekeeper; ~ **de leche** nurse.

**amabilidad** f kindness, niceness.

**amable** adj kind, nice.

**amaestrado/da** adj performing.

**amaestrar** vt to teach; to instruct; to train.

**amagar** vt to threaten; to shake one's fist at; * vi to feint.

**amago** m threat; indication; symptom.

**amalgama** f amalgam.

**amalgamar** vt to amalgamate.

**amamantar** vt to suckle.

**amanecer** vi to dawn; **al** ~ at daybreak.

**amanerado/da** adj affected.

**amansar** vt to tame; to soften; to subdue; ~**se** vr to calm down.

**amante** m/f lover.

**amanuense** m amanuensis, clerk, copyist.

**amapola** f (bot) poppy.

**amar** vt to love.

**amargar** vt to make bitter; to exasperate; ~**se** vr to be bitter.

**amargo/ga** adj bitter, acrid; painful; * m bitterness.

**amargor** m bitterness; sorrow, distress.

**amargura** f bitterness; sorrow.

**amarillear** vi to turn yellow.

**amarillento/ta** adj yellowish.

**amarillo/lla** adj yellow; * m yellow.

**amarra** f mooring rope.

**amarrar** vt to moor; to tie, to fasten.

**amartelar** vt to court, to woo; ~**se** vr to fall in love with.

**amartillar** vt to hammer; to cock (a gun/pistol).

**amasar** vt to knead; (fig) to arrange, to settle; to prepare.

**amasijo** m dough; mixed mortar; medley.

**amateur** m/f amateur.

**amatista** f amethyst.

**amatorio/ria** adj relating to love.

**amazona** f amazon; masculine woman.

**ambages** mpl: **sin** ~ in plain language.

**ámbar** m amber.

**ambición** f ambition.

**ambicionar** vt to crave, to covet.

**ambicioso/sa** adj ambitious.

**ambidextro/tra** adj ambidextrous.

**ambientación** f setting; sound effects pl.

**ambiente** m atmosphere; environment.

**ambigüedad** f ambiguity.

**ambiguo/gua** adj ambiguous; doubtful, equivocal.

**ámbito** m circuit, circumference; field; scope.

**ambos/bas** adj, pn both.

**ambrosía** f ambrosia.

**ambulancia** f ambulance.

**ambulante** adj travelling.

**ambulatorio** m state-run clinic.

**ameba** f amoeba.

**amedrentar** vt to frighten, to terrify; to intimidate.

**amén** f amen; so be it; ~ **de** besides; except.

**amenaza** f threat.

**amenazar** vt to threaten.

**amenizar** vt to make pleasant.

**ameno/na** adj pleasant; delicious; flowery (of language).

**América** f America; ~ **del Norte/del Sur** North/South America.

**americano/na** adj, m/f (Latin) American.

**ametralladora** f machine gun.

**amianto** m asbestos.

**amiga** f (female) friend.

**amigable** adj amicable, friendly; suitable.

**amigo** m friend; comrade; lover; ~/**ga** adj friendly.

**amilanar** vt to frighten, to terrify; ~**se** vr to get scared.

**aminorar** vt to diminish; to reduce.

**amistad** f friendship.

**amistoso/sa** adj friendly, cordial.

**amnesia** f amnesia.

**amnistía** f amnesty.

**amo** m owner; boss.

**amodorrarse** vr to grow sleepy.

**amohinar** vt to annoy; ~**se** vr to sulk.

**amoldar** vt to mould; to adapt; ~**se** vr to adapt oneself.

**amonestación** f advice; admonition; ~**ones** fpl publication of marriage banns.

**amonestar** vt to advise; to admonish; to publish banns of marriage of.

**amoníaco** m ammoniac.

**amor** m love; fancy; lover; ~ **mío** my love; **por** ~ **de Dios** for God's sake; ~ **propio** self-love.

**amoratado** adj livid.

**amordazar** vt to muzzle; to gag.

**amorfo/fa** adj shapeless.

**amorío** m love affair.

**amoroso/sa** adj affectionate, loving; lovely.

**amortajar** vt to shroud.

**amortiguador** m shock absorber.

**amortiguadores** mpl suspension.

**amortiguar** vt to mortify; to deaden; to temper; to muffle.

**amortización** *f* repayment; redemption.

**amortizar** *vt* to entail (an estate), to render inalienable; to pay, to liquidate, to discharge (a debt).

**amotinamiento** *m* mutiny.

**amotinar** *vt* to incite rebellion; ~se *vr* to mutiny.

**amparar** *vt* to shelter, to protect; to favour; ~se *vr* to claim protection.

**amparo** *m* protection, support; help; refuge, asylum.

**amperio** *m* amp.

**ampliación** *f* amplification, enlargement.

**ampliar** *vt* to amplify, to enlarge; to extend; to expand.

**amplificación** *f* enlargement.

**amplificador** *m* amplifier.

**amplificar** *vt* to amplify.

**amplio/lia** *adj* ample, extensive.

**amplitud** *f* amplitude, extension, largeness.

**ampolla** *f* blister; ampoule.

**ampuloso/sa** *adj* pompous.

**amputación** *f* amputation.

**amputar** *vt* to amputate.

**amueblar** *vt* to furnish.

**amuleto** *m* amulet.

**amurallar** *vt* to surround with walls.

**anacoreta** *m* anchorite, hermit.

**anacronismo** *m* anachronism.

**ánade** *m/f* duck.

**anadear** *vi* to waddle.

**anagrama** *f* anagram.

**anales** *mpl* annals *pl*.

**analfabetismo** *m* illiteracy.

**analfabeto/ta** *adj* illiterate.

**analgésico** *m* painkiller.

**análisis** *m* analysis.

**analista** *m/f* analyst.

**analítico/ca** *adj* analytical.

**analizar** *vt* to analyze.

**analogía** *f* analogy.

**analógico/ca, análogo/ga** *adj* analogous; (*comput*) analog.

**ananá** *m* pineapple.

**anaquel** *m* shelf (in a bookcase).

**anaranjado/da** *adj* orange-coloured.

**anarquía** *f* anarchy.

**anárquico/ca** *adj* anarchic, chaotic.

**anarquismo** *m* anarchism.

**anarquista** *m/f* anarchist.

**anatema** *f* anathema.

**anatomía** *f* anatomy.

**anatómico/ca** *adj* anatomical.

**anca** *f* rump.

**ancho/cha** *adj* broad, wide, large; * *m* breadth, width.

**anchoa** *f* anchovy.

**anchura** *f* width, breadth.

**anciano/na** *adj* old; * *m/f* old man/woman.

**ancla** *f* anchor.

**ancladero** *m* anchorage.

**anclaje** *m* anchorage.

**anclar** *vi* to anchor.

**andaderas** *fpl* baby walker.

**andadura** *f* walk; pace; amble.

**andamio** *m* scaffold.

**andamiaje** *m* scaffolding.

**andanada** *f* (*mar*) broadside.

**andar** *vi* to go, to walk; to fare; to act, to proceed, to work; to behave; to elapse; to move; * *vt* to go, to travel; * *m* walk, pace.

**andariego/ga** *adj* wandering.

**andarín** *m* fast walker.

**andas** *fpl* stretcher.

**andén** *m* pavement, sidewalk; (*rail*) platform; quayside.

**andrajo** *m* rag.

**andrajoso/sa** *adj* ragged.

**andurriales** *mpl* byways *pl*.

**anécdota** *f* anecdote.

**anegar** *vt* to inundate, to submerge; ~se *vr* to drown; to sink.

**anejo/ja** *adj* attached.

**anemia** *f* anaemia.

**anestésico** *m* anaesthetic.

**anexar** *vt* to annex; to join.

**anexión** *f* annexation.

**anexionamiento** *m* annexation.

**anexo/xa** *adj* annexed.

**anfibio/bia** *adj* amphibious.

**anfiteatro** *m* amphitheatre.

**anfitrión/ona** *m/f* host/ess.

**ángel** *m* angel.

**angelical** *adj* angelic, heaven-born.

**angélico/ca** *adj* angelic.

**angina** *f* angina.

**anglicano/na** *adj, m/f* Anglican.

**anglicismo** *m* anglicism.

**angosto/ta** *adj* narrow, close.

**anguila** *f* eel.

**angula** *f* elver.

**angular** *adj* angular; **piedra ~** *f* cornerstone.

**ángulo** *m* angle, corner.

**anguloso/sa** *adj* angled, cornered.

**angustia** *f* anguish; heartache.

**angustiar** *vt* to cause anguish.

**anhelante** *adj* eager; longing.

**anhelar** *vi* to gasp; * *vt* to long for.

**anhelo** *m* desire, longing.

**anidar** *vi* to nestle, to make a nest; to dwell, to inhabit.
**anillo** *m* ring.
**ánima** *f* soul.
**animación** *f* liveliness; activity.
**animado/da** *adj* lively.
**animador/ora** *m/f* host(ess).
**animadversión** *f* ill-will.
**animal** *adj, m* animal.
**animar** *vt* to animate, to liven up; to comfort; to revive; **~se** *vr* to cheer up.
**ánimo** *m* soul; courage; mind; intention, meaning; will; thought; * *excl* come on!
**animosidad** *f* valour, courage; boldness.
**animoso/sa** *adj* courageous, spirited.
**aniñarse** *vr* to act in a childish manner.
**aniquilar** *vt* to annihilate, to destroy; **~se** *vr* to decline, to decay.
**anís** *m* aniseed; anisette.
**aniversario/ria** *adj* annual; * *m* anniversary.
**ano** *m* anus.
**anoche** *adv* last night.
**anochecer** *vi* to grow dark; * *m* nightfall.
**anodino/na** *adj* (*med*) anodyne.
**anomalia** *f* anomaly.
**anómalo/la** *adj* anomalous.
**anonadar** *vt* to annihilate; to lessen; **~se** *vr* to humble oneself.
**anonimato** *m* anonymity.
**anónimo/ma** *adj* anonymous.
**anormal** *adj* abnormal.
**anotación** *f* annotation, note.
**anotar** *vt* to comment, to note.
**anquilosamiento** *m* paralysis.
**ánsar** *m* goose.
**ansia** *f* anxiety, eagerness, hankering.
**ansiar** *vt* to desire.
**ansiedad** *f* anxiety.
**ansioso/sa** *adj* anxious, eager.
**antagónico/ca** *adj* antagonistic; opposed.
**antagonista** *m* antagonist.
**antaño** *adv* formerly.
**antártico/ca** *adj* antarctic; * *m*: **el A~** the Antarctic.
**ante** *m* suede; * *prep* before; in the presence of; faced with.
**anteanoche** *adv* the night before last.
**anteayer** *adv* the day before yesterday.
**antebrazo** *m* forearm.
**antecámara** *f* antechamber.
**antecedente** *adj, m* antecedent.
**anteceder** *vt* to precede.
**antecesor/ra** *m/f* predecessor; * *m* forefather.
**antedicho/cha** *adj* aforesaid.
**antelación** *f* ; **con ~** in advance.

**antemano** *adv*: **de ~** beforehand.
**antena** *f* feeler, antenna; aerial; **~ parabólica** satellite dish.
**anteojo** *m* eyeglass; **~ de larga vista** telescope; **~s** *mpl* glasses *pl*.
**antepasado/da** *adj* passed, elapsed; **~s** *mpl* ancestors *pl*.
**antepecho** *m* (*mil*) parapet; ledge.
**anteponer** *vt* to place in front; to prefer.
**anteproyecto** *m* sketch; blueprint.
**anterior** *adj* preceding; former.
**anterioridad** *f* priority; preference.
**antes** *prep, adv* before; * *conj* before.
**antesala** *f* antechamber.
**antiaéreo/rea** *adj* anti-aircraft.
**antibalas** *adj* bullet-proof.
**antibiótico** *m* antibiotic.
**anticiclón** *m* anticyclone.
**anticipación** *f* anticipation.
**anticipado/da** *adj* advance.
**anticipar** *vt* to anticipate; to forestall; to advance.
**anticipo** *m* advance.
**anticonceptivo** *m* contraceptive.
**anticongelante** *m* antifreeze.
**anticuado/da** *adj* antiquated.
**anticuario** *m* antiquary, antiquarian.
**anticuerpo** *m* antibody.
**antídoto** *m* antidote.
**antífona** *f* antiphony; anthem.
**antiestético/ca** *adj* unsightly.
**antifaz** *m* mask.
**antigualla** *f* monument of antiquity; antique.
**antiguamente** *adv* in ancient times, of old.
**antigüedad** *f* antiquity, oldness.
**antiguo/gua** *adj* antique, old, ancient; * *m* senior; **~s** *mpl*: **los ~s** the ancients.
**antílope** *m* antelope.
**antinatural** *adj* unnatural.
**antimonio** *m* antimony.
**antipatía** *f* antipathy.
**antipático/ca** *adj* unpleasant.
**antípodas** *mpl* antipodes.
**antirrobo** *adj* anti-theft.
**antisemita** *adj* anti-Semitic.
**antiséptico/ca** *adj* antiseptic.
**antítesis** *f* (*gr*) antithesis.
**antojadizo/za** *adj* capricious, fanciful.
**antojarse** *vr* to long, to desire; to itch.
**antojo** *m* whim, fancy; longing.
**antología** *f* anthology.
**antorcha** *f* torch; taper.
**antro** *m* (*poet*) cavern, den, grotto.
**antropófago** *m* cannibal.
**antropología** *f* anthropology.

**antropólogo/ga** *m/f* anthropologist.
**anual** *adj* annual.
**anualidad** *f* annuity.
**anublar** *vt* to cloud, to obscure; **~se** *vr* to become clouded.
**anudar** *vt* to knot; to join; **~se** *vr* to get into knots.
**anulación** *f* annulment; cancellation.
**anular** *vt* to annul; to revoke; to cancel; * *adj* annular.
**anunciación** *f* announcement.
**anunciante** *m/f* advertiser.
**anunciar** *vt* to announce; to advertise.
**anuncio** *m* advertisement.
**anverso** *m* obverse.
**anzuelo** *m* hook; allurement.
**añadidura** *f* addition.
**añadir** *vt* to add.
**añejo/ja** *adj* old; stale, musty.
**añicos** *mpl* bits *pl*, small pieces *pl*; **hacer ~** to shatter.
**añil** *m* indigo plant; indigo.
**año** *m* year.
**añojo** *m* yearling calf.
**añoranza** *f* longing.
**aorta** *f* aorta.
**aovar** *vi* to lay eggs.
**apabullar** *vt* to squash.
**apacentar** *vt* to graze.
**apacible** *adj* affable; gentle; placid, quiet.
**apaciguar** *vt* to appease; to pacify, to calm.
**apadrinar** *vt* to support, to favour; to be godfather to.
**apagado/da** *adj* dull; quiet; muted; listless.
**apagar** *vt* to put out; to turn off; to quench, to extinguish; to damp; to destroy; to soften.
**apagón** *m* power cut, outage.
**apalabrar** *vt* to agree to; to engage.
**apalancar** *vt* to lever.
**apalear** *vt* to cane, to drub; to winnow.
**apañado/da** *adj* skilful; suitable.
**apañar** *vt* to grasp; to pick up; to patch; **~se** *vr* to manage.
**aparador** *m* sideboard; store window.
**aparato** *m* apparatus; machine; ostentation, show.
**aparatoso/sa** *adj* showy; spectacular.
**aparcamiento** *m* car park.
**aparcar** *vt*, *vi* to park.
**aparcería** *f* partnership in a farm (*or* other business).
**aparcero/ra** *m/f* partner; associate.
**aparecer** *vi* to appear; **~se** *vr* to appear.
**aparecido/da** *m/f* ghost.

**aparejar** *vt* to prepare; to harness (horses); to rig (a ship).
**aparejo** *m* preparation; harness, gear; (*mar*) tackle, rigging; **~s** *mpl* tools *pl*, implements *pl*.
**aparentar** *vt* to look; to pretend; to deceive.
**aparente** *adj* apparent; convenient.
**aparición** *f* apparition; appearance.
**apariencia** *f* outward appearance.
**apartadero** *m* (*rail*) siding.
**apartado** *m* paragraph; **~ de correos/postal** P O Box.
**apartamento** *m* flat, apartment.
**apartamiento** *m* isolation; separation; flat, apartment.
**apartar** *vt* to separate, to divide; to remove; to sort; **~se** *vr* to go away; to be divorced; to desist.
**aparte** *m* aside; new paragraph; * *adv* apart, separately; besides; aside.
**apasionado/da** *adj* passionate; devoted; fond; biased.
**apasionar** *vt* to excite; **~se** *vr* to get excited.
**apatía** *f* apathy.
**apático/ca** *adj* apathetic, indifferent.
**apeadero** *m* halt, stopping place; station.
**apearse** *vr* to dismount; to get down/out/off.
**apechugar** *vt* to face up to.
**apedrear** *vt* to stone; * *vi* to hail.
**apegarse** *vr*: **~ a** to become fond of.
**apego** *m* attachment, fondness.
**apelación** *f* (*law*) appeal.
**apelar** *vi* (*law*) to appeal; **~ a** to have recourse to.
**apelativo** *adj* (*gr*): **nombre ~** *m* generic name.
**apellidar** *vt* to call by name; to proclaim; **~se** *vr* to be called.
**apellido** *m* surname; family name; epithet.
**apelmazar** *vt* to compress.
**apenar** *vt* to grieve; to embarrass; **~se** *vr* to grieve; to be embarrassed.
**apenas** *adv* scarcely, hardly; * *conj* as soon as.
**apéndice** *m* appendix, supplement.
**apendicitis** *f* appendicitis.
**apercibido/da** *adj* provided; ready.
**apercibirse** *vr* to notice.
**aperitivo** *m* aperitif; appetizer.
**apero** *m* agricultural implement.
**apertura** *f* aperture, opening, chink; cleft.
**apesadumbrar** *vt* to sadden.
**apestar** *vt* to infect; * *vi*: **~ a** to stink of.

**apetecer** *vt* to fancy.
**apetecible** *adj* desirable; appetizing.
**apetito** *m* appetite.
**apetitoso/sa** *adj* pleasing to the taste, appetizing; tempting.
**apiadarse** *vr* to take pity.
**ápice** *m* summit, point; smallest part of a thing.
**apilar** *vt* to pile up; **~se** *vr* to pile up.
**apiñado/da** *adj* crowded; pyramidal; pine-shaped.
**apiñarse** *vr* to clog, to crowd.
**apio** *m* (*bot*) celery.
**apisonadora** *f* steamroller.
**apisonar** *vt* to ram down.
**aplacar** *vt* to appease, to pacify; **~se** *vr* to calm down.
**aplanar** *vt* to level, to flatten.
**aplastar** *vt* to flatten, to crush.
**aplatanarse** *vr* to get weary.
**aplaudir** *vt* to applaud; to extol.
**aplauso** *m* applause; approbation, praise.
**aplazamiento** *m* postponement.
**aplazar** *vt* to postpone.
**aplicable** *adj* applicable.
**aplicación** *f* application; effort.
**aplicado/da** *adj* studious; industrious.
**aplicar** *vt* to apply; to clasp; to attribute; **~se** *vr*: **~ a** to devote oneself to.
**aplique** *m* wall light.
**aplomo** *m* self-assurance.
**apocado/da** *adj* timid.
**Apocalipsis** *m* Apocalypse.
**apocamiento** *m* timidity; depression.
**apocar** *vt* to lessen, to diminish; to contract; **~se** *vr* to feel humiliated.
**apócrifo/fa** *adj* apocryphal; fabulous.
**apodar** *vt* to nickname.
**apoderado/da** *m/f* proxy, attorney; agent.
**apoderar** *vt* to authorize; to give the power of attorney to; **~se** *vr*: **~ de** to take possession of.
**apodo** *m* nickname, sobriquet.
**apogeo** *m* peak.
**apolillar** *vt* to gnaw/eat (clothes); **~se** *vr* to be moth-eaten.
**apología** *f* eulogy; defence.
**apoltronarse** *vr* to grow lazy; to loiter.
**apoplejía** *f* apoplexy.
**apoplético/ca** *adj* apoplectic.
**apoquinar** *vt* (*col*) to fork out.
**aporrear** *vt* to beat up.
**aportar** *vi* to arrive at a port; to arrive; * *vt* to contribute.
**aposentar** *vt* to harbour; to put up.

**aposento** *m* room.
**aposición** *f* (*gr*) apposition.
**apósito** *m* (*med*) external dressing.
**aposta** *adv* on purpose.
**apostar** *vt* to bet, to wager; to post soldiers; * *vi* to bet.
**apostasia** *f* apostasy.
**apóstata** *m* apostate.
**apostatar** *vi* to apostatize.
**apostilla** *f* marginal note; postscript.
**apóstol** *m* apostle.
**apostolado** *m* apostleship.
**apostólico/ca** *adj* apostolical.
**apostrofar** *vt* to apostrophize.
**apóstrofe** *m* apostrophe.
**apóstrofo** *m* (*gr*) apostrophe.
**apostura** *f* neatness.
**apoteosis** *f* apotheosis.
**apoyar** *vt* to rest; to favour, to patronize, to support; **~se** *vr* to lean.
**apoyo** *m* support; protection.
**apreciable** *adj* appreciable; valuable; respectable.
**apreciar** *vt* to appreciate; to estimate, to value.
**aprecio** *m* appreciation; esteem.
**aprehender** *vt* to apprehend, to seize.
**aprehensión** *f* apprehension, seizure.
**apremiante** *adj* urgent.
**apremiar** *vt* to press; to compel.
**apremio** *m* pressure, constriction; judicial compulsion.
**aprender** *vt* to learn; **~ de memoria** to learn by heart.
**aprendiz/za** *m/f* apprentice.
**aprendizaje** *m* apprenticeship.
**aprensión** *f* apprehension.
**aprensivo/va** *adj* apprehensive.
**apresar** *vt* to seize, to grasp.
**apresurado/da** *adj* hasty.
**apresuramiento** *m* hurry.
**apresurar** *vt* to accelerate, to hasten, to expedite; **~se** *vr* to hurry.
**apretado/da** *adj* tight; cramped;, difficult.
**apretar** *vt* to compress, to tighten; to constrain; to distress; to urge earnestly; * *vi* to be too tight.
**apretón** *m* squeeze.
**apretura** *f* squeeze.
**aprieto** *m* conflict; tight spot.
**aprisa** *adv* quickly, swiftly; promptly.
**aprisco** *m* sheepfold.
**aprisionar** *vt* to imprison.
**aprobación** *f* approbation, approval.
**aprobar** *vt* to approve; to pass; * *vi* to pass.

**apropiación** *f* appropriation, assumption.
**apropiado/da** *adj* appropriate.
**apropiarse** *vr* to appropriate.
**aprovechable** *adj* profitable.
**aprovechado/da** *adj* industrious; thrifty; selfish.
**aprovechamiento** *m* use; exploitation.
**aprovechar** *vt* to use; to exploit; to profit from; to take advantage of; * *vi* to be useful; to progress; ~**se** *vr*: ~ **de** to use; to take advantage of.
**aproximación** *f* approximation; closeness.
**aproximado/da** *adj* approximate.
**aproximar** *vt* to approach; ~**se** *vr* to approach.
**aptitud** *f* aptitude, fitness, ability.
**apto/ta** *adj* apt; fit, able; clever.
**apuesta** *f* bet, wager.
**apuesto/ta** *adj* neat.
**apuntado/da** *adj* pointed.
**apuntador** *m* prompter.
**apuntalar** *vt* to prop up.
**apuntar** *vt* to aim; to level, to point at; to mark; * *vi* to begin to appear/show itself; to prompt (theatre); ~**se** *vr* to score; to enrol.
**apunte** *m* annotation; prompting (theatre).
**apuñalar** *vt* to stab.
**apurado/da** *adj* poor, destitute of means; exhausted; hurried.
**apurar** *vt* to purify; to clear up, to verify; to exhaust; to tease and perplex; ~**se** *vr* to worry; to hurry.
**apuro** *m* want; pain, affliction; haste; jam.
**aquejado/da** *adj* afflicted.
**aquel/~la** *adj* that; ~ **los/~ las** *pl* those.
**aquél/~la;** *pn* that (one); ~ **los/~ las** *pl* those (ones).
**aquello** *pn* that.
**aquí** *adv* here; now.
**aquietar** *vt* to quiet, to appease.
**aquilino** *adj* aquiline.
**aquilón** *m* north wind.
**ara** *f* altar.
**árabe** *adj*, *m/f* Arabic (the language).
**arabesco** *m* arabesque.
**arado** *m* plough.
**arancel** *m* tariff.
**arándano** *m* bilberry; blueberry.
**arandela** *f* washer.
**araña** *f* spider; chandelier.
**arañar** *vt* to scratch; to scrape; to corrode.
**arar** *vt* to plough.
**arbitraje** *m* arbitration.
**arbitrar** *vt*, *vi* to arbitrate; to referee.

**arbitrariedad** *f* arbitrariness.
**arbitrario/ria** *adj* arbitrary.
**arbitrativo/va** *adj* arbitrary.
**arbitrio** *m* free will; arbitration.
**árbitro** *m* arbitrator; referee; umpire.
**árbol** *m* tree; (*mar*) mast; shaft.
**arbolado/da** *adj* forested; wooded; * *m* woodland.
**arboladura** *f* rigging; masts *pl*.
**arbolar** *vt* to hoist, to set upright.
**arboleda** *f* grove.
**arbusto** *m* shrub.
**arca** *f* chest, wooden box.
**arcada** *f* arch; arcade; ~**s** *fpl* retching.
**arcaico/ca** *adj* archaic.
**arcaísmo** *m* archaism.
**arcángel** *m* archangel.
**arce** *m* maple tree.
**archipiélago** *m* archipelago.
**archivador** *m* filing cabinet.
**archivar** *vt* to file.
**archivero, archivista** *m* keeper of records, archivist.
**archivo** *m* file(s) (*pl*); archives *pl*.
**arcilla** *f* clay.
**arcilloso/sa** *adj* clayey.
**arcipreste** *m* archpriest.
**arco** *m* arc; arch; fiddle bow; hoop; ~ **iris** rainbow.
**arder** *vi* to burn, to blaze.
**ardid** *m* stratagem, artifice; cunning.
**ardiente** *adj* burning; ardent, passionate; active; fiery.
**ardilla** *f* squirrel.
**ardor** *m* heat; valour; vivacity; fieriness, fervour.
**ardoroso/sa** *adj* fiery; restless.
**arduo/dua** *adj* arduous, difficult; high.
**área** *f* area.
**arena** *f* sand; grit; arena.
**arenal** *m* sandy ground.
**arenga** *f* harangue; speech.
**arengar** *vi* to harangue.
**arenisca** *f* sandstone; grit.
**arenoso/sa** *adj* sandy.
**arenque** *m* herring; ~ **ahumado** smoked herring, kipper.
**argamasa** *f* mortar.
**argamasar** *vi* to mix mortar.
**argolla** *f* large ring.
**argot** *m* slang.
**argucia** *f* subtlety.
**argüir** *vi* to argue, to dispute; * *vt* to deduce; to argue; to imply.
**argumentación** *f* argumentation.

**argumentar** *vt*, *vi* to argue, to dispute; to conclude.
**argumento** *m* argument.
**aria** *f* (*mus*) aria; tune, air.
**aridez** *f* drought, want of rain.
**árido/da** *adj* dry; barren.
**Aries** *m* Aries (sign of the zodiac).
**ariete** *m* battering ram.
**ario/a** *adj* Aryan.
**arisco/ca** *adj* fierce; rude; intractable.
**aristocracia** *f* aristocracy.
**aristócrata** *m* aristocrat.
**aristocrático/ca** *adj* aristocratic.
**aritmética** *f* arithmetic.
**arlequín** *m* harlequin, buffoon.
**arma** *f* weapon, arm.
**armada** *f* fleet, armada.
**armadillo** *m* armadillo.
**armado/da** *adj* armed; reinforced.
**armador** *m* ship owner; privateer; jacket, jerkin.
**armadura** *f* armour; framework; skeleton; armature.
**armamento** *m* armament.
**armar** *vt* to man; to arm; to fit; **~la** to kick up a fuss.
**armario** *m* wardrobe; cupboard.
**armatoste** *m* hulk; contraption.
**armazón** *f* chassis; skeleton; frame.
**armería** *f* arsenal; heraldry; gunsmith's.
**armero** *m* gunsmith.
**armiño** *m* ermine.
**armisticio** *m* armistice.
**armonía** *f* harmony.
**armonioso/sa** *adj* harmonious.
**armonizar** *vt* to harmonize; to reconcile.
**arnés** *m* harness; **~eses** *mpl* gear, trappings *pl*.
**aro** *m* ring; earring.
**aroma** *m* aroma, fragrance.
**aromaterapia** *f* aromatherapy.
**aromático/ca** *adj* aromatic.
**arpa** *f* harp.
**arpegio** *m* (*mus*) arpeggio.
**arpía** *f* (*poet*) shrew.
**arpillera** *f* sackcloth.
**arpón** *m* harpoon.
**arqueado/da** *adj* arched, vaulted.
**arquear** *vt* to arch; to bend.
**arqueo** *m* arching; gauging (of a ship).
**arqueología** *f* archaeology.
**arqueólogo/ga** *m/f* archaeologist.
**arquero** *m* archer.
**arqueta** *f* small trunk.
**arquetipo** *m* archetype.

**arquitecto** *m* architect.
**arquitectónico/ca** *adj* architectural.
**arquitectura** *f* architecture.
**arrabal** *m* suburb; slum.
**arrabalero** *m* suburbanite.
**arraigado** *adj* deep-rooted; established.
**arraigar** *vi* to root; to establish; * *vt* to establish; **~se** *vr* to take root; to settle.
**arrancar** *vt* to pull up by the roots; to pull out; to wrest; to extract; * *vi* to start; to move.
**arranque** *m* sudden start; start; outburst.
**arras** *fpl* security.
**arrasar** *vt* to demolish, to destroy.
**arrastrado/da** *adj* miserable; painstaking; servile.
**arrastrar** *vt* to drag; * *vi* to creep, to crawl; to lead a trump at cards; **~se** *vr* to crawl; to grovel.
**arrastre** *m* dragging.
**¡arre!** *excl* gee!, go on!
**arrear** *vt* to drive on; * *vi* to hurry along.
**arrebañar** *vt* to scrape together; to pick up.
**arrebatado/da** *adj* rapid; violent, impetuous; rash, inconsiderate.
**arrebatar** *vt* to carry off, to snatch; to enrapture.
**arrebato** *m* fury; rapture.
**arrebol** *m* rouge.
**arrebujar** *vt* to crumple; to wrap up.
**arrecife** *m* reef.
**arrecirse** *vr* to grow stiff with cold.
**arreglado** *adj* neat; regular, moderate.
**arreglar** *vt* to regulate; to tidy; to adjust; **~se** *vr* to come to an understanding.
**arreglo** *m* rule, order; agreement; arrangement.
**arrellanarse** *vr* to sit at ease; to make oneself comfortable.
**arremangar** *vt* to roll up; **~se** *vr* to roll up one's sleeves.
**arremeter** *vi* to attack; to seize suddenly.
**arremetida** *f* attack, assault.
**arrendador** *m* landlord.
**arrendamiento** *m* leasing; hire; lease.
**arrendar** *vt* to rent, to let out, to lease.
**arrendatario/ria** *m/f* tenant.
**arreo** *m* dress, ornament; **~s** *mpl* harness.
**arrepentido/da** *adj* repentant.
**arrepentimiento** *m* repentance, penitence.
**arrepentirse** *vr* to repent.
**arrestar** *vt* to arrest; to imprison.
**arresto** *m* boldness; prison; arrest.
**arriada** *f* flood, overflowing.
**arriar** *vt* (*mar*) to lower, to strike; to pay out.

**arriate** *m* bed; causeway.

**arriba** *adv* above, over, up; high, on high, overhead; aloft.

**arribada** *f* (*mar*) arrival (of a vessel) in port.

**arribar** *vi* (*mar*) to put into harbour.

**arribista** *m/f* upstart.

**arriendo** *m* lease; farm rent.

**arriero** *m* muleteer.

**arriesgado/da** *adj* risky; daring.

**arriesgar** *vt* to risk, to hazard; to expose to danger; ~**se** *vr* to take a chance.

**arrimar** *vt* to approach, to draw near; (*mar*) to stow (cargo); ~**se** *vr* to side up; to lean.

**arrinconar** *vt* to put in a corner; to lay aside.

**arrobado/da** *adj* enchanted.

**arrobamiento** *m* rapture; amazement.

**arrobarse** *vr* to be totally amazed; to be out of one's senses.

**arrocero/ra** *adj* rice-producing.

**arrodillarse** *vr* to kneel down.

**arrogancia** *f* arrogance, haughtiness.

**arrogante** *adj* arrogant; haughty, proud; stout.

**arrojadizo/za** *adj* easily thrown.

**arrojar** *vt* to throw, to fling; to dash; to emit; to shoot, to sprout; ~**se** *vr* to hurl oneself.

**arrojo** *m* boldness, fearlessness.

**arrollador/ra** *adj* overwhelming.

**arrollar** *vt* to run over; to defeat heavily.

**arropar** *vt* to clothe, to dress; ~**se** *vr* to wrap up.

**arrostrar** *vt* to face (up to).

**arroyo** *m* stream; gutter.

**arroz** *m* rice.

**arrozal** *m* rice field.

**arruga** *f* wrinkle; rumple.

**arrugar** *vt* to wrinkle; to rumple; to fold; ~ **la frente** to frown; ~**se** *vr* to shrivel.

**arruinar** *vt* to demolish; to ruin; ~**se** *vr* to go bankrupt.

**arrullador/ra** *adj* flattering, cajoling.

**arrullar** *vt* to lull; * *vi* to coo.

**arrullo** *m* cooing (of pigeons); lullaby.

**arrumaco** *m* caress.

**arsenal** *m* arsenal; dockyard.

**arsénico** *m* arsenic.

**arte** *m/f* art; skill; artfulness.

**artefacto** *m* appliance.

**arteria** *f* artery.

**artero/ra** *adj* dexterous, cunning, artful.

**artesa** *f* kneading trough.

**artesanía** *f* craftsmanship.

**artesano** *m* artisan, workman.

**ártico/ca** *adj* arctic; * *m*: **el A~** the Arctic.

**articulación** *f* articulation; joint.

**articulado/da** *adj* articulated; jointed.

**articular** *vt* to articulate; to joint.

**artículo** *m* article; clause; point; (*gr*) article; condition.

**artífice** *m* artisan; artist.

**artificial** *adj* artificial.

**artificio** *m* workmanship, craft; artifice, cunning trick.

**artificioso/sa** *adj* skilful, ingenious; artful, cunning.

**artillería** *f* gunnery; artillery.

**artillero** *m* artillery man.

**artimaña** *f* trap; cunning.

**artista** *m* artist; craftsman.

**artístico/ca** *adj* artistic.

**artritis** *f* arthritis.

**arzobispado** *m* archbishopric.

**arzobispo** *m* archbishop.

**as** *m* ace.

**asa** *f* handle; lever.

**asado** *m* roast meat; barbecue.

**asador** *m* spit.

**asadura** *f* offal.

**asalariado/da** *adj* salaried.

**asaltador/a** *m/f* assailant.

**asaltante** *m/f* assailant.

**asaltar** *vt* to assault; to storm (a position); to assail.

**asalto** *m* assault, attack.

**asamblea** *f* assembly, meeting.

**asar** *vt* to roast.

**asbesto** *m* asbestos.

**ascendencia** *f* ascendancy; ancestry.

**ascendente** *adj* ascending; (*rail*) **tren ~** *m* up train.

**ascender** *vi* to be promoted; to rise; * *vt* to promote.

**ascendiente** *m* forefather; influence.

**Ascensión** *f* feast of the Ascension.

**ascenso** *m* promotion; ascent.

**ascensor** *m* elevator.

**asceta** *m* ascetic.

**ascético/ca** *adj* ascetic.

**asco** *m* nausea; loathing.

**ascua** *f* red-hot coal.

**aseado/da** *adj* clean; elegant; neat.

**asear** *vt* to clean; to tidy.

**asediar** *vt* to besiege; to chase.

**asedio** *m* siege.

**asegurado/da** *adj* insured.

**asegurador** *m* insurer.

**asegurar** *vt* to secure; to insure; to affirm; to bail; ~**se** *vr* to make sure.

**asemejarse** *vr* to be like, to resemble.

**asentado/da** *adj* established.
**asentar** *vt* to sit down; to affirm, to assure; to note; * *vi* to suit.
**asentir** *vi* to acquiesce, to concede.
**aseo** *m* cleanliness; neatness; ~s *mpl* toilets *pl*.
**aséptico/ca** *adj* germ-free.
**asequible** *adj* attainable; obtainable.
**aserción** *f* assertion, affirmation.
**aserradero** *m* sawmill.
**aserrar** *vt* to saw.
**aserrín** *m* sawdust.
**asertivo/va** *adj* affirmative.
**asesinar** *vt* to assassinate; to murder.
**asesinato** *m* assassination; murder.
**asesino** *m* assassin; murderer.
**asesor** *m* counsellor, adviser, consultant.
**asesorar** *vt* to advise; to act as consultant to; ~se *vr* to consult.
**asestar** *vt* to aim, to point; to strike.
**aseverar** *vt* to affirm.
**asfalto** *m* asphalt.
**asfixia** *f* suffocation.
**asfixiar** *vt* to suffocate; ~se *vr* to suffocate.
**así** *adv* so, thus, in this manner; like this; therefore; so that; also; ~ **que** so that; therefore; **así, así** so-so; middling.
**asidero** *m* handle.
**asiduidad** *f* assiduousness.
**asiduo/dua** *adj* assiduous.
**asiento** *m* chair; bench, stool; seat; contract; entry; residence.
**asignación** *f* assignation; destination.
**asignar** *vt* to assign, to attribute.
**asignatura** *f* subject; course.
**asilado/da** *m/f* inmate; refugee.
**asilo** *m* asylum, refuge; ~ **político** political asylum.
**asimilación** *f* assimilation.
**asimilar** *vt* to assimilate.
**asimismo** *adv* similarly, in the same manner.
**asir** *vt* to grasp, to seize; to hold, to grip; * *vi* to take root.
**asistencia** *f* audience; presence; assistance, help.
**asistente** *m* assistant, helper.
**asistir** *vi* to be present; to assist; * *vt* to help.
**asma** *f* asthma.
**asmático/ca** *adj* asthmatic.
**asno** *m* ass.
**asociación** *f* association; partnership.
**asociado** *m* associate.
**asociar** *vt* to associate; ~se *vr* to associate.
**asolar** *vt* to destroy; to devastate.

**asolear** *vt* to expose to the sun; ~se *vr* to sunbathe.
**asomar** *vi* to appear; ~se *vr* to appear, to show up.
**asombrar** *vt* to amaze; to astonish; ~se *vr* to be amazed; to get a fright.
**asombro** *m* dread, terror; astonishment.
**asombroso/sa** *adj* astonishing, marvellous.
**asomo** *m* mark, token, indication; conjecture.
**asonancia** *f* assonance; harmony.
**aspa** *f* cross; sail.
**aspaviento** *m* astonishment; fuss.
**aspecto** *m* appearance; aspect.
**aspereza** *f* roughness; surliness.
**áspero/ra** *adj* rough, rugged; craggy, knotty; horrid; harsh, hard; severe, austere; gruff.
**asperón** *m* grindstone.
**aspersión** *f* sprinkling; aspersion.
**áspid** *m* asp.
**aspiración** *f* breath; pause.
**aspirante** *m* aspirant, aspirer.
**aspirar** *vt* to breathe; to aspire; (*gr*) to aspirate.
**aspirina** *f* aspirin.
**asquear** *vt* to sicken; * *vi* to be sickening; ~se *vr* to feel disgusted.
**asqueroso/sa** *adj* disgusting.
**asta** *f* lance; horn; handle.
**astado/da** *adj* horned.
**asterisco** *m* asterisk.
**astilla** *f* chip (of wood), splinter.
**astillero** *m* dockyard.
**astral** *adj* astral.
**astringente** *adj* astringent.
**astro** *m* star.
**astrología** *f* astrology.
**astrológico/ca** *adj* astrological.
**astrólogo/ga** *m/f* astrologer.
**astronauta** *m/f* astronaut.
**astronave** *f* spaceship.
**astronomía** *f* astronomy.
**astronómico/ca** *adj* astronomical.
**astrónomo/ma** *m/f* astronomer.
**astucia** *f* cunning, slyness.
**astuto/ta** *adj* cunning, sly; astute.
**asueto** *m* time off; holiday, vacation.
**asumir** *vt* to assume.
**Asunción** *f* Assumption.
**asunto** *m* subject, matter; affair, business.
**asustar** *vt* to frighten; ~se *vr* to be frightened.
**atacar** *vt* to attack.
**atajo** *m* short cut.
**atalaya** *f* watchtower.
**atañer** *vi*: ~ **a** to concern.

**ataque** *m* attack.
**atar** *vt* to tie; to fasten.
**atardecer** *vi* to get dark; * *m* dusk; evening.
**atareado/da** *adj* busy.
**atascar** *vt* to jam; to hinder; **~se** *vr* to become bogged down.
**atasco** *m* traffic jam.
**ataúd** *m* coffin.
**ataviar** *vt* to dress up, to trim, to adorn.
**atavío** *m* dress; ornament; **~s** *mpl* finery.
**ateísmo** *m* atheism.
**atemorizar** *vt* to frighten; **~se** *vr* to get scared.
**atenazar** *vt* to grip; to torment.
**atención** *f* attention, heedfulness; civility; observance, consideration.
**atender** *vi* to be attentive; * *vt* to attend to; to heed, to expect, to wait for; to look at.
**atenerse** *vr:* **~ a** to adhere to.
**atentado** *m* terrorist attack; transgression, offence.
**atentamente** *adv* observantly; **le saluda ~** yours faithfully.
**atentar** *vt* to attempt; to commit.
**atento/ta** *adj* attentive; heedful; observing; mindful; polite, courteous, mannerly.
**atenuante** *adj* extenuating.
**atenuar** *vt* to diminish; to lessen.
**ateo/a** *adj, m/f* atheist.
**aterciopelado/da** *adj* velvety.
**aterido/da** *adj* frozen stiff.
**aterirse** *vr* to grow stiff with cold.
**aterrador/a** *adj* frightening.
**aterrar** *vt* to terrify; **~se** *vr* to be terrified.
**aterrizaje** *m* landing.
**aterrizar** *vi* to land.
**aterrorizar** *vt* to frighten, to terrify.
**atesorar** *vt* to treasure/hoard up (riches).
**atestación** *f* testimony, evidence.
**atestado/da** *adj* packed; * *m* affidavit.
**atestar** *vt* to cram, to stuff; to attest, to witness.
**atestiguar** *vt* to witness, to attest.
**atiborrar** *vt* to stuff; **~se** *vr* to stuff oneself.
**ático** *m* attic.
**atildar** *vt* to punctuate with a tilde; to censure.
**atinado/da** *adj* wise; correct.
**atisbar** *vt* to pry into; to examine closely.
**atizar** *vt* to stir (the fire) with a poker; to stir up.
**atlántico/ca** *adj* atlantic; * *m:* **el A~** the Atlantic.
**atlas** *m* atlas.
**atleta** *m/f* athlete.

**atlético/ca** *adj* athletic.
**atletismo** *m* athletics.
**atmósfera** *f* atmosphere.
**atmosférico/ca** *adj* atmospheric.
**atolladero** *m* bog; obstacle; impediment.
**atollar** *vi* to stick; **~se** *vr* to get stuck.
**atolondramiento** *m* stupefaction, consternation.
**atolondrar** *vt* to stun, to stupefy; **~se** *vr* to be stupefied.
**atómico/ca** *adj* atomic.
**atomizador** *m* spray.
**átomo** *m* atom.
**atónito/ta** *adj* astonished, amazed.
**atontado/da** *adj* stunned; silly.
**atontar** *vt* to stun, to stupefy; **~se** to grow stupid.
**atormentar** *vt* to torture; to harass; to torment.
**atornillar** *vt* to screw on; to screw down.
**atosigar** *vt* to poison; to harass; to oppress.
**atracadero** *m* landing-place.
**atracador/a** *m/f* robber.
**atracar** *vt* to moor; to rob; **~se** *vr:* **~ (de)** to stuff oneself (with).
**atracción** *f* attraction.
**atraco** *m* hold-up, robbery.
**atractivo/va** *adj* attractive; magnetic; * *m* charm.
**atraer** *vt* to attract, to allure.
**atragantarse** *vr* to stick in the throat, to choke.
**atrancar** *vt* to bar (a door).
**atrapar** *vt* to trap; to nab; to deceive.
**atrás** *adv* backward(s); behind; previously, **hacia ~** backward(s).
**atrasado/da** *adj* slow; backward; in arrears.
**atrasar** *vi* to be slow; * *vt* to postpone; **~ el reloj** to put back a watch; **~se** *vr* to stay behind; to be late.
**atraso** *m* backwardness; slowness; delay.
**atravesado/da** *adj* oblique; cross; perverse; mongrel; degenerate.
**atravesar** *vt* to cross; to pass over; to pierce; to go through; **~se** *vr* to get in the way; to meddle.
**atrayente** *adj* attractive.
**atreverse** *vr* to dare, to venture.
**atrevido/da** *adj* bold, audacious, daring.
**atrevimiento** *m* boldness, audacity.
**atribución** *f* attribution, imputation.
**atribuir** *vt* to attribute, to ascribe; to impute.
**atribular** *vt* to vex, to afflict.
**atributivo/va** *adj* attributive.

**atributo** *m* attribute.
**atrición** *f* attrition.
**atril** *m* lectern; music stand.
**atrio** *m* porch; portico.
**atrocidad** *f* atrocity.
**atrochar** *vi* to take a short cut.
**atropellado/da** *adj* hasty, precipitate.
**atropellar** *vt* to trample; to run down; to hurry; to insult; ~**se** *vr* to hurry.
**atropello** *m* accident; push; outrage.
**atuendo** *m* attire.
**atroz** *adj* atrocious, heinous; cruel.
**atufar** *vt* to vex, to plague; ~**se** *vr* turn sour; to get mad.
**atún** *m* tuna (fish).
**aturdido/da** *adj* hare-brained.
**aturdimiento** *m* stupefaction; astonishment; dullness.
**aturdir** *vt* to stun, to confuse; to stupefy.
**atusar** *vt* to smooth.
**audacia** *f* audacity, boldness.
**audaz** *adj* audacious, bold.
**audible** *adj* audible.
**audiencia** *f* audience.
**auditivo/va** *adj* auditory.
**auditor** *m* auditor.
**auditoría** *f* audit.
**auditorio** *m* audience; auditorium.
**auge** *m* boom; climax.
**augurar** *vt* to predict.
**augurio** *m* omen.
**aula** *f* lecture room.
**aullar** *vi* to howl.
**aullido/aullo** *m* howling.
**aumentar** *vt* to augment, to increase; to magnify; to put up; * *vi* to increase; to grow larger.
**aumento** *m* increase; promotion, advancement.
**aún** *adv* even; ~ **así** even so.
**aun** *adv* still; yet.
**aunar** *vt* to unite, to assemble.
**aunque** *adv* though, although.
**¡aúpa!** *excl* come on!
**áureo/rea** *adj* golden, gilt *compd*.
**aureola** *f* glory; nimbus.
**auricular** *m* receiver; ~**es** *mpl* headphones *pl*.
**aurora** *f* dawn.
**auscultar** *vt* to sound.
**ausencia** *f* absence.
**ausentarse** *vr* to go out.
**ausente** *adj* absent.
**auspicio** *m* auspice; prediction; protection.

**austeridad** *f* austerity.
**austero/ra** *adj* austere, severe.
**austral** *adj* southern.
**autenticar** *vt* to authenticate.
**autenticidad** *f* authenticity.
**auténtico/ca** *adj* authentic.
**autillo** *m* brown owl.
**auto** *m* judicial sentence; car; edict, ordinance; ~ **de fe** auto-da-fé.
**autoadhesivo/va** *adj* self-adhesive.
**autobiografía** *f* autobiography.
**autobús** *m* bus.
**autocar** *m* bus.
**autocracia** *f* autocracy.
**autócrata** *m* autocrat.
**autóctono/na** *adj* native.
**autodefensa** *f* self defence.
**autodeterminación** *f* self-determination.
**autoedición** *f* desktop publishing.
**autoescuela** *f* driving school.
**autoestop, autostop** *f* hitchhiking; **hacer** ~ to hitchhike.
**autoestopista, autostopista** *m/f* hitchhiker.
**autógrafo** *m* autograph.
**autómata** *m* automaton.
**automático/ca** *adj* automatic.
**automatización** *f* automation.
**automedicación** *f* self-medication.
**automotor** *m* diesel train.
**automóvil** *m* automobile.
**automovilismo** *m* motoring; motor racing.
**automovilista** *m/f* motorist, driver.
**automovilístico/ca** *adj* car *compd*.
**autonomía** *f* autonomy.
**autónomo/ma** *adj* autonomous.
**autonómico/ca** *adj* autonomous.
**autopista** *f* motorway; ~ **de la información** information superhighway.
**autopsía** *f* post mortem, autopsy.
**autor/ra** *m/f* author; maker; writer.
**autoridad** *f* authority.
**autorización** *f* authorization.
**autorizar** *vt* to authorize.
**autorradio** *m* car radio.
**autorretrato** *m* self-portrait.
**autoservicio** *m* self-service store; restaurant.
**autosuficiencia** *f* self-sufficiency.
**autovía** *f* state highway.
**auxiliar** *vt* to aid, to help, to assist; to attend; * *adj* auxiliary.
**auxilio** *m* aid, help, assistance.
**aval** *m* guarantee; guarantor.

**avalancha** *f* avalanche.

**avance** *m* advance; attack; trailer(for a film).

**avanzada** *f* (*mil*) vanguard.

**avanzar** *vt*, *vi* to advance.

**avaricia** *f* avarice.

**avaricioso/sa** *adj* avaricious, covetous.

**avaro/ra** *adj* miserly; * *m/f* miser.

**avasallar** *vt* to subdue; to enslave.

**ave** *f* bird; fowl.

**avecinarse** *vr* to be on the way.

**avellana** *f* hazelnut.

**avellano** *m* hazelnut tree.

**ave maría** *f* Hail Mary.

**avena** *f* oats *pl*.

**avenencia** *f* agreement, bargain; union.

**avenida** *f* avenue.

**avenido/da** *adj* agreed.

**avenir** *vt* to reconcile; **~se** *vr* to reach a compromise.

**aventajado/da** *adj* advantageous, profitable; beautiful; excellent.

**aventajar** *vt* to surpass, to excel.

**aventar** *vt* to fan; to expel.

**aventura** *f* adventure; event, incident.

**aventurado/da** *adj* risky.

**aventurar** *vt* to venture, to risk.

**aventurero/ra** *adj* adventurous.

**avergonzar** *vt* to shame, to abash; **~se** *vr* to be ashamed.

**avería** *f* breakdown.

**averiado/da** *adj* broken down; out of order.

**averiarse** *vr* to break down.

**averiguación** *f* discovery; investigation.

**averiguar** *vt* to inquire into; to investigate, to explore.

**aversión** *f* aversion, dislike; abhorrence.

**avestruz** *m* ostrich.

**aviación** *f* aviation; air force.

**aviador/a** *m/f* aviator.

**avicultura** *f* poultry farming.

**avidez** *f* covetousness.

**ávido/da** *adj* (*poet*) greedy, covetous.

**avieso/sa** *adj* irregular, out of the way; mischievous, perverse.

**avinagrado/da** *adj* sour.

**avinagrarse** *vr* to go sour.

**avío** *m* preparation, provision.

**avión** *m* aeroplane.

**avioneta** *f* light aircraft.

**avisado/da** *adj* prudent, cautious; **mal ~** ill-advised.

**avisar** *vt* to inform; to warn; to advise.

**aviso** *m* notice; warning; hint.

**avispa** *f* wasp.

**avispado/da** *adj* lively, brisk; vivacious.

**avisparse** *vr* to worry.

**avispero** *m* wasp's nest.

**avispón** *m* hornet.

**avistar** *vt* to sight.

**avituallar** *vt* (*mil*) to supply (with food).

**avivar** *vt* to quicken, to enliven; to encourage.

**avutarda** *f* bustard.

**axioma** *m* axiom, maxim.

**¡ay!** *excl* ouch!; ow! **¡~ de mí!** alas! poor me!

**aya** *f* governess, instructress.

**ayer** *adv* yesterday.

**ayuda** *f* help, aid; support; * *m* deputy, assistant.

**ayudante** *m* (*mil*) adjutant; assistant.

**ayudar** *vt* to help, to assist; to further.

**ayunar** *vi* to fast, to abstain from food.

**ayuno** *m* fasting, abstinence from food.

**ayuntamiento** *m* town/city hall.

**azabache** *m* jet.

**azada** *f* spade; hoe.

**azafata** *f* air hostess.

**azafrán** *m* saffron.

**azahar** *m* orange/lemon blossom.

**azar** *m* unforeseen disaster; unexpected accident; fate; **por ~** by chance; **al ~** at random.

**azaroso/sa** *adj* unlucky, ominous; risky.

**azogue** *m* mercury.

**azor** *m* goshawk.

**azorar** *vt* to frighten, to terrify.

**azotaina** *f* drubbing, sound flogging.

**azotar** *vt* to whip, to lash.

**azote** *m* whip.

**azotea** *f* flat roof of a house.

**azteca** *m/f* Aztec.

**azúcar** *m/f* sugar.

**azucarado/da** *adj* sugared; sugary.

**azucarar** *vt* to sugar, to sweeten.

**azucarero** *m* sugar bowl.

**azucena** *f* white lily.

**azufre** *m* sulphur, brimstone.

**azul** *adj* blue; **~ celeste** sky blue.

**azulado/da** *adj* azure, bluish.

**azulejo** *m* tile.

**azuzar** *vt* to irritate, to stir up.

# B

**baba** *f* dribble, spittle.
**babear** *vi* to dribble, to drool.
**babel** *m* bedlam.
**babero** *m* bib.
**babia** *f*: **estar en ~** to be absent-minded/ dreaming.
**baboso/sa** *adj* dribbling, drooling.
**babucha** *f* slipper.
**baca** *f* (*auto*) roof rack.
**bacalao** *m* cod.
**bache** *m* pothole.
**bachillerato** *m* baccalaureate.
**báculo** *m* stick.
**bagaje** *m* baggage.
**bagatela** *f* trifle.
**bahía** *f* bay.
**bailador/ra** *m/f* dancer.
**bailar** *vi* to dance.
**bailarín/ina** *m/f* dancer.
**baile** *m* dance, ball; **~ de disfraces** fancy-dress ball.
**baja** *f* fall; casualty.
**bajada** *f* descent; inclination; slope; ebb.
**bajamar** *f* low tide, low water.
**bajar** *vt* to lower, to let down; to lessen; to humble; to go/come down; to bend downward(s); * *vi* to descend; to go/come down; to grow less; **~se** *vr* to crouch; to lessen.
**bajeza** *f* meanness; lowliness.
**bajío** *m* shoal, sandbank; lowlands *pl*.
**bajo/ja** *adj* low; abject, despicable; common; dull (of colours); deep; humble; * *prep* under, underneath, below; * *adv* softly; quietly; * *m* (*mus*) bass; low place.
**bajón** *m* fall.
**bakalao** *m* (*col*) rave music.
**bala** *f* bullet.
**baladronada** *f* boast, brag; bravado.
**balance** *m* hesitation; balance sheet; balance; rocking chair; rolling (of a ship).
**balancear** *vt*, *vi* to balance; to roll; to waver; **~se** *vr* to swing.
**balancín** *m* balance beam; rocker arm; seesaw; balancing pole.
**balanza** *f* scale; balance.
**balar** *vi* to bleat.
**balaustrada** *f* balustrade, banister.
**balazo** *m* shot.
**balbucear** *vt*, *vi* to stutter.
**balbuciente** *adj* stammering, stuttering.

**balcón** *m* balcony.
**baldar** *vt* to cripple.
**balde** *m* bucket; **de ~** *adv* gratis, for nothing; **en ~** in vain.
**baldío/día** *adj* waste; uncultivated.
**baldosa** *f* floor; tile; flagstone.
**balido** *m* bleating, bleat.
**balín** *m* buckshot.
**balística** *f* ballistics *pl*.
**ballena** *f* whale; whalebone.
**ballenato** *m* calf of a whale.
**ballenero** *m* (*mar*) whaler.
**ballesta** *f* crossbow; **a tiro de ~** at a great distance.
**ballestero** *m* archer; crossbow-maker.
**ballet** *m* ballet.
**balneario** *m* spa.
**balón** *m* ball.
**baloncesto** *m* basketball.
**balonmano** *m* handball.
**balonvolea** *m* volleyball.
**balsa**[1] *f* balsa wood; raft, float.
**balsa**[2] *f* pool, pond.
**bálsamo** *m* balsam, balm.
**baluarte** *m* bastion; bulwark.
**bamba** *f* fat; (*bot*) swelling; flabbiness.
**bambolear** *vi* to reel; **~se** *vr* to sway.
**bamboleo** *m* reeling, staggering.
**bambú** *m* bamboo.
**banana** *f* banana; plantain.
**banano** *m* banana tree.
**banasta** *f* large basket.
**banca** *f* bench; banking; **~ electrónica** electronic banking.
**bancario/ria** *adj* bank(ing) *compd*.
**bancarrota** *f* bankruptcy.
**banco** *m* bench; work bench; bank.
**banda** *f* band; sash; ribbon; troop; party; gang; touchline.
**bandada** *f* flock; shoal.
**bandearse** *vr* to move to and fro.
**bandeja** *f* tray, salver.
**bandera** *f* banner, standard; flag.
**banderilla** *f* small decorated dart used at a bullfight.
**banderillear** *vt* to plant banderillas in a bull's neck/shoulder.
**banderillero** *m* thrower of banderillas.
**banderín** *m* small flag, pennant.
**bandido** *m* bandit, outlaw.
**bando** *m* faction, party; edict.

**bandolera** *f* bandoleer.
**bandolero** *m* bandit.
**bandurria** *f* bandore (musical instrument resembling a lute).
**banquero/ra** *m/f* banker.
**banqueta** *f* three-legged stool; pavement.
**banquete** *m* banquet; formal dinner.
**banquillo** *m* dock; bench.
**bañador** *m* swimsuit.
**bañar** *vt* to bathe; to dip; to coat (with varnish); ~**se** *vr* to bathe; to swim.
**bañera** *f* bath (tub).
**bañero** *m* lifeguard.
**bañista** *m/f* bather.
**baño** *m* bath; dip; bathtub; varnish; coating.
**baptista** *m/f* Baptist.
**bar** *m* bar.
**baraja** *f* pack of cards.
**barajar** *vt* to shuffle (cards); to jumble up.
**baranda** *f* rail.
**barandilla** *f* small balustrade, small railing.
**baratijas** *fpl* trifles *pl*, toys *pl*; trash, junk.
**baratillo** *m* second-hand goods *pl*; junk shop; bargain sale.
**barato/ta** *adj* cheap; **de** ~ gratis; * *m* cheapness; bargain sale; money extracted from winning gamblers.
**baraúnda** *f* noise, hurly-burly.
**barba** *f* chin; beard; ~ **a** ~ face to face; * *m* actor who impersonates old men.
**barbacoa** *f* barbecue.
**barbaridad** *f* barbarity, barbarism; outrage.
**barbarie** *f* barbarism; savagery.
**barbarismo** *m* barbarism (form of speech).
**bárbaro/ra** *adj* barbarous; cruel; rude; rough.
**barbecho** *m* first ploughing, fallow land.
**barbería** *f* barber's shop.
**barbero** *m* barber.
**barbilampiño/ña** *adj* clean-shaven; (*fig*) inexperienced.
**barbilla** *f* (tip of the) chin.
**barbo** *m* barbel.
**barbudo/da** *adj* bearded.
**barca** *f* boat.
**barco** *m* boat; ship.
**barítono** *m* (*mus*) baritone.
**barman** *m* barman.
**barniz** *m* varnish; glaze.
**barnizar** *vt* to varnish.
**barómetro** *m* barometer.
**barón** *m* baron.
**baronesa** *f* baroness.
**barquero** *m* boatman.
**barquilla** *f* (*mar*) log; basket (of an air balloon).

**barquillo** *m* wafer; cornet, cone.
**barra** *m* bar; rod; lever; French loaf; sandbank; **de** ~ **a** ~ from place to place.
**barrabasada** *f* trick, plot.
**barraca** *f* hut.
**barranco** *m* gully, ravine; (*fig*) great difficulty.
**barranquismo** *m* (*sport*) canyoning.
**barrena** *f* drill, bit, auger.
**barrenar** *vt* to drill, to bore; (*fig*) to frustrate.
**barrendero** *m* sweeper.
**barreno** *m* large drill; borehole.
**barreño** *m* tub.
**barrer** *vt* to sweep; to overwhelm.
**barrera** *f* barrier; turnpike, claypit.
**barriada** *f* suburb, area of a city.
**barricada** *f* barricade.
**barrido** *m* sweep.
**barriga** *f* abdomen; belly.
**barrigudo/da** *adj* pot-bellied.
**barril** *m* barrel; cask.
**barrio** *m* area, district.
**barrizal** *m* claypit.
**barro** *m* clay, mud.
**barroco/ca** *adj* baroque.
**barrote** *m* ironwork (of doors, windows, tables); crosspiece.
**barruntar** *vt* to guess; to foresee; to conjecture.
**barrunto** *m* conjecture.
**bártulos** *mpl* gear, belongings *pl*.
**barullo** *m* uproar.
**basamento** *m* base.
**basalto** *m* basalt.
**basar** *vt* to base; ~**se** *vr* ~ **en** to be based on.
**basca** *f* squeamishness, nausea.
**báscula** *f* scales *pl*.
**base** *f* base, basis.
**básico/ca** *adj* basic.
**basílica** *f* basilica.
**basilisco** *m* basilisk.
**bastante** *adj* sufficient, enough; * *adv* quite.
**bastar** *vi* to be sufficient, to be enough.
**bastardo/da** *adj*, *m/f* bastard.
**bastidor** *m* embroidery frame; ~**es** *mpl* scenery (on stage).
**bastión** *m* bastion.
**basto/ta** *adj* coarse, rude, unpolished.
**bastón** *m* cane, stick; truncheon; (*fig*) command.
**bastonazo** *m* beating.
**bastos** *mpl* clubs *pl* (one of the four suits at cards).
**basura** *f* rubbish, trash, refuse; dung.

**basurero** *m* refuse collector, dustman;dunghill.
**bata** *f* dressing gown; overall; laboratory coat.
**batacazo** *m* noise of a fall.
**batalla** *f* battle, combat; fight.
**batallador/a** *adj* battling.
**batallar** *vi* to battle, to fight; to fence with foils; to waver.
**batallón** *m* (*mil*) battalion.
**batata** *f* sweet potato.
**bate** *m* bat.
**batería** *m* battery; percussion.
**batida** *f* beating (of woodland/moorland); search; chase.
**batido/da** *adj* shot (of silk); well-trodden (of roads); * *m* batter; **~ de leche** milk shake.
**batidora** *f* food mixer; whisk.
**batir** *vt* to beat; to whisk; to dash; to demolish; to defeat.
**batista** *f* fine cotton cloth, cambric.
**batuta** *f* baton.
**baúl** *m* trunk; (*col*) belly.
**bautismal** *adj* baptismal.
**bautismo** *m* baptism.
**bautizar** *vt* to baptize, to christen.
**bautizo** *m* baptism.
**baya** *f* berry.
**bayeta** *f* cloth.
**bayo/ya** *adj* bay (colour of a horse).
**bayoneta** *f* bayonet.
**bayonetazo** *m* thrust with a bayonet.
**baza** *f* card trick.
**bazar** *m* bazaar.
**bazo** *m* spleen.
**bazofia** *f* refuse; hogwash.
**be** *m* baa (cry of sheep).
**beatificación** *f* beatification.
**beatificar** *vt* to beatify; to hallow, to sanctify, to make blessed.
**beato/ta** *adj* happy; blessed; devout; * *m* lay brother; *m/f* pious person; beatified person.
**bebé** *m/f* baby.
**bebedero** *m* drinking trough.
**bebedizo** *m* (love) potion.
**bebedor/ra** *m/f* (hard) drinker.
**beber** *vt*, *vi* to drink.
**bebida** *f* drink, beverage.
**beca** *f* fellowship; grant, bursary, scholarship; sash; hood.
**becada** *f* woodcock.
**becerro** *m* yearling calf.
**bedel** *m* janitor; uniformed employee.
**befa** *f* jeer, taunt.
**befarse** *vr*: **~ de** to mock, to ridicule.

**beldad** *f* beauty.
**belén** *m* nativity scene.
**bélico/ca** *adj* warlike, martial.
**belicoso/sa** *adj* warlike; aggressive.
**beligerante** *adj* belligerent.
**bellaco/ca** *adj* artful; cunning.
**belladona** *f* (*bot*) deadly nightshade.
**belleza** *f* beauty.
**bello/lla** *adj* beautiful; handsome; lovely; fine.
**bellota** *f* acorn; (*med*) Adam's apple; pomander.
**bemol** *m* (*mus*) flat.
**bencina** *f* benzine.
**bendecir** *vt* to bless; to consecrate; to praise.
**bendición** *f* blessing, benediction.
**bendito/ta** *adj* saintly; blessed; simple; happy.
**benedictino/na, benito/ta** *adj*, *m/f* Benedictine.
**beneficiado** *m* incumbent; beneficiary.
**beneficiar** *vt* to benefit; to be of benefit to.
**beneficiario/ra** *m/f* beneficiary.
**beneficio** *m* benefit, advantage; profit; benefit night.
**beneficioso/sa** *adj* beneficial.
**benéfico/ca** *adj* beneficent, kind.
**benemérito/ta** *adj* worthy, meritorious.
**beneplácito** *m* consent, approbation.
**benevolencia** *f* benevolence.
**benévolo/la** *adj* benevolent, kind-hearted.
**benigno/na** *adj* benign; kind; mild.
**beodo/da** *adj* drunk, drunken.
**berberecho** *m* cockle.
**berenjena** *f* eggplant.
**bergantín** *m* (*mar*) brig.
**bermejo/ja** *adj* red.
**berrear** *vi* to low, to bellow.
**berrido** *m* bellowing (of a calf).
**berrinche** *m* anger, rage, tantrum (applied to children).
**berro** *m* watercress.
**berza** *f* cabbage.
**besamanos** *m invar* levee; royal audience.
**besamel** *f* white sauce.
**besar** *vt* to kiss; to graze; **~se** *vr* to kiss.
**beso** *m* kiss; collision of persons/things.
**bestia** *f* beast, animal; idiot.
**bestial** *adj* bestial; (*col*) marvellous, great.
**bestialidad** *f* bestiality.
**besugo** *m* sea bream.
**besuquear** *vt* to cover with kisses.
**besuqueo** *m* repeated kisses *pl*.
**betún** *m* shoe polish.
**bezo** *m* thick lip; swollen tissue in a wound.

**biberón** *m* feeding bottle.
**Biblia** *f* Bible.
**bíblico/ca** *adj* biblical.
**bibliófilo/la** *m/f* book-lover, bookworm.
**bibliografía** *f* bibliography.
**bibliográfico/ca** *adj* bibliographical.
**bibliógrafo/fa** *m/f* bibliographer.
**biblioteca** *f* library.
**bibliotecario/ria** *m/f* librarian.
**bicarbonato** *m* bicarbonate.
**bicho** *m* small animal; bug; **mal ~** villain.
**bici** *f* (*col*) bike.
**bicicleta** *f* bicycle; **~ de montaña** mountain bike.
**bidé** *m* bidet.
**bielda** *f* pitchfork.
**bien** *m* good, benefit; profit; **~es** *mpl* goods *pl*, property; wealth; **~es raíces** *mpl* landed property, real estate; * *adv* well, right; very; willingly; easily; **~ que** *conj* although; **está ~** he is well.
**bienal** *adj* biennial.
**bienaventuranza** *f* blessedness; bliss; happiness; prosperity; **~s** *fpl* the Beatitudes.
**bienestar** *m* wellbeing.
**bienhablado/da** *adj* well-spoken.
**bienhecho/cha** *adj* well-shaped.
**bienhechor/ra** *m/f* benefactor.
**bienio** *m* space of two years.
**bienvenida** *f* welcome.
**bifurcación** *f* fork.
**bigamia** *f* bigamy.
**bígamo/ma** *m/f* bigamist.
**bigote** *m* moustache; whiskers *pl*.
**bigotudo/da** *adj* with a big moustache.
**bikini** *m* bikini.
**bilingüe** *adj* bilingual.
**bilioso/sa** *adj* bilious.
**bilis** *f* bile.
**billar** *m* billiards *pl*.
**billete** *m* note, banknote; ticket; (*rail*) ticket; **~ sencillo** single ticket; **~ de ida y vuelta** return ticket.
**billetero** *m* wallet.
**bimensual** *adj* twice monthly.
**bimotor** *m* twin-engined plane.
**binario** *m* binary.
**binoculares** *mpl* binoculars *pl*; opera glasses *pl*.
**biodegradable** *adj* biodegradable.
**biodiversity** *f* biodiversity.
**biografía** *f* biography.
**biógrafo/fa** *m/f* biographer.
**biología** *f* biology.
**biológico/ca** *adj* biological.

**biólogo/ga** *m/f* biologist.
**biombo** *m* screen.
**biopsia** *f* biopsy.
**bípedo** *m* biped.
**birlar** *vt* to knock down at one blow; (*col*) to pinch.
**birreta** *f* biretta.
**bis** *excl* encore.
**bisabuela** *f* great-grandmother.
**bisabuelo** *m* great-grandfather.
**bisagra** *f* hinge.
**bisexual** *adj* bisexual.
**bisexualidad** *f* bisexuality.
**bisiesto** *adj*: **año ~** leap year.
**bisnieto/ta** *m/f* great-grandson/daughter.
**bisoño/na** *adj* raw, inexperienced; novice.
**bisonte** *m* bison.
**bistec** *m* steak.
**bisturí** *m* scalpel.
**bisutería** *f* costume jewellery.
**bizarro/rra** *adj* brave, gallant; generous.
**bizco/ca** *adj* cross-eyed.
**bizcocho** *m* sponge cake; biscuit; ship's biscuit.
**bizquear** *vi* to squint.
**blanco/ca** *adj* white; blank; * *m* whiteness; white person; blank, blank space; target (to shoot at).
**blancura** *f* whiteness.
**blandir** *vt* to brandish a sword; **~se** *vr* to swing.
**blando/da** *adj* soft, smooth; mild, gentle; (*col*) cowardly.
**blanducho/cha** *adj* flabby.
**blandura** *f* softness; gentleness, mildness.
**blanquear** *vt* to bleach; to whitewash; to launder (money); * *vi* to show white.
**blanquecino/na** *adj* whitish.
**blanqueo** *m* laundering (of money).
**blasfemador/ra** *m/f* blasphemer.
**blasfemar** *vi* to blaspheme.
**blasfemia** *f* blasphemy; verbal insult.
**blasfemo/ma** *adj* blasphemous; * *m* blasphemer.
**blasón** *m* heraldry, honour, glory.
**blasonar** *vt* to emblazon; to praise highly.
**bledo** *m*: **me importa un ~** (*col*) I don't give a damn.
**blindado/da** *adj* armour-plated; bulletproof.
**bloc** *m* writing pad.
**bloque** *m* block.
**bloquear** *vt* to block; to blockade.
**bloqueo** *m* blockade.
**blusa** *f* blouse.

**boato** *m* ostentation, pompous show.
**bobada** *f* folly, foolishness.
**bobear** *vt* to act/talk in a stupid manner.
**bobería** *f* silliness, foolishness.
**bobina** *f* bobbin.
**bobo/ba** *m/f* idiot, fool; clown, funny man; * *adj* stupid, silly.
**boca** *f* mouth; entrance, opening; mouth of a river; ~ **en** ~ *adv* by word of mouth; **a pedir de** ~ to one's heart's content.
**bocacalle** *f* entrance to a street.
**bocadillo** *m* sandwich, roll.
**bocado** *m* mouthful.
**bocal** *m* pitcher; mouthpiece of a trumpet.
**bocamanga** *f* cuff.
**bocanada** *f* mouthful (of liquor); gust.
**bocazas** *m/f invar* loudmouth.
**boceto** *m* sketch.
**bochorno** *m* sultry weather, scorching heat; blush.
**bochornoso/sa** *adj* sultry; shameful.
**bocina** *f* trumpet; megaphone; horn (of a car).
**boda** *f* wedding.
**bodega** *f* wine cellar; warehouse; bar.
**bodegón** *m* cheap restaurant; still life (in art).
**bodoque** *m* pellet; lump; (*col*) idiot.
**bodorrio** *m* quiet wedding.
**bofes** *mpl* lungs; lights.
**bofetada** *f* slap (in the face).
**bofetón** *m* hard slap.
**boga** *f* fashion; (*rail*) bogie/bogy; rower; rowing; **estar en** ~ to be fashionable.
**bogar** *vi* to row, to paddle.
**bohemio** *m/f* Bohemian.
**boicot** *m* boycott.
**boicotear** *vt* to boycott.
**boina** *f* beret.
**boj** *m* box; boxwood; box tree.
**bola** *f* ball; marble; globe; slam (in cards); shoe polish; (*col*) lie, fib.
**bolazo** *m* blow with a ball.
**bolchevique** *adj* Bolshevik.
**bolear** *vi* to knock balls about (billiards); * *vt* to throw (a ball).
**bolera** *f* bowling alley.
**bolero** *m* bolero jacket; bolero dance.
**boleta** *f* entrance ticket; pass, permit.
**boletín** *m* bulletin; journal, review.
**boleto** *m* ticket.
**boli** *m* (*col*) (ballpoint) pen.
**boliche** *m* jack (at bowls); bowls, bowling alley; dragnet.
**bolígrafo** *m* (ballpoint) pen.

**bolillo** *m* bobbin.
**bollo** *m* bread roll; lump.
**bolo** *m* skittle; (large) pill.
**bolsa** *f* handbag; bag; pocket; sac; stock exchange.
**bolsillo** *m* pocket; purse.
**bolsista** *m/f* stockbroker.
**bolso** *m* purse.
**bomba** *f* pump; bomb; surprise; **dar a la** ~ to pump; ~ **de gasolina** petrol pump.
**bombardear** *vt* to bombard.
**bombardeo** *m* bombardment.
**bombardero** *m* bomber.
**bombazo** *m* explosion; bombshell.
**bombero** *m* fireman.
**bombilla** *f* light bulb.
**bombín** *m* bowler hat.
**bombo** *m* large drum.
**bombón** *m* sweet; chocolate.
**bonachón/ona** *adj* good-natured.
**bonanza** *f* fair weather (at sea); prosperity; bonanza.
**bondad** *f* goodness, kindness; courtesy.
**bondadoso/sa** *adj* good, kind.
**bonete** *m* clerical hat; college cap.
**bonito** *adj* pretty, nice-looking; pretty good, passable; * *m* tuna (fish).
**bono** *m* (financial) bond.
**boñiga** *f* cow pat.
**bonsái** *m* bonsai.
**boqueada** *f* act of opening the mouth; **la última** ~ the last gasp.
**boquear** *vi* to gape;, to gasp; to breathe one's last; * *vt* to pronounce, to utter (a word).
**boquerón** *m* anchovy; large hole.
**boquete** *m* gap, narrow entrance.
**boquiabierto/ta** *adj* open-mouthed; gaping.
**boquilla** *f* mouthpiece of a musical instrument; nozzle.
**borbollón/borbotón** *m* bubbling; **salir a borbollones** to gush forth.
**borda** *f* (*mar*) gunwale; hut.
**bordado** *m* embroidery.
**bordadora** *f* embroiderer.
**bordar** *vt* to embroider; to do anything very well.
**borde** *m* border; margin; (*mar*) board.
**bordear** *vi* (*mar*) to tack; * *vt* to go along the edge of; to flank.
**bordillo** *m* kerb.
**bordo** *m* (*mar*) board of a ship.
**boreal** *adj* boreal, northern.
**borgoña** *m* burgundy wine.

**borla** *f* tassel; tuft.

**borona** *f* millet; corn; corn bread.

**borrachera** *f* drunkenness; hard drinking; spree.

**borracho/cha** *adj* drunk, intoxicated; blind with passion; * *m/f* drunk, drunkard.

**borrador** *m* first draft; scribbling pad; eraser.

**borraja** *f* (*bot*) borage.

**borrar** *vt* to erase, to rub out; to blur; to obscure.

**borrasca** *f* storm; violent squall of wind; hazard; danger.

**borrascoso/sa** *adj* stormy.

**borrego/ga** *m/f* yearling lamb; simpleton, blockhead.

**borrico/ca** *m/f* donkey, ass; blockhead.

**borrón** *m* blot, blur; rough draft of a writing; first sketch of a painting; stain, blemish.

**borronear** *vt* to sketch.

**boscaje** *m* grove, small wood; landscape (in painting).

**bosque** *m* forest; wood.

**bosquejar** *vt* to make a sketch of (a painting); to make a rough model of (a figure).

**bosquejo** *m* sketch (of a painting); unfinished work.

**bostezar** *vi* to yawn; to gape.

**bostezo** *m* yawn; yawning.

**bota** *f* leather wine-bag; boot.

**botánica** *f* botany.

**botánico/ca** *adj* botanic; * *m/f* botanist.

**botanista** *m/f* botanist.

**botar** *vt* to cast, to fling; to launch.

**bote** *m* bounce; thrust; tin, can; boat.

**botella** *f* bottle.

**botica** *f* pharmacy.

**boticario/ria** *m/f* pharmacist.

**botijo** *m* earthenware jug.

**botín** *m* high boot, half-boot; gaiter; booty.

**botiquín** *m* medicine chest.

**botón** *m* button; knob (of a radio etc); (*bot*) bud.

**botonadura** *f* set of buttons.

**botones** *m invar* bellboy.

**bóveda** *f* arch; vault, crypt.

**boxeador** *m* boxer.

**boxeo** *m* boxing.

**boya** *f* (*mar*) buoy.

**boyante** *adj* buoyant, floating; (*fig*) fortunate, successful.

**bozal** *m* muzzle.

**bozo** *m* down (on the upper lip/chin); head collar (of a horse).

**braceada** *f* violent movement of the arms.

**bracear** *vi* to swing the arms.

**bracero** *m* day-labourer; farm hand.

**braga** *f* sling, rope; nappy; **~s** *fpl* panties *pl.*

**bragazas** *m invar* henpecked husband.

**braguero** *m* truss.

**bragueta** *f* fly, flies *pl* (of trousers).

**braille** *m* braille.

**bramante** *m* twine, string.

**bramar** *vi* to roar, to bellow; to storm, to bluster.

**bramido** *m* roar, bellow, howl.

**brasa** *f* live coal; **estar hecho una ~** to be very flushed.

**brasero** *m* brazier.

**bravamente** *adv* bravely, gallantly; fiercely; roughly; extremely well.

**bravío/vía** *adj* ferocious, savage, wild; coarse; * *m* fierceness, savageness.

**bravo/va** *adj* brave, valiant; bullying; savage, fierce; rough; sumptuous; excellent, fine; * *excl* well done!

**bravura** *f* ferocity; courage.

**braza** *f* fathom.

**brazada** *f* extension of the arms; armful.

**brazado** *m* armful.

**brazal** *m* armband; irrigation channel.

**brazalete** *m* bracelet.

**brazo** *m* arm; branch (of a tree); enterprise; courage; **luchar a ~ partido** to fight hand to hand.

**brea** *f* pitch; tar.

**brear** *vt* to pitch; to tar; to abuse, to illtreat; to play a joke on.

**brebaje** *m* potion.

**brecha** *f* (*mil*) breach; gap, opening; **batir en ~** (*mil*) to make a breach.

**bregar** *vi* to struggle; to quarrel; to slog away.

**breva** *f* early fig; early large acorn.

**breve** *m* papal brief; * *f* (*mus*) breve; * *adj* brief, short; **en ~** shortly.

**brevedad** *f* brevity, shortness, conciseness.

**breviario** *m* breviary; (*fig*) daily reading.

**brezo** *m* (*bot*) heather.

**bribón/ona** *adj* dishonest, rascally.

**bribonear** *vi* to be idle; to play dirty tricks.

**bricolaje** *m* do-it-yourself.

**brida** *f* bridle; clamp, flange.

**bridge** *m* bridge (cards).

**brigada** *f* brigade; squad, gang.

**brigadier** *m* brigadier.

**brillante** *adj* brilliant; bright, shining; * *m* diamond.

**brillar** *vi* to shine; to sparkle, to glisten; to shine, to be outstanding.

**brillo** *m* brilliance, brightness.
**brincar** *vi* to skip; to leap, to jump; to gambol; to fly into a passion.
**brinco** *m* leap, jump; bounce.
**brindar** *vi* : ~ **a la salud de/~ por** to drink the health of, to toast; * *vt* to offer, to present.
**brindis** *m invar* toast.
**brío** *m* spirit, dash.
**briosamente** *adv* spiritedly, dashingly.
**brioso/sa** *adj* dashing, full of spirit; lively.
**brisa** *f* breeze.
**brisca** *f* card game.
**broca** *f* reel; drill; shoemaker's tack.
**brocado** *m* gold/silver brocade; ~/**da** *adj* embroidered; like brocade.
**brocal** *m* rim, mouth; curb.
**brocha** *f* large brush; ~ **de afeitar** shaving brush.
**brochada** *f* brushstroke.
**broche** *m* clasp; brooch; cufflink.
**broma** *f* joke.
**bromear** *vi* to joke.
**bromista** *m/f* joker.
**bronca** *f* row.
**bronce** *m* bronze.
**bronceado/da** *adj* tanned; * *m* bronzing, suntan.
**broncearse** *vr* to get a suntan.
**bronco/ca** *adj* rough, coarse; rude; harsh.
**bronquitis** *f* bronchitis.
**broquel** *m* shield.
**brotar** *vi* (*bot*) to bud, to germinate; to gush, to rush out; (*med*) to break out.
**brote** *m* (*bot*) shoot; (*med*) outbreak.
**bruces** *adv*: **de ~** face downward(s).
**bruja** *f* witch.
**brujería** *f* witchcraft.
**brujo** *m* sorcerer, magician, wizard.
**brújula** *f* compass.
**bruma** *f* mist; (*mar*) sea mist.
**brumoso/sa** *adj* misty.
**bruñido** *m* polish.
**bruñir** *vt* to polish; to put rouge on.
**brusco/ca** *adj* rude; sudden; brusque.
**brutal** *adj* brutal, brutish.
**brutalidad** *f* brutality; brutal action.
**bruto** *m* brute, beast; ~/**ta** *adj* stupid; gross; brutish.
**buba** *f* tumour.
**bucal** *adj* oral.
**bucear** *vi* to dive.
**buceo** *m* diving.
**bucle** *m* curl.
**bucólica** *f* pastoral poetry; (*col*) food.

**buche** *m* craw, maw; (*col*) guts *pl*; mouthful; crease (in clothes).
**budismo** *m* Buddhism.
**buen** *adj* (before *m* nouns) good.
**buenamente** *adv* easily; willingly.
**buenaventura** *f* fortune, good luck.
**bueno/na** *adj* good, perfect; fair; fit, proper; good-looking; ¡**buenos días!** good morning!; ¡**buenas tardes!** good afternoon!; ¡**buenas noches!** good night!; ¡~! right!
**buey** *m* ox, bullock.
**bufa** *f* joke, mock.
**búfalo** *m* buffalo.
**bufanda** *f* scarf.
**bufar** *vi* to choke with anger; to snort.
**bufete** *m* desk, writing-table; lawyer's office.
**bufido** *m* snorting (of an animal).
**bufo/fa** *adj* comic; **ópera** ~**a** *f* comic opera.
**bufón** *m* buffoon; jester; ~/**ona** *adj* funny, comical.
**bufonada** *f* buffoonery; joke.
**buhardilla** *f* attic.
**búho** *m* owl; unsociable person.
**buhonero** *m* pedlar.
**buitre** *m* vulture.
**bujía** *f* candle; spark plug.
**bula** *f* papal bull.
**bulbo** *m* (*bot*) bulb.
**bulboso/sa** *adj* bulbous.
**bulevar** *m* boulevard.
**bulla** *f* confused noise, clatter; crowd; **meter** ~ to make a noise.
**bullicio** *m* bustle; uproar.
**bullicioso/sa** *adj* lively, restless, noisy, busy; turbulent; boisterous.
**bulto** *m* bulk; tumour, swelling; bust; baggage.
**buñuelo** *m* doughnut; fritter.
**buque** *m* vessel, ship, tonnage, capacity( of a ship); hull (of a ship).
**burbuja** *f* bubble.
**burbujear** *vi* to bubble.
**burdel** *m* brothel.
**burdo/da** *adj* coarse, rough.
**burgués/esa** *adj* bourgeois.
**burguesía** *f* bourgeoisie.
**buril** *m* engraver's chisel.
**burla** *f* trick; gibe; joke; **de ~s** in fun.
**burlar** *vt* to hoax; to defeat; to play tricks on, to deceive; to frustrate; ~**se** *vr* to joke, to laugh at.
**burlesco/ca** *adj* burlesque; comical, funny.
**burlón/ona** *m/f* joker.

**burocracia** *f* bureaucracy.
**burócrata** *m/f* bureaucrat.
**burrada** *f* drove of asses; stupid action.
**burro** *m* ass, donkey; idiot; saw-horse.
**bursátil** *adj* stock exchange *compd*.
**bus** *m* bus.
**busca** *f* search, hunt; bleeper.
**buscapiés** *m invar* jumping jack, (fireworks).
**buscar** *vt* to seek, to search for; to look for; to hunt after; * *vi* to look, to search, to seek.

**buscavidas** *m* prying person, busybody.
**buscón** *m* petty thief, small-time crook.
**búsqueda** *f* search.
**busto** *m* bust.
**butaca** *f* armchair; seat.
**butano** *m* butane.
**butifarra** *f* Catalan sausage.
**buzo** *m* diver.
**buzón** *m* letter box, postbox; conduit, canal; cover of a jar.

# C

**cabal** *adj* just, exact; right; complete; accomplished.

**cábalas** *fpl* intrigue.

**cabalgada** *f* cavalcade; (*mil*) cavalry raid.

**cabalgadura** *f* mount, horse, beast of burden.

**cabalgar** *vi* to ride, to go riding.

**cabalgata** *f* procession.

**cabalístico/ca** *adj* cabalistic.

**caballa** *f* mackerel.

**caballar** *adj* equine.

**caballería** *f* mount, steed; cavalry; cavalry horse; chivalry; knighthood.

**caballeriza** *f* stable; stud; stableboys *pl*.

**caballerizo** *m* groom.

**caballero** *m* knight; gentleman; rider, horseman; horse soldier; ~ **andante** knight errant.

**caballerosidad** *f* chivalry.

**caballeroso/sa** *adj* noble; gentlemanlike.

**caballete** *m* ridge of a roof; painter's easel; trestle; bridge (of the nose).

**caballo** *m* horse; ~ **de carreras** racehorse; knight (at chess); queen (in cards); **a ~** on horseback.

**cabaña** *f* hut, cabin; hovel; livestock; balk (in billiards).

**cabaré** *m* cabaret.

**cabecear** *vi* to nod (with sleep); to shake one's head; (*mar*) to pitch.

**cabeceo** *m* nod; shaking (of the head).

**cabecera** *f* headboard; head; far end; pillow; headline; vignette.

**cabecilla** *m* ringleader.

**cabellera** *f* head of hair; wig; tail of a comet.

**cabello** *m* hair.

**cabelludo/da** *adj* hairy, shaggy.

**caber** *vi* to fit.

**cabestrillo** *m* sling.

**cabestro** *m* halter; leading/bell ox.

**cabeza** *f* head; chief, leader; main town, chief centre.

**cabezada** *f* butt; nod/shake of the head.

**cabezal** *m* pillow; compress.

**cabezón** *m* collar (of a shirt); opening in a garment for the head.

**cabezudo/da** *adj* big-headed; pig-headed.

**cabida** *f* room, capacity; **tener ~ con una persona** to have influence with someone.

**cabildo** *m* chapter (of a church); meeting of a chapter; town council.

**cabina** *f* cabin; telephone booth.

**cabizbajo/ja, cabizcaído/da** *adj* crestfallen; pensive, thought- ful.

**cable** *m* cable, lead, wire.

**cabo** *m* end, extremity; cape, headland; (*mar*) cable, rope.

**cabra** *f* goat.

**cabrero** *m* goatherd.

**cabrío/a** *adj* goatish.

**cabriola** *f* caper; gambol.

**cabritilla** *f* kidskin.

**cabrito** *m* kid.

**cabrón** *m* cuckold; ¡~! (*col*) bastard!

**cacahuete** *m* peanut.

**cacao** *m* (*bot*) cacao tree; cocoa.

**cacarear** *vi* to crow; to brag, to boast.

**cacareo** *m* crowing of a cock, cackling of a hen; boast, brag.

**cacería** *f* hunting-party.

**cacerola** *f* pan, saucepan; casserole.

**cachalote** *m* sperm whale.

**cacharro** *m* pot; piece of junk.

**cachear** *vt* to frisk.

**cachemir** *m* cashmere.

**cacheo** *m* frisking.

**cachete** *m* cheek; slap in the face.

**cachiporra** *f* truncheon.

**cachivache** *m* pot; piece of junk.

**cacho** *m* crumb, bit, small slice, piece; horn (of an animal).

**cachondeo** *m* (*col*) farce.

**cachondo/da** *adj* randy; funny.

**cachorro/ra** *m/f* puppy; cub (of any animal).

**cacique** *m* chief; local party boss.

**caco** *m* pickpocket; coward.

**cacofonía** *f* cacophony.

**cacto/cactus** *m* cactus.

**cada** *adj invar* each; every.

**cadalso** *m* scaffold.

**cadáver** *m* corpse, cadaver.

**cadavérico/ca** *adj* cadaverous.

**cadena** *f* chain; series, link; radio/TV network.

**cadencia** *f* cadence.

**cadente** *adj* harmonious.

**cadera** *f* hip.

**cadete** *m* (*mil*) cadet.

**caducar** *vi* to become senile; to expire, to lapse; to deteriorate.

**caducidad** *f* expiry.

**caduco/ca** *adj* worn out; decrepit; perishable; expired, lapsed.

**caer** *vi* to fall; to tumble down; to lapse; to happen; to die; **~se** *vr* to fall down.

**café** *m* coffee; cafe, coffee house.

**cafetera** *f* coffee pot.

**cafetería** *f* cafe.

**cafetero/ra** *m/f* coffee merchant; cafe owner.

**cafre** *adj* savage, inhuman; rude.

**cagar** *vi* (*col*) to have a shit.

**caída** *f* fall, falling; slope, descent.

**caimán** *m* caiman, alligator.

**caja** *f* box, case; casket; cashbox; cash desk; check-out, till; **~ de ahorros** savings bank; **~ de cambios** gearbox; **~ negra** black box.

**cajero/ra** *m/f* cashier, teller.

**cajero automático** *m* cash machine, ATM.

**cajetilla** *f* packet.

**cajón** *m* chest of drawers; locker.

**cal** *f* lime; **~ viva** quick lime.

**cala** *f* creek, small bay; small piece of melon etc; (*mar*) hold; dipstick.

**calabacín** *m* small marrow, courgette.

**calabaza** *f* pumpkin, squash.

**calabozo** *m* prison; cell.

**calada** *f* soaking; lowering of nets; puff, drag; swoop.

**calado** *m* openwork in metal, wood/linen.

**calafatear** *vt* (*mar*) to caulk.

**calamar** *m* squid.

**calambre** *m* cramp.

**calamidad** *f* calamity, disaster.

**calamitoso/sa** *adj* calamitous.

**calaña** *f* model; pattern.

**calandria** *f* lark.

**calar** *vt* to soak, to drench; to penetrate, to pierce; to see through; to lower; **~se** *vr* to stall (of a car).

**calavera** *f* skull; madcap.

**calaverada** *f* ridiculous/foolish action.

**calcañar** *m* heel.

**calcar** *vt* to trace, to copy.

**calcáreo/rea** *adj* chalky, calcareous.

**calceta** *f* (knee-length) stocking.

**calcetín** *m* sock.

**calcio** *m* calcium.

**calco** *m* tracing.

**calcomanía** *f* transfer.

**calculable** *adj* calculable.

**calculadora** *f* calculator.

**calcular** *vt* to calculate, to reckon; to compute.

**cálculo** *m* calculation, estimate; calculus; (*med*) gallstone.

**caldear** *vt* to weld; to warm, to heat up.

**caldera** *f* kettle, boiler; **las ~s de Pero Botero** (*col*) hell.

**calderada** *f* stew.

**calderilla** *f* holy-water vessel; small change.

**caldero** *m* small boiler.

**caldo** *m* stock; broth.

**caldoso/sa** *adj* having too much broth/gravy.

**calefacción** *f* heating.

**calendario** *m* calendar.

**calentador** *m* heater.

**calentamiento global** *m* global warming.

**calentar** *vt* to warm up, to heat up; **~se** *vr* to grow hot; to dispute.

**calentura** *f* fever.

**calenturiento/ta** *adj* feverish.

**calesa** *f* calash, cab.

**calibre** *m* calibre; (*fig*) calibre.

**calidad** *f* grade, quality, condition; kind.

**cálido/da** *adj* hot; (*fig*) warm.

**caliente** *adj* hot; fiery; **en ~** in the heat of the moment.

**califa** *m* caliph.

**califato** *m* caliphate.

**calificación** *f* qualification; grade.

**calificar** *vt* to qualify; to assess, to mark; **~se** *vr* to register as a voter.

**caligrafía** *f* calligraphy.

**calistenia** *f* callisthenics.

**cáliz** *m* chalice.

**caliza** *f* limestone.

**calizo/za** *adj* limy (of ground).

**callado/da** *adj* silent, quiet.

**callandico** *adv* softly, silently.

**callar** *vi*, **~se** *vr* to be silent, to keep quiet.

**calle** *f* street; road.

**calleja** *f* lane, narrow passage.

**callejear** *vi* to loiter about the streets.

**callejero/ra** *adj* loitering.

**callejón** *m* alley.

**callejuela** *f* lane, narrow passage; subterfuge.

**callista** *m/f* chiropodist, podiatrist.

**callo** *m* corn; callus; **~s** *mpl* tripe.

**callosidad** *f* hard patch, callosity.

**calloso/sa** *adj* callous; horny.

**calma** *f* calm, calmness.

**calmante** *m* (*med*) sedative.

**calmar** *vt* to calm, to quiet, to pacify. * *vi* to become calm.

**calmoso/sa** *adj* calm; tranquil.

**calor** *m* heat, warmth; ardour, passion.

**caloría** *f* calorie.

**calumnia** *f* calumny, slander.

**calumniar** *vt* to slander.
**calumnioso/sa** *adj* slanderous.
**caluroso/sa** *adj* warm; hot; lively.
**calva** *f* bald patch.
**calvario** *m* Calvary; (*fig*) debts *pl*.
**calvicie** *f* baldness.
**calvinismo** *m* Calvinism.
**calvinista** *m/f* Calvinist.
**calvo/va** *adj* bald; bare, barren.
**calza** *f* wedge.
**calzado** *m* footwear.
**calzador** *m* shoehorn.
**calzar** *vt* to put on (shoes); to wear (shoes); to stop (a wheel); **~se** *vr* to put on one's shoes.
**calzón** *m* shorts *pl*; pants *pl*; panties *pl*.
**calzonazos** *m invar* stupid guy; **es un ~** he is a weak-willed guy.
**calzoncillos** *mpl* underpants *pl*, shorts *pl*.
**cama** *f* bed; **hacer la ~** to make the bed.
**camada** *f* litter (of animals); **~ de ladrones** gang of thieves.
**camafeo** *m* cameo.
**camaleón** *m* chameleon.
**camandulero/ra** *adj* prudish; hypocritical; sly, tricky.
**cámara** *f* hall; chamber; room; camera; cine camera.
**camarada** *m/f* comrade, companion.
**camarera** *f* waitress; maid.
**camarero** *m* waiter.
**camarilla** *f* clique; lobby.
**camarín** *m* dressing room; lift car.
**camarón** *m* shrimp, prawn.
**camarote** *m* berth, cabin.
**cambalache** *m* exchange, swap.
**cambalachear** *vt* to exchange, to swap.
**cambiable** *adj* changeable, variable; interchangeable.
**cambiar** *vt* to exchange; to change. * *vi* to change, to alter; **~se** *vr* to move house.
**cambio** *m* change, exchange; rate of exchange; bureau de change.
**cambista** *m/f* exchange broker.
**camelar** *vt* to flirt with.
**camello** *m* camel.
**camilla** *f* couch; cot; stretcher.
**caminante** *m/f* traveller, walker.
**caminar** *vi* to travel; to walk, to go.
**caminata** *f* long walk; hike.
**camino** *m* road; way.
**camión** *m* truck.
**camioneta** *f* van.
**camisa** *f* shirt; chemise.
**camiseta** *f* T-shirt; vest.

**camisón** *m* nightgown.
**camorra** *f* quarrel, dispute.
**camorrista** *m/f* quarrelsome person.
**campamento** *m* (*mil*) encampment, camp.
**campana** *f* bell.
**campaña** *f* countryside; level country, plain; (*mil*) campaign.
**campanada** *f* peal of a bell; (*fig*) scandal.
**campanario** *m* belfry.
**campaneo** *m* bellringing, chime.
**campanero** *m* bell founder; bellringer.
**campanilla** *f* handbell; (*med*) uvula.
**campante** *adj* excelling, outstanding; smug.
**campánula** *f* bellflower.
**campear** *vi* to go out to pasture; to work in the fields.
**campechano/na** *adj* open.
**campeón/ona** *m/f* champion.
**campeonato** *m* championship.
**campesino/na, campestre** *adj* rural.
**campiña** *f* flat tract of cultivated farmland.
**camping** *m* camping, campsite.
**campista** *m/f* camper.
**campo** *m* country; countryside; field; camp; ground; pitch; scope, range; **~ de refugiados** refugee camp; **~ abierto** open countryside.
**campus** *m invar* campus.
**camuflaje** *m* camouflage.
**caña** *f* cane, reed; stalk; shinbone; glass of beer; **~ dulce** sugar cane.
**canal** *m* channel, canal.
**canalla** *f* mob, rabble.
**canalón** *m* large gutter.
**cáñamo** *m* hemp.
**cañamón** *m* hemp seed.
**canana** *f* cartridge belt.
**canapé** *f* couch, sofa.
**canario** *m* canary.
**canas** *fpl* grey hair; **peinar ~** to grow old.
**canasta** *f* basket, hamper.
**canastilla** *f* small basket.
**canasto** *m* large basket.
**cañaveral** *m* reedbed.
**cancel** *m* storm door.
**cancelación** *f* cancellation.
**cancelar** *vt* to cancel; to write off.
**Cáncer** *m* Cancer (sign of the zodiac).
**cáncer** *m* cancer.
**cancerígeno/na** *adj* carcinogenic.
**canceroso/sa** *adj* cancerous.
**cancha** *f* (tennis) court.
**canciller** *m* chancellor; foreign minister.
**canción** *f* song.
**cancionero** *m* songbook.

**candado** *m* padlock.
**candela** *f* candle.
**candelabro** *m* candlestick.
**candente** *adj* red-hot.
**candidato/ta** *m/f* candidate.
**cándido/da** *adj* simple, naive; white, snowy.
**candil** *m* oil lamp.
**candilejas** *fpl* footlights *pl*.
**candor** *m* candour; innocence.
**canela** *f* cinnamon.
**canelón** *m* icicle.
**cañería** *f* conduit of water, water pipe.
**cangrejo** *m* crab; crayfish.
**canguro** *m* kangaroo; * *f* baby-sitter.
**caníbal** *m/f* cannibal, man-eater.
**canica** *f* marble.
**canícula** *f* dog days *pl*.
**canijo/ja** *adj* weak, sickly.
**canilla** *f* shinbone; arm-bone; tap of a cask; spool.
**canino/na** *adj* canine; **hambre ~a** *f* ravenous hunger.
**canje** *m* exchange.
**canjear** *vt* to exchange.
**caño** *m* tube, pipe; sewer.
**cano/na** *adj* grey-haired; white-haired.
**canoa** *f* canoe.
**canon** *m* canon; tax; royalty; rent.
**cañón** *m* tube, pipe; barrel; gun; canyon.
**cañonazo** *m* gunshot; (*fig*) bombshell.
**cañonear** *vt* to shell, to bombard.
**cañoneo** *m* shelling, gunfire.
**cañonera** *f* gunboat.
**canónico/ca** *adj* canonical.
**canónigo** *m* canon, prebendary.
**canonización** *f* canonization.
**canonizar** *vt* to canonize.
**canoso/sa** *adj* grey-haired; white-haired.
**cansado/da** *adj* weary, tired; tedious, tiresome.
**cansancio** *m* tiredness, fatigue.
**cansar** *vt* to tire, to tire out; to bore; **~se** *vr* to get tired, to grow weary.
**cantable** *adj* suitable for singing.
**cantante** *m/f* singer.
**cantar** *m* song. * *vt* to sing; to chant. * *vi* to sing; to chirp.
**cántara** *f* pitcher.
**cantarín/ina** *m/f* someone who sings a lot.
**cántaro** *m* pitcher; jug; **llover a ~s** to rain heavily, to pour.
**cantera** *f* quarry.
**cantero** *m* quarryman.
**cántico** *m* canticle.
**cantidad** *f* quantity, amount; number.

**cantimplora** *f* water bottle; hip flask.
**cantina** *f* buffet, refreshment room; canteen; cellar; snack bar; bar.
**cantinela** *f* ballad, song.
**canto** *m* stone; singing; song; edge.
**cantón** *m* corner; canton.
**cantonear** *vi* to loaf around.
**cantor/ra** *m/f* singer.
**canuto** *m* (*col*) joint, marijuana cigarette.
**caoba** *f* mahogany.
**caos** *m* chaos; confusion.
**capa** *f* cloak; cape; layer, stratum; cover; pretext; **~ de ozono** ozone layer.
**capacho** *m* hamper; big basket.
**capacidad** *f* capacity; extent; talent.
**capar** *vt* to geld; to castrate; (*fig*) to curtail.
**caparazón** *m* caparison.
**capataz** *m* foreman, overseer.
**capaz** *adj* capable; capacious, spacious, roomy.
**capazo** *m* large basket; carrycot.
**capcionar** *vt* to seize, to arrest.
**capcioso/sa** *adj* wily, deceitful.
**capear** *vt* to flourish (one's cloak in front of a bull); * *vi* (*mar*) to ride out/weather (a storm).
**capellán** *m* chaplain.
**capeo** *m* challenging of a bull with a cloak.
**caperuza** *f* hood.
**capilar** *adj* capillary.
**capilla** *f* hood, cowl; chapel.
**capirote** *m* hood.
**capital** *m* capital; capital sum; * *f* capital, capital city; * *adj* capital; principal.
**capitalismo** *m* capitalism.
**capitalista** *m/f* capitalist.
**capitalizar** *vt* to capitalize.
**capitán** *m* captain.
**capitana** *f* flagship; (woman) captain (in sport).
**capitanear** *vt* to captain; to command.
**capitanía** *f* captaincy.
**capitel** *m* capital (of a column).
**capitolio** *m* capitol.
**capitulación** *f* capitulation; agreement; **~ones** *fpl* marriage contract.
**capitular** *vi* to come to terms, to make an agreement.
**capítulo** *m* chapter of a cathedral; chapter (of a book).
**capó** *m* (*auto*) bonnet.
**capón** *m* capon.
**caporal** *m* chief, ringleader.
**capota** *f* hat, bonnet; (*auto*) hood.
**capote** *m* greatcoat; bullfighter's cloak.
**capricho** *m* caprice, whim, fancy.

**caprichoso/sa** *adj* capricious, whimsical; obstinate.

**Capricornio** *m* Capricorn (sign of the zodiac).

**cápsula** *f* capsule.

**captar** *vt* to captivate; to understand; (*rad*) to tune in to, to receive.

**captura** *f* capture, arrest.

**capturar** *vt* to capture.

**capucha** *f* circumflex (accent); cap, cowl, hood of a cloak.

**capuchino** *m* Capuchin monk; (**café**) ~ cappuccino (coffee).

**capullo** *m* cocoon of a silkworm; rosebud; coarse cloth made of spun silk.

**caqui** *m, adj* khaki.

**cara** *f* face; appearance; ~ **a** ~ face to face.

**carabina** *f* carbine, rifle.

**carabinero** *m* carabineer.

**caracol** *m* snail; seashell; spiral.

**caracola** *f* shell.

**caracolear** *vi* to prance about (of a horse).

**carácter** *m* character; quality; condition; handwriting.

**característico/ca** *adj* characteristic.

**caracterizar** *vt* to characterize.

**caradura** *m/f*: **es un** ~ he's got a nerve.

**caramba** *excl* well!

**carámbano** *m* icicle.

**carambola** *f* cannon (at billiards); trick.

**caramelo** *m* candy.

**caramente** *adv* dearly.

**caramillo** *m* small flute; piece of gossip.

**carantoña** *f* hideous mask; dressed-up old woman (mutton dressed as lamb); ~**s** *fpl* caresses *pl*.

**carátula** *f* pasteboard mask; **la** ~ the stage.

**caravana** *f* group of wagons, camels, pack mules etc travelling in single file ; tailback (of traffic); caravan.

**caray** *excl* well!

**carbón** *m* coal; charcoal; carbon; carbon paper.

**carbonada** *f* grill; kind of pancake.

**carboncillo** *m* charcoal.

**carbonera** *f* coal tip; coal mine.

**carbonería** *f* coalyard.

**carbonero** *m* coal merchant; (*mar*) collier.

**carbónico/ca** *adj* carbonic.

**carbonilla** *f* coaldust.

**carbonizar** *vt* to carbonize.

**carbono** *m* (*chem*) carbon.

**carbunclo/carbunco** *m* carbuncle.

**carburador** *m* carburettor.

**carcaj** *m* quiver.

**carcajada** *f* (loud) laugh.

**carcamal** *m* nickname for an old person.

**cárcel** *f* prison; jail.

**carcelero** *m* warder, jailer.

**carcoma** *f* deathwatch beetle; woodworm; anxious concern.

**carcomer** *vt* to gnaw, to corrode; ~**se** *vr* to grow worm-eaten.

**carcomido/da** *adj* worm-eaten.

**cardar** *vt* to card (wool).

**cardenal** *m* cardinal; cardinal bird; (*med*) bruise, weal.

**cardenalicio/cia** *adj* belonging to a cardinal.

**cárdeno/na** *adj* purple; livid.

**cardíaco/ca, cardiaco/ca** *adj* cardiac. * heart *compd*.

**cardinal** *adj* cardinal, principal.

**cardo** *m* thistle.

**carear** *vt* to bring face to face; to compare; ~**se** *vr* to come face to face.

**carecer** *vi*: ~ **de** to want, to lack.

**carencia** *f* lack.

**careo** *m* confrontation.

**carero/ra** *adj* pricey.

**carestía** *f* scarcity, want; famine.

**careta** *f* pasteboard mask.

**carga** *f* load; freight, cargo; (*mil*) charge; duty, obligation; tax.

**cargadero** *m* loading place.

**cargado/da** *adj* loaded; live (electricity).

**cargador** *m* loader; carrier; longshoreman.

**cargamento** *m* cargo.

**cargar** *vt* to load, to burden; to charge; * *vi* to charge; to load (up); to lean.

**cargo** *m* burden, loading; employment, post; office; charge, care; obligation; accusation.

**carguero** *m* freighter.

**cariarse** *vr* to decay.

**caricatura** *f* caricature.

**caricia** *f* caress.

**caridad** *f* charity.

**caries** *f* (*med*) tooth decay, caries.

**carilargo/ga** *adj* long-faced.

**carilla** *f* side (of paper); beekeeper's mask.

**cariño** *m* fondness, tenderness; love.

**cariñoso/sa** *adj* affectionate; loving.

**caritativo/va** *adj* charitable.

**cariz** *m* look.

**carmelita** *adj, m/f* Carmelite.

**carmesí** *adj, m* crimson.

**carmín** *m* carmine; rouge; lipstick.

**carnada** *f* bait, lure.

**carnal** *adj* carnal, of the flesh; **primo** ~ first cousin.

**carnaval** *m* carnival.

**carn** *f* flesh; meat; pulp (of fruit).

**carné, carnet** *m* driving licence; ~ **de identidad** identity card.

**carnero** *m* sheep; mutton.

**carnicería** *f* butcher's shop; carnage, slaughter.

**carnicero/ra** *m/f* butcher. * *adj* carnivorous.

**carnívoro/ra** *adj* carnivorous.

**carnoso/sa, carnudo** *adj* beefy, fat; fleshy.

**caro/ra** *adj* dear; affectionate; dear, expensive; * *adv* dearly.

**carótida** *f* carotid artery.

**carpa** *f* carp (fish); tent.

**carpeta** *f* table cover; folder, file, portfolio.

**carpintería** *f* carpentry; carpenter's shop.

**carpintero** *m* carpenter.

**carraca** *f* carrack (ship); rattle.

**carrasco/ca** *m/f* evergreen oak.

**carraspera** *f* hoarseness.

**carrera** *f* career; course; race; run, running; route; journey; **a ~ abierta** at full speed.

**carreta** *f* long narrow cart.

**carrete** *m* reel, spool, bobbin.

**carretera** *f* road; ~ **de circunvalación** ring road.

**carretero** *m* carter, cartwright.

**carretilla** *f* carter; truck; trolley; go-cart; squib, cracker; wheel barrow.

**carretón** *m* small cart.

**carril** *m* lane (of highway); furrow; ~ **bus** bus lane.

**carrillo** *m* cheek; pulley.

**carro** *m* cart; car.

**carrocería** *f* bodywork, coachwork.

**carromato** *m* covered wagon, (Gipsy) caravan.

**carroña** *f* carrion.

**carroza** *f* state coach; (*mar*) awning.

**carruaje** *m* carriage; vehicle.

**carrusel** *m* merry-go-round.

**carta** *f* letter; map; document; playing card; menu; ~ **blanca** carte blanche; ~ **bomba** letter-bomb; ~ **credencial/de creencia** credentials *pl*; ~ **certificada** registered letter.

**cartabón** *m* square (tool).

**cartapacio** *m* notebook; folder.

**cártel** *m* cartel.

**cartel** *m* placard; poster; wall chart; cartel.

**cartera** *f* satchel; handbag; wallet; briefcase; postwoman.

**carterista** *m/f* pickpocket.

**cartero** *m* postman.

**cartilaginoso/sa** *adj* cartilaginous.

**cartílago** *m* cartilage.

**cartilla** *f* first reading book, primer.

**cartón** *m* cardboard, pasteboard; cartoon.

**cartuchera** *f* (*mil*) cartridge belt.

**cartucho** *m* (*mil*) cartridge.

**cartuja** *f* Carthusian order.

**cartujo** *m* Carthusian monk.

**cartulina** *f* card, pass; thin cardboard.

**casa** *f* house; home; firm, company; ~ **de campo** country house; ~ **de moneda** mint; ~ **de huéspedes** boarding house.

**casaca** *f* coat.

**casación** *f* abrogation.

**casadero/ra** *adj* marriageable.

**casado/da** *adj* married.

**casamentero/ra** *m/f* marriage-maker, matchmaker.

**casamiento** *m* marriage, wedding.

**casar** *vt* to marry; to couple; to abrogate; to annul; ~**se** *vr* to marry, to get married.

**cascabel** *m* small bell; rattlesnake.

**cascada** *f* cascade, waterfall.

**cascanueces** *m invar* nutcracker.

**cascar** *vt* to crack, to break into pieces; (*col*) to beat; ~**se** *vr* to be broken open.

**cáscara** *f* rind, peel; husk, shell; bark.

**cascarón** *m* eggshell.

**casco** *m* skull; helmet; fragment; shard; hulk (of a ship); crown (of a hat); hoof; empty bottle, returnable bottle; ~**s azules** blue berets.

**cascote** *m* rubble, fragment of material used in building.

**casera** *f* landlady.

**caserío** *m* country house; small village.

**casero** *m* landlord; janitor; * ~/**ra**, *adj* domestic; household *compd*; home-made.

**caset(t)e** *m* cassette; * *f* cassette-player.

**casi** *adv* almost, nearly; ~ **nada** next to nothing; ~ **nunca** hardly ever, almost never.

**casilla** *f* hut, cabin; box office; square (on a chess board); pigeonhole, compartment.

**casillero** *m* (set of) pigeonholes *pl*; luggage locker.

**casino** *m* club, social club.

**caso** *m* case; occurrence, event; happening, casualty; occasion; (*gr*) case; **en ese ~** in that case; **en todo ~** in any case; ~ **que** in case.

**casorio** *m* unwise marriage.

**caspa** *f* dandruff.

**casquete** *m* helmet.

**casquillo** *m* bottle top; tip, cap; point.

**casta** f caste; race; lineage; breed; kind, quality.

**castaña** f chestnut; demijohn.

**castañar** m chestnut grove.

**castañetear** vi to play the castanets.

**castáño** m chestnut tree; ~/na adj brown, chestnut(-coloured).

**castañuela** f castanet.

**castellano** m Castilian, Spanish.

**castidad** f chastity.

**castigar** vt to castigate, to punish; to afflict.

**castigo** m punishment; correction; penalty.

**castillo** m castle.

**castizo/za** adj pure, thoroughbred.

**casto/ta** adj pure, chaste.

**castor** m beaver.

**castrar** vt to geld, to castrate; to prune; to cut the honeycombs out of (beehives).

**casual** adj casual, accidental.

**casualidad** f chance, accident.

**casucha** f hovel; slum.

**casulla** f chasuble.

**cata** f tasting.

**catacumbas** fpl catacombs pl.

**catador/ra** m/f wine tester.

**catadura** f looks pl, face.

**catalejo** m telescope.

**catalizador** m catalyst; catalytic converter.

**catálogo** m catalogue.

**catamarán** m catamaran.

**cataplasma** f poultice.

**catapulta** f catapult.

**catar** vt to taste; to inspect, to examine; to look at; to esteem.

**catarata** f (med) cataract; waterfall.

**catarro** m catarrh.

**catarroso/sa** adj catarrhal.

**catástrofe** f catastrophe.

**catavino** m small cup for tasting wine; ~s m/f invar wine-taster; tippler.

**catecismo** m catechism.

**cátedra** f professor's chair.

**catedral** f cathedral.

**catedrático/ca** m/f professor (of a university).

**categoría** f category; rank.

**categórico/ca** adj categorical, decisive.

**catequismo** m catechism.

**caterva** f mob.

**catolicismo** m catholicism.

**católico/ca** adj, m/f catholic.

**catorce** adj, m fourteen.

**catre** m cot.

**cauce** m riverbed; (fig) channel.

**caucho** m rubber; tyre.

**caución** f caution; (law) security, bail.

**caucionar** vt to prevent, to guard against; (law) to bail.

**caudal** m volume, flow; property, wealth; plenty.

**caudaloso/sa** adj carrying much water (of rivers); wealthy, rich.

**caudillo** m leader.

**causa** f cause; motive, reason; lawsuit; a ~ de considering, because of.

**causal** adj causal.

**causante** m/f originator; * adj causing, originating.

**causar** vt to cause; to produce; to occasion.

**cáustico** m caustic; ~/ca adj caustic.

**cautela** f caution, cautiousness.

**cauteloso/sa** adj cautious, wary.

**cauterizar** vt (med) to cauterize; to apply a drastic remedy to.

**cautivar** vt to take prisoner in war; to captivate, to charm.

**cautiverio** m captivity.

**cautividad** f captivity.

**cautivo/va** adj, m/f captive.

**cauto/ta** adj cautious, wary.

**cava** f digging and earthing of vines; wine cellar; sparkling wine.

**cavar** vt to dig up, to excavate; * vi to dig, to delve; to think profoundly.

**caverna** f cavern, cave.

**cavernoso/sa** adj cavernous.

**cavidad** f cavity, hollow.

**cavilación** f deep thought.

**cavilar** vt to ponder, to consider carefully.

**caviloso/sa** adj obsessed; suspicious.

**cayada** f, **cayado** m shepherd's crook.

**caza** f hunting; shooting; chase; game; * m fighter-plane.

**cazador/ra** m/f hunter; m huntsman; ~ furtivo poacher.

**cazamoscas** m invar flycatcher (bird).

**cazar** vt to chase, to hunt; to catch.

**cazo** m saucepan; ladle.

**cazuela** f casserole; pan.

**cazurro/rra** adj silent, taciturn.

**cebada** f barley.

**cebar** vt to feed (animals), to fatten.

**cebo** m feed, food; bait, lure; priming.

**cebolla** f onion; bulb.

**cebolleta** f spring onion, scallion.

**cebollino** m onion seed; chive.

**cebón** m fattened pig.

**cebra** f zebra.

**cecear** vt to pronounce s the same as c; to lisp.

**cecina** *f* dried meat; salt beef.

**cedazo** *m* sieve, strainer.

**ceder** *vt* to hand over; to transfer, to make over; to yield, to give up; * *vi* to submit, to comply, to give in; to diminish, to grow less.

**cederrón** *m* CD-ROM.

**cedro** *m* cedar.

**cédula** *f* certificate; document; slip of paper; bill; ~ **de cambio** bill of exchange.

**cegar** *vi* to grow blind; * *vt* to blind; to block up.

**cegato/ta** *adj* short-sighted.

**ceguera** *f* blindness.

**ceja** *f* eyebrow; edging of clothes; (*mus*) bridge of a stringed instrument; brow of a hill.

**cejar** *vi* to go backward(s); to slacken, to give in.

**celada** *f* helmet; ambush; trick.

**celador** *m* watchman.

**celda** *f* cell.

**celdilla** *f* cell; cavity.

**celebración** *f* celebration; praise.

**celebrar** *vt* to celebrate; to praise; ~ **misa** to say mass.

**célebre** *adj* famous, renowned; witty, funny.

**celebridad** *f* celebrity, fame.

**celeridad** *f* speed, velocity.

**celeste** *adj* heavenly; sky-blue.

**celestial** *adj* heavenly; delightful.

**celibato** *m* celibacy.

**célibe** *m/f* bachelor, spinster.

**celo** *m* zeal; rut (in animals); Sellotape™; **~s** *mpl* jealousy.

**celofán** *m* Cellophane™.

**celosía** *f* lattice (of a window).

**celoso/sa** *adj* zealous; jealous.

**célula** *f* cell.

**celular** *adj* cellular.

**celulitis** *f* cellulitis.

**celuloide** *m* celluloid.

**cementerio** *m* graveyard.

**cemento** *m* cement.

**cena** *f* dinner, supper.

**cenador** *m* arbour.

**cenagoso/sa** *adj* miry, marshy.

**cenagal** *m* quagmire.

**cenar** *vt* to have for dinner; * *vi* to have supper, to have dinner.

**cencerro** *m* jangle, clatter.

**cenicero** *m* ashtray.

**ceniciento/ta** *adj* ash-coloured.

**ceñido/da** *adj* tight-fitting; sparing, frugal.

**ceñir** *vt* to surround, to circle; to abbreviate, to abridge; to fit tightly.

**cenit** *m* zenith.

**ceniza** *f* ashes *pl*; **miércoles de ~** Ash Wednesday.

**ceño** *m* frown.

**censo** *m* census; tax; ground rent; ~ **electoral** electoral roll.

**censor/ra** *m/f* censor; reviewer, critic.

**censura** *f* censorship; review; censure, blame.

**censurar** *vt* to review, to criticize; to censure, to blame.

**centella** *f* lightning; spark.

**centellear** *vi* to sparkle.

**centena** *f* hundred.

**centenadas** *adv*: **a ~** by hundreds.

**centenar** *m* hundred.

**centenario/ia** *adj* centenary; * *m* centenary.

**centeno** *m* rye.

**centésimo/ma** *adj* hundredth; * *m* hundredth.

**centígrado** *m* centigrade.

**centímetro** *m* centimetre.

**céntimo** *m* cent.

**centinela** *f* sentry, guard; lookout.

**central** *adj* central; * *f* head office, headquarters; (telephone) exchange; ~ **nuclear** nuclear power station.

**centralización** *m* centralization.

**centralizar** *vt* to centralize.

**céntrico** *adj* central.

**centrífugo/ga** *adj* centrifugal.

**centrista** *adj* centrist.

**centro** *m* centre; ~ **comercial** shopping centre.

**centuplicar** *vt* to increase a hundredfold.

**céntuplo/pla** *adj* one hundredfold.

**ceñudo/da** *adj* frowning, grim.

**cepa** *f* stock (of a vine); origin (of a family).

**cepillar** *vt* to brush.

**cepillo** *m* brush; plane (tool).

**cepo** *m* branch, bough; trap; snare; poor box.

**cera** *f* wax; **~s** *fpl* honeycomb.

**cerámica** *f* pottery.

**cerca** *f* enclosure; fence; **~s** *mpl* objects *pl* in the foreground of a painting; * *adv* near, at hand, close by; ~ **de** close, near.

**cercanías** *fpl* outskirts.

**cercano/na** *adj* near, close by; neighbouring, adjoining.

**cercar** *vt* to enclose, to circle; to fence in.

**cerciorar** *vt* to assure, to ascertain, to affirm; **~se** *vr* to find out.

**cerco** *m* enclosure; fence; (*mil*) siege.

**cerdo** *m* pig.

**cereal** *m* cereal.

**cerebelo** *m* cerebellum.

**cerebro** *m* brain.

**ceremonia** *f* ceremony.
**ceremonial** *adj, m* ceremonial.
**ceremonioso/sa** *adj* ceremonious.
**cereza** *f* cherry.
**cerezo** *m* cherry tree.
**cerilla** *f* wax taper; ear wax; match, safety match.
**cerner** *vt* to sift; * *vi* to bud, to blossom; to drizzle; **~se** *vr* to hover; to swagger.
**cernido** *m* sifting.
**cero** *m* nothing, zero.
**cerquita** *adv* close by.
**cerrado/da** *adj* closed, shut; locked; overcast, cloudy; broad (of accent).
**cerradura** *f* locking-up; lock.
**cerrajería** *f* trade of a locksmith; locksmith's shop.
**cerrajero** *m* locksmith.
**cerrar** *vt* to close, to shut; to block up; to lock; **~ una cuenta** to close an account; **~se** *vr* to close; to heal; to cloud over; *vi* to close, to shut; to lock.
**cerril** *adj* mountainous; rough, wild, untamed.
**cerro** *m* hill; neck (of an animal); backbone; combed flax/hemp; **en ~** bareback.
**cerrojo** *m* bolt (of a door).
**certamen** *m* competition, contest.
**certero** *adj* accurate; well-aimed.
**certeza, certidumbre** *f* certainty.
**certificación** *f* certificate.
**certificado** *m* certificate; **~/da** *adj* registered (of a letter).
**certificar** *vt* to certify, to affirm.
**cervato** *m* fawn.
**cervecería** *f* bar; brewery.
**cervecero** *m* brewer.
**cerveza** *m* beer.
**cerviz** *f* nape of the neck; cervix.
**cesación** *f* cessation, stoppage.
**cesar** *vt* to cease, to stop; to fire; to remove from office; * *vi* to cease, to stop; to retire.
**cese** *m* suspension; dismissal.
**cesión** *f* cession; transfer.
**césped** *m* grass; lawn.
**cesta** *f* basket, pannier.
**cestería** *f* basket shop; basketwork.
**cesto** *m* (large) basket.
**cetrino/na** *adj* greenish-yellow; sallow; jaundiced, melancholic.
**cetro** *m* sceptre.
**chabacano/na** *adj* coarse, vulgar; shoddy.
**chabola** *f* shack.
**cháchara** *f* chitchat, chatter, idle talk.

**chacolí** *m* light white wine with a sharp taste.
**chafar** *vt* to crush; to ruin.
**chal** *m* shawl.
**chalado/da** *adj* crazy.
**chale(t)** *m* detached house.
**chaleco** *m* waistcoat.
**chalupa** *f* (*mar*) boat, launch.
**chamarra** *f* sheepskin jacket.
**champán** *m* champagne.
**champiñón** *m* mushroom.
**champú** *m* shampoo.
**chamuscar** *vt* to singe, to scorch.
**chamusquina** *f* scorching; (*fig*) row, quarrel.
**chanchullo** *m* (*col*) fix, fiddle.
**chanciller** *m* chancellor.
**chancleta** *f* slipper.
**chanclo** *m* clog; galosh.
**chándal** *m* tracksuit.
**chanfaina** *f* cheap stew.
**chantaje** *m* blackmail.
**chanza** *f* joke, jest; **~s** *fpl* fun.
**chapa** *f* metal plate; panel; (*auto*) numberplate.
**chaparrón** *m* heavy shower (of rain).
**chapotear** *vt* to wet with a sponge; * *vi* to paddle (in water).
**chapucear** *vt* to botch, to bungle.
**chapucero** *m* bungler; **~/ra** *adj* clumsy, crude.
**chapurrar** *vt* to speak (a language) badly; to mix (drinks).
**chapuza** *f* badly done job.
**chapuzarse** *vr* to duck; to dive.
**chaqueta** *f* jacket; **~ deportiva** sports jacket.
**charca** *f* pool.
**charco** *m* pool, puddle.
**charcutería** *f* shop selling pork meat products.
**charla** *f* chat, talk.
**charlar** *vi* to chat.
**charlatán/ana** *m/f* chatterbox.
**charlatanería** *f* talkativeness.
**charol** *m* varnish; patent leather.
**charrada** *f* coarse thing; bad breeding; bad taste.
**charretera** *f* shoulder pad.
**charro** *m* coarse individual; **~/rra** *adj* coarse; gaudy.
**charter** *m* charter flight.
**chasco** *m* disappointment; joke, jest.
**chasis** *m invar* (*auto*) chassis.
**chasquear** *vt* to crack (a whip); to disappoint.
**chasquido** *m* crack; click.

**chatarra** *f* scrap.

**chato/ta** *adj* flat, flattish; snub-nosed.

**chaval/la** *m/f* lad/lass.

**cheque** *m* cheque.

**chequeo** *m* check-up; service.

**chequera** *f* chequebook.

**chicano/na** *adj* Chicano.

**chicharra** *f* harvest fly.

**chicharrón** *m* (pork) crackling.

**chichón** *m* lump, bump.

**chichonera** *f* helmet.

**chicle** *m* chewing gum.

**chico/ca** *adj* little, small; * *m/f* boy/girl.

**chifla** *f* whistle; hiss.

**chiflado/da** *adj* crazy.

**chiflar** *vt* to boo.

**chile** *m* chilli pepper.

**chillar** *vi* to scream, to shriek; to howl; to creak.

**chillido** *m* squeak; shriek; howl.

**chillón/ona** *adj* loud, noisy; gaudy; * *m/f* whiner, moaner.

**chimenea** *f* chimney; fireplace.

**china** *f* pebble; porcelain, china-ware; China silk.

**chinche** *f* bug; drawing pin; * *m* nuisance.

**chincheta** *f* drawing pin.

**chinela** *f* slipper.

**chino/na** *adj*, *m/f* Chinese; * *m* Chinese language.

**chiquero** *m* pigsty.

**chiripa** *f* fluke.

**chirla** *f* mussel.

**chirriar** *vi* to hiss; to creak; to chirp.

**chirrido** *m* chirping (of birds); squeaking.

**chis** *excl* sh!

**chisgarabís** *m* (*col*) meddler.

**chisme** *m* tale; thingummyjig.

**chismear** *vi* to tell tales.

**chismoso/sa** *adj* gossiping; * *m/f* gossip.

**chispa** *f* spark; sparkle; wit; drop (of rain); drunkenness.

**chispazo** *m* spark.

**chispeante** *adj* sparkling.

**chispear** *vi* to sparkle; to drizzle.

**chisporrotear** *vi* to crackle; to sparkle; to hiss (of liquids).

**chistar** *vi* to speak.

**chiste** *m* funny story, joke.

**chistoso/sa** *adj* witty; amusing, funny.

**chivato** *m* kid; child.

**chivo/va** *m/f* billy/nanny goat.

**chocante** *adj* startling; odd.

**chocar** *vi* to strike, to knock; to crash; * *vt* to shock.

**chochear** *vi* to dodder, to be senile; to dote.

**chocho** *adj* doddering; doting.

**chocolate** *m* chocolate.

**chocolatera** *f* chocolate pot.

**chófer** *m* driver.

**chollo** *m* bargain.

**chopo** *m* black poplar tree.

**choque** *m* shock; crash, collision; clash, conflict.

**chorizo** *m* pork sausage.

**chorlito** *m* plover.

**chorrear** *vi* to spout, to gush; to drip.

**chorrera** *f* channel; frill.

**chorro** *m* gush; jet; stream; **a ~s** abundantly.

**choto** *m* kid; calf.

**choza** *f* hut, shack.

**chubasco** *m* squall.

**chuchería** *f* trinket.

**chucho** *m* mongrel.

**chufleta** *f* joke; taunt, jeer.

**chulada** *f* funny speech/action.

**chulear** *vi* to brag.

**chuleta** *f* chop.

**chulo** *m* rascal; pimp.

**chunga** *f* fun, joke; **estar de ~** to be in good humour.

**chunguearse** *vr* to be in good humour.

**chupado/da** *adj* skinny; easy.

**chupar** *vt* to suck; to absorb.

**chupete** *m* dummy.

**chupetear** *vi* to suck gently.

**chupón/ona** *m/f* (*col*) swindler, sponger.

**churro** *m* fritter.

**churruscarse** *vr* to scorch.

**churrusco** *m* burnt toast.

**chusco/ca** *adj* pleasant; funny.

**chusma** *f* rabble, mob.

**chuzo** *m* little spear/spike; **llover a ~s** to pour heavily.

**cianuro** *m* cyanide.

**ciática** *f* sciatica.

**ciático/ca** *adj* sciatic.

**cibercafé** *m* Internet café.

**ciberespacio** *m* cyberspace.

**cicatear** *vi* to be mean.

**cicatriz** *f* scar.

**cicatrizar** *vt* to heal.

**ciclismo** *m* cycling.

**ciclista** *m/f* cyclist.

**ciclo** *m* cycle.

**ciclón** *m* cyclone.

**cicloturismo** *m* bicycle touriism.

**cicuta** *f* (*bot*) hemlock.

**ciegamente** *adv* blindly.

**ciego/ga** *adj* blind.

**cielo** *m* sky; heaven; atmosphere; climate.

**cien** *adj, m* a hundred.

**ciénaga** *f* swamp.

**ciencia** *f* science.

**cieno** *m* mud; mire.

**cienpiés** *m invar* centipede.

**científico/ca** *adj* scientific.

**ciento** *adj, m* a hundred.

**cierne** *m*: **en ~** in blossom; **estar en ~** to be in its infancy.

**cierre de cremallera** *m*.zip, zip fastener.

**cierto/ta** *adj* certain, sure; right, correct; **por ~** certainly.

**cierva** *f* hind.

**ciervo** *m* deer, hart, stag; **~ volante** stag beetle.

**cierzo** *m* cold northerly wind.

**cifra** *f* number, numeral; quantity; cipher; abbreviation.

**cifrar** *vt* to write in code; to abridge.

**cigala** *f* langoustine.

**cigarra** *f* cicada.

**cigarrera** *m* cigar case.

**cigarrillo** *m* cigarette.

**cigarro** *m* cigar; cigarette.

**cigüeña** *f* stork; crank (of a bell).

**cilicio** *m* hair shirt; spiked belt.

**cilíndrico/ca** *adj* cylindrical.

**cilindro** *m* cylinder.

**cima** *f* summit; peak; top.

**címbalo** *m* cymbal.

**cimbor(r)io** *m* cupola, dome.

**cimbr(e)ar** *vt* to shake, to swish, to swing; **~ a uno** to give one a clout (with a stick); **~se** *vr* to sway.

**cimentado** *m* refinement of gold.

**cimentar** *vt* to lay the foundation of (a building); to found; to refine (metals); to strengthen, to cement.

**cimiento** *m* foundation, groundwork; basis, origin.

**cinc** *m* zinc.

**cincel** *m* chisel.

**cincelar** *vt* to chisel, to engrave.

**cincha** *f* girth.

**cinchar** *vt* to girth.

**cinco** *adj, m* five.

**cincuenta** *adj, m* fifty.

**cine** *m* cinema.

**cineasta** *m/f* film maker.

**cinematográfico/ca** *adj* cinematographic.

**cínico/ca** *adj* cynical.

**cinismo** *m* cynicism.

**cinta** *f* band, ribbon; reel.

**cinto** *m* belt.

**cintura** *f* waist.

**cinturón** *m* belt, girdle; (*fig*) zone; **~ de seguridad** seatbelt.

**ciprés** *m* cypress tree.

**circo** *m* circus.

**circuito** *m* circuit; circumference.

**circulación** *f* circulation; traffic.

**circular** *adj* circular; circulatory; * *vt* to circulate; * *vi* (*auto*) to drive.

**círculo** *m* circle; (*fig*) scope, compass.

**circuncidar** *vt* to circumcize.

**circuncisión** *f* circumcision.

**circundar** *vt* to surround, to encircle.

**circunferencia** *f* circumference.

**circunflejo/ja** *adj*: **acento ~** *m* circumflex.

**circunscribir** *vt* to circumscribe.

**circunscripción** *f* division; electoral district.

**circunspección** *f* circumspection.

**circunspecto/ta** *adj* circumspect, cautious.

**circunstancia** *f* circumstance.

**circunstante** *m/f* bystander.

**circunvalación** *f*: **carretera de ~** bypass.

**cirio** *m* wax candle.

**ciruela** *f* plum; **~ pasa** prune.

**ciruelo** *m* plum tree.

**cirugía** *f* surgery.

**cirujano** *m* surgeon.

**cisco** *m* coaldust.

**cisma** *m* schism; discord.

**cismático/ca** *adj* schismatic.

**cisne** *m* swan.

**cisterna** *f* cistern.

**cisura** *f* incision.

**cita** *f* quotation; appointment, meeting.

**citación** *f* quotation; (*law*) summons.

**citar** *vt* to make an appointment with; to quote; (*law*) to summon.

**cítrico/ca** *adj* citric; **~s** *mpl* citric fruits *pl*.

**ciudad** *f* city; town.

**ciudadanía** *f* citizenship.

**ciudadano/na** *m/f* citizen; * *adj* civic.

**ciudadela** *f* citadel.

**cívico/ca** *adj* civic.

**civil** *adj* civil; polite, courteous; * *m* Civil Guard; civilian.

**civilización** *f* civilization.

**civilizar** *vt* to civilize.

**civismo** *m* public spirit; patriotism.

**cizaña** *f* discord.

**clamar** *vt* to clamour for.

**clamor** *m* clamour, outcry; peal of bells.

**clamoroso/sa** *adj* noisy, loud.

**clandestino/na** *adj* clandestine, secret, concealed.

**clara** *f* egg-white.

**claraboya** *f* skylight.

**clarear** *vi* to dawn; **~se** *vr* to be transparent.

**clarete** *adj*, *m* claret.

**claridad** *f* brightness, clearness.

**clarificar** *vt* to brighten; to clarify.

**clarín** *m* bugle; bugler.

**clarinete** *m* clarinet; * *m/f* clarinetist.

**claro/ra** *adj* clear, bright; evident, manifest; * *m* opening; clearing (in a wood); skylight.

**claroscuro** *m* chiaroscuro (in painting).

**clase** *f* class; rank; order.

**clásico/ca** *adj* classical.

**clasificación** *f* classification.

**clasificar** *vt* to classify.

**claudicar** *vi* to limp; to act deceitfully; to back down.

**claustro** *m* cloister; faculty (of a university); womb, uterus.

**cláusula** *f* clause.

**clausura** *f* closure, closing.

**clavado/da** *adj* tight-fitting; nailed.

**clavar** *vt* to nail; to fasten in, to force in; to drive in; (*col*) to cheat, to deceive; **~se** *vr* to penetrate.

**clave** *f* key; (*mus*) clef; * *m* harpsichord.

**clavel** *m* (*bot*) carnation.

**clavetear** *vt* to decorate with studs.

**clavicordio** *m* clavichord.

**clavícula** *f* clavicle, collar bone.

**clavija** *f* pin, peg.

**clavo** *m* nail; corn (on the feet); clove.

**claxon** *m* horn.

**clemencia** *f* clemency.

**clemente** *adj* clement, merciful.

**cleptómano/na** *m/f* kleptomaniac.

**clerecía** *f* clergy.

**clerical** *adj* clerical.

**clérigo** *m* priest; clergyman.

**clero** *m* clergy.

**clic, click** *m* click.

**cliché** *m* cliché; negative (of a photo).

**cliente** *m/f* client.

**clientela** *f* clientele.

**clima** *m* climate.

**climatizado/da** *adj* air-conditioned.

**clínica** *f* clinic; private hospital.

**clínico/ca** *adj* clinical.

**clip** *m* paperclip.

**cloaca** *f* sewer.

**cloquear** *vi* to cluck.

**clon** *m* clone.

**clonación** *f* cloning.

**clonar** *vt* to clone.

**clónico/ca** *adj* cloned.

**club** *m* club.

**clueca** *f* broody hen.

**coacción** *f* coercion, compulsion.

**coactivo/va** *adj* coercive.

**coadjutor/ra** *m/f* coadjutor (a bishop appointed as an assistant to a diocesan bishop).

**coagular** *vt*, **~se** *vr* to coagulate; to curdle.

**coágulo** *m*: **~ sanguíneo** blood clot.

**coalición** *f* coalition.

**coartada** *f* (*law*) alibi.

**coartar** *vt* to limit, to restrict, to restrain.

**cobalto** *m* cobalt.

**cobarde** *adj* cowardly, timid.

**cobardía** *f* cowardice.

**cobaya** *f* guinea pig.

**cobertizo** *m* small shed; shelter.

**cobertura** *f* cover; coverage; bedspread.

**cobijar** *vt* to cover; to shelter.

**cobra** *f* cobra.

**cobrador/ra** *m/f* conductor/conductress; collector.

**cobrar** *vt* to recover; **~se** *vr* (*med*) to come to.

**cobre** *m* copper; kitchen utensils *pl*; (*mus*) brass.

**cobrizo/za** *adj* coppery.

**cobro** *m* encashment; payment; recovery.

**cocaína** *f* cocaine.

**cocción** *f* cooking.

**cocear** *vt* to kick; (*fig*) to resist.

**cocer** *vt* to boil; to bake (bricks); * *vi* to boil; to ferment; **~se** *vr* to suffer intense pain.

**cochambre** *m* dirty, stinking object.

**cochambroso/sa** *adj* nasty; filthy, stinking.

**coche** *m* car; coach, carriage; pram; **~ bomba** car bomb; (*rail*) **~ cama** sleeping car; **~ restaurante** restaurant car.

**cochera** *f* garage, lockup, carport, depot.

**cochero** *m* coachman.

**cochinilla** *f* woodlouse; cochineal.

**cochino/na** *adj* dirty, filthy; nasty; * *m* pig.

**cochiquera** *f* pigsty.

**cocido/da** *adj* boiled; (*fig*) skilled, experienced; * *m* stew.

**cocina** *f* kitchen; cooker; cookery.

**cocinero/ra** *m/f* cook.

**coco** *m* coconut; bogeyman.

**cocodrilo** *m* crocodile.

**codazo** *m* blow given with the elbow.

**codear** *vt*, *vi* to elbow; **~se** *vr*: **~se con** to rub shoulders with.

**códice** *m* codex, old manuscript.

**codicia** *m* covetousness, greediness.
**codiciable** *adj* covetable.
**codiciar** *vt* to covet, to desire.
**codicilo** *m* (*law*) codicil.
**codicioso/sa** *adj* greedy, covetous.
**código** *m* law; set of rules; code; ~ **postal** post code.
**codillo** *m* knee (animal); (*bot*) stump; (*tec*) elbow (joint), bend; angle iron.
**codo** *m* elbow.
**codorniz** *f* quail.
**coerción** *f* coercion; restraint.
**coercitivo/va** *adj* coercive.
**coetáneo/nea** *adj* contemporary.
**coexistencia** *f* coexistence.
**coexistente** *adj* coexistent.
**coexistir** *vi* to coexist.
**cofia** *f* (nurse's) cap.
**cofrade** *m* member (of a brotherhood).
**cofradía** *f* brotherhood, fraternity.
**cofre** *m* trunk.
**cogedor** *m* shovel; dustpan.
**coger** *vt* to catch, to take hold of; to occupy, to take up; ~**se** *vr* to catch.
**cognitivo/va** *adj* cognitive.
**cogollo** *m* heart of a lettuce/cabbage; shoot of a plant.
**cogote** *m* back of the neck.
**cohabitar** *vi* to cohabit, to live together.
**cohechar** *vt* to bribe, to suborn.
**cohecho** *m* bribery.
**coherencia** *f* coherence.
**coherente** *adj* coherent.
**cohete** *m* rocket.
**cohibido/da** *adj* shy.
**cohibir** *vt* to prohibit; to restrain.
**cohorte** *m* cohort.
**coincidencia** *f* coincidence.
**coincidente** *adj* coincidental.
**coincidir** *vi* to coincide.
**coito** *m* intercourse, coitus.
**cojear** *vi* to limp, to hobble; (*fig*) to go astray.
**cojera** *f* lameness; limp.
**cojín** *m* cushion.
**cojo/ja** *adj* lame, crippled.
**col** *f* cabbage.
**cola**[1] *f* tail; queue; last place.
**cola**[2] *f* glue.
**colaborador/ra** *m/f* collaborator; contributor.
**colaborar** *vi* to collaborate.
**colación** *f* comparison; light meal, snack; buffet meal.
**colada** *f* wash, washing; (*chem*) bleach; sheep run.

**coladero** *m* colander, strainer.
**colador** *m* sieve.
**colapso** *m* collapse.
**colar** *vt* to strain, to filter; * *vi* to ooze; ~**se en** to get into without paying.
**colateral** *adj* collateral.
**colcha** *f* bedspread, counterpane.
**colchón** *m* mattress.
**colchoneta** *f* mattress.
**coleada** *f* wagging (of an animal's tail).
**colear** *vi* to wag the tail.
**colección** *f* collection.
**coleccionar** *vt* to collect.
**coleccionista** *m/f* collector.
**colecta** *f* collection (for charity).
**colectar** *vt* to collect (taxes).
**colectivo/va** *adj* collective.
**colector** *m* collector; sewer.
**colega** *m/f* colleague.
**colegial** *m* schoolboy.
**colegiala** *f* schoolgirl.
**colegiata** *f* collegiate church.
**colegio** *m* college; school.
**colegir** *vt* to collect; to deduce, to infer.
**cólera** *f* bile; anger; fury, rage.
**coléricamente** *adv* in a rage.
**colérico/ca** *adj* angry; furious; bad-tempered.
**colesterol** *m* cholesterol.
**coleta** *f* pigtail.
**colgadero** *m* hook, hanger, peg.
**colgadura** *f* tapestry; hangings *pl*, drapery.
**colgajo** *m* tatter, rag.
**colgante** *adj* hanging; * *m* pendant.
**colgar** *vt* to hang; to suspend; to decorate with tapestry; * *vi* to be suspended.
**colibrí** *m* hummingbird.
**cólico** *m* colic.
**coliflor** *m* cauliflower.
**colilla** *f* end/butt of a cigarette.
**colina** *f* hill.
**colindante** *adj* neighbouring.
**colindar** *vi* to adjoin.
**coliseo** *m* coliseum; opera house; theatre.
**colisión** *f* collision; friction.
**collar** *m* necklace; (dog) collar.
**colmar** *vt* to heap up; * *vi* to fulfil, to realize.
**colmena** *f* hive, beehive.
**colmenar** *m* apiary.
**colmillo** *m* eyetooth; tusk.
**colmo** *m* height, summit; extreme; **a ~** plentifully.
**colocación** *f* employment; placing; situation.
**colocar** *vt* to arrange; to place; to provide with a job; ~**se** *vr* to get a job.

**colon** *m* (*med*) colon.
**colonia** *f* colony; silk ribbon.
**colonial** *adj* colonial.
**colonización** *f* colonization.
**colonizador/a** *m/f* settler; * *adj* colonizing.
**colonizar** *vt* to colonize.
**colono** *m* colonist; farmer.
**coloquio** *m* conversation; conference.
**color** *m* colour, hue; dye; rouge; suit (of cards).
**coloración** *f* colouring, coloration.
**colorado/da** *adj* ruddy; red.
**colorar** *vt* to colour; to dye.
**colorear** *vt* to colour; to excuse.
**colorete** *m* rouge.
**colorido** *m* colouring.
**colosal** *adj* colossal.
**columna** *f* column.
**columnata** *f* colonnade.
**columpiar** *vt*, **~se** *vr* to swing to and fro.
**columpio** *m* swing, seesaw.
**colusión** *f* collusion.
**colza** *f* (*bot*) rape; rape seed.
**coma** *f* (*gr*) comma; * *m* (*med*) coma.
**comadre** *f* midwife; godmother; neighbour.
**comadreja** *f* weasel.
**comadrón/ona** *m/f* midwife.
**comandancia** *f* command.
**comandante** *m* commander.
**comandar** *vt* to command.
**comarca** *f* territory, district.
**comba** *f* curve; warp (of timber); skipping rope.
**combar** *vt* to bend; **~se** *vr* to warp.
**combate** *m* combat, conflict; fighting.
**combatiente** *m* combatant.
**combatir** *vt* to combat, to fight; to attack; * *vi* to fight.
**combinación** *f* combination; (*chem*) compound; cocktail; scheme.
**combinar** *vi* to combine.
**combustible** *adj* combustible; * *m* fuel.
**combustión** *f* combustion.
**comedero** *m* dining room; trough.
**comedia** *f* comedy; play, drama.
**comediante** *m/f* player, actor/actress.
**comedido/da** *adj* moderate, restrained.
**comedirse** *vr* to restrain oneself.
**comedor/ra** *m/f* glutton; * *m* dining room.
**comendatorio/ria** *adj* introductory (of letters).
**comensal** *m/f* fellow diner.
**comentar** *vt* to comment on, to expound.
**comentario** *m* comment, remark; commentary.

**comentarista** *m/f* commentator.
**comenzar** *vi* to commence, to begin.
**comer** *vt* to eat; to take (a piece at chess); * *vi* to have lunch.
**comercial** *adj* commercial.
**comerciante** *m/f* trader, merchant, dealer.
**comerciar** *vi* to trade, to do business.
**comercio** *m* trade, commerce; business; **~ electrónico** e-commerce; **~ justo** fair trade.
**comestible** *adj* eatable; * *mpl* **~s** food, foodstuffs *pl*.
**cometa** *m* comet; * *f* kite.
**cometer** *vt* to commit, to charge; to entrust.
**cometido** *m* task.
**comezón** *f* itch; itching.
**comicios** *mpl* elections *pl*.
**cómico/ca** *adj* comic, comical.
**comida** *f* food; eating; meal; lunch; **~ basura** junk food.
**comienzo** *m* beginning.
**comillas** *fpl* quotation marks *pl*.
**comilón/ona** *m/f* great eater, glutton; * *f* blow-out.
**comino** *m* cumin (plant/seed).
**comisaría** *f* police station; commissariat.
**comisario/-a** *m/f* commissioner.
**comisión** *f* commission; committee.
**comisionado/da** *m/f*; commissioner; committee member.
**comisionar** *vt* to commission.
**comité** *m* committee.
**comitiva** *f* suite, retinue, followers *pl*.
**como** *adv* as; like; such as.
**cómo** *adv* how?; why? * *excl* what?
**cómoda** *f* chest of drawers.
**comodidad** *f* comfort; convenience; **~es** *fpl* wealth, comforts *pl*.
**comodín** *m* joker.
**cómodo/da** *adj* convenient; comfortable.
**compact disc** *m* compact disc.
**compacto/ta** *adj* compact; close, dense.
**compadecer** *vt* to pity; **~se** *vr* to agree with each other.
**compadre** *m* godfather; friend.
**compaginar** *vt* to arrange, to put in order; **~se** *vr* to tally.
**compañero/ra** *m/f* companion, friend; comrade; partner.
**compañía** *f* company.
**comparación** *f* comparison.
**comparar** *vt* to compare.
**comparativo/va** *adj* comparative.
**comparecer** *vi* to appear in court.

**comparsa** *m/f* extra (in the theatre).
**compartimento** *m* compartment.
**compartir** *vt* to divide into equal parts.
**compás** *m* compass; pair of compasses; (*mus*) measure, beat.
**compasión** *f* compassion, commiseration.
**compasivo/va** *adj* compassionate.
**compatibilidad** *f* compatibility.
**compatible** *adj*: ~ **con** compatible with, consistent with.
**compatriota** *m/f* countryman; countrywoman; fellow citizen.
**compeler** *vt* to compel, to constrain.
**compendiar** *vt* to abridge.
**compendio** *m* abridgement; summary.
**compensación** *f* compensation; recompense.
**compensar** *vt* to compensate; to recompense.
**competencia** *f* competition, rivalry; competence.
**competente** *adj* competent; adequate.
**competer** *vi* to be one's responsibility.
**competición** *f* competition.
**competidor/ra** *m/f* competitor, contestant; rival.
**competir** *vi* to vie; ~ **con** to compete with, to rival.
**compilación** *f* compilation.
**compilador** *m* compiler.
**compilar** *vt* to compile.
**compinche** *m* (*col*) pal, mate.
**complacencia** *f* pleasure; indulgence.
**complacer** *vt* to please; ~**se** *vr* to be pleased with.
**complaciente** *adj* pleasing.
**complejo** *m* complex; ~**ja** *adj* complex.
**complementario/ria** *adj* complementary.
**complemento** *m* complement.
**completar** *vt* to complete.
**completo/ta** *adj* complete; perfect.
**complexión** *f* constitution, temperament; build.
**complicado/da** *adj* complicated.
**complicar** *vt* to complicate.
**cómplice** *m/f* accomplice.
**complicidad** *f* complicity.
**complot** *m* plot.
**componer** *vt* to compose; to constitute; to mend, to repair; to strengthen, to restore; to adorn; to adjust; to reconcile; to compose, to calm; ~**se** *vr*: ~**se de** to consist of.
**comportamiento** *m* behaviour.
**comportarse** *vr* to behave.
**composición** *f* composition; composure; agreement; settlement.

**compositor/ra** *m/f* composer; compositor.
**compostura** *f* composition, composure; mending, repairing; discretion; modesty, demureness.
**compota** *f* stewed fruit.
**compra** *f* purchase; ~ **a plazos** hire purchase.
**comprador/ra** *m/f* buyer; customer, shopper.
**comprar** *vt* to buy, to purchase.
**comprender** *vt* to include, to contain; to comprehend, to understand.
**comprensible** *adj* comprehensible.
**comprensión** *f* comprehension, understanding.
**comprensivo/va** *adj* comprehensive.
**compresa** *f* sanitary towel.
**compresión** *f* compression.
**comprimido** *m* pill.
**comprimir** *vt* to compress; to repress, to restrain.
**comprobante** *m* receipt; voucher.
**comprobar** *vt* to verify, to confirm; to prove.
**comprometer** *vt* to compromise; to embarrass; to implicate; to put in danger; ~**se** *vr* to compromise oneself.
**compromiso** *m* compromise.
**compuerta** *f* hatch; sluice.
**compuesto** *m* compound; ~**ta** *adj* composed; made up of.
**compulsar** *vt* to collate; to compare; to make an authentic copy.
**compulsivo/va** *adj* compulsive.
**compunción** *f* compunction, regret.
**compungirse** *vr* to feel remorseful.
**computador** *m*, **computadora** *f* computer.
**computar** *vt* to calculate; to compute.
**cómputo** *m* computation; calculation.
**comulgar** *vt* to administer communion to; * *vi* to receive communion.
**común** *adj* common, usual, general; * *m* community; public; **en** ~ in common.
**comunal** *adj* communal.
**comunicación** *f* communication; report.
**comunicado** *m* announcement.
**comunicar** *vt* to communicate; ~**se** *vr* to communicate (with each other).
**comunicativo/va** *adj* communicative.
**comunidad** *f* community; **Comunidad Europea** European Community.
**comunión** *f* communion.
**comunismo** *m* communism.
**comunista** *adj*, *m/f* communist.
**comunitario/ria** *adj* of the European Union.

**con** prep with; by; ~ **que** so then, providing that.

**coñac** m brandy, cognac.

**conato** m endeavour; effort; attempt.

**concavidad** f concavity.

**cóncavo/va** adj concave.

**concebir** vt to conceive; * vi to become pregnant.

**conceder** vt to give; to grant; to concede, to allow.

**concejal/la** m/f member of a council.

**concejo** m council.

**concentración** f concentration.

**concentrar** vt, ~**se** vr to concentrate.

**concéntrico/ca** adj concentric.

**concepción** f conception; idea.

**concepto** m conceit, thought; judgement, opinion.

**concerniente** adj: ~ **a** concerning, relating to.

**concernir** v imp to regard, to concern.

**concertar** vt to coordinate; to settle; to adjust; to agree; to arrange, to fix up; * vi (mus) to harmonize, to be in tune.

**concesión** f concession.

**concesionario** m agent.

**concha** f shell; tortoiseshell.

**conchabar** vt to mix, to blend; ~**se** vr to plot, to conspire.

**conciencia** f conscience.

**concienciar** vt to make aware; ~**se** vr to become aware.

**concierto** m concert; agreement; concerto; **de** ~ in agreement, in concert.

**conciliación** f conciliation, reconciliation.

**conciliar** vt to reconcile; * adj of a council.

**conciliatorio/ra** adj conciliatory.

**concilio** m council.

**concisión** f conciseness.

**conciso/sa** adj concise, brief.

**conciudadanía** f joint-citizenship.

**conciudadano/na** m/f fellow citizen.

**cónclave** m conclave.

**concluir** vt to conclude, to end, to complete; to infer, to deduce; ~**se** vr to conclude.

**conclusión** f conclusion.

**concluyente** adj conclusive.

**concordancia** f concordance, concord; harmony.

**concordar** vt to reconcile, to make agree; * vi to agree, to correspond.

**concordato** m concordat.

**concordia** f conformity, agreement.

**concretar** vt to make concrete; to specify.

**concreto/ta** adj concrete.

**concubina** f concubine.

**concupiscencia** f lust.

**concurrencia** f concurrence; coincidence; competition; crowd, gathering.

**concurrido/da** adj busy.

**concurrir** vi to meet; to contribute; to coincide; to compete.

**concursante** m/f competitor.

**concurso** m crowd; competition; help, cooperation.

**concusión** f concussion.

**condado** m county.

**conde** m earl, count.

**condecoración** f medal.

**condecorar** vt to adorn; (mil) to decorate.

**condena** f condemnation.

**condenable** adj culpable.

**condenar** vt to condemn; to find guilty; ~**se** vr to blame oneself; to confess (one's guilt).

**condenatorio/ria** adj condemnatory.

**condensación** f condensation.

**condensar** vt to condense.

**condesa** f countess.

**condescendencia** f helpfulness, willingness; acquiescence; compliance.

**condescender** vi to acquiesce, to comply.

**condición** f condition, state; quality; status; rank; stipulation.

**condicionado/da** adj conditioned.

**condicional** adj conditional.

**condimentar** vt to flavour, to season.

**condimento** m condiment, seasoning.

**condiscípulo/la** m/f fellow pupil; fellow student.

**condolerse** vr to sympathize.

**condón** m condom.

**condonar** vt to condone; to forgive.

**conducción** f conveyance; management; (auto) driving.

**conducente** adj: ~ **a** leading to.

**conducir** vt to convey, to conduct; to drive; to manage; * vi to drive; ~ (**a**) to lead (to); ~**se** vr to conduct oneself.

**conducta** f conduct, behaviour; management.

**conducto** m conduit, pipe; drain; (fig) channel.

**conductor/ra** m/f conductor, guide; (rail) guard; driver.

**conectado/da** adj on-line.

**conectar** vt to connect.

**conejera** f warren, burrow.

**conejo** m rabbit.

**conexión** f connection; plug; relationship.

**conexo/xa** *adj* connected, related.
**confabularse** *vr* to conspire.
**confección** *f* preparation; clothing industry.
**confeccionar** *vt* to make up.
**confederación** *f* confederacy.
**confederado/da** *adj* confederate.
**confederarse** *vr* to confederate.
**conferencia** *f* conference; telephone call.
**conferenciar** *vi* to confer; to be in conference.
**conferir** *vt* to award; to compare.
**confesar** *vt* to confess; to admit.
**confesión** *f* confession.
**confesionario** *m* confessional.
**confeso/sa** *adj* (*law*) self-confessed.
**confesonario** *m* confessional.
**confesor** *m* confessor.
**confeti** *m* confetti.
**confiado/da** *adj* trusting; confident; arrogant.
**confianza** *f* trust; confidence; conceit; familiarity; **en ~** confidential.
**confiar** *vt* to confide, to entrust; * *vi* to trust.
**confidencia** *f* confidence.
**confidencial** *adj* confidential.
**confidente** *m/f* confidante; informer.
**configurar** *vt* to shape, to form.
**confín** *m* limit, boundary.
**confinar** *vt* to confine; * *vi*: **~ con** to border upon.
**confirmación** *f* confirmation.
**confirmar** *vt* to confirm; to corroborate.
**confiscación** *f* confiscation.
**confiscar** *vt* to confiscate.
**confite** *m* candy.
**confitería** *f* sweet shop.
**confitero/ra** *m/f* confectioner.
**confitura** *f* preserve; jam.
**conflagración** *f* conflagration.
**conflictivo/va** *adj* controversial.
**conflicto** *m* conflict.
**confluencia** *f* confluence.
**confluir** *vi* to join (applied to rivers); to gather (applied to people).
**conformar** *vt* to shape; to adjust, to adapt; * *vi* to agree; **~se** *vr* to conform; to resign oneself.
**conforme** *adj* alike, similar; agreed; * *prep* according to.
**conformidad** *f* similarity; agreement; resignation.
**conformista** *m/f* conformist.
**confortable** *adj* comfortable.
**confortar** *vt* to comfort; to strengthen; to console.

**confortativo/va** *adj* comforting.
**confraternidad** *f* fraternity.
**confrontación** *f* confrontation.
**confrontar** *vt* to confront.
**confundir** *vt* to confound, to jumble; to confuse; **~se** *vr* to make a mistake.
**confusamente** *adv* confusedly.
**confusión** *f* confusion.
**confuso/sa** *adj* confused.
**congelación** *f* freezing.
**congelado/da** *adj* frozen; * *mpl*: **~s** frozen food.
**congelador** *m* freezer.
**congelar** *vt* to freeze; **~se** *vr* to congeal.
**congeniar** *vi* to get on well.
**congestión** *f* congestion.
**congestionar** *vt* to congest.
**congoja** *f* anguish, distress, grief.
**congraciarse** *vr* to ingratiate oneself.
**congratulación** *f* congratulation.
**congratular** *vt* to congratulate.
**congregación** *f* congregation, assembly.
**congregar(se)** *vt* (*vr*) to assemble, to meet, to collect.
**congresista** *m/f* delegate.
**congreso** *m* congress.
**cónico/ca** *adj* conical.
**conjetura** *f* conjecture, guess.
**conjeturar** *vt* to conjecture, to guess.
**conjugación** *f* (*gr*) conjugation.
**conjugar** *vt* (*gr*) to conjugate; to combine.
**conjunción** *f* conjunction.
**conjuntamente** *adv* together.
**conjunto/ta** *adj* united, joint; * *m* whole; (*mus*) ensemble, band; team.
**conjuración** *f* conspiracy, plot.
**conjurado/da** *m/f* conspirator.
**conjurar** *vt* to exorcize; * *vi* to conspire, to plot.
**conjuro** *m* incantation, exorcism.
**conmemoración** *f* commemoration.
**conmemorar** *vt* to commemorate.
**conmigo** *pn* with me.
**conminación** *f* threat.
**conminar** *vt* to threaten.
**conminatorio/ria** *adj* threatening.
**conmiseración** *f* commiseration, pity, sympathy.
**conmoción** *f* shock; upheaval; commotion; (*med*) concussion.
**conmovedor/ra** *adj* touching.
**conmover** *vt* to move; to disturb.
**conmutación** *f* commutation, exchange.
**conmutador** *m* switch.
**conmutar** *vt* (*law*) to commute; to exchange.

**connotar** *vt* to imply.
**coño** *excl* (*col*) hell!, damn!
**cono** *m* cone.
**conocedor/ra** *m/f* connoisseur.
**conocer** *vt* to know, to understand; **~se** *vr* to know one another.
**conocido/da** *m/f* acquaintance.
**conocimiento** *m* knowledge, understanding; (*med*) consciousness; acquaintance; (*mar*) bill of lading.
**conque** *m* condition.
**conquista** *f* conquest.
**conquistador** *m* conqueror; * *adj* **~/ra** conquering.
**conquistar** *vt* to conquer.
**consabido/da** *adj* well known; above mentioned.
**consagración** *f* consecration.
**consagrar** *vt* to consecrate.
**consanguíneo/nea** *adj* related by blood.
**consanguinidad** *f* blood relationship.
**consecución** *f* acquisition; attainment.
**consecuencia** *f* consequence; conclusion; consistency; **por ~** therefore.
**consecuente** *adj* consistent.
**consecutivo/va** *adj* consecutive.
**conseguir** *vt* to attain; to get, to obtain.
**consejero/ra** *m/f* adviser; councillor.
**consejo** *m* advice; council.
**consenso** *m* consensus.
**consentido/da** *adj* spoiled (of children).
**consentimiento** *m* consent.
**consentir** *vt* to consent to; to allow; to admit; to spoil (a child).
**conserje** *m/f* doorman, porter; caretaker; janitor.
**conservación** *f* conservation.
**conservante** *m* preservative.
**conservar** *vt* to conserve; to keep; to preserve (fruit).
**conservas** *fpl* canned food.
**conservatorio** *m* (*mus*) conservatoire.
**considerable** *adj* considerable.
**consideración** *f* consideration; respect.
**consideradamente** *adv* considerately.
**considerado/da** *adj* respected; considerate.
**considerar** *vt* to consider.
**consigna** *f* (*mil*) watchword; order, instruction; (*rail*) left-luggage office.
**consignación** *f* consignment.
**consignar** *vt* to consign, to dispatch; to assign; to record, to register.
**consignatario/ria** *m/f* consignee.
**consigo** *pn* with him; with her; with you; with oneself.

**consiguiente** *adj* consequent.
**consistencia** *f* consistence, consistency.
**consistente** *adj* consistent; firm, solid.
**consistir** *vi*: **~ en** to consist of; to be due to.
**consistorio** *m* town council; town hall.
**consocio/cia** *m/f* fellow member; partner.
**consola** *f* control panel; console.
**consolación** *f* consolation.
**consolador/ra** *adj* consoling, comforting.
**consolar** *vt* to console, to comfort, to cheer.
**consolidar** *vt* to consolidate.
**consomé** *m* consommé.
**consonancia** *f* consonance.
**consonante** *m* rhyme; * *f* (*gr*) consonant; * *adj* consonant, harmonious.
**consorcio** *m* partnership.
**consorte** *m/f* consort, companion, partner; accomplice.
**conspiración** *f* conspiracy, plot.
**conspirador/ra** *m/f* conspirator, plotter.
**conspirar** *vi* to conspire, to plot.
**constancia** *f* constancy; steadiness.
**constante** *adj* constant; firm.
**constar** *vi* to be evident, to be certain; to be composed of, to consist of.
**constatar** *vt* to note; to check.
**constelación** *f* constellation.
**consternación** *f* consternation.
**consternar** *vt* to dismay; to shock.
**constipado/da**: **estar ~** to have a cold.
**constiparse** *vr* to catch a cold.
**constitución** *f* constitution.
**constitucional** *adj* constitutional.
**constituir** *vt* to constitute; to establish; to appoint.
**constitutivo/va** *adj* constitutive; essential.
**constituyente** *adj* constituent.
**constreñimiento** *m* constraint.
**constreñir** *vt* to restrict; to force; (*med*) to constipate; to constrict.
**constricción** *f* constriction, contraction.
**construcción** *f* construction.
**constructor/ra** *m/f* builder.
**construir** *vt* to form; to build, to construct; to construe.
**consuegro/gra** *m/f* father-in-law/mother-in-law of one's son/daughter.
**consuelo** *m* consolation, comfort.
**cónsul** *m* consul.
**consulado** *m* consulate.
**consulta** *f* consultation.
**consultar** *vt* to consult, to ask for advice.
**consultivo/va** *adj* consultative.
**consultor/ra** *m/f* adviser, consultant.
**consultorio** *m* (*med*) surgery.

**consumación** *f* consummation, finishing.
**consumado/da** *adj* consummate; complete; accomplished; perfect.
**consumar** *vt* to consummate, to finish; to carry out.
**consumición** *f* consumption; drink.
**consumidor/ra** *m/f* consumer.
**consumir** *vt* to consume; to burn, to use; to waste, to exhaust; ~**se** *vr* to waste away, to be consumed.
**consumismo** *m* consumerism.
**consumo** *m* consumption.
**contabilidad** *f* accounting; bookkeeping.
**contable** *m/f* accountant.
**contacto** *m* contact; (*auto*) ignition.
**contado/da** *adj*: ~**s** scarce, few; * *m*: **pagar al** ~ to pay (in) cash.
**contador** *m* meter; counter in a cafe; ~/~**a** *m/f* accountant.
**contaduría** *f* accountancy; accountant's office.
**contagiar** *vt* to infect; ~**se** *vr* to get infected.
**contagio** *m* contagion.
**contagioso/sa** *adj* contagious.
**contaminación** *f* contamination; pollution.
**contaminar** *vt* to contaminate; to pollute; to corrupt.
**contante** *m* cash.
**contar** *vt* to count, to reckon; to tell; * *vi* to count; ~ **con** to rely upon.
**contemplación** *f* contemplation.
**contemplar** *vt* to look at; to contemplate, to consider; to meditate.
**contemplativo/va** *adj* contemplative.
**contemporáneo/nea** *adj* contemporary.
**contemporizar** *vi* to temporize.
**contencioso/sa** *adj* contentious; quarrelsome.
**contender** *vi* to contend, to compete.
**contendiente** *m/f* competitor.
**contenedor** *m* container.
**contener** *vt* to contain, to hold; to hold back; to repress; ~**se** *vr* to control oneself.
**contenido/da** *adj* moderate, restrained; * *m* contents *pl*.
**contentar** *vt* to content, to satisfy; to please; ~**se** *vr* to be pleased/satisfied.
**contento/ta** *adj* glad; pleased; content; * *m* contentment; (*law*) release.
**contestación** *f* answer, reply.
**contestador** *m*: ~ **automático** answering machine.
**contestar** *vt* to answer, to reply; to prove, to corroborate.
**contexto** *m* context.

**contienda** *f* contest, dispute.
**contigo** *pn* with you.
**contigüidad** *f* contiguity.
**contiguo/gua** *adj* contiguous, close.
**continencia** *f* continence, abstinence, moderation.
**continental** *adj* continental.
**continente** *m* continent, mainland; * *adj* continent.
**contingencia** *f* risk; contingency.
**contingente** *adj* contingent, accidental; * *m* contingent.
**continuación** *f* continuation; sequel.
**continuar** *vt, vi* to continue.
**continuidad** *f* continuity.
**continuo/nua** *adj* continuous.
**contonearse** *vr* to walk affectedly.
**contoneo** *m* affected manner of walking.
**contorno** *m* environs *pl*; contour, outline; **en** ~ round about.
**contorsión** *f* contortion.
**contra** *prep* against; contrary to; opposite.
**contraataque** *m* counter-attack.
**contrabajo** *m* (*mus*) double bass; bass guitar; low bass.
**contrabandista** *m/f* smuggler.
**contrabando** *m* contraband; smuggling.
**contracción** *f* contraction.
**contrachapado** *m* plywood.
**contradecir** *vt* to contradict.
**contradicción** *f* contradiction.
**contradictorio/ria** *adj* contradictory.
**contraer** *vt* to contract, to shrink; to make (a bargain); ~**se** *vr* to shrink, to contract.
**contrafuerte** *m* buttress; foothill; heel-pad.
**contragolpe** *m* backlash.
**contrahecho/cha** *adj* deformed; hunchbacked; counterfeit, fake, false.
**contralto** *m* (*mus*) contralto.
**contramaestre** *m* (*mar*) boatswain; foreman.
**contrapartida** *f* (*com*) balancing entry.
**contrapaso** *m* back step.
**contrapelo** *adv*: **a** ~ against the grain.
**contrapesar** *vi* to counterbalance.
**contrapeso** *m* counterpoise; counterweight.
**contraponer** *vt* to compare, to oppose.
**contraposición** *f* comparison; contrast.
**contraproducente** *adj* counterproductive.
**contraprogramación** *f* competitive scheduling.
**contrapunto** *m* (*mus*) counterpoint.
**contrariar** *vt* to contradict, to oppose; to vex.
**contrariedad** *f* opposition; setback; annoyance.

**contrario/ria** *m/f* opponent; * *adj* contrary, opposite; **por el ~** on the contrary.

**contrarreloj** *f* time trial.

**contrarrestar** *vt* to return a ball; (*fig*) to counteract.

**contrarrevolución** *f* counter-revolution.

**contraseña** *f* countersign; (*mil*) watchword.

**contrasentido** *m* contradiction.

**contrastar** *vt* to resist; to contradict; to assay (metals); to verify (measures and weights); * *vi* to contrast.

**contraste** *m* contrast.

**contrata** *f* contract.

**contratación** *f* signing-up, hiring.

**contratar** *vt* to contract; to hire, to engage.

**contratiempo** *m* setback; accident.

**contratista** *m* contractor.

**contrato** *m* contract, agreement.

**contravención** *f* contravention.

**contraveneno** *m* antidote.

**contravenir** *vi* to contravene, to transgress; to violate.

**contraventana** *f* shutter.

**contribución** *f* contribution; tax.

**contribuir** *vt*, *vi* to contribute.

**contribuyente** *m/f* contributor; taxpayer.

**contrincante** *m* competitor.

**contrito/ta** *adj* contrite, penitent.

**controlador/ra** *m/f* controller.

**controlar** *vt* to control; to check.

**controversia** *f* controversy, dispute.

**contumacia** *f* obstinacy, stubbornness; (*law*) contempt of court.

**contumaz** *adj* obstinate, stubborn; (*law*) guilty of contempt of court.

**contundente** *adj* overwhelming; blunt.

**contusión** *f* bruise.

**convalecencia** *f* convalescence.

**convalecer** *vi* to recover from sickness, to convalesce.

**convaleciente** *m/f*, *adj* convalescent.

**convalidar** *vt* to recognize.

**convencer** *vt* to convince.

**convencimiento** *m* conviction.

**convención** *f* convention, pact.

**convencional** *adj* conventional.

**conveniencia** *f* suitability; usefulness; agreement; **~s** *fpl* property.

**conveniente** *adj* useful; suitable.

**convenio** *m* convention, agreement, treaty.

**convenir** *vi* to agree, to suit.

**convento** *m* convent, nunnery; monastery.

**conventual** *adj* monastic.

**convergencia** *f* convergence.

**converger** *vi* to converge.

**conversación** *f* conversation, talk; communication.

**conversar** *vi* to talk, to converse.

**conversión** *f* conversion, change.

**converso/sa** *m/f* convert.

**convertir** *vt*, **~se** *vr* to convert.

**convexo/xa** *adj* convex.

**convicción** *f* conviction.

**convicto/ta** *adj* convicted (found guilty).

**convidado/da** *m/f* guest.

**convidar** *vt* to invite.

**convincente** *adj* convincing.

**convite** *m* invitation; banquet.

**convivencia** *f* living together.

**convocar** *vt* to convoke, to assemble.

**convocatoria** *f* summons; notice of a meeting.

**convoy** *m* convoy.

**convulsión** *f* convulsion.

**convulsivo/va** *adj* convulsive.

**conyugal** *adj* conjugal, married.

**cónyuge** *m/f* spouse.

**cooperar** *vi* to cooperate.

**cooperativa** *f* cooperative.

**cooperativo/va** *adj* cooperative.

**coordinadora** *f* coordinating committee.

**coordinar** *vt* to arrange, to coordinate.

**copa** *f* cup; glass; top of a tree; crown of a hat; **~s** *fpl* hearts *pl* (at cards).

**copete** *m* quiff; pride.

**copia** *f* plenty, abundance; copy, duplicate.

**copiador/ra** *m/f* copyist; copier.

**copiar** *vt* to copy; to imitate.

**copioso/sa** *adj* copious, abundant, plentiful.

**copla** *f* verse; (*mus*) popular song, folk song.

**copo** *m* small bundle; flake of snow.

**copropietario/ria** *m/f* joint owner.

**cópula** *f* copulation; conjunction; (*gr*) copula.

**copulativo/va** *adj* copulative.

**coqueta** *f* coquette, flirt.

**coquetear** *vi* to flirt.

**coquetería** *f* coquetry, flirtation.

**coraje** *m* courage; anger, passion.

**coral** *m* coral; choir; * *adj* choral.

**coraza** *f* cuirass; armor-plating.

**corazón** *m* heart; core; **de ~** willingly.

**corazonada** *f* feeling; inspiration; quick decision; presentiment.

**corbata** *f* tie.

**corbeta** *f* corvette.

**corcel** *m* steed, charger.

**corchea** *f* (*mus*) quaver.

**corchete** *m* clasp; hook and eye.

**corcho** *m* cork; float (for fishing); cork bark.

**cordel** *m* cord, rope; (*mar*) line.

**cordero** *m* lamb; lambskin; meek/gentle person.

**cordial** *adj* cordial, affectionate; * *m* cordial.

**cordialidad** *f* cordiality.

**cordillera** *f* range of mountains.

**cordón** *m* cord, string; lace; cordon.

**cordura** *f* prudence, good sense, wisdom.

**corista** *m/f* chorister.

**cornada** *f* thrust with a bull's horn.

**cornadura** *f* horns *pl*.

**cornamenta** *f* horns of an animal *pl*.

**córnea** *f* cornea.

**cornear** *vt* to gore.

**córneo/ea** *adj* horny, corneous.

**corneta** *f* bugle.

**cornisa** *f* cornice.

**cornudo/da** *adj* horned.

**coro** *m* choir; chorus.

**corona** *f* crown; coronet; top of the head; crown (of a tooth); tonsure; halo.

**coronación** *f* coronation.

**coronar** *vt* to crown; to complete, to perfect.

**coronario/ria** *adj* coronary.

**coronel** *m* (*mil*) colonel.

**coronilla** *f* crown of the head.

**corpiño** *m* bodice.

**corporación** *f* corporation.

**corporal** *adj* corporal.

**corpóreo/rea** *adj* corporeal.

**corpulencia** *f* corpulence.

**corpulento/ta** *adj* corpulent, bulky.

**Corpus** *m* Corpus Christi.

**corral** *m* yard; farmyard; corral; playpen.

**correa** *f* leather strap, thong; flexibility.

**correaje** *m* leather straps *pl*.

**corrección** *f* correction; reprehension; amendment.

**correccional** *m* reformatory.

**correctivo/va** *adj* corrective.

**correcto/ta** *adj* exact, correct.

**corrector/ra** *m/f* proof-reader.

**corredizo/za** *adj* sliding; easy to be untied.

**corredor/ra** *adj* running; * *m/f* broker, runner; *m* corridor.

**corregir** *vt* to correct, to amend; to reprehend; **~se** *vr* to reform.

**correlación** *f* correlation.

**correo** *m* post, mail; courier; postman; **~ electrónico** e-mail; **a vuelta de ~** by return of post; **~s** *mpl* post office.

**correoso/sa** *adj* flexible, leathery.

**correr** *vt* to run; to flow; to travel over; to pull (a drape); * *vi* to run, to rush; to flow; to blow (applied to the wind); **~se** *vr* to be ashamed; to slide, to move; to run (of colours).

**correría** *f* incursion.

**correspondencia** *f* correspondence; communication; agreement.

**corresponder** *vi* to correspond; to answer; to be suitable; to belong; to concern; **~se** *vr* to love one another.

**correspondiente** *adj* corresponding, suitable.

**corresponsal** *m/f* correspondent.

**corretear** *vi* to rush around; to hang about the streets.

**corrida** *f* run, dash; bullfight.

**corrido/da** *adj* expert; knowing; ashamed.

**corriente** *f* current; course, progression; (electric) current; * *adj* current; common, ordinary, general; fluent; flowing, running.

**corrillo** *m* circle of persons; clique.

**corro** *m* circle of people.

**corroborar** *vt* to corroborate.

**corroer** *vt* to corrode, to erode.

**corromper** *vt* to corrupt; to rot; to turn bad; to seduce; to bribe; **~se** *vr* to rot; to become corrupted; * *vi* to stink.

**corrosión** *f* corrosion.

**corrosivo/va** *adj* corrosive.

**corrupción** *f* corruption; rot, decay.

**corruptible** *adj* corruptible.

**corrupto/ta** *adj* corrupted, corrupt.

**corruptor/ra** *m/f* corruptor, perverter.

**corrusco** *m* broken bread.

**corsé** *m* corset.

**cortacésped** *m* lawn mower.

**cortado** *m* coffee with a little milk; **~/da** *adj* cut; sour; embarrassed.

**cortadura** *f* cut; cutting; incision; fissure; **~s** *fpl* shreds *pl*, cuttings *pl*, parings *pl*.

**cortafuegos** *m invar* firebreak, fire lane.

**cortaplumas** *m invar* penknife.

**cortar** *vt* to cut; to cut off, to curtail; to intersect; to carve; to chop; to cut (at cards); to interrupt; **~se** *vr* to be ashamed/embarrassed; to curdle.

**cortauñas** *m invar* nail clippers *pl*.

**corte**[1] *m* cutting; cut; section; length (of cloth); style.

**corte**[2] *f* (royal) court; capital city; **C~s** *fpl* Spanish Parliament.

**cortedad** *f* shortness, smallness; stupidity; bashfulness.

**cortejar** *vt* to court.

**cortejo** *m* entourage; courtship; procession; lover.

**cortés/esa** *adj* courteous, polite.

**cortesana** *f* courtesan.

**cortesía** *f* courtesy, good manners *pl*.

**corteza** *f* bark; peel; crust; (*fig*) outward appearance.

**cortina** *f* curtain.

**cortinaje** *m* set of curtains.

**corto/ta** *adj* short; scanty, small; stupid; bashful; **a la ~a/a la larga** sooner/later.

**corvo/va** *adj* bent, crooked.

**corzo/za** *m/f* roe deer, fallow deer.

**cosa** *f* thing; matter, affair; **¡no hay tal ~!** nothing of the sort!

**cosaco** *m* cossack.

**cosecha** *f* harvest; harvest time; **de su ~** of one's own invention.

**cosechar** *vt* to harvest, to reap.

**coser** *vt* to sew; to join.

**cosido** *m* stitching, sewing.

**cosmético/a** *adj, m* cosmetic.

**cosmopolita** *adj, m* cosmopolitan.

**cosquillas** *fpl* tickling; (*fig*) agitation.

**costa** *f* cost, price; charge, expense; coast, shore; **a toda ~** at all events.

**costado** *m* side; (*mil*) flank; side of a ship.

**costal** *m* sack, large bag.

**costalada** *f* heavy fall.

**costar** *vt* to cost; to need.

**coste** *m* cost, expense.

**costear** *vt* to pay for.

**costera** *f* side; slope; coast.

**costero/ra** *adj* coastal; (*mar*) coasting.

**costilla** *f* rib; (*fig*) wife; cutlet; **~s** *fpl* back, shoulders *pl*.

**costillar** *m* human ribs *pl*.

**costo** *m* cost, price; expense.

**costoso/sa** *adj* costly, dear, expensive.

**costra** *f* crust; (*med*) scab.

**costumbre** *f* custom, habit.

**costura** *f* sewing; seam; needlework.

**costurera** *f* seamstress.

**costurero** *m* sewing box.

**cotejar** *vt* to compare.

**cotejo** *m* comparison, collation.

**cotidiano/na** *adj* daily.

**cotilla** *m/f* gossip.

**cotización** *f* quotation.

**cotizar** *vt* to quote; **~se** *vr*: **~ a** to sell at; to be quoted at.

**coto** *m* enclosure; reserve; boundary stone.

**cotorra** *f* magpie; small parrot; (*col*) chatterbox.

**covacha** *f* small cave, grotto.

**coyote** *m* coyote.

**coyuntura** *f* joint, articulation; juncture.

**coz** *f* kick; recoil (of a gun); ebbing (of a flood); (*fig*) insult.

**cráneo** *m* skull.

**cráter** *m* crater.

**creación** *f* creation.

**creador/ra** *adj* creative; * *m/f* creator.

**crear** *vt* to create, to make; to establish.

**crecer** *vi* to grow, to increase; to rise.

**creces** *fpl* increase.

**crecida** *f* swell (of rivers).

**crecido/da** *adj* full-grown (of a person); large; (*fig*) vain.

**creciente** *f* crescent (moon); (*mar*) flood tide; * *adj* growing; crescent.

**crecimiento** *m* increase; growth.

**credenciales** *fpl* credentials *pl*.

**credibilidad** *f* credibility.

**crédito** *m* credit; belief, faith; reputation.

**credo** *m* creed.

**credulidad** *f* credulity.

**crédulo/la** *adj* credulous.

**creencia** *f* credence, belief.

**creer** *vt, vi* to believe; to think; to consider.

**crema** *f* cream; custard.

**cremallera** *f* zip, zip fastener.

**crepúsculo** *m* twilight.

**crespo/pa** *adj* curled; angry, displeased.

**crespón** *m* crepe.

**cresta** *f* crest (of birds).

**creyente** *m/f* believer.

**cría** *f* breeding; young.

**criada** *f* servant, maid.

**criadero** *m* (*bot*) nursery; breeding place.

**criadilla** *f* testicle; small loaf; truffle.

**criado/da** *m/f* servant; *adj* reared, brought up, bred.

**criador** *f* creator; breeder.

**crianza** *f* breeding, rearing.

**criar** *vt* to create, to produce; to breed; to nurse; to breast-feed; to bring up, to raise.

**criatura** *f* creature; child.

**criba** *f* sieve.

**cribar** *vt* to sift.

**crimen** *m* crime.

**criminal** *adj, m/f* criminal.

**criminalista** *m/f* criminologist; criminal lawyer.

**crin** *f* mane; horsehair.

**crío/a** *m/f* (*col*) kid.

**criollo/lla** *adj, m/f* Creole.

**cripta** *f* crypt.

**crisis** *f invar* crisis.

**crisma** *f* chrism.

**crisol** *m* crucible; melting pot.
**crispar** *vt* to set on edge; to tense up.
**cristal** *m* crystal; glass; pane; lens.
**cristalino/na** *adj* crystalline.
**cristalización** *f* crystallization.
**cristalizar** *vt* to crystallize.
**cristiandad** *f* Christianity.
**cristianismo** *m* Christianity.
**cristiano/na** *adj*, *m/f* Christian.
**Cristo** *m* Christ.
**criterio** *m* criterion.
**crítica** *m/f* criticism.
**criticar** *vt* to criticize.
**crítico/ca** *m/f* critic; * *adj* critical.
**croar** *vi* to croak.
**cromo** *m* chrome.
**crónica** *f* chronicle; news report; feature.
**crónico/ca** *adj* chronic.
**cronista** *m/f* chronicler; reporter, columnist.
**cronología** *f* chronology.
**cronológico/ca** *adj* chronological.
**cronómetro** *m* stopwatch.
**cruce** *m* crossing; crossroads.
**crucero** *m* cruiser; cruise; transept; crossing; Southern Cross (constellation).
**crucificar** *vt* to crucify; to torment.
**crucifijo** *m* crucifix.
**crucigrama** *m* crossword.
**crudeza** *f* unripeness; crudeness; undigested food (in the stomach).
**crudo/da** *adj* raw; green, unripe; crude; cruel; hard to digest.
**cruel** *adj* cruel.
**crueldad** *f* cruelty.
**cruento/ta** *adj* bloody; cruel.
**crujido** *m* crack; creak; clash; crackling.
**crujiente** *adj* crunchy.
**crujir** *vi* to crackle; to rustle.
**crustáceo** *m* crustacean.
**cruz** *f* cross; tails (of a coin).
**cruzada** *f* crusade.
**cruzado** *m* crusader; ~/**da** *adj* crossed.
**cruzar** *vt* to cross; (*mar*) to cruise. ~**se** *vr* to cross; to pass each other.
**cuaderna** *f* fourth part; timber; rib.
**cuaderno** *m* notebook; exercise book; logbook.
**cuadra** *f* block; stable.
**cuadrado/da** *adj*, *m* square.
**cuadragenario/ria** *adj* forty- year-old.
**cuadragésimo/ma** *adj*, *m* fortieth.
**cuadrangular** *adj* quadrangular, four-cornered.
**cuadrángulo** *m* quadrangle.

**cuadrante** *m* quadrant; dial.
**cuadrar** *vt*, *vi* to square; to fit, to suit, to correspond.
**cuadricular** *adj* squared.
**cuadrilátero/ra** *adj*, *m* quadrilateral.
**cuadrilla** *f* party, group; gang, crew.
**cuadro** *m* square; picture, painting; window frame; scene; chart; (*sport*) team; executive.
**cuadrúpedo/da** *adj* quadruped.
**cuádruple** *adj* quadruple.
**cuádruplo/pla** *adj* quadruple, fourfold.
**cuajada** *f* curd.
**cuajar** *vt* to coagulate; to thicken; to adorn; to set; ~**se** *vr* to coagulate, to curdle; to set; to fill up.
**cuál** *pn* which (one).
**cual** *pn* which; who; whom; * *adv* as; like; * *adj* such as.
**cualidad** *f* quality.
**cualquier** *adj* any.
**cualquiera** *adj* anyone, anybody; someone, somebody; whoever; whichever.
**cuándo** *adv* when; ¿**de ~ acá?** since when?
**cuando** *adv* when; if; even; * *conj* since; **de ~ en ~** from time to time; **~ más, ~ mucho** at most, at best; **~ menos** at least.
**cuantía** *f* quantity, amount; importance.
**cuantioso/sa** *adj* numerous; substantial.
**cuantitativo/va** *adj* quantitative, quantitive.
**cuánto** *adj* what a lot of; how much?; ¿**~s?** how many?; * *pn*, *adv* how; how much; how many.
**cuanto/ta** *adj* as many as; as much as; all; whatever; * *adv* **en ~** as soon as; **en ~ a** as regards; **~ más** moreover, the more as.
**cuarenta** *adj*, *m* forty.
**cuarentena** *f* space of forty days; Lent; quarantine.
**cuaresma** *f* Lent.
**cuarta** *f* fourth; span; (*mar*) point (of the compass).
**cuartear** *vt* to quarter, to divide up; ~**se** *vr* to split into pieces.
**cuartel** *m* quarter, district; barracks *pl*.
**cuarteta** *f* (*poet*) quatrain.
**cuartilla** *f* fourth part; sheet of paper.
**cuarto** *m* fourth part; quarter; room, apartment; span; ~**s** *mpl* cash, money; ~/**ta** *adj* fourth.
**cuarzo** *m* quartz.
**cuatrero** *m* horse thief.
**cuatro** *adj*, *m* four.
**cuatrocientos/tas** *adj* four hundred.
**cuba** *f* cask; tub; (*fig*) drunkard.

**cubeta** *f* small cask.

**cúbico/ca** *adj* cubic.

**cubierta** *f* cover; deck of a ship; (*auto*) bonnet; tyre; pretext.

**cubierto** *m* cover; shelter; place at table; meal at a fixed charge; ~s *mpl* cutlery.

**cubil** *m* lair.

**cubilete** *m* tumbler; dice box.

**cubo** *m* cube; bucket.

**cubo de la basura** *m* dustbin.

**cubrecama** *m* bedspread.

**cubrir** *vt* to cover; to disguise; to protect; to roof a building; ~se *vr* to become overcast.

**cucaña** *f* (*col*) soft job; bargain; cinch.

**cucaracha** *f* cockroach.

**cuchara** *f* spoon.

**cucharada** *f* spoonful; ladleful.

**cucharadita** *f* teaspoonful.

**cucharita** *f* teaspoon.

**cucharón** *m* ladle; large spoon.

**cuchichear** *vi* to whisper.

**cuchicheo** *m* whispering.

**cuchilla** *f* large kitchen knife; chopping knife; blade.

**cuchillada** *f* cut; gash; ~s *fpl* wrangles, quarrels.

**cuchillo** *m* knife.

**cuchitril** *m* pigsty.

**cuclillas** *adv*: **en ~** squatting.

**cuclillo** *m* cuckoo; (*fig*) cuckold.

**cuco** *m* cuckoo; ~/ca *adj* sharp.

**cucurucho** *m* paper cornet.

**cuello** *m* neck; collar.

**cuenca** *m* bowl, deep valley; hollow; socket of the eye.

**cuenco** *m* earthenware bowl.

**cuenta** *f* calculation; account; bill (in a restaurant); count, counting; bead; importance.

**cuentakilómetros** *m invar* mileometer.

**cuentarrevoluciones** *m invar* rev counter, tachometer.

**cuentista** *m/f* storyteller.

**cuento** *m* tale, story, narrative.

**cuerda** *f* rope; string; spring.

**cuerdo/da** *adj* sane; prudent, judicious.

**cuerno** *m* horn.

**cuero** *m* hide, skin, leather.

**cuerpo** *m* body; cadaver, corpse.

**cuervo** *m* raven.

**cuesta** *f* slope, hill; incline; **ir ~ abajo** to go downhill; **~ arriba** uphill.

**cuestión** *f* question, matter; dispute; quarrel; problem.

**cuestionable** *adj* questionable, problematic.

**cuestionar** *vt* to question, to dispute.

**cueva** *f* cave; cellar.

**cuidado** *m* care, worry, concern; charge.

**cuidadosamente** *adv* observantly.

**cuidadoso/sa** *adj* careful; anxious.

**cuidar** *vt* to care for; to mind, to look after.

**culata** *f* butt, breech (of a gun); hindquarters *pl* (of an animal); rear of a horse.

**culebra** *f* snake.

**culinario/ria** *adj* culinary.

**culminación** *f* culmination.

**culo** *m* bottom, backside; (*col*) bum.

**culpa** *f* fault, blame; guilt.

**culpabilidad** *f* guilt.

**culpable** *adj* culpable; guilty; * *m/f* culprit.

**culpar** *vt* to accuse, to blame.

**cultivación** *f* cultivation, culture.

**cultivar** *vt* to cultivate.

**cultivo** *m* cultivation; crop.

**culto/ta** *adj* cultivated, cultured; refined; civilized; * *m* culture; worship.

**cultura** *f* culture.

**cumbre** *f* top, summit.

**cumpleaños** *m invar* birthday.

**cumplido/da** *adj* large, plentiful; complete, perfect, courteous; * *m* compliment.

**cumplidor/ora** *adj* reliable.

**cumplimentar** *vt* to compliment.

**cumplimiento** *m* fulfilment; accomplishment; completion.

**cumplir** *vt* to carry out, to fulfil; to serve (a prison sentence); to carry out (death penalty); to attain, to reach (a certain age); ~se *vr* to be fulfilled; to expire, to be up.

**cúmulo** *m* heap, pile.

**comunicado** *m* communiqué.

**cuna** *f* cradle.

**cuña** *f* wedge.

**cuñado/da** *m/f* brother/sister-in-law.

**cundir** *vi* to spread; to grow, to increase.

**cuneta** *f* ditch.

**cuota** *f* quota; fee.

**cupé** *m* (*auto*) coupé.

**cupo** *m* share.

**cupón** *m* coupon.

**cúpula** *f* cupola, dome.

**cura** *m* priest; * *f* cure; treatment.

**curable** *adj* curable.

**curación** *f* cure; curing.

**curandero** *m* quack (doctor).

**curar** *vt* to cure; to treat, to dress (a wound); to salt; to dress; to tan.

**curativo/va** *adj* curative, healing.

**curia** *f* ecclesiastical court.

**curiosear** *vt* to glance at; * *vi* to look round.

**curiosidad** *f* curiosity.
**curioso/sa** *adj* curious; * *m/f* bystander.
**currante** *m/f* (*col*) worker.
**currar** *vi* (*col*) to work.
**currículum** *m* curriculum vitae.
**cursado/da** *adj* skilled; versed.
**cursar** *vt* to frequent a place; to send, to dispatch; to study.
**cursillo** *m* short course of lectures (in a university).
**cursivo/va** *adj* italic (type).
**curso** *m* course, direction; year (at university); subject.
**cursor** *m* cursor.
**curtidor** *m* tanner.
**curtidos** *mpl* tanned leather.

**curtir** *vt* to tan leather; ~**se** *vr* to become sunburned; to become inured.
**curva** *f* curve, bend.
**curvatura** *f* curvature.
**curvilíneo/nea** *adj* curvilinear.
**curvo/va** *adj* curved, bent.
**cuscurro** *m* little crust of bread.
**cúspide** *f* summit, peak; apex.
**custodia** *f* custody, safekeeping, care; monstrance.
**custodio** *m* guard, keeper; watchman.
**cutáneo/nea** *adj* cutaneous.
**cutícula** *f* cuticle.
**cutis** *m* skin.
**cutre** *adj* (*col*) mean, grotty.
**cuyo/ya** *pn* whose, of which, of whom.

# D

**dactilógrafo/fa** *m/f* typist.
**dádiva** *f* gift, present; donation.
**dadivoso/sa** *adj* generous, open-handed.
**dado** *m* die; **~s** dice.
**daga** *f* dagger.
**dale** *excl* come on!
**daltónico/ca** *adj* colour-blind.
**dama** *f* lady, gentlewoman; mistress; queen; actress who performs principal parts.
**damasco** *m* damask (fabric); damson (plum).
**damasquino/na** *adj* damask.
**damero** *m* checkers board.
**damnificar** *vt* to hurt, to injure, to damage.
**danza** *f* dance.
**danzar** *vi* to dance; to meddle.
**danzarín** *m* fine dancer; meddler.
**dañar** *vt* to hurt, to injure, to damage.
**dañino/na** *adj* harmful; noxious; mischievous.
**daño** *m* harm, damage; prejudice; loss.
**dar** *vt* to give; to supply, to administer, to afford; to deliver; to bestow; to strike, to beat, to knock; to communicate; **~se** *vr* to conform (to the will of another); to give oneself up; **~se prisa** to hurry.
**dardo** *m* dart.
**datar** *vt* to date.
**dátil** *m* (*bot*) date.
**dativo** *m* (*gr*) dative.
**dato** *m* fact.
**de** *prep* of; from; for; by; on; to; with.
**deambular** *vi* to stroll.
**deán** *m* dean.
**debajo** *adv* under, underneath, below.
**debate** *m* debate, discussion; contest; altercation.
**debatir** *vt* to debate, to argue, to discuss.
**debe** *m* (*com*) debit; **~ y haber** debit and credit.
**deber** *m* obligation, duty; debt; * *vt* to owe; to be obliged to; * *vi*: **debe (de)** it must, it should.
**debidamente** *adv* justly, duly; exactly, perfectly.
**débil** *adj* feeble, weak; sickly; frail.
**debilidad** *f* dimness; weakness.
**debilitar** *vt* to debilitate, to weaken.
**débito** *m* debt; duty.
**debutar** *vi* to make one's debut.
**década** *f* decade.
**decadencia** *f* decay, decline.
**decaer** *vi* to decay, to moulder; to decline, to fade.

**decaimiento** *m* decay, decline.
**decálogo** *m* Decalogue.
**decano** *m* senior; dean.
**decantar** *vt* to decant.
**decapitación** *f* decapitation, beheading.
**decapitar** *vt* to behead.
**decena** *f* ten.
**decencia** *f* decency.
**decente** *adj* decent; honest.
**decepción** *f* disappointment.
**decidir** *vt* to decide, to determine.
**decimal** *adj* decimal.
**décimo/ma** *adj*, *m* tenth.
**decir** *vt* to say; to tell; to speak; to name.
**decisión** *f* decision; determination, resolution; sentence.
**decisivo/va** *adj* decisive; final.
**declamación** *f* declamation, discourse, oration.
**declamar** *vi* to declaim; to harangue.
**declaración** *f* declaration; explanation, interpretation; (*law*) deposition.
**declarar** *vt* to declare; to manifest; to expound; to explain; (*law*) to decide; **~se** *vr* to declare one's opinion; * *vi* to testify.
**declinación** *f* declination, descent; decline.
**declinar** *vi* to decline; to decay, to degenerate; * *vt* (*gr*) to decline.
**declive** *m* slope; decline.
**decolorarse** *vr* to become discoloured.
**decomiso** *m* confiscation.
**decoración** *f* decoration.
**decorado** *m* scenery.
**decorar** *vt* to decorate, to adorn; to illustrate.
**decorativo/va** *adj* decorative.
**decoro** *m* honour, respect; circumspection; honesty; decency.
**decoroso/sa** *adj* decorous, decent.
**decrecer** *vi* to decrease.
**decrépito/ta** *adj* decrepit, worn out with age.
**decrepitud** *f* decrepitude.
**decretar** *vt* to decree, to determine.
**decreto** *m* decree; decision; judicial decree.
**dechado** *m*: **~ de virtudes** model of virtue and perfection.
**dedal** *m* thimble; very small drinking glass.
**dedicación** *f* dedication; consecration.
**dedicar** *vt* to dedicate, to devote; to consecrate; **~se** *vr* to apply oneself to.

**dedicatoria** *f* dedication.

**dedo** *m* finger; toe; small bit; ~ **meñique** little finger; ~ **pulgar** thumb; ~ **índice** index finger; ~ **corazón** middle finger; ~ **anular** ring finger.

**deducción** *f* deduction, inference; derivation.

**deducir** *vt* to deduce, to infer; to allege in pleading; to subtract.

**defección** *f* defection; apostasy.

**defectivo/va** *adj* defective.

**defecto** *m* defect; defectiveness.

**defectuoso/sa** *adj* defective, imperfect, faulty.

**defender** *vt* to defend, to protect; to justify, to assert, to maintain; to prohibit, to forbid; to resist, to oppose.

**defensa** *f* defence, justification, apology; guard, shelter, protection, fence.

**defensiva** *f* defensive.

**defensivo** *m* defence, safeguard; ~/**va** *adj* defensive.

**defensor/ra** *m/f* defender, protector; lawyer, defence counsel.

**deferente** *adj* pliant, docile, yielding.

**deferir** *vi* to defer; to yield (to another's opinion); * *vt* to communicate.

**deficiencia** *f* deficiency.

**deficiente** *adj* defective.

**déficit** *m* deficit.

**definición** *f* definition; decision.

**definir** *vt* to define, to describe, to explain; to decide.

**definitivo/va** *adj* definitive; positive.

**deformar** *vt* to deform; ~**se** *vr* to become deformed.

**deforme** *adj* deformed; ugly.

**deformidad** *f* deformity; ugliness; gross error.

**defraudación** *f* fraud; usurpation.

**defraudar** *vt* to defraud, to cheat; to usurp; to disturb.

**defunción** *f* death; funeral.

**degeneración** *f* degeneration; degeneracy.

**degenerar** *vi* to degenerate.

**degollación** *f* beheading.

**degollar** *vt* to behead; to destroy, to ruin.

**degradación** *f* degradation.

**degradar** *vt* to degrade; ~**se** *vr* to degrade/demean oneself.

**degustar** *vt* to taste.

**dehesa** *f* pasture, field.

**deidad** *f* deity, divinity; goddess.

**dejadez** *f* slovenliness, neglect.

**dejado/da** *adj* slovenly, idle, indolent; dejected.

**dejar** *vt* to leave, to quit; to omit; to let; to permit, to allow; to leave, to forsake; to bequeath; to pardon; ~ **de** to stop; to fail to; ~**se** *vr* to abandon oneself.

**dejo** *m* accent; aftertaste, tang.

**del** *adj* of the (contraction of *de* and *el*).

**delantal** *m* apron.

**delante** *adv* in front; opposite; ahead; ~ **de** in front of; before.

**delantera** *f* front, forepart (of something); advantage; forward line.

**delantero/ra** *adj* front; * *m/f* forward.

**delatar** *vt* to accuse; to denounce.

**delator** *m* accuser; informer, denouncer.

**delegación** *f* delegation; substitution.

**delegado/da** *m/f* delegate; deputy.

**delegar** *vt* to delegate; to substitute.

**deleitar** *vt* to delight.

**deletrear** *vt* to spell; to examine; to conjecture.

**delfín** *m* dolphin; dauphin.

**delgadez** *f* thinness.

**delgado/da** *adj* thin; delicate, fine; light; slender, lean; acute; ingenious; little, scanty.

**deliberación** *f* deliberation; resolution.

**deliberadamente** *adv* deliberately.

**deliberar** *vi* to consider, to deliberate; * *vt* to debate; to consult.

**delicadeza** *f* tenderness, softness; delicacy, daintiness; subtlety.

**delicado/da** *adj* delicate, tender; faint; exquisite; delicious, dainty; slender, subtle.

**delicia** *f* delight, pleasure.

**delicioso/sa** *adj* delicious; delightful.

**delincuencia** *f* delinquency.

**delincuente** *m* delinquent.

**delineante** *m/f* draftsman/woman.

**delinear** *vt* to delineate, to sketch; to describe.

**delinquir** *vi* to offend.

**delirante** *adj* delirious.

**delirar** *vi* to rave; to talk nonsense.

**delirio** *m* delirium; dotage; nonsense.

**delito** *m* offence; crime.

**demacrado/da** *adj* pale and drawn.

**demagogia** *f* demagogy.

**demagogo** *m* demagogue.

**demanda** *f* demand, claim; pretension, complaint; challenge; request.

**demandado/da** *m/f* defendant.

**demandante** *m/f* claimant.

**demandar** *vt* to demand; to ask; to claim; to sue.

**demarcación** *f* demarcation; boundary line.

**demarcar** *vt* to mark out (limits).

**demás** *adj* other; remaining; * *pn* los/las ~ the others, the rest; **estar** ~ to be over and above; to be useless/superfluous; **por** ~ in vain, to no purpose.

**demasía** *f* excess; arduous enterprise; rudeness; want of respect; abundance, plenty; **en** ~ excessively.

**demasiado/da** *adj* too; excessive; * *adv* too, too much.

**demencia** *f* madness.

**demente** *adj* mad, insane.

**democracia** *f* democracy.

**demócrata** *m/f* democrat.

**democrático/ca** *adj* democratic.

**demoler** *vt* to demolish; to destroy.

**demolición** *f* demolition.

**demonio** *m* demon.

**demora** *f* delay; demurrage.

**demorar** *vt* to delay; ~se *vr* to be delayed; * *vi* to linger.

**demostrable** *adj* demonstrable.

**demostración** *f* demonstration; manifestation.

**demostrar** *vt* to prove, to demonstrate; to manifest.

**demostrativo/va** *adj* demonstrative.

**denegación** *f* denial; refusal.

**denegar** *vt* to deny; to refuse.

**dengue** *m* prudery.

**denigración** *f* defamation; stigma, disgrace.

**denigrar** *vt* to blacken; to insult.

**denominación** *f* denomination.

**denominar** *vt* to name; to designate.

**denotar** *vt* to denote; to express.

**densidad** *f* density; obscurity.

**denso/sa** *adj* dense, thick; compact.

**dentado/da** *adj* jagged, toothed; perforated (of stamps).

**dentadura** *f* set of teeth.

**dentellada** *f* gnashing of the teeth; nip; pinch with the teeth; **a** ~s snappishly, peevishly.

**dentera** *f* (*fig*) the shivers *pl*.

**dentición** *f* dentition, teething.

**dentífrico** *m* toothpaste.

**dentista** *m/f* dentist.

**dentro** *adv* within; * *pn*: ~ **de** in, inside.

**denuncia** *f* denunciation; accusation; report.

**denunciar** *vt* to advise; to denounce; to report.

**deparar** *vt* to offer, to present.

**departamento** *m* department; (*rail*) compartment; apartment.

**dependencia** *f* dependency; relation, affinity; dependence; office; business, affair.

**depender** *vi*: ~ **de** to depend on, to be dependent on.

**dependienta** *f* saleswoman.

**dependiente** *m* shop assistant; * *adj* dependent.

**depilar** *vt* to depilate, remove hair from.

**depilatorio** *m* hair remover.

**deplorable** *adj* deplorable, lamentable.

**deplorar** *vt* to deplore.

**deponer** *vt* to depose; to declare; to displace; to deposit.

**deportación** *f* deportation.

**deportar** *vt* to deport.

**deporte** *m* sport.

**deportista** *m/f* sportsman/woman.

**deportivo/va** *adj* sports *compd*.

**deposición** *f* deposition; assertion, affirmation; (*law*) deposition upon oath.

**depositar** *vt* to deposit; to confide; to put away for safekeeping.

**depósito** *m* deposit; warehouse; tank.

**depravación** *f* depravity.

**depravar** *vt* to deprave, to corrupt.

**depreciar** *vt* to depreciate.

**depredador/ra** *adj* predatory; * *m* predator.

**depresión** *f* depression.

**deprimido/da** *adj* depressed.

**deprimir** *vt* to depress; ~se *vr* to become depressed.

**deprisa** *adv* quickly.

**depuración** *f* purification.

**depuradora** *f* purifier.

**depurar** *vt* to cleanse; to purify; to filter.

**de quitapón** *adj* detachable, removable.

**derecha** *f* right hand, right side; right.

**derecho/cha** *adj* right; straight; just; perfect; certain; * *m* right, justice; law; tax, duty; fee; * *adv* straight.

**derivación** *f* derivation; source; origin.

**derivado/da** *adj* derivative; * *m* derivative; by-product.

**derivar** *vt*, *vi* to derive; (*mar*) to drift.

**dermatología** *f* dermatology.

**dermatólogo/ga** *m/f* dermatologist.

**derogar** *vt* to derogate, to abolish; to reform.

**derogatorio/ria** *adj* derogatory.

**derramamiento** *m* effusion; waste; dispersion; ~ **de sangre** bloodshed.

**derramar** *vt* to drain off (water); to spread; to spill, to scatter; to waste, to shed; ~se *vr* to pour out.

**derrame** *m* spelling; overflow; discharge; leakage.

**derredor** *m* circumference, circuit; **al ~, en ~** around, about.

**derrengado/da** *adj* bent, crooked.

**derrengar** *vt* to sprain.

**derretir** *vt* to melt; to consume; to thaw; **~se** *vr* to melt.

**derribar** *vt* to demolish; to flatten.

**derribo** *m* demolition; ruins of a demolished building *pl*.

**derrocar** *vt* to pull down, to demolish.

**derrochador** *m* spendthrift.

**derrochar** *vt* to dissipate; to squander.

**derroche** *m* waste.

**derrota** *f* ship's course; road, path; defeat.

**derrotar** *vt* to destroy; to defeat.

**derrotero** *m* collection of sea charts; ship's course; (*fig*) course, way.

**derruir** *vt* to demolish.

**derrumbar** *vt* to throw down; **~se** *vr* to collapse.

**desabastecer** *vt* to cut off supplies from.

**desabillé** *m* deshabille, dishabille.

**desabollar** *vt* to take bulges out of.

**desabotonar** *vt* to unbutton; **~se** *vr* to come undone.

**desabrido/da** *adj* tasteless, insipid; rude; unpleasant.

**desabrigado/da** *adj* uncovered; unsheltered.

**desabrigar** *vt* to uncover; to deprive of clothes/shelter.

**desabrochar** *vt* to undo; **~se** *vr* to come undone.

**desacatar** *vt* to treat in a disrespectful manner.

**desacato** *m* disrespect, incivility.

**desacertado/da** *adj* mistaken; unwise; inconsiderate.

**desacierto** *m* error, gross mistake, blunder.

**desaconsejado/da** *adj* inconsiderate; ill-advised.

**desaconsejar** *vt* to advise against.

**desacorde** *adj* discordant.

**desacostumbrado/da** *adj* unusual.

**desacreditar** *vt* to discredit.

**desacuerdo** *m* blunder; disagreement; forgetfulness.

**desafiar** *vt* to challenge; to defy.

**desafilado/da** *adj* blunt.

**desafinado/da** *adj* out of tune.

**desafinar** *vi* to be out of tune.

**desafío** *m* challenge; struggle; contest, combat.

**desaforado/da** *adj* huge; disorderly, lawless; impudent.

**desafortunadamente** *adv* unfortunately.

**desafortunado/da** *adj* unfortunate, unlucky.

**desafuero** *m* outrage; excess.

**desagradable** *adj* disagreeable, unpleasant.

**desagradar** *vt* to displease; to pester.

**desagradecido/da** *adj* ungrateful.

**desagradecimiento** *m* ingratitude.

**desagrado** *m* harshness; displeasure.

**desagraviar** *vt* to make amends for.

**desagravio** *m* amends *pl*; satisfaction.

**desaguar** *vt* to drain; * *vi* to drain off.

**desagüe** *m* channel, drain; drainpipe; drainage.

**desaguisado** *m* outrage.

**desahogado/da** *adj* comfortable; roomy.

**desahogar** *vt* to ease; to vent; **~se** *vr* to recover; to relax; to let off steam.

**desahogo** *m* ease, relief; freedom.

**desahuciar** *vt* to cause to despair; to give up; to evict.

**desahucio** *m* eviction.

**desairado/da** *adj* disregarded; slighted.

**desairar** *vt* to disregard, to take no notice of.

**desaire** *m* disdain, disrespect; unattractiveness.

**desajustar** *vt* to make uneven; to unbalance; **~se** *vr* to get out of order.

**desajuste** *m* disorder; imbalance.

**desalentador/ra** *adj* disheartening.

**desalentar** *vt* to put out of breath; to discourage.

**desaliento** *m* dismay.

**desaliño** *m* slovenliness; carelessness.

**desalinizadora** *f* desalination plant.

**desalinizar** *vt* to desalinate.

**desalmado/da** *adj* cruel, inhuman.

**desalojar** *vt* to eject; to move out; * *vi* to move out.

**desamarrar** *vt* to cast off (a ship); to untie; to remove.

**desamor** *m* indifference.

**desamparado/da** *adj* helpless.

**desamparar** *vt* to forsake, to abandon; to relinquish.

**desamparo** *m* abandonment; helplessness; dereliction.

**desamueblar** *vt* to remove the furniture from.

**desandar** *vt* to retrace; to go back the same road.

**desangrar** *vt* to bleed; to drain (a pond); (*fig*) to exhaust (one's means); **~se** *vr* to lose a lot of blood.

**desanimado/da** *adj* downhearted.

**desanimar** *vt* to discourage; **~se** *vr* to lose heart.

**desapacible** *adj* disagreeable; unpleasant, harsh.

**desaparecer** *vi* to disappear.

**desaparecido/da** *adj* missing; * *mpl* ~s missing people.

**desaparejar** *vt* to unharness, unhitch (beasts); (*mar*) to unrig (a ship).

**desaparición** *f* disappearance.

**desapego** *m* coolness; lack of interest.

**desapercibido/da** *adj* unnoticed.

**desaplicado/da** *adj* lazy; careless, neglectful.

**desapolillar** *vt* to free from moths; ~se *vr* (*fig*) to get rid of the cobwebs.

**desaprensivo/va** *adj* unscrupulous.

**desaprobación** *f* disapproval.

**desaprobar** *vt* to disapprove; to condemn; to reject.

**desaprovechado/da** *adj* useless; unprofitable; backward; slack.

**desaprovechar** *vt* to waste, to turn to a bad use.

**desarmar** *vt* to disarm; to disband (troops); to dismantle; (*fig*) to pacify.

**desarme** *m* disarmament.

**desarraigar** *vt* to uproot; to root out; to extirpate.

**desarraigo** *m* eradication.

**desarrapado/da** *adj* ragged.

**desarreglado/da** *adj* untidy.

**desarreglar** *vt* to disorder, to upset.

**desarreglo** *m* disorder; untidiness.

**desarrollar** *vt* to develop; to unroll; to unfold; ~se *vr* to develop; to be unfolded; to open.

**desarrollo** *m* development.

**desarropar** *vt* to undress.

**desarticular** *vt* to take apart.

**desasir** *vt* to loosen, to disentangle; ~se *vr* to extricate oneself.

**desasosegar** *vt* to disquiet, to disturb.

**desasosiego** *m* restlessness; anxiety.

**desastrado/da** *adj* wretched, miserable; ragged.

**desastre** *m* disaster; misfortune.

**desastroso/sa** *adj* disastrous.

**desatado/da** *adj* untied; wild.

**desatar** *vt* to untie, to loose; to separate; to solve; ~se *vr* to come undone; to break.

**desatascar** *vt* to unblock; to clear.

**desatender** *vt* to pay no attention to; to disregard.

**desatinado/da** *adj* foolish; extravagant; * *m* fool, madman.

**desatinar** *vi* to talk nonsense; to reel, to stagger.

**desatino** *m* blunder; nonsense.

**desatornillar** *vt* to unscrew.

**desatrancar** *vt* to unbar; to unblock.

**desautorizado/da** *adj* unauthorized.

**desautorizar** *vt* to deprive of authority; to deny.

**desavenencia** *f* discord, disagreement.

**desavenido/da** *adj* contrary, disagreeing.

**desaventajado/da** *adj* disadvantageous, unprofitable.

**desayunar** *vt* to have for breakfast; ~se *vr* to breakfast; * *vi* to have breakfast;

**desayuno** *m* breakfast.

**desazón** *f* disgust; uneasiness; annoyance.

**desazonado/da** *adj* ill-adapted; ill-humoured.

**desazonar** *vt* to annoy; ~se *vr* to be annoyed; to be anxious.

**desbancar** *vt* to break (the bank in gambling); (*fig*) to supplant.

**desbandarse** *vr* to disband; to go off in all directions.

**desbarajuste** *m* confusion.

**desbaratar** *vt* to destroy.

**desbarrar** *vi* to talk rubbish.

**desbastar** *vt* to smooth; to polish; to waste.

**desbloquear** *vt* to unblock.

**desbocado/da** *adj* open-mouthed; wild (applied to a horse); foul-mouthed; indecent.

**desbocarse** *vr* to bolt.

**desbordar** *vt* to exceed; ~se *vr* to overflow.

**descabalgar** *vi* to dismount.

**descabellado/da** *adj* dishevelled; disorderly; wild, unrestrained; disproportional; violent.

**descabellar** *vt* to ruffle.

**descafeinado/da** *adj* decaffeinated.

**descalabrado/da** *adj* wounded on the head; imprudent.

**descalabrar** *vt* to wound on the head; to smash.

**descalabro** *m* blow; misfortune; considerable loss.

**descalificar** *vt* to disqualify; to discredit.

**descalzar** *vt*, ~se *vr* to take off one's shoes.

**descalzo/za** *adj* barefooted; (*fig*) destitute.

**descambiar** *vt* to exchange.

**descaminado/da** *adj* (*fig*) misguided.

**descaminar** *vt* to misguide, to lead astray.

**descamisado/da** *adj* shirtless.

**descampado/da** *adj* disengaged; free; open; * *m* open space.

**descansado/da** *adj* rested, refreshed; quiet.

**descansar** *vt* to rest; * *vi* to rest; to lie down.

**descansillo** *m* landing.

**descanso** *m* rest, repose; break; interval.

**descapotable** *m* convertible.
**descarado/da** *adj* cheeky, barefaced.
**descararse** *vr* to behave insolently.
**descarga** *f* unloading; volley, discharge.
**descargar** *vt* to unload, to discharge; ~se *vr* to unburden oneself.
**descargo** *m* discharge; evidence; receipt.
**descarnado/da** *adj* scrawny.
**descarnar** *vt* to strip the flesh from; to clean away the flesh from; to corrode; ~se *vr* to grow thin.
**descarado/da** *adj* cheeky.
**descaro** *m* nerve.
**descarriar** *vt* to lead astray; to misdirect; ~se *vr* to lose one's way; to stray; to err.
**descarrilamiento** *m* (*rail*) derailment.
**descarrilar** *vi* (*rail*) to leave/run off the rails.
**descarrío** *m* losing of one's way.
**descartar** *vt* to discard; to dismiss; to rule out; ~se *vr* to excuse oneself.
**descascarillado/da** *adj* peeling.
**descastado** *adj* degenerate; ungrateful.
**descendencia** *f* descent, offspring.
**descendente** *adj* descending; **tren** ~ *m* (*rail*) down train.
**descender** *vt* to take down; * *vi* to descend, to walk down; to flow; to fall; ~ **de** to be derived from.
**descendiente** *adj* descending; * *m/f* descendant.
**descenso** *m* descent; drop; relegation.
**descerrajar** *vt* to force the lock (of a door etc); to discharge firearms.
**descifrar** *vt* to decipher; to unravel.
**desclavar** *vt* to draw out nails (from).
**descocado/da** *adj* bold, impudent.
**descodificador** *m* decoder (for TV).
**descolgar** *vt* to take down; to pick up; ~se *vr* to let oneself down.
**descollar** *vi* to excel.
**descolorido/da** *adj* pale, colourless.
**descomedido/da** *adj* impudent, insolent; huge.
**descompaginar** *vt* to disarrange.
**descomponer** *vt* to discompose, to set at odds; to disconcert; (*chem*) to decompose.
**descomposición** *f* disagreement; discomposure; decomposition.
**descompuesto/ta** *adj* decomposed; broken.
**descomunal** *adj* uncommon; huge.
**desconcertado/da** *adj* disconcerted; bewildered.
**desconcertar** *vt* to disturb; to confound; to disconcert; ~se *vr* to be bewildered; to be upset.

**desconchado/da** *adj* peeling.
**desconchar** *vt* to peel off.
**desconcierto** *m* disorder, confusion; uncertainty.
**desconectar** *vt* to disconnect.
**desconfiado/da** *adj* mistrustful, distrustful.
**desconfianza** *f* distrust; jealousy.
**desconfiar** *vi*: ~ **de** to mistrust, to suspect.
**descongelar** *vt* to defrost.
**descongestionar** *vt* to clear.
**desconocer** *vt* to disown, to disavow; to be totally ignorant of (a thing); not to know (a person); not to acknowledge (a favour received).
**desconocido/da** *adj* unknown; disguised; * *m/f* stranger.
**desconocimiento** *m* ignorance.
**desconsiderado/da** *adj* inconsiderate; imprudent.
**desconsolado/da** *adj* disconsolate; painful; sad.
**desconsolar** *vt* to distress.
**desconsuelo** *m* distress; trouble; despair.
**descontado** *adj*: **por** ~ of course; **dar por** ~ to take for granted.
**descontar** *vt* to discount; to deduct.
**descontento** *m* dissatisfaction; disgust.
**descorazonar** *vt* to dishearten, to discourage.
**descorchar** *vt* to uncork.
**descorrer** *vt* to draw.
**descortés/esa** *adj* impolite, rude.
**descortesía** *f* rudeness.
**descoser** *vt* to undo, take apart; to separate; ~se *vr* to come apart at the seams.
**descosido/da** *adj* unstitched; disjointed.
**descoyuntar** *vt* to dislocate; to vex, to annoy.
**descrédito** *m* discredit.
**descreído/da** *adj* incredulous.
**descremado/da** *adj* skimmed.
**describir** *vt* to describe; to draw, to delineate.
**descripción** *f* description; delineation; inventory.
**descriptivo/va** *adj* descriptive.
**descuartizar** *vt* to quarter; to carve.
**descubierto** *m* deficit; overdraft; ~/**ta** *adj* uncovered.
**descubrimiento** *m* discovery; revelation.
**descubrir** *vt* to discover, to disclose; to uncover; to reveal; to show; ~se *vr* to reveal oneself; to take off one's hat; to confess.
**descuento** *m* discount; decrease.
**descuida** *excl* don't worry!

**descuidado/da** *adj* careless, negligent.

**descuidar** *vt* to neglect; * *vi*, **~se** *vr* to be careless.

**descuido** *m* carelessness, negligence; forgetfulness; incivility; improper action.

**desde** *prep* since; after; from; **~ luego** of course; **~ entonces** since then.

**desdecirse** *vr* to retract one's words.

**desdén** *m* disdain, scorn.

**desdentado/da** *adj* toothless.

**desdentar** *vt* to draw out (teeth).

**desdeñable** *adj* contemptible, despicable.

**desdeñar** *vt* to disdain, to scorn; **~se** *vr* to be disdainful.

**desdeñoso/sa** *adj* disdainful; contemptuous.

**desdicha** *f* misfortune, calamity; great poverty.

**desdichado/da** *adj* unfortunate; wretched, miserable.

**desdoblar** *vt* to unfold, to spread open.

**desear** *vt* to desire, to wish; to require, to demand.

**desecación** *f* desiccation.

**desecar** *vt* to dry up.

**desechar** *vt* to depreciate; to reject; to refuse; to throw away.

**desecho** *m* residue; **~s** *mpl* rubbish.

**desembalar** *vt* to unpack.

**desembarazado/da** *adj* free.

**desembarazar** *vt* to free; to clear; **~se** *vr*: **~ de** to get rid of.

**desembarcadero** *m* landing stage.

**desembarcar** *vt* to unload, to disembark; * *vi* to disembark, to land.

**desembarco** *m* landing.

**desembargo** *m* (*law*) raising an embargo.

**desembarque** *m* landing.

**desembocadura** *f* mouth.

**desembocar** *vi*: **~ en** to flow into.

**desembolsar** *vt* to pay out.

**desembolso** *m* expenditure.

**desembragar** *vi* to declutch.

**desembuchar** *vt* to disgorge; to tell all.

**desempaquetar** *vt* to unpack.

**desempatar** *vi* to hold a play-off.

**desempate** *m* play-off.

**desempeñar** *vt* to redeem; to extricate from debt; to fulfil (any duty/promise); to acquit; **~se** *vr* to get out of debt.

**desempeño** *m* redeeming a pledge; occupation.

**desempleado/da** *adj* unemployed; * *m/f* unemployed person.

**desempleo** *m* unemployment.

**desempolvorar** *vt* to dust.

**desencadenar** *vt* to unchain; **~se** *vr* to break loose; to burst.

**desencajar** *vt* to disjoint; to dislocate; to disconnect.

**desencallar** *vt* to refloat.

**desencanto** *m* disenchantment.

**desenchufar** *vt* to unplug.

**desenfadado/da** *adj* free; unembarrassed.

**desenfado** *m* ease; facility; calmness, relaxation.

**desenfocado/da** *adj* out of focus.

**desenfrenado/da** *adj* outrageous; ungovernable.

**desenfreno** *m* wildness; lack of self-control.

**desenganchar** *vt* to unhook; to uncouple.

**desengañado/da** *adj* disillusioned.

**desengañar** *vt* to disillusion; **~se** *vr* to become disillusioned.

**desengaño** *m* disillusionment; disappointment.

**desengrasar** *vt* to take the grease off.

**desenhebrar** *vt* to unthread; to unravel.

**desenlace** *m* climax; outcome.

**desenmarañar** *vt* to disentangle; to unravel.

**desenmascarar** *vt* to unmask.

**desenredar** *vt* to disentangle.

**desenrollar** *vt* to unroll.

**desenroscar** *vt* to untwist; to unroll.

**desentenderse** *vr* to feign not to understand; to pass by without noticing.

**desenterrar** *vt* to exhume; to dig up.

**desentonar** *vi* to be out of tune; to clash.

**desentrañar** *vt* to unravel.

**desentumecer** *vt* to stretch; to loosen up.

**desenvainar** *vt* to unsheathe; to show.

**desenvoltura** *f* sprightliness; cheerfulness; impudence, boldness.

**desenvolver** *vt* to unfold; to unroll; to decipher, to unravel; to develop; **~se** *vr* to develop; to cope.

**desenvuelto/ta** *adj* forward; natural.

**deseo** *m* desire, wish.

**deseoso/sa** *adj* anxious.

**desequilibrado/da** *adj* unbalanced.

**deserción** *f* desertion; defection.

**desertar** *vt* to desert; (*law*) to abandon (a cause).

**desertificación** *f* desertification.

**desertor** *m* deserter; fugitive.

**desesperación** *f* despair, desperation; anger, fury.

**desesperado/da** *adj* desperate, hopeless.

**desesperar** *vi*, **~se** *vr* to despair; * *vt* to make desperate.

**desestabilizar** *vt* to destabilize.
**desestimar** *vt* to disregard, to reject.
**desfachatez** *f* impudence.
**desfalcar** *vt* to embezzle.
**desfalco** *m* embezzlement.
**desfallecer** *vi* to get weak; to faint.
**desfallecimiento** *m* fainting.
**desfasado/da** *adj* old-fashioned.
**desfase** *m* gap.
**desfavorable** *adj* unfavorable.
**desfigurar** *vt* to disfigure, to deform; to disguise.
**desfiladero** *m* gorge.
**desfilar** *vi* (*mil*) to parade.
**desfogarse** *vr* to give vent to one's passion/anger.
**desforestación** *f* deforestation.
**desgajar** *vt* to tear off; to break in pieces; ~**se** *vr* to be separated; to be torn to pieces.
**desgana** *f* disgust; loss of appetite; aversion, reluctance.
**desganado/da** *adj* not hungry; half-hearted; **estar** ~ to lose all pleasure in doing a thing; to lose one's appetite.
**desgañitarse** *vr* to scream, to bawl.
**desgarrador/a** *adj* heartrending.
**desgarrar** *vt* to tear; to shatter.
**desgarro** *m* tear; grief; impudence.
**desgarrón** *m* large tear.
**desgastar** *vt* to waste; to corrode; ~**se** *vr* to get worn out.
**desgaste** *m* wear (and tear).
**desglosar** *vt* to break down.
**desgracia** *f* misfortune; disgrace; accident; setback.
**desgraciado/da** *adj* unfortunate; unhappy; miserable; out of favour; disagreeable.
**desgreñado/da** *adj* dishevelled.
**desgreñar** *vt* to dishevel (the hair); to disorder.
**desguarnecer** *vt* to strip down; to dismantle.
**deshabitado/da** *adj* deserted, uninhabited; desolate.
**deshacer** *vt* to undo, to destroy; to cancel, to efface; to rout (an army); to solve; to melt; to break up, to divide; to dissolve in a liquid; to violate (a treaty); to diminish; to disband (troops); ~**se** *vr* to melt; to come apart.
**desharrapado/da** *adj* shabby; ragged, in tatters.
**deshecho/cha** *adj* undone, destroyed; wasted; melted; in pieces.
**deshelar** *vt* to thaw; ~**se** *vr* to thaw, to melt.
**desheredar** *vt* to disinherit.

**deshidratado/da** *adj* dehydrated.
**deshidratar** *vt* to dehydrate.
**deshielo** *m* thaw.
**deshilachar** *vt* to unravel.
**deshilar** *vt* to fray.
**deshinchar** *vt* to deflate; ~**se** *vr* to go flat, to go down.
**deshojar** *vt* to strip the leaves off.
**deshollinador** *m* chimney sweep.
**deshonesto/ta** *adj* indecent.
**deshonra** *f* dishonour; shame.
**deshonrar** *vt* to affront, to insult, to defame; to dishonour.
**deshonroso/sa** *adj* dishonourable, indecent.
**deshora** *f* unseasonable time.
**deshuesar** *vt* to rid of bones; to stone.
**desidia** *f* idleness, indolence.
**desierto/ta** *adj* deserted; solitary; * *m* desert; wilderness.
**designación** *f* designation.
**designar** *vt* to design; to intend; to appoint; to express, to name.
**designio** *m* design, purpose; road, course.
**desigual** *adj* unequal, unlike; uneven, craggy.
**desigualdad** *f* inequality, dissimilitude; inconstancy; roughness, unevenness.
**desilusión** *f* disappointment.
**desilusionar** *vt* to disappoint; ~**se** *vr* to become disillusioned.
**desinfección** *f* disinfection.
**desinfectar** *vt* to disinfect.
**desinflar** *vt* to deflate.
**desintegración** *f* disintegration.
**desinterés** *m* unselfishness; disinterestedness.
**desinteresado/da** *adj* disinterested; unselfish.
**desistir** *vi* to desist, to cease.
**desleal** *adj* disloyal; unfair.
**deslealtad** *f* disloyalty, breach of faith.
**desleír** *vt* to dilute; to dissolve.
**deslenguado/da** *adj* foul-mouthed.
**desligar** *vt* to separate; to loosen, to unbind; ~**se** *vr* to extricate oneself.
**desliz** *m* slip, sliding; lapse, weakness.
**deslizadizo/za** *adj* slippery, slippy; glib.
**deslizar** *vt* to slip, to slide; to let slip (a comment); ~**se** *vr* to slip; to skid; to flow softly; to creep in.
**deslucido/da** *adj* tarnished; dull; shabby.
**deslucir** *vt* to tarnish; to damage; to discredit.
**deslumbramiento** *m* glare; confusion.
**deslumbrar** *vt* to dazzle; to puzzle.
**desmán** *m* outrage; disaster; misconduct.

**desmandarse** *vr* to behave badly.

**desmantelar** *vt* to dismantle; to abandon, to forsake.

**desmaquillador** *m* make-up remover.

**desmarañar** *vt* to disentangle.

**desmayado/da** *adj* unconscious; dismayed; appalled; weak.

**desmayar** *vi* to be dispirited/faint-hearted; ~se *vr* to faint.

**desmayo** *m* unconsciousness; faint, swoon; dismay.

**desmedido/da** *adj* disproportionate.

**desmejorar** *vt* to impair; to weaken.

**desmembrar** *vt* to dismember; to separate.

**desmemoriado/da** *adj* forgetful.

**desmentir** *vt* to give the lie to; ~se *vr* to contradict oneself.

**desmenuzar** *vt* to crumble; to chip at; to fritter away; to examine minutely.

**desmerecer** *vt* to be unworthy of; * *vi* to deteriorate.

**desmesurado/da** *adj* excessive; huge; immeasurable.

**desmontar** *vt* to level; to remove (a heap of rubbish); to dismantle; * *vi* to dismount.

**desmoralización** *f* demoralization.

**desmoralizar** *vt* to demoralize.

**desmoronar** *vt* to destroy little by little; ~se *vr* to fall into disrepair.

**desnatado/da** *adj* skimmed.

**desnatar** *vt* to skim (milk); to take the choicest part of.

**desnaturalizar** *vt* to divest of naturalization rights; ~se *vr* to forsake one's country.

**desnivel** *m* unevenness of the ground.

**desnucar** *vt* to break (one's neck).

**desnudar** *vt* to undress; to strip; to discover, to reveal; ~se *vr* to undress.

**desnudez** *f* nakedness.

**desnudo/da** *adj* naked; bare, uncovered; ill-clothed; (*fig*) plain, evident.

**desnutrición** *f* malnutrition.

**desnutrido/da** *adj* undernourished.

**desobedecer** *vt, vi* to disobey.

**desobediencia** *f* disobedience; insubordination.

**desobediente** *adj* disobedient.

**desocupado/da** *adj* empty; at leisure.

**desocupar** *vt* to vacate; to empty; ~se *vr* to retire from a business; to withdraw from an arrangement.

**desodorante** *m* deodorant.

**desolación** *f* destruction; affliction.

**desolado/da** *adj* desolate, disconsolate.

**desolar** *vt* to lay waste; to harass.

**desollar** *vt* to flay, to skin; (*fig*) to extort.

**desorden** *m* disorder, confusion.

**desordenado/da** *adj* disorderly; untidy.

**desordenar** *vt* to disorder; to untidy; ~se *vr* to get out of order.

**desorganización** *f* disorganization.

**desorganizar** *vt* to disorganize.

**desorientar** *vt* to mislead; to confuse; ~se *vr* to lose one's way.

**desovar** *vi* to spawn.

**despabilado/da** *adj* watchful, vigilant; wide-awake.

**despabilar** *vt* to snuff (a candle); (*fig*) to dispatch quickly; to sharpen; ~se *vr* to wake up.

**despacio** *adv* slowly, leisurely; little by little; ¡~! softly!, gently!

**despachar** *vt* to dispatch; to expedite; to sell; to send.

**despacho** *m* dispatch, expedition; cabinet; office; commission; warrant, patent; expedient; smart answer.

**despachurrar** *vt* to squash, to crush; to mangle.

**desparejar** *vt* to make unequal/uneven.

**desparpajo** *m* ease; savoir-faire.

**desparramar** *vt* to disseminate, to spread; to spill; to squander, to lavish; ~se *vr* to be dissipated.

**despavorido** *adj* frightened.

**despectivo/va** *adj* pejorative, derogatory.

**despecho** *m* indignation; displeasure; spite; dismay, despair; deceit; derision, scorn; a ~ de in spite of.

**despedazar** *vt* to tear into pieces; to mangle.

**despedida** *f* farewell; sacking.

**despedir** *vt* to discharge; to dismiss (from office); to see off; ~se *vr*: ~ de to say goodbye to.

**despegado/da** *adj* cold; detached.

**despegar** *vt* to unglue; to take off; ~se *vr* to come loose.

**despego** *m* detachment; coolness.

**despegue** *m* take-off.

**despeinado/da** *adj* dishevelled.

**despeinar** *vt* to ruffle.

**despejado/da** *adj* sprightly, quick; clear.

**despejar** *vt* to clear away; ~se *vr* to cheer up; to clear; * *vi* to clear.

**despellejar** *vt* to skin.

**despensa** *f* pantry, larder; provisions *pl*.

**despeñadero** *m* precipice.

**despeñar** *vt* to precipitate; ~se *vr* to throw oneself headlong.

**despepitarse** *vr* to bawl.

**desperdiciar** *vt* to squander.

**desperdicio** *m* waste; **~s** *mpl* rubbish; waste.

**desperdigar** *vt* to separate; to scatter.

**desperezarse** *vr* to stretch oneself.

**desperfecto** *m* slight damage; flaw.

**despertador** *m* alarm clock.

**despertar** *vt* to wake up, to rouse from sleep; to excite; * *vi* to wake up; to grow lively/ sprightly; **~se** *vr* to wake up.

**despiadado/da** *adj* heartless; merciless.

**despido** *m* dismissal.

**despierto/ta** *adj* awake; vigilant; fierce; brisk, sprightly.

**despilfarrar** *vt* to waste.

**despilfarro** *m* slovenliness; waste; mismanagement.

**despintar** *vt* to deface (a painting); to obscure (things); to mislead; **~se** to lose its colour.

**despistar** *vt* to mislead; to throw off the track; **~se** *vr* to take the wrong way; to become confused.

**desplante** *m* bold statement; wrong stance; insolence.

**desplazamiento** *m* displacement.

**desplazar** *vt* to move; to scroll; **~se** *vr* to travel.

**desplegar** *vt* to unfold, to display; to explain, to elucidate; (*mar*) to unfurl; **~se** *vr* to open out; to travel.

**despliegue** *m* display.

**desplomarse** *vr* to fall to the ground; to collapse.

**desplumar** *vt* to fleece; to pluck.

**despoblado** *m* desert.

**despoblar** *vt* to depopulate; to desolate; **~se** *vr* to become depopulated.

**despojar** *vt*: **~ (de)** to strip (of); to deprive (of); **~se** *vr* to undress.

**despojo** *m* plunder; loot; **~s** *mpl* giblets *pl*; remains *pl*; offal.

**desposado/da** *adj* newlywed.

**desposar** *vt* to marry, to betroth; **~se** *vr* to be betrothed/married.

**desposeer** *vt* to dispossess.

**desposeimiento** *m* dispossession.

**déspota** *m* despot.

**despótico/ca** *adj* despotic.

**despotismo** *m* despotism.

**despreciable** *adj* contemptible, despicable.

**despreciar** *vt* to offend; to despise.

**desprecio** *m* scorn, contempt.

**desprender** *vt* to unfasten, to loosen; to separate; **~se** *vr* to give way; to fall down; to extricate oneself.

**desprendimiento** *m* alienation, disinterestedness.

**despreocupado/da** *adj* careless; unworried.

**despreocuparse** *vr* to be carefree.

**desprestigiar** *vt* to run down.

**desprevenido/da** *adj* unawares, unprepared.

**desproporción** *f* disproportion.

**desproporcionado/da** *adj* disproportionate.

**desproporcionar** *vt* to disproportion.

**despropósito** *m* absurdity.

**desprovisto/ta** *adj* unprovided.

**después** *adv* after, afterwards; next.

**despuntar** *vt* to blunt; * *vi* to sprout; to dawn; **al ~ del día** at break of day.

**desquiciar** *vt* to upset; to discompose; to disorder.

**desquitar** *vt* to retrieve (a loss); **~se** *vr* to win one's money back again; to return by giving like for like; to take revenge.

**desquite** *m* recovery of a loss; revenge, retaliation.

**desrizar** *vt* to uncurl.

**destacamento** *m* (*mil*) detachment.

**destacar** *vt* to emphasize; (*mil*) to detach (a body of troops); **~se** *vr* to stand out.

**destajo** *m* piecework; **trabajar a ~** to do piecework.

**destapar** *vt* to uncover; to open; **~se** *vr* to be uncovered.

**destartalado/da** *adj* untidy.

**destello** *m* signal light; sparkle.

**destemplado/da** *adj* out of tune; badly blended (applied to paintings); intemperate.

**desteñir** *vt* to discolour; **~se** *vr* to fade.

**desternillarse** *vr*: **~ de risa** to roar with laughter.

**desterrar** *vt* to banish; to expel, to drive away.

**destetar** *vt* to wean.

**destete** *m* weaning.

**destierro** *m* exile, banishment.

**destilación** *f* distillation.

**destilar** *vt, vi* to distil.

**destinar** *vt* to destine for, to intend for.

**destinatario/a** *m/f* addressee.

**destino** *m* destiny; fate, doom; destination; office.

**destitución** *f* destitution, abandonment.

**destituir** *vt* to dismiss.

**destornillador** *m* screwdriver.

**destornillar** *vt* to unscrew.

**destreza** *f* dexterity, cleverness, cunning, expertness, skill.

**destripar** *vt* to disembowel; to trample.

**destronar** *vt* to dethrone.

**destrozar** *vt* to destroy, to break into pieces; (*mil*) to defeat.

**destrozo** *m* destruction; (*mil*) defeat, massacre.

**destrucción** *f* destruction, ruin.

**destructivo/va** *adj* destructive.

**destruir** *vt* to destroy.

**desunir** *vt* to separate, to disunite; to cause discord between.

**desuso** *m* disuse.

**desvaído/da** *adj* tall and graceless.

**desvalido/da** *adj* helpless; destitute.

**desvalijar** *vt* to rob; to burgle.

**desván** *m* garret.

**desvanecer** *vt* to dispel; ~**se** *vr* to grow vapid, to become insipid; to vanish; to be affected with giddiness.

**desvanecimiento** *m* pride, haughtiness; giddiness; swoon.

**desvariar** *vi* to be delirious.

**desvarío** *m* delirium; giddiness; inconstancy, caprice; extravagance.

**desvelar** *vt* to keep awake; ~**se** *vr* to stay awake.

**desvelo** *m* want of sleep; watchfulness.

**desvencijado/da** *adj* broken down, rickety.

**desvencijar** *vt* to disunite, to divide; to weaken; ~**se** *vr* to be ruptured; to come apart.

**desventaja** *f* disadvantage; damage.

**desventura** *f* misfortune; calamity.

**desventurado/da** *adj* unfortunate; calamitous.

**desvergonzado/da** *adj* impudent, shameless.

**desvergonzarse** *vr* to behave in an impudent manner.

**desvergüenza** *f* impudence; shamelessness.

**desvestir** *vt*, ~**se** *vr* to undress.

**desviar** *vt* to divert; to dissuade; to parry (at fencing); ~**se** *vr* to go off course.

**desvío** *m* turning away, going astray; aversion; disdain; indifference.

**desvivirse** *vr*: ~ **por** to long for.

**detallar** *vt* to detail, to relate minutely.

**detalle** *m* detail.

**detallista** *m* retailer.

**detención** *f* detention; delay.

**detener** *vt* to stop, to detain; to arrest; to keep back; to reserve; to withhold; ~**se** *vr* to stop; to stay.

**detenidamente** *adv* carefully.

**detenido/da** *adj* detailed; sparing, niggardly; slow, inactive.

**detergente** *m* detergent.

**deterioración** *f* deterioration; damage.

**deteriorar** *vt* to damage.

**deterioro** *m* deterioration.

**determinación** *f* determination, resolution; boldness.

**determinado/da** *adj* determined; resolute.

**determinar** *vt* to determine; ~**se** *vr* to decide.

**detestable** *adj* detestable.

**detestar** *vt* to detest, to abhor.

**detonación** *f* detonation.

**detonar** *vi* to detonate.

**detractar** *vt* to denigrate, to defame, to slander.

**detrás** *adv* behind; at the back, in the back.

**detrimento** *m* detriment; damage; loss.

**deuda** *f* debt; fault; offence.

**deudor/ra** *m/f* debtor.

**devaluación** *f* devaluation.

**devanar** *vt* to reel; to wrap up.

**devastación** *f* devastation, desolation.

**devastador/ra** *adj* devastating.

**devastar** *vt* to devastate.

**devengar** *vt* to accrue.

**devoción** *f* devotion, piety; strong affection; ardent love.

**devolución** *f* return; (*law*) devolution.

**devolutivo/va** *adj* (*law*) transferable.

**devolver** *vt* to return; to send back; to refund; to throw up; * *vi* to be sick.

**devorar** *vt* to devour, to swallow up.

**devoto/ta** *adj* devout, pious; devotional; strongly attached.

**día** *m* day.

**diablo** *m* devil.

**diablura** *f* prank.

**diabólico/ca** *adj* diabolical; devilish.

**diácono** *m* deacon.

**diadema** *m/f* diadem; halo.

**diafragma** *m* diaphragm; midriff.

**diagnosis** *f invar* diagnosis.

**diagnóstico** *m* diagnosis.

**diagonal** *adj* diagonal.

**diagrama** *m* diagram.

**dialecto** *m* dialect.

**diálisis** *f invar* dialysis.

**diálogo** *m* dialogue.

**diamante** *m* diamond.

**diámetro** *m* diameter.

**diana** *f* (*mil*) reveille; bull's-eye.

**diapasón** *m* (*mus*) diapason, octave.

**diapositiva** *f* transparency, slide.

**diario** *m* journal, diary; daily newspaper; daily expenses *pl*; ~**/ria** *adj* daily.

**diarrea** *f* diarrhoea.

**dibujar** *vt* to draw, to design.
**dibujo** *m* drawing; sketch, draft; description.
**dicción** *f* diction; style; expression.
**diccionario** *m* dictionary.
**diciembre** *m* December.
**dictado** *m* dictation.
**dictador** *m* dictator.
**dictadura** *f* dictatorship.
**dictamen** *m* opinion, notion; suggestion, insinuation; judgement.
**dictar** *vt* to dictate.
**dicha** *f* happiness, good fortune; **por ~** by chance.
**dicho** *m* saying; sentence; declaration; promise of marriage; **~/cha** *adj* said.
**dichoso/sa** *adj* happy, prosperous.
**diecinueve** *adj*, *m* nineteen.
**dieciocho** *adj*, *m* eighteen.
**dieciséis** *adj*, *m* sixteen.
**diecisiete** *adj*, *m* seventeen.
**diente** *m* tooth; fang; tusk.
**diestro/tra** *adj* right; dexterous, skilful, clever; sagacious, prudent; sly, cunning; * *m* skilful fencer; halter; bridle.
**diesel, diésel** *adj* diesel *compd*.
**dieta** *f* diet, regimen; diet, assembly; daily salary of judges.
**diez** *adj*, *m* ten.
**diezmar** *vt* to decimate.
**diezmo** *m* tithe.
**difamación** *f* defamation.
**difamar** *vt* to defame, to libel.
**difamatorio/ria** *adj* defamatory, calumnious.
**diferencia** *f* difference.
**diferencial** *adj* differential.
**diferenciar** *vt* to differentiate, to distinguish; **~se** *vr* to differ, to distinguish oneself.
**diferente** *adj* different, unlike.
**diferido/da** *adj* recorded.
**diferir** *vt* to defer, to put off; to differ.
**difícil** *adj* difficult.
**dificultad** *f* difficulty.
**dificultar** *vt* to put difficulties in the way of; to render difficult.
**dificultoso/sa** *adj* difficult; painful.
**difundir** *vt* to diffuse, to spread; to divulge; **~se** *vr* to spread (out).
**difunto/ta** *adj* dead, deceased; late.
**difusión** *f* diffusion.
**difuso/sa** *adj* diffusive, copious; large; long-winded; circumstantial.
**digerir** *vt* to digest; to bear with patience; to adjust, to arrange; (*chem*) to digest.

**digestión** *f* digestion; concoction.
**digestivo/va** *adj* digestive.
**digital** *adj* digital.
**digitalizar** *vt* to digitize.
**dignarse** *vr* to condescend, to deign.
**dignidad** *f* dignity, rank.
**digno/na** *adj* worthy; suitable.
**dije** *m* relic; trinket.
**dilapidar** *vt* to squander, to waste.
**dilatación** *f* dilation, extension; greatness of mind; calmness.
**dilatado/da** *adj* large; numerous; prolix; spacious, extensive.
**dilatar** *vt* to dilate, to expand; to spread out; to defer, to protract.
**dilatorio/ria** *adj* dilatory.
**dilema** *m* dilemma.
**diligencia** *f* diligence; affair, business; call of nature; stage coach.
**diligente** *adj* diligent, assiduous, prompt, swift.
**dilucidar** *vt* to elucidate, to explain.
**diluir** *vt* to dilute.
**diluviar** *vi* to rain in torrents.
**diluvio** *m* flood, deluge, inundation; abundance.
**dimensión** *f* dimension; extent; capacity, bulk.
**diminutivo/va** *adj* diminutive.
**diminuto/ta** *adj* defective, faulty; minute, small.
**dimisión** *f* resignation.
**dimitir** *vt* to give up, to abdicate; * *vi* to resign.
**dinámica** *f* dynamics.
**dinámico/ca** *adj* dynamic.
**dinamita** *f* dynamite.
**dínamo, dinamo** *f* dynamo.
**dinastía** *f* dynasty.
**dineral** *m* large sum of money.
**dinero** *m* money.
**diocesano/na** *adj* diocesan.
**diócesis** *f* diocese.
**Dios** *m* God.
**diosa** *f* goddess.
**diploma** *m* diploma, patent.
**diplomacia, diplomática** *f* diplomacy.
**diplomado/da** *adj* qualified.
**diplomático/ca** *adj* diplomatic; * *m/f* diplomat.
**diptongo** *m* diphthong.
**diputación** *f* deputation.
**diputado** *m* deputy.
**diputar** *vt* to depute.
**dique** *m* dike, dam.

**dirección** *f* direction, guidance; administration; steering.

**directivo/va** *adj* governing.

**directo/ta** *adj* direct, straight; apparent, evident; live.

**director/ra** *m/f* director; conductor; president; manager; headmaster.

**dirigir** *vt* to direct; to conduct; to regulate, to govern; **~se** *vr* to go toward(s); to address oneself to.

**discernimiento** *m* discernment.

**discernir** *vt* to discern, to distinguish.

**disciplina** *f* discipline.

**discípulo** *m* disciple; scholar.

**disco** *m* disc; record; discus; light; face (of the sun/moon); lens (of a telescope) ; **~ compacto** compact disc.

**díscolo/la** *adj* ungovernable; peevish.

**disconforme** *adj* differing.

**discordancia** *f* disagreement, discord.

**discordante** *adj* dissonant, discordant.

**discordar** *vi* to clash, to disagree.

**discorde** *adj* discordant; (*mus*) dissonant.

**discordia** *f* discord, disagreement.

**discoteca** *m* discotheque, disco.

**discreción** *f* discretion; acuteness of mind.

**discrecional** *adj* discretionary.

**discrepancia** *f* discrepancy.

**discrepar** *vi* to differ.

**discreto/ta** *adj* discreet; ingenious; witty, eloquent.

**discriminación** *f* discrimination.

**disculpa** *f* apology; excuse.

**disculpar** *vt* to exculpate, to excuse; to acquit, to absolve; **~se** *vr* to apologize; to excuse oneself.

**discurrir** *vi* to ramble about; to run to and fro; to discourse (upon a subject); * *vt* to invent, to contrive; to meditate.

**discurso** *m* speech; conversation; dissertation; space of time.

**discusión** *f* discussion.

**discutir** *vt, vi* to discuss.

**disecar** *vt* to dissect; to stuff.

**disección** *f* dissection.

**diseminar** *vt* to scatter; to disseminate, to propagate.

**disentería** *f* dysentery.

**disentir** *vi* to dissent, to disagree.

**diseñador/ra** *m/f* designer.

**diseñar** *vt* to draw; to design.

**diseño** *m* design; draft; description; picture.

**disfraz** *m* disguise; mask.

**disfrazar** *vt* to disguise, to conceal; to cloak, to dissemble; **~se** *vr* to disguise oneself as.

**disfrutar** *vt* to enjoy; **~se** *vr* to enjoy oneself.

**disgustar** *vt* to disgust; to offend; **~se** *vr* to be displeased; to fall out.

**disgusto** *m* disgust, aversion; quarrel; annoyance; grief, sorrow.

**disidente** *adj* dissident; * *m/f* dissident, dissenter.

**disimular** *vt* to hide; to tolerate.

**disimulo** *m* dissimulation; tolerance.

**disipado/da** *adj* prodigal, lavish.

**disipar** *vt* to dissipate, to disperse, to scatter; to lavish.

**dislocación** *f* dislocation.

**dislocarse** *vr* to be dislocated/out of joint.

**disminución** *f* diminution.

**disminuir** *vt* to diminish; to decrease.

**disolución** *f* dissolution; liquidation.

**disolver** *vt* to loosen, to untie; to dissolve; to disunite; to melt, to liquefy; to interrupt.

**disonancia** *f* dissonance; disagreement, discord.

**disparar** *vt* to shoot, to discharge, to fire; to let off; to throw with violence; * *vi* to shoot, to fire.

**disparatado/da** *adj* inconsistent; absurd, extravagant.

**disparate** *m* nonsense, absurdity, extravagance.

**disparo** *m* shot; discharge; explosion.

**dispensar** *vt* to dispense; to excuse; to dispense with; to distribute.

**displicencia** *f* displeasure; dislike.

**disponer** *vt* to arrange, to prepare; to dispose.

**disponible** *adj* available; disposable.

**disposición** *f* disposition, order; resolution; command; power, authority.

**dispositivo** *m* device.

**dispuesto/ta** *adj* disposed; fit, ready.

**disputa** *f* dispute, controversy.

**disputar** *vt* to dispute, to controvert, to question; * *vi* to debate, to argue.

**disquete** *m* floppy disk.

**distancia** *f* distance; interval; difference.

**distanciarse** *vr* to become estranged.

**distante** *adj* distant, far off.

**distinción** *f* distinction; difference; prerogative.

**distinguido/da** *adj* distinguished, conspicuous.

**distinguir** *vt* to distinguish; to discern; **~se** *vr* to distinguish oneself.

**distintivo** *m* distinctive mark; particular attribute.

**distinto/ta** *adj* distinct, different; clear.
**distracción** *f* distraction, want of attention.
**distraer** *vt* to distract; **~se** *vr* to be absent-minded, to be inattentive.
**distraído/da** *adj* absent-minded, inattentive.
**distribución** *f* distribution; division, separation; arrangement.
**distribuidor** *m* distributor.
**distribuir** *vt* to distribute.
**distrito** *m* district; territory.
**disturbar** *vt* to disturb, to interrupt.
**disturbio** *m* riot; disturbance, interruption.
**disuadir** *vt* to dissuade.
**disuasión** *f* dissuasion.
**diurno/na** *adj* daily.
**diva** *f* prima donna.
**divagar** *vt* to digress.
**diván** *m* divan.
**divergencia** *f* divergence.
**divergente** *adj* divergent.
**diversidad** *f* diversity; variety of things.
**diversificar** *vt* to diversify; to vary.
**diversión** *f* diversion; sport; amusement; (*mil*) diversion.
**diverso/sa** *adj* diverse, different; several, sundry.
**divertido/da** *adj* amused; amusing.
**divertir** *vt* to divert (the attention); to amuse, to entertain; (*mil*) to draw off; **~se** *vr* to amuse oneself.
**dividir** *vt* to divide; to disunite; to separate; to share out.
**divieso** *m* (*med*) boil.
**divinidad** *f* divinity.
**divino/na** *adj* divine, heavenly; excellent.
**divisa** *f* emblem.
**divisar** *vt* to perceive.
**divisible** *adj* divisible.
**división** *f* division; partition; separation; difference.
**divorciar** *vt* to divorce; to separate; **~se** *vr* to get divorced.
**divorcio** *m* divorce; separation, disunion.
**divulgación** *f* publication; dissemination.
**divulgar** *vt* to publish, to divulge.
**dobladillo** *m* hem; turn-up; cuff.
**dobladura** *f* fold.
**doblar** *vt* to double; to fold; to bend; * *vi* to turn; to toll (of a bell); **~se** *vr* to bend, to bow, to submit.
**doble** *adj* double; dual; deceitful; **al ~** doubly; * *m* double.
**doblegar** *vt* to bend; **~se** *vr* to yield.
**doblez** *m* crease; fold; turn-up; * *f* duplicity.
**doce** *adj*, *m* twelve.

**docena** *f* dozen.
**docente** *adj* teaching.
**dócil** *adj* docile, tractable.
**docilidad** *f* docility, gentleness; compliance.
**doctor/ra** *m/f* doctor.
**doctorado** *m* doctorate.
**doctrina** *f* doctrine, instruction; science.
**doctrinal** *m* catechism; * *adj* doctrinal.
**documentación** *f* documentation.
**documento** *m* document; record.
**dogma** *m* dogma.
**dólar** *m* dollar.
**dolencia** *f* disease; affliction.
**doler** *vi* to feel pain; to ache; **~se** *vr* to feel for the sufferings of others; to complain.
**dolor** *m* pain; aching, ache; affliction.
**doloroso/sa** *adj* painful.
**domador/ra** *m/f* trainer; tamer.
**domar** *vt* to tame; to subdue, to master.
**domesticar** *vt* to domesticate.
**domiciliarse** *vr* to establish oneself in a residence.
**domicilio** *m* domicile; home, abode.
**dominación** *f* domination; dominion; authority, power.
**dominante** *adj* dominant; domineering.
**dominar** *vt* to dominate; to be fluent in; **~se** *vr* to moderate one's passions.
**domingo** *m* Sunday; (Christian) Sabbath.
**dominguero/ra** *adj* done/worn on Sunday; * *m/f* Sunday driver.
**dominical** *adj* Sunday.
**dominio** *m* dominion; domination; power, authority; domain.
**donación** *f* donation; gift.
**donar** *vt* to donate; to bestow.
**donativo** *m* contribution.
**doncella** *f* virgin, maiden; lady's maid.
**donde** *adv* where.
**dónde** *adv* where; **¿de ~?** from where?; **¿por ~?** where?
**dónde?** where?
**dondequiera** *adv* anywhere.
**dorado/da** *adj* gilt *compd*; golden; * *m* gilding.
**dorar** *vt* to gild; (*fig*) to palliate.
**dormilón/ona** *m/f* dull, sleepy person.
**dormir** *vi* to sleep; **~se** *vr* to fall asleep.
**dormitorio** *m* dormitory.
**dorsal** *adj* dorsal.
**dos** *adj*, *m* two.
**doscientos/tas** *adj pl* two hundred.
**dosis** *f invar* dose.
**dotado/da** *adj* gifted.
**dotar** *vt* to endow.

**dote** *f* dowry; **~s** *fpl* gifts *pl* of nature; endowments *pl*.

**dragón** *m* dragon; (*mil*) dragoon.

**drama** *m* drama.

**dramático/ca** *adj* dramatic.

**dramatizar** *vt* to dramatize.

**dramaturgo/ga** *m/f* dramatist.

**droga** *f* drug; stratagem; artifice, deceit.

**drogadicción** *f* drug addiction.

**drogadicto/ta** *m/f* drug addict.

**droguería** *f* hardware store.

**dromedario** *m* dromedary.

**dubitativo/va** *adj* doubtful, dubious; uncertain.

**ducado** *m* duchy; ducat.

**ducha** *f* shower; (*med*) douche.

**ducharse** *vr* to have a shower.

**ducho/cha** *adj* skilled, experienced.

**duda** *f* doubt; suspense; hesitation.

**dudar** *vt* to doubt.

**dudoso/sa** *adj* doubtful, dubious.

**duelo** *m* grief, affliction; mourning.

**duende** *m* elf, hobgoblin.

**dueño/ña** *m/f* owner; landlord/lady; employer.

**dulce** *adj* sweet; mild, gentle, meek; soft; * *m* sweet, candy.

**dulcificar** *vt* to sweeten.

**dulzura** *f* sweetness; gentleness; softness.

**dúo** *m* (*mus*) duo, duet.

**duodécimo/ma** *adj* twelfth.

**duplicación** *f* duplication.

**duplicado** *m* duplicate.

**duplicar** *vt* to duplicate, to double; to repeat.

**duplicidad** *f* duplicity; falseness.

**duplo** *m* double.

**duque** *m* duke.

**duquesa** *f* duchess.

**duración** *f* duration.

**duradero/ra** *adj* lasting, durable.

**durante** *adv* during.

**durar** *vi* to last, to continue.

**durazno** *m* peach; peach tree.

**duraznero** *m* peach tree.

**dureza** *f* hardness; harshness; **~ de oído** hardness of hearing.

**durmiente** *adj* sleeping; * *m* (*rail*) sleeper.

**duro/ra** *adj* hard; cruel; harsh, rough; * *m* five peseta coin; * *adv* hard.

**duunviro** *m* magistrate in ancient Rome.

# E

**e** *conj* and (before words starting with *i* and *hi*).

**ea** *interj* hey!, come on!; **¡~ pues!** well then!, let's see!

**ebanista** *m* cabinet-maker, carpenter.

**ébano** *m* ebony.

**ebrio/ia** *adj* drunk.

**ebullición** *f* boiling.

**eccema** *m* eczema.

**echar** *vt* to throw; to add; to fire; to pour out; to mail; to give off; to bud; **~se** *vr* to lie down; to rest; to stretch out.

**eclesiástico/ca** *adj* ecclesiastical.

**eclipsar** *vt* to eclipse; to outshine.

**eclipse** *m* eclipse.

**eco** *m* echo.

**ecografía** *f* ultrasound scan.

**ecología** *f* ecology.

**ecologismo** *m* green movement.

**ecologista** *m/f* ecologist, environmentalist.

**economato** *m* cut-price store.

**economía** *f* economy.

**económico/ca** *adj* economic; cheap; thrifty; financial; avaricious.

**economista** *m/f* economist.

**ecosistema** *m* ecosystem.

**ecotasa** *f* ecotax.

**ecoturismo** *m* ecotourism.

**ecuación** *f* equation.

**ecuador** *m* equator.

**ecuánime** *adj* level-headed.

**ecuestre** *adj* equestrian.

**ecuménico/ca** *adj* ecumenical; universal.

**edad** *f* age.

**edecán** *m* (*mil*) aide-de-camp.

**edición** *f* edition; publication.

**edicto** *m* edict.

**edificación** *f* construction.

**edificante** *adj* edifying, instructive.

**edificar** *vt* to build, to construct; to edify.

**edificio** *m* building; structure.

**editar** *vt* to edit; to publish.

**editor/ra** *m/f* editor; publisher.

**educación** *f* education; upbringing; (good) manners *pl*.

**educador/ra** *m/f* teacher, educator.

**educando/da** *m/f* pupil.

**educar** *vt* to educate, to instruct; to bring up.

**efectivamente** *adv* exactly; really; in fact.

**efectivo/va** *adj* effective; true; certain.

**efecto** *m* effect; consequence; purpose; **~ invernadero** greenhouse effect **~s** *mpl* effects *pl*, goods *pl*; **en ~** in fact, really.

**efectuar** *vt* to effect, to carry out.

**efeméride** *f* event (remembered on its anniversary).

**efervescencia** *f* effervescence, fizziness.

**eficacia** *f* effectiveness, efficacy.

**eficaz** *adj* efficient; effective.

**eficiente** *adj* efficient.

**efigie** *f* effigy, image.

**efímero/ra** *adj* ephemeral.

**efluvio** *m* outflow.

**efusión** *f* effusion.

**efusivo/va** *adj* effusive.

**égloga** *f* (*poet*) eclogue.

**egoísmo** *m* selfishness.

**egoísta** *m/f* self-seeker; * *adj* selfish.

**egregio/gia** *adj* eminent, remarkable.

**eje** *m* axle; axis.

**ejecución** *f* execution.

**ejecutar** *vt* to execute, to carry out, to perform; to put to death; (*law*) to attach, to seize.

**ejecutivo/va** *adj* executive; * *m/f* executive.

**ejecutor/ra** *m/f* executor.

**ejecutoria** *f* (*law*) writ of execution.

**ejecutorio/ria** *adj* (*law*) executory.

**ejemplar** *m* specimen; copy; example; * *adj* exemplary.

**ejemplificar** *vt* to exemplify.

**ejemplo** *m* example; **por ~** for example, for instance.

**ejercer** *vt* to exercise.

**ejercicio** *m* exercise.

**ejercitación** *f* exercise, practice.

**ejercitar** *vt* to exercise; **~se** *vr* to train.

**ejército** *m* army.

**ejote** *m* green bean.

**el** *art*, *m* the.

**él** *pn* he, it.

**elaboración** *f* elaboration.

**elaborado/da** *adj* elaborate.

**elaborar** *vt* to elaborate.

**elasticidad** *f* elasticity.

**elástico/ca** *adj* elastic.

**elección** *f* election; choice.

**elector/ra** *m/f* elector.

**electorado** *m* electorate.

**electoral** *adj* electoral.

**electricidad** *f* electricity.

**electricista** *m/f* electrician.
**eléctrico/ca** *adj* electric, electrical.
**electrización** *f* electrification.
**electrizar** *vt* to electrify.
**electrocardiograma** *m* electrocardiogram.
**electrocutar** *vt* to electrocute.
**electrodoméstico** *m* (electrical) domestic appliance.
**electrónico/ca** *adj* electronic.
**electrotecnia** *f* electrical engineering.
**elefante** *m* elephant.
**elegancia** *f* elegance.
**elegante** *adj* elegant, fine.
**elegía** *f* elegy.
**elegir** *vt* to choose, to elect.
**elemental** *adj* elemental; elementary.
**elemento** *m* element; ~s *mpl* elements *pl*, rudiments *pl*, first principles *pl*.
**elevación** *f* elevation; highness; rise; haughtiness, pride; height; altitude.
**elevar** *vt* to raise; to elevate; ~se *vr* to rise; to be enraptured; to be conceited.
**eliminar** *vt* to eliminate, to remove.
**eliminatoria** *f* preliminary (round).
**elipse** *f* ellipse.
**elipsis** *f* (*gr*) ellipsis.
**elite, élite** *f* elite.
**elixir** *m* elixir.
**ella** *pn* she; it.
**ello** *pn* it.
**elocución** *f* elocution.
**elocuencia** *f* eloquence.
**elocuente** *adj* eloquent.
**elogiar** *vt* to praise, to eulogize.
**elogio** *m* eulogy, praise.
**elote** *m* corn on the cob.
**elucidación** *f* elucidation, explanation.
**eludir** *vt* to elude, to escape.
**emanación** *f* emanation.
**emanar** *vi* to emanate.
**emancipación** *f* emancipation.
**emancipar** *vt* to emancipate, to set free.
**embadurnar** *vt* to smear, to bedaub.
**embajada** *f* embassy.
**embajador/ra** *m/f* ambassador.
**embalaje** *m* packing, package.
**embalar** *vt* to bale, to pack in bales.
**embaldosar** *vt* to pave with tiles.
**embalsamador** *m* embalmer.
**embalsamar** *vt* to embalm.
**embalse** *m* reservoir.
**embarazada** *f* pregnant woman; * *adj* pregnant.
**embarazar** *vt* to embarrass; to make pregnant; ~se *vr* to become intricate.

**embarazo** *m* pregnancy; embarrassment; obstacle.
**embarazoso/sa** *adj* difficult; intricate, entangled.
**embarcación** *f* embarkation; any vessel/ship.
**embarcadero** *m* quay, wharf; port; harbour.
**embarcar** *vt* to embark; ~se *vr* to go on board; (*fig*) to get involved (in a matter).
**embargar** *vt* to lay on an embargo; to impede, to restrain.
**embargo** *m* embargo; sin ~ still, however.
**embarque** *m* embarkation.
**embastar** *vt* to stitch, to tack.
**embate** *m* breakers *pl*, surf, surge; sudden attack.
**embaucador/ra** *m/f* swindler; impostor.
**embaucar** *vt* to deceive; to trick.
**embebecer** *vt* to fascinate; ~se *vr* to be fascinated.
**embebecimiento** *m* amazement, astonishment; fascination.
**embeber** *vt* to soak; to saturate; * *vi* to shrink; ~se *vr* to be enraptured; to be absorbed.
**embelesamiento** *m* rapture.
**embelesar** *vt* to amaze, to astonish.
**embeleso** *m* amazement, enchantment.
**embellecer** *vt* to embellish, to beautify.
**emberrincharse** *vr* to have a tantrum.
**embestida** *f* assault, violent attack.
**embestir** *vt* to assault, to attack.
**emblanquecer** *vt* to whiten; ~se *vr* to grow white; to bleach.
**emblema** *m* emblem.
**embobado/da** *adj* amazed; fascinated.
**embobamiento** *m* astonishment; fascination.
**embobar** *vt* to amaze; to fascinate; ~se *vr* to be amazed; to stand gaping.
**embobecer** *vt* to make silly; ~se *vr* to get silly.
**embobecimiento** *m* silliness.
**émbolo** *m* plunger; piston.
**embolsar** *vt* to put money into (a purse); to pocket.
**emborrachar** *vt* to intoxicate, to inebriate; ~se *vr* to get drunk.
**emboscada** *f* (*mil*) ambush.
**emboscarse** *vr* (*mil*) to lie in ambush.
**embotar** *vt* to blunt; ~se *vr* to go numb.
**embotellamiento** *m* traffic jam.
**embotellar** *vt* to bottle (wine).
**embozado/da** *adj* covered; covert.
**embozar** *vt* to muffle (the face); (*fig*) to cloak, to conceal.

**embozo** *m* part of a cloak, veil/anything with which the face is muffled; covering of one's face.

**embrague** *m* clutch.

**embrear** *vt* to cover with tar/pitch.

**embriagar** *vt* to intoxicate, to inebriate; to transport, to enrapture.

**embriaguez** *f* intoxication, drunkenness; rapture, delight.

**embrión** *m* embryo.

**embrollador/ra** *m/f* troublemaker.

**embrollar** *vt* to muddle; to entangle, to embroil.

**embrollo** *m* muddle.

**embromar** *vt* to tease; to cajole, to wheedle.

**embrujar** *vt* to bewitch.

**embrutecer** *vt* to brutalize; ~**se** *vr* to become depraved.

**embudo** *m* funnel.

**embuste** *m* fraud; lie, (*col*) fib.

**embustero/ra** *m/f* impostor, cheat; liar; * *adj* deceitful.

**embutido** *m* sausage; inlay.

**embutir** *vt* to insert; to stuff; to inlay; to cram, to scoff.

**emergencia** *f* emergency.

**emerger** *vi* to emerge, to appear.

**emético/ca** *adj* emetic.

**emigración** *f* emigration; migration.

**emigrado/da** *adj* emigrated; * *m/f* emigrant.

**emigrante** *m/f* emigrant.

**emigrar** *vi* to emigrate.

**eminencia** *f* eminence.

**eminente** *adj* eminent, high; excellent, conspicuous.

**emisario** *m* emissary.

**emisión** *f* emission; broadcasting; programme; issue.

**emisora** *f* broadcasting station.

**emitir** *vt* to emit, to send forth; to issue; to broadcast.

**emoción** *f* emotion; feeling; excitement.

**emocionante** *adj* exciting.

**emocionar** *vt* to excite; to move, to touch.

**emoliente** *adj* emollient, softening.

**emolumento** *m* emolument.

**emotivo/va** *adj* emotional.

**empacar** *vt* to pack; to crate.

**empachar** *vt* to give indigestion; ~**se** *vr* to have indigestion.

**empacho** *m* (*med*) indigestion.

**empachoso/sa** *adj* indigestible.

**empadronamiento** *m* register; census.

**empadronarse** *vr* to register.

**empalagar** *vt* to sicken; to disgust.

**empalago** *m* disgust; boredom.

**empalagoso/sa** *adj* cloying; tiresome.

**empalizada** *f* (*mil*) palisade.

**empalmadura** *f* join; weld; splice.

**empalmar** *vt* to join.

**empalme** *m* (*rail*) junction; connection.

**empanada** *f* (meat) pie.

**empanar** *vt* to cover with breadcrumbs.

**empantanarse** *vr* to get swamped; to get bogged down.

**empañar** *vt* to put a nappy on; to mist; to steam up; ~**se** *vr* to steam up; to tarnish one's reputation.

**empapar** *vt* to soak; to soak up; ~**se** *vr* to soak.

**empapelar** *vt* to paper.

**empaquetar** *vt* to pack, to parcel up.

**emparedado** *m* sandwich.

**emparejar** *vt* to level; to match, to fit; to equalize.

**emparentar** *vi* to be related by marriage.

**emparrado** *m* vine arbour.

**empastar** *vt* to paste; (*med*) to fill (a tooth).

**empaste** *m* (*med*) filling.

**empatar** *vi* to draw.

**empate** *m* draw.

**empedernido/da** *adj* inveterate; heartless.

**empedernir** *vt* to harden; ~**se** to be inflexible.

**empedrado** *m* paving.

**empedrador** *m* paver.

**empedrar** *vt* to pave.

**empeine** *m* instep.

**empellón** *m* push; heavy blow.

**empeñado/da** *adj* determined; pawned.

**empeñar** *vt* to pawn, to pledge; ~**se** *vr* to pledge oneself to pay debts; to get into debt; ~**se en algo** to insist on something.

**empeño** *m* obligation; determination; perseverance.

**empeorar** *vt* to make worse; * *vi*, ~**se** *vr* to grow worse.

**empequeñecer** *vt* to dwarf; (*fig*) to belittle.

**emperador** *m* emperor.

**emperatriz** *f* empress.

**emperifollarse** *vt* to dress oneself up.

**empero** *conj* yet, however.

**emperrarse** *vr* to get stubborn; to be obstinate.

**empezar** *vt* to begin, to start.

**empinado/da** *adj* high; proud.

**empinar** *vt* to raise; to exalt; * *vi* to drink heavily; ~**se** *vr* to stand on tiptoe; to soar.

**empírico/ca** *adj* empirical.

**empirismo** *m* empiricism.

**empizarrado** *m* slate roofing.

**empizarrar** *vt* to slate, to roof with slate.

**emplasto** *m* plaster.

**emplazamiento** *m* summons; location.

**emplazar** *vt* to summon; to locate.

**empleado/da** *m/f* official; employee.

**emplear** *vt* to employ; to occupy; to commission.

**empleo** *m* employ, employment, occupation.

**empobrecer** *vt* to reduce to poverty; * *vi* to become poor.

**empobrecimiento** *m* impoverishment.

**empollar** *vt* to incubate; to hatch; (*col*) to swot (up).

**empolvar** *vt* to powder; to sprinkle powder upon.

**emponzoñador/ra** *m/f* poisoner.

**emponzoñamiento** *m* poisoning.

**emponzoñar** *vt* to poison; to taint, to corrupt.

**emporio** *m* emporium.

**empotrado/da** *adj* built-in.

**empotrar** *vt* to embed; to build in.

**emprendedor/ra** *m/f* entrepreneur.

**emprender** *vt* to embark on; to tackle; to undertake.

**empresa** *f* (*com*) company; enterprise, undertaking.

**empresario/ria** *m/f* manager.

**empréstito** *m* loan.

**empujar** *vt* to push; to press forward.

**empuje** *m* thrust; pressure; (*fig*) drive.

**empujón** *m* push; impulse; **a ~ones** in fits and starts.

**empuñadura** *f* hilt (of a sword).

**empuñar** *vt* to clench, to grip with the fist; to clutch.

**emulación** *f* emulation.

**emular** *vt* to emulate, to rival.

**emulsión** *f* emulsion.

**en** *prep* in; for; on, upon.

**enaguas** *fpl* petticoat.

**enajenación** *f* alienation; absentmindedness.

**enajenamiento** *m* alienation; absentmindedness.

**enajenar** *vt* to alienate; **~se** *vr* to fall out.

**enamoradamente** *adv* lovingly.

**enamoradizo/za** *adj* inclined to fall in love.

**enamorado/da** *adj* in love, lovesick.

**enamoramiento** *m* falling in love.

**enamorar** *vt* to inspire love in; **~se** *vr* to fall in love.

**enano/na** *adj* dwarfish; * *m* dwarf.

**enarbolar** *vt* to hoist, to raise high.

**enardecer** *vt* to fire with passion, to inflame.

**enarenar** *vt* to fill with sand.

**encabezamiento** *m* heading; foreword.

**encabezar** *vt* to head; to put a heading to; to lead.

**encabritarse** *vr* to rear (of horses).

**encadenamiento** *m* linking together, chaining.

**encadenar** *vt* to chain, to link together; to connect, to unite.

**encajadura** *f* insertion; socket; groove.

**encajar** *vt* to insert; to drive in; to encase; to intrude; **~se** *vr* to squeeze; to gatecrash; * *vi* to fit (well).

**encaje** *m* encasing; joining; socket; groove; inlaid work.

**encajera** *f* lacemaker.

**encajonamiento** *m* packing into boxes etc.

**encajonar** *vt* to pack up in a box.

**encalabrinar** *vt* to make confused; **~se** *vr* to become obstinate.

**encaladura** *f* whitening, whitewash.

**encalar** *vt* to whitewash.

**encallar** *vi* (*mar*) to run aground.

**encallecer** *vi* to get corns.

**encamarse** *vr* to take to one's bed.

**encaminar** *vt* to guide, to show the way; **~se** *vr*: **~ a** to take the road to.

**encandilar** *vt* to dazzle.

**encanecer** *vi* to grow grey; to grow old.

**encantado/da** *adj* bewitched; delighted; pleased.

**encantador/ra** *adj* charming; *m/f* magician.

**encantamiento** *m* enchantment.

**encantar** *vt* to enchant, to charm; (*fig*) to delight.

**encanto** *m* enchantment; spell, charm.

**encañonar** *vt* to hold up; to point a gun at; * *vi* to grow feathers.

**encapotar** *vt* to cover with a cloak; **~se** *vr* to be cloudy.

**encapricharse** *vr* to become stubborn.

**encapuchar** *vt* to cover with a hood.

**encaramar** *vt* to raise; to extol.

**encararse** *vr*: **~ a** to come face to face with.

**encarcelación** *f* incarceration.

**encarcelar** *vt* to imprison.

**encarecer** *vt* to raise the price of; **~se** *vr* to get dearer.

**encarecimiento** *m* price increase; **con ~** insistently.

**encargado/da** *adj* in charge; * *m/f* representative; person in charge.

**encargar** *vt* to charge; to commission.

**encargo** *m* charge; commission; job; order.

**encariñarse** *vr*: ~ **con** to grow fond of.

**encarnación** *f* incarnation, embodiment.

**encarnado/da** *adj* incarnate; flesh-coloured; * *m* flesh colour.

**encarnar** *vt* to embody, to personify.

**encarnizado/da** *adj* bloodshot, inflamed; bloody, fierce.

**encarrilar** *vt* to put back on the rails; to put on the right track.

**encasillar** *vt* to pigeonhole; to typecast.

**encasquetar** *vt* to pull on (a hat).

**encastillarse** *vr* to refuse to yield.

**encauzar** *vt* to channel.

**encebollado** *m* casserole of beef/lamb and onions, seasoned with spice.

**encenagado/da** *adj* muddy, mud-stained.

**encenagamiento** *m* wallowing in mud.

**encenagarse** *vr* to wallow in mud.

**encendedor** *m* lighter.

**encender** *vt* to kindle, to light, to set on fire; to inflame, to incite; to switch on, to turn on; ~**se** *vr* to catch fire; to flare up.

**encendido/da** *adj* inflamed; high-coloured; * *m* ignition (of car).

**encerado** *m* blackboard.

**encerar** *vt* to wax; to polish.

**encerrar** *vt* to shut up, to confine; to contain; ~**se** *vr* to withdraw from the world.

**encespedar** *vt* to turf.

**enchapar** *vt* to veneer.

**encharcarse** *vr* to be flooded.

**enchufar** *vt* to plug in; to connect.

**enchufe** *m* plug; socket; connection; (*col*) contact, connection.

**encía** *f* gum (of the teeth).

**encíclica** *f* encyclical.

**enciclopedia** *f* encyclopedia.

**enciclopédico/ca** *adj* encyclopedic.

**encierro** *m* confinement; enclosure; prison; penning (of bulls).

**encima** *adv* above; over; at the top; besides; ~ **de** *prep* above; over; at the top of; besides.

**encina** *f* holm oak, evergreen oak.

**encinar** *m* holm oak wood; oak grove.

**encinta** *adj* pregnant.

**enclaustrado/da** *adj* cloistered; hidden away.

**enclenque** *adj* weak, sickly; * *m* weakling.

**encoger** *vt* to contract, to shorten; to shrink; to discourage; ~**se** *vr* to shrink; (*fig*) to cringe.

**encogidamente** *adv* shyly, timidly, bashfully.

**encogido/da** *adj* shy, timid, bashful.

**encogimiento** *m* contraction; shrinkage; shyness; timidness; bashfulness.

**encoladura** *f* gluing.

**encolar** *vt* to glue.

**encolerizar** *vt* to provoke, to irritate; ~**se** *vr* to get angry.

**encomendar** *vt* to recommend; to entrust; ~**se** *vr*: ~ **a** to entrust oneself to; to put one's trust in.

**encomiar** *vt* to praise.

**encomienda** *m* commission, charge; message; (*mil*) command; patronage, protection; parcel post.

**encomio** *m* eulogy, praise; commendation.

**enconar** *vt* to inflame; to irritate.

**encono** *m* ill-feeling, rancour.

**enconoso/sa** *adj* hurtful, prejudicial; malevolent.

**encontrado/da** *adj* conflicting; hostile.

**encontrar** *vt* to meet, to encounter; *vr*: ~**se con** to run into; * *vi* to assemble, to come together.

**encopetado/da** *adj* presumptuous, boastful.

**encorvadura** *f* curvature; crookedness.

**encorvar** *vt* to bend, to curve.

**encrespar** *vt* to curl, to frizzle (hair); (*fig*) to anger; ~**se** *vr* to get rough (of the sea); (*fig*) to get cross.

**encrucijada** *f* crossroads; junction.

**encuadernación** *f* binding.

**encuadernador/ra** *m/f* bookbinder.

**encuadernar** *vt* to bind (books).

**encubiertamente** *adv* secretly; deceitfully.

**encubierto/ta** *adj* hidden, concealed.

**encubridor/ra** *m/f* concealer, harbourer; receiver of stolen goods.

**encubrimiento** *m* concealment, hiding; receiving of stolen goods.

**encubrir** *vt* to hide, to conceal.

**encuentro** *m* meeting; collision, crash; match, game.

**encuesta** *f* inquiry; opinion poll.

**encumbrado/da** *adj* high; elevated.

**encumbramiento** *m* elevation; height.

**encumbrar** *vt* to raise, to elevate; ~**se** *vr* to be raised; (*fig*) to become conceited.

**encurtir** *vt* to pickle.

**endeble** *adj* feeble, weak.

**endecasílabo/ba** *adj* consisting of eleven syllables.

**endecha** *f* dirge, lament.

**endemoniado/da** *adj* possessed with the devil; devilish.

**enderezamiento** *m* guidance, direction.

**enderezar** *vt* to straighten out; to set right; ~**se** *vr* to stand upright.

**endeudarse** *vr* to get into debt.

**endiablado/da** *adj* devilish, diabolical; ugly.

**endiosar** *vt* to deify; ~**se** *vr* to be high and mighty.

**endosar** *vt* to endorse.

**endoso** *m* endorsement.

**endrina** *f* sloe, fruit of the blackthorn.

**endrino** *m* blackthorn, sloe.

**endulzar** *vt* to sweeten; to soften.

**endurecer** *vt* to harden, to toughen; ~**se** *vr* to become cruel; to grow hard.

**endurecidamente** *adv* cruelly.

**endurecimiento** *m* hardness; obstinacy; hard-heartedness.

**enebro** *m* (*bot*) juniper.

**enemigo/ga** *adj* hostile; * *m* enemy.

**enemistad** *f* enmity.

**enemistar** *vt* to make an enemy; ~**se** *vr* to become enemies; to fall out.

**energía** *f* energy, power, drive; strength of will; ~ **nuclear** nuclear power; ~ **solar** solar energy; ~ **renovables** renewable forms of energy.

**enérgico/ca** *adj* energetic; forceful.

**energúmeno/na** *m/f* (*col*) madman/woman.

**enero** *m* January.

**enervar** *vt* to enervate.

**enfadadizo/za** *adj* irritable, crotchety.

**enfadar** *vt* to anger, to irritate; to trouble; ~**se** *vr* to become angry.

**enfado** *m* trouble; anger.

**enfadoso/sa** *adj* annoying, troublesome.

**énfasis** *m* emphasis.

**enfático/ca** *adj* emphatic.

**enfermar** *vi* to fall ill; * *vt* to make sick; to weaken.

**enfermedad** *f* illness.

**enfermería** *f* infirmary; sick bay.

**enfermero/ra** *m/f* nurse.

**enfermizo/za** *adj* infirm, sickly.

**enfermo/ma** *adj* sick, ill; * *m/f* invalid, sick person; patient.

**enfervorizar** *vt* to arouse; to inflame, to incite.

**enflaquecer** *vt* to weaken; to make thin.

**enflaquecimiento** *m* loss of weight; (*fig*) weakening.

**enfocar** *vt* to focus; to consider (a problem).

**enfoque** *m* focus.

**enfrascarse** *vr* to be deeply embroiled.

**enfrentar** *vt* to confront; to put face to face; ~**se** *vr* to face each other; to meet (two teams).

**enfrente** *adv* over against, opposite; in front.

**enfriamiento** *m* refrigeration; (*med*) cold, chill.

**enfriar** *vt* to cool; to refrigerate; ~**se** *vr* to cool down; (*med*) to catch a cold/chill.

**enfurecer** *vt* to madden, to enrage; ~**se** *vr* to get rough (of the wind and sea); to become furious/enraged.

**enfurruñarse** *vr* to get sulky; to frown.

**engalanar** *vt* to adorn, to deck.

**engallarse** *vr* to be arrogant.

**engañabobos** *m invar* trickster; trick, trap.

**engañadizo/za** *adj* gullible, easily deceived.

**engañador/ra** *adj* cheating; deceptive; * *m/ f* cheat, impostor, deceiver.

**engañar** *vt* to deceive, to cheat; ~**se** *vr* to be deceived; to make a mistake.

**enganchar** *vt* to hook, to hang up; to hitch up; to couple, to connect; to recruit into military service; ~**se** *vr* (*mil*) to enlist.

**engañifa** *f* deceit, trick.

**engaño** *m* mistake; misunderstanding; deceit, fraud.

**engañoso/sa** *adj* deceitful, artful, false.

**engarzar** *vt* to thread; to link; to curl.

**engastar** *vt* to set, to mount.

**engaste** *m* setting, mount.

**engatusamiento** *m* deception, coaxing.

**engatusar** *vt* to coax.

**engendrar** *vt* to beget, to engender; to produce.

**engendro** *m* foetus, embryo; (*fig*) monstrosity; brainchild.

**englobar** *vt* to include.

**engolfarse** *vr* (*mar*) to sail out to sea; ~ **en** to be deeply involved in.

**engolosinar** *vt* to entice; ~**se** *vr* to find delight in.

**engomadura** *f* gluing.

**engomar** *vt* to glue.

**engordar** *vt* to fatten; * *vi* to grow fat; to put on weight.

**engorro** *m* nuisance, bother.

**engorroso/sa** *adj* troublesome, cumbersome.

**engranaje** *m* gear; gearing.

**engrandecer** *vt* to augment; to magnify; to speak highly of; to exaggerate.

**engrandecimiento** *m* increase; aggrandizement; exaggeration.

**engrasar** *vt* to grease, to lubricate.

**engreído/da** *adj* conceited, vain.

**engreimiento** *m* presumption, vanity.

**engreír** *vt* to make proud; **~se** *vr* to grow proud.

**engrosar** *vt* to enlarge; to increase.

**engrudo** *m* paste.

**engullidor/ra** *m/f* devourer; guzzler.

**engullir** *vt* to swallow; to gobble, to devour.

**enharinar** *vt* to cover/sprinkle with flour.

**enhebrar** *vt* to thread.

**enhilar** *vt* to thread.

**enhorabuena** *f* congratulations *pl*; * *interj* congratulations.

**enhoramala** *interj* good riddance.

**enigma** *m* enigma, riddle.

**enigmático/ca** *adj* enigmatic; dark, obscure.

**enjabonar** *vt* to soap; (*col*) to soft soap; (*col*) to tick off.

**enjaezar** *vt* to harness (a horse).

**enjalbegar** *vt* to whitewash.

**enjambre** *m* swarm (of bees); crowd, multitude.

**enjaular** *vt* to shut up in a cage; to imprison.

**enjoyar** *vt* to adorn with jewels.

**enjuagar** *vt* to rinse out; to wash out.

**enjuague** *m* (*med*) mouthwash; rinsing, rinse.

**enjugar** *vt* to dry (the tears); to wipe off.

**enjuiciar** *vt* to prosecute, to try; to pass judgement on, to judge.

**enjuto/ta** *adj* dried up; (*fig*) lean.

**enlace** *m* connection, link; relationship.

**enladrillado** *m* brick paving.

**enladrillador** *m* bricklayer.

**enladrillar** *vt* to pave with bricks.

**enlazable** *adj* able to be fastened together.

**enlazar** *vt* to join, to unite; to tie.

**enlodar** *vt* to cover in mud; (*fig*) to stain.

**enloquecer** *vt* to madden, to drive crazy; * *vi* to go mad.

**enloquecimiento** *m* madness.

**enlosar** *vt* to pave with flagstones.

**enlutar** *vt* to put into mourning; **~se** *vr* to go into mourning.

**enmaderar** *vt* to roof with timber.

**enmarañar** *vt* to entangle; to complicate; to confuse; **~se** *vr* to become entangled; to get confused.

**enmascarar** *vt* to mask; **~se** *vr* to go in disguise, to masquerade.

**enmendar** *vt* to correct; to reform; to repair, to compensate for; to amend; **~se** *vr* to mend one's ways.

**enmienda** *f* correction, amendment.

**enmohecer** *vt* to make mouldy; to rust; **~se** *vr* to grow mouldy/musty; to rust.

**enmohecido/da** *adj* mouldy.

**enmudecer(se)** *vt* to silence; **~se** *vr* to grow dumb; to be silent.

**ennegrecer** *vt* to blacken; to darken; to obscure.

**ennoblecer** *vt* to ennoble.

**ennoblecimiento** *m* ennoblement.

**enojadizo/za** *adj* peevish; short-tempered, irritable.

**enojar** *vt* to irritate, to make angry; to annoy; to upset; to offend; **~se** *vr* to get angry.

**enojo** *m* anger, annoyance.

**enojoso/sa** *adj* offensive, annoying.

**enorgullecerse** *vr*: **~ (de)** to be proud (of).

**enorme** *adj* enormous, vast, huge; horrible.

**enormidad** *f* enormity; monstrousness.

**enramar** *vt* to cover with the branches of trees.

**enranciarse** *vr* to grow rancid.

**enrarecer** *vt* to thin, to rarefy.

**enredadera** *f* climbing plant; bindweed.

**enredador/ra** *m/f* gossip; troublemaker; busybody.

**enredar** *vt* to entangle, to ensnare, to confound, to perplex; to puzzle; to sow discord among; **~se** *vr* to get entangled; to get complicated; to get embroiled.

**enredo** *m* entanglement; mischievous lie; plot of a play.

**enredoso/sa** *adj* complicated.

**enrejado** *m* trelliswork.

**enrejar** *vt* to fix a grating to (a window); to grate, to lattice.

**enrevesado/da** *adj* complicated.

**enriquecer** *vt* to enrich; to adorn; **~se** *vr* to grow rich.

**enristrar** *vt* to string (garlic); to straighten out; to go straight to.

**enrobustecer** *vt* to strengthen.

**enrojecer** *vt* to redden; * *vi* to blush.

**enrolar** *vt* to recruit; **~se** *vr* (*mil*) to join up.

**enrollar** *vt* to roll (up).

**enronquecer** *vt* to make hoarse; * *vi* to grow hoarse.

**enroscadura** *f* twist.

**enroscar** *vt* to twist; **~se** *vr* to curl/roll up.

**ensalada** *f* salad.

**ensaladera** *f* salad bowl.

**ensaladilla (rusa)** *f* Russian salad.

**ensalmar** *vt* to set (dislocated bones); to heal by spells.

**ensalmo** *m* enchantment, spell.

**ensalzar** *vt* to exalt, to aggrandize; to exaggerate.

**ensamblador/ra** *m/f* joiner.
**ensamblar** *vt* to assemble.
**ensanchar** *vt* to widen; to extend; to enlarge; **~se** *vr* to expand; to assume an air of importance.
**ensanche** *m* dilation, augmentation; widening; expansion.
**ensangrentar** *vt* to stain with blood.
**ensañar** *vr* to irritate, to enrage; **~se con** *vr* to treat brutally.
**ensartar** *vt* to string (beads etc).
**ensayar** *vt* to test; to rehearse.
**ensayo** *m* test, trial; rehearsal of a play; essay.
**ensenada** *f* inlet, cove.
**enseña** *f* colours *pl*, standard.
**enseñanza** *f* teaching, instruction; education.
**enseñar** *vt* to teach, to instruct; to show.
**enseres** *mpl* belongings *pl*.
**ensillar** *vt* to saddle.
**ensimismarse** *vr* to be/become lost in thought.
**ensoberbecer** *vt* to make proud; **~se** *vr* to become proud; (*mar*) to get rough.
**ensordecer** *vt* to deafen; * *vi* to grow deaf.
**ensordecimiento** *m* deafness.
**ensortijar** *vt* to fix a ring in (nose); to curl the hair.
**ensuciar** *vt* to stain, to soil; to defile; **~se** *vr* to wet oneself; to dirty oneself.
**ensueño** *m* fantasy; daydream; illusion.
**entablar** *vt* to board (up); to strike up (conversation).
**entablillar** *vt* (*med*) to put in a splint.
**entallar** *vt* to tailor (a suit); * *vi* to fit.
**ente** *m* organization; entity, being; (*col*) odd character.
**entendederas** *fpl* understanding; brains *pl*.
**entender** *vt*, *vi* to understand, to comprehend; to remark, to take notice (of); to reason, to think; **a mi ~** in my opinion; **~se** *vr* to understand each other.
**entendido/da** *adj* understood; wise; learned, knowing.
**entendimiento** *m* understanding; knowledge; judgement.
**enteramente** *adv* entirely, completely.
**enterar** *vt* to inform; to instruct; **~se** *vr* to find out.
**entereza** *f* entireness, integrity; firmness of mind.
**enternecer** *vt* to soften; to move (to pity); **~se** *vr* to be moved.
**enternecimiento** *m* compassion, pity.
**entero/ra** *adj* entire, complete; perfect; honest; resolute; **por ~** entirely, completely.

**enterrador** *m* gravedigger.
**enterrar** *vt* to inter, to bury.
**entibiar** *vt* to cool.
**entidad** *f* entity; company; body; society.
**entierro** *m* burial; funeral.
**entoldar** *vt* to cover with an awning.
**entomología** *f* entomology.
**entonación** *f* intonation; modulation; (*fig*) presumption, pride.
**entonar** *vt* to tune, to intone; to tone; * *vi* to be in tune; **~se** *vr* to give oneself airs.
**entonces** *adv* then, at that time.
**entontecer** *vt* to fool; * *vi*, **~se** *vr* to get silly.
**entontecimiento** *m* silliness.
**entornar** *vt* to half close.
**entorpecer** *vt* to dull; to make lethargic; to hinder; to delay.
**entorpecimiento** *m* numbness; lethargy.
**entrada** *f* entrance, entry; (*com*) receipts *pl*; entree; ticket (for cinema, theatre etc).
**entrambos/bas** *pn*, *pl* both.
**entrampar** *vt* to trap, to snare; to mess up; to burden with debts; **~se** *vr* get into debt.
**entrañable** *adj* intimate; affectionate.
**entrañas** *fpl* entrails *pl*, intestines *pl*.
**entrante** *adj* coming, next.
**entrar** *vi* to enter, to go in; to commence.
**entre** *prep* between; among(st); in; **~ manos** in hand.
**entreabrir** *vt* to half open (a door), to leave ajar.
**entrecano/na** *adj* grey-black, greyish.
**entrecejo** *m* space between the eyebrows; frown.
**entrecortado/da** *adj* faltering; difficult.
**entredicho** *m* (*law*) injunction; **estar en ~** to be banned; **poner en ~** to cast doubt on.
**entrega** *f* delivery; instalment.
**entregar** *vt* to deliver; to hand over; **~se** *vr* to surrender; to devote oneself.
**entrelazar** *vt* to interlace.
**entremedias** *adv* in the meantime.
**entremeses** *mpl* hors d'oeuvres.
**entremeter** *vt* to put (one thing) between (others); **~se** *vr* to interfere, to meddle.
**entremetido/da** *m/f* meddler; * *adj* meddling.
**entremetimiento** *m* insertion; meddling.
**entrenador/ra** *m/f* trainer, coach.
**entrenar** *vt* to train; **~se** *vr* to train.
**entreoír** *vt* to half hear.
**entrepaño** *m* panel.
**entrepierna** *f* crotch.
**entresaca** *f* thinning out (of trees).

**entresacar** *vt* to thin out; to sift, to separate.

**entresuelo** *m* mezzanine floor, entresol.

**entretanto** *adv* meanwhile.

**entretejer** *vt* to interweave.

**entretela** *f* interfacing, stiffening, interlining.

**entretener** *vt* to amuse; to entertain, to divert; to hold up; to maintain; ~**se** *vr* to amuse oneself; to linger.

**entretenido/da** *adj* pleasant; amusing; entertaining.

**entretenimiento** *m* amusement, entertainment.

**entrever** *vt* to have a glimpse of.

**entreverado/da** *adj* patchy; streaky.

**entrevista** *f* interview.

**entrevistar** *vt* to interview; ~**se** *vr* to have an interview.

**entristecer** *vt* to sadden.

**entrometer** *vt* to put (one thing) between (others); ~**se** *vr* to interfere, to meddle.

**entrometido/da** *m/f* meddler; * *adj* meddling.

**entroncar** *vi* to be related/connected.

**entronización** *f* enthronement.

**entronizar** *vt* to enthrone.

**entumecer** *vt* to swell; to numb; ~**se** *vr* to become numb.

**entumecido/da** *adj* numb, stiff.

**entumecimiento** *m* numbness.

**enturbiar** *vt* to make cloudy; to obscure, to confound; ~**se** *vr* to become cloudy; (*fig*) to get confused.

**entusiasmar** *vt* to excite, to fill with enthusiasm; to delight.

**entusiasmo** *m* enthusiasm.

**entusiasta** *m/f* enthusiast.

**enumeración** *f* enumeration.

**enumerar** *vt* to enumerate.

**enunciación** *f*, **enunciado** *m* enunciation, declaration.

**enunciar** *vt* to enunciate, to declare.

**envainar** *vt* to sheath(e).

**envalentonar** *vt* to give courage to; ~**se** *vr* to boast.

**envanecer** *vt* to make vain; to swell with pride; ~**se** *vr* to become proud.

**envaramiento** *m* stiffness; numbness.

**envarar** *vt* to numb.

**envasar** *vt* to pack; to bottle; to can.

**envase** *m* packing; bottling; canning; container; package; bottle; can.

**envejecer** *vt* to make old; * *vi*, ~**se** *vr* to grow old.

**envenenador/ra** *m/f* poisoner.

**envenenar** *vt* to poison; to embitter.

**envenenamiento** *m* poisoning.

**envergadura** *f* (*fig*) scope.

**envés** *m* wrong side (of material).

**enviado/da** *m/f* envoy, messenger.

**enviar** *vt* to send, to transmit, to convey, to dispatch.

**enviciar** *vt* to vitiate, to corrupt; ~**se** *vr* to get corrupted.

**envidia** *f* envy; jealousy.

**envidiable** *adj* enviable.

**envidiar** *vt* to envy; to grudge; to be jealous of.

**envidioso/sa** *adj* envious; jealous.

**envilecer** *vt* to vilify, to debase; ~**se** *vr* to degrade oneself.

**envío** *m* (*com*) dispatch, remittance of goods; consignment.

**enviudar** *vi* to become a widower/widow.

**envoltorio** *m* bundle of clothes.

**envoltura** *f* cover; wrapping.

**envolver** *vt* to involve; to wrap up.

**enyesar** *vt* to plaster; (*med*) to put in a plaster cast.

**enzarzarse** *vr* to get involved in a dispute; to get oneself into trouble.

**épico/ca** *adj* epic.

**epicúreo/rea** *adj* Epicurean.

**epidemia** *f* epidemic.

**epidémico/ca** *adj* epidemic.

**epidermis** *f* epidermis; cuticle.

**Epifanía** *f* Epiphany.

**epígrafe** *f* epigraph, inscription; motto; headline.

**epigrama** *m* epigram.

**epilepsia** *f* epilepsy.

**epílogo** *m* epilogue.

**episcopado** *m* episcopacy; bishopric.

**episcopal** *adj* Episcopal.

**episódico/ca** *adj* episodic.

**episodio** *m* episode, instalment.

**epístola** *f* epistle, letter.

**epistolar** *adj* epistolary.

**epistolario** *m* collected letters *pl*.

**epitafio** *m* epitaph.

**epíteto** *m* epithet.

**epítome** *m* epitome; compendium.

**época** *f* epoch; period, time.

**epopeya** *f* epic.

**equidad** *f* equity, honesty; impartiality, justice.

**equidistar** *vi* to be equidistant.

**equilátero/ra** *adj* equilateral.

**equilibrar** *vt* to balance; to poise.

**equilibrio** *m* balance, equilibrium.
**equinoccial** *adj* equinoctial.
**equinoccio** *m* equinox.
**equipaje** *m* luggage; equipment.
**equipar** *vt* to fit out, to equip, to furnish.
**equipararse** *vr*: ~ **con** to be on a level with.
**equipo** *m* equipment; team; shift.
**equitación** *f* horsemanship; riding.
**equitativo/va** *adj* equitable; just.
**equivalencia** *f* equivalence.
**equivalente** *adj* equivalent.
**equivaler** *vi* to be of equal value.
**equivocación** *f* mistake, error; misunderstanding.
**equivocado/da** *adj* mistaken, wrong.
**equivocar** *vt* to mistake; ~**se** *vr* to make a mistake, to be wrong.
**equívoco/ca** *adj* equivocal, ambiguous; * *m* equivocation; quibble.
**era** *f* era, age; threshing floor.
**erario** *m* treasury, public funds *pl*.
**erección** *f* foundation, establishment; erection, elevation.
**erguir** *vt* to erect, to raise up straight; ~**se** *vr* to straighten up.
**erial** *m* fallow land.
**erigir** *vt* to erect, to raise, to build; to establish.
**erizamiento** *m* standing on end (of hair etc).
**erizarse** *vr* to bristle; to stand on end.
**erizo** *m* hedgehog; ~ **de mar** sea urchin.
**ermita** *f* hermitage.
**ermitaño** *m* hermit.
**erosionar** *vt* to erode.
**erótico/ca** *adj* erotic.
**erotismo** *m* eroticism.
**errante** *adj* errant; stray; roving.
**errar** *vi* to be mistaken; to wander.
**errata** *f* misprint.
**erre** ~ **que** ~ *adv* obstinately.
**erróneo/nea** *adj* erroneous.
**error** *m* error, mistake, fault.
**eructar** *vi* to belch, to burp.
**eructo** *m* belch, burp.
**erudición** *f* erudition, learning.
**erudito/ta** *adj* learned, erudite.
**erupción** *f* eruption, outbreak.
**esa:** *f* of **ese**.
**ésa:** *f* of **ése**.
**esbelto/ta** *adj* slim, slender.
**esbirro** *m* bailiff; henchman; killer.
**esbozo** *m* outline.
**escabechar** *vt* to marinate; to pickle.
**escabeche** *m* pickle; pickled fish.

**escabel** *m* footstool.
**escabrosidad** *f* unevenness, roughness; harshness.
**escabroso/sa** *adj* rough, uneven; craggy; rude, risqué, blue.
**escabullirse** *vr* to escape, to evade; to slip through one's fingers.
**escafandra** *f* diving suit; space suit.
**escala** *f* ladder; (*mus*) scale; port of call; stopover.
**escalador/ra** *m/f* climber.
**escalar** *vt* to climb.
**escaldado/da** *adj* cautious, suspicious, wary.
**escaldar** *vt* to scald.
**escalera** *f* staircase; ladder.
**escalfar** *vt* to poach (eggs).
**escalofríos** *mpl* shivers *pl*.
**escalofriante** *adj* chilling.
**escalón** *m* step of a stair; rung.
**escama** *f* (fish) scale.
**escamado/da** *adj* wary, cautious.
**escamar** *vt* to scale, to take off the scales; ~**se** *vr* to flake off; to become suspicious.
**escamoso/sa** *adj* scaly.
**escamotear** *vt* to swipe; to make disappear.
**escampar** *vi* to stop raining.
**escanciador** *m* wine waiter; cupbearer.
**escanciar** *vt* to pour (wine).
**escandalizar** *vt* to scandalize; ~**se** *vr* to be shocked.
**escándalo** *m* scandal; uproar.
**escandaloso/sa** *adj* scandalous; shocking.
**escanear** *vt* to scan.
**escáner** *m* scanner.
**escaño** *m* bench with a back; seat (parliament).
**escapada** *f* escape, flight.
**escapar** *vi* to escape; ~**se** *vr* to get away; to leak (water etc).
**escaparate** *m* shop window; wardrobe.
**escapatoria** *f* escape, flight; excuse.
**escape** *m* escape, flight; leak; exhaust (of motor); **a todo** ~ at full speed.
**escapulario** *m* scapulary.
**escarabajo** *m* beetle.
**escaramuza** *f* skirmish; dispute, quarrel.
**escaramuzar** *vt* to skirmish.
**escarbadura** *f* act and effect of scratching.
**escarbar** *vt* to scratch (the earth as hens do); to inquire into.
**escarcha** *f* white frost.
**escarchar** *vi* to be frosty.
**escardador** *m* weeding hoe.
**escardillo** *m* small weeding hoe.
**escarlata** *adj* scarlet.

**escarlatina** *f* scarlet fever.

**escarmentar** *vi* to learn one's lesson; * *vt* to punish severely.

**escarmiento** *m* warning, caution; punishment.

**escarnecer** *vt* to mock, to ridicule.

**escarnio** *m* gibe, ridicule.

**escarola** *f* (*bot*) endive.

**escarpa** *f* slope; escarpment.

**escarpado/da** *adj* sloped; craggy.

**escarpín** *m* sock; pump (shoe).

**escasear** *vi* to be scarce.

**escasez** *f* shortage; poverty.

**escaso/sa** *adj* small, short, little; sparing; scarce; scanty.

**escatimar** *vt* to curtail, to lessen; to be scanty with.

**escena** *f* stage; scene.

**escenario** *m* stage; set.

**escepticismo** *m* scepticism.

**escéptico/ca** *adj* sceptical.

**esclarecer** *vt* to lighten; to illuminate; to illustrate; to shed light on (problem etc).

**esclarecido/da** *adj* illustrious, noble.

**esclarecimiento** *m* clarification; enlightenment.

**esclavina** *f* short cloak/cape.

**esclavitud** *f* slavery, servitude.

**esclavizar** *vt* to enslave.

**esclavo/va** *m/f* slave; captive.

**esclusa** *f* sluice, floodgate.

**escoba** *f* broom, brush.

**escobazo** *m* blow given with a broom.

**escobilla** *f* brush, small broom; blade.

**escocer** *vt* to sting; to burn; ~se *vr* to chafe.

**escoger** *vt* to choose, to select.

**escolar** *m/f* schoolboy/girl; * *adj* scholastic.

**escolástico/ca** *adj* scholastic; * *m* scholar.

**escollo** *m* reef, rock.

**escolta** *f* escort.

**escoltar** *vt* to escort.

**escombros** *mpl* rubbish; debris.

**esconder** *vt* to hide, to conceal; ~se *vr* to be hidden.

**escondidas**: a ~ *adv* in a secret manner.

**escondite** *m* hiding place; **juego del** ~ hide-and-seek.

**escondrijo** *m* hiding place.

**escopeta** *f* shotgun; **a tiro de** ~ within gunshot.

**escopetazo** *m* gunshot; gunshot wound.

**escopetero** *m* gunsmith.

**escoplo** *m* chisel.

**escorbuto** *m* scurvy.

**escoria** *f* dross; scum; dregs *pl*.

**Escorpio** *m* Scorpio (sign of the zodiac).

**escorpión** *m* scorpion.

**escotado/da** *adj* low-cut.

**escotadura** *f* low neck(line).

**escotar** *vt* to cut low in front.

**escote** *m* low neck (of a dress).

**escotilla** *f* (*mar*) hatchway.

**escozor** *m* smart; burning pain; sting(ing).

**escriba** *m* scribe (of the Hebrews).

**escribanía** *f* clerk's office; writing desk.

**escribano** *m* court clerk; notary.

**escribiente** *m* transcriber; clerk; copyist.

**escribir** *vt* to write; to spell; * *vi* to write.

**escrito** *m* document; manuscript, text.

**escritor/ra** *m/f* writer, author.

**escritorio** *m* writing desk; office, study.

**escritura** *f* writing; deed.

**escrúpulo** *m* doubt, scruple, scrupulousness.

**escrupulosidad** *f* scrupulousness.

**escrupuloso/sa** *adj* scrupulous; exact.

**escrutar** *vt* to examine; to count (ballot papers).

**escrutinio** *m* scrutiny, inquiry.

**escrutiñador** *m* scrutinizer, inquirer.

**escuadra** *f* square; squadron; squad.

**escuadrar** *vt* to square.

**escuadrón** *m* squadron.

**escuálido/da** *adj* skinny; squalid.

**escucha** *f* listening(-in); * *m* scout.

**escuchar** *vt* to listen to, to heed.

**escudar** *vt* to shield; to guard from danger; ~se *vr* to protect oneself.

**escudero** *m* squire; page.

**escudilla** *f* bowl.

**escudo** *m* shield.

**escudriñamiento** *m* investigation, scrutiny.

**escudriñar** *vt* to search, to examine; to pry into.

**escuela** *f* school; ~ **primaria** primary school; ~ **secundaria** secondary school.

**escueto/ta** *adj* plain; simple.

**esculpir** *vt* to sculpt.

**escultor/ra** *m/f* sculptor.

**escultura** *f* sculpture.

**escupidera** *f* cuspidor.

**escupidura** *f* spit.

**escupir** *vt* to spit.

**escurreplatos** *m invar* plate rack.

**escurridizo/za** *adj* slippery.

**escurrir** *vt* to drain; to drip; ~se *vr* to slip away; to slip, to slide; * *vi* to wring out.

**ese/esa** *adj* that; **esos/as** *pl* those.

**ése/ésa** *pn* that (one); **ésos/as** *pl* those (ones).

**esencia** *f* essence.
**esencial** *adj* essential; principal.
**esfera** *f* sphere; globe.
**esférico/ca** *adj* spherical.
**esferoide** *f* spheroid.
**esfinge** *f* sphinx.
**esforzado/da** *adj* strong, vigorous; valiant.
**esforzarse** *vr* to exert oneself, to make an effort.
**esfuerzo** *m* effort.
**esfumarse** *vr* to fade away.
**esgrima** *f* fencing.
**esgrimidor** *m* fencer.
**esgrimir** *vi* to fence.
**esguince** *m* (*med*) sprain.
**eslabón** *m* link of a chain; steel; shackle.
**eslabonar** *vt* to link; to unite.
**esmaltador** *m* enameller.
**esmaltar** *vt* to enamel.
**esmalte** *m* enamel.
**esmerado/da** *adj* careful, neat.
**esmeralda** *f* emerald.
**esmerar** *vt* to polish; ~se *vr* to take great care; to work hard.
**esmeril** *m* emery.
**esmerillar** *vt* to polish with emery.
**esmero** *m* careful attention, great care.
**esnob** *adj* snobbish; posh; * *m/f* snob.
**eso** *pn* that.
**esófago** *m* oesophagus; throat.
**esos, ésos** *pl* of **ese, ése.**
**espabilar** *vt* to wake up; ~se *vr* to wake up; (*fig*) to get a move on.
**espacial** *adj* space *compd.*
**espaciar** *vt* to spread out; to space (out).
**espacio** *m* space; (*rad/TV*) programme.
**espaciosidad** *f* spaciousness, capacity.
**espacioso/sa** *adj* spacious, roomy.
**espada** *f* sword; ace of spades.
**espadachín** *m* bully.
**espadaña** *f* (*bot*) bulrush.
**espadín** *m* small short sword.
**espaguetis** *mpl* spaghetti.
**espalda** *f* back, back-part; ~s *fpl* shoulders *pl.*
**espaldilla** *f* shoulder blade.
**espantadizo/za** *adj* timid, easily frightened.
**espantajo** *m* scarecrow; bogeyman.
**espantapájaros** *m invar* scarecrow.
**espantar** *vt* to frighten; to chase/drive away.
**espanto** *m* fright; menace, threat; astonishment.
**espantoso/sa** *adj* frightful, dreadful; amazing.
**español/la** *adj* Spanish; * *m/f* Spaniard; * *m* Spanish (language).
**esparadrapo** *m* sticking plaster.

**esparcir** *vt* to scatter; to divulge; ~se *vr* to amuse oneself.
**espárrago** *m* asparagus.
**esparto** *m* (*bot*) esparto.
**espasmo** *m* spasm.
**espátula** *f* spatula.
**especia** *f* spice.
**especial** *adj* special; particular; **en** ~ especially.
**especialidad** *f* speciality.
**especie** *f* species; kind, sort; matter.
**especificación** *f* specification.
**especificar** *vt* to specify.
**específico/ca** *adj* specific.
**espectáculo** *m* spectacle; show.
**espectador/ra** *m/f* spectator.
**espectro** *m* spectre, phantom, ghost, apparition.
**especulación** *f* speculation; contemplation; venture.
**especulador/ra** *m/f* speculator.
**especular** *vt* to speculate.
**especulativo/va** *adj* speculative; thoughtful.
**espejismo** *m* mirage.
**espejo** *m* mirror.
**espeluznante** *adj* horrifying.
**espera** *f* stay, waiting; (*law*) respite, adjournment, delay.
**esperanza** *f* hope.
**esperanzar** *vt* to give hope to.
**esperar** *vt* to hope; to expect, to wait for.
**esperma** *f* sperm.
**espesar** *vt* to thicken; to condense; ~se *vr* to grow thick; to solidify.
**espeso/sa** *adj* thick, dense.
**espesor** *m* thickness.
**espesura** *f* thickness; density, solidity.
**espía** *m/f* spy.
**espiar** *vt* to spy.
**espiga** *f* ear (of corn).
**espigón** *m* ear of corn; sting; (*mar*) breakwater.
**espina** *f* thorn; fishbone.
**espinaca** *f* (*bot*) spinach.
**espinazo** *m* spine, backbone.
**espinilla** *f* shinbone.
**espino** *m* hawthorn.
**espinoso/sa** *adj* thorny; dangerous.
**espionaje** *m* spying, espionage.
**espiral** *adj*, *f* spiral.
**espirar** *vt* to exhale.
**espíritu** *m* spirit, soul; mind; intelligence; **el E~ Santo** the Holy Ghost; ~s *pl* demons *pl*, hobgoblins *pl.*

**espiritual** *adj* spiritual; ghostly.
**espiritualidad** *f* spirituality.
**espiritualizar** *vt* to spiritualize.
**esplendidez** *f* splendour.
**espléndido/da** *adj* splendid.
**esplendor** *m* splendour.
**espliego** *m* (*bot*) lavender.
**espolear** *vt* to spur, to instigate, to incite.
**espolón** *m* spur (of a cock); spur (of a mountain range); sea wall; jetty; (*mar*) buttress.
**espolvorear** *vt* to sprinkle.
**espondeo** *m* (*poet*) spondee.
**esponja** *f* sponge.
**esponjar** *vt* to sponge; **~se** *vr* to be puffed up with pride.
**esponjoso/sa** *adj* spongy.
**esponsales** *mpl* betrothal.
**espontaneidad** *f* spontaneity.
**espontáneo/nea** *adj* spontaneous.
**esposa** *f* wife.
**esposar** *vt* to handcuff.
**esposas** *fpl* handcuffs *pl*.
**esposo** *m* husband.
**espuela** *f* spur; stimulus; (*bot*) larkspur.
**espuerta** *f* pannier, basket.
**espulgar** *vt* to delouse; to examine closely.
**espuma** *f* froth, foam.
**espumadera** *f* skimmer.
**espumajear** *vi* to foam at the mouth.
**espumar** *vt* to skim, to take the scum off.
**espumarajo** *m* foam, froth (from the mouth).
**espumoso/sa** *adj* frothy, foamy; sparkling (wine).
**espurio/ria** *adj* spurious; adulterated; illegitimate.
**esputo** *m* spit, saliva.
**esqueje** *m* cutting (of plant).
**esquela** *f* note, slip of paper.
**esqueleto** *m* skeleton.
**esquema** *m* scheme; diagram; plan.
**esquí** *m* ski; skiing.
**esquiar** *vi* to ski.
**esquife** *m* skiff, small boat.
**esquilador** *m* sheep-shearer.
**esquilar** *vt* to shear sheep.
**esquina** *f* corner, angle.
**esquinado/da** *adj* cornered, angled.
**esquinar** *vt* to form a corner with.
**esquirol** *m* blackleg; scab.
**esquivar** *vt* to shun, to avoid, to evade.
**esquivez** *f* disdain; shyness.
**esquivo/va** *adj* scornful; shy, reserved.
**esta**: *f* of **este**.
**ésta**: *f* of **éste**.

**estabilidad** *f* stability.
**estable** *adj* stable.
**establecer** *vt* to establish.
**establecimiento** *m* establishment.
**establo** *m* stable.
**estaca** *f* stake; stick; post.
**estacada** *f* fence; fencing; stockade.
**estacazo** *m* blow with a stick.
**estación** *f* season (of the year); station; railroad station, terminus; **~ de autobuses** bus station; **~ de servicio** filling station.
**estacional** *adj* seasonal.
**estacionamiento** *m* parking; car park; (*mil*) stationing.
**estacionar** *vt* to park; (*mil*) to station.
**estacionario/ria** *adj* stationary.
**estadio** *m* phase; stadium.
**estadista** *m* statesman; statistician.
**estadística** *f* statistics *pl*.
**estadístico/ca** *adj* statistical.
**estado** *m* state, condition.
**Estados Unidos** *mpl* United States (of America).
**estafa** *f* trick, fraud.
**estafador/ra** *m/f* swindler, racketeer.
**estafar** *vt* to deceive, to defraud.
**estafeta** *f* post office.
**estallar** *vi* to crack; to burst; to break out.
**estallido** *m* explosion; (*fig*) outbreak.
**estambre** *m* stamen.
**estamento** *m* estate; body; layer; class.
**estameña** *f* serge.
**estampa** *f* print; engraving; appearance.
**estampado/da** *adj* printed; * *m* printing; print; stamping.
**estampar** *vt* to print.
**estampida** *f* stampede.
**estampido** *m* report (of a gun); crack.
**estampilla** *f* seal, stamp.
**estancar** *vt* to check (a current); to monopolize; to prohibit, to suspend; **~se** *vr* to stagnate.
**estancia** *f* stay; bedroom; ranch; (*poet*) stanza.
**estanco** *m* tobacconist's (shop); **~/ca** *adj* watertight.
**estándar** *adj*, *m* standard.
**estandarizar** *vt* to standardize.
**estandarte** *m* banner, standard.
**estanque** *m* pond, pool; reservoir.
**estanquero/ra** *m/f* tobacconist.
**estante** *m* shelf (for books).
**estantería** *f* shelves *pl*, shelving.
**estaño** *m* tin.
**estar** *vi* to be; to be (in a place).

**estatal** *adj* state *compd*.
**estática** *f* statics *pl*.
**estático/ca** *adj* static.
**estatua** *f* statue.
**estatura** *f* stature.
**estatuto** *m* statute, law.
**este**[1] *m* east.
**este/ta**[2] *adj* this; **estos/tas** *pl* these.
**éste** *pn m* this (one); **éstos/tas** *pl* these (ones).
**estera** *f* mat.
**estercolar** *vt* to manure.
**estercolero** *m* dunghill.
**estéreo** *adj invar*, *m* stereo.
**estereotipar** *vt* to stereotype.
**estereotipo** *m* stereotype.
**estéril** *adj* sterile, infertile.
**esterilidad** *f* sterility, infertility.
**esterilla** *f* mat; (*comput*) mouse mat.
**esterlina** *adj*: **libra ~** pound sterling.
**estético/ca** *adj* aesthetic; * *f* aesthetics.
**estiércol** *m* dung; manure.
**estilar(se)** *vi* (*vr*) to be in fashion; to be used.
**estilo** *m* style; fashion; stroke (in swimming).
**estima** *f* esteem.
**estimable** *adj* estimable, worthy of esteem.
**estimación** *f* estimation, valuation.
**estimar** *vt* to estimate, to value; to esteem; to judge; to think.
**estimulante** *adj* stimulating; * *m* stimulant.
**estimular** *vt* to stimulate, to excite; to goad.
**estímulo** *m* stimulus.
**estío** *m* summer.
**estipendiario** *m* stipendiary.
**estipulación** *f* stipulation.
**estipular** *vt* to stipulate.
**estirado/da** *adj* stretched tight; (*fig*) pompous.
**estirar** *vt* to stretch out.
**estirón** *m* pulling; tugging; **dar un ~** to grow rapidly.
**estirpe** *f* race, origin, stock.
**estival** *adj* summer *compd*.
**esto** *pn* this.
**estocada** *f* stab.
**estofa** *f*: **de baja ~** poor quality.
**estofado** *m* stew.
**estola** *f* stole.
**estolidez** *f* stupidity.
**estólido/da** *adj* stupid.
**estomacal** *adj* stomach *compd*.
**estómago** *m* stomach.
**estopa** *f* tow.

**estoque** *m* rapier, sword.
**estorbar** *vt* to hinder; (*fig*) to bother; * *vi* to be in the way.
**estorbo** *m* obstacle, hindrance, impediment.
**estornudar** *vi* to sneeze.
**estornudo** *m* sneeze.
**estos, éstos** *pl* of **este, éste**.
**estrada** *f* highway.
**estrado** *m* drawing room; stage, platform; **~ de los testigos** witness box.
**estrafalario/ria** *adj* slovenly; eccentric.
**estrago** *m* ruin, destruction; havoc.
**estrambótico/ca** *adj* eccentric, odd.
**estrangulador/ra** *m/f* strangler.
**estrangulamiento** *m* bottleneck.
**estrangular** *vt* to strangle; (*med*) to strangulate.
**estraperlo** *m* black market.
**estratagema** *f* stratagem, trick.
**estrategia** *f* strategy.
**estratégico/ca** *adj* strategic.
**estrato** *m* stratum, layer.
**estraza** *f* rag; **papel de ~** brown paper.
**estrechar** *vt* to tighten; to contract, to constrain; to compress; **~se** *vr* to grow narrow; to embrace; **~ la mano** to shake hands.
**estrechez** *f* strictness, narrowness; shortage of money.
**estrecho** *m* straits *pl*; **~/cha** *adj* narrow, close; tight; intimate; rigid, austere; short (of money).
**estrella** *f* star.
**estrellado/da** *adj* starry; **huevos ~s** fried eggs.
**estrellar** *vt* to dash to pieces; **~se** *vr* to smash; to crash; to fail.
**estremecer** *vt* to shake, to make tremble; **~se** *vr* to shake, to tremble.
**estremecimiento** *m* trembling, shaking.
**estrenar** *vt* to wear for the first time; to move into (a house); to show (a film) for the first time; **~se** *vr* to make one's debut.
**estreñido/da** *adj* constipated.
**estreñimiento** *m* constipation.
**estrépito** *m* noise, racket; fuss.
**estrepitoso/sa** *adj* noisy.
**estribar** *vi*: **~ en** to be supported by; to be based on.
**estribillo** *m* chorus.
**estribo** *m* buttress; stirrup; bracket; brace; **perder los ~s** (*col*) to fly off the handle.
**estribor** *m* (*mar*) starboard.
**estricto/ta** *adj* strict; severe.
**estrofa** *f* (*poet*) verse, strophe.

**estropajo** *m* scourer.
**estropajoso/sa** *adj* tough, leathery; despicable; mean; stammering.
**estropear** *vt* to spoil; to damage; **~se** *vr* to get damaged.
**estructura** *f* structure.
**estruendo** *m* clamour, noise; confusion, uproar; pomp, ostentation.
**estrujar** *vt* to press, to squeeze.
**estrujón** *m* pressing, squeezing.
**estuario** *m* estuary.
**estuche** *m* case (for scissors etc); sheath.
**estudiante** *m/f* student.
**estudiantil** *adj* student *compd*.
**estudiar** *vt* to study.
**estudio** *m* study; studio; **~s** *mpl* studies *pl*; learning.
**estudioso/sa** *adj* studious.
**estufa** *f* heater, fire.
**estufilla** *f* muff; small stove.
**estupefacción** *f* stupefaction.
**estupefaciente** *m* narcotic.
**estupefacto** *adj* speechless; thunderstruck.
**estupendo/da** *adj* terrific, marvellous.
**estupidez** *f* stupidity.
**estúpido/da** *adj* stupid.
**estupor** *m* stupor; astonishment.
**estupro** *m* rape.
**etapa** *f* stage; stopping place; (*fig*) phase.
**etcétera** *adv* etcetera, and so on.
**éter** *m* ether.
**etéreo/rea** *adj* ethereal.
**eternidad** *f* eternity.
**eternizar** *vt* to eternalize, to perpetuate.
**eterno/na** *adj* eternal.
**ética** *f* ethics.
**ético/ca** *adj* ethical, moral.
**etimología** *f* etymology.
**etimológico/ca** *adj* etymological.
**etiqueta** *f* etiquette; label, tag.
**Eucaristía** *f* Eucharist.
**eufemismo** *m* euphemism.
**euforia** *f* euphoria.
**euro** *m* euro.
**eurocámara** *f* European Parliament.
**eurodiputado/da** *m/f* Euro-MP.
**euroescéptico/ca** *m/f* Eurosceptic.
**Europa** *f* Europe.
**eurotúnel** *m* Eurotunnel, Channel tunnel.
**evacuación** *f* evacuation.
**evacuar** *vt* to evacuate, to empty.
**evadir** *vt* to evade, to escape.
**evaluar** *vt* to evaluate.
**evangélico/ca** *adj* evangelical.
**evangelio** *m* gospel.

**evangelista** *m* evangelist.
**evangelizar** *vt* to evangelize.
**evaporar** *vt* to evaporate; **~se** *vr* to vanish.
**evasión** *f* evasion, escape.
**evasivo/va** *adj* evasive; * *f* excuse.
**eventual** *adj* possible; temporary, casual (worker).
**evidencia** *f* evidence, proof.
**evidente** *adj* evident, clear.
**evitable** *adj* avoidable.
**evitar** *vt* to avoid.
**evocación** *f* evocation; invocation.
**evocar** *vt* to call out; to invoke.
**evolución** *f* evolution, development; change; (*mil*) manoeuvre.
**evolucionar** *vi* to evolve.
**ex** *adj* ex.
**exacción** *f* exaction; extortion.
**exacerbar** *vt* to exacerbate; to irritate.
**exactamente** *adv* exactly.
**exactitud** *f* exactness.
**exacto/ta** *adj* exact; punctual; accurate.
**exageración** *f* exaggeration.
**exagerar** *vt* to exaggerate.
**exaltación** *f* exaltation, elation.
**exaltar** *vt* to exalt, to elevate; to praise, to extol; **~se** *vr* to get excited.
**examen** *m* exam, examination, test, inquiry.
**examinador** *m* examiner.
**examinar** *vt* to examine.
**exánime** *adj* lifeless, weak.
**exasperación** *f* exasperation.
**exasperar** *vt* to exasperate, to irritate.
**excavación** *f* excavation.
**excavadora** *f* excavator; digger.
**excavar** *vt* to excavate, to dig out.
**excedente** *adj* excessive.
**exceder** *vt* to exceed, to surpass, to excel, to outdo.
**excelencia** *f* excellence.
**Excelencia** *f* Excellency (title).
**excelente** *adj* excellent.
**excelso/sa** *adj* elevated, sublime, lofty.
**excentricidad** *f* eccentricity.
**excéntrico/ca** *adj* eccentric.
**excepción** *f* exception.
**excepto** *adv* excepting, except (for).
**exceptuar** *vt* to except, to exempt.
**excesivo/va** *adj* excessive.
**exceso** *m* excess.
**excitación** *f* excitement; excitation.
**excitar** *vt* to excite; **~se** *vr* to get excited.
**exclamación** *f* exclamation.
**exclamar** *vt* to exclaim, to cry out.
**excluir** *vt* to exclude.

**exclusión** *f* exclusion.
**exclusiva** *f* exclusive; (*com*) sole right.
**exclusivamente, exclusive** *adv* exclusively.
**exclusivo/va** *adj* exclusive.
**excomulgar** *vt* to excommunicate.
**excomunión** *f* excommunication.
**excremento** *m* excrement.
**excursión** *f* excursion, trip.
**excusa** *f* excuse, apology.
**excusable** *adj* excusable.
**excusado** *m* toilet, lavatory.
**excusar** *vt* to excuse; to avoid; ~ **de** to exempt from; ~**se** *vr* to apologize.
**execrable** *adj* execrable, abhorrent.
**execrar** *vt* to execrate, to curse.
**exención** *f* exemption; immunity, privilege.
**exento/ta** *adj* exempt, free.
**exequias** *fpl* funeral rites *pl*, obsequies *pl*.
**exhalación** *f* exhalation; fumes *pl*, vapour.
**exhalar** *vt* to exhale; to give off; to heave (a sigh).
**exhausto/ta** *adj* exhausted.
**exhibición** *f* exhibition, display.
**exhibir** *vt* to exhibit.
**exhortación** *f* exhortation.
**exhortar** *vt* to exhort.
**exhumación** *f* exhumation.
**exhumar** *vt* to disinter, to exhume.
**exigencia** *f* demand, requirement.
**exigir** *vt* to demand, to require.
**exiguo/gua** *adj* meagre, small.
**exiliado/da** *adj* exiled; * *m/f* exile.
**exilio** *m* exile.
**eximir** *vt* to exempt, to free; to excuse.
**existencia** *f* existence, being.
**existente** *adj* existing, in existence.
**existir** *vi* to exist, to be.
**éxito** *m* outcome; success; (*mus* etc) hit; **tener** ~ to be successful.
**exoneración** *f* exoneration.
**exonerar** *vt* to exonerate.
**exorbitante** *adj* exhorbitant, excessive.
**exorcismo** *m* exorcism.
**exorcista** *m* exorcist.
**exorcizar** *vt* to exorcize.
**exótico/ca** *adj* exotic.
**expandir** *vt* to expand.
**expansión** *f* expansion; extension.
**expansivo/va** *adj* expansive.
**expatriarse** *vr* to emigrate; to go into exile.
**expectativa** *f* expectation; prospect.
**expectoración** *f* expectoration.
**expectorar** *vt* to expectorate.
**expedición** *f* expedition.

**expedicionario/ria** *adj* expeditionary.
**expediente** *m* expedient; means; (*law*) proceedings *pl*; dossier, file.
**expedir** *vt* to send, to forward, to dispatch.
**expeditivo/va** *adj* expeditious.
**expedito/ta** *adj* speedy; clear, free.
**expeler** *vt* to expel.
**expensas** *fpl*: **a** ~ **de** at the expense of.
**experiencia** *f* experience; trial.
**experimentado/da** *adj* experienced; expert.
**experimental** *adj* experimental.
**experimentar** *vt* to experience; * *vi*: ~ **con** to experiment with.
**experimento** *m* experiment, trial.
**experto/ta** *adj* expert; experienced.
**expiación** *f* expiation; purification.
**expiar** *vt* to atone for; to purify.
**expiatorio/ria** *adj* expiatory.
**expirar** *vi* to expire.
**explanada** *f* esplanade.
**explayarse** *vr* to speak at length.
**explicación** *f* explanation.
**explicar** *vt* to explain, to expound; ~**se** *vr* to explain oneself.
**explícito/ta** *adj* explicit.
**exploración** *f* exploration.
**explorador/ra** *m/f* explorer.
**explorar** *vt* to explore.
**explosión** *f* explosion.
**explotación** *f* exploitation; running.
**explotar** *vt* to exploit; to run; * *vi* to explode.
**exponente** *m* (*math*) exponent.
**exponer** *vt* to expose; to explain.
**exportación** *f* export; exports *pl*.
**exportar** *vt* to export.
**exposición** *f* exposure; exhibition; explanation; account.
**expresar** *vt* to express.
**expresión** *f* expression.
**expresivo/va** *adj* expressive; energetic.
**expreso/sa** *adj* express, clear, specific; fast (train).
**express** *m* (*rail*) express train.
**exprimidor** *m* squeezer.
**exprimir** *vt* to squeeze out.
**ex profeso** *adv* on purpose.
**expropriar** *vt* to expropriate.
**expuesto/ta** *adj* exposed; on display.
**expulsar** *vt* to expel, to drive out.
**expulsión** *f* expulsion.
**exquisito/ta** *adj* exquisite; excellent.
**éxtasis** *m* ecstasy, enthusiasm.
**extático/ca** *adj* ecstatic.

**extender** *vt* to extend, to stretch out; **~se** *vr* to extend; to spread.

**extensión** *f* extension; extent.

**extensivo/va** *adj* extensive.

**extenso/sa** *adj* extensive.

**extenuación** *f* emaciation; debility, exhaustion.

**extenuar** *vt* to exhaust, to debilitate.

**exterior** *adj* exterior, external; * *m* exterior, outward appearance.

**exteriormente** *adv* externally.

**exterminador** *m* exterminator.

**exterminar** *vt* to exterminate.

**exterminio** *m* extermination.

**externo/na** *adj* external, outer; * *m/f* day pupil.

**extinción** *f* extinction.

**extinguir** *vt* to wipe out; to extinguish.

**extintor** *m* (fire) extinguisher.

**extirpación** *f* extirpation, extermination.

**extirpar** *vt* to extirpate, to root out.

**extorsión** *f* extortion.

**extra** *adj invar* extra; good quality; * *m/f* extra; * *m* bonus.

**extracción** *f* extraction.

**extracto** *m* extract.

**extradición** *f* extradition.

**extraditar** *vt* to extradite.

**extraer** *vt* to extract.

**extranjero/ra** *m/f* stranger; foreigner; * *adj* foreign, alien.

**extrañar** *vt* to find strange; to miss; **~se** *vr* to be surprised; to grow apart.

**extrañeza** *f* strangeness; surprise.

**extraño/ña** *adj* foreign; rare; singular, strange, odd.

**extraordinario/ria** *adj* extraordinary, uncommon, odd.

**extravagancia** *f* extravagance.

**extravagante** *adj* extravagant.

**extraviado/da** *adj* lost, missing.

**extraviar** *vt* to mislead; **~se** *vr* to lose one's way.

**extravío** *m* deviation; loss.

**extremado/da** *adj* extreme; accomplished.

**extremaunción** *f* extreme unction.

**extremidad** *f* extremity; brim; tip; **~es** *fpl* extremities *pl*.

**extremo/ma** *adj* extreme, last; * *m* extreme, highest degree; **en ~**extremely.

**extrínseco/ca** *adj* extrinsic, external.

**extrovertido/da** *adj*, *m/f* extrovert.

**exuberancia** *f* exuberance; luxuriance.

# F

**fábrica** *f* factory.

**fabricación** *f* manufacture, production.

**fabricante** *m/f* producer, manufacturer.

**fabricar** *vt* to build, to construct; to manufacture; (*fig*) to fabricate.

**fabril** *adj* manufacturing *compd*, industrial.

**fábula** *f* fable; fiction; rumour, common talk.

**fabulista** *m/f* writer of fables.

**fabuloso/sa** *adj* fabulous, fictitious.

**facción** *f* (political) faction; feature.

**faccioso/sa** *adj* factious, turbulent.

**facha** *f* appearance, look; face.

**fachada** *f* facade, face, front.

**fácil** *adj* facile, easy.

**facilidad** *f* facility, easiness; **con ~** *adv* cosily, easily.

**facilitar** *vt* to facilitate.

**fácilmente** *adv* easily.

**facineroso** *adj* wicked, criminal.

**facsímil** *m* facsimile, fax.

**factible** *adj* feasible, practicable.

**factor** *m* (*math*) factor; (*com*) factor, agent.

**factoría** *f* agency; factory.

**factura** *f* invoice.

**facultad** *f* faculty.

**facultativo/va** *adj* optional; * *m/f* doctor, practitioner.

**faena** *f* task, job; hard work.

**faisán** *m* pheasant.

**faja** *f* band, sash; strip (of land); corset.

**fajo** *m* bundle; wad.

**falacia** *f* fallacy; fraud.

**falange** *f* phalanx.

**falaz** *adj* deceitful, fraudulent; fallacious.

**falda** *f* skirt; lap; flap; train; slope, hillside.

**faldero/ra** *adj*: **hombre ~** ladies' man; **perrito ~** lap-dog.

**faldón** *m* coat-tails *pl*; skirt.

**falible** *adj* fallible.

**fallar** *vt* (*law*) to pronounce sentence on, to judge; * *vi* to fail.

**fallecer** *vi* to die.

**fallecimiento** *m* decease, death.

**fallido/da** *adj* unsuccessful, frustrated.

**fallo** *m* judgement, sentence; failure.

**falsamente** *adv* falsely.

**falsario/ria** *adj* falsifying, forging.

**falsear** *vt* to falsify, to counterfeit.

**falsedad** *f* falsehood; untruth, (*col*) fib; hypocrisy.

**falsete** *m* (*tec*) plug; bung; (*mus*) falsetto.

**falsificación** *f* falsification.

**falsificador/ora** *m/f* forger, counterfeiter.

**falsificar** *vt* to falsify, to forge, to counterfeit.

**falso/sa** *adj* false, untrue; deceitful; fake.

**falta** *f* fault, defect; want; flaw, mistake; (*sport*) foul.

**faltar** *vi* to be wanting; to fail; not to fulfil one's promise; to need; to be missing.

**falto/ta** *adj* wanting, deficient, lacking; miserable, wretched.

**faltriquera** *f* pocket.

**fama** *f* fame; reputation, name.

**famélico/ca** *adj* starving.

**familia** *f* family.

**familiar** *adj* familiar; homely, domestic; * *m/f* relative, relation.

**familiaridad** *f* familiarity.

**familiarizarse** *vr*: **~ con** to familiarize oneself with.

**famoso/sa** *adj* famous.

**fan** *m/f* fan.

**fanático/ca** *adj* fanatical; enthusiastic; * *m/f* fanatic; fan.

**fandango** *m* fandango.

**fanfarrón/ona** *m/f* bully, braggart.

**fanfarronada** *f* boast, brag.

**fanfarronear** *vi* to bully, to brag.

**fanfarronería** *f* boast, brag.

**fango** *m* mire, mud.

**fangoso/sa** *adj* muddy, miry.

**fantasía** *f* fancy; fantasy; caprice; presumption.

**fantasma** *f* phantom, ghost.

**fantástico/ca** *adj* fantastic, whimsical; presumptuous.

**fardo** *m* bale, parcel.

**farfullar** *vi* to talk with a stammer.

**farisaico/ca** *adj* pharisaical; hypocritical.

**fariseo** *m* Pharisee; hypocrite.

**farmacéutico/ca** *adj* pharmaceutical; * *m/f* pharmacist.

**farmacia** *f* pharmacy.

**faro** *m* (*mar*) lighthouse; (*auto*) headlamp/light; floodlight.

**farol** *m* lantern.

**farola** *f* street light.

**farsa** *f* farce.

**farsante** *m/f* fraud, fake.

**fascículo** *m* part, instalment.

**fascinación** *f* fascination.

**fascinar** *vt* to fascinate; to enchant.
**fascismo** *m* fascism.
**fascista** *adj*, *m/f* fascist.
**fase** *f* phase.
**fastidiar** *vt* to annoy; to offend; to spoil.
**fastidio** *m* annoyance; boredom; disgust.
**fastidioso/sa** *adj* annoying; tedious.
**fatal** *adj* fatal; mortal; awful.
**fatalidad** *f* fatality; mischance, ill-luck.
**fatalismo** *m* fatalism.
**fatalista** *m/f* fatalist.
**fatiga** *f* weariness, fatigue.
**fatigar** *vt* to fatigue, to tire; to harass.
**fatigoso/sa** *adj* tiresome, troublesome.
**fatuidad** *f* fatuity, foolishness, silliness.
**fatuo/tua** *adj* fatuous, stupid, foolish; conceited.
**fauces** *fpl* jaws *pl*; gullet.
**fausto/ta** *adj* happy, fortunate; * *m* splendour, pomp.
**favor** *m* favour; protection; good turn.
**favorable** *adj* favourable.
**favorecer** *vt* to favour, to protect.
**favorito/ta** *adj* favourite.
**fax** *m* fax.
**faz** *f* face.
**fe** *f* faith, belief.
**fealdad** *f* ugliness.
**febrero** *m* February.
**febril** *adj* feverish.
**fecha** *f* date (of a letter etc).
**fechar** *vt* to date.
**fechoría** *f* misdeed; exploit.
**fecundar** *vt* to fertilize.
**fecundidad** *f* fecundity, fertility.
**fecundo/da** *adj* fruitful, fertile.
**federación** *f* federation.
**felicidad** *f* happiness.
**felicitar** *vt* to congratulate.
**feligrés/esa** *m/f* parishioner.
**feliz** *adj* happy, fortunate.
**felpa** *f* plush; towelling.
**felpudo** *m* doormat.
**femenil** *adj* feminine, womanly.
**femenino/na** *adj* feminine; female.
**feminismo** *m* feminism.
**feminista** *adj*, *m/f* feminist.
**fenómeno** *m* phenomenon; (*fig*) freak, accident; * *adj* (*col*) great, marvellous.
**feo/ea** *adj* ugly; bad, nasty.
**feracidad** *f* productivity, fertility.
**feraz** *adj* fertile, fruitful.
**féretro** *m* bier, coffin.
**feria** *f* fair, rest day; village market.
**fermentación** *f* fermentation.

**fermentar** *vi* to ferment.
**fermento** *m* ferment; leaven.
**ferocidad** *f* ferocity, wildness; cruelty.
**feroz** *adj* ferocious, savage; cruel.
**ferretería** *f* ironmonger's (shop).
**ferrocarril** *m* railway.
**ferroviario/ria** *adj* rail *compd*.
**ferry** *m* ferry.
**fértil** *adj* fertile, fruitful.
**fertilidad** *f* fertility, fruitfulness.
**fertilización** *f* fertilization.
**fertilizar** *vt* to fertilize.
**férula** *f* ferule; (*med*) splint.
**ferviente** *adj* fervent; ardent.
**fervor** *m* fervour, zeal; ardour.
**fervoroso/sa** *adj* fervent, ardent, passionate.
**festejar** *vt* to feast; to court, to woo.
**festejo** *m* courtship; feast.
**festín** *m* feast.
**festividad** *f* festivity.
**festivo/va** *adj* festive, merry; witty; **día ~** holiday.
**festón** *m* garland; festoon.
**festonear** *vt* to decorate with garlands.
**fétido/da** *adj* foetid, stinking.
**feto** *m* foetus.
**feudal** *adj* feudal.
**fiable** *adj* trustworthy; reliable.
**fiador/ra** *m/f* guarantor; (*com*) backer.
**fiambre** *m* cold meat.
**fiambrera** *f* lunch basket.
**fianza** *f* (*law*) surety.
**fiar** *vt* to entrust, to confide; to bail; to sell on credit; to buy on credit; * *vi* to trust.
**fibra** *f* fibre.
**fibroso/sa** *adj* fibrous.
**ficción** *f* fiction.
**ficha** *f* token, counter (at games); (index) card.
**ficticio/cia** *adj* fictitious.
**fidedigno/na** *adj* reliable, trustworthy.
**fideicomisario/ria** *m/f* trustee.
**fideicomiso** *f* trust.
**fidelidad** *f* fidelity; loyalty.
**fideos** *mpl* vermicelli *pl*.
**fiebre** *f* fever.
**fiel** *adj* faithful, loyal; * *mpl* **los ~es** the faithful *pl*.
**fieltro** *m* felt.
**fiera** *f* wild beast.
**fiereza** *f* fierceness, ferocity; cruelty.
**fiero/ra** *adj* fierce, ferocious; cruel; rough, harsh.
**fiesta** *f* party; festivity; **~s** *fpl* feast days *pl*; holidays *pl*.

**figura** 90 **florido**

**figura** *f* figure, shape.
**figurado/da** *adj* figurative.
**figurar** *vt* to figure; **~se** *vr* to fancy, to imagine.
**figurilla** *f* ridiculous little figure.
**fijador** *m* fixative; gel (for the hair).
**fijar** *vt* to fix, to fasten; **~se** *vr* to become fixed; to establish oneself; **~se en** to notice.
**fijo/ja** *adj* fixed, firm; settled, permanent.
**fila** *f* row, line; (*mil*) rank; **en ~** in a line, in a row.
**filamento** *m* filament.
**filantropía** *f* philanthropy.
**filántropo/pa** *m/f* philanthropist.
**filete** *m* fillet; fillet steak.
**filiación** *f* lineage; personal description, personal particulars *pl*.
**filial** *adj* filial; * *f* (*com*) subsidiary.
**filibustero** *m* pirate.
**filigrana** *f* filigree.
**filmar** *vt* to film.
**filo** *m* edge, blade.
**filología** *f* philology.
**filológico/ca** *adj* philological.
**filólogo/ga** *m/f* philologist.
**filosofar** *vt* to philosophize.
**filosofía** *f* philosophy.
**filosófico/ca** *adj* philosophical.
**filósofo/fa** *m/f* philosopher.
**filtración** *f* filtration.
**filtrar** *vt* to filter, to strain.
**filtro** *m* filter.
**fin** *m* end; termination, conclusion; aim, purpose; **al ~** at last; **en ~** (*fig*) well then; **por ~** finally, lastly.
**final** *adj* final; * *m* end; termination, conclusion; * *f* (*sport*) final.
**finalizar** *vt* to finish, to conclude; * *vi* to be finished.
**finalmente** *adv* finally, at last.
**financiar** *vt* to finance.
**finca** *f* land, property, real estate; country house; farm.
**fineza** *f* fineness, perfection; elegance; courtesy; small gift.
**fingido/da** *adj* feigned, fake, sham.
**fingimiento** *m* simulation, pretence.
**fingir** *vt* to feign, to fake; to invent; to imitate; **~se** *vr* to pretend to be; * *vi* to pretend.
**finito/ta** *adj* finite.
**fino/na** *adj* fine, pure; slender; polite; acute; dry (of sherry).
**finura** *f* fineness.
**firma** *f* signature; (*com*) company.

**firmamento** *m* firmament, sky, heaven.
**firmar** *vt* to sign.
**firme** *adj* firm, stable, strong, secure; constant; resolute; * *m* road surface.
**firmeza** *f* firmness, stability, constancy.
**fiscal** *adj* fiscal.
**fiscalizar** *vt* to inspect; to criticize.
**fisco** *m* treasury; exchequer.
**fisgar** *vt* to pry into.
**fisgón/ona** *m/f* prying person, (*col*) snooper.
**física** *f* physics.
**físico/ca** *adj* physical; * *m/f* physicist; * *m* physique.
**fisonomía** *f* physiognomy.
**fisonomista** *m/f*: **ser buen ~** to have a good memory for faces.
**flaco/ca** *adj* lean, skinny; feeble.
**flagelación** *f* flagellation.
**flagrante** *adj* flagrant.
**flamante** *adj* flaming, bright; brand-new.
**flan** *m* crème caramel.
**flanco** *m* flank.
**flanquear** *vt* (*mil*) to flank.
**flaquear** *vi* to flag; to weaken.
**flaqueza** *f* thinness, leanness; feebleness, weakness.
**flash** *m* flash.
**flato** *m* (*med*) flatulence; depression.
**flatulento/ta** *adj* flatulent.
**flauta** *f* (*mus*) flute.
**flautista** *m/f* flute player, flautist.
**flecha** *f* arrow.
**fleco** *m* hair cut straight across the forehead, fringe.
**flema** *f* phlegm.
**flemático/ca** *adj* phlegmatic.
**flemón** *m* ulcer in the gums.
**flequillo** *m* hair cut straight across the forehead, fringe.
**fletar** *vt* to freight (a ship).
**flete** *m* (*mar*) freight; charter.
**flexibilidad** *f* flexibility.
**flexible** *adj* flexible; compliant; docile.
**flojedad** *f* feebleness; laxity, laziness; negligence.
**flojera** *f*: **me da ~** I can't be bothered.
**flojo/ja** *adj* loose; flexible; lax, slack; lazy.
**flor** *f* flower.
**florecer** *vi* to blossom.
**florero** *m* vase.
**floresta** *f* wood, grove; beauty spot.
**florete** *m* fencing foil.
**florido/da** *adj* full of flowers; in bloom; choice.

**florista** *m/f* florist.
**flota** *f* fleet.
**flotador** *m* float.
**flotante** *adj* floating.
**flotar** *vi* to float.
**flote** *m*: **a ~** afloat.
**flotilla** *f* small fleet, flotilla.
**fluctuación** *f* fluctuation; uncertainty.
**fluctuar** *vi* to fluctuate; to waver.
**fluidez** *f* fluidity; fluency.
**fluido/da** *adj* fluid; (*fig*) fluent; * *m* fluid.
**fluir** *vi* to flow.
**flujo** *m* flux; flow; **~ de sangre** (*med*) loss of blood.
**fluvial** *adj* fluvial, river *compd*.
**foca** *f* seal.
**foco** *m* focus; centre; source; floodlight; (light)bulb.
**fofo/fa** *adj* spongy; soft; bland.
**fogata** *f* blaze; bonfire.
**fogón** *m* stove; hearth.
**fogonazo** *m* flash; explosion.
**fogosidad** *f* dash, verve; fieriness.
**fogoso/sa** *adj* fiery; ardent, fervent; impetuous, boisterous.
**folk** *m* folk music.
**follaje** *m* foliage.
**folletista** *m/f* pamphleteer.
**folleto** *m* pamphlet; folder, brochure.
**follón** *m* (*col*) mess; fuss.
**fomentar** *vt* to encourage; to promote.
**fomento** *m* promotion.
**fonda** *f* hotel; inn; boarding house.
**fondeadero** *m* anchorage.
**fondear** *vi* to drop anchor.
**fondista** *m/f* innkeeper.
**fondo** *m* bottom; back; background; space; **~s** *mpl* stock, funds *pl*, capital; **a ~** perfectly, completely.
**fontanería** *f* plumbing.
**fontanero/ra** *m/f* plumber.
**footing** *m* jogging.
**forajido** *m* outlaw.
**foral** *adj* belonging to the statute law of a country.
**forastero/ra** *adj* strange, exotic; * *m/f* stranger.
**forcejear** *vi* to struggle.
**forense** *adj* forensic; * *m/f* forensic scientist.
**forjador/ra** *m/f* framer; forger.
**forjadura** *f* forging.
**forjar** *vt* to forge; to frame; to invent.
**forma** *f* form, shape; pattern; (*med*) fitness; (*sport*) form; means, method; **de ~ que** in such a manner that.

**formación** *f* formation; form, figure; education; training.
**formal** *adj* formal; proper, genuine; serious, grave.
**formalidad** *f* formality; gravity.
**formalizar** *vt* (*law*) to formalize; to regularize; **~se** *vr* to be regularized.
**formar** *vt* to form, to shape.
**formidable** *adj* formidable, dreadful; (*col*) terrific.
**fórmula** *f* formula.
**formulario** *m* formulary.
**fornicación** *f* fornication.
**fornicador** *m* fornicator.
**fornicar** *vi* to commit fornication.
**fornido/da** *adj* well-built.
**foro** *m* court of justice; forum.
**forraje** *m* forage.
**forrajear** *vt* to forage.
**forrar** *vt* to line; to face; to cover.
**forro** *m* lining; book jacket.
**fortalecer** *vt* to fortify, to strengthen.
**fortaleza** *f* courage; strength, vigour; (*mil*) fortress, stronghold.
**fortificación** *f* fortification.
**fortificar** *vt* to strengthen; to fortify (a place).
**fortín** *m* (*mil*) small fort.
**fortuito/ta** *adj* fortuitous.
**fortuna** *f* fortune; wealth.
**forzar** *vt* to force.
**forzoso/sa** *adj* indispensable, necessary.
**forzudo/da** *adj* strong, vigorous.
**fosa** *f* grave; pit.
**fósforo** *m* phosphorus; **~s** *mpl* matches *pl*.
**fósil** *adj*, *m* fossil.
**foso** *vt* pit; moat, ditch, fosse.
**foto** *f* photo.
**fotocopia** *f* photocopy.
**fotografía** *f* photography; photograph.
**fotógrafo/fa** *m/f* photographer.
**frac** *m* tails, dress coat.
**fracasar** *vi* to fail.
**fracaso** *m* failure.
**fracción** *f* fraction.
**fractura** *f* fracture.
**fracturar** *vt* to break (a bone).
**fragancia** *f* fragrance, sweetness of smell.
**fragante** *adj* fragrant, scented.
**fragata** *f* (*mar*) frigate.
**frágil** *adj* fragile, frail.
**fragilidad** *f* fragility, brittleness; frailty.
**fragmento** *m* fragment.
**fragosidad** *f* roughness; denseness.
**fragoso/sa** *adj* craggy, rough, uneven.

**fragua** f forge.

**fraguar** vt to forge; to contrive; * vi to solidify, to harden.

**fraile** m friar, monk.

**frambuesa** f raspberry.

**francés/sa** adj French; * m French (language); * m/f Frenchman/woman.

**franco/ca** adj frank; candid; free, gratis.

**franela** f flannel; vest.

**franja** f strip, band, fringe.

**franquear** vt to clear; to overcome; to stamp (letters); ~se to unbosom oneself.

**franqueo** m postage.

**franqueza** f frankness.

**franquicia** f immunity from taxes.

**frasco** m flask.

**frase** f phrase.

**fraternal** adj fraternal, brotherly.

**fraternidad** f fraternity, brotherhood.

**fratricida** m/f fratricide (person).

**fratricidio** m fratricide (murder).

**fraude** m fraud, deceit; cheat.

**fraudulento/ta** adj fraudulent, deceitful.

**frazada** f blanket.

**frecuencia** f frequency.

**frecuentar** vt to frequent.

**frecuente** adj frequent.

**fregadero** m (kitchen) sink.

**fregado** m scouring, scrubbing; (fig) intrigue; underhand work.

**fregar** vt to scrub; to wash up.

**fregona** f kitchen maid; (perj) skivvy.

**freír** vt to fry.

**frenar** vt to brake; (fig) to check.

**frenesí** m frenzy.

**frenético/ca** adj frantic; frenzied, wild.

**frenillo** m speech impediment.

**freno** m bit; brake; (fig) check.

**frente** f front; face; ~ a ~ face to face; en ~ opposite; (mil) front; * m forehead.

**fresa** f strawberry.

**fresal** m strawberry plant; ground bearing strawberry plants.

**fresco/ca** adj fresh; cool; new; ruddy; * m fresh air; * m/f (col) shameless/impudent person.

**frescura** f freshness; frankness; cheek, nerve.

**fresno** m ash tree.

**frialdad** f coldness; indifference.

**fricción** f friction.

**friega** f rubbing; nuisance.

**frígido/da** adj frigid.

**frigorífico** m refrigerator.

**frijol** m bean.

**frío/fría** adj cold; indifferent; * m cold; indifference.

**friolento/ta** adj chilly.

**friolera** f trifle

**friso** m frieze; wainscot.

**fritada** f dish of fried meat/fish.

**frito/ta** adj fried.

**frivolidad** f frivolity.

**frívolo/la** adj frivolous.

**frondosidad** f foliage.

**frondoso/sa** adj leafy.

**frontera** f frontier.

**fronterizo/za** adj frontier compd; bordering.

**frontón** m (sport) pelota court; pelota.

**frotación, frotadura** f friction, rubbing.

**frotar** vt to rub.

**fructífero/ra** adj fruit-bearing, fruitful.

**fructificar** vi to bear fruit; to come to fruition.

**fructuoso/sa** adj fruitful.

**frugal** adj frugal, sparing.

**frugalidad** f frugality, parsimony.

**fruncir** vt to pleat; to knit; to contract; ~ las cejas to knit the eyebrows.

**frustrar** vt to frustrate.

**fruta** f fruit; ~ del tiempo seasonal fruit.

**frutal** m fruit tree.

**frutera** f fruit dish.

**frutería** f. fruit shop, greengrocer's shop.

**frutero/ra** m/f fruiterer, fruit seller, greengrocer; * m fruit basket.

**frutilla** f strawberry.

**fruto** m fruit; benefit, profit.

**fuego** m fire.

**fuelle** m bellows pl.

**fuente** f fountain; spring; source; large dish.

**fuera** adv out(side); away; ~ de prep outside; ¡~! out of the way!

**fueraborda** m outboard motor.

**fuero** m statute law of a country; jurisdiction.

**fuerte** m (mil) fortification, fort; forte; * adj vigorous, tough; strong; loud; heavy; * adv strongly; hard.

**fuerza** f force, strength; (electric) power; violence; a ~ de by dint of; ~s mpl troops pl.

**fuga** f flight, escape; leak (of gas).

**fugarse** vr to escape, to flee.

**fugaz** adj fleeting.

**fugitivo/va** adj, m/f fugitive.

**fulano/na** m/f so-and-so, what's-his-name/ what's-her-name.

**fulgurar** vi to flash.

**fullería** *f* cheating.

**fullero** *m* cardsharp, cheat.

**fulminar** *vt* to fulminate; * *vi* to explode.

**fumador/ra** *m/f* smoker.

**fumar** *vt, vi* to smoke.

**fumigación** *f* fumigation.

**funambulista** *m/f* tightrope walker.

**función** *f* function; duties *pl*; show, performance.

**funcionar** *vi* to function; to work (of a machine).

**funcionario/ria** *m/f* official; civil servant.

**funda** *f* case, sheath; **~ de almohada** pillowcase.

**fundación** *f* foundation.

**fundador/ra** *m/f* founder.

**fundamental** *adj* fundamental.

**fundamentalismo** *m* fundamentalism.

**fundamentalista** *adj, m/f* fundamentalist.

**fundamento** *m* foundation; groundwork; reason, cause.

**fundar** *vt* to found; to establish; to ground.

**fundición** *f* fusion; foundry.

**fundir** *vt* to fuse; to melt; to smelt; **~se** *vr* (*com*) to merge; to bankrupt; to blow (of a fuse).

**fúnebre** *adj* mournful, sad; funereal.

**funeral** *m* funeral; **~es** *mpl* funeral, funeral rites *pl*, obsequies *pl*.

**funerario/ria** *adj* funeral *compd*, funereal.

**funesto/ta** *adj* ill-fated, unfortunate; fatal.

**furgón** *m* wagon.

**furgoneta** *f* pick-up (truck).

**furia** *f* fury, rage.

**furibundo/da** *adj* furious; frenzied.

**furioso/sa** *adj* furious.

**furor** *m* fury, rage.

**furtivamente** *adv* furtively.

**furtivo/va** *adj* furtive.

**furúnculo** *m* (*med*) boil.

**fusible** *m* fuse.

**fusil** *m* rifle.

**fusilar** *vt* to shoot.

**fusilero** *m* rifleman.

**fusión** *f* fusion; (*com*) merger.

**fusta** *f* riding crop.

**fútbol** *m* football.

**futbolista** *m/f* footballer.

**fútil** *adj* futile; trifling.

**futilidad** *f* futility.

**futuro/ra** *adj, m* future.

# G

**gabán** *m* overcoat.
**gabardina** *f* gabardine; raincoat.
**gabarra** *f* (*mar*) lighter.
**gabinete** *m* (*pol*) cabinet, study; office (of solicitors etc).
**gaceta** *f* gazette.
**gachas** *fpl* soft/semi-liquid food; porridge.
**gacho/cha** *adj* curved, bent downward.
**gafas** *fpl* glasses *pl*, spectacles *pl*.
**gafe** *m* jinx.
**gaita** *f* bagpipe; flageolet.
**gaitero/ra** *m/f* bagpiper, bagpipe player.
**gaje** *m*: **~s del oficio** occupational hazards *pl*.
**gajo** *m* segment (of orange).
**gala** *f* full dress; (*fig*) cream, flower; **~s** *fpl* finery; **hacer ~ de** to display, to show off.
**galán** *m* lover; handsome young man; (*teat*) male lead.
**galante** *adj* gallant.
**galanteador** *m* lover, suitor.
**galantear** *vt* to court, to woo.
**galanteo** *m* gallantry, courtship.
**galantería** *f* gallantry; politeness; compliment.
**galápago** *m* tortoise.
**galardón** *m* reward, prize.
**galardonar** *vt* to reward, to recompense.
**galaxia** *f* galaxy.
**galbana** *f* laziness, idleness.
**galeón** *m* (*mar*) galleon.
**galera** *f* (*mar*) galley; wagon.
**galería** *f* gallery.
**galgo** *m* greyhound.
**gallardete** *m* (*mar*) pennant, streamer.
**gallardía** *f* fineness, elegance, gracefulness; dash.
**gallardo/da** *adj* graceful, elegant; brave, daring.
**galleta** *f* biscuit.
**gallina** *f* hen; * *m/f* (*fig*) coward; **~ ciega** blindman's buff.
**gallinero** *m* henhouse, coop; poulterer; (*teat*) top gallery; hubbub.
**gallineta** *f* woodcock (bird).
**gallo** *m* cock.
**galón** *m* (*mil*) stripe; braid; galloon.
**galopar** *vi* to gallop.
**galope** *m* gallop.
**galvánico/ca** *adj* galvanic.
**galvanismo** *m* galvanism.

**gama**[1] *f* (*mus*) scale; (*fig*) range, gamut.
**gama**[2] *f* doe (of the fallow deer).
**gamba** *f* shrimp; prawn.
**gamberro/rra** *m/f* hooligan.
**gamo** *m* buck (of the fallow deer).
**gamuza** *f* chamois (goat antelope); chamois leather.
**gana** *f* desire, wish; appetite; will, longing; **de buena ~** with pleasure, voluntarily; **de mala ~** unwillingly, with reluctance.
**ganadería** *f* cattle raising; cattle; livestock.
**ganadero** *m* rancher; cattle dealer.
**ganado** *m* livestock, cattle *pl*; **~ mayor** horses and mules *pl*; **~ menor** sheep, goats and pigs *pl*.
**ganancia** *f* gain, profit; increase.
**ganancial** *adj* lucrative.
**ganar** *vt* to gain; to win; to earn; * *vi* to win.
**gancho** *m* hook; crook.
**gandul** *adj*, *m/f* layabout, lazy person.
**ganga** *f* bargain.
**gangoso/sa** *adj* nasal.
**gangrena** *f* gangrene.
**gangrenarse** *vr* to become gangrenous.
**gangrenoso/sa** *adj* gangrenous.
**ganso/sa** *m/f* gander; goose; (*col*) idiot.
**garabatear** *vi*, *vt* to scrawl, to scribble.
**garabatos** *mpl* scrawling letters/characters *pl*.
**garaje** *m* garage.
**garante** *m/f* guarantor; * *adj* responsible.
**garantía** *f* warranty, guarantee.
**garañón** *m* jackass, male donkey.
**garapatear** *vi*, *vt* to scrawl, to scribble.
**garapiñar** *vt* to freeze; to ice.
**garbanzo** *m* chickpea.
**garbo** *m* gracefulness, elegance; stylishness; generosity.
**garboso/sa** *adj* graceful; elegant, stylish; generous.
**garduña** *f* marten.
**gargajo** *m* phlegm, spit.
**garganta** *f* throat, gullet; instep; neck (of a bottle); narrow pass between mountains/rivers.
**gargantilla** *f* necklace.
**gárgara** *f* noise made by gargling.
**gargarismo** *m* gargling, gargle.
**gargarizar** *vi* to gargle.
**garita** *f* (*mil*) sentry box; (*rail*) signal box.
**garra** *f* claw; talon; paw.
**garrafa** *f* carafe; (gas) cylinder.

**garrafal** *adj* great, vast, huge.
**garrapata** *f* tick (insect).
**garrotazo** *m* blow with a stick/club.
**garrote** *m* stick, club, cudgel; (*med*) tourniquet; (*law*) garrotte.
**garrotillo** *m* (*med*) croup.
**garrucha** *f* pulley.
**garza** *f* heron.
**garzo/za** *adj* blue-eyed.
**gas** *m* gas.
**gasa** *f* gauze.
**gaseoso/sa** *adj* fizzy; * *f* lemonade.
**gasfitero/ra** *m/f* plumber.
**gasoil** *m* diesel (oil).
**gasolina** *f* petrol.
**gasolinera** *f* filling station, petrol station.
**gasómetro** *m* gasometer.
**gastador/ra** *m/f* spendthrift.
**gastar** *vt* to spend; to expend; to waste; to wear away; to use up; ~**se** *vr* to wear out; to waste.
**gasto** *m* expense, expenditure; use.
**gastronomía** *f* gastronomy.
**gata** *f* she-cat; **a** ~**s** on all fours.
**gatear** *vi* to go on all fours.
**gatera** *f* catlover; (*mar*) cat hole.
**gatillazo** *m* click of the trigger in firing.
**gatillo** *m* trigger of a gun; (*med*) dental forceps.
**gato** *m* tomcat; jack, clamp, vice.
**gatuno/na** *adj* catlike, feline.
**gaveta** *f* drawer of a desk, locker.
**gavilán** *m* sparrow hawk.
**gavilla** *f* sheaf of corn.
**gaviota** *f* seagull.
**gay** *adj invar*, *m* (*col*) gay, homosexual.
**gazapo** *m* young rabbit; liar; lie.
**gazmoñada, gazmoñería** *f* prudery; hypocrisy.
**gazmoñero/ra, gazmoño/ña** *adj* hypocritical.
**gaznate** *m* gullet, wind pipe.
**gazpacho** *m* Spanish cold tomato soup.
**gazuza** *f* ravenous hunger.
**gelatina** *f* jelly; gelatine.
**gemelo/la** *m/f* twin.
**gemido** *m* groan, moan, howl.
**Géminis** *m* Gemini (sign of the zodiac).
**gemir** *vi* to groan, to moan.
**genciana** *f* (*bot*) gentian.
**gendarme** *m* policeman.
**gendarmería** *f* police.
**genealogía** *f* genealogy.
**genealógico/ca** *adj* genealogical.
**generación** *f* generation; progeny, race.

**general** *m* general; * *adj* general; **en** ~ generally, in general.
**generalidad** *f* generality.
**generalizar** *vt* to generalize.
**generalmente** *adv* generally.
**genérico/ca** *adj* generic.
**género** *m* genus; kind, type; gender; (*com*) cloth, material; ~**s** *mpl* goods *pl*, commodities *pl*.
**generosidad** *f* generosity.
**generoso/sa** *adj* noble, generous.
**Génesis** *f* Genesis.
**genial** *adj* inspired, brilliant; genial.
**genio** *m* nature, character; genius.
**genital** *adj* genital; * *mpl* ~**es** genitals *pl*.
**genitivo** *m* (*gr*) genitive case.
**gente** *f* people; nation; family.
**gentil** *m/f* pagan, heathen; * *adj* elegant; graceful; charming.
**gentileza** *f* grace; charm; politeness.
**gentilhombre** *m* gentleman.
**gentío** *m* crowd, throng.
**genuflexión** *f* genuflection.
**genuino/na** *adj* genuine; pure.
**geografía** *f* geography.
**geográfico/ca** *adj* geographical.
**geógrafo/fa** *m/f* geographer.
**geología** *f* geology.
**geólogo/ga** *m/f* geologist.
**geometría** *f* geometry.
**geométrico/ca** *adj* geometrical, geometric.
**geranio** *m* (*bot*) geranium.
**gerente** *m/f* manager; director.
**geriatría** *f* (*med*) geriatrics.
**germen** *m* germ, bud; source, origin.
**germinar** *vi* to germinate, to bud.
**gerundio** *m* (*gr*) gerund.
**gesticular** *vi* to gesticulate.
**gestión** *f* management; negotiation.
**gesto** *m* face; grimace; gesture.
**giganta** *f* giantess.
**gigante** *m* giant; * *adj* gigantic.
**gigantesco/ca** *adj* gigantic, giant.
**gilipollas** *adj invar* (*col*) stupid; * *m/f invar* (*col*) wimp.
**gimnasia** *f* gymnastics.
**gimnasio** *m* gymnasium.
**gimnasta** *m/f* gymnast.
**gimnástico/ca** *adj* gymnastic.
**ginebra** *f* gin.
**ginecólogo/ga** *m/f* gynaecologist.
**gira** *f* trip, tour.
**girar** *vt* to turn around; to swivel; (*com*) to draw, to issue; * *vi* to go round, to revolve; (*com*) to do business; to draw.

**giratorio/ria** *adj* revolving.
**girasol** *m* sunflower.
**giro** *m* turning round; tendency; change; (*com*) draft.
**gitano/na** *m/f* Gypsy.
**glacial** *adj* icy.
**glaciar** *m* glacier.
**glándula** *f* gland.
**glandular** *adj* glandular.
**globalización** *f* globalization.
**globo** *m* globe; sphere; orb; balloon; ~ **aerostático** air balloon.
**glóbulo** *m* globule; corpuscle.
**gloria** *f* glory.
**gloriarse** *vr*: ~ **en** to glory in, to take pride in; to take delight in.
**glorieta** *f* bower, arbour; roundabout.
**glorificación** *f* glorification; praise.
**glorificar** *vt* to glorify.
**glorioso/sa** *adj* glorious.
**glosa** *f* gloss; comment.
**glosar** *vt* to gloss; to comment on.
**glotón/ona** *m/f* glutton.
**glotonería** *f* gluttony.
**gobernación** *f* government.
**gobernador/ra** *m/f* governor.
**gobernar** *vt* to govern; to regulate; to direct.
**gobierno** *m* government.
**goce** *m* enjoyment.
**gol** *m* goal.
**goleta** *f* schooner.
**golf** *m* golf.
**golfa** *f* (*col*) slut.
**golfo**[1] *m* gulf, bay.
**golfo**[2] (*col*) urchin; lout.
**golondrina** *f* swallow.
**golosina** *f* delicacy, tidbit; bauble, trifle; sweet tooth.
**goloso/sa** *adj* sweet-toothed.
**golpe** *m* blow, stroke, hit; knock; clash; coup; **de** ~ suddenly.
**golpear** *vt* to beat, to knock; to punch.
**goma** *f* gum; rubber; elastic.
**gomosidad** *f* stickiness, viscosity.
**gomoso/sa** *adj* gummy, viscous.
**góndola** *f* gondola; (*rail*) goods wagon.
**gondolero** *m* gondolier.
**gordinflón/ona** *m/f* very fat person.
**gordo/da** *adj* fat, plump, big-bellied; first, main; (*col*) enormous.
**gordura** *f* grease; fatness, corpulence, obesity.
**gorgojo** *m* grub, weevil.
**gorgorito** *m* trill, warble.

**gorila** *m* gorilla.
**gorjear** *vi* to twitter, to chirp.
**gorjeo** *m* chirping.
**gorra** *f* cap; bonnet; (*mil*) bearskin.
**gorrión** *m* sparrow.
**gorro** *m* cap; bonnet.
**gorrón/ona** *m/f* scrounger.
**gota** *f* drop; (*med*) gout.
**gotear** *vt* to drip; to drizzle.
**gotera** *f* leak.
**gótico/ca** *adj* Gothic.
**gotoso/sa** *adj* gouty.
**gozar** *vt* to enjoy, to have, to possess; ~**se** *vr* to enjoy oneself, to rejoice.
**gozne** *m* hinge.
**gozo** *m* joy, pleasure.
**gozoso/sa** *adj* joyful, cheerful; content, glad, pleased.
**grabación** *f* recording.
**grabado** *m* engraving.
**grabador** *m* engraver.
**grabadora** *f* tape recorder.
**grabar** *vt* to engrave; to record.
**gracejo** *m* wit;, charm; gracefulness.
**gracia** *f* grace, gracefulness; wit; ¡(**muchas**) ~**s!** thanks (very much); **tener** ~ to be funny.
**gracioso/sa** *adj* graceful; beautiful; funny; pleasing; * *m* comic character.
**grada** *f* step of a staircase; tier, row; ~**s** *fpl* seats *pl* of a stadium/theatre.
**gradería** *f* (flight of) steps *pl*; row of seats.
**grado** *m* step; degree; **de buen** ~ willingly.
**graduación** *f* graduation; (*mil*) rank.
**gradual** *adj* gradual.
**graduar** *vt* to graduate.
**gráfico/ca** *adj* graphic; * *m* diagram; * *f* graph.
**grajo/ja** *m/f* rook.
**grama** *f* grass.
**gramática** *f* grammar.
**gramatical** *adj* grammatical.
**gramático/ca** *m/f* grammarian.
**gramo** *m* gram.
**gran** *adj* = **grande**.
**grana** *f* grain; scarlet.
**granada** *f* (*mil*) grenade; pomegranate.
**granadero** *m* (*mil*) grenadier.
**granadilla** *f* passionflower; passion fruit.
**granado** *m* pomegranate tree.
**granate** *m* garnet (precious stone).
**grande** *adj* great; big; tall; grand; * *m/f* adult.
**grandeza** *f* greatness; grandeur; size.
**grandiosidad** *f* greatness; grandeur, magnificence.
**grandioso/sa** *adj* grand, magnificent.

**granel** *adv*: **a ~** in bulk.
**granero** *m* granary.
**granito** *m* granite.
**granizada** *f* hail; hailstorm; shower, volley.
**granizado** *m* iced drink.
**granizar** *vi* to hail.
**granizo** *m* hail.
**granja** *f* farm.
**granjero/ra** *m/f* farmer.
**grano** *m* grain.
**granuja** *m* rogue; urchin.
**grapa** *f* staple; clamp.
**grasa** *f* suet, fat; grease.
**grasiento/ta** *adj* greasy; rusty; filthy.
**gratificación** *f* gratification; recompense.
**gratificar** *vt* to gratify; to reward, to recompense.
**gratis** *adj* free; *adv* freely.
**gratitud** *f* gratitude, gratefulness.
**grato/ta** *adj* pleasant, agreeable.
**gratuito/ta** *adj* gratuitous; free.
**gravamen** *m* charge, obligation; nuisance; tax.
**gravar** *vt* to burden; (*com*) to tax.
**grave** *adj* weighty, heavy; grave, important;
serious.
**gravedad** *f* gravity; graveness.
**gravemente** *adv* gravely, seriously.
**gravilla** *f* gravel.
**gravitación** *f* gravitation.
**gravitar** *vt* to gravitate; to weigh down on.
**gravoso/sa** *adj* onerous, burdensome; costly.
**graznar** *vi* to croak; to cackle; to quack.
**graznido** *m* croak; cackle; quack.
**greda** *f* clay.
**gremio** *m* union, guild; society; company,
corporation.
**greña** *f* tangle; shock of hair.
**greñudo/da** *adj* dishevelled.
**gresca** *f* clatter; outcry; confusion; wrangle,
quarrel.
**grieta** *f* crevice, crack, chink.
**grifo** *m* tap; petrol station.
**grilletes** *mpl* shackles *pl*; fetters *pl*.
**grillo** *m* cricket; bud, shoot; **~s** *mpl* fetters
*pl*, irons *pl*.
**grima** *f* disgust; annoyance.
**gripe** *f* flu, influenza.
**gris** *adj* grey.
**gritar** *vi* to cry out, to shout, to yell.
**gritería** *f* shouting, clamour, uproar.
**grito** *m* shout, cry, scream.
**grosella** *f* redcurrant; **~ negra** blackcurrant.
**grosellero** *m* currant bush.
**grosería** *f* coarseness, rudeness; vulgar comment.

**grosero/ra** *adj* coarse; rude, bad-mannered.
**grosor** *m* thickness.
**grotesco/ca** *adj* grotesque.
**grúa** *f* crane (machine); derrick.
**grueso/sa** *adj* thick; bulky; large; coarse;
\* *m* bulk.
**grulla** *f* crane (bird).
**grumo** *m* clot; curd.
**grumoso/sa** *adj* clotted.
**gruñido** *m* grunt; growl.
**gruñidor/ra** *m/f* grunter, mumbler; (*fig*)
grumbler.
**gruñir** *vi* to grunt; to grumble; to creak (of
hinges etc).
**grupa** *f* rump.
**grupo** *m* group.
**gruta** *f* grotto.
**guadaña** *f* scythe.
**guagua** *f* trifle, small thing.
**gualdrapa** *f* trappings *pl* (of a horse); tatter, rag.
**guantada** *f* slap.
**guante** *m* glove.
**guapo/pa** *adj* good-looking; handsome;
smart.
**guarda** *m/f* guard, keeper; \* *f* custody, keep-
ing.
**guardaagujas** *m invar* (*rail*) pointsman.
**guardabosque** *m* gamekeeper; ranger, forester.
**guardacostas** *m invar* coastguard vessel.
**guardaespaldas** *m/f invar* bodyguard.
**guardafuegos** *m invar* fireguard, fender.
**guardameta** *m/f* goalkeeper.
**guardapolvo** *m* dust cover; overalls *pl*.
**guardar** *vt* to keep, to preserve; to save
(money); to guard; **~se** *vr* to be on one's
guard; **~se de** to avoid, to abstain from.
**guardarropa** *f* wardrobe; cloakroom.
**guardia** *f* guard; (*mar*) watch; care, custody;
\* *m/f* guard; policeman/woman; \* *m* (*mil*)
guardsman.
**guardián/ana** *m/f* keeper; guardian.
**guardilla** *f* garret, attic.
**guarecer** *vt* to protect; to shelter; **~se** *vr* to
take refuge.
**guarida** *f* den, lair; shelter; hiding place.
**guarismo** *m* figure, numeral.
**guarnecer** *vt* to provide, to equip; to reinforce; to garnish, to set (in gold etc); to
adorn.
**guarnición** *f* trimming; gold setting; sword
guard; garnish; (*mil*) garrison.
**guasa** *f* joke.
**guasón/ona** *m/f* joker, jester.

**gubernativo/va** *adj* governmental.
**guedeja** *f* lock of hair.
**guerra** *f* war; hostility.
**guerrear** *vi* to fight, to wage war.
**guerrero/ra** *m/f* warrior; * *adj* martial, warlike.
**guerrilla** *f* guerrilla warfare; guerrilla group.
**gueto** *m* ghetto.
**guía** *m/f* guide; * *f* guidebook.
**guiar** *vt* to guide; (*auto*) to steer.
**guijarral** *m* stony place.
**guijarro** *m* pebble.
**guillotina** *f* guillotine.
**guillotinar** *vt* to guillotine.
**guinda** *f* cherry.
**guindal** *m* cherry tree.
**guindilla** *f* chilli pepper.
**guiñapo** *m* tatter, rag; rogue.
**guiñar** *vt* to wink.

**guión** *m* hyphen (in writing); script (of film).
**guirigay** *m* gibberish, confused language.
**guirnalda** *f* garland, wreath.
**guisado** *m* stew.
**guisante** *m* (*bot*) pea.
**guisar** *vt* to cook.
**guiso** *m* cooked dish; stew; seasoning.
**guisote** *m* hash, poor quality stew; (*col*) grub.
**guitarra** *f* guitar.
**guitarrista** *m/f* guitar player.
**gula** *f* gluttony.
**gusano** *m* maggot, worm.
**gustar** *vt* to taste; to sample; * *vi* to please, to be pleasing; **me gusta** . . . I like . . .
**gusto** *m* taste; pleasure, delight; liking.
**gustosamente** *adv* gladly, with pleasure.
**gustoso/sa** *adj* pleasant; tasty.
**gutural** *adj* guttural.

# H

**haba** *f* broad bean.

**haber** *vt* to get, to lay hands on; to occur; * *v imp*: **hay** there is, there are; * *v aux* to have; **~se** *vr*: **habérselas con uno** to have it out with somebody; * *m* income, salary; assets *pl*; (*com*) credit.

**habichuela** *f* bean.

**hábil** *adj* able, clever, skilful, dexterous, apt.

**habilidad** *f* ability, ableness, dexterity, aptitude.

**habilitación** *f* entitlement, qualification.

**habilitar** *vt* to qualify, to enable; to finance.

**habitable** *adj* inhabitable.

**habitación** *f* habitation, abode, lodging, dwelling, residence; room.

**habitante** *m/f* inhabitant, occupant.

**habitar** *vt* to inhabit, to live in.

**hábito** *m* dress; habit, custom.

**habitual** *adj* habitual, customary.

**habituar** *vt* to accustom; **~se** *vr* to become accustomed to.

**habla** *f* speech; language; dialect.

**hablador/ra** *m/f* talkative person.

**habladuría** *f* rumour; **~s** *fpl* gossip.

**hablante** *adj* speaking; * *m/f* speaker.

**hablar** *vt*, *vi* to speak; to talk.

**hacedor/ra** *m/f* maker; author.

**hacendado** *m* propery owner; landowner; rancher.

**hacendoso/sa** *adj* industrious.

**hacer** *vt* to make; to do; to put into practice; to perform; to effect; to prepare; to imagine; to force; (*mathh*) to amount to, to make; * *vi* to act, to behave; **~se** *vr* to become.

**hacha** *f* torch; axe, hatchet.

**hachazo** *m* blow with an axe.

**hacia** *adv* toward(s); about; **~ arriba/abajo** up(wards)/down- (wards).

**hacienda** *f* property; large farm; ranch; **H~** Treasury, Exchequer.

**hacinar** *vt* to stack/pile up; to hoard.

**hada** *f* fairy.

**hado** *m* fate, destiny.

**halagar** *vt* to cajole, to flatter.

**halago** *m* cajolery; pleasure.

**halagüeño** *adj* attractive, flattering.

**halcón** *m* falcon.

**halconero** *m* falconer.

**hálito** *m* breath; gentle breeze.

**hall** *m* hall; (theatre) foyer.

**hallar** *vt* to find; to meet with; to discover; **~se** *vr* to find oneself; to be.

**hallazgo** *m* finding, discovery.

**hamaca** *f* hammock.

**hambre** *f* hunger; famine; longing.

**hambriento/ta** *adj* hungry; starved.

**hamburguesa** *f* hamburger.

**haragán/ana** *m/f* idler, good-for-nothing.

**haraganear** *vi* to idle, to loiter.

**haraganería** *f* idleness, laziness.

**harapo** *m* rag, tatter.

**haraposo** *adj* ragged.

**hardware** *m* (*comput*) hardware.

**harina** *f* flour; **~ de maíz** cornflour.

**harinoso/sa** *adj* floury.

**hartar** *vt* to satiate; to glut; to tire, to sicken; **~se** *vr* to gorge oneself (with food); to get fed up.

**harto/ta** *adj* full; fed up; * *adv* enough.

**hartura** *f* surfeit; plenty, abundance.

**hasta** *prep* up to; down to; until, as far as; * *adv* even.

**hastío** *m* loathing; disgust; boredom.

**hatajo** *m* lot, collection.

**hato** *m* clothes *pl*; herd of cattle, flock of sheep; provisions *pl*; crowd, gang, collection.

**haya** *f* beech tree.

**haz** *m* bunch, bundle; beam (of light).

**hazaña** *f* exploit, achievement.

**hazmerreír** *m invar* ridiculous person, laughing stock.

**hebilla** *f* buckle.

**hebra** *f* thread; vein of minerals/metals; grain of wood.

**hebraico/ca** *adj* belonging to the Hebrews.

**hebreo/ea** *m/f* Hebrew; Israeli; * *m* Hebrew language; * *adj* Hebrew; Israeli.

**hechicería** *f* witchcraft; charm.

**hechicero/ra** *adj* charming, bewitching; * *m/f* sorcerer/ sorceress.

**hechizar** *vt* to bewitch, to enchant; to charm.

**hechizo** *m* bewitchment, enchantment.

**hecho/cha** *adj* made; done; mature; ready-to-wear; cooked; * *m* action; act; fact; matter; event.

**hechura** *f* form, shape; fashion; making; workmanship; creature.

**hectárea** *f* hectare.

**heder** *vi* to stink, to smell bad.

**hediondez** *f* strong stench.
**hediondo/da** *adj* foetid, stinking.
**hedor** *m* stench, stink.
**helada** *f* frost; freeze-up.
**helado/da** *adj* frozen; glacial, icy; astonished; astounded; * *m* ice cream.
**helar** *vt* to freeze; to congeal; to astonish, to amaze; ~**se** *vr* to be frozen; to turn into ice; to congeal; * *vi* to freeze; to congeal.
**helecho** *m* fern.
**hélice** *f* spiral, helix; propeller.
**helicóptero** *m* helicopter.
**hembra** *f* female.
**hemisferio** *m* hemisphere.
**hemorragia** *f* haemorrhage.
**hemorroides** *fpl* haemorrhoids *pl*, piles *pl*.
**henchir** *vt* to fill up; ~**se** *vr* to fill/stuff oneself.
**hendedura** *f* fissure, chink, crevice.
**hender** *vt* to crack, to split; to go through; to open a passage.
**hendidura** *f* = **hendedura**.
**heno** *m* hay.
**heraldo** *m* herald.
**herborizar** *vi* to pick herbs; to collect plants.
**heredad** *f* inherited property; country estate, farm.
**heredar** *vt* to inherit.
**heredera** *f* heiress.
**heredero** *m* heir.
**hereditario/ria** *adj* hereditary.
**hereje** *m/f* heretic.
**herejía** *f* heresy.
**herencia** *f* inheritance, heritage, heredity.
**herida** *f* wound, injury.
**herido/da** *adj* wounded, hurt.
**herir** *vt* to wound, to hurt; to beat, to strike; to affect, to touch, to move; to offend.
**hermafrodita** *m* hermaphrodite.
**hermana** *f* sister.
**hermanar** *vt* to match, to suit, to harmonize.
**hermanastra** *f* step-sister, half-sister.
**hermanastro** *m* step-brother, half-brother.
**hermandad** *f* fraternity; brotherhood.
**hermano** *m* brother; ~/**na** *adj* matched; resembling.
**hermético/ca** *adj* hermetic, watertight.
**hermoso/sa** *adj* beautiful, handsome, lovely; large, robust.
**hermosura** *f* beauty.
**hernia** *f* hernia, rupture.
**héroe** *m* hero.
**heroicidad** *f* heroism; heroic deed.
**heroico/ca** *adj* heroic.

**heroína**[1] *f* heroine.
**heroína**[2] *f* heroin (drug).
**heroísmo** *m* heroism.
**herpes** *m* herpes; * *fpl* (*med*) shingles.
**herrador** *m* farrier, blacksmith.
**herradura** *f* horseshoe.
**herramienta** *f* tool.
**herrar** *vt* to shoe (horses).
**herrería** *f* ironworks; forge.
**herrero** *m* smith, blacksmith.
**hervidero** *m* boiling; unrest; swarm.
**hervir** *vt* to boil; to cook; * *vi* to boil; to bubble; to seethe.
**hervor** *m* boiling; fervour, passion.
**heterogeneidad** *f* heterogeneousness.
**heterogéneo/nea** *adj* heterogeneous.
**heterosexual** *adj*, *m/f* heterosexual.
**heterosexualidad** *f* heterosexuality.
**hexámetro** *m* hexameter.
**hez** *f* sediment, dregs *pl*.
**hidalgo** *m* nobleman.
**hidalguía** *f* nobility.
**hidra** *f* hydra.
**hidráulica** *f* hydraulics.
**hidráulico/ca** *adj* hydraulic.
**hidroavión** *m* seaplane.
**hidrofobia** *f* hydrophobia.
**hidrógeno** *m* (*chem*) hydrogen.
**hidromasaje** *m* whirlpool bath.
**hiedra** *f* ivy.
**hiel** *f* gall, bile.
**hielo** *m* frost; ice.
**hiena** *f* hyena.
**hierba** *f* grass; herb.
**hierro** *m* iron.
**hígado** *m* liver; (*fig*) courage, pluck.
**higiene** *f* hygiene.
**higiénico/ca** *adj* hygienic.
**higo** *m* fig.
**higuera** *f* fig tree.
**hijastro/tra** *m/f* stepson/daughter.
**hijo/ja** *m/f* son/daughter; child; offspring.
**hilandero/ra** *m/f* spinner.
**hilar** *vt* to spin.
**hilera** *f* row, line, file.
**hilo** *m* thread; wire.
**hilván** *m* tacking.
**hilvanar** *vt* to tack; to perform in a hurry.
**himno** *m* hymn.
**hincapié** *m*: **hacer** ~ **en** to emphasize.
**hincar** *vt* to thrust in, to drive in.
**hincha** *m/f* (*col*) fan, supporter.
**hinchado/da** *adj* swollen; vain, arrogant.
**hinchar** *vt* to swell; to inflate; (*fig*) to exaggerate; ~**se** *vr* to swell; to become vain.

**hinchazón** *f* swelling, lump.
**hinojo** *m* (*bot*) fennel.
**hipar** *vi* to hiccup.
**hipérbola** *f* hyperbola, section of a cone.
**hipérbole** *f* hyperbole, exaggeration.
**hiperbólico/ca** *adj* hyperbolic, hyperbolical.
**hipermercado, híper** *m* hypermarket; supermarket
**hípica** *f* horseracing; showjumping.
**hipnotismo** *m* hypnotism.
**hipo** *m* hiccups *pl*.
**hipocondria** *f* hypochondria.
**hipocondríaco/ca** *adj* hypochondriac.
**hipocresía** *f* hypocrisy.
**hipócrita** *adj* hypocritical; * *m/f* hypocrite.
**hipódromo** *m* racetrack.
**hipopótamo** *m* hippopotamus.
**hipoteca** *f* mortgage.
**hipotecar** *vt* to mortgage.
**hipotecario/ria** *adj* belonging to a mortgage.
**hipótesis** *f* hypothesis.
**hipotético/ca** *adj* hypothetical.
**hisopo** *m* (*bot*) hyssop; water sprinkler; paintbrush.
**hispano/na** *adj* Hispanic.
**Hispanoamérica** *f* Spanish America.
**hispanoamericano/na** *adj,n* Spanish American.
**histeria** *f* hysteria.
**histérico/ca** *adj* hysterical.
**historia** *f* history; tale, story.
**historiador/ra** *m/f* historian.
**histórico/ca** *adj* historical; historic.
**historieta** *f* short story; short novel; comic strip.
**hito** *m* landmark; boundary post; target.
**hocico** *m* snout; **meter el ~ en todo** to meddle in everything.
**hogar** *m* hearth, fireplace; (*fig*) house, home; family life.
**hogaza** *f* large loaf of bread.
**hoguera** *f* bonfire; blaze.
**hoja** *f* leaf; petal; sheet of paper; blade.
**hojalata** *f* tin plate.
**hojaldre** *f* puff pastry.
**hojarasca** *f* dead leaves *pl*; rubbish.
**hojear** *vt* to turn the pages of.
**hola** *excl* hello!
**holgado/da** *adj* loose, wide, baggy; at leisure; idle, unoccupied, well-to-do; well-off.
**holgar** *vi* to rest; to be out of work; to be superfluous.
**holgazán/ana** *m/f* idler, slacker.
**holgazanear** *vt* to idle, to loaf around, to lounge around.

**holgazanería** *f* idleness, laziness.
**holgura** *f* looseness, bagginess; leisure; comfort; enjoyment.
**hollín** *m* soot.
**holocausto** *m* holocaust.
**hombre** *m* man; human being.
**hombrera** *f* shoulder pad.
**hombro** *m* shoulder.
**hombruno/na** *adj* manlike; virile, manly.
**homenaje** *m* homage.
**homicida** *m/f* murderer; * *adj* murderous, homicidal.
**homicidio** *m* murder.
**homilía** *f* homily.
**homogeneidad** *f* homogeneity.
**homogéneo/nea** *adj* homogeneous.
**homólogo/ga** *adj* homologous; synonymous.
**homosexual** *adj*, *m/f* homosexual.
**honda** *f* sling, catapult.
**hondazo** *m* throw with a sling.
**hondo/da** *adj* deep; profound; intense.
**hondonada** *f* dale, hollow; ravine.
**hondura** *f* depth, profundity.
**honestidad** *f* honesty; modesty; decency.
**honesto/ta** *adj* honest; modest.
**hongo** *m* mushroom; fungus; bowler hat.
**honor** *m* honour.
**honorable** *adj* honourable.
**honorario/ria** *adj* honorary; **~s** *mpl* fees *pl*.
**honorífico/ca** *adj* creditable, honourable.
**honra** *f* honour, reverence; self-esteem; reputation; integrity; **~s funebres** *pl* funeral honours *pl*.
**honradez** *f* honesty, integrity.
**honrado/da** *adj* honest; honourable; reputable.
**honrar** *vt* to honour.
**honroso/sa** *adj* honourable; respectable; honest.
**hora** *f* hour; time.
**horadar** *vt* to drill, to bore.
**horario/ria** *adj* hourly, hour *compd*; * *m* timetable.
**horca** *f* gallows; pitchfork; string (of onions etc).
**horcajadas** *adv*: **a ~** astride.
**horchata** *f* a drink made from almonds/barley and orange flower water.
**horizontal** *adj* horizontal.
**horizonte** *m* horizon.
**horma** *f* mould, form.
**hormiga** *f* ant.
**hormigón** *m* concrete.

**hormiguear** *vi* to itch; to swarm, to team.
**hormiguero** *m* anthill; place swarming with people.
**hormona** *f* hormone.
**hornada** *f* batch.
**horno** *m* oven; furnace.
**horóscopo** *m* horoscope.
**horquilla** *f* pitchfork; hairpin.
**horrendo/da** *adj* horrible; frightful.
**hórreo** *m* granary.
**horrible** *adj* horrid, horrible.
**horripilante** *adj* hair-raising.
**horror** *m* horror, fright; atrocity.
**horrorizar** *vt* to horrify; **~se** *vr* to be terrified.
**horroroso/sa** *adj* horrid, hideous, frightful.
**hortaliza** *f* vegetable.
**hortelano/na** *m/f* gardener; market gardener.
**hortera** *m* shop assistant; (*fig*) coarse person.
**hosco/ca** *adj* sullen, gloomy.
**hospedaje** *m* board and lodging.
**hospedar** *vt* to put up, to lodge; to entertain.
**hospedería** *f* inn; guest room; hospice.
**hospedero/ra** *m/f* landlord/lady; host/hostess.
**hospicio** *m* orphanage; hospice.
**hospital** *m* hospital.
**hospitalario/ria** *adj* hospitable.
**hospitalidad** *f* hospitality.
**hostal** *m* small hotel.
**hostelería** *f* hotel business/trade.
**hostería** *f* inn, tavern, hostelry.
**hostia** *f* host; wafer; (*col*) whack, punch.
**hostigar** *vt* to lash, to whip; to trouble, to pester, to bore.
**hostil** *adj* hostile; adverse.
**hostilidad** *f* hostility.
**hostilizar** *vt* (*mil*) to harry, to harass.
**hotel** *m* hotel.
**hoy** *adv* today; now, nowadays; **de ~ en adelante** as from today.
**hoya** *f* hole, pit.
**hoyo** *m* hole, pit; excavation.
**hoz** *f* sickle; gorge.
**hozar** *vi* to grub (of pigs).
**hucha** *f* money-box.

**hueco/ca** *adj* hollow, concave; empty; vain, ostentatious; * *m* interval; gap, hole; vacancy.
**huelga** *f* strike.
**huella** *f* track, footstep.
**huérfano/na** *adj, m/f* orphan.
**huero/ra** *adj* empty; addled.
**huerta** *f* market garden; irrigated region.
**huerto** *m* orchard; kitchen garden; **~ de hortalizas** market garden.
**hueso** *m* bone; stone, core.
**huésped/da** *m/f* guest, lodger; inn-keeper.
**hueste** *f* army; crowd.
**huesudo/da** *adj* bony.
**huevera** *f* eggcup.
**huevo** *m* egg.
**huida** *f* flight, escape.
**huir** *vi* to flee, to escape.
**hule** *m* oilcloth.
**humanidad** *f* humanity; corpulence; **~es** *fpl* humanities *pl*.
**humano/na** *adj* human; humane, kind.
**humareda** *f* cloud of smoke.
**humeante** *adj* smoking; steaming.
**humear** *vi* to smoke.
**humedad** *f* humidity, moisture; wetness.
**humedecer** *vt* to moisten; to wet; to soak.
**húmedo/da** *adj* humid; wet; moist, damp.
**humildad** *f* humility, humbleness; submission.
**humilde** *adj* humble.
**humillación** *f* humiliation, submission.
**humillar** *vt* to humble; to subdue; **~se** *vr* to humble oneself.
**humo** *m* smoke; fumes *pl*.
**humor** *m* mood, temper; humour.
**hundir** *vt* to submerge; to sink; to ruin; **~se** *vr* to sink, to go to the bottom; to collapse; to be ruined.
**huracán** *m* hurricane.
**huraño/ña** *adj* shy; unsociable.
**hurgar** *vt* to stir; to poke.
**hurón** *m* ferret; (*fig*) shy person; busybody.
**huronear** *vt* to ferret out.
**hurtadillas** *adv*: **a ~** by stealth.
**hurtar** *vt* to steal, to rob.
**hurto** *m* theft, robbery.
**húsar** *m* hussar.
**husmear** *vt* to scent; to pry into.
**huso** *m* spindle.

# I

**ictericia** _f_ jaundice.

**ida** _f_ departure, going; (**viaje de**) ~ outward journey; ~ **y vuelta** round trip; ~**s y venidas** comings and goings _pl_.

**idea** _f_ idea; scheme.

**ideal** _adj_ ideal.

**idealmente** _adv_ ideally.

**idear** _vt_ to conceive; to think, to contrive.

**ídem** _pn_ ditto.

**idéntico/ca** _adj_ identical.

**identidad** _f_ identity.

**identificar** _vt_ to identify.

**ideología** _f_ ideology.

**idilio** _m_ idyll.

**idioma** _m_ language.

**idiosincrasia** _f_ idiosyncrasy.

**idiota** _m/f_ idiot.

**idiotez** _f_ idiocy.

**idólatra** _m/f_ idolater.

**idolatrar** _vt_ to idolize; to worship.

**idolatría** _f_ idolatry.

**ídolo** _m_ idol.

**idoneidad** _f_ aptitude, fitness.

**idóneo/nea** _adj_ suitable, fit.

**iglesia** _f_ church.

**ignominia** _f_ ignominy; infamy.

**ignominioso/sa** _adj_ ignominious.

**ignorancia** _f_ ignorance.

**ignorante** _adj_ ignorant, uninformed.

**ignorar** _vt_ to be ignorant of, not to know.

**igual** _adj_ equal; similar; the same; **al** ~ equally.

**igualar** _vt_ to equalize, to equal; to match; to level off; ~**se** _vr_ to be equal; to agree.

**igualdad** _f_ equality.

**igualmente** _adv_ equally.

**ijar** _m_ flank.

**ilegal** _adj_ illegal, unlawful.

**ilegalidad** _f_ illegality.

**ilegitimidad** _f_ illegitimacy.

**ilegítimo/ma** _adj_ illegal; illegitimate.

**ileso/sa** _adj_ unhurt.

**ilícito/ta** _adj_ illicit, unlawful.

**ilimitado/da** _adj_ unlimited.

**illustrar** _vt_ to illustrate; to instruct.

**iluminación** _f_ illumination.

**iluminar** _vt_ to illumine, to illuminate, to enlighten.

**ilusión** _f_ illusion; hope; **hacerse** ~**ones** to build up one's hopes.

**ilusionista** _m/f_ conjurer.

**iluso/sa** _adj_ easily deceived.

**ilusorio/ria** _adj_ illusory.

**ilustración** _f_ illustration; enlightenment.

**ilustre** _adj_ illustrious, famous.

**imagen** _f_ image.

**imaginable** _adj_ imaginable.

**imaginación** _f_ imagination; fancy.

**imaginar** _vt_ to imagine; to think up; _vi_, ~**se** _vr_ to imagine.

**imán** _m_ magnet.

**imbécil** _m/f_ imbecile, idiot.

**imbecilidad** _f_ imbecility.

**imbuir** _vt_ to imbue; to infuse.

**imitable** _adj_ imitable.

**imitación** _f_ imitation; **a** ~ **de** in imitation of.

**imitador/ra** _m/f_ imitator.

**imitar** _vt_ to imitate, to copy; to counterfeit.

**impaciencia** _f_ impatience.

**impacientar** _vt_ to make impatient; to irritate.

**impaciente** _adj_ impatient.

**impacto** _m_ impact.

**impar** _adj_ odd.

**imparcial** _adj_ impartial.

**imparcialidad** _f_ impartiality.

**impasibilidad** _f_ impassivity.

**impasible** _adj_ impassive.

**impavidez** _f_ intrepidity; cheek(iness).

**impávido/da** _adj_ dauntless, intrepid; cheeky.

**impecable** _adj_ impeccable.

**impedimento** _f_ impediment, obstacle.

**impedir** _vt_ to impede, to hinder; to prevent.

**impeler** _vt_ to drive, to propel; to impel; to incite, to stimulate.

**impenetrable** _adj_ impenetrable, impervious; incomprehensible.

**impenitente** _adj_ impenitent.

**impensado/da** _adj_ impenitent.

**imperativo/va** _adj, m_ imperative.

**imperceptible** _adj_ imperceptible.

**imperdible** _m_ safety pin.

**imperdonable** _adj_ unforgivable.

**imperfección** _f_ imperfection.

**imperfecto/ta** _adj_ imperfect.

**imperial** _adj_ imperial.

**impericia** _f_ lack of experience.

**imperio** _m_ empire.

**imperioso/sa** _adj_ imperious; arrogant, haughty; urgent.

**impermeable** *adj* waterproof; * *m* rain-coat.
**impermutable** *adj* immutable.
**impersonal** *adj* impersonal.
**impertérrito/ta** *adj* intrepid, fearless.
**impertinencia** *f* impertinence; irrelevance.
**impertinente** *adj* not pertinent; touchy; impertinent.
**imperturbable** *adj* imperturbable; un-ruffled.
**ímpetu** *m* impetus; impetuosity.
**impetuoso/sa** *adj* impetuous.
**implacable** *adj* implacable, inexorable.
**implicación** *f* implication.
**implicar** *vt* to implicate, to involve.
**implícito/ta** *adj* implicit.
**implorar** *vt* to beg, to implore.
**imponderable** *adj* imponderable; (*fig*) priceless.
**imponer** *vt* to impose; to command; ~se *vr* to assert oneself; to prevail.
**impopular** *adj* unpopular.
**importación** *f* importing; imports *pl*.
**importancia** *f* importance; significance, weight; size.
**importante** *adj* important, considerable.
**importar** *vi* to be important, to matter; * *vt* to import; to be worth.
**importe** *m* amount, cost.
**importunar** *vt* to bother, to pester.
**importunidad** *f* pestering; annoyance.
**importuno/na** *adj* annoying; unreasonable.
**imposibilidad** *f* impossibility.
**imposibilitar** *vt* to make impossible.
**imposible** *adj* impossible; extremely diffi-cult; slovenly.
**imposición** *f* imposition; tax; deposit.
**impostor/ra** *m/f* impostor, fraud.
**impostura** *f* imposture, fraud; slur, slander.
**impotencia** *f* impotence.
**impotente** *adj* impotent.
**impracticable** *adj* impracticable, un-workable.
**imprecación** *f* curse.
**imprecar** *vt* to curse.
**imprecatorio/ria** *adj* containing curses, wishes full of evil.
**impreciso/sa** *adj* imprecise, vague.
**impregnarse** *vr* to be impregnated.
**imprenta** *f* printing; press; printing office.
**imprescindible** *adj* essential.
**impresión** *f* impression; stamp; print; edi-tion.
**impresionante** *adj* impressive; marvellous; tremendous.

**impresionar** *vt* to move; to impress; ~se *vr* to be impressed; to be moved.
**impreso** *m* printed paper; printed book.
**impresor** *m* printer.
**impresora** *f* printer; ~ láser laser printer.
**imprevisto/ta** *adj* unforeseen, unexpected.
**imprimir** *vt* to print; to imprint; to stamp.
**improbable** *adj* improbable, unlikely.
**improperio** *m* insult, taunt.
**impropio/pia** *adj* improper; unfit; un-becoming.
**improvisar** *vt* to extemporize; to im-provize.
**improviso/sa** *adj*: de ~ unexpectedly.
**imprudencia** *f* imprudence; indiscretion; carelessness.
**imprudente** *adj* imprudent; indiscreet; un-wise.
**impudencia** *f* shamelessness.
**impudente** *adj* shameless.
**impúdico/ca** *adj* shameless; lecherous.
**impuesto/ta** *adj* imposed; * *m* tax, duty.
**impugnación** *f* opposition, contradiction.
**impugnar** *vt* to oppose; challenge; impugn.
**impulsivo/va** *adj* impulsive.
**impulso** *m* impulse; thrust; (*fig*) impulse.
**impune** *adj* unpunished.
**impunidad** *f* impunity.
**impureza** *f* impurity.
**impuro/ra** *adj* impure; foul.
**imputable** *adj* attributable, chargeable.
**imputar** *vt* to impute, to attribute.
**inaccesible** *adj* inaccessible.
**inacción** *f* inaction, inactivity.
**inadmisible** *adj* inadmissible.
**inadvertencia** *f* carelessness, inadvertence.
**inadvertido/da** *adj* unnoticed.
**inagotable** *adj* inexhaustible.
**inaguantable** *adj* unbearable, intolerable.
**inalterable** *adj* unalterable.
**inapelable** *adj* without appeal.
**inapreciable** *adj* imperceptible; invaluable.
**inaudito/ta** *adj* unheard-of.
**inauguración** *f* inauguration, opening.
**inaugurar** *vt* to inaugurate.
**incalculable** *adj* incalculable.
**incandescente** *adj* incandescent.
**incansable** *adj* untiring, tireless.
**incapacidad** *f* incapacity, inability.
**incapaz** *adj* incapable, unable.
**incauto/ta** *adj* incautious, unwary.
**incendiar** *vt* to kindle, to set on fire.
**incendiario/ria** *adj* incendiary; * *m/f* ar-sonist.
**incendio** *m* fire.

**incentivo** *m* incentive.
**incertidumbre** *f* doubt, uncertainty.
**incesante** *adj* incessant, continual.
**incesto** *m* incest.
**incestuoso/sa** *adj* incestuous.
**incidencia** *f* incidence; incident.
**incidente** *m* incident.
**incidir** *vi*: ~ **en** to fall upon; to influence, to affect.
**incienso** *m* incense.
**incierto/ta** *adj* uncertain, doubtful.
**incineración** *f* incineration; cremation.
**incipiente** *adj* incipient.
**incisión** *f* incision, cut.
**incisivo/va** *adj* incisive.
**inciso** *m* (*gr*) comma.
**incitación** *f* incitement.
**incitar** *vt* to incite, to excite.
**incivil** *adj* uncivil, rude.
**inclemencia** *f* inclemency, severity; ~ **del tiempo** inclemency of the weather.
**inclinación** *f* inclination.
**inclinar** *vt* to incline; to nod, to bow (the head); ~**se** *vr* to bow; to stoop.
**incluir** *vt* to include, to comprise; to incorporate; to enclose.
**inclusión** *f* inclusion.
**inclusive** *adv* inclusive.
**incluso/sa** *adj* included; * *adv* inclusively; even.
**incógnito/ta** *adj* unknown; **de** ~ incognito.
**incoherencia** *f* incoherence.
**incoherente** *adj* incoherent.
**incombustible** *adj* incombustible, fireproof.
**incomodar** *vt* to inconvenience; to bother, to annoy.
**incomodidad** *f* inconvenience; annoyance; discomfort.
**incómodo/da** *adj* uncomfortable; annoying; inconvenient.
**incomparable** *adj* incomparable, matchless.
**incompatibilidad** *f* incompatibility.
**incompatible** *adj* incompatible.
**incompetencia** *f* incompetence.
**incompetente** *adj* incompetent.
**incompleto/ta** *adj* incomplete.
**incomprehensible** *adj* incomprehensible.
**incomunicación** *f* isolation; lack of communication.
**incomunicado/da** *adj* isolated, cut off; in solitary confinement.
**inconcebible** *adj* inconceivable.
**incondicional** *adj* unconditional; wholehearted; staunch.

**inconexo/xa** *adj* unconnected, disconnected.
**inconfundible** *adj* unmistakable.
**incongruencia** *adj* incongruity, incongruence.
**incongruo/grua** *adj* incongruous.
**inconmensurable** *adj* immeasurable.
**inconsciencia** *f* unconsciousness; thoughtlessness.
**inconsciente** *adj* unconscious; thoughtless.
**inconsecuencia** *f* inconsequence.
**inconsiderado/da** *adj* inconsiderate, thoughtless.
**inconsolable** *adj* inconsolable.
**inconstancia** *f* inconstancy, unsteadiness.
**inconstante** *adj* inconstant, variable, fickle.
**incontestable** *adj* indisputable, incontrovertible, undeniable.
**incontinencia** *f* incontinence.
**incontinente** *adj* incontinent.
**inconveniencia** *f* inconvenience; impoliteness; unsuitability.
**inconveniente** *adj* inconvenient, unsuitable; impolite.
**incorporación** *f* incorporation, involvement.
**incorporar** *vt* to incorporate; ~**se** *vr* to sit up; to join (an organization), to become incorporated.
**incorrecto/ta** *adj* incorrect.
**incorregible** *adj* incorrigible.
**incorruptible** *adj* incorruptible.
**incredulidad** *f* incredulity.
**incrédulo/la** *adj* incredulous.
**increíble** *adj* incredible.
**incremento** *m* increment, increase; growth; rise.
**increpar** *vt* to reprehend, to reprimand.
**incruento/ta** *adj* bloodless.
**inculcar** *vt* to inculcate.
**inculpar** *vt* to accuse, to blame.
**inculto/ta** *adj* uncultivated; uneducated; uncouth.
**incumbencia** *f* obligation; duty.
**incumbir** *vi*: ~ **a uno** to be incumbent upon one.
**incurable** *adj* incurable; irremediable.
**incurrir** *vt*: ~ **en** to incur; to commit (a crime).
**incursión** *f* incursion, raid.
**indagación** *f* search, inquiry.
**indagar** *vt* to inquire into.
**indebido/da** *adj* undue; illegal, unlawful.
**indecencia** *f* indecency.
**indecente** *adj* indecent.
**indecible** *adj* unspeakable, unutterable.

**indecisión** *f* hesitation; indecision.
**indeciso/sa** *adj* hesitant; undecided.
**indecoroso/sa** *adj* unseemly, unbecoming.
**indefectible** *adj* infallible.
**indefenso/sa** *adj* defenceless.
**indefinible** *adj* indefinable.
**indefinido/da** *adj* indefinite.
**indeleble** *adj* indelible.
**indemnización** *f* indemnification, compensation.
**indemnizar** *vt* to indemnify, to compensate.
**independencia** *f* independence.
**independiente** *adj* independent.
**indestructible** *adj* indestructible.
**indeterminado/da** *adj* indeterminate; indefinite.
**indicación** *f* indication.
**indicador** *m* indicator; gauge.
**indicar** *vt* to indicate.
**indicativo/va** *adj*, *m* indicative.
**índice** *m* ratio, rate; hand (of a watch/clock); index, table of contents; catalogue; forefinger, index finger.
**indicio** *m* indication, mark; sign, token; clue.
**indiferencia** *f* indifference, apathy.
**indiferente** *adj* indifferent.
**indígena** *adj* indigenous, native; * *m/f* native.
**indigencia** *f* indigence, poverty, need.
**indigente** *adj* indigent, poor, destitute.
**indigestión** *f* indigestion.
**indigesto/ta** *adj* undigested; indigestible.
**indignación** *f* indignation, anger.
**indignar** *vt* to irritate; to provoke, to tease; ~se *vr*: ~ por to get indignant about.
**indigno/na** *adj* unworthy, contemptible, low.
**indirecta** *f* innuendo, hint.
**indirecto/ta** *adj* indirect.
**indisciplinado/da** *adj* undisciplined.
**indiscreción** *f* indiscretion, tactlessness; gaffe.
**indiscreto/ta** *adj* indiscreet, tactless.
**indisoluble** *adj* indissoluble.
**indispensable** *adj* indispensable.
**indisponer** *vt* to spoil, to upset; to make ill; ~se *vr* to fall ill.
**indisposición** *f* indisposition, slight illness.
**indispuesto/ta** *adj* indisposed.
**indisputable** *adj* indisputable, incontrovertible.
**indistinto/ta** *adj* indistinct.
**individual** *adj* individual; single (of a room); * *m* (*sport*) singles match.
**individualidad** *f* individuality.

**individualizar** *vt* to specify individually.
**individuo** *m* individual.
**indivisible** *adj* indivisible.
**indocilidad** *f* disobedience.
**índole** *f* disposition, nature, character; soft, kind.
**indolencia** *f* indolence, laziness.
**indolente** *adj* indolent, lazy.
**indómito/ta** *adj* untamed, ungoverned.
**inducción** *f* induction, persuasion.
**inducir** *vt* to induce, to persuade.
**inductivo/va** *adj* inductive.
**indudable** *adj* undoubted; unquestionable.
**indulgencia** *f* indulgence.
**indulgente** *adj* indulgent.
**indultar** *vt* to pardon; to exempt.
**indulto** *m* pardon; exemption.
**industria** *f* industry; skill.
**industrial** *adj* industrial.
**industrialización** *f* industrialization.
**inédito/ta** *adj* unpublished; (*fig*) new.
**inefable** *adj* ineffable, unspeakable, indescribable.
**ineficacia** *f* inefficacy.
**ineficaz** *adj* ineffective; inefficient.
**ineptitud** *f* inability; unfitness, ineptitude.
**inepto/ta** *adj* inept, unfit, useless.
**inercia** *f* inertia, inactivity.
**inerme** *adj* unarmed; defenceless.
**inerte** *adj* inert; dull; sluggish, motionless.
**inescrutable** *adj* inscrutable.
**inesperado/da** *adj* unexpected, unforeseen.
**inestable** *adj* unstable.
**inestimable** *adj* inestimable.
**inevitable** *adj* unavoidable.
**inexactitud** *f* inaccuracy.
**inexacto/ta** *adj* inaccurate, untrue.
**inexorable** *adj* inexorable.
**inexperto/ta** *adj* inexperienced.
**infalibilidad** *f* infallibility.
**infalible** *adj* infallible.
**infame** *adj* infamous.
**infancia** *f* infancy, childhood.
**infanta** *f* infanta, princess.
**infante** *m* infante, prince; (*mil*) infantryman.
**infantería** *f* infantry.
**infanticida** *m/f* infanticide (person).
**infanticidio** *m* infanticide (murder).
**infantil** *adj* infantile; childlike; children's.
**infarto** *m* heart attack; ~ de miocardio heart attack.
**infatigable** *adj* tireless, untiring.
**infección** *f* infection.
**infectar** *vt* to infect.

**infeliz** *adj* unhappy, unfortunate.
**inferior** *adj* inferior.
**inferioridad** *f* inferiority.
**inferir** *vt* to infer.
**infernal** *adj* infernal, hellish.
**infestar** *vt* to harass; to infest.
**infidelidad** *f* infidelity, unfaithfulness.
**infiel** *adj* unfaithful; disloyal; inaccurate.
**infierno** *m* hell.
**infiltración** *f* infiltration.
**infiltrarse** *vr* to infiltrate.
**ínfimo/ma** *adj* lowest; of very poor quality.
**infinidad** *f* infinity; immensity.
**infinitivo** *m* (*gr*) infinitive.
**infinito/ta** *adj* infinite; immense.
**inflación** *f* inflation.
**inflamable** *adj* flammable.
**inflamación** *f* ignition; inflammation.
**inflamar** *vt* to inflame; to excite, to arouse; **~se** *vr* to catch fire.
**inflamatorio/ria** *adj* inflammatory.
**inflar** *vt* to inflate, to blow up; (*fig*) to exaggerate.
**inflexibilidad** *f* inflexibility.
**inflexible** *adj* inflexible.
**influencia** *f* influence.
**influir** *vt* to influence.
**influjo** *m* influence.
**infografía** *f* computer graphics.
**información** *f* information; news; (*mil*) intelligence; investigation, judicial inquiry.
**informal** *adj* irregular, incorrect; untrustworthy; informal.
**informalidad** *f* irregularity; untrustworthiness; informality.
**informar** *vt* to inform; to reveal, to make known; **~se** *vr* to find out; * *vi* to report; (*law*) to plead; to inform.
**informática** *f* computer science, information technology.
**informe** *m* report, statement; piece of information, account; * *adj* shapeless, formless.
**infortunio** *m* misfortune, ill luck.
**infracción** *f* infraction; breach, infringement.
**infractor/ra** *m/f* offender.
**infructuoso/sa** *adj* fruitless, unproductive, unprofitable.
**infundado/da** *adj* groundless.
**infundir** *vt* to infuse, to instil.
**infusión** *f* infusion.
**infuso/sa** *adj* infused; introduced.
**ingeniar** *vt* to devise; **~se** *vr*: **~ para** to manage to.

**ingeniería** *f* engineering; **~ genética** genetic engineering.
**ingeniero/ra** *m/f* engineer.
**ingenio** *m* talent; wit; ingenuity; engine; mill; **~ de azúcar** sugar mill.
**ingenioso/sa** *adj* ingenious, clever; witty.
**ingenuidad** *f* ingenuousness; candour, frankness.
**ingenuo/nua** *adj* ingenuous.
**ingerir** *vt* to ingest; to swallow; to consume.
**ingle** *f* groin.
**inglés/esa** *adj* English; * *m* English (language); * *m/f* Englishman/woman.
**ingratitud** *f* ingratitude, unthankfulness.
**ingrato/ta** *adj* ungrateful, thankless; disagreeable.
**ingrediente** *m* ingredient.
**ingresar** *vt* to deposit; * *vi* to come in.
**ingreso** *m* entry; admission; **~s** *mpl* income; takings *pl*.
**inhabilitar** *vt* to disqualify, to disable.
**inhabitable** *adj* uninhabitable.
**inherente** *adj* inherent.
**inhibición** *f* inhibition.
**inhibir** *vt* to inhibit; to restrain.
**inhumano/na** *adj* inhuman.
**inicial** *adj*, *f* initial.
**iniciar** *vt* to initiate; to begin.
**iniciativa** *f* initiative.
**inimaginable** *adj* unimaginable, inconceivable.
**inimitable** *adj* inimitable.
**ininteligible** *adj* unintelligible.
**iniquidad** *f* iniquity, injustice.
**injertar** *vt* to graft.
**injerto** *m* graft.
**injuria** *f* offence; insult.
**injuriar** *vt* to insult, to wrong.
**injurioso/sa** *adj* insulting; offensive.
**injusticia** *f* injustice.
**injusto/ta** *adj* unjust.
**inmaculado/da** *adj* immaculate.
**inmadurez** *f* immaturity.
**inmediaciones** *fpl* neighbourhood; surrounding area.
**inmediatamente** *adv* immediately, at once.
**inmediato/ta** *adj* immediate.
**inmemorial** *adj* immemorial.
**inmensidad** *f* immensity.
**inmenso/sa** *adj* immense.
**inmensurable** *adj* immeasurable.
**inmigración** *f* immigration.
**inmigrante** *m/f* immigrant.

**inmigrar** *vi* to immigrate.
**inminente** *adj* imminent.
**inmobiliario/ria** *adj* estate *compd*; * *f* estate agency.
**inmoral** *adj* immoral.
**inmortal** *adj* immortal.
**inmortalidad** *f* immortality.
**inmortalizar** *vt* to immortalize.
**inmóvil** *adj* immovable.
**inmovilidad** *f* immobility.
**inmueble** *m* property; * *adj*: **bienes ~s** real property/estate.
**inmundicia** *f* nastiness, filth.
**inmundo/da** *adj* filthy, dirty; nasty.
**inmune** *adj* (*med*) immune; free, exempt.
**inmunidad** *f* immunity; exemption.
**inmutabilidad** *f* immutability.
**inmutable** *adj* immutable.
**inmutarse** *vr* to turn pale.
**innato/ta** *adj* inborn, innate.
**innecesario/ria** *adj* unnecessary.
**innegable** *adj* undeniable.
**innovación** *f* innovation.
**innovador/ra** *m/f* innovator.
**innovar** *vt* to innovate.
**innumerable** *adj* innumerable, countless.
**inocencia** *f* innocence.
**inocentada** *f* practical joke.
**inocente** *adj* innocent.
**inoculación** *f* inoculation.
**inocular** *vt* to inoculate.
**inodoro** *m* toilet, lavatory.
**inofensivo/va** *adj* harmless.
**inolvidable** *adj* unforgettable.
**inopinado/da** *adj* unexpected.
**inoxidable** *adj*: **acero ~** stainless steel.
**inquietar** *vt* to worry, to disturb; **~se** *vr* to worry, to get worried.
**inquieto/ta** *adj* anxious, worried.
**inquietud** *f* uneasiness, anxiety.
**inquilino/na** *m/f* tenant; lodger.
**inquirir** *vt* to inquire into, to investigate.
**insaciable** *adj* insatiable.
**insalubre** *adj* unhealthy.
**insalubridad** *f* unhealthiness.
**insano/na** *adj* insane, mad.
**inscribir** *vt* to inscribe; to list, to register.
**inscripción** *f* inscription; enrolment, registration.
**insecticida** *m* insecticide.
**insecto** *m* insect.
**inseguridad** *f* insecurity.
**inseminación** *f* insemination; **~ artificial** artificial insemination.
**insensatez** *f* stupidity, folly.

**insensato/ta** *adj* senseless, stupid; mad.
**insensibilidad** *f* insensitivity; callousness.
**insensible** *adj* insensitive; imperceptible; numb.
**insensiblemente** *adv* insensitively; imperceptibly.
**inseparable** *adj* inseparable.
**inserción** *f* insertion.
**insertar** *vt* to insert.
**inservible** *adj* useless.
**insidioso/sa** *adj* insidious.
**insigne** *adj* notable.
**insignificante** *adj* insignificant.
**insignia** *f* badge; **~s** *fpl* insignia *pl*.
**insinuación** *f* insinuation.
**insinuar** *vt* to insinuate; **~se** *vr*: to make advances; **~ en** to worm one's way into.
**insipidez** *f* insipidness.
**insípido/da** *adj* insipid.
**insistencia** *f* persistence; insistence.
**insistir** *vi* to insist.
**insolación** *f* (*med*) sunstroke.
**insolencia** *f* insolence, rudeness, effrontery.
**insolente** *adj* insolent, rude.
**insólito/ta** *adj* unusual.
**insolvencia** *f* insolvency.
**insolvente** *adj* insolvent.
**insomnio** *m* insomnia.
**insondable** *adj* unfathomable; inscrutable.
**insoportable** *adj* unbearable.
**inspección** *f* inspection, survey; check.
**inspeccionar** *vt* to inspect; to supervise.
**inspector/ra** *m/f* inspector; superintendent.
**inspiración** *f* inspiration.
**inspirar** *vt* to inspire; (*med*) to inhale.
**instalación** *f* installation.
**instalar** *vt* to install.
**instancia** *f* instance.
**instantáneo/nea** *adj* instantaneous; * *f* snap(shot); **café ~** instant coffee.
**instante** *m* instant; **al ~** immediately, instantly.
**instar** *vt* to press, to urge.
**instigación** *f* instigation.
**instigar** *vt* to instigate.
**instinto** *m* instinct.
**institución** *f* institution.
**instituir** *vt* to institute.
**instituto** *m* institute.
**institutriz** *f* governess.
**instrucción** *f* instruction.
**instructivo/va** *adj* instructive; educational.
**instructor/ra** *m/f* instructor, teacher.
**instruir** *vt* to instruct, to teach.

**instrumento** *m* instrument; tool, implement.

**insuficiencia** *f* lack, inadequacy.

**insuficiente** *adj* insufficient, inadequate.

**insufrible** *adj* insufferable, insupportable.

**insulina** *f* insulin.

**insulso/sa** *adj* insipid; dull.

**insultar** *vt* to insult.

**insulto** *m* insult.

**insuperable** *adj* insuperable, insurmountable.

**insurgente** *m/f* insurgent.

**insurrección** *f* insurrection.

**intacto/ta** *adj* untouched; entire; intact.

**integral** *adj* integral, whole; **pan ~** wholemeal bread.

**integrar** *vt* to make up; to integrate.

**integridad** *f* integrity; completeness.

**íntegro/gra** *adj* integral, entire.

**intelectual** *adj*, *m/f* intellectual.

**inteligencia** *f* intelligence; understanding.

**inteligente** *adj* intelligent.

**inteligible** *adj* intelligible.

**intemperie** *f*: **a la ~** out in the open.

**intempestivo/va** *adj* untimely.

**intención** *f* intention, purpose; plan.

**intencionado/da** *adj* meaningful; deliberate.

**intendencia** *f* administration, management.

**intendente** *m* manager.

**intensidad** *f* intensity; strength.

**intenso/sa** *adj* intense, strong; deep.

**intentar** *vt* to try, to attempt.

**intento** *m* intent, purpose; attempt.

**intercalación** *f* insertion.

**intercalar** *vt* to insert.

**intercambio** *m* exchange, swap.

**interceder** *vi* to intercede.

**interceptar** *vt* to intercept.

**intercesión** *f* intercession, mediation.

**intercesor/ra** *m/f* intercessor, mediator.

**interés** *m* interest; share, part; concern, advantage; profit.

**interesado/da** *adj* interested; prejudiced; mercenary.

**interesante** *adj* interesting; useful, convenient.

**interesar** *vt* to be of interest to, to interest; **~se** *vr*: **~ en**, **por** to take an interest in; * *vi* to be of interest.

**interfaz, interface** *f* interface.

**interferir** *vt* to interfere (with); upset; (*radio*) to jam; * *vi* to interfere (in).

**interfono** *m* intercom.

**interinidad** *f* temporary holding of office.

**interino/na** *adj* provisional, temporary; * *m/f* temporary holder of a post; stand-in.

**interior** *adj* interior, internal; * *m* interior, inside.

**interioridad** *f* inwardness.

**interiorismo** *m* interior design.

**interiorista** *m/f* interior designer.

**interjección** *f* (*gr*) interjection.

**interlocutor/ra** *m/f* speaker.

**intermediar** *vt* to interpose.

**intermedio/dia** *adj* intermediate; * *m* interval.

**interminable** *adj* interminable, endless.

**intermitente** *adj* intermittent; *m* (*auto*) indicator.

**internacional** *adj* international.

**internado** *m* boarding school.

**internar** *vt* to intern; to commit; **~se** *vr* to penetrate.

**interno/na** *adj* interior, internal; * *m/f* boarder.

**interpelación** *f* interpellation, appeal, plea.

**interpelar** *vt* to appeal to.

**interpolar** *vt* to interpolate; to interrupt.

**interponer** *vt* to interpose, to put in.

**interposición** *f* insertion; interjection.

**interpretación** *f* interpretation.

**interpretar** *vt* to interpret, to explain; (*teat*) to perform; to translate.

**intérprete** *m/f* interpreter; translator; (*teat*) performer.

**interracial** *adj* interracial.

**interrogación** *f* interrogation; question mark.

**interrogante** *adj* questioning.

**interrogar** *vt* to interrogate.

**interrogatorio** *m* questioning; (*law*) examination; questionnaire.

**interrumpir** *vt* to interrupt.

**interrupción** *f* interruption.

**interruptor** *m* switch.

**intervalo** *m* interval.

**intervención** *f* supervision, control; (*com*) auditing; (*med*) operation; intervention.

**intervenir** *vt* to control, to supervise; (*com*) to audit; (*med*) to operate on; * *vi* to participate; to intervene.

**interventor/ra** *m/f* inspector; (*com*) auditor.

**interviú** *f* interview.

**intestino/na** *adj* internal, interior; * *m* intestine.

**intimar** *vt* to intimate; * *vi* to become friendly.

**intimidad** *f* intimacy; private life.

**intimidar** *vt* intimidate.

**íntimo/ma** *adj* internal, innermost; intimate, private.

**intolerable** *adj* intolerable, insufferable.
**intolerancia** *f* intolerance.
**intolerante** *adj* intolerant.
**intranquilizarse** *vr* to get anxious/worried.
**intranquilo/la** *adj* worried.
**intransigente** *adj* intransigent.
**intransitable** *adj* impassable.
**intransitivo/va** *adj* (*gr*) intransitive.
**intratable** *adj* intractable, difficult.
**intrepidez** *f* intrepidity; fearlessness.
**intrépido/da** *adj* intrepid, daring.
**intriga** *f* intrigue.
**intrigante** *m/f* intriguer.
**intrigar** *vt*, *vi* to intrigue.
**intrínseco/ca** *adj* intrinsic.
**introducción** *f* introduction.
**introducir** *vt* to introduce; to insert.
**introductor/ra** *m/f* introducer.
**introvertido/da** *adj*, *m/f* introvert.
**intrusión** *f* intrusion.
**intruso/sa** *adj* intrusive; * *m/f* intruder.
**intuición** *f* intuition.
**intuitivo/va** *adj* intuitive.
**inundación** *f* inundation, flood(ing).
**inundar** *vt* to inundate, to overflow; to flood.
**inusitado/da** *adj* unusual.
**inútil** *adj* useless.
**inutilidad** *f* uselessness.
**inutilizar** *vt* to render useless.
**invadir** *vt* (*mil*) to invade; to overrun.
**invalidar** *vt* to invalidate, to render null and void.
**inválido/da** *adj* invalid, null and void; * *m/f* invalid.
**invariable** *adj* invariable.
**invasión** *f* invasion.
**invasor/ra** *adj* invading; * *m/f* invader.
**invencible** *adj* invincible.
**invención** *f* invention.
**inventar** *vt* to invent.
**inventario** *m* inventory.
**invento** *m* invention.
**inventor/ra** *m/f* inventor.
**invernadero** *m* greenhouse.
**invernar** *vi* to pass the winter.
**inverosímil** *adj* unlikely, improbable.
**inverosimilitud** *f* unlikeliness, improbability.
**inversión** *f* (*com*) investment; inversion.
**inverso/sa** *adj* inverse; inverted; contrary.
**invertir** *vt* (*com*) to invest; to invert.
**investidura** *f* investiture.
**investigación** *f* investigation, research.

**investigar** *vt* to investigate; to do research into.
**investir** *vt* to confer.
**invicto/ta** *adj* unconquerable.
**invierno** *m* winter.
**inviolabilidad** *f* inviolability.
**inviolable** *adj* inviolable.
**invisible** *adj* invisible.
**invitado/da** *m/f* guest.
**invitar** *vt* to invite; to entice; to pay for.
**invocación** *f* invocation.
**invocar** *vt* to invoke.
**involuntario/ria** *adj* involuntary.
**invulnerable** *adj* invulnerable.
**inyección** *f* injection.
**ir** *vi* to go; to walk; to travel; ~se *vr* to go away, to depart.
**ira** *f* anger, wrath.
**iracundo/da** *adj* irate; irascible.
**iris** *m* iris (eye); **arco** ~ rainbow.
**ironía** *f* irony.
**irónico/ca** *adj* ironic(al).
**irracional** *adj* irrational.
**irradiación** *f* irradiation.
**irrazonable** *adj* unreasonable.
**irreal** *adj* unreal.
**irreconciliable** *adj* irreconcilable.
**irreflexión** *f* rashness, thoughtlessness.
**irregular** *adj* irregular; abnormal.
**irregularidad** *f* irregularity; abnormality.
**irremediable** *adj* irremediable; incurable.
**irremisible** *adj* irretrievable; unpardonable.
**irreparable** *adj* irreparable.
**irresistible** *adj* irresistible.
**irresoluto/ta** *adj* irresolute; hesitant.
**irreverencia** *f* irreverence; disrespect.
**irreverente** *adj* irreverent; disrespectful.
**irrevocable** *adj* irrevocable.
**irrisorio/ria** *adj* derisory, ridiculous.
**irritación** *f* irritation.
**irritar** *vt* to irritate, to exasperate; to stir up; to inflame.
**irrupción** *f* irruption; invasion.
**isla** *f* island, isle.
**Islam** *m* Islam.
**islámico/ca** *adj* Islamic.
**islote** *m* small island.
**istmo** *m* isthmus.
**italiano/na** *adj* Italian; * *m* Italian (language); * *m/f* Italian man/woman.
**ítem** *m* item.
**itinerario** *m* itinerary.
**izar** *vt* (*mar*) to hoist.
**izquierdo/da** *adj* left; left-handed; * *f* left; left(-wing).

# J

**jabalí** m wild boar.

**jabalina** f wild sow; *(sport)* javelin.

**jabón** m soap.

**jabonar** vt to soap.

**jaca** f pony.

**jacinto** m hyacinth.

**jacuzzi** m jacuzzi.

**jactancia** f boasting.

**jactancioso/sa** adj boastful.

**jactarse** vr to boast.

**jadear** vi to pant.

**jaguar** m jaguar.

**jalea** f jelly.

**jaleo** m racket, uproar.

**jalón** m pull, tug.

**jamás** adv never; **para siempre ~** for ever.

**jamón** m ham; **~ de York** (cooked) ham; **~ serrano** cured ham.

**jaque** m check (at game of chess); **~ mate** checkmate.

**jaqueca** f migraine.

**jarabe** m syrup.

**jarcia** f *(mar)* ropes pl, rigging.

**jardín** m garden.

**jardinería** f gardening.

**jardinero/ra** m/f gardener.

**jarra** f jug, jar, pitcher; **en ~s, de ~s** with arms akimbo; with hands to the sides.

**jarro** m jug.

**jarrón** m vase.

**jaspe** m jasper.

**jaspear** vt to marble; to speckle.

**jaula** f cage; cell for mad people; police wagon.

**jauría** f pack of hounds.

**jazmín** m jasmine.

**jazz** m jazz.

**jefatura** f: **~ de policía** police headquarters.

**jefe** m chief, head, leader; *(rail)* **~ de tren** guard, conductor.

**jengibre** m ginger.

**jerarquía** f hierarchy.

**jerárquico/ca** adj hierarchical.

**jerga** f coarse cloth; jargon.

**jergón** m coarse mattress.

**jerigonza** f jargon, gibberish.

**jeringa** f syringe.

**jeroglífico/ca** adj hieroglyphic; * m hieroglyph, hieroglyphic.

**jersey** m sweater, pullover.

**Jesucristo** m Jesus Christ.

**jesuita** m Jesuit.

**jesuítico/ca** adj jesuitical.

**jibia** f cuttlefish.

**jícara** f small cup (for chocolate).

**jilguero** m goldfinch.

**jinete/ta** m/f horseman/woman, rider.

**jipijapa** m straw hat.

**jirafa** f giraffe.

**jirón** m rag, shred.

**jocosidad** f humour, jocularity.

**jocoso/sa** adj good-humoured.

**jornada** f journey; day's journey; working day.

**jornal** m day's wage.

**jornalero** m (day) labourer.

**joroba** f hump; * m/f hunchback.

**jorobado/da** adj hunchbacked.

**jorobar** vt to pester, to annoy.

**jota** f jot, iota; Spanish dance.

**joven** adj young; * m/f youth; young woman.

**jovial** adj jovial, cheerful.

**jovialidad** f joviality, cheerfulness.

**joya** f jewel; **~s** fpl jewellery.

**joyería** f jewellery; jeweller's shop.

**joyero/ra** m/f jeweller.

**juanete** m *(med)* bunion.

**jubilación** f retirement.

**jubilado/da** adj retired; * m/f senior citizen.

**jubilar** vt to pension off; to superannuate; to discard; **~se** vr to retire.

**jubileo** m jubilee.

**júbilo** m joy, rejoicing.

**judaico/ca** adj Judaic, Jewish.

**judaísmo** m Judaism.

**judía** f bean; **~ verde** green bean, French bean.

**judicatura** f judicature; office of a judge.

**judicial** adj judicial.

**judío/día** adj Jewish; * m/f Jewish man/woman.

**juego** m play; amusement; sport; game; gambling; **~s Olímpicos** Olympic Games.

**juerga** f binge; party.

**jueves** m invar Thursday.

**juez** m/f judge.

**jugada** f playing of a card; stroke, shot.

**jugador/ra** m/f player; gambler.

**jugar** vt, vi to play, to sport, to gamble.

**jugarreta** f bad play, unskilful play.

**jugo** *m* sap, juice.
**jugoso/sa** *adj* juicy, succulent.
**juguete** *m* toy, plaything.
**juguetear** *vi* to play.
**juguetón/ona** *adj* playful.
**juicio** *m* judgement, reason; sanity; opinion.
**juicioso/sa** *adj* judicious, prudent.
**julio** *m* July.
**junco** *m* (*bot*) rush; junk (small Chinese ship).
**jungla** *f* jungle.
**junio** *m* June.
**junta** *f* meeting; assembly; congress; council.
**juntamente** *adv* jointly; at the same time.
**juntar** *vt* to join; to unite; ~**se** *vr* to meet, to assemble; to draw closer.
**junto/ta** *adj* joined; united; near; adjacent; ~**s** together; * *adv*: **todo** ~ all at once.
**juntura** *f* junction; joint.

**Júpiter** *m* Jupiter (planet).
**jurado** *m* jury; juror; member of a panel.
**juramento** *m* oath; curse.
**jurar** *vt*, *vi* to swear.
**jurídico/ca** *adj* lawful, legal; juridical.
**jurisdicción** *f* jurisdiction; district.
**jurisprudencia** *f* jurisprudence.
**jurista** *m/f* jurist.
**justa** *f* joust, tournament.
**justamente** *adv* justly; just.
**justicia** *f* justice; equity.
**justificación** *f* justification.
**justificante** *m* voucher; receipt.
**justificar** *vt* to justify.
**justo/ta** *adj* just; fair, right; exact, correct; tight; * *adv* exactly, precisely; just in time.
**juvenil** *adj* youthful.
**juventud** *f* youthfulness, youth; young people *pl*.
**juzgado** *m* tribunal; court.
**juzgar** *vt*, *vi* to judge.

# K

**karaoke** *m* karaoke.
**ketchup** *m* ketchup.
**kilogramo** *m* kilogram.
**kilometraje** *m* distance in kilometres.

**kilómetro** *m* kilometre.
**kilovatio** *m* kilowatt.
**kiosco** *m* kiosk.

# L

**la** *art f* the; * *pn* her; you; it.
**laberinto** *m* labyrinth.
**labia** *f* fluency; (*col*) the gift of the gab.
**labio** *m* lip; edge.
**labor** *f* labour, task; needlework; farmwork; ploughing.
**laboratorio** *m* laboratory.
**laboriosidad** *f* laboriousness.
**laborioso/sa** *adj* laborious; hard-working.
**labrado/da** *adj* worked; carved; wrought; * *m* cultivated land.
**labrador/ra** *m/f* farmer; peasant.
**labranza** *f* farming; cultivation; farmland.
**labrar** *vt* to work; to carve; to farm; (*fig*) to bring about.
**labriego/ga** *m/f* peasant.
**laca** *f* lacquer; hairspray.
**lacayo** *m* lackey, footman.
**lacerar** *vt* to tear to pieces, to lacerate.
**lacio/cia** *adj* faded, withered; languid; lank (hair).
**lacónico/ca** *adj* laconic.
**laconismo** *m* laconic style, terseness.
**lacra** *f* scar; blot, blemish.
**lacrar** *vt* to seal (with sealing wax).
**lacre** *m* sealing wax.
**lactancia** *f* lactation; breast-feeding.
**lácteo/tea** *adj*: productos ~s dairy products.
**ladear** *vt* to move to one side; to incline; ~se *vr* to lean; to tilt.
**ladera** *f* slope.
**ladino/na** *adj* cunning, crafty.
**lado** *m* side; faction, party; favour, protection; (*mil*) flank; **al ~ de** beside; **poner a un ~** to put aside; **por todos ~s** on all sides.
**ladrar** *vt* to bark.
**ladrido** *m* bark, barking.
**ladrillo** *m* brick.
**ladrón/ona** *m/f* thief, robber, burglar.
**lagar** *m* wine press.
**lagartija** *f* (small) lizard.
**lagarto** *m* lizard.
**lago** *m* lake.
**lágrima** *f* tear.
**lagrimal** *m* corner of the eye.
**lagrimoso/sa** *adj* weeping, shedding tears.
**laguna** *f* lake; lagoon; gap.
**laico/ca** *adj* lay; * *m* layman.
**lamedura** *f* licking.
**lamentable** *adj* lamentable, deplorable; pitiable.

**lamentación** *f* lamentation.
**lamentar** *vt* to be sorry about; to lament, to regret; * *vi*, ~se *vr* to lament, to complain; to mourn.
**lamento** *m* lament.
**lamer** *vt* to lick, to lap.
**lámina** *f* plate, sheet of metal; engraving.
**lámpara** *f* lamp.
**lamparilla** *f* nightlight.
**lamparón** *m* grease spot.
**lampiño/na** *adj* beardless.
**lamprea** *f* lamprey (fish).
**lana** *f* wool.
**lance** *m* cast, throw; move, play (in a game); event, incident.
**lancero** *m* (*mil*) lancer.
**lancha** *f* barge, lighter; launch.
**langosta** *f* locust; lobster.
**langostino** *m* king prawn.
**languidez** *f* langour.
**lánguido/da** *adj* languid, faint, weak.
**lanudo/da** *adj* woolly, fleecy.
**lanza** *f* lance, spear.
**lanzada** *f* stroke with a lance.
**lanzadera** *f* shuttle.
**lanzamiento** *m* throwing; (*mar*, *com*) launch, launching.
**lanzar** *vt* to throw; (*sport*) to bowl, to pitch; to launch, to fling; (*law*) to evict.
**lapicero** *m* pencil, ballpoint pen.
**lápida** *f* flat stone, tablet.
**lapidario** *m*; ~/ria *adj* lapidary.
**lápiz** *m* pencil; propelling pencil.
**lapso** *m* interval; error.
**lapsus** *m* error, mistake.
**largamente** *adv* for a long time.
**largar** *vt* to loosen, to slacken; to let go; to launch; to throw out; ~se *vr* (*col*) to beat it.
**largo/ga** *adj* long; lengthy, generous; copious; **a la ~a** in the end, eventually.
**largueza** *f* liberality, generosity.
**largura** *f* length.
**laringe** *f* larynx.
**laringitis** *f* laryngitis.
**las** *art fpl* the; * *pn* them; you.
**lascivia** *f* lasciviousness; lewdness.
**lascivo/va** *adj* lascivious; lewd.
**láser** *m* laser.
**lasitud** *f* lassitude, weariness.
**lástima** *f* compassion, pity; shame.

**lastimar** *vt* to hurt; to wound; to feel pity for; **~se** *vr* to hurt oneself.
**lastimero/ra** *adj* pitiful, pathetic.
**lastimoso/sa** *adj* pathetic, mournful.
**lastrar** *vt* to ballast (a ship).
**lastre** *m* ballast; good sense.
**lata** *f* tin; can; (*col*) nuisance.
**lateral** *adj* lateral.
**latido** *m* (heart)beat.
**latifundio** *m* large estate.
**latigazo** *m* lash, crack (of a whip).
**látigo** *m* whip.
**latín** *m* Latin.
**latinizar** *vt* to Latinize.
**latino/na** *adj* Latin.
**Latinoamérica** *f* Latin America.
**latinoamericano/na** *adj, m/f* Latin American.
**latir** *vi* to beat, to palpitate.
**latitud** *f* latitude.
**latón** *m* brass.
**latoso/sa** *adj* annoying; boring.
**latrocinio** *m* theft, robbery.
**laúd** *f* lute (musical instrument).
**laudable** *adj* laudable, praiseworthy.
**láudano** *m* laudanum.
**laureado/da** *adj* honoured; * *m* laureate.
**laurel** *m* (*bot*) laurel; reward.
**lava** *f* lava.
**lavabo** *m* washbasin; lavatory, toilet.
**lavadero** *m* washing place; laundry.
**lavado** *m* washing; laundry.
**lavadora** *f* washing machine.
**lavanda** *f* lavender.
**lavandera** *f* laundress.
**lavandería** *f* laundry; **~ automática** Launderetteä.
**lavaparabrisas** *m invar* windscreen washer.
**lavaplatos** *m invar* dishwasher.
**lavar** *vt* to wash; to wipe away; **~se** *vr* to wash oneself.
**lavativa** *f* (*med*) enema; (*fig*) nuisance.
**laxante** *m* (*med*) laxative.
**laxitud** *f* laxity, slackness, laxness.
**laxo/xa** *adj* lax, slack.
**lazada** *f* bow, knot.
**lazarillo** *m*: **perro ~** guide dog.
**lazo** *m* knot; bow; snare, trap; tie; bond.
**le** *pn* him; you; (*dative*) to him; to her; to it; to you.
**leal** *adj* loyal; faithful.
**lealtad** *f* loyalty.
**lebrel** *m* greyhound.
**lebrillo** *m* glazed earthenware pan.
**lección** *f* reading; lesson; lecture; class.

**leche** *f* milk.
**lechera** *f* milkmaid, dairymaid; milk churn, milk can.
**lechería** *f* dairy.
**lecho** *m* bed; layer.
**lechón** *m* sucking pig.
**lechuga** *f* lettuce.
**lechuza** *f* owl.
**lector/ra** *m/f* reader.
**lectura** *f* reading.
**leer** *vt, vi* to read.
**legado** *m* bequest, legacy; legate.
**legajo** *m* file.
**legal** *adj* legal; trustworthy.
**legalidad** *f* legality.
**legalización** *f* legalization.
**legalizar** *vt* to legalize.
**legaña** *f* sleep (in eyes).
**legar** *vt* to leave, to bequeath.
**legible** *adj* legible.
**legión** *f* legion.
**legionario/ria** *m&f* legionary.
**legislación** *f* legislation.
**legislador/ra** *m/f* legislator, lawmaker.
**legislar** *vt* to legislate.
**legislativo/va** *adj* legislative.
**legislatura** *f* legislature.
**legitimar** *vt* to legitimize.
**legitimidad** *f* legitimacy.
**legítimo/ma** *adj* legitimate, lawful; authentic.
**legua** *f* league.
**legumbres** *fpl* pulses *pl*.
**leído/da** *adj* well-read.
**lejano/na** *adj* distant, remote; far.
**lejía** *f* bleach.
**lejos** *adv* at a great distance, far off.
**lelo/la** *adj* stupid, ignorant; * *m/f* idiot.
**lema** *m* motto; slogan.
**lencería** *f* linen, drapery.
**lengua** *f* tongue; language.
**lenguado** *m* sole.
**lenguaje** *m* language.
**lente** *m/f* lens; **~ de contacto** contact lens.
**lenteja** *f* lentil.
**lentilla** *f* contact lens.
**lentitud** *f* slowness.
**lento/ta** *adj* slow.
**leña** *f* wood, timber.
**leñador** *m* forester, woodcutter.
**leño** *m* block, log; trunk of a tree.
**leñoso/sa** *adj* woody.
**Leo** *m* Leo (sign of the zodiac).
**león** *m* lion.
**leona** *f* lioness.

**leonado/da** *adj* lion-coloured, tawny.

**leopardo** *m* leopard.

**leotardos** *mpl* tights.

**lepra** *f* leprosy.

**leproso/sa** *adj* leprous; * *m/f* leper.

**lerdo/da** *adj* slow, heavy; dull; slow-witted.

**les** *pn* them; you; (*dative*) to them; to you.

**lesbiana** *adj*, *f* lesbian.

**lesión** *f* wound; injury; damage.

**letal** *adj* mortal, deadly.

**letanía** *f* litany.

**letárgico/ca** *adj* lethargic.

**letargo** *m* lethargy.

**letra** *f* letter; handwriting; printing type; draft of a song; bill, draft; **~s** *fpl* letters *pl*, learning.

**letrado/da** *adj* learned, lettered; * *m/f* lawyer; counsel.

**letrero** *m* sign; label.

**letrina** *f* latrine.

**leucemia** *f* leukaemia.

**leva** *m* (*mar*) weighing anchor; (*mil*) levy.

**levadizo/za** *adj* that can be lifted/raised; **puente ~** drawbridge.

**levadura** *f* yeast; brewer's yeast.

**levantamiento** *m* raising; insurrection.

**levantar** *vt* to raise, to lift up; to build; to elevate; to hearten, to cheer up; **~se** *vr* to get up; to stand up.

**levante** *m* Levant; east; east wind.

**leve** *adj* light; trivial.

**levita** *f* a heavy overcoat; greatcoat, frock coat.

**léxico** *m* vocabulary.

**ley** *f* law; standard (for metal).

**leyenda** *f* legend.

**liar** *vt* to tie, to bind; to confuse.

**libelo** *m* petition; satire, lampoon.

**libélula** *f* dragonfly.

**liberación** *f* liberation; release.

**liberal** *adj* liberal, generous; * *m/f* liberal.

**liberalidad** *f* liberality, generosity.

**libertad** *f* liberty, freedom.

**libertador/ra** *m/f* liberator.

**libertar** *vt* to free, to set at liberty; to exempt, to clear from an obligation/debt.

**libertinaje** *m* licentiousness.

**libertino/na** *m/f* permissive person.

**libra** *f* pound; **~ esterlina** pound sterling.

**Libra** *f* Libra (sign of the zodiac).

**librar** *vt* to free, to deliver; (*com*) to draw; to make out (a cheque); (*law*) to exempt; to fight (a battle); **~se** *vr* to escape.

**libre** *adj* free; exempt; vacant.

**libremente** *adv* freely.

**librería** *f* bookshop.

**librero/ra** *m/f* bookseller.

**libreta** *f* notebook; **~ de ahorros** savings book.

**libro** *m* book.

**licencia** *f* licence; licentiousness.

**licenciado/da** *adj* licensed; * *m/f* graduate.

**licenciar** *vt* to permit, to allow; to license; to discharge; to confer a degree upon; **~se** *vr* to graduate.

**licencioso/sa** *adj* licentious, dissolute.

**liceo** *m* lyceum; secondary school.

**lícitamente** *adv* lawfully.

**lícito/ta** *adj* lawful, fair; permissible.

**licor** *m* liquor.

**licuadora** *f* blender, liquidizer.

**lid** *m* contest, fight; dispute.

**líder** *m/f* leader.

**liderazgo** *m* leadership.

**liebre** *f* hare.

**lienzo** *f* linen; canvas; face/front of a building.

**liga** *f* suspender; birdlime; league; coalition; alloy.

**ligadura** *f* (*med, mus*) ligature; binding; bond, tie.

**ligamento** *m* ligament; tie; bond.

**ligar** *vt* to tie, to bind, to fasten; **~se** *vr* to commit oneself; * *vi* to mix, blend; (*col*) to pick up.

**ligazón** *f* union, connection.

**ligereza** *f* lightness; swiftness; agility; superficiality.

**ligero/ra** *adj* light, swift; agile; superficial.

**liguero** *m* suspender belt.

**lija** *f* dogfish; sandpaper.

**lijar** *vt* to smooth, to sandpaper.

**lila** *f* lilac.

**lima** *f* file.

**limadura** *f* filing.

**limar** *vt* to file; to polish.

**limitación** *f* limitation, restriction.

**limitado/da** *adj* limited.

**limitar** *vt* to limit; to restrict; to cut down.

**límite** *m* limit, boundary.

**limítrofe** *adj* neighbouring, bordering.

**limón** *m* lemon.

**limonada** *f* lemonade.

**limonar** *m* plantation/orchard of lemon trees.

**limosna** *f* alms *pl*, charity.

**limpiaparabrisas** *m invar* windscreen wiper.

**limpiar** *vt* to clean; to cleanse; to purify; to polish; (*fig*) to clean up.

**limpieza** f cleanliness; cleaning; cleansing; polishing; purity.
**limpio/pia** adj clean; neat; pure.
**linaje** m lineage, family, descent.
**linaza** f linseed.
**lince** m lynx.
**linchar** vt to lynch.
**lindar** vi to be adjacent.
**linde** m boundary.
**lindero** m edge; boundary.
**lindo/da** adj pretty; lovely.
**línea** f line; cable; outline.
**lineal** adj linear.
**lingote** m ingot.
**lingüista** m/f linguist.
**lino** m flax.
**linterna** f torch; lantern, lamp; flashlight.
**lío** m bundle, parcel; (col) muddle, mess.
**liposucción** f liposuction.
**liquidación** f liquidation.
**liquidar** vt to liquidate; to settle (accounts).
**líquido/da** adj liquid.
**lira** f (mus) lyre.
**lirio** m (bot) iris.
**lirón** m dormouse; (fig) sleepyhead.
**lisiado/da** adj injured; * m/f cripple.
**lisiar** vt to injure; to hurt.
**liso/sa** adj plain, even, flat, smooth.
**lisonja** f adulation, flattery.
**lisonjear** vt to flatter.
**lisonjero/ra** m/f flatterer; * adj flattering; pleasing.
**lista** f list; school register; catalogue; menu.
**lista de correos** f poste restante.
**listo/ta** adj ready; smart, clever.
**listón** m ribbon; strip (of wood/metal).
**litera** f berth; bunk, bunk bed.
**literal** adj literal.
**literario/ria** adj literary.
**literato/ta** adj literary; * m/f writer, literary person; ~s mpl literati pl.
**literatura** f literature.
**litigar** vt to fight; * vi (law) to go to law; (fig) to dispute.
**litigio** m lawsuit.
**litografía** f lithography.
**litográfico/ca** adj lithographic.
**litoral** adj coastal; * m coast.
**litro** m litre (measure).
**liturgia** f liturgy.
**litúrgico/ca** adj liturgical.
**liviandad** f fickleness; triviality; lightness.
**liviano/na** adj light; fickle; trivial.
**lívido/da** adj livid.
**llaga** f wound; sore.

**llama** f flame; llama (animal).
**llamada** f call.
**llamador** m knocker (door).
**llamamiento** m call.
**llamar** vt to call; to name; to summon; to ring up, to telephone; * vi to knock at the door; to ring up, to telephone; ~se vr to be named.
**llamarada** f blaze; outburst.
**llamativo/va** adj showy; loud (colour).
**llano/na** adj plain; even, level, smooth; clear, evident; * m plain.
**llanta** f (wheel) rim; tyre; inner tube.
**llanto** m flood of tears, crying.
**llanura** f evenness, flatness; plain, prairie.
**llave** f tap; key; ~ **maestra** master key.
**llavero** m key ring.
**llegada** f arrival, coming.
**llegar** vi to arrive; ~ **a** to reach; ~se vr to come near, to approach.
**llenar** vt to fill; to cover; to fill out (a form); to satisfy, to fulfil; ~se vr to gorge oneself.
**lleno/na** adj full, full up; complete.
**llevadero/ra** adj tolerable.
**llevar** vt to take; to wear; to carry; to convey, to transport; to drive; to lead; to bear; ~se vr to carry off, to take away.
**llorar** vt, vi to weep, to cry.
**lloriquear** vt to whine.
**lloro** m weeping, crying.
**llorón/ona** m/f tearful person; crybaby.
**lloroso/sa** adj mournful, full of tears.
**llover** vi to rain.
**lloviznar** vi to drizzle.
**lluvia** f rain; ~ **ácida** acid rain.
**lluvioso/sa** adj rainy.
**lo** pn it; him; you; * art the.
**loable** adj laudable.
**loar** vt to praise.
**lobato** m young wolf.
**lobo** m wolf.
**lóbrego/ga** adj murky, dark, gloomy.
**lóbulo** m lobe.
**local** adj local; * m place, site.
**localidad** f locality; location.
**localizar** vt to localize.
**loción** f lotion.
**loco/ca** adj mad; * m/f mad person.
**locomotora** f locomotive.
**locuacidad** f loquacity.
**locuaz** adj loquacious, talkative.
**locución** f expression.
**locura** f madness, folly.
**locutor/ra** m/f (rad) announcer; (TV) newsreader.

**locutorio** *m* telephone booth.

**lodazal** *m* muddy place.

**lodo** *m* mud, mire.

**logaritmo** *m* logarithm.

**lógica** *f* logic.

**lógico/ca** *adj* logical.

**lograr** *vt* to achieve; to gain, to obtain.

**logro** *m* achievement; success.

**loma** *f* small hill, hillock.

**lombarda** *f* red cabbage.

**lombriz** *f* worm.

**lomo** *m* loin; back (of an animal); spine (of a book); **llevar, traer a ~** to carry on the back.

**lona** *f* canvas.

**loncha** *f* slice; rasher.

**longaniza** *f* pork sausage.

**longitud** *f* length; longitude.

**lonja**[1] *f* slice; rasher.

**lonja**[2] *f* market, exchange; **~ de pescado** fish market.

**loro** *m* parrot.

**los** *art mpl* the; * *pn* them; you.

**losa** *f* flagstone.

**lote** *m* lot; portion.

**lotería** *f* lottery.

**loza** *f* crockery.

**lozanía** *f* luxuriance, lushness; vigour; self-assurance.

**lozano/na** *adj* luxuriant, lush; sprightly.

**lubricante** *m* lubricant.

**lucero** *m* bright star; **~ del alba** morning star.

**lucha** *f* struggle, fight.

**luchador/ra** *m/f* fighter; * *m* wrestler.

**luchar** *vi* to struggle; to wrestle.

**lúcido/da** *adj* lucid.

**luciérnaga** *f* glowworm.

**lucimiento** *m* splendour, lustre; brightness.

**lución** *m* slowworm.

**lucir** *vt* to light (up); to show off; * *vi* to shine; **~se** *vr* to make a fool of oneself.

**lucrativo/va** *adj* lucrative.

**lucro** *m* gain, profit.

**luego** *adv* next; afterward(s); **desde ~** of course.

**lugar** *m* place, spot; village; reason; **en ~ de** instead of, in lieu of.

**lugareño/ña** *adj* belonging to a village; * *m/f* inhabitant of a village.

**lugarteniente** *m* deputy.

**lúgubre** *adj* lugubrious; sad, gloomy.

**lujo** *m* luxury; abundance.

**lujoso/sa** *adj* luxurious; showy; profuse, lavish.

**lujuria** *f* lust.

**lujurioso/sa** *adj* lustful, lewd.

**lumbre** *f* fire; light.

**lumbrera** *f* luminary; skylight.

**luminaria** *f* illumination.

**luminoso/sa** *adj* luminous, shining.

**luna** *f* moon; glass plate for mirrors; lens.

**lunar** *m* mole, spot; * *adj* lunar.

**lunático/ca** *adj, m/f* lunatic.

**lunes** *m invar* Monday.

**lupa** *f* magnifying glass, magnifier.

**lupanar** *m* brothel.

**lustre** *m* gloss, lustre; splendour.

**lustro** *m* lustrum (space of five years).

**lustroso/sa** *adj* bright, brilliant.

**luteranismo** *m* Lutheranism.

**luterano/na** *adj, m/f* Lutheran.

**luto** *m* mourning (dress); grief.

**luz** *f* light.

# M

**macarrones** *mpl* macaroni.
**macedonia** *f*: ~ **de frutas** fruit salad.
**macerar** *vt* to macerate, to soften.
**maceta** *f* flowerpot.
**machacar** *vt* to pound, to crush; * *vi* to insist, to go on.
**machacón/ona** *adj* wearisome, tedious.
**machete** *m* machete, cutlass.
**machista** *adj*, *m* sexist.
**macho** *adj* male; (*fig*) virile; * *m* male; (*fig*) he-man.
**machucar** *vt* to pound, to bruise.
**macilento/ta** *adj* lean; haggard, withered.
**macizo/za** *adj* massive; solid; * *m* mass, chunk.
**madeja** *f* skein of thread; mop of hair.
**madera** *f* timber, wood.
**madero** *m* beam of timber.
**madrastra** *f* stepmother.
**madraza** *f* loving mother.
**madre** *f* mother; womb.
**madreperla** *f* mother-of-pearl.
**madreselva** *f* honeysuckle.
**madrigal** *m* madrigal.
**madriguera** *f* burrow; den.
**madrina** *f* godmother.
**madroño** *m* strawberry plant.
**madrugada** *f* dawn; **de** ~ at day break.
**madrugador/ra** *m/f* early riser.
**madrugar** *vi* to get up early; to get ahead.
**madurar** *vt* to ripen; * *vi* to ripen, to grow ripe; to mature.
**madurez** *f* maturity; ripeness; wisdom.
**maduro/ra** *adj* ripe, mature.
**maestra** *f* mistress; schoolmistress; teacher.
**maestría** *f* mastery, skill.
**maestro** *m* master; teacher; ~/**tra** *adj* masterly, skilled; principal.
**magia** *f* magic.
**mágico/ca** *adj* magical.
**magisterio** *m* teaching; teaching profession; teachers *pl*.
**magistrado/da** *m/f* magistrate.
**magistral** *adj* magisterial; masterly.
**magistratura** *f* magistracy.
**magnanimidad** *f* magnanimity.
**magnánimo/ma** *adj* magnanimous.
**magnate** *m* magnate.
**magnético/ca** *adj* magnetic.
**magnetismo** *m* magnetism.
**magnetizar** *vt* to magnetize.

**magnetofón, magnetófono** *m* tape recorder.
**magnetofónico/ca** *adj*: **cinta magnetofónica** recording tape.
**magnificencia** *f* magnificence, splendour.
**magnífico/ca** *adj* magnificent, splendid.
**magnitud** *f* magnitude.
**mago/ga** *m/f* magician.
**magro/gra** *adj* thin, lean; meagre.
**magulladura** *f* bruise.
**magullar** *vt* to bruise; to damage; (*col*) to bash.
**mahometano/na** *m/f*, *adj* Muslim.
**mahometanismo** *m* Islam.
**mahonesa** *f* mayonnaise.
**maíz** *m* maize, Indian corn.
**maizal** *m* maize field.
**majada** *f* sheepfold.
**majadería** *f* absurdity; silliness.
**majadero/ra** *adj* dull; silly, stupid; * *m* idiot.
**majestad** *f* majesty.
**majestuoso/sa** *adj* majestic.
**majo/ja** *adj* nice; attractive; smart.
**majuelo** *m* vine newly planted; hawthorn.
**mal** *m* evil; hurt; harm, damage; misfortune; illness; * *adj* (before masculine nouns) bad.
**malamente** *adv* badly.
**malaria** *f* malaria.
**malcriado/da** *adj* rude, ill-behaved; naughty; spoiled.
**maldad** *f* wickedness.
**maldecir** *vt* to curse.
**maldición** *f* curse.
**maldito/ta** *adj* wicked; damned, cursed.
**malear** *vt* to damage; to corrupt.
**malecón** *m* pier.
**maledicencia** *f* slander; scandal.
**maleducado/da** *adj* bad-mannered, rude.
**maleficio** *m* curse; spell; witchcraft.
**maléfico/ca** *adj* harmful, damaging, evil.
**malestar** *m* discomfort; (*fig*) uneasiness; unrest.
**maleta** *f* suitcase; (*auto*) boot.
**maletero** *f* (*auto*) boot.
**malevolencia** *f* malevolence.
**malévolo/la** *adj* malevolent.
**maleza** *f* weeds *pl*; thicket.
**malgastar** *vt* to waste, to ruin.
**malhablado/da** *adj* foul-mouthed.
**malhechor/ra** *m/f* malefactor; criminal.

**malhumorado/da** *adj* cross, bad-tempered.

**malicia** *f* malice, wickedness; suspicion; cunning.

**malicioso/sa** *adj* malicious, wicked, evil; sly, crafty; spiteful.

**malignidad** *f* (*med*) malignancy; evil nature; malice.

**maligno/na** *adj* malignant; malicious.

**malla** *f* mesh, network; ~s *fpl* leotard.

**malo/la** *adj* bad; ill; wicked; * *m/f* villain.

**malograr** *vt* to spoil; to upset (a plan); to waste; ~se *vr* to fail; to die early.

**malparado/da** *adj*: salir ~ to come off badly.

**malparida** *f* woman who has had a miscarriage.

**malparir** *vi* to miscarry, to have a miscarriage.

**malsano/na** *adj* unhealthy.

**malteada** *f* milk shake.

**maltratamiento** *m* ill-treatment.

**maltratar** *vt* to ill-treat, to abuse, to mistreat.

**malva** *f* (*bot*) mallow.

**malvado/da** *adj* wicked, villainous.

**malversación** *f* embezzlement.

**malversador/ra** *m/f* embezzler.

**malversar** *vt* to embezzle.

**mama** *f* teat; breast.

**mamá** *f* (*col*) mum, mummy.

**mamar** *vt, vi* to suck.

**mamarrachada** *f* ridiculous sight.

**mamarracho** *m* mess, botch-up.

**mamífero** *m* mammal.

**mamón/ona** *m/f* small baby; scrounger.

**mampara** *f* partition; screen.

**mampostería** *f* masonry; stonemasonry.

**maná** *m* manna.

**manada** *f* flock, herd; pack; crowd.

**manantial** *m* source, spring; origin.

**manar** *vt* to run with, to flow; * *vi* to spring from; to flow; to abound.

**mancha** *f* stain, spot.

**manchado/da** *adj* spotted.

**manchar** *vt* to stain, to soil.

**mancilla** *f* spot, blemish.

**manco/ca** *adj* one-armed; one-handed; maimed; faulty.

**mancomunar** *vt* to associate, to unite; to make jointly responsible.

**mancomunidad** *f* union, fellowship; community; (*law*) joint responsibility.

**mandado** *m* command; errand, message.

**mandamiento** *m* order, command; commandment.

**mandar** *vt* to command, to order; to bequeath; to send.

**mandarín** *m* mandarin.

**mandarina** *f* tangerine, mandarin orange.

**mandatario/ria** *m/f* agent; leader.

**mandato** *m* mandate, order; term of office.

**mandíbula** *f* jaw.

**mandil** *m* apron.

**mando** *m* command, authority, power; term of office; ~ a distancia remote control.

**mandón/ona** *adj* bossy, domineering.

**manecilla** *f* small hand (of a watch/meter); book-clasp.

**manejable** *adj* manageable.

**manejar** *vt* to manage; to operate; to handle; (*auto*) to drive; ~se *vr* to manage; to behave.

**manejo** *m* management; handling; driving; confidence.

**manera** *f* manner, way; fashion; kind.

**manga** *f* sleeve; hose, hosepipe.

**mango**¹ *m* handle.

**mango**² *m* mango.

**mangonear** *vi* to interfere; * *vt* to boss about.

**manguera** *f* hose; hosepipe.

**manguito** *m* muff.

**maní** *m* peanut.

**manía** *f* mania; craze; dislike; spite.

**maniatar** *vt* to tie the hands of; to handcuff.

**maniático/ca** *adj* maniac, mad, frantic; * *m/f* maniac.

**manicomio** *m* mental home, lunatic asylum.

**manicura** *f* manicure.

**manifestación** *f* manifestation; show; demonstration; mass meeting.

**manifestar** *vt* to manifest, to declare.

**manifiesto/ta** *adj* manifest, open, clear; * *m* manifesto.

**manija** *f* handle.

**maniobra** *f* manoeuvring; handling; (*mil*) manoeuvre.

**maniobrar** *vt* to manoeuvre; to handle.

**manipulación** *f* manipulation.

**manipular** *vt* to manipulate.

**maniquí** *m* dummy; * *m/f* model.

**manirroto/ta** *adj* lavish, extravagant.

**manivela** *f* crank.

**manjar** *m* (tasty) dish.

**mano** *f* hand; hand (of a clock/watch); foot, paw (of an animal); coat (of paint); lot, series; hand (at game); a ~ by hand; a ~s llenas liberally, generously.

**manojo** *m* handful, bunch.

**manopla** *f* gauntlet; glove; face cloth.

**manosear** vt to handle; to finger, to mess up.
**manoseo** m handling; fingering.
**manotazo** m slap, smack.
**manoteo** m gesticulation.
**mansalva** f: a ~ adv indiscriminately.
**mansedumbre** f meekness, gentleness.
**mansión** f mansion.
**manso/sa** adj tame; gentle, soft.
**manta** f blanket.
**manteca** f fat; ~ de cerdo lard.
**mantecado** m cake eaten at Christmas; ice cream.
**mantecoso/sa** adj greasy.
**mantel** m tablecloth.
**mantelería** f table linen.
**mantener** vt to maintain, to support; to nourish; to keep; ~se vr to hold one's ground; to support oneself.
**mantenimiento** m maintenance; subsistence.
**mantequilla** f butter.
**mantilla** f mantilla (head covering for women); ~s fpl baby clothes pl.
**manto** m mantle; cloak, robe.
**mantón** m shawl.
**manual** adj manual; * m manual, handbook.
**manufactura** f manufacture.
**manufacturar** vt to manufacture.
**manuscrito** m manuscript; * adj handwritten.
**manutención** f support, maintenance.
**manzana** f apple.
**manzanilla** f camomile; camomile tea; manzanilla sherry.
**manzano** m apple tree.
**maña** f handiness, dexterity, cleverness, cunning; habit, custom; trick.
**mañana** f morning; * adv tomorrow.
**mañoso/sa** adj skilful, handy; cunning.
**mapa** m map.
**mapamundi** f map of the world.
**maquillaje** m make-up; making up.
**maquillar** vt to make up; ~se vr to put on make-up.
**máquina** f machine; (rail) engine; camera; (fig) machinery; plan, project.
**maquinación** f machination.
**maquinador/ra** m/f schemer, plotter.
**maquinalmente** adv mechanically.
**maquinar** vt, vi to machinate; to conspire.
**maquinaria** f machinery; mechanism.
**maquinilla** f: ~ de afeitar razor.
**maquinista** m (rail) train driver; operator; (mar) engineer.
**mar** m/f sea.

**maraña** f shrub, thicket; tangle.
**maravilla** f wonder.
**maravillar** vt to astonish, to amaze; ~se vr to be amazed, to be astonished.
**maravilloso/sa** adj wonderful, marvellous.
**marca** f mark; stamp; (com) make, brand.
**marcado/da** adj strong, marked.
**marcador** m scoreboard; scorer.
**marcar** vt to mark; to dial; to score; to record; to set (hair); * vi to score; to dial.
**marcha** f march; running; gear; speed; (fig) progress.
**marchar** vi to go; to work; ~se vr to go away.
**marchitar** vt to wither; to fade.
**marchito/ta** adj faded; withered.
**marcial** adj martial, warlike.
**marciano/na** adj Martian.
**marco** m frame; framework; (sport) goalposts pl.
**marea** f tide; ~ negra oil slick.
**marear** vt (mar) to sail, to navigate; to annoy, to upset; ~se vr to feel sick; to feel faint; to feel dizzy.
**marejada** f swell, heavy sea, surge.
**mareo** m sick feeling; dizziness; nuisance.
**marfil** m ivory.
**margarina** f margarine.
**margarita** f daisy.
**margen** m margin; border; * f bank (of river).
**marginal** adj marginal.
**marginar** vt to exclude; to leave margins on (a page); to make notes in the margin of.
**marica** m (col) sissy.
**maricón** m (col) queer.
**marido** m husband.
**mariguana, marihuana** f cannabis.
**marimacho** f (col) mannish woman.
**marina** f navy.
**marinero/ra** adj sea compd; seaworthy; * m sailor.
**marino/na** adj marine; * m sailor, seaman.
**marioneta** f puppet.
**mariposa** f butterfly.
**mariquita** f ladybird.
**mariscal** m marshal.
**marisco** m shellfish.
**marital** adj marital.
**marítimo/ma** adj maritime, marine.
**marmita** f pot.
**mármol** m marble.
**marmóreo/rea** adj marbled, marble compd.
**marmota** f marmot.
**maroma** f rope.
**marqués** m marquis.

**marquesa** *f* marchioness.
**marrano** *m* pig, boar.
**marrón** *adj* brown.
**marrullería** *f* plausibility; plausible excuse; **~s** *fpl* cajolery.
**marrullero/ra** *adj* crafty, cunning.
**marta** *f* marten, sable.
**Marte** *m* Mars (planet).
**martes** *m invar* Tuesday.
**martillar** *vt* to hammer.
**martillo** *m* hammer.
**mártir** *m/f* martyr.
**martirio** *m* martyrdom.
**martirizar** *vt* to martyr.
**marxismo** *m* Marxism.
**marxista** *adj*, *m/f* Marxist.
**marzo** *m* March.
**mas** *adv* but, yet.
**más** *adv* more; most; besides, moreover; **a ~ tardar** at latest; **sin ~ ni ~** without more ado.
**masa** *f* dough, paste; mortar; mass.
**masacre** *m* massacre.
**masaje** *m* massage.
**mascar** *vt* to chew.
**máscara** *m/f* masked person; * *f* mask.
**mascarada** *f* masquerade.
**mascarilla** *f* (*med*) mask.
**masculino/na** *adj* masculine, male.
**mascullar** *vt* to mumble, to mutter.
**masivo/va** *adj* massive, en masse.
**masoquista** *m/f* masochist.
**masticación** *f* mastication.
**masticar** *vt* to masticate, to chew.
**mástil** *m* (*mar*) mast.
**mastín** *m* mastiff.
**masturbación** *f* masturbation.
**masturbarse** *vr* to masturbate.
**mata** *f* shrub; sprig; blade; grove, group of trees; mop of hair.
**matadero** *m* slaughterhouse.
**matador/ra** *adj* killing; * *m/f* killer; * *m* bullfighter.
**matanza** *f* slaughtering; massacre.
**matar** *vt* to kill; to execute; to murder; **~se** *vr* to kill oneself, to commit suicide.
**matasanos** *m invar* quack (doctor).
**matasellos** *m invar* postmark.
**mate**[1] *m* checkmate.
**mate**[2] *adj* matte.
**matemáticas** *fpl* mathematics.
**matemático/ca** *adj* mathematical; * *m/f* mathematician.
**materia** *m* matter, materials *pl*; subject.
**material** *adj* material, physical; * *m* equipment, materials *pl*.

**materialidad** *f* outward appearance.
**materialismo** *m* materialism.
**materialista** *m/f* materialist.
**maternal** *adj* maternal, motherly.
**maternidad** *f* motherhood.
**materno/na** *adj* maternal.
**matinal** *adj* morning *compd*.
**matiz** *m* shade of colour; shading.
**matizar** *vt* to mix colours; to tinge, to tint.
**matón** *m* bully.
**matorral** *m* shrub, thicket.
**matraca** *f* rattle.
**matricida** *m/f* matricide (person).
**matricidio** *m* matricide (act).
**matrícula** *f* register, list; (*auto*) registration number; numberplate.
**matricular** *vt* to register, to enrol.
**matrimonial** *adj* matrimonial.
**matrimonio** *m* marriage, matrimony.
**matriz** *f* matrix; womb; mould, form.
**matrona** *f* matron.
**matutino/na** *adj* morning.
**maullar** *vi* to mew.
**maullido** *m* mew (of a cat).
**mausoleo** *m* mausoleum.
**máxima** *f* maxim.
**máxime** *adv* principally.
**máximo/ma** *adj* maximum; top; highest.
**mayo** *m* May.
**mayonesa** *f* mayonnaise.
**mayor** *adj* main, chief; (*mus*) major; biggest; eldest; greater, larger; elderly; * *m* chief, boss; adult; **al por ~** wholesale; **~es** *mpl* forefathers.
**mayoral** *m* foreman.
**mayordomo** *m* steward.
**mayoría** *f* majority, greater part; **~ de edad** coming of age.
**mayorista** *m/f* wholesaler.
**mayormente** *adv* principally, chiefly.
**mayúsculo/la** *adj* (*fig*) tremendous; * *f* capital letter.
**maza** *f* club; mace.
**mazada** *f* blow with a club.
**mazapán** *m* marzipan.
**mazmorra** *f* dungeon.
**mazo** *m* bunch, handful; club, mallet; bat.
**mazorca** *f* ear; cob; **maíz en la ~** corn on the cob.
**me** *pn* me; to me.
**mear** *vi* (*col*) to pee, to piss.
**mecánica** *f* mechanics.
**mecánico/ca** *adj* mechanical; * *m/f* mechanic.
**mecanismo** *m* mechanism.

**mecanografía** f typing.
**mecanógrafo/fa** m/f typist.
**mecate** m rope.
**mecedora** f rocking chair.
**mecer** vt to rock; to dandle (a child).
**mecha** f wick; fuse.
**mechar** vt to lard; to stuff.
**mechero** m (cigarette) lighter.
**mechón** m lock of hair; large bundle of threads/fibres.
**medalla** f medal.
**medallón** m medallion.
**media** f stocking; sock; average.
**mediación** f mediation, intervention.
**mediado/da** adj half-full; half-complete; **a ~s de** in the middle of.
**mediador/ra** m/f mediator; go-between.
**mediana** f central reserve.
**medianero/ra** adj dividing; adjacent.
**mediano/na** adj medium; middling; mediocre.
**medianoche** f midnight.
**mediante** prep by means of.
**mediar** vi to intervene; to mediate.
**medias** fpl tights pl.
**medicación** f medication.
**medicamento** m medicine.
**medicina** f medicine.
**medicinal** adj medicinal.
**médico/ca** adj medical; * m/f doctor.
**medida** f measure.
**medio/dia** adj half; **a medias** partly; * m middle; average; way, means; medium.
**mediocre** adj middling; moderate; mediocre.
**mediocridad** f mediocrity.
**mediodía** m noon, midday.
**medir** vt to measure; **~se** vr to be moderate.
**meditación** f meditation.
**meditar** vt to meditate.
**mediterráneo/nea** adj Mediterranean; * m: **el M~** the Mediterranean.
**medrar** vi to grow, to thrive, to prosper; to improve.
**medroso/sa** adj fearful, timid.
**médula** f marrow; essence, substance; pith.
**medusa** f jellyfish.
**megafonía** f public-address system.
**megáfono** m megaphone.
**mejilla** f cheek.
**mejillón** m mussel.
**mejor** adj, adv better; best.
**mejora** f improvement.
**mejorar** vt to improve, to ameliorate; to enhance; * vi to improve; (med) to recover, to get better; **~se** vr to improve, to get better.

**mejoría** f improvement; recovery.
**melancolía** f melancholy.
**melancólico/ca** adj melancholy, sad, gloomy.
**melena** f long hair, loose hair; mane.
**melenudo/da** adj long-haired.
**melindroso/sa** adj prudish, finicky.
**mella** f notch in edged tools; gap.
**mellado/da** adj jagged; gap-toothed.
**mellar** vt to notch.
**mellizo/za** adj, m/f twin.
**melocotón** m peach.
**melodía** f melody.
**melodioso/sa** adj melodious.
**melodrama** f melodrama.
**melón** m melon.
**melosidad** f sweetness.
**meloso/sa** adj honeyed; mellow.
**membrana** f membrane.
**membranoso/sa** adj membranous.
**membrete** m letterhead.
**membrillo** m quince; quince tree.
**membrudo/da** adj strong, robust; burly.
**memorable** adj memorable.
**memorándum** m notebook; memorandum.
**memoria** f memory; report; record; **~s** fpl memoirs pl.
**memorial** m memorial; petition.
**mención** f mention.
**mencionar** vt to mention.
**mendigar** vt to beg.
**mendigo/ga** m/f beggar.
**mendrugo** m crust.
**menear** vt to move from place to place; (fig) to handle; **~se** vr to move; to shake; to sway.
**meneo** m movement; shake; swaying.
**menester** m necessity; need; want; **~es** mpl duties pl.
**menesteroso/sa** adj needy.
**menestra** f vegetable soup/stew.
**menguante** f decreasing.
**menguar** vi to diminish; to discredit.
**menopausia** f menopause.
**menor** m/f young person, juvenile; * adj less; smaller; minor; **al por ~** retail.
**menoría** f: **a ~** retail.
**menos** adv less; least; **a lo ~/por lo ~** at least; * prep except; minus.
**menoscabar** vt to damage; to harm; to lessen; to discredit.
**menoscabo** m damage; harm; loss.
**menospreciar** vt to undervalue; to despise, to scorn.
**menosprecio** m contempt, scorn; undervaluation.
**mensaje** m message.

**mensajero/ra** *m/f* messenger; courier.
**menstruación** *f* menstruation.
**mensual** *adj* monthly.
**menta** *f* mint.
**mental** *adj* mental; intellectual.
**mentar** *vt* to mention.
**mente** *f* mind; understanding.
**mentecato/ta** *adj* silly, stupid; * *m/f* idiot.
**mentir** *vt* to feign; to pretend; * *vi* to lie.
**mentira** *f* lie, falsehood.
**mentiroso/sa** *adj* lying; * *m/f* liar.
**menú** *m* menu; set meal.
**menudencia** *f* trifle, small thing; minuteness; ~s *fpl* odds and ends *pl*.
**menudillos** *mpl* giblets *pl*.
**menudo/da** *adj* small; minute; petty, insignificant; **a** ~ frequently, often.
**meñique** *m* little finger.
**meollo** *m* marrow; (*fig*) core.
**mequetrefe** *m* good-for-nothing; busybody.
**meramente** *adv* merely, solely.
**mercader** *m* dealer, trader.
**mercadería** *f* commodity; trade; ~s *fpl* merchandise.
**mercado** *m* market; marketplace.
**mercancía** *f* commodity; ~s *fpl* goods *pl*, merchandise.
**mercantil** *adj* commercial, mercantile.
**mercenario/ria** *adj* mercenary; * *m* mercenary; labourer.
**mercería** *f* haberdashery, draper's shop.
**mercurio** *m* mercury.
**Mercurio** *m* Mercury (planet).
**merecedor/ra** *adj* deserving.
**merecer** *vt* to deserve, to merit.
**merecido/da** *adj* deserved.
**merendar** *vi* to have tea; to have a picnic.
**merengue** *m* meringue.
**meridiano** *m* meridian.
**meridional** *adj* southern.
**merienda** *f* (light) tea; afternoon snack; picnic.
**mérito** *m* merit; worth, value.
**meritorio/ria** *adj* meritorious.
**merluza** *f* hake.
**merma** *f* waste, leakage.
**mermar** *vi* to waste, to diminish.
**mermelada** *f* jam.
**mero** *m* pollack (fish); ~/ra *adj* mere, pure.
**merodeador** *m* (*mil*) marauder.
**merodear** *vi* to pillage, to go marauding.
**mes** *m* month.
**mesa** *f* table; desk; plateau; ~ **redonda** round table.
**meseta** *f* meseta, tableland, plateau.

**mesón** *m* inn.
**mestizo/za** *adj* of mixed race; crossbred; * *m/f* half-caste.
**mesura** *f* gravity; politeness; moderation.
**mesurado/da** *adj* moderate; dignified; courteous.
**meta** *f* goal; finish.
**metabolismo** *m* metabolism.
**metafísica** *f* metaphysics.
**metafísico/ca** *adj* metaphysical.
**metáfora** *f* metaphor.
**metafórico/ca** *adj* metaphorical.
**metal** *m* metal; (*mus*) brass; timbre (of the voice).
**metálico/ca** *adj* metallic.
**metalurgia** *f* metallurgy.
**metamorfosis** *f invar* metamorphosis; transformation.
**meteoro** *m* meteor.
**meteorología** *f* meteorology.
**meter** *vt* to place, to put; to insert, to put in; to involve; to make, to cause; ~se *vr* to meddle, to interfere.
**metódico/ca** *adj* methodical.
**método** *m* method.
**metralla** *f* (*mil*) shrapnel.
**metralleta** *f* submachine-gun.
**métrico/ca** *adj* metric.
**metro**[1] *m* metre.
**metro**[2] *m* underground; tube.
**metrópoli** *f* metropolis; mother country.
**mezcla** *f* mixture; medley.
**mezclar** *vt* to mix; ~se *vr* to mix; to mingle.
**mezquindad** *f* meanness; pettiness; wretchedness.
**mezquino/na** *adj* mean; small-minded, petty; wretched.
**mezquita** *f* mosque.
**mi** *adj* my.
**mí** *pn* me; myself.
**microbio** *m* microbe.
**microbús** *m* minibus.
**microchip** m microchip.
**micrófono** *m* microphone.
**microondas** *m inv* microwave oven.
**microplaqueta** f microchip.
**microscópico/ca** *adj* microscopic.
**microscopio** *m* microscope.
**miedo** *m* fear, dread.
**miel** *f* honey.
**miembro** *m* member.
**mientras** *adv* meanwhile; * *conj* while; as long as.
**miércoles** *m invar* Wednesday.
**mierda** *f* (*col*) shit.

**mies** *f* harvest.
**miga** *f* crumb; **~s** *fpl* fried breadcrumbs *pl.*
**migaja** *f* scrap, crumb.
**migración** *f* migration.
**mijo** *m* (*bot*) millet.
**mil** *m* one thousand.
**milagro** *m* miracle, wonder.
**milagroso/sa** *adj* miraculous.
**milano** *m* kite (bird).
**milésimo/ma** *adj, m* thousandth.
**mili** *f*: **hacer la ~** (*col*) to do one's military service.
**milicia** *f* militia; military service.
**miliciano** *m* militiaman.
**milímetro** *m* millimeter.
**militante** *adj* militant.
**militar** *adj* military; * *m* soldier; * *vi* to serve in the army; (*fig*) to be a member of a party.
**milla** *f* mile.
**millar** *m* thousand.
**millón** *m* million.
**millonario/ria** *m/f* millionaire.
**mimar** *vt* to spoil, pamper.
**mimbre** *m* wicker.
**mímica** *f* sign language; mimicry.
**mimo** *m* caress; spoiling; mime.
**mimoso/sa** *adj* spoilt, pampered; delicate.
**mina** *f* mine; underground passage.
**minar** *vt* to undermine; to mine.
**mineral** *m* mineral; * *adj* mineral.
**mineralogía** *f* mineralogy.
**minero/ra** *m/f* miner.
**miniatura** *f* miniature.
**minicadena** *f* midi system.
**minifalda** *f* miniskirt.
**mínimo/ma** *adj* minimum.
**ministerio** *m* ministry.
**ministro/ra** *m/f* minister.
**minoría** *f* minority.
**minucioso/sa** *adj* meticulous; very detailed.
**minúsculo/la** *adj* minute; * *f* small letter.
**minusválido/da** *adj* (physically) handicapped; * *m/f* (physically) handicapped person.
**minuta** *f* minute, first draft; menu.
**minutero** *m* minute hand (of a watch/clock).
**minuto** *m* minute.
**mío/mía** *adj* mine.
**miope** *adj* short-sighted.
**mira** *f* sight of a gun; (*fig*) aim.
**mirada** *f* glance; gaze.
**mirador** *m* viewpoint, vantage point.
**miramiento** *m* consideration; circumspection.

**mirar** *vt* to look at; to observe; to consider; * *vi* to look; **~se** *vr* to look at oneself; to look at one another.
**mirilla** *f* peephole.
**mirlo** *m* blackbird.
**mirón/ona** *m/f* spectator, onlooker, bystander; voyeur.
**misa** *f* mass; **~ del gallo** midnight mass.
**misal** *m* missal.
**misantropía** *f* misanthropy.
**misántropo/pa** *m/f* misanthropist.
**miserable** *adj* miserable; mean; squalid (place); (*col*) despicable; * *m/f* rotter.
**miseria** *f* misery; poverty; meanness; squalor.
**misericordia** *f* mercy.
**misil** *m* missile.
**misión** *f* mission.
**misionero/ra** *m/f* missionary.
**mismo/ma** *adj* same; very.
**misterio** *m* mystery.
**misterioso/sa** *adj* mysterious.
**mística** *f* mysticism.
**místico/ca** *adj* mystic(al); * *m/f* mystic.
**mitad** *f* half; middle.
**mitigación** *f* mitigation.
**mitigar** *vt* to mitigate.
**mitin** *m* (political) rally.
**mito** *m* myth.
**mitología** *f* mythology.
**mitológico/ca** *adj* mythological.
**mitones** *mpl* mittens *pl.*
**mixto/ta** *adj* mixed.
**mobiliario** *m* furniture.
**mochila** *f* backpack.
**mochuelo** *m* red owl.
**moción** *f* motion.
**moco** *m* (*col*) snot, mucus.
**moda** *f* fashion, style.
**modales** *mpl* manners *pl.*
**modalidad** *f* kind, variety.
**modelar** *vt* to model, to form.
**modelo** *m* model, pattern.
**módem** *m* modem.
**moderación** *f* moderation.
**moderado/da** *adj* moderate.
**moderar** *vt* to moderate.
**moderno/na** *adj* modern.
**modestia** *f* modesty, decency.
**modesto,ta** *adj* modest.
**módico/ca** *adj* moderate.
**modificación** *f* modification.
**modificar** *vt* to modify.
**modisto/ta** *m/f* dressmaker.
**modo** *m* mode, method, manner.
**modorra** *f* drowsiness.

**modulación** *f* modulation.
**modular** *vt* to modulate.
**mofa** *f* mockery.
**mofarse** *vr*: ~ **de** to mock, to scoff at.
**moflete** *m* fat cheek.
**moho** *m* rust; mould, mildew.
**mohoso/sa** *adj* mouldy, musty.
**mojar** *vt* to wet, to moisten; ~**se** *vr* to get wet.
**mojigato** *adj* hypocritical.
**mojón** *m* landmark.
**molde** *m* mould; pattern; model.
**moldura** *f* moulding.
**mole** *f* bulk; pile.
**molécula** *f* molecule.
**moler** *vt* to grind, to pound; to tire out; to annoy, to bore.
**molestar** *vt* to annoy, to bother; to trouble; * *vi* to be a nuisance.
**molestia** *f* trouble; inconvenience; (*med*) discomfort.
**molesto/ta** *adj* annoying; inconvenient; uncomfortable; annoyed.
**molinero** *m* miller.
**molinillo** *m*: ~ **de café** coffee grinder.
**molino** *m* mill.
**molusco** *m* mollusc.
**momentáneo/nea** *adj* momentary.
**momento** *m* moment.
**momia** *f* mummy.
**monacal** *adj* monastic.
**monaguillo** *m* acolyte.
**monarca** *m/f* monarch.
**monarquía** *f* monarchy.
**monárquico/ca** *adj* monarchical; * *m/f* royalist, monarchist.
**monasterio** *m* monastery, convent.
**monástico/ca** *adj* monastic.
**mondadientes** *m invar* toothpick.
**mondar** *vt* to clean; to cleanse; to peel; ~**se** *vr*: ~ **de risa** (*col*) to split one's sides laughing.
**mondo/da** *adj* clean; pure; ~ **y lirondo** bare, plain; pure and simple.
**moneda** *f* money; currency; coin.
**monedero** *m* purse.
**monería** *f* funny face; mimicry; prank; trifle.
**monetario/ria** *adj* monetary, financial.
**monitor** *m* monitor.
**monja** *f* nun.
**monje** *f* monk.
**mono**[1] *m* monkey; ape.
**mono**[2] *m* coveralls *pl*, overalls *pl*.
**mono/na**[3] *adj* lovely; pretty; nice.
**monólogo** *m* monologue.

**monopolio** *m* monopoly.
**monopolista** *m* monopolist.
**monosílabo/ba** *adj* monosyllabic.
**monotonía** *f* monotony.
**monótono/na** *adj* monotonous.
**monovolumen** *m* people mover.
**monstruo** *m* monster.
**monstruosidad** *f* monstrosity.
**monstruoso/sa** *adj* monstrous.
**monta** *f* amount, sum total.
**montaje** *m* assembly; decor (of theatre); montage.
**montaña** *f* mountain.
**montañés/esa** *adj* mountain *compd*; * *m/f* highlander.
**montañoso/sa** *adj* mountainous.
**montar** *vt* to mount, to get on (a bicycle, horse etc); to assemble, to put together; to overlap; to set up (a business); to beat, to whip (in cooking); * *vi* to mount; to ride; ~ **a** to amount to.
**montaraz** *adj* mountainous; wild, untamed.
**monte** *m* mountain; woodland; ~ **alto** forest; ~ **bajo** scrub.
**montería** *f* hunting, chase.
**montés/esa** *adj* wild, untamed.
**montón** *m* heap, pile; mass; **a** ~**ones**, abundantly, by the score.
**montura** *f* mount; saddle.
**monumento** *m* monument.
**monzón** *m* monsoon.
**moño** *m* bun (hair); chignon.
**moquillo** *m* distemper (disease in dogs).
**mora** *f* blackberry.
**morada** *f* home, abode, residence.
**morado/da** *adj* violet, purple.
**morador/ra** *m/f* inhabitant.
**moral**[1] *m* mulberry tree.
**moral**[2] *f* morals *pl*, ethics *pl*; * *adj* moral.
**moraleja** *f* moral.
**moralidad** *f* morality.
**moralista** *m/f* moralist.
**moralizar** *vi* to moralize.
**moralmente** *adv* morally.
**morar** *vi* to inhabit, to dwell.
**moratoria** *f* moratorium.
**mórbido/da** *adj* morbid, diseased.
**morboso/sa** *adj* diseased, morbid.
**morcilla** *f* black pudding, blood sausage.
**mordacidad** *f* sharpness, pungency.
**mordaz** *adj* biting, scathing; pungent.
**mordaza** *f* gag; clamp.
**mordedura** *f* bite.
**morder** *vt* to bite; to nibble; to corrode, to eat away.

**mordisco** *m* bite.

**moreno/na** *adj* brown; swarthy; dark-skinned.

**moribundo/da** *adj* dying.

**morigeración** *f* temperance.

**morir** *vi* to die; to expire; to die down; **~se** *vr* to die; (*fig*) to be dying.

**morisco/ca** *adj* Moorish.

**moro/ra** *adj* Moorish.

**morosidad** *f* slowness, sluggishness.

**moroso/sa** *adj* slow, sluggish; (*com*) slow to pay up.

**morral** *m* haversack.

**morriña** *f* depression; sadness.

**morro** *m* snout; nose (of car, plane etc).

**morsa** *f* walrus.

**mortaja** *f* shroud.

**mortal** *adj* mortal; fatal, deadly.

**mortalidad** *f* mortality.

**mortandad** *f* death toll.

**mortero** *m* mortar (cannon).

**mortífero/ra** *adj* deadly, fatal.

**mortificación** *f* mortification.

**mortificar** *vt* to mortify.

**mortuorio** *m* mortuary.

**moruno/na** *adj* Moorish.

**mosca** *f* fly.

**moscarda** *f* bluebottle, blowfly.

**moscardón** *m* botfly, hornet; (*col*) pest, bore.

**moscatel** *adj, m* muscatel.

**moscón** *m* (*col*) pest, bore.

**mosquearse** *vr* (*col*) to get cross; (*col*) to take offence.

**mosquetero** *m* musketeer.

**mosquitero** *m* mosquito net.

**mosquito** *m* gnat, mosquito.

**mostaza** *f* mustard.

**mosto** *m* must, new wine.

**mostrador** *m* counter, bar.

**mostrar** *vt* to show, to exhibit; to explain; **~se** *vr* to appear, to show oneself.

**mota** *f* speck, tiny piece; dot; defect, fault.

**mote** *m* nickname.

**motejar** *vt* to nickname.

**motín** *m* revolt; mutiny.

**motivar** *vt* to motivate; to explain, to justify.

**motivo** *m* motive, cause, reason.

**moto** f (*col*)motor scooter, motorbike.

**motocicleta** *f* motorcycle.

**motor** *m* engine, motor.

**movedizo/za** *adj* movable; variable, changeable; fickle.

**mover** *vt* to move; to shake; to drive; (*fig*) to cause; **~se** *vr* to move; (*fig*) to get a move on.

**móvil** *adj* mobile, movable; moving; * *m* motive; mobile phone.

**movilidad** *f* mobility.

**movimiento** *m* movement, motion.

**mozo/za** *adj* young; * *m/f* youth, young man/girl; waiter/waitress.

**muchacho/a** *m/f* boy/girl; * *f* maid(servant).

**muchedumbre** *f* crowd.

**mucho/cha** *adj* a lot of, much; * *adv* much, a lot; long.

**muda** *f* change of clothes.

**mudable** *adj* changeable, variable; mutable.

**mudanza** *f* change; move.

**mudar** *vt* to change; to shed, to moult; **~se** *vr* to change one's clothes; to change house; * *vi* to change;

**mudo/da** *adj* dumb; silent, mute.

**mueble** *m* piece of furniture; **~s** *mpl* furniture.

**mueca** *f* grimace, funny face.

**muela** *f* tooth, molar.

**muelle** *m* spring; regulator; quay, wharf.

**muérdago** *m* (*bot*) mistletoe.

**muerte** *f* death.

**muerto** *m* corpse; **~/ta** *adj* dead.

**muesca** *f* notch, groove.

**muestra** *f* pattern; indication; demonstration; proof; sample; token; model.

**mugido** *m* lowing (of cattle).

**mugir** *vi* to low, to bellow.

**mugre** *m* dirt, filth.

**mugriento/ta** *adj* greasy; dirty, filthy.

**mujer** *f* woman.

**mulato/ta** *adj* mulatto.

**muleta** *f* crutch.

**mullido/da** *adj* soft; springy.

**mulo/la** *m/f* mule.

**multa** *f* fine, penalty.

**multar** *vt* to fine.

**multimedia** *adj* multimedia.

**múltiple** *adj* multiple; **~s** many, numerous.

**multiplicación** *f* multiplication.

**multiplicado** *m* (*math*) multiplicand.

**multiplicar** *vt* to multiply.

**multiplicidad** *f* multiplicity.

**multitud** *f* multitude.

**mundano/na** *adj* worldly; mundane.

**mundial** *adj* worldwide; world *compd*.

**mundo** *m* world.

**munición** *f* ammunition.

**municipio** *m* town council; municipality.

**municipal** *adj* municipal.

**muñeca** *f* wrist; child's doll.

**muñeco** *m* scarecrow, puppet.
**muñón** *m* stump.
**muralla** *f* rampart, wall.
**murciélago** *m* bat (animal).
**murmullo** *m* murmur, mutter.
**murmuración** *f* backbiting, gossip.
**murmurador/ra** *m/f* detractor, backbiter.
**murmurar** *vi* to murmur; to gossip, to backbite.
**muro** *m* wall.
**muscular** *adj* muscular.
**músculo** *m* muscle.
**muselina** *f* muslin.
**museo** *m* museum.
**musgo** *m* moss.

**música** *f* music.
**musical** *adj* musical.
**músico/ca** *m/f* musician; * *adj* musical.
**muslo** *m* thigh.
**mustio/tia** *adj* parched, withered; sad, sorrowful.
**musulmán/ana** *adj, m/f* Muslim.
**mutabilidad** *f* mutability.
**mutación** *f* mutation, change.
**mutilación** *f* mutilation.
**mutilar** *vt* to mutilate, to maim.
**mutuo/tua** *adj* mutual, reciprocal.
**mutuamente** *adv* mutually.
**muy** *adv* very; too; greatly; ~ **ilustre** most illustrious.

# N

**nabo** *m* turnip.

**nácar** *m* mother-of-pearl, nacre.

**nacarado/da** *adj* mother-of-pearl *compd*; pearl-coloured.

**nacer** *vi* to be born; to bud, to shoot (of plants); to rise; to grow.

**nacido/da** *adj* born; **recién ~** newborn.

**nacimiento** *m* birth; nativity.

**nación** *f* nation.

**nacional** *adj* national.

**nacionalidad** *f* nationality.

**nacionalizar** *vt* to nationalize; **~se** to become naturalized.

**nada** *f* nothing; * *adv* no way, not at all, by no means.

**nadador/ra** *m/f* swimmer.

**nadar** *vi* to swim.

**nadie** *pn* nobody, no one.

**nado** *adv*: **a ~** afloat.

**naipe** *m* (playing) card.

**nalgas** *fpl* buttocks *pl*.

**naranja** *f* orange.

**naranjada** *f* orangeade.

**naranjal** *m* orange grove.

**naranjo** *m* orange tree.

**narciso** *m* (*bot*) daffodil; narcissus (flower); fop.

**narcótico/ca** *adj* narcotic; * *m* drug, narcotic.

**narcotraficante** *m/f* drug trafficker.

**nardo** *m* (*bot*) spikenard, nard.

**narigón/ona, narigudo/da** *adj* big-nosed.

**nariz** *f* nose; sense of smell.

**narración** *f* narration.

**narrar** *vt* to narrate, to tell.

**narrativa** *f* narrative; story.

**nata** *f* cream.

**natación** *f* swimming.

**natal** *adj* natal, native.

**natalicio** *m* birthday.

**natillas** *fpl* custard.

**natividad** *f* nativity.

**nativo/va** *adj*, *m/f* native.

**natural** *m* temperament, natural disposition; native; inhabitant; * *adj* natural; native; common, usual; **al ~** unaffectedly.

**naturaleza** *f* nature.

**naturalidad** *f* naturalness.

**naturalista** *m* naturalist.

**naturalizar** *vi* to naturalize; **~se** *vr* to become naturalized; to become acclimatized.

**naturalmente** *adv* in a natural way; **¡~!** of course!

**naturópata** *m/f* naturopath.

**naufragar** *vi* to be shipwrecked; to suffer ruin in one's affairs.

**naufragio** *m* shipwreck.

**náufrago/ga** *adj* shipwrecked.

**nauseabundo/da** *adj* nauseating.

**náuseas** *fpl* nauseousness, nausea.

**náutica** *f* navigation.

**navaja** *f* penknife, pocketknife; razor.

**naval** *adj* naval.

**nave** *f* ship; nave.

**navegable** *adj* navigable.

**navegación** *f* navigation; sea journey.

**navegador** *m* (*comput*) browser.

**navegante** *m* navigator.

**navegar** *vt*, *vi* to navigate; to sail; to fly.

**navidad** *f* Christmas.

**navideño/ña** *adj* Christmas *compd*.

**navío** *m* ship.

**nazi** *adj*, *m/f* Nazi.

**neblina** *f* mist; fine rain, drizzle.

**nebuloso/sa** *adj* misty; cloudy; nebulous; foggy; hazy; drizzling; * *f* nebula.

**necedad** *f* gross ignorance, stupidity; imprudence.

**necesario/ria** *adj* necessary.

**neceser** *m* toilet bag; holdall.

**necesidad** *f* necessity, need, want.

**necesitado/da** *adj* necessitous, very needy.

**necesitar** *vt* to need; * *vi* to want, to need.

**necio/cia** *adj* ignorant; stupid, foolish; imprudent.

**necrología** *f* obituary.

**nectarina** *f* nectarine.

**néctar** *m* nectar.

**nefando/da** *adj* base, nefarious, abominable.

**nefasto/ta** *adj* unlucky.

**negación** *f* negation; denial.

**negado/da** *adj* incapable, unfit.

**negar** *vt* to deny; to refuse; **~se** *vr*: **~ a hacer** to refuse to do.

**negativo/va** *adj*, *m* negative; * *f* negative; refusal.

**negligencia** *f* negligence.

**negligente** *adj* negligent; careless, heedless.

**negociación** *f* negotiation; commerce.

**negociante** *m/f* trader, dealer.

**negociar** *vt, vi* to negotiate.

**negocio** *m* business, affair; transaction; firm; place of business.

**negro/gra** *adj* black; dark; * *m* black; * *m/f* black person, Negro/Negress.

**negrura** *f* blackness.

**negruzco/ca** *adj* blackish.

**nene** *m*, **nena** *f* baby.

**nenúfar** *m* water lily.

**neófito** *m* neophyte.

**Neptuno** *m* Neptune (planet).

**nervio** *m* nerve.

**nervioso/sa** *adj* nervous.

**neto/ta** *adj* neat, pure; net.

**neumático/ca** *adj* pneumatic; * *m* tyre.

**neurona** *f* neurone.

**neutral** *adj* neutral; neuter.

**neutralidad** *f* neutrality.

**neutralizar** *vt* to neutralize; to counteract.

**neutro/tra** *adj* neutral; neuter.

**neutrón** *m* neutrone.

**nevada** *f* heavy fall of snow.

**nevar** *vi* to snow.

**nevera** *f* icebox.

**nevería** *f* ice-cream shop.

**nexo** *m* link.

**ni** *conj* neither, nor.

**nicho** *m* niche.

**nido** *m* nest; hiding place.

**niebla** *f* fog; mist.

**nieta** *f* granddaughter.

**nieto** *m* grandson.

**nieve** *f* snow.

**nigromancia** *f* necromancy.

**nimiedad** *f* small-mindedness; triviality.

**nimio/mia** *adj* trivial.

**ninfa** *f* nymph.

**ningún, ninguno/na** *adj* no; * *pn* nobody; none; not one; neither.

**niña** *f* little girl; pupil, (of eye).

**niñera** *f* nursemaid.

**niñería** *f* childishness; childish act.

**niñero/ra** *adj* fond of children.

**niñez** *f* childhood.

**niño/ña** *adj* childish; * *m/f* child; infant; **desde ~** from infancy, from a child; * *m* boy.

**níspero** *m* medlar.

**nitidez** *f* clarity; brightness; sharpness.

**nitrato** *m* (*chem*) nitrate.

**nitrógeno** *m* nitrogen.

**nivel** *m* level; standard; height; **a ~** perfectly level.

**niveladora** *f* bulldozer.

**nivelar** *vt* to level; to even up; to balance.

**no** *adv* no; not; * *excl* no!

**noble** *adj* noble, illustrious; generous.

**nobleza** *f* nobleness, nobility.

**noción** *f* notion, idea.

**nocivo/va** *adj* harmful.

**nocturno/na** *adj* nocturnal, nightly; * *m* nocturne.

**noche** *f* night; evening; darkness;**¡buenas ~s!** good night!

**Nochebuena** *f* Christmas Eve.

**Nochevieja** *f* New Year's Eve.

**nodriza** *f* nurse.

**nogal** *m* walnut tree.

**nómada** *adj* nomadic; * *m/f* nomad.

**nombramiento** *m* nomination; appointment.

**nombrar** *vt* to name; to nominate; to appoint.

**nombre** *m* name; title; reputation.

**nomenclatura** *f* nomenclature.

**nómina** *f* list; (*com*) payroll.

**nominador** *m* nominator.

**nominal** *adj* nominal.

**nominativo** *m* (*gr*) nominative.

**non** *adj* odd, uneven; * *m* odd number.

**nonagenario/ria** *adj* ninety-year-old; * *m/f* nonagenarian.

**no obstante** *adv* nevertheless, notwithstanding.

**nor(d)este** *adj* northeast, northeastern; * *m* northeast.

**nórdico/ca** *adj* northern; Nordic.

**noria** *f* water wheel; big wheel.

**normal** *adj* normal; usual.

**normalizar** *vt* to normalize; to standardize; **~se** *vr* to return to normal.

**noroeste** *adj* northwest, northwestern; * *m* northwest.

**norte** *adj* north, northern; * *m* north; (*fig*) rule, guide.

**nos** *pn* us; to us; for us; from us; to ourselves.

**nosotros/tras** *pn* we; us.

**nostalgia** *f* homesickness.

**nota** *f* note; notice, remark; mark.

**notable** *adj* notable, remarkable.

**notar** *vt* to note; to mark; to remark; **~se** *vr* to be obvious.

**notaría** *f* notary profession; notary's office.

**notario** *m* notary.

**noticia** *f* notice; knowledge, information; note; **~s** *fpl* news.

**noticiario** *m* newsreel; news bulletin.

**noticiero** *m* news bulletin.

**notificación** *f* notification.
**notificar** *vt* to notify, to inform.
**notoriedad** *f* notoriety.
**notorio/ria** *adj* notorious.
**novato/ta** *adj* inexperienced; * *m/f* beginner; fresher.
**novecientos/tas** *adj* nine hundred.
**novedad** *f* novelty; modernness; newness; piece of news; change.
**novela** *f* novel.
**novelero/ra** *adj* highly imaginative.
**novelesco/ca** *adj* fictional; romantic; fantastic.
**noveno/na** *adj* ninth.
**noventa** *adj. m* ninety.
**novia** *f* bride; girlfriend; fiancée.
**noviazgo** *m* engagement.
**novicio** *m* novice.
**noviembre** *m* November.
**novilla** *f* heifer.
**novillada** *f* drove of young bulls; fight of young bulls.
**novillo** *m* young bull/ox.
**novio** *m* bridegroom; boyfriend; fiancé.
**nubarrón** *m* large cloud.
**nube** *f* cloud.
**nublado/da** *adj* cloudy; * *m* storm cloud.
**nublarse** *vr* to grow dark.
**nuca** *f* nape (of the neck); scruff of the neck.
**nuclear** *adj* nuclear.
**núcleo** *m* core; nucleus.
**nudillo** *m* knuckle.
**nudo** *m* knot.
**nuera** *f* daughter-in-law.

**nuestro/tra** *adj* our; * *pn* ours.
**nuevamente** *adv* again; anew.
**nueve** *m, adj* nine.
**nuevo/va** *adj* new; modern; fresh; * *f* piece of news; ¿qué hay de ~? is there any news?, what's new?
**nuez** *f* nut; walnut; Adam's apple; ~ moscada nutmeg.
**nulidad** *f* incompetence; nullity.
**nulo/la** *adj* useless; drawn; null.
**numeración** *f* numeration.
**numerador** *m* numerator.
**numeral** *m* numeral.
**numerar** *vt* to number.
**numérico/ca** *adj* numerical.
**número** *m* number; cipher.
**numeroso/sa** *adj* numerous.
**nunca** *adv* never.
**nuncio** *m* nuncio.
**nupcial** *adj* nuptial.
**nupcias** *fpl* nuptials *pl*, wedding.
**nutria** *f* otter.
**nutrición** *f* nutrition.
**nutrir** *vt* to nourish; to feed.
**nutritivo/va** *adj* nutritious, nourishing.
**nylon** *m* nylon.

# Ñ

**ñato/ta** *adj* snub-nosed.
**ñoñería** *f* insipidness.
**ñoño/ña** *adj* insipid; spineless; silly.

# O

**o** *conj* or; either.

**oasis** *m invar* oasis.

**obcecación** *f* obduracy.

**obcecar** *vt* to blind; to darken.

**obedecer** *vt* to obey.

**obediencia** *f* obedience.

**obediente** *adj* obedient.

**obelisco** *m* obelisk.

**obertura** *f* (*mus*) overture.

**obesidad** *f* obesity.

**obeso/sa** *adj* obese, fat.

**obispado** *m* bishopric, episcopate.

**obispo** *m* bishop.

**objeción** *f* objection, opposition, exception.

**objetar** *vi* to object.

**objetor** *m* ~ **de conciencia** conscientious objector.

**objetivo/va** *adj*, *m* objective.

**objeto** *m* object; aim.

**oblea** *f* wafer.

**oblicuo/cua** *adj* oblique.

**obligación** *f* obligation; (*com*) bond.

**obligar** *vt* to force; ~se *vr* to bind oneself.

**obligatorio/ria** *adj* obligatory.

**oblongo/ga** *adj* oblong.

**oboe** *m* oboe.

**obra** *f* work; building, construction; play; **por ~ de** thanks to.

**obrar** *vt* to work, to operate; to put into practice; * *vi* to behave, to act; to have an effect.

**obrero/ra** *adj* working; labour *compd*; * *m/f* workman; labourer.

**obscenidad** *f* obscenity.

**obsceno/na** *adj* obscene.

**obsequiar** *vt* to lavish attention on; ~ **con** to present with.

**obsequio** *m* gift; courtesy.

**obsequioso/sa** *adj* obsequious, compliant; officious.

**observación** *f* observation; remark.

**observador/ra** *m/f* observer.

**observancia** *f* observance.

**observar** *vt* to observe; to notice.

**observatorio** *m* observatory.

**obsesión** *f* obsession.

**obsesionar** *vt* to obsess.

**obstáculo** *m* obstacle, impediment, hindrance.

**obstar** *vi*: ~ **a**, ~ **para** to oppose, to obstruct, to hinder.

**obstetricia** *f* obstetrics.

**obstinación** *f* obstinacy, stubbornness.

**obstinado/da** *adj* obstinate.

**obstinarse** *vr* to be obstinate; ~ **en** to persist in.

**obstrucción** *f* obstruction.

**obstruir** *vt* to obstruct; ~se *vr* to be blocked up, to be obstructed.

**obtener** *vt* to obtain; to gain.

**obtuso/sa** *adj* obtuse, blunt.

**obús** *m* (*mil*) shell.

**obviar** *vt* to obviate, to remove.

**obvio/via** *adj* obvious, evident.

**ocasión** *f* occasion, opportunity.

**ocasional** *adj* occasional.

**ocasionar** *vt* to cause, to occasion.

**ocaso** *m* (*fig*) decline.

**occidental** *adj* occidental, western.

**occidente** *m* occident, west.

**océano** *m* ocean.

**ochenta** *m*, *adj* eighty.

**ocho** *m*, *adj* eight.

**ochocientos** *m*, *adj* eight hundred.

**ocio** *m* leisure; pastime.

**ociosidad** *f* idleness, leisure.

**ocioso/sa** *adj* idle; useless.

**ocre** *m* ochre.

**octavilla** *f* pamphlet.

**octavo/va** *adj* eighth.

**octogenario/ria** *adj*, *m/f* octogenarian.

**octubre** *m* October.

**ocular** *adj* ocular; eye *compd*.

**oculista** *m/f* oculist.

**ocultar** *vt* to hide, to conceal.

**oculto/ta** *adj* hidden, concealed; secret.

**ocupación** *f* occupation; business; employment.

**ocupado/da** *adj* busy; occupied; engaged.

**ocupar** *vt* to occupy; to hold (an office); ~se *vr*: ~ **de**, ~ **en** to concern oneself with; to look after.

**ocurrencia** *f* event; bright idea.

**ocurrir** *vi* to occur, to happen.

**oda** *f* ode.

**odiar** *vt* to hate; ~se *vr* to hate one another.

**odio** *m* hatred.

**odioso/sa** *adj* odious, hateful.

**odontólogo/ga** *m/f* dentist.

**odorífero/ra** *adj* odoriferous, odorous.

**oeste** *adj* west, western; * *m* west.

**ofender** *vt* to offend; to injure ~**se** *vr* to be vexed; to take offence.

**ofensa** *f* offence; injury.

**ofensivo/va** *adj* offensive, injurious.

**ofensor** *m* offender.

**oferta** *f* offer; offering.

**oficial** *adj* official; * *m* officer; official.

**oficiar** *vi* to officiate, to minister (of clergymen etc).

**oficina** *f* office.

**oficio** *m* office; employment, occupation; ministry; function; trade, business;~**s** *mpl* divine service.

**oficiosidad** *f* diligence; officiousness; importunity.

**oficioso/sa** *adj* officious; diligent; unofficial, informal.

**ofrecer** *vt* to offer; to present; to exhibit; ~**se** *vr* to offer oneself; to occur, to present itself.

**ofrecimiento** *m* offer, promise.

**ofrenda** *f* offering, oblation.

**ofrendar** *vt* to offer, to contribute.

**oftalmólogo/ga** *m/f* ophthalmologist.

**ofuscación** *f* dimness of sight; obfuscation.

**ofuscar** *vt* to darken, to render obscure; to bewilder.

**oídas** *fpl*: **de ~** by hearsay.

**oído** *m* hearing; ear.

**oír** *vt, vi* to hear; to listen (to).

**ojal** *m* buttonhole.

**¡ojalá!** *conj* if only!, would that!

**ojeada** *f* glance.

**ojear** *vt* to eye, to view; to glance.

**ojera** *f* bag under the eyes.

**ojeriza** *f* spite, grudge, ill-will.

**okupa** *m/f* (*col*) squatter.

**ojo** *m* eye; sight; eye of a needle; arch of a bridge.

**ola** *f* wave.

**oleada** *f* surge; violent emotion.

**oleaje** *m* succession of waves, sea swell.

**óleo** *m* oil.

**oler** *vt* to smell, to scent; * *vi* to smell; ~ **a** to smack of.

**olfatear** *vt* to smell; (*fig*) to sniff out.

**olfato** *m* sense of smell.

**oligarquía** *f* oligarchy.

**oligárquico/ca** *adj* oligarchical.

**olimpíada** *f*: **las O~s** the Olympics.

**olímpico/ca** *adj* Olympic.

**oliva** *f* olive.

**olivar** *m* olive grove.

**olivo** *m* olive tree.

**olla** *f* pan; stew; ~ **podrida** dish composed of different boiled meats and vegetables; ~ **exprés/~ a presión** pressure cooker.

**olmo** *m* elm tree.

**olor** *m* smell, odour; scent.

**oloroso/sa** *adj* fragrant; odorous.

**olvidadizo/za** *adj* forgetful.

**olvidar** *vt* to forget.

**olvido** *m* forgetfulness.

**ombligo** *m* navel.

**omisión** *f* omission.

**omitir** *vt* to omit.

**omnipotencia** *f* omnipotence.

**omnipotente** *adj* omnipotent, almighty.

**once** *m, adj* eleven.

**onda** *f* wave.

**ondear** *vi* to undulate; to fluctuate.

**ondulado/da** *adj* wavy.

**oneroso/sa** *adj* burdensome.

**opa** *f* takeover bid.

**opacidad** *f* opacity; gloom, darkness.

**opaco/ca** *adj* opaque; dark.

**opción** *f* option, choice.

**ópera** *f* opera.

**operación** *f* operation; ~ **de cesárea** *f* caesarean section, caesarean operation.

**operador/ra** *m/f* operator; projectionist; cameraman/woman.

**operar** *vi* to operate; to act.

**opinar** *vt* to think; * *vi* to give one's opinion.

**opinión** *f* opinion.

**opio** *m* opium.

**oponente** *m/f* opponent.

**oponer** *vt* to oppose; ~**se** *vr* to be opposed, ~ **a** to oppose.

**oportunidad** *f* opportunity.

**oportunismo** *m* opportunism.

**oportuno/na** *adj* seasonable, opportune.

**oposición** *f* opposition; ~**ones** *fpl* public examinations *pl*.

**opositor/ra** *m/f* opponent; candidate (in public examination).

**opresión** *f* oppression.

**opresivo/va** *adj* oppressive.

**opresor** *m* oppressor.

**oprimir** *vt* to oppress; to crush; to press; to squeeze.

**optar** *vt* to choose, to elect.

**optativo/va** *adj* optional.

**óptica** *f* optics.

**óptico/ca** *adj* optical; * *m/f* optician.

**optimista** *m/f* optimist.

**óptimo/ma** *adj* best.

**opuesto/ta** *adj* opposite; contrary; adverse.

**opulencia** *f* wealth, riches *pl*.

**opulento/ta** *adj* opulent, wealthy.
**oración** *f* oration, speech; prayer.
**orador/ra** *m/f* orator.
**oral** *adj* oral.
**orangután** *m* orang-utan.
**orar** *vi* to pray.
**oratoria** *f* oratory, rhetorical skill.
**órbita** *f* orbit.
**orden** *m/f* order; ~ **del día** order of the day.
**ordenación** *f* arrangement; ordination; edict, ordinance.
**ordenado/da** *adj* methodical; orderly.
**ordenador** *m* computer.
**ordenanza** *f* order; statute, ordinance; ordination.
**ordenar** *vt* to arrange; to order; to ordain; ~**se** *vr* to take holy orders.
**ordeñar** *vt* to milk.
**órdenes sagradas** *fpl* holy orders *pl*.
**ordinal** *adj* ordinal.
**ordinario/ria** *adj* ordinary, common; **de ~** regularly, commonly, ordinarily.
**orégano** *m* oregano.
**oreja** *f* ear.
**orejera** *f* earflap.
**orfanato** *m* orphanage.
**orfandad** *f* orphanhood.
**orgánico/ca** *adj* organic; harmonious.
**organigrama** *m* flowchart.
**organismo** *m* organism; organization.
**organista** *m/f* organist.
**organización** *f* organization; arrangement.
**organizar** *vt* to organize.
**órgano** *m* organ.
**orgasmo** *m* orgasm.
**orgía** *f* orgy.
**orgullo** *m* pride, haughtiness.
**orgulloso/sa** *adj* proud, haughty.
**orientación** *f* position; direction.
**oriental** *adj* oriental, eastern.
**orientar** *vt* to orient; to point; to direct; to guide; ~**se** *vr* to get one's bearings; to decide on a course of action.
**oriente** *m* orient.
**orificio** *m* orifice; mouth; aperture.
**origen** *m* origin, source; native country; family, extraction.
**original** *adj* original, primitive; * *m* original, first copy.
**originalidad** *f* originality.
**originar** *vt, vi* to originate.
**originario/ria** *adj* original.
**orilla** *f* limit, border, margin; edge (of cloth); shore.
**orín** *m* rust.

**orina** *f* urine.
**orinal** *m* chamber pot.
**orinar** *vi* to pass water, urinate.
**oriundo/da** *adj*: ~ **de** native of.
**ornamento** *m* ornament, embellishment.
**ornitología** *f* ornithology.
**oro** *m* gold.
**oros** *mpl* diamonds *pl* (at cards).
**orquesta** *f* orchestra.
**orquídea** *f* orchid.
**ortiga** *f* (*bot*) nettle.
**ortodoxia** *f* orthodoxy.
**ortodoxo/xa** *adj* orthodox.
**ortografía** *f* orthography.
**ortográfico/ca** *adj* orthographic(al).
**oruga** *f* (*bot*) caterpillar.
**orza** *f* jar.
**orzuelo** *m* (*med*) stye.
**os** *pn* you; to you.
**osa** *f* she-bear; **O~ Mayor/Menor** Great/ Little Bear.
**osadamente** *adv* boldly, daringly.
**osadía** *f* boldness, intrepidity; zeal, fervour.
**osamenta** *f* skeleton.
**osar** *vi* to dare, to venture.
**óscar** *m* Oscar.
**oscilación** *f* oscillation.
**oscilar** *vi* to oscillate.
**oscurecer** *vt* to obscure; to darken; * *vi* to grow dark; ~**se** *vr* to disappear.
**oscuridad** *f* obscurity; darkness.
**oscuro/ra** *adj* obscure; dark.
**osificarse** *vr* to ossify.
**oso** *m* bear; ~ **blanco** polar bear.
**ostensible** *adj* ostensible, apparent.
**ostentación** *f* ostentation, ambitious display, show.
**ostentar** *vt* to show; * *vi* to boast, to brag.
**ostentoso/sa** *adj* sumptuous, ostentatious.
**ostra** *f* oyster.
**otitis** *f* earache.
**otoñal** *adj* autumnal.
**otoño** *m* autumn.
**otorgamiento** *m* granting; execution.
**otorgar** *vt* to concede; to grant.
**otorrino/na, otorrinolaringólogo/ga** *m/ f* ear, nose and throat specialist.
**otro/tra** *adj* another; other.
**ovación** *f* ovation.
**ovalado/da** *adj* oval.
**óvalo** *m* oval.
**ovario** *m* ovary.
**oveja** *f* sheep.
**overol** *m* overalls *pl*.
**ovillo** *m* ball of wool.

**ovíparo/ra** *adj* oviparous, egg-bearing.
**ovulación** *f* ovulation.
**óvulo** *m* ovum.
**oxidación** *f* rusting.

**oxidar** *vt* to rust; **~se** *vr* to go rusty.
**óxido** *f* (*chem*) oxide.
**oxígeno** *m* (*chem*) oxygen.
**oyente** *m/f* listener, hearer.

# P

**pabellón** *m* pavilion; summer house; block, section.

**pábilo** *m* wick.

**pacer** *vt* to pasture, to graze.

**paciencia** *f* patience.

**paciente** *adj*, *m/f* patient.

**pacificación** *f* pacification.

**pacificar** *vt* to pacify, to appease.

**pacífico/ca** *adj* pacific, peaceful; * *m*: el P~ the Pacific.

**pacotilla** *f*: **de ~** third-rate; cheap.

**pactar** *vt* to covenant; to contract; to stipulate.

**pacto** *m* contract, pact.

**padecer** *vt* to suffer; to sustain (an injury); to put up with.

**padecimiento** *m* suffering, sufferance.

**padrastro** *m* stepfather.

**padrazo** *m* loving, over-indulgent father.

**padre** *m* father; **~s** *mpl* parents *pl*.

**padrino** *m* godfather.

**padrón** *m* census; register; pattern; model.

**paella** *f* paella (dish of rice with shellfish, meat etc).

**paga** *f* payment, fee.

**pagadero/ra** *adj* payable.

**paganismo** *m* paganism, heathenism.

**pagano/na** *adj*, *m/f* heathen, pagan.

**pagar** *vt* to pay; to pay for; (*fig*) to repay; * *vi* to pay.

**pagaré** *m* bond, note of hand, promissory note, IOU (I owe you).

**página** *f* page.

**pago** *m* payment; reward.

**país** *m* country; region.

**paisaje** *m* landscape.

**paisano/na** *adj* of the same country; * *m/f* fellow countryman/woman.

**paja** *f* straw; (*fig*) trash.

**pajar** *m* straw loft.

**pajarita** *f* bow tie.

**pájaro** *m* bird; sly, acute fellow.

**pajarraco** *m* large bird; cunning fellow.

**paje** *m* page.

**pajita** *f* (drinking) straw.

**pajizo/za** *adj* straw-coloured.

**pala** *f* spade, shovel.

**palabra** *f* word; **de ~** by word of mouth.

**palabrota** *f* swearword.

**palaciego/ga** *adj* pertaining/relating to the palace; * *m* courtier.

**palacio** *m* palace.

**paladar** *m* palate; taste, relish.

**paladear** *vt* to taste.

**palanca** *f* lever.

**palanca de cambios** *f* gear lever.

**palangana** *f* basin.

**palco** *m* box (in a theatre).

**paleta** *f* bat; palette; trowel.

**paleto/ta** *m/f* rustic.

**paliar** *vt* to mitigate.

**paliativo/va** *adj*, *m* palliative.

**palidecer** *vi* to turn pale.

**palidez** *f* paleness, wanness.

**pálido/da** *adj* pallid, pale.

**palillo** *m* small stick; toothpick; **~s** *mpl* chopsticks *pl*.

**paliza** *f* beating, thrashing.

**palma** *f* palm tree; palm of the hand; palm leaf.

**palmada** *f* slap, clap; **~s** *fpl* clapping of hands, applause.

**palmatoria** *f* candlestick; cane.

**palmear** *vi* to slap; to clap.

**palmera** *f* palm tree.

**palmeta** *f* cane.

**palmo** *m* palm; small amount.

**palmotear** *vi* to slap; to applaud.

**palmoteo** *m* clapping of hands.

**palo** *m* stick; cudgel; blow given with a stick; post; mast; bat; suit (at cards).

**paloma** *f* pigeon, dove; **~ torcaz** ring dove/ wood pigeon; **~ mensajera** carrier pigeon, homing pigeon.

**palomar** *m* pigeon house/loft.

**palomilla** *f* moth; wing nut; angle iron.

**palomino** *m* young pigeon.

**palomitas** *fpl* popcorn.

**palpable** *adj* palpable, evident.

**palpar** *vt* to feel, to touch.

**palpitación** *f* palpitation; panting.

**palpitante** *adj* palpitating; (*fig*) burning.

**palta** *f* avocado (pear).

**paludismo** *m* malaria.

**palpitar** *vi* to palpitate.

**palurdo/da** *adj* rustic, clownish, rude.

**pampa** *f* pampa(s), prairie.

**pámpano** *m* vine branch.

**pamplina** *f* trifle.

**pan** *m* bread; loaf.

**pana** *f* corduroy.

**panacea** *f* panacea, universal medicine.

**panadería** f baker's (shop).
**panadero/ra** m/f baker.
**panal** m honeycomb; sweet rusk.
**pañal** m nappy; ~ **desechable** disposable nappy.
**pancarta** f placard.
**panda** m panda.
**pandereta** f tambourine.
**pandilla** f group; gang; clique.
**panegírico/ca** adj panegyrical; * m eulogy.
**panel** m panel.
**panfleto** m pamphlet.
**pánico** m panic.
**panorama** m panorama.
**pantalla** f screen; lampshade.
**pantalón** m, **pantalones** mpl trousers pl, women's panties/knickers pl.
**pantano** m fen; marsh; reservoir; obstacle, difficulty.
**pantanoso/sa** adj marshy, fenny, boggy.
**panteísta** f pantheist.
**panteón** m: ~ **familiar** family tomb.
**pantera** f panther.
**pantomima** f pantomime.
**pantorrilla** f calf (of the leg).
**pantufla** m slipper.
**panza** f belly, paunch.
**panzada** f bellyful of food.
**panzudo/da** adj big-bellied.
**pañal** m nappy.
**paño** m cloth; piece of cloth; duster, rag.
**pañuelo** m handkerchief.
**papa** f potato; * m: **el P~** the Pope.
**papá** m (col) dad, pop.
**papada** f double chin.
**papagayo** m parrot.
**papal** adj papal.
**papanatas** m invar (col) simpleton.
**paparrucha** f piece of nonsense.
**papaya** f papaya, pawpaw.
**papel** m paper; writing; part, role (acted in a play); ~ **de estraza** brown paper; ~ **sellado** stamped paper.
**papeleo** m red tape.
**papelera** f writing desk; wastepaper basket.
**papelería** f stationer's (shop).
**papeleta** f slip of paper; ballot paper; report.
**paperas** fpl mumps.
**papilla** f baby food.
**papista** m papist.
**paquete** m packet; parcel; package tour.
**par** adj equal; alike; even; * m pair; couple; peer; **sin** ~ matchless.
**para** prep for; to, in order to; toward(s).

**parabién** m congratulations pl; felicitations pl.
**parábola** f parable; parabola.
**parabólico/ca** adj parabolic(al).
**parabrisas** m invar windscreen.
**paracaídas** m invar parachute.
**paracaidista** m/f parachutist; (mil) paratrooper.
**parachoques** m invar bumper; shock absorber.
**parada** f halt; suspension; pause; stop; shutdown; stopping place; ~ **a petición** request stop; ~ **de autobús** bus stop.
**paradero** m halting place; term, end.
**parado/da** adj motionless; at a standstill; stopped; standing (up); unemployed; * m/f unemployed person.
**paradoja** f paradox.
**parador** m parador, state-owned hotel.
**parafrasear** vt to paraphrase.
**paráfrasis** f invar paraphrase.
**paraguas** m invar umbrella.
**paraíso** m paradise.
**paraje** m place, spot.
**paralelo/la** adj, m parallel.
**paralítico/ca** adj paralytic, palsied.
**paralizar** vt to paralyse; ~**se** vr to become paralysed; (fig) to come to a standstill.
**páramo** m desert; wilderness.
**parangón** m paragon, model; comparison.
**paranoico/ca** m/f paranoiac.
**parapente** m paragliding.
**parapeto** m parapet.
**parar** vi to stop, to halt; * vt to stop, to detain; **sin** ~ instantly, without delay; ~**se** vr to stop, to halt; to stand up.
**pararrayos** m invar lightning conductor/rod.
**parásito** m parasite; (fig) sponger.
**parasol** m parasol.
**parcela** f piece of ground.
**parche** m patch.
**parcial** adj partial.
**parcialidad** f prejudice; bias.
**parco/ca** adj sober, moderate.
**pardo/da** adj grey.
**parear** vt to match, to pair, to couple.
**parecer** m opinion, advice, counsel; countenance, air, mien; * vi to appear; to seem; ~**se** vr: ~ **a** to resemble.
**parecido/da** adj resembling, like.
**pared** f wall; (law) ~ **medianera** party-wall.
**pareja** f pair, couple; a timber beam that serves as a support, brace.
**parejo/ja** adj equal; even.

**parentela** f parentage, kindred.
**parentesco** m relationship.
**paréntesis** m invar parenthesis.
**parida** f woman who has recently given birth.
**paridad** f parity, equality.
**pariente/ta** m/f relative, relation.
**parir** vt to give birth to; * vi to give birth.
**parking** m car park.
**parlamentar** vi to parley.
**parlamentario/ria** m/f member of parliament; * adj parliamentary.
**parlamento** m parliament.
**parlanchín/ina** adj, m/f chatterer, jabberer.
**parlotear** vi to prattle, to chatter, to gossip.
**paro** m strike; unemployment.
**parodia** f parody.
**parpadear** vi to blink; to flicker.
**párpado** m eyelid.
**parque** m park; ~ **eólico** wind farm.
**parque de bomberos** m.fire station.
**parquímetro** m parking meter.
**parra** f vine raised on stakes/nailed to a wall.
**párrafo** m paragraph.
**parricida** m/f parricide (person).
**parricidio** m parricide (act).
**parrilla** f grill; grille; steakhouse.
**párroco** m parish priest.
**parroquia** f parish; customers pl.
**parroquial** adj parochial.
**parroquiano** m parishioner; customer; ~/na adj parochial.
**parsimonia** f parsimony.
**parte** m message; report; * f part; side; party; **de ocho días a esta ~** within these last eight days; **de ~ a ~** from side to side, through and through.
**partera** f midwife.
**partición** f partition, division.
**participación** f participation.
**participante** m/f participant.
**participar** vi to participate, to partake.
**partícipe** m/f participant.
**participio** m participle.
**partícula** f particle.
**particular** adj particular, special; * m private individual; particular matter/subject.
**particularidad** f particularity.
**particularizar** vt, vr to particularize; to distinguish; to specify.
**partida** f departure; party; item in an account; parcel; game.
**partidario/ria** adj partisan; * m/f supporter.
**partido** m party; match; team.

**partidor** m apportioner, divider.
**partir** vt to part; to divide, to separate; to cut; to break; * vi to depart; ~**se** vr to break (in two etc).
**parto** m birth.
**parvulario** m nursery school, kindergarten.
**pasa** f raisin.
**pasada** f passage, passing; **de ~** on the way, in passing.
**pasadizo** m narrow passage; narrow, covered way.
**pasado/da** adj past; bad; overdone; out of date; ~ **mañana** the day after tomorrow; **la semana pasada** last week; * m past.
**pasador** m bolt; hair slide; grip.
**pasaje** m passage; fare; passengers pl.
**pasajero/ra** adj transient; transitory; fugitive; * m/f traveller; passenger.
**pasamanos** m invar (hand)rail; banister.
**pasamontañas** m invar balaclava helmet.
**pasaporte** m passport.
**pasar** vt to pass; to surpass; to suffer; to strain; to dissemble; * vi to pass; to happen; ~**se** vr to go over (to another party); to go bad/off.
**pasarela** f footbridge; gangway.
**pasatiempo** m pastime, amusement.
**Pascua** f Passover; Easter.
**pase** m pass; showing; permit.
**paseante** m walker.
**pasear** vt to walk; vi, ~**se** vr to walk; to walk about.
**paseo** m walk; shopping mall.
**pasillo** m passage.
**pasión** f passion.
**pasionaria** f passionflower, granadilla.
**pasivo/va** adj passive.
**pasmar** vt to amaze; to numb; to chill; ~**se** vr to be astonished.
**pasmo** m astonishment, amazement.
**pasmoso/sa** adj marvellous, wonderful.
**paso** m pace, step; passage; manner of walking; flight of steps; accident; (rail) ~ **a nivel** level crossing; **al ~** on the way, in passing.
**paso de peatones** m pedestrian crossing.
**pasota** adj, m/f (col) dropout; **ser un ~** not to care about anything.
**pasta** f paste; dough; pastry; (col) dough, money; ~**s** fpl pastries pl; pasta; ~ **de dientes** toothpaste.
**pastar** vt to pasture, to graze.
**pastel** m cake; pie; pastel drawing; crayon.
**pastelería** f cake shop.
**pasteurizado/da** adj pasteurized.
**pastilla** f bar (of soap); tablet, pill.

**pasto** *m* pasture; field; **a ~** abundantly.

**pastor** *m* shepherd; pastor.

**pastoso/sa** *adj* mellow, pleasant (voice); soft, doughy.

**pata** *f* leg (of animal/furniture); foot; **a la ~ coja** hopscotch (children's game); **a ~** (*col*) on foot; **meter la ~** to put one's foot in it.

**patada** *f* kick.

**patalear** *vi* to kick violently.

**pataleo** *m* act of stamping one's foot.

**pataleta** *f* fit, convulsion; swoon.

**patán** *m* clown; churl, surly person

**patata** *f* potato.

**patatús** *m* dizzy spell, fainting fit.

**paté** *m* pâté.

**patear** *vt* to kick; to stamp on.

**patente** *adj* patent, manifest, evident; * *f* patent; warrant.

**paternal** *adj* paternal, fatherly.

**paternidad** *f* paternity, fatherhood.

**paterno/na** *adj* paternal, fatherly.

**patético/ca** *adj* pathetic.

**patíbulo** *m* scaffold, gallows.

**patillas** *fpl* sideburns *pl*.

**patín** *m* skate; runner.

**patinaje** *m* skating.

**patinar** *vi* to skate; to skid; (*col*) to blunder.

**patinete** *m* scooter (child's).

**patio** *m* courtyard; playground (in schools).

**patizambo/ba** *adj* knock-kneed.

**pato** *m* duck.

**patochada** *f* blunder, folly; nonsense.

**patología** *f* pathology.

**patológico/ca** *adj* pathological.

**patoso/sa** *adj* (*col*) clumsy.

**patraña** *f* lie.

**patria** *f* native country.

**patriarca** *m* patriarch.

**patriarcado** *m* patriarchy.

**patriarcal** *adj* patriarchal.

**patrimonial** *adj* patrimonial.

**patrimonio** *m* patrimony.

**patrio/tria** *adj* native; paternal.

**patriota** *m/f* patriot.

**patriótico/ca** *adj* patriotic.

**patriotismo** *m* patriotism.

**patrocinar** *vt* to sponsor; to back, to support.

**patrocinio** *m* sponsorship; backing, support.

**patrón/ona** *m/f* boss, master/mistress; landlord/lady; patron saint; * *m* pattern.

**patronal** *adj*: **la clase ~** management.

**patronato** *m* patronage, sponsorship; trust, foundation.

**patronímico** *m* patronymic.

**patrulla** *f* patrol.

**patrullar** *vi* to patrol.

**paulatino/na** *adj* gradual, slow.

**pausa** *f* pause; repose.

**pausado/da** *adj* slow, deliberate; calm, quiet.

**pausar** *vi* to pause.

**pauta** *f* guideline.

**pavesa** *f* embers *pl*, hot cinders *pl*.

**pavimento** *m* pavement; paving.

**pavo** *m* turkey; **~ real** peacock.

**pavonearse** *vr* to strut, to walk with affected dignity.

**pavor** *m* dread, terror.

**pavoroso/sa** *adj* awful, formidable.

**payaso/sa** *m/f* clown.

**payo/ya** *m/f* non-Gypsy (for a Gypsy).

**paz** *f* peace; tranquillity, ease.

**peaje** *m* toll.

**peana** *f* pedestal; footstool.

**peatón** *m* pedestrian.

**peca** *f* freckle; spot.

**pecado** *m* sin.

**pecador/ra** *m/f* sinner.

**pecaminoso/sa** *adj* sinful.

**pecar** *vi* to sin.

**pecho** *m* chest; breast(s) (*pl*); teat; bosom; (*fig*) courage, valour; **dar el ~ a** to breastfeed; **tomar a ~** to take to heart.

**pechuga** *f* breast (of a fowl); (*col*) bosom.

**pecoso/sa** *adj* freckled.

**peculiar** *adj* peculiar; special.

**pecuniario/ria** *adj* pecuniary.

**pedagogía** *f* pedagogy.

**pedagógico/ca** *adj* pedagogic.

**pedagogo/ga** *m/f* pedagogue.

**pedal** *m* pedal.

**pedalear** *vi* to pedal.

**pedante** *adj* pedantic; * *m/f* pedant.

**pedantería** *f* pedantry.

**pedazo** *m* piece, titbit.

**pedernal** *m* flint.

**pedestal** *m* pedestal, foot.

**pediatra** *m/f* paediatrician.

**pediatría** *f*. paediatrics *pl*.

**pedicuro/ra** *m/f* chiropodist, podiatrist.

**pedido** *m* (*com*) order; request.

**pedir** *vt* to ask for; to petition; to beg; to order; to need; to solicit; * *vi* to ask.

**pedo** *m* (*col*) fart; **tirarse un ~** to fart.

**pedrada** *f* throw (of a stone).

**pedregal** *m* stony place.

**pedregoso/sa** *adj* stony.

**pedrería** *f* precious stones *pl* (collection of).

**pedrisco** *m* hailstone.

**pedrusco** *m* rough piece of stone.

**pegadizo/za** *adj* clammy, sticky; catchy; contagious.

**pegajoso/sa** *adj* sticky, viscous; contagious; attractive.

**pegamento** *m* glue.

**pegar** *vt* to cement; to join, to unite; to beat; ~ **fuego a** to set fire to; * *vi* to stick; to match; ~**se** *vr* to intrude; to steal in.

**pegatina** *f* sticker.

**pegote** *m* sticking plaster; intruder; hanger-on, (*col*) sponger.

**peinado** *m* hairstyle.

**peinar** *vt* to comb; to style.

**peine** *m* comb.

**peineta** *f* convex comb for women.

**peladilla** *f* sugared almond, burnt almond; small pebble.

**pelado/da** *adj* peeled; shorn; bare; broke; * *m* (*col*) haircut.

**peladura** *f* peeling; plucking.

**pelaje** *m* fur coat; (*fig*) appearance.

**pelar** *vt* to cut (hair); to strip off (feathers); to peel; ~**se** *vr* to peel off; to have one's hair cut.

**peldaño** *m* step (of a flight of stairs).

**pelea** *f* battle, fight; quarrel.

**pelear** *vt* to fight, to combat; ~**se** *vr* to scuffle.

**pelele** *m* dummy; man of straw.

**peletería** *f* fur shop.

**peletero** *m* furrier.

**peliagudo/da** *adj* tricky; arduous, difficult.

**pelícano** *m* pelican.

**película** *f* film; pellicle.

**peligrar** *vi* to be in danger; ~ **de** to risk.

**peligro** *m* danger, peril; risk.

**peligroso/sa** *adj* dangerous, perilous.

**pelirrojo/ja** *m/f* redhead; * *adj* red-haired.

**pellejo** *m* skin; hide, pelt; peel; wine skin, leather bag for wine; oilskin; drunkard.

**pelliza** *f* fur jacket.

**pellizcar** *vt* to pinch.

**pellizco** *m* pinch; nip; small bit; (*fig*) remorse.

**pelmo/ma, pelmazo/za** *m/f* (*col*) pain (in the neck).

**pelo** *m* hair; pile; flaw (in precious stones).

**pelón/ona** *adj* hairless, bald.

**pelota** *f* ball.

**pelotazo** *m* blow with a ball.

**pelotera** *f* quarrel.

**pelotón** *m* large ball; crowd; posse; (*mil*) platoon.

**peluca** *f* wig.

**peluche** *m*: **muñeco de ~** soft toy.

**peludo/da** *adj* hairy.

**peluquería** *f* hairdresser's (shop); barber's (shop).

**peluquero/ra** *m/f* hairdresser; barber.

**pelusa** *f* bloom (on fruit); fluff.

**pena** *f* punishment, pain; **a duras ~s** with great difficulty/trouble.

**penacho** *m* tuft on the heads of some birds; crest.

**penal** *adj* penal.

**penalidad** *f* suffering, trouble; hardship; penalty.

**penalti/penalty** *m* penalty (kick).

**penar** *vi* to suffer pain; * *vt* to chastise.

**pendencia** *f* quarrel, dispute.

**pendenciero/ra** *adj* quarrelsome.

**pender** *vi* to hang; to be pending; to depend.

**pendiente** *f* slope, declivity; * *m* earring; * *adj* pending; unsettled.

**pendón** *m* standard; banner.

**péndulo** *m* pendulum.

**pene** *m* penis.

**penetración** *f* penetration; perception.

**penetrante** *adj* deep; sharp; piercing; searching; biting.

**penetrar** *vt* to penetrate.

**penicilina** *f* penicillin.

**península** *f* peninsula.

**penique** *m* penny.

**penitencia** *f* penitence; penalty, fine.

**penitenciaría** *f* prison.

**penitente** *adj* penitent, repentant; * *m* penitent.

**penoso/sa** *adj* painful.

**pensador/ra** *m/f* thinker.

**pensamiento** *m* thought, thinking.

**pensar** *vi* to think.

**pensativo/va** *adj* pensive, thoughtful.

**pensión** *f* pension; guest-house; worry; regret.

**pensionista** *m/f* pensioner; lodger.

**Pentecostés** *m* Pentecost, Whitsuntide.

**penúltimo/ma** *adj* penultimate, last but one.

**penumbra** *f* half-light.

**penuria** *f* penury, poverty, neediness, extreme want.

**peña** *f* rock, large stone.

**peñasco** *m* large rock.

**peñón** *m* rocky mountain.

**peón** *m* (day)labourer; foot soldier; pawn (at chess).

**peonía** *f* (*bot*) peony.

**peonza** *f* spinning top.

**peor** *adj, adv* worse; **cada vez ~** worse and worse.

**pepinillo** *m* gherkin.

**pepino** *m* cucumber.

**pepita** *f* kernel; pip.

**pepitoria** *f* fricassee.

**pequeñez** *f* smallness; childhood, infancy; triviality.

**pequeño/ña** *adj* little, small; young.

**pera** *f* pear.

**peral** *m* pear tree.

**percance** *m* perquisite (perk); bad luck, setback.

**percatarse** *vr*: **~ de** to notice.

**percepción** *f* perception; notion.

**perceptible** *adj* perceptible, perceivable.

**percha** *f* coat hook; coat hanger; perch.

**percibir** *vt* to receive; to perceive, to comprehend.

**percusión** *f* percussion.

**perder** *vt* to lose; to waste; to miss; **~se** *vr* to go astray; to be lost; to be spoiled.

**perdición** *f* loss, losing; perdition, ruin.

**pérdida** *f* loss, damage; lost object.

**perdido/da** *adj* lost; stray.

**perdigón** *m* young partridge; **~ones** *mpl* buckshot, pellets.

**perdiz** *f* partridge.

**perdón** *m* pardon; mercy; **¡~!** sorry!; excuse me!

**perdonable** *adj* pardonable.

**perdonar** *vt* to pardon, to forgive; to excuse.

**perdurable** *adj* perpetual, everlasting.

**perdurar** *vi* to last; to still exist.

**perecedero/ra** *adj* perishable.

**perecer** *vi* to perish, to die; to shatter (an object).

**peregrinación** *f* pilgrimage.

**peregrinar** *vi* to go on a pilgrimage.

**peregrino/na** *adj* (*fig*) strange; * *m/f* pilgrim.

**perejil** *m* parsley.

**perenne** *adj* perennial; perpetual.

**perentorio/ria** *adj* peremptory; urgent.

**pereza** *f* laziness, idleness.

**perezoso/sa** *adj* lazy, idle.

**perfección** *f* perfection.

**perfeccionar** *vt* to perfect; to complete, to finish.

**perfecto/ta** *adj* perfect; complete.

**perfidia** *f* perfidy.

**pérfido/da** *adj* perfidious.

**perfil** *m* profile.

**perfilado/da** *adj* well-formed, delicate (of features).

**perfilar** *vt* to outline; **~se** *vr*: **~ en** to show up against.

**perforar** *vt* to perforate; to drill; to punch a hole in; * *vi* to drill.

**perfumador** *m* perfumer.

**perfumar** *vt* to perfume.

**perfume** *m* perfume.

**perfumería** *f* perfumery.

**pergamino** *m* parchment.

**pericia** *f* skill, knowledge; expertise.

**periferia** *f* periphery; outskirts *pl*.

**periférico** *m* ring-road.

**perífrasis** *f invar* periphrasis, circumlocution.

**perímetro** *m* perimeter; circumference.

**periódico/ca** *adj* periodical; * *m* newspaper.

**periodista** *m/f* journalist.

**período/periodo** *m* period.

**peripecia** *f* vicissitude; sudden change.

**peripuesto/ta** *adj* dressed up, very spruce.

**periquito** *m* budgie.

**perito/ta** *adj* skilful, experienced; * *m/f* expert; skilled worker; technician.

**perjudicar** *vt* to prejudice, to damage; to injure, to hurt.

**perjudicial** *adj* prejudicial, damaging.

**perjuicio** *m* damage, harm.

**perjurar** *vi* to perjure, to swear falsely; to swear.

**perjurio** *m* perjury; false oath.

**perjuro/ra** *adj* perjured; * *m/f* perjurer.

**perla** *f* pearl; **de ~s** fine.

**permanecer** *vi* to stay; to continue to be.

**permanencia** *f* permanence; stay.

**permanente** *adj* permanent.

**permiso** *m* permission, leave, licence.

**permitir** *vt* to permit, to allow.

**permuta** *f* permutation, exchange.

**permutar** *vt* to exchange, to permute.

**pernera** *f* trouser leg.

**pernicioso/sa** *adj* pernicious, destructive; wicked.

**pernio** *m* hinge.

**perno** *m* bolt.

**pernoctar** *vi* to spend the night.

**pero** *m* kind of apple; * *conj* but, yet.

**perogrullada** *f* truism, platitude.

**perol** *m* large metal pan.

**perorata** *f* harangue, speech.

**perpendicular** *adj* perpendicular.

**perpetrar** *vt* to perpetrate, to commit (a crime).

**perpetuar** *vt* to perpetuate.

**perpetuidad** *f* perpetuity.

**perpetuo/tua** *adj* perpetual.
**perplejidad** *f* perplexity.
**perplejo/ja** *adj* perplexed.
**perra** *f* bitch; (*col*) money.
**perrera** *f* kennel.
**perro** *m* dog.
**persecución** *f* persecution; toil, trouble; fatigue.
**perseguidor** *m* persecutor.
**perseguir** *vt* to pursue; to persecute; to chase after.
**perseverancia** *f* perseverance, constancy.
**perseverante** *adj* persistent.
**perseverar** *vi* to persevere, to persist.
**persiana** *f* (Venetian) blind.
**persignarse** *vr* to make the sign of the cross.
**persistencia** *f* persistence; steadiness.
**persistir** *vi* to persist.
**persona** *f* person; **de ~ a ~** from person to person.
**personaje** *m* celebrity; character.
**personal** *adj* personal; single; * *m* personnel.
**personalidad** *f* personality.
**personarse** *vr* to appear in person.
**personificar** *vt* to personify.
**perspectiva** *f* perspective; view; outlook.
**perspicacia** *f* perspicacity, clear-sightedness.
**perspicaz** *adj* perspicacious, clear-sighted.
**persuadir** *vt* to persuade; **~se** *vr* to be persuaded.
**persuasión** *f* persuasion.
**persuasivo/va** *adj* persuasive.
**pertenecer** *vi:* **~ a** to belong to; to appertain, to concern.
**pertenencia** *f* ownership; **~s** *fpl* possessions *pl*.
**perteneciente** *adj:* **~ a** belonging to.
**pértiga** *f* long pole/rod.
**pertinacia** *f* pertinacity; obstinacy, stubbornness.
**pertinaz** *adj* pertinacious; obstinate.
**pertinente** *adj* relevant; appropriate.
**pertrechar** *vt* to supply with ammunition and other warlike stores; to dispose; to arrange, to prepare; **~se** *vr* to be provided with the necessary defensive stores and arms.
**pertrechos** *mpl* tools *pl*, instruments *pl*; ammunition.
**perturbación** *f* perturbation; disturbance.
**perturbado/da** *adj* mentally unbalanced.
**perturbador** *m* disturber.
**perturbar** *vt* to perturb, to disturb.
**perversidad** *f* perversity.

**perversión** *f* perversion; depravation, corruption.
**perverso/sa** *adj* perverse; extremely wicked.
**pervertido/da** *adj* perverted; * *m/f* pervert.
**pervertir** *vt* to pervert; to corrupt.
**pesa** *f* weight.
**pesadez** *f* heaviness, weight; gravity; slowness; peevishness, fretfulness; trouble; fatigue.
**pesadilla** *f* nightmare.
**pesado/da** *adj* peevish; troublesome; cumbersome; tedious; heavy, weighty.
**pesadumbre** *f* weightiness; gravity; quarrel, dispute; grief; trouble.
**pésame** *m* message of condolence.
**pesar** *m* sorrow, grief; repentance; **a ~ de** in spite of, notwithstanding; * *vi* to weigh; to repent; * *vt* to weigh.
**pesario** *m* pessary.
**pesaroso/sa** *adj* sorrowful, full of repentance; restless, uneasy.
**pesca** *f* fishing.
**pescadería** *f* fish market, fishmonger's (shop), fish shop.
**pescado** *m* fish (in general).
**pescador** *m* fisher, fisherman.
**pescar** *vt* to fish for, to catch (fish); * *vi* to fish.
**pescuezo** *m* neck.
**pesebre** *m* crib, manger.
**peseta** *f* peseta.
**pesimista** *m* pessimist.
**pésimo/ma** *adj* very bad.
**peso** *m* weight, heaviness; balance scales *pl*.
**pespunte** *m* back-stitching.
**pesquero/ra** *adj* fishing *compd*.
**pesquisa** *f* inquiry, examination.
**pestaña** *f* eyelash.
**pestañear** *vi* to blink.
**pestañeo** *m* blink.
**peste** *f* pest, plague, pestilence.
**pesticida** *m* pesticide.
**pestífero/ra** *adj* pestilential.
**pestilencia** *f* pestilence.
**pestillo** *m* bolt.
**petaca** *f* covered hamper; tobacco pouch.
**pétalo** *m* petal.
**petardo** *m* petard; cheat, fraud; imposition.
**petate** *m* straw bed; sleeping mat of the Indians; (*mar*) sailors' bedding on board ship; (*mar*) passengers' baggage; poor fellow.
**petición** *f* petition, demand.
**peto** *m* breastplate; bodice.
**petrificar(se)** *vt, vr* to petrify.
**petróleo** *m* oil, petroleum.

**petrolero/ra** *adj* petroleum *compd*; * *m* (oil) tanker; (*com*) oil man.

**petulancia** *f* petulance; insolence.

**petulante** *adj* petulant; insolent.

**peyorativo/va** *adj* pejorative.

**pez**[1] *m* fish.

**pez**[2] *f* pitch.

**pezón** *m* nipple.

**pezuña** *f* hoof.

**piadoso/sa** *adj* pious; mild; merciful; moderate.

**pianista** *m/f* pianist.

**piano** *m* piano.

**piar** *vi* to squeak; to chirp.

**piara** *f* herd (of swine); flock (of sheep).

**pibe/ba** *m/f* boy/girl.

**pica** *f* pike.

**picacho** *m* sharp point.

**picadero** *m* riding school.

**picadillo** *m* minced meat.

**picado/da** *adj* pricked; minced, chopped; bad (tooth); cross.

**picador** *m* riding master; picador.

**picadura** *f* prick; puncture.

**picante** *adj* hot, spicy; racy.

**picapedrero** *m* stonecutter.

**picaporte** *m* door handle; latch.

**picar** *vt* to prick; to sting; to mince; to nibble; * *vi* to prick; to sting; to itch; **~se** *vr* to be piqued; to take offence; to be moth-eaten; to begin to rot.

**picardía** *f* roguery; deceit; malice; lewdness.

**picaresco/ca** *adj* roguish; picaresque.

**pícaro/ra** *adj* roguish; mischievous, malicious; sly; * *m/f* rogue, knave.

**picazón** *f* itching; stinging; displeasure.

**pichón** *m* young pigeon.

**pico** *m* beak; bill, nib; peak; pick-axe.

**picotazo** *m* peck (of a bird).

**picotear** *vt* to peck (of birds).

**picudo/da** *adj* with a beak; sharp-pointed.

**pie** *m* foot; leg; basis; trunk (of trees); foundation; occasion; **a ~** on foot.

**piedad** *f* piety; mercy, pity.

**piedra** *f* stone.

**piel** *f* skin; hide; peel.

**pienso** *m* fodder.

**pierna** *f* leg.

**pieza** *f* piece; room.

**pigmeo/mea** *m/f, adj* pigmy.

**pijama** *m* pyjamas *pl*.

**pila** *f* battery; trough; font; sink; pile, heap; **nombre de ~** first name.

**pilar**[1] *m* basin.

**pilar**[2] *m* pillar, column; pillar box; mainstay.

**píldora** *f* pill.

**pileta** *f* basin; swimming pool.

**pillaje** *m* pillage, plunder.

**pillar** *vt* to pillage, to plunder, to foray, to seize; to catch onto; to catch.

**pillo/lla** *m, adj* rascal, scoundrel.

**pilotaje** *m* pilotage.

**piloto** *m/f* pilot.

**piltrafa** *f* piece of meat that is nearly all skin.

**pimentón** *m* paprika.

**pimienta** *f* allspice, pepper, pimento.

**pimiento** *m* sweet pepper, pimiento.

**pinacoteca** *f* art gallery.

**pináculo** *m* pinnacle.

**pinar** *m* grove of pine trees.

**pincel** *m* paintbrush.

**pincelada** *f* dash with a paintbrush.

**pinchar** *vt* to prick; to puncture.

**pinchazo** *m* prick; puncture; (*fig*) prod.

**pinchito** *m* small snack.

**pincho** *m* thorn; snack.

**pingajo** *m* rag, tatter.

**ping-pong** *m* table tennis.

**pingüe** *adj* fat, greasy; fertile.

**pingüino** *m* penguin.

**pino** *m* pine tree.

**pinta** *f* spot, blemish; scar; mark (on playing cards); pint.

**pintado/da** *adj* painted, mottled; **venir ~** to fit exactly.

**pintar** *vt* to paint; to picture; to describe; to exaggerate; * *vi* to paint; (*col*) to count, to be important; **~se** *vr* to put on make-up.

**pintarrajear** *vt* to daub.

**pintarrajo** *m* daub.

**pintor/-ra** *m/f* painter.

**pintoresco/ca** *adj* picturesque.

**pintura** *f* painting.

**pinza** *f* claw; clothes peg; pincers *pl*; **~s** *fpl* tweezers *pl*.

**piña** *f* pineapple; fir cone; group.

**piñón** *m* pine nut; pinion.

**pío/pía** *adj* pious, devout; merciful.

**piojo** *m* louse; troublesome hanger-on.

**piojoso/sa** *adj* lousy; miserable, stingy.

**pionero/ra** *adj* pioneering; *m/f* pioneer.

**pipa** *f* pipe (for smoking); seed; sunflower seed.

**pipí** *m* (*col*): **hacer ~** to have to go (wee-wee).

**pique** *m* pique, offence taken; rivalry; **echar a ~** to sink a ship; **a ~** in danger; **a ~ de** on the point of.

**piquete** *m* slight prick/sting; picket.
**pira** *f* funeral pyre.
**piragua** *f* canoe.
**piragüismo** *m* canoeing.
**piramidal** *adj* pyramidal.
**pirámide** *f* pyramid.
**pirata** *m* pirate.
**piropo** *m* compliment; flattery.
**pirotecnia** *f* fireworks *pl*.
**pirueta** *f* pirouette.
**pisada** *f* footstep; footprint.
**pisar** *vt* to tread, to trample; to stamp on (the ground); to hammer down; * *vi* to tread, to walk.
**piscina** *f* swimming pool; ~ **para niños** paddling pool.
**Piscis** *m* Pisces (sign of the zodiac).
**piso** *m* flat, apartment; tread, trampling; floor, pavement; floor, storey.
**pisotear** *vt* to trample, to tread under foot.
**pista** *f* trace, footprint; clue.
**pisto** *m* thick broth.
**pistola** *f* pistol.
**pistolera** *f* pistol holster.
**pistolero/ra** *m/f* gunman/woman, gangster.
**pistoletazo** *m* pistol shot.
**pistón** *m* piston; (musical) key.
**pita** *f* (*bot*) any plant of the family *Agavaceae* with tall flowers and thick, fleshy leaves.
**pitar** *vt* to blow; to whistle at; * *vi* to whistle; to toot one's horn; to smoke.
**pitillo** *m* cigarette.
**pito** *m* whistle; horn.
**pitón** *m* python.
**pitonisa** *f* sorceress, enchantress.
**pitorreo** *m* joke; **estar de** ~ to be joking.
**pizarra** *f* slate.
**pizarral** *m* slate quarry, slate pit.
**pizca** *f* mite; pinch.
**placa** *f* plate; badge; ~ **de matrícula** numberplate.
**placentero/ra** *adj* joyful, merry.
**placer** *m* pleasure; delight; * *vt* to please.
**plácido/da** *adj* placid.
**plaga** *f* plague.
**plagar** *vt* to plague, to torment.
**plagio** *m* plagiarism.
**plan** *m* plan; design; plot.
**plana** *f* trowel; page (of a book); level; ~ **mayor** (*mil*) staff.
**plancha** *f* plate; iron; gangway; press-up.
**planchar** *vt* to iron.
**planchuela** *n* nameplate *f*.
**planeador** *m* glider.

**planear** *vt* to plan; * *vi* to glide.
**planeta** *m* planet.
**planetario/ria** *adj* planetary.
**planicie** *f* plain.
**planificación** *f* planning; ~ **familiar** family planning, birth control.
**plano/na** *adj* plain, level, flat; * *m* plan; ground plot; ~ **inclinado** (*rail*) dead level.
**planta** *f* plant; plantation.
**plantación** *f* plantation.
**plantar** *vt* to plant; to fix upright; to strike/hit (a blow); to found; to establish; ~**se** *vr* to stand upright.
**plantear** *vt* to plan; to implant.
**plantilla** *f* personnel; insole of a shoe.
**plantón** *m* long wait; (*mil*) sentry.
**plañir** *vi* to lament, to grieve, to bewail.
**plasmar** *vt* to mould; to represent.
**plasta** *f* paste, soft clay; mess.
**plástico/ca** *adj* plastic; * *m* plastic; * *f* (art of) sculpture.
**plata** *f* silver; silverware; cash; **en** ~ briefly.
**plataforma** *f* platform; ~ **giratoria** (*rail*) turntable.
**plátano** *m* banana; plane tree.
**plateado/da** *adj* silvered; silver-plated.
**platería** *f* silversmith's shop; trade of silversmithing.
**plática** *f* discourse, conversation.
**platicar** *vi* to converse.
**platillo** *m* saucer; ~**s** *mpl* cymbals *pl*; ~ **volador,** ~ **volante** flying saucer.
**platino** *m* platinum; ~**s** *mpl* contact points *pl*.
**plato** *m* dish; plate.
**platónico/ca** *adj* platonic.
**plausible** *adj* plausible.
**playa** *f* beach.
**playera** *f* T-shirt; ~**s** *fpl* canvas shoes *pl*.
**plaza** *f* square; place; office, employment; room; seat.
**plazo** *m* term; instalment; expiry date.
**pleamar** *f* (*mar*) high water.
**plebe** *f* common people *pl*, populace.
**plebeyo/ya** *adj* plebeian; * *m* commoner.
**plebiscito** *m* plebiscite.
**plegable** *adj* pliable; folding.
**plegar** *vt* to fold; to plait.
**plegaria** *f* prayer.
**pleitear** *vi* to plead, to litigate.
**pleito** *m* contract, bargain; dispute, controversy, debate; lawsuit.
**plenamente** *adv* fully; completely.
**plenario/ria** *adj* complete; full.
**plenilunio** *m* full moon.

**plenipotenciario** *m* plenipotentiary.
**plenitud** *f* fullness; abundance.
**pleno/na** *adj* full; complete; * *m* plenum.
**pliego** *m* sheet of paper.
**pliegue** *m* fold; plait.
**plisado/da** *adj* pleated; * *m* pleating.
**plomero** *m* plumber.
**plomizo/za** *adj* leaden.
**plomo** *m* lead; **a ~** perpendicularly.
**pluma** *f* feather, plume.
**plumaje** *m* plumage; plume.
**plumero** *m* bunch of feathers; feather duster.
**plumón** *m* felt-tip pen; marker; down (feathers).
**plural** *adj* (*gr*) plural.
**pluralidad** *f* plurality.
**Plutón** *m* Pluto (planet).
**población** *f* population; town.
**poblado** *m* town; village; inhabited place.
**poblador/ra** *m/f* populator, founder.
**poblar** *vt* to populate, to people; to fill, to occupy.
**pobre** *adj* poor.
**pobreza** *f* poverty, poorness.
**pocilga** *f* pig sty.
**pocillo** *m* coffee cup.
**pócima, poción** *f* potion.
**poco/ca** *adj* little, scanty; (*pl*) few; * *adv* little; **~ a ~** gently; little by little; * *m* small part; little.
**poda** *f* pruning (of trees).
**podadera** *f* pruning knife.
**podar** *vt* to prune.
**podenco** *m* hound.
**poder** *m* power, authority; command; force; * *vi* to be able to; to possess the power of doing/performing.
**poderío** *m* power, authority; wealth, riches *pl*.
**poderoso/sa** *adj* powerful; eminent, excellent.
**podredumbre** *f* putrid matter; grief.
**podrido/da** *adj* rotten, bad; (*fig*) rotten.
**podrir** *vt* to rot, to putrefy; **~se** *vr* to rot, to decay.
**poema** *m* poem.
**poesía** *f* poetry.
**poeta** *m* poet.
**poético/ca** *adj* poetical.
**poetisa** *f* poetess.
**poetizar** *vt* to poetize.
**polar** *adj* polar.
**polea** *f* pulley; (*mar*) tackle-block.
**polémica** *f* polemic.

**polémico/ca** *adj* polemical.
**polen** *m* pollen.
**policía** *f* police; * *m/f* policeman/woman.
**polideportivo** *m* sports centre.
**poligamia** *f* polygamy.
**polígamo** *m* polygamist.
**polígono** *m* polygon.
**polilla** *f* moth.
**polio** *f* polio.
**pólipo** *m* polypus.
**politécnico/ca** *adj* polytechnic.
**politeísmo** *m* polytheism.
**política** *f* politics; policy.
**político/ca** *adj* political; * *m/f* politician.
**póliza** *f* written order; policy.
**polizón** *m* stowaway.
**pollera** *f* skirt.
**pollería** *f* poulterer's (shop).
**pollo** *m* chicken.
**polo** *m* pole; ice lolly; polo; polo neck.
**polución** *f* pollution.
**polvareda** *f* cloud of dust.
**polvera** *f* powder compact.
**polvo** *m* powder, dust.
**pólvora** *f* gunpowder.
**polvoriento/ta** *adj* dusty.
**polvorín** *m* powder reduced to the finest dust; powder flask.
**pomada** *f* cream, ointment.
**pomelo** *m* grapefruit.
**pómez** *f*: **piedra ~** pumice stone.
**pompa** *f* pomp; bubble.
**pomposo/sa** *adj* pompous.
**pómulo** *m* cheekbone.
**ponche** *m* punch.
**poncho/cha** *adj* soft, mild; * *m* poncho.
**ponderación** *f* pondering, considering; exaggeration.
**ponderar** *vt* to ponder, to weigh; to exaggerate.
**ponedero/ra** *adj* egg-laying; capable of being laid/placed; * *m* nest; nest egg.
**poner** *vt* to put, to place; to put on; to impose; to lay (eggs); **~se** *vr* to oppose; to set (of stars); to become.
**poniente** *m* west; west wind.
**pontificado** *m* pontificate.
**pontífice** *m* Pope, pontiff.
**pontificio/cia** *adj* pontifical.
**pontón** *m* pontoon.
**ponzoña** *f* poison.
**ponzoñoso/sa** *adj* poisonous.
**popa** *f* (*mar*) poop, stern.
**populacho** *m* populace, mob.
**popular** *adj* popular.

**popularidad** *f* popularity.
**popularizarse** *vr* to become popular.
**populoso/sa** *adj* populous.
**poquedad** *f* paucity, smallness; cowardice.
**por** *prep* for; by; about; by means of; through; on account of.
**porcelana** *f* porcelain, china.
**porcentaje** *m* percentage.
**porción** *f* part, portion; lot.
**porcuno/na** *adj* hoggish.
**pordiosero/ra** *m/f* beggar.
**porfiar** *vt* to dispute obstinately; to persist in a pursuit.
**pormenor** *f* detail.
**pornografía** *f* pornography.
**poro** *m* pore.
**porosidad** *f* porosity.
**poroso/sa** *adj* porous.
**porque** *conj* because; since; so that.
**porqué** *m* cause, reason.
**porquería** *f* nastiness, foulness; brutishness, rudeness; trifle; dirty action.
**porqueriza** *f* pigsty.
**porra** *f* cudgel.
**porrillo: a ~** *adv* copiously, abundantly.
**porrón** *m* spouted wine jar.
**portada** *f* portal, porch; frontispiece.
**portador/ra** *m/f* carrier, porter.
**portaequipajes** *m invar* (*auto*) boot; luggage rack.
**portal** *m* porch; portal.
**portamonedas** *m invar* purse.
**portarse** *vr* to behave.
**portátil** *adj* portable; * *m* laptop.
**portaaviones** *m invar* aircraft carrier.
**portavoz** *m/f* spokesman/woman.
**portazo** *m* bang of a door; banging a door in one's face.
**porte** *m* transportation (charges *pl*); deportment, demeanour, conduct.
**portento** *m* prodigy, portent.
**portentoso/sa** *adj* prodigious, marvellous, strange.
**portería** *f* porter's office; goal (sport).
**portero/ra** *m/f* porter; caretaker; gatekeeper; goalkeeper.
**portezuela** *f* little door.
**pórtico** *m* portico, porch, lobby.
**portilla** *f*, **portillo** *m* aperture in a wall; gate; gap, breach.
**portón** *m* main door (of a house).
**porvenir** *m* future.
**pos** *prep*: **en ~ de** after, behind; in pursuit of.
**posada** *f* shelter; inn, hotel.

**posaderas** *fpl* buttocks *pl*.
**posadero** *m* innkeeper.
**posar** *vi* to sit, to pose; * *vt* to lay down (a burden); **~se** *vr* to settle; to perch; to land.
**posdata** *f* postcript.
**pose** *f* pose.
**poseedor/ra** *m/f* owner, possessor; holder.
**poseer** *vt* to hold, to possess.
**poseído/da** *adj* possessed by the devil.
**posesión** *f* possession.
**posesivo/va** *adj* possessive.
**posesor/ra** *m/f* possessor.
**posibilidad** *f* possibility.
**posibilitar** *vt* to make possible; to make feasible.
**posible** *adj* possible.
**posición** *f* position; posture; situation.
**positivo/va** *adj* positive.
**poso** *m* sediment, dregs *pl*.
**posponer** *vt* to postpone.
**posta** *f*: **a ~** on purpose.
**postal** *adj* postal; * *f* postcard.
**poste** *m* post, pillar.
**póster** *m* poster.
**postergación** *f* missing out, passing over; putting over.
**postergar** *vt* to leave behind; to postpone.
**posteridad** *f* posterity.
**posterior** *adj* posterior.
**posterioridad** *f*: **con ~** subsequently, later.
**postigo** *m* postern; small door; shutter (of a window).
**postizo/za** *adj* artificial (not natural); * *m* wig.
**postor** *m* bidder at a public sale; better.
**postración** *f* prostration.
**postrar** *vt* to humble, to humiliate; **~se** *vr* to prostrate oneself.
**postre** *m* dessert.
**postrer(o)/ra** *adj* last, hindmost.
**postrimerías** *fpl* dying moments; final stages.
**póstumo/ma** *adj* posthumous.
**postura** *f* posture, position; attitude; bet, wager; agreement, convention.
**potable** *adj* drinkable.
**potaje** *m* pottage; drink made up of several ingredients; medley of various useless things.
**pote** *m* pot, jar; flower pot.
**potencia** *f* power; mightiness.
**potencial** *m* potential.
**potentado** *m* potentate; prince.
**potente** *adj* potent, powerful, mighty.
**potestad** *f* power; dominion; jurisdiction.

**potro/ra** *m/f* colt; foal.
**poyo** *m* stone seat/bench.
**pozo** *m* well.
**práctica** *f* practice.
**practicable** *adj* practicable, feasible.
**practicante** *adj* practising; * *m/f* practitioner.
**practicar** *vt* to practise.
**práctico/ca** *adj* practical; skilful, experienced.
**pradera** *f* meadow.
**prado** *m* lawn; meadow.
**pragmático/ca** *adj* pragmatic.
**preámbulo** *m* preamble; circumlocution.
**prebenda** *f* prebend.
**precampaña** *f* run-up to an election campaign.
**precario/ria** *adj* precarious.
**precaución** *f* precaution.
**precaver** *vt* to prevent; to guard against.
**precedencia** *f* precedence; preference; superiority.
**precedente** *adj* preceding, foregoing.
**preceder** *vt* to precede, to go before.
**precepto** *m* precept, order.
**preceptor/ra** *m/f* master, teacher, preceptor.
**preciado/da** *adj* esteemed, valued.
**preciarse** *vr* to boast; ~ **de** to take pride in.
**precinto** *m* seal.
**precio** *m* price; value.
**preciosidad** *f* excellence; preciousness.
**precioso/sa** *adj* precious; (*col*) beautiful.
**precipicio** *m* precipice; violent, sudden fall; ruin, destruction.
**precipitación** *f* precipitation, rush.
**precipitado/da** *adj* precipitate, headlong, hasty.
**precipitar** *vt* to precipitate; ~**se** *vr* to act hastily; to rush.
**precisamente** *adv* precisely; exactly.
**precisar** *vt* to compel, to oblige; to need.
**precisión** *f* necessity, compulsion; preciseness.
**preciso/sa** *adj* necessary, requisite; precise, exact; abstracted.
**precocidad** *f* precocity.
**preconizar** *vt* to proclaim; to recommend.
**precoz** *adj* precocious.
**precursor/ra** *m/f* harbinger, forerunner.
**predecesor/ra** *m/f* predecessor.
**predecir** *vt* to foretell.
**predestinación** *f* predestination.
**predestinar** *vt* to predestine.
**predicación** *f* preaching; sermon.
**predicado** *m* predicate.

**predicador** *m* preacher.
**predicar** *vt* to preach.
**predicción** *f* prediction.
**predilección** *f* predilection.
**predilecto/ta** *adj* darling, favourite.
**predisponer** *vt* to predispose; to prejudice.
**predisposición** *f* inclination; prejudice.
**predominar** *vi* to predominate, to prevail.
**predominio** *m* predominant power, superiority.
**preeminencia** *f* pre-eminence; superiority.
**preeminente** *adj* pre-eminent; superior.
**preescolar** *adj* pre-school.
**preestreno** *m* preview.
**preexistencia** *f* pre-existence.
**preexistente** *adj* pre-existent.
**preexistir** *vt* to pre-exist, to exist before.
**prefabricado/da** *adj* prefabricated.
**prefacio** *m* preface.
**prefecto** *m* prefect.
**prefectura** *f* prefecture.
**preferencia** *f* preference.
**preferible** *adj* preferable.
**preferir** *vt* to prefer.
**prefijar** *vt* (*gr*) to prefix; to fix beforehand.
**prefijo** *m* dialling code.
**pregón** *m* proclamation; hue and cry.
**pregonar** *vt* to proclaim.
**pregonero** *m* town crier.
**pregunta** *f* question; inquiry.
**preguntar** *vt* to ask; to question; to demand; to inquire.
**preguntón/ona** *m/f* inquisitive person.
**prehistórico/ca** *adj* prehistoric.
**prejuicio** *m* prejudgement; preconception; prejudice.
**prelado** *m* prelate.
**preliminar** *adj, m* preliminary.
**preludio** *m* prelude.
**prematuro/ra** *adj* premature.
**premeditación** *f* premeditation, forethought.
**premeditar** *vt* to premeditate, to think out.
**premiar** *vt* to reward, to remunerate.
**premio** *m* reward, recompense; premium.
**premisa** *f* premise.
**premura** *f* pressure, haste, hurry.
**prenatal** *adj* pre-natal.
**prenda** *f* pledge; garment; sweetheart; person/thing dearly loved; ~**s** *fpl* accomplishments *pl*, talents *pl*.
**prendar** *vt* to enchant; ~**se** *vr*: ~ **de** to fall in love with.
**prendedor** *m* brooch.
**prender** *vt* to seize, to catch, to lay hold of;

to imprison; ~se *vr* to catch fire; * *vi* to take root.

**prendimiento** *m* seizure; capture.

**prensa** *f* press.

**prensar** *vt* to press.

**preñado/da** *adj* pregnant.

**preñez** *f* pregnancy.

**preocupación** *f* worry, preoccupation.

**preocupado/da** *adj* worried, anxious.

**preocupar(se)** *vt* (*vr*) to worry.

**preparación** *f* preparation.

**preparador/ra** *m/f* trainer.

**preparar** *vt* to prepare; ~se *vr* to be prepared.

**preparativo/va** *adj* preparatory; preliminary; qualifying; * *m* preparation.

**preparatorio/ria** *adj* preparatory.

**preponderancia** *f* preponderance.

**preponderar** *vi* to preponderate, to prevail.

**preposición** *f* (*gr*) preposition.

**prepucio** *m* foreskin.

**prerrogativa** *f* prerogative, privilege.

**presa** *f* capture, seizure; dyke, dam.

**presagiar** *vt* to presage, to forebode.

**presagio** *m* omen.

**presbítero** *m* priest, clergyman.

**presciencia** *f* prescience, foreknowledge.

**prescindir** *vi*: ~ **de** to do without; to dispense with.

**prescribir** *vt* to prescribe.

**prescripción** *f* prescription.

**presencia** *f* presence.

**presenciar** *vt* to attend; to be present at; to witness.

**presentación** *f* presentation.

**presentador/ra** *m/f* (*rad*, *TV*) presenter; compere.

**presentar** *vt* to present; to introduce; to offer; to show; ~se *vr* to present oneself; to appear; to run (as candidate); to apply.

**presente** *m* present, gift; * *adj* present.

**presentemente** *adv* presently, now.

**presentimiento** *m* presentiment.

**presentir** *vt* to have a premonition of.

**preservación** *f* preservation.

**preservar** *vt* to preserve; to defend.

**preservativo** *m* condom, sheath.

**presidencia** *f* presidency.

**presidente/ta** *m/f* president.

**presidiario/ria** *m/f* convict.

**presidio** *m* penitentiary, prison.

**presidir** *vt* to preside at.

**presilla** *f* clip; loop (in clothes).

**presión** *f* pressure, pressing; ~ **de los neumáticos** tyre pressure.

**presionar** *vt* to press; (*fig*) to put pressure on.

**preso/sa** *m/f* prisoner.

**prestado/da** *adj* on loan; **pedir** ~ to borrow.

**prestamista** *m* borrower, lender.

**préstamo** *m* loan.

**prestar** *vt* to lend.

**presteza** *f* quickness; haste, speed.

**prestigio** *m* prestige.

**presto/ta** *adj* quick; prompt; ready; * *adv* soon; quickly.

**presumible** *adj* presumable.

**presumido/da** *adj* presumptous, arrogant.

**presumir** *vt* to presume, to conjecture; * *vi* to be conceited.

**presunción** *f* presumption, conjecture; conceit.

**presunto/ta** *adj* supposed; so-called.

**presuntuoso/sa** *adj* presumptuous.

**presuponer** *vt* to presuppose.

**presupuesto** *m* estimate; budget.

**presuroso/sa** *adj* hasty, quick; prompt; nimble.

**pretencioso/sa** *adj* pretentious.

**pretender** *vt* to pretend, to claim; to try, to attempt.

**pretendiente** *m* pretender; suitor.

**pretensión** *f* pretension.

**pretérito/ta** *adj* past.

**pretextar** *vt* to plead, use as an excuse.

**pretexto** *m* pretext, pretence; plea, excuse.

**prevalacer** *vi* to prevail; to triumph; to take root.

**prevención** *f* disposition, preparation; supply of provisions; foresight; prevention; (*mil*) guardroom/house.

**prevenido/da** *adj* prepared; careful, cautious; foreseeing.

**prevenir** *vt* to prepare; to foresee, to know in advance; to prevent; to warn; ~se *vr* to be prepared; to be predisposed.

**preventivo/va** *adj* preventive.

**prever** *vt* to foresee, to forecast.

**previo/via** *adj* previous.

**previsión** *f* foresight, prevision; forecast.

**previsor/ra** *adj* far-sighted.

**prima** *f* bonus; (female) cousin.

**primacía** *f* priority; primacy.

**primado** *m* primate.

**primario/ria** *adj* primary.

**primavera** *f* spring (the season).

**primeramente** *adv* in the first place, mainly.

**primer(o)/ra** *adj* first; prior; former; * *adv* first; rather, sooner.

**primicias** *fpl* first fruits *pl.*
**primitivo/va** *adj* primitive; original.
**primo/ma** *m* cousin.
**primogénito/ta** *adj, m/f* first-born.
**primogenitura** *f* primogeniture.
**primor** *m* beauty; dexterity, ability.
**primordial** *adj* basic, fundamental.
**primoroso/sa** *adj* neat, elegant; fine, excellent; handsome.
**princesa** *f* princess.
**principal** *adj, m* principal, chief.
**príncipe** *m* prince.
**principiante** *m* beginner, learner.
**principiar** *vt, vi* to commence, to begin.
**principio** *m* beginning, commencement; principle.
**pringoso/sa** *adj* greasy; sticky.
**pringue** *m/f* grease; lard; dripping.
**prioridad** *f* priority.
**prisa** *f* speed; hurry; urgency; promptness.
**prisión** *f* prison; imprisonment.
**prisionero** *m* prisoner.
**prisma** *m* prism.
**prismáticos** *mpl* binoculars *pl.*
**privación** *f* deprivation, want.
**privado/da** *adj* private; particular.
**privar** *vt* to deprive; to prohibit; ~se *vr* to deprive oneself.
**privativo/va** *adj* private, one's own; particular, peculiar.
**privilegiado/da** *adj* privileged; very good.
**privilegiar** *vt* to privilege.
**privilegio** *m* privilege.
**pro** *m/f* profit; benefit; advantage.
**proa** *f* (*mar*) prow.
**probabilidad** *f* probability, likelihood.
**probable** *adj* probable, likely.
**probado/da** *adj* proved, tried.
**probador** *m* fitting room.
**probar** *vt* to try; to prove; to taste; * *vi* to try.
**probeta** *f* test tube.
**problema** *m* problem.
**problemático/ca** *adj* problematic.
**procedencia** *m* derivation.
**procedente** *adj* reasonable; proper; ~ de coming from.
**proceder** *m* procedure; * *vi* to proceed, to go on; to act.
**procedimiento** *m* proceeding; legal procedure.
**procesado/da** *m/f* accused.
**procesador** *m*: ~ de textos word processor.
**procesar** *vt* to put on trial.
**procesión** *f* procession.

**proceso** *m* process; lawsuit.
**proclama** *f* proclamation, publication.
**proclamación** *f* proclamation; acclamation.
**proclamar** *vt* to proclaim.
**procreación** *f* procreation, generation.
**procrear** *vt* to procreate, to generate.
**procurador/ra** *m/f* procurer; attorney; solicitor.
**procurar** *vt* to try; to obtain; to produce.
**prodigalidad** *f* plenty, abundance.
**prodigar** *vt* to waste, to lavish.
**prodigio** *m* prodigy; monster.
**prodigioso/sa** *adj* prodigious, monstrous; exquisite; excellent.
**pródigo/ga** *adj* prodigal.
**producción** *f* production.
**producir** *vt* to produce; (*law*) to produce as evidence; ~se *vr* to come about; to arise; to be made; to break out.
**productividad** *f* productivity.
**productivo/va** *adj* productive.
**producto** *m* product.
**productor/ra** *adj* productive; * *m/f* producer.
**proeza** *f* prowess, valour, bravery.
**profanación** *f* desecration.
**profanar** *vt* to profane, to desecrate.
**profano/na** *adj* profane.
**profecía** *f* prophecy.
**profesar** *vt* to profess, to practise.
**profesión** *f* profession.
**profesional** *adj, m/f* professional.
**profeso/sa** *adj* professed.
**profesor/ra** *m/f* teacher; lecturer.
**profesorado** *m* teaching profession.
**profeta** *m* prophet.
**profético/ca** *adj* prophetic.
**profetizar** *vt* to prophesy.
**prófugo/ga** *m/f* fugitive.
**profundidad** *f* profundity, profoundness; depth; grandeur.
**profundizar** *vt* to go deeply into; to deepen; to penetrate.
**profundo/da** *adj* profound.
**profusamente** *adv* profusely.
**profusión** *f* profusion; prodigality.
**progenie** *f* progeny, offspring; race; generation.
**progenitor** *m* progenitor, ancestor, forefather.
**programa** *m* program(me).
**programación** *f* computer programming.
**programador/ra** *m/f* programmer.
**programar** *vt* to program(me).
**progresar** *vi* to progress.

**progresión** *f* progression.
**progresista** *adj*, *m/f* progressive.
**progreso** *m* progress.
**progresivo/va** *adj* progressive.
**prohibición** *f* prohibition, ban.
**prohibir** *vt* to prohibit, to forbid; to hinder.
**prójimo** *m* fellow creature; neighbour.
**prole** *f* offspring, progeny; race.
**proletariado** *m* proletariat.
**proletario/ria** *adj* proletarian.
**proliferación** *f* proliferation.
**proliferar** *vi* to proliferate.
**prolífico/ca** *adj* prolific.
**prolijidad** *f* prolixity; minute attention to detail.
**prolijo/ja** *adj* long-winded; tedious.
**prólogo** *m* prologue.
**prolongación** *f* prolongation.
**prolongar** *vt* to prolong.
**promedio** *m* average; middle.
**promesa** *f* promise.
**prometer** *vt* to promise; to assure; **~se** *vr* to become engaged.
**prometido/da** *adj* promised; engaged; * *m/f* fiancé/fiancée.
**prominencia** *f* protuberance.
**prominente** *adj* prominent, jutting out.
**promiscuo/cua** *adj* promiscuous; confusedly mingled; ambiguous.
**promoción** *f* promotion.
**promontorio** *m* promontory, cape.
**promotor** *m* promoter.
**promover** *vt* to promote, to advance; to stir up.
**promulgación** *f* promulgation.
**promulgar** *vt* to promulgate, to publish.
**pronombre** *m* (*gr*) pronoun.
**pronosticar** *vt* to predict, to foretell; to conjecture.
**pronóstico** *m* prediction; forecast.
**prontitud** *f* promptness.
**pronto/ta** *adj* prompt; ready; * *adv* promptly.
**pronunciación** *f* pronunciation.
**pronunciamiento** *m* (*law*) publication; insurrection, sedition.
**pronunciar** *vt* to pronounce; to deliver; **~se** *vr* to rebel.
**propagación** *f* propagation; extension.
**propagador/ra** *m/f* propagator.
**propaganda** *f* propaganda; advertising.
**propagar** *vt* to propagate.
**propasar** *vt* to go beyond, to exceed.
**propender** *vi* to incline.
**propensión** *f* propensity, inclination.
**propenso/sa** *adj* prone, inclined.

**propiamente** *adv* properly; really.
**propiciar** *vt* to favour; to cause.
**propiciatorio/ria** *adj* propitiatory.
**propicio/cia** *adj* propitious.
**propiedad** *f* property, possessions *pl*; right of property; propriety.
**propietario/ria** *adj* proprietary; * *m/f* proprietor.
**propina** *f* tip.
**propinar** *vt* to hit; to give.
**propio/pia** *adj* proper; own; typical; very.
**proponer** *vt* to propose.
**proporción** *f* proportion; symmetry.
**proporcionado/da** *adj* proportionate; fit; **bien ~** well-proportioned.
**proporcional** *adj* proportional.
**proporcionar** *vt* to provide; to adjust, to adapt.
**proposición** *f* proposition.
**propósito** *m* aim, purpose; **a ~** on purpose.
**propuesta** *f* proposal, offer; representation.
**propulsar** *vt* to propel; (*fig*) to promote.
**prórroga** *f* prolongation; extension; extra time.
**prorrogable** *adj* extendable.
**prorrogar** *vt* to extend; to postpone.
**prorrumpir** *vi* to break forth, to burst forth.
**prosa** *f* prose.
**prosaico/ca** *adj* prosaic.
**proscribir** *vt* to proscribe, to outlaw.
**proscripción** *f* proscription.
**proscrito/ta** *adj* banned.
**prosecución** *f* continuation.
**proseguir** *vt* to continue; * *vi* to continue, to go on.
**prospección** *f* exploration; prospecting.
**prospecto** *m* prospectus.
**prosperar** *vi* to prosper, to thrive.
**prosperidad** *f* prosperity.
**próspero/ra** *adj* prosperous.
**prostíbulo** *m* brothel.
**prostitución** *f* prostitution.
**prostituir** *vt* to prostitute.
**prostituta** *f* prostitute.
**protagonista** *m/f* protagonist.
**protagonizar** *vt* to take the chief role in.
**protección** *f* protection.
**protector** *m* to protect.
**proteger** *vt* protector.
**proteína** *f* protein.
**protesta** *f* protest.
**protestante** *m/f* Protestant.
**protestar** *vt* to protest; to make public declaration (of faith); * *vi* to protest.
**protocolo** *m* protocol.

**prototipo** *m* prototype.
**provecho** *m* profit; advantage.
**provechoso/sa** *adj* profitable; advantageous.
**proveedor/ra** *m/f* purveyor.
**proveer** *vt* to provide; to provision; to decree.
**provenir** *vi* to arise, to originate; to issue.
**proverbial** *adj* proverbial.
**proverbio** *m* proverb; ~s *mpl* Book of Proverbs.
**providencia** *f* providence; foresight; divine providence.
**providencial** *adj* providential.
**provincia** *f* province.
**provincial** *adj*, *m* provincial.
**provinciano/na** *adj* provincial; country *compd*.
**provisión** *f* provision; store.
**provisional** *adj* provisional.
**provisionalmente** *adv* provisionally.
**provocación** *f* provocation.
**provocador/ra** *adj* provocative.
**provocar** *vt* to provoke; to lead to; to excite.
**provocativo/va** *adj* provocative.
**próximamente** *adv* soon.
**proximidad** *f* proximity, closeness.
**próximo/ma** *adj* next; neighbouring; close, nearby.
**proyección** *f* projection; showing; influence.
**proyectar** *vt* to throw; to cast; to screen; to plan.
**proyectil** *m* projectile, missile.
**proyecto** *m* plan; project.
**proyector** *m* projector.
**prudencia** *f* prudence, wisdom.
**prudente** *adj* prudent.
**prueba** *f* proof; reason; argument; token; experiment; essay; attempt; relish, taste.
**prurito** *m* itching.
**psicoanálisis** *m* psychoanalysis.
**psicoanalista** *m/f* psychoanalist.
**psicología** *f* psychology.
**psicólogo/ga** *m/f* psychologist.
**psiquiatra** *m/f* psychiatrist.
**psiquiátrico/ca** *adj* psychiatric.
**psíquico/ca** *adj* psychic(al).
**púa** *f* sharp point, prickle; shoot; pick.
**pubertad** *f* puberty.
**publicación** *f* publication.
**publicar** *vt* to publish; to make public.
**publicidad** *f* publicity.
**público/ca** *adj* public; * *m* public; audience; crowd.
**puchero** *m* pot; stew.

**púdico/ca** *adj* chaste, pure.
**pudiente** *adj* rich, opulent.
**pudor** *m* bashfulness.
**pudrir** *vt* to rot, to putrefy; ~se *vr* to decay, to rot.
**pueblo** *m* people *pl*; town, village; population; populace.
**puente** *m* bridge.
**puenting** *m* bungee-jumping.
**puerco/ca** *adj* nasty; filthy, dirty; rude, coarse; * *m* pig, hog; ~ espín porcupine.
**pueril** *adj* childish; peurile.
**puerilidad** *f* puerility.
**puerro** *m* leek.
**puerta** *f* door; doorway; gateway; ~ trasera back door.
**puerto** *m* port, harbour; haven; pass; narrow pass.
**pues** *adv* then; therefore; well; ¡~! well, then.
**puesto** *m* place; particular spot; post, employment; barracks *pl*; stand.
**púgil** *m* boxer.
**pugilato** *m* boxing.
**pugna** *f* combat, battle.
**pugnar** *vi* to fight, to combat; to struggle.
**pujante** *adj* powerful, strong; robust; stout; strapping.
**pujanza** *f* power, strength.
**pujar** *vt* to outbid; to strain.
**pulcritud** *f* beauty.
**pulcro/cra** *adj* beautiful; affected.
**pulga** *f* flea; tener malas ~s to be easily piqued; to be ill-tempered.
**pulgada** *f* inch.
**pulgar** *m* thumb.
**pulir** *vt* to polish; to put the last touches to.
**pulla** *f* smart repartee; obscene expression.
**pulmón** *m* lung.
**pulmonía** *f* pneumonia.
**pulpa** *f* pulp; soft part (of fruit).
**pulpería** *f* small grocery shop.
**púlpito** *m* pulpit.
**pulpo** *m* octopus.
**pulsación** *f* pulsation.
**pulsador** *m* push button.
**pulsar** *vt* to touch; to play; to press.
**pulsera** *f* bracelet.
**pulso** *m* pulse; wrist; firmness/steadiness of the hand.
**pulular** *vi* to swarm.
**pulverización** *f* pulverization.
**pulverizador** *m* spray gun.
**pulverizar** *vt* to pulverize.
**puna** *f* (*med*) mountain sickness.
**pungir** *vt* to punch, to prick.

**punición** *f* punishment, chastisement.
**punitivo/va** *adj* punitive.
**punta** *f* point; end; trace.
**puntada** *f* stitch.
**puntal** *m* prop, stay; buttress.
**puntapié** *m* kick.
**puntear** *vt* to tick; to pluck (the guitar); to stitch.
**puntería** *f* aiming.
**puntero** *m* pointer; ~/ra *adj* leading.
**puntiagudo/da** *adj* sharp-pointed.
**puntilla** *f* narrow lace edging; **de ~s** on tip-toe.
**punto** *m* point; end; spot; stitch.
**puntuación** *f* punctuation.
**puntual** *adj* punctual; exact; reliable.
**puntualidad** *f* punctuality.
**puntualizar** *vt* to fix; to specify.
**puntuar** *vt* to punctuate; to evaluate.
**punzada** *f* prick; sting; pain; compunction.
**punzante** *adj* sharp.
**punzar** *vt* to punch; to prick; to sting.
**punzón** *m* punch.
**puñado** *m* handful.
**puñal** *m* dagger.
**puñalada** *f* stab.
**puñetazo** *m* punch.
**puño** *m* fist; handful; wrist-band; cuff; handle.

**pupila** *f* pupil (of eye).
**pupitre** *m* desk.
**puré** *m* puree; (thick) soup; **~ de patatas** mashed potatoes *pl*.
**pureza** *f* purity, chastity.
**purga** *f* purge.
**purgante** *m* purgative.
**purgar** *vt* to purge; to purify; to atone, to expiate.
**purgativo/va** *adj* purgative, purging.
**purgatorio** *m* purgatory.
**purificación** *f* purification.
**purificador/ra** *m/f* purifier; * *adj* purifying.
**purificar** *vt* to purify.
**purismo** *m* purism.
**purista** *m* purist.
**puritano/na** *adj* puritanical; * *m/f* Puritan.
**puro/ra** *adj* pure; mere; clear; genuine.
**púrpura** *f* purple.
**purpúreo/rea** *adj* purple.
**purulento/ta** *adj* purulent.
**pus** *m* pus.
**pusilánime** *adj* pusillanimous, fainthearted.
**pusilanimidad** *f* pusillanimity.
**pústula** *f* pustule, pimple.
**puta** *f* whore.
**putrefacción** *f* putrefaction.
**pútrido/da** *adj* putrid, rotten.

# Q

**que** *pn* that; who; which; what; * *conj* that; than.

**qué** *adj* what; which; * *pn* what; which.

**quebrada** *f* broken, uneven ground.

**quebradero** *m* breaker; ~ **de cabeza** worry.

**quebradizo/za** *adj* brittle; flexible.

**quebrado** *m* (*math*) fraction.

**quebradura** *f* fracture; rupture, hernia.

**quebrantamiento** *m* fracture; rupture; breaking; weariness, fatigue; violation (of the law).

**quebrantar** *vt* to break; to crack; to burst; to pound, to grind; to violate; to fatigue; to weaken.

**quebranto** *m* weakness; great loss, severe damage.

**quebrar** *vt* to break; to transgress; to violate (a law); * *vi* to go bankrupt; ~**se** *vr* to break into pieces; to be ruptured.

**queda** *f* resting time; (*mil*) tattoo.

**quedar** *vi* to stay; ~**se** *vr* to remain.

**quedo/da** *adj* quiet, still; * *adv* softly, gently.

**quehacer** *m* task.

**queja** *f* complaint.

**quejarse** *vr* to complain of.

**quejido** *m* complaint.

**quejoso/sa** *adj* complaining, querulous.

**quejumbroso/sa** *adj* complaining, plaintive.

**quema** *f* burning, combustion; fire.

**quemador** *m* burner.

**quemadura** *f* burn.

**quemar** *vt* to burn; to kindle; ~**se** *vr* to be parched with heat; to burn oneself; * *vi* to be too hot.

**quemarropa** *f*: **a ~** *adv* point-blank.

**quemazón** *f* burn; itch.

**querella** *f* charge; dispute; complaint.

**querellarse** *vr* to complain; to file a complaint.

**querer** *vt* to want; to desire; to will; to love; * *m* will, desire.

**querido/da** *adj* dear, beloved; * *m/f* darling; lover; ~ **mío**, ~**da mía** my dear, my love, my darling.

**queroseno** *n* paraffin *m*.

**querubín** *m* cherub.

**quesería** *f* cheesemonger, cheese shop.

**queso** *m* cheese.

**quicio** *m* hook, hinge (of a door).

**quiebra** *f* break, fracture; bankruptcy; slump.

**quien** *pn* who; whom.

**quién** *pn* who; whom.

**quienquiera** *adj* whoever.

**quieto/ta** *adj* still, peaceable.

**quietud** *f* quietness, peace, tranquillity, calmness.

**quijada** *f* jaw; jawbone.

**quijotada** *f* quixotic action.

**quijote** *m* quixotic person.

**quijotesco/ca** *adj* quixotic.

**quilate** *m* carat.

**quilla** *f* keel.

**quimera** *f* chimera.

**quimérico/ca** *adj* chimerical, fantastic.

**química** *f* chemistry.

**químico/ca** *m/f* chemist; * *adj* chemical.

**quimioterapia** *f* chemotherapy.

**quina** *f* Peruvian bark, quinine.

**quincalla** *f* hardware.

**quince** *adj*, *m* fifteen; fifteenth.

**quincena** *f* fortnight.

**quiniela** *f* pools coupon ; ~**s** *fpl* football pools *pl*.

**quinientos/tas** *adj* five hundred.

**quinina** *f* quinine.

**quinquenal** *adj* quinquennial.

**quinquenio** *m* space of five years.

**quinqui** *m* delinquent.

**quinta** *f* country house; levy, drafting of soldiers.

**quintaesencia** *f* quintessence.

**quintilla** *f* (*poet*) metrical composition of five verses.

**quinto** *adj* fifth; * *m* fifth; drafted soldier.

**quíntuplo/pla** *adj* quintuple, fivefold.

**quiosco** *m* bandstand; bookstall.

**quirófano** *m* operating theatre.

**quiromancia** *f* palmistry.

**quirúrgico/ca** *adj* surgical.

**quisquilloso/sa** *adj* difficult, touchy; peevish, irritable.

**quiste** *m* cyst.

**quitaesmalte** *m* nail-polish remover.

**quitamanchas** *m invar* stain remover.

**quitanieves** *m invar* snowplough.

**quitar** *vt* to take away, to remove; to take off; to relieve; to annul; ~**se** *vr* to take off (clothes etc); to withdraw.

**quitasol** *m* parasol.

**quizá, quizás** *adv* perhaps.

# R

**rabadilla** *f* coccyx; rump, croup (of a horse/other four-legged animal).

**rábano** *m* radish.

**rabí** *m* rabbi.

**rabia** *f* rage, fury.

**rabiar** *vt* to be furious, to rage.

**rabieta** *f* touchiness, petulance; fit of bad temper.

**rabino** *m* rabbi.

**rabioso/sa** *adj* rabid; furious.

**rabo** *m* tail.

**racha** *f* gust of wind; **buena/mala ~** spell of good/bad luck.

**racial** *adj* racial, race *compd*.

**racimo** *m* bunch of grapes.

**raciocinio** *m* reasoning; argument.

**ración** *f* ration.

**racional** *adj* rational; reasonable.

**racionalidad** *f* rationality.

**racionar** *vt* to ration (out).

**racismo** *m* racialism.

**racista** *adj*, *m/f* racist.

**radar** *m* radar.

**radiación** *f* radiation.

**radiactivo/va, radioactivo/va** *adj* radioactive.

**radiador** *m* radiator.

**radiante** *adj* radiant.

**radiar** *vt* to radiate.

**radicación** *f* taking root; becoming rooted (of a habit).

**radical** *adj* radical.

**radicar** *vt* to take root; **~se** *vr* to establish oneself.

**radio** *f* radio; radio (set); * *m* radius; ray.

**radiografía** *f* radiography; X-ray.

**radioterapia** *f* radiotherapy.

**raer** *vt* to scrape; to grate; to erase.

**ráfaga** *f* gust; flash; burst.

**rafting** *m* rafting.

**raído/da** *adj* scraped; worn-out; impudent.

**raíz** *f* root; base, basis; origin.

**raja** *f* splinter, chip (of wood); chink, fissure.

**rajar** *vt* to split; to chop, to cleave.

**rajatabla** *f*: **a ~** *adv* strictly.

**ralea** *f* race; breed, species.

**rallador** *m* grater.

**rallar** *vt* to grate.

**ralo/la** *adj* thin, rare.

**rama** *f* branch (of a tree, of a family).

**ramadán** *m* Ramadan.

**ramaje** *m* branches *pl*.

**rambla** *f* avenue.

**ramera** *f* whore, prostitute.

**ramificación** *f* ramification.

**ramificarse** *vr* to ramify.

**ramillete** *m* bunch.

**ramo** *m* branch (of a tree).

**rampa** *f* ramp.

**rampante** *adj* rampant.

**rana** *f* frog.

**ranchera** *f* estate car.

**ranchero** *m* rancher;farmer.

**rancho** *m* grub; farm, ranch; smallholding; settlement, camp.

**rancio/cia** *adj* rank; rancid.

**rango** *m* rank, standing.

**ranúnculo** *m* (*bot*) buttercup.

**ranura** *f* groove; slot.

**rapacidad** *f* rapacity.

**rapadura** *f* shaving; baldness.

**rapar** *vt* to shave; to plunder.

**rapaz/za** *adj* rapacious; * *m/f* young boy/girl.

**rape** *m* quick shave; monkfish.

**rapé** *m* snuff.

**rapidez** *f* speed, rapidity.

**rápido/da** *adj* quick, rapid, swift.

**rapiña** *f* robbery.

**rappel** *m* abseiling.

**raptar** *vt* to kidnap.

**rapto** *m* kidnapping; (*fig*) ecstasy, rapture.

**raqueta** *f* racket.

**raquítico/ca** *adj* stunted; (*fig*) inadequate.

**rareza** *f* rarity, rareness.

**raro/ra** *adj* rare, scarce; extraordinary.

**ras** *m*: **a ~ de** level with; **a ~ de tierra** at ground level.

**rasar** *vt* to level.

**rascacielos** *m invar* skyscraper.

**rascar** *vt* to scratch, to scrape.

**rasgar** *vt* to tear, to rip.

**rasgo** *m* dash, stroke; grand/magnanimous action; **~s** *mpl* features *pl*.

**rasguear** *vi* to form bold strokes with a pen; (*mus*) to strum.

**rasguñar** *vt* to scratch, to scrape.

**rasguño** *m* scratch.

**raso/sa** *adj* plain; flat; * *m* satin; **al raso** in the open air.

**raspa** *f* beard (of an ear of corn); backbone (of fish); stalk (of grapes); rasp.

**raspadura** *f* filing, scraping; filings *pl*.
**raspar** *vt* to scrape, to rasp.
**rastra** *f* rake; **a ~s** by dragging.
**rastreador** *m* tracker.
**rastrear** *vt* to trace; to inquire into; * *vi* to skim along close to the ground (of birds).
**rastrero/ra** *adj* creeping; low, humble, cringing.
**rastrillar** *vt* to rake.
**rastrillo** *m* rake.
**rastro** *m* track; rake; trace.
**rastrojera** *f* stubble field.
**rastrojo** *m* stubble.
**rasurador** *m*, **rasuradora** *f* electric shaver.
**rasurarse** *vr* to shave.
**rata** *f* rat.
**ratería** *f* larceny, petty theft.
**ratero/ra** *adj* creeping, mean, vile; * *m/f* pickpocket; burglar.
**ratificación** *f* ratification.
**ratificar** *vt* to ratify; to approve of.
**rato** *m* moment; **a ~s perdidos** in leisure time.
**ratón** *m* mouse.
**ratonera** *f* mousetrap.
**raudal** *m* torrent.
**raya** *f* stroke; line; part; frontier; ray (fish); roach (fish).
**rayado/da** *adj* ruled; crossed; striped.
**rayar** *vt* to draw lines on; to cross out; to underline; to cross; to rifle.
**rayo** *m* ray, beam (of light).
**rayón** *m* rayon.
**raza** *f* race, lineage; quality.
**razón** *f* reason; right; reasonableness; account; calculation.
**razonable** *adj* reasonable.
**razonado/da** *adj* rational; prudent.
**razonamiento** *m* reasoning; discourse.
**razonar** *vi* to reason; to discourse, to talk.
**reacción** *f* reaction.
**reaccionar** *vi* to react.
**reaccionario/ria** *adj* reactionary.
**reacio/cia** *adj* stubborn.
**reactor** *m* reactor.
**reajuste** *m* readjustment.
**real** *adj* real, actual; royal; * *m* (*mil*) camp.
**realce** *m* embossment; flash; lustre, splendour.
**realidad** *f* reality; sincerity.
**realista** *m* realist; royalist.
**realizador/ra** *m/f* producer (in TV etc).
**realizar** *vt* to realize; to achieve; to undertake.
**realmente** *adv* really, actually.

**realzar** *vt* to raise, to elevate; to emboss; to heighten.
**reanimar** *vt* to cheer, to encourage; to reanimate.
**reanudar** *vt* to renew; to resume.
**reaparición** *f* reappearance.
**reasumir** *vt* to retake, to resume.
**reata** *f* collar, leash; string (of horses).
**rebaja** *f* abatement; deduction; **~s** *fpl* sale.
**rebajar** *vt* to abate, to lessen, to diminish; to lower.
**rebanada** *f* slice.
**rebaño** *m* flock (of sheep), herd (of cattle).
**rebasar** *vt* to exceed.
**rebatir** *vt* to resist; to parry, to ward off; to refute; to repress.
**rebeca** *f* cardigan.
**rebelarse** *vr* to revolt; to rebel; to resist.
**rebelde** *m/f* rebel; * *adj* rebellious.
**rebeldía** *f* rebelliousness, disobedience; (*law*) contumacy; **en ~** by default.
**rebelión** *f* rebellion, revolt.
**rebosar** *vi* to run over, to overflow; to abound.
**rebotar** *vt* to bounce; to clinch; to repel; * *vi* to rebound.
**rebote** *m* rebound; **de ~** on the rebound.
**rebozado/da** *adj* fried in batter/breadcrumbs.
**rebozar** *vt* to wrap up; to fry in batter/breadcrumbs.
**rebullir** *vi* to stir, to begin to move.
**rebuscado/da** *adj* affected; recherché; far-fetched.
**rebuznar** *vi* to bray.
**rebuzno** *m* braying (of an ass).
**recabar** *vt* to obtain by entreaty.
**recado** *m* message; gift.
**recaer** *vi* to fall back.
**recaída** *f* relapse.
**recalcar** *vt* to stress, to emphasize.
**recalcitrante** *adj* recalcitrant.
**recalentamiento** *m* overheating.
**recalentar** *vt* to heat again; to overheat.
**recámara** *f* bedroom.
**recambio** *m* spare; refill.
**recapacitar** *vt* to reflect.
**recapitulación** *f* recapitulation.
**recapitular** *vt* to recapitulate.
**recargado/da** *adj* overloaded.
**recargar** *vt* to overload; to recharge; to charge again.
**recargo** *m* extra load; new charge/accusation.
**recatado/da** *adj* prudent; circumspect; modest

**recato** *m* prudence; circumspection; modesty; bashfulness.

**recaudación** *f* take, income; recovery of debts; tax collector's office.

**recaudador** *m* tax collector.

**recelar** *vt* to gather; to obtain; to recover.

**recelar** *vt* to fear; to suspect, to doubt.

**recelo** *m* dread; suspicion, mistrust.

**receloso/sa** *adj* mistrustful; shy.

**recepción** *f* reception.

**recepcionista** *m/f* receptionist.

**receptáculo** *m* receptacle.

**receptor** *m* receiver; investigating official.

**recesión** *f* (*com*) recession.

**receta** *f* recipe; prescription.

**recetar** *vt* to prescribe.

**rechazar** *vt* to refuse; to repulse; to contradict.

**rechazo** *m* rebound; denial; recoil.

**rechifla** *f* booing; (*fig*) derision.

**rechiflar** *vt* to boo.

**rechinar** *vi* to gnash (teeth).

**rechistar** *vi*: **sin ~** without a murmur.

**rechoncho/cha** *adj* chubby.

**recibidor** *m* entrance hall.

**recibimiento** *m* reception.

**recibir** *vt* to receive, to accept; to let in; to go to meet; **~se** *vr*: **~ de** to qualify as.

**recibo** *m* receipt.

**reciclado/da** *adj* recycled.

**reciclar** *vt* to recycle.

**recién** *adv* recently, lately.

**reciente** *adj* recent; new, fresh; modern.

**recinto** *m* district, precinct.

**recio/cia** *adj* stout; strong, robust; coarse, thick; rude; arduous, rigid; * *adv* strongly, stoutly; **hablar ~** to talk loud.

**recipiente** *m* container.

**reciprocidad** *f* reciprocity.

**recíproco/ca** *adj* reciprocal, mutual.

**recitación** *f* recitation.

**recital** *m* recital; reading.

**recitar** *vt* to recite.

**recitativo/va** *adj* recitative.

**reclamación** *f* claim; reclamation; protest.

**reclamar** *vt* to claim.

**reclamo** *m* claim; advertisement; attraction; decoy bird; catchword (in printing).

**reclinar** *vt* to recline; **~se** *vr* to lean back.

**recluir** *vt* to shut up.

**reclusión** *f* seclusion; prison.

**recluta** *f* recruitment; * *m/f* recruit.

**reclutador** *m* recruitment officer.

**reclutar** *vt* to recruit.

**recobrar** *vt* to recover; **~se** *vr* to recover (from sickness).

**recodo** *m* corner/angle jutting out.

**recogedor** *m* scraper (instrument).

**recoger** *vt* to collect; to retake, to take back; to get; to gather; to shelter; to compile; **~se** *vr* to take shelter/refuge; to retire; to withdraw from the world.

**recogido/da** *adj* retired, secluded; quiet.

**recogimiento** *m* collection; retreat; shelter; abstraction from all worldly concerns.

**recolección** *f* summary; recollection.

**recomendación** *f* recommendation.

**recomendar** *vt* to recommend.

**recompensa** *f* compensation; recompense, reward.

**recompensar** *vt* to recompense, to reward.

**recomponer** *vt* to recompose; to mend.

**reconcentrar** *vt* to concentrate on.

**reconciliación** *f* reconciliation.

**reconciliar** *vt* to reconcile; **~se** *vr* to make one's peace.

**recóndito/ta** *adj* recondite, secret, concealed.

**reconfortar** *vt* to comfort.

**reconocer** *vt* to recognize; to examine closely; to acknowledge; to consider; (*mil*) to reconnoitre.

**reconocido/da** *adj* recognized; grateful.

**reconocimiento** *m* recognition; acknowledgement; gratitude; confession; search; submission; inquiry; (*mil*) reconnaissance.

**reconquista** *f* reconquest.

**reconquistar** *vt* to reconquer.

**reconstituyente** *m* tonic.

**reconstruir** *vt* to reconstruct.

**reconvenir** *vt* to return the accusations of.

**reconversión** *f*: **~ industrial** industrial rationalization.

**recopilación** *f* summary, abridgement.

**recopilador** *m* compiler.

**recopilar** *vt* to compile.

**récord** *adj invar* record; * *m* record.

**recordar** *vt* to remember; to remind; * *vi* to remember.

**recorrer** *vt* to run over, to peruse; to cover.

**recortar** *vt* to cut out.

**recorte** *m* cutting; trimming.

**recostar** *vt* to lean, to recline; **~se** *vr* to lie down.

**recoveco** *m* cubbyhole; bend.

**recrear** *vt* to amuse, to entertain; to delight.

**recreativo/va** *adj* recreational.

**recreo** *m* recreation; playtime (at school).

**recriminación** *f* recrimination.

**recriminar** *vt* to recriminate.

**recrudecer** *vt, vi,* ~**se** *vr* to worsen.

**recrudecimiento** *m* upsurge.

**recta** *f* straight line.

**rectángulo/la** *adj* rectangular; * *m* rectangle.

**rectificación** *f* rectification.

**rectificar** *vt* to rectify.

**rectilíneo/nea** *adj* rectilinear.

**rectitud** *f* straightness; rectitude; justness, honesty; exactitude.

**recto/ta** *adj* straight; right; just, honest; * *m* rectum.

**rector/ra** *m/f* superior of a community/establishment; vice-chancellor (of a university); curate, rector; * *adj* governing.

**rectorado** *m* rectorship; vice-chancellorship.

**rectoría** *f* rectory; rectorship.

**recua** *f* train (of mules, pack animals).

**recuadro** *m* box; inset.

**recuento** *m* inventory.

**recuerdo** *m* souvenir; memory.

**recular** *vi* to fall back, to recoil.

**recuperable** *adj* recoverable.

**recuperación** *f* recovery.

**recuperar** *vt* to recover; ~**se** *vr* to recover (from sickness).

**recurrir** *vi*: ~ **a** to resort to.

**recurso** *m* recourse.

**recusación** *f* refusal.

**recusar** *vt* to refuse; to refuse to admit.

**red** *f* net; network; snare.

**redacción** *f* editing; editor's office.

**redactar** *vt* to draft; to edit.

**redactor/ra** *m/f* editor.

**redada** *f*: ~ **policial** police raid.

**redecilla** *f* hairnet.

**rededor** *m* environs *pl*; **al** ~ round about.

**redención** *f* redemption.

**redentor/ra** *m/f* redeemer.

**redescubrir** *vt* to rediscover.

**redicho/cha** *adj* affected.

**redil** *m* sheepfold.

**redimible** *adj* redeemable.

**redimir** *vt* to redeem; to ransom.

**rédito** *m* revenue, rent.

**redoblado/da** *adj* redoubled; stout and thick; reinforced.

**redoblar** *vt* to redouble; to rivet.

**redoble** *m* doubling, repetition; (*mil*) roll of a drum.

**redomado/da** *adj* sly; out-and-out.

**redondear** *vt* to round.

**redondel** *m* circle; traffic roundabout.

**redondez** *f* roundness, circular form.

**redondo/da** *adj* round; complete.

**reducción** *f* reduction.

**reducible** *adj* reducible; convertible.

**reducido/da** *adj* reduced; limited; small.

**reducir** *adj* to reduce; to limit; ~**se** *vr* to diminish.

**reducto** *m* (*mil*) redoubt.

**redundancia** *f* superfluity, redundancy, excess.

**redundar** *vi* to contribute.

**reelegir** *vt* to re-elect, to elect again.

**reembolsar** *vt* to refund; to reimburse.

**reembolso** *m* reimbursement; refund; **contra** ~ C.O.D.

**reemplazar** *vt* to replace; to restore.

**reemplazo** *m* replacement; reserve.

**reenganchar** *vt* (*mil*) to re-enlist; ~**se** *vr* to enlist again.

**referencia** *f* reference.

**referéndum** *m* referendum.

**referir** *vt* to refer, to relate, to report; ~**se** *vr* to refer/relate to.

**refilón** *m*: **de** ~ *adv* obliquely.

**refinado/da** *adj* refined; subtle, artful.

**refinar** *vt* to refine.

**refinería** *f* refinery.

**reflejar** *vt* to reflect.

**reflejo** *m* reflex; reflection.

**reflexión** *f* meditation, reflection.

**reflexionar** *vt* to reflect on; * *vi* to reflect, to meditate.

**reflexivo/va** *adj* reflexive; thoughtful.

**reflujo** *m* reflux, ebb; **flujo y** ~ the tides *pl*.

**reforma** *f* reform; correction; repair.

**reformar** *vt* to reform; to correct; to restore; ~**se** *vr* to mend.

**reformatorio** *m* reformatory.

**reforzar** *vt* to strengthen, to fortify; to encourage.

**refracción** *f* refraction.

**refractario/ria** *adj* refractory.

**refrán** *m* proverb.

**refregar** *vt* to scrub.

**refrenar** *vt* to refrain; to check.

**refrendar** *vt* to countersign; to approve.

**refrescante** *adj* refreshing.

**refrescar** *vt* to refresh; ~**se** *vr* to get cooler; to go out for a breath of fresh air; * *vi* to cool down.

**refresco** *m* refreshment.

**refriega** *f* affray, skirmish, fray.

**refrigerador** *m*, **refrigeradora** *f* refrigerator, fridge.

**refrigerar** *vt* to cool; to refresh; to refrigerate; to comfort.

**refrigerio** *m* refrigeration; refreshment; consolation, comfort.

**refuerzo** *m* reinforcement.

**refugiado/da** *m/f* refugee.

**refugiar** *vt* to shelter; **~se** *vr* to take refuge.

**refugio** *m* refuge, asylum.

**refulgir** *vi* to shine.

**refunfuñar** *vi* to snarl; to growl; to grumble.

**refutación** *f* refutation.

**refutar** *vt* to refute.

**regadera** *f* watering can.

**regadío** *m* irrigated land.

**regalar** *vt* to give (as present); to give away; to pamper; to caress.

**regalía** *f* regalia; bonus; royalty; privilege.

**regaliz** *m* liquorice.

**regalo** *m* present, gift; pleasure; comfort.

**regañadientes**: **a ~** *adv* reluctantly.

**regañar** *vt* to scold; * *vi* to growl; to grumble; to quarrel.

**regañón/ona** *adj* snarling, growling; grumbling; troublesome.

**regar** *vt* to water, to irrigate.

**regata** *f* irrigation ditch; regatta.

**regatear** *vt* (*com*) to bargain over; to be mean with; * *vi* to haggle; to dribble (in sport).

**regateo** *m* haggling; bartering; dribbling.

**regazo** *m* lap.

**regencia** *f* regency.

**regeneración** *f* regeneration.

**regenerar** *vt* to regenerate.

**regentar** *vt* to rule; to govern.

**regente** *m* regent; manager.

**régimen** *m* regime, management; diet; (*gr*) rules *pl* of verbs.

**regimiento** *m* regime; (*mil*) regiment.

**regio/gia** *adj* royal, regal.

**región** *f* region.

**regir** *vt* to rule, to govern; to direct; * *vi* to apply.

**registrador/ra** *m/f* registrar; controller.

**registrar** *vt* to survey; to inspect, to examine; to record, to enter in a register; **~se** *vr* to register; to happen.

**registro** *m* examining; enrolling office; register; registration.

**regla** *f* rule, ruler; period.

**reglamentar** *vt* to regulate.

**reglamentario/ria** *adj* statutory.

**reglamento** *m* regulation; bylaw/bye-law.

**regocijar** *vt* to gladden; **~se** *vr* to rejoice.

**regocijo** *m* joy, pleasure; merriment, rejoicing.

**regodearse** *vr* to be delighted; to trifle, to play the fool; to joke, to jest.

**regodeo** *m* joy, merriment.

**regordete** *adj* chubby, plump.

**regresar** *vi* to return, to go back.

**regreso** *m* return, regression.

**reguero** *m* small rivulet; trickle of spilt liquid; drain, gutter.

**regulación** *f* regulation.

**regulador/ra** *m/f* regulator; knob, control.

**regular** *vt* to regulate, to adjust; * *adj* regular; ordinary.

**regularidad** *f* regularity.

**regularizar** *vt* to regularize.

**rehabilitación** *f* rehabilitation.

**rehabilitar** *vt* to rehabilitate.

**rehacer** *vt* to repair, to make again; to redo; **~se** *vr* to recover; (*mil*) to rally.

**rehén** *m* hostage.

**rehuir** *vt* to avoid.

**rehusar** *vt* to refuse, to decline.

**reimpresión** *f* reprint.

**reimprimir** *vt* to reprint.

**reina** *f* queen.

**reinado** *m* reign.

**reinante** *adj* (*fig*) prevailing.

**reinar** *vi* to reign; to govern.

**reincidencia** *f* relapse.

**reincidir** *vi*: **~ en** to relapse into, to fall back into.

**reino** *m* kingdom, reign.

**reintegración** *f* reintegration, restoration.

**reintegrar** *vt* to reintegrate, to restore; **~se** *vr* to be reinstated/restored.

**reintegro** *m* reintegration.

**reír(se)** *vi* (*vr*) to laugh.

**reiteración** *f* repetition, reiteration.

**reiterar** *vt* to reiterate, to repeat.

**reivindicación** *f* claim; vindication.

**reivindicar** *vt* to claim.

**reja** *f* ploughshare; lattice, grating.

**rejilla** *f* grating, grille; vent; luggage rack.

**rejoneador** *m* mounted bullfighter.

**rejonear** *vt* to spear (bulls).

**rejuvenecer** *vt*, *vi* to rejuvenate.

**relación** *f* relation; relationship; report; account.

**relacionar** *vt* to relate.

**relajación** *f* relaxation; remission; laxity.

**relajar** *vt* to relax, to slacken; **~se** *vr* to relax.

**relamerse** *vr* to lick one's lips; to relish.

**relamido/da** *adj* affected; overdressed.

**relámpago** *m* flash of lightning.

**relampaguear** *vi* to flash.

**relatar** *vt* to relate, to tell.

**relativo/va** *adj* relative.

**relato** *m* story; recital.

**relax** *m* relaxation.

**releer** *vt* to reread.

**relegación** *f* relegation; exile.

**relegar** *vt* to relegate; to banish, to exile.

**relente** *m* evening dew.

**relevante** *adj* excellent, great; eminent.

**relevar** *vt* to emboss, to work in relief; to exonerate; to relieve; to assist.

**relevo** *m* (*mil*) relief.

**relicario** *m* reliquary.

**relieve** *m* relief; (*fig*) prominence.

**religión** *f* religion.

**religiosidad** *f* religiousness.

**religioso/sa** *adj* religious.

**relinchar** *vi* to neigh.

**relincho** *m* neigh, neighing.

**reliquia** *f* residue, remains *pl*; (saintly) relic.

**rellano** *m* landing (of stairs).

**rellenar** *vt* to fill up; to stuff.

**relleno/na** *adj* satiated, full up; stuffed; * *m* stuffing.

**reloj** *m* clock; watch.

**relojero** *m* watchmaker.

**relucir** *vi* to shine, to glitter; to excel, to be brilliant.

**relumbrar** *vi* to sparkle, to shine.

**remachar** *vt* to rivet; (*fig*) to drive home.

**remanente** *m* remainder; (*com*) balance; surplus.

**remangar** *vt* to roll up.

**remansarse** *vr* to form a pool.

**remanso** *m* stagnant water; quiet place.

**remar** *vi* to row.

**rematadamente** *adv* entirely, totally.

**rematado/da** *adj* utter, complete.

**rematar** *vt* to terminate, to finish; to sell off cheaply; * *vi* to end.

**remate** *m* end, conclusion; shot; tip; last/best bid.

**remedar** *vt* to copy, to imitate; to mimic.

**remediable** *adj* remediable.

**remediar** *vt* to remedy; to assist, to help; to free from danger; to avoid.

**remedio** *m* amendment, correction; recourse; refuge.

**remedo** *m* imitation, copy.

**remendar** *vt* to patch, to mend; to correct.

**remero** *m* rower, oarsman.

**remesa** *f* shipment; remittance.

**remiendo** *m* patch; mend.

**remilgado/da** *adj* prim; affected.

**remilgo** *m* primness, affectation.

**reminiscencia** *f* reminiscence, recollection.

**remiso/sa** *adj* remiss, careless; indolent.

**remitente** *m* sender.

**remitir** *vt* to remit, to send; to pardon (a fault); to suspend, to put off; * *vi*, ~**se** *vr* to slacken.

**remo** *m* oar; rowing.

**remojar** *vt* to steep; to dunk.

**remojo** *m* steeping, soaking.

**remolacha** *f* beet (as in sugar beet).

**remolcar** *vt* to tow.

**remolino** *m* whirlwind; whirlpool; crowd.

**remolón/ona** *adj* stubborn; lazy.

**remolque** *m* tow, towing; tow rope.

**remontar** *vt* to mend; ~**se** *vr* to tower, to soar.

**remorder** *vt* to disturb.

**remordimiento** *m* remorse.

**remoto/ta** *adj* remote, distant; far.

**remover** *vt* to stir; to move around.

**remozar** *vt* to rejuvenate; to renovate.

**remuneración** *f* remuneration, recompense.

**remunerador/ra** *m/f* remunerator.

**remunerar** *vt* to reward, to remunerate.

**renacer** *vi* to be born again; to revive.

**renacimiento** *m* regeneration; rebirth.

**renacuajo** *m* tadpole.

**renal** *adj* renal, kidney *compd*.

**rencilla** *f* quarrel.

**rencor** *m* rancour, grudge.

**rencoroso/sa** *adj* rancorous.

**rendición** *f* surrender; profit.

**rendido/da** *adj* submissive; exhausted.

**rendija** *f* crevice, crack, cleft.

**rendimiento** *m* output; efficiency.

**rendir** *vt* to subject, to subdue; ~**se** *vr* to yield; to surrender; to be tired out.

**renegado** *m* apostate; wicked person.

**renegar** *vt* to deny; to disown; to detest, to abhor; * *vi* to apostatize; to blaspheme, to curse.

**renglón** *m* line; item.

**reno** *m* reindeer.

**renombrado/da** *adj* renowned.

**renombre** *m* renown.

**renovación** *f* renovation; renewal.

**renovar** *vt* to renew; to renovate; to reform.

**renquear** *vi* to limp.

**renta** *f* income; rent; profit.

**renuncia** *f* renunciation; resignation.

**renunciar** *vt* to renounce; * *vi* to resign.

**reñido/da** *adj* at variance, at odds; hard-fought.

**reñir** *vt*, *vi* to wrangle, to quarrel; to scold, to chide.

**reo** *m* offender, criminal.

**reojo** *m*: **mirar de ~** to look at furtively.

**reparación** *f* repair; reparation.

**reparar** *vt* to repair; to consider, to observe; to parry; * *vi*: **~ en** to notice; to pass (at cards).

**reparo** *m* repair, reparation; consideration; difficulty.

**repartición** *f* distribution.

**repartidor** *m/f* distributor; assessor of taxes.

**repartir** *vt* to distribute; to deliver.

**reparto** *m* distribution; delivery; cost; property development.

**repasar** *vt* to pass again; to revise; to check; to mend.

**repaso** *m* revision; check-up.

**repatriar** *vt* to repatriate.

**repecho** *m* slope.

**repelente** *adj* repellent, repulsive.

**repeler** *vt* to repel; to refute, to reject.

**repente**: **de ~** *adv* suddenly.

**repentino/na** *adj* sudden, unforeseen.

**repercusión** *f* reverberation.

**repercutir** *vi* to reverberate; to rebound.

**repertorio** *m* repertory; index; list.

**repetición** *f* repetition; (*mus*) encore.

**repetidor/ra** *m/f* repeater.

**repetir** *vt*, *vi* to repeat.

**repicar** *vt* to ring.

**repique** *m* chime.

**repiquetear** *vt* to ring merrily.

**repisa** *f* pedestal, stand; shelf; windowsill.

**replegar** *vt* to redouble; to fold over; **~se** *vr* (*mil*) to fall back.

**repleto/ta** *adj* replete, very full.

**réplica** *f* reply, answer; repartee.

**replicar** *vi* to reply.

**repoblación** *f* repopulation; restocking; **~ forestal** reforestation.

**repoblar** *vt* to repopulate; to reforest.

**repollo** *m* cabbage.

**reponer** *vt* to replace; to restore; **~se** *vr* to recover lost health/property.

**reportaje** *m* report, article.

**reportero/ra** *m/f* reporter.

**reposado/da** *adj* quiet, peaceful; settled (wine).

**reposar** *vi* to rest, to repose.

**reposición** *f* replacement; remake.

**reposo** *m* rest, repose.

**repostería** *f* confectioner's (shop).

**repostero** *m* confectioner.

**reprender** *vt* to reprimand.

**represa** *f* dam; lake.

**represalia** *f* reprisal.

**representación** *f* representation; authority.

**representante** *m/f* representative; understudy (theatre).

**representar** *vt* to represent; to play on the stage; to look (age).

**representativo/va** *adj* representative.

**represión** *f* repression.

**reprimenda** *f* reprimand.

**reprimir** *vt* to repress; to check; to contain.

**reprobable** *adj* reprehensible.

**reprobación** *f* reprobation, reproof.

**reprobar** *vt* to reject; to condemn, to upbraid.

**réprobo** *m* reprobate.

**reprochar** *vt* to reproach.

**reproche** *m* reproach.

**reproducción** *f* reproduction.

**reproducir** *vt* to reproduce.

**reptil** *m* reptile.

**república** *f* republic.

**republicano/na** *adj*, *m/f* republican.

**repudiar** *vt* to repudiate.

**repudio** *m* repudiation.

**repuesto** *m* supply; spare part.

**repugnancia** *f* reluctance; repugnance.

**repugnante** *adj* repugnant.

**repugnar** *vt* to disgust.

**repulsa** *f* refusal.

**repulsar** *vt* to reject; to decline, to refuse.

**repulsión** *f* repulsion.

**repulsivo/va** *adj* repulsive.

**reputación** *f* reputation, renown.

**reputar** to consider.

**requebrar** *vt* to woo, to court.

**requerimiento** *m* request; requisition; intimation; summons.

**requerir** *vt* to intimate, to notify; to request; to require, to need; to summon.

**requesón** *m* cottage cheese.

**requiebro** *m* endearing expression.

**réquiem** *m* requiem.

**requisa** *f* inspection; (*mil*) requisition.

**requisito** *m* requisite.

**res** *f* animal; 100 **~es** 100 head of cattle.

**resabio** *m* (unpleasant) aftertaste; vicious habit, bad custom.

**resaca** *f* surge, surf; (*fig*) backlash; (*col*) hangover.

**resaltar** *vi* to rebound; to jut out; to be evident; to stand out.

**resarcimiento** *m* compensation, reparation.

**resarcir** vt to compensate, to make amends for.

**resbaladizo/za** adj slippery.

**resbalar(se)** vi (vr) to slip, to slide.

**resbalón** m slip, slide.

**rescatar** vt to ransom, to redeem.

**rescate** m ransom.

**rescindir** vt to rescind, to annul.

**rescisión** f rescindment, revocation.

**rescoldo** m embers pl, cinders pl.

**resecarse** vr to dry up.

**reseco/ca** adj very dry.

**resentido/da** adj resentful.

**resentimiento** m resentment.

**resentirse** vr: ~ de to suffer; ~ con to resent.

**reseña** f review; account.

**reseñar** vt to describe; to review.

**reserva** f reserve; reservation.

**reservado/da** adj reserved, cautious, circumspect.

**reservar** vt to keep; to reserve; ~se vr to preserve oneself; to keep to oneself.

**resfriado** m cold.

**resfriarse** vr to catch cold.

**resguardar** vt to preserve, to defend; ~se vr to be on one's guard.

**resguardo** m guard; security, safety; voucher; receipt.

**residencia** f residence.

**residente** adj residing, resident; * m/f resident.

**residir** vi to reside, to dwell.

**residuo** m residue, remainder.

**resignación** f resignation.

**resignadamente** adv resignedly.

**resignarse** vr to resign oneself.

**resina** f resin.

**resinoso/sa** adj resinous.

**resistencia** f resistance, opposition.

**resistente** adj strong; resistant.

**resistir** vt to resist, to oppose; to put up with; * vi to resist; to hold out.

**resma** f ream (of paper).

**resol** m glare (of the sun).

**resollar** vi to wheeze; to breath with difficulty.

**resolución** f resolution, boldness; decision.

**resolver** vt to resolve, to decide; to analyse; ~se vr to resolve, to determine.

**resonar** vi to resound.

**resoplar** vi to snore; to snort.

**resoplido** m heavy breathing.

**resorte** m spring.

**respaldar** vt to endorse; ~se vr to lean back.

**respaldo** m backing; endorsement; back of a seat.

**respectivo/va** adj respective.

**respecto** m respect; relation; **al** ~ on this matter.

**respetable** adj respectable.

**respetar** vt to respect; to revere.

**respeto** m respect, regard, consideration; homage.

**respetuoso/sa** adj respectful.

**respingar** vi to shy.

**respingo** m start; jump.

**respiración** f respiration, breathing.

**respiradero** m vent, breathing hole; rest, repose.

**respirar** vi to breathe.

**respiratorio/ria** adj respiratory.

**respiro** m breathing; (fig) respite.

**resplandecer** vi to shine; to glisten.

**resplandeciente** adj resplendent.

**resplandor** m splendour, brilliance.

**responder** vt to answer; * vi to answer; to correspond; ~ de to be responsible for.

**respondón/ona** adj ever ready to reply; cheeky.

**responsable** adj responsible; accountable, answerable.

**responsabilidad** f responsibility.

**responsabilizarse** vr to take charge.

**responso** m prayer for the dead.

**respuesta** f answer, reply.

**resquemor** m resentment.

**resquicio** m crack, cleft; (fig) chance.

**restablecer** vt to re-establish; ~se vr to recover.

**restablecimiento** m re-establishment.

**restallar** vi to crack; to click.

**restante** adj remaining.

**restar** vt to subtract, to take away; * vi to be left.

**restauración** f restoration.

**restaurante** m restaurant.

**restaurar** vt to restore.

**restitución** f restitution.

**restituir** vt to restore; to return.

**resto** m remainder, rest.

**restregar** vt to scrub, to rub.

**restricción** f restriction, limitation.

**restringir** vt to restrict, to limit; to restrain.

**resucitar** vt to resuscitate, to revive; to renew.

**resuello** m breath, breathing.

**resuelto/ta** adj resolute, determined; prompt.

**resultado** *m* result, consequence.
**resultar** *vi* to be; to turn out; to amount to.
**resumen** *m* summary.
**resumidamente** *adv* summarily.
**resumir** *vt* to abridge; to sum up; to summarize.
**resurrección** *f* resurrection, revival.
**retablo** *m* picture drawn on a board; splendid altarpiece.
**retaguardia** *f* rearguard.
**retahíla** *f* range, series.
**retal** *m* remnant.
**retar** *vt* to challenge.
**retardar** *vt* to retard; to delay.
**retardo** *m* delay.
**retazo** *m* remnant; cutting.
**retención** *f* retention.
**retener** *vt* to retain, to keep back.
**retentiva** *f* memory.
**reticencia** *f* reticence.
**retina** *f* retina.
**retintín** *m* tinkling sound; affected tone of voice.
**retirada** *f* (*mil*) retreat, withdrawal; recall.
**retirar** *vt* to withdraw, to retire; to remove; **~se** *vr* to retire, to retreat; to go to bed.
**retiro** *m* retreat, retirement; pension.
**reto** *m* challenge; threat, menace.
**retocar** *vt* to retouch; to mend; to finish off (work).
**retoñar** *vi* to sprout.
**retoño** *m* sprout; offspring.
**retoque** *m* finishing stroke; retouching.
**retorcer** *vt* to twist; to wring.
**retorcimiento** *m* twisting, contortion.
**retórica** *f* rhetoric.
**retórico/ca** *adj* rhetorical; * *f* rhetoric; affectedness.
**retornar** *vt, vi* to return.
**retorno** *m* return; barter, exchange.
**retortero: andar al ~** to bustle about.
**retortijón** *m* twisting; **~ de tripas** stomach cramp.
**retozar** *vi* to frisk, to skip.
**retozo** *m* romp.
**retozón/ona** *adj* wanton; romping.
**retracción** *f* retraction.
**retractar** *vt* to retract.
**retraer** *vt* to draw back; to dissuade; **~se** *vr* to take refuge; to flee.
**retraído/da** *adj* shy.
**retransmisión** *f* broadcast.
**retransmitir** *vt* to broadcast; to relay; to retransmit.

**retrasado/da** *adj* late; (*med*) mentally retarded; backward.
**retraso** *m* delay; slowness; backwardness; lateness; (*rail*): **el tren ha tenido ~** the train is overdue/late.
**retratar** *vt* to portray; to photograph; to describe.
**retrato** *m* portrait, effigy.
**retreta** *f* (*mil*) retreat.
**retrete** *m* toilet, lavatory.
**retribución** *f* retribution.
**retribuir** *vt* to repay.
**retroacción** *f* retroaction.
**retroactivo/va** *adj* retroactive.
**retroceder** *vi* to go backward(s), to fly back; to back down.
**retrógrado/da** *adj* retrograde; reactionary.
**retrospectivo/va** *adj* retrospective.
**retrovisor** *m* rear-view mirror.
**retumbar** *vi* to resound, to jingle.
**reuma** *f* rheumatism.
**reumático/ca** *adj* rheumatic.
**reumatismo** *m* rheumatism.
**reunión** *f* reunion, meeting.
**reunir** *vt* to reunite; to unite; **~se** *vr* to gather, to meet.
**revalidación** *f* confirmation, ratification.
**revalidar** *vt* to ratify, to confirm.
**revancha** *f* revenge.
**revelación** *f* revelation.
**revelado** *m* developing.
**revelar** *vt* to reveal; to develop (photographs).
**reventar** *vi* to burst, to explode; to toil, to overwork.
**reventón** *m* (*auto*) blow-out.
**reverberación** *f* reverberation.
**reverberar** *vi* to reverberate.
**reverdecer** *vi* to grow green again; to revive.
**reverencia** *f* reverence, veneration; respect.
**reverenciar** *vt* to venerate, to revere.
**reverendo/da** *adj* reverend.
**reverente** *adj* respectful, reverent.
**reverso** *m* reverse.
**revés** *m* back; wrong side; disappointment, setback.
**revestir** *vt* to put on; to coat, to cover.
**revisar** *vt* to revise, to review.
**revisión** *f* revision.
**revisor/ra** *m/f* inspector; ticket collector.
**revista** *f* magazine; review, revision.
**revivir** *vi* to revive.
**revocación** *f* revocation.
**revocar** *vt* to revoke.
**revolcarse** *vr* to wallow.

**revolotear** *vi* to flutter.
**revoloteo** *m* fluttering.
**revoltijo** *m* confusion, disorder.
**revoltoso/sa** *adj* rebellious, unruly.
**revolución** *f* revolution.
**revolucionario/ria** *adj*, *m/f* revolutionary.
**revolver** *vt* to move about; to turn around; to mess up; to revolve; ~se *vr* to turn round; to change (of the weather).
**revólver** *m* revolver.
**revuelo** *m* fluttering; (*fig*) commotion.
**revuelta** *f* turn; disturbance, revolt.
**rey** *m* king; king (in cards/chess).
**reyerta** *f* quarrel, brawl.
**rezagar** *vt* to leave behind; to defer; ~se *vr* to remain behind.
**rezar** *vi* to pray, to say one's prayers.
**rezo** *m* prayer.
**rezongar** *vi* to grumble.
**rezumar** *vt* to ooze, to leak.
**ría** *f* estuary.
**riada** *f* flood.
**ribera** *f* shore, bank.
**ribereño/ña** *adj* coastal; riverside.
**ribete** *m* trimming; seam, border.
**ribetear** *vt* to hem, to border.
**ricino** *m*: **aceite de ~** castor oil.
**rico/ca** *adj* rich; delicious; lovely; cute.
**ridiculez** *f* absurdity.
**ridiculizar** *vt* to ridicule.
**ridículo/la** *adj* ridiculous.
**riego** *m* irrigation.
**riel** *m* (*rail*) rail.
**rienda** *f* rein of a bridle; **dar ~ suelta** to give free rein to.
**riesgo** *m* risk, danger.
**rifa** *f* raffle, lottery.
**rifar** *vt* to raffle.
**rifle** *m* rifle.
**rigidez** *f* rigidity.
**rígido/da** *adj* rigid, inflexible; severe.
**rigor** *m* rigour.
**riguroso/sa** *adj* rigorous.
**rima** *f* rhyme.
**rimar** *vi* to rhyme.
**rimbombante** *adj* pompous.
**rímel, rimmel** *m* mascara.
**rincón** *m* (inside) corner.
**rinoceronte** *m* rhinoceros.
**riña** *f* quarrel, dispute.
**riñón** *m* kidney.
**río** *m* river, stream.
**rioja** *m* rioja (wine).
**riqueza** *f* riches *pl*, wealth.
**risa** *f* laugh, laughter.

**risco** *m* steep rock.
**risible** *adj* risible, laughable.
**risotada** *f* loud laugh.
**ristra** *f* string.
**risueño/na** *adj* smiling.
**rítmico/ca** *adj* rhythmic.
**ritmo** *m* rhythm.
**rito** *m* rite, ceremony.
**ritual** *adj*, *m* ritual.
**rival** *adj*, *m/f* rival.
**rivalidad** *f* rivalry.
**rivalizar** *vi*: ~ **con** to rival, to vie with.
**rizado/da** *adj* curly.
**rizar** *vt* to curl (hair).
**rizo** *m* curl; ripple (on water).
**robar** *vt* to rob; to steal; to break into.
**roble** *m* oak tree.
**robledal** *m* oakwood.
**robo** *m* robbery; theft.
**robot** *m* robot.
**robustez** *f* robustness.
**robusto/ta** *adj* robust, strong.
**roca** *f* rock.
**rocalla** *f* pebbles *pl*.
**roce** *m* rub; brush; friction.
**rociada** *f* sprinkling; spray, shower.
**rociar** *vt* to sprinkle; to spray.
**rocín** *m* nag; hack; stupid person.
**rocío** *m* dew.
**rocoso/sa** *adj* rocky.
**rodada** *f* rut, track of a wheel.
**rodadura** *f* act of rolling.
**rodaja** *f* slice.
**rodaje** *m* filming; **en ~** (*auto*) running in.
**rodar** *vi* to roll.
**rodear** *vi* to make a detour; * *vt* to surround, to enclose.
**rodeo** *m* detour; subterfuge; evasion; rodeo.
**rodilla** *f* knee; **de ~s** on one's knees.
**rodillo** *m* roller.
**roedor/ra** *adj* gnawing; * *m* rodent.
**roedura** *f* gnawing.
**roer** *vt* to gnaw; to corrode.
**rogar** *vt*, *vi* to ask for; to beg, to entreat; to pray.
**rogativa** *f* supplication, prayer.
**rojez** *f* redness.
**rojizo/za** *adj* reddish.
**rojo/ja** *adj* red; ruddy.
**rol** *m* list, roll, catalogue; role.
**rollizo/za** *adj* round; plump, chubby.
**rollo** *m* roll; coil.
**romance** *m* Romance language; romance.
**romancero** *m* collection of romances/ballads.

**romanticismo** *m* romanticism.
**romántico/ca** *adj* romantic.
**rombo** *m* rhombus.
**romboide** *m* rhomboid.
**romería** *f* pilgrimage.
**romero** *m* (*bot*) rosemary.
**romo/ma** *adj* blunt; snub-nosed.
**rompecabezas** *m invar* riddle; jigsaw.
**romper** *vt* to break; to tear up; to wear out; to break up (land); * *vi* to break (of waves); to break through.
**rompimiento** *m* tearing, breaking; crack.
**ron** *m* rum.
**roncar** *vi* to snore; to roar.
**roncha** *f* weal, bruise.
**ronco/ca** *adj* hoarse; husky; raucous.
**ronda** *f* night patrol; round (of drinks, cards etc).
**rondar** *vt*, *vi* to patrol; to prowl around.
**ronquera** *f* hoarseness.
**ronquido** *m* snore; roar.
**ronzal** *m* halter.
**ronronear** *vi* to purr.
**roña** *f* scab, mange; grime; rust.
**roñoso/sa** *adj* filthy; mean.
**ropa** *f* clothes *pl*; clothing; dress.
**ropaje** *m* gown, robes *pl*; drapery.
**ropero** *m* linen cupboard; closet.
**rosa** *f* rose; birthmark.
**rosado/da** *adj* pink; rosy.
**rosal** *m* rosebush.
**rosario** *m* rosary.
**rosca** *f* thread (of a screw); coil, spiral.
**rosetón** *m* rosette; rose window, wheel window.
**rosquilla** *f* doughnut.
**rostro** *m* face.
**rotación** *f* rotation.
**roto/ta** *adj* broken, destroyed; debauched.
**rótula** *f* kneecap; ball-and-socket joint.
**rotulador** *m* felt-tip/fibre-tip pen.
**rotular** *vt* to inscribe, to label.
**rótulo** *m* inscription; label, ticket; placard, poster.
**rotundo/da** *adj* round; emphatic.
**rotura** *f* breaking; crack; tear.
**roturar** *vt* to plough.
**rozadura** *f* graze, scratch.
**rozar** *vt* to rub; to chafe; to nibble (the grass); to scrape; to touch lightly.

**rubí** *m* ruby.
**rubicundo/da** *adj* reddish.
**rubio/bia** *adj* fair-haired, blond/blonde; * *m/f* blond/blonde.
**rubor** *m* blush; bashfulness.
**rúbrica** *f* red mark; flourish at the end of a signature; title, heading, rubric.
**rubricar** *vt* to sign with a flourish; to sign and seal.
**rudeza** *f* roughness, rudeness; stupidity.
**rudimento** *m* principle; beginning; ~s *mpl* rudiments *pl*.
**rudo/da** *adj* rough, coarse; plain, simple; stupid.
**rueca** *f* distaff.
**rueda** *f* wheel; circle; slice, round.
**ruedo** *m* rotation; border, selvage; arena, bullring.
**ruego** *m* request, entreaty.
**rufián** *m* pimp, pander; lout.
**rugby** *m* rugby.
**rugido** *m* roar.
**rugir** *vi* to roar, to bellow.
**rugoso/sa** *adj* wrinkled.
**ruibarbo** *m* rhubarb.
**ruido** *m* noise, sound; din, row; fuss.
**ruidoso/sa** *adj* noisy, loud.
**ruin** *adj* mean, despicable; mean, stingy.
**ruina** *f* ruin, collapse; downfall, destruction; ~s *fpl* ruins *pl*.
**ruindad** *f* meanness, lowness; mean act.
**ruinoso/sa** *adj* ruinous, disastrous.
**ruiseñor** *m* nightingale.
**ruleta** *f* roulette.
**rulo** *m* rolling pin; hair curler.
**rumba** *f* rumba.
**rumbo** *m* (*mar*) course, bearing; road, route, way; course of events, pomp, ostentation.
**rumboso/sa** *adj* generous, lavish.
**rumiante** *m* ruminant.
**rumiar** *vt* to chew; * *vi* to ruminate.
**rumor** *m* rumour; murmur.
**runrún** *m* rumour; sound of voices, whirr.
**ruptura** *f* rupture.
**rural** *adj* rural.
**rusticidad** *f* rusticity; coarseness.
**rústico/ca** *adj* rustic; * *m/f* peasant.
**ruta** *f* route, itinerary.
**rutina** *f* routine; habit.

# S

**sábado** *m* Saturday; (Jewish) Sabbath.

**sábana** *f* sheet; altar cloth.

**sabandija** *f* insect.

**sabañón** *m* chilblain.

**sabelotodo** *m/f invar* know-all.

**saber** *vt* to know; to be able to; to find out, to learn; to experience; * *vi*: ~ **a** to taste of; * *m* learning, knowledge.

**sabiduría** *f* learning, knowledge; wisdom.

**sabiendas** *adv*: **a** ~ knowingly.

**sabihondo/da** *adj* know-all; pedantic.

**sabio/bia** *adj* sage, wise; * *m/f* sage, wise person.

**sablazo** *m* sword wound; (*col*) sponging, scrounging.

**sable** *m* sabre, cutlass.

**sabor** *m* taste, savour, flavour.

**saborear** *vt* to savour, to taste; to enjoy.

**sabotaje** *m* sabotage.

**saboteador/ora** *m/f* saboteur.

**sabotear** *vt* to sabotage.

**sabroso/sa** *adj* tasty, delicious; pleasant; salted.

**sabueso** *m* bloodhound.

**sacacorchos** *m invar* corkscrew.

**sacapuntas** *m invar* pencil sharpener.

**sacar** *vt* to take out, to extract; to get out; to bring out (a book etc); to take off (clothes); to receive, to get; (*sport*) to serve.

**sacarina** *f* saccharin.

**sacerdotal** *adj* priestly.

**sacerdote** *m* priest.

**sacerdotisa** *f* priestess.

**saciar** *vt* to satiate.

**saciedad** *f* satiety.

**saco** *m* bag, sack; jacket; ~ **de dormir** sleeping bag.

**sacramental** *adj* sacramental.

**sacramento** *m* sacrament.

**sacrificar** *vt* to sacrifice.

**sacrificio** *m* sacrifice.

**sacrilegio** *m* sacrilege.

**sacrílego/ga** *adj* sacrilegious.

**sacristán** *m* sacristan, sexton.

**sacristía** *f* sacristy, vestry.

**sacro/cra** *adj* holy, sacred.

**sacrosanto/ta** *adj* sacrosanct.

**sacudida** *f* shake, jerk.

**sacudir** *vt* to shake, to jerk; to beat, to hit.

**sádico/ca** *adj* sadistic; * *m/f* sadist.

**sadismo** *m* sadism.

**saeta** *f* arrow, dart.

**sagacidad** *f* shrewdness, cleverness, sagacity.

**sagaz** *adj* shrewd, clever, sagacious.

**Sagitario** *m* Sagittarius (sign of the zodiac).

**sagrado/da** *adj* sacred, holy.

**sagrario** *m* shrine; tabernacle.

**sainete** *m* (*teat*) farce; flavour, relish; seasoning.

**sal** *f* salt.

**sala** *f* large room; (*teat*) house, auditorium; public hall; (*law*) court; (*med*) ward.

**salado/da** *adj* salted; witty, amusing.

**salamandra** *f* salamander.

**salar** *vt* to salt.

**salarial** *adj* wage *compd*, salary *compd*.

**salario** *m* salary.

**salazón** *f* salting.

**salchicha** *f* sausage.

**salchichón** *m* salami-type sausage.

**saldar** *vt* to pay; to sell off; (*fig*) to settle.

**saldo** *m* settlement; balance; remainder; ~**s** *mpl* sale.

**saledizo/za** *adj* projecting, salient.

**salero** *m* salt cellar.

**saleroso** *adj* witty, amusing.

**salida** *f* exit, way out; leaving, departure; production, output; (*com*) sale; sales outlet.

**saliente** *adj* projecting; rising; (*fig*) outstanding.

**salina** *f* saltworks, salt mine.

**salino/na** *adj* saline.

**salir** *vi* to go out, to leave; to depart, to set out; to appear; to turn out, to prove; ~**se** *vr* to escape, to leak.

**salitre** *m* saltpetre.

**saliva** *f* saliva.

**salmo** *m* psalm.

**salmón** *m* salmon.

**salmonete** *m* red mullet.

**salmuera** *f* brine.

**salobre** *adj* brackish, salty.

**salón** *m* living room, lounge; public hall.

**salpicadero** *m* dashboard.

**salpicar** *vt* to sprinkle, to splash, to spatter.

**salpimentar** *vt* to season with pepper and salt.

**salsa** *f* sauce.

**salsera** *f* sauce boat; gravy boat.

**saltamontes** *m invar* grasshopper.

**saltar** *vt* to jump, to leap; to skip, to miss

out; * *vi* to leap, to jump; to bounce; (*fig*) to explode, to blow up.

**salteador** *m* highwayman.

**saltear** *vt* to rob in a hold-up; to assault; to sauté (in cooking).

**saltimbanqui** *m/f* acrobat.

**salto** *m* leap, jump.

**saltón/ona** *adj* bulging; protruding.

**salubre** *adj* healthy.

**salubridad** *f* healthiness.

**salud** *f* health.

**saludable** *adj* healthy.

**saludar** *vt* to greet; (*mil*) to salute.

**saludo** *m* greeting.

**salutación** *f* salutation, greeting.

**salva** *f* (*mil*) salute, salvo.

**salvación** *f* salvation; rescue.

**salvado** *m* bran.

**salvaguardar** *vt* to safeguard.

**salvaguardia** *m* safeguard.

**salvaje** *adj* savage.

**salvajismo** *m* savagery.

**salvar** *vt* to save; to rescue; to overcome; to cross, to jump across; to cover, to travel; to exclude; ~se *vr* to escape from danger.

**salvavidas** *adj invar*: **bote** ~ lifeboat; **chaleco** ~ life jacket.

**salvia** *f* (*bot*) sage.

**salvo/va** *adj* safe; * *adv* save, except (for).

**salvoconducto** *m* safe-conduct.

**san** *adj* saint (as title).

**sanamente** *adv* healthily.

**sanar** *vt, vi* to heal.

**sanatorio** *m* sanatorium; nursing home.

**sanción** *f* sanction.

**sancionar** *vt* to sanction.

**sandalia** *f* sandal.

**sándalo** *m* sandal, sandalwood.

**sandez** *f* folly, stupidity.

**sandía** *f* watermelon.

**sandwich** *m* sandwich.

**saneamiento** *m* sanitation.

**sanear** *vt* to drain.

**sangrar** *vt, vi* to bleed.

**sangre** *f* blood; **a** ~ **fría** in cold blood; **a** ~ **y fuego** without mercy.

**sangría** *f* sangria (drink); bleeding.

**sangriento/ta** *adj* bloody, blood-stained, gory; cruel.

**sanguijuela** *f* leech.

**sanguinario/ria** *adj* bloodthirsty, cruel.

**sanguíneo/nea** *adj* blood *compd*.

**sanidad** *f* sanitation; health.

**sanitario/ria** *adj* sanitary; health; ~s *mpl* toilets *pl*.

**sano/na** *adj* healthy, fit; intact, sound.

**santiamén** *m*: **en un** ~ in no time at all.

**santidad** *f* sanctity.

**santificar** *vt* to sanctify; to make holy.

**santiguarse** *vr* to make the sign of the cross.

**santo/ta** *adj* holy; sacred; * *m/f* saint; ~ **y seña** password, watchword.

**santuario** *m* sanctuary.

**saña** *f* anger, passion.

**sañudo/da** *adj* furious, enraged.

**sapo** *m* toad.

**saque** *m* (*sport*) serve, service, throw-in.

**saqueador/ra** *m/f* ransacker, looter.

**saquear** *vt* to ransack, to plunder.

**saqueo** *m* looting, sacking.

**sarampión** *m* measles.

**sarao** *m* evening party, soiree.

**sarcasmo** *m* sarcasm.

**sarcástico/ca** *adj* sarcastic.

**sarcófago** *m* sarcophagus.

**sardina** *f* sardine.

**sardónico/ca** *adj* sardonic; ironic(al).

**sargento** *m* sergeant.

**sarmiento** *m* vine shoot.

**sarna** *f* itch; mange; (*med*) scabies.

**sarnoso/sa** *adj* itchy, scabby, mangy.

**sarpullido** *m* (*med*) rash.

**sarro** *m* (*med*) tartar.

**sarta** *f* string of beads etc; string, row.

**sartén** *f* frying pan.

**sastre** *m* tailor.

**sastrería** *f* tailor's shop.

**Satanás** *m* Satan.

**satélite** *m* satellite.

**sátira** *f* satire.

**satírico/ca** *adj* satirical.

**satirizar** *vt* to satirize.

**sátiro** *m* satyr.

**satisfacción** *f* satisfaction; apology.

**satisfacer** *vt* to satisfy; to pay (a debt); ~se *vr* to satisfy oneself; to take revenge.

**satisfactorio/ria** *adj* satisfactory.

**satisfecho/cha** *adj* satisfied.

**saturación** *f* (*chem*) saturation.

**Saturno** *m* Saturn (planet).

**sauce** *m* (*bot*) willow.

**saúco** *m* (*bot*) elder.

**sauna** *f* sauna.

**savia** *f* sap.

**saxofón** *m* saxophone.

**sazonado/da** *adj* flavoured, seasoned.

**sazonar** *vt* to ripen; to season.

**se** *pn reflexivo*: himself; herself; itself; yourself; themselves; yourselves; each other; one another; oneself.

**sebo** *m* fat, grease.

**seboso/sa** *adj* fat, greasy.

**secador** *m*: ~ **de pelo** hairdryer/drier.

**secadora** *f* tumble dryer/drier.

**secamente** *adv* drily/dryly, curtly.

**secano** *m* dry, arable land which is not irrigated.

**secar** *vt* to dry; ~**se** *vr* to dry up; to dry oneself.

**sección** *f* section.

**seco/ca** *adj* dry; dried up; skinny; cold (of character); brusque, sharp; bare.

**secretaría** *f* secretariat.

**secretario/ria** *m/f* secretary.

**secreto/ta** *adj* secret; hidden; * *m* secret; secrecy.

**secta** *f* sect.

**sectario/ria** *adj*, *m/f* sectarian.

**sector** *m* sector.

**secuela** *f* sequel; consequence.

**secuencia** *f* sequence.

**secuestrador/ra** *m/f* kidnapper.

**secuestrar** *vt* to kidnap; to confiscate.

**secuestro** *m* kidnapping; confiscation.

**secular** *adj* secular.

**secularización** *f* secularization.

**secularizar** *vt* to secularize.

**secundar** *vt* to second.

**secundario/ria** *adj* secondary.

**sed** *f* thirst; **tener** ~ to be thirsty.

**seda** *f* silk.

**sedal** *m* fishing line.

**sedante** *m* sedative.

**sede** *f* see; seat; headquarters.

**sedentario/ria** *adj* sedentary.

**sedición** *f* sedition.

**sedicioso/sa** *adj* seditious, mutinous.

**sediento/ta** *adj* thirsty; eager.

**sedoso/sa** *adj* silky.

**seducción** *f* seduction.

**seducir** *vt* to seduce; to bribe; to charm, to attract.

**seductor/ra** *adj* seductive; charming; attractive; * *m/f* seducer.

**segador/ra** *m/f* reaper, harvester.

**segadora-trilladora** *f* combine (harvester).

**segar** *vt* to reap, to harvest; to mow.

**seglar** *adj* secular, lay.

**segmento** *m* segment.

**segregación** *f* segregation, separation.

**segregar** *vt* to segregate, to separate.

**seguido/da** *adj* continuous; successive; long-lasting; * *adv* straight (on); after; often.

**seguidor/ra** *m/f* follower; supporter.

**seguimiento** *m* pursuit; continuation.

**seguir** *vt* to follow, to pursue; to continue; * *vi* to follow; to carry on; ~**se** *vr* to follow, to ensue.

**según** *prep* according to.

**segundo/da** *adj* second; * *m* second (of time).

**seguramente** *adv* surely; for sure.

**seguridad** *f* security; certainty; safety; confidence; stability.

**seguro/ra** *adj* safe, secure; sure, certain; firm, constant; * *adv* for sure; * *m* safety device; insurance; safety, certainty.

**seis** *adj*, *m* six; sixth.

**seiscientos/tas** *adj* six hundred.

**seísmo** *m* earthquake.

**selección** *f* selection, choice.

**seleccionar** *vt* to select, to choose.

**selecto/ta** *adj* select, choice.

**sellar** *vt* to seal; to stamp (a document).

**sello** *m* seal; stamp.

**selva** *f* forest.

**semáforo** *m* traffic lights *pl*; signal.

**semana** *f* week.

**semanal** *adj* weekly.

**semanario/ria** *m* weekly (magazine).

**semblante** *m* face; (*fig*) look; appearance.

**sembrado** *m* sown field.

**sembrar** *vt* to sow; to sprinkle, to scatter.

**semejante** *adj* similar, like; * *m* fellow man.

**semejanza** *f* resemblance, likeness.

**semejar** *vi* to resemble; ~**se** *vr* to look alike.

**semen** *m* semen.

**semental** *m* stud.

**sementera** *f* sowing time; land sown with seed.

**semestral** *adj* half-yearly.

**semicircular** *adj* semicircular.

**semicírculo** *m* semicircle.

**semifinal** *f* semifinal.

**semilla** *f* seed, bean.

**semilla de soja** *f* soya bean.

**semillero** *m* seed plot.

**seminario** *m* seedbed; seminary.

**seminarista** *m* seminarist.

**semitono** *m* (*mus*) semitone.

**sémola** *f* semolina.

**sempiterno/na** *adj* everlasting.

**senado** *m* senate.

**senador/ra** *m/f* senator.

**sencillez** *f* plainness; simplicity; naturalness.

**sencillo/lla** *adj* simple; natural; unaffected; single.

**senda** *f m* path, footpath.

**senderismo** *m* hillwalking.
**senderista** *m/f* hillwalker.
**sendero** *m* path, footpath.
**senil** *adj* senile.
**seno** *m* bosom; lap; womb; hole, cavity; sinus; **~s** *mpl* breasts *pl*.
**sensación** *f* sensation, feeling; sense.
**sensacional** *adj* sensational.
**sensato/ta** *adj* sensible.
**sensibilidad** *f* sensibility, sensitivity.
**sensible** *adj* sensitive; perceptible, appreciable; regrettable.
**sensitivo/va** *adj* sense *compd*, sensitive.
**sensorial** *adj* sensorial, sensory.
**sensual** *adj* sensuous, sensual.
**sensualidad** *f* sensuousness; sensuality; sexiness.
**sentado/da** *adj* sitting, seated; sedate; settled.
**sentar** *vt* to seat; (*fig*) to establish; * *vi* to suit; **~se** *vr* to sit down.
**sentencia** *f* (*law*) sentence; opinion; saying.
**sentenciar** *vt* (*law*) to sentence, to pass judgement on; * *vi* to give one's opinion.
**sentencioso/sa** *adj* sententious.
**sentido** *m* sense; feeling; meaning; **~/da** *adj* regrettable; sensitive.
**sentimental** *adj* sentimental.
**sentimiento** *m* feeling, emotion, sentiment; sympathy; regret, grief.
**sentir** *vt* to feel; to hear; to perceive; to sense; to suffer from; to regret, to be sorry for; **~se** *vr* to feel; to feel pain; to crack (of walls etc); * *m* opinion, judgement.
**seña** *f* sign, mark, token; signal; (*mil*) password; **~s** *fpl* address.
**señal** *f* sign, token; symptom; signal; landmark; (*com*) deposit.
**señalado/da** *adj* distinct; special; distinguished, notable.
**señalar** *vt* to stamp, to mark; to signpost; to point out; to fix, to settle; **~se** *vr* to distinguish oneself, to excel.
**señor** *m* man; gentleman; master; Mr; sir.
**señora** *f* lady; Mrs; madam; wife.
**señorita** *f* Miss; young lady.
**señorito** *m* Master, young gentleman; rich kid.
**señuelo** *m* decoy; bait, lure.
**separable** *adj* separable.
**separación** *f* separation.
**separar** *vt* to separate; **~se** *vr* to separate; to come away, to come apart; to withdraw.
**septentrional** *adj* north, northern.
**séptico** *adj* septic.

**septiembre** *m* September.
**séptimo/ma** *adj* seventh.
**sepulcral** *adj* sepulchral.
**sepulcro** *m* sepulchre, grave, tomb.
**sepultar** *vt* to bury, to inter.
**sepultura** *f* burial, interment; grave, tomb.
**sepulturero** *m* gravedigger, sexton.
**sequedad** *f* dryness; brusqueness.
**sequía** *f* dryness; thirst; drought.
**séquito** *m* retinue, suite; group of supporters; aftermath.
**ser** *vi* to be; to exist; **~ de** to come from; to be made of; to belong to; * *m* being.
**serenarse** *vr* to calm down.
**serenata** *f* (*mus*) serenade.
**serenidad** *f* serenity.
**sereno** *m* night watchman; **~/na** *adj* serene, calm, quiet.
**serial** *m* serial.
**serie** *f* series; sequence.
**seriedad** *f* seriousness, gravity; reliability; sincerity.
**serio/ria** *adj* serious; grave; reliable.
**sermón** *m* sermon.
**sermonear** *vt* to lecture; * *vi* to sermonize.
**seronegativo/va** *adj* HIV-negative.
**seropositivo/va** *adj* HIV-positive.
**serpentear** *vi* to wriggle; to wind, to snake.
**serpentina** *f* streamer.
**serpiente** *f* snake.
**serranía** *f* range of mountains; mountainous country.
**serrano/na** *m/f* highlander.
**serrar** *vt* to saw.
**serrín** *m* sawdust.
**serrucho** *m* handsaw.
**servible** *adj* serviceable.
**servicial** *adj* helpful, obliging.
**servicio** *m* service; service charge; service, set of dishes; **~s** *mpl* toilet facilities *pl*.
**servidor/ra** *m/f* servant.
**servidumbre** *f* servitude; servants *pl*, staff.
**servil** *adj* servile.
**servilleta** *f* napkin, serviette.
**servir** *vt* to serve; to wait on; * *vi* to serve; to be of use; to be in service; **~se** *vr* to serve oneself; to help oneself; to deign, to please; to make use of.
**sesenta** *m*, *adj* sixty; sixtieth.
**sesentón/ona** *m/f* person of about sixty years of age.
**sesgar** *vt* to slope, to slant.
**sesgo** *m* slope.
**sesión** *f* session; sitting; performance; showing.

**seso** *m* brain.
**sestear** *vi* to take a nap.
**sesudo/da** *adj* sensible, prudent.
**seta** *f* mushroom.
**setecientos/tas** *adj* seven hundred.
**setenta** *adj, m* seventy.
**setiembre** *m* September.
**seto** *m* fence; enclosure; hedge.
**seudo-** *pref* pseudo-.
**seudónimo** *m* pseudonym.
**severidad** *f* severity.
**severo/ra** *adj* severe, strict; grave, serious.
**sexagenario/ria** *adj* sixty years old.
**sexagésimo/ma** *adj* sixtieth.
**sexenio** *m* space of six years.
**sexo** *m* sex.
**sexto/ta** *adj, m* sixth.
**sexual** *adj* sexual.
**si** *conj* whether; if.
**sí** *adv* yes; certainly; indeed; * *pn* oneself; himself; herself; itself; yourself; themselves; yourselves; each other; one another.
**siderúrgico/ca** *adj* iron and steel *compd*.
**sidra** *f* cider.
**siega** *f* harvest, mowing.
**siembra** *f* sowing time.
**siempre** *adv* always; all the time; ever; still; ~ **jamás** for ever and ever.
**sien** *f* temple (of the head).
**sierra** *f* saw; range of mountains.
**siervo/va** *m/f* slave.
**siesta** *f* siesta, afternoon nap.
**siete** *adj, m* seven.
**sietemesino/na** *adj* born seven months after conception; premature; (*fig*) half-witted.
**sífilis** *f* syphilis.
**sifón** *m* siphon/syphon; soda.
**sigilo** *m* secrecy.
**sigiloso/sa** *adj* reserved; silent.
**sigla** *f* acronym; abbreviation.
**siglo** *m* century.
**significación** *f* significance, meaning.
**significado** *m* significance, meaning.
**significar** *vt* to signify, to mean; to make known, to express.
**significativo/va** *adj* significant.
**signo** *m* sign, mark.
**siguiente** *adj* following, successive, next.
**sílaba** *f* syllable.
**silbar** *vt, vi* to hiss; to whistle.
**silbato** *m* whistle.
**silbido/silbo** *m* hiss; whistling.
**silencio** *m* silence; ¡~! silence! quiet!
**silencioso/sa** *adj* silent.

**silla** *f* chair; saddle; seat; ~ **de ruedas** wheelchair.
**sillón** *m* armchair, easy chair; rocking chair.
**silo** *m* silo.
**silogismo** *m* syllogism.
**silueta** *f* silhouette; outline; figure.
**silvestre** *adj* wild, uncultivated; rustic.
**sima** *f* abyss; pothole, cavern.
**simbólico/ca** *adj* symbolic.
**simbolizar** *vt* to symbolize.
**símbolo** *m* symbol.
**simetría** *f* symmetry.
**simétrico/ca** *adj* symmetrical.
**simiente** *f* seed.
**similar** *adj* similar.
**similitud** *f* similarity, similitude.
**simio** *m* ape.
**simpatía** *f* liking; kindness; solidarity; affection.
**simpático/ca** *adj* pleasant; kind.
**simpatizante** *m/f* sympathizer.
**simpatizar** *vi*: ~ **con** to get on well with.
**simple** *adj* single; simple, easy; mere; sheer; silly; * *m/f* simpleton.
**simpleza** *f* simpleness, gullibility; silliness.
**simplicidad** *f* simplicity.
**simplificar** *vt* to simplify.
**simulación** *f* simulation.
**simulacro** *m* simulacrum, idol.
**simuladamente** *adv* deceptively, hypocritically.
**simular** *vt* to simulate.
**simultaneidad** *f* simultaneity.
**simultáneo/nea** *adj* simultaneous.
**sin** *prep* without.
**sinagoga** *f* synagogue.
**sinceridad** *f* sincerity.
**sincero/ra** *adj* sincere.
**síncope** *f* (*med*) syncope, fainting fit.
**sincronizar** *vt* to synchronize.
**sindical** *adj* union *compd*.
**sindicato** *m* trade(s) union; syndicate.
**sinfín** *m*: **un** ~ **de** a great many.
**sinfonía** *f* symphony.
**singular** *adj* singular; exceptional; peculiar, odd.
**singularidad** *f* singularity.
**singularizar** *vt* to distinguish; to singularize; ~**se** *vr* to distinguish oneself; to stand out.
**siniestro/tra** *adj* left; (*fig*) sinister; * *m* accident.
**sinnúmero** *m* = **sinfín**.
**sino** *conj* but; except; save; only; * *m* fate.
**sinónimo/ma** *adj* synonymous; * *m* synonym.

**sinsabor** *m* unpleasantness; disgust.
**sintaxis** *f* syntax.
**síntesis** *f* synthesis.
**sintético/ca** *adj* synthetic.
**sintetizar** *vt* synthesize.
**síntoma** *m* symptom.
**sinuosidad** *f* sinuosity; curve, wave.
**sinuoso/sa** *adj* sinuous; wavy.
**sinvergüenza** *m/f* rogue.
**siquiera** *conj* even if, even though; * *adv* at least.
**sirena** *f* siren; mermaid; car hooter/horn.
**sirviente/ta** *m/f* servant.
**sisa** *f* petty theft; cut, percentage.
**sisear** *vt, vi* to hiss.
**sistema** *m* system.
**sistemático/ca** *adj* systematic.
**sitiar** *vt* to besiege.
**sitio** *m* place; spot; site, location; room, space; job, post; (*mil*) siege, blockade.
**situación** *f* situation, position; standing.
**situar** *vt* to place, to situate; to invest; **~se** *vr* to be established in place/business.
**slip** *m* underpants *pl*, briefs *pl*.
**smoking** *m* dinner-jacket.
**sobaco** *m* armpit, armhole.
**sobar** *vt* to handle, to soften; to knead; to massage, to rub hard; to rumple (clothes); to fondle.
**soberanía** *f* sovereignty.
**soberano/na** *adj, m/f* sovereign.
**soberbia** *f* pride, haughtiness; magnificence.
**soberbio/bia** *adj* proud, haughty; magnificent.
**sobornar** *vt* to suborn, to bribe.
**soborno** *m* subornation, bribery; bribe.
**sobra** *f* surplus, excess; **de ~** spare, surplus, extra.
**sobradamente** *adv* too; amply.
**sobrante** *adj* remaining; * *m* surplus, remainder.
**sobrar** *vt* to exceed, to surpass; * *vi* to be more than enough; to remain, to be left.
**sobrasada** *f* pork sausage spread.
**sobre** *prep* on; on top of; above, over; more than; besides; * *m* envelope.
**sobreabundancia** *f* superabundance.
**sobreabundar** *vi* to superabound.
**sobrecarga** *f* extra load; (*com*) surcharge.
**sobrecargar** *vt* to overload; (*com*) to surcharge.
**sobrecoger** *vt* to surprise.
**sobredosis** *f invar* overdose.
**sobreentender** *vt* to deduce; **~se** *vr*: **se sobreentiende que . . .** it is implied that.

**sobrehumano/na** *adj* superhuman.
**sobrellevar** *vt* to carry; to tolerate.
**sobremanera** *adv* excessively.
**sobremesa** *f*: **de ~** immediately after dinner.
**sobrenatural** *adj* supernatural.
**sobrenaturalmente** *adv* supernaturally.
**sobrenombre** *m* nickname.
**sobrepasar** *vt* to surpass.
**sobreponer** *vt* to put (something) over/on top of; **~se** *vr* to pull through.
**sobresaliente** *adj* projecting; (*fig*) outstanding.
**sobresalir** *vi* to project; (*fig*) to stand out.
**sobresaltar** *vt* to frighten.
**sobresalto** *m* start, scare; sudden shock.
**sobreseer** *vt*: **~ una causa** (*law*) to stay a case; * *vi*: **~ de** to desist from.
**sobreseimiento** *m* dismissal, suspension.
**sobrevenir** *vi* to happen, to come unexpectedly; to supervene.
**sobreviviente** *adj* surviving; * *m/f* survivor.
**sobrevivir** *vi* to survive.
**sobrevolar** *vt* to fly over.
**sobriedad** *f* sobriety.
**sobrino/na** *m/f* nephew/niece.
**sobrio/ria** *adj* sober, frugal.
**socarrón/ona** *adj* sarcastic; ironic(al).
**socarronería** *f* sarcasm; irony.
**socavar** *vt* to undermine.
**socavón** *m* hole.
**sociabilidad** *f* sociability.
**sociable** *adj* sociable.
**social** *adj* social.
**socialdemócrata** *adj, m/f* social democrat.
**socialista** *adj, m/f* socialist.
**sociedad** *f* society.
**socio/cia** *m/f* associate, member.
**sociología** *f* sociology.
**sociólogo/ga** *m/f* sociologist.
**socorrer** *vt* to help.
**socorrido/da** *adj* well-stocked/supplied.
**socorrista** *m/f* first aider; lifeguard.
**socorro** *m* help, aid, assistance, relief.
**soda** *f* soda; soda water.
**sodomía** *f* sodomy.
**sodomita** *m* sodomite.
**soez** *adj* dirty, obscene.
**sofá** *m* sofa.
**sofisma** *m* sophism.
**sofista** *m/f* sophist.
**sofisticación** *f* sophistication.
**sofocar** *vt* to suffocate.
**software** *m* software.
**soga** *f* rope.
**sojuzgar** *vt* to conquer, to subdue.

**sol** m sun; sunshine, sunlight.

**solamente** adv only, solely.

**solapa** f lapel.

**solapado/da** adj cunning, crafty, artful.

**solar** m building site; piece of land; ancestral home of a family; * adj solar.

**solariego/ga** adj belonging to the ancestral home of a family.

**solaz** m recreation, relaxation; solace, consolation.

**solazar** vt to provide relaxation for; to comfort.

**soldada** f wages pl.

**soldadesca** f military profession.

**soldado** m/f soldier; ~ **raso** private.

**soldador** m welder; soldering iron.

**soldadura** f soldering; solder.

**soldar** vt to solder; to weld; to unite.

**soleado/da** adj sunny.

**soledad** f solitude; loneliness.

**solemne** adj solemn; impressive, grand.

**solemnidad** f solemnity.

**solemnizar** vt to solemnize; to praise.

**soler** vi to be accustomed to, to be in the habit of.

**solfeo** m (mus) solfa.

**solicitar** vt to ask for, to seek; to apply for (a job); to canvass for; to chase after, to pursue.

**solícito/ta** adj diligent; solicitous.

**solicitud** f care, solicitude; request, petition.

**solidaridad** f solidarity.

**solidario/ria** adj joint; mutually binding.

**solidez** f solidity.

**sólido/da** adj solid.

**soliloquio** m soliloquy, monologue.

**solista** m/f soloist.

**solitario/ria** adj lonely, solitary; * m solitaire; * m/f hermit.

**sollozar** vi to sob.

**sollozo** m sob.

**solo** m (mus) solo; ~/la adj alone, single; **a solas** alone, unaided.

**sólo** adv only.

**solomillo** m sirloin.

**solsticio** m solstice.

**soltar** vt to untie, to loosen; to set free, to let out; ~**se** vr to get loose; to come undone.

**soltero/ra** m/f bachelor/single woman; * adj single, unmarried.

**soltura** f looseness, slackness; agility, activity; fluency.

**soluble** adj soluble; solvable.

**solución** f solution; denouement.

**solucionar** vt to solve; to resolve.

**solvente** adj, m solvent.

**sombra** f shade; shadow.

**sombrear** vt to shade.

**sombrero** m hat.

**sombrilla** f parasol.

**sombrío/bría** adj shady, gloomy; sad.

**somero/ra** adj superficial.

**someter** vt to conquer (a country); to subject to one's will; to submit; to subdue; ~**se** vr to give in, to submit.

**sometimiento** m submission.

**somnífero** m sleeping pill.

**somnolencia** f sleepiness, drowsiness.

**son** m sound; rumour.

**sonado/da** adj celebrated; famous; generally reported.

**sonaja** f (mus) timbrel.

**sonajero** m (mus) small timbrel.

**sonámbulo/la** m/f sleepwalker; somnambulist.

**sonar** vt to ring; * vi to sound; to make a noise; to be pronounced; to be talked of; to sound familiar; ~**se** vr to blow one's nose.

**sonata** f (mus) sonata.

**sonda** f sounding; (med) probe.

**sondear** vt (mar) to sound; to probe; to bore.

**sondeo** m sounding; boring; (fig) poll.

**soneto** m sonnet.

**sónico/ca** adj sonic.

**sonido** m sound.

**sonoro/ra** adj sonorous.

**sonreír(se)** vi (vr) to smile.

**sonrisa** f smile.

**sonrojarse** vr to blush.

**sonrojo** m blush.

**sonsacar** vt to wheedle, cajole; to obtain by cunning.

**sonsonete** m tapping noise; monotonous voice.

**soñador/ra** m/f dreamer.

**soñar** vt, vi to dream.

**soñoliento/ta** adj sleepy, drowsy.

**sopa** f soup; sop.

**sopapo** m punch, thump.

**sopera** f soup dish.

**sopero** m soup plate.

**sopetón** m: **de ~** suddenly.

**soplar** vt to blow away, to blow off; to blow up, to inflate; * vi to blow, to puff.

**soplete** m blowlamp.

**soplo** m blowing; puff of wind; (col) tip-off.

**soplón/ona** m/f telltale.

**sopor** *m* drowsiness, sleepiness.
**soporífero/ra** *adj* soporific; * *m* sleeping pill.
**soportable** *adj* tolerable, bearable.
**soportal** *m* portico.
**soportar** *vt* to suffer, to tolerate; to support.
**sorber** *vt* to sip; to inhale; to swallow; to absorb.
**sorbete** *m* sorbet, a fruit water ice
**sorbo** *m* sip; gulp, swallow.
**sordera** *f* deafness.
**sordidez** *f* sordidness; dirtiness; meanness.
**sórdido/da** *adj* sordid; dirty; mean.
**sorda/da** *adj* deaf; silent, quiet; * *m/f* deaf person.
**sordomudo/da** *adj* deaf and dumb.
**sorna** *f* slyness; sarcasm; slowness.
**soroche** *m* mountain sickness.
**sorprender** *vt* to surprise.
**sorpresa** *f* surprise.
**sortear** *vt* to draw/cast (lots); to raffle; to avoid.
**sorteo** *m* draw; raffle.
**sortija** *f* ring; ringlet, curl.
**sortilegio** *m* sorcery.
**sosegado/da** *adj* quiet, peaceful.
**sosegar** *vt* to appease, to calm; * *vi* to rest.
**sosería** *f* insipidness; dullness.
**sosiego** *m* tranquillity, calmness.
**soslayar** *vt* to do/place (something) obliquely.
**soslayo** *adv:* **al/de ~** obliquely, sideways.
**soso/sa** *adj* insipid, tasteless; dull.
**sospecha** *f* suspicion.
**sospechar** *vt* to suspect.
**sospechoso/sa** *adj* suspicious; suspect; * *m/f* suspect.
**sostén** *m* support; bra; sustenance.
**sostener** *vt* to sustain, to maintain; **~se** *vr* to support/maintain oneself; to contrive, to remain.
**sostenimiento** *m* support; maintenance; sustenance.
**sota** *f* jack, knave (at cards).
**sotana** *f* cassock.
**sótano** *m* basement, cellar.
**sotavento** *m* (*mar*) leeward, lee.
**soto** *m* grove, thicket.
**squash** *m* squash.
**status** *m invar* status.
**su** *pn* his, her, its, one's; their; your.
**suave** *adj* smooth, soft; delicate; gentle; mild, meek.
**suavidad** *f* softness, sweetness; suavity.

**suavizar** *vt* to soften.
**subalterno/na** *adj* secondary; auxiliary.
**subasta** *f* auction.
**subastar** *vt* to sell by auction.
**subcampeón/ona** *m/f* runner-up.
**subconsciente** *adj, m* subconscious.
**subdesarrollado/da** *adj* underdeveloped.
**subdesarrollo** *m* underdevelopment.
**subdirector/ora** *m/f* assistant director.
**súbdito/ta** *adj, m/f* subject.
**subdividir** *vt* to subdivide.
**subdivisión** *f* subdivision.
**subestimar** *vt* to underestimate.
**subida** *f* climb, ascent, rise in value/price.
**subido/da** *adj* deep-coloured; high (price).
**subir** *vt, vi* to raise, to lift up; to go up; to climb, to ascend; to increase, to swell; to get in, to get on, to board; to rise (in price).
**súbito/ta** *adj* sudden, hasty; unforeseen.
**subjetivo/va** *adj* subjective.
**subjuntivo** *m* (*gr*) subjunctive.
**sublevación** *f* sedition, revolt.
**sublevar** *vt* to excite (a rebellion); to incite (a revolt); **~se** *vr* to revolt.
**sublime** *adj* sublime.
**sublimidad** *f* sublimity.
**submarino/na** *adj* underwater; * *m* submarine.
**subnormal** *adj* subnormal; * *m/f* subnormal person.
**subordinación** *f* subordination.
**subrayar** *vt* to underline.
**subrepticio/cia** *adj* surreptitious.
**subsanar** *vt* to excuse; to mend, to repair; to overcome.
**subsidio** *m* subsidy, aid; benefit, allowance.
**subsistencia** *f* subsistence.
**subsistir** *vi* to subsist.
**su(b)stancia** *f* substance.
**su(b)stancial** *adj* substantial.
**su(b)stancioso/sa** *adj* substantial; nutritious.
**su(b)stracción** *f* removal; (*math*) subtraction.
**su(b)straer** *vt* to remove; (*math*) to subtract; **~se** *vr* to avoid; to withdraw.
**subterfugio** *f* subterfuge.
**subterráneo/nea** *adj* subterranean; underground; * *m* underground passage; (*rail*) underground.
**suburbio** *m* slum quarter; suburbs *pl.*
**subvencionar** *vt* to subsidize.
**subversión** *f* subversion, overthrow.
**subversivo/va** *adj* subversive.
**subvertir** *vt* to subvert, to overthrow.

**subyugar** *vt* to subdue, to subjugate.

**sucedáneo/nea** *adj* substitute; * *m* substitute (food).

**suceder** *vt* to succeed, to inherit; * *vi* to happen.

**sucesión** *f* succession; issue, offspring; inheritance.

**sucesivamente** *adv*: **y así ~** and so on.

**sucesivo/va** *adj* successive.

**suceso** *m* event; incident.

**sucesor/ra** *m/f* successor; heir.

**suciedad** *f* dirtiness, filthiness; dirt.

**sucinto/ta** *adj* succinct, concise.

**sucio/cia** *adj* dirty, filthy; obscene; dishonest.

**suculento/ta** *adj* succulent, juicy.

**sucumbir** *vt* to succumb.

**sucursal** *f* branch (office).

**sudar** *vt, vi* to sweat.

**sudeste** *adj* southeast, southeastern; * *m* southeast.

**sudoeste** *adj* southwest, southwestern; * *m* southwest.

**sudor** *m* sweat.

**sudorífico/ca** *adj* sweaty.

**suegra** *f* mother-in-law.

**suegro** *m* father-in-law.

**suela** *f* sole (shoe).

**sueldo** *m* wages *pl*, salary.

**suelo** *m* ground; floor; soil, surface.

**suelto/ta** *adj* loose; free; detached; swift; * *m* loose change.

**sueño** *m* sleep; dream.

**suero** *m* (*med*) serum; whey.

**suerte** *f* fate, destiny, chance, lot, fortune, good luck; kind, sort.

**suéter** *m* sweater.

**suficiencia** *f* sufficiency, competence, fitness.

**suficiente** *adj* enough, sufficient; fit, capable.

**sufragar** *vt* to aid, to assist.

**sufragio** *m* vote, suffrage; aid, assistance.

**sufrible** *adj* bearable.

**sufrido/da** *adj* long-suffering, patient; hard-wearing.

**sufrimiento** *m* suffering; patience.

**sufrir** *vt* to suffer; to bear, to put up with; to support.

**sugerencia** *f* suggestion.

**sugerir** *vt* to suggest.

**sugestión** *f* suggestion.

**suicida** *adj* suicidal; * *m/f* suicide; suicidal person.

**suicidio** *m* suicide.

**sujeción** *f* subjection.

**sujetador** *m* fastener; bra.

**sujetar** *vt* to fasten, to hold down; to subdue; to subject; **~se** *vr* to subject oneself.

**sujeto/ta** *adj* fastened, secure; subject, liable; * *m* subject; individual.

**sulfúrico** *adj* sulphuric.

**sultán** *m* sultan.

**sultana** *f* sultana.

**suma** *f* total, sum; adding up; summary.

**sumamente** *adv* extremely.

**sumar** *vt* to add, to add up; to collect, to gather; * *vi* to add up.

**sumario/ria** *adj* brief, concise; * *m* summary.

**sumergir** *vt* to submerge, to sink; to immerse.

**sumidero** *m* sewer, drain.

**suministrador/ra** *m/f* provider, supplier.

**suministrar** *vt* to supply, to furnish.

**sumir** *vt* to sink, to submerge; (*fig*) to plunge.

**sumisión** *f* submission.

**sumiso/sa** *adj* submissive, docile.

**sumo/ma** *adj* great, extreme; highest, greatest; **a lo ~** at most.

**suntuosidad** *f* sumptuousness.

**suntuoso/sa** *adj* sumptuous.

**súper** *f* four-star (petrol).

**superable** *adj* surmountable.

**superabundancia** *f* superabundance.

**superabundar** *vi* to superabound.

**superar** *vt* to surpass; to overcome; to exceed, to go beyond.

**superficial** *adj* superficial; shallow.

**superficie** *f* surface; area.

**superfluo/ua** *adj* superfluous.

**superintendencia** *f* supervision.

**superintendente** *m/f* superintendent, supervisor; shopwalker.

**superior** *adj* superior; upper; higher; better; * *m/f* superior.

**superioridad** *f* superiority.

**superlativo/va** *adj, m* (*gr*) superlative.

**supermercado** *m* supermarket.

**superstición** *f* superstition.

**supersticioso/sa** *adj* superstitious.

**supervisor/ra** *m/f* supervisor.

**supervivencia** *f* survival.

**superviviente** *m/f* survivor; * *adj* surviving.

**suplantación** *f* supplanting.

**suplantar** *vt* to supplant.

**suplemento** *m* supplement.

**suplente** *m/f* substitute.

**supletorio/ria** *adj* supplementary.
**súplica** *f* petition, request; supplication.
**suplicante** *adj, m/f* applicant; supplicant.
**suplicar** *vt* to beg (for), to plead (for); to beg; to plead with.
**suplicio** *m* torture.
**suplir** *vt* to supply; to make good, to make up for; to replace.
**suponer** *vt* to suppose; * *vi* to have authority.
**suposición** *f* supposition; authority.
**supremo/ma** *adj* supreme.
**supresión** *f* suppression; abolition; removal; deletion.
**suprimir** *vt* to suppress; to abolish; to remove; to delete.
**supuesto** *m* assumption; ~/ta *adj* supposed; ~ que *conj* since, granted that.
**supuración** *f* suppuration.
**supurar** *vt* to suppurate.
**sur** *adj* south, southern; * *m* south; south wind.
**surcar** *vt* to furrow; to cut, to score.
**surco** *m* furrow; groove.
**surgir** *vi* to emerge; to crop up.
**surtido** *m* assortment, supply.
**surtir** *vt* to supply, to furnish, to provide; * *vi* to spout, to spurt.
**susceptible** *adj* susceptible; impressionable.
**suscitar** *vt* to excite, to stir up.
**suscribir** *vt* to sign; to subscribe to.
**suscripción** *f* subscription.

**suscriptor/ra** *m/f* subscriber.
**susodicho/cha** *adj* above-mentioned.
**suspender** *vt* to suspend, to hang up; to stop; to fail (an exam etc).
**suspensión** *f* suspension; stoppage.
**suspenso/sa** *adj* hanging; suspended, failed.
**suspicacia** *f* suspicion, mistrust.
**suspicaz** *adj* suspicious, mistrustful.
**suspirar** *vi* to sigh.
**suspiro** *m* sigh.
**sustancia** *f* = **substancia**.
**sustancial** *adj* = **substancial**.
**sustancioso** *adj* = **substancioso**.
**sustantivo/va** *adj, m (gr)* substantive, noun.
**sustentar** *vt* to sustain; to support, to nourish.
**sustento** *m* food, sustenance; support.
**sustitución** *f* substitution.
**sustituir** *vt* to substitute.
**sustituto/ta** *adj, m/f* substitute.
**susto** *m* fright, scare.
**sustracción** *f* subtraction.
**sustraer** *vt* to take away; to subtract.
**susurrar** *vi* to whisper; to murmur; to rustle; ~se *vr* to be whispered about.
**susurro** *m* whisper; murmur.
**sutil** *adj* subtle; thin; delicate; very soft; keen, observant.
**sutileza** *f* subtlety; thinness; keenness.
**suyo/ya** *adj* his; hers; theirs; one's; his; her; its own; one's own; their own; **de ~** per se; **los ~s** *mpl* his own, near friends, relations, family, supporters.

# T

**tabaco** *m* tobacco; (*col*) cigarettes *pl*.
**tábano** *m* horsefly.
**taberna** *f* bar, tavern.
**tabernero/ra** *m/f* barman/barmaid, bartender.
**tabicar** *vt* to wall up.
**tabique** *m* thin wall; partition wall.
**tabla** *f* board; shelf; plank; slab; index of a book; bed of earth in a garden.
**tablado** *m* scaffold; platform; stage.
**tablero** *m* plank, board; chessboard; draughtboard; (*auto*) dashboard; bulletin board; gambling den.
**tableta** *f* tablet; (chocolate) bar.
**tablilla** *f* small board; (*med*) splint.
**tablón** *m* plank; beam; ~ **de anuncios** bulletin board.
**tabú** *m* taboo.
**taburete** *m* stool.
**tacañería** *f* meanness; craftiness.
**tacaño/ña** *adj* mean, stingy; crafty.
**tacha** *f* fault, defect; small nail.
**tachar** *vt* to find fault with; to cross out, to erase.
**tachuela** *f* tack, nail.
**tácito/ta** *adj* tacit, silent; implied.
**taciturno/na** *adj* tacit, silent; sulky.
**taco** *m* stopper, plug; heel (of a shoe); wad; book of coupons; billiard cue.
**tacón** *m* heel.
**taconear** *vi* to stamp with one's heels; to walk on one's heels.
**taconeo** *m* stamping of the heels in dancing.
**táctica** *f* tactics *pl*.
**tacto** *m* touch, feeling; tact.
**tafetán** *m* taffeta.
**tafilete** *m* morocco leather.
**tahona** *f* bakery.
**tahúr** *m* gambler; cheat.
**taimado/da** *adj* sly, cunning, crafty.
**tajada** *f* slice; (*med*) hoarseness.
**tajante** *adj* sharp.
**tajar** *vt* to cut; to chop; to slice.
**tajo** *m* cut, incision; cleft, sheer drop; working area; chopping block.
**tal** *adj* such; **con ~ que** provided that; **no hay ~** no such thing.
**tala** *f* felling of trees.
**taladrar** *vt* to bore; to pierce.
**taladro** *m* drill; borer, gimlet.

**talante** *m* mood; appearance; aspect; will.
**talar** *vt* to fell (trees); to desolate.
**talco** *m* talc.
**talega** *f*, **talego** *m* bag; bagful.
**talento** *m* talent.
**talismán** *m* talisman.
**talla** *f* raised work; sculpture; stature, size; measure (of anything); hand, draw, turn (at cards).
**tallado/da** *adj* cut; carved; engraved.
**tallador** *m* engraver.
**tallar** *vt* to cut, to chop; to carve in wood; to engrave; to measure.
**tallarines** *mpl* noodles.
**talle** *m* shape; size; proportion; waist.
**taller** *m* workshop, laboratory.
**tallo** *m* shoot, sprout.
**talón** *m* heel; receipt; cheque.
**talonario** *m* cheque book; receipt book.
**tamaño** *m* size, shape, bulk.
**tamarindo** *m* tamarind tree.
**tambalearse** *vr* to stagger, to waver.
**tambaleo** *m* staggering, reeling.
**también** *adv* also, as well; likewise; besides.
**tambor** *m* drum; drummer; eardrum.
**tamborilear** *vi* to drum.
**tamborilero** *m* drummer.
**tamiz** *m* fine sieve.
**tampoco** *adv* neither, nor.
**tampón** *m* tampon.
**tan** *adv* so.
**tanda** *f* turn; rotation; task; gang; number of persons employed in a workforce.
**tangente** *f* tangent.
**tangible** *adj* tangible.
**tanque** *m* tank; tanker.
**tantear** *vt* to reckon (up); to measure, to proportion; to consider; to examine.
**tanteo** *m* computation, calculation; valuation; test; scoring.
**tanto** *m* certain sum/quantity; point; goal; ~**/ta** *adj* so much, as much; very great; * *adv* so much, as much; so long, as long.
**tañido** *m* tune; sound; clink.
**tapa** *f* lid, cover; snack; (*col*) ~ **de los sesos** skull.
**tapadera** *f* lid (of a pot), cover.
**tapar** *vt* to stop up, to cover; to conceal, to hide.
**taparrabo** *m* loincloth.
**tapete** *m* tablecloth.

**tapia** *f* wall.

**tapiar** *vt* to brick up; to stop up (a passage).

**tapicería** *f* tapestry; upholstery; upholsterer's shop.

**tapicero** *m* tapestry-maker; upholsterer.

**tapiz** *m* tapestry; carpet.

**tapizar** *vt* to upholster.

**tapón** *m* cork, plug, bung.

**taquigrafía** *f* shorthand, stenography.

**taquígrafo/fa** *m/f* shorthand typist.

**taquilla** *f* booking office; takings *pl*.

**taquillero/ra** *m/f* ticket clerk.

**tara** *f* (*com*) tare.

**tarántula** *f* tarantula.

**tardanza** *f* slowness, delay.

**tardar** *vi* to delay; to take a long time; to be late.

**tarde** *f* afternoon; evening; * *adv* late.

**tardío/dia** *adj* late; slow, tardy.

**tardo/da** *adj* sluggish, tardy.

**tarea** *f* task.

**tarifa** *f* tariff; price list.

**tarima** *f* platform; step.

**tarjeta** *f* card; visiting card; ~ **postal** postcard; ~ **de crédito** credit card.

**tarro** *m* pot.

**tarta** *f* tart; cake.

**tartamudear** *vi* to stutter, to stammer.

**tartamudo/da** *adj* stammering.

**tarugo** *m* wooden peg/pin.

**tasa** *f* rate; measure, rule; valuation; ~s **de aeropuerto** airport tax.

**tasación** *f* valuation, appraisal.

**tasador** *m* appraiser.

**tasar** *vt* to appraise, to value.

**tasca** *f* (*col*) pub, bar, dive.

**tatarabuelo/la** *m/f* great-great-grandfather/mother.

**tataranieto/ta** *m/f* great-great-grandson/daughter.

**tatuaje** *m* tattoo; tattooing.

**tatuar** *vt* to tattoo.

**taurino/na** *adj* bullfighting *compd*.

**Tauro** *m* Taurus (sign of the zodiac).

**taxi** *m* taxi.

**taxista** *m/f* taxi driver.

**taza** *f* cup; basin of a fountain.

**té** *m* (*bot*) tea.

**te** *pn* you.

**tea** *f* torch.

**teatral** *adj* theatrical.

**teatro** *m* theatre, playhouse.

**tebeo** *m* comic.

**techo** *m* roof; ceiling.

**techumbre** *f* upper roof, ceiling.

**tecla** *f* key (of an organ, piano etc).

**teclado** *m* keyboard.

**técnico/ca** *adj* technical.

**tecnología** *f* technology.

**tedio** *m* boredom; dislike, abhorrence.

**teja** *f* tile.

**tejado** *m* roof covered with tiles.

**tejanos** *mpl* jeans *pl*.

**tejar** *vt* to tile.

**tejedor** *m* weaver.

**tejemaneje** *m* artfulness, cleverness; restlessness.

**tejer** *vt* to weave.

**tejido** *m* texture; web.

**tejo** *m* quoit (a ring of iron, plastic etc used in the game of quoits); hopscotch; (*bot*) yew tree.

**tejón** *m* badger.

**tela** *f* cloth; material.

**telar** *m* loom.

**telaraña** *f* cobweb.

**tele** *f* (*col*) telly.

**telebanca** *f* telephone banking.

**telecomedia** *f* sitcom.

**telediario** *m* television news.

**telefax** *m invar* fax; fax (machine).

**telefonear** *vt* to telephone.

**telefónico/ca** *adj* telephone *compd*.

**teléfono** *m* (tele)phone.

**teléfono público** *m* payphone.

**telegráfico/ca** *adj* telegraphic.

**telégrafo** *m* telegraph.

**telegrama** *m* telegram.

**telescopio** *m* telescope.

**teletienda** *f* home shopping programme.

**teletrabajador/ra** *m/f* teleworker.

**teletrabajo** *m* teleworking.

**televidente** *m/f* viewer.

**televisar** *vt* to televise.

**televisión** *f* television; ~ **por cable** cable television.

**televisor** *m* television set.

**télex** *m* telex.

**telón** *m* curtain.

**tema** *m* theme.

**temblar** *vi* to tremble.

**temblón/ona** *adj* trembling.

**temblor** *m* trembling; earthquake.

**temer** *vt* to fear, to doubt; * *vi* to be afraid.

**temerario/ria** *adj* rash.

**temeridad** *f* temerity, imprudence.

**temeroso/sa** *adj* timid; frightful.

**temible** *adj* dreadful, terrible.

**temor** *m* dread, fear.

**témpano** *m* ice-floe.

**temperamento** *m* temperament.
**temperatura** *f* temperature.
**tempested** *f* tempest, storm; violent commotion.
**tempestuoso/sa** *adj* tempestuous, stormy.
**templado/da** *adj* temperate, tempered.
**templanza** *f* temperance, moderation.
**templar** *vt* to temper, to moderate, to cool; to tune; ~se *vr* to be moderate.
**temple** *m* temperature; tempera; temperament; tuning; **al** ~ painted in distemper.
**templo** *m* temple.
**temporada** *f* time, season; epoch, period.
**temporal** *adj* temporary, temporal; * *m* tempest, storm.
**temprano/na** *adj* early, anticipated; * *adv* early; very early, prematurely.
**tenacidad** *f* tenacity; obstinacy.
**tenacillas** *fpl* small tongs *pl*.
**tenaz** *adj* tenacious; stubborn.
**tenaza(s)** *f* (*pl*) tongs *pl*, pincers *pl*.
**tenazmente** *adv* tenaciously; obstinately.
**tendedero** *m* clothes line.
**tendencia** *f* tendency.
**tender** *vt* to stretch out; to expand; to extend; to hang out; to lay; ~se *vr* to stretch oneself out.
**tenderete** *m* stall; display of goods.
**tendero/ra** *m/f* shopkeeper.
**tendido/da** *adj* lying down; hanging; * *m* row of seats for the spectators at a bullfight.
**tendón** *m* tendon, sinew.
**tenebroso/sa** *adj* dark, obscure.
**tenedor** *m* holder, keeper, tenant; fork.
**tenencia** *f* possession; tenancy; tenure.
**tener** *vt* to have; to take; to hold; to possess; ~se *vr* to stand upright; to stop, to halt; to resist; to adhere.
**tenia** *f* tapeworm.
**teniente** *m* lieutenant.
**tenis** *m* tennis.
**tenista** *m/f* tennis player.
**tenor** *m* meaning; (*mus*) tenor.
**tensar** *vt* to tauten; to draw.
**tensión** *f* tension.
**tenso/sa** *adj* tense.
**tentación** *f* temptation.
**tentador/ra** *m/f* tempter.
**tentar** *vt* to touch; to try; to tempt; to attempt.
**tentativa** *f* attempt.
**tentempié** *m* (*col*) snack.
**tenue** *adj* thin; tenuous, slender.
**tenuidad** *f* slenderness; weakness; trifle.
**teñir** *vt* to tinge, to dye.

**teología** *f* theology, divinity.
**teológico/ca** *adj* theological.
**teólogo** *m* theologian, divine.
**teorema** *f* theorem.
**teoría, teórica** *f* theory.
**teórico/ca** *adj* theoretical.
**terapéutico/ca** *adj* therapeutic.
**terapia** *f* therapy.
**tercermundista** *adj* Third World *compd*.
**tercer(o)/ra** *adj* third; * *m* (*law*) third party.
**terceto** *m* (*mus*) trio.
**terciar** *vt* to put on sideways; to divide into three parts; to plough the third time; * *vi* to mediate; to take part.
**tercio/cia** *adj* third; * *m* third part.
**terciopelo** *m* velvet.
**terco/ca** *adj* obstinate.
**tergiversación** *f* distortion; evasion.
**tergiversar** *vt* to distort.
**termal** *adj* thermal.
**termas** *fpl* thermal waters *pl*.
**terminación** *f* termination; conclusion; last syllable of a word.
**terminal** *adj*, *m/f* terminal.
**terminante** *adj* decisive; categorical.
**terminar** *vt* to finish; to end; to terminate; * *vi* to end; to stop.
**término** *m* term; end; boundary; limit; terminus.
**terminología** *f* terminology.
**termodinámico/ca** *adj* thermodynamic.
**termómetro** *m* thermometer.
**termo** *m* flask.
**termostato** *m* thermostat.
**ternero/ra** *m/f* calf; veal; heifer.
**ternilla** *f* gristle.
**ternilloso/sa** *adj* gristly.
**terno** *m* three-piece suit.
**ternura** *f* tenderness.
**terquedad** *f* stubbornness, obstinacy.
**terrado** *m* terrace.
**terraplén** *m* terrace; platform.
**terrateniente** *m/f* landowner.
**terraza** *f* balcony; (flat) roof; terrace (in fields).
**terremoto** *m* earthquake.
**terrenal** *adj* terrestrial, earthly.
**terreno/na** *adj* earthly, terrestrial; * *m* land, ground, field.
**terrestre** *adj* terrestrial.
**terrible** *adj* terrible, dreadful; ferocious.
**territorial** *adj* territorial.
**territorio** *m* territory.
**terrón** *m* clod of earth; lump; ~ones *mpl* landed property.

**terror** *m* terror, dread.
**terrorismo** *m* terrorism.
**terrorista** *m/f* terrorist.
**terso/sa** *adj* smooth, glossy.
**tersura** *f* smoothness; shine.
**tertulia** *f* club, assembly, circle.
**tesis** *f invar* thesis.
**tesón** *m* tenacity, firmness.
**tesorero** *m* treasurer.
**tesoro** *m* treasure; exchequer.
**testamentaría** *f* testamentary execution.
**testamentario** *m* executor of a will; **~/ria** *adj* testamentary.
**testamento** *m* will, testament.
**testar** *vt, vi* to make one's will.
**testarudo/da** *adj* obstinate.
**testículo** *m* testicle.
**testificación** *f* attestation.
**testificar** *vt* to attest, to witness.
**testigo** *m* witness, deponent.
**testimoniar** *vt* to attest, to bear witness to.
**testimonio** *m* testimony.
**teta** *f* teat.
**tétanos** *m* tetanus.
**tetera** *f* teapot.
**tetilla** *f* nipple; teat (of a bottle).
**tétrico/ca** *adj* gloomy, sullen, surly.
**textil** *adj* textile *compd*.
**texto** *m* text.
**textual** *adj* textual.
**textura** *f* texture.
**tez** *f* complexion, hue.
**ti** *pn* you; yourself.
**tía** *f* aunt; (*col*) bird.
**tiara** *f* tiara.
**tibieza** *f* lukewarmness.
**tibio/bia** *adj* lukewarm.
**tiburón** *m* shark.
**tiempo** *m* time; term; weather; (*gr*) tense; occasion, opportunity; season.
**tienda** *f* tent; awning; tilt; shop.
**tiento** *m* touch; circumspection; **a ~/a tientas** gropingly.
**tierno/na** *adj* tender.
**tierra** *f* earth; land, ground; native country.
**tieso/sa** *adj* stiff, hard, firm; robust; valiant; stubborn.
**tiesto** *m* large earthenware pot.
**tifón** *m* typhoon.
**tifus** *m* typhus.
**tigre** *m* tiger.
**tijeras** *fpl* scissors *pl*.
**tijeretada** *f* cut (with scissors), clip.
**tijereta** *f* earwig.
**tijeretear** *vt* to cut (with scissors).

**tildar** *vt* to brand, to stigmatize.
**tilde** *f* tilde (ñ).
**tilo** *m* lime tree.
**timar** *vt* to steal; to swindle.
**timbrar** *vt* to stamp.
**timbre** *m* stamp; bell; timbre; stamp duty.
**timidez** *f* timidity.
**tímido/da** *adj* timid; cowardly.
**timo** *m* swindle.
**timón** *m* helm, rudder.
**tímpano** *m* eardrum; small drum.
**tina** *f* tub; bath(tub).
**tinaja** *f* large earthenware jar.
**tinglado** *m* shed; trick; intrigue.
**tinieblas** *fpl* darkness; shadows *pl*.
**tino** *m* skill; judgement, prudence.
**tinta** *f* ink; tint, dye; colour.
**tinte** *m* tint, dye; dry cleaner's (place of business).
**tintero** *m* inkwell.
**tinto/ta** *adj* dyed; * *m* red wine.
**tintorería** *f* dry cleaner's (place of business).
**tintura** *f* tincture; dyeing.
**tiña** *f* scab.
**tiñoso/sa** *adj* scabby, scurvy; niggardly.
**tío** *m* uncle; (*col*) bloke, chap.
**tiovivo** *m* merry-go-round, roundabout.
**típico/ca** *adj* typical.
**tiple** *m* (*mus*) treble; * *f* soprano.
**tipo** *m* type; norm; pattern; (*col*) bloke, chap.
**tipografía** *f* typography.
**tipográfico/ca** *adj* typographical.
**tipógrafo** *m* printer.
**tiquet** *m* ticket; cash slip.
**tiquismiquis** *m invar* fussy person.
**tira** *f* abundance; strip.
**tirabuzón** *m* curl.
**tirachinas** *m invar* catapult.
**tirado/da** *adj* dirt-cheap; (*col*) very easy; * *f* cast; distance; series; edition.
**tirador** *m* handle.
**tiranía** *f* tyranny.
**tiránico/ca** *adj* tyrannical.
**tiranizar** *vt* to tyrannize.
**tirano/na** *m/f* tyrant.
**tirante** *m* joist; stay; strap; brace; * *adj* taut, extended, drawn.
**tirantez** *f* tension; tautness.
**tirar** *vt* to throw; to pull; to draw; to drop; to tend, to aim at; * *vi* to shoot; to pull; to go; to tend to.
**Tirita**™ *f* (sticking) plaster.
**tiritar** *vi* to shiver.
**tiritona** *f* shiver; shaking with cold.

**tiro** *m* throw, shot; prank; set of coach horses; **errar el ~** to miss (at shooting).

**tirón** *m* pull, haul, tug.

**tirotear** *vt* to shoot at.

**tiroteo** *m* shooting; sharpshooting.

**tirria** *f* antipathy.

**tísico/ca** *adj* consumptive.

**tisis** *f* tuberculosis.

**títere** *m* puppet; ridiculous little fellow.

**titiritero/ra** *m/f* puppeteer.

**titubear** *vi* to stammer; to stagger; to hesitate.

**titubeo** *m* staggering; hesitation.

**titular** *adj* titular; * *m/f* occupant; * *m* headline; * *vt* to title; **~se** *vr* to obtain a title.

**título** *m* title; name; **a ~** on pretence, under pretext.

**tiza** *f* chalk.

**tiznar** *vt* to stain; to tarnish.

**tizne** *m* soot; smut.

**tiznón** *m* spot, stain.

**tizón** *m* half-burnt wood.

**toalla** *f* towel.

**tobillo** *m* ankle.

**tobogán** *m* toboggan; roller-coaster; slide.

**toca** *f* headdress.

**tocadiscos** *m invar* record player.

**tocado** *m* headdress, headgear.

**tocador** *m* dressing table; dressing room.

**tocante** *prep*: **~ a** concerning, relating to.

**tocar** *vt* to touch; to strike; (*mus*) to play; to ring (a bell); * *vi* to belong; to concern; to knock; to call; to be a duty/obligation.

**tocayo/ya** *m/f* namesake.

**tocino** *m* bacon.

**todavía** *adv* even; yet, still.

**todo/da** *adj* all, entire; every; * *pn* everything, all; * *m* whole.

**todopoderoso/sa** *adj* almighty.

**todoterreno** *m* all-terrain vehicle.

**toga** *f* toga; gown.

**toldo** *m* awning; parasol.

**tolerable** *adj* tolerable.

**tolerancia** *f* tolerance, indulgence.

**tolerante** *adj* tolerant.

**tolerar** *vt* to tolerate, to suffer.

**toma** *f* taking (as in the taking of vows); (*med*) dose; plug, socket.

**tomar** *vt* to take; to seize, to grasp; to understand; to interpret, to perceive; to drink; to acquire; * *vi* to drink; to take.

**tomate** *m* tomato.

**tomillo** *m* thyme.

**tomo** *m* bulk; tome; volume.

**ton** *m*: **sin ~ ni son** without rhyme/reason.

**tonada** *f* tune, melody.

**tonadilla** *f* interlude of music; short tune.

**tonalidad** *f* tone.

**tonel** *m* cask, barrel.

**tonelada** *f* ton; (*mar*) tonnage duty.

**tónico/ca** *adj* tonic, strengthening; * *m* tonic; * *f* tonic (water); (*mus*) tonic; (*fig*) keynote.

**tonificar** *vt* to tone up.

**tono** *m* tone.

**tono de marcar** *m* dialling tone.

**tontada** *f* nonsense.

**tontear** *vi* to talk nonsense; to act foolishly.

**tontería** *f* foolery, nonsense.

**tonto/ta** *adj* stupid, foolish.

**topacio** *m* topaz.

**topar** *vt* to run into; to find.

**tope** *m* butt; scuffle; **~s** *mpl* (*rail*) buffers *pl*.

**topera** *f* molehill.

**tópico/ca** *adj* topical.

**topo** *m* mole; stumbler.

**topografía** *f* topography.

**topográfico/ca** *adj* topographical.

**toque** *m* touch; bell-ringing; crisis.

**toquilla** *f* headscarf; shawl.

**tórax** *m* thorax.

**torbellino** *m* whirlwind.

**torcedura** *f* twisting.

**torcer** *vt* to twist, to curve; to turn; to sprain; **~se** *vr* to bend; to go wrong; * *vi* to turn off.

**torcido/da** *adj* oblique; crooked.

**torcimiento** *m* bending; deflection; circumlocution.

**tordo** *m* thrush; **~/da** *adj* speckled black and white.

**torear** *vt* to avoid; to tease; * *vi* to fight bulls.

**toreo** *m* bullfighting.

**torero** *m* bullfighter.

**toril** *m* bull pen (at bullfight).

**tormenta** *f* storm, tempest.

**tormento** *m* torment, pain, anguish; torture.

**tornar** *vt* to return; to restore; **~se** *vr* to become; * *vi* to return; **~ a hacer** to do again.

**tornasolado** *adj* iridescent; shimmering.

**torneo** *m* tournament.

**tornillo** *m* screw.

**torniquete** *m* turnstile; (*med*) tourniquet.

**torno** *m* winch; revolution.

**toro** *m* bull.

**toronja** *f* grapefruit.

**torpe** *adj* dull, heavy; stupid.

**torpedo** *m* torpedo.

**torpeza** *f* heaviness, dullness; torpor; stupidity.

**torre** *f* tower; turret; steeple of a church.

**torrefacto/ta** *adj* roasted.

**torrente** *m* torrent.

**tórrido/da** *adj* torrid, parched, hot.

**torrija** *f* French toast.

**torso** *m* torso.

**torta** *f* cake; (*col*) slap.

**tortícolis** *f invar* stiff neck.

**tortilla** *f* omelette; pancake.

**tórtola** *f* turtledove.

**tortuga** *f* tortoise.

**tortuoso/sa** *adj* tortuous, circuitous.

**tortura** *f* torture.

**torvo/va** *adj* stern, grim.

**tos** *f* cough.

**toscamente** *adv* coarsely, grossly.

**tosco/ca** *adj* coarse, ill-bred, clumsy.

**toser** *vi* to cough.

**tostada** *f* slice of toast.

**tostado/da** *adj* parched; sunburnt; light-yellow; light-brown.

**tostador** *m* toaster.

**tostar** *vt* to toast, to roast.

**total** *m* whole, totality; * *adj* total, entire; * *adv* in short.

**totalidad** *f* totality.

**totalitario/ria** *adj* totalitarian.

**tóxico/ca** *adj* toxic; * *m* poison.

**toxicómano/na** *m/f* drug addict.

**tozudo/da** *adj* obstinate.

**traba** *f* obstacle, impediment; trammel, fetter.

**trabajador/ra** *adj* working; * *m/f* worker.

**trabajar** *vt* to work, to labour; to persuade; to push; * *vi* to strive.

**trabajo** *m* work, labour, toil; difficulty; ~s *mpl* troubles *pl*.

**trabajoso/sa** *adj* laborious; painful.

**trabalenguas** *m invar* tongue twister.

**trabar** *vt* to join, to unite; to take hold of; to fetter, to shackle.

**trabucarse** *vr* to mistake.

**tracción** *f* traction; ~ delantera/trasera front-wheel/rear-wheel drive.

**tractor** *m* tractor.

**tradición** *f* tradition.

**traducción** *f* translation.

**traducir** *vt* to translate.

**traductor,ra** *m/f* translator.

**traer** *vt* to bring, to carry; to attract; to persuade; to wear; to cause.

**traficante** *m* merchant, dealer.

**traficar** *vi* to trade, to do business, to deal.

**tráfico** *m* traffic, trade.

**tragaldabas** *m/f invar* glutton.

**tragaluz** *m* skylight.

**tragaperras** *m/f invar* slot machine.

**tragar** *vt* to swallow; to swallow up.

**tragedia** *f* tragedy.

**trágico/ca** *adj* tragic.

**trago** *m* drink; gulp; adversity, misfortune.

**tragón/ona** *adj* gluttonous.

**traición** *f* treason.

**traicionar** *vt* to betray.

**traicionero/ra** *adj* treacherous.

**traidor/ra** *m/f* traitor; * *adj* treacherous.

**traje** *m* dress, costume; suit.

**trajín** *m* haulage; (*col*) bustle.

**trajinar** *vt* to carry; * *vi* to bustle about; to travel around.

**trama** *f* weft, woof; (*fig*) plot; intrigue.

**tramar** *vt* to weave; to plot.

**tramitar** *vt* to transact; to negotiate; to handle.

**trámite** *m* path; (*law*) procedure.

**tramo** *m* section; piece of ground; flight of stairs.

**tramoya** *f* scene, theatrical decoration; trick.

**tramoyista** *m* scene-painter; swindler.

**trampa** *f* trap, snare; trapdoor; fraud.

**trampear** *vt* to swindle, to deceive; * *vi* to cheat.

**trampolín** *m* trampoline; diving board.

**tramposo/sa** *adj* deceitful, swindling.

**tranca** *f* bar, crossbeam.

**trance** *m* danger; last stage of life; trance.

**tranco** *m* long step/stride.

**tranquilidad** *f* tranquillity; repose, heart's ease.

**tranquilizar** *vt* to calm; to reassure.

**tranquilo/la** *adj* tranquil, calm, quiet.

**transacción** *f* transaction.

**transbordador** *m* ferry.

**transbordar** *vt* to transfer.

**transbordo** *m* transfer; **hacer ~** to change (trains).

**transcribir** *vt* to transcribe; to copy.

**transcurrir** *vi* to pass; to turn out.

**transcurso** *m*: ~ **del tiempo** course of time.

**transeúnte** *adj* transitory; * *m* passerby.

**transferencia** *f* transference; (*com*) transfer.

**transferir** *vt* to transfer; to defer.

**transfiguración** *f* transformation, transfiguration.

**transformación** *f* transformation.

**transformador** *m* transformer.

**transformar** *vt* to transform; ~se *vr* to change one's sentiments/manners.

**tránsfuga, tránsfugo** *m* deserter; fugitive; defector.

**transfusión** *f* transfusion.

**transgresión** *f* transgression.

**transgresor** *m* transgressor.

**transición** *f* transition.

**transido/da** *adj* worn out with anguish; overcome.

**transigir** *vi* to compromise.

**transistor** *m* transistor.

**transitar** *vi* to travel, to pass through a place.

**transitivo/va** *adj* transitive.

**tránsito** *m* passage; transition; road, way; change; removal; death of holy/virtuous persons.

**transitorio/ria** *adj* transitory.

**transmisión** *f* transmission; transfer; broadcast.

**transmitir** *vt* to transmit; to broadcast.

**transmutación** *f* transmutation.

**transmutar** *vt* to transmute.

**transparencia** *f* transparency; clearness; slide.

**transparentarse** *vr* to be transparent; to shine through.

**transparente** *adj* transparent.

**transpiración** *f* perspiration; transpiration.

**transpirar** *vt* to perspire; to transpire.

**transportar** *vt* to transport, to convey.

**transporte** *m* transportation.

**transposición** *f* transposition, transposal.

**transversal** *adj* transverse; collateral.

**tranvía** *m* tram/tramcar.

**trapacería** *f* fraud, deceit.

**trapacero/ra** *adj* deceitful.

**trapecio** *m* trapeze.

**trapecista** *m/f* trapeze artist.

**trapero/ra** *m/f* ragman, rag-and-bone man; dealer in rags.

**trapicheo** *m* (*col*) fiddle.

**trapo** *m* rag, tatter.

**tráquea** *f* windpipe.

**traqueteo** *m* rattling.

**tras** *prep* after, behind.

**trascendencia** *f* transcendency; penetration.

**trascendental** *adj* transcendental.

**trascender** *vi* to smell; to come out; **~ de** to go beyond.

**trasegar** *vt* to move about; to decant.

**trasero/ra** *adj* back; * *m* bottom.

**trasfondo** *m* background.

**trasgredir** *vt* to contravene.

**trashumante** *adj* migrating.

**trasiego** *m* removal; decanting (of drinks).

**trasladar** *vt* to transport; to transfer; to postpone; to transcribe, to copy; **~se** *vr* to move.

**traslado** *m* move; removal.

**traslucirse** *vr* to be transparent; to conjecture.

**trasluz** *m* reflected light.

**trasnochar** *vi* to watch, to sit up the whole night.

**traspaperlarse** *vr* to get mislaid among other papers.

**traspasar** *vt* to remove, to transport; to transfix, to pierce; to return; to exceed (the proper bounds); to transfer.

**traspaso** *m* transfer, sale.

**traspié** *m* trip; slip, stumble.

**trasplantar** *vt* to transplant.

**trasplante** *m* transplant.

**trasquilar** *vt* to shear (sheep); to clip.

**trasquilón** *m* cut (of the shears); badly cut hair.

**traste** *m* fret (of a guitar); **dar al ~ con algo** to ruin something.

**trastear** *vt* to move (furniture).

**trastera** *f* lumber.

**trastero** *m* lumber room.

**trastienda** *f* back room behind a shop.

**trasto** *m* piece of junk; useless person.

**trastornado/da** *adj* crazy.

**trastornar** *vt* to overthrow, to overturn; to confuse; **~se** *vr* to go crazy.

**trastorno** *m* overturning; confusion.

**trastrocar** *vt* to invert (the order of things).

**tratable** *adj* friendly.

**tratado** *m* treaty, convention; treatise.

**tratamiento** *m* treatment; style of address.

**tratante** *m* dealer.

**tratar** *vt* to traffic, to trade; to use; to treat; to handle; to address; **~se** *vr* to treat each other.

**trato** *m* treatment; manner, address; trade, traffic; conversation; (*com*) agreement.

**trauma** *m* trauma.

**través** *m* (*fig*) reverse; **de/al ~** across, crossways; **a ~ de** *prep* across; over; through.

**travesaño** *m* crossbeam; transom.

**travesía** *f* crossing; side road/street; trajectory; (*mar*) crosswind.

**travesura** *f* wit; wickedness.

**travieso/sa** *adj* restless, uneasy, fidgety; turbulent; lively; naughty.

**trayecto** *m* road; journey, stretch; course.

**trayectoria** *f* trajectory; path.

**traza** *f* first sketch; trace, outline; project; manner; means; appearance.

**trazar** *vt* to plan out; to project; to trace.

**trazo** *m* sketch, plan, design.

**trébedes** *fpl* trivet, tripod.

**trébol** *m* trefoil, clover.

**trece** *adj, m* thirteen; thirteenth.

**trecho** *m* space, distance of time/place; **a ~s** at intervals.

**tregua** *f* truce, cessation of hostilities.

**treinta** *adj, m* thirty.

**tremendo/da** *adj* terrible, formidable; awful, grand.

**tremolar** *vt* to hoist (the colours); to wave.

**trémulo/la** *adj* tremulous, trembling.

**tren** *m* train, retinue; baggage; (*rail*) train; **~ de alta velocidad** high-speed train; **~ de mercancías** freight train.

**trenza** *f* plait (in hair); braid.

**trenzar** *vt* to braid.

**trepar** *vi* to climb; to crawl.

**tres** *adj, m* three.

**tresillo** *m* three-piece suite; (*mus*) triplet.

**treta** *f* thrust (fencing); trick.

**triangular** *adj* triangular.

**triángulo** *m* triangle.

**tribu** *f* tribe.

**tribulación** *f* tribulation, affliction.

**tribuna** *f* tribune.

**tribunal** *m* tribunal, court of justice.

**tributar** *vt* to pay; to contribute to; to pay (homage, respect).

**tributario/ria** *adj* tributary.

**tributo** *m* tribute.

**tricolor** *adj* tricoloured.

**tricotar** *vi* to knit.

**tridente** *m* trident.

**trienal** *adj* triennial.

**trienio** *m* period of three years.

**trigal** *m* wheat field.

**trigésimo/ma** *adj, m* thirtieth.

**trigo** *m* wheat.

**trigueño/ña** *adj* corn-coloured; olive-skinned.

**trillado/da** *adj* beaten; trite, stale, hackneyed; **camino ~** common routine.

**trilladora** *f* threshing machine.

**trillar** *vt* to thresh.

**trillón** *m* trillion.

**trimestral** *adj* quarterly, three-monthly.

**trimestre** *m* period of three months.

**trinar** *vi* to trill, to quaver; to be angry.

**trincar** *vt* to tie up; to pinion.

**trinchante** *m* carver; carving knife.

**trinchar** *vt* to carve, to cut up (meat).

**trinchera** *f* trench, entrenchment.

**trineo** *m* sledge, sleigh.

**Trinidad** *f* Trinity.

**trino** *m* trill.

**trío** *m* (*mus*) trio.

**tripa** *f* gut, intestine; **~s** *fpl* guts; tripe.

**triple** *adj* triple, treble.

**triplicar** *vt* to treble.

**trípode** *m* tripod, trivet.

**tripulación** *f* crew.

**tripulante** *m/f* crewman/woman.

**tripular** *vt* to man; to drive.

**triquiñuela** *f* trick.

**triquitraque** *m* clack, clatter; clashing.

**tris** *m invar*: **estar en un ~ de** to be on the point of.

**triste** *adj* sad, mournful, melancholy.

**tristeza** *f* sadness, mourning.

**trituración** *f* pulverization.

**triturar** *vt* to reduce to powder; to grind, to pound.

**triunfal** *adj* triumphal.

**triunfar** *vi* to triumph; to trump (at cards).

**triunfo** *m* triumph; trump (at cards).

**trivial** *adj* trivial.

**trivialidad** *f* triviality.

**triza** *f*: **hacer ~s** to smash to bits; to tear to shreds.

**trocar** *vt* to exchange.

**trocha** *f* short cut.

**troche**: **a ~ y moche** *adv* helter-skelter.

**trofeo** *m* trophy.

**tromba** *f* whirlwind.

**trombón** *m* trombone.

**trombosis** *f invar* thrombosis.

**trompa** *f* trumpet; proboscis; spinning top.

**trompazo** *m* heavy blow; accident.

**trompeta** *f* trumpet; * *m* trumpeter.

**trompetilla** *f* small trumpet; speaking-trumpet.

**trompicón** *m* stumble.

**trompo** *m* spinning top.

**tronar** *vi* to thunder; to rage.

**troncar** *vt* to truncate, to mutilate.

**tronchar** *vt* to cut off; to shatter; to tire out.

**troncho** *m* sprig, stem/stalk.

**tronco** *m* trunk (of the body, tree); log; stock.

**tronera** *f* loophole; small window; pocket (of a billiard table).

**trono** *m* throne.

**tropa** *f* troop.

**tropel** *m* confused noise; hurry; bustle, confusion; heap of things; crowd; **en ~** in a tumultuous and confused manner.

**tropelía** *f* outrage.

**tropezar** *vi* to stumble; * *vt* to meet accidentally.

**tropezón/ona** *adj* stumbling; * *m* trip; **a ~ones** by fits and starts.
**tropical** *adj* tropical.
**trópico** *m* tropic.
**tropiezo** *m* stumble, trip; obstacle; slip, fault; quarrel; dispute.
**trotamundos** *m invar* globetrotter.
**trotar** *vi* to trot.
**trote** *m* trot; travelling.
**trovador/ra** *m/f* troubadour.
**trozo** *m* piece.
**trucha** *f* trout.
**truco** *m* knack; trick.
**trueno** *m* thunderclap.
**trueque** *m* exchange.
**trufa** *f* truffle.
**truhán** *adj* rogue.
**truncado/da** *adj* truncated.
**truncamiento** *m* truncation.
**truncar** *vt* to truncate, to maim.
**tu** *adj* your.
**tú** *pn* you.
**tubérculo** *m* tuber.
**tuberculosis** *f* tuberculosis.
**tubería** *f* pipe; pipeline.
**tubo** *m* tube.
**tuerca** *f* screw.
**tuerto/ta** *adj* one-eyed; squint-eyed; * *m/f* one-eyed person.
**tuétano** *m* marrow.
**tufarada** *f* strong scent/smell.
**tufo** *m* warm vapour arising from the earth; offensive smell.
**tugurio** *m* slum.
**tul** *m* tulle.
**tulipán** *m* tulip.
**tullido/da** *adj* crippled, maimed.
**tumba** *f* tomb.
**tumbar** *vt* to knock down; * *vi* to tumble (to fall down); **~se** *vr* to lie down to sleep.

**tumbo** *m* fall; jolt.
**tumbona** *f* easy chair; beach chair.
**tumor** *m* tumour, growth.
**túmulo** *m* tomb; sepulchral monument.
**tumulto** *m* tumult, uproar.
**tumultuoso/sa** *adj* tumultuous.
**tuna** *f* (*bot*) prickly pear.
**tunda** *f* beating.
**túnel** *m* tunnel.
**túnica** *f* tunic.
**tuno** *m* rogue.
**tupé** *m* toupee, wig/hairpiece.
**tupido/da** *adj* dense.
**tupir** *vt* to press close; **~se** *vr* to stuff oneself.
**turbación** *f* perturbation, confusion; trouble, disorder.
**turbado/da** *adj* disturbed.
**turbante** *m* turban.
**turbar** *vt* to disturb, to trouble; **~se** *vr* to be disturbed.
**turbina** *f* turbine.
**turbio/bia** *adj* muddy; troubled.
**turbulencia** *f* turbulence; disturbance.
**turbulento/ta** *adj* muddy; turbulent.
**turismo** *m* tourism; **~ rural** rural tourism.
**turista** *m/f* tourist, holiday-maker.
**turístico/ca** *adj* tourist *compd*.
**turnar** *vi* to alternate.
**turno** *m* turn; shift; opportunity.
**turquesa** *f* turquoise.
**turrón** *m* nougat (almond cake).
**tutear** *vt* to address as *tu*.
**tutela** *f* guardianship, tutelage.
**tutelar** *adj* tutelar, tutelary.
**tutor** *m* guardian, tutor.
**tutora** *f* tutoress.
**tutoría** *f* tutelage.
**tuyo/ya** *adj* yours; **~s** *pl* friends and relations of the party addressed.

# U

**u** *conj*/(instead of/before *an* o/*ho*).
**ubicar** *vt* to place; **~se** *vr* to be located.
**ubre** *f* udder.
**ufanarse** *vr* to boast.
**ufano/na** *adj* haughty, arrogant.
**ujier** *m* usher.
**úlcera** *f* ulcer.
**ulcerar** *vi* to ulcerate.
**ulterior** *adj* ulterior; farther, further.
**últimamente** *adv* lately.
**ultimar** *vt* to finalize; to finish.
**ultimátum** *m* ultimatum.
**último/ma** *adj* last; latest; bottom; top.
**ultrajar** *vt* to outrage; to despise; to abuse.
**ultraje** *m* outrage.
**ultramar** *adj*, *m* overseas.
**ultramarinos** *mpl* groceries.
**ultrasónico/ca** *adj* ultrasonic.
**umbilical** *adj* umbilical.
**umbral** *m* threshold.
**un/una** *art* a, an; * *adj*, *m* one (for **uno**).
**unánime** *adj* unanimous.
**unanimidad** *f* unanimity.
**unción** *f* unction; extreme/last unction.
**ungir** *vt* to anoint.
**ungüento** *m* ointment.
**únicamente** *adv* only, simply.
**único/ca** *adj* only; singular, unique.
**unicornio** *m* unicorn.
**unidad** *f* unity; unit; conformity; union.
**unificar** *vt* to unite.
**uniformar** *vt* to make uniform.
**uniforme** *adj* uniform; * *m* (*mil*) uniform, regimentals *pl*.
**uniformidad** *f* uniformity.
**unilateral** *adj* unilateral.
**unión** *f* union; **U~ Europea** European Union.
**unir** *vt* to join, to unite; to mingle; to bind, to tie; **~se** *vr* to associate.
**unísono/na** *adj* unison.
**universal** *adj* universal.
**universalidad** *f* universality.
**universidad** *f* university.
**universitario/ria** *adj* university *compd*; * *m/f* student.

**universo** *m* universe.
**uno** *m* one; **~/una** *adj* one; sole, only; **~ a otro** one another; **~ a ~** one by one; **a una** jointly together.
**untar** *vt* to anoint; to grease; (*col*) to bribe.
**uña** *f* nail; hoof; claw, talon.
**¡upa!** up! up!
**urbanidad** *f* urbanity, politeness.
**uranio** *m* uranium.
**Urano** *m* Uranus (planet).
**urbanismo** *m* town planning.
**urbanización** *f* urban development; housing estate.
**urbano/na** *adj* urban; urbane, polite.
**urdimbre** *f* warp; intrigue.
**urdir** *vt* to warp; to contrive.
**urgencia** *f* urgency; emergency; need, necessity.
**urgente** *adj* urgent.
**urgentemente** *adv* urgently.
**urgir** *vi* to be urgent.
**urinario/ria** *adj* urinary; * *m* urinal.
**urna** *f* urn; ballot box.
**urraca** *f* magpie.
**usado/da** *adj* used; experienced; worn.
**usanza** *f* usage, use, custom.
**usar** *vt* to use, to make use of; to wear; **~se** *vr* to be used.
**uso** *m* use, service; custom; mode.
**usted** *pn* you.
**usuario** *m* user.
**usufructo** *m* (*law*) usufruct, use.
**usura** *f* usury.
**usurario/ria** *adj* usurious.
**usurero** *m* usurer.
**usurpación** *f* usurpation.
**usurpar** *vt* to usurp.
**utensilio** *m* utensil.
**uterino/na** *adj* uterine.
**útero** *m* uterus, womb.
**util** *adj* useful, profitable; * *m* utility.
**utilidad** *f* utility.
**utilizar** *vt* to use; to make useful.
**utopía** *f* Utopia.
**utópico/ca** *adj* Utopian.
**uva** *f* grape.

# V

**vaca** *f* cow; beef.
**vacaciones** *fpl* vacation; holidays *pl*.
**vacante** *adj* vacant; * *f* vacancy.
**vaciar** *vt* to empty, to clear; to mould; * *vi* to fall, to decrease (of waters); **~se** *vr* to empty.
**vacilación** *f* hesitation; irresolution.
**vacilar** *vi* to hesitate; to falter; to fail.
**vacío/cía** *adj* void, empty; unoccupied; concave; vain; presumptuous; * *m* vacuum; emptiness.
**vacuna** *f* vaccine.
**vacunar** *vt* to vaccinate.
**vacuno/na** *adj* bovine, cow *compd*.
**vadear** *vt* to wade, to ford.
**vagabundo/da** *adj* wandering; * *m* vagrant, bum, tramp.
**vagancia** *f* vagrancy.
**vagar** *vi* to rove/loiter about; to wander.
**vagido** *m* cry of a child; convulsive sob.
**vagina** *f* vagina.
**vago/ga** *adj* vagrant; restless; vague.
**vagón** *m* (*rail*) wagon; carriage; **~ de mercancías** goods wagon.
**vaguear** *vi* to rove, to loiter; to wander.
**vahído** *m* vertigo, giddiness.
**vaho** *m* steam, vapour.
**vaina** *f* scabbard (of a sword); pod, husk.
**vainilla** *f* (*bot*) vanilla.
**vaivén** *m* fluctuation, instability; giddiness.
**vajilla** *f* crockery.
**vale** *m* farewell; promissory note, IOU.
**valedero/ra** *adj* valid; efficacious; binding.
**valentía** *f* valour, courage.
**valentón** *m* braggart.
**valentonada** *f* brag, boast.
**valer** *vi* to be valuable; to be deserving; to cost; to be valid; to be worth; to produce; to be current; * *vt* to protect, to favour; to be worth; to be equivalent to; **~se** *vr* to employ, to make use of; to have recourse to.
**valeroso/sa** *adj* valiant, brave; strong, powerful.
**valía** *f* valuation; worth.
**validar** *vt* to validate.
**validez** *f* validity; stability.
**válido/da** *adj* valid.
**valiente** *adj* robust, vigorous; valiant, brave; boasting.
**valija** *f* suitcase.

**valioso/sa** *adj* valuable.
**valla** *f* fence; hurdle; barricade.
**vallar** *vt* to fence in.
**valle** *m* valley.
**valor** *m* value; price; validity; force; power; courage, valour.
**valoración** *f* valuation.
**valorar** *vt* to value; to evaluate.
**valuación** *f* valuation.
**vals** *m invar* waltz.
**válvula** *f* valve.
**vampiro** *m* vampire.
**vanagloriarse** *vr* to boast.
**vandalismo** *m* vandalism.
**vándalo/la** *m*, *adj* vandal.
**vanguardia** *f* vanguard.
**vanidad** *f* vanity; ostentation.
**vanidoso/sa** *adj* vain, showy; haughty; conceited.
**vano/na** *adj* vain; useless, frivolous; arrogant; futile; **en ~** in vain.
**vapor** *m* vapour, steam; breath; steamer, steamboat, steamship.
**vaporizador** *m* atomizer.
**vaporizar** *vt* to vaporize.
**vaporoso/sa** *adj* vaporous.
**vapular** *vt* to whip, to flog.
**vaquerizo/za** *adj* cattle *compd*; * *m* cowherd, cowman
**vaquero** *m* cowherd, cowman; **~/ra** *adj* belonging to a cowherd; **~s** *mpl* jeans *pl*.
**vara** *f* rod; pole, staff; stick.
**variable** *adj* variable, changeable.
**variación** *f* variation.
**variado/da** *adj* varied; variegated.
**variar** *vt* to vary; to modify; to change; * *vi* to vary.
**varices** *fpl* varicose veins *pl*.
**variedad** *f* variety; inconstancy.
**varilla** *f* small rod; curtain rod; spindle; pivot.
**vario/ria** *adj* varied, different; vague; variegated; **~s** *pl* some; several.
**varón** *m* man, male.
**varonil** *adj* male, masculine; manly.
**vasco/ca** *adj*, *m/f* Basque.
**vascuence** *m* Basque.
**Vaselina**™ *f* Vaseline™.
**vasija** *f* vessel.
**vaso** *m* glass; vessel; vase.
**vástago** *m* bud, shoot; offspring.

**vasto/ta** *adj* vast, huge.
**vaticinar** *vt* to divine, to foretell.
**vaticinio** *m* prophecy.
**vatio** *m* watt.
**vecindad** *f* inhabitants of a place; neighbourhood.
**vecindario** *m* number of inhabitants of a place; neighbourhood.
**vecino/na** *adj* neighbouring; near; * *m* neighbour, inhabitant.
**veda** *f* prohibition.
**vedar** *vt* to prohibit, to forbid; to impede.
**vegetación** *f* vegetation.
**vegetal** *adj* vegetable.
**vegetar** *vi* to vegetate.
**vegetariano/na** *adj, m/f* vegetarian.
**vehemencia** *f* vehemence, force.
**vehemente** *adj* vehement, violent.
**vehículo** *m* vehicle.
**veinte** *adj, m* twenty.
**veintena** *f* twentieth part; score.
**vejación** *f* vexation; embarrassment.
**vejar** *vt* to vex; to humiliate.
**vejestorio** *m* old man.
**vejez** *f* old age.
**vejiga** *f* bladder.
**vela** *f* wakefulness; vigil; night work; candle; sail; **hacerse a la ~** to set sail.
**velado/da** *adj* veiled; blurred; * *f* soirée.
**velador** *m* night watchman; observer; candlestick; pedestal table.
**velar** *vi* to stay awake; to be attentive; * *vt* to guard, to watch.
**veleidad** *f* feeble will; inconstancy.
**velero/ra** *adj* swift-sailing.
**veleta** *f* weather cock, weather vane.
**vello** *m* down; gossamer; short downy hair.
**vellón** *m* fleece.
**velludo/da** *adj* shaggy, woolly.
**velo** *m* veil; pretext.
**velocidad** *f* speed; velocity.
**velocímetro** *m* speedometer.
**veloz(mente)** *adj (adv)* swift(ly), fast.
**vena** *f* vein.
**venado** *m* deer; venison.
**vencedor/ra** *m/f* conqueror, victor, winner.
**vencer** *vt* to defeat; to conquer, to vanquish; * *vi* to win; to expire.
**vencido/da** *adj* defeated; due.
**vencimiento** *m* victory; maturity.
**vendaje** *m* bandage, dressing for wounds.
**vendal** *f* bandage.
**vendar** *vt* to bandage; to hoodwink.
**vendaval** *m* gale.

**vendedor/ra** *m/f* seller; **~ de periódicos** newsagent; **~ ambulante** pedlar.
**vender** *vt* to sell.
**vendimia** *f* grape harvest; vintage.
**vendimiador/ra** *m/f* vintager.
**vendimiar** *vt* to harvest; to pick (grapes); (*col*) to make a killing with.
**veneno** *m* poison, venom.
**venenoso/sa** *adj* venomous, poisonous.
**venerable** *adj* venerable.
**veneración** *f* veneration, worship.
**venerar** *vt* to venerate, to worship.
**venéreo/rea** *adj* venereal.
**venganza** *f* revenge, vengeance.
**vengar** *vt* to revenge, to avenge; **~se** *vr* to take revenge.
**vengativo/va** *adj* revengeful.
**venia** *f* pardon; leave, permission; bow.
**venial** *adj* venial.
**venida** *f* arrival; return; overflow of a river.
**venidero/ra** *adj* future; **~s** *mpl* posterity.
**venir** *vi* to come, to arrive; to follow, to succeed; to happen; to spring from; **~se** *vr* to ferment.
**venta** *f* sale.
**ventaja** *f* advantage.
**ventajoso/sa** *adj* advantageous.
**ventana** *f* window; window shutter; nostril.
**ventanilla** *f* window.
**venta por correo** *f* mail order.
**ventarrón** *m* violent wind.
**ventilación** *f* ventilation; draught.
**ventilar** *vt* to ventilate; to fan; to discuss.
**ventisca** *f*, **ventisco** *m* snowstorm.
**ventiscar** *vi* to drift, to lie in drifts (snow).
**ventisquero** *m* snowdrift; **~s** *mpl* glaciers *pl*.
**ventolera** *f* gust; pride, loftiness.
**ventosidad** *f* flatulence.
**ventoso/sa** *adj* windy; flatulent.
**ventrículo** *m* ventricle.
**ventrílocuo** *m* ventriloquist.
**ventura** *f* happiness; luck, chance, fortune; **por ~** by chance.
**venturoso/sa** *adj* lucky, fortunate, happy.
**Venus** *f* Venus (planet).
**ver** *vt* to see, to look at; to observe; to visit; * *vi* to understand; to see; **~se** *vr* to be seen; to be conspicuous; to find oneself; **~se con uno** to have a bone to pick with someone; * *m* sense of sight; appearance.
**vera** *f* edge; bank.
**veracidad** *f* truth; veracity.
**veranear** *vi* to spend the summer holiday.
**veraneo** *m* summer holiday.

**veraniego/ga** *adj* summer.
**verano** *m* summer.
**veras** *fpl* truth, sincerity; **de ~** in truth, really.
**veraz** *adj* truthful.
**verbal** *adj* verbal.
**verbena** *f* fair; dance.
**verbo** *m* word, term; (*gr*) verb.
**verbosidad** *f* verbosity.
**verdad** *f* truth, veracity; reality; reliability.
**verdaderamente** *adv* truly, in fact.
**verdadero/ra** *adj* true; real; sincere.
**verde** *m, adj* green.
**verdear, verdecer** *vi* to turn green.
**verdín** *m* bright green; verdure.
**verdor** *m* greenness; verdure; youth.
**verdoso/sa** *adj* greenish, greeny.
**verdugo** *m* hangman; very cruel person.
**verdulero/ra** *m/f* greengrocer.
**verdura** *f* verdure; vegetables *pl*, greens *pl*.
**vereda** *f* path; pavement.
**veredicto** *m* verdict.
**vergel** *m* orchard.
**vergonzoso/sa** *adj* bashful; shamefaced.
**vergüenza** *f* shame; bashfulness; confusion.
**vericueto** *m* rough road.
**verídico/ca** *adj* truthful.
**verificación** *f* verification.
**verificar** *vt* to check, to verify; **~se** *vr* to happen.
**verisímil** *adj* probable.
**verja** *f* grate, lattice.
**vermut** *m* vermouth.
**verosímil** *adj* likely; credible.
**verosimilitud** *f* likeliness; credibility.
**verraco** *m* boar.
**verruga** *f* wart, pimple.
**versado/da** *adj* versed.
**versátil** *adj* versatile.
**versículo** *m* versicle; short verse.
**versificar** *vt* to versify.
**versión** *f* translation, version.
**verso** *m* verse.
**vértebra** *f* vertebra.
**vertedero** *m* sewer, drain; tip.
**verter** *vt* to pour; to spill; to empty; * *vi* to flow.
**vertical** *adj* vertical.
**vértice** *m* vertex, zenith; crown of the head.
**vertiente** *f* slope; waterfall, cascade.
**vertiginoso/sa** *adj* giddy.
**vértigo** *m* giddiness, vertigo.
**vesícula** *f* blister.
**vespertino/na** *adj* evening *compd*.
**vestíbulo** *m* vestibule, lobby; foyer.

**vestido** *m* dress; clothes *pl*.
**vestidura** *f* dress; clothing.
**vestigio** *m* vestige; footstep; trace.
**vestimenta** *f* clothing.
**vestir** *vt* to put on; to wear; to dress; to adorn; to cloak, to disguise; * *vi* to dress; **~se** to get dressed.
**vestuario** *m* clothes *pl*; uniform; vestry; changing room.
**veta** *f* vein (in mines, wood etc); streak; grain.
**vetado/da** *adj* striped, veined.
**vetar** *vt* to veto.
**veterano/na** *adj* experienced, practised; * *m* veteran, old soldier.
**veterinario/ria** *adj* veterinary; * *m/f* veterinary surgeon; * *f* veterinary science.
**veto** *m* veto.
**vez** *f* time; turn; return; **cada ~** each time; **una ~** once; **a veces** sometimes, by turns.
**vía** *f* way; road, route; mode, manner, method; (*rail*) railway line.
**viajante** *m* sales representative.
**viajar** *vi* to travel.
**viaje** *m* journey; voyage; travel.
**viajero/ra** *m/f* traveller.
**vial** *adj* road *compd*.
**viático** *m* viaticum; travel allowance.
**víbora** *f* viper.
**vibración** *f* vibration.
**vibrador** *m* vibrator.
**vibrante** *adj* vibrant.
**vibrar** *vt, vi* to vibrate.
**vicaría** *f* vicarship; vicarage.
**vice-** *pref* vice- (deputy etc).
**vicealmirante** *m* vice-admiral.
**viceconsulado** *m* vice-consulate.
**vicepresidente/ta** *m/f* vice-president.
**viciar** *vt* to vitiate, to corrupt; to invalidate.
**vicio** *m* vice.
**vicioso/sa** *adj* vicious; depraved.
**vicisitud** *f* vicissitude.
**víctima** *f* victim; sacrifice.
**victoria** *f* victory.
**victorioso/sa** *adj* victorious.
**vicuña** *m* vicuna.
**vid** *f* (*bot*) vine.
**vida** *f* life.
**vidriado** *m* glazed earthenware, crockery.
**vídeo** *m* video.
**videocámara** *f* video camera, camcorder.
**videocasete** *m* video cassette.
**videoclip** *m* pop video.
**videojuego** *m* video game.

**vidriar** *vt* to glaze.
**vidriera** *f* stained-glass window; shop window.
**vidriero** *m* glazier.
**vidrio** *m* glass.
**vidrioso/sa** *adj* glassy; brittle; slippery; very delicate.
**vieira** *f* scallop.
**viejo/ja** *adj* old; ancient, antiquated.
**viento** *m* wind; air.
**vientre** *m* belly.
**viernes** *m invar* Friday; **V~ Santo** Good Friday.
**viga** *f* beam; girder.
**vigencia** *f* validity.
**vigente** *adj* in force.
**vigésimo/ma** *adj, m* twentieth.
**vigía** *f* (*mar*) lookout; * *m* watchman, guard.
**vigilancia** *f* vigilance, watchfulness.
**vigilante** *adj* watchful, vigilant.
**vigilar** *vt* to watch over; * *vi* to keep watch.
**vigilia** *f* vigil; watch.
**vigor** *m* vigour, strength.
**vigoroso/sa** *adj* vigorous.
**vil** *adj* mean, sordid, low; worthless; infamous; ungrateful.
**vileza** *f* meanness, lowness; abjectness.
**vilipendiar** *vt* to despise, to revile.
**villa** *f* villa; small town.
**villancico** *m* Christmas carol.
**villano/na** *adj* rustic, clownish; villainous; * *m* villain; rustic.
**villorio** *m* one horse town; (*col*) dump; shanty town.
**vilo: en ~** *adv* in the air; in suspense.
**vinagre** *m* vinegar.
**vinagrera** *f* vinegar cruet.
**vinagreta** *f* vinaigrette sauce.
**vinculación** *f* link; linking.
**vincular** *vt* to link.
**vínculo** *m* tie, link, chain; entail.
**vindicación** *f* revenge.
**vindicar** *vt* to avenge.
**vindicativo/va** *adj* vindictive.
**vinicultura** *f* wine growing.
**vino** *m* wine; ~ **tinto** red wine.
**viña** *f* vineyard.
**viñedo** *m* vineyard.
**viñeta** *f* vignette.
**viola** *f* viola.
**violación** *f* violation; rape.
**violado/da** *adj* violet-coloured; violated.
**violador/ra** *m/f* rapist; violator; profaner.
**violar** *vt* to rape; to violate; to profane.
**violencia** *f* violence.

**violentar** *vt* to force.
**violento/ta** *adj* violent; forced; absurd; embarrassing.
**violeta** *f* violet.
**violín** *m* violin, fiddle.
**violinista** *m* violinist.
**violón** *m* double bass.
**violoncelo, violonchelo** *m* violoncello (full name for cello).
**vip** *m/f* VIP.
**viperino/na** *adj* viperish.
**viraje** *m* turn; bend.
**virar** *vi* to swerve.
**virgen** *m/f* virgin.
**virginidad** *f* virginity.
**Virgo** *f* Virgo (sign of the zodiac).
**viril** *adj* virile, manly.
**virilidad** *f* virility, manhood.
**virrey** *m* viceroy.
**virtual** *adj* virtual.
**virtud** *f* virtue.
**virtuoso/sa** *adj* virtuous.
**viruela** *f* smallpox.
**virulencia** *f* virulence.
**virulento/ta** *adj* virulent.
**virus** *m invar* virus.
**visa** *f*, **visado** *m* visa.
**viscosidad** *f* viscosity.
**viscoso/sa** *adj* viscous, glutinous.
**visera** *f* visor.
**visibilidad** *f* visibility.
**visible** *adj* visible; apparent.
**visillos** *mpl* lace curtains *pl*.
**visión** *f* sight, vision; fantasy.
**visionario/ria** *adj* visionary.
**visita** *f* visit; visitor.
**visitar** *vt* to visit.
**vislumbrar** *vt* to catch a glimpse of; to perceive indistinctly.
**visón** *m* mink.
**víspera** *f* eve; evening before; **~s** *pl* vespers.
**vista** *f* sight, view; vision; eyesight; appearance; looks *pl*; prospect; intention; (*law*) trial; * *m* customs officer.
**vistazo** *m* glance.
**visto: ~ que** *conj* considering that.
**vistoso/sa** *adj* colourful, attractive, lively.
**visual** *adj* visual.
**vital** *adj* life *compd*; vital.
**vitalicio/cia** *adj* for life.
**vitalidad** *f* vitality.
**vitamina** *f* vitamin.
**viticultor/ra** *m/f* wine grower.
**viticultura** *f* wine growing.
**vitorear** *vt* to shout, to applaud.

**vítreo/trea** *adj* vitreous.
**vitriolo** *m* vitriol.
**vitrina** *f* showcase.
**vituperación** *f* condemnation, censure.
**vituperar** *vt* to condemn, to censure.
**vituperio** *m* condemnation, censure; insult.
**viuda** *f* widow.
**viudedad** *f* widowhood; widow's pension.
**viudez** *f* widowhood.
**viudo** *m* widower.
**vivacidad** *f* vivacity, liveliness.
**vivamente** *adv* in lively fashion.
**vivaracho/cha** *adj* lively, sprightly; bright.
**vivaz** *adj* lively.
**víveres** *mpl* provisions.
**vivero** *m* plant nursery; fish farm.
**viveza** *f* liveliness; sharpness.
**vividor/ra** *adj* (*perj*) sharp, clever; unscrupulous.
**vivienda** *f* housing; flat.
**viviente** *adj* living.
**vivificar** *vt* to vivify, to enliven.
**vivíparo/ra** *adj* viviparous.
**vivir** *vt* to live through; to go through; * *vi* to live; to last.
**vivo/va** *adj* living; lively; **al ~** to the life; very realistically.
**vizconde** *m* viscount.
**vocablo** *m* word, term.
**vocabulario** *m* vocabulary.
**vocación** *f* vocation.
**vocacional** *adj* vocational.
**vocal** *f* vowel; * *m/f* member (of a committee); * *adj* vocal, oral.
**vocativo** *m* (*gr*) vocative.
**vocear** *vt* to cry; to shout; to cheer; to shriek; * *vi* to yell.
**vocería** *f*, **vocerío** *m* shouting.
**vociferar** *vt* to shout; to proclaim in a loud voice; * *vi* to yell.
**vodka** *m/f* vodka.
**volador/ra** *adj* flying; fast.
**volandas**: **en ~** *adv* in the air; (*fig*) swiftly.
**volante** *adj* flying; * *m* (*auto*) steering wheel; note; pamphlet; shuttlecock.
**volar** *vi* to fly; to pass swiftly (of time); to rush, to hurry; * *vt* to blow up, to explode.
**volatería** *f* falconry; fowling; birds *pl*.
**volátil** *adj* volatile; changeable.

**volatilizar** *vt* to volatilize, to vaporize.
**volcán** *m* volcano.
**volcánico** *adj* volcanic.
**volcar** *vt* to upset, to overturn; to make giddy; to empty out; to exasperate; **~se** *vr* to tip over.
**voleibol** *m* volleyball.
**voleo** *m* volley.
**volquete** *m* tipper truck; dump truck.
**voltaje** *m* voltage.
**voltear** *vt* to turn over; to overturn; * *vi* to roll over, to tumble.
**voltereta** *f* tumble; somersault.
**voltio** *m* volt.
**voluble** *adj* unpredictable; fickle.
**volumen** *m* volume; size.
**voluminoso/sa** *adj* voluminous.
**voluntad** *f* will, willpower; wish, desire.
**voluntario/ria** *adj* voluntary; * *m/f* volunteer.
**voluptuoso/sa** *adj* voluptuous.
**volver** *vt* to turn (over); to turn upside down; to turn inside out; * *vi* to return, to go back; **~se** *vr* to turn around.
**vomitar** *vt*, *vi* to vomit.
**vómito** *m* vomiting; vomit.
**vomitona** *f* violent vomiting.
**voracidad** *f* voracity.
**voraz** *adj* voracious; **~mente** *adv* voraciously.
**vórtice** *m* whirlpool.
**vos** *pn* you.
**vosotros/tras** *pn pl* you.
**votación** *f* voting; vote.
**votar** *vi* to vow; to vote.
**voto** *m* vow; vote; opinion, advice; swearword; curse; **~s** *mpl* good wishes *pl*.
**voz** *f* voice; shout; rumour; word, term.
**vuelco** *m* overturning.
**vuelo** *m* flight; wing; projection of a building; ruffle, frill; **cazar al ~** to catch in flight; **~ chárter** charter flight.
**vuelta** *f* turn; circuit; return; row of stitches; cuff; change; bend, curve; reverse, other side; return journey.
**vuestro/tra** *adj* your; * *pn* yours.
**vulgar** *adj* vulgar, common.
**vulgaridad** *f* vulgar, common.
**vulgaridad** *f* vulgarity, commonness.
**vulgo** *m* common people *pl*.
**vulnerable** *adj* vulnerable.

# W X Y

**wáter** *m* toilet.
**whisky** *m* whisky.
**windsurf** *m* windsurfing.
**windsurfista** *m/f* windsurfer.

**xenofobia** *f* xenophobia.
**xilófono** *m* xylophone.
**xilógrafo** *m* xylographer; wood engraver.

**y** *conj* and.
**ya** *adv* already; now; immediately; at once;
soon; * *conj*: ~ **que** since, seeing that; ¡~!
of course!, sure!
**yacer** *vi* to lie, to lie down.
**yacimiento** *m* deposit.
**yanqui** *m/f* Yankee.
**yate** *m* yacht, sailing boat.
**yedra** *f* ivy.
**yegua** *f* mare.

**yema** *f* bud; leaf; yolk; ~ **del dedo** tip of the
finger.
**yermo** *m* wasteland, wilderness; ~/**ma** *adj*
waste; (*fig*) barren.
**yerno** *m* son-in-law.
**yerro** *m* error, mistake, fault.
**yerto/ta** *adj* stiff, inflexible; rigid.
**yesca** *f* tinder.
**yeso** *m* gypsum; plaster; ~ **mate** plaster of
Paris.
**yo** *pn* I; ~ **mismo** I myself.
**yodo** *m* iodine.
**yogur** *m* yoghurt.
**yugo** *m* yoke.
**yugular** *adj* jugular.
**yunque** *m* anvil.
**yunta** *f* yoke; ~**s** *fpl* couple, pair.
**yute** *m* jute.
**yuxtaponer** *vt* to juxtapose.
**yuxtaposición** *f* juxtaposition.

# Z

**zafar** *vt* to loosen, to untie; to lighten (a ship); **~se** *vr* to escape; **~se de** to avoid; to free oneself from (trouble).

**zafio/fia** *adj* uncouth, coarse.

**zafiro** *m* sapphire.

**zaga** *f* rear; **a la ~** behind.

**zagal/la** *m/f* boy/girl.

**zaguán** *m* porch, entrance hall.

**zaherir** *vt* to criticize; to upbraid.

**zahorí** *m* clairvoyant.

**zalamería** *f* flattery.

**zalamero/ra** *adj* flattering; * *m/f* wheedler, flatterer.

**zamarra** *f* sheepskin; sheepskin jacket.

**zambo/ba** *adj* knock-kneed.

**zambomba** *f* rural drum.

**zambullida** *f* plunge, dive; dipping, submersion.

**zambullirse** *vr* to plunge/dive into water.

**zampar** *vt* to gobble down; to put away hurriedly; **~se** *vr* to thrust oneself suddenly into any place; to crash, to hurtle.

**zanahoria** *f* carrot.

**zancada** *f* stride.

**zancadilla** *f* trip; trick.

**zanco** *m* stilt.

**zancudo/da** *adj* long-legged; * *m* mosquito.

**zángano** *m* drone; idler, slacker.

**zanja** *f* ditch, trench.

**zanjar** *vt* to dig (ditches); (*fig*) to surmount; to resolve.

**zapador** *m* (*mil*) sapper.

**zapata** *f* boot; **~ de freno** (*auto*) brake shoe.

**zapatazo** *m* stamp (dancing).

**zapatear** *vt* to tap with the shoe; to beat time with the sole of the shoe.

**zapatería** *f* shoemaking; shoe shop; shoe factory.

**zapatero/ra** *m/f* shoemaker; **~ de viejo** cobbler.

**zapatilla** *f* slipper; pump (shoe); (*sport*) **~s de lona** *fpl* trainers *pl*.

**zapato** *m* shoe.

**zapping** *m* channel-hopping.

**zar** *m* czar.

**zarandear** *vt* to shake vigorously.

**zarcillo** *m* earring; tendril.

**zarpa** *f* dirt on clothes; claw.

**zarpar** *vi* to weigh anchor.

**zarpazo** *m* thud.

**zarrapastroso/sa** *adj* shabby, rough-looking.

**zarza** *f* bramble.

**zarzal** *m* bramble patch.

**zarzamora** *f* blackberry.

**zarzuela** *f* Spanish light opera.

**zigzag** *adj* zigzag.

**zigzaguear** *vi* to zigzag.

**zinc** *m* zinc.

**zócalo** *m* plinth, base; skirting board.

**zodiaco** *m* zodiac.

**zona** *f* zone; area, belt.

**zoo** *m* zoo.

**zoología** *f* zoology.

**zoológico/ca** *adj* zoological; * *m* zoo.

**zoólogo/ga** *m/f* zoologist.

**zopenco/ca** *adj* dull, very stupid.

**zoquete** *m* block; crust of bread; (*col*) blockhead.

**zorra** *f* fox; vixen; (*col*) whore, tart.

**zorro** *m* male fox; cunning person.

**zozobra** *f* (*mar*) capsizing; uneasiness, anxiety.

**zozobrar** *vi* (*mar*) to founder; to capsize; (*fig*) to fail; to be anxious.

**zueco** *m* wooden shoe; clog.

**zumba** *f* banter, teasing; beating.

**zumbar** *vt* to hit; **~se** *vr* to hit each other; * *vi* to buzz.

**zumbido** *m* humming, buzzing sound.

**zumbón/ona** *adj* waggish, funny, teasing.

**zumo** *m* juice.

**zurcir** *vt* to darn; (*fig*) to join, to unite; to hatch (lies).

**zurdo/da** *adj* left; left-handed.

**zurra** *f* flogging; drudgery.

**zurrar** *vt* (*col*) to flog, to lay into; (*fig*) to criticize harshly.

**zurrón** *m* pouch.

**zutano/na** *m/f* so-and-so; **~ y fulano** such and such a one, so-and-so.

# English–Spanish Dictionary

## A

**a** *art* un, uno, una; * *prep* a, al, en.

**aback** *adv* detrás, atrás; **to be taken ~** quedar consternado/da.

**abacus** *n* ábaco *m*.

**abandon** *vt* abandonar, dejar.

**abandonment** *n* abandono *m*; desamparo *m*.

**abase** *vt* abatir, humillar.

**abasement** *n* abatimiento *m*; humillación *f*.

**abash** *vt* avergonzar, causar confusión.

**abate** *vt* disminuir, rebajar; * *vi* disminuirse.

**abatement** *n* rebaja, disminución *f*.

**abbess** *n* abadesa *f*.

**abbey** *n* abadía *f*.

**abbot** *n* abad *m*.

**abbreviate** *vt* abreviar, acortar.

**abbreviation** *n* abreviatura *f*.

**abdicate** *vt* abdicar; renunciar.

**abdication** *n* abdicación *f*; renuncia *f*.

**abdomen** *n* abdomen *m*.

**abdominal** *adj* abdominal.

**abduct** *vt* secuestrar.

**abductor** *n* músculo abductor *m*.

**abed** *adv* en (la) cama.

**aberrant** *adj* anormal.

**aberration** *n* error *m*; aberración *f*.

**abet** *vt*: **to aid and ~** ser cómplice de.

**abeyance** *n* desuso *m*.

**abhor** *vt* aborrecer, detestar.

**abhorrence** *n* aborrecimiento, odio *m*.

**abhorrent** *adj* repugnante.

**abide** *vt* soportar, sufrir.

**abilities** *npl* talento *m*.

**ability** *n* habilidad, capacidad, aptitud *f*.

**abject** *adj* vil, despreciable, bajo/ja; **~ly** *adv* vilmente, bajamente.

**abjure** *vt* abjurar; renunciar.

**ablative** *n* (*gr*) ablativo *m*.

**ablaze** *adj* en llamas.

**able** *adj* capaz, hábil; **to be ~** poder.

**able-bodied** *adj* robusto/ta, vigoroso/sa.

**ablution** *n* ablución *f*.

**ably** *adv* con habilidad.

**abnegation** *n* abnegación, resignación *f*.

**abnormal** *adj* anormal.

**abnormality** *n* anormalidad *f*.

**aboard** *adv* a bordo.

**abode** *n* domicilio *m*.

**abolish** *vt* abolir, anular, revocar.

**abolition** *n* abolición, anulación *f*.

**abominable** *adj* abominable, detestable; **~bly** *adv* abominablemente.

**abomination** *n* abominación *f*.

**aboriginal** *adj* aborigen.

**aborigines** *npl* aborígenes *mpl*.

**abort** *vi* abortar.

**abortion** *n* aborto *m*.

**abortive** *adj* fracasado/da.

**abound** *vi* abundar; **to ~ with** abundar en.

**about** *prep* acerca de, acerca; **I carry no money ~ me** no traigo dinero; * *adv* aquí y allá; **to be ~ to** estar a punto de; **to go ~** andar acá y acullá; **to go ~ a thing** emprender alguna cosa; **all ~** en todo lugar.

**above** *prep* encima; * *adv* arriba; **~ all** sobre todo, principalmente; **~ mentioned** ya mencionado.

**aboveboard** *adj* legítimo/ma.

**abrasion** *n* abrasión *f*.

**abrasive** *adj* abrasivo/va.

**abreast** *adv* de costado.

**abridge** *vt* abreviar, compendiar; acortar.

**abridgement** *n* compendio *m*, recopilación *f*.

**abroad** *adv* en el extranjero; **to go ~** salir del país.

**abrogate** *vt* abrogar, anular.

**abrogation** *n* abrogación, anulación *f*.

**abrupt** *adj* brusco/ca; **~ly** *adv* precipitadamente; bruscamente.

**abscess** *n* absceso *m*.

**abscond** *vi* esconderse; huir.

**abseiling** *n* rappel *m*.

**absence** *n* ausencia *f*.

**absent** *adj* ausente; * *vi* ausentarse.

**absentee** *n* ausente *m*.

**absenteeism** *n* absentismo *m*.

**absent-minded** *adj* distraído/da.

**absolute** *adj* absoluto/ta; categórico/ca; **~ly** *adv* totalmente.

**absolution** *n* absolución *f*.

**absolutism** *n* absolutismo *m*.

**absolve** *vt* absolver.

**absorb** *vt* absorber.

**absorbent** *adj* absorbente.

**absorbent cotton** *n* algodón hidrófilo *m*.

**absorption** *n* absorción *f*.

**abstain** *vi* abstenerse, privarse.

**abstemious** *adj* abstemio/mia, sobrio/ria; **~ly** *adv* moderadamente.

**abstemiousness** *n* sobriedad, abstinencia *f*.

**abstinence** *n* abstinencia *f*; templanza *f*.

**abstinent** *adj* abstinente, sobrio/ria.

**abstract** *adj* abstracto/ta; * *n* extracto *m*; sumario *m*; **in the ~** de modo abstracto.

**abstraction** *n* abstracción *f*.

**abstractly** *adv* en abstracto.

**abstruse** *adj* oscuro/ra; **~ly** *adv* oscuramente.

**absurd** *adj* absurdo/da; **~ly** *adv* absurdamente.

**absurdity** *n* absurdidad *f*.

**abundance** *n* abundancia *f*.

**abundant** *adj* abundante; **~ly** *adv* abundantemente.

**abuse** *vt* abusar; maltratar; * *n* abuso *m*; injurias *fpl*.

**abusive** *adj* abusivo/va, ofensivo/va; **~ly** *adv* abusivamente.

**abut** *vi* confinar.

**abysmal** *adj* abismal; insondable.

**abyss** *n* abismo *m*.

**acacia** *n* acacia *f*.

**academic** *adj* académico/ca.

**academician** *n* académico *m*.

**academy** *n* academia *f*.

**accede** *vi* acceder.

**accelerate** *vt* acelerar.

**accelerator** *n* acelerador *m*.

**acceleration** *n* aceleración *f*.

**accent** *n* acento *m*; tono *m*; * *vt* acentuar.

**accentuate** *vt* acentuar.

**accentuation** *n* acentuación *f*.

**accept** *vt* aceptar; admitir.

**acceptable** *adj* aceptable.

**acceptability** *n* aceptabilidad *f*.

**acceptance** *n* aceptación *f*.

**access** *n* acceso *m*; entrada *f*.

**accessible** *adj* accesible.

**accession** *n* acceso *m*.

**accessory** *n* accesorio *m*; (*law*) cómplice *m*.

**accident** *n* accidente *m*; casualidad *f*.

**accidental** *adj* casual; **~ly** *adv* por casualidad.

**acclaim** *vt* aclamar, aplaudir.

**acclamation** *n* aclamación *f*; aplauso *m*.

**acclimatize** *vt* aclimatar.

**accommodate** *vt* alojar; complacer.

**accommodating** *adj* servicial.

**accommodations** *npl* alojamiento *m*.

**accompaniment** *n* (*mus*) acompañamiento *m*.

**accompanist** *n* (*mus*) acompañante *m*.

**accompany** *vt* acompañar.

**accomplice** *n* cómplice *m*.

**accomplish** *vt* efectuar, completar.

**accomplished** *adj* elegante, consumado/da.

**accomplishment** *n* cumplimiento *m*; **~s** *pl* talentos, conocimientos *mpl*.

**accord** *n* acuerdo, convenio *m*; **with one ~** unánimemente; **of one's own ~** espontáneamente.

**accordance** *n*: **in ~ with** de acuerdo con.

**according** *prep* según, conforme; **~ as** según que, como; **~ly** *adv* por consiguiente.

**accordion** *n* (*mus*) acordeón *m*.

**accost** *vt* trabar conversación con.

**account** *n* cuenta *f*; **on no ~** de ninguna manera; bajo ningún concepto; **on ~ of** por motivo de; **to call to ~** pedir cuenta; **to turn to ~** hacer provechoso; * *vt* **to ~ for** explicar.

**accountability** *n* responsabilidad *f*.

**accountable** *adj* responsable.

**accountancy** *n* contabilidad *f*.

**accountant** *n* contable, contador *m*.

**account book** *n* libro de cuentas *m*.

**account number** *n* número de cuenta *m*.

**accrue** *vi* resultar, provenir.

**accumulate** *vt* acumular; amontonar; * *vi* crecer.

**accumulation** *n* acumulación *f*; amontonamiento *m*.

**accuracy** *n* exactitud *f*.

**accurate** *adj* exacto/ta; **~ly** *adv* exactamente.

**accursed** *adj* maldito/ta.

**accusation** *n* acusación *f*.

**accusative** *n* (*gr*) acusativo *m*.

**accusatory** *adj* acusatorio/ria.

**accuse** *vt* acusar; culpar.

**accused** *n* acusado *m*.

**accuser** *n* acusador/a *m/f*.

**accustom** *vt* acostumbrar.

**accustomed** *adj* acostumbrado/da, habitual.

**ace** *n* as *m*; **within an ~ of** . . . casi, por poco no . . . .

**acerbic** *adj* mordaz.

**acetate** *n* (*chem*) acetato *m*.

**ache** *n* dolor *m*; * *vi* doler.

**achieve** *vt* realizar; obtener.

**achievement** *n* realización *f*; hazaña *f*.

**acid** *adj* ácido/da; agrio/ria; * *n* ácido *m*.

**acid rain** *n* lluvia ácida *f*.

**acidity** *n* acidez *f.*
**acknowledge** *vt* reconocer, confesar.
**acknowledgement** *n* reconocimiento *m;* gratitud *f.*
**acme** *n* apogeo *m.*
**acne** *n* acne *m.*
**acorn** *n* bellota *f.*
**acoustics** *n* acústica *f.*
**acquaint** *vt* informar, avisar.
**acquaintance** *n* conocimiento *m;* conocido *m.*
**acquiesce** *vi* someterse, consentir, asentir.
**acquiescence** *n* consentimiento *m.*
**acquiescent** *adj* deferente.
**acquire** *vt* adquirir.
**acquisition** *n* adquisición, obtención *f.*
**acquit** *vt* absolver.
**acquittal** *n* absolución *f.*
**acre** *n* acre *m.*
**acrid** *adj* acre.
**acrimonious** *adj* mordaz.
**acrimony** *n* acrimonia, acritud *f.*
**across** *adv* de una parte a otra; * *prep* a través de; **to come ~** toparse con.
**act** *vt* representar; * *vi* hacer; * *n* acto, hecho *m;* acción *f;* **~s of the apostles** Hechos *mpl* de los Apóstoles.
**acting** *adj* interino/na.
**action** *n* acción *f;* batalla *f.*
**action replay** *n* repetición *f.*
**activate** *vt* activar.
**active** *adj* activo/va; **~ly** *adv* activamente.
**activity** *n* actividad *f.*
**actor** *n* actor *m.*
**actress** *n* actriz *f.*
**actual** *adj* real; efectivo/va; **~ly** *adv* en efecto, realmente.
**actuary** *n* actuario de seguros *m.*
**acumen** *n* agudeza, perspicacia *f.*
**acupuncture** *n* acupuntura *f.*
**acute** *adj* agudo/da; ingenioso/sa; **~ly** *adv* con agudeza; **~ accent** *n* acento agudo *m;* **~ angle** *n* ángulo agudo *m.*
**acuteness** *n* perspicacia, sagacidad *f.*
**adage** *n* proverbio *m.*
**adamant** *adj* inflexible.
**adapt** *vt* adaptar, acomodar; ajustar.
**adaptability** *n* facilidad de adaptarse *f.*
**adaptable** *adj* adaptable.
**adaptation** *n* adaptación *f.*
**adaptor** *n* adaptador *m.*
**add** *vt* añadir, agregar; **to ~ up** sumar.
**addendum** *n* suplemento *m.*
**adder** *n* culebra *f;* víbora *f.*
**addict** *n* drogadicto *m.*

**addiction** *n* dependencia *f.*
**addictive** *adj* que crea dependencia.
**addition** *n* adición *f.*
**additional** *adj* adicional; **~ly** *adv* en/por adición.
**additive** *n* aditivo *m.*
**address** *vt* dirigir; * *n* dirección *f;* discurso *m.*
**adduce** *vt* alegar, aducir.
**adenoids** *npl* vegetaciones adenoideas *fpl.*
**adept** *adj* hábil.
**adequacy** *n* suficiencia *f.*
**adequate** *adj* adecuado/da; suficiente; **~ly** *adv* adecuadamente.
**adhere** *vi* adherir.
**adherence** *n* adherencia *f.*
**adherent** *n* adherente, partidario *m.*
**adhesion** *n* adhesión *f.*
**adhesive** *adj* pegajoso/sa.
**adhesiveness** *n* adhesividad *f.*
**adieu** *adv* adiós; * *n* despedida *f.*
**adipose** *adj* adiposo/sa.
**adjacent** *adj* adyacente, contiguo/gua.
**adjectival** *adj* adjetivado/da; **~ly** *adv* como adjetivo.
**adjective** *n* adjetivo *m.*
**adjoin** *vi* estar contiguo/gua.
**adjoining** *adj* contiguo/gua.
**adjourn** *vt* aplazar.
**adjournment** *n* prórroga *f.*
**adjudicate** *vt* adjudicar.
**adjunct** *n* adjunto *m.*
**adjust** *vt* ajustar, acomodar.
**adjustable** *adj* ajustable.
**adjustment** *n* ajustamiento, arreglo *m.*
**adjutant** *n (mil)* ayudante *m.*
**ad lib** *vt* improvisar.
**administer** *vt* administrar; gobernar; **to ~ an oath** prestar juramento.
**administration** *n* administración *f;* gobierno *m.*
**administrative** *adj* administrativo/va.
**administrator** *n* administrador/a *m/f.*
**admirable** *adj* admirable; **~bly** *adv* admirablemente.
**admiral** *n* almirante *m.*
**admiralship** *n* almirante *f.*
**admiralty** *n* almirantazgo *m.*
**admiration** *n* admiración *f.*
**admire** *vt* admirar.
**admirer** *n* admira/a *m/f.*
**admiringly** *adv* con admiración.
**admissible** *adj* admisible.
**admission** *n* entrada *f.*
**admit** *vt* admitir; **to ~ to** confesarse culpable de.

**admittance** *n* entrada *f*.
**admittedly** *adj* de acuerdo que.
**admixture** *n* mixtura, mezcla *f*.
**admonish** *vt* amonestar, reprender.
**admonition** *n* amonestación *f*; consejo, aviso *m*.
**admonitory** *adj* exhortatorio/ria.
**ad nauseam** *adv* hasta el cansancio.
**adolescence** *n* adolescencia *f*.
**adopt** *vt* adoptar.
**adopted** *adj* adoptivo/va.
**adoption** *n* adopción *f*.
**adoptive** *adj* adoptivo/va.
**adorable** *adj* adorable.
**adorably** *adv* de modo adorable.
**adoration** *n* adoración *f*.
**adore** *vt* adorar.
**adorn** *vt* adornar.
**adornment** *n* adorno *m*.
**adrift** *adv* a la deriva.
**adroit** *adj* diestro/tra, hábil.
**adroitness** *n* destreza *f*.
**adulation** *n* adulación, zalamería *f*.
**adulatory** *adj* lisonjero/ra.
**adult** *adj* adulto/ta; * *n* adulto *m*; adulta *f*.
**adulterate** *vt* adulterar, corromper; * *adj* adulterado/da, falsificado/da.
**adulteration** *n* adulteración, corrupción *f*.
**adulterer** *n* adúltero *m*.
**adulteress** *n* adúltera *f*.
**adulterous** *adj* adúltero/ra.
**adultery** *n* adulterio *m*.
**advance** *vt* avanzar; promover; pagar por adelantado; * *vi* hacer progresos; **to make ~s** insinuarse; * *n* avance *m*; paga adelantada *f*.
**advanced** *adj* avanzado/da.
**advancement** *n* adelantamiento *m*; progreso *m*; promoción *f*.
**advantage** *n* ventaja *f*; **to take ~ of** sacar provecho de.
**advantageous** *adj* ventajoso/sa; **~ly** *adv* ventajosamente.
**advantageousness** *n* ventaja, utilidad *f*.
**advent** *n* venida *f*; **Advent** *n* Adviento *m*.
**adventitious** *adj* adventicio/cia.
**adventure** *n* aventura *f*.
**adventurer** *n* aventurero *m*.
**adventurous** *adj* intrépido/da; valeroso/sa; **~ly** *adv* arriesgadamente.
**adverb** *n* adverbio *m*.
**adverbial** *adj* adverbial; **~ly** *adv* como adverbio.
**adversary** *n* adversario, enemigo *m*.
**adverse** *adj* adverso/sa, contrario/ria.

**adversity** *n* calamidad *f*; infortunio *m*.
**advertise** *vt* anunciar.
**advertisement** *n* anuncio *m*.
**advertising** *n* publicidad *f*.
**advice** *n* consejo *m*; aviso *m*.
**advisability** *n* prudencia, conveniencia *f*.
**advisable** *adj* prudente, conveniente.
**advise** *vt* aconsejar; avisar.
**advisedly** *adv* prudentemente, avisadamente.
**advisory** *adj* consultivo/va.
**advocacy** *n* defensa *f*.
**advocate** *n* abogado *m*; protector *m*; * *vt* abogar por.
**advocateship** *n* abogacía *f*.
**aerial** *n* antena *f*.
**aerobics** *npl* aerobic *m*.
**aerometer** *n* areómetro *m*.
**aeroplane** *n* avión *m*.
**aerosol** *n* aerosol *m*.
**aerostat** *n* globo aerostático *m*.
**aesthetic** *adj* estético/ca; **~s** *npl* estética *f*.
**afar** *adv* lejos, distante; **from ~** desde lejos.
**affability** *n* afabilidad, urbanidad *f*.
**affable** *adj* afable, complaciente; **~bly** *adv* afablemente.
**affair** *n* asunto *m*; negocio *m*.
**affect** *vt* conmover; afectar.
**affectation** *n* afectación *f*.
**affected** *adj* afectado/da, lleno/na de afectación; **~ly** *adv* con afectación.
**affectingly** *adv* con afecto.
**affection** *n* cariño *m*.
**affectionate** *adj* afectuoso/sa; **~ly** *adv* cariñosamente.
**affidavit** *n* declaración jurada *f*.
**affiliate** *vt* afiliar.
**affiliation** *n* afiliación *f*.
**affinity** *n* afinidad *f*.
**affirm** *vt* afirmar, declarar.
**affirmation** *n* afirmación *f*.
**affirmative** *adj* afirmativo/va; **~ly** *adv* afirmativamente.
**affix** *vt* pegar; * *n* (*gr*) afijo *m*.
**afflict** *vt* afligir.
**affliction** *n* aflicción *f*; dolor *m*.
**affluence** *n* abundancia *f*.
**affluent** *adj* opulento/ta.
**afflux** *n* confluencia, afluencia *f*.
**afford** *vt* dar; proveer.
**affray** *n* asalto *m*; tumulto *m*.
**affront** *n* afrenta, injuria *f*; * *vt* afrentar, insultar, ultrajar.
**aflame** *adv* en llamas.
**afloat** *adv* flotante, a flote.

**afraid** *adj* espantado/da, tímido/da; **I am ~** temo.

**afresh** *adv* de nuevo, otra vez.

**aft** *adv* (*mar*) a popa.

**after** *prep* después; detrás; según; * *adv* después; **~ all** después de todo.

**afterbirth** *n* secundinas *fpl*.

**after-effects** *npl* consecuencias *fpl*.

**afterlife** *n* vida venidera *f*.

**aftermath** *n* consecuencias *fpl*.

**afternoon** *n* tarde *f*.

**aftershave** *n* aftershave *m*.

**aftertaste** *n* resabio *m*.

**afterwards** *adv* después.

**again** *adv* otra vez; **~ and ~** muchas veces; **as much ~** otra vez tanto.

**against** *prep* contra; **~ the grain** a contrapelo; de mala gana.

**agate** *n* ágata *f*.

**age** *n* edad *f*; **under ~** menor; * *vt* envejecer.

**aged** *adj* viejo/ja, anciano/na.

**agency** *n* agencia *f*.

**agenda** *n* orden del día *m*.

**agent** *n* agente *m*.

**agglomerate** *vt* aglomerar.

**agglomeration** *n* aglomeración *f*.

**aggrandizement** *n* engrandecimiento *m*.

**aggravate** *vt* agravar, exagerar.

**aggravation** *n* agravación *f*.

**aggregate** *n* agregado *m*.

**aggregation** *n* agregación *f*.

**aggression** *n* agresión *f*.

**aggressive** *adj* ofensivo/va.

**aggressor** *n* agresor *m*.

**aggrieved** *adj* ofendido/da.

**aghast** *adj* horrorizado/da.

**agile** *adj* ágil; diestro/tra.

**agility** *n* agilidad *f*; destreza *f*.

**agitate** *vt* agitar.

**agitation** *n* agitación *f*; perturbación *f*.

**agitator** *n* agitador, incitador *m*.

**ago** *adv* pasado, largo tiempo; después; **how long ~?** ¿cuánto hace?

**agog** *adj* emocionado/da.

**agonizing** *adj* atroz.

**agony** *n* agonía *f*.

**agree** *vt* convenir; * *vi* estar de acuerdo/da.

**agreeable** *adj* agradable; amable; **~bly** *adv* agradablemente; **~ with** según, conforme a.

**agreeableness** *n* amabilidad, gracia *f*.

**agreed** *adj* establecido/da, convenido/da; **~!** *adv* ¡de acuerdo!

**agreement** *n* acuerdo *m*.

**agricultural** *adj* agrario/ria.

**agriculture** *n* agricultura *f*.

**agriculturist** *n* agricultor *m*.

**agronomy** *n* agronomía *f*.

**aground** *adv* (*mar*) encallado.

**ah!** *excl* ¡ah!, ¡ay!

**ahead** *adv* más allá, delante de otro; (*mar*) por la proa.

**ahoy!** *excl* (*mar*) ¡ohe!

**aid** *vt* ayudar, socorrer; **to ~ and abet** ser cómplice de; * *n* ayuda *f*; auxilio, socorro *m*.

**aide-de-camp** *n* (*mil*) ayudante de campo *m*.

**AIDS** *n* SIDA *m*.

**ail** *vt* afligir, molestar.

**ailing** *adj* doliente.

**ailment** *n* dolencia, indisposición *f*.

**aim** *vt* apuntar aspirar a; intentar; * *n* designio *m*; puntería *f*.

**aimless** *adj* sin designio, sin objeto; **~ly** a la deriva.

**air** *n* aire *m*; * *vt* airear; ventilar.

**airbag** *n* airbag *m*.

**air balloon** *n* globo aerostático *m*.

**airborne** *adj* aerotransportado/da.

**air-conditioned** *adj* climatizado/da.

**air conditioning** *n* aire acondicionado *m*.

**aircraft** *n* avión *m*.

**air cushion** *n* cojinete rellenado de aire *m*.

**air force** *n* fuerzas aéreas *fpl*.

**air freshener** *n* ambientador *m*.

**air gun** *n* escopeta de aire comprimido *f*.

**air hole** *n* respiradero *m*.

**airless** *adj* falto de ventilación, sofocado/da.

**airlift** *n* puente aéreo *m*.

**airline** *n* línea aérea *f*.

**airmail** *n*: **by ~** por avión.

**airport** *n* aeropuerto *m*.

**airport tax** *n* tasas de aeropuerto *f*.

**air pump** *n* bomba de aire *f*.

**airsick** *adj* mareado/da.

**airstrip** *n* pista de aterrizaje *f*.

**air terminal** *n* terminal *f*.

**airtight** *adj* herméticamente cerrado/da.

**airy** *adj* bien ventilado/da.

**aisle** *n* nave de una iglesia *f*.

**ajar** *adj* entreabierto/ta.

**akimbo** *adj* corvo/va.

**akin** *adj* parecido/da.

**alabaster** *n* alabastro *m*; * *adj* alabastrino/na.

**alacrity** *n* presteza *f*.

**alarm** *n* alarma *f*; * *vt* alarmar; inquietar.

**alarm bell** *n* timbre de alarma *m*.

**alarmist** *n* alarmista *m*.

**alas** *adv* desgraciadamente.

**albeit** *conj* aunque.

**album** *n* álbum *m*.
**alchemist** *n* alquimista *m*.
**alchemy** *n* alquimia *f*.
**alcohol** *n* alcohol *m*.
**alcoholic** *adj* alcohólico/ca; * *n* alcohol-
izado *m*.
**alcove** *n* nicho *m*.
**alder** *n* aliso *m*.
**ale** *n* cerveza *f*.
**alert** *adj* vigilante; alerto/ta; * *n* alerta *f*.
**alertness** *n* cuidado *m*; vigilancia *f*.
**algae** *npl* alga *f*.
**algebra** *n* álgebra *f*.
**algebraic** *adj* algebraico/ca.
**alias** *adj* alias.
**alibi** *n* (*law*) coartada *f*.
**alien** *adj* ajeno/na; * *n* forastero *m*.
**alienate** *vt* enajenar.
**alienation** *n* enajenación *f*.
**alight** *vi* apearse; * *adj* encendido/da.
**align** *vt* alinear.
**alike** *adj* semejante, igual; * *adv* igualmente.
**alimentation** *n* alimentación *f*.
**alimony** *n* alimentos *mpl*.
**alive** *adj* vivo/va, viviente; activo/va.
**alkali** *n* álcali *m*.
**alkaline** *adj* alcalino/na.
**all** *adj* todo/da; * *adv* totalmente; ~ **at once,**
~ **of a sudden** de repente; ~ **the same** sin
embargo; ~ **the better** tanto mejor; **not**
**at ~!** ¡no hay de qué!; **once for ~** una vez
por todas; * *n* todo *m*.
**allay** *vt* aliviar.
**all clear** *n* luz verde *f*.
**allegation** *n* alegación *f*.
**allege** *vt* alegar; declarar.
**allegiance** *n* lealtad, fidelidad *f*.
**allegorical** *adj* alegórico/ca; ~**ly** *adv*
alegóricamente.
**allegory** *n* alegoría *f*.
**allegro** *n* (*mus*) alegro *m*.
**allergy** *n* alergia *f*.
**alleviate** *vt* aliviar, aligerar.
**alleviation** *n* alivio *m*; mitigación *f*.
**alley** *n* callejuela *f*.
**alliance** *n* alianza *f*.
**allied** *adj* aliado/da.
**alligator** *n* caimán *m*.
**alliteration** *n* aliteración *f*.
**all-night** *adj* abierto/ta toda la noche.
**allocate** *vt* repartir.
**allocation** *n* cuota *f*.
**allot** *vt* asignar.
**allow** *vt* conceder; permitir; dar, pagar; **to ~**
**for** tener en cuenta.

**allowable** *adj* admisible, permitido/da.
**allowance** *n* concesión *f*.
**alloy** *n* liga, mezcla, aleación *f*.
**all right** *adv* bien.
**all-round** *adj* completo/ta.
**allspice** *n* pimienta de Jamaica *f*.
**allude** *vt* aludir.
**allure** *n* fascinación *f*.
**alluring** *adj* seductor/a; ~**ly** *adv* seductora-
mente.
**allurement** *n* aliciente, atractivo *m*.
**allusion** *n* alusión *f*.
**allusive** *adj* alusivo/va; ~**ly** *adv* de modo
alusivo.
**alluvial** *adj* aluvial.
**ally** *n* aliado *m*; * *vt* aliar.
**almanac** *n* almanaque *m*.
**almighty** *adj* omnipotente, todopoderoso/
sa.
**almond** *n* almendra *f*.
**almond tree** *n* almendro *m*.
**almost** *adv* casi; cerca de.
**alms** *n* limosna *f*.
**aloft** *prep* arriba.
**alone** *adj* solo; * *adv* solamente, sólo; **to**
**leave ~** dejar en paz.
**along** *adv* a lo largo; ~ **side** al lado.
**aloof** *adv* lejos.
**aloud** *adj* en voz alta.
**alphabet** *n* alfabeto *m*.
**alphabetical** *adj* alfabético/ca; ~**ly** *adv* por
orden alfabético.
**alpine** *adj* alpino/na.
**already** *adv* ya.
**also** *adv* también, además.
**altar** *n* altar *m*.
**altarpiece** *n* retablo *m*.
**alter** *vt* modificar.
**alteration** *n* alteración *f*.
**altercation** *n* altercado *m*.
**alternate** *adj* alterno/na; * *vt* alternar,
variar; ~**ly** *adv* alternativamente.
**alternating** *adj* alterno/na.
**alternation** *n* alternación *f*.
**alternator** *n* alternador *m*.
**alternative** *n* alternativa *f*; * *adj* alternative; ~**ly** *adv* si no.
**although** *conj* aunque, no obstante.
**altitude** *n* altitud, altura *f*.
**altogether** *adv* del todo.
**alum** *n* alumbre *m*.
**aluminium** *n* aluminio *m*.
**aluminous** *adj* aluminoso/sa.
**always** *adv* siempre, constantemente.
**a.m.** *adv* de la mañana.

**amalgam** *n* amalgama *f.*
**amalgamate** *vt* (*vi*) amalgamar(se).
**amalgamation** *n* amalgamación *f.*
**amanuensis** *n* amanuense, secretario *m.*
**amaryllis** *n* (*bot*) amarillas *f.*
**amass** *vt* acumular, amontonar.
**amateur** *n* aficionado *m,* amateur *m/f.*
**amateurish** *adj* torpe.
**amatory** *adj* amatorio/ria; erótico/ca.
**amaze** *vt* asombrar.
**amazement** *n* asombro *m.*
**amazing** *adj* pasmoso/sa; ~ly *adv* extraordinariamente.
**amazon** *n* amazona *f.*
**ambassador** *n* embajador *m.*
**ambassadress** *n* embajadora *f.*
**amber** *n* ámbar *m;* * *adj* ambarino/na.
**ambidextrous** *adj* ambidextro/tra, ambidiestro/tra.
**ambient** *adj* ambiente.
**ambiguity** *n* ambigüedad, duda *f.*
**ambiguous** *adj* ambiguo; ~ly *adv* ambiguamente.
**ambition** *n* ambición *f.*
**ambitious** *adj* ambicioso/sa; ~ly *adv* ambiciosamente.
**amble** *vi* andar sin prisa.
**ambulance** *n* ambulancia *f.*
**ambush** *n* emboscada *f;* **to lie in** ~ estar emboscado/da; * *vt* tender una emboscada a.
**ameliorate** *vt* mejorar.
**amelioration** *n* mejoramiento *m.*
**amenable** *adj* sensible.
**amend** *vt* enmendar.
**amendable** *adj* reparable, corregible.
**amendment** *n* enmienda *f.*
**amends** *npl* compensación *f.*
**amenities** *npl* comodidades *fpl.*
**America** *n* América *f.*
**American** *adj* americano/na.
**amethyst** *n* amatista *f.*
**amiability** *n* amabilidad *f.*
**amiable** *adj* amable.
**amiableness** *n* amabilidad *f.*
**amiably** *adv* amablemente.
**amicable** *adj* amigable, amistoso/sa; ~bly *adv* amistosamente.
**amid(st)** *prep* entre, en medio de.
**amiss** *adv:* **something's** ~ algo pasa.
**ammonia** *n* amoniaco *m.*
**ammunition** *n* municiones *fpl.*
**amnesia** *n* amnesia *f.*
**amnesty** *n* amnistía *f.*
**among(st)** *prep* entre, en medio de.
**amoral** *adv* amoral.

**amorous** *adj* amoroso/sa; ~ly *adv* amorosamente.
**amorphous** *adj* informe.
**amount** *n* importe *m;* cantidad *f;* * *vi* sumar.
**amp(ere)** *n* amperio *m.*
**amphibian** *n* anfibio *m.*
**amphibious** *adj* anfibio/bia.
**amphitheatre** *n* anfiteatro *m.*
**ample** *adj* amplio/lia.
**ampleness** *n* amplitud, abundancia *f.*
**amplification** *n* amplificación *f;* extensión *f.*
**amplifier** *n* amplificador *m*
**amplify** *vt* ampliar, extender.
**amplitude** *n* amplitud, extensión *f.*
**amply** *adv* ampliamente.
**amputate** *vt* amputar.
**amputation** *n* amputación *f.*
**amulet** *n* amuleto *m.*
**amuse** *vt* entretener, divertir.
**amusement** *n* diversión *f,* pasatiempo, entretenimiento *m.*
**amusing** *adj* divertido/da; ~ly *adv* entretenidamente.
**an** *art* un, uno, una.
**anachronism** *n* anacronismo *m.*
**anaemia** *n* anemia *f.*
**anaemic** *adj* (*med*) anémico/ca.
**anaesthetic** *n* anestesia *f.*
**analog** *adj* (*comput*) analógico/ca.
**analogous** *adj* análogo.
**analogy** *n* analogía *f.*
**analyse** *vt* analizar.
**analysis** *n* análisis *m invar.*
**analyst** *n* analizador/a *m/f.*
**analytical** *adj* analítico/ca; ~ly *adv* analíticamente.
**anarchic** *adj* anárquico/ca.
**anarchist** *adj* anarquista.
**anarchy** *n* anarquía *f.*
**anatomical** *adj* anatómico/ca; ~ly *adv* anatómicamente.
**anatomize** *vt* anatomizar.
**anatomy** *n* anatomía *f*
**ancestor** *n:* ~s *pl* antepasados *mpl.*
**ancestral** *adj* hereditario/ria.
**ancestry** *n* raza, alcurnia *f.*
**anchor** *n* ancla *f;* * *vi* anclar; **to weigh** ~ zarpar.
**anchorage** *n* fondeadero *m.*
**anchovy** *n* anchoa *f.*
**ancient** *adj* antiguo.
**ancillary** *adj* auxiliar.
**and** *conj* y, e.
**anecdotal** *adj* anecdótico/ca.

**anecdote** n anécdota f
**anemone** n (bot) anémona f
**anew** adv de nuevo, nuevamente.
**angel** n ángel m
**angelic** adj angélico/ca.
**anger** n cólera f; * vt enojar, irritar.
**angle** n ángulo m; * vt pescar con caña.
**angled** adj anguloso/sa.
**angler** n pescador/a de caña m/f.
**anglicism** n anglicismo m.
**angling** n pesca con caña f
**angrily** adv enojado.
**angry** adj enojado/da.
**anguish** n ansia, angustia f
**angular** adj angular.
**angularity** n forma angular f.
**animal** n adj animal m.
**animate** vt animar; * adj viviente.
**animated** adj vivo/va.
**animation** n animación f
**animosity** n rencor m.
**animus** n odio m
**anise** n anís m
**aniseed** n anís m
**ankle**   n   tobillo   m; ~ **bone** hueso deltobillo m
**annals** n anales mpl.
**annex** vt anejar; * n anejo m.
**annexation** n anexión f.
**annihilate** vt aniquilar.
**annihilation** n aniquilación f.
**anniversary** n aniversario m.
**annotate** vi anotar.
**annotation** n anotación f.
**announce** vt anunciar, publicar.
**announcement** n anuncio m.
**announcer** n locutor/a m/f.
**annoy** vt molestar.
**annoyance** n molestia f.
**annoying** adj molesto/ta; fastidioso/sa.
**annual** adj anual; ~**ly** adv anualmente, cada año.
**annuity** n renta vitalicia f.
**annul** vt anular.
**annulment** n anulación f.
**annunciation** n anunciación f
**anodyne** adj anodino/na.
**anoint** vt untar, ungir.
**anomalous** adj anómalo.
**anomaly** n anomalía, irregularidad f.
**anon** adv más tarde.
**anonymity** n anonimato m.
**anonymous** adj anónimo/ma; ~**ly** adj anónimamente.
**anorexia** n anorexia f.

**another** adj otro/tra, diferente; **one** ~ uno a otro.
**answer** vt responder, replicar; corresponder; **to** ~ **for** responder de/por; **to** ~ **to** corresponder a; * n respuesta, réplica f.
**answerable** adj responsable.
**answering machine** n contestador automático m.
**ant** n hormiga f.
**antagonism** n antagonismo m; rivalidad f.
**antagonist** n antagonista m.
**antagonize** vt provocar.
**antarctic** adj antártico/ca.
**anteater** n oso hormiguero m
**antecedent** n: ~**s** pl antecedentes mpl.
**antechamber** n antecámara f
**antedate** vt antedatar.
**antelope** n antílope m.
**antenna** npl antena f.
**anterior** adj anterior, precedente.
**anthem** n himno m.
**ant hill** n hormiguero m.
**anthology** n antología f.
**anthracite** n antracita f.
**anthropologist** n antropólogo/ga m/f.
**anthropology** n antropología f
**anti-aircraft** adj antiaéreo/rea.
**antibiotic** n antibiótico m.
**antibody** n anticuerpo m.
**Antichrist** n Anticristo m.
**anticipate** vt anticipar, prevenir.
**anticipation** n anticipación f.
**anticlockwise** adv en sentido contrario al de las agujas del reloj.
**antidote** n antídoto m.
**antifreeze** n anticongelante m.
**antimony** n antimonio m.
**antipathy** n antipatía f.
**antipodes** npl antípodas fpl
**antiquarian** n anticuario m.
**antiquated** adj antiguo/gua; * n antigüedad f.
**antiquity** n antigüedad f.
**antiseptic** adj antiséptico/ca.
**antisocial** adj antisocial.
**antithesis** n antítesis f.
**antler** n cuerna f.
**anvil** n yunque m.
**anxiety** n ansiedad f, ansia f; afán m, zozobra f.
**anxious** adj ansioso/sa; ~**ly** adv ansiosamente; **to be** ~ vi zozobrar.
**any** adj pn cualquier, cualquiera; alguno, alguna; todo; ~**body** alguien, nadie, cualquiera; ~**how** de cualquier manera; ~**more** más; ~**place** en ninguna parte; ~**thing** algo, nada, cualquier cosa.

**apace** *adv* rápidamente.
**apart** *adv* aparte, separadamente.
**apartment** *n* apartamento, departamento *m*.
**apartment house** *n* casa de apartamentos *f*.
**apathetic** *adj* apático/ca.
**apathy** *n* apatía *f*.
**ape** *n* mono *m*; * *vt* remedar.
**aperture** *n* abertura *f*.
**apex** *n* ápice *m*.
**aphorism** *n* aforismo *m*; máxima *f*.
**apiary** *n* colmenar *m*.
**apiece** *adv* por cabeza, por persona.
**aplomb** *n* aplomo *m*.
**Apocalypse** *n* Apocalipsis *m*.
**apocrypha** *npl* libros apócrifos *mpl*.
**apocryphal** *adj* apócrifo/fa, no canónico/ca.
**apologetic** *adj* de disculpa.
**apologist** *n* apologista *m*.
**apologize** *vt* disculpar.
**apology** *n* apología, defensa *f*.
**apoplexy** *n* apoplejía *f*
**apostle** *n* apóstol *m*.
**apostolic** *adj* apostólico/ca.
**apostrophe** *n* apóstrofe *m*.
**apotheosis** *n* apoteosis *f*.
**appal** *vt* espantar, aterrar.
**appalling** *adj* espantoso/sa.
**apparatus** *n* aparato *m*.
**apparel** *n* traje, vestido *m*.
**apparent** *adj* evidente, aparente; ~ly *adv* por lo visto.
**apparition** *n* aparición, visión *f*.
**appeal** *vi* apelar, recurrir a un tribunal superior; * *n* (*law*) apelación *f*.
**appealing** *adj* atractivo/va.
**appear** *vi* aparecer.
**appearance** *n* apariencia *f*.
**appease** *vt* aplacar.
**appellant** *n* (*law*) apelante *m*.
**append** *vt* anejar.
**appendage** *n* cosa accesoria *f*.
**appendicitis** *n* apendicitis *f*.
**appendix** *n* apéndice *m*.
**appertain** *vi* tocar a.
**appetite** *n* apetito *m*.
**appetizing** *adj* apetitivo/va.
**applaud** *vi* aplaudir.
**applause** *n* aplausos *mpl*
**apple** *n* manzana *f*.
**apple pie** *n* pastelillo de manzanas *m*; **in ~ order** en sumo orden.
**apple tree** *n* manzano *m*.
**appliance** *n* aparato *m*.
**applicability** *n* aplicabilidad *f*.

**applicable** *adj* aplicable.
**applicant** *n* aspirante, candidato *m*.
**application** *n* aplicación *f*; solicitud *f*.
**applied** *adj* aplicado/da.
**apply** *vt* aplicar; * *vi* dirigirse a, recurrir a.
**appoint** *vt* nombrar.
**appointee** *n* persona nombrada *f*.
**appointment** *n* cita *f*; nombramiento *m*.
**apportion** *vt* repartir.
**apportionment** *n* repartición *f*.
**apposite** *adj* adaptado/da.
**apposition** *n* aposición *f*.
**appraisal** *n* estimación *f*.
**appraise** *vt* tasar; estimar.
**appreciable** *adj* sensible.
**appreciably** *adv* sensiblemente.
**appreciate** *vt* apreciar; agradecer.
**appreciation** *n* aprecio *m*.
**appreciative** *adj* agradecido/da.
**apprehend** *vt* arrestar.
**apprehension** *n* aprensión *f*.
**apprehensive** *adj* aprensivo/va, tímido/da.
**apprentice** *n* aprendiz *m*; * *vt* poner de aprendiz.
**apprenticeship** *n* aprendizaje *m*.
**apprise** *vt* informar.
**approach** *v* (*vi*) aproximar(se); * *n* acceso *m*.
**approachable** *adj* accesible.
**approbation** *n* aprobación *f*.
**appropriate** *vt* apropiarse de; * *adj* apropiado/da.
**approval** *n* aprobación *f*.
**approve (of)** *vt* aprobar.
**approximate** *vi* acercarse; * *adj* aproximativo/va; ~ly *adv* aproximadamente.
**approximation** *n* aproximación *f*.
**apricot** *n* damasco, albaricoque *m*.
**April** *n* abril *m*.
**apron** *n* delantal *m*.
**apse** *n* ábside *m*.
**apt** *adj* apto/ta, idóneo/nea; ~ly *adv* oportunamente.
**aptitude** *n* aptitud *f*.
**aqualung** *n* escafandra autónoma *f*.
**aquarium** *n* acuario *m*.
**Aquarius** *n* Acuario *m*.
**aquatic** *adj* acuático/ca.
**aqueduct** *n* acueducto *m*.
**aquiline** *adj* aguileño/ña.
**arabesque** *n* arabesco *m*.
**arable** *adj* labrantío/tía.
**arbiter** *n* árbitro *m*.
**arbitrariness** *n* arbitrariedad *f*.
**arbitrary** *adj* arbitrario/ria.

**arbitrate** *vt* arbitrar, juzgar como árbitro.
**arbitration** *n* arbitrio *m*.
**arbitrator** *n* árbitro *m*.
**arbour** *n* emparrado *m*; enramada *f*.
**arcade** *n* galería *f*.
**arch** *n* arco *m*; * *adj* malicioso/sa.
**archaeological** *adj* arqueológico/ca.
**archaeologist** *n* arqueólogo/ga *m/f*.
**archaeology** *n* arqueología *f*.
**archaic** *adj* arcaico/ca.
**archangel** *n* arcángel *m*.
**archbishop** *n* arzobispo *m*.
**archbishopric** *n* arzobispado *m*.
**archer** *n* arquero *m*.
**archery** *n* tiro con arco *m*.
**architect** *n* arquitecto/ta *m/f*.
**architectural** *adj* arquitectónico/ca.
**architecture** *n* arquitectura *f*.
**archives** *npl* archivos *mpl*.
**archivist** *n* archivero/ra *m/f*.
**archly** *adv* maliciosamente.
**archway** *n* arcada, bóveda *f*.
**arctic** *adj* ártico/ca.
**ardent** *adj* apasionado/da; **~ly** *adv* con pasión.
**ardour** *n* ardor *m*; vehemencia *f*; pasión *f*.
**arduous** *adj* arduo, difícil.
**area** *n* área *f*; espacio *m*, zona *f*.
**arena** *n* arena *f*.
**arguably** *adv* posiblemente.
**argue** *vi* discutir; * *vt* sostener.
**argument** *n* argumento *m*, controversia *f*.
**argumentation** *n* argumentación *f*.
**argumentative** *adj* discutidor/a.
**aria** *n* (*mus*) aria *f*.
**arid** *adj* árido/da, estéril.
**aridity** *n* sequedad *f*.
**Aries** *n* Aries *m*.
**aright** *adv* bien; **to set ~** rectificar.
**arise** *vi* levantarse; nacer.
**aristocracy** *n* aristocracia *f*.
**aristocrat** *n* aristócrata *m/f*.
**aristocratic** *adj* aristocrático/ca; **~ally** *adv* aristocráticamente.
**arithmetic** *n* aritmética *f*.
**arithmetical** *adj* aritmético/ca; **~ly** *adv* aritméticamente.
**ark** *n* arca *f*.
**arm** *n* brazo *m*; arma *f*, * *vt* (*vi*) armar(se).
**armament** *n* armamento *m*.
**armchair** *n* sillón *m*.
**armed** *adj* armado/da.
**armful** *n* brazada *f*.
**armhole** *n* sobaco *m*.
**armistice** *n* armisticio *m*.

**armour** *n* armadura *f*.
**armoured car** *n* carro blindado *m*.
**armoury** *n* arsenal *m*.
**armpit** *n* sobaco *m*.
**armrest** *n* apoyabrazos *m invar*.
**army** *n* ejército *m*; tropas *fpl*.
**aroma** *n* aroma *m*.
**aromatherapy** *n* aromaterapia *f*.
**aromatic** *adj* aromático/ca.
**around** *prep* alrededor de; * *adv* alrededor.
**arouse** *vt* despertar; excitar.
**arraign** *vt* acusar.
**arraignment** *n* acusación *f*; proceso criminal *m*.
**arrange** *vt* organizar.
**arrangement** *n* colocación *f*; arreglo.
**arrant** *adj* consumado/da.
**array** *n* serie *f*.
**arrears** *npl* resto de una deuda *m*; atraso *m*.
**arrest** *n* arresto *m*; * *vt* detener, arrestar.
**arrival** *n* llegada *f*.
**arrive** *vi* llegar.
**arrogance** *n* arrogancia, presunción *f*.
**arrogant** *adj* arrogante, presuntuoso/sa; **~ly** *adv* arrogantemente.
**arrogate** *vt* arrogarse.
**arrogation** *n* arrogación *f*.
**arrow** *n* flecha *f*.
**arsenal** *n* (*mil*) arsenal *m*; (*mar*) atarazana, armería *f*.
**arsenic** *n* arsénico *m*.
**arson** *n* fuego incendiario *m*.
**art** *n* arte *m*.
**arterial** *adj* arterial.
**artesian well** *n* pozo artesiano *m*.
**artery** *n* arteria *f*.
**artful** *adj* ingenioso/sa.
**artfulness** *n* astucia, habilidad *f*.
**art gallery** *n* pinacoteca *f*.
**arthritis** *n* artritis *f*.
**artichoke** *n* alcachofa *f*.
**article** *n* artículo *m*.
**articulate** *vt* articular, pronunciar distintamente.
**articulated** *adj* articulado/da.
**articulation** *n* articulación *f*.
**artifice** *n* artificio, fraude *m*.
**artificial** *adj* artificial; artificioso/sa; **~ly** *adv* artificialmente; artificiosamente.
**artificial insemination** *n* inseminación artificial *f*.
**artificiality** *n* artificialidad *f*.
**artillery** *n* artillería *f*.
**artisan** *n* artesano/na *m/f*.
**artist** *n* artista *m*.

**artistic** *adj* artístico/ca.
**artistry** *n* habilidad *f*.
**artless** *adj* sencillo, simple; **~ly** *adv* sencillamente, naturalmente.
**artlessness** *n* sencillez *f*.
**as** *conj* como; mientras; también; visto que, puesto que; **~ for, ~ to** en cuanto a.
**asbestos** *n* asbesto, amianto *m*.
**ascend** *vi* ascender, subir.
**ascendancy** *n* dominio *m*.
**ascension** *n* ascensión *f*.
**ascent** *n* subida *f*.
**ascertain** *vt* establecer.
**ascetic** *adj* ascético/ca; * *n* asceta *m*.
**ascribe** *vt* atribuir.
**ash** *n* (*bot*) fresno *m*; ceniza *f*
**ashamed** *adj* avergonzado/da.
**ashore** *adv* en tierra, a tierra; **to go ~** desembarcar.
**ashtray** *n* cenicero *m*.
**Ash Wednesday** *n* miércoles de ceniza *m*.
**aside** *adv* a un lado.
**ask** *vt* pedir, rogar; **to ~ after** preguntar por; **to ~ for** pedir; **to ~ out** invitar.
**askance** *adv* desconfiado/da.
**askew** *adv* de lado.
**asleep** *adj* dormido/da; **to fall ~** dormirse.
**asparagus** *n* espárrago *m*.
**aspect** *n* aspecto *m*.
**aspen** *n* álamo temblón *m*.
**aspersion** *n* calumnia *f*.
**asphalt** *n* asfalto *m*.
**asphyxia** *n* (*med*) asfixia *f*.
**asphyxiate** *vt* asfixiar.
**asphyxiation** *n* asfixia *f*.
**aspirant** *n* aspirante *m*.
**aspirate** *vt* aspirar, pronunciar con aspiración; * *n* sonido aspirado *m*.
**aspiration** *n* aspiración *f*.
**aspire** *vi* aspirar, desear.
**aspirin** *n* aspirina *f*.
**ass** *n* asno *m*; **she ~** burra *f*.
**assail** *vt* asaltar, atacar.
**assailant** *n* asaltante m/f, agresor/a *m/f*.
**assassin** *n* asesino/na *m/f*.
**assassinate** *vt* asesinar.
**assassination** *n* asesinato *m*.
**assault** *n* asalto *m*; * *vt* acometer, asaltar.
**assemblage** *n* multitud *f*.
**assemble** *vt* reunir, convocar; * *vi* juntarse.
**assembly** *n* asamblea, junta *f*; congreso *m*.
**assembly line** *n* cadena de montaje *f*.
**assent** *n* asentimiento *m*; * *vi* asentir.
**assert** *vt* sostener, mantener; afirmar.
**assertion** *n* aserción *f*.

**assertive** *adj* perentorio/ria.
**assess** *vt* valorar.
**assessment** *n* valoración *f*.
**assessor** *n* asesor/a *m/f*.
**assets** *npl* bienes *mpl*.
**assiduous** *adj* diligente, aplicado/da; **~ly** *adv* diligentemente.
**assign** *vt* asignar.
**assignation** *n* cita *f*.
**assignment** *n* asignación *f*; tarea *f*.
**assimilate** *vt* asimilar.
**assimilation** *n* asimilación *f*.
**assist** *vt* asistir, ayudar, socorrer.
**assistance** *n* asistencia *f*; socorro *m*.
**assistant** *n* asistente, ayudante *m*.
**associate** *vt* asociar; * *adj* asociado/da; * *n* socio *m*.
**association** *n* asociación, sociedad *f*.
**assonance** *n* asonancia *f*.
**assorted** *adj* surtido/da.
**assortment** *n* surtido *m*.
**assuage** *vt* mitigar, suavizar.
**assume** *vt* asumir; suponer.
**assumption** *n* supuesto *m*.
**Assumption** *n* Asunción *f*.
**assurance** *n* seguro *m*.
**assure** *vt* asegurar.
**assuredly** *adv* sin duda.
**asterisk** *n* asterisco *m*.
**astern** *adv* (*mar*) a popa.
**asthma** *n* asma *f*.
**asthmatic** *adj* asmático/ca.
**astonish** *vt* pasmar, sorprender.
**astonishing** *adj* asombroso/sa; **~ly** *adv* asombrosamente.
**astonishment** *n* asombro *m*.
**astound** *vt* pasmar.
**astray** *adv*: **to go ~** extraviarse; **to lead ~** llevar por mal camino.
**astride** *adv* a horcajadas.
**astringent** *adj* astringente.
**astrologer** *n* astrólogo/ga *m/f*.
**astrological** *adj* astrológico/ca.
**astrology** *n* astrología *f*.
**astronaut** *n* astronauta *m/f*.
**astronomer** *n* astrónomo *m*.
**astronomical** *adj* astronómico/ca.
**astronomy** *n* astronomía *f*.
**astute** *adj* astuto/ta.
**asylum** *n* asilo, refugio *m*.
**at** *prep* a; en; **~ once** en seguida; ya; **~ all** en absoluto; **~ all events** en todo caso; **~ first** al principio; **~ last** por fin.
**atheism** *n* ateísmo *m*.
**atheist** *n* ateo *m*, atea *f*.

**athlete** *n* atleta *m/f*.
**athletic** *adj* atlético/ca.
**atlas** *n* atlas *m invar*.
**atmosphere** *n* atmósfera *f*.
**atmospheric** *adj* atmosférico/ca.
**atom** *n* átomo *m*.
**atom bomb** *n* bomba atómica *f*.
**atomic** *adj* atómico/ca.
**atone** *vt* expiar.
**atonement** *n* expiación *f*.
**atop** *adv* encima.
**atrocious** *adj* atroz; **~ly** *adv* atrozmente.
**atrocity** *n* atrocidad, enormidad *f*.
**atrophy** *n* (*med*) atrofia *f*.
**attach** *vt* adjuntar.
**attaché** *n* agregado *m*.
**attachment** *n* afecto *m*.
**attack** *vt* atacar; acometer; * *n* ataque *m*.
**attacker** *n* asaltante *m*.
**attain** *vt* conseguir, obtener.
**attainable** *adj* asequible.
**attempt** *vt* intentar; probar, experimentar; * *n* intento *m*, tentativa *f*.
**attend** *vt* servir; asistir; **to ~ to** ocuparse de; * *vi* prestar atención.
**attendance** *n* presencia *f*.
**attendant** *n* sirviente *m*.
**attention** *n* atención *f*; cuidado *m*.
**attentive** *adj* atento/ta; cuidadoso/sa; **~ly** *adv* con atención.
**attenuate** *vt* atenuar, disminuir.
**attest** *vt* atestiguar.
**attic** *n* desván *m*; guardilla *f*.
**attire** *n* atavío *m*.
**attitude** *n* actitud, postura *f*.
**attorney** *n* abogado/da *m/f*.
**attract** *vt* atraer.
**attraction** *n* atracción *f*; atractivo *m*.
**attractive** *adj* atractivo/va.
**attribute** *vt* atribuir; * *n* atributo *m*.
**attrition** *n* agotamiento *m*.
**auburn** *adj* moreno/na, castaño/ña.
**auction** *n* subasta *f*.
**auctioneer** *n* subastador/a, rematador/a *m/f*.
**audacious** *adj* audaz, temerario/ria; **~ly** *adv* atrevidamente.
**audacity** *n* audacia, osadía *f*.
**audible** *adj* perceptible al oído; **~ly** *adv* de manera audible.
**audience** *n* audiencia *f*; auditorio *m*.
**audit** *n* auditoría *f*; * *vt* auditar.
**auditor** *n* censor/a de cuentas *m/f*.
**auditory** *adj* auditivo/va.
**augment** *vt* aumentar, acrecentar; * *vi* crecer.

**augmentation** *n* aumentación *f*; aumento *m*.
**August** *n* agosto *m*.
**august** *adj* majestuoso/sa.
**aunt** *n* tía *f*.
**au pair** *n* au pair *f*.
**aura** *n* aura *f*.
**auspices** *npl* auspicios *mpl*.
**auspicious** *adj* propicio/cia; **~ly** *adv* favorablemente.
**austere** *adj* austero/ra, severo/ra; **~ly** *adv* austeramente.
**austerity** *n* austeridad *f*.
**authentic** *adj* auténtico/ca; **~ly** *adv* auténticamente.
**authenticate** *vt* autenticar.
**authenticity** *n* autenticidad *f*.
**author** *n* autor/a *m/f*; escritor/a *m/f*.
**authoress** *n* autora; escritora *f*.
**authoritarian** *adj* autoritario/ria.
**authoritative** *adj* autoritativo/va; **~ly** *adv* autoritativamente, con autoridad.
**authority** *n* autoridad *f*.
**authorization** *n* autorización *f*.
**authorize** *vt* autorizar.
**authorship** *n* autoría *f*.
**autocrat** *n* autócrata *m*.
**autocratic** *adj* autocrático/ca.
**autograph** *n* autógrafo *m*.
**automated** *adj* automatizado/da.
**automatic** *adj* automático/ca.
**automaton** *n* autómata *m*.
**autonomy** *n* autonomía *f*.
**autopsy** *n* autopsia *f*.
**autumn** *n* otoño *m*.
**autumnal** *adj* otoñal.
**auxiliary** *adj* auxiliar, asistente.
**avail** *vt*: **to ~ oneself of** aprovecharse de; * *n*: **to no ~** en vano.
**available** *adj* disponible.
**avalanche** *n* alud *m*.
**avarice** *n* avaricia *f*.
**avaricious** *adj* avaro/ra.
**avenge** *vt* vengarse, castigar.
**avenue** *n* avenida *f*.
**aver** *vt* afirmar, declarar.
**average** *vt* tomar un término medio; * *n* término medio *m*.
**aversion** *n* aversión *f*, disgusto *m*.
**avert** *vt* desviar, apartar.
**aviary** *n* pajarera *f*.
**avoid** *vt* evitar, escapar, huir; * *vr* zafarse de.
**avoidable** *adj* evitable.
**await** *vt* aguardar.
**awake** *vt* despertar; * *vi* despertarse; * *adj* despierto/ta.

**awakening** *n* despertar.

**award** *vt* otorgar; * *n* premio *m*; sentencia, decisión *f*.

**aware** *adj* consciente; vigilante.

**awareness** *n* conciencia *f*.

**away** *adv* ausente, fuera; ~! ¡fuera! , ¡quita de ahí!, ¡marcha! **far and ~** de mucho, con mucho.

**away game** *n* partido fuera de casa *m*.

**awe** *n* miedo, temor *m*.

**awe-inspiring, awesome** *adj* imponente.

**awful** *adj* tremendo/da; horroroso/sa; ~**ly** *adv* terriblemente.

**awhile** *adv* un rato, algún tiempo.

**awkward** *adj* torpe, rudo/da, poco diestro/tra; ~**ly** *adv* groseramente, toscamente.

**awkwardness** *n* tosquedad, grosería, poca habilidad *f*.

**awl** *n* lezna *f*.

**awning** *n* (*mar*) toldo *m*.

**awry** *adv* oblicuamente, torcidamente, al través.

**axe** *n* hacha *f*; * *vt* despedir; cortar.

**axiom** *n* axioma *m*.

**axis** *n* eje *m*.

**axle** *n* eje *m*.

**ay(e)** *excl* sí.

# B

**baa** n balido m; * vi balar.
**babble** vi charlar, parlotear; * n ~ , **babbling** charla, cháchara f.
**babbler** n charlador/a, charlatán/ana m/f.
**babe**, **baby** n niño/a, pequeño/a, nene/a m/f; **small** ~ mamón/ona m/f.
**baboon** n babuino m.
**babyhood** n niñez f.
**babyish** adj niñero/ra; pueril.
**baby carriage** n cochecito m.
**baby linen** n ropita de niño f.
**bachelor** n soltero m; bachiller m.
**bachelorship** n soltería f; bachillerato m.
**back** n dorso m; revés de la mano m; * adv atrás, detrás; **a few years** ~ hace algunos años; * vt sostener, apoyar, favorecer.
**backbite** vt hablar mal del que está ausente; difamar.
**backbiter** n detractor/a m/f.
**backbone** n hueso dorsal, espinazo m.
**backdate** vt antedatar.
**backdoor** n puerta trasera f.
**backer** n partidario/ria m/f.
**backgammon** n backgammon m.
**background** n fondo m.
**backlash** n reacción f.
**backlog** n trabajo acumulado m.
**back number** n número atrasado m.
**backpack** n mochila f.
**back payment** n paga atrasada f.
**backside** n trasero m.
**backward** adj tardo/da, lento/ta; * adv hacia atrás.
**bacon** n tocino m.
**bad** adj mal/malo; perverso/sa; infeliz; dañoso/sa; indispuesto/ta; ~**ly** adv malamente.
**badge** n señal f; símbolo m; divisa f.
**badger** n tejón m; * vt fatigar; cansar, atormentar.
**badminton** n bádminton m.
**badness** n maldad, mala calidad f.
**baffle** vt confundir, hundir; acosar.
**bag** n saco m; bolsa f.
**baggage** n bagaje, equipaje m.
**bagpipe** n gaita f.
**bail** n fianza, caución (juratoria) f; fiador m; * vt caucionar, fiar.
**bailiff** n alguacil m; mayordomo m.
**bait** vt cebar; atraer; * n cebo m; anzuelo m.
**baize** n bayeta f.

**bake** vt cocer en horno.
**bakery** n panadería f.
**baker** n hornero/ra, panadero/ra m/f; ~**'s dozen** trece piezas.
**baking** n cocción f.
**baking powder** n levadura f.
**balance** n balanza f; equilibrio m; saldo de una cuenta m; **to lose one's** ~ caerse, dar en tierra; * vt pesar en balanza; contrapesar; saldar; considerar, examinar.
**balance sheet** n balance m.
**balcony** n balcón m.
**bald** adj calvo/va.
**baldness** n calvicie f.
**bale** n bala f; * vt embalar; tirar el agua del bote.
**baleful** adj triste, funesto/ta; ~**ly** adv tristemente; míseramente.
**ball** n bola f; pelota f; baile m, balón m.
**ballad** n balada f.
**ballast** n lastre, m * vt lastrar.
**ballerina** n bailarina f.
**ballet** n ballet m.
**ballistic** adj balístico/ca.
**balloon** n globo m.
**ballot** n voto m; escrutinio m; * vi votar.
**ballpoint (pen)** n bolígrafo m.
**ballroom** n salón de baile m.
**balm**, **balsam** n bálsamo m; * vt untar con bálsamo.
**balmy** adj balsámico/ca; fragante.
**balustrade** n balaustrada f.
**bamboo** n bambú m.
**bamboozle** vt (col) engañar.
**ban** n prohibición f; * vt prohibir.
**banal** adj vulgar.
**banana** n plátano m.
**band** n faja f; cuadrilla f; banda (de soldados) f; orquesta f.
**bandage** n venda f, vendaje m; * vt vendar.
**bandit** n bandido/da m/f.
**bandstand** n quiosco m.
**bandy** vt pelotear; discutir.
**bandy-legged** adj patizambo/ba.
**bang** n golpe m; * vt golpear; cerrar con violencia.
**bangle** n brazalete m.
**bangs** npl flequillo m.
**banish** vt desterrar, echar fuera, proscribir, expatriar.
**banishment** n destierro m.

**banister(s)** *n(pl)* pasamanos *m*.
**banjo** *n* banjo *m*.
**bank** *n* orilla (de río) *f*; montón de tierra *m*; banco *m*; dique *m*; escollo *m*; * *vt* poner dinero en un banco; **to ~ on** contar con.
**bank account** *n* cuenta de banco *f*.
**bank card** *n* tarjeta bancaria *f*.
**banker** *n* banquero/ra *m/f*.
**banking** *n* banca *f*; **electronic ~** banca electrónica.
**banknote** *n* billete de banco *m*.
**bankrupt** *adj* insolvente; * *n* fallido/da, quebrado/da *m*.
**bankruptcy** *n* bancarrota, quiebra *f*.
**bank statement** *n* detalle de cuenta *m*.
**banner** *n* bandera *f*; estandarte *m*.
**banquet** *n* banquete *m*.
**banter** *n* zumba *f*.
**baptism** *n* bautismo *m*.
**baptismal** *adj* bautismal.
**baptistery** *n* bautisterio *m*.
**baptize** *vt* bautizar.
**bar** *n* bar *m*; barra *f*; tranca *f*; obstáculo *m*; (*law*) abogacía *f*; * *vt* impedir; prohibir; excluir.
**barbarian** *n* bárbaro/ra *m/f*, * *adj* bárbaro/ra, cruel.
**barbaric** *adj* bárbaro/ra.
**barbarism** *n* (*gr*) barbarismo *m*; crueldad *f*.
**barbarity** *n* barbaridad, inhumanidad *f*.
**barbarous** *adj* bárbaro/ra, cruel.
**barbecue** *n* barbacoa *f*.
**barber** *n* peluquero *m*.
**barber's (shop)** *n* peluquería *f*.
**bar code** *n* código de barras *m*.
**bard** *n* bardo *m*; poeta *m*.
**bare** *adj* desnudo/da, descubierto/ta; simple; puro/ra; * *vt* desnudar, descubrir.
**barefaced** *adj* desvergonzado/da, impudente.
**barefoot(ed)** *adj* descalzo, sin zapatos.
**bareheaded** *adj* descubierto/ta.
**barelegged** *adj* con las piernas desnudas.
**barely** *adv* apenas, solamente.
**bareness** *n* desnudez *f*.
**bargain** *n* ganga *f*; contrato, pacto *m*; * *vi* pactar; negociar; **to ~ for** esperar.
**barge** *n* barcaza *f*.
**baritone** *n* (*mus*) barítono *m*.
**bark** *n* corteza *f*; ladrido *m* (del perro); * *vi* ladrar.
**barley** *n* cebada *f*.
**barmaid** *n* camarera *f*.
**barman** *n* barman *m*.
**barn** *n* granero, pajar *m*.
**barnacles** *npl* percebe *m*.

**barometer** *n* barómetro *m*.
**baron** *n* barón *m*.
**baroness** *n* baronesa *f*.
**baronial** *adj* de barón.
**barracks** *npl* cuartel *m*.
**barrage** *n* descarga *f*; (*fig*) lluvia *f*.
**barrel** *n* barril *m*; cañón de escopeta *m*.
**barrel organ** *n* organillo de cilindro *m*.
**barren** *adj* estéril, infructuoso/sa; (*fig*) yermo/ma.
**barricade** *n* barricada *f*; estacada *f*; barrera *f*; * *vt* cerrar con barreras, empalizar.
**barrier** *n* barrera *f*; obstáculo *m*.
**barring** *adv* excepto, fuera de.
**barrow** *n* carretilla *f*.
**bartender** *n* barman *m*.
**barter** *vi* baratar; * *vt* cambiar, trocar.
**base** *n* fondo *m*; base *f*; basa *f*; pedestal *m*; zócalo *m*; * *vt* apoyar; * *adj* bajo/ja, vil.
**baseball** *n* béisbol *m*.
**baseless** *adj* sin fondo/base.
**basement** *n* sótano *m*.
**baseness** *n* bajeza, vileza *f*.
**bash** *vt* golpear.
**bashful** *adj* vergonzoso/sa, modesto/ta, tímido/da; **~ly** *adv* vergonzosamente.
**basic** *adj* básico/ca; **~ally** *adv* básicamente.
**basilisk** *n* basilisco *m*.
**basin** *n* jofaina, bacía *f*.
**basis** *n* base *f*; fundamento *m*.
**bask** *vi* ponerse a tomar el sol.
**basket** *n* cesta, canasta *f*.
**basketball** *n* baloncesto *m*.
**bass** *n* (*mus*) contrabajo *m*.
**bassoon** *n* bajón *m*.
**bass viol** *n* viola *f*.
**bass voice** *n* bajo cantante *m*.
**bastard** *n*, *adj* bastardo/da *m/f*.
**baste** *vt* pringar; hilvanar.
**basting** *n* hilván *m*; apaleamiento *m*; paliza *f*.
**bastion** *n* (*mil*) bastión *m*.
**bat** *n* murciélago *m*.
**batch** *n* serie *f*.
**bath** *n* baño *m*.
**bathe** *vt* (*vi*) bañar(se).
**bathing suit** *n* traje de baño *m*.
**bathos** *n* estilo bajo en la poesía *m*.
**bathroom** *n* (cuarto de) baño *m*.
**baths** *npl* piscina *f*.
**bathtub** *n* baño *m*, bañera *f*.
**baton** *n* batuta *f*.
**battalion** *n* (*mil*) batallón *m*.
**batter** *vt* apalear; batir, cañonear; * *n* batido *m*.

**battering ram** n (*mil*) ariete m.
**battery** n batería f.
**battle** n combate m; batalla f; * vi batallar,
combatir.
**battle array** n orden de batalla f.
**battlefield** n campo de batalla m.
**battlement** n muralla almenada f.
**battleship** n acorazado m.
**bawdy** adj indecente.
**bawl** vi gritar, vocear.
**bay** n bahía f; laurel, lauro m; * vi balar;
* adj bayo.
**bayonet** n bayoneta f.
**bay window** n ventana salediza f.
**bazaar** n bazar m.
**be** vi ser; estar.
**beach** n playa, orilla f.
**beacon** n almenara f.
**bead** n cuenta f; ~s npl rosario m.
**beagle** n sabueso m.
**beak** n pico m.
**beaker** n taza con pico f.
**beam** n rayo de luz m; travesaño m; pareja
f; * vi brillar.
**bean** n alubia f, frijol m, judía f; **green ~**,
**French ~** judía verde f.
**beansprouts** npl brotes de soja mpl.
**bear** vt llevar; sostener; soportar; producir;
parir; * vi sufrir (algún dolor).
**bear** n oso m; **she ~** osa f.
**bearable** adj soportable.
**beard** n barba f.
**bearded** adj barbado/da.
**bearer** n portador/a m/f; árbol fructífero m.
**bearing** n relación f.
**beast** n bestia f; hombre brutal m; ~ **of burden** acémila f.
**beastliness** n bestialidad, brutalidad f.
**beastly** adj bestial, brutal; * adv brutalmente.
**beat** vt golpear; tocar (un tambor); **to ~ time**
(with the sole of the shoe) zapatear; * vi
pulsar, palpitar; * n golpe m; pulsación f.
**beatific** adj beatífico/ca.
**beatify** vt beatificar, santificar.
**beating** n paliza, zurra f; pulsación f,
zumba f.
**beatitude** n beatitud, felicidad f.
**beautiful** adj hermoso/sa, bello; ~**ly** adv
con belleza/perfección.
**beautify** vt hermosear; embellecer; adornar.
**beauty** n hermosura, belleza f; ~ **salon** n
salón de belleza m; ~ **spot** n lunar m.
**beaver** n castor m.
**because** conj porque, a causa de.
**beckon** vi hacer seña con la cabeza/la mano.

**become** vt convenir; estar bien; * vi hacerse,
convertirse, venir a parar.
**becoming** adj decente, conveniente.
**bed** n cama f.
**bedclothes** npl cobertores npl, mantas/
colchas fpl.
**bedding** n ropa de cama f.
**bedecked** adj adornado/da.
**bedlam** n manicomio m.
**bedpost** n pilar de cama m.
**bedridden** adj postrado/da en cama,
encamado/da.
**bedroom** n dormitorio m.
**bedspread** n colcha f.
**bedtime** n hora de irse a la cama f.
**bee** n abeja f.
**beech** n haya f.
**beef** n carne de vaca f.
**beefburger** n hamburguesa f.
**beefsteak** n bistec m.
**beehive** n colmena f.
**beeline** n línea recta f.
**beer** n cerveza f.
**beeswax** n cera f.
**beet** n remolacha f.
**beetle** n escarabajo m.
**befall** vi suceder, acontecer, sobrevenir.
**befit** vt convenir, acomodarse a.
**before** adv, prep antes de; delante, enfrente;
ante.
**beforehand** adv de antemano, anticipadamente.
**befriend** vt proteger, amparar.
**beg** vt mendigar, rogar; suplicar; suponer;
* vi vivir de limosna.
**beget** vt engendrar.
**beggar** n mendigo/ga m/f.
**begin** vt, vi comenzar, empezar.
**beginner** n principiante m; novicio/cia m/f.
**beginning** n principio, origen m.
**begrudge** vt envidiar.
**behalf** n **on ~ of** de parte de.
**behave** vi comportarse, portarse, conducirse.
**behaviour** n conducta f; modo de portarse m.
**behead** vt decapitar, cortar la cabeza.
**behind** prep detrás; atrás; a la, en zaga; * adv
atrasadamente.
**behold** vt ver, contemplar, observar.
**behove** vi importar, ser útil; incumbir.
**beige** adj color beige.
**being** n existencia f; estado m; ser m.
**belated** adj atrasado/da.
**belch** vi eructar, vomitar; * n eructo m.
**belfry** n campanario m.
**belie** vt desmentir, calumniar.

**belief** *n* fe, creencia *f*; opinión *f*; credo *m*.
**believable** *adj* creíble.
**believe** *vt* creer; * *vi* pensar, imaginar.
**believer** *n* creyente, fiel, cristiano/na *m/f*.
**belittle** *vt* minimizar.
**bell** *n* campana *f*.
**bellicose** *adj* belicoso/sa.
**belligerent** *adj* beligerante.
**bellow** *vi* bramar; rugir; vociferar; * *n* bramido *m*.
**bellows** *npl* fuelle *m*.
**belly** *n* vientre *m*; panza *f*.
**bellyful** *n* panzada *f*; hartura *f*.
**belong** *vi* pertenecer.
**belongings** *npl* pertenencias *fpl*.
**beloved** *adj* querido/da, amado/da.
**below** *adv*, *prep* debajo, inferior; abajo.
**belt** *n* cinturón, cinto *m*; zona *f*.
**bemoan** *vt* deplorar, lamentar.
**bemused** *adj* confundido/da.
**bench** *n* banco *m*, banquillo *m*.
**bend** *vt* encorvar, inclinar, plegar; hacer una reverencia; * *vi* encorvarse, inclinarse; * *n* curva *f*.
**beneath** *adv*, *prep* debajo, abajo.
**benediction** *n* bendición *f*.
**benefactor** *n* bienhechor *m*.
**benefice** *n* beneficio *m*; beneficio eclesiástico *m*.
**beneficent** *adj* benéfico/ca.
**beneficial** *adj* beneficioso/sa, provechoso/sa, útil.
**beneficiary** *n* beneficiario/ria *m*.
**benefit** *n* beneficio *m*; utilidad *f*; provecho *m*; * *vt* beneficiar; * *vi* utilizarse; prevalerse.
**benefit night** *n* representación dramática a beneficio de un actor/de una actriz *f*.
**benevolence** *n* benevolencia *f*; donativo gratuito *m*.
**benevolent** *adj* benévolo/la.
**benign** *adj* benigno/na; afable; liberal.
**bent** *n* inclinación *f*.
**benzine** *n* (*chem*) bencina *f*.
**bequeath** *vt* legar en testamento.
**bequest** *n* legado *m*.
**bereave** *vt* privar.
**bereavement** *n* pérdida *f*.
**beret** *n* boina *f*.
**berm** *n* arcén *m*.
**berry** *n* baya *f*.
**berserk** *adj* loco/ca.
**berth** *n* (*mar*) amarradero *m*, camarote *m*.
**beseech** *vt* suplicar, implorar, conjurar, rogar.
**beset** *vt* acosar.

**beside(s)** *prep* al lado de; excepto; sobre; fuera de; * *adv* por otra parte.
**besiege** *vt* sitiar, bloquear.
**best** *adj* mejor; * *adv* (lo) mejor; * *n* lo mejor *m*.
**bestial** *adj* bestial, brutal; **~ly** *adv* bestialmente.
**bestiality** *n* bestialidad, brutalidad *f*.
**bestow** *vt* dar, conferir; otorgar.
**bestseller** *n* bestseller *m*.
**bet** *n* apuesta *f*; * *vt* apostar.
**betray** *vt* traicionar; divulgar algún secreto.
**betrayal** *n* traición *f*.
**betroth** *vt* contraer esponsales.
**betrothal** *n* esponsales *mpl*.
**better** *adj*, *adv* mejor; **so much the ~** tanto mejor; * *vt* mejorar, reformar.
**betting** *n* juego *m*.
**between** *prep* entre, en medio de.
**bevel** *n* cartabón *m*.
**beverage** *n* bebida *f*; trago *m*.
**bevy** *n* bandada (de aves) *f*.
**beware** *vi* guardarse.
**bewilder** *vt* pasmar.
**bewilderment** *n* perplejidad *f*.
**bewitch** *vt* encantar, hechizar.
**beyond** *prep* más allá, más adelante, fuera de.
**bias** *n* propensión, inclinación *f*; sesgo *m*; prejuicio *m*.
**bib** *n* babador *m*.
**Bible** *n* Biblia *f*.
**biblical** *adj* bíblico/ca.
**bibliography** *n* bibliografía *f*.
**bicarbonate of soda** *n* bicarbonato de soda *m*.
**bicker** *vi* escaramucear, reñir, disputar.
**bicycle** *n* bicicleta *f*.
**bid** *vt* mandar, ordenar; ofrecer; * *n* oferta *f*; tentativa *f*.
**bidding** *n* orden *f*; mandato *m*; ofrecimiento *m*.
**bide** *vt* sufrir, aguantar.
**biennial** *adj* bienal.
**bifocals** *npl* gafas bifocales *fpl*.
**bifurcated** *adj* bifurcado/da.
**big** *adj* grande, lleno/na; inflado/da.
**bigamist** *n* bígamo/ma *m/f*.
**bigamy** *n* bigamia *f*.
**big dipper** *n* montaña rusa *f*.
**bigheaded** *adj* engreído/da.
**bigness** *n* grandeza *f*.
**bigot** *n* fanático/ca *m/f*.
**bigoted** *adj* fanático/ca.
**bike** *n* bici *f*; bicicleta *f*; **mountain ~** bicicleta de montaña.

**bikini** *n* bikini *m*.
**bilberry** *n* arándano *m*.
**bile** *n* bilis *f*.
**bilingual** *adj* bilingüe.
**bilious** *adj* bilioso/sa.
**bill** *n* pico de ave *m*; billete *m*; cuenta *f*.
**billboard** *n* cartelera *f*.
**billet** *n* alojamiento *m*.
**billiards** *npl* billar *m*.
**billiard-table** *n* mesa de billar *f*.
**billion** *n* mil millones *mpl*, millardo *m*.
**bin** *n* cubo de la basura *m*.
**bind** *vt* atar; unir; encuadernar.
**binder** *n* encuadernador/a *m/f*.
**binding** *n* venda, faja *f*.
**binge** *n* juerga *f*.
**bingo** *n* bingo *m*.
**biochemistry** *n* bioquímica *f*.
**biodegradable** *adj* biodegradable.
**biodiversity** *n* biodiversity *f*.
**binoculars** *npl* prismáticos *mpl*.
**biographer** *n* biógrafo/fa *m/f*.
**biographical** *adj* biográfico/ca.
**biography** *n* biografía *f*.
**biological** *adj* biológico/ca.
**biology** *n* biología *f*.
**biped** *n* bípedo *m*.
**birch** *n* abedul *m*.
**bird** *n* ave *f*; pájaro *m*.
**bird's-eye view** *n* vista de pájaro *f*.
**bird-watcher** *n* ornitólogo/ga *m/f*.
**birth** *n* nacimiento *m*; origen *m*; parto *m*.
**birth certificate** *n* partida de nacimiento *f*.
**birth control** *n* control de natalidad *m*.
**birthday** *n* cumpleaños *m invar*.
**birthplace** *n* lugar de nacimiento *m*.
**birthright** *n* derechos de nacimiento *mpl*; primogenitura *f*.
**biscuit** *n* bizcocho *m*; galleta *f*.
**bisect** *vt* bisecar.
**bishop** *n* obispo *m*.
**bison** *n* bisonte *m*.
**bit** *n* bocado *m*; pedacito *m*.
**bitch** *n* perra *f*; (*fig*) zorra *f*.
**bite** *vt* morder; picar; ~ **the dust** (*col*) morder la tierra, morir; * *n* mordedura *f*.
**bitter** *adj* amargo/ga, áspero/ra; mordaz, satírico/ca; penoso/sa; ~**ly** *adv* amargamente; con pena; severamente.
**bitterness** *n* amargor *m*; rencor *m*; pena *f*; dolor *m*.
**bitumen** *n* betún *m*.
**bizarre** *adj* raro/ra, extravagante.
**blab** *vi* chismear.

**black** *adj* negro/gra, oscuro/ra; funesto/ta; * *n* color negro *m*.
**blackberry** *n* zarzamora *f*.
**blackbird** *n* mirlo *m*.
**blackboard** *n* pizarra *f*.
**black box** *n* caja negra *f*.
**blacken** *vt* teñir de negro; ennegrecer.
**black ice** *n* hielo invisible *m*.
**blackjack** *n* veintiuna *f*.
**blackleg** *n* esquirol *m*.
**blacklist** *n* lista negra *f*.
**blackmail** *n* chantaje *m*; * *vt* chantajear.
**black market** *n* mercado negro *m*.
**blackness** *n* negrura *f*.
**black pudding** *n* morcilla *f*.
**black sheep** *n* oveja negra *f*.
**blacksmith** *n* herrero *m*.
**blackthorn** *n* endrino *m*.
**bladder** *n* vejiga *f*.
**blade** *n* hoja *f*; filo *m*; escobilla *f*.
**blame** *vt* culpar; * *n* culpa *f*.
**blameless** *adj* inocente, irreprensible, puro/ra; ~**ly** *adv* inocentemente.
**blanch** *vt* blanquear.
**bland** *adj* blando/da, suave, dulce, apacible.
**blank** *adj* blanco/ca; pálido/da; * *n* blanco *m*.
**blank cheque** *n* cheque en blanco *m*.
**blanket** *n* manta *f*.
**blare** *vi* resonar.
**blasé** *adj* indiferente.
**blaspheme** *vt* blasfemar, jurar, decir blasfemias.
**blasphemous** *adj* blasfemo/ma.
**blasphemy** *n* blasfemia *f*.
**blast** *n* soplo de aire *m*; carga explosiva *f*; * *vt* volar.
**blast-off** *n* lanzamiento *m*.
**blatant** *adj* obvio.
**blaze** *n* llama *f*; * *vi* encenderse en llamas; brillar, resplandecer.
**bleach** *vt* blanquear al sol; * *vi* blanquear; * *n* lejía *f*.
**bleached** *adj* teñido/da de rubio; descolorado/da.
**bleachers** *npl* gradas al sol *fpl*.
**bleak** *adj* pálido/da, descolorido/da; frío, helado/da.
**bleakness** *n* frialdad *f*; palidez *f*.
**bleary(-eyed)** *adj* legañoso/sa.
**bleat** *n* balido *m*; * *vi* balar.
**bleed** *vi*, *vt* sangrar.
**bleeding** *n* sangría *f*.
**bleeper** *n* busca *m*.
**blemish** *vt* manchar, ensuciar; infamar; * *n* tacha *f*; deshonra, infamia *f*.

**blend** vt mezclar.

**bless** vt bendecir.

**blessing** n bendición f; beneficio m; ventaja f.

**blight** vt arruinar.

**blind** adj ciego/ga; ~ **alley** n callejón sin salida m; * vt cegar; deslumbrar; * n velo m; **Venetian** ~ persiana f.

**blinders** npl anteojeras fpl.

**blindfold** vt vendar los ojos; ~**ed** adj con los ojos vendados.

**blindly** adv ciegamente, a ciegas.

**blindness** n ceguera f.

**blind side** n punto ciego m.

**blind spot** n punto ciego m.

**blink** vi parpadear.

**blinkers** npl anteojeras fpl.

**bliss** n felicidad (eterna) f.

**blissful** adj feliz en sumo grado; beato/ta, bienaventurado/da; ~**ly** adv felizmente.

**blissfulness** n suprema felicidad f.

**blister** n ampolla f; * vi ampollarse.

**blitz** n bombardeo aéreo m.

**blizzard** n ventisca f.

**bloated** adj hinchado/da.

**blob** n gota f.

**bloc** n bloque m.

**block** n bloque m; obstáculo m; zoquete m; manzana f; ~ (**up**) vt bloquear.

**blockade** n bloqueo m; * vt bloquear.

**blockage** n obstrucción f.

**blockbuster** n éxito de público m.

**blockhead** n bruto, necio, zopenco m; (col) zoquete m.

**blond** adj rubio/bia; * n rubio/bia m/f.

**blood** n sangre f.

**blood donor** n donante de sangre m/f.

**blood group** n grupo sanguíneo m.

**bloodhound** n sabueso m.

**bloodily** adv sangrientamente, inhumanamente.

**bloodiness** n (fig) crueldad f.

**bloodless** adj exangüe; sin efusión de sangre.

**blood poisoning** n septicemia f.

**blood pressure** n presión sanguínea f.

**blood sausage** n morcilla f.

**bloodshed** n efusión de sangre f; matanza f, derramamiento de sangre m.

**bloodshot** adj ensangrentado/da.

**bloodstream** n corriente sanguínea f.

**bloodsucker** n sanguijuela f; (fig) desollador/a m/f.

**blood test** n análisis de sangre m invar.

**bloodthirsty** adj sanguinario/ria.

**blood transfusion** n transfusión sanguínea f.

**blood vessel** n vena f; vaso sanguíneo m.

**bloody** adj sangriento/ta, ensangrentado/da; cruel; ~ **minded** adj sanguinario/ria.

**bloom** n flor f; (also fig); * vi florecer.

**blossom** n flor f.

**blot** vt manchar (lo escrito); cancelar; denigrar; * n mancha f.

**blotchy** adj muy manchado/da.

**blotting paper** n papel secante m.

**blouse** n blusa f.

**blow** vi soplar; sonar; * vt soplar; inflar; **to** ~ **up** volar; * n golpe m.

**blowout** n pinchazo m.

**blowpipe** n soplete m.

**blubber** n grasa de ballena f; * vi lloriquear.

**bludgeon** n cachiporra f; palocorto m.

**blue** adj azul.

**bluebell**, **harebell** n (bot) campanilla f.

**blue berets** npl cascos azules mpl.

**bluebottle** n moscarda f.

**blueness** n color azul m.

**blueprint** n (fig) anteproyecto m.

**bluff** n farol m; * vt farolear.

**bluish** adj azulado/da.

**blunder** n metedura de pata f; error craso m; * vi meter la pata.

**blunt** adj obtuso/sa; grosero/ra; * vt embotar.

**bluntly** adv sin artificio; claramente; obtusamente.

**bluntness** n embotadura, franqueza f.

**blur** n contorno borroso m; * vt hacer borroso.

**blurt out** vt descolgarse con.

**blush** n rubor m; sonrojo m; * vi ponerse colorado/da, sonrojarse.

**blustery** adj tempestuoso/sa.

**boa** n boa f (serpiente).

**boar** n verraco m; **wild** ~ jabalí m.

**board** n tabla f; mesa f; consejo m; * vt embarcarse en; subir a.

**boarder** n pensionista m/f.

**boarding card** n tarjeta de embarque f.

**boarding house** n pensión f, casa de huéspedes f.

**boarding school** n internado m.

**boast** vi jactarse; * n jactancia f; ostentación f.

**boastful** adj jactancioso/sa.

**boat** n barco m; bote m; barca f.

**boating** n canotaje m; paseo en barquilla m; regata f.

**bobsleigh** n bob m.

**bode** vt presagiar, pronosticar.

**bodice** n corsé m.

**bodily** adj, adv corpóreo/rea; corporalmente.

**body** *n* cuerpo *m*; individuo *m*; gremio *m*; **any ~** cualquier; **every ~** cada uno.

**body-building** *n* culturismo *m*.

**bodyguard** *n* guardaespaldas *m/f invar*.

**bodywork** *n* (*auto*) carrocería *f*.

**bog** *n* pantano *m*.

**boggy** *adj* pantanoso/sa, palustre.

**bogus** *adj* postizo.

**boil** *vi* hervir; bullir; hervirle a uno la sangre; * *vt* cocer; * *n* furúnculo *m*.

**boiled egg** *n* huevo duro *m*, huevo pasado por agua *m*.

**boiled potatoes** *npl* patatas hervidas *fpl*.

**boiler** *n* marmita *f*; caldero *m*.

**boiling point** *n* punto de ebullición *m*.

**boisterous** *adj* borrascoso/sa, tempestuoso/sa; violento/ta; **~ly** *adv* tumultuosamente, furiosamente.

**bold** *adj* ardiente, valiente; audaz; temerario/ria; impudente; **~ly** *adv* descaradamente.

**boldness** *n* intrepidez *f*; valentía *f*; osadía *f*.

**bolster** *n* travesero *m*; cabezal *m*; * *vt* reforzar.

**bolt** *n* cerrojo *m*; * *vt* cerrar con cerrojo.

**bomb** *n* bomba *f*; **~ disposal** desactivación de explosivos *f*.

**bombard** *vt* bombardear.

**bombardier** *n* bombardero *m*.

**bombardment** *n* bombardeo *m*.

**bombshell** *n* (*fig*) bomba *f*.

**bond** *n* ligadura *f*; vínculo *m*; vale *m*; obligación *f*.

**bondage** *n* esclavitud, servidumbre *f*.

**bond holder** *n* titular de bonos *m/f*.

**bone** *n* hueso *m*; * *vt* desosar.

**boneless** *adj* sin huesos; desosado/da.

**bonfire** *n* hoguera *f*.

**bonnet** *n* gorra *f*; bonete *m*; (*auto*) capo *m*; capucha *f*.

**bonny** *adj* bonito/ta.

**bonsai** *n* bonsái *m*.

**bonus** *n* cuota, prima *f*.

**bony** *adj* osudo/da.

**boo** *vt* abuchear.

**booby trap** *n* trampa explosiva *f*.

**book** *n* libro *m*; **to bring to ~** *vt* pedir cuentas a alguien.

**bookbinder** *n* encuadernador/a *m/f*.

**bookcase** *n* estantería *f*.

**bookkeeper** *n* tenedor/a de libros *m/f*.

**bookkeeping** *n* teneduría de libros *f*.

**bookmaker** *n* corredor de apuestas *m*.

**bookmarker** *n* registro de un libro *m*.

**bookseller** *n* librero/ra *m/f*.

**bookstore** *n* librería *f*.

**bookworm** *n* polilla *f*; ratón de biblioteca *m*.

**boom** *n* trueno *m*; boom *m*; * *vi* retumbar.

**boon** *n* presente, regalo *m*; favor *m*.

**boor** *n* patán, villano/na *m/f*.

**boorish** *adj* rústico/ca, agreste.

**boost** *n* estímulo *m*; * *vt* estimular.

**booster** *n* reinyección *f*.

**boot** *n* (*aut*) maletero *m*; bota *f*; zapata *f*; **to ~** *adv* además.

**booth** *n* barraca, cabaña *f*.

**booty** *n* botín *m*; presa *f*, saqueo *m*.

**booze** *vi* emborracharse; * *n* bebida *f*.

**border** *n* orilla *f*; borde *m*; margen *f*, frontera *f*; * *vt* lindar con.

**borderline** *n* frontera *f*.

**bore** *vt* taladrar; barrenar; fastidiar; * *n* taladro *m*; calibre *m*; pelmazo/za m/f.

**boredom** *n* aburrimiento *m*.

**borehole** *n* barreno *m*.

**boring** *adj* aburrido/da.

**born** *adj* nacido/da; destinado/da.

**borrow** *vt* pedir prestado/da.

**borrower** *n* prestamista *m*.

**bosom** *n* seno, pecho *m*.

**bosom friend** *n* amigo/ga íntimo/ma *m/f*.

**boss** *n* jefe *m*; patrón/ona *m/f*.

**botanic(al)** *adj* botánico/ca.

**botanist** *n* botánico *m*.

**botany** *n* botánica *f*.

**botch** *vt* chapuzar.

**botch-up** *n* mamarracho *m*.

**both** *adj* ambos, entrambos; ambas, entrambas; * *conj* tanto como.

**bother** *vt* preocupar; fastidiar; * *n* molestia *f*.

**bottle** *n* botella *f*; * *vt* embotellar.

**bottleneck** *n* embotellamiento *m*.

**bottle-opener** *n* abrebotellas *m invar*.

**bottom** *n* fondo *m*; fundamento *m*; * *adj* más bajo/ja; último/ma.

**bottomless** *adj* insondable; excesivo/va; impenetrable.

**bough** *n* brazo del árbol *m*; ramo *m*.

**boulder** *n* canto rodado *m*.

**bounce** *vi* rebotar; ser rechazado/da; * *n* rebote *m*.

**bound** *n* límite *m*; salto *m*; repercusión *f*; * *vi* resaltar; * *adj* destinado/da.

**boundary** *n* límite *m*; frontera *f*.

**boundless** *adj* ilimitado/da, infinito/ta.

**bounteous, bountiful** *adj* liberal, generoso/sa, bienhechor.

**bounty** *n* liberalidad, bondad *f*.

**bouquet** *n* ramillete de flores *m*.

**bourgeois** *adj* burgués/esa.

**bout** *n* ataque *m*; encuentro *m*.

**bovine** *adj* bovino/na.

**bow**[1] *vt* encorvar, doblar; * *vi* encorvarse; hacer una reverencia; * *n* reverencia, inclinación *f*.

**bow**[2] *n* arco *m*; arco de violín; corbata *f*; nudo *m*.

**bowels** *npl* intestinos *mpl*; entrañas *fpl*.

**bowl** *n* taza, cajita *f*, * *vi* jugar a las bochas.

**bowler hat** *n* hongo *m*.

**bowling** *n* bolos *mpl*.

**bowling alley** *n* bolera *f*.

**bowling-green** *n* campo *m* para jugar a las bochas.

**bowstring** *n* cuerda del arco *f*.

**bow tie** *n* pajarita *f*.

**box** *n* caja, cajita *f*; palco de teatro *m*; ~ **on the ear** bofetada *f*; * *vt* encajonar; * *vi* boxear.

**boxer** *n* boxeador *m*.

**boxing** *n* boxeo *m*.

**boxing gloves** *npl* guantes de boxeo *mpl*.

**boxing ring** *n* cuadrilátero *m*.

**box office** *n* taquilla *f*.

**box-seat** *n* asiento de palco *m*.

**boy** *n* muchacho *m*; niño *m*; zagal *m*.

**boycott** *vt* boicotear; * *n* boicot *m*.

**boyfriend** *n* novio *m*.

**boyish** *adj* pueril; frívolo.

**bra** *n* sujetador *m*.

**brace** *n* abrazadera *f*; corrector *m*.

**bracelet** *n* brazalete *m*.

**bracing** *adj* vigorizante.

**bracken** *n* (*bot*) helecho *m*.

**bracket** *n* puntal *m*; paréntesis *m*; corchete *m*; **to ~ with** *vt* unir, ligar.

**bracing** *adj* vigorizante.

**brag** *n* jactancia *f*, * *vi* jactarse, fanfarronear.

**braid** *n* trenza *f*; * *vt* trenzar.

**brain** *n* cerebro *m*; seso, juicio *m*; * *vt* descerebrar, matar a uno.

**brainchild** *n* parto del ingenio *m*.

**brainwash** *vt* lavar el cerebro.

**brainwave** *n* idea luminosa *f*.

**brainy** *adj* inteligente.

**brainless** *adj* tonto/ta, insensato/ta.

**brake** *n* freno *m*; * *vt*, *vi* frenar.

**brake fluid** *n* liquido de frenos *m*.

**brake light** *n* luz de frenado *f*.

**brake shoe** *n* (*auto*) zapata de freno *f*.

**bramble** *n* zarza, espina *f*.

**bramble patch** *n* zarzal *m*.

**bran** *n* salvado *m*.

**branch** *n* ramo *m*; rama *f*; * *vt* (*vi*) ramificar(se).

**branch line** *n* (*rail*) empalme, ramal *m*.

**brand** *n* marca *f*; hierro *m*; * *vt* marcar (con un hierro incandescente).

**brandish** *vt* blandir, ondear.

**brand-new** *adj* flamante.

**brandy** *n* coñac *m*.

**brash** *adj* tosco/ca; descarado/da.

**brass** *n* bronce *m*.

**brassiere** *n* sujetador *m*.

**brat** *n* crío *m*.

**bravado** *n* baladronada *f*.

**brave** *adj* bravo/va, valiente, atrevido/da; * *vt* desafiar; * *n* bravo *m*; ~**ly** *adv* bravamente.

**bravery** *n* valor *m*; magnificencia *f*.

**brawl** *n* pelea, camorra *f*; * *vi* pelearse.

**brawn** *n* fuerza muscular *f*; carne de verraco *f*.

**bray** *vi* rebuznar; * *n* rebuzno (del asno) *m*.

**braze** *vt* soldar con latón; broncear.

**brazen** *adj* de latón; desvergonzado/da; impudente; * *vi* hacerse descarado/da.

**brazier** *n* brasero *m*.

**breach** *n* rotura *f*; brecha *f*; violación *f*.

**bread** *n* pan *m*; (*fig*) sustento *m*; **brown ~** pan moreno *m*.

**breadbox** *n* panera *f*.

**breadcrumbs** *npl* migajas *fpl*.

**breadth** *n* anchura *f*.

**breadwinner** *n* sostén de la familia *m*.

**break** *vt* romper; quebrantar; violar; arruinar; interrumpir; * *vi* romperse; **to ~ into** forzar; **to ~ out** abrirse salida; * *n* rotura, abertura *f*; interrupción *f*; ~ **of day** despuntar del día *m*, aurora *f*.

**breakage** *n* rotura *f*.

**breakdown** *n* avería *f*; descalabro *m*.

**breakfast** *n* desayuno *m*; * *vi* desayunar.

**breaking** *n* rompimiento *m*; principio de las vacaciones en las escuelas *m*; fractura *f*.

**breakthrough** *n* avance *m*.

**breakwater** *n* rompeolas *m invar*.

**breast** *n* pecho, seno *m*; pechuga *f* corazón *m*.

**breastbone** *n* esternón *m*.

**breastplate** *n* peto *m*; pectoral *m*; coraza *f*.

**breaststroke** *n* braza *f*.

**breath** *n* aliento *m*, respiración *f*; soplo de aire *m*.

**breathe** *vt*, *vi* respirar; exhalar.

**breathing** *n* respiración *f*; aliento *m*.

**breathing space** *n* descanso, reposo *m*.

**breathless** *adj* falto/ta de aliento; desalentado/da.

**breathtaking** *adj* pasmoso/sa.

**breed** *n* casta, raza *f*; * *vt* procrear, engendrar; producir; educar; * *vi* multiplicarse.

**breeder** *n* criador/a *m/f*.

**breeding** n crianza f; buena educación f.
**breeze** n brisa f.
**breezy** adj refrescado/da con brisas.
**brethren** n pl de **brother** hermanos mpl (en estilo grave).
**breviary** n breviario m.
**brevity** n brevedad, concisión f.
**brew** vt hacer; tramar, mezclar; * vi hacerse; tramarse; * n brebaje m.
**brewer** n cervecero m.
**brewery** n cervecería f.
**briar**, **brier** n zarza f, espino m.
**bribe** n cohecho, soborno m; * vt cohechar, corromper, sobornar.
**bribery** n cohecho, soborno m.
**bric-a-brac** n baratijas fpl.
**brick** n ladrillo m; * vt enladrillar.
**bricklayer** n albañil m.
**bricklaying** n albañilería f.
**bridal** adj nupcial.
**bride** n novia f.
**bridegroom** n novio m.
**bridesmaid** n madrina de boda f.
**bridge** n puente m/f; caballete de la nariz m; puente de violín m; **to build a ~ (over)** vt construir un puente (sobre).
**bridle** n brida f freno m; * vt embridar; reprimir, refrenar.
**brief** adj breve, conciso/sa, sucinto/ta; * n compendio m; breve m.
**briefcase** n cartera f.
**briefly** adv brevemente, en pocas palabras.
**brier** n = **briar**.
**brigade** n (mil) brigada f.
**brigadier** n (mil) general de brigada m.
**brigand** n bandido m.
**bright** adj claro/ra, luciente, brillante; ~ly adv espléndidamente.
**brighten** vt pulir, dar lustre; ilustrar; * vi aclararse.
**brightness** n esplendor m, brillantez f; agudeza f, claridad f.
**brilliance** n brillo m.
**brilliant** adj brillante; ~ly adv espléndidamente.
**brim** n borde extremo m; orilla f.
**brimful(l)** adj lleno/na hasta el borde.
**bring** vt llevar, traer; conducir; inducir, persuadir; **to ~ about** efectuar; **to ~ forth** producir; parir; **to ~ up** educar.
**brink** n orilla f; margen m/f, borde m.
**brisk** adj vivo/va, alegre, jovial; fresco/ca.
**brisket** n pecho (de un animal) m.
**briskly** adj vigorosamente; alegremente; vivamente.

**bristle** n cerda, seta f; * vi erizarse.
**bristly** adj cerdoso/sa, lleno/na de cerdas.
**brittle** adj quebradizo, frágil.
**broach** vt comenzar a hablar de.
**broad** adj ancho.
**broad bean** n (bot) haba f; ~s haba gruesa fpl.
**broadcast** n emisión f; * vt, vi emitir; transmitir.
**broadcasting** n radiodifusión f.
**broaden** vt (vi) ensanchar(se).
**broadly** adv anchamente.
**broad-minded** adj tolerante.
**broadness** n ancho m; anchura f.
**broadside** n costado de navío m; andanada f.
**broadways** adv a lo ancho, por lo ancho.
**brocade** n brocado m.
**broccoli** n brécol m.
**brochure** n folleto m.
**brogue** n abarca f; acento irlandés m.
**broil** vt asar a la parrilla.
**broken** adj roto/ta, interrumpido/da; ~ **English** inglés mal articulado m.
**broker** n corredor/a m/f.
**brokerage** n corretaje m.
**bronchial** adj bronquial.
**bronchitis** n bronquitis f.
**bronze** n bronce m; * vt broncear.
**brooch** n broche m.
**brood** vi empollar; meditar; * n raza f; nidada f.
**brood-hen** n empolladora f.
**brook** n arroyo m.
**broom** n retama f, escoba f.
**broomstick** n palo de escoba m.
**broth** n caldo m.
**brothel** n burdel m.
**brother** n hermano m.
**brotherhood** n hermandad f; fraternidad f.
**brother-in-law** n cuñado m.
**brotherly** adj, adv fraternal; fraternalmente.
**brow** n caja f; frente f; cima f.
**browbeat** vt intimidar.
**brown** adj moreno/na; castaño/ña; ~ **paper** n papel de estraza m; ~ **bread** n pan moreno m; ~ **sugar** n azúcar terciado m; * n color moreno m; * vt volver moreno/na.
**browse** vt ramonear; * vi pacer la hierba.
**browser** n navegador m.
**bruise** vt magullar; * n magulladura, contusión f; roncha f.
**brunch** n desayuno-almuerzo m.
**brunette** n morena f.
**brunt** n choque m.
**brush** n cepillo m; escobilla f; combate m; * vt cepillar.

**brushwood** n breñal, zarzal m.
**brusque** adj brusco/ca.
**Brussels sprout** n col de Bruselas f.
**brutal** adj brutal; **~ly** adv brutalmente.
**brutality** n brutalidad f.
**brutalize** vt (vi) embrutecer(se).
**brute** n bruto m; * adj feroz, bestial; irracional.
**brutish** adj brutal, bestial; feroz; **~ly** adv brutalmente.
**bubble** n burbuja f; * vi burbujear, bullir.
**bubblegum** n chicle m.
**bucket** n cubo, pozal m.
**buckle** n hebilla f; * vt hebillar; abrochar; * vi encorvarse.
**buckshot** n perdigones mpl.
**bucolic** adj bucólico/ca.
**bud** n pimpollo, botón, capullo m; yema f; * vi brotar.
**Buddhism** n Budismo m.
**budding** adj en ciernes.
**buddy** n compañero m.
**budge** vi moverse, menearse.
**budgerigar** n periquito m.
**budget** n presupuesto m.
**buff** n entusiasta m.
**buffalo** n búfalo m.
**buffers** npl (rail) parochoques m invar, topes mpl.
**buffet** n buffet m; * vt abofetear.
**buffoon** n bufón, chocarrero m.
**bug** n chinche m.
**bugbear** n espantajo, coco m.
**bugle(horn)** n trompa de caza f.
**build** vt edificar; construir.
**builder** n constructor/a m/f; maestro/tra de obras m/f.
**building** n edificio m; construcción f.
**bulb** n bulbo m; cebolla f.
**bulbous** adj bulboso/sa.
**bulge** vi combarse; * n bombeo m.
**bulk** n masa f; volumen m; grosura f; mayor parte f; capacidad de un buque f; **in ~** a granel.
**bulky** adj grueso/sa, grande.
**bull** n toro m.
**bulldog** n dogo m.
**bulldozer** n aplanadora f.
**bullet** n bala f.
**bulletin board** n tablón de anuncios m.
**bulletproof** adj a prueba de balas.
**bullfight** n corrida de toros f.
**bullfighter** n torero m.
**bullfighting** n toreo m.
**bullion** n oro/plata en barras m/f.

**bullock** n novillo capado m.
**bullring** n plaza de toros f.
**bull's-eye** n centro del blanco m.
**bully** n valentón m; * vt tiranizar.
**bulwark** n baluarte m.
**bum** n vagabundo/da m/f.
**bumblebee** n abejorro, zángano m.
**bump** n hinchazón f; jiba f; bollo m; barriga f; * vt chocar contra.
**bumper** n parachoques m invar.
**bumpkin** n patán m; villano/na m/f.
**bumpy** adj bacheado/da.
**bun** n bollo m; mono m.
**bunch** n ramo m; grupo m.
**bundle** n fardo m, haz m (de leña etc); paquete m; rollo m; * vt atar, hacer un lío.
**bung** n tapón m; * vt atarugar.
**bungalow** n bungalow m.
**bungee-jumping** n puenting m.
**bungle** vt chapucear; * vi hacer algo chabacanamente.
**bunion** n juanete m.
**bunk** n litera f.
**bunker** n refugio m; búnker m.
**buoy** n (mar) boya f.
**buoyancy** n capacidad para flotar f.
**buoyant** adj boyante.
**burden** n carga f; * vt cargar.
**bureau** n armario m; escritorio m.
**bureaucracy** n burocracia f.
**bureaucrat** n burócrata m/f.
**burglar** n ladrón/ona m/f.
**burglar alarm** n alarma antirrobo f.
**burglary** n robo en una casa m.
**burial** n enterramiento m; exequias fpl; sepultura f.
**burial place** n cementerio m.
**burlesque** n, adj lengua burlesca f; burlesco/ca m/f.
**burly** adj fornido/da.
**burn** vt quemar, abrasar, incendiar; * vi arder; * n quema dura f.
**burner** n quemador m; mechero m.
**burning** adj ardiente.
**burrow** n madriguera f; * vi esconderse en la madriguera.
**bursar** n tesorero/ra m/f.
**burse** n bolsa, lonja f.
**burst** vi reventar; abrirse; **to ~ into tears** prorrumpir en lágrimas; **to ~ out laughing** estallarse de risa; * vt **to ~ into** irrumpir en; * n reventón m; rebosadura f.
**bury** vt enterrar, sepultar; esconder.
**bus** n autobús m.
**bush** n arbusto, espinal m; cola de zorro f.

**bushy** *adj* espeso/sa, lleno/na de arbustos.
**busily** *adv* diligentemente, apresuradamente.
**business** *n* asunto *m*; negocios *mpl*; empleo *m*; ocupación *f*.
**businesslike** *adj* serio/ria.
**businessman** *n* hombre de negocios *m*.
**business trip** *n* viaje de negocios *m*.
**businesswoman** *n* mujer de negocios *f*.
**bus lane** *n* carril bus *m*.
**bust** *n* busto *m*.
**bus stop** *n* parada de autobuses *f*.
**bustle** *vi* hacer ruido; menearse; andar al retortero; * *n* baraúnda *f*; ruido *m*.
**bustling** *adj* animado/da.
**busy** *adj* ocupado/da; entrometido/da.
**busybody** *n* entrometido *m*.
**but** *conj* pero; mas; excepto, menos; solamente.
**butcher** *n* carnicero/ra *m/f*; * *vt* matar atrozmente.
**butcher's** (**shop**) *n* carnicería *f*.
**butchery** *n* matadero *m*.
**butler** *n* mayordomo *m*.
**butt** *n* colilla *f*; cabo, extremo *m*; * *vt* topar.
**butter** *n* mantequilla *f*; * *vt* untar con mantequilla.

**buttercup** *n* (*bot*) ranúnculo *m*.
**butterfly** *n* mariposa *f*.
**buttermilk** *n* suero de manteca *m*.
**buttocks** *npl* posaderas *fpl*.
**button** *n* botón *m*; * *vt* abotonar.
**buttonhole** *n* ojal *m*.
**buttress** *n* estribo *m*; apoyo *m*; * *vt* estribar.
**buxom** *adj* frescachona, rolliza.
**buy** *vt* comprar.
**buyer** *n* comprador/a *m/f*.
**buzz, buzzing** *n* susurro, zumbido *m*; * *vi* zumbar.
**buzzard** *n* ratonero *m* común.
**buzzer** *n* timbre *m*.
**by** *prep* por; a, en; de; cerca, al lado de; ~ **and** ~ de aquí a poco, ahora; ~ **the** ~ de paso; ~ **much** con mucho; ~ **all means** por supuesto.
**bygone** *adj* pasado/da.
**by-law** *n* ordenanza municipal *f*.
**bypass** *n* carretera de circunvalación *f*.
**by-product** *n* derivado *m*.
**by-road** *n* camino secundario *m*.
**bystander** *n* mirador *m*.
**byte** *n* (*comput*) byte *m*.
**byword** *n* proverbio, refrán *m*.

# C

cab *n* taxi *m*.

cabbage *n* berza, col *f*.

cabin *n* cabaña, cámara de navío *f*.

cabinet *n* consejo de ministros *m*; gabinete *m*; escritorio *m*.

cabinet-maker *n* ebanista *m*.

cable *n* cable *m*.

cable car *n* teleférico *m*.

cable television *n* televisión por cable *f*.

caboose *n* (*mar*) cocina *f*.

cache *n* alijo *m*.

cackle *vi* cacarear, graznar; * *n* cacareo *m*; charla *f*.

cactus *n* cacto *m*, cactus *m invar*.

cadence *n* (*mus*) cadencia *f*.

cadet *n* cadete *m*.

cadge *vt* mangar.

caesarean section/operation *n* (*med*) (operación de) cesárea *f*.

café *n* café *m*.

cafeteria *n* café *m*.

caffeine *n* cafeína *f*.

cage *n* jaula *f*; prisión *f*; * *vt* enjaular.

cagey *adj* cauteloso/sa.

cajole *vt* lisonjear, adular; sonsacar.

cake *n* bollo *m*; tortita *f*.

calamitous *adj* calamitoso/sa.

calamity *n* calamidad, miseria *f*.

calculable *adj* calculable.

calculate *vt* calcular, contar.

calculation *n* cálculo *m*.

calculator *n* calculadora *f*.

calculus *n* cálculo *m*.

calendar *n* calendario *m*.

calf *n* ternero *m*; ternera *f*; carne de ternero *f*.

calibre *n* calibre *m*.

call *vt* llamar, nombrar; llamar por teléfono; convocar, citar; apelar; to ~ for preguntar por, ir a buscar; to ~ on visitar; to ~ attention llamar la atención; to ~ names insultar; * *n* llamada *f*; instancia *f*; invitación *f*; urgencia *f*; vocación *f*; profesión *f*.

caller *n* visitador/a *m/f*.

calligraphy *n* caligrafía *f*.

calling *n* profesión, vocación *f*.

callisthenics *n* calistenia *f*.

callous *adj* calloso/sa, endurecido/da; insensible.

calm *n* calma, tranquilidad *f*; * *adj* quieto/ta, tranquilo/la; * *vt* calmar; aplacar, aquietar; ~ly *adv* tranquilamente.

calmness *n* tranquilidad, calma *f*.

calorie *n* caloría *f*.

calumny *n* calumnia *f*.

Calvary *n* calvario *m*.

calve *vi* parir.

Calvinist *n* calvinista *m/f*.

camcorder *n* videocámara *f*.

camel *n* camello *m*.

cameo *n* camafeo *m*.

camera *n* máquina fotográfica *f*; cámara *f*.

cameraman *n* cámara *m*.

camomile *n* manzanilla *f*.

camouflage *n* camuflaje *m*.

camp *n* campo *m*; * *vi* acampar; refugee ~ campo de refugiados.

campaign *n* campana *f*; run-up-to-the-election ~ precampaña *f*; * *vi* hacer campana.

campaigner *n* defensor/a *m/f*.

camper *n* campista *m/f*.

camping *n* camping *m*.

camphor *n* alcanfor *m*.

campsite *n* camping *m*.

campus *n* ciudad universitaria *f*, campus *m invar*.

can *vi* poder; * *n* lata *f*.

canal *n* estanque *m*; canal *m*.

cancel *vt* cancelar; anular, invalidar.

cancellation *n* cancelación *f*.

cancer *n* cáncer *m*.

Cancer *n* Cáncer *m* (signo del zodiaco).

cancerous *adj* canceroso/sa.

candid *adj* cándido/da, sencillo/lla, sincero/ra; ~ly *adv* cándidamente, francamente.

candidate *n* candidato/ta *m/f*.

candied *adj* azucarado/da.

candle *n* candela *f*; vela *f*.

candlelight *n* luz de candela *f*.

candlestick *n* candelero *m*.

candour *n* candor *m*; sinceridad *f*.

candyfloss *n* algodón azucarado *m*.

cane *n* cana *f*; bastón *m*.

canine *adj* canino/na, perruno/na.

canister *n* bote *m*.

cannabis *n* cannabis *m*.

cannibal *n* caníbal *m/f*; antropófago/ga *m/f*.

cannibalism *n* canibalismo *m*.

cannon *n* cañón *m*.

cannonball *n* bala de artillería *f*.

canny *adj* cuerdo/da, discreto/ta.

canoe *n* canoa *f*.

**canon** n canon m; regla f; ~ **law** derecho canónico m.
**canonization** n canonización f.
**canonize** vt canonizar.
**can opener** n abrelatas m invar.
**canopy** n dosel, pabellón m.
**cantankerous** adj áspero/ra, fastidioso/sa.
**canteen** n cantina f.
**canter** n medio galope m.
**canvas** n cañamazo m.
**canvass** vt escudriñar, examinar; controvertir; * vi solicitar votos; pretender.
**canvasser** n solicitador/a m/f.
**canyon** n cañón m.
**canyoning** n barranquismo m.
**cap** n gorra f.
**capability** n capacidad, aptitud, inteligencia f.
**capable** adj capaz.
**capacitate** vt hacer capaz.
**capacity** n capacidad f; inteligencia, habilidad f.
**cape** n cabo, promontorio m.
**caper** n cabriola f; alcaparra f; * vi hacer cabriolas.
**capillary** adj capilar.
**capital** adj capital; principal; * n capital f (la ciudad principal); capital, fondo m; mayúscula f.
**capitalism** n capitalismo m.
**capitalist** n capitalista m.
**capitalize** vt capitalizar; **to ~ on** aprovechar.
**capital punishment** n pena de muerte f.
**Capitol** n Capitolio m.
**capitulate** vi capitular.
**capitulation** n capitulación f.
**caprice** n capricho m; extravagancia f.
**capricious** adj caprichoso/sa; ~**ly** adv caprichosamente.
**Capricorn** n Capricornio m (signo del zodiaco).
**capsize** vt (mar) volcar, zozobrar.
**capsizing** n (mar) zozobra f.
**capsule** n cápsula f.
**captain** n capitán/ana m/f.
**captaincy**, **captainship** n capitanía f.
**captivate** vt cautivar.
**captivation** n atractivo m.
**captive** n cautivo/va, esclavo/va m/f.
**captivity** n cautividad, esclavitud f, cautiverio m.
**capture** n captura f; presa f; * vt apresar, capturar.
**car** n coche, carro m; vagón m.
**carafe** n garrafa f.
**caramel** n caramelo m.

**carat** n quilate m.
**caravan** n caravana f.
**caraway** n (bot) alcaravea f.
**carbohydrates** npl hidratos de carbono mpl.
**car bomb** n coche bomba m.
**carbon** n carbono m, carbón m.
**carbon copy** n copia al carbón f.
**carbonize** vt carbonizar.
**carbon paper** n papel carbón m.
**carbuncle** n carbúnculo, rubí m; carbunco, tumor maligno m.
**carburettor** n carburador m.
**carcass** n cadáver m.
**carcinogenic** adj cancerígeno/na.
**card** n naipe m; carta f; **pack of ~s** baraja f.
**cardboard** n cartón m.
**card game** n juego de naipes m.
**cardiac** adj cardíaco/ca, cardiaco/ca.
**cardinal** adj cardinal, principal; * n cardenal m.
**card table** n mesa para jugar f.
**care** n cuidado m; solicitud f; * vi cuidar, tener cuidado/pena, inquietarse; **what do I ~?** ¿a mí que me importa?; **to ~ for** vt cuidar a; querer.
**career** n carrera f; curso m; * vi correr a carrera tendida.
**carefree** n despreocupado/da.
**careful** adj cuidadoso/sa, diligente, prudente; ~**ly** adv cuidadosamente.
**careless** adj descuidado/da, negligente; indolente; ~**ly** adv descuidadamente.
**carelessness** n negligencia, indiferencia f.
**caress** n caricia f; * vt acariciar, halagar.
**caretaker** n portero m, conserje m/f.
**car-ferry** n transbordador para coches m.
**cargo** n cargamento m.
**car hire** n alquiler de coches m.
**caricature** n caricatura f; * vt hacer caricaturas, ridiculizar.
**caries** n caries f.
**caring** adj humanitario/ria.
**Carmelite** n carmelita m.
**carnage** n carnicería, matanza f.
**carnal** adj carnal; sensual; ~**ly** adv carnalmente.
**carnation** n clavel m.
**carnival** n carnaval m.
**carnivorous** adj carnívoro/ra.
**carol** n villancico m, canción de alegría/piedad f.
**car park** n aparcamiento, estacionamiento m.
**carpenter** n carpintero m; ~**'s bench** banco de carpintero m.

**carpentry** *n* carpintería *f*.
**carpet** *n* alfombra *f*; * *vt* cubrir con alfombras.
**carpeting** *n* alfombrado *m*.
**car radio** *n* autorradio *m*.
**carriage** *n* porte *m*; coche *m*; vehículo *m*.
**carriage-free** *adj* franco de porte.
**carrier** *n* portador, carretero *m*.
**carrier pigeon** *n* paloma correo/mensajera *f*.
**carrion** *n* carroña *f*.
**carrot** *n* zanahoria *f*.
**carry** *vt* llevar, conducir; **to ~ out** ejecutar; * *vi* oírse; **to ~ the day** quedar victorioso/sa; **to ~ on** seguir.
**cart** *n* carro *m*; carreta *f*; * *vt* llevar (en carro).
**cartel** *n* cartel *m*.
**carthorse** *n* caballo de tiro *m*.
**Carthusian** *n* cartujo (monje) *m*.
**cartilage** *n* cartílago *m*.
**cartload** *n* carretada *f*.
**carton** *n* caja *f*.
**cartoon** *n* dibujo animado *m*; tira cómica *f*.
**cartridge** *n* cartucho *m*.
**carve** *vt* cincelar; trinchar; grabar.
**carving** *n* escultura *f*.
**carving knife** *n* cuchillo de trinchar *m*.
**car wash** *n* lavado de coches *m*.
**case** *n* caja *f*; maleta *f*; caso *m*; estuche *m*; vaina *f*; **in ~** por si acaso.
**cash** *n* dinero contante *m*; * *vt* cobrar.
**cash card** *n* tarjeta de cajero automático *f*.
**cash dispenser**, **cash machine** *n* cajero automático *m*.
**cashier** *n* cajero *m*.
**cashmere** *n* cachemira *f*.
**casing** *n* forro *m*; cubierta *f*.
**casino** *n* casino *m*.
**cask** *n* barril, tonel *m*.
**casket** *n* ataúd *m*.
**casserole** *n* cazuela *f*.
**cassette** *n* cassette *m*.
**cassette player**, **recorder** *n* cassette *m*.
**cassock** *n* sotana *f*.
**cast** *vt* tirar, lanzar; modelar; * *n* reparto *m*; forma *f*.
**castanets** *npl* castañuelas *fpl*.
**castaway** *n* réprobo *m*.
**caste** *n* casta *f*.
**castigate** *vt* castigar.
**casting vote** *n* voto de calidad *m*.
**cast iron** *n* hierro colado *m*.
**castle** *n* castillo *m*; fortaleza *f*.
**castor oil** *n* aceite de ricino *m*.
**castrate** *vt* castrar.

**castration** *n* capadura *f*.
**cast steel** *n* acero fundido *m*.
**casual** *adj* casual, fortuito/ta; **~ly** *adv* casualmente, fortuitamente.
**casualty** *n* víctima *f*; baja *f*.
**cat** *n* gato *m*; gata *f*.
**catalogue** *n* catálogo *m*.
**catalyst** *n* catalizador *m*.
**catalytic converter** *n* catalizador *m*.
**catamaran** *n* catamarán *m*.
**catapult** *n* catapulta, honda *f*.
**cataract** *n* cascada *f*; catarata *f*.
**catarrh** *n* catarro *m*; reuma *f*.
**catastrophe** *n* catástrofe *f*.
**catcall** *n* silbido *m*; reclamo *m*.
**catch** *vt* coger, agarrar, asir; atrapar; pillar; sorprender; **to ~ cold** resfriarse; **to ~ fire** encenderse; * *n* presa *f*; captura *f*; (*mus*) canon *m*; trampa *f*.
**catching** *adj* contagioso/sa.
**catch phrase** *n* lema *m*.
**catchword** *n* reclamo *m*.
**catchy** *adj* pegadizo/za.
**catechism** *n* catecismo *m*.
**catechize** *vt* catequizar, examinar.
**categorical** *adj* categórico/ca; **~ly** *adv* categóricamente.
**categorize** *vt* clasificar.
**category** *n* categoría *f*.
**cater** *vi* abastecer, proveer.
**caterer** *n* proveedor/a, abastecedor/a *m/f*.
**catering** *n* alimentación *f*.
**caterpillar** *n* oruga *f*.
**catgut** *n* cuerda de violón *f*.
**cathedral** *n* catedral *f*.
**catholic** *adj*, *n* católico/ca *m/f*.
**Catholicism** *n* catolicismo *m*.
**cattle** *n* ganado *m*.
**cattle show** *n* feria de ganado *f*.
**caucus** *n* junta electoral *f*.
**cauliflower** *n* coliflor *f*.
**cause** *n* causa *f*; razón *f*; motivo *m*; proceso *m*; * *vt* causar.
**causeway** *n* arrecife *m*.
**caustic** *adj*, *n* cáustico *m*.
**cauterize** *vt* cauterizar.
**caution** *n* prudencia, precaución *f*; aviso *m*; * *vt* avisar; amonestar; advertir.
**cautionary** *adj* de escarmiento.
**cautious** *adj* prudente, circunspecto/ta, cauto/ta.
**cavalier** *adj* arrogante.
**cavalry** *n* caballería *f*.
**cave** *n* caverna *f*; bodega *f*.

**caveat** *n* aviso *m*; advertencia *f*; (*law*) notificación *f*.
**cavern** *n* caverna *f*; bodega *f*.
**cavernous** *adj* cavernoso/sa.
**caviar** *n* caviar *m*.
**cavity** *n* hueco *m*; caries *f invar*.
**CD-ROM** *n* cederrón *m*.
**cease** *vt* parar, suspender; * *vi* desistir.
**cease-fire** *n* alto el fuego *m*.
**ceaseless** *adj* incesante, continuo/nua; ~**ly** *adv* perpetuamente.
**cedar** *n* cedro *m*.
**cede** *vt* ceder, transferir.
**ceiling** *n* techo *m*.
**celebrate** *vt* celebrar.
**celebration** *n* celebración *f*.
**celebrity** *n* celebridad, fama *f*.
**celery** *n* apio *m*.
**celestial** *adj* celeste, divino/na.
**celibacy** *n* celibato *m*, soltería *f*.
**celibate** *adj* soltero; soltera.
**cell** *n* celdilla *f*; célula *f*; cueva *f*.
**cellar** *n* sótano *m*; bodega *f*.
**cello** *n* violoncelo *m*.
**Cellophane**™ *n* celofán *m*.
**cellular** *adj* celular.
**cellulitis** *n* celulitis *f*.
**cellulose** *n* (*chém*) celulosa *f*.
**cement** *n* cemento; (*fig*) vínculo *m*; * *vt* pegar con cemento.
**cemetery** *n* cementerio *m*.
**cenotaph** *n* cenotafio *m*.
**censor** *n* censor/a *m/f*; crítico/ca *m/f*.
**censorious** *adj* severo/ra, crítico/ca.
**censorship** *n* censura *f*.
**censure** *n* censura, reprensión *f*; * *vt* censurar, reprender; criticar.
**census** *n* censo *m*.
**cent** *n* centavo *m*.
**centenarian** *n* centenario *m*; centenaria *f*.
**centenary** *n* centena *f*; * *adj* centenario/ria.
**centennial** *adj* centenario/ria.
**centigrade** *n* centígrado *m*.
**centilitre** *n* centilitro *m*.
**centimetre** *n* centímetro *m*.
**centipede** *n* escolopendra *f*.
**central** *adj* central; ~**ly** *adv* centralmente, en el centro.
**central reserve** *n* mediana *f*.
**centralize** *vt* centralizar.
**centre** *n* centro *m*; * *vt* centrar; concentrar; * *vi* concentrarse.
**centrifugal** *adj* centrífugo/ga.
**century** *n* siglo *m*.

**ceramic** *adj* cerámico/ca.
**cereals** *npl* cereales *fpl*.
**cerebral** *adj* cerebral.
**ceremonial** *adj*, *n* ceremonial *m*; rito externo *m*.
**ceremonious** *adj* ceremonioso/sa; ~**ly** *adv* ceremoniosamente.
**ceremony** *n* ceremonia *f*.
**certain** *adj* cierto/ta, evidente; seguro/ra; ~**ly** *adv* ciertamente, sin duda.
**certainty**, **certitude** *n* certeza *f*; seguridad *f*.
**certificate** *n* certificado, testimonio *m*.
**certification** *n* certificado *m*.
**certified mail** *n* correo certificado *m*.
**certify** *vt* certificar, afirmar.
**cervical** *adj* cervical.
**cessation** *n* cesación *f*.
**cesspool** *n* cloaca *f*; sumidero *m*.
**chafe** *vt* frotar; enojar, irritar.
**chaff** *n* paja menuda *f*.
**chaffinch** *n* pinzón *m*.
**chagrin** *n* disgusto *m*.
**chain** *n* cadena *f*; serie, sucesión *f*; * *vt* encadenar, atar con cadena.
**chain reaction** *n* reacción en cadena *f*.
**chain store** *n* gran almacén *m*.
**chair** *n* silla *f*; * *vt* presidir.
**chairman** *n* presidente *m*.
**chalice** *n* cáliz *m*.
**chalk** *n* creta *f*; tiza *f*.
**challenge** *n* desafío *m*; * *vt* desafiar, impugnar.
**challenger** *n* desafiador/a *m/f*.
**challenging** *adj* desafiante.
**chamber** *n* cámara *f*; aposento *m*.
**chambermaid** *n* moza de cámara *f*.
**chameleon** *n* camaleón *m*.
**chamois leather** *n* gamuza *f*.
**champagne** *n* champaña *m*.
**champion** *n* campeón *m*; * *vt* defender.
**championship** *n* campeonato *m*.
**chance** *n* ventura, suerte *f*; oportunidad *f*; **by** ~ por acaso; * *vt* arriesgar.
**chancellor** *n* canciller *m*.
**chancery** *n* chancillería *f*.
**chandelier** *n* araña de luces *f*; candelero *m*.
**change** *vt* cambiar; * *vi* variar, alterarse; * *n* mudanza, variedad *f*; vicisitud *f*; cambio *m*.
**changeable** *adj* variable, inconstante; mudable.
**changeless** *adj* constante, inmutable.
**changing** *adj* cambiante.
**channel** *n* canal *m*; estrecho *m*; * *vt* encauzar.
**channel-hopping** *n* zapping *m*.

**chant** n canto (llano) m; * vt cantar.

**chaos** n caos m; confusión f.

**chaotic** adj confuso/sa.

**chapel** n capilla f.

**chaplain** n capellán m.

**chapter** n capítulo m.

**char** vt chamuscar.

**character** n carácter m; personaje m.

**characteristic** adj característico/ca; **~ally** adv característicamente.

**characterize** vt caracterizar.

**characterless** adj sin carácter.

**charade** n charada f.

**charcoal** n carbón de leña m.

**chard** n (bot) acelga f.

**charge** vt cargar; acusar, imputar; * n cargo m; acusación f; (mil) ataque m; depósito m; carga f.

**chargeable** adj imputable.

**charge card** n tarjeta de compra f.

**charitable** adj caritativo/va; benigno/na, clemente; **~bly** adv caritativamente.

**charity** n caridad, benevolencia f; limosna f.

**charlatan** n charlatán/tana m/f.

**charm** n encanto m; atractivo m; * vt encantar, embelesar, atraer.

**charming** adj encantado/da.

**chart** n carta de navegar f.

**charter** n carta f; privilegio m; * vt fletar un buque; alquilar.

**charter flight** n vuelo chárter m, charter m.

**chase** vt cazar; perseguir; * n caza f.

**chasm** n vacío m.

**chaste** adj casto/ta; puro/ra; honesto/ta.

**chasten** vt corregir, castigar.

**chastise** vt castigar, reformar, corregir.

**chastisement** n castigo m.

**chastity** n castidad, pureza f.

**chat** vi charlar; * n charla, cháchara f.

**chatter** vi cotorrear; rechinar; charlar; * n chirrido m; charla f.

**chatterbox** n parlero/ra, hablador/a, gárrulo/la m/f.

**chatty** adj locuaz, parlanchín/china.

**chauffeur** n chófer m.

**chauvinist** n machista m.

**cheap** adj barato/ta; **~ly** adv a bajo precio.

**cheapen** vt regatear; abaratar.

**cheaper** adj más barato/ta.

**cheat** vt engañar, defraudar; * n trampa f; fraude, engaño m; tramposo/sa m/f.

**check** vt comprobar; contar; reprimir, refrenar; regañar; registrar; * n restricción f; freno m.

**checkmate** n mate m.

**checkout** n caja f.

**checkpoint** n control m.

**check-up** n reconocimiento médico m.

**cheek** n mejilla f; (col) desvergüenza f; atrevimiento m.

**cheekbone** n hueso del carrillo m.

**cheeky** adj descarado/da.

**cheer** n alegría f; aplauso m; buen humor m; * vt animar, alentar.

**cheerful** adj alegre, vivo/va, jovial; **~ly** adv alegremente.

**cheerfulness, cheeriness** n alegría f; buen humor m.

**cheese** n queso m.

**cheesemonger's (shop)** n quesería f.

**chef** n jefe de cocina m.

**chemical** adj químico/ca.

**chemist** n químico m.

**chemistry** n química f.

**chemotherapy** n quimioterapia f.

**cheque** n cheque m.

**cheque account** n cuenta corriente f.

**chequerboard, draughtboard** n tablero de damas m.

**chequered** adj accidentado/da.

**cherish** vt fomentar, proteger.

**cheroot** n puro m.

**cherry** n cereza f; * adj bermejo/ja.

**cherry tree** n cerezo m.

**cherub** n querubín m.

**chess** n ajedrez m.

**chessboard** n tablero de ajedrez m.

**chessman** n pieza de ajedrez f.

**chest** n pecho m; arca f; **~ of drawers** cómoda f.

**chestnut** n castaña f; color de castaña m.

**chestnut tree** n castaño m.

**chew** vt mascar, masticar.

**chewing gum** n chicle m.

**chic** adj elegante.

**chicanery** n quisquilla f.

**chick** n polluelo m; (col) chica f.

**chicken** n pollo m.

**chickenpox** n varicela f.

**chickpea** n garbanzo m.

**chicory** n achicoria f.

**chide** vt reprobar, regañar.

**chief** adj principal, capital; **~ly** adv principalmente; * n jefe, principal m.

**chief executive** n director/a general m/f.

**chieftain** n jefe, comandante m.

**chiffon** n gasa f.

**chilblain** n sabañón m.

**child** n niño m; niña f; hijo m; hija f; **from a ~** desde niño/ña; **with ~** preñada, embarazada.

**childbirth** n parto m.
**childhood** n infancia, niñez f; pequeñez f.
**childish** adj frívolo/la, pueril; ~**ly** adv puerilmente.
**childishness** n puerilidad f.
**childless** adj sin hijos.
**childlike** adj pueril.
**children** npl de **child** niños mpl.
**chill** adj frío/ría, friolero/ra; * n frío m; * vt enfriar; helar.
**chilly** adj friolero/ra.
**chime** n armonía f; clave m; * vi sonar con armonía; concordar.
**chimney** n chimenea f.
**chimpanzee** n chimpancé m.
**chin** n barbilla f.
**chinaware** n porcelana f.
**chink** n grieta, hendedura f; * vi resonar.
**chip** vt astillar; * vi picarse; * n astilla f; chip m; patata/papa frita f.
**chiropodist, podiatrist** n pedicuro/ra m/f.
**chirp** vi chirriar, gorjear; * n gorjeo, chirrido m.
**chirping** n canto de las aves m.
**chisel** n cincel m; * vt cincelar, grabar.
**chitchat** n charla f.
**chivalrous** adj caballeresco/ca.
**chivalry** n caballería f.
**chives** npl cebollinos f.
**chlorine** n cloro m.
**chloroform** n cloroformo m.
**chock-full** adj de bote en bote, completamente lleno/na.
**chocolate** n chocolate m.
**choice** n elección, preferencia f; selecto m; * adj selecto/ta, exquisito/ta, excelente.
**choir** n coro m.
**choke** vt sofocar; oprimir; tapar.
**cholera** n cólera m.
**choose** vt escoger, elegir.
**chop** vt tajar, cortar; * n chuleta f; ~**s** pl (col) quijadas fpl.
**chopper** n helicóptero m.
**chopping block** n tajo de cocina m.
**chopsticks** npl palillos mpl.
**chore** n faena f.
**choral** adj coral.
**chord** n cuerda f.
**chorist, chorister** n corista m.
**chorus** n coro m.
**Christ** n Cristo m.
**christen** vt bautizar.
**Christendom** n cristianismo m; cristiandad f.
**christening** n bautismo m.

**Christian** adj, n cristiano/na m/f; ~ **name** nombre de pila m.
**Christianity** n cristianismo m; cristiandad f.
**Christmas** n Navidad f.
**Christmas card** n tarjeta de Navidad f.
**Christmas Eve** n Nochebuena f.
**chrome** n cromo m.
**chronic** adj crónico/ca.
**chronicle** n crónica f.
**chronicler** n cronista m.
**chronological** adj cronológico/ca; ~**ly** adv cronológicamente.
**chronology** n cronología f.
**chronometer** n cronómetro m.
**chubby** adj gordo/da.
**chuck** vt lanzar.
**chuckle** vi reírse a carcajadas.
**chug** vi resoplar.
**chum** n compañero/ra, compinche m/f.
**chunk** n trozo m.
**church** n iglesia f.
**churchyard** n cementerio m.
**churlish** adj hosco/ca, grosero/ra; tacaño/ña.
**churn** n mantequera f; * vt batir la leche para hacer manteca.
**cider** n sidra f.
**cigar** n cigarro m.
**cigarette** n cigarrillo m.
**cigarette case** n pitillera f.
**cigarette end** n colilla f.
**cigarette holder** n boquilla f.
**cinder** n carbonilla f.
**cinema** n cine m.
**cinnamon** n canela f.
**cipher** n cifra f.
**circle** n círculo m; corrillo m; asamblea f; * vt circundar; cercar; * vi circular.
**circuit** n circuito m; recinto m.
**circuitous** adj circular, tortuoso/sa.
**circular** adj circular, redondo/da; * n carta circular f.
**circulate** vi circular; moverse alrededor.
**circulation** n circulación f.
**circumcise** vt circuncidar.
**circumcision** n circuncisión f.
**circumference** n circunferencia f; circuito m.
**circumflex** n acento circunflejo m.
**circumlocution** n circunlocución f.
**circumnavigate** vt circunnavegar.
**circumnavigation** n circunnavegación f.
**circumscribe** vt circunscribir.
**circumspect** adj circunspecto/ta, prudente, reservado/da.

**circumspection** n circunspección, pru–
dencia f.
**circumstance** n circunstancia, condición f;
incidente m.
**circumstantial** adj accidental; accesorio/
ria.
**circumstantiate** vt circunstanciar, detallar.
**circumvent** vt burlar.
**circumvention** n evasión f.
**circus** n circo m.
**cistern** n cisterna f.
**citadel** n ciudadela, fortaleza f.
**citation** n citación, cita f.
**cite** vt citar (a juicio); alegar; referirse a.
**citizen** n ciudadano/na m/f.
**citizenship** n ciudadanía f.
**city** n ciudad f.
**civic** adj cívico/ca.
**civil** adj civil, cortés; ~ly adv civilmente.
**civil defence** n protección civil f.
**civil engineer** n ingeniero/ra civil m/f.
**civilian** n paisano m.
**civility** n civilidad, urbanidad, cortesía f.
**civilization** n civilización f.
**civilize** vt civilizar.
**civil law** n derecho civil m.
**civil war** n guerra civil f.
**clad** adj vestido/da, cubierto/ta.
**claim** vt pedir en juicio, reclamar; * n
demanda f; derecho m.
**claimant** n reclamante m; demandador/a m/f.
**clairvoyant** n clarividente m/f; zahorí m.
**clam** n almeja f.
**clamber** vi gatear, trepar.
**clammy** adj viscoso/sa.
**clamour** n clamor, grito m; * vi vociferar,
gritar.
**clamp** n abrazadera f; * vt afianzar; **to ~
down on** reforzar la lucha contra.
**clan** n familia, tribu, raza f.
**clandestine** adj clandestino/na, oculto/ta.
**clang** n rechino, sonido desapacible m; * vi
rechinar.
**clap** vt aplaudir.
**clapping** n palmada f; aplauso, palmoteo m.
**claret** n clarete m.
**clarification** n clarificación f.
**clarify** vt clarificar, aclarar.
**clarinet** n clarinete m.
**clarity** n claridad f.
**clash** vi chocar; * n estruendo m; choque m.
**clasp** n broche m; hebilla f; abrazo m; * vt
abrochar; abrazar.
**class** n clase f; orden f; * vt clasificar,
coordinar.

**classic(al)** adj clásico/ca; * n autor
clásico m.
**classification** n clasificación f.
**classified advertisement** n anuncio por
palabras m.
**classify** vt clasificar.
**classmate** n compañero/ra de clase m/f.
**classroom** n aula f.
**clatter** vi resonar; hacer ruido; * n ruido m.
**clause** n cláusula f; artículo m; estipulación f.
**claw** n garra f; zarpa f; * vt desgarrar, arañar.
**clay** n arcilla f.
**clean** adj limpio/pia; casto/ta; * vt limpiar.
**cleaning** n limpieza f.
**cleanliness** n limpieza f.
**cleanly** adj limpio/pia; * adv limpiamente,
aseadamente.
**cleanness** n limpieza f; pureza f.
**cleanse** vt limpiar, purificar; purgar.
**clear** adj claro/ra; neto/ta; diáfano/na;
evidente; * adv claramente; * vt clarificar,
aclarar; justificar, absolver; * vi aclararse.
**clearance** n despeje m; acreditación f.
**clear-cut** adj bien definido/da.
**clearly** adv claramente, evidentemente.
**cleaver** n cuchillo de carnicero m.
**clef** n clave f.
**cleft** n hendedura, abertura f.
**clemency** n clemencia f.
**clement** adj clemente, benigno/na.
**clenched** adj cerrado/da.
**clergy** n clero m.
**clergyman** n eclesiástico m.
**clerical** adj clerical, eclesiástico/ca.
**clerk** n dependiente m; oficinista m.
**clever** adj listo/ta; hábil, mañoso/sa; ~ly adv
diestramente, hábilmente.
**click** vt chasquear; * vi taconear.
**client** n cliente m/f.
**cliff** n acantilado m.
**climate** n clima m; temperatura f.
**climatic** adj climático/ca.
**climax** n clímax m.
**climb** vt escalar, trepar; * vi subir.
**climber** n alpinista m/f.
**climbing** n alpinismo m.
**clinch** vt cerrar; remachar.
**cling** vi colgar, adherirse, pegarse.
**clinic** n clínica f.
**clink** vt hacer resonar; * vi resonar; * n
retintín m.
**clip** vt cortar; * n clip m; horquilla f.
**clipping** n recorte m.
**clique** n camarilla f.
**cloak** n capa f; pretexto m; * vi encapotar.

**cloakroom** n guardarropa m; aseos mpl.
**clock** n reloj m.
**clockwork** n mecanismo de un reloj m; * adj sumamente exacto y puntual.
**clod** n terrón m.
**clog** n zueco m; * vi atascarse.
**cloister** n claustro, monasterio m.
**clone** n clon m; * vt clonar.
**cloned** adj clónico/ca.
**cloning** n clonación f.
**close** vt cerrar; concluir, terminar; * vi cerrarse; * n fin m; conclusión f; * adj cercano/na; estrecho/cha; ajustado/da; denso/sa; reservado/da; * adv de cerca; ~ **by** muy cerca; junto.
**closed** adj cerrado/da.
**closely** adv estrechamente; de cerca.
**closeness** n proximidad f; estrechez; reclusión f.
**closet** n armario m.
**close-up** n primer plano m.
**closure** n cierre m; conclusión f.
**clot** n grumo m; embolia f.
**cloth** n paño m; mantel m; vestido m; lienzo m.
**clothe** vt vestir, cubrir.
**clothes** npl ropa f; ropaje m; ropa de cama f; **bed** ~ cobertores mpl.
**clothes basket** n cesta grande f.
**clotheshorse** n tendedero m.
**clothesline** n cuerda (de tendedero) f.
**clothes peg** n pinza f.
**clothing** n vestidos mpl.
**cloud** n nube f; nublado m; (fig) adversidad f; * vt anublar; oscurecer; * vi anublarse; oscurecerse.
**cloudiness** n nubosidad f; oscuridad f.
**cloudy** adj nublado/da; oscuro/ra; sombrío/ría, melancólico/ca.
**clout** n tortazo m.
**clove** n clavo m.
**clover** n trébol m.
**clown** n payaso m.
**club** n cachiporra f.
**club car** n (rail) coche restaurante m.
**clue** n pista f, indicios m; idea f.
**clump** n grupo m.
**clumsily** adv torpemente.
**clumsiness** n torpeza f.
**clumsy** adj torpe, pesado/da; sin arte.
**cluster** n racimo m; manada f; pelotón m; * vt agrupar; * vi arracimarse.
**clutch** n embrague m; apretón m; * vt empuñar.
**clutter** vt atestar.

**coach** n autocar, autobús m; vagón m; entrenador/a m/f; * vt entrenar; enseñar.
**coach trip** n excursión en autocar f.
**coagulate** vt coagular, cuajar; * vi coagularse, cuajarse, espesarse.
**coal** n carbón m.
**coalesce** vi juntarse, incorporarse.
**coalfield** n yacimiento de carbón m.
**coalition** n coalición, confederación f.
**coalman** n carbonero m.
**coalmine** n mina de carbón, carbonería f.
**coarse** adj basto/ta; grosero/ra; zafio/fia; ~**ly** adv groseramente.
**coast** n costa f.
**coastal** adj costero/ra; ribereño/ña.
**coastguard** n guardacostas m invar.
**coastline** n litoral m.
**coat** n chaqueta f; abrigo m; capa f; * vt cubrir.
**coat hanger** n percha f.
**coat hook** n percha f.
**coating** n revestimiento m.
**coax** vt lisonjear.
**cob** n mazorca de maíz f.
**cobbler** n zapatero/ra m/f.
**cobbles, cobblestones** npl adoquines mpl.
**cobweb** n telaraña f.
**cocaine** n cocaína f.
**coccyx** n rabadilla f.
**cock** n gallo m; macho m; * vt armar el sombrero; amartillar, montar una escopeta.
**cock-a-doodle-doo** n quiquiriquí m.
**cockcrow** n canto del gallo m.
**cockerel** n gallito m.
**cockfight(ing)** n pelea de gallos f.
**cockle** n berberecho m.
**cockpit** n cabina f.
**cockroach** n cucaracha f.
**cocktail** n cóctel m.
**cocoa** n coco m; cacao m.
**coconut** n coco m.
**cocoon** n capullo (del gusano de seda) m.
**cod** n bacalao m.
**code** n código m; prefijo m.
**cod-liver oil** n aceite de hígado de bacalao m.
**coefficient** n coeficiente m.
**coercion** n coerción f.
**coexistence** n coexistencia f.
**coffee** n café m.
**coffee break** n descanso m.
**coffee house** n café m.
**coffee-pot** n cafetera f.
**coffee table** n mesita f.
**coffer** n cofre m; caja f.
**coffin** n ataúd m.
**cog** n diente (de rueda) m.

**cogency** *n* fuerza, urgencia *f*.

**cogent** *adj* convincente, urgente; **~ly** *adv* de modo convincente.

**cognac** *n* coñac *m*.

**cognate** *adj* cognado/da.

**cognition** *n* conocimiento *m*; convicción *f*.

**cognizance** *n* conocimiento *m*; competencia *f*.

**cognizant** *adj* informado/da; (*law*) competente.

**cogwheel** *n* rueda dentada *f*.

**cohabit** *vi* cohabitar.

**cohabitation** *n* cohabitación *f*.

**cohere** *vi* pegarse; unirse.

**coherence** *n* coherencia, conexión *f*.

**coherent** *adj* coherente; consiguiente.

**cohesion** *n* coherencia *f*.

**cohesive** *adj* cohesivo/va.

**coil** *n* rollo *m*; bobina *f*; * *vt* enrollar.

**coin** *n* moneda *f*; * *vt* acuñar.

**coincide** *vi* coincidir, concurrir, convenir.

**coincidence** *n* coincidencia *f*.

**coincidental** *adj* coincidente.

**coke**[1] *n* coque *m*.

**Coke**[2] *n* Coca-Cola™ *f*.

**colander** *n* colador, pasador *m*.

**cold** *adj* frío/ría; indiferente, insensible; reservado/da; **~ly** *adv* fríamente; indiferentemente; * *n* frío *m*; frialdad *f*; resfriado *m*.

**cold-blooded** *adj* impasible.

**coldness** *n* frialdad *f*; indiferencia, insensibilidad, apatía *f*.

**cold sore** *n* herpes labial *m*.

**coleslaw** *n* ensalada de col *f*.

**colic** *n* cólico *m*.

**collaborate** *vt* cooperar.

**collaboration** *n* cooperación *f*.

**collapse** *vi* hundirse; * *n* hundimiento; (*med*) colapso *m*.

**collapsible** *adj* plegable.

**collar** *n* cuello *m*.

**collarbone** *n* clavícula *f*.

**collate** *vt* comparar, confrontar.

**collateral** *adj* colateral; * *n* garantía subsidiaria *f*.

**collation** *n* colación *f*.

**colleague** *n* colega, compañero/ra *m/f*.

**collect** *vt* recoger; coleccionar.

**collection** *n* colección *f*; compilación *f*.

**collective** *adj* colectivo/va, congregado/da; **~ly** colectivamente.

**collector** *n* coleccionista *m/f*.

**college** *n* colegio *m*.

**collide** *vi* chocar.

**collision** *n* choque *m*, colisión *f*.

**colloquial** *adj* familiar; coloquial; **~ly** *adv* familiarmente.

**colloquialism** *n* lengua usual *f*.

**collusion** *n* colusión *f*.

**colon** *n* dos puntos *mpl*; (*med*) colon *m*.

**colonel** *n* (*mil*) coronel *m*.

**colonial** *adj* colonial.

**colonist** *n* colono *m*.

**colonize** *vt* colonizar.

**colony** *n* colonia *f*.

**colossal** *adj* colosal.

**colossus** *n* coloso *m*.

**colour** *n* color *m*; **~s** *pl* bandera *f*; * *vt* colorar; pintar; * *vi* ponerse colorado/da.

**colour-blind** *adj* daltónico/ca.

**colourful** *adj* lleno de color.

**colouring** *n* colorido *m*.

**colourless** *adj* descolorido/da, sin color.

**colour television** *n* televisión en color *f*.

**colt** *n* potro *m*.

**column** *n* columna *f*.

**columnist** *n* columnista *m*.

**coma** *n* coma *f*.

**comatose** *adj* comatoso/sa.

**comb** *n* peine *m*; * *vt* peinar.

**combat** *n* combate *m*; batalla *f*; **single ~** duelo *m*; * *vt* combatir.

**combatant** *n* combatiente *m*.

**combative** *adj* combativo/va.

**combination** *n* combinación, coordinación *f*.

**combine** *vt* combinar; * *vi* unirse.

**combustion** *n* combustión *f*.

**come** *vi* venir; **to ~ across/upon** *vt* topar con; dar con; **to ~ by** *vt* conseguir; **to ~ down** *vi* bajar; ser derribado/da; **to ~ from** *vt* ser de; **to ~ in for** *vt* merecer; **to ~ into** *vt* heredar; **to ~ round/to** *vi* volver en sí; **to ~ up with** *vt* sugerir.

**comedian** *n* comediante, cómico *m*.

**comedienne** *n* cómica *f*.

**comedy** *n* comedia *f*.

**comet** *n* cometa *m*.

**comfort** *n* confort *m*; ayuda *f*; consuelo *m*; comodidad *f*; * *vt* confortar; alentar, consolar.

**comfortable** *adj* cómodo/da.

**comfortably** *adv* agradablemente; cómodamente.

**comforter** *n* chupete *m*.

**comic(al)** *adj* cómico/ca, burlesco/ca; **~ly** *adv* cómicamente.

**coming** *n* venida, llegada *f*; * *adj* venidero/ra.

**comma** *n* (*gr*) coma *f*.

**command** *vt* comandar, ordenar; * *n* orden *f.*

**commander** *n* comandante *m.*

**commandment** *n* mandamiento, precepto *m.*

**commando** *n* comando *m.*

**commemorate** *vt* conmemorar; celebrar.

**commemoration** *n* conmemoración *f.*

**commence** *vt, vi* comenzar.

**commencement** *n* principio *m.*

**commend** *vt* encomendar; alabar; enviar.

**commendable** *adj* recomendable.

**commendably** *adv* loablemente.

**commendation** *n* recomendación *f.*

**commensurate** *adj* proporcionado/da.

**comment** *n* comentario *m;* * *vt* comentar; glosar.

**commentary** *n* comentario *m;* interpretación *f.*

**commentator** *n* comentarista *m/f.*

**commerce** *n* comercio, tráfico, trato, negocio *m.*

**commercial** *adj* comercial.

**commiserate** *vt* compadecer, tener compasión.

**commiseration** *n* conmiseración, piedad *f.*

**commissariat** *n* comisaría *f.*

**commission** *n* comisión *f;* * *vt* comisionar; encargar.

**commissioner** *n* comisionado/da, delegado/da *m/f.*

**commit** *vt* cometer; depositar; encargar.

**commitment** *n* compromiso *m.*

**committee** *n* comité *m.*

**commodity** *n* comodidad *f.*

**common** *adj* común; bajo/ja; **in ~** comúnmente; * *n* pastos comunales *mpl.*

**commoner** *n* plebeyo *m.*

**common law** *n* derecho consuetudinario *m.*

**commonly** *adv* comúnmente, frecuentemente.

**commonplace** *n* lugar común *m;* * *adj* trivial.

**common sense** *n* sentido común *m.*

**commonwealth** *n* república *f.*

**commotion** *n* tumulto *m;* perturbación del ánimo *f.*

**commune** *vt* conversar, conferir.

**communicable** *adj* comunicable, impartible.

**communicate** *vt* comunicar, participar; * *vi* comunicarse.

**communication** *n* comunicación *f.*

**communicative** *adj* comunicativo/va.

**communion** *n* comunión *f.*

**communiqué** *n* comunicado *m.*

**communism** *n* comunismo *m.*

**communist** *n* comunista *m/f.*

**community** *n* comunidad *f;* colectividad *f.*

**community centre** *n* centro social *m.*

**community chest** *n* arca comunitaria *f.*

**commutable** *adj* conmutable, cambiable.

**commutation ticket** *n* billete de abono *m.*

**commute** *vt* conmutar.

**compact** *adj* compacto/ta, sólido/da, denso/sa; * *n* pacto, convenio *m;* **~ly** *adv* estrechamente; en pocas palabras.

**compact disc, CD** *n* compact disc *m,* disco compacto *m.*

**companion** *n* compañero/ra, socio/cia, compinche *m/f.*

**companionship** *n* sociedad, compañía *f.*

**company** *n* compañía, sociedad *f;* compañía de comercio *f.*

**comparable** *adj* comparable.

**comparative** *adj* comparativo/va; **~ly** *adv* comparativamente.

**compare** *vt* comparar.

**comparison** *n* comparación *f.*

**compartment** *n* compartimento *m.*

**compass** *n* brújula *f.*

**compassion** *n* compasión, piedad *f.*

**compassionate** *adj* compasivo/va.

**compatibility** *n* compatibilidad *f.*

**compatible** *adj* compatible.

**compatriot** *n* compatriota *m/f.*

**compel** *vt* compeler, obligar, constreñir.

**compelling** *adj* convicente.

**compensate** *vt* compensar.

**compensation** *n* compensación *f;* resarcimiento *m.*

**compere** *n* (*rad, TV*) presentador/a *m/f.*

**compete** *vi* concurrir, competir.

**competence** *n* competencia *f;* suficiencia *f.*

**competent** *adj* competente, adecuado/da; **~ly** *adv* competentemente.

**competition** *n* competencia *f;* concurrencia *f.*

**competitive** *adj* competitivo/va.

**competitive scheduling** *n* contraprogramación *f.*

**competitor** *n* competidor/a *m/f,* rival *m.*

**compilation** *n* compilación *f.*

**compile** *vt* compilar.

**complacency** *n* autocomplacencia *f.*

**complacent** *adj* complaciente.

**complain** *vi* quejarse, lamentarse, lastimarse, dolerse.

**complaint** *n* queja *f;* reclamación *f.*

**complement** *n* complemento *m.*

**complementary** *adj* complementario/ria.

**complete** *adj* completo/ta, perfecto/ta; ~ly *adv* completamente; * *vt* completar, acabar.
**completion** *n* terminación *f*.
**complex** *adj* complejo/ja.
**complexion** *n* tez *f*; aspecto *m*.
**complexity** *n* complejidad *f*.
**compliance** *n* complacencia, sumisión *f*.
**compliant** *adj* complaciente, oficioso/sa.
**complicate** *vt* complicar.
**complication** *n* complicación *f*.
**complicity** *n* complicidad *f*.
**compliment** *n* cumplido *m*; * *vt* cumplimentar; hacer cumplidos.
**complimentary** *adj* elogioso/sa, ceremonioso/sa.
**comply** *vi* cumplir; condescender, conformarse.
**component** *adj* componente.
**compose** *vt* componer; sosegar.
**composed** *adj* compuesto/ta, moderado/da.
**composer** *n* compositor/a *m/f*.
**composite** *adj* compuesto/ta.
**composition** *n* composición *f*.
**compositor** *n* cajista *m*.
**compost** *n* abono, estiércol *m*.
**composure** *n* composición *f*; tranquilidad, sangre fría *f*.
**compound** *vt* componer, combinar; * *adj*, *n* compuesto *m*.
**comprehend** *vt* comprender, contener; entender.
**comprehensible** *adj* comprensible; ~ly *adv* comprensiblemente.
**comprehension** *n* comprensión *f*; inteligencia *f*.
**comprehensive** *adj* comprensivo/va; ~ly *adv* comprensivamente.
**compress** *vt* comprimir, estrechar; * *n* cabezal *m*.
**comprise** *vt* comprender, incluir.
**compromise** *n* compromiso *m*; * *vt* comprometer.
**compulsion** *n* compulsión *f*; apremio *m*.
**compulsive** *adj* compulsivo/va; ~ly *adv* compulsivamente.
**compulsory** *adj* obligatorio/ria.
**compunction** *n* compunción, contrición *f*.
**computable** *adj* computable, calculable.
**computation** *n* computación *f*, cómputo *m*.
**compute** *vt* computar, calcular.
**computer** *n* ordenador *m*.
**computer graphics** *n* infografía *f*.
**computerize** *vt* computerizar, informatizar.

**computer programming** *n* programación *f*.
**computer science** *n* informática *f*.
**computing** *n* informática *f*.
**comrade** *n* camarada, compañero/ra *m/f*.
**comradeship** *n* compañerismo *m*.
**con** *vt* estafar; * *n* estafa *f*.
**concave** *adj* cóncavo/va.
**concavity** *n* concavidad *f*.
**conceal** *vt* ocultar, esconder.
**concealment** *n* ocultación *f*; encubrimiento *m*.
**concede** *vt* conceder, asentir.
**conceit** *n* concepto *m*; capricho *m*; pensamiento *m*; presunción *f*.
**conceited** *adj* afectado/da, vano/na, presumido/da.
**conceivable** *adj* concebible, inteligible.
**conceive** *vt* concebir, comprender; * *vi* concebir.
**concentrate** *vt* concentrar.
**concentration** *n* concentración *f*.
**concentration camp** *n* campo de concentración *m*.
**concentric** *adj* concéntrico/ca.
**concept** *n* concepto *m*.
**conception** *n* concepción *f*; sentimiento *m*.
**concern** *vt* concernir, importar; * *n* negocio *m*; asunto *m*; preocupación *f*.
**concerning** *prep* tocante a.
**concert** *n* concierto *m*.
**concerto** *n* concierto *m*.
**concession** *n* concesión *f*; privilegio *m*.
**conciliate** *vt* conciliar.
**conciliation** *n* conciliación *f*.
**conciliatory** *adj* conciliador/a.
**concise** *adj* conciso/sa, sucinto/ta; ~ly *adv* concisamente.
**conclude** *vt* concluir; decidir; determinar.
**conclusion** *n* conclusión, determinación *f*; fin *m*.
**conclusive** *adj* decisivo/va, conclusivo/va; ~ly *adv* concluyentemente.
**concoct** *vt* cocer, digerir; (*fig*) zurcir.
**concoction** *n* confección *f*; cocción *f*.
**concomitant** *adj* concomitante.
**concord** *n* concordia, armonía *f*.
**concordance** *n* concordancia *f*.
**concordant** *adj* concordante, conforme.
**concourse** *n* concurso *m*; multitud *f*; gentío *m*.
**concrete** *n* hormigón *m*; * *vt* concretar.
**concubine** *n* concubina *f*.
**concur** *vi* concurrir; juntarse.
**concurrence** *n* concurrencia *f*; unión *f*; asistencia *f*.

**concurrently** *adv* al mismo tiempo.
**concussion** *n* conmoción cerebral *f*.
**condemn** *vt* condenar; desaprobar; vituperar.
**condemnation** *n* condena *f*.
**condensation** *n* condensación *f*.
**condense** *vt* condensar.
**condescend** *vi* condescender; consentir.
**condescending** *adj* condescendiente.
**condescension** *n* condescendencia *f*.
**condiment** *n* condimento *m*; salsa *f*.
**condition** *vt* condicionar; *\*n* situación, condición, calidad *f*; estado *m*.
**conditional** *adj* condicional, hipotético/ca; **~ly** *adv* condicionalmente.
**conditioned** *adj* condicionado/da.
**conditioner** *n* acondicionador *m*.
**condolences** *npl* pésame *m*.
**condom** *n* condón *m*.
**condominium** *n* condominio *m*.
**condone** *vt* perdonar.
**conducive** *adj* conducente, oportuno/na.
**conduct** *n* conducta *f*; manejo, proceder *m*; *\* vt* conducir, guiar.
**conductor** *n* conductor *m*; guía, director *m*; conductor de electricidad *m*.
**conduit** *n* conducto *m*; cano *m*.
**cone** *n* cono *m*.
**confection** *n* confitura *f*; confección *f*.
**confectioner** *n* confitero/ra *m/f*.
**confectioner's** (**shop**) *n* pastelería *f*; confitería *f*.
**confectionery** (**sweets**) *n* caramelo *m*.
**confederacy** *n* confederación *f*.
**confederate** *vi* confederarse; *\* adj, n* confederado/da *m/f*.
**confer** *vi* conferenciar; *\* vt* conferir, comparar.
**conference** *n* conferencia *f*.
**confess** *vt* (*vi*) confesar(se).
**confession** *n* confesión *f*.
**confessional** *n* confesionario *m*.
**confessor** *n* confesor *m*.
**confetti** *n* confeti *m*.
**confidant** *n* confidente, amigo/ga íntimo/ma *m/f*.
**confide** *vt, vi* confiar; fiarse.
**confidence** *n* confianza, seguridad *f*.
**confidence trick** *n* timo *m*.
**confident** *adj* cierto/ta, seguro/ra; confiado/da.
**confidential** *adj* confidencial.
**configuration** *n* configuración *f*.
**confine** *vt* limitar; aprisionar.
**confinement** *n* prisión *f*; confinación *f*.
**confirm** *vt* confirmar; ratificar.

**confirmation** *n* confirmación *f*; ratificación *f*; prueba *f*.
**confirmed** *adj* empedernido/da.
**confiscate** *vt* confiscar.
**confiscation** *n* confiscación *f*.
**conflagration** *n* conflagración *f*; incendio *m*.
**conflict** *n* conflicto *m*; combate *m*; pelea *f*.
**conflicting** *adj* contradictorio/ria.
**confluence** *n* confluencia *f*; concurso *m*.
**conform** *vt* (*vi*) conformar(se).
**conformity** *n* conformidad, conveniencia *f*.
**confound** *vt* turbar, confundir.
**confront** *vt* afrontar; confrontar; comparar.
**confrontation** *n* enfrentamiento *m*.
**confuse** *vt* confundir; desordenar.
**confusing** *adj* confuso/sa.
**confusion** *n* confusión *f*; perturbación *f*; desorden *m*.
**congeal** *vt, vi* helar, congelar(se).
**congenial** *adj* congenial.
**congenital** *adj* congénito/ta.
**congested** *adj* atestado/da.
**congestion** *n* congestión *f*; acumulación *f*.
**conglomerate** *vt* conglomerar, aglomerar; *\* adj* aglomerado/da; *\* n* (*com*) conglomerado *m*.
**conglomeration** *n* aglomeración *f*.
**congratulate** *vt* congratular, felicitar.
**congratulations** *npl* felicidades *fpl*; *\* interj* enhorabuena.
**congratulatory** *adj* congratulatorio/ria.
**congregate** *vt* congregar, reunir.
**congregation** *n* congregación, reunión *f*.
**congress** *n* congreso *m*; conferencia *f*.
**congressman** *n* miembro del Congreso *m*.
**congruity** *n* congruencia *f*.
**congruous** *adj* idóneo/nea, congruo/rua, apto/ta.
**conic(al)** *adj* cónico/ca.
**conifer** *n* conífera *f*.
**coniferous** *adj* (*bot*) conífero/ra.
**conjecture** *n* conjetura, apariencia *f*; *\* vt* conjeturar; pronosticar.
**conjugal** *adj* conyugal, matrimonial.
**conjugate** *vt* (*gr*) conjugar.
**conjugation** *n* conjugación *f*.
**conjunction** *n* conjunción *f*; unión *f*.
**conjuncture** *n* coyuntura *f*; ocasión *f*; tiempo crítico *m*.
**conjure** *vi* conjurar, suplicar.
**conjurer** *n* conjurado/a, encantador/a *m/f*.
**con man** *n* timador *m*.
**connect** *vt* juntar, unir, enlazar.
**connection** *n* conexión *f*.

**connivance** n connivencia f.
**connive** vi tolerar.
**connoisseur** n conocedor/a m/f.
**conquer** vt conquistar; vencer.
**conqueror** n vencedor/a, conquistador/a m/f.
**conquest** n conquista f.
**conscience** n conciencia f; escrúpulo m.
**conscientious** adj concienzudo/da, escrupuloso/sa; ~**ly** adv concienzudamente.
**conscientious objector** n objetor de conciencia m.
**conscious** adj sabedor, consciente; ~**ly** adv a sabiendas.
**consciousness** n conciencia f.
**conscript** n conscripto m.
**conscription** n reclutamiento m.
**consecrate** vt consagrar; dedicar.
**consecration** n consagración f.
**consecutive** adj consecutivo/va; ~**ly** adv consecutivamente.
**consensus** n consenso m.
**consent** n consentimiento m; aprobación f, * vi consentir; aprobar.
**consequence** n consecuencia f; importancia f.
**consequent** adj consecutivo/va, concluyente; ~**ly** adv consiguientemente.
**conservation** n conservación f.
**conservative** adj conservador/a m/f.
**conservatory** n conservatorio m.
**conserve** vt conservar; * n conserva f.
**consider** vt considerar, examinar; * vi pensar, deliberar.
**considerable** adj considerable; importante; ~**bly** adv considerablemente.
**considerate** adj considerado/da, prudente, discreto/ta; ~**ly** adv juiciosamente; prudentemente.
**consideration** n consideración f; deliberación f; importancia f, valor, mérito m.
**considering** conj en vista de; ~ **that** a causa de; visto que, en razón a.
**consign** vt consignar.
**consignment** n consignación f.
**consist** vi consistir.
**consistency** n consistencia f.
**consistent** adj consistente; conveniente, conforme; solido/da, estable; ~**ly** adv conformemente.
**console** n consola f.
**consolable** adj consolable.
**consolation** n consolación f; consuelo m.
**consolatory** adj consolatorio/ria.
**console** vt consolar.
**consolidate** vt (vi) consolidar(se).

**consolidation** n consolidación f.
**consonant** adj consonante, conforme; * n (gr) consonante f.
**consort** n consorte, socio m.
**conspicuous** adj conspicuo/cua, aparente; notable; ~**ly** adv claramente.
**conspiracy** n conspiración f.
**conspirator** n conspirador/a m/f.
**conspire** vi conspirar, maquinar.
**constancy** n constancia, perseverancia, persistencia f.
**constant** adj constante; perseverante; ~**ly** adv constantemente.
**constellation** n constelación f.
**consternation** n consternación f; terror m.
**constipated** adj estreñido/da.
**constituency** n circunscripción electoral f.
**constituent** n constitutivo m; * adj constituyente.
**constitute** vt constituir; establecer.
**constitution** n constitución f; estado m; temperamento m.
**constitutional** adj constitucional.
**constrain** vt constreñir, forzar; restringir.
**constraint** n constreñimiento m; fuerza, violencia f.
**constrict** vt constreñir, estrechar.
**construct** vt construir, edificar.
**construction** n construcción f.
**construe** vt construir; interpretar.
**consul** n cónsul m.
**consular** adj consular.
**consulate, consulship** n consulado m.
**consult** vt (vi) consultar(se); aconsejar(se).
**consultant** n asesor m.
**consultation** n consulta, deliberación f.
**consume** vt consumir; disipar; * vi consumirse.
**consumer** n consumidor/a m/f.
**consumer goods** npl bienes de consumo mpl.
**consumerism** n consumismo m.
**consumer society** n sociedad de consumo f.
**consummate** vt consumar, acabar, perfeccionar; * adj cumplido/da, consumado/da.
**consummation** n consumación, perfección f.
**consumption** n consumo m.
**contact** n contacto m.
**contact lenses** npl lentes de contacto fpl.
**contagious** adj contagioso/sa.
**contain** vt contener, comprender; caber, reprimir, refrenar.
**container** n recipiente m.

**contaminate** *vt* contaminar; corromper; **~d** *adj* contaminado/da, corrompido/da.
**contamination** *n* contaminación *f*.
**contemplate** *vt* contemplar.
**contemplation** *n* contemplación *f*.
**contemplative** *adj* contemplativo/va.
**contemporaneous, contemporary** *adj* contemporáneo/nea.
**contempt** *n* desprecio, desdén *m*.
**contemptible** *adj* despreciable, vil; **~bly** *adv* vilmente.
**contemptuous** *adj* desdeñoso/sa, insolente; **~ly** *adv* con desdén.
**contend** *vi* contender, disputar, afirmar.
**content** *adj* contento/ta, satisfecho/cha; * *vt* contentar, satisfacer; * *n* contenido *m*; **~s** *pl* contenido *m*; tabla de materias *f*.
**contentedly** *adv* de un modo satisfecho/ cha; con paciencia.
**contention** *n* contención, altercación *f*.
**contentious** *adj* contencioso/sa, litigioso/ sa; **~ly** *adv* contenciosamente.
**contentment** *n* contentamiento, placer *m*.
**contest** *vt* contestar, disputar, litigar; * *n* concurso *m*; contestación, altercación *f*.
**contestant** *n* concursante/ta *m/f*.
**context** *n* contexto *m*; contextura *f*.
**contiguous** *adj* contiguo/gua, vecino/na.
**continent** *adj* continente; * *n* continente *m*.
**continental** *adj* continental.
**contingency** *n* contingencia *f*; acontecimiento *m*; eventualidad *f*.
**contingent** *n* contingente *m*; cuota *f*; * *adj* contingente, casual; **~ly** *adv* casualmente.
**continual** *adj* continuo/nua; **~ly** *adv* continuamente.
**continuation** *n* continuación, serie *f*.
**continue** *vt* continuar; * *vi* durar, perseverar, persistir.
**continuity** *n* continuidad *f*.
**continuous** *adj* continuo/nua, unido/da; **~ly** *adv* continuadamente.
**contort** *vt* torcer.
**contortion** *n* contorsión *f*.
**contour** *n* contorno *m*.
**contraband** *n* contrabando *m*; * *adj* prohibido/da, ilegal.
**contraception** *n* contracepción *f*.
**contraceptive** *n* anticonceptivo *m*; * *adj* anticonceptivo/va.
**contract** *vt* contraer; abreviar; contratar; * *vi* contraerse; * *n* contrato, pacto *m*.
**contraction** *n* contracción *f*; abreviatura *f*.
**contractor** *n* contratante *m/f*.

**contradict** *vt* contradecir.
**contradiction** *n* contradicción, oposición *f*.
**contradictory** *adj* contradictorio/ria.
**contraption** *n* artilugio *m*.
**contrariness** *n* contrariedad, oposición *f*.
**contrary** *adj* contrario/ria, opuesto/ta; * *n* contrario *m*; **on the ~** al contrario.
**contrast** *n* contraste *m*; oposición *f*; * *vt* contrastar, oponer.
**contrasting** *adj* opuesto/ta.
**contravention** *n* contravención *f*.
**contributory** *adj* contributario/ria.
**contribute** *vt* contribuir, ayudar.
**contribution** *n* contribución *f*; tributo *m*.
**contributor** *n* contribuidor/a *m/f*.
**contributory** *adj* contribuyente.
**contrite** *adj* contrito/ta, arrepentido/da.
**contrition** *n* penitencia, contrición *f*.
**contrivance** *n* designio *m*; invención *f*; concepto *m*.
**contrive** *vt* inventar, trazar, maquinar; manejar; combinar.
**control** *n* control *m*; inspección *f*; * *vt* controlar; manejar; restringir; gobernar.
**control room** *n* sala de mando *f*.
**control tower** *n* torre de control *f*.
**controversial** *adj* polémico/ca.
**controversy** *n* controversia *f*.
**contusion** *n* contusión *f*, magullamiento *m*.
**conundrum** *n* problema *m*.
**conurbation** *n* conurbación *f*.
**convalesce** *vi* convalecer.
**convalescence** *n* convalecencia *f*.
**convalescent** *adj* convaleciente.
**convene** *vt* convocar; juntar, unir; * *vi* convenir, juntarse.
**convenience** *n* conveniencia, comodidad, conformidad *f*.
**convenient** *adj* conveniente, apto/ta, cómodo/da, propio/pia; **~ly** *adv* cómodamente, oportunamente.
**convent** *n* convento, claustro, monasterio *m*.
**convention** *n* convención *f*; contrato, tratado *m*.
**conventional** *adj* convencional, estipulado/ da.
**converge** *vi* converger.
**convergence** *n* convergencia *f*.
**convergent** *adj* convergente.
**conversant** *adj* versado en; íntimo/ma.
**conversation** *n* conversación *f*.
**converse** *vi* conversar; platicar.
**conversely** *adv* mutuamente, recíprocamente.

**conversion** *n* conversión, transmutación *f*.

**convert** *vt* (*vi*) convertir(se); * *n* converso, convertido *m*.

**convertible** *adj* convertible, transmutable; * *n* descapotable *m*.

**convex** *adj* convexo/xa.

**convexity** *n* convexidad *f*.

**convey** *vt* transportar; transmitir, transferir.

**conveyance** *n* transporte *m*; conducción *f*; escritura de traspaso *f*.

**conveyancer** *n* notario *m*.

**convict** *vt* probar un delito; * *n* convicto/ta *m*/*f*.

**conviction** *n* convicción *f*.

**convince** *vt* convencer, poner en evidencia.

**convincing** *adj* convincente.

**convincingly** *adv* de modo convincente.

**convivial** *adj* sociable; hospitalario/ria.

**conviviality** *n* sociabilidad *f*.

**convoke** *vt* convocar, reunir.

**convoy** *n* convoy *m*.

**convulse** *vt* conmover, convulsionar.

**convulsion** *n* convulsión *f*; conmoción *f*; tumulto *m*.

**convulsive** *adj* convulsivo/va; ~**ly** *adv* convulsivamente.

**coo** *vi* arrullar.

**cook** *n* cocinero/ra *m*/*f*; * *vt* cocinar; * *vi* cocinar; guisar.

**cookbook** *n* libro de cocina *m*.

**cooker** *n* cocina *f*.

**cookery** *n* arte culinario *m*, cocina *f*.

**cool** *adj* fresco/ca; indiferente; * *n* frescura *f*; * *vt* enfriar, refrescar.

**coolly** *adv* frescamente; indiferentemente.

**coolness** *n* fresco *m*; frialdad *f*, frescura *f*.

**cooperate** *vi* cooperar.

**cooperation** *n* cooperación *f*.

**cooperative** *adj* cooperativo/va; co-operante.

**coordinate** *vt* coordinar.

**coordination** *n* coordinación, elección *f*.

**cop** *n* (*col*) poli *m*.

**copartner** *n* compañero/ra, socio/cia *m*/*f*.

**cope** *vi* arreglárselas.

**copier** *n* copiadora *f*.

**copious** *adj* copioso/sa, abundante; ~**ly** *adv* en abundancia.

**copper** *n* cobre *m*.

**coppice, copse** *n* bosquecillo *m*.

**copulate** *vi* copular.

**copy** *n* copia *f*; original *m*; ejemplar *m*; * *vt* copiar; imitar.

**copybook** *n* copiador de cartas (libro) *m*.

**copying machine** *n* copiadora *f*.

**copyist** *n* copista *m*/*f*.

**copyright** *n* propiedad de una obra literaria *f*; derechos de autor *mpl*.

**coral** *n* coral *m*.

**coral reef** *n* arrecife de coral *m*.

**cord** *n* cuerda *f*, cable *m*.

**cordial** *adj* cordial, de corazón, amistoso/sa; ~**ly** *adv* cordialmente.

**corduroy** *n* pana *f*.

**core** *n* cuesco *m*; interior, centro, corazón *m*; materia *f*.

**cork** *n* alcornoque *m*; corcho *m*; * *vt* encorchar.

**corkscrew** *n* sacacorchos *m invar*.

**corn**[1] *n* trigo *m*; granos *mpl*; maíz *m*.

**corn**[2] *n* callo *m*.

**corncob** *n* mazorca *f*.

**cornea** *n* córnea *f*.

**corned beef** *n* carne acecinada *f*.

**corner** *n* rincón *m*; esquina *f*.

**cornerstone** *n* piedra angular *f*.

**cornet** *n* corneta *f*.

**cornfield** *n* maizal *m*.

**cornflakes** *npl* copos de maíz *mpl*.

**cornflour** *n* harina de maíz *f*.

**cornice** *n* cornisa *f*.

**corollary** *n* corolario *m*.

**coronary** *n* infarto *m*.

**coronation** *n* coronación *f*.

**coroner** *n* oficial que hace la inspección jurídica de los cadáveres *m*.

**coronet** *n* corona pequeña *f*.

**corporal** *n* cabo *m*.

**corporate** *adj* corporativo/va.

**corporation** *n* corporación *f*; gremio *m*.

**corporeal** *adj* corpóreo/rea.

**corps** *n* cuerpo (de ejército) *m*; regimiento *m*.

**corpse** *n* cadáver *m*.

**corpulent** *adj* corpulento/ta, gordo/da.

**corpuscle** *n* corpúsculo, átomo *m*.

**corral** *n* corral *m*.

**correct** *vt* corregir; enmendar; * *adj* correcto/ta, justo/ta; ~**ly** *adv* correctamente.

**correction** *n* corrección *f*; enmienda *f*; censura *f*.

**corrective** *adj* correctivo/va; * *n* correctivo *m*; restricción *f*.

**correctness** *n* exactitud *f*.

**correlation** *n* correlación *f*.

**correlative** *adj* correlativo/va.

**correspond** *vi* corresponder; corresponderse.

**correspondence** *n* correspondencia *f*.

**correspondent** *adj* correspondiente, conforme; * *n* corresponsal *m*.

**corridor** n pasillo m.
**corroborate** vt corroborar.
**corroboration** n corroboración f.
**corroborative** adj corroborativo/va.
**corrode** vt corroer.
**corrosion** n corrosión f.
**corrosive** adj, n corrosivo m.
**corrugated iron** n chapa ondulada f.
**corrupt** vt corromper; sobornar; * vi corromperse, pudrirse; * adj corrompido/da; depravado/da.
**corruptible** adj corruptible.
**corruption** n corrupción f; depravación f.
**corruptive** adj corruptivo/va.
**corset** n corsé, corpiño m.
**cortege** n cortejo m.
**cosily** adv cómodamente, con facilidad.
**cosmetic** adj cosmético/ca; * n cosmético m.
**cosmic** adj cósmico/ca.
**cosmonaut** n cosmonauta m/f.
**cosmopolitan** adj cosmopolita.
**cosset** vt mimar.
**cost** n coste, precio m; * vi costar.
**costly** adj costoso/sa, caro/ra.
**costume** n traje m.
**cosy** adj cómodo/da.
**cottage** n casita, casucha f.
**cotton** n algodón m.
**cotton mill** n hilandería de algodón.
**cotton wool** n algodón hidrófilo m.
**couch** n sofá m.
**couchette** n litera f.
**cough** n tos f; * vi toser.
**council** n concilio, consejo m.
**councillor** n concejal/a m/f.
**counsel** n consejo, aviso m; abogado/da m/f.
**counsellor** n consejero/ra m/f; abogado/da m/f.
**count** vt contar, numerar; calcular; **to ~ on** contar con; * n cuenta f; cálculo m; conde m.
**countdown** n cuenta atrás f.
**countenance** n rostro m; aspecto m; (buena/mala) cara f.
**counter** n mostrador m; ficha f.
**counteract** vt contrariar, impedir, estorbar; frustrar.
**counterbalance** vt contrapesar; igualar, compensar; * n contrapeso m.
**counterfeit** vt contrahacer, imitar, falsear; * adj falsificado/da; fingido/da.
**countermand** vt contramandar; revocar.
**counterpart** n parte correspondiente f.
**counterproductive** adj contraproducente.
**countersign** vt refrendar; firmar un decreto.

**countess** n condesa f.
**countless** adj innumerable.
**countrified** adj rústico/ca; tosco/ca, rudo/da.
**country** n país m; campo m; región f; patria f; * adj rústico/ca; campestre, rural.
**country house** n casa de campo, granja f.
**countryman** n paisano m; compatriota m.
**county** n condado m.
**coup** n golpe m.
**coupé** n (auto) cupé m.
**couple** n par m; lazo m; yuntas fpl; * vt unir, parear; casar.
**couplet** n copla f; par m.
**coupon** n cupón m.
**courage** n coraje; valor f.
**courageous** adj corajudo/da, valeroso/sa; **~ly** adv valerosamente.
**courier** n correo, mensajero/ra m/f, expreso m.
**course** n curso m; carrera f; camino m; ruta f; método m; **of ~** por supuesto, sin duda.
**court** n corte f; palacio m; tribunal de justicia m; * vt cortejar; solicitar, adular.
**courteous** adj cortés; benévolo/la; **~ly** adv cortésmente.
**courtesan** n cortesana f.
**courtesy** n cortesía f; benignidad f.
**courthouse** n palacio de justicia m.
**courtly** adj cortesano/na, elegante.
**court martial** n consejo de guerra m.
**courtroom** n sala de justicia f.
**courtyard** n patio m.
**cousin** n primo m; prima f; **first ~** primo hermano m.
**cove** n (mar) ensenada, caleta f.
**covenant** n contrato m; convención f; * vi pactar, estipular.
**cover** n cubierta f; abrigo m; pretexto m; * vt cubrir; tapar; ocultar; proteger.
**coverage** n alcance m.
**coveralls** npl mono m.
**covering** n ropa f; vestido m.
**cover letter** n carta de explicación f.
**covert** adj cubierto/ta; oculto/ta, secreto/ta; **~ly** adv secretamente.
**cover-up** n encubrimiento m.
**covet** vt codiciar, desear con ansia.
**covetous** adj avariento/ta, sórdido/da.
**cow** n vaca f.
**coward** n cobarde m/f.
**cowardice** n cobardía, timidez f.
**cowardly** adj, adv cobarde; pusilánime.
**cowboy, cowhand** n vaquero m.
**cower** vi agacharse.

**cowherd** *n* vaquero *m*; vaquerizo *m*.
**coy** *adj* recatado/da, modesto/ta; esquivo/va;
~**ly** *adv* con esquivez.
**coyness** *n* esquivez, modestia *f*.
**crab** *n* cangrejo *m*; manzana silvestre *f*.
**crab apple** *n* manzana silvestre *f*; ~ **tree** *n*
manzano silvestre *m*.
**crack** *n* crujido *m*; hendedura, quebraja *f*;
* *vt* hender, rajar; romper; **to ~ down on**
reprimandar fuertemente;* *vi* reventar.
**cracker** *n* buscapiés *m invar*; galleta *f*.
**crackle** *vi* crujir, chillar.
**crackling** *n* estallido, crujido *m*.
**cradle** *n* cuna *f*; * *vt* acunar.
**craft** *n* arte *m*; artificio *m*; barco *m*.
**craftily** *adv* astutamente.
**craftiness** *n* astucia, estratagema *f*.
**craftsman** *n* artífice, artesano *m*.
**craftsmanship** *n* artesanía *f*.
**crafty** *adj* astuto/ta, artificioso/sa.
**crag** *n* despeñadero *m*.
**cram** *vt* embutir; engordar; empujar; * *vi*
empollar.
**crammed** *adj* atestado/da.
**cramp** *n* calambre *m*; * *vt* constreñir.
**cramped** *adj* apretado/da.
**crampon** *n* crampón *m*.
**cranberry** *n* arándano agrio *m*.
**crane** *n* grulla *f*; grúa *f*.
**crash** *vi* estallar; * *vr* zamparse; * *n* estallido
*m*; choque *m*.
**crash helmet** *n* casco *m*.
**crash landing** *n* aterrizaje forzoso *m*.
**crass** *adj* craso/sa, grueso/sa, basto/ta, tosco/
ca, grosero/ra.
**crate** *n* cesta grande *f*.
**crater** *n* cráter *m*; boca de volcán *f*.
**cravat** *n* pañuelo *m*.
**crave** *vt* rogar, suplicar.
**craving** *adj* insaciable, pedigüeño/ña; * *n*
deseo ardiente *m*.
**crawl** *vi* arrastrar; **to ~ with** hormiguear.
**crayfish** *n* cangrejo de río *m*.
**crayon** *n* lápiz *m*.
**craze** *n* manía *f*.
**craziness** *n* locura *f*.
**crazy** *adj* loco/ca.
**creak** *vi* crujir, chirriar.
**cream** *n* crema *f*; * *adj* color crema.
**creamy** *adj* cremoso/sa.
**crease** *n* pliegue *m*; * *vt* plegar.
**create** *vt* crear; causar.
**creation** *n* creación *f*; elección *f*.
**creative** *adj* creativo/va.
**creator** *n* creador/a *m/f*.

**creature** *n* criatura *f*.
**credence** *n* creencia, fe *f*; renombre *m*.
**credentials** *npl* (cartas) credenciales *fpl*.
**credibility** *n* credibilidad *f*.
**credible** *adj* creíble.
**credit** *n* crédito *m*; reputación *f*; autoridad *f*;
* *vt* creer, fiar, acreditar.
**creditable** *adj* estimable, honorífico/ca;
~**bly** *adv* honorablemente.
**credit card** *n* tarjeta de crédito *f*.
**creditor** *n* acreedor *m*.
**credulity** *n* credulidad *f*.
**credulous** *adj* crédulo/la; ~**ly** *adv* con
credulidad.
**creed** *n* credo *m*.
**creek** *n* arroyo *m*.
**creep** *vi* arrastrar, serpear; complacer
bajamente.
**creeper** *n* (*bot*) enredadera *f*.
**creepy** *adj* horripilante.
**cremate** *vt* incinerar cadáveres.
**cremation** *n* cremación *f*.
**crematorium** *n* crematorio *m*.
**crescent** *adj* creciente; * *n* cuarto creciente *m*.
**cress** *n* berro *m*.
**crest** *n* cresta *f*.
**crested** *adj* crestado/da.
**crestfallen** *adj* acobardado/da, abatido/da
de espíritu.
**crevasse** *n* grieta (de glaciar) *f*.
**crevice** *n* raja, hendedura *f*.
**crew** *n* banda, tropa *f*; tripulación *f*.
**crib** *n* cuna *f*; pesebre *m*.
**cricket** *n* grillo *m*; críquet *m*.
**crime** *n* crimen *m*; culpa *f*.
**criminal** *adj* criminal, reo/rea; ~**ly** *adv*
criminalmente; * *n* criminal *m/f*.
**criminality** *n* criminalidad *f*.
**crimson** *adj*, *n* carmesí *m*.
**cripple** *vt* lisiar; (*fig*) estropear.
**crisis** *n* crisis *f invar*.
**crisp** *adj* crujiente.
**crispness** *n* sequedad *f*.
**criss-cross** *adj* entrelazado/da.
**criterion** *n* criterio *m*.
**critic** *n* crítico *m*; crítica *f*.
**critic(al)** *adj* crítico/ca; exacto/ta; delicado/
da; ~**ally** *adv* exactamente, rigurosamente.
**criticism** *n* crítica *f*.
**criticize** *vt* criticar, censurar; zaherir; (*fig*)
zurrar.
**croak** *vi* graznar.
**crochet** *n* ganchillo *m*; * *vt*, *vi* hacer
ganchillo.

**crockery** *n* loza *f*; vasijas de barro *fpl*.
**crocodile** *n* cocodrilo *m*.
**crony** *n* amigote *m*; compinche *m*.
**crook** *n* (*col*) ladrón *m*; cayado *m*.
**crooked** *adj* torcido/da; perverso/sa.
**crop** *n* cultivo *m*; cosecha *f*; * *vt* recortar.
**cross** *n* cruz *f*, carga *f*; * *adj* mal humorado/da; * *vt* atravesar, cruzar; **to ~ over** traspasar.
**crossbar** *n* travesaño *m*.
**crossbreed** *n* raza cruzada *f*.
**cross-country** *n* carrera a campo traviesa *f*.
**cross-examine** *vt* preguntar a un testigo.
**crossfire** *n* fuego cruzado *m*.
**crossing** *n* cruce *m*; paso a nivel *m*.
**cross-purpose** *n* disposición contraria *f*; contradicción *f*; **to be at ~s** entenderse mal.
**cross-reference** *n* remisión *f*.
**crossroad** *n* encrucijada *f*.
**crotch** *n* entrepierna *f*.
**crouch** *vi* agacharse, bajarse.
**crow** *n* cuervo *m*; canto del gallo *m*; * *vi* cantar el gallo.
**crowd** *n* público *m*; muchedumbre *f*; * *vt* amontonar; * *vi* reunirse.
**crown** *n* corona *f*; cumbre *f*; * *vt* coronar.
**crown prince** *n* príncipe real *m*.
**crucial** *adj* crucial.
**crucible** *n* crisol *m*.
**crucifix** *n* crucifijo *m*.
**crucifixion** *n* crucifixión *f*.
**crucify** *vt* crucificar; atormentar.
**crude** *adj* crudo/da, imperfecto/ta; **~ly** *adv* crudamente.
**cruel** *adj* cruel, inhumano/na; **~ly** *adv* cruelmente.
**cruelty** *n* crueldad *f*.
**cruet set/stand** *n* vinagreras *fpl*.
**cruise** *n* crucero *m*; * *vi* hacer un crucero.
**cruiser** *n* crucero *m*.
**crumb** *n* miga *f*.
**crumble** *vt* desmigajar, desmenuzar; * *vi* desmigajarse.
**crumple** *vt* arrugar.
**crunch** *vt* ronzar; * *n* (*fig*) crisis *f invar*.
**crunchy** *adj* crujiente.
**crusade** *n* cruzada *f*.
**crush** *vt* apretar, oprimir; * *n* choque *m*.
**crust** *n* costra *f*; corteza *f*; zoquete *m*.
**crusty** *adj* costroso/sa; bronco/ca, áspero/ra.
**crutch** *n* muleta *f*.
**crux** *n* lo esencial.
**cry** *vt*, *vi* gritar; exclamar; llorar; * *n* grito *m*; lloro *m*; clamor *m*.

**crypt** *n* cripta *f*.
**cryptic** *adj* enigmático/ca.
**crystal** *n* cristal *m*.
**crystal-clear** *adj* claro/ra como el agua.
**crystalline** *adj* cristalino/na; transparente.
**crystallize** *vt* (*vi*) cristalizar(se).
**cub** *n* cachorro *m*.
**cube** *n* cubo *m*.
**cubic** *adj* cúbico/ca.
**cuckoo** *n* cuco *m*.
**cucumber** *n* pepino *m*.
**cud** *n*: **to chew the ~** rumiar; (*fig*) reflexionar.
**cuddle** *vt* abrazar; * *vi* abrazarse; * *n* abrazo *m*.
**cudgel** *n* garrote, palo *m*.
**cue** *n* taco (de billar) *m*.
**cuff**[1] *n* puño *m*, bocamanga *f*, vuelta *f*.
**cuff**[2] *n* puñada *f*.
**culinary** *adj* culinario/ria, de la cocina.
**cull** *vt* escoger, elegir.
**culminate** *vi* culminar.
**culmination** *n* colmo *m*.
**culpability** *n* culpabilidad *f*.
**culpable** *adj* culpable, criminal; **~bly** *adv* culpablemente, criminalmente.
**culprit** *n* culpable *m/f*.
**cult** *n* culto *f*.
**cultivate** *vi* cultivar, mejorar; perfeccionar.
**cultivation** *n* cultivo *m*.
**cultural** *adj* cultural.
**culture** *n* cultura *f*.
**cumbersome** *adj* engorroso/sa, pesado/da, confuso/sa.
**cumulative** *adj* cumulativo/va.
**cunning** *adj* astuto/ta; intrigante; **~ly** *adv* astutamente; expertamente; * *n* astucia, sutileza *f*; **~ person** zorro *m*.
**cup** *n* taza, jícara *f*; (*bot*) cáliz *m*.
**cupboard** *n* armario *m*.
**curable** *adj* curable.
**curate** *n* teniente de cura *m*; párroco *m*.
**curator** *n* curador/a *m/f*; guardián/ana *m/f*.
**curb** *n* freno *m*; * *vt* refrenar, contener, moderar.
**curd** *n* cuajada *f*.
**curdle** *vt* (*vi*) cuajar(se), coagular(se).
**cure** *n* cura *f*; remedio *m*; * *vt* curar, sanar.
**curfew** *n* toque de queda *m*.
**curing** *n* curación *f*.
**curiosity** *n* curiosidad *f*; rareza *f*.
**curious** *adj* curioso/sa; **~ly** *adv* curiosamente.
**curl** *n* rizo de pelo *m*; * *vt* rizar; ondear; * *vi* rizarse.
**curling iron** *n*, **curling tongs** *npl* tenacillas de rizar *fpl*.

**curly** *adj* rizado/da.

**currant** *n* pasa *f*.

**currency** *n* moneda *f*; circulación *f*; duración *f*.

**current** *adj* corriente, común; * *n* curso, progreso *m*; marcha *f*; corriente *f*.

**current affairs** *npl* actualidades *fpl*.

**currently** *adv* actualmente.

**curriculum vitae** *n* currículum *m*.

**curry** *n* curry *m*.

**curse** *vt* maldecir; * *vi* imprecar; blasfemar; * *n* maldición *f*.

**cursor** *n* cursor *m*.

**cursory** *adj* precipitado/da, inconsiderado/da.

**curt** *adj* sucinto/ta.

**curtail** *vt* acortar.

**curtain** *n* cortina *f*; telón (en teatro) *m*.

**curtain rod** *n* varilla de cortinaje *f*.

**curtsy** *n* reverencia *f*; * *vi* hacer una reverencia.

**curvature** *n* curvatura *f*.

**curve** *vt* encorvar; * *n* curva *f*.

**cushion** *n* cojín *m*; almohada *f*.

**custard** *n* natillas *fpl*.

**custodian** *n* custodio *m*.

**custody** *n* custodia *f*; prisión *f*.

**custom** *n* costumbre *f*, uso *m*.

**customary** *adj* usual, acostumbrado/da, ordinario/ria.

**customer** *n* cliente *m/f*.

**customs** *npl* aduana *f*.

**customs duty** *n* derechos de aduana *mpl*.

**customs officer** *n* aduanero/ra *m/f*.

**cut** *vt* cortar; separar; herir; dividir; cortar los naipes; **to ~ short** interrumpir, cortar la palabra; **to ~ teeth** nacerle los dientes (a un niño); * *vi* traspasar; cruzarse; * *n* corte *m*; cortadura *f*; herida *f*; **~ and dried** *adj* rutinario/ria.

**cutback** *n* reducción *f*.

**cute** *adj* lindo/da.

**cutlery** *n* cuchillería *f*.

**cutlet** *n* chuleta *f*.

**cut-rate** *adj* a precio reducido.

**cut-throat** *n* asesino *m*; * *adj* encarnizado/da.

**cutting** *n* cortadura *f*; * *adj* cortante; mordaz.

**cyanide** *n* cianuro *m*.

**cyberspace** *n* ciberespacio *m*.

**cycle** *n* ciclo *m*; bicicleta *f*; * *vi* ir en bicicleta.

**cycling** *n* ciclismo *m*.

**cyclist** *n* ciclista *m/f*.

**cyclone** *n* ciclón *m*.

**cygnet** *n* pollo del cisne *m*.

**cylinder** *n* cilindro *m*; rollo *m*.

**cylindric(al)** *adj* cilíndrico/ca.

**cymbals** *n* címbalo *m*.

**cynic(al)** *adj* cínico/ca; obsceno/na; * *n* cínico *m* (filósofo).

**cynicism** *n* cinismo *m*.

**cypress** *n* ciprés *m*.

**cyst** *n* quiste *m*.

**czar** *n* zar *m*.

# D

dab *n* pedazo pequeño *m*; toque *m*.
dabble *vi* chapotear.
dad(dy) *n* papa *m*.
daddy-long-legs *n* típula *f*.
daffodil *n* narciso *m*.
dagger *n* puñal *m*.
daily *adj* diario/ria, cotidiano/na; * *adv* diariamente, cada día; * *n* diario *m*.
daintily *adv* delicadamente.
daintiness *n* elegancia *f*; delicadeza *f*.
dainty *adj* delicado/da, elegante.
dairy *n* lechería *f*.
dairy farm *n* vaquería *f*.
dairy produce *n* productos lácteos *mpl*.
daisy *n* margarita, maya *f*.
dale *n* valle *m*.
dally *vi* tardar.
dam *n* presa *f*; * *vt* represar.
damage *n* daño *m*; perjuicio *m*; * dañar; perjudicar.
damask *n* damasco *m*; * *adj* de damasco.
dame *n* dama *f*.
damn *vt* condenar; * *adj* maldito/ta.
damnable *adj* maldito/ta; ~bly *adv* terriblemente.
damnation *n* perdición *f*.
damning *adj* irrecusable.
damp *adj* húmedo/da; * *n* humedad *f*; * *vt* mojar.
dampen *vt* mojar.
dampness *n* humedad *f*.
damson *n* damascena *f* (ciruela).
dance *n* danza *f*; baile *m*; * *vi* bailar.
dance hall *n* salón de baile *m*.
dancer *n* bailarín *m*, bailarina *f*.
dandelion *n* diente de león *m*.
dandruff *n* caspa *f*.
dandy *adj* mono/na.
danger *n* peligro, riesgo *m*.
dangerous *adj* peligroso/sa; ~ly *adv* peligrosamente.
dangle *vi* estar colgado/da.
dank *adj* húmedo/da.
dapper *adj* apuesto/ta.
dappled *adj* rodado/da.
dare *vi* atreverse; * *vt* desafiar.
daredevil *n* atrevido *m*.
daring *n* osadía *f*; * *adj* atrevido/da; ~ly *adv* atrevidamente, osadamente.
dark *adj* oscuro/ra; negro/gra; * *n* oscuridad *f*; ignorancia *f*.

darken *vt* (*vi*) oscurecer(se).
dark glasses *npl* gafas de sol *fpl*.
darkness *n* oscuridad *f*.
darkroom *n* cuarto oscuro *m*.
darling *n*, *adj* querido *m*.
darn *vt* zurcir.
dart *n* dardo *m*.
dartboard *n* diana *f*.
dash *vi* irse de prisa; * *n* pizca *f*; at one ~ de un golpe.
dashboard *n* tablero de instrumentos *m*.
dashing *adj* gallardo/da.
dastardly *adj* cobarde.
data *n* datos *mpl*.
database *n* base de datos *f*.
data processing *n* proceso de datos *m*.
date *n* fecha *f*; cita *f*; (*bot*) dátil *m*; * *vt* fechar; salir con.
dated *adj* anticuado/da.
dative *n* dativo *m*.
daub *vt* manchar.
daughter *n* hija *f*; ~ in-law nuera *f*.
daunting *adj* desalentador/a.
dawdle *vi* gastar tiempo.
dawn *n* alba *f*; * *vi* amanecer.
day *n* día *m*; luz *f*; by ~ de día; ~ by ~ de día en día.
daybreak *n* alba *f*.
day labourer *n* jornalero *m*.
daylight *n* luz del día, luz natural *f*; ~ saving time *n* hora de verano *f*.
daytime *n* día *m*.
daze *vt* aturdir.
dazed *adj* aturdido/da.
dazzle *vt* deslumbrar.
dazzling *adj* deslumbrante.
deacon *n* diácono *m*.
dead *adj* muerto/ta, marchito/ta; ~wood *n* lastre *m*; ~ silence *n* silencio profundo *m*; the ~ *npl* los muertos.
dead-drunk *adj* borracho como una cuba.
deaden *vt* amortiguar.
dead heat *n* empate *m*.
deadline *n* fecha tope *f*.
deadlock *n* punto muerto *m*.
deadly *adj* mortal; * *adv* terriblemente.
dead march *n* marcha fúnebre *f*.
deadness *n* inercia *f*.
deaf *adj* sordo/da.
deafen *vt* ensordecer.
deaf-mute *n* sordomudo/da *m/f*.

**deafness** n sordera f.

**deal** n convenio m; transacción f; **a great ~** mucho; **a good ~** bastante; * vt distribuir; dar; * vi comerciar; **to ~ in/with** tratar en/con.

**dealer** n comerciante m/f; traficante m/f; mano f.

**dealings** npl trato m.

**dean** n deán m.

**dear** adj querido/da, caro/ra, costoso/sa; **~ly** adv caro.

**dearness** n carestía f.

**dearth** n escasez f.

**death** n muerte f.

**deathbed** n lecho de muerte m.

**deathblow** n golpe mortal m.

**death certificate** n partida de defunción f.

**death penalty** n pena de muerte f.

**death throes** npl agonía f.

**death warrant** n sentencia de muerte f.

**debacle** n desastre m.

**debar** vt excluir, no admitir.

**debase** vt degradar.

**debasement** n degradación f.

**debatable** adj discutible.

**debate** n debate m; polémica f; * vt discutir; examinar.

**debauched** adj vicioso/sa.

**debauchery** n libertinaje m.

**debilitate** vt debilitar.

**debit** n debe m; * vt (com) cargar en una cuenta.

**debt** n deuda f; obligación f; **to get into ~** contraer deudas.

**debtor** n deudor/a m/f.

**debunk** vt desacreditar.

**decade** n década f.

**decadence** n decadencia f.

**decaffeinated** adj descafeinado/da.

**decanter** n garrafa f.

**decapitate** vt decapitar, degollar.

**decapitation** n decapitación f.

**decay** vi decaer; pudrirse; * n decadencia f; caries f.

**deceased** adj muerto/ta.

**deceit** n engaño m.

**deceitful** adj engañoso/sa; **~ly** adv falsamente.

**deceive** vt engañar.

**December** n diciembre m.

**decency** n decencia f; modestia f.

**decent** adj decente, razonable; **~ly** adv decentemente.

**deception** n engaño m.

**deceptive** adj engañoso/sa.

**decibel** n decibelio m.

**decide** vt, vi decidir; resolver.

**decided** adj decidido/da.

**decidedly** adv decididamente.

**deciduous** adj (bot) de hoja caduca.

**decimal** adj decimal.

**decimate** vt diezmar.

**decipher** vt descifrar.

**decision** n decisión, determinación f.

**decisive** adj decisivo/va; **~ly** adv de modo decisivo.

**deck** n cubierta f; * vt adornar.

**deckchair** n tumbona f.

**declaim** vi declamar.

**declamation** n declamación f.

**declaration** n declaración f.

**declare** vt declarar, manifestar.

**declension** n declinación f.

**decline** vt (gr) declinar; evitar; * vi decaer; * n decadencia f.

**declutch** vi desembragar.

**decode** vt descifrar.

**decoder** n (TV) descodificador m.

**decompose** vt descomponer.

**decomposition** n descomposición f.

**decor** n decoración f.

**decorate** vt decorar, adornar.

**decoration** n decoración f.

**decorative** adj decorativo/va.

**decorator** n pintor (decorador) m.

**decorous** adj decoroso/sa; **~ly** adv decorosamente.

**decorum** n decoro, garbo m.

**decoy** n señuelo m.

**decrease** vt disminuir; * n disminución f.

**decree** n decreto m; * vt decretar; ordenar.

**decrepit** adj decrépito/ta.

**decry** vt desacreditar, censurar.

**dedicate** vt dedicar; consagrar.

**dedication** n dedicación f; dedicatoria f.

**deduce** vt deducir; concluir.

**deduct** vt restar.

**deduction** n deducción f; descuento m.

**deed** n acción f; hecho m; hazaña f.

**deem** vi juzgar.

**deep** adj profundo/da.

**deepen** vt profundizar.

**deep-freeze** n congeladora f.

**deeply** adv profundamente.

**deepness** n profundidad f.

**deer** n ciervo m.

**deface** vt desfigurar, afear.

**defacement** n desfiguración f.

**defamation** n difamación f.

**default** n defecto m; falta f; * vi faltar.

**defaulter** n (law) moroso/sa m/f.
**defeat** n derrota f; * vt derrotar; frustrar.
**defect** n defecto m; falta f.
**defection** n deserción f.
**defective** adj defectuoso/sa.
**defend** vt defender; proteger.
**defendant** n acusado/da m/f.
**defence** n defensa f; protección f.
**defenceless** adj indefenso/sa.
**defensive** adj defensivo/va; ~ly adv de modo defensivo.
**defer** vt aplazar.
**deference** n deferencia f; respeto m.
**deferential** adj respetuoso/sa.
**defiance** n desafío m.
**defiant** adj insolente.
**deficiency** n defecto m; falta f.
**deficient** adj insuficiente.
**deficit** n déficit m.
**defile** vt ensuciar.
**definable** adj definible.
**define** vt definir.
**definite** adj definido/da; preciso/sa; ~ly adv no cabe duda.
**definition** n definición f.
**definitive** adj definitivo/va; ~ly adv definitivamente.
**deflate** vt desinflar.
**deflect** vt desviar.
**deflower** vt desvirgar.
**deform** vt desfigurar.
**deformity** n deformidad f.
**defraud** vt estafar.
**defray** vt costear.
**defrost** vt deshelar; descongelar.
**defroster** n luneta térmica f.
**deft** adj diestro/tra; ~ly adv hábilmente.
**defunct** adj difunto/ta.
**defuse** vt desactivar.
**degenerate** vi degenerar; * adj degenerado/da.
**degeneration** n degeneración f.
**degradation** n degradación f.
**degrade** vt degradar.
**degree** n grado m; título m.
**dehydrated** adj deshidratado/da.
**de-ice** vt deshelar.
**deign** vi dignarse.
**deity** n deidad, divinidad f.
**dejected** adj desanimado/da.
**dejection** n desaliento m.
**delay** vt demorar; * n retraso m.
**delectable** adj deleitoso/sa.
**delegate** vt delegar; * n delegado m.
**delegation** n delegación f.

**delete** vt tachar; borrar.
**deliberate** vt deliberar; * adj intencionado/da; ~ly adv a propósito.
**deliberation** n deliberación f.
**deliberative** adj deliberativo/va.
**delicacy** n delicadeza f.
**delicate** adj delicado/da; exquisito/ta; ~ly adv delicadamente.
**delicious** adj delicioso/sa; exquisito/ta; ~ly adv deliciosamente.
**delight** n delicia f; gozo, encanto m; * vt (vi) deleitar(se).
**delighted** adj encantado/da.
**delightful** adj encantador/a; ~ly adv en forma encantadora.
**delineate** vt delinear.
**delineation** n delineación f.
**delinquency** n delincuencia f.
**delinquent** n delincuente m/f.
**delirious** adj delirante.
**delirium** n delirio m.
**deliver** vt entregar; pronunciar.
**deliverance** n liberación f.
**delivery** n entrega f; parto m.
**delude** vt engañar.
**deluge** n diluvio m.
**delusion** n engaño m; ilusión f.
**delve** vi hurgar.
**demagogue** n demagogo/a m/f.
**demand** n demanda f; reclamación f; * vt exigir; reclamar.
**demanding** adj exigente.
**demarcation** n demarcación f.
**demean** vi rebajarse.
**demeanour** n conducta f.
**demented** adj demente.
**demise** n desaparición f.
**democracy** n democracia f.
**democrat** n demócrata m/f.
**democratic** adj democrático/ca.
**demolish** vt demoler.
**demolition** n demolición f.
**demon** n demonio, diablo m.
**demonstrable** adj demostrable; ~bly adv manifiestamente.
**demonstrate** vt demostrar, probar; * vi manifestarse.
**demonstration** n demostración f; manifestación f.
**demonstrative** adj demostrativo/va.
**demonstrator** n manifestante m/f.
**demoralization** n desmoralización f.
**demoralize** vt desmoralizar.
**demote** vt degradar.
**demur** vi objetar.

**demure** *adj* modesto/ta; **~ly** *adv* modestamente.

**den** *n* guarida *f.*

**denatured alcohol** *n* alcohol desnaturalizado *m.*

**denial** *n* negación *f.*

**denims** *npl* vaqueros *mpl.*

**denomination** *n* valor *m.*

**denominator** *n* (*math*) denominador *m.*

**denote** *vt* denotar, indicar.

**denounce** *vt* denunciar.

**dense** *adj* denso/sa, espeso/sa.

**density** *n* densidad *f.*

**dent** *n* abolladura *f*; * *vt* abollar.

**dental** *adj* dental.

**dentifrice** *n* dentífrico *m.*

**dentist** *n* dentista *m/f.*

**dentistry** *n* odontología *f.*

**denture** *npl* dentadura postiza *f.*

**denude** *vt* desnudar, despojar.

**denunciation** *n* denuncia *f.*

**deny** *vt* negar.

**deodorant** *n* desodorante *m.*

**deodorize** *vt* desodorizar.

**depart** *vi* partir.

**department** *n* departamento *m.*

**department store** *n* gran almacén *m.*

**departure** *n* partida *f.*

**departure lounge** *n* sala de embarque *f.*

**depend** *vi* depender; **~ on/upon** contar con.

**dependable** *adj* seguro/ra, serio/ria.

**dependant** *n* dependiente *m.*

**dependency** *n* dependencia *f.*

**dependent** *adj* dependiente.

**depict** *vt* pintar, retratar; describir.

**depleted** *adj* reducido/da.

**deplorable** *adj* deplorable, lamentable; **~bly** *adv* deplorablemente.

**deplore** *vt* deplorar, lamentar.

**deploy** *vt* (*mil*) desplegar.

**depopulated** *adj* despoblado/da.

**depopulation** *n* despoblación *f.*

**deport** *vt* deportar.

**deportation** *n* deportación *f*; destierro *m.*

**deportment** *n* conducta *f.*

**deposit** *vt* depositar; * *n* depósito *m*; yacimiento *m.*

**deposition** *n* deposición *f.*

**depositor** *n* depositante *m.*

**depot** *n* depósito *m.*

**deprave** *vt* depravar, corromper.

**depraved** *adj* depravado/da.

**depravity** *n* depravación *f.*

**deprecate** *vt* lamentar.

**depreciate** *vi* depreciarse.

**depreciation** *n* depreciación *f.*

**depredation** *n* pillaje *m.*

**depress** *vt* deprimir.

**depressed** *adj* deprimido/da.

**depression** *n* depresión *f.*

**deprivation** *n* privación *f.*

**deprive** *vt* privar.

**deprived** *adj* necesitado/da.

**depth** *n* profundidad *f.*

**deputation** *n* diputación *f.*

**depute** *vt* diputar, delegar.

**deputize** *vi* suplir a.

**deputy** *n* diputado/da *m/f.*

**derail** *vt* descarrilar.

**deranged** *adj* trastornado/da.

**derelict** *adj* abandonado/da.

**deride** *vt* burlar.

**derision** *n* mofa *f.*

**derisive** *adj* irrisorio/ria.

**derivable** *adj* deducible.

**derivation** *n* derivación *f.*

**derivative** *n* derivado *m.*

**derive** *vt* (*vi*) derivar(se).

**dermatologist** *n* dermatólogo/ga *m/f.*

**dermatology** *n* dermatología *f.*

**derogatory** *adj* despectivo/va.

**derrick** *n* torre de perforación *f.*

**desalinate** *vt* desalinizar.

**desalination plant** *n* desalinizadora *f.*

**descant** *n* (*mus*) discante *m.*

**descend** *vi* descender.

**descendant** *n* descendiente *m.*

**descent** *n* descenso *m.*

**describe** *vt* describir.

**description** *n* descripción *f.*

**descriptive** *adj* descriptivo/va.

**descry** *vt* divisar.

**desecrate** *vt* profanar.

**desecration** *n* profanación *f.*

**desert**[1] *n* desierto *m*; * *adj* desierto/ta.

**desert**[2] *vt* abandonar; desertar; * *n* mérito *m.*

**deserter** *n* desertor/a *m/f.*

**desertion** *n* deserción *f.*

**deserve** *vt* merecer; ser digno/na.

**deservedly** *adv* merecidamente.

**deserving** *adj* meritorio/ria.

**deshabille, dishabille** *n* deshabillé *m.*

**desideratum** *n* desiderátum *m.*

**design** *vt* diseñar; * *n* diseño *m*; dibujo *m.*

**designate** *vt* nombrar; designar.

**designation** *n* designación *f.*

**designedly** *adv* a propósito.

**designer** *n* diseñador *m*; modisto *m.*

**desirability** *n* conveniencia *f.*

**desirable** *adj* deseable.

**desire** n deseo m; * vt desear.
**desirous** adj deseoso/sa, ansioso/sa.
**desist** vi desistir.
**desk** n escritorio m.
**desktop publishing** n autoedición f.
**desolate** adj desierto/ta.
**desolation** n desolación f.
**despair** n desesperación f; * vi desesperarse.
**despairingly** adj desesperadamente.
**despatch = dispatch**.
**desperado** n bandido/da m/f.
**desperate** adj desesperado/da; ~ly adv desesperadamente; sumamente.
**desperation** n desesperación f.
**despicable** adj despreciable.
**despise** vt despreciar.
**despite** prep a pesar de.
**despoil** vt despojar.
**despondency** n abatimiento m.
**despondent** adj abatido/da.
**despot** n déspota m/f.
**despotic** adj despótico/ca, absoluto/ta; ~ally adv despóticamente.
**despotism** n despotismo m.
**dessert** n postre m.
**destination** n destino m.
**destine** vt destinar.
**destiny** n destino m; suerte f.
**destitute** adj indigente.
**destitution** n miseria f.
**destroy** vt destruir, arruinar.
**destruction** n destrucción, ruina f.
**destructive** adj destructivo/va.
**desultory** adj irregular; sin método.
**detach** vt separar.
**detachable** adj desmontable; de quita-pón.
**detachment** n (mil) destacamento m.
**detail** n detalle m; **in ~** detalladamente; * vt detallar.
**detain** vt retener; detener.
**detect** vt detectar.
**detection** n descubrimiento m.
**detective** n detective m/f.
**detector** n detector m.
**detention** n detención f.
**deter** vt disuadir.
**detergent** n detergente m.
**deteriorate** vt deteriorar.
**deterioration** n deterioro m.
**determination** n resolución f.
**determine** vt determinar, decidir.
**determined** adj resuelto/ta.
**deterrent** n fuerza de disuasión f.
**detest** vt detestar, aborrecer.

**detestable** adj detestable, abominable.
**dethrone** vt destronar.
**dethronement** n destronamiento m.
**detonate** vi detonar.
**detonation** n detonación f.
**detour** n desviación f.
**detract** vt desvirtuar.
**detriment** n perjuicio m.
**detrimental** adj perjudicial.
**deuce** n deuce m.
**devaluation** n devaluación f.
**devastate** vt devastar.
**devastating** adj devastador.
**devastation** n devastación, ruina f.
**develop** vt desarrollar.
**development** n desarrollo m.
**deviate** vi desviarse.
**deviation** n desviación f.
**device** n mecanismo m.
**devil** n diablo, demonio m.
**devilish** adj diabólico/ca; ~ly adv diabólica-mente.
**devious** adj taimado/da.
**devise** vt inventar; idear.
**devoid** adj desprovisto/ta.
**devolve** vt delegar.
**devote** vt dedicar; consagrar.
**devoted** adj fiel.
**devotee** n partidario/a m/f.
**devotion** n devoción f.
**devotional** adj devoto/ta.
**devour** vt devorar.
**devout** adj devoto/ta, piadoso/sa; ~ly adv piadosamente.
**dew** n rocío m.
**dewy** adj rociado/da.
**dexterity** n destreza f.
**dexterous** adj diestro/tra, hábil.
**diabetes** n diabetes f.
**diabetic** n diabético/ca m/f.
**diabolic** adj diabólico/ca; ~ally adv diabólicamente.
**diadem** n diadema f.
**diagnosis** n (med) diagnóstico m.
**diagnostic** adj, n diagnóstico m; ~s pl diagnóstica f.
**diagonal** adj, n diagonal f; ~ly adv diagonalmente.
**diagram** n diagrama m.
**dial** n cuadrante m; disco m.
**dialect** n dialecto m.
**dialling code** n prefijo m.
**dialling tone** n tono de marcar m.
**dialogue** n diálogo m.
**diameter** n diámetro m.

**diametrical** *adj* diametral; **~ly** *adv* diametralmente.

**diamond** *n* diamante *m*.

**diamond-cutter** *n* diamantista *m/f*.

**diamonds** *npl* (cards) diamantes *mpl*.

**diaphragm** *n* diafragma *m*.

**diarrhoea** *n* diarrea *f*.

**diary** *n* diario *m*.

**dice** *npl* dados *mpl*.

**dictate** *vt* dictar; * *n* dictado *m*.

**dictation** *n* dictado *m*.

**dictatorial** *adj* autoritativo/va, magistral.

**dictatorship** *n* dictadura *f*.

**diction** *n* dicción *f*

**dictionary** *n* diccionario *m*.

**didactic** *adj* didáctico/ca.

**die**[1] *vi* morir; **to ~ away** perderse; **to ~ down** apagarse.

**die**[2] *n* dado *m*.

**diehard** *n* reaccionario/ria *m/f*.

**diesel** *n* diesel *m*.

**diet** *n* dieta *f*; régimen *m*; * *vi* estar a dieta.

**dietary** *adj* dietético/ca.

**differ** *vi* diferenciarse.

**difference** *n* diferencia, disparidad *f*.

**different** *adj* diferente; **~ly** *adv* diferentemente.

**differentiate** *vt* diferenciar.

**difficult** *adj* difícil.

**difficulty** *n* dificultad *f*.

**diffidence** *n* timidez *f*.

**diffident** *adj* desconfiado/da; **~ly** *adv* desconfiadamente.

**diffraction** *n* difracción *f*.

**diffuse** *vt* difundir, esparcir; * *adj* difuso/sa.

**diffusion** *n* difusión *f*.

**dig** *vt* cavar; **to ~ ditches** zanjar; * *n* empujón *m*.

**digest** *vt* digerir.

**digestible** *adj* digerible.

**digestion** *n* digestión *f*.

**digestive** *adj* digestivo/va.

**digger** *n* excavadora *f*.

**digit** *n* dígito *m*.

**digital** *adj* digital.

**digitize** *vt* digitalizar.

**dignified** *adj* grave.

**dignitary** *n* dignatario *m*.

**dignity** *n* dignidad *f*.

**digress** *vi* divagar.

**digression** *n* digresión *f*.

**dike** *n* dique *m*.

**dilapidated** *adj* desmoronado/da.

**dilapidation** *n* ruina *f*.

**dilate** *vt* (*vi*) dilatar(se).

**dilemma** *n* dilema *m*.

**diligence** *n* diligencia *f*.

**diligent** *adj* diligente, asiduo/dua; **~ly** *adv* diligentemente.

**dilute** *vt* diluir.

**dim** *adj* turbio/bia; lerdo/da; oscuro/ra; * *vt* bajar.

**dime** *n* moneda de diez centavos *f*.

**dimension** *n* dimensión, extensión *f*.

**diminish** *vt* (*vi*) disminuir(se).

**diminution** *n* disminución *f*.

**diminutive** *n* diminutivo *m*.

**dimly** *adv* indistintamente.

**dimmer** *n* interruptor *m*.

**dimple** *n* hoyuelo *m*.

**din** *n* alboroto *m*.

**dine** *vi* cenar.

**dinghy** *n* lancha neumática *f*.

**dingy** *adj* sombrío/ría.

**dinner** *n* cena *f*.

**dinner-jacket** *n* smoking *m*.

**dinner time** *n* hora de comer *f*.

**dinosaur** *n* dinosaurio *m*.

**dint** *n*: **by ~ of** a fuerza de.

**diocese** *n* diócesis *f invar*.

**dip** *vt* mojar; * *n* zambullida *f*.

**diphtheria** *n* difteria *f*.

**diphthong** *n* diptongo *m*.

**diploma** *n* diploma *m*.

**diplomacy** *n* diplomacia *f*.

**diplomat** *n* diplomático/ca *m/f*.

**diplomatic** *adj* diplomático/ca.

**dipsomania** *n* dipsomanía *f*.

**dipstick** *n* (*auto*) varilla de nivel *f*.

**dire** *adj* calamitoso/sa.

**direct** *adj* directo/ta; * *vt* dirigir.

**direction** *n* dirección *f*; instrucción *f*.

**directly** *adj* directamente; inmediatamente.

**director** *n* director/a *m/f*.

**directory** *n* guía *f*.

**dirt** *n* suciedad *f*; **~ on clothes** zarpa *f*.

**dirtiness** *n* suciedad *f*.

**dirty** *adj* sucio/cia; vil, bajo/ja.

**disability** *n* discapacidad *f*.

**disabled** *adj* discapacitado/da.

**disabuse** *vt* desengañar.

**disadvantage** *n* desventaja *f*; * *vt* perjudicar.

**disadvantageous** *adj* desventajoso/sa.

**disaffected** *adj* descontento/ta.

**disagree** *vi* no estar de acuerdo.

**disagreeable** *adj* desagradable; **~bly** *adv* desagradablemente.

**disagreement** *n* desacuerdo *m*.

**disallow** *vt* rechazar.

**disappear** *vi* desaparecer; ausentarse.

**disappearance** *n* desaparición *f*.
**disappoint** *vt* decepcionar.
**disappointed** *adj* decepcionado/da.
**disappointing** *adj* decepcionante.
**disappointment** *n* decepción *f*.
**disapproval** *n* desaprobación, censura *f*.
**disapprove** *vt* desaprobar.
**disarm** *vt* desarmar.
**disarmament** *n* desarme *m*.
**disarray** *n* desarreglo *m*.
**disaster** *n* desastre *m*.
**disastrous** *adj* desastroso/sa, calamitoso/sa.
**disband** *vt* disolver.
**disbelief** *n* incredulidad *f*.
**disbelieve** *vt* desconfiar.
**disburse** *vt* desembolsar, pagar.
**disc, disk** *n* disco.
**discard** *vt* descartar.
**discern** *vt* discernir, percibir.
**discernible** *adj* perceptible.
**discerning** *adj* perspicaz.
**discernment** *n* perspicacia *f*.
**discharge** *vt* descargar; pagar (una deuda); cumplir; * *n* descarga *f*; descargo *m*.
**disciple** *n* discípulo/la *m/f*.
**discipline** *n* disciplina *f*, * *vt* disciplinar.
**disclaim** *vt* negar.
**disclaimer** *n* negación *f*.
**disclose** *vi* revelar.
**disclosure** *n* revelación *f*.
**discolour** *vt* descolorar.
**discolouration** *n* descolorimiento *m*.
**discomfort** *n* incomodidad *f*.
**disconcert** *vt* desconcertar.
**disconnect** *vt* desconectar.
**disconsolate** *adj* inconsolable; ~**ly** *adv* desconsoladamente.
**discontent** *n* descontento/ta *m/f*; * *adj* descontento/ta.
**discontented** *adj* descontento/ta.
**discontinue** *vi* interrumpir.
**discord** *n* discordia *f*.
**discordant** *adj* discordante.
**discotheque, disco** *n* discoteca *f*.
**discount** *n* descuento *m*; rebaja *f*; * *vt* descontar.
**discourage** *vt* desalentar, desanimar.
**discouraged** *adj* desalentado/da.
**discouragement** *n* desaliento *m*.
**discouraging** *adj* desalentador/a.
**discourse** *n* discurso *m*.
**discourteous** *adj* descortés, grosero/ra; ~**ly** *adv* descortésmente.
**discourtesy** *n* descortesía *f*.
**discover** *vt* descubrir.

**discovery** *n* descubrimiento *m*; revelación *f*.
**discredit** *vt* desacreditar.
**discreditable** *adj* ignominioso/sa.
**discreet** *adj* discreto/ta; ~**ly** *adv* discretamente.
**discrepancy** *n* discrepancia, diferencia *f*.
**discretion** *n* discreción *f*.
**discretionary** *adj* discrecional.
**discriminate** *vt* distinguir.
**discrimination** *n* discriminación *f*.
**discursive** *adj* discursivo/va.
**discuss** *vt* discutir.
**discussion** *n* discusión *f*.
**disdain** *vt* desdeñar; * *n* desdén, desprecio *m*.
**disdainful** *adj* desdeñoso/sa; ~**ly** *adv* desdeñosamente.
**disease** *n* enfermedad *f*.
**diseased** *adj* enfermo/ma.
**disembark** *vt*, *vi* desembarcar.
**disembarkation** *n* desembarco *m*.
**disenchant** *vt* desencantar.
**disenchanted** *adj* desilusionado/da.
**disenchantment** *n* desilusión *f*.
**disengage** *vt* soltar.
**disentangle** *vt* desenredar.
**disfigure** *vt* desfigurar, afear.
**disgrace** *n* ignominia *f*; escándalo *m*; * *vt* deshonrar.
**disgraceful** *adj* ignominioso/sa; ~**ly** *adv* vergonzosamente.
**disgruntled** *adj* descontento/ta.
**disguise** *vt* disfrazar; * *n* disfraz *m*.
**disgust** *n* aversión *f*; * *vt* repugnar.
**disgusting** *adj* repugnante.
**dish** *n* fuente *f*; plato *m*; taza *f*; * *vt* servir en fuente; **to ~ up** servir.
**dishcloth** *n* paño de cocina *m*.
**dishearten** *vt* desalentar.
**dishevelled** *adj* desarreglado/da.
**dishonest** *adj* deshonesto/ta; ~**ly** *adv* deshonestamente.
**dishonesty** *n* falta de honradez *f*.
**dishonour** *n* deshonra, ignominia *f*; * *vt* deshonrar.
**dishonourable** *adj* deshonroso/sa; ~**bly** *adv* deshonrosamente.
**dishtowel** *n* trapo de fregar *m*.
**dishwarmer** *n* escalfador *m*.
**dishwasher** *n* lavaplatos *m/f*; lavavajillas *m invar*.
**disillusion** *vt* desilusionar.
**disillusioned** *adj* desilusionado/da.
**disincentive** *n* freno *m*.
**disinclination** *n* aversión *f*.
**disinclined** *adj* reacio/cia.

**disinfect** *vt* desinfectar.
**disinfectant** *n* desinfectante *m*.
**disinherit** *vt* desheredar.
**disintegrate** *vi* disgregarse.
**disinterested** *adj* desinteresado/da; **~ly** *adv* desinteresadamente.
**disjointed** *adj* inconexo/xa.
**diskette** *n* disco, disquete *m*.
**dislike** *n* aversión *f*; * *vt* tener antipatía.
**dislocate** *vt* dislocar.
**dislocation** *n* dislocación *f*.
**dislodge** *vt, vi* desalojar.
**disloyal** *adj* desleal; **~ly** *adv* deslealmente.
**disloyalty** *n* deslealtad *f*.
**dismal** *adj* triste.
**dismantle** *vt* desmontar.
**dismay** *n* consternación *f*.
**dismember** *vt* despedazar.
**dismiss** *vt* despedir.
**dismissal** *n* despedida *f*.
**dismount** *vt* desmontar; * *vi* apearse.
**disobedience** *n* desobediencia *f*.
**disobedient** *adj* desobediente.
**disobey** *vt* desobedecer.
**disorder** *n* desorden *m*; confusión *f*.
**disorderly** *adj* desarreglado/da, confuso/sa.
**disorganization** *n* desorganización *f*.
**disorganized** *adj* desorganizado/da.
**disorientated** *adj* desorientado/da.
**disown** *vt* desconocer.
**disparage** *vt* despreciar.
**disparaging** *adj* despreciativo/va.
**disparity** *n* disparidad *f*.
**dispassionate** *adj* desapasionado/da.
**dispatch** *vt* enviar; * *n* envío *m*; informe *m*.
**dispel** *vt* disipar.
**dispensary** *n* dispensario *m*.
**dispense** *vt* dispensar; distribuir.
**disperse** *vt* dispersar.
**dispirited** *adj* desalentado/da.
**displace** *vt* desplazar.
**display** *vt* exponer; * *n* ostentación *f*; despliegue *m*.
**displeased** *adj* disgustado/da.
**displeasure** *n* disgusto *m*.
**disposable** *adj* desechable.
**disposal** *n* disposición *f*.
**dispose** *vt* disponer; arreglar.
**disposed** *adj* dispuesto/ta.
**disposition** *n* disposición *f*.
**dispossess** *vt* desposeer.
**disproportionate** *adj* desproporcionado/da.
**disprove** *vt* refutar.
**dispute** *n* disputa, controversia *f*; * *vt* disputar.

**disqualify** *vt* incapacitar.
**disquiet** *n* inquietud *f*.
**disquieting** *adj* inquietante.
**disquisition** *n* disquisición *f*.
**disregard** *vt* desatender; * *n* desdén *m*.
**disreputable** *adj* de mala fama.
**disrespect** *n* irreverencia *f*.
**disrespectful** *adj* irreverente; **~ly** *adv* irreverentemente.
**disrobe** *vt* desnudar.
**disrupt** *vt* interrumpir.
**disruption** *n* interrupción *f*.
**dissatisfaction** *n* descontento/ta, disgusto *m*.
**dissatisfied** *adj* insatisfecho/cha.
**dissect** *vt* disecar.
**dissection** *n* disección *f*.
**disseminate** *vt* diseminar.
**dissension** *n* disensión *f*.
**dissent** *vi* disentir; * *n* disensión *f*.
**dissenter** *n* disidente *m*.
**dissertation** *n* disertación *f*.
**dissident** *n* disidente *m*.
**dissimilar** *adj* distinto/ta.
**dissimilarity** *n* disimilitud *f*.
**dissimulation** *n* disimulo *m*.
**dissipate** *vt* disipar.
**dissipation** *n* disipación *f*.
**dissociate** *vt* disociar.
**dissolute** *adj* libertino/na.
**dissolution** *n* disolución *f*.
**dissolve** *vt* disolver; * *vi* disolverse, derretirse.
**dissonance** *n* disonancia *f*.
**dissuade** *vt* disuadir.
**distance** *n* distancia *f*; **at a ~** de lejos; * *vt* apartar.
**distant** *adj* distante.
**distaste** *n* disgusto *m*.
**distasteful** *adj* desagradable.
**distend** *vt* hinchar.
**distil** *vt* destilar.
**distillation** *n* destilación *f*.
**distillery** *n* destilería *f*.
**distinct** *adj* distinto/ta, diferente; claro/ra; **~ly** *adv* distintamente.
**distinction** *n* distinción *f*.
**distinctive** *adj* distintivo/va.
**distinctness** *n* claridad *f*.
**distinguish** *vt* distinguir; discernir.
**distort** *vt* retorcer.
**distorted** *adj* distorsionado/da.
**distortion** *n* distorsión *f*.
**distract** *vt* distraer.
**distracted** *adj* distraído/da; **~ly** *adj* distraídamente.

**distraction** *n* distracción *f*; confusión *f*.
**distraught** *adj* enloquecido/da.
**distress** *n* angustia *f*; * *vt* angustiar.
**distressing** *adj* penoso/sa.
**distribute** *vt* distribuir, repartir.
**distribution** *n* distribución *f*.
**distributor** *n* distribuidor *m*.
**district** *n* distrito *m*.
**distrustful** *adj* desconfiado/da; sospechoso/sa.
**disturb** *vt* molestar.
**disturbance** *n* disturbio *m*.
**disturbed** *adj* preocupado/da.
**disturbing** *adj* inquietante.
**disuse** *n* desuso *m*.
**disused** *adj* abandonado/da.
**ditch** *n* zanja *f*.
**dither** *vi* vacilar.
**ditto** *adv* ídem.
**ditty** *n* cancioneta *f*.
**diuretic** *adj* (*med*) diurético/ca.
**dive** *vi* bucear; *vr* zambullirse; sumergirse; * *n* zambullida *f*.
**diver** *n* buzo *m*.
**diverge** *vi* divergir.
**divergence** *n* divergencia *f*.
**divergent** *adj* divergente.
**diverse** *adj* diverso/sa, diferente; **~ly** *adv* diversamente.
**diversion** *n* diversión *f*.
**diversity** *n* diversidad *f*.
**divert** *vt* desviar; divertir.
**divest** *vt* desnudar; despojar.
**divide** *vt* dividir; * *vi* dividirse.
**dividend** *n* dividendo *m*.
**dividers** *npl* (*math*) compás de puntas *m*.
**divine** *adj* divino/na.
**divinity** *n* divinidad *f*.
**diving** *n* salto *m*; buceo *m*.
**diving board** *n* trampolín *m*.
**divisible** *adj* divisible.
**division** *n* (*math*) división *f*; desunión *f*.
**divisor** *n* (*math*) divisor *m*.
**divorce** *n* divorcio *m*; * *vi* divorciarse.
**divorced** *adj* divorciado/da.
**divulge** *vt* divulgar, publicar.
**dizziness** *n* vértigo *m*.
**dizzy** *adj* mareado/da.
**DJ** *n* pinchadiscos *m*.
**do** *vt* hacer, obrar.
**docile** *adj* dócil, apacible.
**dock** *n* muelle *m*; * *vi* atracar.
**docker** *n* estibador *m*.
**dockyard** *n* (*mar*) astillero *m*.
**doctor** *n* médico/ca *m/f*.

**doctrinal** *adj* doctrinal.
**doctrine** *n* doctrina *f*.
**document** *n* documento *m*.
**documentary** *adj* documental.
**dodge** *vt* esquivar.
**doe** *n* gama *f*; **~ rabbit** coneja *f*.
**dog** *n* perro *m*.
**dogged** *adj* tenaz; **~ly** *adv* tenazmente.
**dog kennel** *n* perrera *f*.
**dogmatic** *adj* dogmático/ca; **~ly** *adv* dogmáticamente.
**doings** *npl* hechos *mpl*; eventos *mpl*.
**do-it-yourself** *n* bricolaje *m*.
**doleful** *adj* lúgubre, triste.
**doll** *n* muñeca *f*.
**dollar** *n* dólar *m*.
**dolphin** *n* delfín *m*.
**domain** *n* campo *m*.
**dome** *n* cúpula *f*.
**domestic** *adj* doméstico/ca.
**domesticate** *vt* domesticar.
**domestication** *n* domesticación *f*.
**domesticity** *n* domesticidad *f*.
**domicile** *n* domicilio *m*.
**dominant** *adj* dominante.
**dominate** *vi* dominar.
**domination** *n* dominación *f*.
**domineer** *vi* dominar.
**domineering** *adj* dominante.
**dominion** *n* dominio *m*.
**dominoes** *npl* dominó *m*.
**donate** *vt* donar.
**donation** *n* donación *f*.
**done** *adj* hecho/cha; cocido/da.
**donkey** *n* asno, borrico *m*.
**donor** *n* donante *m/f*.
**doodle** *vi* garabatear.
**doom** *n* suerte *f*.
**door** *n* puerta *f*.
**doorbell** *n* timbre *m*.
**door handle** *n* tirador *m*.
**doorman** *n* portero *m*.
**doormat** *n* felpudo *m*.
**doorstep** *n* peldaño *m*.
**doorway** *n* entrada *f*.
**dormant** *adj* latente.
**dormer window** *n* buhardilla *f*.
**dormitory** *n* dormitorio *m*.
**dormouse** *n* lirón *m*.
**dosage** *n* dosis *f invar*.
**dose** *n* dosis *f invar*; * *vt* disponer la dosis de.
**dossier** *n* expediente *m*.
**dot** *n* punto *m*.
**dote** *vi* adorar.
**dotingly** *adv* con cariño excesivo.

**double** *adj* doble; * *vt* doblar; duplicar; * *n* doble *m*.

**double bed** *n* cama matrimonial *f*.

**double-breasted** *adj* cruzado/da.

**double chin** *n* papada *f*.

**double-dealing** *n* duplicidad *f*.

**double-edged** *adj* de doble filo.

**double entry** *n* (*com*) partida doble *f*.

**double-lock** *vt* echar la segunda vuelta a la llave a.

**double room** *n* habitación doble *f*.

**doubly** *adj* doblemente.

**doubt** *n* duda, sospecha *f*; * *vt* dudar; sospechar.

**doubtful** *adj* dudoso/sa.

**doubtless** *adv* sin duda.

**dough** *n* masa *f*.

**douse** *vt* apagar.

**dove** *n* paloma *f*.

**dovecot(e)** *n* palomar *m*.

**dowdy** *adj* mal vestido/da.

**down** *n* plumón *m*; flojel *m*; * *prep* abajo; **to sit ~** sentarse; **upside ~** al revés.

**downcast** *adj* cabizbajo/ja.

**downfall** *n* ruina *f*.

**downhearted** *adj* desanimado/da.

**downhill** *adv* cuesta abajo/ja.

**down payment** *n* entrada *f*.

**downpour** *n* aguacero *m*.

**downright** *adj* manifiesto/ta.

**downstairs** *adv* abajo/ja.

**down-to-earth** *adj* práctico/ca.

**downtown** *adv* al centro (de la ciudad).

**downward(s)** *adv* hacia abajo.

**dowry** *n* dote *f*.

**doze** *vi* dormitar.

**dozen** *n* docena *f*.

**dozy** *adj* somnoliento/ta.

**drab** *adj* gris.

**draft** *n* borrador *m*; quinta *f*; corriente de aire *f*.

**drafty** *adj* expuesto/ta al aire.

**drag** *vt* arrastrar; tirar con fuerza; * *n* lata *f*.

**dragnet** *n* red barredera *f*.

**dragon** *n* dragón *m*.

**dragonfly** *n* libélula *f*.

**drain** *vt* desaguar; secar; * *n* desaguadero *m*.

**drainage** *n* desagüe *m*.

**draining board** *n* escurridor *m*.

**drainpipe** *n* desagüe *m*.

**drake** *n* ánade macho *m*.

**dram** *n* traguito *m*.

**drama** *n* drama *m*.

**dramatic** *adj* dramático/ca; **~ally** *adv* dramáticamente.

**dramatist** *n* dramaturgo/ga *m/f*.

**dramatize** *vt* dramatizar.

**drape** *vt* cubrir; * *n* cortina *f*; telon *m* (en teatro); **~s** *npl* cortinas *fpl*.

**drastic** *adj* drástico/ca.

**draughtboard** *n* tablero de damas *m*.

**draughts** *npl* juego de damas *m*.

**draw** *vt* tirar; dibujar; **to ~ nigh** acercarse.

**drawback** *n* desventaja *f*.

**drawer** *n* cajón *m*.

**drawing** *n* dibujo *m*.

**drawing board** *n* tablero de dibujo *m*.

**drawing pin** *n* chincheta *f*.

**drawing room** *n* salón *m*.

**drawl** *vi* hablar con pesadez.

**dread** *n* terror, espanto *m*; * *vt* temer.

**dreadful** *adj* espantoso/sa; **~ly** *adv* terriblemente.

**dream** *n* sueño *m*; * *vi* sonar.

**dreary** *adj* triste.

**dredge** *vt* dragar.

**dregs** *npl* heces *fpl*.

**drench** *vt* empapar.

**dress** *vt* vestir; vendar; * *vi* vestirse; * *n* vestido *m*.

**dresser** *n* aparador *m*.

**dressing** *n* vendaje *m*; aliño *m*.

**dressing gown** *n* bata *f*.

**dressing room** *n* tocador *m*.

**dressing table** *n* tocador *m*.

**dressmaker** *n* modista *f*.

**dressy** *adj* elegante.

**dribble** *vi* caer gota a gota, babear.

**dribbling** *n* regateo *m*.

**dried** *adj* seco/ca.

**drift** *n* montón *m*; ventisquero *m*; significado *m*; * *vi* ir a la deriva.

**driftwood** *n* madera de deriva *f*.

**drill** *n* taladro *m*; (*mil*) instrucción *f*; * *vt* taladrar.

**drink** *vt, vi* beber; * *n* bebida *f*.

**drinkable** *adj* potable.

**drinker** *n* bebedor/a *m/f*.

**drinking bout** *n* borrachera *f*.

**drinking water** *n* agua potable *f*.

**drip** *vi* gotear; * *n* gota *f*; goteo *m*.

**dripping** *n* pringue *m/f*.

**drive** *vt* conducir, empujar; * *vi* conducir, manejar; * *n* paseo en coche *m*; entrada *f*.

**drivel** *n* baba *f*; * *vi* babear.

**driver** *n* conductor/a *m/f*; chofer *m*.

**driver's licence** *n* carnet *m* de conducir, carnet *m* de manejar.

**driveway** *n* entrada *f*.

**driving** *n* conducción *f*, manejo *m*.

**driving instructor** *n* profesor/a de auto-escuela *m/f*.
**driving school** *n* autoescuela *f*.
**driving test** *n* examen de conducir, examen de manejo *m*.
**drizzle** *vi* lloviznar.
**droll** *adj* gracioso/sa.
**drone** *n* zumbido *m*; zángano *m*.
**drool** *vi* babear.
**droop** *vi* decaer.
**drop** *n* gota *f*; * *vt* dejar caer; * *vi* bajar; **to ~ out** retirarse.
**drop-out** *n* marginado *m*.
**dropper** *n* cuentagotas *m invar*.
**dross** *n* escoria *f*.
**drought** *n* sequía *f*.
**drove** *n*: **in ~s** en tropel.
**drown** *vt* anegar; * *vi* anegarse.
**drowsiness** *n* somnolencia *f*.
**drowsy** *adj* somnoliento/ta.
**drudgery** *n* trabajo monótono *m*; zurra *f*.
**drug** *n* droga *f*; * *vt* drogar.
**drug addict** *n* drogadicto/ta *m/f*.
**drug addiction** *n* drogadicción *f*.
**drug trafficker** *n* narcotraficante *m/f*.
**drum** *n* tambor *m*; **rural ~** zambomba *f*; * *vi* tocar el tambor.
**drum majorette** *n* batonista *f*.
**drummer** *n* batería *m*.
**drumstick** *n* palillo de tambor *m*.
**drunk** *adj* borracho/cha.
**drunkard** *n* borracho *m*.
**drunken** *adj* borracho/cha.
**drunkenness** *n* borrachera *f*.
**dry** *adj* seco/ca; * *vt* secar; * *vi* secarse.
**dry-cleaning** *n* lavado en seco *m*.
**dryness** *n* sequedad *f*.
**dry rot** *n* podredumbre *f*.
**dual** *adj* doble.
**dual-purpose** *adj* de doble uso.
**dubbed** *adj* doblado/da.
**dubious** *adj* dudoso/sa.
**duck** *n* pato *m*; * *vt* (*vr*) zambullir(se).
**duckling** *n* patito *m*.
**dud** *adj* estropeado/da.
**due** *adj* debido/da, apto/ta; * *adv* exacta-mente; * *n* derecho *m*.
**duel** *n* duelo *m*.
**duet** *n* (*mus*) dúo *m*.
**dull** *adj* lerdo/da; insípido/da; zopenco/ca; gris; * *vt* aliviar.
**duly** *adv* debidamente; puntualmente.
**dumb** *adj* mudo/da; **~ly** *adv* sin chistar.

**dumbbell** *n* pesa *f*.
**dumbfounded** *adj* pasmado/da.
**dummy** *n* chupete *m*.
**dump** *n* montón *m*; * *vt* dejar.
**dumping** *n* (*com*) dumping *m*.
**dumpling** *n* bola de masa *f*.
**dumpy** *adj* gordito/ta.
**dunce** *n* zopenco *m*.
**dune** *n* duna *f*.
**dung** *n* estiércol *m*.
**dungarees** *npl* mono *m*.
**dungeon** *n* calabozo *m*.
**dupe** *n* bobo *m*; * *vt* engañar, embaucar.
**duplex** *n* dúplex *m*.
**duplicate** *n* duplicado *m*; copia *f*; * *vt* multicopiar.
**duplicity** *n* duplicidad *f*.
**durability** *n* durabilidad *f*.
**durable** *adj* duradero/ra.
**duration** *n* duración *f*.
**during** *prep* mientras, durante el tiempo que.
**dusk** *n* crepúsculo *m*.
**dust** *n* polvo *m*; * *vt* desempolvar.
**dustbin** *n* cubo de la basura *m*.
**dustbin man**, **dustman** *n* basurero *m*.
**duster** *n* plumero *m*.
**dusty** *adj* polvoriento/ta.
**Dutch courage** *n* valor fingido *m*.
**duteous** *adj* fiel, leal.
**dutiful** *adj* obediente, sumiso/sa; **~ly** *adv* obedientemente.
**duty** *n* deber *m*; obligación *f*.
**duty-free** *adj* libre de derechos de aduana.
**dwarf** *n* enano *m*; enana *f*; * *vt* em-pequeñecer.
**dwell** *vi* habitar, morar.
**dwelling** *n* habitación *f*; domicilio *m*.
**dwindle** *vi* mermar, disminuirse.
**dye** *vt* teñir; * *n* tinte *m*.
**dyer** *n* tintorero/ra *m/f*.
**dyeing** *n* tintorería *f*; tintura *f*.
**dye-works** *npl* taller del tintorero *m*.
**dying** *adj* agonizante, moribundo/da; * *n* muerte *f*; **~ moments** postrimerías *fpl*.
**dynamic** *adj* dinámico/ca.
**dynamics** *n* dinámica *f*.
**dynamite** *n* dinamita *f*.
**dynamiter** *n* dinamitero/ra *m/f*.
**dynamo** *n* dinamo *f*.
**dynasty** *n* dinastía *f*.
**dysentery** *n* disentería *f*.
**dyspepsia** *n* (*med*) dispepsia *f*.
**dyspeptic** *adj* dispéptico/ca.

# E

**each** *pn* cada uno, cada una; ~ **other** unos a otros, unas a otras, mutuamente.

**eager** *adj* entusiasmado/da; **~ly** *adv* con entusiasmo.

**eagerness** *n* ansia *f*; anhelo *m*.

**eagle** *n* águila *f*.

**eagle-eyed** *adj* con vista de lince.

**eaglet** *n* aguilucho *m*.

**ear** *n* oreja *f*; oído *m*; espiga *f*; **by ~** de oreja.

**earache** *n* dolor de oídos *m*.

**eardrum** *n* tímpano (del oído) *m*.

**early** *adj* temprano/na; *adv* temprano.

**earmark** *vt* destinar a.

**earn** *vt* ganar; conseguir.

**earnest** *adj* serio/ria; en serio; **~ly** *adv* seriamente.

**earnestness** *n* seriedad *f*.

**earnings** *npl* ingresos *mpl*.

**earphones** *npl* auriculares *mpl*.

**earring** *n* zarcillo, pendiente *m*.

**earth** *n* tierra *f*; * *vt* conectar a tierra.

**earthen** *adj* de tierra.

**earthenware** *n* loza de barro *f*.

**earthquake** *n* terremoto *m*.

**earthworm** *n* lombriz *f*.

**earthy** *adj* sensual.

**earwig** *n* tijereta *f*.

**ease** *n* comodidad *f*; facilidad *f*; **at ~** con desahogo; * *vt* aliviar; mitigar.

**easel** *n* caballete *m*.

**easily** *adv* fácilmente.

**easiness** *n* facilidad *f*.

**east** *n* este *m*; oriente *m*.

**Easter** *n* Pascua de Resurrección; Semana Santa *f*.

**Easter egg** *n* huevo de Pascua *m*.

**easterly** *adj* del este.

**eastern** *adj* del este, oriental.

**eastward(s)** *adv* hacia el este.

**easy** *adj* fácil; cómodo/da, ~ **going** acomodadizo/za.

**easy chair** *n* sillón *m*.

**eat** *vt* comer; * *vi* alimentarse.

**eatable** *adj* comestible; * **~s** *npl* víveres *mpl*.

**eaves** *npl* alero *m*.

**eau de Cologne** *n* agua de Colonia *f*.

**eavesdrop** *vt* escuchar a escondidas.

**ebb** *n* reflujo *m*; * *vi* menguar; decaer, disminuir.

**ebony** *n* ébano *m*.

**eccentric** *adj* excéntrico/ca.

**eccentricity** *n* excentricidad *f*.

**ecclesiastic** *adj* eclesiástico/ca.

**echo** *n* eco *m*; * *vi* resonar, repercutir.

**eclectic** *adj* ecléctico/ca.

**eclipse** *n* eclipse *m*; * *vt* eclipsar.

**ecologist**, **environmentalist** *n* ecologista *m/f*.

**ecology** *n* ecología *f*.

**e-commerce** *n* comercio electrónico *m*.

**economic(al)** *adj* económico/ca, frugal, moderado/da.

**economics** *npl* economía *f*.

**economist** *n* economista *m/f*.

**economize** *vt* economizar.

**economy** *n* economía *f*; frugalidad *f*.

**ecosystem** *n* ecosistema *m*.

**ecotax** *n* ecotasa *f*.

**ecotourism** *n* ecoturismo *m*.

**ecstasy** *n* éxtasis *m*; rapto *m*.

**ecstatic** *adj* extático/ca; **~ally** *adv* en éxtasis.

**eczema** *n* eczema *m*.

**eddy** *n* reflujo de agua *m*; remolino *m*; * *vi* arremolinarse.

**edge** *n* filo *m*; punta *f*; margen *m/f*; acrimonia *f*; * *vt* ribetear; introducir.

**edgeways**, **edgewise** *adv* de lado.

**edging** *n* orla, orilla *f*.

**edgy** *adj* nervioso/sa.

**edible** *adj* comestible.

**edict** *n* edicto, mandato *m*.

**edification** *n* edificación *f*.

**edifice** *n* edificio *m*; fábrica *f*.

**edify** *vt* edificar.

**edit** *vt* dirigir; redactar; cortar.

**edition** *n* edición *f*; publicación *f*; impresión *f*.

**editor** *n* director/a *m/f*; redactor/a *m/f*.

**editorial** *adj*, *n* editorial *m*.

**educate** *vt* educar; enseñar.

**education** *n* educación *f*.

**eel** *n* anguila *f*.

**eerie** *adj* espeluznante.

**efface** *vt* borrar, destruir.

**effect** *n* efecto *m*; realidad *f*; **~s** *npl* efectos, bienes *mpl*; * *vt* efectuar, ejecutar.

**effective** *adj* eficaz; efectivo/va; **~ly** *adv* efectivamente, en efecto.

**effectiveness** *n* eficacia *f*.

**effectual** *adj* eficiente, eficaz; **~ly** *adv* eficazmente.

**effeminacy** *n* afeminación *f*.
**effeminate** *adj* afeminado/da.
**effervescence** *n* efervescencia *f*; hervor *m*.
**effete** *adj* estéril.
**efficacy** *n* eficacia *f*.
**efficiency** *n* eficiencia, virtud *f*.
**efficient** *adj* eficaz.
**effigy** *n* efigie, imagen *f*; retrato *m*.
**effort** *n* esfuerzo, empeño *m*.
**effortless** *adj* sin esfuerzo.
**effrontery** *n* descaro *m*; impudencia, desvergüenza *f*.
**effusive** *adj* efusivo/va.
**egg** *n* huevo *m*; * **to ~ on** *vt* animar.
**eggcup** *n* huevera *f*.
**eggplant** *n* berenjena *f*.
**eggshell** *n* cáscara de huevo *f*.
**ego(t)ism** *n* egoísmo *m*.
**ego(t)ist** *n* egoísta *m*/*f*.
**ego(t)istical** *adj* egotista.
**eiderdown** *n* edredón *m*.
**eight** *adj*, *n* ocho.
**eighteen** *adj*, *n* dieciocho.
**eighteenth** *adj*, *n* decimoctavo.
**eighth** *adj*, *n* octavo.
**eightieth** *adj*, *n* octogésimo/ma.
**eighty** *adj*, *n* ochenta.
**either** *pn* cualquiera; * *conj* o, sea, ya.
**ejaculate** *vt* exclamar; eyacular.
**ejaculation** *n* exclamación *f*; eyaculación *f*.
**eject** *vt* expeler, desechar.
**ejection** *n* expulsión *f*.
**ejector seat** *n* asiento eyectable *m*.
**eke** *vt* alargar; prolongar; hacer crecer.
**elaborate** *vt* elaborar; * *adj* elaborado/da; **~ly** *adv* cuidadosamente.
**elapse** *vi* pasar, correr (el tiempo).
**elastic** *adj* elástico/ca.
**elasticity** *n* elasticidad *f*.
**Elastoplast™** *n* Tirita™ *f*.
**elated** *adj* regocijado/da.
**elation** *n* regocijo *m*.
**elbow** *n* codo *m*; * *vt* codear.
**elbow-room** *n* anchura *f*; espacio suficiente *m*; (*fig*) libertad, latitud *f*.
**elder** *n* saúco *m* (árbol); * *adj* mayor.
**elderly** *adj* anciano/na.
**elders** *npl* ancianos, antepasados *mpl*.
**eldest** *adj* el mayor, la mayor.
**elect** *vt* elegir; * *adj* elegido/da, escogido/da.
**election** *n* elección *f*.
**electioneering** *n* electoralismo *m*.
**elective** *adj* facultativo/va.
**elector** *n* elector/a *m*/*f*.
**electoral** *adj* electoral.

**electorate** *n* electorado *m*.
**electric(al)** *adj* eléctrico/ca; **~ domestic appliance** electrodoméstico *m*.
**electric blanket** *n* manta eléctrica *f*.
**electric cooker** *n* cocina eléctrica *f*.
**electric fire** *n* estufa eléctrica *f*.
**electrician** *n* electricista *m*/*f*.
**electricity** *n* electricidad *f*.
**electrify** *vt* electrizar.
**electrocardiogram** *n* electrocardiograma *m*.
**electron** *n* electrón *m*.
**electronic** *adj* electrónico/ca; **~s** *npl* electrónica *f*.
**elegance** *n* elegancia *f*.
**elegant** *adj* elegante, delicado/da; **~ly** *adv* elegantemente.
**elegy** *n* elegía *f*.
**element** *n* elemento *m*; fundamento *m*.
**elemental**, **elementary** *adj* elemental.
**elephant** *n* elefante *m*.
**elephantine** *adj* inmenso/sa.
**elevate** *vt* elevar, alzar, exaltar.
**elevation** *n* elevación *f*; altura *f*; alteza (de pensamientos) *f*.
**elevator** *n* ascensor *m*.
**eleven** *adj*, *n* once.
**eleventh** *adj*, *n* undécimo.
**elf** *n* duende *m*.
**elicit** *vt* sacar de.
**eligibility** *n* elegibilidad *f*.
**eligible** *adj* elegible.
**eliminate** *vt* eliminar, descartar.
**elk** *n* alce *m*.
**elliptic(al)** *adj* elíptico/ca.
**elm** *n* olmo *m*.
**elocution** *n* elocución *f*.
**elocutionist** *n* profesor de elocución *m*.
**elongate** *vt* alargar.
**elope** *vi* escapar, huir, evadirse.
**elopement** *n* fuga, huida, evasión *f*.
**eloquence** *n* elocuencia *f*.
**eloquent** *adj* elocuente; **~ly** *adv* elocuentemente.
**else** *pn* otro/ra.
**elsewhere** *adv* en otra parte.
**elucidate** *vt* explicar.
**elucidation** *n* elucidación, explicación *f*.
**elude** *vt* eludir, evitar.
**elusive** *adj* esquivo/va.
**emaciated** *adj* demacrado/da.
**e-mail** *n* correo electrónico *m*.
**emanate (from)** *vi* emanar.
**emancipate** *vt* emancipar; dar libertad.
**emancipation** *n* emancipación *f*.

**embalm** *vt* embalsamar.
**embankment** *n* terraplén *m*.
**embargo** *n* embargo *m*.
**embark** *vt* embarcar.
**embarkation** *n* embarque *m*.
**embarrass** *vt* avergonzar.
**embarrassed** *adj* avergonzado/da.
**embarrassing** *adj* violento/ta; embarazoso/sa.
**embarrassment** *n* desconcierto *m*.
**embassy** *n* embajada *f*.
**embed** *vt* empotrar; clavar.
**embellish** *vt* hermosear, adornar.
**embellishment** *n* adorno *m*.
**embers** *npl* rescoldo *m*.
**embezzle** *vt* desfalcar.
**embezzlement** *n* desfalco *m*.
**embitter** *vt* amargar.
**emblem** *n* emblema *m*.
**emblematic(al)** *adj* emblemático/ca, simbólico/ca.
**embodiment** *n* incorporación *f*.
**embody** *vt* incorporar.
**embrace** *vt* abrazar; contener; * *n* abrazo *m*.
**embroider** *vt* bordar.
**embroidery** *n* bordado *m*; bordadura *f*.
**embroil** *vt* embrollar; confundir.
**embryo** *n* embrión *m*.
**emendation** *n* enmienda, corrección *f*.
**emerald** *n* esmeralda *f*.
**emerge** *vi* salir, proceder.
**emergency** *n* emergencia *f*; necesidad urgente *f*.
**emergency cord** *n* timbre de alarma *m*.
**emergency exit** *n* salida de emergencia *f*.
**emergency landing** *n* aterrizaje forzoso *m*.
**emergency meeting** *n* reunión extraordinaria *f*.
**emery** *n* esmeril *m*.
**emigrant** *n* emigrante *m/f*.
**emigrate** *vi* emigrar.
**emigration** *n* emigración *f*.
**eminence** *n* altura *f*; eminencia, excelencia *f*.
**eminent** *adj* eminente, elevado/da; distinguido/da; **~ly** *adv* eminentemente.
**emission** *n* emisión *f*.
**emit** *vt* emitir; arrojar, despedir.
**emolument** *n* emolumento, provecho *m*.
**emotion** *n* emoción *f*.
**emotional** *adj* emocional.
**emotive** *adj* emotivo/va.
**emperor** *n* emperador *m*.
**emphasis** *n* énfasis *m*.
**emphasize** *vt* hablar con énfasis.

**emphatic** *adj* enfático/ca; **~ally** *adv* enfáticamente.
**empire** *n* imperio *m*.
**employ** *vt* emplear, ocupar.
**employee** *n* empleado/da *m/f*.
**employer** *n* patrón *m*; empresario/ria *m/f*.
**employment** *n* empleo *m*; trabajo *m*.
**emporium** *n* emporio *m*.
**empress** *n* emperatriz *f*.
**emptiness** *n* vaciedad *f*; futilidad *f*.
**empty** *adj* vacío/cia; vano/na; ignorante; * *vt* vaciar, evacuar.
**empty-handed** *adj* con las manos vacías.
**emulate** *vt* emular, competir; imitar.
**emulsion** *n* emulsión *f*.
**enable** *vt* capacitar.
**enact** *vt* promulgar; representar; hacer.
**enamel** *n* esmalte *m*; * *vt* esmaltar.
**enamour** *vt* enamorar.
**encamp** *vi* acamparse.
**encampment** *n* campamento *m*.
**encase** *vt* encajar, encajonar.
**enchant** *vt* encantar.
**enchanting** *adj* encantador/a.
**enchantment** *n* encanto *m*.
**encircle** *vt* cercar, circundar.
**enclose** *vt* cercar, circunvalar, circundar; incluir.
**enclosure** *n* cercamiento *m*; cercado *m*.
**encompass** *vt* abarcar.
**encore** *adv* otra vez, de nuevo.
**encounter** *n* encuentro *m*; duelo *m*; pelea *f*; * *vt* encontrar.
**encourage** *vt* animar, alentar.
**encouragement** *n* estímulo, patrocinio *m*.
**encroach** *vt* usurpar, avanzar gradualmente.
**encroachment** *n* usurpación, intrusión *f*.
**encrusted** *adj* incrustado/da.
**encumber** *vt* embarazar, cargar.
**encumbrance** *n* embarazo, impedimento *m*.
**encyclical** *adj* encíclico/ca, circular.
**encyclopaedia** *n* enciclopedia *f*.
**end** *n* fin *m*; extremidad *f*; término *m*; resolución *f*; **to the ~ that** para que; **to no ~** en vano; **on ~** en pie, de pie; * *vt* terminar, concluir, fenecer; * *vi* acabar, terminar.
**endanger** *vt* peligrar, arriesgar.
**endear** *vt* encarecer.
**endearing** *adj* simpático/ca.
**endearment** *n* ternura *f*.
**endeavour** *vi* esforzarse; intentar; * *n* esfuerzo *m*.
**endemic** *adj* endémico/ca.

**ending** *n* conclusión; *f*; desenlace *m*; terminación *f*.

**endive** *n* (*bot*) endibia *f*.

**endless** *adj* infinito/ta, perpetuo/tua; **~ly** *adv* sin fin, perpetuamente.

**endorse** *vt* endosar; aprobar.

**endorsement** *n* endoso *m*; aprobación *f*.

**endow** *vt* dotar.

**endowment** *n* dote, dotación *f*.

**endurable** *adj* sufrible, tolerable.

**endurance** *n* duración *f*; paciencia *f*; sufrimiento *m*.

**endure** *vt* sufrir, soportar; * *vi* durar.

**endways, endwise** *adv* de punta, derecho.

**enemy** *n* enemigo/ga, antagonista *m/f*.

**energetic** *adj* enérgico/ca, vigoroso/sa.

**energy** *n* energía, fuerza *f*; **renewable forms of ~** energía renovables.

**enervate** *vt* enervar, debilitar.

**enfeeble** *vt* debilitar.

**enfold** *vt* envolver.

**enforce** *vt* hacer cumplir.

**enforced** *adj* forzoso/sa.

**enfranchise** *vt* emancipar.

**engage** *vt* llamar; abordar; contratar.

**engaged** *adj* prometido/da.

**engagement** *n* empeño *m*; combate *m*; pelea *f*; obligación *f*.

**engagement ring** *n* anillo de prometida *m*.

**engaging** *adj* atractivo/va.

**engender** *vt* engendrar; producir.

**engine** *n* motor *m*; locomotora *f*.

**engine driver** *n* maquinista *m/f*.

**engineer** *n* ingeniero/ra *m/f*, maquinista *m/f*.

**engineering** *n* ingeniería *f*.

**engrave** *vt* grabar; esculpir; tallar.

**engraving** *n* grabado *m*; estampa *f*.

**engrossed** *adj* absorto/ta.

**engulf** *vt* sumergir.

**enhance** *vt* aumentar, realzar.

**enigma** *n* enigma *m*.

**enjoy** *vt* gozar; poseer.

**enjoyable** *adj* agradable; divertido/da.

**enjoyment** *n* disfrute *m*; placer *m*; fruición *f*.

**enlarge** *vt* engrandecer, dilatar, extender.

**enlargement** *n* aumento *m*; ampliación *f*, soltura *f*.

**enlighten** *vt* iluminar; instruir.

**enlightened** *adj* iluminado/da.

**Enlightenment** *n*: **the ~** el Siglo de las Luces *m*, la Ilustración *f*.

**enlist** *vt* alistar.

**enlistment** *n* alistamiento *m*.

**enliven** *vt* animar; avivar; alegrar.

**enmity** *n* enemistad *f*; odio *m*.

**enormity** *n* enormidad *f*; atrocidad *f*.

**enormous** *adj* enorme; **~ly** *adv* enormemente.

**enough** *adv* bastante; basta; * *n* bastante *m*.

**enounce** *vt* declarar.

**enquire, inquire** *vt*, *vi* preguntar; **to ~ about** informarse de; **to ~ after** *vt* preguntar por; **to ~ into** *vt* investigar, indagar, inquirir.

**enquiry, inquiry** *n* pesquisa *f*.

**enrage** *vt* enfurecer, irritar.

**enrapture** *vt* arrebatar, entusiasmar; encantar.

**enrich** *vt* enriquecer; adornar.

**enrichment** *n* enriquecimiento *m*.

**enrol** *vt* registrar; arrollar.

**enrolment** *n* inscripción *f*.

**en route** *adv* durante el viaje.

**ensign** *n* (*mil*) bandera *f*; abanderado *m*; (*mar*) alférez *m*.

**enslave** *vt* esclavizar, cautivar.

**ensue** *vi* seguirse; suceder.

**ensure** *vt* asegurar.

**entail** *vt* suponer.

**entangle** *vt* enmarañar, embrollar.

**entanglement** *n* enredo *m*.

**enter** *vt* entrar; admitir; registrar; **to ~ for** presentarse para; **to ~ into** establecer; formar parte de/en; firmar.

**enterprise** *n* empresa *f*.

**enterprising** *adj* emprendedor/a.

**entertain** *vt* divertir; hospedar; mantener.

**entertainer** *n* artista *m/f*.

**entertaining** *adj* divertido/da.

**entertainment** *n* entretenimiento, pasatiempo *m*.

**enthralled** *adj* encantado/da.

**enthralling** *adj* cautivador/a.

**enthrone** *vt* entronizar.

**enthusiasm** *n* entusiasmo *m*.

**enthusiast** *n* entusiasta *m/f*.

**enthusiastic** *adj* entusiasta.

**entice** *vt* tentar; seducir.

**entire** *adj* entero/ra, completo/ta, perfecto/ta; **~ly** *adv* enteramente.

**entitle** *vt* intitular; conferir algún derecho.

**entitled** *adj* titulado/da.

**entity** *n* entidad, existencia *f*.

**entourage** *n* séquito *m*.

**entrails** *npl* entrañas *fpl*; asadura *f*.

**entrance** *n* entrada *f*; admisión *f*; principio *m*.

**entrance examination** *n* examen de ingreso *m*.

**entrance fee** *n* cuota *f*.

**entrance hall** *n* pórtico, vestíbulo *m*.
**entrant** *n* participante *m*; candidato *m*.
**entrap** *vt* enredar; engañar.
**entreat** *vt* rogar, suplicar.
**entreaty** *n* petición, suplica, instancia *f*.
**entrepreneur** *n* empresario/ria *m/f*.
**entrust** *vt* confiar.
**entry** *n* entrada *f*.
**entry phone** *n* portero automático *m*.
**entwine** *vt* entrelazar, enroscar, torcer.
**enumerate** *vt* enumerar, numerar.
**enunciate** *vt* enunciar, declarar.
**enunciation** *n* enunciación *f*.
**envelop** *vt* envolver.
**envelope** *n* sobre *m*.
**enviable** *adj* envidiable.
**envious** *adj* envidioso/sa; ~**ly** *adv* envidiosamente.
**environment** *n* medio ambiente *m*.
**environmental** *adj* ambiental, medioambiental.
**environs** *npl* vecindad *f*; contornos *mpl*.
**envisage** *vt* prever; concebir.
**envoy** *n* enviado/da *m/f*; mensajero/ra *m/f*.
**envy** *n* envidia, malicia *f*; * *vt* envidiar.
**ephemeral** *adj* efímero/ra.
**epic** *adj* épico/ca; * *n* épica *f*.
**epidemic** *adj* epidémico/ca; * *n* epidemia *f*.
**epilepsy** *n* epilepsia *f*.
**epileptic** *adj* epiléptico/ca.
**epilogue** *n* epílogo *m*.
**Epiphany** *n* Epifanía *f*.
**episcopacy** *n* episcopado *m*.
**Episcopal** *adj* episcopal.
**Episcopalian** *n* anglicano/na *m/f*.
**episode** *n* episodio *m*.
**epistle** *n* epístola *f*.
**epistolary** *adj* epistolar.
**epithet** *n* epíteto *m*.
**epitome** *n* epítome, compendio *m*.
**epitomize** *vt* epitomar, abreviar.
**epoch** *n* época *f*.
**equable** *adj* uniforme; ~**bly** *adv* uniformemente.
**equal** *adj* igual; justo/ta; semejante; * *n* igual *m*; compañero *m*; * *vt* igualar; compensar.
**equalize** *vt* igualar.
**equalizer** *n* igualada *f*.
**equality** *n* igualdad, uniformidad *f*.
**equally** *adv* igualmente.
**equanimity** *n* ecuanimidad *f*.
**equate** *vt* equiparar (con).
**equation** *n* ecuación *f*.
**equator** *n* ecuador *m*.
**equatorial** *adj* ecuatorial, ecuatorio/ria.

**equestrian** *adj* ecuestre.
**equilateral** *adj* equilátero/ra.
**equilibrium** *n* equilibrio *m*.
**equinox** *n* equinoccio *m*.
**equip** *vt* equipar, pertrechar.
**equipment** *n* equipaje *m*.
**equitable** *adj* equitativo/va, imparcial; ~**bly** *adv* equitativamente.
**equity** *n* equidad, justicia, imparcialidad *f*.
**equivalent** *adj, n* equivalente *m*.
**equivocal** *adj* equívoco/ca, ambiguo/gua; ~**ly** *adv* equivocadamente, ambiguamente.
**equivocate** *vt* equivocar, usar equívocos.
**equivocation** *n* equívoco *m*.
**era** *n* era *f*.
**eradicate** *vt* desarraigar, extirpar.
**eradication** *n* extirpación *f*.
**erase** *vt* borrar.
**eraser** *n* goma de borrar *f*.
**erect** *vt* erigir; establecer; * *adj* derecho/ha, erguido/da, vertical.
**erection** *n* establecimiento *m*; estructura *f*; erección *f*.
**ermine** *n* armiño *m*.
**erode** *vt* erosionar; corroer.
**erotic** *adj* erótico/ca.
**err** *vi* vagar, errar; desviarse.
**errand** *n* recado, mensaje *m*.
**errand boy** *n* recadero *m*.
**errata** *npl* fe de erratas *f*.
**erratic** *adj* errático/ca, errante; irregular.
**erroneous** *adj* erróneo/nea; falso/sa; ~**ly** *adv* erróneamente.
**error** *n* error *m*; yerro *m*.
**erudite** *adj* erudito/ta.
**erudition** *n* erudición *f*; doctrina *f*.
**erupt** *vi* entrar en erupción; hacer erupción.
**eruption** *n* erupción *f*.
**escalate** *vi* extenderse.
**escalation** *n* intensificación *f*.
**escalator** *n* escalera mecánica *f*.
**escapade** *n* travesura *f*.
**escape** *vt* evitar; escapar; * *vi* evadirse, salvarse; * *vr* zafarse; * *n* escapada, huida, fuga *f*; inadvertencia *f*; **to make one's ~** poner los pies en polvorosa.
**escapism** *n* escapismo *m*.
**eschew** *vt* huir, evitar, evadir.
**escort** *n* escolta *f*; * *vt* escoltar.
**esoteric** *adj* esotérico/ca.
**especial** *adj* especial; ~**ly** *adv* especialmente.
**espionage** *n* espionaje *m*.
**esplanade** *n* (*mil*) esplanada *f*.
**espouse** *vt* desposar.

**essay** *n* ensayo *m*.

**essence** *n* esencia *f*.

**essential** *n* esencia *f*; * *adj* esencial, substancial, principal; ~**ly** *adv* esencialmente.

**establish** *vt* establecer, fundar, fijar; confirmar.

**establishment** *n* establecimiento *m*; fundación *f*; institución *f*.

**estate** *n* estado *m*; hacienda *f*; bienes *mpl*.

**estate car** *n* ranchera *f*.

**esteem** *vt* estimar, apreciar; pensar; * *n* estima *f*; consideración *f*.

**estimate** *vt* estimar, apreciar, tasar; * *n* presupuesto *m*.

**estimation** *n* estimación, valuación *f*; opinión *f*.

**estrange** *vt* extrañar, apartar, enajenar.

**estranged** *adj* separado/da.

**estrangement** *n* enajenación *f*; extrañeza, distancia *f*.

**estuary** *n* estuario *m*, ría *f*.

**etch** *vt* grabar al aguafuerte.

**etching** *n* grabado al aguafuerte *m*.

**eternal** *adj* eterno/na, perpetuo/tua, inmortal; ~**ly** *adv* eternamente.

**eternity** *n* eternidad *f*.

**ether** *n* éter *m*.

**ethical** *adj* ético/ca; ~**ly** *adv* moralmente.

**ethics** *npl* ética *f*.

**ethnic** *adj* étnico/ca.

**ethos** *n* genio *m*.

**etiquette** *n* etiqueta *f*.

**etymological** *adj* etimológico/ca.

**etymologist** *n* etimólogo/ga *m/f*, etimologista *m/f*.

**etymology** *n* etimología *f*.

**Eucharist** *n* Eucaristía *f*.

**eulogy** *n* elogio, encomio *m*; alabanza *f*.

**eunuch** *n* eunuco *m*.

**euphemism** *n* eufemismo *m*.

**euro** *n* euro *m*.

**Euro MP** *n* eurodiputado/da *m/f*.

**Europe** *n* Europa *f*.

**European Community** *n* Comunidad Europea *f*.

**European Parliament** *n* eurocámara *f*.

**European Union** *n* unión Europea *f*.

**Eurosceptic** *n* euroescéptico/ca *m/f*.

**Eurotunnel, Channel Tunnel** *n* eurotúnel *m*.

**evacuate** *vt* evacuar.

**evacuation** *n* evacuación *f*.

**evade** *vt* evadir, escapar, evitar.

**evaluate** *vt* evaluar; interpretar.

**evangelic(al)** *adj* evangélico/ca.

**evangelist** *n* evangelista *m*.

**evaporate** *vt* evaporar; * *vi* evaporarse; disiparse.

**evaporated milk** *n* leche evaporada *f*.

**evaporation** *n* evaporación *f*.

**evasion** *n* evasión *f*; escape *m*.

**evasive** *adj* evasivo/va; ~**ly** *adv* con evasivas.

**eve** *n* víspera *f*.

**even** *adj* llano/na, igual; par, semejante; * *adv* aun; aun cuando, supuesto que; no obstante; * *vt* igualar, allanar; * *vi*: **to ~ out** nivelarse.

**even-handed** *adj* imparcial, equitativo/va.

**evening** *n* tarde *f*.

**evening class** *n* clase nocturna *f*.

**evening dress** *n* traje de etiqueta *m*; traje de noche *m*.

**evenly** *adv* igualmente, llanamente.

**evenness** *n* igualdad *f*; uniformidad *f*; llanura *f*; imparcialidad *f*.

**event** *n* acontecimiento, evento *m*; suceso *m*.

**eventful** *adj* lleno de acontecimientos.

**eventual** *adj* final; ~**ly** *adv* por fin.

**eventuality** *n* eventualidad *f*.

**ever** *adv* siempre; **for ~ and ~** siempre jamás, eternamente; **~ since** después.

**evergreen** *adj* de hoja perenne; * *n* árbol de hoja perenne *m*.

**everlasting** *adj* eterno/na.

**evermore** *adv* eternamente, para siempre jamás.

**every** *adj* cada uno, cada una; **~ where** en/por todas partes; **~ thing** todo; **~ one, ~ body** todos, todo el mundo.

**evict** *vt* desahuciar.

**eviction** *n* desahucio *m*.

**evidence** *n* evidencia *f*; testimonio *m*; prueba *f*; * *vt* evidenciar.

**evident** *adj* evidente; patente, manifiesto/ta; ~**ly** *adv* evidentemente.

**evil** *adj* malo/la, depravado/da, pernicioso/sa; dañoso/sa; * *n* mal *m*; maldad *f*.

**evil-minded** *adj* malicioso/sa, mal intencionado/da.

**evocative** *adj* sugestivo/va.

**evoke** *vt* evocar.

**evolution** *n* evolución *f*.

**evolve** *vt*, *vi* evolucionar; desenvolver; desplegarse.

**ewe** *n* oveja *f*.

**exacerbate** *vt* exacerbar.

**exact** *adj* exacto/ta; * *vt* exigir.

**exacting** *adj* exigente.

**exaction** n exacción, extorsión f.
**exactly** adj exactamente.
**exactness, exactitude** n exactitud f.
**exaggerate** vt exagerar.
**exaggeration** n exageración f.
**exalt** vt exaltar, elevar; alabar; realzar.
**exaltation** n exaltación, elevación f.
**exalted** adj exaltado/da; muy animado/da.
**examination** n examen m.
**examine** vt examinar; escudriñar.
**examiner** n inspector/a m/f.
**example** n ejemplar m; ejemplo m.
**exasperate** vt exasperar, irritar, enojar, provocar; agravar; amargar.
**exasperation** n exasperación, irritación f.
**excavate** vt excavar, ahondar.
**excavation** n excavación f.
**exceed** vt exceder; sobrepujar.
**exceedingly** adv extremamente, en sumo grado.
**excel** vt sobresalir, exceder; * vi descollar.
**excellence** n excelencia f; preeminencia f.
**Excellency** n Excelencia (título) f.
**excellent** adj excelente; ~ly adv excelentemente.
**except** vt exceptuar, excluir; ~(ing) prep excepto, a excepción de.
**exception** n excepción, exclusión f.
**exceptional** adj excepcional.
**excerpt** n extracto m.
**excess** n exceso m.
**excessive** adj excesivo/va; ~ly adv excesivamente.
**exchange** vt cambiar; trocar, permutar; * n cambio m; bolsa f.
**exchange rate** n tipo de cambio m.
**excise** n impuestos sobre el consumo mpl.
**excitability** n excitabilidad f.
**excitable** adj excitable.
**excite** vt excitar; estimular.
**excited** adj emocionado/da.
**excitement** n estímulo, excitación f.
**exciting** adj emocionante.
**exclaim** vi exclamar.
**exclamation** n exclamación f; clamor m.
**exclamation mark** n punto de admiración m.
**exclamatory** adj exclamatorio/ria.
**exclude** vt excluir; exceptuar.
**exclusion** n exclusión, exclusiva, excepción f.
**exclusive** adj exclusivo/va; ~ly adv exclusivamente.
**excommunicate** vt excomulgar.
**excommunication** n excomunión f.

**excrement** n excremento m.
**excruciating** adj atroz, enorme, grave.
**exculpate** vt disculpar; justificar.
**excursion** n excursión f; digresión f.
**excusable** adj excusable.
**excuse** vt disculpar; perdonar; * n disculpa, excusa f, pretexto m; ~ me! interj ¡perdón!
**execute** vt ejecutar.
**execution** n ejecución f.
**executioner** n ejecutor/a m/f; verdugo m.
**executive** adj ejecutivo/va.
**executor** n testamentario/ria, albacea m/f.
**exemplary** adj ejemplar.
**exemplify** vt ejemplificar.
**exempt** adj exento/ta.
**exemption** n exención f.
**exercise** n ejercicio m; ensayo m; tarea f; practica f; * vi hacer ejercicio; * vt ejercer; valerse de.
**exercise book** n cuaderno m.
**exert** vt emplear; to ~ oneself esforzarse.
**exertion** n esfuerzo m.
**exhale** vt exhalar.
**exhaust** n escape m; * vt agotar.
**exhausted** adj agotado/da.
**exhaustion** n agotamiento m; extenuación f.
**exhaustive** adj comprensivo/va.
**exhibit** vt exhibir; mostrar; * n (law) objeto expuesto m.
**exhibition** n exposición, presentación f.
**exhilarating** adj estimulante.
**exhilaration** n alegría f; buen humor, regocijo m.
**exhort** vt exhortar, excitar.
**exhortation** n exhortación f.
**exhume** vt exhumar, desenterrar.
**exile** n destierro m; * vt desterrar, deportar.
**exist** vi existir.
**existence** n existencia f.
**existent** adj existente.
**existing** adj actual, presente.
**exit** n salida f; * vi hacer mutis.
**exodus** n éxodo m.
**exonerate** vt exonerar, descargar.
**exoneration** n exoneración f.
**exorbitant** adj exorbitante, excesivo/va.
**exorcise** vt exorcizar, conjurar.
**exorcism** n exorcismo m.
**exotic** adj exótico/ca, extranjero/ra.
**expand** vt extender, dilatar.
**expanse** n extensión f.
**expansion** n expansión f.
**expansive** adj expansivo/va.
**expatriate** vt expatriar.
**expect** vt esperar, aguardar.

**expectance**, **expectancy** n expectación, esperanza f.

**expectant** adj expectante.

**expectant mother** n mujer encinta f.

**expectation** n expectación, expectativa f.

**expediency** n conveniencia, oportunidad f.

**expedient** adj oportuno/na, conveniente; * n expediente m; ~**ly** adv convenientemente.

**expedite** vt acelerar; expedir.

**expedition** n expedición f.

**expeditious** adj pronto/ta, expedito/ta; ~**ly** adv prontamente.

**expel** vt expeler, desterrar.

**expend** vt expender; desembolsar.

**expendable** adj prescindible.

**expenditure** n gasto, desembolso m.

**expense** n gasto m; coste m.

**expense account** n cuenta de gastos f.

**expensive** adj caro/ra; costoso/sa; ~**ly** adv costosamente.

**experience** n experiencia f; práctica f; * vt experimentar.

**experienced** adj experimentado/da.

**experiment** n experimento m; * vt experimentar.

**experimental** adj experimental; ~**ly** adv experimentalmente.

**expert** adj experto/ta, diestro/tra.

**expertise** n pericia f.

**expiration** n expiración f; muerte f.

**expire** vi expirar.

**explain** vt explanar, explicar.

**explanation** n explicación f.

**explanatory** adj explicativo/va.

**expletive** adj expletivo/va.

**explicable** adj explicable.

**explicit** adj explícito/ta; ~**ly** adv explícitamente.

**explode** vt, vi estallar, explotar.

**exploit** vt explotar; * n hazaña f; hecho heroico m.

**exploitation** n explotación f.

**exploration** n exploración f; examen m.

**exploratory** adj exploratorio/ria.

**explore** vt explorar, examinar; sondear.

**explorer** n explorador/a m/f.

**explosion** n explosión f.

**explosive** adj, n explosivo m.

**exponent** n (math) exponente m.

**export** vt exportar.

**export**, **exportation** n exportación f.

**exporter** n exportador/a m/f.

**expose** vt exponer; mostrar; descubrir; poner en peligro.

**exposed** adj expuesto/ta.

**exposition** n exposición f; interpretación f.

**expostulate** vi debatir, contender.

**exposure** n exposición f; velocidad de obturación f; fotografía f.

**exposure meter** n fotómetro m.

**expound** vt exponer; interpretar.

**express** vt exprimir; representar; * adj expreso/sa, claro/ra; a propósito; * n expreso, correo m; (rail) tren expreso m.

**expression** n expresión f; locución f.

**expressionless** adj sin expresión (cara).

**expressive** adj expresivo/va; ~**ly** adv expresivamente.

**expressly** adv expresamente.

**expressway** n autopista f.

**expropriate** vt expropiar (por causa de utilidad pública).

**expropriation** n (law) expropiación f.

**expulsion** n explosión f.

**expurgate** vt expurgar.

**exquisite** adj exquisito/ta, perfecto/ta, excelente; ~**ly** adv exquisitamente.

**extant** adj existente.

**extempore** adv de improviso.

**extemporize** vi improvisar.

**extend** vt extender; amplificar; * vi extenderse.

**extension** n extensión f.

**extensive** adj extenso/sa, dilatado/da; ~**ly** adv extensivamente.

**extent** n extensión f.

**extenuate** vt extenuar, disminuir, atenuar.

**extenuating** adj atenuante.

**exterior** adj, n exterior m.

**exterminate** vt exterminar; extirpar.

**extermination** n exterminación, extirpación f.

**external** adj externo/na; ~**ly** adv exteriormente; ~**s** npl exterior m.

**extinct** adj extinto/ta; abolido/da.

**extinction** n extinción f; abolición f.

**extinguish** vt extinguir; suprimir.

**extinguisher** n extintor m.

**extirpate** vt extirpar.

**extol** vt alabar, magnificar, alzar, exaltar.

**extort** vt sacar por la fuerza.

**extortion** n extorsión f.

**extortionate** adj excesivo/va.

**extra** adv extra; * n extra m.

**extract** vt extraer; extractar; * n extracto m; compendio m.

**extraction** n extracción f; descendencia f.

**extracurricular** adj extraescolar.

**extradite** vt extraditar.

**extradition** *n* (*law*) extradición *f*.
**extramarital** *adj* extramatrimonial.
**extramural** *adj* extraescolar.
**extraneous** *adj* extraño/ña, ajeno/na.
**extraordinarily** *adv* extraordinariamente.
**extraordinary** *adj* extraordinario/ria.
**extravagance** *n* extravagancia *f*; gastos, excesivos *mpl*.
**extravagant** *adj* extravagante, exorbitante; pródigo/ga; **~ly** *adv* extravagantemente.
**extreme** *adj* extremo/ma, supremo/ma; último/ma; * *n* extremo *m*; **~ly** *adv* extremamente.
**extremist** *adj*, *n* extremista *m/f*.
**extremity** *n* extremidad *f*.
**extricate** *vt* desembarazar, desenredar.
**extrinsic(al)** *adj* extrínseco/ca, exterior.

**extrovert** *adj*, *n* extrovertido *m*.
**exuberance** *n* exuberancia, suma abundancia *f*.
**exuberant** *adj* exuberante, abundantísimo/ma; **~ly** *adv* exuberantemente.
**exude** *vi* transpirar.
**exult** *vt* exultar, regocijarse, triunfar.
**exultation** *n* exultación *f*; regocijo *m*.
**eye** *n* ojo *m*; * *vt* ojear, contemplar, observar.
**eyeball** *n* globo del ojo *m*.
**eyebrow** *n* ceja *f*.
**eyelash** *n* pestaña *f*.
**eyelid** *n* párpado *m*.
**eyesight** *n* vista *f*.
**eyesore** *n* monstruosidad *f*.
**eyetooth** *n* colmillo *m*.
**eyewitness** *n* testigo ocular *m*.
**eyrie** *n* nido de águila *m*.

# F

**fable** *n* fábula *f*; ficción *f*.
**fabric** *n* tejido *m*.
**fabricate** *vt* fabricar, edificar.
**fabrication** *n* fabricación *f*.
**fabulous** *adj* fabuloso/sa; **~ly** *adv* fabulosamente.
**facade** *n* fachada *f*.
**face** *n* cara, faz *f*; superficie *f*; fachada *f*; aspecto *m*; apariencia *f*; * *vt* encararse; hacer frente; **to ~ up to** hacer frente a.
**face cloth** *n* manopla *f*.
**face cream** *n* crema facial *f*.
**face-lift** *n* lifting *m*.
**face powder** *n* polvos *mpl*.
**facet** *n* faceta *f*.
**facetious** *adj* chistoso/sa, alegre, gracioso/sa; **~ly** *adv* chistosamente.
**face value** *n* valor nominal *m*.
**facial** *adj* facial.
**facile** *adj* fácil, afable.
**facilitate** *vt* facilitar.
**facility** *n* facilidad, ligereza *f*; afabilidad *f*.
**facing** *n* paramento *m*; * *prep* enfrente.
**facsimile** *n* facsímil *m*; fax *m*.
**fact** *n* hecho *m*; realidad *f*; **in ~** en efecto.
**faction** *n* facción *f*; disensión *f*.
**factor** *n* factor *m*.
**factory** *n* fábrica *f*.
**factual** *adj* basado/da en hechos reales.
**faculty** *n* facultad *f*; personal docente *m*.
**fad** *n* moda *f*.
**fade** *vi* decaer, marchitarse, fallecer.
**fail** *vt* suspender; fallar a; * *vi* suspender; fracasar; fallar; (*fig*) zozobrar.
**failing** *n* falta *f*; defecto *m*.
**failure** *n* falta *f*; culpa *f*; descuido *m*; quiebra, bancarrota *f*.
**faint** *vi* desmayarse, debilitarse; * *n* desmayo *m*; * *adj* débil; **~ly** *adv* débilmente.
**fainthearted** *adj* cobarde, medroso/sa, pusilánime.
**faintness** *n* flaqueza *f*; desmayo *m*.
**fair** *adj* hermoso/sa, bello/la; blanco/ca; rubio/bia; claro/ra, sereno/na; favorable; recto/ta, justo/ta; franco/ca; * *adv* limpio; * *n* feria *f*.
**fairly** *adv* justamente; completamente.
**fairness** *n* hermosura *f*; justicia *f*.
**fair play** *n* juego limpio *m*.
**fair trade** *n* comercio justo *m*.
**fairy** *n* hada *f*.

**fairy tale** *n* cuento de hadas *m*.
**faith** *n* fe *f*; dogma de fe *m*; fidelidad *f*.
**faithful** *adj* fiel, leal; **~ly** *adv* fielmente.
**faithfulness** *n* fidelidad, lealtad *f*.
**fake** *n* falsificación *f*; impostor/a *m/f*; * *adj* falso/sa; * *vt* fingir; falsificar.
**falcon** *n* halcón *m*.
**falconry** *n* cetrería *f*.
**fall** *vi* caer(se); perder el poder; disminuir, decrecer en precio; **to ~ asleep** dormirse; **to ~ back** retroceder; **to ~ back on** recurrir a; **to ~ behind** quedarse atrás; **to ~ down** caerse; **to ~ for** dejarse engañar; enamorarse de; **to ~ in** hundirse; **to ~ short** faltar; **to ~ sick** enfermar; **to ~ in love** enamorarse; **to ~ off** caerse; disminuir; **to ~ out** reñir, disputar; * *n* caída *f*; otoño *m*.
**fallacious** *adj* falaz, fraudulento/ta; **~ly** *adv* falazmente.
**fallacy** *n* falacia, sofistería *f*; engaño *m*.
**fallibility** *n* falibilidad *f*.
**fallible** *adj* falible.
**fallow** *adj* en barbecho; **~ deer** *n* gamo *m*.
**false** *adj* falso/sa; **~ly** *adv* falsamente.
**false alarm** *n* falsa alarma *f*.
**falsehood, falseness** *n* falsedad *f*.
**falsify** *vt* falsificar.
**falsity** *n* falsedad, mentira *f*.
**falter** *vi* tartamudear; faltar.
**faltering** *adj* vacilante.
**fame** *n* fama *f*; renombre *m*.
**famed** *adj* celebrado/da, famoso/sa.
**familiar** *adj* familiar; casero/ra; **~ly** *adv* familiarmente.
**familiarity** *n* familiaridad *f*.
**familiarize** *vt* familiarizar.
**family** *n* familia *f*; linaje *m*; clase, especie *f*.
**family business** *n* negocio familiar *m*.
**family doctor** *n* médico de familia *m*.
**famine** *n* hambre *f*; carestía *f*.
**famished** *adj* hambriento/ta.
**famous** *adj* famoso/sa, afamado/da; **~ly** *adv* famosamente.
**fan** *n* abanico *m*; aficionado *m*; fan *m/f*; * *vt* abanicar; atizar.
**fanatic** *adj*, *n* fanático/ca *m/ca*.
**fanaticism** *n* fanatismo *m*.
**fan belt** *n* correa del ventilador *f*.
**fanciful** *adj* imaginativo/va, caprichoso/sa; **~ly** *adv* caprichosamente.

**fancy** n fantasía, imaginación f; capricho m; * vt tener ganas de; imaginarse.

**fancy-goods** npl novedades, modas fpl.

**fancy-dress ball** n baile de disfraces m.

**fanfare** n (mus) fanfarria f.

**fang** n colmillo m.

**fantastic** adj fantástico/ca; caprichoso/sa; **~ally** adv fantásticamente.

**fantasy** n fantasía f.

**far** adv lejos, a una gran distancia; * adj lejano/na, distante, remoto/ta; **~ and away** con mucho, de mucho; **~ off** lejano/na.

**faraway** adj remoto/ta.

**farce** n farsa f.

**farcical** adj burlesco/ca.

**fare** n precio m; tarifa f; comida f; viajero m; pasaje m.

**farewell** n despedida f; **~!** excl ¡adiós!

**farm** n finca f, granja f; * vt cultivar.

**farmer** n agricultor/a m/f; granjero/ra m/f.

**farmhand** n peón m.

**farmhouse** n casa de hacienda f, granja f.

**farming** n agricultura f.

**farmland** n tierra de cultivo f.

**farmyard** n corral m.

**far-reaching** adj de gran alcance.

**fart** n (col) pedo; * vi tirarse un pedo.

**farther** adv más lejos; más adelante; * adj más lejos, ulterior.

**farthest** adv lo más lejos; lo más tarde; a lo más.

**fascinate** vt fascinar, encantar.

**fascinating** adj fascinante.

**fascination** n fascinación f; encanto m.

**fascism** n fascismo.

**fascist** n fascista m/f.

**fashion** n moda f; forma, figura f; uso m; manera f; estilo m; **people of ~** gente de tono f; * vt formar, amoldar.

**fashionable** adj a la moda; elegante; **the ~ world** el gran mundo; **~bly** adv a/segun la moda.

**fashion show** n desfile de modelos m.

**fast** vi ayunar; * n ayuno m; * adj rápido/da; firme, estable; * adv rápidamente; firmemente; estrechamente.

**fasten** vt abrochar; afirmar, asegurar, atar; fijar; * vi fijarse, establecerse.

**fastener, fastening** n cierre m; cerrojo m.

**fast food** n comida rápida f.

**fastidious** adj fastidioso/sa, desdeñoso/sa; **~ly** adv fastidiosamente.

**fat** adj gordo/da; * n grasa f; pringue m/f.

**fatal** adj fatal; funesto/ta; **~ly** adv fatalmente.

**fatalism** n fatalismo m.

**fatalist** n fatalista m/f.

**fatality** n fatalidad, predestinación f.

**fate** n hado, destino m.

**fateful** adj fatídico/ca.

**father** n padre m; **loving (over-indulgent) ~** padrazo m.

**fatherhood** n paternidad f.

**father-in-law** n suegro m.

**fatherland** n patria f.

**fatherly** adj paternal.

**fathom** n braza (medida) f; * vt sondar; penetrar.

**fatigue** n fatiga f; * vt fatigar, cansar.

**fatten** vt, vi engordar.

**fatty** adj graso/sa.

**fatuous** adj fatuo/tua, tonto/ta, imbécil.

**fault** n falta, culpa f; delito m; defecto m; yerro m.

**faultfinder** n censurador/a m/f.

**faultless** adj perfecto/ta, cumplido/da.

**faulty** adj defectuoso/sa.

**fauna** n fauna f.

**faux pas** n metedura de pata f.

**favour** n favor, beneficio m; patrocinio m; blandura f; * vt favorecer, proteger.

**favourable** adj favorable, propicio/cia; **~bly** adv favorablemente.

**favoured** adj favorecido/da.

**favourite** n favorito/ta m/f; * adj favorecido/da.

**favouritism** n favoritismo m.

**fawn** n cervatillo m; * vi adular servilmente.

**fawningly** adv lisonjeramente, con adulación servil.

**fax** n facsímil(e) m; fax m; * vt mandar por fax.

**fear** vi temer; * n miedo m.

**fearful** adj medroso/sa, temeroso/sa; tímido/da; **~ly** adv medrosamente, temerosamente.

**fearless** adj intrépido/da, atrevido/da; **~ly** adv sin miedo.

**fearlessness** n intrepidez f.

**feasibility** n posibilidad f.

**feasible** adj factible, viable.

**feast** n banquete, festín m; fiesta f; * vi banquetear.

**feat** n hecho m; acción, hazaña f.

**feather** n pluma f;.

**feather bed** n plumón m.

**feature** n característica f; rasgo m; forma f; * vi figurar.

**feature film** n largometraje m.

**February** n febrero m.

**federal** *adj* federal.

**federalist** *n* federalista *m/f.*

**federate** *vt (vi)* federar(se).

**federation** *n* federación *f.*

**fed-up** *adj* harto/ta.

**fee** *n* honorarios *mpl*; cuota *f.*

**feeble** *adj* flaco/ca, débil.

**feebleness** *n* debilidad *f.*

**feebly** *adv* débilmente.

**feed** *vt* nutrir; alimentar; **to ~ on** alimentarse de; * *vi* nutrirse; engordar; * *n* comida *f*; pasto *m.*

**feedback** *n* reacción *f.*

**feel** *vt* sentir; tocar; creer; **to ~ around** tantear; * *n* sensación *f*; tacto, sentido *m.*

**feeler** *n* antena *f*; (*fig*) tentativa *f.*

**feeling** *n* tacto *m*; sensibilidad *f*; corazonada *f.*

**feelingly** *adv* sensiblemente.

**feign** *vt* inventar, fingir; disimular.

**feline** *adj* felino/na.

**fellow** *n* tipo, tío *m*; socio/cia *m/f.*

**fellow citizen** *n* conciudadano/na *m/f.*

**fellow countryman** *n* compatriota *m/f.*

**fellow feeling** *n* simpatía *f.*

**fellow men** *npl* semejantes *mpl.*

**fellowship** *n* compañerismo *m*; beca (en un colegio) *f.*

**fellow student** *n* compañero/ra de curso *m/f.*

**fellow traveller** *n* compañero/ra de viaje *m/f.*

**felon** *n* criminal *m/f.*

**felony** *n* crimen *m.*

**felt** *n* fieltro *m.*

**felt-tip pen, fibre-tip pen** *n* rotulador *m.*

**female** *n* hembra *f*; * *adj* femenino/na.

**feminine** *adj* femenino/na.

**feminism** *n* feminismo *m.*

**feminist** *n* feminista *m/f.*

**fen** *n* pantano *m.*

**fence** *n* cerca *f*; defensa *f*; * *vt* cercar; * *vi* esgrimir.

**fencing** *n* esgrima *f.*

**fennel** *n* (*bot*) hinojo *m.*

**ferment** *n* agitación *f*; * *vi* fermentar.

**fern** *n* (*bot*) helecho *m.*

**ferocious** *adj* feroz; fiero/ra; **~ly** *adv* ferozmente.

**ferocity** *n* ferocidad, fiereza *f.*

**ferret** *n* hurón *m*; * *vt* huronear; **to ~ out** descubrir, echar fuera.

**ferry** *n* transbordador, ferry *m*; * *vt* transportar.

**fertile** *adj* fértil, fecundo/da.

**fertility** *n* fertilidad, fecundidad *f.*

**fertilization** *n* fertilización *f.*

**fertilize** *vt* fertilizar.

**fertilizer** *n* abono *m.*

**fervent** *adj* ferviente; fervoroso/sa; **~ly** *adv* con fervor.

**fervid** *adj* ardiente, vehemente.

**fervour** *n* fervor, ardor *m.*

**fester** *vi* enconarse, inflamarse.

**festival** *n* fiesta *f*; festival *m.*

**festive** *adj* festivo/va.

**festivity** *n* festividad *f.*

**fetch** *vt* ir a buscar.

**fetching** *adj* atractivo/va.

**fete** *n* fiesta *f.*

**fetid, foetid** *adj* fétido/da, hediondo/da.

**feud** *n* riña, contienda *f.*

**feudal** *adj* feudal.

**feudalism** *n* feudalismo *m.*

**fever** *n* fiebre *f.*

**feverish** *adj* febril.

**few** *adj* poco/ca; **a ~** algunos; **~ and far between** pocos.

**fewer** *adj* menor; * *adv* menos.

**fewest** *adj* los menos.

**fiancé** *n* novio *m.*

**fiancée** *n* novia *f.*

**fib** *n* mentira *f*; * *vi* mentir.

**fibre** *n* fibra, hebra *f.*

**fibreglass** *n* fibra de vidrio *f.*

**fickle** *adj* voluble, inconstante, mudable, ligero/ra.

**fiction** *n* ficción *f*; invención *f.*

**fictional** *adj* novelesco/ca.

**fictitious** *adj* ficticio/cia; fingido/da; **~ly** *adv* fingidamente.

**fiddle** *n* violín *m*; trampa *f*; * *vi* tocar el violín.

**fiddler** *n* violinista *m/f.*

**fidelity** *n* fidelidad, lealtad *f.*

**fidget** *vi* inquietarse.

**fidgety** *adj* inquieto/ta, impaciente.

**field** *n* campo *m*; campaña *f*; espacio *m.*

**field day** *n* (*mil*) día de maniobras *m.*

**fieldmouse** *n* ratón de campo *m.*

**fieldwork** *n* trabajo de campo *m.*

**fiend** *n* enemigo *m*; demonio *m.*

**fiendish** *adj* demoniaco/ca.

**fierce** *adj* fiero/ra, feroz; cruel, furioso/sa; **~ly** *adv* furiosamente.

**fierceness** *n* fiereza, ferocidad *f.*

**fiery** *adj* ardiente; apasionado/da.

**fifteen** *adj, n* quince.

**fifteenth** *adj, n* decimoquinto/ta.

**fifth** *adj, n* quinto/ta; **~ly** *adv* en quinto lugar.

**fiftieth** *adj, n* quincuagésimo/ma.

**fifty** *adj, n* cincuenta.

**fig** *n* higo *m*.

**fight** *vt, vi* reñir; batallar; combatir; * *n* batalla *f*; combate *m*; pelea *f*.

**fighter** *n* combatiente *m*; luchador/a *m/f*; caza *m*.

**fighting** *n* combate *m*.

**fig-leaf** *n* hoja de higuera *f*.

**fig tree** *n* higuera *f*.

**figurative** *adj* figurativo/va; ~**ly** *adv* figuradamente.

**figure** *n* figura, forma *f*; imagen *f*; cifra *f*; * *vi* figurar; ser lógico/ca; **to ~ out** comprender.

**figurehead** *n* testaferro *m*.

**filament** *n* filamento *m*; fibra *f*.

**filch** *vi* ratear.

**filcher** *n* ratero/ra, ladroncillo/lla *m/f*.

**file** *n* hilo *m*; lista *f*; (*mil*) fila, hilera *f*; lima *f*; carpeta *f*; fichero *m*; * *vt* enhilar; limar; clasificar; presentar; * *vi* **to ~ in/out** entrar/ salir en fila; **to ~ past** desfilar ante.

**filing cabinet** *n* archivador *m*.

**fill** *vt* llenar; hartar; **to ~ in** rellenar; **to ~ up** llenar (hasta el borde).

**fillet** *n* filete *m*.

**fillet steak** *n* filete de ternera *m*.

**filling station** *n* estación de servicio *f*; gasolinera *f*.

**fillip** *n* (*fig*) estímulo *m*.

**filly** *n* potra *f*.

**film** *n* película *f*; film *m*; capa *f*; * *vt* filmar; * *vi* rodar.

**film star** *n* estrella de cine *f*.

**film strip** *n* tira de película *f*.

**filter** *n* filtro *m*; * *vt* filtrar.

**filter-tipped** *adj* con filtro.

**filth(iness)** *n* inmundicia, porquería *f*; fango, lodo *m*.

**filthy** *adj* sucio/cia, puerco/ca.

**fin** *n* aleta *f*.

**final** *adj* final, último/ma; ~**ly** *adv* final- mente; ~ **stages** postrimerías *fpl*.

**finale** *n* final *m*.

**finalist** *n* finalista *m/f*.

**finalize** *vt* concluir.

**finance** *n* fondos *mpl*.

**financial** *adj* financiero/ra.

**financier** *n* financiero/ra *m/f*.

**find** *vt* hallar, descubrir; **to ~ out** averiguar; descubrir; **to ~ one's self** hallarse; * *n* hallazgo *m*.

**findings** *npl* fallo *m*; recomendaciones *fpl*.

**fine** *adj* fino/na; agudo/da, cortante; claro/ ra, trasparente; delicado/da; astuto/ta; elegante; bello/la; * *n* multa *f*; * *vt* multar.

**fine arts** *npl* bellas artes *fpl*.

**finely** *adv* con elegancia.

**finery** *n* adorno, atavío *m*.

**finesse** *n* sutileza *f*.

**finger** *n* dedo *m*; * *vt* tocar, manosear; manejar.

**fingernail** *n* uña *f*.

**fingerprint** *n* huella dactilar *f*.

**fingertip** *n* yema del dedo *f*.

**finicky** *adj* delicado/da.

**finish** *vt* acabar, terminar, concluir; **to ~ off** acabar (con); **to ~ up** terminar; * *vi*: **to ~ up** ir a parar.

**finishing line** *n* línea de llegada, línea de meta *f*.

**finishing school** *n* academia para señoritas *f*.

**finite** *adj* finito/ta; conjugado/da.

**fir tree** *n* abeto *m*

**fire** *n* fuego *m*; incendio *m*; * *vt* disparar; incendiar; despertar; * *vi* encenderse.

**fire alarm** *n* alarma de incendios *f*.

**firearm** *n* arma de fuego *f*.

**fireball** *n* bola *f* de fuego.

**firebreak, fire line** *n* cortafuegos *m*.

**fire engine** *n* coche de bomberos *m*.

**fire escape** *n* escalera de incendios *f*.

**fire extinguisher** *n* extintor *m*.

**firefly** *n* luciérnaga *f*.

**fireman** *n* bombero *m*.

**fireplace** *n* hogar, fogón *m*.

**fireproof** *adj* a prueba de fuego.

**fireside** *n* chimenea *f*.

**fire station** *n* parque de bomberos *m*.

**firewater** *n* aguardiente *m*.

**firewood** *n* leña *f*.

**fireworks** *npl* fuegos artificiales *mpl*.

**firing** *n* disparos *mpl*.

**firing squad** *n* pelotón de ejecución *m*.

**firm** *adj* firme, estable, constante; * *n* (*com*) firma *f*; ~**ly** *adv* firmemente.

**firmament** *n* firmamento *m*.

**firmness** *n* firmeza *f*; constancia *f*.

**first** *adj* primero/ra; * *adv* primeramente; **at ~** al principio; ~**ly** *adv* en primer lugar.

**first aid** *n* primeros auxilios *mpl*.

**first-aid kit** *n* botiquín *m*.

**first-class** *adj* de primera (clase).

**first-hand** *adj* de primera mano.

**first name** *n* nombre de pila *m*.

**first-rate** *adj* de primera (clase).

**fiscal** *adj* fiscal.

**fish** *n* pez *m*; * *vi* pescar.

**fishbone** *n* espina *f*.

**fisherman** n pescador m.
**fish farm** n piscifactoría f.
**fishing** n pesca f.
**fishing line** n sedal m.
**fishing rod** n caña de pescar f.
**fishing tackle** n aparejo m.
**fish market** n lonja de pescado f.
**fishmonger** n pescadero/ra m/f.
**fishmonger's (shop)** n pescadería f.
**fishy** adj (fig) sospechoso/sa.
**fissure** n grieta, hendedura f.
**fist** n puño m.
**fit** n paroxismo m; convulsión f; * adj en forma; apto/ta, idóneo/nea, justo/ta; * vt ajustar, acomodar, adaptar; **to ~ out** proveer; * vi convenir; **to ~ in** encajarse; llevarse bien (con todos).
**fitness** n salud f; aptitud, conveniencia f.
**fitted carpet** n moqueta f.
**fitted kitchen** n cocina amueblada f.
**fitter** n ajustador m.
**fitting** adj conveniente, idóneo/nea, justo/ta; * n conveniencia f; **~s** pl guarnición f.
**five** adj, n cinco.
**fix** vt fijar, establecer; **to ~ up** arreglar.
**fixation** n obsesión f.
**fixed** adj fijo/ja.
**fixture** n encuentro m.
**fizz(le)** vi silbar.
**fizzy** adj gaseoso/sa.
**flabbergasted** adj pasmado/da.
**flabby** adj blando/da, flojo/ja, lacio/cia.
**flaccid** adj flojo/ja, flaco/ca; fláccido/da.
**flag** n bandera f; losa f; * vi debilitarse.
**flagpole** n asta de bandera f.
**flagrant** adj flagrante; notorio/ria.
**flagship** n buque insignia m.
**flair** n aptitud especial f.
**flak** n fuego antiaéreo m; lluvia de críticas.
**flake** n copo m; lámina f; * vi romperse en láminas.
**flaky** adj escamoso/sa, desmenuzable.
**flamboyant** adj vistoso/sa.
**flame** n llama f; fuego (del amor) m.
**flamingo** n flamenco m.
**flammable** adj inflamable.
**flank** n ijada f; (mil) flanco m; * vt flanquear.
**flannel** n franela, flanela f.
**flap** n solapa f; hoja f; aletazo m; * vt aletear; * vi ondear.
**flare** vi lucir, brillar; **to ~ up** encenderse; encolerizarse; estallar; * n llama f.
**flash** n flash m; relámpago m; * vt **to ~ on and off** encender y apagar.
**flashbulb** n bombilla de flash f.

**flash cube** n cubo de flash m.
**flashy** adj superficial.
**flask** n frasco m; botella f.
**flat**[1] adj llano/na, plano/na; insípido/da; * n llanura f; plano m; (mus) bemol m; **~ly** adv horizontalmente; llanamente; enteramente; de plano, de nivel; francamente.
**flat**[2] n apartamento, departamento m.
**flatness** n llanura f; insipidez f.
**flatten** vt allanar; abatir.
**flatter** vt adular, lisonjear.
**flattering** adj halagüeño/ña, zalamero/ra.
**flattery** n adulación, lisonja f; zalamería f.
**flatulence** n (med) flatulencia f.
**flaunt** vt ostentar.
**flavour** n sabor m; * vt sazonar.
**flavoured** adj con sabor (a).
**flavourless** adj soso/sa.
**flaw** n falta, tacha f; defecto m.
**flawless** adj sin defecto.
**flax** n lino m.
**flea** n pulga f.
**flea bite** n picadura de pulga f.
**fleck** n mota f; punto m.
**flee** vt huir de; * vi escapar; huir.
**fleece** n vellón m; * vt (col) pelar.
**fleet** n flota f; escuadra f.
**fleeting** adj pasajero/ra, fugitivo/va.
**flesh** n carne f.
**flesh wound** n herida superficial f.
**fleshy** adj carnoso/sa, pulposo/sa.
**flex** n cordón m; * vt tensar.
**flexibility** n flexibilidad f.
**flexible** adj flexible.
**flick** n golpecito m; * vt dar un golpecito a.
**flicker** vt aletear; fluctuar.
**flier** n aviador/a m/f.
**flight** n vuelo m; huida, fuga f; bandada (de pájaros) f; (fig) elevación f.
**flight attendant** n auxiliar de vuelo m/f.
**flight deck** n cabina de mandos f.
**flimsy** adj débil; fútil.
**flinch** vi encogerse.
**fling** vt lanzar, echar.
**flint** n pedernal m.
**flip** vt arrojar, lanzar.
**flippant** adj petulante, locuaz.
**flipper** n aleta f.
**flirt** vi coquetear; * n coqueta f.
**flirtation** n coquetería f.
**flit** vi volar, huir; aletear.
**float** vt hacer flotar; lanzar; * vi flotar; * n flotador m; carroza f; reserva f.
**flock** n manada f; rebaño m; gentío m; * vi congregarse.

**flog** *vt* azotar; (*col*) zurrar.

**flogging** *n* tunda, zurra *f*.

**flood** *n* diluvio *m*; inundación *f*; flujo *m*; * *vt* inundar.

**flooding** *n* inundación *f*.

**floodlight** *n* foco *m*.

**floor** *n* suelo, piso *m*; piso (de una casa); * *vt* dejar sin respuesta.

**floorboard** *n* tabla *f*.

**floor lamp** *n* lámpara de pie *f*.

**floor show** *n* cabaret *m*.

**flop** *n* fracaso *m*.

**floppy** *adj* flojo/ja.

**floppy disk** *n* floppy *m*, disquete *m*.

**flora** *n* flora *f*.

**floral** *adj* floral.

**florescence** *n* florescencia *f*.

**florid** *adj* florido/da.

**florist** *n* florista *m/f*.

**florist's** (**shop**) *n* floristería *f*.

**flotilla** *n* (*mar*) flotilla *f*.

**flounder** *n* platija (pez de mar) *f*; * *vi* tropezar.

**flour** *n* harina *f*.

**flourish** *vi* florecer; gozar de prosperidad; * *n* belleza *f*; lazo *m*; (*mus*) floreo, preludio *m*.

**flourishing** *adj* floreciente.

**flout** *vt* burlarse de.

**flow** *vi* fluir, manar; crecer la marea; ondear; * *n* flujo de la marea *m* ; abundancia *f*; flujo *m*.

**flow chart** *n* organigrama *m*.

**flower** *n* flor *f*; * *vi* florear; florecer.

**flowerbed** *n* parterre *m*.

**flowerpot** *n* tiesto *m*, maceta *f*.

**flowery** *adj* florido/da.

**flower show** *n* exposición de flores *f*.

**fluctuate** *vi* fluctuar.

**fluctuation** *n* fluctuación *f*.

**fluency** *n* fluidez *f*.

**fluent** *adj* fluido/da; fácil; ~ly *adv* con fluidez.

**fluff** *n* pelusa *f*; ~y *adj* velloso/sa.

**fluid** *adj*, *n* fluido/da *m*.

**fluidity** *n* fluidez *f*.

**fluke** *n* (*col*) chiripa *f*.

**fluoride** *n* fluoruro *m*.

**flurry** *n* ráfaga *f*; agitación *f*.

**flush** *vt*: to ~ out levantar; desalojar; * *vi* ponerse colorado/da; * *n* rubor *m*; resplandor *m*.

**flushed** *adj* ruborizado/da.

**fluster** *vt* confundir.

**flustered** *adj* aturdido/da.

**flute** *n* flauta *f*.

**flutter** *vi* revolotear; estar en agitación; * *n* confusión *f*; agitación *f*.

**flux** *n* flujo *m*.

**fly** *vt* pilotar; transportar; * *vi* volar; huir, escapar; to ~ away/off emprender el vuelo; * *n* mosca *f*; bragueta *f*.

**flying** *n* aviación *f*.

**flying saucer** *n* platillo volante *m*.

**flypast** *n* desfile aéreo *m*.

**flysheet** *n* doble techo *m*.

**foal** *n* potro *m*.

**foam** *n* espuma *f*; * *vi* espumar.

**foam rubber** *n* espuma de caucho *f*.

**foamy** *adj* espumoso/sa.

**focus** *n* foco *m*.

**fodder** *n* forraje *m*.

**foe** *n* adversario/ria *m/f*, enemigo/ga *m/f*.

**foetus** *n* feto *m*.

**fog** *n* niebla *f*.

**foggy** *adj* nebuloso/sa, brumoso/sa.

**fog light** *n* faro antiniebla *m*.

**foible** *n* debilidad, parte flaca *f*.

**foil** *vt* frustrar; * *n* hoja *f*; florete *m*.

**fold** *n* redil *m*; pliegue *m*; * *vt* plegar; * *vi*: to ~ up plegarse, doblarse; quebrar.

**folder** *n* carpeta *f*; folleto *m*.

**folding** *adj* plegable.

**folding chair** *n* silla de tijera *f*.

**foliage** *n* follaje *m*.

**folio** *n* folio *m*.

**folk** *n* gente *f*.

**folklore** *n* folklore *m*.

**folk music** *n* folk *m*.

**folk song** *n* canción folklórica *f*.

**follow** *vt* seguir; acompañar; imitar; to ~ up responder a; investigar; * *vi* seguir, resultar, provenir.

**follower** *n* seguidor/a *m/f*; imitador/a *m/f*; secuaz, partidario/ria *m/f*; adherente *m*; compañero/ra *m/f*.

**following** *adj* siguiente; * *n* afición *f*.

**folly** *n* extravagancia, bobería *f*.

**foment** *vt* fomentar; proteger.

**fond** *adj* cariñoso/sa; ~ly *adv* cariñosamente.

**fondle** *vt* acariciar.

**fondness** *n* gusto *m*; cariño *m*.

**font** *n* pila bautismal *f*.

**food** *n* comida *f*.

**food mixer** *n* batidora *f*.

**food poisoning** *n* intoxicación alimentaria *f*.

**food processor** *n* robot de cocina *m*.

**foodstuffs** *npl* comestibles *mpl*.

**fool** *n* loco/ca, tonto/ta *m/f*; * *vt* engañar.

**foolhardy** *adj* temerario/ria.

**foolish** *adj* bobo/ba, tonto/ta; **~ly** *adv* tontamente.

**foolproof** *adj* infalible.

**foolscap** *n* papel tamaño folio *m*.

**foot** *n* pie *m*; pata *f*; paso *m*; **on, by ~** a pie.

**footage** *n* imágenes *fpl*.

**football** *n* balón *m*; fútbol *m*.

**footballer** *n* futbolista *m/f*; jugador/a de fútbol *m/f*.

**football pools** *npl* quinielas *fpl*.

**football pools coupon** *n* quiniela *f*.

**footbrake** *n* freno de pie *m*.

**footbridge** *n* puente peatonal *m*.

**foothills** *npl* estribaciones *fpl*.

**foothold** *n* pie firme *m*.

**footing** *n* base *f*; estado *m*; condición *f*; fundamento *m*.

**footlights** *npl* candilejas *fpl*.

**footman** *n* lacayo *m*; soldado de infantería *m*.

**footnote** *n* nota de pie *f*.

**footpath** *n* senda *f*.

**footprint** *n* huella, pisada *f*.

**footsore** *adj* con los pies doloridos.

**footstep** *n* paso *m*; huella *f*.

**footwear** *n* calzado *m*.

**for** *prep* por, a causa de; para; * *conj* porque, para que; por cuanto; **as ~ me** tocante a mí; **what ~?** ¿para qué?

**forage** *n* forraje *m*; * *vt* forrajear; saquear.

**foray** *n* incursión *f*.

**forbid** *vt* prohibir, vedar; impedir; **God ~!** ¡Dios no quiera!

**forbidding** *adj* inhóspito/ta; severo/ra.

**force** *n* fuerza *f*; poder, vigor *m*; violencia *f*; necesidad *f*; **~s** *pl* tropas *fpl*; * *vt* forzar, violentar; esforzar; constreñir.

**forced** *adj* forzado/da.

**forced march** *n* (*mil*) marcha forzada *f*.

**forceful** *adj* enérgico/ca.

**forceps** *n* fórceps *m*.

**forcible** *adj* fuerte, eficaz, poderoso/sa; **~bly** *adv* fuertemente, forzadamente.

**ford** *n* vado *m*; * *vt* vadear.

**fore** *n*: **to the ~** en evidencia.

**forearm** *n* antebrazo *m*.

**foreboding** *n* presentimiento *m*.

**forecast** *vt* pronosticar; * *n* pronóstico *m*.

**forecourt** *n* patio *m*.

**forefather** *n* abuelo, antecesor *m*.

**forefinger** *n* índice *m*.

**forefront** *n*: **in the ~ of** en la vanguardia de.

**forego** *vt* ceder, abandonar; preceder.

**foregone** *adj* pasado/da; anticipado/da.

**foreground** *n* delantera *f*.

**forehead** *n* frente *f*; insolencia *f*.

**foreign** *adj* extranjero/ra; extraño/ña.

**foreigner** *n* extranjero/ra, forastero/ra *m/f*.

**foreign exchange** *n* divisas *fpl*.

**foreleg** *n* pata delantera *f*.

**foreman** *n* capataz *m*; (*law*) presidente del jurado *m*.

**foremost** *adj* principal.

**forenoon** *n* mañana *f*.

**forensic** *adj* forense; **~ scientist** *n* forense *m/f*.

**forerunner** *n* precursor/a *m/f*; predecesor/a *m/f*.

**foresee** *vt* prever.

**foreshadow** *vt* pronosticar; simbolizar.

**foresight** *n* previsión *f*; presciencia *f*.

**forest** *n* bosque *m*; selva *f*.

**forestall** *vt* anticipar; prevenir.

**forester** *n* guardabosque *m/f*.

**forestry** *n* silvicultura *f*.

**foretaste** *n* muestra *f*.

**foretell** *vt* predecir, profetizar.

**forethought** *n* providencia *f*; premeditación *f*.

**forever** *adv* para siempre.

**forewarn** *vt* prevenir de antemano.

**foreword** *n* prefacio *m*.

**forfeit** *n* confiscación *f*; * *vt* perder derecho a.

**forge** *n* fragua *f*; fábrica de metales *f*; * *vt* forjar; falsificar; inventar; * *vi*: **to ~ ahead** avanzar constantemente.

**forger** *n* falsificador/a *m/f*.

**forgery** *n* falsificación *f*.

**forget** *vt* olvidar; * *vi* olvidarse.

**forgetful** *adj* olvidadizo/za; descuidado/da.

**forgetfulness** *n* olvido *m*; negligencia *f*.

**forget-me-not** *n* (*bot*) nomeolvides *m*.

**forgive** *vt* perdonar.

**forgiveness** *n* perdón *m*; remisión *f*.

**fork** *n* tenedor *m*; horca *f*; * *vi* bifurcarse; **to ~ out** (*col*) desembolsar.

**forked** *adj* horcado/da.

**fork-lift truck** *n* carretilla elevadora *f*.

**forlorn** *adj* abandonado/da, perdido/da.

**form** *n* forma *f*; modelo *m*; modo *m*; formalidad *f*; método *m*; molde *m*; * *vt* formar.

**formal** *adj* formal, metódico/ca; ceremonioso/sa; **~ly** *adv* formalmente.

**formality** *n* formalidad *f*; ceremonia *f*.

**format** *n* formato *m*; * *vt* formatear.

**formation** *n* formación *f.*
**formative** *adj* formativo/va.
**former** *adj* precedente; anterior, pasado/da; **~ly** *adv* antiguamente, en tiempos pasados.
**formidable** *adj* formidable, terrible.
**formula** *n* fórmula *f.*
**formulate** *vt* formular, articular.
**forsake** *vt* dejar, abandonar.
**fort** *n* castillo *m;* fortaleza *f.*
**forte** *adj* fuerte.
**forthcoming** *adj* venidero/ra.
**forthright** *adj* franco/ca.
**forthwith** *adj* inmediatamente, sin tardanza.
**fortieth** *adj, n* cuadragésimo *m.*
**fortification** *n* fortificación *f.*
**fortify** *vt* fortificar; corroborar.
**fortitude** *n* fortaleza *f;* valor *m.*
**fortnight** *n* quince días *mpl;* dos semanas *fpl;* **~ly** *adj, adv* cada quince días.
**fortress** *n* (*mil*) fortaleza *f.*
**fortuitous** *adj* impensado/da; casual; **~ly** *adv* fortuitamente.
**fortunate** *adj* afortunado/da; **~ly** *adv* felizmente.
**fortune** *n* fortuna, suerte *f.*
**fortune-teller** *n* sortílego/ga, adivino/na *m/f.*
**forty** *adj, n* cuarenta.
**forum** *n* foro *m.*
**forward** *adj* avanzado/da; delantero/ra; presumido/da; **~(s)** *adv* adelante, más allá; * *vt* remitir; promover, patrocinar.
**forwardness** *n* precocidad *f;* audacia *f.*
**fossil** *adj, n* fósil *m.*
**foster** *vt* criar, nutrir.
**foster child** *n* hijo/ja adoptivo/va *m/f.*
**foster father** *n* padre adoptivo *m.*
**foster mother** *n* madre adoptiva *f.*
**foul** *adj* sucio/cia, puerco/ca; impuro/ra, detestable; **~ copy** *n* borrador *m;* **~ly** *adv* suciamente; ilegítimamente; * *vt* ensuciar.
**foul play** *n* mala jugada *f;* muerte violenta *f.*
**found** *vt* fundar, establecer; edificar; fundir.
**foundation** *n* fundación *f;* fundamento *m.*
**founder** *n* fundador/a *m/f;* fundidor *m;* * *vi* (*mar*) irse a pique; zozobrar.
**foundling** *n* niño/ña expósito/ta *m/f.*
**foundry** *n* fundición *f.*
**fount, fountain** *n* fuente *f.*
**fountainhead** *n* origen de fuente *m.*
**four** *adj, n* cuatro.
**fourfold** *adj* cuádruple.
**four-poster (bed)** *n* cama de dosel *f.*
**foursome** *n* grupo de cuatro personas *m.*
**fourteen** *adj, n* catorce.

**fourteenth** *adj, n* decimocuarto/ta.
**fourth** *adj, n* cuarto/ta; * *n* cuarto *m;* **~ly** *adv* en cuarto lugar.
**fowl** *n* ave *f* de corral.
**fox** *n* zorra *f;* (*fig*) zorro *m.*
**foyer** *n* vestíbulo *m.*
**fracas** *n* riña *f.*
**fraction** *n* fracción *f.*
**fracture** *n* fractura *f;* * *vt* fracturar, romper.
**fragile** *adj* frágil; débil.
**fragility** *n* fragilidad *f;* debilidad, flaqueza *f.*
**fragment** *n* fragmento *m.*
**fragmentary** *adj* fragmentario/ria.
**fragrance** *n* fragancia *f.*
**fragrant** *adj* fragante, oloroso/sa; **~ly** *adv* con fragancia.
**frail** *adj* frágil, débil.
**frailty** *n* fragilidad *f;* debilidad *f.*
**frame** *n* armazón *m;* marco, cerco *m;* cuadro de vidriera *m;* estructura *f;* montura *f;* * *vt* encuadrar; componer, construir, formar.
**frame of mind** *n* estado de ánimo *m.*
**framework** *n* estructura *f;* esqueleto *m,* armazón *f.*
**franchise** *n* sufragio *m;* concesión *f.*
**frank** *adj* franco/ca, liberal.
**frankly** *adv* francamente.
**frankness** *n* franqueza *f.*
**frantic** *adj* frenético/ca, furioso/sa.
**fraternal** *adj* fraternal; **~ly** *adv* fraternalmente.
**fraternity** *n* fraternidad *f.*
**fraternize** *vi* hermanarse.
**fratricide** *n* fratricidio *m;* fratricida *m/f.*
**fraud** *n* fraude, engaño *m.*
**fraudulence** *n* fraudulencia *f.*
**fraudulent** *adj* fraudulento/ta; **~ly** *adv* fraudulentamente.
**fraught** *adj* cargado/da, lleno/na.
**fray** *n* riña, disputa, querella *f.*
**freak** *n* fantasía *f;* fenómeno *m.*
**freckle** *n* peca *f.*
**freckled** *adj* pecoso/sa.
**free** *adj* libre; liberal; suelto/ta; exento/ta; desocupado/da; gratis; * *vt* soltar; librar; eximir; * *vr:* **to ~ oneself from trouble** zafarse de.
**freedom** *n* libertad *f.*
**freehold** *n* propiedad absoluta *f.*
**free-for-all** *n* trifulca *f.*
**free gift** *n* prima *f.*
**free kick** *n* tiro libre *m.*
**freelance** *adj, adv* por cuenta propia.
**freely** *adv* libremente; espontáneamente; liberalmente, gratis.

**freemason** n francmasón m, masón m.
**freemasonry** n francmasonería f, masonería f.
**Freepost**™ n franqueo pagado m.
**free-range** adj de granja.
**freethinker** n librepensador/a m/f.
**freethinking** n librepensamiento m.
**free trade** n libre comercio m.
**freeway** n autopista f.
**freewheel** vi ir en punto muerto.
**free will** n libre albedrío m.
**freeze** vi helar(se); * vt congelar; helar.
**freeze-dried** adj liofilizado/da.
**freezer** n congelador m.
**freezing** adj helado/da.
**freezing point** n punto de congelación m.
**freight** n carga f; flete m.
**freighter** n fletador m.
**freight train** n tren de mercancías m.
**French bean** n judía verde f.
**French fries** npl patatas/papas fritas fpl.
**French window** n puertaventana f.
**frenzied** adj loco/ca, delirante.
**frenzy** n frenesí m; locura f.
**frequency** n frecuencia f.
**frequent** adj frecuente; **~ly** adv frecuentemente; * vt frecuentar.
**fresco** n fresco m.
**fresh** adj fresco/ca; nuevo/va, reciente; **~ water** n agua dulce f.
**freshen** vt (vi) refrescar(se).
**fresher** n novato m.
**freshly** adv nuevamente; recientemente.
**freshness** n frescura f; fresco m.
**freshwater** adj de agua dulce.
**fret** vi agitarse, enojarse.
**friar** n fraile m.
**friction** n fricción f.
**Friday** n viernes m; **Good ~** Viernes Santo m.
**friend** n amigo/ga m/f.
**friendless** adj sin amigos.
**friendliness** n amistad, benevolencia, bondad f.
**friendly** adj amistoso/sa.
**friendship** n amistad f.
**frieze** n friso m.
**frigate** n (mar) fragata f.
**fright** n espanto, terror m.
**frighten** vt espantar.
**frightened** adj asustado/da.
**frightening** adj espantoso/sa.
**frightful** adj espantoso/sa, horrible; **~ly** adv espantosamente, terriblemente.
**frigid** adj frío/ría, frígido/da; **~ly** adv fríamente.

**fringe** n franja f.
**fringe benefits** npl ventajas adicionales fpl.
**frisk** vt cachear.
**frisky** adj juguetón/ona.
**fritter** vt: **to ~ away** desperdiciar.
**frivolity** n frivolidad f.
**frivolous** adj frívolo/la, vano/na.
**frizz(le)** vt frisar; rizar.
**frizzy** adj rizado/da.
**fro** adv: **to go to and ~** ir y venir.
**frog** n rana f.
**frolic** vi juguetear.
**frolicsome** adj juguetón/ona, travieso/sa.
**from** prep de; después; desde.
**front** n parte delantera f; fachada f; paseo marítimo m; frente m; apariencias fpl; * adj delantero/ra; primero/ra.
**frontal** adj de frente.
**front door** n puerta principal f.
**frontier** n frontera f.
**front page** n primera plana f.
**front-wheel drive** n (auto) tracción delantera f.
**frost** n helada f; hielo m; * vt escarchar.
**frostbite** n congelación f.
**frostbitten** adj helado/da, con síntomas de congelación.
**frosted** adj deslustrado/da.
**frosty** adj helado/da, frío/ría como el hielo.
**froth** n espuma (de algún líquido) f; * vi espumar.
**frothy** adj espumoso/sa.
**frown** vt mirar con ceño; * n ceño m.
**frozen** adj helado/da.
**frugal** adj frugal; económico/ca; sobrio/ria; **~ly** adv frugalmente.
**fruit** n fruta f; fruto m; producto m.
**fruiterer** n frutero/ra m/f.
**fruitful** adj fructífero/ra, fértil; provechoso/sa, útil; **~ly** adv con fertilidad.
**fruitfulness** n fertilidad f.
**fruition** n realización f.
**fruit juice** n zumo de fruta m.
**fruitless** adj estéril; inútil; **~ly** adv vanamente, inútilmente.
**fruit salad** n ensalada de frutas f, macedonia f.
**fruit seller, greengrocer** n frutero/ra m.
**fruit shop, greengrocer's shop** n frutería f.
**fruit tree** n frutal m.
**frustrate** vt frustrar; anular.
**frustrated** adj frustrado/da.
**frustration** n frustración f.
**fry** vt freír.
**frying pan** n sartén f.

**fuchsia** n (bot) fucsia f.

**fudge** n caramelo blando m.

**fuel** n combustible m.

**fuel tank** n depósito m de combustible.

**fugitive** adj, n fugitivo/va m/f.

**fugue** n (mús) fuga f.

**fulcrum** n fulcro m.

**fulfil** vt cumplir; realizar.

**fulfilment** n cumplimiento m.

**full** adj lleno/na, repleto/ta, completo/ta; perfecto/ta; * adv enteramente, del todo.

**full-blown** adj hecho/cha y derecho/cha.

**full-fledged** adj hecho/cha y derecho/cha.

**full-length** adj de cuerpo entero/ra; completo/ta.

**full moon** n plenilunio m; luna llena f.

**fullness** n plenitud, abundancia f.

**full-scale** adj en gran escala; de tamaño natural.

**full-time** adj de tiempo completo.

**fully** adv llenamente, enteramente, ampliamente.

**fulsome** adj exagerado/da.

**fumble** vi manejar torpemente.

**fume** vi humear; encolerizarse.

**fumes** npl humo m.

**fumigate** vt fumigar.

**fun** n diversión f; alegría f.

**function** n función f.

**functional** adj funcional.

**fund** n fondo m; fondos públicos mpl; * vt costear.

**fundamental** adj fundamental; ~ly adv fundamentalmente.

**fundamentalism** n fundamentalismo m.

**fundamentalist** n fundamentalista m/f.

**funeral service** n misa de difuntos f, funeral m.

**funeral** n funeral m.

**funereal** adj funeral, fúnebre.

**fungus** n hongo m; seta f.

**funnel** n embudo m; cañón (de chimenea) m.

**funny** adj divertido/da; curioso/sa; zumbón/ona.

**fur** n piel f.

**fur coat** n abrigo de pieles m.

**furious** adj furioso/sa, frenético/ca; ~ly adv con furia.

**furlong** n estadio m (octava parte de una milla).

**furlough** n (mil) licencia f; permiso m.

**furnace** n horno m; hornaza f.

**furnish** vt amueblar; facilitar; suministrar.

**furnishings** npl muebles mpl.

**furniture** n muebles mpl.

**furrow** n surco m; * vt surcar; estriar.

**furry** adj peludo/da.

**further** adj nuevo/va; más lejano/na; * adv más lejos, más allá; aún; además; * vt adelantar, promover, ayudar.

**further education** n educación para adultos f.

**furthermore** adv además.

**furthest** adv lo más lejos, lo más remoto.

**furtive** adj furtivo/va; secreto/ta; ~ly adv furtivamente.

**fury** n furor m; furia f; ira f.

**fuse** vt, vi fundir; derretirse; * n fusible m; n mecha f.

**fuse box** n caja de fusibles f.

**fusion** n fusión f.

**fuss** n lío m; alboroto m.

**fussy** adj jactancioso/sa.

**futile** adj fútil, frívolo/la.

**futility** n futilidad, vanidad f.

**future** adj futuro/ra; * n futuro m; porvenir m.

**fuzzy** adj borroso/sa; muy rizado/da.

# G

**gab** n (col) charla f.
**gabble** vi charlar, parlotear; * n algarabía f.
**gable** n gablete m.
**gadget** n dispositivo m.
**gaffe** n plancha f.
**gag** n mordaza f; chiste m; * vt amordazar.
**gaiety** n alegría f.
**gaily** adv alegremente.
**gain** n ganancia f; interés, provecho m; * vt ganar; conseguir.
**gait** n marcha f; porte m.
**gala** n fiesta f.
**galaxy** n galaxia f.
**gale** n vendaval m.
**gall** n hiel f.
**gallant** adj galante.
**gall bladder** n vesícula biliar f.
**gallery** n galería f.
**galley** n cocina f; galera f.
**gallon** n galón m.
**gallop** n galope m; * vi galopar.
**gallows** n horca f.
**gallstone** n cálculo biliar m.
**galore** adv en abundancia.
**galvanize** vt galvanizar.
**gambit** n estrategia f.
**gamble** vi jugar; especular; * n riesgo m; apuesta f.
**gambler** n jugador/a m/f.
**gambling** n juego m.
**game** n juego m; pasatiempo m; partido m; partida f, caza f; * vi jugar.
**gamekeeper** n guardabosques m invar.
**gaming** n juego m.
**gammon** n jamón m.
**gamut** n (mus) gama f.
**gander** n ganso m.
**gang** n pandilla, banda f.
**gangrene** n gangrena f.
**gangster** n gángster m.
**gangway** n pasarela f.
**gap** n hueco m; claro m; intervalo m.
**gape** vi boquear; estar con la boca abierta.
**gaping** adj muy abierto/ta.
**garage** n garaje m.
**garbled** adj falsificado/da.
**garden** n jardín m.
**garden-hose** n regadera f.
**gardener** n jardinero/ra m/f.
**gardening** n jardinería f.
**gargle** vi hacer gárgaras.

**gargoyle** n gárgola f.
**garish** adj ostentoso/sa.
**garland** n guirnalda f.
**garlic** n ajo m.
**garment** n prenda f.
**garnish** vt guarnecer, adornar; * n guarnición f; adorno m.
**garret** n guardilla f; desván m.
**garrison** n (mil) guarnición f; * vt (mil) guarnecer.
**garrotte, garrote** vt estrangular.
**garrulous** adj gárrulo/la, locuaz, charlador/a.
**garter** n liga f.
**gas** n gas m.
**gas burner** n mechero de gas m.
**gas cylinder** n bombona de gas f.
**gaseous** adj gaseoso/sa.
**gas fire** n estufa de gas f.
**gash** n cuchillada f; raja f, * vt acuchillar.
**gasket** n junta de culata f.
**gas mask** n careta antigás f.
**gas meter** n contador de gas m.
**gasp** vi jadear; * n boqueada f.
**gas ring** n hornillo de gas m.
**gassy** adj gaseoso/sa.
**gas tap** n llave del gas f.
**gastric** adj gástrico/ca.
**gastronomic** adj gastronómico/ca.
**gasworks** npl fábrica de gas f.
**gate** n puerta f.
**gateway** n puerta f.
**gather** vt recoger, amontonar; entender; plegar; * vi juntarse.
**gathering** n reunión f, colecta f.
**gauche** adj torpe.
**gaudy** adj chillón/ona.
**gauge** n calibre m; entrevía f; indicador m; * vt medir.
**gaunt** adj flaco/ca, delgado/da.
**gauze** n gasa f.
**gay** adj alegre; vivo/va; gay.
**gaze** vi contemplar, considerar; * n mirada f.
**gazelle** n gacela f.
**gazette** n gaceta f.
**gazetteer** n gacetero m; diccionario geográfico m.
**gear** n atavío m; vestido m; aparejo m; tirantes mpl; velocidad f.
**gearbox** n caja de cambios f.
**gear lever** n palanca de cambios f.
**gear wheel** n rueda dentada f.

**gel** *n* gel *m*.

**gelatin(e)** *n* gelatina, jalea *f*.

**gelignite** *n* gelignita *f*.

**gem** *n* gema *f*.

**Gemini** *n* Géminis *m* (signo del zodiaco).

**gender** *n* género *m*.

**gene** *n* gen *m*.

**genealogical** *adj* genealógico/ca.

**genealogy** *n* genealogía *f*.

**general** *adj* general, común, usual; **in ~** por lo general; **~ly** *adv* generalmente; * *n* general *m*; generala *f*.

**general election** *n* elecciones generales *fpl*.

**generality** *n* generalidad, mayor parte *f*.

**generalization** *n* generalización *f*.

**generalize** *vt* generalizar.

**generate** *vt* engendrar; producir; causar.

**generation** *n* generación *f*.

**generator** *n* generador *m*.

**generic** *adj* genérico/ca.

**generosity** *n* generosidad, liberalidad *f*.

**generous** *adj* generoso/sa.

**genetic engineering** *n* ingeniería genética *f*.

**genetics** *npl* genética *f*.

**genial** *adj* genial, natural; alegre.

**genitals** *npl* genitales *mpl*.

**genitive** *n* genitivo *m*.

**genius** *n* genio *m*.

**genteel** *adj* refinado/da, elegante.

**gentile** *n* gentil, pagano/na *m/f*.

**gentle** *adj* suave, dócil, manso/sa, moderado/da; benigno/na.

**gentleman** *n* caballero *m*.

**gentleness** *n* dulzura, suavidad *f*.

**gently** *adv* suavemente.

**gentry** *n* alta burguesía *f*.

**gents** *n* aseos *mpl*.

**genuflection** *n* genuflexión *f*.

**genuine** *adj* genuino/na, puro/ra; **~ly** *adv* puramente, naturalmente.

**genus** *n* género *m*.

**geographer** *n* geógrafo/fa *m/f*.

**geographical** *adj* geográfico/ca.

**geography** *n* geografía *f*.

**geological** *adj* geológico/ca.

**geologist** *n* geólogo/ga *m/f*.

**geology** *n* geología *f*.

**geometric(al)** *adj* geométrico/ca.

**geometry** *n* geometría *f*.

**geranium** *n* (*bot*) geranio *m*.

**geriatric** *n*, *adj* geriátrico/ca *m/f*.

**germ** *n* germen *m*.

**germinate** *vi* brotar.

**gesticulate** *vi* gesticular.

**gesture** *n* gesto, movimiento expresivo *m*.

**get** *vt* ganar; conseguir, obtener, alcanzar; coger; agarrar; * *vi* hacerse, ponerse; prevalecer; introducirse; **to ~ the better** salir vencedor/a, sobrepujar.

**geyser** *n* géiser *m*; calentador de agua *m*.

**ghastly** *adj* espantoso/sa.

**gherkin** *n* pepinillo, cohombrillo *m*.

**ghetto** *n* gueto *m*.

**ghost** *n* fantasma *m*; espectro *m*.

**ghostly** *adj* fantasmal.

**giant** *n* gigante *m*.

**gibberish** *n* jerigonza *f*.

**gibe** *vi* escarnecer, burlarse, mofar; * *n* mofa, burla *f*.

**giblets** *npl* menudillos *mpl*.

**giddiness** *n* vértigo *m*.

**giddy** *adj* vertiginoso/sa.

**gift** *n* regalo *m*; don *m*; dádiva *f*; talento *m*.

**gifted** *adj* dotado/da.

**gift voucher** *n* vale de regalo *m*.

**gigantic** *adj* gigantesco/ca.

**giggle** *vi* reírse tontamente.

**gild** *vt* dorar.

**gilding**, **gilt** *n* doradura *f*.

**gill** *n* cuarta parte de pinta *f*; **~s** *pl* agallas *fpl*.

**gilt-edged** *adj* de máxima garantía.

**gimmick** *n* truco *m*.

**gin** *n* ginebra *f*.

**ginger** *n* jengibre *m*.

**gingerbread** *n* pan de jengibre *m*.

**ginger-haired** *adj* pelirrojo/ja.

**giraffe** *n* jirafa *f*.

**girder** *n* viga *f*.

**girdle** *n* faja *f*; cinturón *m*.

**girl** *n* muchacha, chica *f*, zagala *f*.

**girlfriend** *n* amiga; novia *f*.

**girlish** *adj* de niña.

**giro** *n* giro postal *m*.

**girth** *n* cincha *f*; circunferencia *f*.

**gist** *n* punto principal *m*.

**give** *vt*, *vi* dar, donar; conceder; abandonar; pronunciar; aplicarse, dedicarse; **to ~ away** regalar; traicionar; revelar; **to ~ back** devolver; **to ~ in** *vi* ceder; *vt* entregar; **to ~ off** despedir; **to ~ out** distribuir; **to ~ up** *vi* rendir; *vt* renunciar a.

**gizzard** *n* molleja *f*.

**glacial** *adj* glacial.

**glacier** *n* glaciar *m*.

**glad** *adj* alegre, contento/ta, agradable; **I am ~ to see** me alegro de ver; **~ly** *adv* alegremente.

**gladden** *vt* alegrar.

**gladiator** n gladiador m.

**glamorous** adj atractivo/va.

**glamour** n encanto, atractivo m.

**glance** n ojeada f; * vi mirar; echar una ojeada.

**glancing** adj oblicuo/cua.

**gland** n glándula f.

**glare** n deslumbramiento m; mirada feroz y penetrante f; * vi deslumbrar, brillar; echar miradas de indignación.

**glaring** adj deslumbrante; manifiesto/ta; notorio/ria.

**glass** n vidrio m, cristal m; telescopio m; vaso m; espejo m; ~es pl gafas fpl; * adj vítreo/rea.

**glassware** n cristalería f.

**glassy** adj vítreo/rea, cristalino/na, vidrioso/sa.

**glaze** vt vidriar; embarnizar.

**glazier** n vidriero m, cristalero m.

**gleam** n relámpago, rayo m; * vi relampaguear, brillar.

**gleaming** adj reluciente.

**glean** vt espigar; recoger.

**glee** n alegría f; gozo m; jovialidad f.

**glen** n valle m; llanura f.

**glib** adj con lab; ~ly adv con labia.

**glide** vi resbalar; planear.

**gliding** n vuelo sin motor m.

**glimmer** n vislumbre f; * vi vislumbrarse.

**glimpse** n vislumbre f; relámpago m; ojeada f; * vt entrever, percibir.

**glint** vi centellear.

**glisten**, **glitter** vi relucir, brillar.

**gloat** vi relamerse; saborear.

**global** adj mundial.

**globalization** n globalización f.

**global warming** n calentamiento global m.

**globe** n globo m; esfera f.

**gloom**, **gloominess** n oscuridad f; melancolía, tristeza f; ~ily adv oscuramente; tristemente.

**gloomy** adj sombrío/ría, oscuro/ra; cubierto de nubes; triste, melancólico/ca.

**glorification** n glorificación, alabanza f.

**glorify** vt glorificar, celebrar.

**glorious** adj glorioso/sa, ilustre; ~ly adv gloriosamente.

**glory** n gloria, fama, celebridad f.

**gloss** n glosa f; lustre m; * vt glosar, interpretar; **to ~ over** encubrir.

**glossary** n glosario m.

**glossy** adj lustroso/sa, brillante.

**glove** n guante m.

**glove compartment** n guantera f.

**glow** vi arder; inflamarse; relucir; * n color vivo m; viveza de color f; vehemencia de una pasión f.

**glower** vi mirar con ceño.

**glue** n cola f; cemento m; * vt pegar.

**gluey** adj viscoso/sa, pegajoso/sa.

**glum** adj abatido/da, triste.

**glut** n hartura, abundancia f.

**glutinous** adj glutinoso/sa, viscoso/sa.

**glutton** n glotón/ona, tragón/ona m/f.

**gluttony** n glotonería f.

**glycerine** n glicerina f.

**gnarled** adj nudoso/sa.

**gnash** vt, vi rechinar.

**gnat** n mosquito m.

**gnaw** vt roer.

**gnome** n gnomo m.

**go** vi ir, irse, andar, caminar; partir(se), marchar; huir; pasar; **to ~ ahead** seguir adelante; **to ~ away** marcharse; **to ~ back** volver; **to ~ by** pasar; **to ~ for** ir por; gustar; **to ~ in** entrar; **to ~ off** irse; pasarse; **to ~ on** seguir; pasar; **to ~ out** salir; apagarse; **to ~ up** subir.

**goad** n aguijada, aijada f; * vt aguijar; estimular, incitar.

**go-ahead** adj emprendedor/a; * n luz verde f.

**goal** n meta f; fin m.

**goalkeeper** n portero/ra m/f.

**goalpost** n poste (de la portería) m.

**goatherd** n cabrero/ra m/f.

**gobble** vt engullir, tragar; **to ~ down** zampar.

**go-between** n mediador/a m/f.

**goblet** n copa f.

**goblin** n espíritu ambulante, duende m.

**God** n Dios m.

**godchild** n ahijado, hijo de pila m.

**goddaughter** n ahijada, hija de pila f.

**goddess** n diosa f.

**godfather** n padrino m.

**godforsaken** adj dejado/da de la mano de Dios.

**godhead** n deidad, divinidad f.

**godless** adj infiel, impío/pía, sin Dios, ateo/tea.

**godlike** adj divino/na.

**godliness** n piedad, devoción, santidad f.

**godly** adj piadoso/sa, devoto/ta, religioso/sa; recto/ta, justificado/da.

**godmother** n madrina f.

**godsend** n don del cielo m.

**godson** n ahijado m.

**goggle-eyed** adj con ojos desorbitados.

**goggles** npl gafas fpl; gafas de bucear fpl.

**going** n ida f; salida f; partida f; progreso m.

**gold** n oro m.

**golden** adj áureo/rea, de oro; excelente; ~ **rule** n regla de oro f.

**goldfish** n pez de colores m.

**gold-plated** adj chapado/da en oro.

**goldsmith** n orfebre m.

**golf** n golf m.

**golf ball** n pelota de golf f.

**golf club** n club de golf m.

**golf course** n campo de golf m.

**golfer** n golfista m/f.

**gondolier** n gondolero/ra m/f.

**gone** adj ido/da; perdido/da; pasado/da; gastado/da; muerto/ta.

**gong** n atabal chino, gong m.

**good** adj bueno/na, benévolo/la, cariñoso/sa; conveniente, apto/ta; * adv bien; * n bien m; prosperidad, ventaja f; ~s pl bienes muebles mpl; mercaderías fpl.

**goodbye !** excl ¡adiós!

**Good Friday** n Viernes Santo m.

**goodies** npl golosinas fpl.

**good-looking** adj guapo/pa.

**good nature** n bondad f.

**good-natured** adj bondadoso/sa.

**goodness** n bondad f.

**goodwill** n benevolencia, bondad f.

**goose** n ganso m; oca f.

**gooseberry** n grosella espinosa f.

**goose bumps, goose flesh** npl carne de gallina f.

**goose-step** n paso de la oca m.

**gore** n sangre cuajada f; * vt cornear.

**gorge** n barranco m; * vt engullir, tragar.

**gorgeous** adj maravilloso/sa.

**gorilla** n gorila m.

**gorse** n aulaga f.

**gory** adj sangriento/ta.

**goshawk** n azor m.

**gospel** n evangelio m.

**gossamer** n vello m; pelusa (de frutas) f.

**gossip** n cotilleo m; * vi cotillear.

**gothic** adj gótico/ca.

**gout** n gota f (enfermedad).

**govern** vt gobernar, dirigir, regir.

**governess** n gobernadora f.

**government** n gobierno m; administración publica f.

**governor** n gobernador/a m/f.

**gown** n toga f; vestido de mujer m; bata f.

**grab** vt agarrar.

**grace** n gracia f; favor m; merced f; perdón m; gracias fpl; **to say ~** bendecir la mesa; * vt adornar; agraciar.

**graceful** adj gracioso/sa, primoroso/sa; ~ly adv elegantemente, con gracia.

**gracious** adj gracioso/sa; favorable; ~ly adv graciosamente.

**gradation** n gradación f.

**grade** n grado m; curso m.

**gradient** n (rail) pendiente.

**gradual** adj gradual; ~ly adv gradualmente.

**graduate** vi graduarse.

**graduation** n graduación f.

**graffiti** n pintadas fpl.

**graft** n injerto m; * vt injertar, ingerir.

**grain** n grano m; semilla f; cereales mpl.

**gram** n gramo m (peso).

**grammar** n gramática f.

**grammatical** adj gramatical; ~ly adv gramaticalmente.

**granary** n granero m.

**grand** adj grande, ilustre.

**grandchild** n nieto/ta m/f.

**grandad** n abuelo m.

**granddaughter** n nieta f; **great ~** bisnieta f.

**grandeur** n grandeza f; pompa f.

**grandfather** n abuelo m; **great ~** bisabuelo m.

**grandiose** adj grandioso/sa.

**grandma** n abuelita f.

**grandmother** n abuela f; **great ~** bisabuela f.

**grandparents** npl abuelos mpl.

**grand piano** n piano de cola m.

**grandson** n nieto m; **great ~** bisnieto m.

**grandstand** n tribuna f.

**granite** n granito m.

**granny** n abuelita f.

**grant** vt conceder; **to take for ~ed** presuponer; * n beca f; concesión f.

**granulate** vt granular.

**granule** n gránulo m.

**grape** n uva f; **bunch of ~s** racimo de uvas m.

**grapefruit** n toronja f, pomelo m.

**graph** n gráfica f.

**graphic(al)** adj gráfico/ca; pintoresco/ca; ~ally adv gráficamente.

**graphics** n artes gráficas fpl; gráficos mpl.

**grapnel** n (mar) arpeo m.

**grasp** vt empuñar, asir, agarrar; * n puño m; comprensión f; poder m.

**grasping** adj avaro/ra.

**grass** n hierba f.

**grasshopper** n saltamontes m invar.

**grassland** n pampa, pradera f.

**grass-roots** adj popular.

**grass snake** n culebra de agua f.

**grassy** adj herboso/sa.

**grate** n reja, verja, rejilla f; * vt rallar; rechinar (los dientes); enrejar.

**grateful** *adj* grato/ta, agradecido/da; **~ly** *adv* agradecidamente.

**gratefulness** *n* gratitud *f*.

**grater** *n* rallador *m*.

**gratification** *n* gratificación *f*.

**gratify** *vt* contentar; gratificar.

**gratifying** *adj* grato/ta.

**grating** *n* rejado *m*; * *adj* áspero/ra; ofensivo/va.

**gratis** *adv* gratis.

**gratitude** *n* gratitud *f*.

**gratuitous** *adj* gratuito/ta, voluntario/ria; **~ly** *adv* gratuitamente.

**gratuity** *n* gratificación, recompensa *f*.

**grave** *n* sepultura *f*; * *adj* grave, serio/ria; **~ly** *adv* con gravedad, seriamente.

**grave digger** *n* sepulturero *m*.

**gravel** *n* cascajo *m*.

**gravestone** *n* lápida *f*.

**graveyard** *n* cementerio *m*.

**gravitate** *vi* gravitar.

**gravitation** *n* gravitación *f*.

**gravity** *n* gravedad *f*.

**gravy** *n* jugo de la carne *f*; salsa *f*.

**graze** *vt* pastorear; tocar ligeramente; * *vi* pacer.

**grease** *n* grasa *f*; pringue *m/f*; * *vt* untar.

**greaseproof** *adj* a prueba de grasa.

**greasy** *adj* grasiento/ta.

**great** *adj* gran, grande; principal; ilustre; noble, magnánimo/ma; **~ly** *adv* muy, mucho.

**greatcoat** *n* sobretodo *m*.

**greatness** *n* grandeza *f*; dignidad *f*; poder *m*; magnanimidad *f*.

**greedily** *adv* vorazmente, ansiosamente.

**greediness, greed** *n* gula *f*; codicia *f*.

**greedy** *adj* avaro/ra, codicioso/sa; goloso/sa, glotón/ona.

**Greek** *n* griego (idioma) *m*.

**green** *adj* verde, fresco/ca, reciente; no maduro/ra; * *n* verde *m*; llanura verde *f*; **~s** *pl* verduras *fpl*.

**green belt** *n* zona verde *f*.

**greenery** *n* verdura *f*.

**greengrocer** *n* verdulero/ra *m/f*.

**greenhouse** *n* invernadero *m*

**greenhouse effect** *n* efecto invernadero *m*.

**greenish** *adj* verdoso/sa.

**green movement** *n* ecologismo *m*.

**greenness** *n* verdor, vigor *m*; frescura, falta de experiencia *f*; novedad *f*.

**greet** *vt* saludar, congratular.

**greeting** *n* saludo *m*.

**greeting(s) card** *n* tarjeta de felicitación *f*.

**grenade** *n* (*mil*) granada *f*.

**grenadier** *n* granadero *m*.

**grey** *adj* gris; cano/na; * *n* gris *m*.

**grey-haired** *adj* canoso/sa.

**greyhound** *n* galgo *m*.

**greyish** *adj* grisáceo/a; entrecano/na.

**greyness** *n* color gris *m*.

**grid** *n* reja *f*; red *f*.

**gridiron** *n* parrilla *f*; campo de fútbol americano *m*.

**grief** *n* dolor *m*; aflicción, pena *f*.

**grievance** *n* pesar *m*; molestia *f*; agravio *m*; injusticia *f*; perjuicio *m*.

**grieve** *vt* agraviar, afligir; * *vi* afligirse; llorar.

**grievous** *adj* doloroso/sa; enorme, atroz; **~ly** *adv* penosamente; cruelmente.

**griffin** *n* grifo *m*.

**grill** *n* parrilla *f*; * *vt* interrogar.

**grille** *n* reja *f*.

**grim** *adj* feo, fea; horrendo/da; ceñudo/da.

**grimace** *n* mueca *f*.

**grime** *n* porquería *f*.

**grimy** *adj* ensuciado/da.

**grin** *n* mueca *f*; * *vi* sonreír.

**grind** *vt* moler; pulverizar; afilar; picar; rechinar los dientes.

**grinder** *n* molinero *m*; molinillo *m*; amolador *m*.

**grip** *n* asimiento *m*; asidero *m*; maletín *m*; * *vt* agarrar.

**gripping** *adj* absorbente.

**grisly** *adj* horroroso/sa.

**gristle** *n* tendón, cartílago *m*.

**gristly** *adj* tendinoso/sa, cartilaginoso/sa.

**grit** *n* gravilla *f*; valor *m*.

**groan** *vi* gemir, suspirar; * *n* gemido, suspiro *m*.

**grocer** *n* tendero/ra, abarrotero/ra *m/f*.

**groceries** *npl* comestibles *mpl*.

**grocer's shop** *n* tienda de comestibles *f*.

**groggy** *adj* atontado/da.

**groin** *n* ingle *f*.

**groom** *n* establero *m*; criado *m*; novio *m*; * *vt* cuidar, almohazar.

**groove** *n* ranura *f*.

**grope** *vt, vi* tentar, buscar a oscuras; andar a tientas.

**gross** *adj* grueso/sa, corpulento/ta, espeso/sa; grosero/ra; estúpido/da; **~ly** *adv* enormemente.

**grotesque** *adj* grotesco/ca.

**grotto** *n* gruta *f*.

**ground** *n* tierra *f*; terreno, suelo, pavimento *m*; fundamento *m*; razón fundamental *f*; campo (de batalla) *m*; fondo *m*; * *vt* mantener en tierra; conectar con tierra.

**ground floor** *n* planta baja *f*.

**grounding** *n* conocimientos básicos *mpl*.

**groundless** *adj* infundado/da; **~ly** *adv* sin motivo.

**ground staff** *n* personal de tierra *m*.

**groundwork** *n* preparación *f*.

**group** *n* grupo *m*; * *vt* agrupar.

**grouse** *n* lagópodo escocés *m*; * *vi* quejarse.

**grove** *n* arboleda *f*.

**grovel** *vi* arrastrarse.

**grow** *vt* cultivar; * *vi* crecer, aumentarse; **~ up** crecer.

**grower** *n* cultivador/a *m/f*; productor/a *m/f*.

**growing** *adj* creciente.

**growl** *vi* regañar, gruñir; * *n* gruñido *m*.

**grown-up** *n* adulto/ta *m/f*.

**growth** *n* crecimiento *m*.

**grub** *n* gusano *m*.

**grubby** *adj* sucio/cia.

**grudge** *n* rencor, odio *m*; envidia *f*; * *vt*, *vi* envidiar.

**grudgingly** *adv* de mala gana.

**gruelling** *adj* penoso/sa, duro/ra.

**gruesome** *adj* horrible.

**gruff** *adj* brusco/ca; **~ly** *adv* bruscamente.

**gruffness** *n* aspereza, severidad *f*.

**grumble** *vi* gruñir; murmurar.

**grumpy** *adj* regañón/ona.

**grunt** *vi* gruñir; * *n* gruñido *m*.

**G-string** *n* taparrabo *m*.

**guarantee** *n* garantía *f*; * *vt* garantizar.

**guard** *n* guardia *f*; * *vt* guardar; defender.

**guarded** *adj* cauteloso/sa, mesurado/da.

**guardroom** *n* (*mil*) cuarto de guardia *m*.

**guardian** *n* tutor/ra *m/f*; curador/a *m/f*; guardián/dana *m/f*.

**guardianship** *n* tutela *f*.

**guerrilla** *n* guerrillero/ra *m/f*.

**guerrilla group** *n* guerrilla *f*.

**guerrilla warfare** *n* guerra de guerrillas *f*.

**guess** *vt*, *vi* conjeturar; adivinar; suponer; * *n* conjetura *f*.

**guesswork** *n* conjeturas *fpl*.

**guest** *n* huésped/a, convidado/da *m/f*.

**guest room** *n* cuarto de huéspedes *m*.

**guffaw** *n* carcajada *f*.

**guidance** *n* gobierno *m*; dirección *f*.

**guide** *vt* guiar, dirigir; * *n* guía *m*.

**guide dog** *n* perro lazarillo *m*.

**guidelines** *npl* directiva *f*.

**guidebook** *n* guía *f*.

**guild** *n* gremio *m*; corporación *f*.

**guile** *n* astucia *f*.

**guillotine** *n* guillotina *f*; * *vt* guillotinar.

**guilt** *n* culpabilidad *f*.

**guiltless** *adj* inocente, libre de culpa.

**guilty** *adj* reo, rea, culpable.

**guinea pig** *n* cobaya *f*, conejillo de Indias *m*.

**guise** *n* manera *f*.

**guitar** *n* guitarra *f*.

**gulf** *n* golfo *m*; abismo *m*.

**gull** *n* gaviota *f*.

**gullet** *n* esófago *m*.

**gullibility** *n* credulidad *f*; simpleza *f*.

**gullible** *adj* crédulo/la.

**gully** *n* barranco *m*.

**gulp** *n* trago *m*; * *vi* tragar saliva; * *vr* tragarse.

**gum** *n* goma *f*; cemento *m*; encía *f*; chicle *m*; * *vt* pegar con goma.

**gum tree** *n* árbol gomero *m*.

**gun** *n* pistola *f*; escopeta *f*.

**gunboat** *n* cañonera *f*.

**gun carriage** *n* cureña *f*.

**gunfire** *n* disparos *mpl*.

**gunman** *n* pistolero *m*.

**gunmetal** *n* bronce de cañones *m*.

**gunner** *n* artillero *m*.

**gunnery** *n* artillería *f*.

**gunpoint** *n*: **at ~** a punta de pistola; a mano armada.

**gunpowder** *n* pólvora *f*.

**gunshot** *n* escopetazo *m*.

**gunsmith** *n* armero/ra *m/f*.

**gurgle** *vi* gorgotear.

**guru** *n* gurú *m*.

**gush** *vi* brotar; chorrear; * *n* chorro *m*.

**gushing** *adj* superabundante.

**gusset** *n* escudete *m*.

**gust** *n* ráfaga *f*; soplo de aire *m*, racha *f*.

**gusto** *n* entusiasmo *m*.

**gusty** *adj* tempestuoso/sa.

**gut** *n* intestino *m*; **~s** *npl* valor *m*; * *vt* destripar.

**gutter** *n* canalón *m*; arroyo *m*.

**guttural** *adj* gutural.

**guy** *n* tío *m*; tipo *m*.

**guzzle** *vt* engullir.

**gym(nasium)** *n* gimnasio *m*.

**gymnast** *n* gimnasta *m/f*.

**gymnastic** *adj* gimnástico/ca; **~s** *npl* gimnástica *f*.

**gynaecologist** *n* ginecólogo/ga *m/f*.

**Gypsy** *n* gitano/na *m/f*.

**gypsum** *n* yeso *m*.

**gyrate** *vi* girar.

# H

haberdasher *n* camisero/ra *m/f*.
haberdashery *n* camisería *f*; mercería *f*; prendas de caballero *fpl*.
habit *n* costumbre *f*.
habitable *adj* habitable.
habitat *n* hábitat *m*.
habitual *adj* habitual; **~ly** *adv* por costumbre.
hack *n* corte *m*; gacetillero/ra *m/f*; * *vt* tajar, cortar.
hackneyed *adj* trillado/da.
haddock *n* especie de bacalao *f*.
haemorrhage *n* hemorragia *f*.
haemorrhoids *npl* hemorroides *mpl*.
hag *n* bruja *f*.
haggard *adj* ojeroso/sa.
haggle *vi* regatear.
hail *n* granizo *m*; * *vt* saludar; * *vi* granizar.
hailstone *n* piedra de granizo *f*.
hair *n* pelo; cabello *m*.
hairbrush *n* cepillo *m*.
haircut *n* corte de pelo *m*.
hairdresser *n* peluquero/ra *m/f*.
hairdryer *n* secador de pelo *m*.
hairless *adj* calvo/va.
hairnet *n* redecilla *f*.
hairpiece *n* tupé *m*.
hairpin *n* horquilla *f*.
hairpin curve *n* curva muy cerrada *f*.
hair remover *n* depilatorio *m*.
hairspray *n* laca *f*.
hairstyle *n* peinado *m*.
hairy *adj* peludo/da, cabelludo/da.
hale *adj* sano/na, vigoroso/sa.
half *n* mitad *f*; * *adj* medio/dia.
half-caste *adj* mestizo/za.
half-hearted *adj* indiferente.
half-hour *n* media hora *f*.
half-moon *n* media luna *f*.
half-price *adj* a mitad de precio.
half-time *n* descanso *m*.
halfway *adv* a medio camino.
hall *n* vestíbulo *m*; hall *m*.
hallmark *n* contraste *m*.
hallow *vt* consagrar, santificar.
hallucination *n* alucinación *f*.
halo *n* halo *m*.
halt *vi* parar; * *n* parada *f*, alto *m*.
halve *vt* partir por la mitad.
ham *n* jamón *m*.
hamburger *n* hamburguesa *f*.
hamlet *n* aldea *f*.

hammer *n* martillo *m*; * *vt* martillar.
hammock *n* hamaca *f*.
hamper *n* cesto *f*; * *vt* estorbar.
hamstring *vt* desjarretar.
hand *n* mano *f*; brazo *m*; aguja *f*; **at ~** a mano; * *vt* alargar.
handbag *n* cartera *f*.
handbell *n* campanilla *f*.
handbook *n* manual *m*.
handbrake *n* freno de mano *m*.
handcuff *n* esposa *f*.
handful *n* puñado *m*.
handicap *n* desventaja *f*.
handicapped *adj* minusválido/da.
handicraft *n* artesanía *f*.
handiwork *n* obra *f*.
handkerchief *n* pañuelo *m*.
handle *n* mango, puño *m*; asa; manija *f*; * *vt* manejar; tratar.
handlebars *npl* manillar *m*.
handling *n* manejo *m*.
handrail *n* pasamanos *m*.
handshake *n* apretón de manos *m*.
handsome *adj* guapo/pa; **~ly** *adv* primorosamente.
handwriting *n* letra *f*.
handy *adj* práctico/ca; diestro/tra.
hang *vt* colgar; ahorcar; * *vi* colgar; ser ahorcado/da.
hanger *n* percha *f*.
hanger-on *n* parásito *m*.
hangings *npl* tapicería *f*.
hangman *n* verdugo *m*.
hangover *n* resaca *f*.
hang-up *n* complejo *m*.
hanker *vi* ansiar, apetecer.
haphazard *adj* fortuito/ta.
hapless *adj* desgraciado/da.
happen *vi* pasar; acontecer, acaecer.
happening *n* suceso *m*.
happily *adv* felizmente.
happiness *n* felicidad *f*.
happy *adj* feliz.
harangue *n* arenga *f*; * *vi* arengar.
harass *vt* cansar, fatigar.
harbinger *n* precursor *m*.
harbour *n* puerto *m*; * *vt* albergar.
hard *adj* duro/ra, firme; difícil; penoso/sa; severo/ra, rígido/da; **~ of hearing** medio sordo/da; **~ by** muy cerca.
harden *vt* (*vi*) endurecer(se).

**hard-headed** *adj* realista.
**hard-hearted** *adj* duro de corazón, insensible.
**hardiness** *n* robustez *f*.
**hardly** *adv* apenas.
**hardness** *n* dureza *f*; dificultad *f*; severidad *f*.
**hardship** *n* penas *fpl*.
**hard-up** *adj* sin plata.
**hardware** *n* hardware *m*; quincallería *f*.
**hardwearing** *adj* resistente.
**hardy** *adj* fuerte, robusto/ta.
**hare** *n* liebre *f*.
**hare-brained** *adj* atolondrado/da.
**hare-lipped** *adj* labihendido/da.
**haricot** *n* alubia *f*.
**harlequin** *n* arlequín *m*.
**harm** *n* mal, daño *m*; perjuicio *m*; * *vt* dañar.
**harmful** *adj* perjudicial.
**harmless** *adj* inocuo/cua.
**harmonic** *adj* armónico/ca.
**harmonious** *adj* armonioso/sa; **~ly** *adv* armoniosamente.
**harmonize** *vt* armonizar.
**harmony** *n* armonía *f*.
**harness** *n* arreos de un caballo *mpl*; * *vt* enjaezar.
**harp** *n* arpa *f*.
**harpist** *n* arpista *m/f*.
**harpoon** *n* arpón *m*.
**harpsichord** *n* clavicordio *m*.
**harrow** *n* grada *f*; rastro *m*.
**harry** *vt* hostigar.
**harsh** *adj* duro/ra; austero/ra; **~ly** *adv* severamente.
**harshness** *n* aspereza, dureza *f*; austeridad *f*.
**harvest** *n* cosecha *f*; * *vt* cosechar.
**harvester** *n* cosechadora *f*.
**hash** *n* hachís *m*; picadillo *m*.
**hassock** *n* cojín de paja *m*.
**haste** *n* apuro *m*; **to be in ~** estar apurado/da.
**hasten** *vt* acelerar, apresurar; * *vi* tener prisa.
**hastily** *adv* precipitadamente.
**hastiness** *n* precipitación *f*.
**hasty** *adj* apresurado/da.
**hat** *n* sombrero *m*.
**hatbox** *n* sombrerera *f*.
**hatch** *vt* incubar; tramar; **to ~ a plot/scheme** zurcir; * *n* escotilla *f*.
**hatchback** *n* tres puertas, cinco puertas *m invar*.
**hatchet** *n* hacha *f*.
**hatchway** *n* (*mar*) escotilla *f*.
**hate** *n* odio, aborrecimiento *m*; * *vt* odiar, detestar.
**hateful** *adj* odioso/sa.

**hatred** *n* odio, aborrecimiento *m*.
**hatter** *n* sombrerero *m*.
**haughtily** *adv* orgullosamente.
**haughtiness** *n* orgullo *m*; altivez *f*.
**haughty** *adj* altanero/ra, orgulloso/sa.
**haul** *vt* tirar; * *n* botín *m*.
**hauler** *n* transportista *m/f*.
**haunch** *n* anca *f*.
**haunt** *vt* frecuentar, rondar; * *n* guarida *f*; costumbre *f*.
**have** *vt* haber; tener, poseer.
**haven** *n* asilo *m*; puerto *m*.
**haversack** *n* mochila *f*.
**havoc** *n* estrago *m*.
**hawk** *n* halcón *m*; * *vi* cazar con halcón.
**hawthorn** *n* espino blanco *m*.
**hay** *n* heno *m*.
**hay fever** *n* fiebre del heno *f*.
**hayloft** *n* henil *m*.
**hayrick**, **haystack** *n* almiar *m*.
**hazard** *n* riesgo *m*; * *vt* arriesgar.
**hazardous** *adj* arriesgado/da, peligroso/sa.
**haze** *n* niebla *f*.
**hazel** *n* avellano *m*; * *adj* castaño/ña.
**hazelnut** *n* avellana *f*.
**hazy** *adj* oscuro/ra.
**he** *pn* él.
**head** *n* cabeza *f*; jefe *m*; juicio *m*; * *vt* encabezar; **to ~ for** dirigirse a.
**headache** *n* dolor de cabeza *m*.
**headdress** *n* cofia *f*; tocado *m*.
**headland** *n* promontorio *m*.
**headlight** *n* faro *m*.
**headline** *n* titular *m*.
**headlong** *adv* precipitadamente.
**headmaster** *n* director *m*.
**head office** *n* oficina central *f*.
**headphones** *npl* auriculares *mpl*.
**headquarters** *npl* (*mil*) cuartel general *m*; sede central *f*.
**headroom** *n* altura *f*.
**headstrong** *adj* testarudo/da, cabezudo/da.
**headwaiter** *n* maître *m*.
**headway** *n* progresos *mpl*.
**heady** *adj* cabezón/ona.
**heal** *vt, vi* curar.
**health** *n* salud *f*; brindis *m invar*.
**healthiness** *n* sanidad *f*.
**healthy** *adj* sano/na.
**heap** *n* montón *m*; * *vt* amontonar.
**hear** *vt* oír; escuchar; * *vi* oír; escuchar.
**hearing** *n* oído *m*.
**hearing aid** *n* audífono *m*.
**hearsay** *n* rumor *m*; fama *f*.
**hearse** *n* coche fúnebre *m*.

**heart** *n* corazón *m*; **by ~** de memoria; **with all my ~** con toda mi alma.

**heart attack** *n* infarto, infarto de miocardio *m*.

**heartbreaking** *adj* desgarrador.

**heartburn** *n* ardor de estómago *m*

**heart failure** *n* fallo cardíaco *m*.

**heartfelt** *adj* sincero/ra.

**hearth** *n* hogar *m*.

**heartily** *adv* sinceramente, cordialmente.

**heartiness** *n* cordialidad, sinceridad *f*.

**heartless** *adj* cruel; **~ly** *adv* cruelmente.

**hearty** *adj* cordial.

**heat** *n* calor *m*; * *vt* calentar.

**heater** *n* calentador *m*.

**heather** *n* (*bot*) brezo *m*.

**heathen** *n* pagano/na *m/f*; **~ish** *adj* salvaje.

**heating** *n* calefacción *f*.

**heat wave** *n* ola de calor *f*.

**heave** *vt* alzar; tirar; * *n* tirón *m*.

**heaven** *n* cielo *m*.

**heavenly** *adj* divino/na.

**heavily** *adv* pesadamente.

**heaviness** *n* pesadez *f*.

**heavy** *adj* pesado/da; opresivo/va.

**Hebrew** *n* hebreo *m*.

**heckle** *vt* interrumpir.

**hectic** *adj* agitado/da.

**hedge** *n* seto *m*; * *vt* cercar con seto.

**hedgehog** *n* erizo *m*.

**heed** *vt* hacer caso de; * *n* cuidado *m*; atención *f*.

**heedless** *adj* descuidado/da, negligente; **~ly** *adv* negligentemente.

**heel** *n* talón *m*; **to take to one's ~s** apretar los talones, huir.

**hefty** *adj* grande.

**heifer** *n* ternera *f*.

**height** *n* altura *f*; altitud *f*.

**heighten** *vt* realzar; adelantar, mejorar; exaltar.

**heinous** *adj* atroz.

**heir** *n* heredero/ra *m/f*; **~ apparent** heredero/ra forzoso/sa *m/f*.

**heiress** *n* heredera *f*.

**heirloom** *n* reliquia de familia *f*.

**helicopter** *n* helicóptero *m*.

**hell** *n* infierno *m*.

**hellish** *adj* infernal.

**helm** *n* (*mar*) timón *m*.

**helmet** *n* casco *m*.

**help** *vt*, *vi* ayudar, socorrer; **I cannot ~ it** no puedo remediarlo; no lo puedo evitar; * *n* ayuda *f*; socorro, remedio *m*.

**helper** *n* ayudante *m/f*.

**helpful** *adj* útil.

**helping** *n* ración *f*.

**helpless** *adj* indefenso/sa; **~ly** *adv* irremediablemente.

**helter-skelter** *adv* a trochemoche, en desorden.

**hem** *n* ribete *m*; * *vt* ribetear.

**he-man** *n* macho *m*.

**hemisphere** *n* hemisferio *m*.

**hemp** *n* cáñamo *m*.

**hen** *n* gallina *f*.

**henchman** *n* secuaz *m*.

**henceforth**, **henceforward** *adv* de aquí en adelante.

**henhouse** *n* gallinero *m*.

**hepatitis** *n* hepatitis *f*.

**her** *pn* su; ella; de ella; a ella.

**herald** *n* heraldo *m*.

**heraldry** *n* heráldica *f*.

**herb** *n* hierba *f*; **~s** *pl* hierbas *fpl*.

**herbaceous** *adj* herbáceo/cea.

**herbalist** *n* herbolario *m*.

**herbivorous** *adj* herbívoro/ra.

**herd** *n* rebaño *m*.

**here** *adv* aquí, acá.

**hereabout(s)** *adv* aquí alrededor.

**hereafter** *adv* en el futuro.

**hereby** *adv* por esto.

**hereditary** *adj* hereditario/ria.

**heredity** *n* herencia *f*.

**heresy** *n* herejía *f*.

**heretic** *n* hereje *m/f*; * *adj* herético/ca.

**herewith** *adv* con esto.

**heritage** *n* patrimonio *m*.

**hermetic** *adj* hermético/ca; **~ly** *adv* herméticamente.

**hermit** *n* ermitaño/ña *m/f*.

**hermitage** *n* ermita *f*.

**hernia** *n* hernia *f*.

**hero** *n* héroe *m*.

**heroic** *adj* heroico/ca; **~ally** *adv* heroicamente.

**heroine** *n* heroína *f*.

**heroism** *n* heroísmo *m*.

**heron** *n* garza *f*.

**herring** *n* arenque *m*.

**hers** *pn* suyo, de ella.

**herself** *pn* ella misma.

**hesitant** *adj* vacilante.

**hesitate** *vt* dudar; tardar.

**hesitation** *n* duda, irresolución *f*.

**heterogeneous** *adj* heterogéneo/nea.

**heterosexual** *adj*, *n* heterosexual *m*.

**hew** *vt* tajar; cortar; picar.

**heyday** *n* apogeo *m*.

**hi** *excl* ¡hola!

**hiatus** n (gr) hiato m.
**hibernate** vi invernar.
**hiccup** n hipo m; * vi tener hipo.
**hickory** n nogal americana m.
**hide** vt esconder; * n cuero m; piel f.
**hideaway** n escondite m.
**hideous** adj horrible; ~ly adv horriblemente.
**hiding place** n escondite, escondrijo m.
**hierarchy** n jerarquía f.
**hieroglyphic** adj jeroglífico/ca; * n jeroglífico m.
**hi-fi** n estéreo, hi-fi m.
**higgledy-piggledy** adv confusamente.
**high** adj alto/ta; elevado/da.
**high altar** n altar mayor m.
**highchair** n silla alta f.
**high-handed** adj despótico/ca.
**highlands** npl tierras montañosas, tierras altas fpl.
**highlight** n punto culminante m.
**highly** adv en sumo grado.
**highness** n altura f; alteza f.
**highly strung** adj hipertenso/sa.
**high water** n marea alta f.
**highway** n carretera f.
**hike** vi ir de excursión.
**hijack** vt secuestrar.
**hijacker** n secuestrador/a m/f.
**hilarious** adj alegre.
**hill** n colina f.
**hillock** n colina f.
**hillside** n ladera f.
**hilly** adj montañoso/sa.
**hilt** n puño de espada m.
**him** pn le, lo, el.
**himself** pn él mismo, se, si mismo.
**hind** adj trasero/ra, posterior; * n cierva f.
**hinder** vt impedir.
**hindrance** n impedimento, obstáculo m.
**hindmost** adj postrero/ra.
**hindquarter** n cuarto trasero m.
**hindsight** n: with ~ en retrospectiva.
**hinge** n bisagra f.
**hint** n indirecta f, * vt insinuar; sugerir.
**hip** n cadera f.
**hippopotamus** n hipopótamo m.
**hire** vt alquilar; * n alquiler m.
**hire purchase** n compra a plazos f.
**his** pn su, suyo, de él.
**Hispanic** adj hispano/na; hispánico/ca; * n hispanoamericano/na m/f.
**hiss** vt, vi silbar.
**historian** n historiador/a m/f.
**historic(al)** adj histórico/ca; ~ally adv históricamente.

**history** n historia f.
**histrionic** adj teatral.
**hit** vt golpear; alcanzar; zumbar; to ~ each other vr zumbarse; * n golpe m; éxito m.
**hitch** vt atar; * n problema m.
**hitchhike** vi hacer autoestop.
**hitchhiker** n autoestopista m/f.
**hitchhiking** n autoestop f.
**hitherto** adv hasta ahora, hasta aquí.
**hive** n colmena f.
**HIV-negative** adj seronegativo/va.
**HIV-positive** adj seropositivo/va.
**hoard** n montón m; tesoro escondido m; * vt acumular.
**hoarfrost** n escarcha f.
**hoarse** adj ronco/ca; ~ly adv roncamente.
**hoarseness** n ronquera, carraspera f.
**hoax** n trampa f; * vt engañar, burlar.
**hobble** vi cojear.
**hobby** n pasatiempo m, afición f.
**hobbyhorse** n caballo de batalla m.
**hockey** n hockey m.
**hodgepodge** n mezcolanza f.
**hoe** n azadón m; * vt azadonar.
**hoist** vt alzar; * n grúa f.
**hold** vt tener; detener; contener; celebrar; to ~ on to agarrarse a; * vi valer; * n presa f; poder m.
**holder** n poseedor/a m/f; titular m/f.
**holding** n tenencia, posesión f.
**hold-up** n atraco m; retraso m.
**hole** n agujero m.
**holiday** n día de fiesta m; ~s pl vacaciones fpl.
**holiday-maker** n turista m/f.
**holiness** n santidad f.
**hollow** adj hueco/ca; * n hoyo m; * vt excavar, ahuecar.
**holly** n (bot) acebo m.
**hollyhock** n malva hortense f.
**holocaust** n holocausto m.
**holster** n pistolera f.
**holy** adj santo/ta, pío, pía; consagrado/da.
**holy water** n agua bendita f.
**holy week** n semana santa f.
**homage** n homenaje m.
**home** n casa f; patria f; domicilio m; ~ly adj casero/ra.
**home address** n domicilio m.
**homeless** adj sin casa.
**homeliness** n simpleza f.
**homely** adj casero/ra.
**home-made** adj casero/ra.
**homeopathist** n homeópata m/f.
**homeopathy** n homeopatía f.

**home shopping programme (TV)** *n* teletienda *f*.

**homesick** *adj* nostálgico/ca.

**homesickness** *n* nostalgia *f*.

**hometown** *n* ciudad natal *f*.

**homeward** *adj* hacia casa; hacia su país.

**homework** *n* deberes *mpl*.

**homicidal** *adj* homicida.

**homicide** *n* homicidio *m*; homicida *m/f*.

**homogeneous** *adj* homogéneo/nea.

**homosexual** *adj, n* homosexual *m*.

**honest** *adj* honrado/da; **~ly** *adv* honradamente.

**honesty** *n* honradez *f*.

**honey** *n* miel *f*.

**honeycomb** *n* panal *m*.

**honeymoon** *n* luna de miel *f*.

**honeysuckle** *n* (*bot*) madreselva *f*.

**honorary** *adj* honorario/ria.

**honour** *n* honra *f*; honor *m*; * *vt* honrar.

**honourable** *adj* honorable; ilustre.

**honourably** *adv* honorablemente.

**hood** *n* capo *m*; capucha *f*.

**hoodlum** *n* matón *m*.

**hoof** *n* pezuña *f*.

**hook** *n* gancho *m*; anzuelo *m*; **by ~/by crook** de un modo u otro; * *vt* enganchar.

**hooked** *adj* encorvado/da.

**hooligan** *n* gamberro/rra *m/f*.

**hoop** *n* aro *m*.

**hooter** *n* sirena *f*.

**hop** *n* (*bot*) lúpulo *m*; salto *m*; * *vi* saltar, brincar.

**hope** *n* esperanza *f*; * *vi* esperar.

**hopeful** *adj* esperanzador/a; **~ly** *adv* con esperanza.

**hopefulness** *n* buena esperanza *f*.

**hopeless** *adj* desesperado/da; **~ly** *adv* sin esperanza.

**hopscotch** *n* tejo *m*.

**horde** *n* horda *f*.

**horizon** *n* horizonte *m*.

**horizontal** *adj* horizontal; **~ly** *adv* horizontalmente.

**hormone** *n* hormona *f*.

**horn** *n* cuerno *m*; (*auto*) sirena *f*.

**horned** *adj* cornudo/da.

**hornet** *n* avispón *m*.

**horny** *adj* calloso/sa.

**horoscope** *n* horóscopo *m*.

**horrendous** *adj* horrendo/da.

**horrible** *adj* horrible, terrible.

**horribly** *adv* horriblemente; enormemente.

**horrid** *adj* horrible.

**horrific** *adj* horroroso/sa.

**horrify** *vt* horrorizar.

**horror** *n* horror, terror *m*.

**horror film** *n* película de horror *f*.

**hors d'oeuvre** *n* entremeses *mpl*.

**horse** *n* caballo *m*; caballete *m*.

**horseback** *adv*: **on ~** a caballo.

**horse-breaker** *n* domador/a de caballos *m/f*.

**horse chestnut** *n* castaño de Indias *m*.

**horsefly** *n* moscarda *f*; moscardón *m*.

**horseman** *n* jinete *m*.

**horsemanship** *n* equitación *f*.

**horsepower** *n* caballo de fuerza *m*.

**horse race** *n* carrera de caballos *f*.

**horseracing** *n* hípica *f*.

**horseradish** *n* rábano silvestre *m*.

**horseshoe** *n* herradura de caballo *f*.

**horsewoman** *n* jineta *f*.

**horticulture** *n* horticultura, jardinería *f*.

**horticulturist** *n* jardinero/ra *m/f*.

**hosepipe** *n* manguera *f*.

**hosiery** *n* calcetería *f*.

**hospitable** *adj* hospitalario/ria.

**hospitably** *adv* con hospitalidad.

**hospital** *n* hospital *m*.

**hospitality** *n* hospitalidad *f*.

**host** *n* anfitrión *m*; hostia *f*.

**hostage** *n* rehén *m*.

**hostess** *n* anfitriona *f*.

**hostile** *adj* hostil.

**hostility** *n* hostilidad *f*.

**hot** *adj* caliente; cálido/da.

**hotbed** *n* semillero *m*.

**hotdog** *n* perro caliente *m*.

**hotel** *n* hotel *m*.

**hotelier** *n* hotelero/ra *m/f*.

**hot-headed** *adj* exaltado/da.

**hothouse** *n* invernadero *m*.

**hotline** *n* línea directa *f*.

**hotplate** *n* hornillo *m*.

**hotly** *adv* con calor; violentamente.

**hound** *n* perro de caza *m*.

**hour** *n* hora *f*.

**hour-glass** *n* reloj de arena *m*.

**hourly** *adv* cada hora.

**house** *n* casa *f*; familia *f*; * *vt* alojar.

**houseboat** *n* casa flotante *f*.

**housebreaker** *n* ladrón/ona de casa *m/f*.

**housebreaking** *n* allanamiento de morada *m*.

**household** *n* familia *f*.

**householder** *n* amo de casa, padre de familia *m*; dueño/ña de la casa *m/f*.

**housekeeper** *n* ama de llaves *f*.

**housekeeping** *n* trabajos domésticos *mpl*.

**house-warming party** *n* fiesta de estreno de una casa *f*.

**housewife** *n* ama de casa *f.*
**housework** *n* faenas de la casa *fpl.*
**housing** *n* vivienda *f.*
**housing development** *n* urbanización *f.*
**hovel** *n* choza, cabaña *f.*
**hover** *vi* flotar.
**how** *adv* cómo, como; ~ **do you do!** ¡encantado!
**however** *adv* comoquiera, comoquiera que sea; aunque; no obstante.
**howl** *vi* aullar; * *n* aullido *m.*
**hub** *n* centro *m.*
**hubbub** *n* barullo *m.*
**hubcap** *n* tapacubos *m invar.*
**hue** *n* color *m*; matiz *m.*
**huff** *n*: in a ~ picado/da.
**hug** *vt* abrazar; * *n* abrazo *m.*
**huge** *adj* vasto/ta, enorme; ~**ly** *adv* inmensamente.
**hulk** *n* (*mar*) casco *m*; armatoste *m.*
**hull** *n* (*mar*) casco *m.*
**hum** *vi* canturrear.
**human** *adv* humano/na.
**humane** *adv* humano/na; benigno/na; ~**ly** *adv* humanamente.
**humanist** *n* humanista *m/f.*
**humanitarian** *adj* humanitario/ria.
**humanity** *n* humanidad *f.*
**humanize** *vt* humanizar.
**humanly** *adv* humanamente.
**humble** *adj* humilde, modesto/ta; * *vt* humillar, postrar.
**humbleness** *n* humildad *f.*
**humbly** *adv* con humildad.
**humbug** *n* tonterías *fpl.*
**humdrum** *adj* monótono/na.
**humid** *adj* húmedo/da.
**humidity** *n* humedad *f.*
**humiliate** *vt* humillar.
**humiliation** *n* humillación *f.*
**humility** *n* humildad *f.*
**humming** *n* zumbido *m.*
**humming-bird** *n* colibrí *m.*
**humorist** *n* humorista *m/f*
**humorous** *adj* gracioso/sa; ~**ly** *adv* con gracia.
**humour** *n* sentido del humor *m*, humor *m*; jocosidad *f*; * *vt* complacer.
**hump** *n* giba, joroba *f.*
**hunch** *n* corazonada *f*; ~**backed** *adj* jorobado/da, jiboso/sa.
**hundred** *adj* ciento; * *n* centenar *m*; un ciento.
**hundredth** *adj* centésimo.
**hundredweight** *n* quintal *m.*
**hunger** *n* hambre *f*; * *vi* hambrear.

**hunger strike** *n* huelga de hambre *f.*
**hungrily** *adv* con apetito.
**hungry** *adj* hambriento/ta.
**hunt** *vt* cazar; perseguir; buscar; * *vi* andar a caza; * *n* caza *f.*
**hunter** *n* cazador/a *m/f.*
**hunting** *n* caza *f.*
**huntsman** *n* cazador *m.*
**hurdle** *n* valla *f.*
**hurl** *vt* tirar con violencia; arrojar.
**hurricane** *n* huracán *m.*
**hurried** *adj* hecho/cha de prisa; ~**ly** *adv* con prisa.
**hurry** *vt* acelerar, apresurar; * *vi* apresurarse; * *n* prisa *f.*
**hurt** *vt* hacer daño; ofender; * *n* mal, daño *m.*
**hurtful** *adj* dañoso/sa; ~**ly** *adv* dañosamente.
**hurtle** *vr* zamparse.
**husband** *n* marido *m.*
**husbandry** *n* agricultura *f.*
**hush!** ¡chitón!, ¡silencio!; * *vt* hacer callar; * *vi* estar quieto/ta.
**husk** *n* cáscara *f.*
**huskiness** *n* ronquedad *f.*
**husky** *adj* ronco/ca.
**hustings** *n* tribuna para las elecciones *f.*
**hustle** *vt* empujar con fuerza.
**hut** *n* cabaña, barraca *f.*
**hutch** *n* conejera *f.*
**hyacinth** *n* jacinto *m.*
**hydrant** *n* boca de incendios *f.*
**hydraulic** *adj* hidráulico/ca; ~**s** *npl* hidráulica *f.*
**hydroelectric** *adj* hidroeléctrico/ca.
**hydrofoil** *n* hidroala *f.*
**hydrogen** *n* hidrógeno *m.*
**hydrophobia** *n* hidrofobia *f.*
**hyena** *n* hiena *f.*
**hygiene** *n* higiene *f.*
**hygienic** *adj* higiénico/ca.
**hymn** *n* himno *m.*
**hyperbole** *n* hipérbole *f*; exageración *f.*
**hypermarket** *n* hipermercado *m.*
**hyphen** *n* (*gr*) guión *m.*
**hypochondria** *n* hipocondria *f.*
**hypochondriac** *adj*, *n* hipocondríaco/ca *m/f.*
**hypocrisy** *n* hipocresía *f.*
**hypocrite** *n* hipócrita *m/f.*
**hypocritical** *adj* hipócrita.
**hypothesis** *n* hipótesis *f.*
**hypothetical** *adj* hipotético/ca; ~**ly** *adv* hipotéticamente.
**hysterical** *adj* histérico/ca.
**hysterics** *npl* histeria *f.*

# I

I *pn* yo; ~ **myself** yo mismo.
**ice** *n* hielo *m*; * *vt* helar.
**ice-axe** *n* piqueta *f*.
**iceberg** *n* iceberg *m*.
**ice-bound** *adj* rodeado/da de hielos.
**icebox** *n* nevera *f*.
**ice cream** *n* helado *m*.
**ice rink** *n* pista de hielo *f*.
**ice skating** *n* patinaje sobre hielo *m*.
**icicle** *n* carámbano *m*.
**iconoclast** *n* iconoclasta *m/f*.
**icy** *adj* helado/da; frío/ría.
**idea** *n* idea *f*.
**ideal** *adj* ideal; ~**ly** *adv* idealmente.
**idealist** *n* idealista *m/f*.
**identical** *adj* idéntico/ca.
**identification** *n* identificación *f*.
**identify** *vt* identificar.
**identity** *n* identidad *f*.
**ideology** *n* ideología *f*.
**idiom** *n* idioma *m*.
**idiomatic** *adj* idiomático/ca.
**idiosyncrasy** *n* idiosincrasia *f*.
**idiot** *n* idiota, necio/cia *m/f*.
**idiotic** *adj* tonto/ta, bobo/ba.
**idle** *adj* desocupado/da; holgazán/zana; inútil.
**idleness** *n* pereza *f*.
**idler** *n* holgazán/zana *m/f*; zángano *m*.
**idly** *adv* ociosamente; vanamente.
**idol** *n* ídolo *m*.
**idolatry** *n* idolatría *f*.
**idolize** *vt* idolatrar.
**idyllic** *adj* idílico/ca.
**i.e.** *adv* esto es.
**if** *conj* si, aunque; ~ **not** si no.
**igloo** *n* iglú *m*.
**ignite** *vt* encender.
**ignition** *n* (*chem*) ignición *f*; encendido *m*.
**ignition key** *n* llave de contacto *f*.
**ignoble** *adj* innoble; bajo/ja.
**ignominious** *adj* ignominioso/sa; ~**ly** *adv* ignominiosamente.
**ignominy** *n* ignominia, infamia *f*.
**ignoramus** *n* ignorante, tonto/ta *m/f*.
**ignorance** *n* ignorancia *f*.
**ignorant** *adj* ignorante; ~**ly** *adv* ignorantemente.
**ignore** *vt* no hacer caso de.
**ill** *adj* malo/la, enfermo/ma; * *n* mal, infortunio *m*; * *adv* mal.
**ill-advised** *adj* imprudente.

**illegal** *adj* ilegal; ~**ly** *adv* ilegalmente.
**illegality** *n* ilegalidad *f*.
**illegible** *adj* ilegible.
**illegibly** *adv* de modo ilegible.
**illegitimacy** *n* ilegitimidad *f*.
**illegitimate** *adj* ilegítimo/ma; ~**ly** *adv* ilegítimamente.
**ill feeling** *n* rencor *m*.
**illicit** *adj* ilícito/ta.
**illiterate** *adj* analfabeto/ta.
**illness** *n* enfermedad *f*.
**illogical** *adj* ilógico/ca.
**ill-timed** *adj* inoportuno/na.
**ill-treat** *vt* maltratar.
**illuminate** *vt* iluminar.
**illumination** *n* iluminación *f*.
**illusion** *n* ilusión *f*.
**illusory** *adj* ilusorio/ria.
**illustrate** *vt* ilustrar; explicar.
**illustration** *n* ilustración *f*; elucidación *f*.
**illustrative** *adj* explicativo/va.
**illustrious** *adj* ilustre, insigne.
**ill-will** *n* rencor *m*.
**image** *n* imagen *f*.
**imagery** *n* imágenes *fpl*.
**imaginable** *adj* concebible.
**imaginary** *adj* imaginario/ria.
**imagination** *n* imaginación *f*.
**imaginative** *adj* imaginativo/va.
**imagine** *vt* imaginarse; idear, inventar.
**imbalance** *n* desequilibrio *m*.
**imbecile** *adj* imbécil, necio/cia.
**imbibe** *vt* beber.
**imbue** *vt* infundir.
**imitate** *vt* imitar, copiar.
**imitation** *n* imitación, copia *f*.
**imitative** *adj* imitativo/va.
**immaculate** *adj* inmaculado/da, puro/ra.
**immaterial** *adj* poco importante.
**immature** *adj* inmaduro/ra.
**immeasurable** *adj* inconmensurable.
**immeasurably** *adv* inmensamente.
**immediate** *adj* inmediato/ta; ~**ly** *adv* inmediatamente; ya.
**immense** *adj* inmenso/sa; vasto/ta; ~**ly** *adv* inmensamente.
**immensity** *n* inmensidad *f*.
**immerse** *vt* sumergir.
**immersion** *n* inmersión *f*.
**immigrant** *n* inmigrante *m/f*.
**immigrate** *vi* inmigrar.

**immigration** *n* inmigración *f*.
**imminent** *adj* inminente.
**immobile** *adj* inmóvil.
**immobility** *n* inmovilidad *f*.
**immoderate** *adj* inmoderado/da, excesivo/va; **~ly** *adv* inmoderadamente.
**immodest** *adj* inmodesto/ta.
**immoral** *adj* inmoral.
**immorality** *n* inmoralidad *f*.
**immortal** *adj* inmortal.
**immortality** *n* inmortalidad *f*.
**immortalize** *vt* inmortalizar, eternizar.
**immune** *adj* inmune.
**immunity** *n* inmunidad *f*.
**immunize** *vt* inmunizar.
**immutable** *adj* inmutable.
**imp** *n* diablillo, duende *m*.
**impact** *n* impacto *m*.
**impair** *vt* disminuir.
**impale** *vt* empalar.
**impalpable** *adj* impalpable.
**impart** *vt* comunicar.
**impartial** *adj* imparcial; **~ly** *adv* imparcialmente.
**impartiality** *n* imparcialidad *f*.
**impassable** *adj* intransitable.
**impasse** *n* punto muerto *m*.
**impassive** *adj* impasible.
**impatience** *n* impaciencia *f*.
**impatient** *adj* impaciente; **~ly** *adv* impacientemente.
**impeach** *vt* acusar, denunciar.
**impeccable** *adj* impecable.
**impecunious** *adj* indigente.
**impede** *vt* estorbar.
**impediment** *n* obstáculo *m*.
**impel** *vt* impeler, impulsar.
**impending** *adj* inminente.
**impenetrable** *adj* impenetrable.
**imperative** *adj* imperativo/va.
**imperceptible** *adj* imperceptible.
**imperceptibly** *adv* imperceptiblemente.
**imperfect** *adj* imperfecto/ta, defectuoso/sa; **~ly** *adv* imperfectamente; * *n* (*gr*) pretérito imperfecto *m*.
**imperfection** *n* imperfección *f*, defecto *m*.
**imperial** *adj* imperial.
**imperialism** *n* imperialismo *m*.
**imperious** *adj* imperioso/sa; arrogante; **~ly** *adv* imperiosamente, arrogantemente.
**impermeable** *adj* impermeable.
**impersonal** *adj* impersonal; **~ly** *adv* impersonalmente.
**impersonate** *vt* hacerse pasar por; imitar.
**impertinence** *n* impertinencia *f*; descaro *m*.

**impertinent** *adj* impertinente; **~ly** *adv* impertinentemente.
**imperturbable** *adj* imperturbable.
**impervious** *adj* impermeable.
**impetuosity** *n* impetuosidad *f*.
**impetuous** *adj* impetuoso/sa; **~ly** *adv* impetuosamente.
**impetus** *n* ímpetu *m*.
**impiety** *n* impiedad *f*.
**impinge** (**on**) *vt* tener influjo en.
**impious** *adj* impío/pía, irreligioso/sa.
**implacable** *adj* implacable.
**implacably** *adv* implacablemente.
**implant** *vt* implantar; plantear.
**implement** *n* herramienta *f*; utensilio *m*.
**implicate** *vt* implicar.
**implication** *n* implicación *f*.
**implicit** *adj* implícito/ta; **~ly** *adv* implícitamente.
**implore** *vt* suplicar.
**imply** *vt* suponer.
**impolite** *adj* maleducado/da.
**impoliteness** *n* falta de educación *f*.
**impolitic** *adj* imprudente; impolítico/ca.
**import** *vt* importar; * *n* importación *f*.
**importance** *n* importancia *f*.
**important** *adj* importante.
**importation** *n* importación *f*.
**importer** *n* importador/a *m/f*.
**importunate** *adj* importuno/na.
**importune** *vt* importunar.
**importunity** *n* importunidad *f*.
**impose** *vt* imponer.
**imposing** *adj* imponente.
**imposition** *n* imposición, carga *f*.
**impossibility** *n* imposibilidad *f*.
**impossible** *adj* imposible.
**impostor** *n* impostor *m*.
**impotence** *n* impotencia *f*.
**impotent** *adj* impotente; **~ly** *adv* sin poder.
**impound** *vt* embargar.
**impoverish** *vt* empobrecer.
**impoverished** *adj* necesitado/da.
**impoverishment** *n* empobrecimiento *m*.
**impracticability** *n* inviabilidad *f*.
**impracticable** *adj* impracticable, inviable.
**impractical** *adj* poco práctico/ca.
**imprecation** *n* imprecación, maldición *f*.
**imprecise** *adj* impreciso/sa.
**impregnable** *adj* inexpugnable.
**impregnate** *vt* impregnar.
**impregnation** *n* fecundación *f*; impregnación *f*.
**impress** *vt* impresionar.
**impression** *n* impresión *f*; edición *f*.

**impressionable** *adj* impresionable.
**impressive** *adj* impresionante.
**imprint** *n* sello *m*; * *vt* imprimir; estampar.
**imprison** *vt* encarcelar.
**imprisonment** *n* encarcelamiento *m*.
**improbability** *n* improbabilidad *f*.
**improbable** *adj* improbable.
**impromptu** *adj* de improviso.
**improper** *adj* impropio/pia, indecente; **~ly** *adv* impropiamente.
**impropriety** *n* impropiedad *f*.
**improve** *vt, vi* mejorar.
**improvement** *n* progreso *m*, mejora *f*.
**improvident** *adj* impróvido/da, imprudente.
**improvise** *vt* improvisar.
**imprudence** *n* imprudencia *f*.
**imprudent** *adj* imprudente.
**impudence** *n* impudencia *f*.
**impudent** *adj* impudente; **~ly** *adv* desvergonzadamente.
**impugn** *vt* impugnar.
**impulse** *n* impulso *m*.
**impulsive** *adj* impulsivo/va.
**impunity** *n* impunidad *f*.
**impure** *adj* impuro/ra; **~ly** *adv* impuramente.
**impurity** *n* impureza *f*.
**in** *prep* en.
**inability** *n* incapacidad *f*.
**inaccessible** *adj* inaccesible.
**inaccuracy** *n* inexactitud *f*.
**inaccurate** *adj* inexacto/ta.
**inaction** *n* inacción *f*.
**inactive** *adj* inactivo/va, perezoso/sa.
**inactivity** *n* inactividad *f*.
**inadequate** *adj* inadecuado/da, defectuoso/sa.
**inadmissible** *adj* inadmisible.
**inadvertently** *adv* sin querer.
**inalienable** *adj* inalienable.
**inane** *adj* necio/cia.
**inanimate** *adj* inanimado/da.
**inapplicable** *adj* inaplicable.
**inappropriate** *adj* impropio/pia.
**inasmuch** *adv* visto que; en tanto en cuanto.
**inattentive** *adj* desatento/ta.
**inaudible** *adj* inaudible.
**inaugural** *adj* inaugural.
**inaugurate** *vt* inaugurar.
**inauguration** *n* inauguración *f*.
**inauspicious** *adj* poco propicio/cia.
**in-between** *adj* intermedio/dia.
**inborn, inbred** *adj* innato/ta.
**incalculable** *adj* incalculable.

**incandescent** *adj* incandescente.
**incantation** *n* conjuro *m*.
**incapable** *adj* incapaz.
**incapacitate** *vt* inhabilitar.
**incapacity** *n* incapacidad *f*.
**incarcerate** *vt* encarcelar.
**incarnate** *adj* encarnado/da.
**incarnation** *n* encarnación *f*.
**incautious** *adj* incauto/ta; **~ly** *adv* incautamente.
**incendiary** *n* bomba incendiaria *f*.
**incense** *n* incienso *m*; * *vt* exasperar.
**incentive** *n* incentivo *m*.
**inception** *n* principio *m*.
**incessant** *adj* incesante, constante; **~ly** *adv* continuamente.
**incest** *n* incesto *m*.
**incestuous** *adj* incestuoso/sa.
**inch** *n* pulgada *f*; **~ by ~** palmo a palmo.
**incidence** *n* frecuencia *f*.
**incident** *n* incidente *m*.
**incidental** *adj* casual; **~ly** *adv* a propósito.
**incinerator** *n* incinerador *m*.
**incipient** *adj* incipiente.
**incise** *vt* tajar, cortar.
**incision** *n* incisión *f*.
**incisive** *adj* incisivo/va.
**incisor** *n* incisivo *m*.
**incite** *vt* incitar, estimular.
**inclement** *adj* feo, fea.
**inclination** *n* inclinación, propensión *f*.
**incline** *vt* (*vi*) inclinar(se); * *n* cuesta *f*.
**include** *vt* incluir, comprender.
**including** *prep* incluso.
**inclusion** *n* inclusión *f*.
**inclusive** *adj* inclusivo/va.
**incognito** *adv* de incógnito.
**incoherence** *n* incoherencia *f*.
**incoherent** *adj* incoherente, inconsecuente; **~ly** *adv* de modo incoherente.
**income** *n* renta *f*; ingresos *mpl*.
**income tax** *n* impuesto sobre la renta *m*.
**incoming** *adj* entrante.
**incomparable** *adj* incomparable.
**incomparably** *adv* incomparablemente.
**incompatibility** *n* incompatibilidad *f*.
**incompatible** *adj* incompatible.
**incompetence** *n* incompetencia *f*.
**incompetent** *adj* incompetente; **~ly** *adv* incompetentemente.
**incomplete** *adj* incompleto/ta.
**incomprehensibility** *n* incomprensibilidad *f*.
**incomprehensible** *adj* incomprensible.
**inconceivable** *adj* inconcebible.

**inconclusive** *adj* no concluyente; * *adv* sin conclusión.

**incongruity** *n* incongruencia *f*.

**incongruous** *adj* incongruo/rua; ~ly *adv* incongruamente.

**inconsequential** *adj* inconsecuente.

**inconsiderate** *adj* desconsiderado/da; ~ly *adv* desconsideradamente.

**inconsistency** *n* inconsecuencia *f*.

**inconsistent** *adj* inconsecuente.

**inconsolable** *adj* inconsolable.

**inconspicuous** *adj* discreto/ta.

**incontinence** *n* incontinencia *f*.

**incontinent** *adj* incontinente.

**incontrovertible** *adj* incontrovertible.

**inconvenience** *n* incomodidad *f*; * *vt* incomodar.

**inconvenient** *adj* incómodo/da; ~ly *adv* incómodamente.

**incorporate** *vt* (*vi*) incorporar(se).

**incorporated company** (**inc**) *n* sociedad anónima *f*.

**incorporation** *n* incorporación *f*.

**incorrect** *adj* incorrecto/ta; ~ly *adv* incorrectamente.

**incorrigible** *adj* incorregible.

**incorruptibility** *n* incorruptibilidad *f*.

**incorruptible** *adj* incorruptible.

**increase** *vt* acrecentar, aumentar; * *vi* crecer; * *n* aumento *m*.

**increasing** *adj* creciente; ~ly *adv* cada vez más.

**incredible** *adj* increíble.

**incredulity** *n* incredulidad *f*.

**incredulous** *adj* incrédulo/la.

**increment** *n* incremento *m*.

**incriminate** *vt* incriminar.

**incrust** *vt* incrustar.

**incubate** *vi* incubar.

**incubator** *n* incubadora *f*.

**inculcate** *vt* inculcar.

**incumbent** *adj* obligatorio/ria; * *n* beneficiado/da *m/f*.

**incur** *vt* incurrir.

**incurability** *n* lo incurable.

**incurable** *adj* incurable.

**incursion** *n* incursión, invasión *f*.

**indebted** *adj* agradecido/da.

**indecency** *n* indecencia *f*.

**indecent** *adj* indecente; ~ly *adv* indecentemente.

**indecision** *n* irresolución *f*.

**indecisive** *adj* indeciso/sa.

**indecorous** *adj* indecente.

**indeed** *adv* verdaderamente, de veras.

**indefatigable** *adj* incansable.

**indefinite** *adj* indefinido/da; ~ly *adv* indefinidamente.

**indelible** *adj* indeleble.

**indelicacy** *n* falta de delicadeza, grosería *f*.

**indelicate** *adj* poco delicado/da.

**indemnify** *vt* indemnizar.

**indemnity** *n* indemnidad *f*.

**indent** *vt* mellar.

**independence** *n* independencia *f*.

**independent** *adj* independiente; ~ly *adv* independientemente.

**indescribable** *adj* indescriptible.

**indestructible** *adj* indestructible.

**indeterminate** *adj* indeterminado/da.

**index** *n* índice *m*.

**index card** *n* ficha *f*.

**indexed** *adj* indexado/da.

**index finger** *n* dedo índice *m*.

**indicate** *vt* indicar.

**indication** *n* indicación *f*; indicio *m*.

**indicative** *adj*, *n* (*gr*) indicativo *m*.

**indicator** *n* indicador *m*.

**indict** *vt* acusar.

**indictment** *n* acusación *f*.

**indifference** *n* indiferencia *f*.

**indifferent** *adj* indiferente; ~ly *adv* indiferentemente.

**indigenous** *adj* indígena.

**indigent** *adj* indigente.

**indigestible** *adj* indigerible.

**indigestion** *n* indigestión *f*.

**indignant** *adj* indignado/da.

**indignation** *n* indignación *f*.

**indignity** *n* indignidad *f*.

**indigo** *n* añil *m*.

**indirect** *adj* indirecto/ta; ~ly *adv* indirectamente.

**indiscreet** *adj* indiscreto/ta; ~ly *adv* indiscretamente.

**indiscretion** *n* indiscreción *f*.

**indiscriminate** *adj* indistinto/ta; ~ly *adv* sin distinción.

**indispensable** *adj* indispensable.

**indisposed** *adj* indispuesto/ta.

**indisposition** *n* indisposición *f*.

**indisputable** *adj* indiscutible.

**indisputably** *adv* indisputablemente.

**indistinct** *adj* indistinto/ta, confuso/sa; ~ly *adv* indistintamente.

**indistinguishable** *adj* indistinguible.

**individual** *adj* individual; ~ly *adv* individualmente; * *n* individuo *m*.

**individuality** *n* individualidad *f*.

**indivisible** *adv* indivisible; **~bly** *adv* indivisiblemente.

**indoctrinate** *vt* adoctrinar.

**indoctrination** *n* adoctrinamiento *m*.

**indolence** *n* indolencia, pereza *f*.

**indolent** *adj* indolente; **~ly** *adv* con negligencia.

**indomitable** *adj* indomable.

**indoors** *adv* dentro.

**indubitably** *adv* indudablemente.

**induce** *vt* inducir, persuadir; causar.

**inducement** *n* aliciente *m*.

**induction** *n* inducción *f*.

**indulge** *vt, vi* conceder; ser indulgente.

**indulgence** *n* indulgencia *f*.

**indulgent** *adj* indulgente; **~ly** *adv* de modo indulgente.

**industrial** *adj* industrial.

**industrialist** *n* industrial *m/f*.

**industrialization** *n* industrialización *f*.

**industrialize** *vt* industrializar.

**industrial park** *n* polígono industrial *m*.

**industrious** *adj* trabajador/a.

**industry** *n* industria *f*.

**inebriated** *adj* embriagado/da.

**inebriation** *n* embriaguez *f*.

**inedible** *adj* incomestible.

**ineffable** *adj* inefable.

**ineffective, ineffectual** *adj* ineficaz; **~ly** *adv* sin efecto.

**inefficiency** *n* ineficacia *f*.

**inefficient** *adj* ineficaz.

**ineligible** *adj* inelegible.

**inept** *adj* incompetente.

**ineptitude** *n* incompetencia *f*.

**inequality** *n* desigualdad *f*.

**inert** *adj* inerte, perezoso/sa.

**inertia** *n* inercia *f*.

**inescapable** *adj* ineludible.

**inestimable** *adj* inestimable, inapreciable.

**inevitable** *adj* inevitable.

**inevitably** *adv* inevitablemente.

**inexcusable** *adj* inexcusable.

**inexhaustible** *adj* inagotable.

**inexorable** *adj* inexorable.

**inexpedient** *adj* imprudente.

**inexpensive** *adj* económico/ca.

**inexperience** *n* inexperiencia *f*.

**inexperienced** *adj* inexperto/ta.

**inexpert** *adj* inexperto/ta.

**inexplicable** *adj* inexplicable.

**inexpressible** *adj* indecible.

**inextricably** *adv* indisolublemente.

**infallibility** *n* infalibilidad *f*.

**infallible** *adj* infalible; indefectible.

**infamous** *adj* vil, infame; **~ly** *adv* infamemente.

**infamy** *n* infamia *f*.

**infancy** *n* infancia *f*; pequeñez *f*.

**infant** *n* niño/ña *m/f*.

**infanticide** *n* infanticidio *m*; infanticida *m/f*.

**infantile** *adj* infantil.

**infantry** *n* infantería *f*.

**infatuated** *adj* chiflado/da.

**infatuation** *n* infatuación *f*.

**infect** *vt* infectar.

**infection** *n* infección *f*.

**infectious** *adj* contagioso/sa; infeccioso/sa.

**infer** *vt* inferir.

**inference** *n* inferencia *f*.

**inferior** *adj* inferior; * *n* subordinado/da *m/f*.

**inferiority** *n* inferioridad *f*.

**infernal** *adj* infernal.

**inferno** *n* infierno *m*.

**infest** *vt* infestar.

**infidel** *n* infiel, pagano *m*.

**infidelity** *n* infidelidad *f*.

**infiltrate** *vi* infiltrarse.

**infinite** *adj* infinito/ta; **~ly** *adv* infinitamente.

**infinitive** *n* infinitivo *m*.

**infinity** *n* infinito *m*; infinidad *f*.

**infirm** *adj* enfermo/ma, débil.

**infirmary** *n* enfermería *f*.

**infirmity** *n* fragilidad, enfermedad *f*.

**inflame** *vt (vi)* inflamar(se).

**inflammation** *n* inflamación *f*.

**inflammatory** *adj* inflamatorio/ria.

**inflatable** *adj* inflable.

**inflate** *vt* inflar, hinchar.

**inflation** *n* inflación *f*.

**inflection** *n* inflexión *f*; modulación de la voz *f*.

**inflexibility** *n* inflexibilidad *f*.

**inflexible** *adj* inflexible; yerto/ta.

**inflexibly** *adv* inflexiblemente.

**inflict** *vt* imponer.

**influence** *n* influencia *f*; * *vt* influir.

**influential** *adj* influyente.

**influenza** *n* gripe *f*.

**influx** *n* afluencia *f*.

**inform** *vt* informar.

**informal** *adj* informal.

**informality** *n* informalidad *f*.

**informant** *n* informante *m/f*.

**information** *n* información *f*; **~ super-highway** autopista de la información *f*.

**infraction** *n* infracción *f*.

**infra-red** *adj* infrarrojo/ja.

**infrastructure** *n* infraestructura *f*.

**infrequent** *adj* raro/ra; **~ly** *adv* raramente.
**infringe** *vt* infringir; violar.
**infringement** *n* infracción *f*.
**infuriate** *vt* enfurecer.
**infuse** *vt* infundir.
**infusion** *n* infusión *f*.
**ingenious** *adj* ingenioso/sa; **~ly** *adv* ingeniosamente.
**ingenuity** *n* ingeniosidad *f*.
**ingenuous** *adj* ingenuo/nua, sincero/ra; **~ly** *adv* ingenuamente.
**inglorious** *adj* ignominioso/sa, vergonzoso/sa; **~ly** *adv* ignominiosamente.
**ingot** *n* lingote *m*.
**ingrained** *adj* inveterado/da.
**ingratiate** *vi* congraciarse.
**ingratitude** *n* ingratitud *f*.
**ingredient** *n* ingrediente *m*.
**inhabit** *vt*, *vi* habitar.
**inhabitable** *adj* habitable.
**inhabitant** *n* habitante *m/f*.
**inhale** *vt* inhalar.
**inherent** *adj* inherente.
**inherit** *vt* heredar.
**inheritance** *n* herencia *f*.
**inheritor** *n* heredero/a *m/f*.
**inhibit** *vt* inhibir.
**inhibited** *adj* cohibido/da.
**inhibition** *n* inhibición *f*.
**inhospitable** *adj* inhospitalario/ria.
**inhospitality** *n* inhospitalidad *f*.
**inhuman** *adj* inhumano/na, cruel; **~ly** *adv* inhumanamente.
**inhumanity** *n* inhumanidad, crueldad *f*.
**inimical** *adj* enemigo/ga.
**inimitable** *adj* inimitable.
**iniquitous** *adj* inicuo/cua, injusto/ta.
**iniquity** *n* iniquidad, injusticia *f*.
**initial** *adj* inicial; * *n* inicial *f*.
**initially** *adv* al principio.
**initiate** *vt* iniciar.
**initiation** *n* principio *m*; iniciación *f*.
**initiative** *n* iniciativa *f*.
**inject** *vt* inyectar.
**injection** *n* inyección *f*.
**injudicious** *adj* poco juicioso/sa.
**injunction** *n* entredicho *m*.
**injure** *vt* herir.
**injury** *n* daño *m*.
**injury time** *n* descuento *m*.
**injustice** *n* injusticia *f*.
**ink** *n* tinta *f*.
**inkling** *n* sospecha *f*.
**inkstand** *n* tintero *m*.
**inlaid** *adj* taraceado/da.

**inland** *adj* interior; * *adv* tierra adentro.
**in-laws** *npl* suegros *mpl*.
**inlay** *vt* taracear.
**inlet** *n* ensenada *f*.
**inmate** *n* preso *m*.
**inmost** *adj* más íntimo/ma.
**inn** *n* posada *f*; mesón *m*.
**innate** *adj* innato/ta.
**inner** *adj* interior.
**innermost** *adj* más íntimo/ma.
**inner tube** *n* cámara *f*.
**innkeeper** *n* posadero/ra, mesonero/ra *m/f*.
**innocence** *n* inocencia *f*.
**innocent** *adj* inocente; **~ly** *adv* inocentemente.
**innocuous** *adj* inocuo/cua; **~ly** *adv* inocentemente.
**innovate** *vt* innovar.
**innovation** *n* innovación *f*.
**innuendo** *n* indirecta, insinuación *f*.
**innumerable** *adj* innumerable.
**inoculate** *vt* inocular.
**inoculation** *n* inoculación *f*.
**inoffensive** *adj* inofensivo/va.
**inopportune** *adj* inconveniente, inoportuno/na.
**inordinately** *adv* desmesuradamente.
**inorganic** *adj* inorgánico/ca.
**inpatient** *n* paciente interno/na *m/f*.
**input** *n* entrada *f*.
**inquest** *n* encuesta judicial *f*.
**inquire** *vt*, *vi* preguntar; **to ~ about** informarse de; **to ~ after** *vt* preguntar por; **to ~ into** *vt* investigar, indagar, inquirir.
**inquiry** *n* pesquisa *f*.
**inquisition** *n* inquisición *f*.
**inquisitive** *adj* curioso/sa.
**inroad** *n* incursión, invasión *f*.
**insane** *adj* loco/ca, demente.
**insanity** *n* locura *f*.
**insatiable** *adj* insaciable.
**inscribe** *vt* inscribir; dedicar.
**inscription** *n* inscripción *f*; dedicatoria *f*.
**inscrutable** *adj* inescrutable.
**insect** *n* insecto *m*.
**insecticide** *n* insecticida *m*.
**insecure** *adj* inseguro/ra.
**insecurity** *n* inseguridad *f*.
**insemination** *n* inseminación *f*.
**insensible** *adj* inconsciente.
**insensitive** *adj* insensible.
**inseparable** *adj* inseparable.
**insert** *vt* introducir.
**insertion** *n* inserción *f*.
**inshore** *adj* costero/ra.

**inside** *n* interior *m*; * *adv* dentro.
**inside out** *adv* al revés; a fondo.
**insidious** *adj* insidioso/sa; ~ly *adv* insidiosamente.
**insight** *n* perspicacia *f*.
**insignia** *npl* insignias *fpl*.
**insignificant** *adj* insignificante, frívolo/la.
**insincere** *adj* poco sincero/ra.
**insincerity** *n* falta de sinceridad *f*.
**insinuate** *vt* insinuar.
**insinuation** *n* insinuación *f*.
**insipid** *adj* insípido/da; insulso/sa; ñoño/ña.
**insipidness** *n* ñoñería *f*.
**insist** *vi* insistir.
**insistence** *n* insistencia *f*.
**insistent** *adj* insistente.
**insole** *n* plantilla *f*.
**insolence** *n* insolencia *f*.
**insolent** *adj* insolente; ~ly *adv* insolentemente.
**insoluble** *adj* insoluble.
**insolvency** *n* insolvencia *f*.
**insolvent** *adj* insolvente.
**insomnia** *n* insomnio *m*.
**insomuch** *conj* puesto que.
**inspect** *vt* examinar, inspeccionar.
**inspection** *n* inspección *f*.
**inspector** *n* inspector, superintendente *m*.
**inspiration** *n* inspiración *f*.
**inspire** *vt* inspirar.
**instability** *n* inestabilidad *f*.
**install**, **instal** *vt* instalar.
**installation** *n* instalación *f*.
**instalment** *n* instalación *f*; plazo *m*.
**instance** *n* ejemplo *m*; **for** ~ por ejemplo.
**instant** *adj* inmediato/ta; ~ly *adv* en seguida; * *n* instante, momento *m*.
**instantaneous** *adj* instantáneo/nea; ~ly *adv* instantáneamente.
**instead (of)** *prep* por, en lugar de, en vez de.
**instep** *n* empeine *m*.
**instigate** *vt* instigar.
**instigation** *n* instigación *f*.
**instil** *vt* inculcar.
**instinct** *n* instinto *m*.
**instinctive** *adj* instintivo/va; ~ly *adv* por instinto.
**institute** *vt* establecer; * *n* instituto *m*.
**institution** *n* institución *f*.
**instruct** *vt* instruir, enseñar; illustrar.
**instruction** *n* instrucción *f*.
**instructive** *adj* instructivo/va.
**instructor** *n* instructor/a *m/f*.
**instrument** *n* instrumento *m*.

**instrumental** *adj* instrumental.
**insubordinate** *adj* insubordinado/da.
**insubordination** *n* insubordinación *f*.
**insufferable** *adj* insoportable.
**insufferably** *adv* de modo insoportable.
**insufficiency** *n* insuficiencia *f*.
**insufficient** *adj* insuficiente; ~ly *adv* insuficientemente.
**insular** *adj* insular.
**insulate** *vt* aislar.
**insulating tape** *n* cinta aislante *f*.
**insulation** *n* aislamiento *m*.
**insulin** *n* insulina *f*.
**insult** *vt* insultar; * *n* insulto *m*.
**insulting** *adj* insultante.
**insuperable** *adj* insuperable.
**insurance** *n* (*com*) seguro *m*.
**insurance policy** *n* póliza de seguros *f*.
**insure** *vt* asegurar.
**insurgent** *n* insurgente, rebelde *m*.
**insurmountable** *adj* insuperable.
**insurrection** *n* insurrección *f*.
**intact** *adj* intacto/ta.
**intake** *n* admisión *f*; entrada *f*.
**integral** *adj* íntegro/gra; (*chem*) integrante; * *n* todo *m*.
**integrate** *vt* integrar.
**integration** *n* integración *f*.
**integrity** *n* integridad *f*.
**intellect** *n* intelecto *m*.
**intellectual** *adj* intelectual.
**intelligence** *n* inteligencia *f*.
**intelligent** *adj* inteligente.
**intelligentsia** *n* intelectualidad *f*.
**intelligible** *adj* inteligible.
**intelligibly** *adv* inteligiblemente.
**intemperate** *adj* inmoderado/da; ~ly *adv* inmoderadamente.
**intend** *vi* tener intención de.
**intendant** *n* intendente *m*.
**intended** *adj* deseado/da.
**intense** *adj* intenso/sa, hondo/da; ~ly *adv* intensamente.
**intensify** *vt* intensificar.
**intensity** *n* intensidad *f*.
**intensive** *adj* intensivo/va.
**intensive care unit** *n* unidad de vigilancia intensiva, unidad de cuidados intensivos *f*.
**intent** *adj* atento/ta, cuidadoso/sa; ~ly *adv* con aplicación; * *n* designio *m*.
**intention** *n* intención *f*; designio *m*.
**intentional** *adj* intencional; ~ly *adv* a propósito.
**inter** *vt* enterrar.
**interaction** *n* interacción *f*.

**intercede** *vi* interceder.
**intercept** *vt* interceptar.
**intercession** *n* intercesión, mediación *f*.
**interchange** *n* intercambio *m*.
**intercom** *n* interfono *m*.
**intercourse** *n* coito *m*.
**interest** *vt* interesar; * *n* interés *m*.
**interesting** *adj* interesante.
**interest rate** *n* tipo de interés *m*.
**interface** *n* interfaz, interface *f*.
**interfere** *vi* entrometerse.
**interference** *n* interferencia *f*.
**interim** *adj* provisional.
**interior** *adj* interior.
**interior design** *n* interiorismo *m*.
**interior designer** *n* interiorista *m/f*.
**interjection** *n* (*gr*) interjección *f*.
**interlock** *vi* endentarse.
**interlocutor** *n* interlocutor/a *m/f*.
**interloper** *n* intruso/sa *m/f*.
**interlude** *n* intermedio *m*.
**intermarriage** *n* matrimonio mixto *m*.
**intermediary** *n* intermediario/ria *m/f*.
**intermediate** *adj* intermedio/dia.
**interment** *n* entierro *m*; sepultura *f*.
**interminable** *adj* inacabable.
**intermingle** *vt, vi* entremezclar; mezclarse.
**intermission** *n* descanso *m*.
**intermittent** *adj* intermitente.
**intern** *n* interno *m*.
**internal** *adj* interno/na; ~**ly** *adv* internamente.
**international** *adj* internacional.
**Internet café** *n* cibercafé *m*.
**interplay** *n* interacción *f*.
**interpose** *vt* interponer.
**interpret** *vt* interpretar.
**interpretation** *n* interpretación *f*.
**interpreter** *n* intérprete *m/f*.
**interracial** *adj* interracial.
**interregnum** *n* interregno *m*.
**interrelated** *adj* interrelacionado/da.
**interrogate** *vt* interrogar.
**interrogation** *n* interrogatorio *m*.
**interrogative** *adj* interrogativo/va.
**interrupt** *vt* interrumpir.
**interruption** *n* interrupción *f*.
**intersect** *vi* cruzarse.
**intersection** *n* cruce *m*.
**intersperse** *vt* esparcir.
**intertwine** *vt* entretejer.
**interval** *n* intervalo *m*.
**intervene** *vi* intervenir; ocurrir.
**intervention** *n* intervención *f*.
**interview** *n* entrevista *f*; * *vt* entrevistar.

**interviewer** *n* entrevistador/a *m/f*.
**interweave** *vt* entretejer.
**intestate** *adj* intestado/da.
**intestinal** *adj* intestinal.
**intestine** *n* intestino *m*.
**intimacy** *n* intimidad *f*.
**intimate** *n* amigo/ga íntimo/ma *m/f*; * *adj* íntimo/ma; ~**ly** *adv* íntimamente; * *vt* insinuar, dar a entender.
**intimidate** *vt* intimidar.
**into** *prep* en, dentro, adentro.
**intolerable** *adj* intolerable.
**intolerably** *adv* intolerablemente.
**intolerance** *n* intolerancia *f*.
**intolerant** *adj* intolerante.
**intonation** *n* entonación *f*.
**intoxicate** *vt* embriagar.
**intoxication** *n* embriaguez *f*.
**intractable** *adj* intratable.
**intransitive** *adj* (*gr*) intransitivo/va.
**intravenous** *adj* intravenoso/sa.
**in-tray** *n* bandeja de entrada *f*.
**intrepid** *adj* intrépido/da; ~**ly** *adv* intrépidamente.
**intrepidity** *n* intrepidez *f*.
**intricacy** *n* complejidad *f*.
**intricate** *adj* intrincado/da, complicado/da; ~**ly** *adv* intrincadamente.
**intrigue** *n* intriga *f*; * *vi* intrigar.
**intriguing** *adj* fascinante.
**intrinsic** *adj* intrínseco/ca; ~**ally** *adv* intrínsecamente.
**introduce** *vt* introducir.
**introduction** *n* introducción *f*.
**introductory** *adj* introductorio/ria.
**introspection** *n* introspección *f*.
**introvert** *n* introvertido/da *m/f*.
**intrude** *vi* entrometerse.
**intruder** *n* intruso/sa *m/f*.
**intrusion** *n* invasión *f*.
**intuition** *n* intuición *f*.
**intuitive** *adj* intuitivo/va.
**inundate** *vt* inundar.
**inundation** *n* inundación *f*.
**inure** *vt* acostumbrar, habituar.
**invade** *vt* invadir.
**invader** *n* invasor/a *m/f*.
**invalid** *adj* inválido/da, nulo/la; * *n* minusválido *m*.
**invalidate** *vt* invalidar, anular.
**invaluable** *adj* inapreciable.
**invariable** *adj* invariable.
**invariably** *adv* invariablemente.
**invasion** *n* invasión *f*.
**invective** *n* invectiva *f*.

**inveigle** vt seducir, persuadir.
**invent** vt inventar.
**invention** n invento m.
**inventive** adj inventivo/va.
**inventor** n inventor m.
**inventory** n inventario m.
**inverse** adj inverso/sa.
**inversion** n inversión f.
**invert** vt invertir.
**invest** vt invertir.
**investigate** vt investigar.
**investigation** n investigación, pesquisa f.
**investigator** n investigador/a m/f.
**investment** n inversión f.
**inveterate** adj inveterado/da.
**invidious** adj odioso/sa.
**invigilate** vt vigilar.
**invigorating** adj vigorizante.
**invincible** adj invencible.
**invincibly** adv invenciblemente.
**inviolable** adj inviolable.
**invisible** adj invisible.
**invisibly** adv invisiblemente.
**invitation** n invitación f.
**invite** vt invitar.
**inviting** adj atractivo/va.
**invoice** n (com) factura f.
**invoke** vt invocar.
**involuntarily** adv involuntariamente.
**involuntary** adj involuntario/ria.
**involve** vt implicar.
**involved** adj complicado/da.
**involvement** n compromiso m.
**invulnerable** adj invulnerable.
**inward** adj interior; interno/na; ~, ~s adv hacia dentro.
**iodine** n (chem) yodo m.
**IOU (I owe you)** n pagaré m.
**irascible** adj irascible.
**irate**, **ireful** adj enojado/da.
**iris** n iris m.
**irksome** adj fastidioso/sa.
**iron** n hierro m, plancha f; * adj férreo/rea; * vt planchar.
**ironic** adj irónico/ca; ~ly adv con ironía.
**ironing** n planchado m.
**ironing board** n tabla de planchar f.
**iron ore** n mineral de hierro m.
**ironwork** n herraje m; ~s pl herrería f.
**irony** n ironía f.

**irradiate** vt irradiar.
**irrational** adj irracional.
**irreconcilable** adj irreconciliable.
**irregular** adj irregular; ~ly adv irregularmente.
**irregularity** n irregularidad f.
**irrelevant** adj impertinente.
**irreligious** adj irreligioso/sa.
**irreparable** adj irreparable.
**irreplaceable** adj irreemplazable.
**irrepressible** adj incontenible.
**irreproachable** adj irreprensible.
**irresistible** adj irresistible.
**irresolute** adj irresoluto/ta; ~ly adv irresolutamente.
**irresponsible** adj irresponsable.
**irretrievably** adv irreparablemente.
**irreverence** n irreverencia f.
**irreverent** adj irreverente; ~ly adv irreverentemente.
**irrigate** vt regar.
**irrigation** n riego m.
**irritability** n irritabilidad f.
**irritable** adj irritable.
**irritant** n (med) irritante m.
**irritate** vt irritar.
**irritating** adj fastidioso/sa.
**irritation** n fastidio m; picazón f.
**Islam** n islam m.
**Islamic** adj islámico/ca.
**island** n isla f.
**islander** n isleño/ña m/f.
**isle** n isla f.
**isolate** vt aislar.
**isolation** n aislamiento m.
**issue** n asunto m; * vt expedir; publicar; repartir.
**isthmus** n istmo m.
**it** pn él, ella, ello, lo, la, le.
**italic** n cursiva f.
**itch** n picazón f; * vi picar.
**item** n artículo m.
**itemize** vt detallar.
**itinerant** n ambulante, errante m.
**itinerary** n itinerario m.
**its** pn su, suyo.
**itself** pn se, por sí mismo.
**ivory** n marfil m.
**ivy** n hiedra f; yedra f.

# J

**jab** *vt* clavar.
**jabber** *vi* farfullar.
**jack** *n* gato *m*; sota *f*.
**jackal** *n* chacal *m*.
**jackboots** *npl* botas militares *fpl*.
**jackdaw** *n* grajo *m*.
**jacket** *n* chaqueta; funda *f*.
**jack-knife** *vi* colear.
**jackpot** *n* premio gordo *m*.
**jacuzzi** *n* jacuzzi *m*.
**jade** *n* jade *m*.
**jagged** *adj* dentado/da.
**jaguar** *n* jaguar *m*.
**jail, gaol** *n* cárcel *f*.
**jailbird** *n* preso/sa *m/f*.
**jailer** *n* carcelero/ra *m/f*.
**jam** *n* conserva *f*; mermelada de frutas *f*;
  (*auto*) embotellamiento *m*
**jangle** *vi* sonar.
**January** *n* enero *m*.
**jar** *vi* chocar; (*mus*) discordar; reñir; * *n*
  jarra *f*.
**jargon** *n* jerigonza *f*.
**jasmine** *n* jazmín *m*.
**jaundice** *n* ictericia *f*.
**jaunt** *n* excursión *f*.
**jaunty** *adj* alegre.
**javelin** *n* jabalina *f*.
**jaw** *n* mandíbula *f*.
**jay** *n* arrendajo *m*.
**jazz** *n* jazz *m*.
**jealous** *adj* celoso/sa; envidioso/sa.
**jealousy** *n* celos *mpl*; envidia *f*.
**jeans** *npl* vaqueros *mpl*.
**Jeep**™ *n* jeep *m*.
**jeer** *vi* befar, mofar; * *n* burla *f*.
**jelly** *n* jalea, gelatina *f*.
**jellyfish** *n* medusa *f*, aguamar *m*.
**jeopardize** *vt* arriesgar, poner en riesgo.
**jerk** *n* sacudida *f*; * *vt* tirar.
**jerky** *adj* espasmódico/ca.
**jersey** *n* jersey *m*.
**jest** *n* broma *f*.
**jester** *n* bufón/ona *m/f*.
**jestingly** *adv* de burlas.
**Jesuit** *n* jesuita *m*.
**Jesus** *n* Jesús *m*.
**jet** *n* avión a reacción *m*; azabache *m*.
**jet engine** *n* motor a reacción *m*, reactor *m*.
**jettison** *vt* desechar.
**jetty** *n* muelle *m*.

**Jew** *n* judío/día *m/f*.
**jewel** *n* joya *f*.
**jeweller** *n* joyero/ra *m/f*.
**jeweller's shop** *n* joyería *f*.
**jewellery** *n* joyería *f*.
**Jewish** *adj* judío/día.
**jib** *n* (*mar*) foque *m*.
**jibe** *n* mofa *f*.
**jig** *n* giga *f*.
**jigsaw** *n* rompecabezas *m invar*.
**jilt** *vt* dejar.
**jinx** *n* gafe *m*.
**job** *n* trabajo *m*.
**jockey** *n* jinete *m/f*.
**jocular** *adj* jocoso/sa, alegre.
**jocularity** *n* jocosidad *f*.
**jog** *vi* hacer footing.
**jogging** *n* footing *m*.
**join** *vt* juntar, unir; (*fig*) zurcir; **to ~ in**
  participar en; * *vi* unirse, juntarse.
**joiner** *n* carpintero/ra *m/f*.
**joinery** *n* carpintería *f*.
**joint** *n* articulación *f*; * *adj* común.
**jointly** *adv* conjuntamente.
**joint-stock company** *n* (*com*) sociedad por
  acciones *f*.
**joke** *n* broma *f*; * *vi* bromear.
**joker** *n* comodín *m*.
**jollity** *n* alegría *f*.
**jolly** *adj* alegre.
**jolt** *vt* sacudir; * *n* sacudida *f*.
**jostle** *vt* codear.
**journal** *n* revista *f*.
**journalism** *n* periodismo *m*.
**journalist** *n* periodista *m/f*.
**journey** *n* viaje *m*; * *vt* viajar.
**jovial** *adj* jovial, alegre; **~ly** *adv* con
  jovialidad.
**joy** *n* alegría *f*; júbilo *m*.
**joyful, joyous** *adj* alegre, gozoso/sa; **~ly**
  *adv* alegremente.
**joystick** *n* palanca de control *f*, joystick *m*.
**jubilant** *adj* jubiloso/sa.
**jubilation** *n* júbilo/la, regocijo *m*.
**jubilee** *n* jubileo *m*.
**Judaism** *n* judaísmo *m*.
**judge** *n* juez/a *m/f*; * *vt* juzgar.
**judgement** *n* juicio *m*.
**judicial** *adj* judicial; **~ly** *adv* judicialmente.
**judiciary** *n* poder judicial *m*, judicatura *f*.
**judicious** *adj* prudente.

**judo** *n* judo *m*.
**jug** *n* jarro *m*.
**juggle** *vi* hacer juegos malabares.
**juggler** *n* malabarista *m/f*.
**jugular** *adj* yugular.
**juice** *n* zumo, jugo *m*.
**juicy** *adj* jugoso/sa.
**jukebox** *n* gramola *f*.
**July** *n* julio *m*.
**jumble** *vt* mezclar; * *n* revoltijo *m*.
**jump** *vi* saltar, brincar; * *n* salto *m*.
**jumper** *n* suéter, jersey *m*.
**jumpy** *adj* nervioso/sa.
**juncture** *n* coyuntura *f*.
**June** *n* junio *m*.
**jungle** *n* selva *f*.
**junior** *adj* más joven.
**juniper** *n* (*bot*) enebro *m*.
**junk** *n* basura *f*; baratijas *fpl*.
**junk food** *n* comida basura f.

**junta** *n* junta *f*.
**jurisdiction** *n* jurisdicción *f*.
**jurisprudence** *n* jurisprudencia *f*.
**jurist** *n* jurista *m/f*.
**juror**, **juryman** *n* jurado/da *m/f*.
**jury** *n* jurado *m*.
**just** *adj* justo/ta; * *adv* justamente, exactamente; ~ **as** como; ~ **now** ahora mismo.
**justice** *n* justicia *f*.
**justifiably** *adv* con justificación.
**justification** *n* justificación *f*.
**justify** *vt* justificar.
**justly** *adv* justamente.
**justness** *n* justicia *f*.
**jut** *vi*; **to ~ out** sobresalir.
**jute** *n* yute *m*.
**juvenile** *adj* juvenil.
**juxtapose** *vt* yuxtaponer.
**juxtaposition** *n* yuxtaposición *f*.

# K

kaleidoscope *n* caleidoscopio *m*.
kangaroo *n* canguro *m*.
karaoke *n* karaoke *m*.
karate *n* kárate *m*.
kebab *n* pincho *m* moruno.
keel *n* (*mar*) quilla *f*.
keen *adj* agudo/da; vivo/va.
keenness *n* entusiasmo *m*.
keep *vt* mantener; guardar; conservar.
keeper *n* guardián/ana *m/f*.
keepsake *n* recuerdo *m*.
keg *n* barril *m*.
kennel *n* perrera *f*.
kerb *n* bordillo *m*.
kernel *n* fruta *f*; meollo *m*.
ketchup *n* catsup, ketchup *m*.
kettle *n* hervidor *m*.
kettle-drum *n* timbal *m*.
key *n* llave *f*; (*mus*) clave *f*; tecla *f*.
keyboard *n* teclado *m*.
keyhole *n* ojo de la cerradura *m*.
keynote *n* (*mus*) tónica *f*.
key ring *n* llavero *m*.
keystone *n* piedra clave *f*.
khaki *n* caqui *m*.
kick *vt*, *vi* patear; * *n* puntapié *m*; patada *f*.
kid *n* chico/ca *m/f*.
kidnap *vt* secuestrar.
kidnapper *n* secuestrador/a *m/f*.
kidnapping *n* secuestro *m*; rapto *m*.
kidney *n* riñón *m*.
killer *n* asesino/na *m/f*.
killing *n* asesinato *m*.
kiln *n* horno *m*.
kilo *n* kilo *m*.
kilobyte *n* kilobyte *m*.
kilogram *n* kilo *m*.
kilometre *n* kilómetro *m*.
kilt *n* falda escocesa *f*.
kin *n* parientes *mpl*; next of ~ pariente próximo *m*, pariente próxima *f*.
kind *adj* cariñoso/sa; * *n* género *m*.
kindergarten *n* jardín de infancia *m*.
kind-hearted *adj* bondadoso/sa.
kindle *vt*, *vi* encender.
kindliness *n* benevolencia *f*.
kindly *adj* bondadoso/sa.
kindness *n* bondad *f*.

kindred *adj* emparentado/da.
kinetic *adj* cinético/ca.
king *n* rey *m*.
kingdom *n* reino *m*.
kingfisher *n* martín pescador *m*.
king prawn *n* langostino *m*.
kiosk *n* quiosco *m*.
kiss *n* beso *m*; * *vt* besar.
kissing *n* besos *mpl*.
kit *n* equipo *m*.
kitchen *n* cocina *f*.
kitchen garden *n* huerta *f*.
kitchen maid *n* fregona *f*.
kite *n* cometa *f*.
kitten *n* gatito *m*.
knack *n* don *m*.
knapsack *n* mochila *f*.
knave *n* bribón, pícaro *m*; (cards) sota *f*.
knead *vt* amasar.
knee *n* rodilla *f*.
knee-deep *adj* metido hasta las rodillas.
kneel *vi* arrodillarse.
knell *n* toque de difuntos *m*.
knife *n* cuchillo *m*.
knight *n* caballero *m*.
knit *vt*, *vi* tejer, tricotear; to ~ the brows fruncir el ceño.
knitter *n* calcetero/ra, mediero/ra *m/f*.
knitting needle *n* aguja de tejer *f*.
knitwear *n* prendas de punto *fpl*.
knob *n* bulto *m*; nudo en la madera *m*; botón de las flores *m*.
knock *vt*, *vi* golpear, tocar; to ~ down derribar; * *n* golpe *m*.
knocker *n* aldaba *f*.
knock-kneed *adj* patizambo/ba; zambo/ba.
knock-out *n* K.O. *m*.
knoll *n* cima de una colina *f*.
knot *n* nudo *m*; lazo *m*; * *vt* anudar.
knotty *adj* escabroso/sa.
know *vt*, *vi* conocer; saber.
know-all *n* sabelotodo *m/f*.
know-how *n* conocimientos *mpl*.
knowing *adj* entendido/da; ~ly *adv* a sabiendas.
knowledge *n* conocimiento *m*.
knowledgeable *adj* bien informado/da.
knuckle *n* nudillo *m*.

# L

**label** *n* etiqueta *f.*
**laboratory** *n* laboratorio *m.*
**laborious** *adj* laborioso/sa; difícil; **~ly** *adv* laboriosamente.
**labour** *n* trabajo *m;* **to be in ~** estar de parto; * *vt* trabajar.
**labourer** *n* peón *m.*
**labyrinth** *n* laberinto *m.*
**lace** *n* cordón; encaje *m;* * *vt* abrochar.
**lacerate** *vt* lacerar.
**lack** *vt, vi* faltar; * *n* falta *f.*
**lackadaisical** *adj* descuidado/da.
**lackey** *n* lacayo *m.*
**laconic** *adj* lacónico/ca.
**lacquer** *n* laca *f.*
**lad** *n* muchacho *m.*
**ladder** *n* escalera *f.*
**ladle** *n* cucharón *m.*
**ladleful** *n* cucharada *f.*
**lady** *n* señora *f.*
**ladybird** *n* mariquita *f.*
**lady-killer** *n* casanova *m.*
**ladylike** *adj* fino/na.
**ladyship** *n* señoría *f.*
**lag** *vi* quedarse atrás.
**lager** *n* cerveza (rubia) *f.*
**lagoon** *n* laguna *f.*
**laid-back** *adj* relajado/da.
**lair** *n* guarida *f.*
**laity** *n* laicado *m.*
**lake** *n* lago *m;* laguna *f.*
**lamb** *n* cordero *m;* * *vi* parir.
**lame** *adj* cojo/ja.
**lament** *vt (vi)* lamentar(se); * *n* lamento *m.*
**lamentable** *adj* lamentable, deplorable.
**lamentation** *n* lamentación *f.*
**laminated** *adj* laminado/da; plastificado/da.
**lamp** *n* lámpara *f.*
**lampoon** *n* sátira *f.*
**lampshade** *n* pantalla *f.*
**lance** *n* lanza *f;* * *vt* abrir con lanceta.
**lancet** *n* lanceta *f.*
**land** *n* país *m;* tierra *f;* * *vt, vi* desembarcar.
**land forces** *npl* tropas de tierra *fpl.*
**land-holder** *n* hacendado *m.*
**landing** *n* desembarco *m.*
**landing strip** *n* pista de aterrizaje *f.*
**landlady** *n* propietaria *f.*
**landlord** *n* propietario *m.*
**landlubber** *n* marinero de agua dulce *m.*
**landmark** *n* lugar conocido; hito *m.*

**landowner** *n* terrateniente *m/f.*
**landscape** *n* paisaje *m.*
**landslide** *n* corrimiento de tierras *m.*
**lane** *n* callejuela *f.*
**langoustine** *n* langostino *m.*
**language** *n* lengua *f;* lenguaje *m.*
**languid** *adj* lánguido/da, débil; **~ly** *adv* lánguidamente, débilmente.
**languish** *vi* languidecer.
**lank** *adj* lacio/cia.
**lanky** *adj* larguirucho/cha.
**lantern** *n* linterna *f;* farol *m.*
**lap** *n* regazo *m;* * *vt* lamer.
**lapdog** *n* perro faldero *m.*
**lapel** *n* solapa *f.*
**lapse** *n* lapso *m;* * *vi* transcurrir.
**laptop** *n* portátil *m.*
**larceny** *n* latrocinio *m.*
**larch** *n* alerce *m.*
**lard** *n* manteca de cerdo *f.*
**larder** *n* despensa *f.*
**large** *adj* grande; **at ~** en libertad; **~ly** *adv* en gran parte.
**large-scale** *adj* en gran escala.
**largesse** *n* liberalidad *f.*
**lark** *n* alondra *f.*
**larva** *n* larva, oruga *f.*
**laryngitis** *n* laringitis *f.*
**larynx** *n* laringe *f.*
**lascivious** *adj* lascivo/va; **~ly** *adv* lascivamente.
**laser** *n* láser *m.*
**laser printer** *n* impresora láser *f.*
**lash** *n* latigazo *m;* * *vt* dar latigazos; atar.
**lasso** *n* lazo *m.*
**last** *adj* último/ma; pasado/da; **at ~** por fin; **~ly** *adv* finalmente; * *n* horma de zapatero *f,* * *vi* durar.
**last-ditch** *adj* último/ma.
**lasting** *adj* duradero/ra, permanente; **~ly** *adv* perpetuamente.
**last-minute** *adj* de última hora.
**latch** *n* picaporte *m.*
**latch-key** *n* llave maestra *f.*
**late** *adj* tarde; difunto/ta; *(rail)* **the train is ten minutes ~** el tren tiene un retraso de diez minutos; * *adv* tarde; **~ly** *adv* recientemente.
**latecomer** *n* recién llegado/da *m/f.*
**latent** *adj* latente.
**lateral** *adj* lateral; **~ly** *adv* lateralmente.

**lathe** *n* torno *m*.
**lather** *n* espuma *f*.
**latitude** *n* latitud *f*.
**latrine** *n* letrina *f*.
**latter** *adj* último/ma; **~ly** *adv* últimamente, recientemente.
**lattice** *n* celosía *f*.
**laudable** *adj* loable.
**laudably** *adv* loablemente.
**laugh** *vi* reir; **to ~ at** *vt* reírse de; * *n* risa *f*.
**laughable** *adj* absurdo/da.
**laughing stock** *n* hazmerreír *m*.
**laughter** *n* risa *f*.
**launch** *vt* (*vi*) lanzar(se); * *n* (*mar*) lancha *f*.
**launching** *n* lanzamiento *m*.
**launching pad** *n* plataforma de lanzamiento *f*.
**launder** *vt* lavar.
**Launderette**™ *n* lavandería automática *f*.
**laundry** *n* lavandería *f*.
**laurel** *n* laurel *m*.
**lava** *n* lava *f*.
**lavatory** *n* cuarto de baño *m*.
**lavender** *n* (*bot*) espliego *m*, lavanda *f*.
**lavish** *adj* pródigo/ga; **~ly** *adv* pródigamente; * *vt* disipar.
**law** *n* ley *f*; derecho *m*.
**law-abiding** *adj* respetuoso/sa con la ley.
**law and order** *n* orden público *m*.
**law court** *n* tribunal *m*.
**lawful** *adj* legal; legítimo/ma; **~ly** *adv* legalmente.
**lawless** *adj* anárquico/ca.
**lawlessness** *n* anarquía *f*.
**lawmaker**, **lawgiver** *n* legislador/a *m/f*.
**lawn** *n* pasto *m*.
**lawnmower** *n* cortacésped *m*.
**law school** *n* facultad de derecho *f*.
**lawsuit** *n* proceso *m*.
**lawyer** *n* abogado/da *m/f*.
**lax** *adj* laxo/xa; flojo/ja.
**laxative** *n* laxante *m*.
**laxity** *n* laxitud *f*; flojedad *f*.
**lay** *vt* poner; **to ~ claim** reclamar; pretender; **to ~ into** (*col*) zurrar; * *vi* poner.
**layabout** *n* vago/ga *m/f*.
**layer** *n* capa *f*.
**layette** *n* ajuar de niño *m*.
**layman** *n* lego, seglar *m*.
**layout** *n* composición *f*.
**laze** *vi* holgazanear.
**lazily** *adv* perezosamente; lentamente.
**laziness** *n* pereza *f*.
**lazy** *adj* perezoso/sa.
**lead**[1] *n* plomo *m*.

**lead**[2] *vt* conducir, guiar; * *vi* mandar.
**leader** *n* jefe/fa *m/f*.
**leadership** *n* dirección *f*; liderazgo *m*.
**leading** *adj* principal; capital; **~ article** *n* artículo principal *m*.
**leaf** *n* hoja *f*, yema *f*.
**leaflet** *n* folleto *m*.
**leafy** *adj* frondoso/sa.
**league** *n* liga, alianza *f*; legua *f*.
**leak** *n* escape *m*; * *vi* (*mar*) hacer agua.
**leaky** *adj* agujereado/da.
**lean** *vt* (*vi*) apoyar(se); * *adj* magro/ra.
**leap** *vi* saltar; * *n* salto *m*.
**leapfrog** *n* pídola *f*.
**leap year** *n* año bisiesto *m*.
**learn** *vt*, *vi* aprender.
**learned** *adj* docto/ta.
**learner** *n* aprendiz *m*.
**learning** *n* erudición *f*.
**lease** *n* arriendo *m*; * *vt* arrendar.
**leasehold** *n* arriendo *m*.
**leash** *n* correa *f*.
**least** *adj* mínimo/ma; **at ~** por lo menos; **not in the ~** en absoluto.
**leather** *n* cuero *m*.
**leathery** *adj* correoso/sa.
**leave** *n* licencia *f*; permiso *m*; **to take ~** despedirse; * *vt* dejar, abandonar.
**leaven** *n* levadura *f*; * *vt* fermentar.
**leavings** *npl* sobras *fpl*.
**lecherous** *adj* lascivo/va.
**lecture** *n* conferencia *f*; * *vt* dar una conferencia.
**lecturer** *n* conferenciante *m/f*; profesor/ra *m/f*.
**ledge** *n* reborde *m*.
**ledger** *n* (*com*) libro mayor *m*.
**lee** *n* (*mar*) sotavento *m*.
**leech** *n* sanguijuela *f*.
**leek** *n* (*bot*) puerro *m*.
**leer** *vt* mirar de manera lasciva.
**lees** *npl* sedimento, poso *m*.
**leeward** *adj* (*mar*) sotavento.
**leeway** *n* libertad de acción *f*.
**left** *adj* izquierdo/da; zurdo/da; **on the ~** a la izquierda.
**left-handed** *adj* zurdo/da.
**left luggage office** *n* consigna *f*.
**leftovers** *npl* sobras *fpl*.
**leg** *n* pierna *f*; pie *m*.
**legacy** *n* herencia *f*.
**legal** *adj* legal, legítimo/ma; **~ly** *adv* legalmente.
**legal holiday** *n* fiesta oficial *f*.
**legality** *n* legalidad, legitimidad *f*.

**legalize** *vt* legalizar.
**legal tender** *n* moneda de curso legal *f*.
**legate** *n* legado *m*.
**legatee** *n* legado *m*.
**legation** *n* legación *f*.
**legend** *n* leyenda *f*.
**legendary** *adj* legendario/ria.
**legible** *adj* legible.
**legibly** *adv* legiblemente.
**legion** *n* legión *f*.
**legislate** *vt* legislar.
**legislation** *n* legislación *f*.
**legislative** *adj* legislativo/va.
**legislator** *n* legislador/a *m/f*.
**legislature** *n* cuerpo legislativo *m*.
**legitimacy** *n* legitimidad *f*.
**legitimate** *adj* legítimo/ma; **~ly** *adv* legítimamente; * *vt* legitimar.
**leisure** *n* ocio *m*; **~ly** *adj* sin prisa; **at ~** desocupado/da.
**lemon** *n* limón *m*.
**lemonade** *n* limonada *f*.
**lemon tea** *n* te con limón *m*.
**lemon tree** *n* limonero *m*.
**lend** *vt* prestar.
**length** *n* largo *m*; duración *f*; **at ~** finalmente.
**lengthen** *vt* alargar; * *vi* alargarse.
**lengthways, lengthwise** *adv* a lo largo.
**lengthy** *adj* largo/ga.
**lenient** *adj* indulgente.
**lens** *n* lente *f*.
**Lent** *n* Cuaresma *f*.
**lentil** *n* lenteja *f*.
**leopard** *n* leopardo *m*; mallas *fpl*.
**leotard** *n* leotardo *m*.
**leper** *n* leproso/sa *m/f*.
**leprosy** *n* lepra *f*.
**lesbian** *n* lesbiana *f*.
**less** *adj* menor; * *adv* menos.
**lessen** *vt* disminuir; * *vi* disminuirse.
**lesser** *adj* más pequeño/ña.
**lesson** *n* lección *f*.
**lest** *conj* para que no.
**let** *vt* dejar, permitir; alquilar.
**lethal** *adj* mortal.
**lethargic** *adj* letárgico/ca.
**lethargy** *n* letargo *m*.
**letter** *n* letra *f*; carta *f*.
**letter bomb** *n* carta bomba *f*.
**letter box, postbox** *n* buzón *m*.
**lettering** *n* letras *fpl*.
**letter of credit** *n* carta de crédito *f*.
**lettuce** *n* lechuga *f*.
**leukaemia** *n* leucemia *f*.

**level** *adj* llano/na, igual; nivelado/da; * *n* nivel *m*; * *vt* allanar; nivelar.
**level crossing** *n* paso a nivel *m*.
**level-headed** *adj* sensato/ta.
**lever** *n* palanca *f*.
**leverage** *n* influencia *f*.
**levity** *n* ligereza *f*.
**levy** *n* leva (de tropas) *f*; * *vt* recaudar.
**lewd** *adj* obsceno/na.
**lexicon** *n* lexicón *m*.
**liability** *n* responsabilidad *f*.
**liable** *adj* sujeto/ta; responsable.
**liaise** *vi* enlazar.
**liaison** *n* enlace *m*.
**liar** *n* embustero *m*.
**libel** *n* difamación *f*; * *vt* difamar.
**libellous** *adj* difamatorio/ria.
**liberal** *adj* liberal, generoso/sa; **~ly** *adv* liberalmente.
**liberality** *n* liberalidad, generosidad *f*.
**liberate** *vt* libertar.
**liberation** *n* liberación *f*.
**libertine** *n* libertino *m*.
**liberty** *n* libertad *f*.
**Libra** *n* Libra *f*.
**librarian** *n* bibliotecario/ria *m/f*.
**library** *n* biblioteca *f*.
**libretto** *n* libreto *m*.
**licence** *n* licencia *f*; permiso *m*.
**license** *vt* autorizar, licenciar.
**licentious** *adj* licencioso/sa.
**lichen** *n* (*bot*) liquen *m*.
**lick** *vt* lamer.
**lid** *n* tapa *f*.
**lie** *n* mentira *f*; * *vi* mentir; echarse.
**lie down** *vi* yacer.
**lieu** *n*: **in ~ of** en vez de.
**lieutenant** *n* lugarteniente *m/f*; teniente *m/f*.
**life** *n* vida *f*; **for ~** para toda la vida.
**lifeboat** *n* lancha de socorro *f*; bote salvavidas *m*.
**lifeguard** *n* socorrista *m/ff*.
**life jacket** *n* chaleco salvavidas *m*.
**lifeless** *adj* muerto/ta; sin vida.
**lifelike** *adj* natural.
**lifeline** *n* cordón umbilical *m*.
**life sentence** *n* cadena perpetua *f*.
**life-sized** *adj* de tamaño natural.
**life span** *n* vida *f*.
**lifestyle** *n* estilo de vida *f*.
**life-support system** *n* sistema de respiración asistida *m*.
**lifetime** *n* vida *f*.
**lift** *vt* levantar.
**ligament** *n* ligamento *m*.

**light** *n* luz *f*; * *adj* ligero/ra; claro/ra; * *vt* encender; alumbrar.
**light bulb** *n* foco *m*; bombilla *f*.
**lighten** *vi* relampaguear; * *vt* iluminar; aligerar; (*mar*) zafar.
**lighter** *n* encendedor *m*.
**light-headed** *adj* mareado/da.
**light-hearted** *adj* alegre.
**lighthouse** *n* (*mar*) faro *m*.
**lighting** *n* iluminación *f*.
**lightly** *adv* ligeramente.
**lightning** *n* relámpago *m*.
**lightning-rod** *n* pararrayos *m invar*.
**light pen** *n* lápiz óptico *m*.
**lightweight** *adj* ligero/ra.
**light year** *n* año luz *m*.
**ligneous** *adj* leñoso/sa.
**like** *adj* semejante; igual; * *adv* como, del mismo modo que; * *vt, vi* gustar.
**likeable** *adj* simpático/ca.
**likelihood** *n* probabilidad *f*.
**likely** *adj* probable, verosímil.
**liken** *vt* comparar.
**likeness** *n* semejanza *f*.
**likewise** *adv* igualmente.
**liking** *n* agrado *m*.
**lilac** *n* lila *f*.
**lily** *n* lirio *m*; ~ **of the valley** lirio de los valles.
**limb** *n* miembro *m*.
**limber** *adj* flexible.
**lime** *n* cal *f*; lima *f*; ~ **tree** tilo *m*.
**limestone** *n* piedra caliza *f*; caliza *f*.
**limit** *n* límite, término *m*; * *vt* restringir.
**limitation** *n* limitación *f*; restricción *f*.
**limitless** *adj* inmenso/sa.
**limousine** *n* limusina *f*.
**limp** *vi* cojear; * *n* cojera *f*; * *adj* flojo/ja.
**limpet** *n* lapa *f*.
**limpid** *adj* claro/ra, transparente.
**line** *n* línea *f*; raya *f*; * *vt* forrar; revestir.
**lineage** *n* linaje *m*; filiación *f*.
**linear** *adj* lineal.
**lined** *adj* rayado/da; arrugado/da.
**linen** *n* lino *m*.
**liner** *n* transatlántico *m*.
**linesman** *n* juez de línea *m*.
**linger** *vi* persistir.
**lingerie** *n* ropa interior *f*.
**lingering** *adj* lento/ta.
**linguist** *n* lingüista *m/f*.
**linguistic** *adj* lingüístico/ca.
**linguistics** *n* lingüística *f*.
**liniment** *n* linimento *m*.
**lining** *n* forro *m*.

**link** *n* eslabón *m*; * *vt* enlazar.
**linnet** *n* pardillo *m*.
**linoleum** *n* linóleo *m*.
**linseed** *n* linaza *f*.
**lint** *n* hilas *fpl*.
**lintel** *n* dintel, tranquero *m*.
**lion** *n* león *m*.
**lioness** *n* leona *f*.
**lip** *n* labio *m*; borde *m*.
**liposuction** *n* liposucción *f*.
**lip read** *vi* leer los labios.
**lipstick** *n* lápiz de labios *m*.
**liqueur** *n* licor *m*.
**liquid** *adj* líquido/da; * *n* líquido *m*.
**liquidate** *vt* liquidar.
**liquidation** *n* liquidación *f*.
**liquidize** *vt* licuar.
**liquor** *n* licor *m*.
**liquorice** *n* regaliz *m*.
**lisp** *vi* cecear; * *n* ceceo *m*.
**list** *n* lista *f*; * *vt* hacer una lista de.
**listen** *vi* escuchar.
**listless** *adj* indiferente.
**litany** *n* letanía *f*.
**literal** *adj* literal; ~**ly** *adv* literalmente.
**literary** *adj* literario/ria.
**literate** *adj* culto/ta.
**literature** *n* literatura *f*.
**lithe** *adj* ágil.
**lithograph** *n* litografía *f*.
**lithography** *n* litografía *f*.
**litigation** *n* litigio *m*.
**litigious** *adj* litigioso/sa.
**litre** *n* litro *m*.
**litter** *n* litera *f*; camada *f*; * *vt* parir.
**little** *adj* pequeño/ña, poco/ca; ~ **by** ~ poco a poco; * *n* poco *m*.
**liturgy** *n* liturgia *f*.
**live** *vi* vivir; habitar; **to** ~ **on** alimentarse de; **to** ~ **up to** *vt* cumplir con; * *adj* vivo/va.
**livelihood** *n* vida *f*.
**liveliness** *n* vivacidad *f*; belleza *f*.
**lively** *adj* vivo/va.
**liven up** *vt* animar.
**liver** *n* hígado *m*.
**livery** *n* librea *f*.
**livestock** *n* ganado *m*.
**livid** *adj* lívido/da, cárdeno/na.
**living** *n* vida *f*; * *adj* vivo/va.
**living room** *n* sala de estar *f*.
**lizard** *n* lagarto *m*.
**load** *vt* cargar; * *n* carga *f*.
**loaded** *adj* cargado/da.
**loaf** *n* pan *m*.
**loafer** *n* holgazán, gandul *m*.

**loam** *n* marga *f*.
**loan** *n* préstamo *m*.
**loathe** *vt* aborrecer; tener hastío; * *vi* fastidiar.
**loathing** *n* aversión *f*.
**loathsome** *adj* asqueroso/sa.
**lobby** *n* vestíbulo *m*.
**lobe** *n* lóbulo *m*.
**lobster** *n* langosta *f*.
**local** *adj* local.
**local anaesthetic** *n* anestesia local *f*.
**local government** *n* gobierno municipal *m*.
**locality** *n* localidad *f*.
**localize** *vt* localizar.
**locally** *adv* en la vecindad.
**locate** *vt* localizar.
**location** *n* situación *f*.
**loch** *n* lago *m*.
**lock** *n* cerradura *f*; * *vt* cerrar con llave.
**locker** *n* vestuario *m*.
**locket** *n* medallón *m*.
**lockout** *n* cierre patronal *m*.
**locksmith** *n* cerrajero *m*.
**lockup** *n* garaje *m*, cochera *f*.
**locomotive** *n* locomotora *f*.
**locust** *n* langosta *f*.
**lodge** *n* casa del guarda *f*; * *vi* alojarse.
**lodger** *n* inquilino/na *m/f*.
**loft** *n* desván *m*.
**lofty** *adj* alto/ta.
**log** *n* leño *m*.
**logbook** *n* (*mar*) diario de a bordo *m*.
**logic** *n* lógica *f*.
**logical** *adj* lógico/ca.
**logo** *n* logotipo *m*.
**loin** *n* lomo *m*.
**loiter** *vi* merodear.
**loll** *vi* repantigarse.
**lollipop** *n* pirulí *m*, piruleta *f*.
**lonely** *adj* solitario/ria; solo/la.
**loneliness** *n* soledad *f*.
**long** *adj* largo/ga; * *vi* anhelar.
**long-distance call** *n* llamada interurbana *f*.
**longevity** *n* longevidad *f*.
**long-haired** *adj* de pelo largo.
**longing** *n* anhelo *m*.
**longitude** *n* longitud *f*.
**longitudinal** *adj* longitudinal.
**long jump** *n* salto de longitud *m*.
**long-legged** *adj* zancudo/da.
**long-playing record** *n* elepé *m*.
**long-range** *adj* de gran alcance.
**long-term** *adj* a largo plazo.
**long wave** *n* onda larga *f*.
**long-winded** *adj* prolijo/ja.

**look** *vi* mirar; parecer; **to ~ after** *vt* cuidar; **to ~ for** *vt* buscar; **to ~ forward to** *vt* esperar con impaciencia; **to ~ out for** *vt* aguardar; * *n* aspecto *m*; mirada *f*.
**looking glass** *n* espejo *m*.
**lookout** *n* (*mil*) centinela *f*; vigía *f*.
**loom** *n* telar *m*; * *vi* amenazar.
**loop** *n* lazo *m*.
**loophole** *n* escapatoria *f*.
**loose** *adj* suelto/ta; flojo/ja; **~ly** *adv* aproximadamente.
**loosen** *vt* aflojar, zafar.
**loot** *vt* saquear; * *n* botín *m*.
**lop** *vt* desmochar.
**lop-sided** *adj* desequilibrado/da.
**loquacious** *adj* locuaz.
**loquacity** *n* locuacidad *f*.
**lord** *n* señor *m*.
**lore** *n* saber popular *m*.
**lose** *vt* perder; * *vi* perder; **to ~ weight** *vi* adelgazar.
**loss** *n* pérdida *f*; **to be at a ~** no saber qué hacer.
**lost and found** *n* objetos perdidos *mpl*.
**lot** *n* suerte *f*; lote *m*; **a ~** mucho.
**lotion** *n* loción *f*.
**lottery** *n* lotería, rifa *f*.
**loud** *adj* fuerte; **~ly** *adv* fuerte.
**loudspeaker** *n* altavoz *m*.
**lounge** *n* salón *m*.
**louse** *n* (*pl* **lice**) piojo *m*.
**lousy** *adj* vil.
**lout** *n* gamberro *m*.
**lovable** *adj* amable.
**love** *n* amor, cariño *m*; **to fall in ~** enamorarse; * *vt* amar; gustar.
**love letter** *n* carta de amor *f*.
**love life** *n* vida sentimental *f*.
**lovely** *adj* hermoso/sa.
**lover** *n* amante *m*.
**lovesick** *adj* enamorado/da.
**loving** *adj* amoroso/sa.
**low** *adj* bajo/ja; * *vi* mugir.
**low-cut** *adj* escotado/da.
**lower** *adj* más bajo/ja; * *vt* bajar.
**lowest** *adj* más bajo/ja, ínfimo/ma.
**lowland** *n* tierra baja *f*.
**lowliness** *n* humildad *f*.
**lowly** *adj* humilde.
**low water, low tide** *n* bajamar *f*.
**loyal** *adj* leal; fiel; **~ly** *adv* lealmente.
**loyalty** *n* lealtad *f*; fidelidad *f*.
**lozenge** *n* pastilla *f*.
**lubricant** *n* lubricante *m*.
**lubricate** *vt* lubricar.

**lucid** *adj* lúcido/da.
**luck** *n* suerte; fortuna *f*.
**luckily** *adv* afortunadamente.
**luckless** *adj* desdichado/da.
**lucky** *adj* afortunado/da.
**lucrative** *adj* lucrativo/va.
**ludicrous** *adj* absurdo/da.
**lug** *vt* arrastrar.
**luggage** *n* equipaje *m*.
**lugubrious** *adj* lúgubre, triste.
**lukewarm** *adj* tibio/bia.
**lull** *vt* acunar; * *n* tregua *f*.
**lullaby** *n* nana *f*.
**lumbago** *n* lumbago *m*.
**lumberjack** *n* maderero/ra *m/f*.
**luminous** *adj* luminoso/sa.
**lump** *n* terrón *m*; bulto *m*; chichón *m*; * *vt* juntar.
**lump sum** *n* suma global *f*.
**lunacy** *n* locura *f*.
**lunar** *adj* lunar.
**lunatic** *adj* loco/ca.
**lunch, luncheon** *n* almuerzo *m*, comida *f*; * *vt, vi* almorzar.
**lungs** *npl* pulmones *mpl*.
**lurch** *n* sacudida *f*.
**lure** *n* señuelo *m*; cebo *m*; * *vt* inducir.

**lurid** *adj* sensacional.
**lurk** *vi* esconderse.
**luscious** *adj* delicioso/sa.
**lush** *adj* exuberante.
**lust** *n* lujuria, sensualidad *f*; concupiscencia *f*; * *vi* lujuriar; **to ~ after** *vt* codiciar.
**lustful** *adj* lujurioso/sa, voluptuoso/sa; **~ly** *adv* lujuriosamente.
**lustily** *adv* vigorosamente.
**lustre** *n* lustre *m*.
**lusty** *adj* fuerte, vigoroso/sa.
**lute** *n* laúd *m*.
**Lutheran** *n* luterano/na *m/f*.
**luxuriance** *n* exuberancia, superabundancia *f*.
**luxuriant** *adj* exuberante, superabundante.
**luxuriate** *vi* crecer con exuberancia.
**luxurious** *adj* lujoso/sa; exuberante; **~ly** *adv* lujosamente.
**luxury** *n* lujo *m*, voluptuosidad *f*; exuberancia *f*.
**lying** *n* mentiras *fpl*.
**lymph** *n* linfa *f*.
**lynch** *vt* linchar.
**lynx** *n* lince *m*.
**lyrical** *adj* lírico/ca.
**lyrics** *npl* letra *f*.

# M

**macaroni** *n* macarrones *mpl*.
**macaroon** *n* almendrado *m*.
**mace** *n* maza *f*; macis *f invar*.
**macerate** *vt* macerar; mortificar.
**machination** *n* maquinación, trama *f*.
**machine** *n* máquina *f*.
**machine gun** *n* ametralladora *f*.
**machinery** *n* maquinaria, mecánica *f*.
**mackerel** *n* caballa *f*.
**mad** *adj* loco/ca, furioso/sa, rabioso/sa, insensato/ta.
**madam** *n* madama, señora *f*.
**madden** *vt* enloquecer.
**madder** *n* (*bot*) rubia *f*.
**madhouse** *n* casa de locos *f*.
**madly** *adv* locamente.
**madman** *n* loco *m*.
**madness** *n* locura *f*.
**magazine** *n* revista *f*; almacén *m*.
**maggot** *n* gusano *m*.
**magic** *n* magia *f*; * *adj* mágico/ca; **~ally** *adv* mágicamente.
**magician** *n* mago/ga *m/f*; prestidigitador/a *m/f*.
**magisterial** *adj* magistral; **~ly** *adv* magistralmente.
**magistracy** *n* magistratura *f*.
**magistrate** *n* magistrado/da *m/f*.
**magnanimity** *n* magnanimidad *f*.
**magnanimous** *adj* magnánimo; **~ly** *adv* magnanimaménte.
**magnet** *n* iman *m*.
**magnetic** *adj* magnetico/ca.
**magnetism** *n* magnetismo *m*.
**magnificence** *n* magnificencia *f*.
**magnificent** *adj* magnifico; **~ly** *adv* magnífcamente.
**magnify** *vt* aumentar; exagerar.
**magnifying glass** *n* lupa *f*.
**magnitude** *n* magnitud *f*.
**magpie** *n* urraca *f*.
**mahogany** *n* caoba *f*.
**maid** *n* criada *f*.
**maiden** *n* doncella *f*.
**maiden name** *n* nombre de soltera *m*.
**mail** *n* correo *m*.
**mailing list** *n* lista de direcciones *f*.
**mail order** *n* venta por correo *f*.
**mail train** *n* (*rail*) tren correo *m*.
**maim** *vt* mutilar.
**main** *adj* principal; esencial; **in the ~** en general.

**mainland** *n* continente *m*.
**main line** *n* (*rail*) línea principal *f*.
**mainly** *adv* principalmente.
**main street** *n* calle mayor *f*.
**maintain** *vt* mantener; sostener.
**maintenance** *n* mantenimiento *m*.
**maize** *n* maíz *m*.
**majestic** *adj* majestuoso/sa; **~ally** *adv* majestuosamente.
**majesty** *n* majestad *f*.
**major** *adj* principal; * *n* (*mil*) comandante/a *m/f*.
**majority** *n* mayoría *f*.
**make** *vt* hacer, crear; **to ~ for** dirigirse hacia; **to ~ up** inventar; **to ~ up for** compensar; **to ~ off with something** alzar; * *n* marca *f*.
**make-believe** *n* invención *f*.
**makeshift** *adj* improvisado.
**make-up** *n* maquillaje *m*.
**make-up remover** *n* desmaquillador *m*.
**malady** *n* enfermedad *f*.
**malaise** *n* malestar *m*.
**malaria** *n* malaria *f*.
**malcontent** *adj*, *n* malcontento/ta *m/f*.
**male** *adj* masculino/na; * *n* macho *m*.
**malevolence** *n* malevolencia *f*.
**malevolent** *adj* malévolo/la; **~ly** *adv* malignamente.
**malfunction** *n* mal funcionamiento, fallo *m*.
**malice** *n* malicia *f*.
**malicious** *adj* malicioso/sa; **~ly** *adv* maliciosamente.
**malign** *adj* maligno; * *vt* calumniar.
**malignant** *adj* maligno/na; **~ly** *adv* malignamente.
**mall (shopping)** *n* centro comercial; paseo *m*.
**malleable** *adj* maleable.
**mallet** *n* mazo *m*.
**mallow** *n* (*bot*) malva *f*.
**malnutrition** *n* desnutrición *f*.
**malpractice** *n* negligencia *f*.
**malt** *n* malta *f*.
**maltreat** *vt* maltratar.
**mammal** *n* mamífero *m*.
**mammoth** *adj* gigantesco/ca.
**man** *n* hombre *m*; * *vt* (*mar*) tripular.
**manacle** *n* manilla *f*; **~s** *npl* esposas *fpl*.
**manage** *vt*, *vi* manejar, dirigir.
**manageable** *adj* manejable.

**management** *n* dirección *f*.
**manager** *n* director/a *m/f*.
**manageress** *n* directora *f*.
**managerial** *adj* directivo/va.
**managing director** *n* director/a general *m/f*.
**mandarin** *n* (*bot*) mandarina *f*; mandarín *m*.
**mandate** *n* mandato *m*.
**mandatory** *adj* obligatorio/ria.
**mane** *n* crines *fpl*, melena *f*.
**manfully** *adv* valerosamente.
**manger** *n* pesebre *m*.
**mangle** *n* rodillo *m*; * *vt* mutilar.
**mangy** *adj* sarnoso/sa.
**manhandle** *vt* maltratar.
**manhood** *n* madurez *f*; hombría *f*.
**man-hour** *n* hora hombre *f*.
**mania** *n* manía *f*.
**maniac** *n* maníaco/ca *m/f*.
**manic** *adj* frenético/ca.
**manicure** *n* manicura *f*.
**manifest** *adj* manifiesto/ta, patente; * *vt* manifestar.
**manifestation** *n* manifestación *f*.
**manifesto** *n* manifiesto *m*.
**manipulate** *vt* manejar; manipular.
**manipulation** *n* manejo; manipulación *f*.
**mankind** *n* género humano *m*.
**manlike** *adj* varonil.
**manliness** *n* valentía, hombría *f*.
**manly** *adj* varonil.
**man-made** *adj* artificial.
**manner** *n* manera *f*; modo *m*; forma *f*; ~s *pl* modales *mpl*.
**manoeuvre** *n* maniobra *f*.
**manpower** *n* mano de obra *f*.
**mansion** *n* palacio *m*, mansión *f*.
**manslaughter** *n* homicidio (sin premeditación) *m*.
**mantelpiece** *n* repisa (de chimenea) *f*.
**manual** *adj*, *n* manual *m*.
**manufacture** *n* fabricación *f*; * *vt* fabricar.
**manufacturer** *n* fabricante *m/f*.
**manure** *n* abono *m*; estiércol *m*; fiemo *m*; * *vt* abonar.
**manuscript** *n* manuscrito *m*.
**many** *adj* muchos, muchas; ~ **a time** muchas veces; **how ~?** ¿cuántos?; **as ~ as** tantos como.
**map** *n* mapa *m*; * *vt* planear, trazar el mapa de; **to ~ out** proyectar.
**maple** *n* arce *m*.
**mar** *vt* estropear.
**marathon** *n* maratón *m*.
**marauder** *n* merodeador/a *m/f*.
**marble** *n* mármol *m*; * *adj* marmóreo/rea.

**March** *n* marzo *m*.
**march** *n* marcha *f*; * *vi* marchar.
**march past** *n* desfile *m*.
**mare** *n* yegua *f*.
**margarine** *n* margarina *f*.
**margin** *n* margen *m*; borde *m*.
**marginal** *adj* marginal.
**marigold** *n* (*bot*) caléndula *f*.
**marijuana** *n* marihuana *f*.
**marinate** *vt* adobar.
**marine** *adj* marino/na; * *n* infante de marina *m*.
**mariner** *n* marinero/ra *m/f*.
**marital** *adj* marital.
**maritime** *adj* marítimo/ma.
**marjoram** *n* mejorana *f*.
**mark** *n* marca *f*; señal *f*; * *vt* marcar.
**marker** *n* registro *m*.
**market** *n* mercado *m*.
**marketable** *adj* vendible.
**market garden** *n* huerto de hortalizas *m*.
**marketing** *n* márketing *m*.
**marketplace** *n* mercado *m*.
**market research** *n* análisis de mercados *m invar*.
**market value** *n* valor de mercado *m*.
**marksman** *n* tirador *m*.
**marmalade** *n* mermelada de naranja *f*.
**maroon** *adj* marrón.
**marquee** *n* entoldado/da *m/f*.
**marriage** *n* matrimonio *m*; casamiento *m*.
**marriageable** *adj* casadero/ra.
**marriage certificate** *n* partida de casamiento *f*.
**married** *adj* casado/da; conyugal.
**marrow** *n* médula *f*.
**marry** *vi* casarse.
**marsh** *n* pantano *m*.
**marshal** *n* mariscal/a *m/f*.
**marshy** *adj* pantanoso/sa.
**marten** *n* marta *f*.
**martial** *adj* marcial; ~ **law** *n* ley marcial *f*.
**martyr** *n* mártir *m*.
**martyrdom** *n* martirio *m*.
**marvel** *n* maravilla *f*; * *vi* maravillar(se).
**marvellous** *adj* maravilloso/sa; ~**ly** *adv* maravillosamente.
**marzipan** *n* mazapán *m*.
**mascara** *n* rímel *m*.
**masculine** *adj* masculino/na, varonil.
**mash** *n* mezcla *f*.
**mask** *n* máscara *f*; * *vt* enmascarar.
**masochist** *n* masoquista *m/f*.
**mason** *n* albañil *m*.
**masonry** *n* mampostería *f*.

**masquerade** *n* mascarada *f*.
**mass** *n* masa *f*; misa *f*; montón *m*.
**massacre** *n* carnicería, matanza *f*; * *vt* hacer una carnicería.
**massage** *n* masaje *m*.
**masseur** *n* masajista *m*.
**masseuse** *n* masajista *f*.
**massive** *adj* enorme.
**mass-media** *npl* medios de comunicación de masas *mpl*.
**mast** *n* mástil *m*.
**master** *n* amo/ma, dueño/ña *m/f*; maestro/ tra *m/f*; * *vt* dominar.
**masterly** *adj* magistral.
**mastermind** *vt* dirigir.
**masterpiece** *n* obra maestra *f*.
**mastery** *n* maestría *f*.
**masticate** *vt* masticar.
**mastiff** *n* mastín *m*.
**mat** *n* estera *f*; felpudo *m*.
**match** *n* fósforo *m*, cerilla *f*; partido *m*; * *vt* igualar; * *vi* hacer juego.
**matchbox** *n* caja de fósforos *f*.
**matchless** *adj* incomparable, sin par.
**matchmaker** *n* casamentero/ra *m/f*.
**mate** *n* compañero/ra *m/f*; * *vt* acoplar.
**material** *adj* material; ~ly *adv* materialmente.
**materialism** *n* materialismo *m*.
**maternal** *adj* maternal.
**maternity clothes** *npl* vestido premamá *m*.
**maternity hospital** *n* hospital de maternidad *m*.
**mathematical** *adj* matemático/ca; ~ly *adv* matemáticamente.
**mathematician** *n* matemático/ca *m/f*.
**mathematics** *npl* matemáticas *fpl*.
**maths** *npl* mates, matemáticas *fpl*.
**matinee** *n* función de la tarde *f*.
**mating** *n* aparejamiento *m*.
**matins** *npl* maitines *mpl*.
**matriculate** *vt* matricular.
**matriculation** *n* matriculación *f*.
**matrimonial** *adj* matrimonial.
**mat, matt(e)** *adj* mate.
**matted** *adj* enmarañado/da.
**matter** *n* materia, substancia *f*; asunto *m*; cuestión *f*; **what is the ~?** ¿qué pasa?; **as a ~ of fact** en realidad; * *vi* importar.
**mattress** *n* colchón *m*.
**mature** *adj* maduro/ra; * *vt* madurar.
**maturity** *n* madurez *f*.
**maul** *vt* magullar.
**mausoleum** *n* mausoleo *m*.
**mauve** *adj* malva.

**maxim** *n* máxima *f*.
**maximum** *n* máximo *m*.
**may** *vi* poder; ~**be** acaso, quizá.
**May** *n* mayo *m*.
**Mayday** *n* primero de mayo *m*.
**mayonnaise** *n* mayonesa *f*.
**mayor** *n* alcalde *m*.
**mayoress** *n* alcaldesa *f*.
**maze** *n* laberinto *m*.
**me** *pn* me; mí.
**meadow** *n* pradera *f*; prado *m*.
**meagre** *adj* pobre.
**meagreness** *n* escasez *f*.
**meal** *n* comida *f*; harina *f*.
**mealtime** *n* hora de comer *f*.
**mean** *adj* tacaño/ña; ~**s** *npl* medios *mpl*; * *vt, vi* significar.
**meander** *vi* serpentear.
**meaning** *n* sentido, significado *m*.
**meaningful** *adj* significativo/va.
**meaningless** *adj* sin sentido.
**meanness** *n* tacañería *f*.
**meantime** (**in the**), **meanwhile** *adv* mientras tanto.
**measles** *npl* sarampión *m*.
**measure** *n* medida *f*; (*mus*) compás *m*; * *vt* medir.
**measurement** *n* medida *f*.
**meat** *n* carne *f*.
**meatball** *n* albóndiga *f*.
**meaty** *adj* sustancioso/sa.
**mechanic** *n* mecánico/ca *m/f*.
**mechanical** *adj* mecánico; ~**ly** *adv* mecánicamente.
**mechanics** *npl* mecánica *f*.
**mechanism** *n* mecanismo *m*.
**medal** *n* medalla *f*.
**medallion** *n* medallón *m*.
**medallist** *n* medallero/ra *m/f*.
**meddle** *vi* entrometerse.
**meddler** *n* entrometido *m*.
**media** *npl* medios de comunicación *mpl*.
**mediate** *vi* mediar.
**mediation** *n* mediación, interposición *f*.
**mediator** *n* intermediario/ria *m/f*.
**medical** *adj* médico/ca.
**medicate** *vt* medicar.
**medicated** *adj* medicinal.
**medicinal** *adj* medicinal.
**medicine** *n* medicina *f*; medicamento *m*.
**medieval** *adj* medieval.
**mediocre** *adj* mediocre.
**mediocrity** *n* mediocridad *f*.
**meditate** *vi* meditar.
**meditation** *n* meditación *f*.

**meditative** *adj* contemplativo/va.
**Mediterranean** *adj* mediterráneo/nea; **the ~** el Mediterráneo/nea *m*.
**medium** *n* medio *m*; * *adj* mediano/na.
**medium wave** *n* onda media *f*.
**medley** *n* mezcla *f*.
**meek** *adj* manso/sa; **~ly** *adv* mansamente.
**meekness** *n* mansedumbre *f*.
**meet** *vt* encontrar; **to ~ with** reunirse con; * *vi* encontrarse; juntarse.
**meeting** *n* reunión *f*; congreso *m*.
**megaphone** *n* megáfono *m*.
**melancholy** *n* melancolía *f*; * *adj* melancólico/ca.
**mellow** *adj* maduro/ra; suave; * *vi* madurar.
**mellowness** *n* madurez *f*.
**melodious** *adj* melodioso/sa; **~ly** *adv* melodiosamente.
**melody** *n* melodía *f*.
**melon** *n* melón *m*.
**melt** *vt* derretir; * *vi* derretirse.
**melting point** *n* punto de fusión *m*.
**member** *n* miembro *m*/*f*.
**membership** *n* número de miembros *m*.
**membrane** *n* membrana *f*.
**memento** *n* recuerdo *m*.
**memo** *n* memorándum *m*.
**memoir** *n* memoria *f*.
**memorable** *adj* memorable.
**memorandum** *n* memorándum *m*.
**memorial** *n* monumento conmemorativo *m*.
**memorize** *vt* memorizar, aprender de memoria.
**memory** *n* memoria *f*; recuerdo *m*.
**menace** *n* amenaza *f*; * *vt* amenazar.
**menacing** *adj* amenazador/ra.
**menagerie** *n* casa de fieras *f*.
**mend** *vt* reparar.
**mending** *n* reparación *f*.
**menial** *adj* doméstico/ca.
**meningitis** *n* meningitis *f*.
**menopause** *n* menopausia *f*.
**menstruation** *n* menstruación *f*.
**mental** *adj* mental, intelectual.
**mentality** *n* mentalidad *f*.
**mentally** *adv* mentalmente, intelectualmente.
**mention** *n* mención *f*; * *vt* mencionar.
**mentor** *n* mentor *m*.
**menu** *n* menú *m*; carta *f*.
**mercantile** *adj* mercantil.
**mercenary** *adj*, *n* mercenario/ria *m*/*f*.
**merchandise** *n* mercancía *f*.
**merchant** *n* comerciante *m*/*f*.

**merchantman** *n* navío mercante *m*.
**merchant marine** *n* marina mercante *f*.
**merciful** *adj* compasivo/va.
**merciless** *adj* despiadado/da; **~ly** *adv* despiadadamente.
**mercury** *n* mercurio *m*.
**mercy** *n* compasión *f*.
**mere** *adj* mero/ra; **~ly** *adv* simplemente.
**merge** *vt* fundir.
**merger** *n* fusión *f*.
**meridian** *n* meridiano *m*.
**meringue** *n* merengue *m*.
**merit** *n* mérito *m*; * *vt* merecer.
**meritorious** *adj* meritorio/ria.
**mermaid** *n* sirena *f*.
**merrily** *adv* alegremente.
**merriment** *n* diversión *f*; regocijo *m*.
**merry** *adj* alegre.
**merry-go-round** *n* tiovivo *m*.
**mesh** *n* malla *f*.
**mesmerize** *vt* hipnotizar.
**mess** *n* lío *m*; mamarracho *m*; (*mil*) comedor *m*; **to ~ up** *vt* desordenar.
**message** *n* mensaje *m*.
**messenger** *n* mensajero/ra *m*/*f*.
**metabolism** *n* metabolismo *n*.
**metal** *n* metal *m*.
**metallic** *adj* metálico/ca.
**metallurgy** *n* metalurgía *f*.
**metamorphosis** *n* metamorfosis *f* *invar*.
**metaphor** *n* metáfora *f*.
**metaphoric(al)** *adj* metafórico/ca.
**metaphysical** *adj* metafísico/ca.
**metaphysics** *npl* metafísica *f*.
**mete (out)** *vt* imponer.
**meteor** *n* meteoro *m*.
**meteorological** *adj* meteorológico/ca.
**meteorology** *n* meteorología *f*.
**meter** *n* contador *m*.
**method** *n* método *m*.
**methodical** *adj* metódico/ca; **~ly** *adv* metódicamente.
**Methodist** *n* metodista *m*/*f*.
**metre** *n* metro *m*.
**metric** *adj* métrico/ca.
**metropolis** *n* metrópoli *f*.
**metropolitan** *adj* metropolitano/na.
**mettle** *n* valor *m*.
**mettlesome** *adj* brioso/sa.
**mew** *vi* maullar.
**mezzanine** *n* entresuelo *m*.
**microbe** *n* microbio *m*.
**microchip** *n* microchip *m*.
**microphone** *n* micrófono *m*.
**microscope** *n* microscopio *m*.

**microscopic** *adj* microscópico/ca.
**microwave** *n* microondas *m invar;* ~ **oven**
microondas *m.*
**mid** *adj* medio/dia.
**midday** *n* mediodía *m.*
**middle** *adj* medio/dia; * *n* medio, centro *m.*
**middle name** *n* segundo nombre *m.*
**middleweight** *n* peso medio *m.*
**middling** *adj* mediano/na.
**midge** *n* mosquito *m.*
**midget** *n* enano/na *m/f.*
**midi system** *n* minicadena *f.*
**midnight** *n* medianoche *f.*
**midriff** *n* diafragma *m.*
**midst** *n* medio, centro *m.*
**midsummer** *n* pleno verano *m.*
**midway** *adv* a medio camino.
**midwife** *n* partera *f.*
**midwifery** *n* obstetricia *f.*
**might** *n* poder *m;* fuerza *f.*
**mighty** *adj* fuerte.
**migraine** *n* jaqueca *f.*
**migrate** *vi* emigrar, migrar.
**migration** *n* emigración, migración *f.*
**migratory** *adj* migratorio/ria.
**mike** *n* micrófono *m.*
**mild** *adj* apacible; suave; ~**ly** *adv* suavemente.
**mildew** *n* moho *m.*
**mildness** *n* dulzura *f.*
**mile** *n* milla *f.*
**mileage** *n* kilometraje *m.*
**mileometer,    milometer** *n* cuentakilómetros *m invar.*
**milieu** *n* ambiente *m.*
**militant** *adj* militante.
**military** *adj* militar.
**militate** *vi* militar.
**militia** *n* milicia *f.*
**milk** *n* leche *f;* * *vt* ordenar.
**milkshake** *n* batido de leche *m,* malteada *f.*
**milky** *adj* lechoso/sa; **M~ Way** *n* Vía Láctea *f.*
**mill** *n* molino *m;* * *vt* moler.
**millennium** *n* milenio *m.*
**miller** *n* molinero/ra *m/f.*
**millet** *n* (*bot*) mijo *m.*
**milligram** *n* miligramo *m.*
**millilitre** *n* mililitro *m.*
**millimetre** *n* milímetro *m.*
**milliner** *n* sombrerero/ra *m/f.*
**millinery** *n* sombrerería *f.*
**million** *n* millón *m.*
**millionaire** *n* millonario/ria *m/f.*
**millionth** *adj, n* millonésimo/ma *m/f.*
**millstone** *n* piedra de molino *f.*

**mime** *n* mimo *m.*
**mimic** *vt* imitar.
**mimicry** *n* mímica *f.*
**mince** *vt* picar.
**mind** *n* mente *f;* * *vt* cuidar; * *vi* molestar.
**minded** *adj* dispuesto/ta.
**mindful** *adj* consciente.
**mindless** *adj* sin motivo.
**mine** *pn* mío, mía, mi; * *n* mina; * *vi* minar.
**minefield** *n* campo de minas *m.*
**miner** *n* minero/ra *m/f.*
**mineral** *adj, n* mineral *m.*
**mineralogy** *n* mineralogía *f.*
**mineral water** *n* agua mineral *f.*
**minesweeper** *n* dragaminas *m invar.*
**mingle** *vt* mezclar.
**miniature** *n* miniatura *f.*
**minimal** *adj* mínimo/ma.
**minimize** *vt* minimizar.
**minimum** *n* mínimo *m.*
**mining** *n* minería *f.*
**minion** *n* favorito/ta *m/f.*
**minister** *n* ministro/tro *m/f;* * *vt* servir.
**ministerial** *adj* ministerial.
**ministry** *n* ministerio *m.*
**mink** *n* visón *m.*
**minnow** *n* vario *m* (pez).
**minor** *adj* menor; * *n* menor (de edad) *m/f.*
**minority** *n* minoría *f.*
**minstrel** *n* juglar *m.*
**mint** *n* (*bot*) menta *f;* casa de la moneda *f;*
* *vt* acuñar.
**minus** *adv* menos.
**minute**[1] *adj* diminuto/ta; ~**ly** *adv* minu-
ciosamente.
**minute**[2] *n* minuto *m.*
**miracle** *n* milagro *m.*
**miraculous** *adj* milagroso/sa.
**mirage** *n* espejismo *m.*
**mire** *n* fango *m.*
**mirky** *adj* turbio/bia.
**mirror** *n* espejo *m.*
**mirth** *n* alegría *f.*
**mirthful** *adj* alegre.
**misadventure** *n* desgracia *f.*
**misanthrope,    misanthropist** *n* mis-
ántropo *m.*
**misapply** *vt* aplicar mal.
**misapprehension** *n* error *m.*
**misbehave** *vi* portarse mal.
**misbehaviour** *n* mala conducta *f.*
**miscalculate** *vt* calcular mal.
**miscarriage** *n* aborto (espontáneo) *m.*
**miscarry** *vi* abortar (espontáneamente);
malograrse.

**miscellaneous** *adj* varios, varias.
**miscellany** *n* miscelánea *f*.
**mischief** *n* mal, daño *m*.
**mischievous** *adj* dañoso/sa; travieso/sa.
**misconception** *n* equivocación *f*.
**misconduct** *n* mala conducta *f*.
**misconstrue** *vt* interpretar mal.
**miscount** *vt* contar mal.
**miscreant** *n* malvado/da *m/f*.
**misdeed** *n* delito *m*.
**misdemeanour** *n* delito *m*.
**misdirect** *vt* dirigir mal.
**miser** *n* avaro/ra *m/f*.
**miserable** *adj* miserable, infeliz.
**miserly** *adj* mezquino/na, tacaño/ña.
**misery** *n* miseria *f*.
**misfit** *n* inadaptado/da *m/f*.
**misfortune** *n* desgracia *f*.
**misgiving** *n* recelo *m*; presentimiento *m*.
**misgovern** *vt* gobernar mal.
**misguided** *adj* equivocado/da.
**mishandle** *vt* manejar mal.
**mishap** *n* desgracia *f*.
**misinform** *vt* informar mal.
**misinterpret** *vt* interpretar mal.
**misjudge** *vi* juzgar mal.
**mislay** *vt* extraviar.
**mislead** *vt* engañar.
**mismanage** *vt* manejar mal.
**mismanagement** *n* mala administración *f*.
**misnomer** *n* nombre inapropiado *m*.
**misogynist** *n* misógino/na *m/f*.
**misplace** *vt* extraviar.
**misprint** *vt* imprimir mal; * *n* errata *f*.
**misrepresent** *vt* representar mal.
**Miss** *n* señorita *f*.
**miss** *vt* perder; echar de menos.
**missal** *n* misal *m*.
**misshapen** *adj* deforme.
**missile** *n* misil *m*.
**missing** *adj* perdido/da; ausente.
**mission** *n* misión *f*.
**missionary** *n* misionero/ra *m/f*.
**misspent** *adj* disipado/da.
**mist** *n* niebla *f*.
**mistake** *vt* entender mal; * *vi* equivocarse, engañarse; to be mistaken equivocarse; * *n* equivocación *f*; error *m*, yerro *m*.
**Mister** *n* Señor *m*.
**mistletoe** *n* (*bot*) muérdago *m*.
**mistress** *n* amante *f*.
**mistrust** *vt* desconfiar; * *n* desconfianza *f*.
**mistrustful** *adj* desconfiado/da.
**misty** *adj* nebuloso/sa.

**misunderstand** *vt* entender mal.
**misunderstanding** *n* malentendido *m*.
**misuse** *vt* maltratar; abusar de.
**mitre** *n* mitra *f*.
**mitigate** *vt* mitigar.
**mitigation** *n* mitigación *f*.
**mittens** *npl* manoplas *fpl*.
**mix** *vt* mezclar.
**mixed** *adj* surtido/da; mixto/ta.
**mixed-up** *adj* confuso/sa.
**mixer** *n* licuadora *f*.
**mixture** *n* mezcla *f*.
**mix-up** *n* confusión *f*.
**moan** *n* gemido *m*; * *vi* gemir; quejarse.
**moat** *n* foso *m*.
**mob** *n* multitud *f*.
**mobile** *adj* móvil; ~ **phone** móvil *m*.
**mobile home** *n* caravana *f*.
**mobility** *n* movilidad *f*.
**mobilize** *vt* (*mil*) movilizar.
**moccasin** *n* mocasín *m*.
**mock** *vt* burlarse.
**mockery** *n* mofa *f*.
**mode** *n* modo *m*.
**model** *n* modelo *m*; * *vt* modelar.
**modem** *n* módem *m*.
**moderate** *adj* moderado/da; **~ly** *adv* medianamente; * *vt* moderar.
**moderation** *n* moderación *f*.
**modern** *adj* moderno/na.
**modernize** *vt* modernizar.
**modest** *adj* modesto/ta; **~ly** *adv* modestamente.
**modesty** *n* modestia *f*.
**modicum** *n* mínimo *m*.
**modification** *n* modificación *f*.
**modify** *vt* modificar.
**modulate** *vt* modular.
**modulation** *n* (*mus*) modulación *f*.
**module** *n* módulo *m*.
**mogul** *n* magnate *m/f*.
**mohair** *n* mohair *m*.
**moist** *adj* húmedo/da.
**moisten** *vt* humedecer.
**moisture** *n* humedad *f*.
**molars** *npl* muelas *fpl*.
**molasses** *npl* melaza *f*.
**mole** *n* topo *m*.
**molecule** *n* molécula *f*.
**molehill** *n* topera *f*.
**molest** *vt* importunar.
**mollify** *vt* apaciguar.
**mollusc** *n* molusco *m*.
**mollycoddle** *vt* mimar.
**molten** *adj* derretido/da.

**moment** n momento m.
**momentarily** adv momentáneamente.
**momentary** adj momentáneo/nea.
**momentous** adj importante.
**momentum** n ímpetu m.
**monarch** n monarca m.
**monarchy** n monarquía f.
**monastery** n monasterio m.
**monastic** adj monástico/ca.
**Monday** n lunes m.
**monetary** adj monetario/ria.
**money** n dinero m.
**money laundering** n blanqueo m.
**money order** n giro m.
**Mongol** n mongólico/ca m/f.
**mongrel** adj, n mestizo/za m/f.
**monitor** n monitor m.
**monk** n monje m.
**monkey** n mono m.
**monochrome** adj monocromo/ma.
**monocle** n monóculo m.
**monologue** n monólogo m.
**monopolize** vt monopolizar.
**monopoly** n monopolio m.
**monosyllable** n monosílabo m.
**monotonous** adj monótono/na.
**monotony** n monotonía f.
**monsoon** n (mar) monzón m.
**monster** n monstruo m.
**monstrosity** n monstruosidad f.
**monstrous** adj monstruoso/sa; **~ly** adv monstruosamente.
**montage** n montaje m.
**month** n mes m.
**monthly** adj mensual; **~ly** adv mensualmente.
**monument** n monumento m.
**monumental** adj monumental.
**moo** vi mugir.
**mood** n humor m.
**moodiness** n mal humor m.
**moody** adj malhumorado/da.
**moon** n luna f.
**moonbeams** npl rayos lunares mpl.
**moonlight** n luz de la luna f.
**moor** vt (mar) atracar.
**mooring rope** n amarra f.
**moorland**, **moor** n páramo m.
**moose** n alce m.
**mop** n fregona f; * vt fregar.
**mope** vi estar triste.
**moped** n ciclomotor m.
**moral** adj moral; **~ly** adv moralmente.
**morals** npl moralidad f.
**morale** n moral f.

**moralist** n moralista m/f.
**morality** n ética, moralidad f.
**moralize** vt, vi moralizar.
**morass** n pantano m.
**morbid** adj morboso/sa.
**more** adj, adv más; **never ~** nunca más; **once ~** otra vez; **~ and ~** más y más, cada vez más; **so much the ~** cuanto más.
**moreover** adv además.
**morgue** n depósito de cadáveres m.
**morning** n mañana f; **good ~** buenos días mpl.
**moron** n imbécil m/f.
**morose** adj hosco/ca.
**morphine** n morfina f.
**morsel** n bocado m.
**mortal** adj mortal; **~ly** adv mortalmente; * n mortal m/f.
**mortality** n mortalidad f.
**mortar** n mortero m.
**mortgage** n hipoteca f; * vt hipotecar.
**mortgage company** n banco hipotecario m.
**mortgager** n deudor hipotecario m, deudora hipotecaria f.
**mortification** n mortificación f.
**mortify** vt mortificar.
**mortuary** n depósito de cadáveres m.
**mosaic** n mosaico m.
**mosque** n mezquita f.
**mosquito** n mosquito m; zancudo/da m.
**moss** n (bot) musgo m.
**mossy** adj cubierto/ta de musgo.
**most** adj la mayoría de; * adv sumamente; **at ~** a lo sumo; **~ly** adv principalmente.
**motel** n motel m.
**moth** n polilla f.
**mothball** n bola de naftalina f.
**mother** n madre f; **loving ~** madraza f.
**motherhood** n maternidad f.
**mother-in-law** n suegra f.
**motherless** adj sin madre.
**motherly** adj maternal.
**mother-of-pearl** n nácar m.
**mother-to-be** n futura madre f.
**mother tongue** n lengua materna f.
**motif** n tema m.
**motion** n movimiento m.
**motionless** adj inmóvil.
**motion picture** n película f.
**motivated** adj motivado/da.
**motive** n motivo m.
**motley** adj abigarrado/da.
**motor** n motor m.
**motorbike** n moto f.
**motorboat** n lancha motora f.

**motorcycle** *n* motocicleta *f.*
**motor scooter** *n* moto *f.*
**motor vehicle** *n* automóvil *m.*
**mottled** *adj* multicolor.
**motto** *n* lema *m.*
**mould** *n* molde *m;* moho *m;* * *vt* moldear.
**moulder** *vi* decaer.
**mouldy** *adj* enmohecido/da.
**moult** *vt* mudar.
**mound** *n* montón *m.*
**mount** *n* monte *m;* * *vt* subir.
**mountain** *n* montaña *f.*
**mountaineer** *n* montañero/ra *m/f.*
**mountaineering** *n* montañismo *m.*
**mountainous** *adj* montañoso/sa.
**mourn** *vt* lamentar.
**mourner** *n* doliente *m/f.*
**mournful** *adj* triste; **~ly** *adv* tristemente.
**mourning** *n* luto *m.*
**mouse** *n* (*pl* **mice**) ratón *m.*
**mouse mat** *n* alfombrilla *f.*
**mousse** *n* mousse *f.*
**moustache** *n* bigote *m.*
**mouth** *n* boca *f;* desembocadura *f.*
**mouthful** *n* bocado *m.*
**mouth organ** *n* harmónica *f.*
**mouthpiece** *n* boquilla *f.*
**mouthwash** *n* enjuague *m.*
**mouthwatering** *adj* apetitoso/sa.
**movable** *adj* movible.
**move** *vt* mover; proponer; * *vi* moverse; * *n* movimiento *m.*
**movement** *n* movimiento *m.*
**movie** *n* película *f.*
**movie camera** *n* cámara cinematográfica *f.*
**moving** *adj* conmovedor/a.
**mow** *vt* segar.
**mower** *n* cortacésped *m.*
**Mrs** *n* señora *f.*
**much** *adj, adv* mucho/cha; con mucho.
**muck** *n* suciedad *f.*
**mucous** *adj* mocoso/sa.
**mucus** *n* moco *m.*
**mud** *n* barro *m.*
**muddle** *vt* confundir; * *n* confusión *f.*
**muddy** *adj* fangoso/sa.
**mudguard** *n* guardabarros *m invar.*
**muffle** *vt* embozar.
**mug** *n* jarra *f.*
**muggy** *adj* bochornoso/sa.
**mulberry** *n* mora *f;* **~ tree** morera *f.*
**mule** *n* mulo *m,* mula *f.*
**mull** *vt* meditar.
**multifarious** *adj* múltiple.
**multimedia** *adj* multimedia.

**multiple** *adj* múltiplo/a; * *n* múltiplo *m.*
**multiplication** *n* multiplicación *f;* **~ table** tabla de multiplicar *f.*
**multiply** *vt* multiplicar.
**multitude** *n* multitud *f.*
**mumble** *vt, vi* refunfuñar.
**mummy**[1] *n* mamá *f.*
**mummy**[2] *n* momia *f.*
**mumps** *npl* paperas *fpl.*
**munch** *vt* mascar.
**mundane** *adj* trivial.
**municipal** *adj* municipal.
**municipality** *n* municipalidad *f.*
**munificence** *n* munificencia *f.*
**munitions** *npl* municiones *fpl.*
**mural** *n* mural *m.*
**murder** *n* asesinato *m;* homicidio *m;* * *vt* asesinar.
**murderer** *n* asesino/na *m/f.*
**murderess** *n* asesina *f.*
**murderous** *adj* homicida.
**murky** *adj* sombrío/ría.
**murmur** *n* murmullo *m;* * *vi* murmurar.
**muscle** *n* músculo *m.*
**muscular** *adj* muscular.
**muse** *vi* meditar.
**museum** *n* museo *m.*
**mushroom** *n* (*bot*) seta *f;* champiñón *m.*
**music** *n* musica *f.*
**musical** *adj* musical; melodioso/sa.
**musician** *n* músico/ca *m/f.*
**musk** *n* almizcle *m.*
**muslin** *n* muselina *f.*
**mussel** *n* mejillón *m.*
**must** *v aux* tener que, deber; deber de.
**mustard** *n* mostaza *f.*
**muster** *vt* agregar.
**musty** *adj* mohoso/sa, añejo/ja.
**mute** *adj* mudo/da, silencioso/sa.
**muted** *adj* callado/da.
**mutilate** *vt* mutilar.
**mutilation** *n* mutilación *f.*
**mutiny** *n* motin, tumulto *m;* * *vi* amotinarse, rebelarse.
**mutter** *vt, vi* murmurar, musitar; * *n* murmuración *f.*
**mutton** *n* carnero *m.*
**mutual** *adj* mutuo/tua, mutual, recíproco/ ca; **~ly** *adv* mutuamente, recíprocamente.
**muzzle** *n* bozal *m;* hocico *m;* * *vt* embozar.
**my** *pn* mi, mis; mio, mia; mios, mias.
**myriad** *n* miríada *f;* gran número *m.*
**myrrh** *n* mirra *f.*
**myrtle** *n* mirto, arrayán *m.*
**myself** *pn* yo mismo/ma.

**mysterious** *adj* misterioso/sa; **~ly** *adv* misteriosamente.
**mystery** *n* misterio *m*.
**mystic(al)** *adj* místico/ca.
**mystify** *vt* dejar perplejo/ja.

**mystique** *n* misterio *m*.
**myth** *n* mito *m*.
**mythology** *n* mitología *f*.

# N

**nab** *vt* agarrar.

**nag** *n* jaca *f*; * *vt* regañar.

**nagging** *adj* persistente; * *npl* quejas *fpl*.

**nail** *n* uña *f*, garra *f*; clavo *m*; * *vt* clavar.

**nailbrush** *n* cepillo de uñas *m*.

**nailfile** *n* lima de uñas *f*.

**nail polish** *n* esmalte de uñas *m*.

**nail scissors** *npl* tijeras de manicura *fpl*.

**naïve** *adj* ingenuo/nua.

**naked** *adj* desnudo/da evidente; puro/ra, simple.

**name** *n* nombre *m*; fama, reputación *f*; * *vt* nombrar; mencionar.

**nameless** *adj* anónimo/ma.

**nameplate** *n* planchuela *f*.

**namely** *adv* a saber.

**namesake** *n* tocayo/ya *m/f*.

**nanny** *n* niñera *f*.

**nap** *n* sueño ligero *m*.

**napalm** *n* napalm *m*.

**nape** *n* nuca *f*.

**napkin** *n* servilleta *f*.

**nappy** *n* pañal *m*; **disposable ~** pañal desechable.

**narcissus** *n* (*bot*) narciso *m*.

**narcotic** *adj* narcótico/ca; * *n* narcótico *m*.

**narrate** *vt* narrar, relatar.

**narrative** *adj* narrativo/va; * *n* narrativa *f*.

**narrow** *adj* angosto/ta, estrecho/cha; **~ly** *adv* estrechamente; * *vt* estrechar; limitar.

**narrow-minded** *adj* estrecho/cha de miras.

**narrow pass** *n* puerto *m*.

**nasal** *adj* nasal.

**nasty** *adj* sucio/cia, puerco/ca; obsceno/na; sórdido/da.

**natal** *adj* nativo/va; natal.

**nation** *n* nación *f*.

**national** *adj* nacional; **~ly** *adv* nacionalmente.

**nationalism** *n* nacionalismo *m*.

**nationalist** *adj*, *n* nacionalista *m/f*.

**nationality** *n* nacionalidad *f*.

**nationalize** *vt* nacionalizar.

**nationwide** *adj* a nivel nacional.

**native** *adj* nativo/va; * *n* natural *m/f*.

**native language** *n* lengua materna *f*.

**Nativity** *n* Navidad *f*.

**natural** *adj* natural; sencillo/lla; **~ly** *adv* naturalmente.

**natural gas** *n* gas natural *m*.

**naturalist** *n* naturalista *m/f*.

**naturalize** *vt* naturalizar.

**nature** *n* naturaleza *f*; índole *f*.

**naturopath** *n* naturópata *m/f*.

**naught** *n* cero *m*.

**naughty** *adj* malo/la, malvado/da.

**nausea** *n* náuseas *fpl*, gana de vomitar *f*.

**nauseate** *vt* dar náuseas a.

**nauseous** *adj* fastidioso/sa.

**nautical, naval** *adj* náutico/ca, naval.

**nave** *n* nave (de la iglesia) *f*.

**navel** *n* ombligo *m*.

**navigate** *vi* navegar.

**navigation** *n* navegación *f*.

**navy** *n* marina *f*; armada *f*.

**Nazi** *n* nazi *m/f*.

**near** *prep* cerca de, junto a; * *adv* casi; cerca, cerca de; * *adj* cercano/na, proximo/ma.

**nearby** *adj* cercano/na.

**nearly** *adv* casi.

**near-sighted** *adj* miope.

**neat** *adj* hermoso/sa, pulido/da; puro/ra; neto/ta; **~ly** *adv* elegantemente.

**nebulous** *adj* nebuloso/sa.

**necessarily** *adv* necesariamente.

**necessary** *adj* necesario/ria.

**necessitate** *vt* necesitar.

**necessity** *n* necesidad *f*.

**neck** *n* cuello *m*; * *vi* besuquearse.

**necklace** *n* collar *m*.

**nectar** *n* néctar *m*.

**née, nee** *adj*: **~ Brown** de soltera Brown.

**need** *n* necesidad *f*, pobreza *f*; * *vt* necesitar.

**needle** *n* aguja *f*.

**needless** *adj* superfluo/lua, inútil.

**needlework** *n* costura *f*; bordado de aguja *m*; obra de punto *m*.

**needy** *adj* necesitado/da, pobre.

**negation** *n* negación *f*.

**negative** *adj* negativo/va; **~ly** *adv* negativamente; * *n* negativa *f*.

**neglect** *vt* descuidar, desatender; * *n* negligencia *f*.

**negligee** *n* salto de cama *m*.

**negligence** *n* negligencia *f*; descuido *m*.

**negligent** *adj* negligente, descuidado/da; **~ly** *adv* negligentemente.

**negligible** *adj* insignificante.

**negotiate** *vt*, *vi* negociar (con).

**negotiation** *n* negociación *f*; negocio *m*.

**Negress** *n* negra *f*.

**Negro** *adj* negro/gra; * *n* negro *m*.

**neigh** vi relinchar; * n relincho m.
**neighbour** n vecino/na m/f; * vt confinar.
**neighbourhood** n vecindad f; vecindario m.
**neighbouring** adj vecino/na.
**neighbourly** adj sociable.
**neither** conj ni; * pn ninguno/na, ni uno ni otro, ni una ni otra.
**neon** n neón m.
**neon light** n luz de neón f.
**nephew** n sobrino m.
**nepotism** n nepotismo m.
**nerve** n nervio m; valor m.
**nerve-racking** adj espantoso/sa.
**nervous** adj nervioso/sa; nervudo/da.
**nervous breakdown** n crisis nerviosa f.
**nest** n nido m; nidada f.
**nest egg** n (fig) ahorros mpl.
**nestle** vt anidarse.
**net** n red f.
**netball** n nétbol m.
**net curtain** n visillo m.
**netting** n mallado m.
**nettle** n ortiga f.
**network** n red f, malla f.
**neurone** n neurona f.
**neurosis** n neurosis f invar.
**neurotic** adj, n neurótico/ca m/f.
**neuter** adj (gr) neutro/tra.
**neutral** adj neutral.
**neutrality** n neutralidad f.
**neutralize** vt neutralizar.
**neutron** n neutrón m.
**neutron bomb** n bomba de neutrones f.
**never** adv nunca, jamás; ~ **mind** no importa.
**never-ending** adj sin fin.
**nevertheless** adv no obstante.
**new** adj nuevo/va, fresco/sca, reciénte; ~**ly** adv nuevamente.
**newborn** adj recién nacido/da.
**newcomer** n recién llegado/da m.
**new-fangled** adj inventado/da por novedad.
**news** npl novedad, noticias fpl.
**news agency** n agencia de noticias f.
**newsagent** n vendedor/a de periódicos m/f.
**newscaster** n presentador/a m/f.
**news flash** n noticia de última hora f.
**newsletter** n boletín n.
**newspaper** n periódico m.
**newsreel** n noticiario m.
**New Year** n Año Nuevo m; ~'s **Day** Día de Año Nuevo m; ~'s **Eve** Nochevieja f.
**next** adj próximo/ma; **the** ~ **day** el día siguiente; * adv luego, inmediatamente después.
**nib** n pico m; punta f.
**nibble** vt picar, mordiscar.

**nice** adj simpático/ca; agradable; lindo/da; ~**ly** adv bien.
**nice-looking** adj guapo/pa.
**niche** n nicho m.
**nick** n mella f; * vt (col) robar.
**nickel** n níquel m; moneda de cinco centavos f.
**nickname** n mote, apodo m; * vt poner apodos.
**nicotine** n nicotina f.
**niece** n sobrina f.
**niggling** adj insignificante.
**night** n noche f; velador m; **by** ~ de noche; **good** ~ buenas noches.
**nightclub** n cabaret m.
**nightfall** n anochecer m.
**nightingale** n ruiseñor m.
**nightly** adv por las noches, todas las noches; * adj nocturno/na.
**nightmare** n pesadilla f.
**night school** n clases nocturnas fpl.
**night shift** n turno de noche m.
**night-time** n noche f.
**night work** n vela f.
**nihilist** n nihilista m/f.
**nimble** adj ligero/ra, activo/va, listo/ta, ágil.
**nine** adj, n nueve.
**nineteen** adj, n diecinueve.
**nineteenth** adj, n decimonoveno/na.
**ninetieth** adj, n nonagésimo/ma.
**ninety** adj, n noventa.
**ninth** adj, n nono/na, noveno/na.
**nip** vt pellizcar; morder.
**nipple** n pezón m; tetilla f.
**nit** n liendre f.
**nitrogen** n nitrógeno m.
**no** adv no; * adj ningún, ninguno/na.
**nobility** n nobleza f.
**noble** adj noble; insigne; * n noble m/f.
**nobleman** n noble m.
**nobody** n nadie, ninguna persona f.
**nocturnal** adj nocturnal, nocturno/na.
**nod** n cabeceo m; señal f; * vi cabecear; amodorrarse.
**noise** n ruido, estruendo m; rumor m.
**noisily** adv con ruido.
**noisiness** n ruido, tumulto, alboroto m.
**noisy** adj ruidoso/sa, turbulento/ta.
**nominal** adj nominal; ~**ly** adv nominalmente.
**nominate** vt nombrar.
**nomination** n nominación f.
**nominative** n (gr) nominativo m.
**nominee** n candidato/ta m/f.
**nonalcoholic** adj no alcóholico/ca.
**nonaligned** adj no alineado/da.

**nonchalant** *adj* indiferente.
**noncommittal** *adj* reservado/da.
**nonconformist** *n* inconformista *m/f*.
**nondescript** *adj* no descrito/ta.
**none** *adj* nadie, ninguno/na.
**nonentity** *n* nulidad *f*.
**nonetheless** *adv* sin embargo.
**nonexistent** *adj* inexistente.
**nonfiction** *n* no ficción *f*.
**nonplussed** *adj* confuso/sa.
**nonsense** *n* disparate, absurdo *m*.
**nonsensical** *adj* absurdo/da.
**nonsmoker** *n* no fumador/a *m/f*.
**nonstick** *adj* antiadherente.
**nonstop** *adj* directo/ta; * *adv* sin parar.
**noodles** *npl* fideos (chinos) *mpl*.
**noon** *n* mediodía *m*.
**noose** *n* nudo corredizo *m*.
**nor** *conj* ni.
**normal** *adj* normal.
**north** *n* norte *m*; * *adj* del norte.
**North America** *n* América del Norte, Norteamérica *f*.
**northeast** *n* nor(d)este *m*.
**northerly, northern** *adj* norteño/ña.
**North Pole** *n* polo norte *m*.
**northward(s)** *adv* hacia el norte.
**northwest** *n* nor(d)oeste *m*.
**nose** *n* nariz *f*; olfato *m*.
**nosebleed** *n* hemorragia nasal *f*.
**nosedive** *n* picado vertical *m*.
**nostalgia** *n* nostalgia *f*.
**nostril** *n* ventana de la nariz *f*.
**not** *adv* no.
**notable** *adj* notable; memorable.
**notably** *adv* especialmente.
**notary** *n* notario/ria *m/f*.
**notch** *n* muesca *f*; * *vt* hacer muescas.
**note** *n* nota, marca *f*; señal *f*; aprecio *m*; billete *m*; consecuen cia *f*; noticia *f*; indirecta *f*; * *vt* notar, marcar; observar.
**notebook** *n* cuaderno *m*, libreta *f*.
**noted** *adj* afamado/da, celebre.
**notepad** *n* bloc *m*.
**notepaper** *n* papel de cartas *m*.
**nothing** *n* nada *f*; **good for ~** lo que sirve para nada.
**notice** *n* noticia *f*; aviso *m*; * *vt* observar.
**noticeable** *adj* notable, reparable.
**notification** *n* notificación *f*.
**notify** *vt* notificar.
**notion** *n* noción *f*; opinión *f*; idea *f*.
**notoriety** *n* mala fama *f*.
**notorious** *adj* tristemente célebre; **~ly** *adv* notoriamente.
**notwithstanding** *conj* no obstante, aunque.
**nougat** *n* turrón *m*.
**nought** *n* cero *m*.
**noun** *n* (*gr*) sustantivo *m*.
**nourish** *vt* nutrir, alimentar.
**nourishing** *adj* nutritivo/va.
**nourishment** *n* nutrimiento, alimento *m*.
**novel** *n* novela *f*.
**novelist** *n* novelista *m/f*.
**novelty** *n* novedad *f*.
**November** *n* noviembre *m*.
**novice** *n* novicio/cia *m/f*.
**now** *adv* ya, ahora, hoy (en) día; **~ and then** de vez en cuando.
**nowadays** *adv* hoy (en) día.
**nowhere** *adv* en ninguna parte.
**noxious** *adj* nocivo/va, dañoso/sa.
**nozzle** *n* boquilla *f*.
**nuance** *n* matiz *m*.
**nuclear** *adj* nuclear; **~ power** energía nuclear *f*; **~ power station** *n* central nuclear *f*.
**nucleus** *n* núcleo *m*.
**nude** *adj* desnudo/da, en carnes, en cueros, sin vestido.
**nudge** *vt* dar un codazo a.
**nudist** *n* nudista *m/f*.
**nudity** *n* desnudez *f*.
**nuisance** *n* daño, perjuicio *m*; incomodidad *f*.
**nuke** *n* (*col*) bomba atómica *f*; * *vt* atacar con arma nuclear.
**null** *adj* nulo/la, inválido/da.
**nullify** *vt* anular, invalidar.
**numb** *adj* entorpecido/da; * *vt* entorpecer.
**number** *n* número *m*; cantidad *f*; * *vt* numerar.
**numberplate** *n* placa de matrícula *f*.
**numbness** *n* entumecimiento *m*.
**numeral** *n* número *m*.
**numerical** *adj* numérico/ca.
**numerous** *adj* numeroso/sa.
**nun** *n* monja, religiosa *f*.
**nunnery** *n* convento de monjas *m*.
**nuptial** *adj* nupcial; **~s** *npl* nupcias *fpl*.
**nurse** *n* enfermera *f*; * *vt* cuidar; amamantar.
**nursery** *n* guardería infantil *f*; criadero *m*.
**nursery rhyme** *n* canción infantil *f*.
**nursery school** *n* parvulario *m*.
**nursing home** *n* clinica de reposo *f*.
**nurture** *vt* criar, educar.
**nut** *n* nuez *f*.
**nutcrackers** *npl* cascanueces *m invar*.
**nutmeg** *n* nuez moscada *f*.
**nutritious** *adj* nutritivo/va.
**nutshell** *n* cascara de nuez *f*.
**nylon** *n* nylon, nailon *m*; * *adj* de nylon, de nailon.

# O

**oak** *n* roble *m*.

**oar** *n* remo *m*.

**oasis** *n* oasis *f invar*.

**oath** *n* juramento *m*.

**oatmeal** *n* harina de avena *f*.

**oats** *npl* avena *f*.

**obedience** *n* obediencia *f*.

**obedient** *adj* obediente; **~ly** *adv* obedientemente.

**obese** *adj* obeso/sa, gordo/da.

**obesity** *n* obesidad *f*.

**obey** *vt* obedecer.

**obituary** *n* necrología *f*.

**object** *n* objeto *m*; * *vt* objetar.

**objection** *n* oposición, objeción, réplica *f*.

**objectionable** *adj* desagradable.

**objective** *adj* objetivo/va; * *n* objetivo *m*.

**obligation** *n* obligación *f*.

**obligatory** *adj* obligatorio/ria.

**oblige** *vt* obligar; complacer, favorecer.

**obliging** *adj* servicial.

**oblique** *adj* oblicuo/cua; indirecto/ta; **~ly** *adv* oblicuamente.

**obliterate** *vt* borrar.

**oblivion** *n* olvido *m*.

**oblivious** *adj* olvidadizo/za.

**oblong** *adj* oblongo/ga.

**obnoxious** *adj* odioso/sa.

**oboe** *n* oboe *m*.

**obscene** *adj* obsceno/na, impúdico/ca.

**obscenity** *n* obscenidad *f*.

**obscure** *adj* oscuro/ra; **~ly** *adv* oscuramente; * *vt* oscurecer.

**obscurity** *n* oscuridad *f*.

**observance** *n* observancia *f*; reverencia *f*.

**observant** *adj* observante, respetuoso/sa.

**observantly** *adv* cuidadosamente, atentamente.

**observation** *n* observación *f*.

**observatory** *n* observatorio *m*.

**observe** *vt* observar, mirar.

**observer** *n* observador/a *m/f*.

**obsess** *vt* obsesionar.

**obsessive** *adj* obsesivo/va.

**obsolete** *adj* obsoleto/ta.

**obstacle** *n* obstáculo *m*.

**obstinacy** *n* tenacidad *f*.

**obstinate** *adj* obstinado/da; **~ly** *adv* obstinadamente.

**obstruct** *vt* obstruir; impedir.

**obstruction** *n* obstrucción *f*; impedimento *m*.

**obtain** *vt* obtener, adquirir; **~ by cunning** sonsacar.

**obtainable** *adj* asequible.

**obtrusive** *adj* intruso/sa, importuno/na.

**obtuse** *adj* obtuso/sa, sin punta; lerdo/da, torpe.

**obvious** *adj* obvio/via, evidente; **~ly** *adv* naturalmente.

**occasion** *n* ocasión *f*; momento oportuno *m*; * *vt* ocasionar, causar.

**occasional** *adj* ocasional, casual; **~ly** *adv* ocasionalmente.

**occupant**, **occupier** *n* ocupante *m/f*; poseedor/a *m/f*; inquilino/na *m/f*.

**occupation** *n* ocupación *f*; empleo *m*.

**occupy** *vt* ocupar, emplear.

**occur** *vi* pasar, ocurrir.

**occurrence** *n* incidente *m*.

**ocean** *n* océano *m*; alta mar *f*.

**ocean-going** *adj* de alta mar.

**oceanic** *adj* oceánico/ca.

**ochre** *n* ocre *m*.

**octave** *n* octava *f*.

**October** *n* octubre *m*.

**octopus** *n* pulpo *m*.

**odd** *adj* impar; particular; extravagante; extraño/ña; **~ly** *adv* extrañamente.

**oddity** *n* singularidad, particularidad, rareza *f*.

**oddness** *n* desigualdad *f*; singularidad *f*.

**odds** *npl* probabilidades *fpl*; apuestas *fpl*.

**odious** *adj* odioso/sa.

**odorous** *adj* odorífero/ra.

**odour** *n* olor *m*; fragancia *f*.

**of** *prep* de; tocante; segun.

**of course!** *interj* ¡naturalmente!

**off** *adj* desconectado/da; apagado/da; cerrado/da; cancelado/da; **~!** *excl* ¡fuera!

**offence** *n* ofensa *f*; injuria *f*.

**offend** *vt* ofender, irritar; injuriar; * *vi* pecar.

**offender** *n* delincuente *m*.

**offensive** *adj* ofensivo/va; injurioso/sa; **~ly** *adv* ofensivamente.

**offer** *vt* ofrecer; * *n* oferta *f*.

**offering** *n* sacrificio *m*; oferta *f*.

**offhand** *adj* descortés; * *adv* de repente.

**office** *n* oficina *f*; oficio, empleo *m*; servicio *m*.

**office building** *n* bloque de oficinas *m*.

**office hours** *npl* horas de oficina *fpl*.

**officer** *n* oficial/a, empleado/da *m/f*.

**office worker** *n* oficinista *m/f*.

**official** *adj* oficial; **~ly** *adv* de oficio; * *n* empleado *m*.

**officiate** *vi* oficiar.

**officious** *adj* oficioso/sa; **~ly** *adv* oficiosamente.

**off-line** *adj*, *adv* fuera de línea.

**off-peak** *adj* de temporada baja.

**off-season** *adj*, *adv* fuera de temporada, en tarifa reducida.

**offset** *vt* contrarrestar.

**offshoot** *n* ramificación *f*.

**offshore** *adj* costero/ra.

**offside** *adj* fuera de juego.

**offspring** *n* prole *f*; linaje *m*; descendencia *f*.

**offstage** *adv* entre bastidores.

**off-the-peg** *adj* confeccionado/da.

**ogle** *vt* comerse con los ojos.

**oil** *n* aceite *m*; óleo *m*; * *vt* engrasar.

**oilcan** *n* lata de aceite *f*.

**oilfield** *n* campo petrolífero *m*.

**oil filter** *n* filtro de aceite *m*.

**oil painting** *n* pintura al óleo *f*.

**oil rig** *n* torre de perforación *f*.

**oil slick** *n* marea negra *f*.

**oil tanker** *n* petrolero *m*.

**oil well** *n* pozo petrolífero *m*.

**oily** *adj* aceitoso/sa; grasiento/ta.

**ointment** *n* ungüento *m*.

**OK, okay** *excl* vale; * *adj* bien; * *vt* dar el visto bueno a.

**old** *adj* viejo/ja; antiguo/gua.

**old age** *n* vejez *f*.

**old-fashioned** *adj* pasado/da de moda.

**olive** *n* olivo *m*; oliva *f*.

**olive oil** *n* aceite de oliva *m*.

**Olympic Games** *n* las Olímpicos *f*.

**omelette** *n* tortilla (francesa) *f*.

**omen** *n* agüero, presagio *m*.

**ominous** *adj* ominoso/sa.

**omission** *n* omisión *f*; descuido *m*.

**omit** *vt* omitir.

**omnipotence** *n* omnipotencia *f*.

**omnipotent** *adj* omnipotente, todopoderoso/sa.

**on** *prep* sobre, encima, en; de; a; * *adj* encendido/da; prendido/da; abierto/ta; puesto/ta.

**once** *adv* una vez; **at ~** en seguida; **all at ~** de una vez, en seguida; **~ more** otra vez.

**oncoming** *adj* que viene de frente.

**one** *adj* un, uno, una; **~ by ~** uno a uno, una a una, uno por uno, una por una.

**one-day excursion** *n* billete de ida y vuelta en un día *m*.

**one-man** *adj* individual.

**onerous** *adj* oneroso/sa, molesto/ta.

**oneself** *pn* sí mismo; sí misma.

**one-sided** *adj* parcial.

**one-to-one** *adj* de uno a uno; cara a cara.

**ongoing** *adj* continuo/nua.

**onion** *n* cebolla *f*.

**on-line** *adj*, *adv* en línea.

**onlooker** *n* espectador/a *m/f*.

**only** *adj* único/ca, solo/la; * *adv* solamente.

**onset, onslaught** *n* acometida *f*; ataque *m*.

**onus** *n* responsabilidad *f*.

**onward(s)** *adv* adelante.

**ooze** *vi* manar suavemente, rezumar.

**opaque** *adj* opaco/ca.

**open** *adj* abierto/ta; patente, evidente; sincero/ra, franco/ca; **~ly** *adv* con franqueza; * *vt* (*vi*) abrir(se); descubrir(se); **to ~ on to** dar a; **to ~ up** *vt* abrir; *vi* abrirse.

**opening** *n* abertura *f*; (*com*) salida *f*; principio *m*.

**open-minded** *adj* de mentalidad abierta.

**openness** *n* claridad *f*; franqueza, sinceridad *f*.

**opera** *n* ópera *f*.

**opera house** *n* teatro de la ópera *m*.

**operate** *vi* obrar, operar.

**operating theatre** *n* quirófano *m*.

**operation** *n* operación *f*; efecto *m*.

**operational** *adj* operacional.

**operative** *adj* operativo/va.

**operator** *n* operario/ria *m/f*; operador/a *m/f*.

**ophthalmic** *adj* oftálmico/ca.

**opine** *vi* opinar, juzgar.

**opinion** *n* opinión *f*; juicio *m*.

**opinionated** *adj* testarudo/da.

**opinion poll** *n* sondeo *m*.

**opponent** *n* antagonista *m/f*; adversario/ria *m/f*.

**opportune** *adj* oportuno/na.

**opportunist** *n* oportunista *m/f*.

**opportunity** *n* oportunidad *f*.

**oppose** *vt* oponerse.

**opposing** *adj* opuesto/ta.

**opposite** *adj* opuesto/ta; contrario/ria; * *adv* enfrente; *prep* frente a; * *n* lo contrario.

**opposition** *n* oposición *f*; resistencia *f*; impedimento *m*.

**oppress** *vt* oprimir.

**oppression** *n* opresión *f*.

**oppressive** *adj* opresivo/va, cruel.

**oppressor** *n* opresor/a *m/f*.

**optic(al)** *adj* óptico/ca; **~s** *npl* óptica *f*.

**optician** *n* óptico/ca *m/f*.

**optimist** *n* optimista *m/f*.

**optimistic** *adj* optimista.

**optimum** *adj* óptimo/ma.
**option** *n* opción *f;* deseo *m.*
**optional** *adj* facultativo/va.
**opulent** *adj* opulento/ta.
**or** *conj* o; u.
**oracle** *n* oráculo *m.*
**oral** *adj* oral, vocal; **~ly** *adv* verbalmente, de palabra.
**orange** *n* naranja *f.*
**orator** *n* orador/a *m/f.*
**orbit** *n* órbita *f.*
**orchard** *n* huerto *m.*
**orchestra** *n* orquesta *f.*
**orchestral** *adj* orquestal.
**orchid** *n* orquídea *f.*
**ordain** *vt* ordenar; establecer.
**ordeal** *n* prueba rigurosa *f.*
**order** *n* orden *m/f;* regla *f;* mandato *m;* serie, clase *f;* * *vt* ordenar, arreglar; mandar.
**order form** *n* hoja de pedido *f.*
**orderly** *adj* ordenado/da, regular.
**ordinarily** *adv* ordinariamente.
**ordinary** *adj* ordinario/ria.
**ordination** *n* ordenación *f.*
**ordnance** *n* armamento *m;* pertrechos *mpl.*
**ore** *n* mineral *m.*
**organ** *n* órgano *m.*
**organic** *adj* orgánico/ca.
**organic farming** *n* agricultura biológica *f.*
**organism** *n* organismo *m.*
**organist** *n* organista *m/f.*
**organization** *n* organización *f.*
**organize** *vt* organizar.
**orgasm** *n* orgasmo *m.*
**orgy** *n* orgía *f.*
**oriental** *adj* oriental.
**orifice** *n* orificio *m.*
**origin** *n* origen, principio *m.*
**original** *adj* original, primitivo/va; **~ly** *adv* originalmente.
**originality** *n* originalidad *f.*
**originate** *vi* originar.
**ornament** *n* ornamento *m;* * *vt* ornamentar, adornar.
**ornamental** *adj* ornamental, decorativo/va.
**ornate** *adj* adornado/da, ataviado/da.
**ornithology** *n* ornitología *f.*
**orphan** *adj, n* huérfano/na *m/f.*
**orphanage** *n* orfanato *m.*
**orthodox** *adj* ortodoxo/xa.
**orthodoxy** *n* ortodoxia *f.*
**orthography** *n* ortografía *f.*
**orthopaedic** *adj* ortopédico/ca.
**Oscar** *n* óscar *m.*

**oscillate** *vi* oscilar, vibrar.
**osprey** *n* águila pescadora *f.*
**ostensibly** *adv* aparentemente.
**ostentatious** *adj* ostentoso/sa.
**osteopath** *n* ostéopata *m/f.*
**ostracize** *vt* condenar al ostracismo.
**ostrich** *n* avestruz *m.*
**other** *pn* otro, otra.
**otherwise** *adv* de otra manera, por otra parte.
**otter** *n* nutria *f.*
**ouch** *excl* ¡ay!
**ought** *v aux* deber, ser menester.
**ounce** *n* onza *f.*
**our**, **ours** *pn* nuestro, nuestra, nuestros, nuestras.
**ourselves** *pn pl* nosotros mismos, nosotras mismas.
**oust** *vt* quitar; desposeer.
**out** *adv* fuera, afuera; apagado/da.
**outboard** *adj:* **~ motor** fueraborda *m.*
**outbreak** *n* erupción *f.*
**outburst** *n* explosión *f.*
**outcast** *n* paria *m/f.*
**outcome** *n* resultado *m.*
**outcry** *n* clamor *m;* griterío *m.*
**outdated** *adj* fuera de moda.
**outdo** *vt* exceder a otro, sobrepujar.
**outdoor** *adj* al aire libre; **~s** *adv* al aire libre.
**outer** *adj* exterior.
**outermost** *adj* extremo/ma; lo más exterior.
**outer space** *n* espacio exterior *m.*
**outfit** *n* vestidos *mpl;* ropa *f.*
**outfitter** *n* sastre *m.*
**outgoing** *adj* extrovertido/da.
**outgrow** *vt* sobrecrecer.
**outhouse** *n* dependencia (de una casa) *f.*
**outing** *n* excursión *f.*
**outlandish** *adj* estrafalario/ria.
**outlaw** *n* bandido *m;* * *vt* proscribir.
**outlay** *n* despensa *f,* gastos *mpl.*
**outlet** *n* salida *f.*
**outline** *n* contorno *m;* bosquejo *m.*
**outlive** *vt* sobrevivir.
**outlook** *n* perspectiva *f.*
**outlying** *adj* distante, lejos.
**outmoded** *adj* anticuado/da.
**outnumber** *vt* superar en número.
**out-of-date** *adj* caducado/da; pasado/da de moda.
**outpatient** *n* paciente externo/na *m/f.*
**outpost** *n* puesto avanzado *m.*
**output** *n* rendimiento *m;* salida *f.*
**outrage** *n* ultraje *m;* * *vt* ultrajar.

**outrageous** *adj* escandaloso/sa; atroz; **~ly** *adv* escandalosamente; injuriosamente; enormemente.

**outright** *adv* absolutamente; * *adj* completo/ta.

**outrun** *vt* correr más que.

**outset** *n* principio *m*.

**outshine** *vt* exceder en brillantez, eclipsar.

**outside** *n* superficie *f*; exterior *m*; apariencia *f*; * *adv* fuera; * *prep* fuera de.

**outsider** *n* forástero *m/f*.

**outsize** *adj* de talla grande.

**outskirts** *npl* alrededores *mpl*.

**outspoken** *adj* muy franco/ca.

**outstanding** *adj* excepcional; pendiente.

**outstretch** *vt* extenderse, alargar.

**outstrip** *vt* dejar atrás; superar.

**out-tray** *n* bandeja de salida *f*.

**outward** *adj* exterior, externo/na; de ida; **~ly** *adv* por fuera; exteriormente.

**outweigh** *vt* pesar más que.

**outwit** *vt* burlar.

**oval** *n* óvalo *m*; * *adj* oval.

**ovary** *n* ovario *m*.

**oven** *n* horno *m*.

**ovenproof** *adj* resistente al horno.

**over** *prep* sobre, encima; más de; durante; **all ~** por todos lados; * *adj* terminado/da; de sobra; **~ again** otra vez; **~ and ~** repetidas veces.

**overall** *adj* total; * *adv* en conjunto; **~s** *npl* overol *m*; mono *m*.

**overawe** *vt* imponer respeto.

**overbalance** *vi* perder el equilibrio.

**overbearing** *adj* despótico/ca.

**overboard** *adv* (*mar*) por la borda, al *mar*.

**overbook** *vt* sobrereservar.

**overcast** *adj* encapotado/da.

**overcharge** *vt* sobrecargar; cobrar de más.

**overcoat** *n* abrigo *m*.

**overcome** *vt* vencer; superar.

**overconfident** *adj* demasiado confiado/da.

**overcrowded** *adj* atestado/da; superpoblado/da.

**overdo** *vi* hacer más de lo necesario; exagerar.

**overdose** *n* sobredosis *f invar*.

**overdraft** *n* saldo deudor, descubierto *m*.

**overdrawn** *adj* en descubierto.

**overdress** *vt* engalanar con exceso.

**overdue** *adj* retrasado/da.

**overeat** *vi* comer demasiado.

**overestimate** *vt* sobreestimar.

**overflow** *vt*, *vi* inundar; rebosar; * *n* inundación *f*; superabundancia *f*.

**overgrown** *adj* invadido/da.

**overgrowth** *n* vegetación exuberante *f*.

**overhang** *vt* colgar sobre.

**overhaul** *vt* revisar; * *n* revisión *f*.

**overhead** *adv* sobre la cabeza, en lo alto.

**overhear** *vt* oír por casualidad.

**overjoyed** *adj* muy gozoso/sa.

**overkill** *n* exceso de medios *m*.

**overland** *adj*, *adv* por tierra.

**overlap** *vi* traslaparse.

**overleaf** *adv* al dorso.

**overload** *vt* sobrecargar.

**overlook** *vt* mirar desde lo alto; examinar; repasar; pasar por alto, tolerar; descuidar.

**overnight** *adv* durante la noche; * *adj* de noche.

**overpass** *n* paso superior *m*.

**overpower** *vt* predominar, oprimir.

**overpowering** *adj* agobiante.

**overrate** *vt* sobrevalorar.

**override** *vt* no hacer caso de; anular.

**overriding** *adj* predominante.

**overrule** *vt* denegar.

**overrun** *vt* inundar; infestar; rebasar.

**overseas** *adv* fuera del país; * *adj* extranjero/ra.

**oversee** *vt* inspeccionar.

**overseer** *n* superintendente *m*.

**overshadow** *vt* eclipsar.

**overshoot** *vt* excederse.

**oversight** *n* yerro *m*; equivocación *f*.

**oversleep** *vi* dormir demasiado.

**overspill** *n* exceso de población *m*.

**overstate** *vi* exagerar.

**overstep** *vt* traspasar, exceder.

**overt** *adj* abierto/ta; publico/ca; **~ly** *adv* abiertamente.

**overtake** *vt* adelantar, sobrepasar.

**overthrow** *vt* trastornar; demoler; destruir; * *n* trastorno *m*; ruina, derrota *f*.

**overtime** *n* horas extra *fpl*.

**overtone** *n* trasfondo *m*.

**overture** *n* abertura *f*; (*mus*) obertura *f*.

**overturn** *vt* subvertir, trastornar.

**overweight** *adj* demasiado pesado/da.

**overwhelm** *vt* abrumar; oprimir; sumergir.

**overwhelming** *adj* arrollador/a; irresistible.

**overwork** *vi* trabajar demasiado.

**owe** *vt* deber, tener deudas; estar obligado/da.

**owing** *adj* que es debido/da; **~ to** por causa de.

**owl** *n* búho *m*.

**own** *adj* propio/pia; **my ~** mío, mía; * *vt* tener; poseer; **to ~ up** *vi* confesar.

**owner** *n* dueño/ña, propietario/ria *m/f*.

**ownership** *n* posesión *f.*
**ox** *n* buey *m;* **~en** *pl* ganado vacuno *m.*
**oxidize** *vt* oxidar.
**oxygen** *n* oxígeno *m.*

**oxygen mask** *n* máscara de oxígeno *f.*
**oxygen tent** *n* tienda de oxígeno *f.*
**oyster** *n* ostra *f.*
**ozone** *n* ozono *m.*

# P

pa n papá m.

pace n paso m; * vt regular el ritmo de; * vi
   pasear.

pacemaker n marcapasos m invar.

pacific adj pacífico/ca; **P~ Ocean** el
   Pacífico m.

pacification n pacificación f.

pacify vt pacificar.

pack n lío, fardo m; baraja (de naipes) f;
   cuadrilla f; * vt empaquetar; hacer la maleta;
   llenar.

package n paquete m; acuerdo m.

package tour n viaje organizado m.

packet n paquete m.

packing n embalaje m.

pact n pacto m.

pad n bloc m; plataforma f; (col) casa f; * vt
   rellenar.

padding n relleno m; paja f.

paddle vi vadear; remar; chapotear; * n
   canalete m.

paddle steamer n vapor de ruedas m.

paddling pool n piscina para niños f.

paddock n corral m.

paddy field n arrozal m.

paediatrics n pediatría f.

pagan adj, n pagano/na m/f.

page n página f; paje m.

pageant n espectáculo público m.

pageantry n pompa f.

pail n cubo, pozal m.

pain n pena f; castigo m; dolor m; * vt afligir.

pained adj afligido/da.

painful adj dolorido/da; penoso/sa; ~ly adv
   dolorosamente, con pena.

painkiller n analgésico m.

painless adj sin pena; indoloro/ra.

painstaking adj laborioso/sa, meticuloso/
   sa.

paint vt pintar.

paintbrush n pincel m; brocha f.

painter n pintor m/f.

painting n pintura f.

paintwork n pintura f.

pair n par m; yuntas fpl.

pal n compañero/ra m/f.

palatable adj sabroso/sa.

palate n paladar m; gusto m.

palatial adj palatino/na.

palaver n lío m.

pale adj palido/da; claro/ra.

palette n paleta f.

paling n estacada, palizada f.

pall n cortina de humo f; * vi perder el sabor.

palliative adj paliativo/va; * n paliativo m.

pallid adj pálido/da.

pallor n palidez f.

palm n (bot) palma f.

palmistry n quiromancia f.

Palm Sunday n Domingo de Ramos m.

palpable adj palpable; evidente.

palpitation n palpitación f.

paltry adj irrisorio/ria; mezquino/na.

pamper vt mimar.

pamphlet n folleto m.

pan n cazuela f; sartén f; olla f.

panacea n panacea f.

panache n estilo m.

pancake n crepe f.

pandemonium n jaleo m.

pane n cristal m.

panel n panel m; paño m.

panelling n paneles mpl.

pang n angustia, congoja f.

panic adj, n pánico/ca m.

panicky adj asustadizo/za.

panic-stricken adj preso/sa del pánico.

pansy n (bot) pensamiento m.

pant vi jadear.

panther n pantera f.

panties npl bragas fpl.

pantry n despensa f.

papacy n papado m.

papal adj papal.

papaw, pawpaw, papaya n papaya f.

paper n papel m; periódico m; examen m;
   estudio m; ~s pl escrituras fpl; (com)
   fondos mpl; * adj de papel; * vt empapelar; tapizar.

paperback n libro en rústica m.

paper bag n bolsa de papel f.

paperclip n clip m.

paperweight n sujetapapeles m invar.

paperwork n papeleo m.

paprika n pimentón m, paprika f.

par n equivalencia f; igualdad f; par m; **at ~**
   (com) a la par.

parable n parábola f.

parachute n paracaídas m invar; * vi
   lanzarse en paracaídas.

parade n ostentación, pompa f; (mil) parada
   f; * vt, vi desfilar; pasear; hacer gala.

**paradise** n paraíso m.

**paradox** n paradoja f.

**paradoxical** adj paradójico/ca.

**paraffin** n queroseno m.

**paragliding** n parapente m.

**paragon** n dechado m.

**paragraph** n párrafo m.

**parallel** adj paralelo/la; * n línea paralela f; * vt paralelizar; parangonar.

**paralyse** vt paralizar.

**paralysis** n parálisis f.

**paralytic** adj paralítico/ca.

**paramedic** n auxiliar sanitario/ria m/f.

**paramount** adj supremo/ma, superior.

**paranoid** adj paranoico/ca.

**paraphernalia** n parafernalia f.

**parasite** n parásito m.

**parasol** n parasol, quitasol m.

**paratrooper** n paracaidista m.

**parcel** n paquete m; porción, cantidad f; equipajes, bultos mpl; * vt empaquetar, embalar.

**parch** vt resecar.

**parched** adj reseco/ca; muerto/ta de sed.

**parchment** n pergamino m.

**pardon** n perdón m; * vt perdonar.

**parent** n padre m; madre f.

**parentage** n parentela f; extracción f.

**parental** adj de los padres.

**parenthesis** n paréntesis m invar.

**parish** n parroquia f; * adj parroquial.

**parishioner** n parroquiano/na m/f.

**parity** n paridad f.

**park** n parque m; * vt, vi aparcar, estacionar.

**parking** n aparcamiento, estacionamiento m.

**parking meter** n parquímetro m.

**parking ticket** n multa de estacionamiento f.

**parlance** n lenguaje m.

**parliament** n parlamento m.

**parliamentary** adj parlamentario/ria.

**parlour** n salón m.

**parody** n parodia f; * vt parodiar.

**parole** n: on ~ en libertad bajo palabra.

**parricide** n parricidio m; parricida m/f.

**parrot** n papagayo m.

**parry** vt parar.

**parsley** n (bot) perejil m.

**parsnip** n (bot) chirivía f.

**part** n parte f; partido m; oficio m; papel (de un actor) m; obligación f; raya f; ~s pl partes fpl; paraje, distrito m; * vt partir, separar, desunir; * vi partirse, separarse; **to ~ with** entregar; pagar; deshacerse de; ~ly adv en parte.

**partial** adj parcial; ~ly adv parcialmente.

**participant** n concursante m.

**participate** vi participar (en).

**participation** n participación f.

**participle** n (gr) participio m.

**particle** n partícula f.

**particular** adj particular, singular; ~ly adv particularmente; * n particular m; particularidad f.

**parting** n separación, partida f; raya (en los cabellos) f.

**partisan** n partidario/ria m/f.

**partition** n partición, separación f; * vt partir, dividir en varias partes.

**partner** n socio/cia, compañero/ra m/f.

**partnership** n compañía, sociedad de comercio f.

**partridge** n perdiz f.

**party** n partido m; fiesta f.

**pass** vt pasar; traspasar; transferir; adelantarse a; * vi pasar, aprobar; * n permiso m; puerto m; **to ~ away** vi fallecer; **to ~ by** vi pasar; vt pasar por alto; **to ~ on** vt transmitir.

**passable** adj pasadero/ra, transitable.

**passage** n pasaje m; travesía f; pasadizo m.

**passbook** n libreta de depósitos f.

**passenger** n pasajero/ra m/f.

**passer-by** n transeúnte m/f.

**passing** adj pasajero/ra.

**passion** n pasión f; amor m; celo, ardor m.

**passionate** adj apasionado/da; ~ly adv apasionadamente; ardientemente.

**passive** adj pasivo/va; ~ly adv pasivamente.

**passkey** n llava maestra f.

**Passover** n Pascua f.

**passport** n pasaporte m.

**passport control** n control de pasaportes m.

**password** n contraseña f.

**past** adj pasado/da; gastado/da; * n (gr) pretérito m; el pasado; * prep más allá de; después de.

**pasta** n pasta f.

**paste** n pasta f; engrudo m; * vt engrudar.

**pasteurized** adj pasteurizado/da.

**pastime** n pasatiempo m; diversión f.

**pastor** n pastor m.

**pastoral** adj pastoril; pastoral.

**pastry** n pastelería f.

**pasture** n pasto m.

**pasty** adj pastoso/sa; pálido/da.

**pat** vt dar golpecillos.

**patch** n remiendo m; parche m; terreno m; * vt remendar; **to ~ up** reparar; hacer las paces en.

**patchwork** n obra de retacitos f, chapucería f.

**pâté** *n* paté *m*.

**patent** *adj* patente; privilegiado/da; * *n* patente *f*; * *vt* privilegiar.

**patentee** *n* poseedor/a de una patente *m/f*.

**patent leather** *n* charol *m*.

**paternal** *adj* paternal.

**paternity** *n* paternidad *f*.

**path** *n* senda *f*.

**pathetic** *adj* patético/ca; **~ally** *adv* patéticamente.

**pathological** *adj* patológico/ca.

**pathology** *n* patología *f*.

**pathos** *n* patetismo *m*.

**pathway** *n* sendero *m*.

**patience** *n* paciencia *f*.

**patient** *adj* paciente, sufrido/da; **~ly** *adv* con paciencia; * *n* enfermo/ma *m/f*.

**patio** *n* patio *m*.

**patriarch** *n* patriarca *m*.

**patriot** *n* patriota *m*.

**patriotic** *adj* patriotico/ca.

**patriotism** *n* patriotismo *m*.

**patrol** *n* patrulla *f*; * *vi* patrullar.

**patrol car** *n* coche patrulla *m*.

**patrolman** *n* policía *m*.

**patron** *n* patrón/ona, protector *m/f*.

**patronage** *n* patrocinio *m*; patronato, patronazgo *m*.

**patronize** *vt* patrocinar, proteger.

**patter** *n* golpeteo *m*; labia *f*; * *vi* tamborilear.

**pattern** *n* patrón *m*; dibujo *m*.

**paunch** *n* panza *f*, vientre *m*.

**pauper** *n* pobre *m/f*.

**pause** *n* pausa *f*; * *vt* pausar; deliberar.

**pave** *vt* empedrar; enlosar, embaldosar.

**pavement** *n* acera *f*.

**pavilion** *n* pabellón *m*.

**paving stone** *n* ladrillo *m*; losa *f*.

**paw** *n* pata *f*, garra *f*; * *vt* manosear.

**pawn** *n* peón *m*; * *vt* empeñar.

**pawnbroker** *n* prestamista *m/f*.

**pawnshop** *n* casa de empeños *f*.

**pay** *vt* pagar; sufrir por; **to ~ back** *vt* reembolsar; **to ~ for** pagar; **to ~ off** *vt* liquidar; *vi* dar resultados; * *n* paga *f*; salario *m*.

**payable** *adj* pagadero/ra.

**payday** *n* día de paga *m*.

**payee** *n* portador/a *m/f*.

**pay envelope** *n* sobre (de paga) *m*.

**paymaster** *n* pagador/a *m/f*.

**payment** *n* paga *f*; pagamento, pago *m*.

**payphone** *n* teléfono público *m*.

**payroll** *n* nómina *f*.

**pea** *n* guisante *m*.

**peace** *n* paz *f*.

**peaceful** *adj* tranquilo/la, pacífico/ca.

**peach** *n* melocotón, durazno *m*.

**peacock** *n* pavón, pavo real *m*.

**peak** *n* cima *f*.

**peak hours**, **peak period** *n* horas punta *fpl*.

**peal** *n* campaneo *m*; estruendo *m*.

**peanut** *n* cacahuete *m*; maní *m*.

**pear** *n* pera *f*.

**pearl** *n* perla *f*.

**peasant** *n* campesino/na *m/f*.

**peat** *n* turba *f*.

**pebble** *n* guija *f*; guijarro *m*.

**peck** *n* picotazo *m*; * *vt* picotear; picar.

**pecking order** *n* orden de jerarquía *m*.

**peculiar** *adj* peculiar, particular, singular; **~ly** *adv* peculiarmente.

**peculiarity** *n* particularidad, singularidad *f*.

**pedal** *n* pedal *m*; * *vi* pedalear.

**pedant** *n* pedante *m/f*.

**pedantic** *adj* pedante.

**pedestal** *n* pedestal *m*.

**pedestrian** *n* peatón/ona *m/f*; * *adj* pedestre.

**pedestrian crossing** *n* paso de peatones *m*.

**pedigree** *n* genealogía *f*; * *adj* de raza.

**pedlar** *n* vendedor/a ambulante *m/f*.

**peek** *vi* mirar de soslayo.

**peel** *vt* pelar; * *vi* desconcharse; * *n* piel *f*; cáscara *f*.

**peer** *n* compañero/ra *m/f*; par *m*.

**peerless** *adj* incomparable.

**peeved** *adj* enojado/da.

**peevish** *adj* regañón/ona, bronco/ca; enojadizo/za.

**peg** *n* clavija *f*; gancho *m*; * *vt* clavar.

**pelican** *n* pelícano *m*.

**pellet** *n* bolita *f*, **~s** perdigones *mpl*.

**pelt** *n* pellejo, cuero *m*; * *vt* arrojar; * *vi* llover a cántaros.

**pen** *n* bolígrafo *m*; pluma *f*; redil *m*.

**penal** *adj* penal.

**penalty** *n* pena *f*; castigo *m*; multa *f*.

**penance** *n* penitencia *f*.

**pence** *n pl* de **penny**.

**pencil** *n* lápiz *m*; lapicero *m*.

**pencil case** *n* estuche *m*.

**pendant** *n* pendiente *m*.

**pending** *adj* pendiente.

**pendulum** *n* péndulo *m*.

**penetrate** *vt* penetrar.

**penguin** *n* pingüino *m*.

**penicillin** *n* penicilina *f*.

**peninsula** *n* península *f*.

**penis** *n* pene *m*.

**penitence** *n* penitencia *f*.
**penitent** *adj, n* penitente *m*.
**penknife** *n* navaja *f*.
**pennant** *n* banderola *f*.
**penniless** *adj* sin dinero.
**penny** *n* penique *m*.
**penpal** *n* amigo/ga por carta *m/f*.
**pension** *n* pensión *f*; * *vt* dar pensión a.
**pensive** *adj* pensativo/va; ~**ly** *adv* pensativamente.
**pentagon** *n*: the **P**~ el Pentágono.
**Pentecost** *n* Pentecostés *m*.
**penthouse** *n* ático *m*.
**pent-up** *adj* reprimido/da.
**penultimate** *adj* penúltimo/ma.
**penury** *n* penuria, carestia *f*.
**people** *n* pueblo *m*; nación *f*; gente *f*; * *vt* poblar.
**people mover** *n* monovolumen *m*.
**pep** *n* enérgia *f*; **to** ~ **up** *vt* animar.
**pepper** *n* pimienta *f*; * *vt* sazonar con pimienta.
**peppermint** *n* menta *f*.
**per** *prep* por.
**per annum** *adv* al año.
**per capita** *adj, adv* per cápita.
**perceive** *vt* percibir, comprender.
**percentage** *n* porcentaje *m*.
**perception** *n* percepción, idea, noción *f*.
**perch** *n* percha *f*.
**perchance** *adv* acaso, quizá.
**percolate** *vt* colar; filtrar.
**percolator** *n* cafetera de filtro *f*.
**percussion** *n* percusión *f*; golpe *m*.
**perdition** *n* pérdida, ruina *f*.
**peremptory** *adj* perentorio/ria; decisivo/va.
**perennial** *adj* perenne; perpetuo/tua.
**perfect** *adj* perfecto/ta, acabado/da; puro/ra; ~**ly** *adv* perfectamente; * *vt* perfeccionar, acabar.
**perfection** *n* perfección *f*.
**perforate** *vt* horadar.
**perforated** *adj* dentado/da.
**perforation** *n* perforación *f*.
**perform** *vt* ejecutar; efectuar; * *vi* representar, hacer papel.
**performance** *n* ejecución *f*; cumplimiento *m*; obra *f*; representación teatral, función *f*.
**performer** *n* ejecutor/a *m/f*; actor *m*, actriz *f*.
**perfume** *n* perfume *m*; fragancia *f*; * *vt* perfumar.
**perhaps** *adv* quizá, quizás.
**peril** *n* peligro, riesgo *m*.
**perilous** *adj* peligroso/sa; ~**ly** *adv* peligrosamente.

**perimeter** *n* perímetro *m*.
**period** *n* período *m*; época *f*; regla *f*.
**periodic** *adj* periódico/ca; ~**ally** *ad* periódicamente.
**periodical** *n* periódico *m*.
**peripheral** *adj* periférico/ca; * *n* peri férico *m*.
**perish** *vi* perecer.
**perishable** *adj* perecedero/ra.
**perjure** *vt* perjurar.
**perjury** *n* perjurio *m*.
**perk** *n* extra *m*.
**perky** *adj* animado/da.
**perm** *n* permanente *f*.
**permanent** *adj* permanente; ~**ly** *ad* permanentemente.
**permeate** *vt* penetrar, atravesar.
**permissible** *adj* lícito/ta, permiso.
**permission** *n* permiso *m*.
**permissive** *adj* permisivo/va.
**permit** *vt* permitir; * *n* permiso *m*.
**permutation** *n* permutación *f*.
**perpendicular** *adj* perpendicular; ~**ly** *ad* perpendicularmente; * *n* línea perpendicu lar *f*.
**perpetrate** *vt* perpetrar, cometer.
**perpetual** *adj* perpetuo/tua; ~**ly** *ad* perpetuamente.
**perpetuate** *vt* perpetuar, eternizar.
**perplex** *vt* confundir.
**persecute** *vt* perseguir, importunar.
**persecution** *n* persecución *f*.
**perseverance** *n* perseverancia *f*.
**persevere** *vi* perseverar.
**persist** *vi* persistir.
**persistence** *adj* persistencia *f*.
**persistent** *adj* persistente.
**person** *n* persona *f*.
**personable** *adj* atractivo/va.
**personage** *n* personaje *m*.
**personal** *adj* personal; ~**ly** *adv* personal mente.
**personal assistant** *n* secretario/ria persona *m/f*.
**personal column** *n* anuncios personale *mpl*.
**personal computer** *n* ordenador persona *m*, computadora personal *f*.
**personality** *n* personalidad *f*.
**personification** *n* personificación *f*.
**personify** *vt* personificar.
**personnel** *n* personal *m*.
**perspective** *n* perspectiva *f*.
**perspiration** *n* transpiración *f*.
**perspire** *vi* transpirar.

**persuade** vt persuadir.

**persuasion** n persuasión f.

**persuasive** adj persuasivo/va; ~ly adv de modo persuasivo.

**pert** adj listo/va, vivo/va; petulante.

**pertaining**: ~ **to** prep relacionado/da con.

**pertinent** adj pertinente; ~ly adv oportunamente.

**pertness** n impertinencia f; vivacidad f.

**perturb** vt perturbar.

**perusal** n lectura, lección f.

**peruse** vt leer; examinar atentamente.

**pervade** vt atravesar, penetrar.

**perverse** adj perverso/sa, depravado/da; ~ly adv perversamente.

**pervert** vt pervertir, corromper.

**pessimist** n pesimista m.

**pest** n plaga f; molestia f.

**pester** vt molestar, cansar.

**pestilence** n pestilencia f.

**pet** n animal doméstico m; favorito/ta m/f; * vt mimar; * vi besuquearse.

**petal** n (bot) pétalo m.

**petite** adj chiquito/ta.

**petition** n presentación, petición f; * vt suplicar; requerir en justicia.

**petrified** adj horrorizado/da.

**petrol** n gasolina f; **four-star** ~ súper f.

**petroleum** n petróleo m.

**petticoat** n enaguas fpl.

**pettiness** n mezquindad f; pequeñez f.

**petty** adj mezquino/na; insignificante.

**petty cash** n dinero para gastos menores m.

**petty officer** n contramaestre m.

**petulant** adj petulante.

**pew** n banco m.

**pewter** n peltre m.

**phantom** n fantasma m.

**pharisee** n fariseo/sea m/f.

**pharmaceutical** adj farmacéutico/ca.

**pharmacist** n farmacéutico/ca m/f.

**pharmacy** n farmacia f.

**phase** n fase f.

**pheasant** n faisán m.

**phenomenal** adj fenomenal.

**phenomenon** n fenómeno m.

**phial** n vial m.

**philanthropic** adj filantrópico/ca.

**philanthropist** n filántropo/pa m/f.

**philanthropy** n filantropía f.

**philologist** n filólogo/ga m/f.

**philology** n filología f.

**philosopher** n filósofo/fa m/f.

**philosophic(al)** adj filosófico/ca; ~ally adv filosóficamente.

**philosophize** vi filosofar.

**philosophy** n filosofía f; **natural** ~ filosofía natural f.

**phlegm** n flema f.

**phlegmatic(al)** adj flemático/ca.

**phobia** n fobia f.

**phone** n teléfono m; * vt telefonear; **to** ~ **back** volver a llamar; **to** ~ **up** llamar por teléfono.

**phone book** n guía telefónica f.

**phone box** n cabina telefónica f.

**phone call** n llamada (telefonica) f.

**phosphorus** n fosforo m.

**photocopier** n fotocopiadora f.

**photocopy** n fotocopia f.

**photograph** n fotografía f; * vt fotografiar.

**photographer** n fotógrafo/fa m/f.

**photographic** adj fotográfico/ca.

**photography** n fotografía f.

**phrase** n frase f; estilo m; * vt expresar.

**phrase book** n libro de frases m.

**physical** adj físico/ca; ~ly adv físicamente.

**physical education** n educación física f.

**physician** n médico/ca m/f.

**physicist** n físico/ca m/f.

**physiological** adj fisiológico/ca.

**physiologist** n fisiólogo/ga m/f.

**physiology** n fisiología f.

**physiotherapy** n fisioterapia f.

**physique** n físico m.

**pianist** n pianista m/f.

**piano** n piano m.

**piccolo** n flautín m.

**pick** vt escoger, elegir; recoger; mondar, limpiar; **to** ~ **on** vt meterse con; **to** ~ **out** vt escoger; **to** ~ **up** vi ir mejor; recobrarse; * vt recoger; comprar; aprender; * n pico m; **the** ~ **of** lo más escogido de.

**pickaxe** n pico m.

**picket** n piquete m.

**pickle** n escabeche m; * vt escabechar.

**pickpocket** n carterista m/f.

**pick-up** n (auto) furgoneta f.

**picnic** n picnic m.

**pictorial** adj pictórico/ca.

**picture** n pintura f; retrato m; * vt pintar; figurar.

**picture book** n libro de dibujos m.

**picturesque** adj pintoresco/ca.

**pie** n pastel m; tarta f; empanada f.

**piece** n pedazo m; pieza, obra f; * vt remendar.

**piecemeal** adv en pedazos; * adj dividido/da.

**piecework** n destajo m; * vi **to do** ~ trabajar a destajo.

**pier** n pilar m; muelle m.
**pierce** vt penetrar, agujerear, taladrar.
**piercing** adj penetrante.
**piety** n piedad, devoción f.
**pig** n cerdo m; (col) cochino m.
**pigeon** n paloma f; **carrier** or **homing ~** paloma mensajera f.
**pigeonhole** n casillero m.
**piggy bank** n hucha f.
**pig-headed** adj terco/ca.
**pigsty** n pocilga f.
**pigtail** n trenza f.
**pike** n lucio m; pica f.
**pile** n estaca f; pila f; montón m; pelo m; pelillo m; **~s** pl almorranas fpl; * vt amontonar, apilar.
**pile-up** n colisión múltiple f.
**pilfer** vt hurtar.
**pilgrim** n peregrino/na m/f.
**pilgrimage** n peregrinación f.
**pill** n píldora f.
**pillage** vt saquear.
**pillar** n pilar m.
**pillion** n asiento trasero m.
**pillow** n almohada f.
**pillowcase** n funda de almohada f.
**pilot** n piloto m/f; * vt pilotar; (fig) guiar.
**pilot light** n piloto m.
**pimp** n chulo, cafiche m.
**pimple** n grano m.
**pin** n alfiler m; **~s and needles** npl hormigueo m; * vt prender con alfileres; fijar con clavija.
**pinafore** n delantal m.
**pinball** n flíper m.
**pincers** n pinzas, tenazuelas fpl.
**pinch** vt pellizcar; (col) birlar; * vi apretar; * n pellizco m.
**pincushion** n acerico m.
**pine**[1] n (bot) pino m.
**pine**[2] vi ansiar por.
**pineapple** n piña f, ananás m invar.
**ping** n sonido agudo m.
**pink** n rosa f; * adj color de rosa.
**pinnacle** n cumbre f.
**pinpoint** vt precisar.
**pint** n pinta f.
**pioneer** n pionero/ra m/f.
**pious** adj pío, pía, devoto/ta; **~ly** adv piadosamente.
**pip** n pepita f.
**pipe** n tubo, caño m; pipa f; **~s** cañería f.
**pipe cleaner** n limpiapipas m invar.
**pipe dream** n sueño imposible m.

**pipeline** n tubería f; oleoducto m; gas oducto m.
**piper** n gaitero/ra m/f.
**piping** adj hirviente.
**pique** n pique m; desazón f; ojeriza f.
**piracy** n piratería f.
**pirate** n pirata m/f.
**pirouette** n pirueta f; vi piruetear.
**Pisces** n Piscis m (signo del zodiaco).
**piss** n (col) meada f; * vi mear.
**pistol** n pistola f.
**piston** n émbolo m.
**pit** n hoyo m; mina f.
**pitch** n lanzamiento m; tono m; * vt tira arrojar; * vi caerse; caer de cabeza.
**pitch-black** adj negro/gra como boca de lob
**pitcher** n cántaro m.
**pitchfork** n horca f.
**pitfall** n trampa f.
**pithy** adj meduloso/sa.
**pitiable** adj lastimoso/sa.
**pitiful** adj lastimoso/sa, compasivo/va; ~▮ adv lastimosamente.
**pittance** n pitanza, ración f; porcioncilla
**pity** n piedad, compasión f; * vt compadece
**pivot** n eje m.
**pizza** n pizza f.
**placard** n pancarta f.
**placate** vt apaciguar.
**place** n lugar, sitio m; rango, empleo m; * ▮ colocar; poner.
**placid** adj plácido/da, quieto/ta; ~ly ad plácidamente.
**plagiarism** n plagio m.
**plague** n peste, plaga f; * vt atormentar infestar, apestar.
**plaice** n platija f (pez).
**plaid** n tartán m.
**plain** adj liso/so, llano/na, abierto/ta sincero/ra; puro/ra, simple, común; claro ra, evidente, distinto/ta; ~ly adv llana mente; claramente; * n llano m.
**plaintiff** n (law) demandante m/f.
**plait** n pliegue m; trenza f; * vt plegar trenzar.
**plan** n plano m; plan m; * vt proyectar.
**plane** n avión m; plano m; cepillo m; * ▮ allanar; acepillar.
**planet** n planeta m.
**planetary** adj planetario/ria.
**plank** n tabla f.
**planner** n planificador/a m/f.
**planning** n planificación f.
**plant** n planta f; fábrica f; maquinaria f; * ▮ plantar.

**plantation** *n* plantación *f*; colonia *f*.

**plaque** *n* placa *f*.

**plaster** *n* yeso *m*; emplasto *m*; * *vt* enyesar; emplastar.

**plastered** *adj* (*col*) borracho/cha.

**plasterer** *n* yesero/ra *m/f*.

**plaster of Paris** *n* yeso mate *m*.

**plastic** *adj* plástico/ca.

**plastic surgery** *n* cirugía plástica *f*.

**plate** *n* plato *m*; lámina *f*; placa *f*.

**plateau** *n* meseta *f*.

**plate glass** *n* vidrio cilindrado *m*.

**platform** *n* plataforma *f*.

**platinum** *n* platino *m*.

**platitude** *n* tópico *m*.

**platoon** *n* (*mil*) pelotón *m*.

**platter** *n* fuente *f*; plato grande *m*.

**plaudit** *n* aplauso *m*.

**plausible** *adj* plausible.

**play** *n* juego *m*; comedia *f*; * *vt*, *vi* jugar; juguetear; representar; (*mus*) tocar; **to ~ down** *vt* quitar importancia a.

**playboy** *n* playboy *m*.

**player** *n* jugador/a *m/f*; comediante/ta *m/f*, actor *m*, actriz *f*.

**playful** *adj* juguetón/ona, travieso/sa; **~ly** *adv* juguetonamente, reto zando.

**playmate** *n* camarada *m/f*.

**playground** *n* patio *m*.

**playgroup** *n* parvulario *m*.

**play-off** *n* desempate *m*.

**playpen** *n* corral (de niños) *m*.

**plaything** *n* juguete *m*.

**playwright** *n* dramaturgo/ga *m/f*.

**plea** *n* defensa *f*; excusa *f*; pretexto *m*; * *vt* pretextar.

**plead** *vt* defender en juicio; alegar.

**pleasant** *adj* agradable; placentero/ra, alegre; **~ly** *adv* alegremente, placenteramente.

**please** *vt* agradar, complacer.

**pleased** *adj* contento/ta.

**pleasing** *adj* agradable, placentero/ra.

**pleasure** *n* gusto, placer *m*; recreo *m*.

**pleat** *n* pliegue *m*.

**pledge** *n* prenda *f*; fianza *f*; * *vt* empeñar, prometer.

**plentiful** *adj* copioso/sa, abundante.

**plenty** *n* copia, abundancia *f*.

**plethora** *n* plétora *f*.

**pleurisy** *n* pleuresía *f*.

**pliable**, **pliant** *adj* flexible, dócil.

**pliers** *npl* alicates *mpl*.

**plight** *n* situación difícil *f*.

**plinth** *n* plinto *m*; zócalo *m*.

**plod** *vi* afanarse mucho, ajetrearse.

**plot** *n* terreno *m*; plano *m*; conspiración, trama *f*; estratagema *f*; * *vi* trazar; conspirar; tramar.

**plough** *n* arado *m*; * *vt* arar, labrar la tierra; **to ~ back** *vt* reinvertir; **to ~ through** abrirse paso; roer.

**ploy** *n* truco *m*.

**pluck** *vt* tirar con fuerza; arrancar; desplumar; * *n* ánimo *m*.

**plucky** *adj* gallardo/da.

**plug** *n* tapón *m*; enchufe *m*; bujía *f*; * *vt* tapar.

**plum** *n* ciruela *f*.

**plumage** *n* plumaje *m*.

**plumb** *n* plomada *f*; * *adv* a plomo; * *vt* aplomar.

**plumber** *n* fontanero/ra, plomero/ra *m/f*.

**plume** *n* pluma *f*.

**plump** *adj* gordo/da, rollizo/za.

**plum tree** *n* ciruelo *m*.

**plunder** *vt* saquear, pillar, robar; * *n* pillaje, botín *m*.

**plunge** *vi* sumergir(se), precipitarse; * *n* zambullida *f*.

**plunger** *n* desatascador *m*.

**pluperfect** *n* (*gr*) pluscuamperfecto *m*.

**plural** *adj*, *n* plural *m*.

**plurality** *n* pluralidad *f*.

**plus** *n* signo de más *m*; * *prep* más, y, además de.

**plush** *adj* de felpa.

**plutonium** *n* plutonio *m*.

**ply** *vt* trabajar con ahínco; * *vi* aplicarse; (*mar*) ir y venir.

**plywood** *n* madera contrachapada *f*.

**pneumatic** *adj* neumático/ca.

**pneumatic drill** *n* martillo neumático *m*.

**pneumonia** *n* pulmonía *f*.

**poach** *vt* escalfar; cazar en vedado; * *vi* cazar en vedado.

**poached** *adj* escalfado/da.

**poacher** *n* cazador furtivo *m*.

**poaching** *n* caza furtiva *f*.

**pocket** *n* bolsillo *m*; bolsa *f*; * *vt* embolsar.

**pocket money** *n* dinero para gastos *m*.

**pod** *n* vaina *f*.

**podgy** *adj* gordinflón/ona.

**poem** *n* poema *m*.

**poet** *n* poeta *m*, poetisa *f*.

**poetic** *adj* poético/ca.

**poetry** *n* poesía *f*.

**poignant** *adj* punzante.

**point** *n* punta *f*; punto *m*; promontorio *m*; puntillo *m*; estado *m*; **~ of view** *n* punto de vista *m*; * *vt* apuntar; aguzar; puntuar; **to ~ a gun** encañonar.

**point-blank** *adv* directamente.

**pointed** *adj* puntiagudo/da; epigramático/ca; **~ly** *adv* sutilmente.

**pointer** *n* apuntador/a *m/f*; perro de muestra *m*.

**pointless** *adj* sin sentido.

**poise** *n* peso *m*; equilibrio *m*.

**poison** *n* veneno *m*; * *vt* envenenar.

**poisoning** *n* envenenamiento *m*.

**poisonous** *adj* venenoso/sa.

**poke** *vt* hurgar; empujar.

**poker** *n* atizador *m*; póker *m*.

**poker-faced** *adj* con cara de póker.

**poky** *adj* estrecho/cha.

**polar** *adj* polar.

**pole** *n* polo *m*; palo *m*; pértiga *f*.

**pole vault** *n* salto con pértiga *m*.

**police** *n* policía *f*.

**police car** *n* coche patrulla *m*.

**policeman** *n* policía *m*.

**police state** *n* estado policial *m*.

**police station** *n* comisaría *f*.

**policewoman** *n* mujer policía *f*.

**policy** *n* política *f*.

**polio** *n* polio *f*.

**polish** *vt* pulir, alisar; limar; **to ~ off** *vt* terminar; despachar; * *n* pulimento *m*.

**polished** *adj* elegante, pulido/da.

**polite** *adj* pulido/da, cortés; **~ly** *adv* cortésmente.

**politeness** *n* cortesía *f*.

**politic** *adj* político/ca; astuto/ta.

**political** *adj* político/ca.

**political asylum** *n* asilo político *m*.

**politician** *n* político/ca *m/f*.

**politics** *npl* política *f*.

**polka** *n* polca *f*; **~ dot** *n* lunar *m*.

**poll** *n* voto *m*; encuesta *f*, sondeo *m*.

**pollen** *n* (*bot*) polen *m*.

**pollute** *vt* contaminar.

**pollution** *n* polución, contaminación *f*.

**polo** *n* polo *m*.

**polyester** *n* poliéster *m*.

**polyethylene, polythene** *n* polietileno *m*.

**polygamy** *n* poligamia *f*.

**polystyrene** *n* poliestireno *m*.

**polytechnic** *n* politécnico *m*.

**pomegranate** *n* granada *f*.

**pomp** *n* pompa *f*; esplendor *m*.

**pompom** *n* borla *f*.

**pompous** *adj* pomposo/sa.

**pond** *n* estanque *m*.

**ponder** *vt* ponderar, considerar.

**ponderous** *adj* ponderoso/sa, pesado/da.

**pontiff** *n* pontífice, papa *m*.

**pontoon** *n* pontón *m*.

**pony** *n* jaca *f*; potro *m*.

**ponytail** *n* cola de caballo *f*.

**pool** *n* charca *f*; piscina, alberca *f*; * *vt* juntar; **to form a ~** remansarse.

**poor** *adj* pobre; humilde; de poco valor; **~ly** *adv* pobremente; **the ~** *n* los pobres *mpl*.

**pop** *n* pop *m*; papá *m*; gaseosa *f*; chasquido *m*; * **to ~ in/out** *vi* entrar/salir un momento.

**pop concert** *n* concierto pop *m*.

**popcorn** *n* palomitas *fpl*.

**Pope** *n* Papa *m*.

**poplar** *n* álamo *m*.

**poppy** *n* (*bot*) amapola *f*.

**populace** *n* populacho *m*.

**popular** *adj* popular; **~ly** *adv* popularmente.

**popularity** *n* popularidad *f*.

**popularize** *vt* popularizar.

**populate** *vi* poblar.

**population** *n* población *f*.

**populous** *adj* populoso/sa.

**pop video** *n* videoclip *m*.

**porcelain** *n* porcelana, china, loza fina *f*.

**porch** *n* pórtico, vestíbulo *m*, zaguán *m*.

**porcupine** *n* puerco espín *m*.

**pore** *n* poro *m*.

**pork** *n* carne de cerdo, carne de puerco *f*.

**pornography** *n* pornografía *f*.

**porous** *adj* poroso/sa.

**porpoise** *n* marsopa *f*.

**porridge** *n* gachas de avena *fpl*.

**port** *n* puerto *m*; (*mar*) babor *m*; vino de Oporto *m*.

**portable** *adj* portátil.

**portal** *n* portal *m*; portada *f*.

**porter** *n* portero *m*; mozo *m*; conserje *m/f*.

**portfolio** *n* cartera *f*.

**porthole** *n* portilla *f*.

**portico** *n* pórtico, portal *m*.

**portion** *n* porción, parte *f*.

**portly** *adj* rollizo/za.

**portrait** *n* retrato *m*.

**portray** *vt* retratar.

**pose** *n* postura *f*; pose *f*; * *vi* posar; * *vt* plantear.

**posh** *adj* elegante.

**position** *n* posición, situación *f*; * *vt* colocar.

**positive** *adj* positivo/va, real, verdadero/ra; **~ly** *adv* positivamente; ciertamente.

**posse** *n* pelotón *m*.

**possess** *vt* poseer; gozar.

**possession** *n* posesión *f.*
**possessive** *adj* posesivo/va.
**possibility** *n* posibilidad *f.*
**possible** *adj* posible; **~ly** *adv* quizá, quizás.
**post** *n* correo *m*; puesto *m*; empleo *m*; poste *m*; * *vt* apostar; fijar.
**postage** *n* franqueo *m.*
**postage stamp** *n* sello de correos *m*; estampilla *f.*
**postal box**, **P O Box** *n* apartado de correos *m.*
**postcard** *n* tarjeta postal *f.*
**post code** *n* código postal *m.*
**postdate** *vt* posfechar.
**poster** *n* cartel *m.*
**poste restante** *n* lista de correos *f.*
**posterior** *n* trasero *m.*
**posterity** *n* posteridad *f.*
**postgraduate** *n* posgraduado/da *m/f.*
**posthumous** *adj* póstumo/ma.
**postman** *n* cartero *m.*
**postmark** *n* matasellos *m.*
**postmaster** *n* administrador/a de correos *m/f.*
**post office** *n* correos *m.*
**postpone** *vt* diferir, suspender; posponer.
**postscript** *n* posdata *f.*
**posture** *n* postura *f.*
**post-war** *adj* de posguerra.
**postwoman** *n* cartera *f.*
**posy** *n* ramillete de flores *m.*
**pot** *n* marmita *f*; olla *f*; (*col*) marihuana *f*; * *vt* preservar en marmitas.
**potato** *n* patata *f*; papa *f.*
**potato peeler** *n* pelapatatas *m invar.*
**potbellied** *adj* panzudo/da.
**potent** *adj* potente, poderoso/sa, eficaz.
**potential** *adj* potencial, poderoso/sa.
**pothole** *n* bache *m.*
**potion** *n* poción, bebida medicinal *f.*
**potted** *adj* en conserva; en tiesto.
**potter** *n* alfarero/ra *m/f.*
**pottery** *n* cerámica *f.*
**potty** *adj* chiflado/da.
**pouch** *n* bolsa *f*; petaca *f*; zurrón *m.*
**poultice** *n* cataplasma *f.*
**poultry** *n* aves de corral *fpl.*
**pound** *n* libra *f*; libra esterlina *f*; corral *m*; * *vt* machacar; * *vi* dar golpes.
**pour** *vt* echar; servir; * *vi* fluir con rapidez; llover a cántaros.
**pout** *vi* fruncir el ceño.
**poverty** *n* pobreza *f.*
**powder** *n* polvo *m*; pólvora *f*; * *vt* polvorear.
**powder compact** *n* polvera *f.*
**powdered milk** *n* leche en polvo *f.*

**powder puff** *n* borla *f.*
**powder room** *n* aseos *mpl.*
**powdery** *adj* polvoriento/ta.
**power** *n* poder *m*; potestad *f*; imperio *m*; potencia *f*; autoridad *f*; fuerza *f*; * *vt* impulsar.
**powerful** *adj* poderoso/sa; **~ly** *adv* poderosamente, con mucha fuerza.
**powerless** *adj* impotente.
**power station** *n* central eléctrica *f.*
**practicable** *adj* factible; viable.
**practical** *adj* práctico/ca; **~ly** *adv* prácticamente.
**practicality** *n* viabilidad *f.*
**practical joke** *n* broma pesada *f.*
**practice** *n* práctica *f*; uso *m*; costumbre *f*; **~s** *pl* intrigas *fpl.*
**practise** *vi* practicar, ejercer.
**practitioner** (**medical**) *n* médico/ca *m/f.*
**pragmatic** *adj* pragmático/ca.
**prairie** *n* pampa *f.*
**praise** *n* renombre *m*; alabanza *f*; * *vt* celebrar, alabar.
**praiseworthy** *adj* digno/na de alabanza; laudable.
**prance** *vi* cabriolar.
**prank** *n* travesura, extravagancia *f.*
**prattle** *vi* charlar; * *n* charla *f.*
**prawn** *n* gamba *f.*
**pray** *vi* rezar; rogar; orar.
**prayer** *n* oración, súplica *f.*
**prayer book** *n* devocionario *m.*
**preach** *vi* predicar.
**preacher** *n* pastor/a; predicador/a *m/f.*
**preamble** *n* preámbulo *m.*
**precarious** *adj* precario, incierto/ta; **~ly** *adv* precariamente.
**precaution** *n* precaución *f.*
**precautionary** *adj* preventivo/va.
**precede** *vt* anteceder, preceder.
**precedence** *n* precedencia *f.*
**precedent** *adj*, *n* precedente *m.*
**precinct** *n* límite, lindero *m*; barrio *m.*
**precious** *adj* precioso/sa.
**precipice** *n* precipicio *m.*
**precipitate** *vt* precipitar; * *adj* precipitado/da.
**precise** *adj* preciso/sa, exacto/ta; **~ly** *adv* precisamente, exactamente.
**precision** *n* precisión, limitación exacta *f.*
**preclude** *vt* prevenir, impedir.
**precocious** *adj* precoz, temprano/na, prematuro/ra.
**preconceive** *vt* preconcebir.
**preconception** *n* preconcepción *f.*

**precondition** *n* condición previa *f.*
**precursor** *n* precursor/a *m/f.*
**predator** *n* depredador/a *m/f.*
**predecessor** *n* predecesor/a, antecesor/a *m/f.*
**predestination** *n* predestinación *f.*
**predicament** *n* aprieto *m*; dilema *m.*
**predict** *vt* predecir.
**predictable** *adj* previsible.
**prediction** *n* predicción *f.*
**predilection** *n* predilección *f.*
**predominant** *adj* predominante.
**predominate** *vt* predominar.
**preen** *vt* limpiarse (las plumas).
**prefab** *n* casa prefabricada *f.*
**preface** *n* prefacio *m.*
**prefer** *vt* preferir.
**preferable** *adj* preferible.
**preferably** *adv* de preferencia.
**preference** *n* preferencia *f.*
**preferential** *adj* preferente.
**preferment** *n* promoción *f*; preferencia *f.*
**prefix** *vt* prefijar; * *n* (*gr*) prefijo *m.*
**pregnancy** *n* embarazo *m.*
**pregnant** *adj* embarazada.
**prehistoric** *adj* prehistórico/ca.
**prejudice** *n* perjuicio, daño *m*; * *vt* perjudicar, hacer daño.
**prejudiced** *adj* predispuesto/ta; parcial.
**prejudicial** *adj* perjudicial, dañoso/sa.
**preliminary** *adj* preliminar.
**prelude** *n* preludio *m.*
**premarital** *adj* premarital.
**premature** *adj* prematuro/ra; **~ly** *adv* anticipadamente.
**premeditation** *n* premeditación *f.*
**premier** *n* primer ministro *m*, primera ministra *f.*
**première** *n* estreno *m.*
**premise** *n* premisa *f.*
**premises** *npl* establecimiento *m.*
**premium** *n* premio *m*; remuneración *f*; prima *f.*
**premonition** *n* presentimiento *m.*
**preoccupied** *adj* preocupado/da; ensimismado/da.
**prepaid** *adj* con el porte pagado.
**preparation** *n* preparación *f*; cosa preparada *f.*
**preparatory** *adj* preparatorio/ria.
**prepare** *vt* (*vi*) preparar(se).
**prepared** *adj* abonado/da.
**preponderance** *n* preponderancia *f.*
**preposition** *n* preposición *f.*
**preposterous** *adj* absurdo/da.
**prerequisite** *n* requisito *m.*

**prerogative** *n* prerrogativa *f.*
**prescribe** *vi* prescribir; recetar.
**prescription** *n* prescripción *f*; receta medicinal *f.*
**presence** *n* presencia *f*; asistencia *f.*
**present** *n* regalo *m*; * *adj* presente; **~ly** *adv* al presente; * *vt* ofrecer, presentar; regalar; acusar.
**presentable** *adj* decente, decoroso/sa.
**presentation** *n* presentación *f.*
**present-day** *adj* actual.
**presenter** *n* presentador/a *m/f.*
**presentiment** *n* presentimiento *m.*
**preservation** *n* preservación *f.*
**preservative** *n* preservativo *m.*
**preserve** *vt* preservar, conservar; poner en conserva; * *n* conserva, confitura *f.*
**preside** *vi* presidir; dirigir.
**presidency** *n* presidencia *f.*
**president** *n* presidente *m/f.*
**presidential** *adj* presidencial.
**press** *vt* empujar; apretar; compeler; * *vi* apretar; * *n* prensa *f*; armario *m*; apretón *m*; imprenta *f.*
**press agency** *n* agencia de prensa *f.*
**press conference** *n* rueda de prensa *f.*
**pressing** *adj* urgente; **~ly** *adv* urgentemente.
**press-up** *n* plancha *f.*
**pressure** *n* presión *f*; opresión *f.*
**pressure cooker** *n* olla exprés, olla a presión *f.*
**pressure group** *n* grupo de presión *m.*
**pressurized** *adj* a presión.
**prestige** *n* prestigio *m.*
**presumable** *adj* presumible.
**presumably** *adv* es de suponer que.
**presume** *vt* presumir, suponer.
**presumption** *n* presunción *f.*
**presumptuous** *adj* presuntuoso/sa.
**presuppose** *vt* presuponer.
**pretence** *n* pretexto *m*; pretensión *f.*
**pretend** *vi* pretender; presumir.
**pretender** *n* pretendiente *m/f.*
**pretension** *n* pretensión *f.*
**pretentious** *adj* presumido/da; ostentoso/sa.
**preterite** *n* pretérito *m.*
**pretext** *n* pretexto *m*; **to find a ~ for** pretextar.
**pretty** *adj* lindo/da, bien parecido/da; hermoso/sa; * *adv* algo, un poco.
**prevail** *vi* prevalecer, predominar.
**prevailing** *adj* dominante (uso, costumbre).
**prevalent** *adj* predominante, eficaz.
**prevent** *vt* prevenir; impedir.

**prevention** *n* prevención *f*.
**preventive** *adj* preventivo/va.
**preview** *n* preestreno *m*.
**previous** *adj* previo/via; antecedente; **~ly** *adv* antes.
**prewar** *adj* de antes de la guerra.
**prey** *n* presa *f*.
**price** *n* precio *m*.
**priceless** *adj* inapreciable.
**price list** *n* tarifa, lista de precios *f*.
**pricey** *adj* carero/ra.
**prick** *vt* punzar, picar; apuntar; excitar; * *n* puntura *f*; pica dura *f*; punzada *f*.
**prickle** *n* pincho *m*; espina *f*.
**prickly** *adj* espinoso/sa.
**pride** *n* orgullo *m*; vanidad *f*; jactancia *f*.
**priest** *n* sacerdote *m*.
**priestess** *n* sacerdotisa *f*.
**priesthood** *n* sacerdocio *m*.
**priestly** *adj* sacerdotal.
**priggish** *adj* afectado/da.
**prim** *adj* peripuesto/ta, afectado/da.
**primacy** *n* primacía *f*.
**primarily** *adv* primariamente, sobre todo.
**primary** *adj* primario/ria, principal, primero/ra.
**primary school** *n* escuela primaria *f*.
**primate** *n* primadoprimate *m*.
**prime** *n* (*fig*) flor, nata *f*; primavera *f*; principio *m*; * *adj* primero/ra; primoroso/sa, excelente; * *vt* cebar.
**prime minister** *n* primer ministro *m*, primera ministra *f*.
**primeval** *adj* primitivo/va.
**priming** *n* cebo *m*; imprimación *f*.
**primitive** *adj* primitivo/va; **~ly** *adv* primitivamente.
**primrose** *n* (*bot*) primavera *f*.
**prince** *n* príncipe *m*.
**princess** *n* princesa *f*.
**principal** *adj* principal; **~ly** *adv* principalmente; * *n* principal, jefe *m*.
**principality** *n* principado/da *m*.
**principle** *n* principio *m*; causa primitiva *f*; fundamento, motivo *m*.
**print** *vt* imprimir; * *n* impresión, estampa, edición *f*; impreso *m*; **out of ~** vendido/da, agotado/da.
**printed matter** *n* impresos *mpl*.
**printer** *n* impresor/a *m/f*.
**printing** *n* imprenta *f*.
**prior** *adj* anterior, precedente; * *n* prior (prelado) *m*.
**priority** *n* prioridad *f*.
**priory** *n* priorato *m*.

**prism** *n* prisma *m*.
**prison** *n* prisión, carcel *f*.
**prisoner** *n* prisionero/ra *m/f*.
**pristine** *adj* prístino/na, antiguo/gua.
**privacy** *n* soledad *f*.
**private** *adj* secreto/ta, privado/da; particular; **~ soldier** *n* soldado raso *m*; **~ly** *adv* en secreto.
**private eye** *n* detective privado/da *m/f*.
**privet** *n* alheña *f*.
**privilege** *n* privilegio *m*.
**prize** *n* premio *m*; presa *f*; * *vt* apreciar, valuar; **to ~ open** abrir por fuerza.
**prize-giving** *n* entrega de premios *f*.
**prizewinner** *n* premiado/da *m/f*.
**pro** *prep* para.
**probability** *n* probabilidad, verosimilitud *f*.
**probable** *adj* probable, verosímil; **~bly** *adv* probablemente.
**probation** *n* prueba *f*.
**probationary** *adj* de prueba.
**probe** *n* sonda *f*; encuesta *f*; * *vt* sondar; investigar.
**problem** *n* problema *m*.
**problematical** *adj* problemático/ca; **~ly** *adv* problemáticamente.
**procedure** *n* procedimiento *m*; progreso, proceso *m*.
**proceed** *vi* proceder; provenir; originarse; **~s** *npl* producto *m*; rédito *m*; **gross ~s** producto íntegro; **net ~s** producto neto.
**proceedings** *n* procedimiento *m*; proceso *m*; conducta *f*.
**process** *n* proceso *m*.
**procession** *n* procesión *f*.
**proclaim** *vt* proclamar, promulgar; publicar.
**proclamation** *n* proclamación *f*; decreto *m*.
**procrastinate** *vt* diferir, retardar.
**proctor** *n* censor/a *m/f*.
**procure** *vt* procurar.
**procurement** *n* procuración *f*.
**prod** *vt* empujar.
**prodigal** *adj* pródigo/ga.
**prodigious** *adj* prodigioso/sa; **~ly** *adv* prodigiosamente.
**prodigy** *n* prodigio *m*.
**produce** *vt* producir, criar; causar; * *n* producto *m*.
**producer** *n* productor/a *m/f*.
**product** *n* producto *m*; obra *f*; efecto *m*.
**production** *n* producción *f*; producto *m*.
**production line** *n* línea de producción *f*.
**productive** *adj* productivo/va.
**productivity** *n* productividad *f*.
**profane** *adj* profano/na.

**profess** vt profesar; ejercer; declarar.
**profession** n profesión f.
**professional** adj profesional.
**professor** n profesor/a, catedratico/ca m/f.
**proficiency** n capacidad f.
**proficient** adj proficiente, adelantado/da.
**profile** n perfil m.
**profit** n ganancia f; provecho m; ventaja f; * vi aprovechar.
**profitability** n rentabilidad f.
**profitable** adj provechoso/sa, ventajoso/sa.
**profiteering** n explotación f.
**profound** adj profundo/da; ~ly adv profundamente.
**profuse** adj profuso/sa, prodigo/ga; ~ly adv profusamente.
**program** n programa m.
**programme** n programa m.
**programmer** n programador/a m/f.
**programming** n programación f.
**progress** n progreso m; curso m; * vi hacer progresos.
**progression** n progresión f; adelantamiento m.
**progressive** adj progresivo/va; ~ly adv progresivamente.
**prohibit** vt prohibir, vedar; impedir.
**prohibition** n prohibición f.
**project** vt proyectar, trazar; * n proyecto m.
**projectile** n proyectil m.
**projection** n proyección f; estimación f.
**projector** n proyector m.
**proletarian** adj proletario/ria.
**proletariat** n proletariado m.
**prolific** adj prolifico/ca, fecundo/da.
**prologue** n prólogo m.
**prolong** vt prolongar; diferir.
**prom** n concierto m.
**promenade** n paseo m.
**prominence** n prominencia f.
**prominent** adj prominente, saledizo/za.
**promiscuous** adj promiscuo/cua.
**promise** n promesa f; * vt prometer.
**promising** adj prometedor/a.
**promontory** n promontorio m.
**promote** vt promover.
**promoter** n promotor/a, promovedor/a m/f.
**promotion** n promoción f.
**prompt** adj pronto/ta; ~ly adv prontamente; * vt sugerir, insinuar; apuntar (en el teatro).
**prompter** n apuntador/a m/f.
**prone** adj inclinado/da.
**prong** n diente m.

**pronoun** n pronombre m.
**pronounce** vt pronunciar; recitar.
**pronounced** adj marcado/da.
**pronouncement** n declaración f.
**pronunciation** n pronunciación f.
**proof** n prueba f; * adj impenetrable; de prueba.
**prop** vt sostener; * n apoyo, puntal m; sostén m.
**propaganda** n propaganda f.
**propel** vt impeler.
**propeller** n hélice f.
**propensity** n propensión, tendencia f.
**proper** adj propio/pia; conveniente; exacto/ta; bien parecido/da; ~ly adv propiamente, justamente.
**property** n propiedad f.
**prophecy** n profecía f.
**prophesy** vt profetizar.
**prophet** n profeta m.
**prophetic** adj profético/ca.
**proportion** n proporción f; simetría f.
**proportional** adj proporcional.
**proportionate** adj proporcionado/da.
**proposal** n propuesta, proposición f; oferta f.
**propose** vt proponer.
**proposition** n proposición, propuesta f.
**proprietor** n propietario/ria m/f.
**propriety** n propiedad f.
**pro rata** adv de forma prorrateada.
**prosaic** adj prosaico/ca, en prosa.
**prose** n prosa f.
**prosecute** vt proseguir.
**prosecution** n prosecución f; acusación f.
**prosecutor** n fiscal m/f.
**prospect** n perspectiva f; esperanza f; * vt explorar; * vi buscar.
**prospecting** n prospección f.
**prospective** adj probable; futuro/ra.
**prospector** n explorador/a m/f.
**prospectus** n prospecto m.
**prosper** vi prosperar.
**prosperity** n prosperidad f.
**prosperous** adj próspero/ra, feliz.
**prostitute** n prostituta f.
**prostitution** n prostitución f.
**prostrate** adj postrado/da.
**protagonist** n protagonista m.
**protect** vt proteger; amparar.
**protection** n protección f.
**protective** adj protectorio/ria.
**protector** n protector/a, patrono/na m/f.
**protégé(e)** n protegido/da m/f.
**protein** n proteína f.

**protest** *vi* protestar; * *n* protesta *f.*
**Protestant** *n* protestante *m/f.*
**protester** *n* manifestante *m/f.*
**protocol** *n* protocolo *m.*
**prototype** *n* prototipo *m.*
**protracted** *adj* prolongado/da.
**protrude** *vi* sobresalir.
**proud** *adj* soberbio/bia, orgulloso/sa; **~ly** *adv* soberbiamente.
**prove** *vt* probar, justificar; * *vi* resultar; salir (bien/mal).
**proverb** *n* proverbio *m.*
**proverbial** *adj* proverbial; **~ly** *adv* proverbialmente.
**provide** *vt* proveer; **to ~ for** mantener a; tener en cuenta.
**provided** *conj*: **~ that** con tal que.
**providence** *n* providencia *f.*
**province** *n* provincia *f*; campo de acción *m.*
**provincial** *adj* provincial; * *n* provincial/a *m/f.*
**provision** *n* provisión *f*; precaución *f.*
**provisional** *adj* provisional; **~ly** *adv* provisionalmente.
**proviso** *n* estipulación *f.*
**provocation** *n* provocación *f*; apelación *f.*
**provocative** *adj* provocativo/va.
**provoke** *vt* provocar; apelar.
**prow** *n* (*mar*) proa *f.*
**prowess** *n* proeza, valentía *f.*
**prowl** *vi* rondar, vagar.
**prowler** *n* merodeador/a *m/f.*
**proximity** *n* proximidad *f.*
**proxy** *n* poder *m*; apoderado/da *m/f.*
**prudence** *n* prudencia *f.*
**prudent** *adj* prudente, circunspecto/ta; **~ly** *adv* con juicio.
**prudish** *adj* gazmoño/ña, mojigato/ta.
**prune** *vt* podar; * *n* ciruela pasa *f.*
**prussic acid** *n* ácido prúsico *m.*
**pry** *vi* espiar, acechar; **to ~ open** *vt* abrir por fuerza.
**psalm** *n* salmo *m.*
**pseudonym** *n* seudónimo *m.*
**psyche** *n* psique *f.*
**psychiatric** *adj* psiquiátrico/ca.
**psychiatrist** *n* psiquiatra *m/f.*
**psychiatry** *n* psiquiatría *f.*
**psychic** *adj* psíquico/ca.
**psychoanalysis** *n* psicoanálisis *m.*
**psychoanalyst** *n* psicoanalista *m/f.*
**psychological** *adj* psicológico/ca.
**psychologist** *n* psicólogo/ga *m/f.*
**psychology** *n* psicología *f.*
**puberty** *n* pubertad *f.*

**public** *adj* público/ca; común; notorio/ria; **~ly** *adv* publicamente; * *n* público *m.*
**public-address system** *n* megafonía *f.*
**publican** *n* publicano *m*; tabernero/ra *m/f.*
**publication** *n* publicación *f*; edición *f.*
**publicity** *n* publicidad *f.*
**publicize** *vt* publicitar; hacer propaganda para.
**public opinion** *n* opinión pública *f.*
**public school** *n* instituto; colegio privado *m.*
**publish** *vt* publicar.
**publisher** *n* editorial *f*; editor/a *m/f.*
**publishing** *n* industria del libro *f.*
**pucker** *vt* arrugar, hacer pliegues.
**pudding** *n* pudín *m*; morcilla *f.*
**puddle** *n* charco *m.*
**puerile** *adj* pueril.
**puff** *n* soplo *m*; bocanada *f*; resoplido *m*; * *vt* chupar; * *vi* bufar; resoplar.
**puff pastry** *n* hojaldre *m.*
**puffy** *adj* hinchado/da, entumecido/da.
**pull** *vt* tirar; coger; rasgar, desgarrar; **to ~ down** derribar; **to ~ in** parar; llegar a la estación; **to ~ off** cerrar; **to ~ out** *vi* irse; salir; * *vt* arrancar; **to ~ through** salir adelante; **to ~ up** *vi* parar; * *vt* arrancar; parar; * *n* tirón *m*; sacudida *f.*
**pulley** *n* polea, garrucha *f.*
**pullover** *n* jersey *m.*
**pulp** *n* pulpa *f*; pasta *f.*
**pulpit** *n* púlpito *m.*
**pulsate** *vi* pulsar, latir.
**pulse** *n* pulso *m*; legumbres *fpl.*
**pulverize** *vt* pulverizar.
**pumice** *n* piedra pómez *f.*
**pummel** *vt* aporrear.
**pump** *n* bomba *f*; (*shoe*) zapatilla *f*; * *vt* bombear; sondear; sonsacar.
**pumpkin** *n* calabaza *f.*
**pun** *n* juego de palabras *m*; * *vi* hacer juegos de palabras.
**punch** *n* puñetazo *m*; punzón *m*; taladro *m*; ponche *m*; * *vt* golpear; perforar.
**punctual** *adj* puntual, exacto/ta; **~ly** *adv* puntualmente.
**punctuate** *vi* puntuar.
**punctuation** *n* puntuación *f.*
**pundit** *n* experto/ta *m/f.*
**pungent** *adj* picante, acre, mordaz.
**punish** *vt* castigar.
**punishment** *n* castigo *m*; pena *f.*
**punk** *n* punk *m/f*; música punk *f*; rufián/fiana *m/f.*
**punt** *n* barco llano *m.*

**puny** *adj* joven, pequeño/ña; inferior.

**pup** *n* cachorro *m*; * *vi* parir (la perra).

**pupil** *n* alumno/na *m/f*; pupila *f*.

**puppet** *n* títere, muñeco *m*.

**puppy** *n* perrito *m*.

**purchase** *vt* comprar; * *n* compra *f*; adquisición *f*.

**purchaser** *n* comprador/a *m/f*.

**pure** *adj* puro/ra; **~ly** *adv* puramente.

**purée** *n* puré *m*.

**purge** *vt* purgar.

**purification** *n* purificación *f*.

**purifier** *n* depuradora *f*.

**purify** *vt* purificar.

**purist** *n* purista *m/f*.

**puritan** *n* puritano/na *m/f*.

**purity** *n* pureza *f*.

**purl** *n* punto del revés *m*.

**purple** *adj* purpureo/rea; * *n* púrpura *f*.

**purport** *vi*: **to ~ to** dar a entender que.

**purpose** *n* intención *f*; designio, proyecto *m*; **to the ~** al propósito; **to no ~** inútilmente; **on ~** a propósito.

**purposeful** *adj* resuelto/ta.

**purr** *vi* ronronear.

**purse** *n* bolsa *f*, cartera *f*.

**purser** *n* comisario *m/f*.

**pursue** *vt* perseguir; seguir, acosar.

**pursuit** *n* perseguimiento *m*; ocupación *f*.

**purveyor** *n* abastecedor *m*.

**push** *vt* empujar; estrechar, apretar; **to ~ aside** apartar; **to ~ off** (*col*) largarse; **to ~ on** seguir adelante; * *n* impulso *m*; empujón *m*; esfuerzo *m*; asalto *m*.

**pusher** *n* traficante de drogas *m/f*.

**put** *vt* poner, colocar; proponer; imponer, obligar; **to ~ away** guardar; **to ~ away hurriedly** zampar; **to ~ down** poner en el suelo; sacrificar; apuntar; sofocar; **to ~ forward** adelantar; **to ~ off** aplazar; desanimar; **to ~ on** ponerse; encender; presentar; ganar; echar; **to ~ out** apagar; extender; molestar; **to ~ up** alzar; aumentar; alojar.

**putrid** *adj* podrido/da.

**putt** *n* putt *m*; *vt* hacer un putt.

**putty** *n* masilla *f*.

**puzzle** *n* acertijo *m*; rompecabezas *m inv ar*.

**puzzling** *adj* extraño/ña.

**pyjamas** *npl* pijama *m*.

**pylon** *n* torre de alta tensión *f*.

**pyramid** *n* pirámide *f*.

**python** *n* pitón *m*.

# Q

**quack** *vi* graznar; * *n* graznido *m*; (*col*) curandero/ra *m/f*.
**quadrangle** *n* cuadrángulo *m*.
**quadrant** *n* cuadrante *m*.
**quadrilateral** *adj* cuadrilátero/ra.
**quadruped** *n* cuadrúpedo *m*.
**quadruple** *adj* cuádruplo.
**quadruplet** *n* cuatrillizo/za *m/f*.
**quagmire** *n* barrizal *m*, cenagal *m*.
**quail** *n* codorniz *f*.
**quaint** *adj* pulido/da; exquisito/ta.
**quake** *vi* temblar; tiritar.
**Quaker** *n* cuáquero/ra *m/f*.
**qualification** *n* calificación *f*; título *m*.
**qualified** *adj* capacitado/da; titulado/da.
**qualify** *vt* calificar; modificar; * *vi* clasificarse.
**quality** *n* calidad *f*.
**qualm** *n* escrupúlo *m*.
**quandary** *n* incertidumbre, duda *f*.
**quantitative** *adj* cuantitativo/va.
**quantity** *n* cantidad *f*.
**quarantine** *n* cuarentena *f*.
**quarrel** *n* riña, contienda *f*; * *vi* reñir, disputar.
**quarrelsome** *adj* pendenciero/ra.
**quarry** *n* cantera *f*.
**quarter** *n* cuarto *m*; cuarta parte *f*, **~ of an hour** cuarto de hora; * *vt* cuartear.
**quarterly** *adj* trimestral; * *adv* trimestralmente.
**quartermaster** *n* (*mil*) comisario/ria *m/f*.
**quartet** *n* (*mus*) cuarteto *m*.
**quartz** *n* cuarzo *m*.
**quash** *vt* fracasar; anular, abrogar.
**quay** *n* muelle *m*.
**queasy** *adj* nauseabundo/da.
**queen** *n* reina *f*; dama *f*.
**queer** *adj* extraño/ña; ridículo/la; *n* (*col*) maricón *m*.
**quell** *vt* calmar; sosegar.

**quench** *vt* apagar; extinguir.
**query** *n* cuestión, pregunta *f*; * *vt* preguntar.
**quest** *n* pesquisa, inquisición, busca *f*.
**question** *n* pregunta *f*; cuestión *f*; asunto *m*; duda *f*; * *vt* dudar de; interrogar.
**questionable** *adj* cuestionable, dudoso/sa.
**questioner** *n* interrogador/a *m/f*.
**question mark** *n* signo de interrogación *m*.
**questionnaire** *n* cuestionario *m*.
**quibble** *vi* buscar evasivas.
**quick** *adj* rapido/da; vivo/va; pronto/ta; ágil; **~ly** *adv* rápidamente.
**quicken** *vt* apresurar; * *vi* darse prisa.
**quicksand** *n* arenas movedizas *f/pl*.
**quicksilver** *n* azogue, mercurio *m*.
**quick-witted** *adj* agudo/da, perspicaz.
**quiet** *adj* callado/da; **~ly** *adv* tranquilamente.
**quietness** *n* tranquilidad *f*.
**quinine** *n* quinina *f*.
**quintet** *n* (*mus*) quinteto *m*.
**quintuple** *adj* quíntuplo.
**quintuplet** *n* quintillizo/za *m/f*.
**quip** *n* indirecta *f*; * *vt* echar pullas.
**quirk** *n* peculiaridad *f*.
**quit** *vt* dejar; desocupar; * *vi* renunciar; irse; * *adj* libre, descargado/da.
**quite** *adv* bastante; totalmente, enteramente, absolutamente.
**quits** *adv* ¡en paz!
**quiver** *vi* temblar.
**quixotic** *adj* quijotesco/ca.
**quiz** *n* concurso *m*; programa concurso *m*; * *vt* interrogar.
**quizzical** *adj* burlón/ona.
**quota** *n* cuota *f*.
**quotation** *n* citación, cita *f*.
**quotation marks** *npl* comillas *fpl*.
**quote** *vt* citar.
**quotient** *n* cociente *m*.

# R

**rabbi** *n* rabino/na *m/f*.
**rabbit** *n* conejo *m*.
**rabbit hutch** *n* conejera *f*.
**rabble** *n* gentuza *f*.
**rabid** *adj* rabioso/sa; furioso/sa.
**rabies** *n* rabia *f*.
**race** *n* raza, casta *f*; carrera *f*; * *vt* hacer correr a; competir contra; acelerar; * *vi* correr; competir; latir rápidamente.
**racehorse** *n* caballo de carreras *m*.
**racial** *adj* racial.
**raciness** *n* vivacidad *f*.
**racing** *n* carreras *fpl*.
**racist** *adj*, *n* racista *m/f*.
**rack** *n* rejilla *f*; estante *m*; * *vt* atormentar; trasegar.
**racket** *n* ruido *m*; raqueta *f*.
**rack-rent** *n* alquiler abusivo *m*.
**racy** *adj* picante, vivo/va.
**radiance** *n* brillantez *f*, resplandor *m*.
**radiant** *adj* radiante, brillante.
**radiate** *vt*, *vi* radiar, irradiar.
**radiation** *n* radiación *f*.
**radiator** *n* radiador *m*.
**radical** *adj* radical; **~ly** *adv* radicalmente.
**radicalism** *n* radicalismo *m*.
**radio** *n* radio *f*.
**radioactive** *adj* radioactivo/va; **~ fallout** lluvia radioactiva *f*.
**radish** *n* rábano *m*.
**radius** *n* radio *f*.
**raffle** *n* rifa *f* (juego); * *vt* rifar.
**raft** *n* balsa, almadía *f*.
**rafter** *n* par *m*; viga *f*.
**rafting** *n* rafting *m*.
**rag** *n* trapo, andrajo *m*.
**ragamuffin** *n* granuja, galopín/ina *m/f*.
**rage** *n* rabia *f*; furor *m*; * *vi* rabiar; encolerizarse.
**ragged** *adj* andrajoso/sa.
**raging** *adj* furioso/sa, rabioso/sa.
**ragman, rag-and-bone man** *n* trapero *m*.
**raid** *n* incursión *f*; * *vt* invadir.
**raider** *n* invasor/a *m/f*.
**rail** *n* baranda, barandilla *f*; (*rail*) raíl, carril *m*; * *vt* cercar con barandillas.
**raillery** *n* burlas *fpl*.
**railway** *n* ferrocarril *m*.
**raiment** *n* vestido *m*.
**rain** *n* lluvia *f*; * *vi* llover.
**rainbow** *n* arco iris *m*.

**rainwater** *n* agua de lluvia *f*.
**rainy** *adj* lluvioso/sa.
**raise** *vt* levantar, alzar; fabricar, edificar; elevar.
**raisin** *n* pasa *f*.
**rake** *n* rastro, rastrillo *m*; libertino/na *m/f*; * *vt* rastrillar.
**rakish** *adj* libertino/na, disoluto/ta.
**rally** *vt* (*mil*) reunir; * *vi* reunirse.
**ram** *n* carnero, morueco *m*; ariete *m*; * *vt* chocar con.
**ramble** *vi* divagar; salir de excursión a pie; * *n* excursión a pie, caminata *f*.
**rambler** *n* excursionista *m/f*.
**ramification** *n* ramificación *f*.
**ramify** *vi* ramificarse.
**ramp** *n* rampa *f*.
**rampant** *adj* exuberante.
**rampart** *n* terraplén *m*; (*mil*) muralla *f*.
**ramrod** *n* baqueta *f*; atacador *m*.
**ramshackle** *adj* en ruina.
**ranch** *n* hacienda, estancia *f*.
**rancid** *adj* rancio/cia.
**rancour** *n* rencor *m*.
**random** *adj* fortuito/ta, sin orden; **at ~** al azar.
**range** *vt* colocar, ordenar; *vi* vagar; * *n* clase *f*; orden *m*; hilera *f*; cordillera *f*; campo de tiro *m*; reja de cocina *f*.
**ranger** *n* guardabosques *m invar*.
**rank** *adj* exuberante; rancio/cia; fétido/da; * *n* fila, hilera, clase *f*.
**rankle** *vi* doler.
**rankness** *n* exuberancia *f*; olor/gusto rancio *m*.
**ransack** *vt* saquear, pillar.
**ransom** *n* rescate *m*.
**rant** *vi* vociferar.
**rap** *vi* dar un golpecito; * *n* golpecito *m*.
**rapacious** *adj* rapaz; **~ly** *adv* con rapacidad.
**rapacity, rapaciousness** *n* rapacidad *f*.
**rape** *n* violación *f*; estupro *m*; (*bot*) colza *f*; * *vt* violar.
**rapid** *adj* rápido/da; **~ly** *adv* rápidamente.
**rapidity** *n* rapidez *f*.
**rapier** *n* espadín *m*.
**rapist** *n* violador *m*.
**rapt** *adj* arrebatado/da; absorto/ta.
**rapture** *n* rapto *m*; éxtasis *m invar*.
**rapturous** *adj* arrebatado/da.
**rare** *adj* raro/ra, extraordinario/ria; **~ly** *adv* raramente.

**rarity** *n* raridad, rareza *f*.
**rascal** *n* pícaro/ra *m/f*.
**rash** *adj* precipitado/da, temerario/ria; ~**ly**
  *adv* temerariamente; * *n* salpullido *m*;
  erupción (cutánea) *f*.
**rashness** *n* temeridad *f*.
**rasp** *n* raspador *m*; * *vt* raspar, escofinar.
**raspberry** *n* frambuesa *f*; ~ **bush** fram-
  bueso *m*.
**rat** *n* rata *f*.
**rate** *n* tasa *f*, precio, valor *m*; grado *m*; * *vt*
  tasar, apreciar.
**rather** *adv* más bien; antes.
**ratification** *n* ratificación *f*.
**ratify** *vt* ratificar.
**rating** *n* tasación *f*; clasificación *f*; índice *m*.
**ratio** *n* razón *f*.
**ration** *n* ración *f*; (*mil*) víveres *mpl*.
**rational** *adj* racional; razonable; ~**ly** *adv*
  racionalmente.
**rationality** *n* racionalidad *f*.
**rattan** *n* (*bot*) rota *f*.
**rattle** *vi* golpear; traquetear; * *vt* sacudir;
  * *n* traqueteo *m*; sonajero *m*.
**rattlesnake** *n* serpiente de cascabel *f*.
**ravage** *vt* saquear, pillar; estragar; * *n*
  saqueo *m*.
**rave** *vi* delirar.
**rave music** *n* (*col*) bakalao *m*.
**raven** *n* cuervo *m*.
**ravenous** *adj* voraz; ~**ly** *adv* vorazmente.
**ravine** *n* barranco *m*.
**ravish** *vt* encantar; raptar.
**ravishing** *adj* encantador/a.
**raw** *adj* crudo/da; puro/ra; novato/ta.
**rawboned** *adj* huesudo/da; magro/gra.
**rawness** *n* crudeza *f*; falta de experiencia *f*.
**ray** *n* rayo de luz *m*; raya *f* (pez).
**raze** *vt* arrasar.
**razor** *n* navaja *f*; máquina de afeitar *f*.
**reach** *vt* alcanzar; llegar hasta; * *vi*
  extenderse, llegar; alcan zar, penetrar; * *n*
  alcance *m*.
**react** *vi* reaccionar.
**reaction** *n* reacción *f*.
**read** *vt* leer; * *vi* estudiar.
**readable** *adj* legible.
**reader** *n* lector/a *m/f*.
**readily** *adv* pronto; de buena gana.
**readiness** *n* voluntad, gana *f*; prontitud *f*.
**reading** *n* lectura *f*.
**reading room** *n* sala de lectura *f*.
**readjust** *vt* reajustar.
**ready** *adj* listo/ta, pronto/ta; inclinado/da;
  abonado/da; fácil.

**real** *adj* real, verdadero/ra; ~**ly** *adv*
  realmente.
**reality** *n* realidad *f*.
**realization** *n* realización *f*.
**realize** *adv* darse cuenta de; realizar.
**realm** *n* reino *m*.
**ream** *n* resma *f*.
**reap** *vt* segar.
**reaper** *n* segador/a *m/f*.
**reappear** *vi* reaparecer.
**rear** *n* parte trasera *f*; retaguardia *f*; zaga *f*;
  * *vt* levantar, alzar.
**rearmament** *n* rearme *m*.
**reason** *n* razon *f*; causa *f*; * *vt*, *vi* razonar.
**reasonable** *adj* razonable.
**reasonableness** *n* lo razonable.
**reasonably** *adv* razonablemente.
**reasoning** *n* razonamiento *m*.
**reassure** *vt* tranquilizar, alentar; (*com*) asegurar.
**rebel** *n* rebelde *m/f*; * *vi* rebelarse.
**rebellion** *n* rebelión *f*.
**rebellious** *adj* rebelde.
**rebound** *vi* rebotar.
**rebuff** *n* desaire *m*; * *vt* rechazar.
**rebuild** *vt* reedificar.
**rebuke** *vt* reprender; * *n* reprensión *f*.
**rebut** *vi* repercutir.
**recalcitrant** *adj* recalcitrante.
**recall** *vt* recordar; retirar; * *n* retirada *f*.
**recant** *vt* retractar, desdecirse.
**recantation** *n* retractación *f*.
**recapitulate** *vt*, *vi* recapitular.
**recapitulation** *n* recapitulación *f*.
**recapture** *n* recobra *f*.
**recede** *vi* retroceder.
**receipt** *n* recibo *m*; recepción *f*; ~**s** *npl*
  ingresos *mpl*.
**receivable** *adj* por cobrar.
**receive** *vt* recibir; aceptar, admitir.
**recent** *adj* reciente, nuevo/va; ~**ly** *adv*
  recientemente.
**receptacle** *n* receptáculo *m*.
**reception** *n* recepción *f*.
**recess** *n* descanso *m*; recreo *m*; hueco *m*.
**recession** *n* retirada *f*; (*com*) recesión *f*.
**recipe** *n* receta *f*.
**recipient** *n* recipiente *m*.
**reciprocal** *adj* recíproco/ca; ~**ly** *adv*
  recíprocamente.
**reciprocate** *vi* reciprocar.
**reciprocity** *n* reciprocidad *f*.
**recital** *n* recital *m*.
**recite** *vt* recitar; referir, relatar.
**reckless** *adj* temerario/ria; ~**ly** *adv* temerariamente.

**reckon** vt contar, computar; * vi calcular.
**reckoning** n cuenta f; cálculo m.
**reclaim** vt reformar; reclamar.
**reclaimable** adj reclamable.
**recline** vt (vi) reclinar(se); recostar(se).
**recluse** n recluso/sa m/f.
**recognition** n reconocimiento; recuerdo m.
**recognize** vt reconocer.
**recoil** vi recular.
**recollect** vt acordarse de; recordar.
**recollection** n recuerdo m.
**recommence** vt empezar de nuevo.
**recommend** vt recomendar.
**recommendation** n recomendación f.
**recompense** n recompensa f; * vt recompensar.
**reconcilable** adj reconciliable.
**reconcile** vt reconciliar.
**reconciliation** n reconciliación f.
**recondite** adj recóndito/ta, reservado/da.
**reconnaissance** n (mil) reconocimiento m.
**reconnoitre** vt (mil) reconocer.
**reconsider** vt reconsiderar.
**reconstruct** vt reedificar.
**record** vt registrar; grabar; * n registro, archivo m; disco; récord m; ~s pl anales mpl.
**recorder** n registrador/a, archivero/ra m/f; (mus) flauta de pico f.
**recount** vt contar de nuevo; relatar.
**recourse** n recurso m; remedio m.
**recover** vt recobrar; recuperar; restablecer; * vi convalecer, restablecerse.
**recoverable** adj recuperable.
**recovery** n convalecencia f; recuperación f.
**recreation** n recreación f; recreo m.
**recriminate** vi recriminar.
**recrimination** n recriminación f.
**recruit** vt reclutar; * n (mil) recluta m/f.
**recruiting** n recluta f.
**rectangle** n rectángulo m.
**rectangular** adj rectangular.
**rectification** n rectificación f.
**rectify** vt rectificar.
**rectilinear** adj rectilíneo/nea.
**rectitude** n rectitud f.
**rector** n rector/a m/f.
**recumbent** adj recostado/da, reclinado/da.
**recur** vi repetirse.
**recurrence** n repetición f.
**recurrent** adj repetido/da.
**recycle** vt reciclar.
**recycled** adj reciclado/da.
**red** adj rojo/ja; tinto/ta; * n rojo m.
**redden** vt enrojecer; * vi ponerse colorado/da.

**reddish** adj rojizo/za.
**redeem** vt redimir, rescatar.
**redeemable** adj redimible.
**redeemer** n redentor/a m/f.
**redemption** n redención f.
**redeploy** vt reorganizar.
**red-handed** adj **to catch somebody ~** pillar a alguien con las manos en la masa.
**red-hot** adj candente, ardiente.
**red-letter day** n día señalado m.
**redness** n rojez, bermejura f.
**redolent** adj fragante, oloroso/sa.
**redouble** vt (vi) redoblar(se).
**redress** vt corregir; reformar; rectificar; * n reparación, compensación f.
**red tape** n (fig) trámites mpl.
**reduce** vt reducir; disminuir; rebajar.
**reducible** adj reducible.
**reduction** n reducción f; rebaja f.
**redundancy** n despido m.
**redundant** adj superfluo/lua.
**reed** n caña f.
**reedy** adj lleno de canas.
**reef** n (mar) rizo m; arrecife m.
**reek** n mal olor m; * vi humear; vahear.
**reel** n carrete m; bobina f; rollo m; * vi tambalear(se).
**re-election** n reelección f.
**re-engage** vt empeñar de nuevo.
**re-enter** vt volver a entrar.
**re-establish** vt restablecer, volver a establecer.
**re-establishment** n restablecimiento m; restauración f.
**refectory** n refectorio; comedor m.
**refer** vt, vi referir, remitir; referirse.
**referee** n árbitro/ra m/f.
**reference** n referencia, relación f.
**refine** vt refinar, purificar.
**refinement** n refinación f; refinadura f; cultura f.
**refinery** n refinería f.
**refit** vt reparar; (mar) reparar.
**reflect** vt, vi reflejar; reflexionar.
**reflection** n reflexión, meditación f.
**reflector** n reflector m; captafaros m invar.
**reflex** adj reflejo.
**reform** vt (vi) reformar(se).
**reform, reformation** n reformación f.
**reformer** n reformador/a m/f.
**reformist** n reformista m/f.
**refract** vt refractar.
**refraction** n refracción f.
**refrain** vi: **to ~ from something** abstenerse de algo.

**refresh** *vt* refrescar.
**refreshment** *n* refresco, refrigerio *m*.
**refrigerator** *n* nevera *f*; refrigerador *m*.
**refuel** *vi* repostar (combustible).
**refuge** *n* refugio, asilo *m*.
**refugee** *n* refugiado/da *m/f*.
**refund** *vt* devolver; * *n* reembolso *m*.
**refurbish** *vt* restaurar, renovar.
**refusal** *n* negativa *f*.
**refuse**[1] *vt* rehusar.
**refuse**[2] *n* basura *f*.
**refuse collector** *n* basurero *m*.
**refute** *vt* refutar.
**regain** *vt* recobrar, recuperar.
**regal** *adj* real.
**regale** *vt* regalar.
**regalia** *n* insignias *fpl*.
**regard** *vt* estimar; considerar; * *n* consideración *f*; respeto *m*.
**regarding** *pr* en cuanto a.
**regardless** *adv* a pesar de todo.
**regatta** *n* regata *f*.
**regency** *n* regencia *f*.
**regenerate** *vt* regenerar; * *adj* regenerado/da.
**regeneration** *n* regeneración *f*.
**regent** *n* regente *m/f*.
**regime** *n* régimen *m*.
**regiment** *n* regimiento *m*.
**region** *n* región *f*.
**register** *n* registro *m*; * *vt* registrar; **~ed letter** *n* carta certificada *f*.
**registrar** *n* registrador/a *m/f*.
**registration** *n* registro *m*.
**registry** *n* registro *m*.
**regressive** *adj* regresivo/va.
**regret** *n* sentimiento *m*; remordimiento *m*; pensión *f*; * *vt* sentir.
**regretful** *adj* pesaroso/sa.
**regular** *adj* regular; ordinario/ria; **~ly** *adv* regularmente; * *n* regular *m*.
**regularity** *n* regularidad *f*.
**regulate** *vt* regular, ordenar.
**regulation** *n* regulación *f*; arreglo *m*.
**regulator** *n* regulador *m*.
**rehabilitate** *vt* rehabilitar.
**rehabilitation** *n* rehabilitación *f*.
**rehearsal** *n* repetición *f*; ensayo *m*.
**rehearse** *vt* repetir; ensayar.
**reign** *n* reinado, reino *m*; * *vi* reinar; prevalecer.
**reimburse** *vt* reembolsar.
**reimbursement** *n* reembolso *m*.
**rein** *n* rienda *f*; * *vt* refrenar.
**reindeer** *n* reno *m*.

**reinforce** *vt* reforzar.
**reinstate** *vt* reintegrar.
**reinsure** *vt* (*com*) reasegurar.
**reissue** *n* reedición *f*.
**reiterate** *vt* reiterar.
**reiteration** *n* reiteración, repetición *f*.
**reject** *vt* rechazar.
**rejection** *n* rechazo *m*.
**rejoice** *vt* (*vi*) regocijar(se).
**rejoicing** *n* regocijo *m*.
**relapse** *vi* recaer; * *n* reincidencia *f*; recaída *f*.
**relate** *vt*, *vi* relatar, referirse.
**related** *adj* emparentado/da.
**relation** *n* relación *f*; pariente *m*.
**relationship** *n* parentesco *m*; relación *f*.
**relative** *adj* relativo/va; **~ly** *adv* relativamente; * *n* pariente *m/f*.
**relax** *vt*, *vi* relajar; descansar.
**relaxation** *n* relajación *f*; descanso *m*; relax *m*.
**relay** *n* relevo *m*; * *vt* retransmitir.
**release** *vt* soltar, libertar; * *n* liberación *f*; descargo *m*.
**relegate** *vt* relegar.
**relegation** *n* relegación *f*, descenso *m*.
**relent** *vi* ablandarse.
**relentless** *adj* implacable.
**relevant** *adj* pertinente.
**reliable** *adj* fiable, de confianza.
**reliance** *n* confianza *f*.
**relic** *n* reliquia *f*.
**relief** *n* relieve *m*; alivio *m*.
**relieve** *vt* aliviar, consolar; socorrer.
**religion** *n* religión *f*.
**religious** *adj* religioso/sa; **~ly** *adv* religiosamente.
**relinquish** *vt* abandonar, dejar.
**relish** *n* sabor *m*; gusto *m*; salsa *f*, * *vt* gustar de, agradar.
**reluctance** *n* repugnancia *f*.
**reluctant** *adj* reticente.
**rely** *vi* confiar en; contar con.
**remain** *vi* quedar, restar, permanecer, durar.
**remainder** *n* resto, residuo *m*.
**remains** *npl* restos, residuos *mpl*; sobras *fpl*.
**remand** *vt*: **to ~ in custody** mantener bajo prisión preventiva.
**remark** *n* observación, nota *f*; * *vt* notar, observar.
**remarkable** *adj* notable, interesante.
**remarkably** *adv* notablemente.
**remarry** *vi* volver a casarse.
**remedial** *adj* curativo/va.
**remedy** *n* remedio, recurso *m*; * *vt* remediar.

**remember** *vt* acordarse de; recordar.
**remembrance** *n* memoria *f*; recuerdo *m*.
**remind** *vt* recordar.
**reminiscence** *n* reminiscencia *f*.
**remiss** *adj* negligente.
**remission** *n* remisión *f*.
**remit** *vt, vi* remitir, perdonar; disminuir.
**remittance** *n* remesa *f*.
**remnant** *n* resto, residuo *m*.
**remodel** *vt* remodelar.
**remonstrate** *vi* protestar.
**remorse** *n* remordimiento *m*; compunción *f*.
**remorseless** *adj* implacable.
**remote** *adj* remoto/ta, lejano/na; **~ly** *adv* remotamente, lejos.
**remote control** *n* mando a distancia *m*.
**remoteness** *n* alejamiento *m*; distancia *f*.
**removable** *adj* de quita y pon, de quitapón.
**removal** *n* remoción *f*; mudanza *f*.
**remove** *vt* quitar; * *vi* mudarse.
**remunerate** *vt* remunerar.
**remuneration** *n* remuneración *f*.
**render** *vt* devolver, restituir; traducir; rendir.
**rendezvous** *n* cita *f*; lugar de encuentro *m*.
**renegade** *n* renegado/da *m/f*.
**renew** *vt* renovar, restablecer.
**renewal** *n* renovación *f*.
**rennet** *n* cuajo *m*.
**renounce** *vt* renunciar.
**renovate** *vt* renovar.
**renovation** *n* renovación *f*.
**renown** *n* renombre *m*; celebridad *f*.
**renowned** *adj* célebre.
**rent** *n* renta *f*; arrendamiento *m*; alquiler *m*; * *vt* alquilar.
**rental** *n* alquiler *m*.
**renunciation** *n* renuncia *f*.
**reopen** *vt* reabrir.
**reorganization** *n* reorganización *f*.
**reorganize** *vt* reorganizar.
**repair** *vt* reparar; resarcir; * *n* reparación *f*.
**reparable** *adj* reparable.
**reparation** *n* reparación *f*.
**repartee** *n* réplica aguda/picante *f*.
**repatriate** *vt* repatriar.
**repay** *vt* devolver; pagar, restituir.
**repayment** *n* pago *m*.
**repeal** *vt* abrogar, revocar; * *n* revocación, anulación *f*.
**repeat** *vt* repetir.
**repeatedly** *adv* repetidamente.
**repeater** *n* reloj de repetición *m*.
**repel** *vt* repeler, rechazar.
**repent** *vi* arrepentirse.

**repentance** *n* arrepentimiento *m*.
**repentant** *adj* arrepentido/da.
**repertory** *n* repertorio *m*.
**repetition** *n* repetición, reiteración *f*.
**replace** *vt* reemplazar; reponer.
**replant** *vt* replantar.
**replenish** *vt* llenar, surtir.
**replete** *adj* repleto/ta, lleno/na.
**reply** *n* respuesta *f*; * *vi* responder.
**report** *vt* referir, contar; dar cuenta de; * *n* informe *m*; repor taje *m*; relación *f*.
**reporter** *n* reportero/ra *m/f*.
**repose** *vt, vi* reposar; * *n* reposo *m*.
**repository** *n* depósito *m*.
**repossess** *vt* reobrar.
**reprehend** *vt* reprender.
**reprehensible** *adj* reprensible.
**represent** *vt* representar.
**representation** *n* representación *f*.
**representative** *adj* representativo/va; * *n* representante *m/f*.
**repress** *vt* reprimir, domar.
**repression** *n* represión *f*.
**repressive** *adj* represivo/va.
**reprieve** *vt* suspender una ejecución; indultar; * *n* indulto *m*.
**reprimand** *vt* reprender, corregir; * *n* reprensión *f*; repri menda *f*.
**reprint** *vt* reimprimir.
**reprisal** *n* represalia *f*.
**reproach** *n* improperio, oprobio *m*; * *vt* hacer reproches a.
**reproachful** *adj* ignominioso/sa; **~ly** *adv* ignominiosamente.
**reproduce** *vt* reproducir.
**reproduction** *n* reproducción *f*.
**reptile** *n* reptil *m*.
**republic** *n* república *f*.
**republican** *adj, n* republicano/a *m/f*.
**republicanism** *n* republicanismo *m*.
**repudiate** *vt* repudiar.
**repugnance** *n* repugnancia *f*.
**repugnant** *adj* repugnante; **~ly** *adv* con repugnancia.
**repulse** *vt* repulsar, desechar; * *n* repulsa *f*; rechazo *m*.
**repulsion** *n* repúlsion, repulsa *f*.
**repulsive** *adj* repulsivo/va.
**reputable** *adj* honroso/sa.
**reputation** *n* reputación *f*.
**repute** *vt* reputar.
**request** *n* petición, súplica *f*; * *vt* rogar, suplicar.
**request stop** *n* parada a petición *f*.
**require** *vt* requerir, demandar.

**requirement** n requisito m; exigencia f.
**requisite** adj necesario/ria, indispensable;
* n requisito m.
**requisition** n petición, demanda f.
**requite** vt recompensar.
**rescind** vt rescindir, abrogar.
**rescue** vt librar, rescatar; * n libramiento,
recobro m.
**research** vt investigar; * n investigación f.
**resemblance** n semejanza f.
**resemble** vt asemejarse.
**resent** vt resentirse.
**resentful** adj resentido/da; vengativo/va;
~ly adv con resentimi ento.
**resentment** n resentimiento m.
**reservation** n reserva f.
**reserve** vt reservar; * n reserva f.
**reservedly** adv con reserva.
**reservoir** n depósito m; pantano m.
**reside** vi residir, morar.
**residence** n residencia, morada f.
**resident** adj residente.
**residuary** adj sobrado/da; ~ **legatee** n (law)
legatario/ria universal m/f.
**residue** n residuo, resto m.
**resign** vt, vi resignar, renunciar, ceder;
resignarse, rendirse.
**resignation** n resignación f; dimisión f.
**resin** n resina f.
**resinous** adj resinoso/sa.
**resist** vt resistir, oponerse.
**resistance** n resistencia f.
**resolute** adj resuelto/ta; ~ly adv resuelta-
mente.
**resolution** n resolución f.
**resolve** vt, vr resolver(se); (fig) zanjar.
**resonance** n resonancia f.
**resonant** adj resonante.
**resort** vi recurrir, frecuentar; * n recurso m;
resorte m.
**resound** vi resonar.
**resource** n recurso m; expediente m.
**respect** n respecto m; respeto m; motivo
m; ~s pl recuerdos mpl; * vt apreciar;
respetar; venerar.
**respectability** n respetabilidad f.
**respectable** adj respetable; considerable;
~bly adv notablemente.
**respectful** adj respetuoso/sa; ~ly adv
respetuosamente.
**respecting** prep con respecto a.
**respective** adj respectivo/va, relativo/va;
~ly adv respectivamente.
**respirator** n respirador m.
**respiratory** adj respiratorio/ria.

**respite** n suspensión f; respiro m; * vt suspender, diferir.
**resplendence** n resplandor, brillo m.
**resplendent** adj resplandeciente.
**respond** vt responder; corresponder.
**respondent** n (law) defensor/a m.
**response** n respuesta, réplica f.
**responsibility** n responsabilidad f.
**responsible** adj responsable.
**responsive** adj sensible.
**rest** n reposo m; sueño m; quietud f; (mus)
pausa f; resto, residuo m; * vt descansar;
apoyar; * vi dormir, reposar; descansarse.
**restaurant** n restaurante (económico) m.
**resting place** n última morada f.
**restitution** n restitución f.
**restive** adj inquieto/ta; obstinado/da.
**restless** adj insomne; inquieto/ta.
**restoration** n restauración f.
**restorative** adj restaurativo/va.
**restore** vt restaurar, restituir.
**restrain** vt restringir, restriñir.
**restraint** n refrenamiento, constreñimiento m.
**restrict** vt restringir, limitar.
**restriction** n restricción f.
**restrictive** adj restrictivo/va.
**result** vi resultar; * n resultado m.
**resume** vt resumir; empezar de nuevo.
**resurrection** n resurrección f.
**resuscitate** vt resucitar.
**retail** vt vender al por menor; * n venta por
menor f.
**retain** vt retener, guardar.
**retainer** n adherente, partidario/ria m/f; ~s
pl comitiva f; séquito m.
**retake** vt volver a tomar.
**retaliate** vt tomar represalias.
**retaliation** n represalias fpl.
**retardation** n retraso m.
**retarded** adj retrasado/da.
**retch** vi tener arcadas.
**retention** n retención f.
**retentive** adj retentivo/va.
**reticence** n reticencia f.
**retina** n retina f.
**retire** vt (vi) retirar(se); jubilar(se).
**retired** adj apartado/da, retirado/da;
jubilado/da.
**retirement** n retiro m, jubilación f.
**retort** vt replicar; * n réplica f.
**retouch** vt retocar.
**retrace** vt volver a trazar.
**retract** vt retraer; retractar.
**retrain** vt reciclar.

**retraining** *n* reciclaje profesional *m*.
**retreat** *n* retirada *f*; * *vi* retirarse.
**retribution** *n* retribución, recompensa *f*.
**retrievable** *adj* recuperable; reparable.
**retrieve** *vt* recuperar, recobrar.
**retriever** *n* sabueso *m*.
**retrograde** *adj* retrógrado/da.
**retrospect, retrospection** *n* reflexión *f*.
**retrospective** *adj* retrospectivo/va.
**return** *vt* retribuir; restituir; devolver; * *n* retorno *m*; vuelta *f*; recompensa, rendimiento *m*; recaída *f*.
**reunion** *n* reunión *f*.
**reunite** *vt* (*vi*) reunir(se).
**rev counter** *n* cuentarrevoluciones *m invar*.
**reveal** *vt* revelar.
**revel** *vi* andar de juerga.
**revelation** *n* revelación *f*.
**reveller** *n* juerguista *m/f*.
**revelry** *n* juerga *f*.
**revenge** *vt* vengar; * *n* venganza *f*.
**revengeful** *adj* vengativo/va.
**revenue** *n* renta *f*; rédito *m*.
**reverberate** *vt, vi* reverberar; resonar, retumbar.
**reverberation** *n* rechazo *m*; reverberación *f*.
**revere** *vt* reverenciar, venerar.
**reverence** *n* reverencia *f*; * *vt* reverenciar.
**reverend** *adj* reverendo/da; venerable; * *n* padre *m*.
**reverent, reverential** *adj* reverencial, respetuoso/sa.
**reversal** *n* revocación *f*; cambio total *m*.
**reverse** *vt* trastrocar; abolir; poner en marcha atrás; * *n* vicisi tud *f*; contrario *m*; reverso *m* (de una moneda).
**reversible** *adj* revocable; reversible.
**reversing lights** *npl* (*auto*) luces de marcha atrás *fpl*.
**reversion** *n* reversión *f*.
**revert** *vt, vi* trastrocar; volverse atrás.
**review** *vt* rever; (*mil*) revistar; * *n* revista *f*; reseña *f*.
**reviewer** *n* revisor/a *m/f*; crítico/ca *m/f*.
**revile** *vt* ultrajar; difamar.
**revise** *vt* rever; repasar.
**reviser** *n* revisor/a *m/f*.
**revision** *n* revisión *f*.
**revisit** *vt* volver a visitar.
**revival** *n* restauración *f*; restablecimiento *m*.
**revive** *vt* avivar; restablecer; * *vi* revivir.
**revocation** *n* revocación *f*.
**revoke** *vt* revocar, anular.
**revolt** *vi* rebelarse; * *n* rebelión *f*.

**revolting** *adj* asqueroso/sa.
**revolution** *n* revolución *f*.
**revolutionary** *adj, n* revolucionario/a *m/f*.
**revolve** *vt* revolver; meditar; * *vi* girar.
**revolver** *n* revólver *m*.
**revolving** *adj* giratorio/ria.
**revue** *n* revista *f*.
**revulsion** *n* revulsión *f*.
**reward** *n* recompensa *f*; * *vt* recompensar.
**rhapsody** *n* rapsodia *f*.
**rhetoric** *n* retórica *f*.
**rhetorical** *adj* retórico/ca.
**rheumatic** *adj* reumático/ca.
**rheumatism** *n* reumatismo *m*.
**rhinoceros** *n* rinoceronte *m*.
**rhomboid** *n* romboide *m*.
**rhombus** *n* rombo *m*.
**rhubarb** *n* ruibarbo *m*.
**rhyme** *n* rima *f*; poema *m*; * *vi* rimar.
**rhythm** *n* ritmo *m*.
**rhythmical** *adj* rítmico/ca.
**rib** *n* costilla *f*.
**ribald** *adj* escabroso/sa.
**ribbon** *n* listón *m*; cinta *f*.
**rice** *n* arroz *m*.
**rich** *adj* rico/ca; opulento/ta; abundante; ~**ly** *adv* ricamente.
**riches** *npl* riqueza *f*.
**richness** *n* riqueza *f*; abundancia *f*.
**rickets** *n* raquitismo *m*.
**rickety** *adj* raquítico/ca.
**rid** *vt* librar, desembarazar.
**riddance** *n*: good ~! ¡enhoramala!
**riddle** *n* enigma *m*; criba *f*; * *vt* cribar.
**ride** *vi* cabalgar; andar en coche; * *n* paseo a caballo/en coche *m*.
**rider** *n* caballero/ra, jinete *m*, amazona *f*.
**ridge** *n* espinazo, lomo *m*; cumbre *f*; * *vt* formar lomos/surcos.
**ridicule** *n* ridiculez *f*; ridiculo *m*; * *vt* ridiculizar.
**ridiculous** *adj* ridículo/la; ~**ly** *adv* ridiculamente.
**riding** *n* equitación *f*.
**riding habit** *n* traje de amazona *m*.
**riding school** *n* picadero *m*.
**rife** *adj* común, frecuente.
**riffraff** *n* desecho, desperdicio *m*.
**rifle** *vt* robar, pillar; estriar, rayar; * *n* rifle *m*.
**rifleman** *n* fusilero *m*.
**rig** *vt* ataviar; (*mar*) aparejar; * *n* torre de perforación *f*; plataforma petrolera *f*.
**rigging** *n* (*mar*) aparejo *m*.
**right** *adj* derecho/cha, recto/ta; justo/ta;

honesto/ta; ~! ¡bien!, ¡bueno!; ~ly *adv*
rectamente, justamente; * *n* justicia *f*;
razón *f*; derecho *m*; mano derecha *f*; * *vt*
hacer justicia.

**righteous** *adj* justo/ta, honrado/da, ~ly *adv*
justamente.

**righteousness** *n* equidad *f*; honradez *f*.

**rigid** *adj* rígido/da; austero/ra, severo/ra;
yerto/ta; ~ly *adv* con rigidez.

**rigidity** *n* rigidez, austeridad *f*.

**rigmarole** *n* galimatías *m*.

**rigorous** *adj* riguroso/sa; ~ly *adv* rigorosa-
mente.

**rigour** *n* rigor *m*; severidad *f*.

**rim** *n* margen *m/f*; orilla *f*.

**rind** *n* corteza *f*.

**ring** *n* círculo, cerco *m*; anillo *m*; campaneo
*m*; * *vt* sonar; * *vi* retiñir, retumbar; **to ~
the bell** pulsar el timbre.

**ringer** *n* campanero/ra *m/f*.

**ringleader** *n* cabecilla *m/f*.

**ringlet** *n* anillejo *m*.

**ring road** *n* periférico *m*; carretera de
circunvalación *f*.

**ringworm** *n* (*med*) tina favosa *f*.

**rink** *n* (*also* **ice ~**) pista de hielo *f*.

**rinse** *vt* lavar, limpiar.

**riot** *n* tumulto, bullicio *m*; * *vi* amotinarse.

**rioter** *n* amotinado/da *m/f*.

**riotous** *adj* bullicioso/sa, sedicioso/sa;
disoluto/ta; ~ly *adv* disolutamente.

**rip** *vt* rasgar, lacerar; descoser.

**ripe** *adj* maduro/ra, sazonado/da.

**ripen** *vt*, *vi* madurar.

**ripeness** *n* madurez *f*.

**rip-off** *n* (*col*): **it's a ~!** ¡es una estafa!

**ripple** *vi* rizarse; * *vt* rizar; * *n* onda *f*,
rizo *m*.

**rise** *vi* levantarse; nacer, salir; rebelarse; ascender; hincharse; elevarse; resucitar; * *n*
levantamiento *m*; elevación *f*; subida *f*;
salida (del sol) *f*; causa *f*.

**rising** *n* salida (del sol) *f*; fin (de una junta/
sesión) *m*.

**risk** *n* riesgo, peligro *m*; * *vt* arriesgar.

**risky** *adj* peligroso/sa.

**rissole** *n* croqueta *f*.

**rite** *n* rito *m*.

**ritual** *adj*, *n* ritual *m*.

**rival** *adj*, *n* rival *m/f*; * *vt* competir, emular.

**rivalry** *n* rivalidad *f*.

**river** *n* río *m*.

**riverside** *adj* ribereño/ña.

**rivet** *n* remache *m*; * *vt* remachar, roblar.

**rivulet** *n* riachuelo *m*.

**road** *n* camino *m*.

**road sign** *n* señal de trafico *f*.

**roadstead** *n* (*mar*) rada *f*.

**roadworks** *npl* obras *fpl*.

**roam** *vt*, *vi* corretear; vagar.

**roan** *adj* ruano/na.

**roar** *vi* rugir, aullar; bramar; * *n* rugido *m*;
bramido, truendo *m*; mugido *m*.

**roast** *vt* asar; tostar.

**roast beef** *n* rosbif *m*.

**rob** *vt* robar, hurtar.

**robber** *n* ladrón/ona *m/f*.

**robbery** *n* robo *m*.

**robe** *n* manto *m*; toga *f*; * *vt* vestir de gala.

**robin** (**redbreast**) *n* petirrojo *m*.

**robust** *adj* robusto/ta.

**robustness** *n* robustez *f*.

**rock** *n* roca *f*; escollo *m*; rueca *f*; * *vt* mecer;
arrullar; ape drear; * *vi* bambolear.

**rock and roll** *n* rocanrol *m*.

**rock crystal** *n* cuarzo *m*.

**rocket** *n* cohete *m*.

**rocking chair** *n* mecedora *f*.

**rock salt** *n* sal gema *f*.

**rocky** *adj* peñascoso/sa.

**rod** *n* varilla, verga, cana *f*.

**rodent** *n* roedor/a *m/f*.

**roe**[1] *n* corzo *m*.

**roe**[2] *n* huevaf *f*.

**roebuck** *n* corzo *m*.

**rogation** *n* rogaciones *fpl*.

**rogue** *n* bribón/ona, pícaro/ra, villano/na *m/f*.

**roguish** *adj* pícaro/ra.

**roll** *vt* rodar; volver; arrollar; * *vi* rodar; girar;
* *n* rodadura *f*; rollo *m*; lista *f*, catalogo *m*;
bollo *m*; panecillo *m*.

**roller** *n* rodillo, cilindro *m*.

**roller skates** *npl* patines de rueda *mpl*.

**rolling pin** *n* rodillo de cocina *m*.

**Roman Catholic** *adj*, *n* católico/ca *m/f*
(romano/na).

**romance** *n* romance *m*; ficción *f*; cuento *m*;
fábula *f*.

**romantic** *adj* romántico/ca.

**romp** *vi* retozar.

**roof** *n* tejado *m*; paladar *m*; * *vt* techar.

**roofing** *n* techado, tejado *m*.

**rook**[1] *n* grajo *m*.

**rook**[2] *n* torre *f* (en el juego de ajedrez).

**room** *n* habitación, sala *f*; lugar, espacio *m*;
aposento *m*.

**roominess** *n* espaciosidad, capacidad *f*.

**roomy** *adj* espacioso/sa.

**roost** *n* pértiga del gallinero *f*; * *vi* dormir en
una pértiga.

**root** *n* raíz *f*; origen *m*; * *vt*, *vi*: **to ~ out** desarraigar; arraigar.

**rooted** *adj* inveterado/da.

**rope** *n* cuerda *f*; cordel *m*; * *vi* hacer hebras.

**rope maker** *n* cordelero/ra *m/f*.

**rosary** *n* rosario *m*.

**rose** *n* rosa *f*.

**rose bed** *n* campo de rosales *m*.

**rosebud** *n* capullo de rosa *m*.

**rosemary** *n* (*bot*) romero *m*.

**rose tree** *n* rosal *m*.

**rosette** *n* roseta *f*.

**rosé wine** *n* vino rosado *m*.

**rosewood** *n* palo de rosa *m*.

**rosiness** *n* color rosado *m*.

**rosy** *adj* rosado/da.

**rot** *vi* pudrirse; * *n* putrefacción *f*.

**rotate** *vt*, *vi* girar.

**rotation** *n* rotación *f*.

**rote** *n* uso *m*; práctica *f*.

**rotten** *adj* podrido/da, corrompido/da.

**rottenness** *n* podredumbre, putrefacción *f*.

**rotund** *adj* rotundo/da, redondo/da, circular, esférico/ca.

**rouble** *n* rublo *m*.

**rouge** *n* arrebol, colorete *m*.

**rough** *adj* áspero/ra, tosco/ca; bronco/ca, bruto/ta, brusco/ca; tempestuoso/sa; **~-looking** zarrapastroso/sa; **~ly** *adv* rudamente.

**roughcast** *n* mezcla gruesa *f*.

**roughen** *vt* poner áspero/ra.

**roughness** *n* aspereza *f*; rudeza, tosquedad *f*; tempestad *f*.

**roulette** *n* ruleta *f*.

**round** *adj* redondo/da; cabal; franco/ca, sincero/ra; * *n* círculo *m*; redondez *f*; vuelta *f*; giro *m*; escalón *m*; ronda *f*; andanada de canones *f*; descarga *f*; * *adv* alrededor; por todos lados; **~ly** *adv* redondamente; francamente; * *vt* cercar, rodear; redondear.

**roundabout** *adj* amplio/lia; indirecto/ta, vago/ga; * *n* tiovivo *m*; glorieta *f*.

**roundness** *n* redondez *f*.

**rouse** *vt* despertar; excitar.

**rout** *n* derrota *f*; * *vt* derrotar.

**route** *n* ruta *f*; camino *m*.

**routine** *adj* rutinario/ria; * *n* rutina *f*; número *m*.

**rove** *vi* vagar, vaguear.

**rover** *n* vagabundo/da *m/f*; pirata *m/f*.

**row**[1] *n* camorra *f*; rina *f*.

**row**[2] *n* hilera, fila *f*.

**row**[3] *vt* (*mar*) remar, bogar.

**rowdy** *n* alborotador/a, bullanguero/ra *m/f*.

**rower** *n* remero/ra *m/f*.

**royal** *adj* real; regio/gia; **~ly** *adv* regiamente.

**royalist** *n* realista *m/f*.

**royalty** *n* realeza, dignidad real *f*; honorarios que paga el editor al autor por cada ejemplar vendido de su obra *mpl*.

**royalties** *npl* regalías *fpl*.

**rub** *vt* estregar, fregar, frotar; raspar; * *n* frotamiento *m*; (*fig*) embarazo *m*; dificultad *f*.

**rubber** *n* caucho *m*, goma *f*, goma de borrar *f*; (*col*) condón *m*.

**rubber-band** *n* goma, gomita *f*.

**rubbish** *n* basura *f*; tonterías *fpl*; escombro *m*; ruinas *fpl*.

**rubric** *n* rúbrica *f*.

**ruby** *n* rubí *m*.

**rucksack** *n* mochila *f*.

**rudder** *n* timón *m*.

**ruddiness** *n* tez encendida; rubicundez *f*.

**ruddy** *adj* colorado/da, rubio/bia.

**rude** *adj* rudo/da, brutal, rústico/ca, grosero/ra; tosco/ca; **~ly** *adv* rudamente, groseramente.

**rudeness** *n* descortesía *f*; rudeza, insolencia *f*.

**rudiment** *n* rudimentos *mpl*.

**rue** *vi* compadecerse; * *n* (*bot*) ruda *f*.

**rueful** *adj* lamentable, triste.

**ruffian** *n* malhechor/a, bandolero/ra *m/f*; * *adj* brutal.

**ruffle** *vt* desordenar, desazonar; rizar.

**rug** *n* alfombra *f*.

**rugby** *n* rugby *m*.

**rugged** *adj* áspero/ra, tosco/ca; brutal; peludo/da.

**ruin** *n* ruina *f*; perdición *f*; escombros *mpl*; * *vt* arruinar; destruir.

**ruinous** *adj* ruinoso/sa.

**rule** *n* mando *m*; regla *f*; regularidad *f*; dominio *m*; * *vt* gobernar; reglar, arreglar, dirigir.

**ruler** *n* gobernador/a *m/f*; regla *f*.

**rum** *n* ron *m*.

**rumble** *vi* crujir, rugir.

**ruminate** *vt* rumiar.

**rummage** *vt* rebuscar.

**rumour** *n* rumor *m*; * *vt* rumorearse.

**rump** *n* ancas *fpl*.

**run** *vt* dirigir; organizar; llevar; pasar; **to ~ the risk** aventurar, arriesgar; * *vi* correr; fluir, manar; pasar rápidamente; proceder; ir; desteñirse; ser candidato/ta; * *n* corrida, carrera *f*; paseo *m*; curso *m*; serie *f*; moda *f*; ataque *m*.

**runaway** *n* fugitivo/va, desertor/a *m/f*.

**rung** *n* escalón, peldaño *m* (de escalera de mano).

**runner** *n* corredor/a *m/f*; correo, mensajero/ra *m/f*.

**running** *n* carrera, corrida *f*; curso *m*.

**runway** *n* pista de aterrizaje *f*.

**rupture** *n* rotura *f*; hernia, quebradura *f*; * *vt* reventar, romper.

**rural** *adj* rural, campestre, rústico/ca.

**ruse** *n* astucia, maña *f*.

**rush** *n* junco *m*; ráfaga *f*; ímpetu *m*; * *vt* apresurar; * *vi* abalanzarse, tirarse.

**rusk** *n* galleta *f*.

**russet** *adj* bermejo/ja.

**rust** *n* herrumbre *f*; * *vi* oxidarse.

**rustic** *adj* rústico/ca; * *n* patán/ana, rústico/ca *m/f*.

**rustiness** *n* herrumbre *f*.

**rustle** *vi* crujir, rechinar; * *vt* hacer crujir.

**rustling** *n* estruendo *m*; crujido *m*.

**rusty** *adj* oriniento/ta, mohoso/sa; oxidado/da.

**rut** *n* celo *m*; carril *m*.

**ruthless** *adj* cruel, insensible; **~ly** *adv* inhumanamente.

**rye** *n* (*bot*) centeno *m*.

# S

**Sabbath** *n* sábado *m*.
**sable** *n* cebellina *f*.
**sabotage** *n* sabotaje *m*.
**sabre** *n* sable *m*.
**saccharin** *n* sacarina *f*.
**sachet** *n* sobrecito *m*.
**sack** *n* saco *m*; * *vt* despedir; saquear.
**sacrament** *n* sacramento *m*; Eucaristía *f*.
**sacramental** *adj* sacramental.
**sacred** *adj* sagrado/da, sacro/cra; inviolable.
**sacredness** *n* santidad *f*.
**sacrifice** *n* sacrificio *m*; * *vt, vi* sacrificar.
**sacrificial** *adj* de sacrificio.
**sacrilege** *n* sacrilegio *m*.
**sacrilegious** *adj* sacrílego/ga.
**sad** *adj* triste, melanólico/ca; infausto/ta;
  obscuro/ra; **~ly** *adv* tristemente.
**sadden** *vt* entristecer.
**saddle** *n* silla *f*; sillín *m*; * *vt* ensillar.
**saddlebag** *n* alforja *f*.
**saddler** *n* sillero *m/f*.
**sadness** *n* tristeza *f*.
**safari** *n* safari *m*.
**safe** *adj* seguro/ra; ileso/sa; fuera de peligro;
  de fiar; **~ly** *adv* seguramente; **~ and sound**
  sano y salvo; * *n* caja fuerte *f*.
**safe-conduct** *n* salvoconducto *m*.
**safeguard** *n* salvaguardia *f*; * *vt* proteger,
  defender.
**safety** *n* seguridad *f*; salvamento *m*.
**safety belt** *n* cinturón (de seguridad) *m*.
**safety match** *n* cerilla *f*.
**safety pin** *n* imperdible, seguro *m*.
**saffron** *n* azafrán *m*.
**sage** *n* (*bot*) salvia *f*; sabio/bia *m/f*; * *adj*
  sabio/bia; **~ly** *adv* sabiamente.
**Sagittarius** *n* Sagitario *m* (signo del
  zodíaco).
**sago** *n* (*bot*) sagú *m*.
**sail** *n* vela *f*; * *vt* gobernar; * *vi* dar a la vela,
  navegar.
**sailing** *n* navegación *f*.
**sailing boat** *n* yate *m*.
**sailor** *n* marinero/ra *m/f*.
**saint** *n* santo/ta *m/f*.
**sainted, saintly** *adj* santo/ta.
**sake** *n* causa, razón *f*; **for God's ~** por amor
  de Dios.
**salad** *n* ensalada *f*.
**salad bowl** *n* ensaladera *f*.
**salad dressing** *n* aliño *m*.

**salad oil** *n* aceite para ensaladas *m*.
**salamander** *n* salamandra *f*.
**salary** *n* sueldo *m*.
**sale** *n* venta *f*, liquidación *f*.
**saleable** *adj* vendible.
**salesman** *n* vendedor *m*.
**saleswoman** *n* vendedora *f*.
**salient** *adj* saliente, saledizo/za.
**saline** *adj* salino/na.
**saliva** *n* saliva *f*.
**sallow** *adj* cetrino/na, pálido/da.
**sally** *n* (*mil*) salida, surtida *f*; * *vi* salir.
**salmon** *n* salmón *m*.
**salmon trout** *n* trucha salmonada *f*.
**saloon** *n* bar *m*.
**salt** *n* sal *f*; * *vt* salar.
**salt cellar** *n* salero *m*.
**salting** *n* saladura *f*.
**saltpetre** *n* salitre *m*.
**saltworks** *npl* salinas *fpl*.
**salubrious** *adj* salubre, saludable.
**salubriousness, salubrity** *n* salubridad *f*.
**salutary** *adj* salubre, salutífero/ra.
**salutation** *n* salutación *f*.
**salute** *vt* saludar; * *n* saludo *m*.
**salvage** *n* (*mar*) salvamento, rescate *m*.
**salvation** *n* salvación *f*.
**salve** *n* emplasto, ungüento *m*.
**salver** *n* salvilla, bandeja *f*.
**salvo** *n* salva, excusa *f*.
**same** *adj* mismo/ma, idéntico/ca.
**sameness** *n* identidad *f*.
**sample** *n* muestra *f*; ejemplo *m*; * *vt* probar.
**sampler** *n* muestra *f*; dechado, modelo *m*.
**sanatorium** *n* sanatorio *m*.
**sanctify** *vt* santificar.
**sanctimonious** *adj* santurrón/ona.
**sanction** *n* sanción *f*; * *vt* sancionar.
**sanctity** *n* santidad *f*.
**sanctuary** *n* santuario *m*; asilo *m*.
**sand** *n* arena *f*; * *vt* lijar.
**sandal** *n* sandalia *f*.
**sandbag** *n* (*mil*) saco de tierra *m*.
**sandpit** *n* arenal *m*.
**sandstone** *n* arenisca *f*.
**sandwich** *n* bocadillo, sandwich *m*.
**sandy** *adj* arenoso/sa.
**sane** *adj* sano/na.
**sanguinary** *adj* sanguinario/ria.
**sanguine** *adj* sanguíneo/nea.
**sanitary towel** *n* compresa *f*.

**sanity** *n* juicio sano, sentido común *m*.
**sap** *n* savia *f*; * *vt* minar.
**sapient** *adj* sabio/bia, cuerdo/da.
**sapling** *n* arbolito *m*.
**sapper** *n* (*mil*) zapador *m*.
**sapphire** *n* zafiro *m*.
**sarcasm** *n* sarcasmo *m*.
**sarcastic** *adj* sarcástico/ca; **~ally** *adv* sarcásticamente.
**sarcophagus** *n* sarcófago, sepulcro *m*.
**sardine** *n* sardina *f*.
**sash** *n* cingulo *m*, cinta *f*.
**sash window** *n* ventana/vidriera corrediza *f*.
**Satan** *n* Satanás *m*.
**satanic(al)** *adj* diabólico/ca.
**satchel** *n* mochila *f*.
**satellite** *n* satélite *m*.
**satellite dish** *n* antena parabólica *f*.
**satiate, sate** *vt* saciar, hartar.
**satin** *n* raso *m*; * *adj* de raso.
**satire** *n* satira *f*.
**satiric(al)** *adj* satírico/ca; **~ly** *adv* satíricamente.
**satirist** *n* autor satírico *m*, autora satírica *f*.
**satirize** *vt* satirizar.
**satisfaction** *n* satisfacción *f*.
**satisfactorily** *adv* satisfactoriamente.
**satisfactory** *adj* satisfactorio/ria.
**satisfy** *vt* satisfacer; convencer.
**saturate** *vt* saturar.
**Saturday** *n* sábado *m*.
**saturnine** *adj* saturnino/na, melancólico/ca.
**satyr** *n* sátiro *m*.
**sauce** *n* salsa *f*, crema *f*; * *vt* condimentar.
**saucepan** *n* cazo *m*.
**saucer** *n* platillo *m*.
**saucily** *adv* desvergonzadamente.
**sauciness** *n* insolencia, impudencia *f*.
**saucy** *adj* insolente.
**saunter** *vi* callejear, corretear.
**sausage** *n* salchicha *f*.
**savage** *adj* salvaje, bárbaro/ra; **~ly** *adv* bárbaramente; * *n* salvaje *m/f*.
**savageness** *n* salvajería, *f*, crueldad *f*.
**savagery** *n* crueldad *f*.
**savanna(h)** *n* sabana *f*.
**save** *vt* salvar; economizar; ahorrar; evitar; conservar; * *adv* salvo, excepto; * *n* parada *f*.
**saveloy (sausage)** *n* chorizo *m*.
**saver** *n* libertador/a *m/f*; ahorrador/a *m/f*.
**saving** *adj* frugal, económico/ca; * *prep* fuera de, excepto; * *n* salvamiento *m*; **~s** *pl* ahorro *m*, economía *f*.
**savings account** *n* cuenta de ahorros *f*.

**savings bank** *n* caja de ahorros *f*.
**Saviour** *n* Salvador *m*.
**savour** *n* olor *m*; sabor *m*; * *vt* gustar, saborear.
**savouriness** *n* paladar; sabor *m*.
**savoury** *adj* sabroso/sa.
**saw** *n* sierra *f*; * *vt* serrar.
**sawdust** *n* serrín *m*.
**sawfish** *n* priste *m*.
**sawmill** *n* aserradero *m*.
**sawyer** *n* aserrador/a *m/f*.
**saxophone** *n* saxofóno *m*.
**say** *vt* decir, hablar.
**saying** *n* dicho, proverbio *m*.
**scab** *n* roña *f*; roñoso *m*.
**scabbard** *n* vaina (de espada) *f*; cobertura *f*.
**scabby** *adj* sarnoso/sa.
**scaffold** *n* tablado *m*; cadalso *m*.
**scaffolding** *n* andamio *m*.
**scald** *vt* escaldar; * *n* escaldadura *f*.
**scale** *n* balanza *f*; escama *f*; escala *f*; gama *f*; * *vt*, *vi* escalar; descostrarse.
**scallop** *n* vieira *f*; festón *m*; * *vt* festonear.
**scalp** *n* cuero cabelludo *m*; * *vt* escalpar.
**scamp** *n* bribón/ona, ladrón/ona *m/f*.
**scamper** *vi* escapar, huir.
**scampi** *npl* gambas *fpl*.
**scan** *vt* escudriñar; registrar; escandir; escanear.
**scandal** *n* escándalo *m*; infamia *f*.
**scandalize** *vt* escandalizar.
**scandalous** *adj* escandaloso/sa; **~ly** *adv* escandalosamente.
**scanner** *n* escáner *m*.
**scant, scanty** *adj* escaso/sa, parco/ca.
**scantily** *adv* escasamente, estrechamente.
**scantiness** *n* estrechez, escasez *f*.
**scapegoat** *n* chivo expiatorio *m*.
**scar** *n* cicatriz *f*; * *vt* dejar cicatriz en.
**scarce** *adj* raro/ra; **~ly** *adv* apenas.
**scarcity** *n* escasez *f*; raridad *f*.
**scare** *vt* espantar; * *n* susto *m*.
**scarecrow** *n* espantapájaros *m invar*.
**scarf** *n* bufanda *f*.
**scarlet** *n* escarlata *f*; * *adj* escarlata.
**scarlet fever** *n* escarlatina *f*.
**scarp** *n* escarpa *f*.
**scat** *interj* (*col*) ¡zape!
**scatter** *vt* esparcir; disipar.
**scavenger** *n* basurero/ra *m/f*; carroñero/ra *m/f*.
**scenario** *n* argumento *m*; guión *m*; (*fig*) escenario *m*.
**scene** *n* escena *f*; panorama *m*; escándalo *m*; paisaje *m*.

**scenery** *n* vista *f*; decoración (de teatro) *f*.
**scenic** *adj* escénico/ca.
**scent** *n* olfato *m*; olor *m*; rastro *m*; * *vt* oler.
**scent bottle** *n* frasco de perfume *m*.
**scentless** *adj* sin olfato; inodoro/ra.
**sceptic** *n* escéptico/ca *m/f*.
**sceptic(al)** *adj* escéptico/ca.
**scepticism** *n* escepticismo *m*.
**sceptre** *n* cetro *m*.
**schedule** *n* horario *m*; programa *m*; lista *f*.
**scheme** *n* proyecto, plan *m*; esquema *m*; sistema *m*; modelo *m*; * *vt* proyectar; * *vi* intrigar.
**schemer** *n* proyectista, intrigante *m/f*.
**schism** *n* cisma *m*.
**schismatic** *adj* cismático/ca.
**scholar** *n* estudiante *m/f*; erudito/ta *m/f*, escolástico/ca *m/f*.
**scholarship** *n* ciencia *f*; erudición *f*.
**scholastic** *adj* escolástico/ca.
**school** *n* escuela *f*, colegio *m*; * *vt* enseñar.
**schoolboy** *n* alumno *m*.
**schoolgirl** *n* alumna *f*.
**schooling** *n* instrucción *f*.
**schoolmaster** *n* maestro de escuela *m*.
**schoolmistress** *n* maestra de niños/niñas *f*.
**schoolteacher** *n* maestro/tra *m/f*; profesor/a *m/f*.
**schooner** *n* (*mar*) goleta *f*.
**sciatica** *n* ciática *f*.
**science** *n* ciencia *f*.
**scientific** *adj* científico/ca; ~ally *adv* científicamente.
**scientist** *n* científico/ca *m/f*.
**scimitar** *n* cimitarra *f*.
**scintillate** *vi* chispear, centellar.
**scintillating** *adj* brillante, ingenioso/sa.
**scission** *n* separación, partición *f*.
**scissors** *npl* tijeras *fpl*.
**scoff** *vi* mofarse, burlarse.
**scold** *vt*, *vi* regañar, reñir, refunfuñar.
**scoop** *n* cucharón *m*; pala *f*, exclusiva *f*; * *vt* cavar, socavar.
**scooter** (**child's**) *n* patinete *m*.
**scope** *n* objeto, intento, designio, blanco, espacio *m*; alcance *m*; libertad *f*.
**scorch** *vt* quemar; tostar; * *vi* quemarse, secarse.
**score** *n* muesca, canalita *f*, consideración *f*; cuenta *f*; puntuación *f*; razón *f*; motivo *m*; veintena *f*; * *vt* ganar; señalar con una línea; * *vi* marcar.
**scoreboard** *n* marcador *m*.
**scorn** *vt*, *vi* despreciar; mofar; * *n* desdén, menosprecio *m*.

**scornful** *adj* desdeñoso/sa; ~ly *adv* con desdén.
**Scorpio** *n* Escorpión *m* (signo del zodíaco).
**scorpion** *n* escorpión *m*.
**scotch** *vt* descartar.
**Scotch** *n* whisky escocés *m*.
**scoundrel** *n* pícaro/ra *m/f*.
**scour** *vt* fregar, estregar; limpiar; * *vi* corretear.
**scourge** *n* azote *m*; castigo *m*; * *vt* azotar, castigar.
**scout** *n* (*mil*) explorador/a *m/f*; espía *m/f*; * *vi* ir de reconocimiento.
**scowl** *vi* fruncir el ceño; * *n* ceño, semblante ceñudo *m*.
**scragginess** *n* flaqueza, aspereza *f*.
**scraggy** *adj* áspero/ra; macilento/ta.
**scramble** *vi* arrapar; trepar; disputar; * *n* disputa *f*; subida *f*.
**scrap** *n* migaja *f*; sobras *fpl*; pedacito *m*; riña *f*; chatarra *f*.
**scrape** *vt*, *vi* raer, raspar; arañar; tocar mal un instrumento; * *n* embarazo *m*; dificultad *f*.
**scraper** *n* rascador *m*.
**scratch** *vt* rascar, raspar; raer, garrapatear; * *n* rasguño *m*.
**scrawl** *vt*, *vi* garrapatear; * *n* garabatos *mpl*.
**scream**, **screech** *vi* chillar, dar alaridos; * *n* chillido, grito, alarido *m*.
**screen** *n* pantalla *f*; biombo *m*; mampara *f*; abanico de chimenea *m*; * *vt* abrigar, esconder; proyectar; cribar, cerner.
**screenplay** *n* guión *m*.
**screw** *n* tornillo *m*; * *vt* atornillar; forzar, apretar, estrechar.
**screwdriver** *n* destornillador *m*.
**scribble** *vt* escarabajear; * *n* escrito de poco mérito *m*.
**scribe** *n* escritor/a *m/f*; escriba *m/f*.
**scrimmage** *n* tumulto *m*.
**script** *n* guión *m*; letra *f*.
**scriptural** *adj* bíblico/ca.
**Scripture** *n* Sagrada Escritura *f*.
**scroll** *n* rollo (de papel/pergamino) *m*.
**scrounger** *n* mamón/ona *m/f*.
**scrub** *vt* restregar; anular; * *n* maleza *f*.
**scruffy** *adj* desaliñado/da.
**scruple** *n* escrúpulo *m*.
**scrupulous** *adj* escrupuloso/sa; ~ly *adv* escrupulosamente.
**scrutinize** *vt* escudriñar, examinar.
**scrutiny** *n* escrutinio, examen *m*.
**scuffle** *n* quimera, riña *f*; * *vi* reñir, pelear.
**scull** *n* barquillo *m*.
**scullery** *n* fregadero *m*.

**sculptor** *n* escultor/a *m/f*.

**sculpture** *n* escultura *f*; * *vt* esculpir.

**scum** *n* espuma *f*, escoria *f*; canalla *m/f*.

**scurrilous** *adj* vil, bajo/ja; injurioso/sa; **~ly** *adv* injuriosamente.

**scurvy** *n* escorbuto *m*; * *adj* escorbútico/ca; vil, despreciable.

**scuttle** *n* carbonera *f*; * *vt* barrenar.

**scythe** *n* guadaña *f*.

**sea** *n* mar *m/f*; * *adj* de mar; **heavy ~** oleada *f*.

**sea breeze** *n* viento de mar *m*.

**seacoast** *n* costa marítima *f*.

**sea fight** *n* combate naval *m*.

**seafood** *n* mariscos *mpl*.

**sea front** *n* paseo marítimo *m*.

**sea-green** *adj* verdemar.

**seagull** *n* gaviota *f*.

**sea horse** *n* caballito de mar *m*.

**seal** *n* sello *m*; foca *f*; * *vt* sellar.

**sealing wax** *n* lacre *m*.

**seam** *n* costura *f*; * *vt* coser.

**seaman** *n* marinero *m*.

**seamanship** *n* pericia en la navegación *m*.

**seamstress** *n* costurera *f*.

**seamy** *adj* sórdido/da.

**seaplane** *n* hidroavión *m*.

**seaport** *n* puerto de mar *m*.

**sear** *vt* cauterizar.

**search** *vt* examinar; escudriñar; inquirir, tentar; investigar, buscar; * *n* pesquisa *f*; busca *f*; buscada *f*.

**searchlight** *n* reflector *m*.

**seashore** *n* ribera *f*, litoral *m*.

**seasick** *adj* mareado/da.

**seasickness** *n* mareo *m*.

**seaside** *n* orilla/ribera del mar *f*.

**season** *n* estación *f*; tiempo oportuno *m*; sazón *f*; * *vt* sazonar; imbuir.

**seasonable** *adj* oportuno/na, a propósito.

**seasonably** *adv* oportunamente.

**seasoning** *n* condimento *m*.

**season ticket** *n* abono *m*.

**season ticket holder** *n* abonado/da *m/f*.

**seat** *n* asiento *m*; silla *f*; escaño *m*; situación *f*; * *vt* situar; colocar; asentar.

**seat belt** *n* cinturón de seguridad *m*.

**seaward** *adj* del litoral; **~s** *adv* hacia el mar.

**seaweed** *n* alga marina *f*.

**seaworthy** *adj* en condiciones de navegar.

**secede** *vi* apartarse, separarse.

**secession** *n* secesión *f*; separación *f*.

**seclude** *vt* apartar, excluir.

**seclusion** *n* separación *f*; exclusión *f*.

**second** *adj* segundo/da; **~ly** *adv* en segundo lugar; * *n* defensor/a *m/f*; segundo *m*; (*mus*) segunda *f*; * *vt* ayudar; segundar.

**secondary** *adj* secundario/ria.

**secondary school** *n* centro de enseñanza secundaria *m*; escuela secundaria *f*.

**second-hand** *adj* de segunda mano.

**secrecy** *n* secreto *m*, confidencialidad *f*.

**secret** *adj* secreto/ta; * *n* secreto *m*; **~ly** *adv* secretamente.

**secretary** *n* secretario/ria *m/f*.

**secrete** *vt* esconder; (*med*) secretar.

**secretion** *n* secreción *f*.

**secretive** *adj* misterioso/sa.

**sect** *n* secta *f*.

**sectarian** *n* sectario/ria *m/f*.

**section** *n* sección *f*.

**sector** *n* sector *m*.

**secular** *adj* secular, seglar.

**secularize** *vt* secularizar.

**secure** *adj* seguro/ra; salvo/va; **~ly** *adv* seguramente; * *vt* asegurar; salvar.

**security** *n* seguridad *f*; defensa *f*; confianza *f*, fianza *f*.

**sedan, saloon** *n* sedán *m*.

**sedate** *adj* sosegado/da, tranquilo/la; **~ly** *adv* tranquilamente.

**sedateness** *n* tranquilidad *f*.

**sedative** *n* sedativo *m*.

**sedentary** *adj* sedentario/ria.

**sedge** *n* (*bot*) juncia *f*.

**sediment** *n* sedimento *m*; hez *f*; poso *m*.

**sedition** *n* sedición *f*; tumulto, alboroto, motín *m*; revuelta *f*.

**seditious** *adj* sedicioso/sa.

**seduce** *vt* seducir; engañar.

**seducer** *n* seductor/a *m/f*.

**seduction** *n* seducción *f*.

**seductive** *adj* seductor/a.

**sedulous** *adj* asiduo/dua; **~ly** *adv* asiduamente.

**see** *vt*, *vi* ver, observar, descubrir; advertir; conocer, juzgar; comprender; **~!** ¡mira!

**seed** *n* semilla, simiente *f*; * *vi* granar.

**seedling** *n* plantón *m*.

**seedsman** *n* tratante en semillas *m*.

**seed time** *n* sementera, siembra *f*.

**seedy** *adj* desaseado/da.

**seeing** *conj*: **~ that** visto que, ya que.

**seek** *vt*, *vi* buscar; pretender.

**seem** *vi* parecer, semejarse.

**seeming** *n* apariencia *f*; **~ly** *adv* al parecer.

**seemliness** *n* decencia *f*.

**seemly** *adj* decente, propio/pia.

**seer** *n* proféta *m*, profetisa *f*.

**seesaw** *n* vaivén *m*; * *vi* balancear.

**seethe** *vi* hervir, bullir.

**segment** *n* segmento *m*.

**seize** *vt* asir, agarrar; secuestrar (bienes/
efectos).

**seizure** *n* captura *f*; secuestro *m*.

**seldom** *adv* raramente, rara vez.

**select** *vt* elegir, escoger; * *adj* selecto/ta,
escogido/da.

**selection** *n* selección *f*.

**self** *n* uno/na mismo/ma; **the ~** el yo; * *pref*
auto-

**self-command** *n* autocontrol *m*.

**self-conceit** *n* presunción *f*.

**self-confident** *adj* que tiene confianza en
sí mismo/ma.

**self-defence** *n* defensa propia *f*.

**self-denial** *n* abnegación de sí mismo/ma *f*.

**self-employed** *adj* autónomo/ma.

**self-evident** *adj* obvio/via.

**self-governing** *adj* autónomo/ma.

**self-interest** *n* interés propio *m*.

**selfish** *adj* egoísta; **~ly** *adv* interesada-
mente.

**selfishness** *n* egoísmo *m*.

**self-medication** *n* automedicación *f*.

**self-pity** *n* lástima de sí mismo/ma *f*.

**self-portrait** *n* autorretrato *m*.

**self-possession** *n* sangre fría, tranquilidad
de ánimo *f*.

**self-reliant** *adj* independiente.

**self-respect** *n* amor propio *m*.

**selfsame** *adj* mismísimo/ma.

**self-satisfied** *adj* pagado/da de sí mismo/
ma.

**self-seeking** *adj* egoísta.

**self-service** *adj* de autoservicio.

**self-styled** *adj* autoproclamado/da.

**self-sufficient** *adj* autosuficiente.

**self-taught** *adj* autodidacta.

**self-willed** *adj* obstinado/da.

**sell** *vt, vi* vender; traficar.

**seller** *n* vendedor/a *m/f*.

**selling-off** *n* privatización *f*.

**Sellotape™** *n* celo *m*.

**semblance** *n* semejanza, apariencia *f*.

**semen** *n* semen *m*.

**semester** *n* semestre *m*.

**semicircle** *n* semicírculo *m*.

**semicircular** *adj* semicircular.

**semicolon** *n* punto y coma *m*.

**semiconductor** *n* semiconductor *m*.

**semifinal** *n* semifinal *f*.

**seminarist** *n* seminarista *m*.

**seminary** *n* seminario *m*.

**semitone** *n* (*mus*) semitono *m*.

**senate** *n* senado *m*.

**senator** *n* senador/a *m/f*.

**senatorial** *adj* senatorio/ria.

**send** *vt* enviar, despachar, mandar; enviar;
producir.

**sender** *n* remitente *m/f*.

**senile** *adj* senil.

**senility** *n* senectud *f*; vejez *f*.

**senior** *n* mayor *m*; * *adj* mayor; superior.

**seniority** *n* antigüedad, ancianidad *f*.

**senna** *n* (*bot*) sena *f*.

**sensation** *n* sensación *f*.

**sense** *n* sentido *m*; entendimiento *m*; razón
*f*; juicio *m*; sentimiento *m*.

**senseless** *adj* insensible; insensato/ta; **~ly**
*adv* insensatamente.

**senselessness** *n* tontería, insensatez *f*.

**sensibility** *n* sensibilidad *f*.

**sensible** *adj* sensato/ta; juicioso/sa.

**sensibly** *adv* sensatamente.

**sensitive** *adj* sensible.

**sensual, sensuous** *adj* sensual; **~ly** *adv*
sensualmente.

**sensuality** *n* sensualidad *f*.

**sentence** *n* oración *f*; sentencia *f*; * *vt*
sentenciar, condenar.

**sententious** *adj* sentencioso/sa; **~ly** *adv*
sentenciosamente.

**sentient** *adj* sensitivo/va.

**sentiment** *n* sentimiento *m*; opinión *f*.

**sentimental** *adj* sentimental.

**sentinel, sentry** *n* centinela *m*.

**sentry box** *n* garita *f*.

**separable** *adj* separable.

**separate** *vt* (*vi*) separar(se); * *adj* separado/
da; distinto/ta; **~ly** *adv* separadamente.

**separation** *n* separación *f*.

**September** *n* septiembre *m*.

**septennial** *adj* sieteñal.

**septuagenarian** *n* septuagenario/ria *m/f*.

**sepulchre** *n* sepulcro *m*.

**sequel** *n* continuación *f*; consecuencia *f*.

**sequence** *n* serie, continuación *f*.

**sequester, sequestrate** *vt* secuestrar.

**sequestration** *n* secuestro *m*.

**seraglio** *n* serallo *m*.

**seraph** *n* serafín *m*.

**serenade** *n* serenata *f*; * *vt* dar serenatas.

**serene** *adj* sereno/na; **~ly** *adv* serenamente.

**serenity** *n* serenidad *f*.

**serf** *n* siervo/va, esclavo/va *m/f*.

**serge** *n* sarga *f*.

**sergeant** *n* sargento/ta *m/f*; alguacil *m/f*.

**serial** *adj* consecutivo/va, en serie; * *n* serial *m*; telenovela *f*.

**series** *n* serie *f*.
**serious** *adj* serio/ria, grave; **~ly** *adv* seriamente.
**sermon** *n* sermón *f*; oración evangélica *f*.
**serous** *adj* seroso/sa.
**serpent** *n* serpiente, sierpe *f*.
**serpentine** *adj* serpentino/na; * *n* (*chem*) serpentina *f*.
**serrated** *adj* serrado/da.
**serum** *n* suero *m*.
**servant** *n* criado *m*; criada *f*.
**servant girl** *n* criada *f*.
**serve** *vt*, *vi* servir; asistir (a la mesa); hacer; cumplir; sacar; ser a propósito; **to ~ a warrant** ejecutar un auto de prisión.
**service** *n* servicio *m*; servidumbre, utilidad *f*; culto divino *m*; acomodo *m*; * *vt* mantener; reparar.
**serviceable** *adj* servible; oficioso/sa.
**servile** *adj* servil.
**servitude** *n* servidumbre, esclavitud *f*.
**session** *n* junta *f*; sesión *f*.
**set** *vt* poner, colocar, fijar; establecer, determinar; * *vi* ponerse (el sol/los astros); cuajarse; aplicarse; * *n* juego, conjunto *m*; servicio (de plata) *m*; conjunto/agregado de muchas cosas; decorado *m*; set *m*; cuadrilla, bandada *f*; * *adj* puesto/ta, fijo/ja; listo/ta; decidido/da.
**settee** *n* sofá *m*.
**setter** *n* setter *m*.
**setting** *n* establecimiento *m*; marco *m*; montadura *f*; **~ of the sun** puesta del sol *f*.
**settle** *vt* colocar, fijar, afirmar; arreglar; calmar; * *vi* repo sarse; establecerse; sosegarse.
**settlement** *n* establecimiento *m*; domicilio *m*; contrato *m*; empleo *m*; poso *m*; colonia *f*.
**settler** *n* colono/na *m/f*.
**set-to** *n* riña *f*; combate *m*.
**seven** *adj*, *n* siete.
**seventeen** *adj*, *n* diecisiete.
**seventeenth** *adj*, *n* decimoséptimo/ma.
**seventh** *adj*, *n* séptimo/ma.
**seventieth** *adj*, *n* septuagésimo/ma.
**seventy** *adj*, *n* setenta.
**sever** *vt*, *vi* separar.
**several** *adj*, *pn* varios/as, algunos/nas.
**severance** *n* separación *f*.
**severe** *adj* severo/ra, riguroso/sa, áspero/ra, duro/ra; **~ly** *adv* severamente.
**severity** *n* severidad *f*.
**sew** *vt*, *vi* coser.
**sewer** *n* alcantarilla *f*.

**sewerage** *n* alcantarillado *m*.
**sewing machine** *n* máquina de coser *f*.
**sex** *n* sexo *m*.
**sexist** *adj*, *n* sexista *m/f*.
**sextant** *n* sextante *m*.
**sexton** *n* sepulturero/ra *m/f*.
**sexual** *adj* sexual.
**sexy** *adj* sexy.
**shabbily** *adv* vilmente, mezquinamente.
**shabbiness** *n* miseria *f*.
**shabby** *adj* desharrapado/da, zarrapastroso/sa.
**shackle** *vt* poner grilletes; **~s** *npl* grilletes *mpl*.
**shade** *n* sombra, oscuridad *f*; matiz *m*; sombrilla *f*; * *vt* dar sombra a; abrigar; proteger.
**shadiness** *n* sombraje *m*; umbría *f*.
**shadow** *n* sombra *f*; protección *f*.
**shadowy** *adj* umbroso/sa; oscuro/ra; quimerico/ca.
**shady** *adj* opaco/ca, oscuro/ra, sombrío/ría.
**shaft** *n* flecha, saeta *f*; fuste de columna *m*; pozo *m*; hueco *m*; rayo *m*.
**shag** *n* tabaco picado *m*; cormorán moñudo *m*.
**shaggy** *adj* lanoso/sa.
**shake** *vt* sacudir; agitar; **to ~ vigorously** zarandear; **to ~ hands** darse las manos; * *vi* vacilar; temblar; * *n* sacudida *f*; vibración *f*.
**shaking** *n* temblor *m*.
**shaky** *adj* titubeante.
**shallow** *adj* somero/ra, superficial; trivial.
**shallowness** *n* poca profundidad *f*; necedad *f*.
**sham** *vt* engañar; * *n* fingimiento *m*; impostura *f*; * *adj* fingido/da, disimulado/da.
**shambles** *npl* confusión *f*.
**shame** *n* vergüenza *f*; deshonra *f*; * *vt* avergonzar, deshonrar.
**shamefaced** *adj* vergonzoso/sa, pudoroso/sa.
**shameful** *adj* vergonzoso/sa; deshonroso/sa; **~ly** *adv* ignominiosamente.
**shameless** *adj* desvergonzado/da; **~ly** *adv* desvergonzadamente.
**shamelessness** *n* desvergüenza, impudencia *f*.
**shammy (chamois)** *n* gamuza *f*.
**shampoo** *vt* lavar con champú; * *n* champú *m*.
**shamrock** *n* trébol *m*.
**shank** *n* caña *f*; asta (de ancla) *f*; cañón (de pipa) *m*.
**shanty** *n* chabola *f*.
**shantytown** *n* barrio de chabolas *m*.

**shape** *vt, vi* formar; proporcionar; concebir; * *n* forma, figura *f*; modelo *m*.
**shapeless** *adj* informe.
**shapely** *adj* bien hecho/cha.
**share** *n* parte, porción *f*; (*com*) acción *f*; reja del arado *f*; * *vt, vi* repartir; compartir.
**sharer** *n* partícipe *m/f*.
**shark** *n* tiburón *m*.
**sharp** *adj* agudo/da, aguzado/da; astuto/ta; perspicaz; penetrante; acre, mordaz, severo/ra, rígido/da; vivo/va, violento/ta; * *n* (*mus*) sostenido *m*; * *adv* en punto.
**sharpen** *vt* afilar, aguzar.
**sharply** *adv* con filo; severamente, agudamente; ingenios amente.
**sharpness** *n* agudeza *f*; sutileza, perspicacia *f*; acrimonia *f*.
**shatter** *vt* destrozar, estrellar; * *vi* hacerse pedazos.
**shave** *vt* afeitar, rasurar; * *vi* afeitarse, rasurarse;* *n* afeite *m*.
**shaver** *n* máquina de afeitar *f*.
**shaving** *n* rasurado *m*.
**shaving brush** *n* brocha de afeitar *f*.
**shaving cream** *n* crema de afeitar *f*.
**shawl** *n* chal *m*.
**she** *pn* ella.
**sheaf** *n* gavilla *f*; haz *m*.
**shear** *vt* atusar; tundir; **~s** *npl* tijeras de podar *fpl*.
**sheath** *n* vaina *f*.
**shed** *vt* verter, derramar; esparcir; * *n* tejadillo *m*; cabaña *f*.
**sheen** *n* resplandor *m*.
**sheep** *n* oveja *f*.
**sheepfold** *n* redil *m*.
**sheepish** *adj* vergonzoso/sa; tímido/da.
**sheepishness** *n* timidez, cortedad de genio *f*.
**sheepskin** *n* piel de carnero *m*; zamarra *f*; **~ jacket** zamarra *f*.
**sheer** *adj* puro/ra, claro/ra, sin mezcla; escarpado/da; * *adv* verticalmente.
**sheet** *n* sábana *f*; lámina *f*; pliego de papel *f*; (*mar*) escota *f*.
**sheet anchor** *n* áncora mayor de un navío *f*.
**sheeting** *n* tela para sábanas *f*.
**sheet iron** *n* chapa de hierro batido *f*.
**sheet lightning** *n* relampagueamiento *m*.
**shelf** *n* anaquel *m*; (*mar*) arrecife *m*; escollera *f*; **on the ~** desecho/cha.
**shell** *n* cáscara *f*; proyectil *m*; concha *f*; corteza *f*; * *vt* descas carar, descortezar; bombardear; * *vi* descascararse.
**shellfish** *npl invar*crustáceo *m*; marisco *m*.

**shelter** *n* guardia *f*; amparo, abrigo *m*; asilo, refugio *m*; * *vt* guarecer, abrigar; acoger; * *vi* abrigarse.
**shelve** *vt* echar a un lado, arrinconar.
**shelving** *n* estantería *f*.
**shepherd** *n* pastor *m*.
**shepherdess** *n* pastora *f*.
**sherbet** *n* sorbete *m*.
**sheriff** *n* sheriff *m/f*.
**sherry** *n* jerez *m*.
**shield** *n* escudo *m*; patrocinio *m*; * *vt* defender.
**shift** *vi* cambiarse; moverse; * *vt* mudar, cambiar; transpor tar; * *n* cambio *m*; turno *m*.
**shinbone** *n* espinilla *f*.
**shine** *vi* lucir, brillar, resplandecer; * *vt* lustrar; * *n* brillo *m*.
**shingle** *n* guijarros *mpl*; **~s** *pl* (*med*) herpes *m invar*.
**shining** *adj* resplandeciente; * *n* esplendor *m*.
**shiny** *adj* brillante, luciente.
**ship** *n* nave *f*; barco *m*; navío, buque *m*; * *vt* embarcar; transportar.
**shipbuilding** *n* construcción naval *f*.
**shipmate** *n* (*mar*) ayudante *m/f*.
**shipment** *n* cargamento *mf*.
**shipowner** *n* naviero/ra *m/f*.
**shipwreck** *n* naufragio *m*.
**shirt** *n* camisa *f*.
**shit** *excl* (*col*) ¡mierda!
**shiver** *vi* tiritar de frío.
**shoal** *n* banco *m*.
**shock** *n* choque *m*; descarga *f*; susto *m*; * *vt* asustar; ofender.
**shock absorber** *n* amortiguador *m*.
**shoddy** *adj* de pacotilla.
**shoe** *n* zapato *m*; herradura *f*; * *vt* calzar; herrar.
**shoe factory** *n* zapatería *f*.
**shoehorn** *n* calzador *m*.
**shoelace** *n* cordón de zapato *m*.
**shoemaker** *n* zapatero/ra *m/f*.
**shoemaking** *n* zapatería *f*.
**shoe shop** *n* zapatería *f*.
**shoestring** *n* lazo de zapato *m*.
**shoot** *vt* tirar, arrojar, lanzar, disparar; * *vi* brotar, germinar; sobresalir; lanzarse; * *n* vástago *m*.
**shooter** *n* tirador *m*.
**shooting** *n* caza con escopeta *f*; tiroteo *m*.
**shop** *n* tienda *f*; taller *m*.
**shop window** *n* escaparate *m*.
**shopkeeper** *n* tendero/ra *m/f*.
**shoplifter** *n* ladrón/ona de tiendas *m/f*.

**shopper** *n* comprador/a *m/f*.

**shopping** *n* compras *fpl*.

**shopping centre** *n* centro comercial *m*.

**shopping mall** *n* paseo *m*.

**shore** *n* costa, ribera, playa *f*.

**short** *adj* corto/ta, breve, sucinto/ta, conciso/sa; **~ly** *adv* brevemente; pronto; en pocas palabras.

**shortcoming** *n* insuficiencia *f*; déficit *m*.

**shorten** *vt* acortar; abreviar.

**shorthand typist** *n* taquígrafo/fa *m/f*.

**shortness** *n* cortedad *f*; brevedad *f*.

**short-sighted** *adj* miope, corto de vista.

**short-sightedness** *n* miopía *f*.

**short wave** *n* onda corta *f*.

**shot** *n* tiro *m*; alcance *m*; perdigones *mpl*; tentativa *f*; toma *f*.

**shotgun** *n* escopeta *f*.

**shoulder** *n* hombro *m*; brazuelo *m*; * *vt* cargar al hombro.

**shout** *vi* gritar, aclamar; * *vt* gritar; * *n* aclamación *f*, grito *m*.

**shouting** *n* gritos *mpl*.

**shove** *vt*, *vi* empujar; impeler; * *n* empujon *m*.

**shovel** *n* pala *f*; * *vt* traspalar.

**show** *vt* mostrar; descubrir, manifestar; probar, ensenar, explicar; * *vi* parecer; * *n* espectaculo *m*; muestra *f*; exposición, parada *f*.

**show business** *n* el mundo del espectaculo *m*.

**shower** *n* nubada *f*; llovizna *f*; ducha *f*; (*fig*) abundancia *f*; * *vi* llover.

**showery** *adj* lluvioso/sa.

**showjumping** *n* hípica *f*.

**showroom** *n* sala de muestras *f*.

**showy** *adj* ostentoso/sa, suntuoso/sa.

**shred** *n* cacho, pedazo pequeño *m*; * *vt* hacer trizas.

**shrew** *n* mujer de mal genio *f*; musaraña *f*.

**shrewd** *adj* astuto/ta; maligno/gna; **~ly** *adv* astutamente.

**shrewdness** *n* astucia *f*.

**shriek** *vt*, *vi* chillar; * *n* chillido *m*.

**shrill** *adj* agudo/da, penetrante.

**shrillness** *n* aspereza (del sonido/de la voz) *f*.

**shrimp** *n* camarón *m*; enano/na *m/f*, hombrecillo *m*.

**shrine** *n* relicario *m*.

**shrink** *vi* encogerse; angostarse, acortarse.

**shrivel** *vi* arrugarse, encogerse; * *vt* encoger.

**shroud** *n* cubierta *f*; mortaja *f*; * *vt* cubrir, defender; amortajar; proteger.

**Shrove Tuesday** *n* martes de carnaval *m*.

**shrub** *n* arbusto *m*.

**shrubbery** *n* plantio de arbustos *m*.

**shrug** *vt* encogerse de hombros; * *n* encogimiento de hombros *m*.

**shudder** *vi* estremecerse; * *n* temblor *m*.

**shuffle** *vt* desordenar; barajar.

**shun** *vt* huir, evitar.

**shunt** *vt* (*rail*) maniobrar.

**shut** *vt* cerrar, encerrar; *vi* cerrarse.

**shutter** *n* contraventana *f*.

**shuttle** *n* lanzadera *f*.

**shuttlecock** *n* volante, rehilete *m*.

**shy** *adj* tímido/da; reservado/da; vergonzoso/sa, contenido/da; **~ly** *adv* tímidamente.

**shyness** *n* timidez *f*.

**sibling** *n* hermano/na *m/f*.

**sibyl** *n* sibila, profetisa *f*.

**sick** *adj* malo/la, enfermo/ma; disgustado/da.

**sicken** *vt* enfermar; * *vi* caer enfermo/ma.

**sickle** *n* hoz *f*.

**sick leave** *n* baja por enfermedad *f*.

**sickliness** *n* indisposición habitual *f*.

**sickly** *adj* enfermizo/za.

**sickness** *n* enfermedad *f*.

**sick pay** *n* subsidio por enfermedad *m*.

**side** *n* lado *m*; costado *m*; facción *f*; partido *m*; * *adj* lateral; oblicuo/cua; * *vi* unirse.

**sideboard** *n* aparador *m*; alacena *f*.

**sidelight** *n* luz lateral *f*.

**sidelong** *adj* lateral.

**sideways** *adv* de lado, al través.

**siding** *n* toma de partido *f*; (*rail*) aguja *f*.

**sidle** *vi* ir de lado.

**siege** *n* (*mil*) sitio *m*.

**sieve** *n* tamiz *m*; criba *f*; colador *m*; * *vt* cribar.

**sift** *vt* cerner; cribar; examinar; investigar.

**sigh** *vi* suspirar, gemir; * *n* suspiro *m*.

**sight** *n* vista *f*; mira *f*; espectáculo *m*.

**sightless** *adj* ciego/ga.

**sightly** *adj* vistoso/sa, hermoso/sa.

**sightseeing** *n* excursionismo, turismo *m*.

**sign** *n* señal *f*, indicio *m*; letrero *m*; signo *m*; firma *f*; seña *f*; * *vt* firmar.

**signal** *n* señal *f*, aviso *m*; * *adj* insigne, señalado/da.

**signalize** *vt* señalar.

**signal lamp** *n* (*rail*) reflector de señales *m*.

**signalman** *n* (*rail*) guardavía *m*.

**signature** *n* firma *f*.

**signet** *n* sello *m*.

**significance** *n* importancia *f*.

**significant** *adj* significante.

**signify** *vt* significar.

**signpost** n indicador m.
**silence** n silencio m; * vt imponer silencio.
**silent** adj silencioso/sa; ~ly adv silenciosamente.
**silex** n sílex m.
**silicon chip** n chip de silicio m.
**silk** n seda f.
**silken** adj hecho/cha de seda; sedeño/ña.
**silkiness** n blandura, molicie f.
**silkworm** n gusano de seda m.
**silky** adj hecho/cha de seda; sedoso/sa.
**sill** n repisa f; umbral de puerta m.
**silliness** n simpleza, bobería, tontería, necedad f.
**silly** adj tonto/ta, imbécil; ñoño/ña.
**silver** n plata f; * adj de plata.
**silversmith** n platero/ra m/f.
**silvery** adj plateado/da.
**similar** adj similar; semejante; ~ly adv del mismo modo.
**similarity** n semejanza f.
**simile** n símil m.
**simmer** vi hervir a fuego lento.
**simony** n simonía f.
**simper** vi sonreír; * n sonrisa f.
**simple** adj simple, puro/ra, sencillo/lla.
**simpleton** n simplón/ona, simplonazo/za m/f.
**simplicity** n sencillez f; simpleza f.
**simplification** n simplificación f.
**simplify** vt simplificar.
**simply** adv sencillamente; solo.
**simulate** vt simular, fingir.
**simulation** n simulación f.
**simultaneous** adj simultáneo/nea.
**sin** n pecado m; * vi pecar, faltar.
**since** adv desde, entonces, después; * prep desde; * conj desde que; ya que.
**sincere** adj sencillo/lla; sincero/ra; ~ly adv sinceramente; **yours ~ly** le saluda atentamente.
**sincerity** n sinceridad f.
**sinecure** n sinecura f.
**sinew** n tendón m; nervio m.
**sinewy** adj nervioso/sa, robusto/ta.
**sinful** adj pecaminoso/sa, malvado/da; ~ly adv malvadamente.
**sinfulness** n corrupción f.
**sing** vi, vt cantar; gorjear; (poet) celebrar.
**singe** vt chamuscar.
**singer** n cantante m/f.
**singing** n canto m.
**single** adj sencillo/lla, simple, solo/la; soltero/ra; * n billete sencillo m; sencillo m; * vt singularizar; separar.
**singly** adv separadamente.

**singular** adj singular, peculiar; * n singular m; ~ly adv singularmente.
**singularity** n singularidad f.
**sinister** adj siniestro/tra, izquierdo/da; infeliz, funesto/ta.
**sink** vi hundirse; sumergirse; bajarse; arruinarse, decaer; * vt hundir, echar a lo hondo; destruir; * n fregadero m.
**sinking fund** n fondo de amortización m.
**sinner** n pecador/a m/f.
**sinuosity** n sinuosidad f.
**sinuous** adj sinuoso/sa.
**sinus** n seno m.
**sip** vt sorber; * n sorbo m.
**siphon** n sifón m.
**sir** n señor m.
**sire** n caballo padre m.
**siren** n sirena f.
**sirloin** n solomillo m.
**sister** n hermana f.
**sisterhood** n hermandad f.
**sister-in-law** n cuñada f.
**sisterly** adj de hermana.
**sit** vi sentarse; estar situado/da; * vt presentarse a.
**sitcom** n telecomedia f.
**site** n sitio m; situación f.
**sit-in** n ocupación f.
**sitting** n sesión, junta f; sentada f.
**sitting room** n sala de estar f.
**situated** adj situado/da.
**situation** n situación f.
**six** adj, n seis.
**sixteen** adj, n dieciséis.
**sixteenth** adj, n decimosexto/ta.
**sixth** adj, n sexto/ta.
**sixtieth** adj, n sexagésimo/ma.
**sixty** adj, n sesenta.
**size** n tamaño, talle m; calibre m; dimensión f; estatura f; condición f.
**sizeable** adj considerable.
**skate** n patín m; * vi patinar.
**skateboard** n monopatín m.
**skating** n patinaje m.
**skating rink** n pista de patinaje f.
**skein** n madeja f.
**skeleton** n esqueleto m.
**skeleton key** n llave maestra f.
**sketch** n esbozo m; esquicio m; * vt esquiciar, bosquejar.
**skewer** n aguja de lardear f; espetón m; * vt espetar.
**ski** n esquí m; * vi esquiar.
**ski boot** n bota de esquí f.
**skid** n patinazo m; * vi patinar.

**skier** *n* esquiador/a *m/f*.

**skiing** *n* esquí *m*.

**skilful** *adj* práctico/ca, diestro/tra; **~ly** *adv* diestramente.

**skilfulness** *n* destreza *f*.

**skill** *n* destreza, arte, pericia *f*.

**skilled** *adj* práctico/ca, instruido/da.

**skim** *vt* espumar; tratar superficialmente.

**skimmed milk** *n* leche desnatada *f*.

**skimmer** *n* espumadera *f*.

**skin** *n* piel *f*; cutis *m*; * *vt* desollar.

**skin diving** *n* buceo *m*.

**skinned** *adj* desollado/da.

**skinny** *adj* flaco/ca, macilento/ta.

**skip** *vi* saltar, brincar; * *vt* pasar, omitir; * *n* salto, brinco *m*; cuba *f*.

**ski pants** *npl* pantalones de esquí *mpl*.

**skipper** *n* capitán/ana *m/f*.

**skirmish** *n* escaramuza *f*; * *vi* escaramuzar.

**skirt** *n* falda, orla *f*; * *vt* orillar.

**skirting board** *n* zócalo *m*.

**skit** *n* burla, zumba *f*.

**skittish** *adj* espantadizo/za, retozón/ona; terco/ca; inconstante; **~ly** *adv* caprichosamente.

**skittle** *n* bolo *m*.

**skulk** *vi* escuchar, acechar.

**skull** *n* cráneo *m*.

**skullcap** *n* casquete *m*.

**sky** *n* cielo, firmamento *m*.

**skylight** *n* claraboya *f*.

**skyrocket** *n* cohete *m*.

**skyscraper** *n* rascacielos *m invar*.

**slab** *n* losa *f*.

**slack** *adj* flojo/ja, perezoso/sa, negligente, lento/ta.

**slack(en)** *vt, vi* aflojar; ablandar; entibiarse; decaer; relajar; aliviar.

**slacker** *n* zángano *m*.

**slackness** *n* flojedad, remisión *f*; descuido *m*.

**slag** *n* escoria *f*.

**slam** *vt* cerrar de golpe; * *vi* cerrarse de golpe.

**slander** *vt* calumniar, infamar; * *n* calumnia *f*.

**slanderer** *n* calumniador/a, maldiciente *m/f*.

**slanderous** *adj* calumnioso/sa; **~ly** *adv* calumniosamente.

**slang** *n* argot *m*; jerigonza *f*.

**slant** *vi* pender oblicuamente; * *n* sesgo *m*; interpretación *f*.

**slanting** *adj* sesgado/da, oblicuo/cua.

**slap** *n* manotazo *m*; bofetada *f*; * *adv* directamente; * *vt* golpear, dar una bofetada.

**slash** *vt* acuchillar; * *n* cuchillada *f*.

**slate** *n* pizarra *f*.

**slater** *n* pizarrero/ra *m/f*.

**slating** *n* techo de pizarras *m*.

**slaughter** *n* carnicería, matanza *f*; * *vt* matar atrozmente; hacer una matanza de.

**slaughterer** *n* matador/a, asesino/na *m/f*.

**slaughterhouse** *n* matadero *m*.

**slave** *n* esclavo/va *m/f*; * *vi* trabajar como esclavo/va.

**slaver** *n* baba *f*; * *vi* babosear.

**slavery** *n* esclavitud *f*.

**slavish** *adj* servil, humilde; **~ly** *adv* servilmente.

**slavishness** *n* bajeza, servidumbre *f*.

**slay** *vt* matar, quitar la vida.

**slayer** *n* matador/a *m/f*.

**sleazy** *adj* de mala fama.

**sledge, sleigh** *n* trineo *m*.

**sledgehammer** *n* mazo *m*.

**sleek** *adj* liso/sa, brunido/da.

**sleep** *vi* dormir; * *n* sueño *m*.

**sleeper** *n* durmiente *m*.

**sleepily** *adv* con somnolencia/torpeza.

**sleepiness** *n* sueño *m*.

**sleeping bag** *n* saco *m* de dormir.

**sleeping pill** *n* somnífero *m*.

**sleepless** *adj* desvelado/da.

**sleepwalking** *n* sonambulismo *m*.

**sleepy** *adj* soñoliento/ta.

**sleet** *n* aguanieve *f*.

**sleeve** *n* manga *f*.

**sleight** *n*: **~ of hand** escamoteo *m*.

**slender** *adj* delgado/da, débil, pequeño/ña, escaso/sa; **~ly** *adv* delgadamente.

**slenderness** *n* delgadez *f*; tenuidad *f*; pequeñez *f*.

**slice** *n* rebanada *f*; espátula *f*; * *vt* rebanar.

**slide** *vi* resbalar, deslizarse; correr por encima del hielo; * *n* resbalón *m*; corredera *f*; diapositiva *f*; tobogán *m*.

**sliding** *adj* corredizo/za.

**slight** *adj* ligero/ra, leve, pequeño/ña; * *n* descuido *m*; * *vt* despreciar.

**slightly** *adv* ligeramente.

**slightness** *n* debilidad *f*; negligencia *f*.

**slim** *adj* delgado/da; * *vi* adelgazar.

**slime** *n* lodo *m*; substancia viscosa *f*.

**sliminess** *n* viscosidad *f*.

**slimming** *n* adelgazamiento *m*.

**slimy** *adj* viscoso/sa, pegajoso/sa.

**sling** *n* honda *f*; cabestrillo *m*; * *vt* tirar.

**slink** *vi* escaparse; esconderse.

**slip** *vi* resbalar; escapar, huirse; * *vt* deslizar; * *n* resbalón *m*; tropiezo *m*; escapada *f*; papelito *m*.

**slipper** *n* zapatilla *f*.

**slippery** *adj* resbaladizo/za.
**slip road** *n* vía de acceso *f*; rampa de acceso *f*.
**slipshod** *adj* descuidado/da.
**slipway** *n* grada *f*, gradas *fpl*.
**slit** *vt* rajar, hender; * *n* raja, hendedura *f*.
**slobber** *n* baba *f*.
**sloe** *n* endrina *f*.
**slogan** *n* eslogan, lema *m*.
**sloop** *n* (*mar*) balandro *m*.
**slop** *n* aguachirle *f*; lodazal *m*; ~s *pl* gachas *fpl*.
**slope** *n* cuesta *f*; sesgo *m*; declivio *m*; escarpa *f*; * *vt* sesgar.
**sloping** *adj* oblicuo/cua; en declive.
**sloppy** *adj* descuidado/da; desaliñado/da.
**sloth** *n* pereza *f*.
**slouch** *vt, vi* estar cabizbajo/ja; bambolearse pesadamente.
**slovenliness** *n* desaliño *m*; porquería *f*.
**slovenly** *adj* desaliñado/da, puerco/ca, sucio/cia.
**slow** *adj* tardío/día, lento/ta, torpe, perezoso/sa; ~ly *adv* lentamente, despacio.
**slowness** *n* lentitud, tardanza, pesadez *f*.
**slowworm** *n* lución *m*.
**slug** *n* holgazán/ana *m/f*, zángano *m*; babosa *f*; ficha *f*; trago *m*.
**sluggish** *adj* perezoso/sa; lento/ta; ~ly *adv* perezosamente.
**sluggishness** *n* pereza *f*.
**sluice** *n* compuerta *f*; * *vt* soltar la compuerta de.
**slum** *n* tugurio *m*; barrio bajo *m*.
**slumber** *vi* dormitar; * *n* sueño ligero *m*.
**slump** *n* depresión *f*.
**slur** *vt* ensuciar; calumniar; pronunciar mal; * *n* calumnia *f*.
**slush** *n* lodo, barro, cieno *m*.
**slut** *n* marrana *f*.
**sly** *adj* astuto/ta; ~ly *adv* astutamente.
**slyness** *n* astucia, maña *f*.
**smack** *n* sabor, gusto *m*; beso fuerte (que se oye) *m*; chasquido de latigo *m*; * *vi* saber; besar con ruido; * *vt* golpear.
**small** *adj* pequeño/ña, menudo/da.
**smallish** *adj* algo pequeño/ña.
**smallness** *n* pequeñez *f*.
**smallpox** *n* viruelas *fpl*.
**small talk** *n* charla, prosa *f*.
**smart** *adj* elegante; listo/ta, ingenioso/sa; vivo/va; * *vi* escocer.
**smartly** *adv* agudamente, vivamente; elegantemente; inteli gentemente.
**smartness** *n* agudeza, viveza, sutileza *f*.
**smash** *vt* romper, quebrantar; estrellar; batir;

* *vi* hacerse pedazos; estrellarse; * *n* fracaso *m*; choque *m*.
**smattering** *n* conocimiento superficial *m*.
**smear** *n* (*med*) frotis *m invar*; * *vt* untar; difamar.
**smell** *vt, vi* oler; * *n* olfato *m*; olor *m*; hediondez *f*.
**smelly** *adj* maloliente.
**smelt** *n* espirenque de *mar m*; * *vt* fundir (el metal).
**smelter** *n* fundidor/a *m/f*.
**smile** *vi* sonreír; * *n* sonrisa *f*.
**smirk** *vi* sonreír.
**smite** *vt* herir; afligir.
**smith** *n* herrero/ra *m/f*.
**smithy** *n* herrería *f*.
**smock** *n* camisa de mujer *f*.
**smoke** *n* humo *m*; vapor *m*; * *vt, vi* ahumar; humear; fumar.
**smoked herring (kipper)** *n* arenque ahumado *m*.
**smokeless** *adj* sin humo.
**smoker** *n* fumador/a *m/f*.
**smoking: no ~** prohibido fumar.
**smoky** *adj* humeante; humoso/sa.
**smooth** *adj* liso/sa, pulido/da, llano/na; suave; afable; * *vt* allanar; alisar; lisonjear.
**smoothly** *adv* llanamente; con blandura.
**smoothness** *n* lisura *f*; llanura *f*; suavidad *f*.
**smother** *vt* sofocar; suprimir.
**smoulder** *vi* arder debajo la ceniza.
**smudge** *vt* manchar; * *n* mancha *f*.
**smug** *adj* presumido/da.
**smuggle** *vt* pasar de contrabando.
**smuggler** *n* contrabandista *m/f*.
**smuggling** *n* contrabando *m*.
**smut** *n* tiznón *m*; suciedad *f*.
**smuttiness** *n* obscenidad *f*.
**smutty** *adj* tiznado/da; obsceno/na.
**snack** *n* bocado, bocadillo *m*, pinchito *m*.
**snack bar** *n* cafetería *f*.
**snag** *n* problema *m*.
**snail** *n* caracol *m*.
**snake** *n* serpiente, culebra *f*.
**snaky** *adj* serpentino/na.
**snap** *vt, vi* romper; agarrar; morder; insultar; **to ~ one's fingers** castañetear; * *n* estallido *m*; foto *f*.
**snapdragon** *n* (*bot*) boca de dragón *f*.
**snare** *n* lazo *m*; trampa *f*.
**snarl** *vi* regañar, gruñir.
**snatch** *vt* arrebatar; agarrar; * *n* arrebatamiento *m*; robo *m*; bocado *m*.
**sneak** *vi* arrastrar; * *n* soplón/ona *m/f*.
**sneer** *vi* hablar con desprecio.

**sneeringly** *adv* con desprecio.
**sneeze** *vi* estornudar.
**sniff** *vt* oler; * *vi* resollar con fuerza.
**snigger** *vi* reír disimuladamente.
**snip** *vt* tijeretear; * *n* tijeretada *f*, pedazo pequeño *m*; porción *f*.
**snipe** *n* agachadiza *f*; zopenco *m*.
**sniper** *n* francotirador/a *m/f*.
**snivel** *n* moquita *f*; * *vi* moquear.
**sniveller** *n* lloraduelos *m invar*.
**snob** *n* (e)snob *m/f*.
**snobbish** *adj* esnob.
**snooze** *n* sueño ligero *m*; * *vi* echar una siesta.
**snore** *vi* roncar.
**snorkel** *n* (tubo)respirador *m*.
**snort** *vi* resoplar.
**snout** *n* hocico *m*; morro *m*.
**snow** *n* nieve *f*; * *vi* nevar.
**snowball** *n* bola de nieve *f*.
**snowdrop** *n* (*bot*) campanilla blanca *f*.
**snowman** *n* muñeco de nieve *m*.
**snowplough** *n* quitanieves *m invar*.
**snowy** *adj* nevoso/sa; nevado/da.
**snub** *vt* reprender, regañar.
**snub-nosed** *adj* chato/ta; ñato/ta.
**snuff** *n* rapé *m*.
**snuffbox** *n* tabaquera *f*.
**snuffle** *vi* ganguear, hablar gangoso.
**snug** *adj* abrigado/da; conveniente, cómodo/da, agradable, grato/ta.
**so** *adv* así; de este modo; tan.
**soak** *vi*, *vt* remojarse; calarse; empapar, remojar.
**so-and-so** *n* zutano/na *m/f*.
**soap** *n* jabón *m*; * *vt* jabonar.
**soap bubble** *n* burbuja de jabón *f*.
**soap opera** *n* telenovela *f*.
**soap powder** *n* jabón en polvo *m*.
**soapsuds** *n* jabonaduras *fpl*.
**soapy** *adj* jabonoso/sa.
**soar** *vi* remontarse, sublimarse.
**sob** *n* sollozo *m*; * *vi* sollozar.
**sober** *adj* sobrio/ria; serio/ria; ~ly *adv* sobriamente; juiciosamente.
**sobriety** *n* sobriedad *f*; seriedad, sangre fría *f*.
**soccer** *n* fútbol *m*.
**sociability** *n* sociabilidad *f*.
**sociable** *adj* sociable, comunicativo/va.
**sociably** *adv* sociablemente.
**social** *adj* social, sociable; ~ly *adv* sociablemente.
**socialism** *n* socialismo *m*.
**socialist** *n* socialista *m/f*.
**social work** *n* asistencia social *f*.

**social worker** *n* asistente/ta social *m/f*.
**society** *n* sociedad *f*; compañía *f*.
**sociologist** *n* sociólogo/ga *m/f*.
**sociology** *n* sociología *f*.
**sock** *n* calcetín *m*; media *f*.
**socket** *n* enchufe *m*.
**sod** *n* césped *m*.
**soda** *n* sosa *f*; gaseosa *f*.
**sofa** *n* sofá *m*.
**soft** *adj* blando/da, suave; benigno/na, tierno/na; afeminado/da; mullido/da; ~ly *adv* suavemente; paso a paso.
**soften** *vt* ablandar, mitigar; enternecer.
**soft-hearted** *adj* compasivo/va.
**softness** *n* blandura, dulzura *f*.
**soft-spoken** *adj* de voz suave.
**software** *n* (*comput*) software *m*.
**soil** *vt* ensuciar, emporcar; * *n* mancha, porquería *f*; terreno *m*; tierra *f*.
**sojourn** *vi* residir, morar; * *n* morada *f*; residencia *f*.
**solace** *vt* solazar, consolar; * *n* consuelo *m*.
**solar** *adj* solar; ~ energy energía solar *f*.
**solder** *vt* soldar; * *n* soldadura *f*.
**soldier** *n* soldado/da *m/f*; militar *m*.
**soldierly** *adj* soldadesco/ca.
**sole** *n* planta (del pie) *f*; suela (del zapato) *f*; lenguado *m*; * *adj* único/ca, solo/la.
**solecism** *n* (*gr*) solecismo *m*.
**solemn** *adj* solemne; ~ly *adv* solemnemente.
**solemnity** *n* solemnidad *f*.
**solemnize** *vt* solemnizar.
**solicit** *vt* solicitar; implorar.
**solicitation** *n* solicitación *f*.
**solicitor** *n* representante, agente *m/f*.
**solicitous** *adj* solícito/ta, diligente; ~ly *adv* solícitamente.
**solicitude** *n* solicitud *f*.
**solid** *adj* sólido/da, compacto/ta; * *n* sólido *m*; ~ly *adv* sólidamente.
**solidify** *vt* solidificar.
**solidity** *n* solidez *f*.
**soliloquy** *n* soliloquio *m*.
**solitaire** *n* solitario *m*.
**solitary** *adj* solitario/ria, retirado/da; * *n* ermitaño/ña *m/f*.
**solitude** *n* soledad *f*; vida solitaria *f*.
**solo** *n* (*mus*) solo/la *m*.
**solstice** *n* solsticio *m*.
**soluble** *adj* soluble.
**solution** *n* solución *f*.
**solve** *vt* resolver.
**solvency** *n* solvencia *f*.
**solvent** *adj* solvente; *n* (*chem*) solvente *m*.

**some** *adj* algo de, un poco, algún, alguno, alguna, unos, pocos, ciertos.

**somebody** *n* alguien *m*.

**somehow** *adv* de algún modo.

**someplace** *adv* en alguna parte; a alguna parte.

**something** *n* alguna cosa, algo.

**sometime** *adv* algún día.

**sometimes** *adv* a veces.

**somewhat** *adv* algo; algún tanto, un poco.

**somewhere** *adv* en alguna parte; a alguna parte.

**somnambulism** *n* sonambulismo *m*.

**somnambulist** *n* sonámbulo/la *m/f*.

**somnolence** *n* somnolencia *f*.

**somnolent** *adj* somnoliento/ta.

**son** *n* hijo *m*.

**sonata** *n* (*mus*) sonata *f*.

**song** *n* canción *f*.

**son-in-law** *n* yerno *m*.

**sonnet** *n* soneto *m*.

**sonorous** *adj* sonoro/ra.

**soon** *adv* ya, pronto; **as ~ as** luego que.

**sooner** *adv* antes, más pronto.

**soot** *n* hollín *m*.

**soothe** *vt* adular; calmar.

**soothsayer** *n* adivino/na *m/f*.

**sop** *n* sopa *f*.

**sophism** *n* sofisma *m*.

**sophist** *n* sofista *m/f*.

**sophistical** *adj* sofístico/ca.

**sophisticate** *vt* sofisticar; falsificar.

**sophisticated** *adj* sofisticado/da.

**sophistry** *n* sofistería *f*.

**soporific** *adj* soporífero/ra.

**sorcerer** *n* hechicero *m*.

**sorceress** *n* hechicera *f*.

**sorcery** *n* hechizo, encanto *m*.

**sordid** *adj* sórdido/da, sucio/cia; asqueroso/sa.

**sordidness** *n* sordidez, suciedad *f*.

**sore** *n* llaga, úlcera *f*; * *adj* doloroso/sa, penoso/sa; resentido/da; ~**ly** *adv* penosamente.

**sorrel** *n* (*bot*) acedera *f*; * *adj* alazán rojo/ja.

**sorrow** *n* pesar *m*; tristeza *f*; * *vi* entristecerse.

**sorrowful** *adj* pesaroso/sa, afligido/da; ~**ly** *adv* con aflicción.

**sorry** *adj* triste, afligido/da; arrepentido/da; **I am ~** lo siento.

**sort** *n* suerte *f*; género *m*; especie *f*; calidad *f*; manera *f*; * *vt* separar en distintas clases; escoger, elegir.

**soul** *n* alma *f*; esencia *f*; persona *f*.

**sound** *adj* sano/na; entero/ra; puro/ra; firme; ~**ly** *adv* sanamente, vigorosamente; * *n* sonido, ruido *m*; estrecho *m*; * *vt* sonar; tocar; celebrar; sondar; * *vi* sonar, resonar; parecer.

**sounding board** *n* diapasón *m*; sombrero de púlpito *m*.

**sound effects** *npl* efectos sonoros *mpl*.

**soundings** *npl* (*mar*) sondeo *m*; (*mar*) surgidero *m*.

**soundness** *n* sanidad *f*; fuerza, solidez *f*.

**soundtrack** *n* banda sonora *f*.

**soup** *n* sopa *f*.

**sour** *adj* agrio/ria, ácido/da; cortado/da; áspero/ra; ~**ly** *adv* agriamente; * *vt*, *vi* agriar, acedar; agriarse.

**source** *n* manantial *m*; principio *m*.

**sourness** *n* acedía, agrura *f*; acrimonia *f*.

**souse** *n* (*col*) borracho/cha *m/f*; * *vt* escabechar; chapuzar.

**souvenir** *n* recuerdo *m*.

**south** *n* sur *m*; * *adj* del sur; * *adv* al sur.

**southerly**, **southern** *adj* del sur, meridional.

**southward(s)** *adv* hacia el sur.

**southwester** *n* (*mar*) viento de sudoeste *m*; sombrero grande de los marineros *m*.

**sovereign** *adj*, *n* soberano/na *m/f*.

**sovereignty** *n* soberanía *f*.

**sow** *n* puerca, marrana *f*.

**sow** *vt* sembrar; esparcir.

**sowing-time** *n* sementera, siembra *f*.

**soya bean** *n* semilla de soja *f*.

**space** *n* espacio *m*; intersticio *m*; * *vt* espaciar.

**spacecraft** *n* nave espacial *f*.

**spaceman** *n* astronauta *m*.

**spacewoman** *n* astronauta *f*.

**spacious** *adj* espacioso/sa, amplio/lia; ~**ly** *adv* con bastante espacio.

**spaciousness** *n* espaciosidad *f*.

**spade** *n* laya, azada *f*; pica *f* (en los naipes).

**spaghetti** *n* espaguetis *mpl*.

**span** *n* palmo *m*; envergadura *f*; * *vt* cruzar; abarcar.

**spangle** *n* lentejuela *f*; * *vt* adornar con lentejuelas.

**spaniel** *n* perro de aguas *m*.

**Spanish** *adj*, *n* español/a *m/f*; ~ **musical comedy/light opera** zarzuela *f*.

**Spanish America** *n* Hispanoamérica *f*.

**Spanish American** *adj*, *n* hispanoamericano/na *m/f*.

**spar** *n* palo *m*; * *vi* entrenarse.

**spare** *vt*, *vi* ahorrar, economizar; perdonar; pasarse sin; vivir con economía; * *adj* de más; de reserva.

**sparing** *adj* escaso/sa, raro/ra, económico/ca; **~ly** *adv* parcamente, frugalmente.

**spark** *n* chispa *f*.

**sparkle** *n* centella, chispa *f*; * *vi* chispear; espumar.

**spark plug** *n* bujía *f*.

**sparrow** *n* gorrión *m*.

**sparrowhawk** *n* gavilán *m*.

**sparse** *adj* delgado/da; tenue; **~ly** *adv* tenuemente.

**spasm** *n* espasmo *m*.

**spasmodic** *adj* espasmódico/ca.

**spatter** *vt* salpicar, manchar.

**spatula** *n* espátula *f*.

**spawn** *n* freza *f*; * *vt, vi* desovar; engendrar.

**spawning** *n* freza *f*.

**speak** *vt, vi* hablar; decir; conversar; pronunciar.

**speaker** *n* altavoz; bafle *m*; orador/a *m/f*.

**spear** *n* lanza *f*; arpón *m*; * *vt* herir con lanza.

**special** *adj* especial, particular; **~ly** *adv* especialmente.

**speciality** *n* especialidad *f*.

**species** *n* especie *f*.

**specific** *adj* específico/ca; * *n* específico *m*.

**specifically** *adv* específicamente.

**specification** *n* especificación *f*.

**specify** *vt* especificar.

**specimen** *n* muestra *f*; prueba *f*.

**specious** *adj* especioso/sa.

**speck(le)** *n* mácula, tacha *f*; * *vt* abigarrar, manchar.

**spectacle** *n* espectáculo *m*.

**spectacles** *npl* gafas *fpl*.

**spectator** *n* espectador/a *m/f*.

**spectral** *adj* espectral; **~ analysis** *n* análisis espectral *m invar*.

**spectre** *n* espectro *m*.

**speculate** *vi* especular; reflexionar.

**speculation** *n* especulación *f*; especulativa *f*; meditación *f*.

**speculative** *adj* especulativo/va, teórico/ca.

**speculum** *n* espéculo *m*.

**speech** *n* habla *m*; discurso *m*; lenguaje *m*; conversación *f*.

**speechify** *vi* arengar.

**speechless** *adj* sin habla.

**speed** *n* prisa *f*; velocidad *f*; * *vt* apresurar; despachar; * *vi* darse prisa.

**speedboat** *n* lancha motora *f*.

**speedily** *adv* aceleradamente, deprisa.

**speediness** *n* celeridad, prontitud, precipitación *f*.

**speed limit** *n* límite de velocidad *m*, velocidad maxima *f*.

**speedometer** *n* velocímetro *m*.

**speedway** *n* pista de carreras *f*.

**speedy** *adj* veloz, pronto/ta, diligente.

**spell** *n* hechizo, encanto *m*; período *m*; * *vt, vi* escribir correc tamente; deletrear; hechizar, encantar.

**spelling** *n* ortografía *f*.

**spend** *vt* gastar; pasar; disipar; consumir.

**spendthrift** *n* despilfarrador/a *m/f*.

**spent** *adj* agotado/da.

**sperm** *n* esperma *f*.

**spermaceti** *n* espermaceti *m*.

**spew** *vi* (*col*) vomitar.

**sphere** *n* esfera *f*.

**spherical** *adj* esférico/ca; **~ly** *adv* en forma esférica.

**spice** *n* especia *f*; * *vt* especiar.

**spick-and-span** *adj* aseado/da, (bien) arreglado/da.

**spicy** *adj* aromático/ca.

**spider** *n* araña *f*.

**spigot** *n* grifo *m*.

**spike** *n* espiga de grano *f*; espigón *m*; * *vi* clavar con espi gones.

**spill** *vt* derramar, verter; * *vi* derramarse.

**spin** *vt* hilar; alargar, prolongar; girar; * *vi* dar vueltas; * *n* vuelta *f*; paseo (en coche) *m*.

**spinach** *n* espinaca *f*.

**spinal** *adj* espinal.

**spindle** *n* huso *m*; quicio *m*.

**spine** *n* espinazo *m*, espina *f*.

**spineless** *adj* ñoño/ña.

**spinet** *n* (*mus*) espineta *f*.

**spinner** *n* hilador/a *m/f*; hilandero/ra *m/f*.

**spinning top** *n* trompa *f*.

**spinning wheel** *n* rueca *f*.

**spin-off** *n* derivado, producto secundario *m*.

**spinster** *n* soltera *f*.

**spiral** *adj* espiral; **~ly** *adv* en figura de espiral.

**spire** *n* espira *f*; pirámide *m*; aguja *f* (de una torre).

**spirit** *n* aliento *m*; espíritu *m*; ánimo, valor *m*; brío *m*; humor *m*; fantasma *m*; * *vt* incitar, animar; **to ~ away** quitar secretamente.

**spirited** *adj* vivo/va, brioso/sa; **~ly** *adv* con espíritu.

**spirit lamp** *n* velón/quinque de alcohol *m*.

**spiritless** *adj* abatido/da, sin espíritu.

**spiritual** *adj* espiritual; **~ly** *adv* espiritualmente.

**spiritualist** n espiritista m/f.
**spirituality** n espiritualidad f.
**spit** n asador m; saliva f; * vt, vi espetar; escupir.
**spite** n rencor m, malevolencia f; **in ~ of** a pesar de, a despe cho; * vt dar pesar.
**spiteful** adj rencoroso/sa, malicioso/sa; **~ly** adv malignamente, con tirria.
**spitefulness** n malicia f; rencor m.
**spittle** n saliva f; baba f, esputo m.
**splash** vt salpicar, enlodar; * vi chapotear; * n chapoteo m; mancha f.
**spleen** n bazo m; esplín m.
**splendid** adj espléndido/da, magnífico/ca; **~ly** adv espléndidamente.
**splendour** n esplendor m; pompa f.
**splice** vt (mar) empalmar, empleitar.
**splint** n tablilla f.
**splinter** n cacho m; astilla f; brisna f; * vt (vi) hender(se).
**split** n hendedura f; división f; * vt hender, rajar; * vi hen derse.
**splutter**, **sputter** vi escupir con frecuencia; babosear; barbotar.
**spoil** vt despojar; arruinar; mimar.
**spoiled** adj pasado/da; cortado/da.
**spoke** n radio (de la rueda) m.
**spokesman** n portavoz m.
**spokeswoman** n portavoz f.
**sponge** n esponja f; * vt limpiar con esponja; * vi meterse de mogollón.
**sponger** n mogollón m.
**sponginess** n esponjosidad f.
**spongy** adj esponjoso/sa.
**sponsor** n patrocinador/a m/f; padrino m; madrina f.
**sponsorship** n patrocinio m.
**spontaneity** n espontaneidad, voluntariedad f.
**spontaneous** adj espontáneo/nea; **~ly** adv espontaneamente.
**spool** n carrete m; canilla f, broca f.
**spoon** n cuchara f.
**spoonful** n cucharada f.
**sporadic(al)** adj esporádico/ca.
**sport** n deporte m; juego, retozo m; juguete, divertimiento, recreo, pasatiempo m.
**sports car** n coche deportivo m.
**sports jacket** n chaqueta deportiva f.
**sportsman** n deportista m.
**sportswear** n ropa de deporte/sport f.
**sportswoman** n deportista f.
**spot** n mancha f; borrón m; sitio, lugar m; grano m; * vt notar; manchar.
**spotless** adj limpio/pia, inmaculado/da.
**spotlight** n foco, reflector m.

**spotted**, **spotty** adj lleno/na de manchas; con granos.
**spouse** n esposo/a m/f.
**spout** vi borbotar; chorrear; * vt arrojar; vomitar; (fig) declamar; * n piton m, pico m.
**sprain** adj descoyuntar; * n dislocación f.
**sprat** n meleta, nuesa f (pez).
**sprawl** vi revolcarse.
**spray** n rociada f; espray m; ramita f; espuma de la mar f.
**spread** vt extender, desplegar; esparcir, divulgar; * vi extenderse, desplegarse; * n extensión, dilatación f.
**spree** n fiesta f; juerga f.
**sprig** n ramito m.
**sprightliness** n alegría, vivacidad f.
**sprightly** adj alegre, despierto/ta, vivaracho/cha.
**spring** vi brotar, arrojar; nacer, provenir; dimanar, origi narse; saltar, brincar; * n primavera f; elasticidad f; muelle, resorte m; salto m; manantial m.
**springiness** n elasticidad f.
**spring onion** n cebolleta f.
**springtime** n primavera f.
**spring water** n agua de fuente f.
**springy** adj elástico/ca; mullido/da.
**sprinkle** vt rociar.
**sprinkling** n rociadura f.
**sprout** n vástago, renuevo m; **~s** npl coles de Bruselas fpl; * vi brotar.
**spruce** adj pulido/da, gentil; **~ly** adv bellamente, lindamente; * vr vestirse con afectación.
**spruceness** n lindeza, hermosura f.
**spur** n espuela f; espolón (del gallo) m; estímulo m; * vt espolear; estimular.
**spurious** adj espurio/ria, falso/sa; contra-hecho/cha; supuesto/ta; bastardo/da.
**spurn** vt despreciar.
**spy** n espía m/f; * vt, vi espiar.
**squabble** vi reñir, disputar; * n riña, disputa f.
**squad** n escuadra f; brigada f; equipo m.
**squadron** n (mil) escuadrón m.
**squalid** adj sucio/cia, puerco/ca.
**squall** n ráfaga f; chubasco m; * vi chillar.
**squally** adj borrascoso/sa.
**squalor** n porquería, suciedad f.
**squander** vt malgastar, disipar.
**square** adj cuadrado/da, cuadrángulo/la; exacto/ta; cabal; * n cuadro m; plaza f; escuadra f; * vt cuadrar; ajustar, arreglar; * vi ajustarse.

**squareness** *n* cuadratura *f.*

**squash** *vt* aplastar; * *n* squash *m.*

**squat** *vi* agacharse; * *adj* agachado/da; rechoncho/cha.

**squatter** *n* ocupante ilegal *m/f;* (*col*) okupa *m/f.*

**squeak** *vi* plañir, chillar; * *n* grito, plañido *m.*

**squeal** *vi* plañir, gritar.

**squeamish** *adj* fastidioso/sa; demasiado delicado/da.

**squeeze** *vt* apretar, comprimir; estrechar; * *n* presión *f;* apre ton *m;* restricción *f.*

**squid** *n* calamar *m.*

**squint** *adj* bizco/ca; * *vi* bizquear; * *n* estrabismo.

**squirrel** *n* ardilla *f.*

**squirt** *vt* jeringar; * *n* jeringa *f;* chorro *m;* pisaverde *m.*

**stab** *vt* apuñalar; * *n* puñalada *f.*

**stability** *n* estabilidad, solidez *f.*

**stable** *n* establo *m;* * *vt* poner en el establo; * *adj* estable.

**stack** *n* pila *f;* * *vt* hacinar.

**staff** *n* personal *m,* plantilla *f;* palo *m;* apoyo *m.*

**stag** *n* ciervo *m.*

**stage** *n* etapa *f;* escena *f;* tablado *m;* teatro *m;* parada *f;* escalón *m.*

**stagger** *vi* vacilar, titubear; estar incierto/ta; * *vt* asustar; esca lonar.

**stagnant** *adj* estancado/da.

**stagnate** *vi* estancarse.

**stagnation** *n* estancamiento *m.*

**staid** *adj* grave, serio/ria.

**stain** *vt* manchar; empañar la reputación de; * *n* mancha *f;* deshonra *f.*

**stainless** *adj* limpio/pia; inmaculado/da.

**stair** *n* escalón *m;* ~s *pl* escalera *f.*

**staircase** *n* escalera *f.*

**stake** *n* estaca *f;* apuesta *f* (en el juego); * *vt* estacar; apostar.

**stale** *adj* añejo/ja, viejo/ja, rancio/cia.

**staleness** *n* vejez *f;* rancidez *f.*

**stalk** *vi* andar con paso majestuoso; * *n* tallo, pie, tronco *m;* troncho *m* (de ciertas hortalizas).

**stall** *n* pesebre *m;* puesto *m;* tabanco *m;* emplazamiento *m;* * *vt* parar; * *vi* pararse; buscar evasivas.

**stallion** *n* semental *m;* caballo entero *m.*

**stalwart** *n* partidario/ria leal *m/f.*

**stamen** *n* estambre *m;* fundamento *m.*

**stamina** *n* resistencia *f.*

**stammer** *vi* tartamudear; * *n* tartamudeo *m.*

**stamp** *vt* patear; estampar, imprimir; acuñar; andar con mucha pesadez; * *vi* patear; * *n* cuño *m;* sello *m;* impresión *f;* huella *f;* estampilla *f;* zapatazo *m.*

**stampede** *n* estampida *f.*

**stand** *vi* estar de pie; ponerse de pie; sostenerse; permanecer; pararse, hacer alto, estar situado/da; hallarse; erizarse (el pelo); * *vt* poner; aguantar; sostener, defender; * *n* puesto, sitio *m;* posición, situación *f;* parada *f;* estado *m* (fijo); tribuna *f;* stand *m.*

**standard** *n* estandarte *m;* modelo *m;* precio ordinario *m;* norma *f;* * *adj* normal.

**standing** *adj* permanente, fijado/da, establecido/da; de pie; estancado/da; * *n* duración *f;* posición *f;* puesto *m.*

**standstill** *n* pausa *f;* alto *m.*

**staple** *n* grapa *f;* * *adj* básico/ca, establecido/da; * *vt* grapar.

**star** *n* estrella *f;* asterisco *m.*

**starboard** *n* estribor *m.*

**starch** *n* almidón *m;* * *vt* almidonar.

**stare** *vi:* **to ~ at** clavar la vista en; * *n* mirada fija *f.*

**stark** *adj* fuerte, áspero/ra; puro/ra; * *adv* del todo.

**starling** *n* estornino *m.*

**starry** *adj* estrellado/da.

**start** *vi* empezar; sobrecogerse, sobresaltarse; levantarse de repente; salir; * *vt* empezar; causar; fundar; poner en marcha; * *n* principio *m;* salida *f;* sobresalto *m;* ímpetu *m;* paso primero *m.*

**starter** *n* estárter *m;* juez de salida *m.*

**starting point** *n* punto de partida *m.*

**startle** *vt* sobresaltar.

**startling** *adj* alarmante.

**starvation** *n* hambre, inanición *f.*

**starve** *vi* pasar hambre.

**state** *n* estado *m;* condición *f;* estado (político); pompa, gran deza *f;* **the S~s** los Estados Unidos *mpl;* * *vt* afirmar; exponer.

**stateliness** *n* grandeza, pompa *f.*

**stately** *adj* augusto/ta, majestuoso/sa.

**statement** *n* afirmación, cuenta *f.*

**statesman** *n* estadista, político *m.*

**statesmanship** *n* política *f.*

**static** *adj* estático/ca; * *n* parásitos *mpl.*

**station** *n* estación *f;* emisora *f;* empleo, puesto *m;* situación *f;* condición *f;* (*rail*) estación; * *vt* apostar.

**stationary** *adj* estacionario/ria, fijo/ja.

**stationer** *n* papelero/ra *m/f.*

**stationery** *n* papelería *f.*

**statistical** *adj* estadístico/ca.
**statistics** *npl* estadística *f*.
**statuary** *n* estatuario/ria, escultor/a *m/f*.
**statue** *n* estatua *f*.
**stature** *n* estatura, talla *f*.
**statute** *n* estatuto *m*; reglamento *m*.
**stay** *n* estancia *f*; ~s *npl* corsé, justillo *m*;
 * *vi* quedarse, estarse; detenerse; esperarse;
 **to ~ in** quedarse en casa; **to ~ on** quedarse;
 **to ~ up** velar.
**steadfast** *adj* firme, estable, sólido/da; ~ly
 *adv* firmemente, con constancia.
**steadily** *adv* firmemente; invariablemente.
**steadiness** *n* firmeza, estabilidad *f*.
**steady** *adj* firme, fijo/ja; * *vt* hacer firme.
**steak** *n* filete *m*; bistec *m*.
**steal** *vt, vi* robar.
**stealth** *n* hurto *m*; **by ~** a hurtadillas.
**stealthily** *adv* furtivamente.
**stealthy** *adj* furtivo/va.
**steam** *n* vapor *m*; humo *m*; * *vt* cocer al
 vapor; * *vi* echar humo.
**steam-engine** *n* máquina de vapor *f*.
**steamer, steamboat** *n* vapor, buque de
 vapor *m*.
**steel** *n* acero *m*; * *adj* de acero.
**steelyard** *n* romana *f*.
**steep** *adj* escarpado/da; excesivo/va; * *vt*
 empapar.
**steeple** *n* torre *f*; campanario *m*.
**steeplechase** *n* carrera de obstáculos *f*.
**steepness** *n* lo escarpado; lo abrupto.
**steer** *n* novillo *m*; * *vt* manejar, conducir;
 dirigir; gobernar; * *vi* conducir.
**steering** *n* dirección *f*.
**steering wheel** *n* volante *m*.
**stellar** *adj* estrellado/da.
**stem** *n* vástago, tallo *m*; estirpe *f*; pie *m*;
 cañón *m*; * *vt* cortar la corriente.
**stench** *n* hedor *m*.
**stencil** *n* cliché *m*.
**stenography** *n* taquigrafía *f*.
**step** *n* paso, escalón *m*; huella *f*; * *vi* dar un
 paso; andar.
**stepbrother** *n* hermanastro *m*.
**stepdaughter** *n* hijastra *f*.
**stepfather** *n* padrastro *m*.
**stepmother** *n* madrastra *f*.
**stepping stone** *n* pasadera *f*.
**stepsister** *n* hermanastra *f*.
**stepson** *n* hijastro *m*.
**stereo** *n* estérreo *m*.
**stereotype** *n* estereotipo *m*; * *vt* estereotipar.

**sterile** *adj* estéril.
**sterility** *n* esterilidad *f*.
**sterling** *adj* esterlín/ina, genuino/na,
 verdadero/ra; * *n* libras esterlinas *fpl*.
**stern** *adj* austero/ra, rígido/da, severo/ra; * *n*
 (*mar*) popa *f*; ~ly *adv* austeramente.
**stethoscope** *n* (*med*) estetoscopio *m*.
**stevedore** *n* (*mar*) estibador/a *m/f*.
**stew** *vt* estofar; * *n* estufa, olla *f*.
**steward** *n* mayordomo *m*; (*mar*) des-
 pensero *m*.
**stewardess** *n* azafata *f*.
**stewardship** *n* mayordomía *f*.
**stick** *n* palo, palillo, bastón *m*; vara *f*; * *vt*
 pegar, hincar; aguantar; picar; * *vi* pegarse;
 detenerse; perseverar; dudar.
**stickiness** *n* viscosidad, gomosidad *f*.
**sticking plaster** *n* esparadrapo *m*.
**sticky** *adj* viscoso/sa, tenaz.
**stiff** *adj* tieso/sa; duro/ra, torpe; rígido/da;
 yerto/ta; obstinado/da; ~ly *adv* obstinadamente.
**stiffen** *vt* atiesar, endurecer; * *vi* endure-
 cerse.
**stiff neck** *n* tortícolis *m*.
**stiffness** *n* tesura, rigidez *f*; obstinación *f*.
**stifle** *vt* suofocar.
**stifling** *adj* bochornoso/sa.
**stigma** *n* estigma *m*.
**stigmatize** *vt* estigmatizar.
**stile** *n* portillo con escalones *m* (para pasar
 de un cercado a otro).
**stiletto** *n* estilete *m*; tacón de aguja *m*.
**still** *vt* aquietar, aplacar; destilar; * *adj*
 silencioso/sa, tranquilo/la; * *n* alambique *m*;
 * *adv* todavía; hasta ahora; no obstante;
 aún así.
**stillborn** *adj* nacido/da muerto/ta.
**stillness** *n* calma, quietud *f*.
**stilts** *npl* zancos *mpl*.
**stimulant** *n* estimulante *m*.
**stimulate** *vt* estimular, aguijonear.
**stimulation** *n* estímulo *m*; estimulación *f*.
**stimulus** *n* estímulo *m*.
**sting** *vt* picar/morder (un insecto); * *vi*
 escocer; * *n* aguijón *m*; punzada, picadura,
 picada *f*; timo *m*.
**stingily** *adv* avaramente.
**stinginess** *n* tacañería, avaricia *f*.
**stingy** *adj* mezquino/na, tacaño/ña, avaro/
 ra.
**stink** *vi* heder; * *n* hedor *m*.
**stint** *n* tarea *f*.
**stipulate** *vt* estipular.
**stipulation** *n* estipulación *f*; condición *f*.

**stir** vt remover; agitar; incitar; * vi moverse; * n tumulto m; turbulencia f.

**stirrup** n estribo m.

**stitch** vt coser; * n punzada f; punto m.

**stoat** n armiño m.

**stock** n existencias fpl; ganado m; caldo m; estirpe f, linaje m; capital, principal m; fondo m; ~s pl acciones en los fondos públicos fpl; * vt proveer, abastecer.

**stockade** n prisión militar f.

**stockbroker** n agente de bolsa m/f.

**stock exchange** n bolsa f.

**stockholder** n accionista m/f.

**stocking** n media f.

**stock market** n bolsa f.

**stoic** n estoico/ca m/f.

**stoical** adj estoico/ca; ~ly adv estoicamente.

**stoicism** n estoicismo m.

**stole** n estola f.

**stomach** n estómago m; apetito m; * vt aguantar.

**stone** n piedra f; pepita f; hueso de fruta m; * adj de piedra; * vt apedrear; deshuesar; empedrar; trabajar de albañil.

**stone deaf** adj sordo/da como una tapia.

**stoning** n apedreamiento m.

**stony** adj de piedra, pétreo/rea; duro/ra.

**stool** n banquillo, taburete m.

**stoop** vi encorvarse, inclinarse; bajarse; * n inclinación hacia abajo f.

**stop** vt detener, parar; tapar; * vi pararse, hacer alto; * n parada f; punto m; pausa f; obstáculo m.

**stopover** n parada; rescala f.

**stoppage** n obstrucción f; impedimento m.

**stopwatch** n cronómetro m.

**storage** n almacenamiento m; almacenaje m.

**store** n abundancia f; provisión f; almacén m, tienda f; * vt surtir, proveer, abastecer.

**storey** n piso m (de una casa).

**stork** n cigüeña f.

**storm** n tempestad, borrasca f; asalto m; * vt tomar por asalto; * vi rabiar.

**stormily** adv violentamente.

**stormy** adj tempestuoso/sa; violento/ta.

**story** n historia f; chiste m.

**stout** adj robusto/ta, corpulento/ta, vigoroso/sa; terco/ca; ~ly adv valientemente; obstinadamente.

**stoutness** n valor m; fuerza f, corpulencia f.

**stove** n cocina f; estufa f.

**stow** vt ordenar, colocar; (mar) estibar.

**straggle** vi rezagarse.

**straggler** n rezagado/da m/f.

**straight** adj derecho/cha; estrecho/cha; franco/ca; * adv directamente.

**straightaway** adv inmediatamente.

**straighten** vt enderezar.

**straightforward** adj derecho/cha; franco/ca; leal.

**straightforwardness** n derechura f, franqueza f.

**strain** vt colar, filtrar; apretar (a uno contra sí); forzar, violen tar; * vi esforzarse; * n tensión f; retorcimiento m; raza f; linaje m; estilo m; sonido m; armonía f.

**strainer** n colador m; coladera f.

**strait** n estrecho m; aprieto, peligro m; penuria f.

**straitjacket** n camisa de fuerza f.

**strand** n hebra f; costa, playa f.

**strange** adj raro/ra; extraño/ña; ~ly adv extrañamente, extraordinariamente.

**strangeness** n rareza f; extrañeza f.

**stranger** n desconocido/da m/f; extranjero/ra m/f.

**strangle** vt estrangular.

**strangulation** n estrangulamiento m.

**strap** n correa, tira de cuero f; tirante de bota m; * vt atar con correa.

**strapping** adj abultado/da, corpulento/ta.

**stratagem** n estratagema f; astucia f.

**strategic** adj estratégico/ca.

**strategy** n estrategia f.

**stratum** n estrato m.

**straw** n paja m; pajita f.

**strawberry** n fresa f.

**stray** vi extraviarse; perder el camino; * adj extraviado/da; perdido/da.

**streak** n raya, lista f, vena f; * vt rayar.

**stream** n arroyo, río, torrente m; * vi correr.

**streamer** n serpentina f.

**street** n calle f.

**strength** n fuerza, robustez f; vigor m; fortaleza f.

**strengthen** vt fortificar; corroborar.

**strenuous** adj arduo/dua; ágil.

**stress** n presión f; estrés m; fuerza f; peso m; importancia f; acento m; * vt subrayar; acentuar.

**stretch** vt, vi extender, alargar; estirar; extenderse; esfor zarse; * n extensión f; trecho m; estirón m.

**stretcher** n camilla f.

**strew** vt esparcir; sembrar.

**strict** adj estricto/ta, estrecho/cha; exacto/ta, riguroso/sa; severo/ra; ~ly adv exactamente, con severidad.

**strictness** *n* exactitud *f*; severidad *f*, estrechez *f*.

**stride** *n* tranco *m*; zancada *f*; * *vi* atrancar.

**strife** *n* contienda, disputa *f*.

**strike** *vt*, *vi* golpear; herir; castigar; tocar; chocar; sonar; cesar de trabajar; * *n* ataque *m*; descubrimiento *m*; huelga *f*.

**striker** *n* huelguista *m/f*.

**striking** *adj* llamativo/va; notorio/ria; ~ly *adv* sorprendentemente.

**string** *n* cordón *m*; hilo *m*; cuerda *f*; hilera *f*, fibra *f*; * *vt* encordar; enhilar; estirar.

**stringent** *adj* astringente.

**stringy** *adj* fibroso/sa.

**strip** *vt* desnudar, despojar; * *vi* desnudarse; * *n* tira *f*; franja *f*; faja *f*; cinta *f*.

**stripe** *n* raya, lista *f*; azote *m*; * *vt* rayar.

**strive** *vi* esforzarse; empeñarse; disputar, contender; oponerse.

**stroke** *n* golpe *m*; toque (en la pintura) *m*; sonido (del reloj) *m*; plumada *f*; acaricia *f*; apoplejía *f*; * *vt* acariciar.

**stroll** *n* paseo *m*; * *vi* dar un paseo.

**strong** *adj* fuerte, vigoroso/sa, robusto/ta; poderoso/sa; violento/ta; ~ly *adv* fuertemente, con violencia.

**strongbox** *n* caja fuerte *f*.

**stronghold** *n* plaza fuerte *f*.

**strophe** *n* estrofa *f*.

**structure** *n* estructura *f*; edificio *m*.

**struggle** *vi* esforzarse; luchar; agitarse; * *n* lucha *f*.

**strum** *vt* (*mus*) rasguear.

**strut** *vi* pavonearse; * *n* contoneo *m*.

**stub** *n* talón *m*; colilla *f*; tronco *m*.

**stubble** *n* rastrojo *m*; cerda *f*.

**stubborn** *adj* obstinado/da; testarudo/da; ~ly *adv* obstinadamente.

**stubbornness** *n* obstinación, pertinacia *f*.

**stucco** *n* estuco *m*.

**stud**[1] *n* corchete *m*; taco *m*.

**stud**[2] caballeriza *f*.

**student** *n* estudiante *m/f*; * *adj* estudiantil.

**studio** *n* estudio *m*.

**studio flat** *n* estudio *m*.

**studious** *adj* estudioso/sa; diligente; ~ly *adv* estudiosamente, diligentemente.

**study** *n* estudio *m*; aplicación *f*; meditación profunda *f*; * *vt* estudiar; observar; * *vi* estudiar; aplicarse.

**stuff** *n* materia *f*; material *m*; estofa *f*; * *vt* henchir, llenar; disecar.

**stuffing** *n* relleno *m*.

**stuffy** *adj* cargado/da; de miras estrechas.

**stumble** *vi* tropezar; * *n* traspié, tropiezo *m*.

**stumbling block** *n* tropiezo *m*; escollo *m*.

**stump** *n* tronco *m*; tocón *m*; muñón *m*.

**stun** *vt* aturdir, ensordecer.

**stunner** *n* cosa estupenda *f*.

**stunt** *n* vuelo acrobático *m*; truco publicitario *m*; * *vt* no dejar crecer.

**stuntman** *n* especialista *m*.

**stuntwoman** *n* especialista *f*.

**stupefy** *vt* atontar, atolondrar.

**stupendous** *adj* estupendo/da, maravilloso/sa.

**stupid** *adj* estúpido/da; **very ~** zopenco/ca; ~ly *adv* estúpidamente.

**stupidity** *n* estupidez *f*.

**stupor** *n* estupor *m*.

**sturdily** *adv* fuertemente.

**sturdiness** *n* fuerza, fortaleza *f*; obstinación *f*.

**sturdy** *adj* fuerte, tieso/sa, robusto/ta; bronco/ca, insolente.

**sturgeon** *n* esturión *m*.

**stutter** *vi* tartamudear.

**sty** *n* zahurda *f*; pocilga *f*.

**sty(e)** *n* orzuelo *m*.

**style** *n* estilo *m*; moda *f*; * *vt* titular; nombrar; estilizar.

**stylish** *adj* elegante, en buen estilo.

**suave** *adj* afable.

**subdivide** *vt* subdividir.

**subdivision** *n* subdivisión *f*.

**subdue** *vt* sojuzgar, sujetar; conquistar; mortificar.

**subject** *adj* sujeto/ta; sometido/da; * *n* sujeto *m*; súbdito/ta *m/f*; tema *m*; * *vt* sujetar; exponer.

**subjection** *n* sujeción *f*.

**subjugate** *vt* sojuzgar, subyugar.

**subjugation** *n* subyugación *f*.

**subjunctive** *n* subjuntivo *m*.

**sublet** *vt* subarrendar.

**sublimate** *vt* sublimar.

**sublime** *adj* sublime, excelso/sa; ~ly *adv* de modo sublime; * *n* sublime *m*.

**sublimity** *n* sublimidad *f*.

**submachine gun** *n* metralleta *f*.

**submarine** *adj* submarino/na; * *n* submarino *m*.

**submerge** *vt* sumergir.

**submersion** *n* inmersión *f*; zambullida *f*.

**submission** *n* sumisión *f*.

**submissive** *adj* sumiso/sa, obsequioso/sa; ~ly *adv* con sumisión.

**submissiveness** *n* obsequio *m*; sumisión *f*.

**submit** *vt*, (*vi*) someter(se).

**subordinate** *adj* subordinado/da, inferior; * *vt* subordinar.

**subordination** *n* subordinación *f*.
**subpoena** *n* citación *f*; * *vt* citar.
**subscribe** *vt, vi* suscribir, certificar con su firma; consentir.
**subscriber** *n* suscriptor/a *m/f*.
**subscription** *n* suscripción *f*.
**subsequent** *adj* subsiguiente; **~ly** *adv* subsiguientemente.
**subservient** *adj* subordinado/da; servil.
**subside** *vi* sumergirse, irse a fondo.
**subsidence** *n* derrumbamiento *m*.
**subsidiary** *adj* subsidiario/ria.
**subsidize** *vt* subvencionar, dar subsidios.
**subsidy** *n* subvención *f*; subsidio, socorro *m*.
**subsist** *vi* subsistir; existir.
**subsistence** *n* existencia *f*; subsistencia *f*.
**substance** *n* substancia *f*; entidad *f*; esencia *f*.
**substantial** *adj* substancial; real, material; substancioso/sa; fuerte; **~ly** *adv* substancialmente.
**substantiate** *vt* probar.
**substantive** *n* sustantivo *m*.
**substitute** *vt* sustituir; * *n* suplente *m/f*.
**substitution** *n* sustitución *f*.
**substratum** *n* sustrato *m*.
**subterfuge** *n* subterfugio *m*; evasión *f*.
**subterranean** *adj* subterráneo/nea.
**subtitle** *n* subtítulo *m*.
**subtle** *adj* sutil, astuto/ta.
**subtlety** *n* sutileza, astucia *f*.
**subtly** *adv* sutilmente.
**subtract** *vt (math)* sustraer.
**suburb** *n* zona residencial *f*.
**suburban** *adj* suburbano/na.
**subversion** *n* subversión *f*.
**subversive** *adj* subversivo/va.
**subvert** *vt* subvertir, destruir.
**succeed** *vt, vi* seguir; conseguir, lograr, tener éxito.
**success** *n* éxito *m*.
**successful** *adj* exitoso/sa; próspero/ra, dichoso/sa; **~ly** *adv* con éxito; prósperamente.
**succession** *n* sucesión *f*; descendencia *f*; herencia *f*.
**successive** *adj* sucesivo/va; **~ly** *adv* sucesivamente.
**successor** *n* sucesor/a *m/f*.
**succinct** *adj* sucinto/ta, compendioso/sa; **~ly** *adv* con brevedad.
**succulent** *adj* suculento/ta, jugoso/sa.
**succumb** *vi* sucumbir.
**such** *adj* tal, semejante; **~ as** tal como.
**such and such a one** *n* zutano/na y fulano *m/f*.

**suck** *vt, vi* chupar; mamar.
**suckle** *vt* amamantar.
**suckling** *n* mamantón/ona *m/f*.
**suction** *n (med)* succión *f*.
**sudden** *adj* repentino/na, no previsto/ta; **~ly** *adv* de repente, súbitamente.
**suddenness** *n* precipitación *f*.
**suds** *npl* jabonaduras *fpl*.
**sue** *vt* demandar.
**suede** *n* ante *m*, gamuza *f*.
**suet** *n* sebo *m*.
**suffer** *vt, vi* sufrir, padecer; tolerar, permitir.
**suffering** *n* pena *f*; dolor *m*.
**suffice** *vi* bastar, ser suficiente.
**sufficiency** *n* suficiencia *f*; capacidad *f*.
**sufficient** *adj* suficiente; **~ly** *adv* bastante.
**suffocate** *vt* asfixiar; sofocar; * *vi* asfixiarse.
**suffocation** *n* asfixia *f*.
**suffrage** *n* sufragio, voto *m*.
**suffuse** *vt* difundir, derramar.
**sugar** *n* azúcar *m*; * *vt* azucarar.
**sugar beet** *n* remolacha *f*.
**sugar cane** *n* caña de azúcar *f*.
**sugar loaf** *n* pan de azúcar *m*.
**sugary** *adj* azucarado/da.
**suggest** *vt* sugerir.
**suggestion** *n* sugestión *f*.
**suicidal** *adj* suicida.
**suicide** *n* suicidio *m*; suicida *m/f*.
**suit** *n* conjunto *m*; petición *f*; traje *m*; pleito *m*; surtido *m*; * *vt* convenir; sentar a; adaptar.
**suitable** *adj* conforme, conveniente.
**suitably** *adv* convenientemente.
**suitcase** *n* maleta, valija *f*.
**suite** *n* suite *f*; serie *f*; tren *m*, comitiva *f*.
**suitor** *n* suplicante *m*; amante, cortejo *m*; pleiteante *m/f*; galanteador *m*.
**sulkiness** *n* mal humor *m*.
**sulky** *adj* regañón, terco/ca.
**sullen** *adj* hosco/ca; intratable; **~ly** *adv* de mal humor; tercamente.
**sullenness** *n* hosquedad *f*; obstinación, pertinacia, terquedad *f*.
**sulphur** *n* azufre *m*.
**sulphurous** *adj* sulfureo, azufroso/sa.
**sultan** *n* sultán *m*.
**sultana** *n* sultana *f*; pasa *f*.
**sultry** *adj* caluroso/sa; sofocante.
**sum** *n* suma *f*; total *m*; * **to ~ up** *vt* sumar; recopilar; * *vi* hacer un resumen.
**summarily** *adv* sumariamente.
**summary** *adj* sumario/ria; * *n* sumario *m*.
**summer** *n* verano, estío *m*.
**summerhouse** *n* glorieta de jardín *f*.

**summit** *n* ápice *m*; cima *f*.
**summon** *vt* citar, requerir por auto de juez; convocar, convidar; (*mil*) intimar la rendición.
**summons** *n* citación *f*; requerimiento *m*.
**sumptuous** *adj* suntuoso/sa; ~ly *adv* suntuosamente.
**sun** *n* sol *m*.
**sunbathe** *vi* tomar el sol.
**sunburnt** *adj* quemado/da por el sol.
**Sunday** *n* domingo *m*; * *adj* dominical; **done/worn on** ~ dominguero/ra.
**Sunday driver** *n* dominguero/ra *m/f*.
**sundial** *n* reloj de sol, cuadrante *m*.
**sundry** *adj* diversos/sas.
**sunflower** *n* girasol *m*.
**sunglasses** *npl* gafas de sol *fpl*.
**sunless** *adj* sin sol; sin luz.
**sunlight** *n* luz del sol *f*.
**sunny** *adj* soleado/da; brillante.
**sunrise** *n* salida del sol *f*; amanecer *m*.
**sunroof** *n* techo corredizo *m*.
**sunset** *n* puesta del sol *f*.
**sunshade** *n* quitasol *m*.
**sunshine** *n* solana *f*; claridad del sol *f*.
**sunstroke** *n* insolación *f*.
**suntan** *n* bronceado *m*.
**suntan oil** *n* aceite bronceador *m*.
**super** *adj* (*col*) bárbaro/ra.
**superannuated** *adj* añejado/da; pensionado/da.
**superannuation** *n* pensión, jubilación *f*; retiro *m*.
**superb** *adj* magnífico/ca; ~ly *adv* magníficamente.
**supercargo** *n* (*mar*) sobrecargo *m*.
**supercilious** *adj* arrogante, altanero/ra; ~ly *adv* con altivez.
**superficial** *adj* superficial; ~ly *adv* superficialmente.
**superfluity** *n* superfluidad *f*.
**superfluous** *adj* superfluo/lua.
**superhuman** *adj* sobrehumano/na.
**superintendent** *n* superintendente *m/f*.
**superior** *adj* superior; * *n* superior/a *m/f*.
**superiority** *n* superioridad *f*.
**superlative** *adj* superlativo/va; * *n* superlativo *m*; ~ly *adv* superlativamente, en sumo grado.
**supermarket** *n* supermercado *m*.
**supernatural** *adj* sobrenatural.
**supernumerary** *adj* supernumerario/ria.
**superpower** *n* superpotencia *f*.
**supersede** *vt* sobreseer; sustituir; invalidar.
**supersonic** *adj* supersónico/ca.

**superstition** *n* superstición *f*.
**superstitious** *adj* supersticioso/sa; ~ly *adv* supersticiosamente.
**superstructure** *n* superestructura *f*.
**supertanker** *n* superpetrolero *m*.
**supervene** *vi* sobrevenir.
**supervise** *vt* supervisar, revistar.
**supervision** *n* supervisión *f*.
**supervisor** *n* supervisor/a *m/f*.
**supine** *adj* supino/na; negligente.
**supper** *n* cena *f*.
**supplant** *vt* suplantar.
**supple** *adj* flexible, manejable; blando/da.
**supplement** *n* suplemento *m*.
**supplementary** *adj* adicional.
**suppleness** *n* flexibilidad *f*.
**suppli(c)ant** *n* suplicante *m/f*.
**supplicate** *vt* suplicar.
**supplication** *n* súplica, suplicación *f*.
**supplier** *n* proveedor/a *m/f*.
**supply** *vt* suministrar; suplir, completar; surtir; * *n* provisión *f*; suministro *m*.
**support** *vt* sostener; soportar, asistir; * *n* apoyo *m*.
**supportable** *adj* soportable.
**supporter** *n* partidario/ria *m/f*; aficionado/da *m/f*.
**suppose** *vt*, *vi* suponer.
**supposition** *n* suposición *f*.
**suppress** *vt* suprimir.
**suppression** *n* supresión *f*.
**supremacy** *n* supremacía *f*.
**supreme** *adj* supremo/ma; ~ly *adv* supremamente.
**surcharge** *vt* sobrecargar; * *n* sobretasa *f*.
**sure**[1] *adj* seguro/ra, cierto/ta; firme; estable; **to be** ~ estar seguro/ra; ~ly *adv* ciertamente, seguramente, sin duda.
**sure!**[2] *interj* ¡ya!
**sureness** *n* certeza, seguridad *f*.
**surety** *n* seguridad *f*; fiador *m/f*.
**surf** *n* (*mar*) resaca *f*.
**surface** *n* superficie *f*; * *vt* revestir; * *vi* salir a la superficie.
**surfboard** *n* plancha de surf *f*.
**surfeit** *n* exceso *m*.
**surge** *n* ola, onda *f*; * *vi* avanzar en tropel.
**surgeon** *n* cirujano/na *m/f*.
**surgery** *n* cirugía *f*.
**surgical** *adj* quirúrgico/ca.
**surliness** *n* mal humor *m*.
**surly** *adj* hosco/ca.
**surmise** *vt* sospechar; * *n* sospecha *f*.
**surmount** *vt* sobrepujar; (*fig*) zanjar.
**surmountable** *adj* superable.

**surname** n apellido, sobrenombre m.
**surpass** vt sobresalir, sobrepujar, exceder, aventajar.
**surpassing** adj sobresaliente.
**surplice** n sobrepelliz f.
**surplus** n excedente m; sobrante m; * adj sobrante.
**surprise** vt sorprender; * n sorpresa f.
**surprising** adj sorprendente.
**surrender** vt, vi rendir; ceder; rendirse; * n rendición f.
**surreptitious** adj subrepticio/cia; ~ly adv subrepticiamente.
**surrogate** vt subrogar; * n subrogado/da m/f.
**surrogate mother** n madre de alquiler f.
**surround** vt circundar, cercar, rodear.
**surrounding area** n inmediaciones fpl.
**survey** vt inspeccionar, examinar; apear; * n inspección f; apeo (de tierras) m.
**survive** vi sobrevivir; * vt sobrevivir a.
**survivor** n superviviente m/f.
**susceptibility** n susceptibilidad f.
**susceptible** adj susceptible.
**suspect** vt, vi sospechar; * n sospechoso/sa m/f.
**suspend** vt suspender.
**suspender belt** n liguero m.
**suspense** n suspense m; detención f; incertidumbre f.
**suspension** n suspensión f.
**suspension bridge** n puente colgante m.
**suspicion** n sospecha f.
**suspicious** adj suspicaz; ~ly adv sospechosamente.
**suspiciousness** n suspicacia f.
**sustain** vt sostener, sustentar, mantener; apoyar; sufrir.
**sustenance** n sostenimiento, sustento m.
**suture** n sutura, costura f.
**swab** n algodón m; frotis m invar.
**swaddle** vt fajar.
**swaddling-clothes** npl pañales mpl.
**swagger** vi baladronear.
**swallow** n golondrina f; * vt tragar, engullir.
**swamp** n pantano m.
**swampy** adj pantanoso/sa.
**swan** n cisne m.
**swap** vt canjear; * n intercambio m.
**swarm** n enjambre m; gentío m; hormiguero m; * vi enjambrar; hormiguear de gente; abundar.
**swarthy** adj atezado/da.
**swarthiness** n tez morena f.
**swashbuckling** adj fanfarrón/ona.
**swathe** vt fajar.

**sway** vt mover; * vi ladearse, inclinarse; * n balanceo m; poder, imperio, influjo m.
**swear** vt, vi jurar; hacer jurar; juramentar.
**sweat** n sudor m; * vi sudar; trabajar con fatiga.
**sweater**, **sweatshirt** n suéter m.
**sweep** vt, vi barrer; arrebatar; deshollinar; pasar/tocar liger amente; oscilar; * n barredura f; vuelta f; giro m.
**sweeping** adj rápido/da; ~s pl barreduras fpl.
**sweepstake** n lotería f.
**sweet** adj dulce, grato/ta, gustoso/sa; suave; oloroso/sa; melodioso/sa; hermoso/sa; amable; * adv dulcemente, suavemente; * n dulce, caramelo m.
**sweetbread** n mellejas de ternera fpl.
**sweeten** vt endulzar; suavizar; aplacar; perfumar.
**sweetener** n edulcorante m.
**sweetheart** n novio/via m/f; querida f.
**sweetmeats** npl dulces secos mpl.
**sweetness** n dulzura, suavidad f.
**swell** vi hincharse; ensoberbecerse; embravecerse; * vt hinchar, inflar, agravar; * n marejada f; * adj (col) estupendo/da, fenomenal.
**swelling** n hinchazón f; tumor m.
**swelter** vi ahogarse de calor.
**swerve** vi vagar; desviarse.
**swift** adj veloz, ligero/ra, rápido/da; * n vencejo m.
**swiftly** adv velozmente.
**swiftness** n velocidad, rapidez f.
**swill** vt beber en exceso; * n bazofia f.
**swim** vi nadar; abundar en; * vt pasar a nado; * n nadada f.
**swimming** n natación f.
**swimming pool** n piscina f.
**swimsuit** n traje de baño m.
**swindle** vt estafar.
**swindler** n estafador/a m/f.
**swine** n puerco, cochino m.
**swing** vi balancear, columpiarse; vibrar; agitarse; * vt colum piar; balancear; girar; * n vibración f; balanceo m.
**swinging door** n puerta giratoria f.
**swirl** n remolino.
**switch** n varilla f; interruptor m; (rail) aguja f; * vt cambiar de; **to ~ off** apagar; parar; **to ~ on** encender, prender.
**switchboard** n centralita f.
**swivel** vt girar.
**swoon** vi desmayarse; * n desmayo, deliquio, pasmo m.

**swoop** *vi* calarse; * *n* calada; redada *f*; **in one** ~ de un golpe.
**sword** *n* espada *f*.
**swordfish** *n* pez espada *f*.
**swordsman** *n* guerrero, espadachín *m*.
**sycamore** *n* sicomoro *m* (árbol).
**sycophant** *n* sicofante *m*.
**syllabic** *adj* silábico/ca.
**syllable** *n* sílaba *f*.
**syllabus** *n* programa de estudios *m*.
**syllogism** *n* silogismo *m*.
**sylph** *n* silfio *m*; sílfide *f*.
**symbol** *n* simbolo *m*.
**symbolic(al)** *adj* simbólico/ca.
**symbolize** *vt* simbolizar.
**symmetrical** *adj* simétrico/ca; ~**ly** *adv* con simetría.
**symmetry** *n* simetría *f*.
**sympathetic** *adj* simpático/ca; ~**ally** *adv* simpáticamente.
**sympathize** *vi* compadecerse.

**sympathy** *n* simpatía *f*.
**symphony** *n* sinfonía *f*.
**symposium** *n* simposio *m*.
**symptom** *n* síntoma *m*.
**synagogue** *n* sinagoga *f*.
**synchronism** *n* sincronismo *m*.
**syndicate** *n* sindicato *m*.
**syndrome** *n* síndrome *m*.
**synod** *n* sínodo *m*.
**synonym** *n* sinónimo *m*.
**synonymous** *adj* sinónimo/ma; ~**ly** *adv* con sinonimia.
**synopsis** *n* sinopsis *f invar*; sumario *m*.
**synoptic** *adj* sinóptico/ca.
**syntax** *n* sintaxis *f*.
**synthesis** *n* síntesis *f invar*.
**syringe** *n* jeringa, lavativa *f*; * *vt* jeringar.
**system** *n* sistema *m*.
**systematic** *adj* sistemático/ca; ~**ally** *adv* sistemáticamente.
**systems analyst** *n* analista de sistemas *m/f*.

# T

**tab** *n* lengüeta *f*; etiqueta *f*.
**tabernacle** *n* tabernáculo *m*.
**table** *n* mesa *f*; tabla *f*; * *vt* someter a discusión; poner sobre la mesa; ~ **d'hôte** menu *m*.
**tablecloth** *n* mantel *m*.
**tablespoon** *n* cuchara para comer *f*.
**tablet** *n* tableta *f*; pastilla *f*; comprimido *m*.
**table tennis** *n* ping-pong, tenis de mesa *m*.
**taboo** *adj* tabú; * *n* tabú *m*; * *vt* interdecir.
**tabular** *adj* tabular.
**tachometer** *n* cuentarrevoluciones *m invar*.
**tacit** *adj* tácito/ta; ~**ly** *adv* tácitamente.
**taciturn** *adj* taciturno/na, callado/da.
**tack** *n* bordo *m*; *n* tachuela *f*; * *vt* atar; pegar; * *vi* virar.
**tackle** *n* equipo *m*, aparejos *mpl*; placaje *m*; (*mar*) cordaje *m*, jarcia *f*.
**tact** *n* tacto *m*.
**tactician** *n* táctico/ca *m/f*.
**tactics** *npl* táctica *f*.
**tadpole** *n* renacuajo *m*.
**taffeta** *n* tafetán *m*.
**tag** *n* herrete *m*; * *vt* herretear.
**tail** *n* cola *f*; rabo *m*; * *vt* vigilar a.
**tailgate** *n* puerta trasera *f*.
**tailor** *n* sastre *m*.
**tailoring** *n* corte *m*.
**tailor-made** *adj* hecho/cha a la medida.
**tailwind** *n* viento de cola *m*.
**taint** *vt* tachar, manchar; viciar; * *n* mancha *f*.
**tainted** *adj* contaminado/da; manchado/da.
**take** *vt* tomar, coger, asir; recibir, aceptar; pillar; prender; admitir; entender; * *vi* prender el fuego; **to ~ apart** *vt* descoser; **to ~ away** quitar; llevar; **to ~ back** devolver; retractar; **to ~ down** derribar; apuntar; **to ~ in** entender, abarcar; acoger; **to ~ off** *vi* despegar; *vt* quitar; imitar; **to ~ on** aceptar; contratar; desafiar; **to ~ out** sacar; quitar; **to ~ to** encariñarse con; **to ~ up** acortar; ocupar; dedicarse a; * *n* toma *f*.
**takeoff** *n* despegue *m*.
**takeover** *n* absorción *f*; ~ **bid** opa *f*.
**takings** *npl* ingresos *mpl*.
**talc** *n* talco *m*.
**talent** *n* talento *m*; capacidad *f*.
**talented** *adj* con talento.
**talisman** *n* talismán *m*.
**talk** *vi* hablar, conversar; charlar; * *n* habla *f*; charla *f*, fama *f*.

**talkative** *adj* locuaz.
**talk show** *n* programa de entrevistas *m*.
**tall** *adj* alto/ta, elevado/da; robusto/ta.
**tally** *vi* corresponder.
**talon** *n* garra *f*.
**tambourine** *n* pandereta *f*.
**tame** *adj* amansado/da, domado/da, domesticado/da; ~**ly** *adv* mansamente; bajamente; * *vt* domar, domesticar.
**tameness** *n* domesticidad *f*; sumisión *f*.
**tamper** *vi* tocar.
**tampon** *n* tampón *m*.
**tan** *vt* broncear; * *vi* broncearse, ponerse moreno/na; * *n* bronceado *m*.
**tang** *n* sabor fuerte *m*.
**tangent** *n* tangente *f*.
**tangerine** *n* mandarina *f*.
**tangible** *adj* tangible.
**tangle** *vt* enredar, embrollar.
**tank** *n* cisterna *f*; aljibe *m*.
**tanker** *n* petrolero *m*; camión cisterna *m*.
**tanned** *adj* bronceado/da.
**tantalizing** *adj* tentador/a.
**tantamount** *adj* equivalente.
**tantrum** *n* rabieta *f*.
**tap** *vt* tocar ligeramente; utilizar; intervenir; zapatear; * *n* grifo *m*; palmada suave *f*; toque ligero *m*; llave *f*; espita *f*.
**tape** *n* cinta *f*; * *vt* grabar.
**tape measure** *n* metro *m*.
**taper** *n* cirio *m*.
**tape recorder** *n* grabadora *f*.
**tapestry** *n* tapiz *m*; tapicería *f*.
**tar** *n* brea *f*.
**target** *n* blanco *m* (para tirar).
**tariff** *n* tarifa *f*.
**Tarmac**™ *n* pista *f*.
**tarnish** *vt* deslustrar.
**tarpaulin** *n* alquitranado *m*.
**tarragon** *n* (*bot*) estragón *m*.
**tart** *adj* acedo/da, acre; * *n* tarta, torta *f*; (*col*) zorra *f*.
**tartan** *n* tela escocesa *f*.
**tartar** *n* tártaro *m*.
**task** *n* tarea *f*.
**tassel** *n* borlita *f*.
**taste** *n* gusto *m*; sabor *m*; saboreo *m*; ensayo *m*; * *vt*, *vi* gustar; probar; experimentar; agradar; tener sabor.
**tasteful** *adj* sabroso/sa; ~**ly** *adv* sabrosamente.

**tasteless** *adj* insípido/da, sin sabor.
**tasty** *adj* sabroso/sa.
**tattoo** *n* tatuaje *m*; * *vt* tatuar.
**taunt** *vt* mofar; ridiculizar; * *n* mofa, burla *f*.
**Taurus** *n* Tauro *m* (signo del zodíaco).
**taut** *adj* tieso/sa.
**tautological** *adj* tautológico/ca.
**tautology** *n* tautología *f*.
**tawdry** *adj* jarifo/fa, vistoso/sa, chabacano/na.
**tax** *n* impuesto *m*; contribución *f*; * *vt* gravar; poner a prueba.
**taxable** *adj* sujeto/ta a impuestos.
**taxation** *n* imposición de impuestos *f*.
**tax collector** *n* recaudador/a *m/f* de impuestos.
**tax-free** *adj* libre de impuestos.
**taxi** *n* taxi *m*; * *vi* rodar por la pista.
**taxi driver** *n* taxista *m/f*.
**taxi rank** *n* parada de taxis *f*.
**tax payer** *n* contribuyente *m/f*.
**tax relief** *n* desgravación fiscal *f*.
**tax return** *n* declaración de la renta *f*.
**tea** *n* té *m*.
**teach** *vt* enseñar, instruir; * *vi* enseñar.
**teacher** *n* profesor/a *m/f*; maestro/tra *m/f*.
**teaching** *n* enseñanza *f*.
**teacup** *n* taza de té *f*.
**teak** *n* teca *f* (árbol).
**team** *n* equipo *m*.
**teamster** *n* camionero/ra *m/f*.
**teamwork** *n* trabajo de equipo *m*.
**teapot** *n* tetera *f*.
**tear**[1] *vt* despedazar, rasgar; **to ~ up** hacer trizas.
**tear**[2] *n* lágrima *f*; gota *f*.
**tearful** *adj* lloroso/sa; **~ly** *adv* con lloro.
**tear gas** *n* gas lacrimógeno *m*.
**tease** *vt* tomar el pelo.
**tea service**, **tea set** *n* servicio para té *m*.
**teasing** *adj* zumbón/ona; * *n* zumba *f*.
**teaspoon** *n* cucharita *f*.
**teat** *n* ubre, teta *f*.
**technical** *adj* técnico/ca.
**technicality** *n* detalle técnico *m*.
**technician** *n* técnico/ca *m*
**technique** *n* técnica *f*.
**technological** *adj* tecnológico/ca.
**technology** *n* tecnología *f*.
**teddy (bear)** *n* osito de felpa *m*.
**tedious** *adj* tedioso/sa, fastidioso/sa; **~ly** *adv* fastidiosamente.
**tedium** *n* tedio, fastidio *m*.
**tee** *n* tee *m*.
**teem** *vi* rebosar de.

**teenage** *adj* juvenil; **~r** *n* adolescente *m/f*.
**teens** *npl* adolescencia *f*.
**tee-shirt**, **T-shirt** *n* camiseta *f*.
**teeth** *n pl* de **tooth**.
**teethe** *vi* echar los dientes.
**teetotal** *adj* abstemio/mia, sobrio/ria.
**teetotaller** *n* abstemio/mia *m/f*.
**telegram** *n* telegrama *m*.
**telegraph** *n* telégrafo *m*.
**telegraphic** *adj* telegráfico/ca.
**telegraphy** *n* telegrafía *f*.
**telepathy** *n* telepatía *f*.
**telephone** *n* teléfono *m*.
**telephone banking** *n* telebanca *f*.
**telephone booth** *n* cabina telefónica *f*.
**telephone call** *n* llamada telefónica *f*.
**telephone directory** *n* guía *f* telefónica.
**telephone number** *n* número de teléfono *m*.
**telescope** *n* telescopio *m*.
**telescopic** *adj* telescópico/ca.
**televise** *vt* televisar.
**television** *n* televisión *f*.
**television news** *n* telediario *m*.
**television set** *n* televisor *m*.
**teleworker** *n* teletrabajador/ra *m/f*.
**teleworking** *n* teletrabajo *m*.
**telex** *n* télex *m*; *vt*, *vi* enviar un télex.
**tell** *vi* decir; informar, contar.
**teller** *n* cajero/ra *m/f*.
**telling** *adj* contundente; revelador/a.
**telltale** *adj* indicador/a.
**telly** *n* (*col*) tele *f*.
**temper** *vt* templar, moderar; * *n* mal genio *m*.
**temperament** *n* temperamento *m*.
**temperance** *n* templanza, moderación *f*.
**temperate** *adj* templado/da, moderado/da, sobrio/ria.
**temperature** *n* temperatura *f*.
**tempest** *n* tempestad *f*.
**tempestuous** *adj* tempestuoso/sa.
**template** *n* plantilla *f*.
**temple** *n* templo *m*; sien *f*.
**temporarily** *adv* temporalmente.
**temporary** *adj* temporal.
**tempt** *vt* tentar; provocar.
**temptation** *n* tentación *f*.
**tempting** *adj* tentador/a.
**ten** *adj*, *n* diez.
**tenable** *adj* defendible.
**tenacious** *adj* tenaz; **~ly** *adv* tenazmente.
**tenacity** *n* tenacidad *f*; porfía *f*.
**tenancy** *n* tenencia *f*.
**tenant** *n* arrendatario/ria, inquilino/na *m/f*.

**tend** *vt* guardar, velar; * *vi* tener tendencia a.

**tendency** *n* tendencia *f*.

**tender** *adj* tierno/na, delicado/da; sensible; **~ly** *adv* tiernamente; * *n* oferta *f*; * *vt* ofrecer; estimar.

**tenderness** *n* ternura *f*.

**tendon** *n* tendón *m*.

**tendril** *n* zarcillo *m*.

**tenement** *n* casa de pisos *f*.

**tenet** *n* dogma *m*; aserción *f*.

**tennis** *n* tenis *m*.

**tennis court** *n* cancha de tenis *f*.

**tennis player** *n* tenista *m/f*.

**tennis racket** *n* raqueta de tenis *f*.

**tennis shoes** *npl* zapatillas de tenis *fpl*.

**tenor** *n* (*mus*) tenor *m*; contenido *m*; substancia *f*.

**tense** *adj* tieso/sa, tenso/sa; * *n* (*gr*) tiempo *m*.

**tension** *n* tensión, tirantez *f*.

**tent** *n* tienda de campaña *f*.

**tentacle** *n* tentáculo *m*.

**tentative** *adj* de ensayo, de prueba; **~ly** *adv* como prueba.

**tenth** *adj*, *n* décimo/ma.

**tenuous** *adj* tenue.

**tenure** *n* tenencia *f*.

**tepid** *adj* tibio/bia.

**term** *n* término *m*; dicción *f*; vocablo *m*; condición, estipulación *f*; * *vt* nombrar, llamar.

**terminal** *adj* mortal; * *n* terminal *m*; terminal *f*.

**terminate** *vt* terminar.

**termination** *n* terminación, conclusión *f*.

**terminus** *n* terminal *f*.

**terrace** *n* terraza *f*.

**terrain** *n* terreno *m*.

**terrestrial** *adj* terrestre, terreno/na.

**terrible** *adj* terrible.

**terribly** *adv* terriblemente.

**terrier** *n* terrier *m*.

**terrific** *adj* fantástico/ca; maravilloso/sa.

**terrify** *vt* aterrar, espantar.

**territorial** *adj* territorial.

**territory** *n* territorio, distrito *m*.

**terror** *n* terror *m*.

**terrorism** *n* terrorismo *m*.

**terrorist** *n* terrorista *m/f*.

**terrorist attack** *n* atentado *m*.

**terrorize** *vt* aterrorizar.

**terse** *adj* tajante.

**test** *n* examen *m*; prueba *f*; * *vt* probar; examinar.

**testament** *n* testamento *m*.

**tester** *n* ensayador/a *m/f*.

**testicles** *npl* testículos *mpl*.

**testify** *vt* testificar, atestiguar.

**testimonial** *n* atestación *f*.

**testimony** *n* testimonio *m*.

**test pilot** *n* piloto de pruebas *m/f*.

**test tube** *n* probeta *f*.

**testy** *adj* tétrico/ca.

**tetanus** *n* tétanos *m invar*.

**tether** *vt* atar.

**text** *n* texto *m*.

**textbook** *n* libro de texto *m*.

**textiles** *npl* textiles *mpl*.

**textual** *adj* textual.

**texture** *n* textura *f*; tejido *m*.

**than** *adv* que, de.

**thank** *vt* agradecer, dar las gracias a.

**thankful** *adj* grato/ta, agradecido/da; **~ly** *adv* con gratitud.

**thankfulness** *n* gratitud *f*.

**thankless** *adj* ingrato/ta.

**thanks** *npl* gracias *fpl*.

**Thanksgiving** *n* día de acción de gracias *m*.

**that** *pn* aquel, aquello, aquella; que; este; * *conj* porque; para que; **so ~** de modo que.

**thatch** *n* techo de paja *m*; * *vt* techar con paja.

**thaw** *n* deshielo *m*; * *vi* deshelarse.

**the** *art* el, la, lo; los, las.

**theatre** *n* teatro *m*.

**theatregoer** *n* aficionado/da al teatro *m/f*.

**theatrical** *adj* teatral.

**theft** *n* robo *m*.

**their** *pn* su, suyo, suya; de ellos, de ellas; **~s** el suyo, la suya, los suyos, las suyas; de ellos, de ellas.

**them** *pn* los, las, les; ellos, ellas.

**theme** *n* tema *m*.

**themselves** *pn pl* ellos mismos, ellas mismas; sí mismos; se.

**then** *adv* entonces, después; en tal caso; * *conj* en ese caso; * *adj* entonces; **now and ~** de vez en cuando.

**theologian** *n* teólogo/ga *m/f*.

**theological** *adj* teológico/ca.

**theology** *n* teología *f*.

**theorem** *n* teorema *m*.

**theoretic(al)** *adj* teórico/ca; **~ly** *adv* teóricamente.

**theorist** *n* teórico/ca *m/f*.

**theorize** *vt* teorizar.

**theory** *n* teoría *f*.

**therapeutics** *n* terapéutica *f*.

**therapist** *n* terapeuta *m/f*.

**therapy** n terapia f.
**there** adv allí, allá.
**thereabout(s)** adv por ahí, acerca de.
**thereafter** adv después; según.
**thereby** adv así; de ese modo.
**therefore** adv por eso, por lo tanto.
**thermal** adj termal.
**thermal printer** n impresora térmica f.
**thermometer** n termómetro m.
**thermostat** n termostato m.
**thesaurus** n diccionario de sinónimos m.
**these** pn pl éstos, éstas; adj estos, estas.
**thesis** n tesis f invar.
**they** pn pl ellos, ellas.
**thick** adj espeso/sa, denso/sa; grueso/sa; torpe.
**thicken** vi espesar, condensar; condensarse.
**thicket** n espesura f.
**thickness** n espesor m.
**thickset** adj grueso/sa; rechoncho/cha.
**thick-skinned** adj duro/ra de pellejo.
**thief** n ladrón/ona m/f.
**thigh** n muslo m.
**thimble** n dedal m.
**thin** adj delgado/da, delicado/da, flaco/ca; claro/ra; * vt atenuar; adelga zar; aclarar.
**thing** n cosa f; objeto m; chisme m.
**think** vi pensar, imaginar, meditar, considerar; creer, juzgar; **to ~ over** reflexionar; **to ~ up** imaginar.
**thinker** n pensador/a m/f.
**thinking** n pensamiento m; juicio m; opinión f.
**third** adj tercero/ra; * n tercio m; **~ly** adv en tercer lugar.
**third rate** adj mediocre.
**thirst** n sed f.
**thirsty** adj sediento/ta.
**thirteen** adj, n trece.
**thirteenth** adj, n decimotercero/ra.
**thirtieth** adj, n trigésimo/ma.
**thirty** adj, n treinta.
**this** adj este, esta; * pn éste, ésta, esto.
**thistle** n cardo m.
**thorn** n espino m; espina f.
**thorny** adj espinoso/sa; arduo/dua.
**thorough** adj entero/ra, perfecto/ta; **~ly** adv enteramente, profundamente.
**thoroughbred** adj de sangre, de casta.
**thoroughfare** n paso, tránsito m.
**those** pn pl ésos, ésas; aquéllos, aquéllas; * adj esos, esas; aquellos, aquellas.
**though** conj aunque, no obstante; * adv sin embargo.
**thought** n pensamiento, juicio m; opinión f; cuidado m.

**thoughtful** adj pensativo/va.
**thoughtless** adj descuidado/da; insensato/ta; **~ly** adv descuidadamente, sin reflexión.
**thousand** adj, n mil.
**thousandth** adj, n milésimo/ma.
**thrash** vt golpear; derrotar.
**thread** n hilo m; rosca f; * vt enhebrar.
**threadbare** adj raído/da, muy usado/da.
**threat** n amenaza f.
**threaten** vt amenazar.
**three** adj, n tres.
**three-dimensional** adj tridimensional.
**three-monthly** adj trimestral.
**three-ply** adj triple.
**threshold** n umbral m.
**thrifty** adj económico/ca.
**thrill** vt emocionar; * n emoción f.
**thriller** n película/novela de suspense f.
**thrive** vi prosperar; crecer.
**throat** n garganta f.
**throb** vi palpitar; vibrar; dar punzadas.
**throne** n trono m.
**throng** n tropel de gente m; * vt venir en tropel.
**throttle** n acelerador m; * vt estrangular.
**through** prep por; durante; mediante; * adj directo/ta; * adv completamente.
**throughout** prep por todo; * adv en todas partes.
**throw** vt echar, arrojar, tirar, lanzar; * n tiro m; golpe m; **to ~ away** tirar; **to ~ off** desechar; **to ~ out** tirar; **to ~ up** vomitar, devolver.
**throwaway** adj desechable.
**thrush** n tordo m (ave).
**thrust** vt empujar, introducir; * vr zamparse; * n empuje m.
**thud** n ruido sordo m; zarpazo m.
**thug** n gamberro/rra m/f.
**thumb** n pulgar m.
**thump** n golpe m; * vt, vi golpear.
**thunder** n trueno m; * vi tronar.
**thunderbolt** n rayo m.
**thunderclap** n trueno m.
**thunderstorm** n tormenta f.
**thundery** adj tormentoso/sa.
**Thursday** n jueves m invar.
**thus** adv así, de este modo.
**thwart** vt frustrar.
**thyme** n (bot) tomillo m.
**thyroid** n tiroides m invar.
**tiara** n tiara f.
**tic** n tic m.
**tick** n tictac m; palomita f; * vt marcar; **to ~ over** girar en marcha; ir tirando.

**ticket** *n* billete, boleto *m*; etiqueta *f*; tarjeta *f*.
**ticket collector** *n* (*rail*) revisor/a *m/f*.
**ticket office** *n* taquilla *f*, boletería *f*; despacho de boletos *m*.
**tickle** *vt* hacer cosquillas.
**ticklish** *adj* con cosquillas.
**tidal** *adj* (*mar*) de marea.
**tidal wave** *n* maremoto *m*.
**tide** *n* curso *m*; marea *f*.
**tidy** *adj* ordenado/da; arreglado/da; aseado/da.
**tie** *vt* anudar, atar; * *vi* empatar; **to ~ up** envolver; atar; amarrar; concluir; * *n* atadura *f*; lazo *m*; corbata *f*; empate *m*.
**tier** *n* grada *f*, piso *m*.
**tiger** *n* tigre *m*.
**tight** *adj* tirante, tieso/sa, tenso/sa; cerrado/da; apretado/da; * *adv* con fuerza.
**tighten** *vt* tirar, estirar.
**tightfisted** *adj* tacaño/ña.
**tightly** *adv* muy fuerte.
**tightrope** *n* cuerda floja *f*.
**tights** *npl* medias *fpl*.
**tigress** *n* tigresa *f*.
**tile** *n* teja *f*; baldosa *f*; azulejo *m*; * *vt* tejar.
**tiled** *adj* embaldosado/da.
**till**[1] *n* caja registradora *f*.
**till**[2] *vt* cultivar, labrar.
**tiller** *n* cana del timón *f*.
**tilt** *vt* inclinar; * *vi* inclinarse.
**timber** *n* madera de construcción *f*, árboles *mpl*.
**time** *n* tiempo *m*; época *f*; hora *f*; momento *m*; (*mus*) compás *m*; **in ~** a tiempo; **from ~ to ~** de vez en cuando; * *vt* medir el tiempo; cronometrar.
**time bomb** *n* bomba de relojería *f*.
**time lag** *n* desfase *m*.
**timeless** *adj* eterno/na.
**timely** *adj* oportuno/na.
**time off** *n* tiempo libre *m*.
**timer** *n* interruptor *m*; programador horario *m*.
**time scale** *n* escala de tiempo *f*.
**time trial** *n* contrarreloj *f*.
**time zone** *n* huso horario *m*.
**timid** *adj* tímido/da, temeroso/sa; **~ly** *adv* con timidez.
**timidity** *n* timidez *f*.
**timing** *n* cronometraje *m*; oportunidad *f*.
**tin** *n* estaño *m*; hojalata *f*.
**tinder** *n* yesca *f*.
**tinfoil** *n* papel de estaño *m*.
**tinge** *n* matiz *m*.
**tingle** *vi* zumbar; latir, punzar.

**tingling** *n* zumbido *m*; latido *m*.
**tinker** *n* calderero remendón *m*; gitano/na *m/f*.
**tinkle** *vi* tintinear.
**tin plate** *n* hojalata *f*.
**tinsel** *n* oropel *m*.
**tint** *n* tinte *m*; * *vt* teñir.
**tinted** *adj* teñido/da; ahumado/da.
**tiny** *adj* pequeño/ña, chico/ca.
**tip**[1] *n* punta, extremidad *f*.
**tip**[2] propina *f*; consejo *m*; * *vt* dar una propina a.
**tip**[3] *vt* inclinar; vaciar.
**tip-off** *n* advertencia *f*.
**tipsy** *adj* alegre.
**tiptop** *adj* excelente, perfecto/ta.
**tirade** *n* invectiva *f*.
**tire** *vt* cansar, fatigar; * *vi* cansarse; fastidiarse.
**tireless** *adj* incansable.
**tiresome** *adj* tedioso/sa, molesto/ta.
**tiring** *adj* cansado/da.
**tissue** *n* tejido *m*; pañuelo de papel *m*.
**tissue paper** *n* papel de seda *m*.
**titbit** *n* golosina *f*; pedazo *m*.
**titillate** *vt* estimular.
**title** *n* título *m*.
**title deed** *n* derecho de propiedad *m*.
**title page** *n* portada *f*.
**titter** *vi* reírse disimuladamente; * *n* risa disimulada *f*.
**titular** *adj* titular.
**to** *prep* a; para; por; de; hasta; en; con; que.
**toad** *n* sapo *m*.
**toadstool** *n* (*bot*) seta venenosa *f*.
**toast** *vt* tostar; brindar; * *n* tostada *f*; brindis *m*.
**toaster** *n* tostadora *f*.
**tobacco** *n* tabaco *m*.
**tobacconist** *n* tabaquero/ra, estanquero/ra *m/f*.
**tobacconist's** (**shop**) *n* estanco *m*, tabaquería *f*.
**tobacco pouch** *n* petaca *f*.
**toboggan** *n* tobogán *m*.
**today** *adv* hoy.
**toddler** *n* niño/ña (que empieza a andar) *m/f*.
**toddy** *n* ponche *m*.
**toe** *n* dedo del pie *m*; punta *f*.
**together** *adv* juntamente, juntos; al mismo tiempo.
**toil** *vi* fatigarse, trabajar mucho; afanarse; * *n* trabajo *m*; fatiga *f*; afán *m*.
**toilet** *n* servicios *mpl*; sanitario *m*; * *adj* de aseo.
**toilet bag** *n* bolsa de aseo *f*.

**toilet bowl** *n* taza del retrete *f*.
**toilet paper** *n* papel higiénico *m*.
**toiletries** *npl* artículos de aseo *mpl*.
**token** *n* señal *f*; muestra *f*; recuerdo *m*; vale *m*; ficha *f*.
**tolerable** *adj* soportable; pasable.
**tolerance** *n* tolerancia *f*.
**tolerant** *adj* tolerante.
**tolerate** *vt* tolerar.
**toll** *n* peaje *m*; número de victimas *m*; * *vi* doblar.
**tomato** *n* tomate *m*.
**tomb** *n* tumba *f*; sepulcro *m*, sepultura *f*.
**tomboy** *n* muchachota *f*.
**tombstone** *n* piedra sepulcral *f*.
**tomcat** *n* gato *m*.
**tomorrow** *adv* mañana; * *n* mañana *f*.
**ton** *n* tonelada *f*.
**tone** *n* tono *m*; acento *m*; * *vi* armonizar; **to ~ down** suavizar.
**tone-deaf** *adj* sin oído musical.
**tongs** *npl* tenacillas *fpl*.
**tongue** *n* lengua *f*.
**tongue-tied** *adj* mudo/da.
**tongue-twister** *n* trabalenguas *m invar*.
**tonic** *n* (*med*) tónico *m*.
**tonight** *adv*, *n* esta tarde (*f*).
**tonnage** *n* tonelaje *m*.
**tonsil** *n* amígdala *f*; **~s** *npl* agallas *fpl*.
**tonsillitis** *n* agalla *f*.
**tonsure** *n* tonsura *f*.
**too** *adv* demasiado; también.
**tool** *n* herramienta *f*; utensilio *m*.
**tool box** *n* caja de herramientas *f*.
**toot** *vi* tocar la bocina.
**tooth** *n* diente *m*.
**toothache** *n* dolor de muelas *m*.
**toothbrush** *n* cepillo de dientes *m*.
**toothless** *adj* desdentado/da.
**toothpaste** *n* pasta de dientes *f*.
**toothpick** *n* palillo *m*.
**top** *n* cima, cumbre *f*; último grado *m*; lo alto; superficie *f*; tapa *f*; cabeza *f*; * *adj* de arriba; primero/ra; * *vt* elevarse por encima; sobrepujar, exceder; **to ~ off** llenar.
**topaz** *n* topacio *m*.
**top floor** *n* último piso *m*.
**top-heavy** *adj* inestable.
**topic** *n* tema *m*; **~al** *adj* actual.
**topless** *adj* topless.
**top-level** *adj* al más alto nivel.
**topmost** *adj* lo más alto.
**topographic(al)** *adj* topográfico/ca.
**topography** *n* topografía *f*.

**topple** *vt* derribar; * *vi* volcarse.
**top-secret** *adj* de alto secreto.
**topsy-turvy** *adv* al revés.
**torch** *n* antorcha *f*; linterna *f*.
**torment** *vt* atormentar; * *n* tormento *m*.
**tornado** *n* tornado *m*.
**torrent** *n* torrente *m*.
**torrid** *adj* apasionado/da.
**tortoise** *n* tortuga *f*.
**tortoiseshell** *adj* de carey.
**tortuous** *adj* tortuoso/sa, sinuoso/sa.
**torture** *n* tortura *f*; * *vt* torturar.
**toss** *vt* tirar, lanzar, arrojar; agitar, sacudir.
**total** *adj* total, entero/ra; **~ly** *adv* totalmente.
**totalitarian** *adj* totalitario/ria.
**totality** *n* totalidad *f*.
**totter** *vi* vacilar.
**touch** *vt* tocar, palpar; **to ~ on** aludir a; **to ~ up** retocar; * *n* contacto *m*; tacto *m*; toque *m*; prueba *f*.
**touch-and-go** *adj* arriesgado/da.
**touchdown** *n* aterrizaje *m*; ensayo *m*.
**touched** *adj* conmovido/da; chiflado/da.
**touching** *adj* patético/ca, conmovedor/a.
**touchstone** *n* piedra de toque *f*.
**touchwood** *n* yesca *f*.
**touchy** *adj* quisquilloso/sa.
**tough** *adj* duro/ra; difícil; resistente; fuerte; * *n* gorila *m*.
**toughen** *vt* endurecer.
**toupee** *n* tupé *m*.
**tour** *n* viaje *m*; visita *f*; * *vt* visitar.
**touring** *n* viajes turísticos *mpl*.
**tourism** *n* turismo *m*; **bicycle ~** cicloturismo; **rural ~** turismo rural.
**tourist** *n* turista *m/f*.
**tourist office** *n* oficina de turismo *f*.
**tournament** *n* torneo *m*.
**tow** *n* remolque *m*; * *vt* remolcar.
**toward(s)** *prep*, *adv* hacia, con dirección a; cerca de, respecto a.
**towel** *n* toalla *f*.
**towelling** *n* toalla *f*.
**towel rack** *n* toallero *m*.
**tower** *n* torre *m*.
**towering** *adj* imponente.
**town** *n* ciudad *f*.
**town clerk** *n* secretario/ria del ayuntamiento *m/f*.
**town hall** *n* ayuntamiento *m*.
**towrope** *n* cable de remolque *m*.
**toy** *n* juguete *m*.
**toyshop** *n* juguetería *f*.
**trace** *n* huella, pisada *f*; * *vt* trazar, delinear; encontrar.

**track** *n* vestigio *m*; huella *f*; camino *m*; vía *f*; pista *f*; canción *f*; * *vt* rastrear.

**tracksuit** *n* chándal *m*.

**tract** *n* región, comarca *f*; serie *f*; tratado *m*.

**traction** *n* tracción *f*.

**trade** *n* comercio, tráfico *m*; negocio, trato *m*; ocupación *f*; * *vi* comerciar, traficar.

**trade fair** *n* feria de muestras *f*.

**trademark** *n* marca comercial *f*.

**trade name** *n* nombre comercial *m*.

**trader** *n* comerciante, traficante *m*.

**tradesman** *n* tendero *m*.

**trade(s) union** *n* sindicato *m*.

**trade unionist** *n* sindicalista *m/f*.

**trading** *n* comercio *m*; * *adj* comercial.

**tradition** *n* tradición *f*

**traditional** *adj* tradicional.

**traffic** *n* tráfico *m*; tránsito *m*; * *vi* traficar, comerciar.

**traffic jam** *n* embotellamiento *m*.

**trafficker** *n* traficante, comerciante *m/f*.

**traffic lights** *npl* semáforo *m*.

**tragedy** *n* tragedia *f*.

**tragic** *adj* trágico/ca; **~ally** *adv* trágicamente.

**tragicomedy** *n* tragicomedia *f*.

**trail** *vt, vi* rastrear; arrastrar; * *n* rastro *m*; pista *f*; cola *f*.

**trailer** *n* remolque *m*; avance *m*.

**trailer** *n* tráiler *m*.

**train** *vt* entrenar; amaestrar, enseñar, criar, adiestrar; disciplinar; *vr* ejercitarse; * *n* tren *m*; cola *f*; serie *f*; **high-speed ~** tren de alta velocidad *m*.

**trained** *adj* cualificado/da; amaestrado/da.

**trainee** *n* aprendiz/a *m/f*.

**trainer** *n* entrenador/a *m/f*.

**trainers** *npl* zapatillas de lona *fpl*.

**training** *n* entrenamiento *m*; formación *f*.

**trait** *n* rasgo *m*.

**traitor** *n* traidor/a *m/f*.

**tram** *n* tranvía *f*.

**tramp** *n* vagabundo/da *m/f*; (*col*) puta *f*; * *vi* andar pesadamente; * *vt* pisotear.

**tramp** *n* vagabundo/da *m/f*.

**trample** *vt* pisotear.

**trampoline** *n* cama elástica *f*.

**trance** *n* rapto *m*; éxtasis *m*.

**tranquil** *adj* tranquilo/la.

**tranquillize** *vt* tranquilizar.

**tranquillizer** *n* tranquilizante *m*.

**transact** *vt* negociar.

**transaction** *n* transacción *f*; negociación *f*.

**transatlantic** *adj* transatlántico/ca.

**transcend** *vt* trascender, pasar; exceder.

**transcription** *n* transcripción *f*.

**transfer** *vt* transferir, trasladar; * *n* transferencia *f*; traspaso *m*; calcomanía *f*.

**transform** *vt* transformar.

**transformation** *n* transformación *f*.

**transfusion** *n* transfusión *f*.

**transient** *adj* pasajero/ra, transitorio/ria.

**transit** *n* tránsito *m*.

**transition** *n* tránsito *m*; transición *f*.

**transitional** *adj* de transición.

**transitive** *adj* transitivo/va.

**translate** *vt* traducir.

**translation** *n* traducción *f*.

**translator** *n* traductor/ra *m/f*.

**transmission** *n* transmisión *f*.

**transmit** *vt* transmitir.

**transmitter** *n* transmisor *m*; emisora *f*.

**transparency** *n* transparencia *f*.

**transparent** *adj* transparente, diáfano/na.

**transpire** *vi* resultar; ocurrir.

**transplant** *vt* trasplantar; * *n* trasplante *m*.

**transport** *vt* transportar; * *n* transporte *m*.

**transportation** *n* transporte *m*.

**trap** *n* trampa *f*; * *vt* atrapar, bloquear.

**trap door** *n* trampilla *f*; escotillón *m*.

**trapeze** *n* trapecio *m*.

**trappings** *npl* adornos *mpl*.

**trash** *n* basura *f*; tonterías *fpl*.

**trash can** *n* cubo de la basura *m*.

**trashy** *adj* vil, despreciable, de ningún valor.

**travel** *vi* viajar; * *vt* recorrer; * *n* viaje *m*.

**travel agency** *n* agencia de viajes *f*.

**travel agent** *n* agente de viajes *m*.

**traveller** *n* viajante, viajero/ra *m/f*.

**traveller's cheque** *n* cheque de viaje *m*.

**travelling** *n* viajes *mpl*.

**travel-sickness** *n* mareo *m*.

**travesty** *n* parodia *f*.

**trawler** *n* arrastrero *m*.

**tray** *n* bandeja *f*; cajón *m*.

**treacherous** *adj* traidor/a, perfido/da.

**treachery** *n* traición *f*.

**tread** *vi* pisar; pistoear; * *n* pisada *f*; ruido de pasos *m*; banda de rodadura *f*.

**treason** *n* traición *f*; **high ~** alta traición *f*.

**treasure** *n* tesoro *m*; * *vt* atesorar.

**treasurer** *n* tesorero/ra *m/f*.

**treat** *vt* tratar; regalar; * *n* regalo *m*; placer *m*.

**treatise** *n* tratado *m*.

**treatment** *n* trato *m*.

**treaty** *n* tratado *m*.

**treble** *adj* triple; * *vt* (*vi*) triplicar(se); * *n* (*mus*) tiple *m*.

**treble clef** *n* clave de sol *f*.

**tree** *n* árbol *m*.

**trek** *n* caminata *f*; expedición *f*.

**trellis** *n* enrejado *m*.

**tremble** *vi* temblar.

**trembling** *n* temor *m*; trino *m*.

**tremendous** *adj* tremendo/da; enorme; estupendo/da.

**tremor** *n* temblor *m*.

**trench** *n* foso *m*; (*mil*) trinchera *f*; zanja *f*.

**trend** *n* tendencia *f*; curso *m*; moda *f*.

**trendy** *adj* de moda.

**trepidation** *n* inquietud *f*.

**trespass** *vt* transpasar, violar.

**tress** *n* trenza *f*; rizo de pelo *m*.

**trestle** *n* caballete de serrador *m*.

**trial** *n* proceso *m*; prueba *f*; ensayo *m*; desgracia *f*.

**triangle** *n* triángulo *m*.

**triangular** *adj* triangular.

**tribal** *adj* tribal.

**tribe** *n* tribu *f*; raza, casta *f*.

**tribulation** *n* tribulación *f*.

**tribunal** *n* tribunal *m*.

**tributary** *adj, n* tributario/ria *m/f*.

**tribute** *n* tributo *m*.

**trice** *n* momento, tris *m*.

**trick** *n* engaño, fraude *m*; burla *f*; baza *f*; zancadilla *f*; * *vt* engañar.

**trickery** *n* engaño *m*.

**trickle** *vi* gotear; * *n* reguero *m*.

**tricky** *adj* difícil; delicado/da.

**tricycle** *n* triciclo *m*.

**trifle** *n* bagatela, nineria *f*; * *vi* bobear; juguetear.

**trifling** *adj* frívolo/la, inútil.

**trigger** *n* gatillo *m*; * **to ~ off** *vt* desencadenar.

**trigonometry** *n* trigonometría *f*.

**trill** *n* trino *m*; * *vi* trinar.

**trillion** *n* trillón *m*.

**trim** *adj* aseado/da; en buen estado; arreglado/da; * *vt* arreglar; recortar; adornar.

**trimester** *n* trimestre *m*.

**trimmings** *npl* accesorios *mpl*.

**Trinity** *n* Trinidad *f*.

**trinket** *n* joya, alhaja *f*; adorno *m*.

**trio** *n* (*mus*) trío *m*.

**trip** *vt* hacer caer; * *vi* tropezar; resbalar; **to ~ up** *vi* caerse; *vt* hacer caer; * *n* resbalón *m*; viaje corto *m*; zancadilla *f*.

**tripe** *n* callos *mpl*; bobadas *fpl*.

**triple** *adj* triple; * *vt* triplicar.

**triplets** *npl* trillizos/zas *m/fpl*.

**triplicate** *n* triplicado *m*.

**trite** *adj* trivial; usado/da.

**triumph** *n* triunfo *m*; * *vi* triunfar.

**triumphal** *adj* triunfal.

**triumphant** *adj* triunfante; victorioso/sa; **~ly** *adv* en triunfo.

**trivia** *npl* trivialidades *fpl*.

**trivial** *adj* trivial, vulgar; **~ly** *adv* trivialmente.

**triviality** *n* trivialidad *f*.

**trolley** *n* carrito *m*.

**trombone** *n* trombón *m*.

**troop** *n* grupo *m*; **~s** *npl* tropas *fpl*.

**trooper** *n* soldado a caballo *m*.

**trophy** *n* trofeo *m*.

**tropical** *adj* trópico/ca.

**trot** *n* trote *m*; * *vi* trotar.

**trouble** *vt* afligir; molestar; * *n* problema *m*; disturbio *m*; inquietud *f*; aflicción, pena *f*.

**troubled** *adj* preocupado/da; agitado/da.

**troublemaker** *n* agitador/a *m/f*.

**troubleshooter** *n* conciliador/a *m/f*.

**troublesome** *adj* molesto/ta.

**trough** *n* abrevadero *m*; comedero *m*.

**troupe** *n* grupo *m*.

**trousers** *npl* bragas *fpl*; pantalones *mpl*.

**trout** *n* trucha *f*.

**trowel** *n* paleta *f*.

**truce** *n* tregua *f*.

**truck** *n* camión *m*; vagón *m*.

**truck driver** *n* camionero/ra *m/f*.

**truculent** *adj* truculento/ta, cruel.

**trudge** *vi* andar fatigosamente, andar con dificultad.

**true** *adj* verdadero/ra, cierto/ta; sincero/ra; exacto/ta.

**truelove** *n* amor verdadero *m*.

**truffle** *n* trufa *f*.

**truly** *adv* en verdad; sinceramente.

**trump** *n* triunfo (en el juego de naipes) *m*.

**trumpet** *n* trompeta *f*.

**trunk** *n* baúl, cofre *m*; trompa *f*.

**truss** *n* braguero *m*; * *vt* atar; espetar.

**trust** *n* confianza *f*; trust *m*; fideicomiso *m*; * *vt* tener confianza en; confiar algo a.

**trusted** *adj* de confianza.

**trustee** *n* fideicomisario/ria, curador/a *m/f*.

**trustful** *adj* fiel; confiado/da.

**trustily** *adv* fielmente.

**trusting** *adj* confiado/da.

**trustworthy** *adj* digno/na de confianza.

**trusty** *adj* fiel, leal; seguro/ra.

**truth** *n* verdad *f*; fidelidad *f*; realidad *f*; **in ~** en verdad.

**truthful** *adj* verídico/ca; veraz.

**truthfulness** *n* veracidad *f*.

**try** *vt* examinar, ensayar, probar; experimentar; tentar; inte ntar; juzgar; * *vi* probar; **to ~ on** probarse; **to ~ out** probar; * *n* tentativa *f*; ensayo *m*.

**trying** *adj* pesado/da; cansado/da.
**tub** *n* balde *m*, barreño *m*, cubo *m*; tina *f*.
**tuba** *n* tuba *f*.
**tube** *n* tubo, cañon, canuto *m*.
**tuberculosis** *n* tuberculosis *f invar*.
**tubing** *n* caería *f*.
**tuck** *n* pliegue *m*; * *vt* poner.
**Tuesday** *n* martes *m invar*.
**tuft** *n* mechón *m*; manojo *m*.
**tug** *vt* remolcar; * *n* remolcador *m*.
**tuition** *n* matrícula *f*; enseñanza *f*.
**tulip** *n* tulipán *m*.
**tumble** *vi* caer, hundirse; revolcarse; * *vt* revolver; volcar; * *n* caída *f*; vuelco *m*.
**tumbledown** *adj* destartalado/da.
**tumbler** *n* vaso *m*.
**tummy** *n* barriga *f*.
**tumour** *n* tumor *m*.
**tumultuous** *adj* tumultuoso/sa.
**tuna** *n* atún *m*.
**tune** *n* tono *m*; armonia *f*; aria *f*; * *vt* afinar; sintonizar.
**tuneful** *adj* armonioso/sa, acorde, melodioso/sa.
**tuner** *n* sintonizador/a *m*.
**tunic** *n* túnica *f*.
**tuning fork** *n* (*mus*) diapasón *m*.
**tunnel** *n* túnel *m*; * *vt* construir un tunel por.
**turban** *n* turbante *m*.
**turbine** *n* turbina *f*.
**turbulence** *n* turbulencia, confusión *f*.
**turbulent** *adj* turbulento/ta, tumultuoso/sa.
**tureen** *n* sopera *f*.
**turf** *n* césped *m*; * *vt* cubrir con césped.
**turgid** *adj* pesado/da.
**turkey** *n* pavo *m*.
**turmoil** *n* disturbio *m*; baraúnda *f*.
**turn** *vi* volver; cambiar; girar; dar vueltas; volverse a, mudarse, transformarse; **to ~ around** volverse; girar; **to ~ back** volverse; **to ~ down** rechazar; doblar; **to ~ in** acostarse; **to ~ off** *vi* desviarse; *vt* apagar; parar; **to ~ on** encender, prender; poner en marcha; **to ~ out** apagar; **to ~ over** *vi* volverse; *vt* volver; **to ~ up** *vi* llegar; aparecer; *vt* subir; * *n* vuelta *f*; giro *m*; rodeo *m*; turno *m*; vez *f*; inclinación *f*.
**turncoat** *n* desertor/a, renegado/da *m/f*.
**turning** *n* vuelta *f*.
**turnip** *n* nabo *m*.
**turn-off** *n* salida *f*.
**turnout** *n* concurrencia *f*.
**turnover** *n* facturación *f*.
**turnstile** *n* torniquete *m*.
**turntable** *n* plato *m*.

**turpentine** *n* trementina *f*.
**turquoise** *n* turquesa *f*.
**turret** *n* torrecilla, torreta *f*.
**turtle** *n* tortuga marina *f*.
**turtledove** *n* tórtola *f*.
**tusk** *n* colmillo *m*.
**tussle** *n* pelea *f*.
**tutor** *n* tutor/a *m/f*; profesor/a *m/f*; * *vt* enseñar, instruir.
**twang** *n* gangueo *m*; sonido agudo *m*.
**tweezers** *npl* tenacillas *fpl*.
**twelfth** *adj*, *n* duodécimo/ma.
**twelve** *adj*, *n* doce.
**twentieth** *adj*, *n* vigésimo/ma.
**twenty** *adj*, *n* veinte.
**twice** *adv* dos veces.
**twig** *n* ramita *f*; * *vi* caer en la cuenta.
**twilight** *n* crepúsculo *m*.
**twin** *n* gemelo/la *m/f*.
**twine** *vi* entrelazarse; caracolear; * *n* bramante *m*.
**twinge** *vt* punzar, pellizcar; * *n* dolor agudo/ punzante *m*; punzada *f*.
**twinkle** *vi* centellear; parpadear.
**twirl** *vt* dar vueltas a; * *vi* piruetear; * *n* rotación *f*.
**twist** *vt* torcer, retorcer; entretejer; * *vi* serpentear; * *n* torsión *f*; vuelta *f*; doblez *f*.
**twit** *n* (*col*) tonto/ta *m/f*.
**twitch** *vi* moverse nerviosamente; * *n* tirón; tic *m*.
**twitter** *vi* gorjear; * *n* gorjeo *m*.
**two** *adj*, *n* dos.
**two-door** *adj* de dos puertas.
**two-faced** *adj* falso/sa.
**twofold** *adj* doble, duplicado/da; * *adv* al doble.
**two-seater** *n* avión/coche de dos plazas *m*.
**twosome** *n* pareja *f*.
**tycoon** *n* magnate *m*.
**type** *n* tipo *m*; letra *f*; modelo *m*; * *vt* escribir a máquina.
**typecast** *adj* encasillado/da.
**typeface** *n* tipo *m*.
**typescript** *n* texto mecanografiado *m*.
**typewriter** *n* máquina de escribir *f*.
**typewritten** *adj* mecanografiado/da.
**typical** *adj* típico/ca.
**typographer** *n* tipógrafo *m*.
**typographical** *adj* tipográfico/ca
**typography** *n* tipografía *f*.
**tyrannical** *adj* tiránico/ca.
**tyranny** *n* tiranía *f*; crueldad *f*.
**tyrant** *n* tirano/na *m/f*.
**tyre** *n* neumático *m*; llanta *f*.
**tyre pressure** *n* presión de los neumáticos *f*.

# U

**ubiquitous** *adj* ubicuo/cua.
**udder** *n* ubre *f*.
**ugh** *excl* ¡puaj!
**ugliness** *n* fealdad *f*.
**ugly** *adj* feo, fea; peligroso/sa.
**ulcer** *n* úlcera *f*.
**ulterior** *adj* ulterior.
**ultimate** *adj* último/ma; **~ly** *adv* al final; a fin de cuentas.
**ultimatum** *n* ultimátum *m*.
**ultramarine** *n* ultramar *m*; * *adj* ultramarino/na.
**ultrasound** *n* ultrasonido *m*.
**ultrasound scan** *n* ecografía *f*.
**umbilical cord** *n* cordón umbilical *m*.
**umbrella** *n* paraguas *m invar*.
**umpire** *n* árbitro/tra *m/f*.
**umpteen** *adj* enésimos/mas.
**unable** *adj* incapaz.
**unaccompanied** *adj* solo/la, sin acompañamiento.
**unaccomplished** *adj* incompleto/ta, no acabado/da.
**unaccountable** *adj* inexplicable, extraño/ña.
**unaccountably** *adv* extrañamente.
**unaccustomed** *adj* desacostumbrado/da, desusado/da.
**unacknowledged** *adj* desconocido/da; negado/da.
**unacquainted** *adj* desconocido/da; ignorado/da.
**unadorned** *adj* sin adorno.
**unadulterated** *adj* genuino/na, puro/ra; sin mezcla.
**unaffected** *adj* sincero/ra, sin afectación.
**unaided** *adj* sin ayuda.
**unaltered** *adj* invariado/da.
**unambitious** *adj* poco/ca ambicioso/sa.
**unanimity** *n* unanimidad *f*.
**unanimous** *adj* unánime; **~ly** *adv* unánimemente.
**unanswerable** *adj* incontrovertible, incontestable.
**unanswered** *adj* no contestado/da.
**unapproachable** *adj* inaccesible.
**unarmed** *adj* inerme, desarmado/da.
**unassuming** *adj* nada presuntuoso/sa, modesto/ta.
**unattached** *adj* independiente; disponible.
**unattainable** *adj* inasequible.

**unattended** *adj* sin atender.
**unauthorized** *adj* no autorizado/da.
**unavoidable** *adj* inevitable.
**unavoidably** *adv* inevitablemente.
**unaware** *adj* ignorante.
**unawares** *adv* inadvertidamente; de improviso.
**unbalanced** *adj* desequilibrado/da; trastornado/da.
**unbearable** *adj* insoportable.
**unbecoming** *adj* indecente, indecoroso/sa.
**unbelievable** *adj* increíble.
**unbend** *vi* relajarse; * *vt* enderezar.
**unbiased** *adj* imparcial.
**unblemished** *adj* sin mancha, sin tacha, irreprensible.
**unborn** *adj* no nacido/da.
**unbreakable** *adj* irrompible.
**unbroken** *adj* intacto/ta; indómito/ta; entero/ra; no batido/da.
**unbutton** *vt* desabotonar.
**uncalled-for** *adj* fuera de lugar.
**uncanny** *adj* extraordinario/ria.
**unceasing** *adj* sin cesar, continuo/nua.
**unceremonious** *adj* brusco/ca.
**uncertain** *adj* incierto/ta, dudoso/sa.
**uncertainty** *n* incertidumbre *f*.
**unchangeable** *adj* inmutable.
**unchanged** *adj* no alterado/da.
**unchanging** *adj* inalterable, immutable.
**uncharitable** *adj* nada caritativo/va, duro/ra.
**unchecked** *adj* desenfrenado/da, incontrolado/da.
**unchristian** *adj* poco cristiano/na.
**uncivil** *adj* grosero/ra, descortés.
**uncivilized** *adj* tosco/ca, salvaje, incivilizado/da.
**uncle** *n* tío.
**uncomfortable** *adj* incómodo/da; molesto/ta.
**uncomfortably** *adv* incómodamente; inquietantemente.
**uncommon** *adj* raro/ra, extraordinario/ria.
**uncompromising** *adj* irreconciliable.
**unconcerned** *adj* indiferente.
**unconditional** *adj* sin condiciones, incondicional.
**unconfined** *adj* libre, ilimitado/da.
**unconfirmed** *adj* no confirmado/da.
**unconnected** *adj* inconexo/xa.
**unconquerable** *adj* invencible, insuperable.

**unconscious** *adj* inconsciente; **~ly** *adv* inconscientemente.

**unconstrained** *adj* libre, voluntario/ria.

**uncontrollable** *adj* incontrolable; desenfrenado/da.

**unconventional** *adj* poco convencional.

**unconvincing** *adj* no convincente.

**uncork** *vt* destapar.

**uncorrected** *adj* sin corregir, no corregido/da.

**uncouth** *adj* grosero/ra, zafio/fia.

**uncover** *vt* descubrir.

**uncultivated** *adj* inculto/ta.

**uncut** *adj* no cortado/da, entero/ra.

**undamaged** *adj* ileso/sa, libre de daño.

**undaunted** *adj* intrépido/da.

**undecided** *adj* indeciso/sa.

**undefiled** *adj* impoluto/ta, puro/ra.

**undeniable** *adj* innegable, incontestable; **~bly** *adv* indubitablemente.

**under** *prep* debajo de; menos de; segun; * *adv* debajo.

**under-age** *adj* menor de edad.

**undercharge** *vt* cobrar de menos.

**underclothing** *n* ropa íntima *f.*

**undercoat** *n* primera mano *f.*

**undercover** *adj* clandestino/na.

**undercurrent** *n* corriente subyacente *f.*

**undercut** *vt* vender más barato que.

**underdeveloped** *adj* subdesarrollado/da.

**underdog** *n* desvalido/da *m/f.*

**underdone** *adj* poco cocido/da.

**underestimate** *vt* subestimar.

**undergo** *vt* sufrir; sostener.

**undergraduate** *n* estudiante universitario/ria *m/f.*

**underground** *n* metro *m*; movimiento clandestino *m.*

**undergrowth** *n* soto *m*, maleza *f.*

**underhand** *adv* clandestinamente; * *adj* secreto/ta, clandestino/na.

**underlie** *vi* estar debajo.

**underline** *vt* subrayar.

**undermine** *vt* minar.

**underneath** *adv* debajo; * *prep* debajo de.

**underpaid** *adj* mal pagado/da.

**underpants** *npl* calzoncillos *mpl.*

**underprivileged** *adj* desvalido/da.

**underrate** *vt* menospreciar.

**undersecretary** *n* subsecretario/ria *m/f.*

**underside** *n* revés *m.*

**understand** *vt* entender, comprender.

**understandable** *adj* comprensible.

**understanding** *n* entendimiento *m*; inteligencia *f*; conocimiento *m*; correspondencia *f*, * *adj* comprensivo/va.

**understatement** *n* subestimación *f*; modestia *f.*

**undertake** *vt*, *vi* emprender.

**undertaker** *n* director de pompas fúnebres.

**undertaking** *n* empresa *f*; empeño *m.*

**undervalue** *vt* menospreciar.

**underwater** *adj* submarino/na; * *adv* bajo el agua.

**underwear** *n* ropa íntima *f.*

**underworld** *n* hampa *f.*

**underwrite** *vt* suscribir; asegurar contra riesgos.

**underwriter** *n* asegurador/a *m/f.*

**undeserved** *adj* inmerecido/da; **~ly** *adv* sin haberlo merecido.

**undeserving** *adj* indigno/na.

**undesirable** *adj* indeseable.

**undetermined** *adj* indeterminado/da, indeciso/sa.

**undigested** *adj* no digerido/da.

**undiminished** *adj* entero/ra, no disminuido/da.

**undisciplined** *adj* indisciplinado/da.

**undisguised** *adj* sin disfraz, cándido/da, sincero/ra.

**undismayed** *adj* intrépido/da.

**undisputed** *adj* incontestable.

**undisturbed** *adj* quieto/ta, tranquilo/la.

**undivided** *adj* indiviso/sa, entero/ra.

**undo** *vt* deshacer, destar, descoser.

**undoing** *n* ruina *f.*

**undoubted** *adj* indudable; **~ly** *adv* indudablemente.

**undress** *vi* desnudarse.

**undue** *adj* indebido/da; injusto/ta.

**undulating** *adj* ondulante.

**unduly** *adv* indebidamente.

**undying** *adj* inmortal.

**unearth** *vt* desenterrar.

**unearthly** *adj* inverosímil.

**uneasiness** *n* inquietud *f*; zozobra *f.*

**uneasy** *adj* inquieto/ta, desasosegado/da; incomodo/da.

**uneducated** *adj* ignorante.

**unemployed** *adj* desmpleado/da, parado/da; **~ person** parado/da *m/f.*

**unemployment** *n* desempleo, paro *m.*

**unending** *adj* interminable.

**unenlightened** *adj* no iluminado/da.

**unenviable** *adj* poco envidiable.

**unequal** *adj* desigual; **~ly** *adv* desigualmente.

**unequalled** *adj* incomparable.

**unerring** *adj* infalible; **~ly** *adv* infaliblemente.

**uneven** *adj* desigual; impar; **~ly** *adv* desigualmente.

**unexpected** *adj* inesperado/da; inopinado/da; **~ly** *adv* de repente; inopinadamente.

**unexplored** *adj* inexplorado/da, no descubierto/ta.

**unfailing** *adj* infalible, seguro/ra.

**unfair** *adj* falso/sa; injusto/ta; **~ly** *adv* injustamente.

**unfaithful** *adj* infiel, pérfido/da.

**unfaithfulness** *n* infidelidad, perfidia *f*.

**unfaltering** *adj* firme, asegurado/da.

**unfamiliar** *adj* desacostumbrado/da, poco común.

**unfashionable** *adj* pasado/da de moda; **~bly** *adv* contra la moda.

**unfasten** *vt* desatar, soltar, aflojar.

**unfathomable** *adj* insondable, impenetrable.

**unfavourable** *adj* desfavorable.

**unfeeling** *adj* insensible, duro/ra de corazón.

**unfinished** *adj* imperfecto/ta, no acabado/da.

**unfit** *adj* indispuesto/ta; incapaz.

**unfold** *vt* desplegar; revelar; * *vi* abrirse.

**unforeseen** *adj* imprevisto/ta.

**unforgettable** *adj* inolvidable.

**unforgivable** *adj* imperdonable.

**unforgiving** *adj* implacable.

**unfortunate** *adj* desafortunado/da, infeliz; **~ly** *adv* por desgracia, infelizmente.

**unfounded** *adj* sin fundamento.

**unfriendly** *adj* antipático/ca.

**unfruitful** *adj* estéril; infructuoso/sa.

**unfurnished** *adj* sin muebles; desprovisto/ta.

**ungainly** *adj* desmañado/da.

**ungentlemanly** *adj* indigno/na de un hombre bien criado.

**ungovernable** *adj* indomable, ingobernable.

**ungrateful** *adj* ingrato/ta; desagradable; **~ly** *adv* ingratamente.

**ungrounded** *adj* infundado/da.

**unhappily** *adv* infelizmente.

**unhappiness** *n* infelicidad *f*.

**unhappy** *adj* infeliz.

**unharmed** *adj* ileso/sa, sano/na y salvo/va.

**unhealthy** *adj* malsano/na; enfermizo/za.

**unheard-of** *adj* inaudito/ta, extraño/ña, sin ejemplo.

**unheeding** *adj* negligente; distraído/da.

**unhitch** *vt* desaparejar.

**unhook** *vt* desenganchar; descolgar; desabrochar.

**unhoped (for)** *adj* inesperado/da.

**unhurt** *adj* ileso/sa.

**unicorn** *n* unicornio *m*.

**uniform** *adj* uniforme; **~ly** *adv* uniformemente; * *n* uniforme *m*.

**uniformity** *n* uniformidad *f*.

**unify** *vt* unificar.

**unimaginable** *adj* inimaginable.

**unimpaired** *adj* no disminuido/da, no alterado/da.

**unimportant** *adj* poco importante.

**uninformed** *adj* desinformado/da.

**uninhabitable** *adj* inhabitable.

**uninhabited** *adj* inhabitado/da, desierto/ta.

**uninjured** *adj* ileso/sa, no dañado/da.

**unintelligible** *adj* ininteligible.

**unintelligibly** *adv* de modo ininteligible.

**unintentional** *adj* involuntario/ria, no intencionado/da.

**uninterested** *adj* desinteresado/da.

**uninteresting** *adj* poco interesante.

**uninterrupted** *adj* sin interrupción, continuo/nua.

**uninvited** *adj* no convivado/da.

**union** *n* unión *f*; sindicato *m*.

**unionist** *n* sindicalista *m/f*.

**unique** *adj* único/ca, uno/na, singular.

**unison** *n* unísono *m*.

**unit** *n* unidad *f*.

**unitarian** *n* unitario/ria *m/f*.

**unite** *vt* (*vi*) unir(se), juntarse; (*fig*) zurcir.

**unitedly** *adv* unidamente, de acuerdo.

**United States (of America)** *npl* Estados Unidos (de América) *mpl*.

**unity** *n* unidad, concordia, conformidad *f*.

**universal** *adj* universal; **~ly** *adv* universalmente.

**universe** *n* universo *m*.

**university** *n* universidad *f*.

**unjust** *adj* injusto/ta; **~ly** *adv* injustamente.

**unkempt** *adj* despeinado/da; descuidado/da.

**unkind** *adj* poco amable; severo/ra.

**unknowingly** *adv* sin saberlo.

**unknown** *adj* incógnito/ta.

**unlawful** *adj* ilegal; **~ly** *adv* ilegalmente.

**unlawfulness** *n* ilegalidad *f*.

**unleash** *vt* desencadenar.

**unless** *conj* a menos que, si no.

**unlicensed** *adj* sin licencia.

**unlike, unlikely** *adj* diferente; improbable; inverosímil.

**unlikelihood** *n* inverisimilitud *f*.

**unlimited** *adj* ilimitado/da.

**unlisted** *adj* que no viene en la guía.

**unload** *vt* descargar.

**unlock** *vt* abrir.

**unluckily** *adv* desafortunadamente.

**unlucky** *adj* desafortunado/da.

**unmanageable** *adj* inmanejable, intratable.

**unmannered** *adj* rudo/da, brutal, grosero/ra.

**unmannerly** *adj* malcriado/da, descortés.

**unmarried** *adj* soltero/ra.

**unmask** *vt* desenmascarar.

**unmentionable** *adj* que no se puede mencionar.

**unmerited** *adj* desmerecido/da.

**unmindful** *adj* olvidadizo/za, negligente.

**unmistakable** *adj* inconfundible; **~ly** *adv* indudablemente.

**unmitigated** *adj* absoluto/ta.

**unmoved** *adj* inmoto, firme.

**unnatural** *adj* antinatural; perverso/sa; afectado/da.

**unnecessary** *adj* inútil, innecesario/ria.

**unneighbourly** *adj* poco atento/ta con sus vecinos; descortés.

**unnoticed** *adj* inadvertido/da.

**unnumbered** *adj* innumerable.

**unobserved** *adj* no observado/da.

**unobtainable** *adj* inconseguible; inexistente.

**unobtrusive** *adj* modesto/ta.

**unoccupied** *adj* desocupado/da.

**unoffending** *adj* sencillo/lla, inocente.

**unofficial** *adj* no oficial.

**unorthodox** *adj* heterodoxo/xa.

**unpack** *vt* desempacar; desenvolver.

**unpaid** *adj* no pagado/da.

**unpalatable** *adj* desabrido/da, desgradable.

**unparalleled** *adj* sin paralelo; sin par.

**unpleasant** *adj* desagradable; **~ly** *adv* desagradablemente.

**unpleasantness** *n* desagrado *m*.

**unplug** *vt* desconectar.

**unpolished** *adj* que no está pulido/da; rudo/da, grosero/ra.

**unpopular** *adj* impopular.

**unpractised** *adj* inexperto/ta, no versado/da.

**unprecedented** *adj* sin precedentes.

**unpredictable** *adj* imprevisible.

**unprejudiced** *adj* imparcial.

**unprepared** *adj* no preparado/da.

**unprofitable** *adj* inútil, vano/na; poco lucrativo/va.

**unprotected** *adj* desvalido/da, sin protección.

**unpublished** *adj* no publicado/da; inédito/ta.

**unpunished** *adj* impune.

**unqualified** *adj* sin títulos; total.

**unquestionable** *adj* indubitable, indisputable; **~ly** *adv* sin duda, sin disputa.

**unquestioned** *adj* incontestable, no preguntado/da.

**unravel** *vt* desenredar.

**unread** *adj* no leído/da; ignorante.

**unreal** *adj* irreal.

**unrealistic** *adj* poco realista.

**unreasonable** *adj* poco razonable; disparatado/da.

**unreasonably** *adv* poco razonablemente; disparatadamente.

**unrelated** *adj* sin relación; inconexo/xa.

**unrelenting** *adj* implacable.

**unreliable** *adj* poco fiable.

**unremitting** *adj* constante, incansable.

**unrepentant** *adj* impenitente.

**unreserved** *adj* sin restricción; franco/ca; **~ly** *adv* abiertamente.

**unrest** *n* malestar *m*; disturbios *mpl*.

**unrestrained** *adj* desenfrenado/da; ilimitado/da.

**unripe** *adj* inmaduro/ra.

**unrivalled** *adj* sin rival, sin igual.

**unroll** *vt* desenrollar.

**unruliness** *n* turbulencia *f*; desenfreno *m*.

**unruly** *adj* desenfrenado/da.

**unsafe** *adj* inseguro/ra, peligroso/sa.

**unsatisfactory** *adj* insatisfactorio/ria.

**unsavoury** *adj* desabrido/da, insípido/da.

**unscathed** *adj* ileso/sa.

**unscrew** *vt* destornillar.

**unscrupulous** *adj* sin escrúpulos.

**unseasonable** *adj* intempestivo/va, fuera de propósito.

**unseemly** *adj* indecente.

**unseen** *adj* invisible.

**unselfish** *adj* desinteresado/da.

**unsettle** *vt* perturbar.

**unsettled** *adj* inquieto/ta; inestable; variable.

**unshaken** *adj* firme, estable.

**unshaven** *adj* sin afeitar.

**unsightly** *adj* desagradable a la vista, feo/a.

**unskilful** *adj* inhábil, poco mañoso/sa.

**unskilled** *adj* no cualificado/da.

**unsociable** *adj* insociable, intratable.

**unspeakable** *adj* inefable, indecible.

**unstable** *adj* instable, inconstante.

**unsteadily** *adv* ligeramente, inconstantemente.

**unsteady** *adj* inestable.

**unstudied** *adj* no estudiado/da; no premeditado/da.

**unsuccessful** *adj* infeliz, desafortunado/da; **~ly** *adv* sin éxito.

**unsuitable** *adj* inapropiado/da; inoportuno/na.

**unsure** *adj* ineguro/ra.

**unsympathetic** *adj* poco comprensivo/va.

**untamed** *adj* indomado/da.

**untapped** *adj* sin explotar.

**untenable** *adj* insostenible.

**unthinkable** *adj* inconcebible.

**unthinking** *adj* desatento/ta, irreflexivo/va.

**untidiness** *n* desaliño *m*.

**untidy** *adj* desordenado/da; sucio/cia.

**untie** *vt* desatar, deshacer, soltar, zafar.

**until** *prep* hasta; * *conj* hasta que.

**untimely** *adj* intempestivo/va.

**untiring** *adj* incansable.

**untold** *adj* nunca dicho/cha; indecible; incalculable.

**untouched** *adj* intacto/ta.

**untoward** *adj* impropio/pia; adverso/sa.

**untried** *adj* no ensayado/da/probado/da.

**untroubled** *adj* no perturbado/da, tranquilo/la.

**untrue** *adj* falso/sa.

**untrustworthy** *adj* indigno/na de confianza.

**untruth** *n* falsedad, mentira *f*.

**unused** *adj* sin usar, no usado/da.

**unusual** *adj* inusual, inusitado/da, raro/ra; **~ly** *adv* inusitadamente, raramente.

**unveil** *vt* quitar el velo, descubrir.

**unwavering** *adj* inquebrantable.

**unwelcome** *adj* desagradable, inoportuno/na.

**unwell** *adj* enfermizo/za, malo/la.

**unwieldy** *adj* pesado/da.

**unwilling** *adj* desinclinado/da; **~ly** *adv* de mala gana.

**unwillingness** *n* mala gana, repugnancia *f*.

**unwind** *vt* desenredar, desenmarañar; * *vi* relajarse.

**unwise** *adj* imprudente.

**unwitting** *adj* inconsciente.

**unworkable** *adj* poco práctico/ca.

**unworthy** *adj* indigno/na.

**unwrap** *vt* desenvolver.

**unwritten** *adj* no escrito/ta.

**up** *adv* arriba, en lo alto; levantado/da; * *prep* hacia; hasta.

**upbraid** *vt* zaherir.

**upbringing** *n* educación *f*.

**update** *vt* poner al día.

**upheaval** *n* agitación *f*.

**uphill** *adj* difícil, penoso/sa; * *adv* cuesta arriba.

**uphold** *vt* sostener, apoyar.

**upholstery** *n* tapicería *f*.

**upkeep** *n* mantenimiento *m*.

**uplift** *vt* levantar.

**upon** *prep* sobre, encima.

**upper** *adj* superior; más elevado/da.

**upper-class** *adj* de la clase alta.

**upper-hand** *n* (*fig*) superioridad *f*.

**uppermost** *adj* más alto/ta, supremo/ma; **to be ~** predominar.

**upright** *adj* derecho/cha, perpendicular, recto/ta; puesto/ta en pie; honrado/da.

**uprising** *n* sublevación *f*.

**uproar** *n* tumulto, alboroto *m*.

**uproot** *vt* desarraigar.

**upset** *vt* trastornar; derramar, volcar; * *n* revés *m*; trastorno *m*; * *adj* molesto/ta; revuelto/ta.

**upshot** *n* remate *m*; fin *m*; conclusión *f*.

**upside-down** *adv* al revés.

**upstairs** *adv* arriba.

**upstart** *n* advenedizo/za *m/f*.

**uptight** *adj* nervioso/sa.

**up-to-date** *adj* al día.

**upturn** *n* mejora *f*.

**upward** *adj* ascendente; **~s** *adv* hacia arriba.

**urban** *adj* urbano/na.

**urbane** *adj* cortés.

**urchin** *n* golfillo/lla *m/f*.

**urge** *vt* animar; * *n* impulso *m*; deseo *m*.

**urgency** *n* urgencia *f*.

**urgent** *adj* urgente.

**urinal** *n* orinal *m*.

**urinate** *vi* orinar.

**urine** *n* orina *f*.

**urn** *n* urna *f*.

**us** *pn* nos; nosotros, nosotras.

**usage** *n* tratamiento *m*; uso *m*.

**use** *n* uso *m*; utilidad, práctica *f*; * *vt* usar, emplear.

**used** *adj* usado/da.

**useful** *adj* , **~ly** *adv* útil(mente).

**usefulness** *n* utilidad *f*.

**useless** *adj* inútil; **~ly** *adv* inútilmente.

**uselessness** *n* inutilidad *f*.

**user-friendly** *adj* fácil de utilizar.

**usher** *n* ujier *m/f*; acomodador/a *m/f*.

**usherette** *n* acomodadora *f*.

**usual** *adj* usual, común, normal; **~ly** *adv* normalmente.

**usurer** *n* usurero/ra *m/f*.

**usurp** *vt* usurpar.

**usury** *n* usura *f*.

**utensil** *n* utensilio *m*.

**uterus** *n* útero *m*.

**utility** *n* utilidad *f*.
**utilize** *vt* utilizar.
**utmost** *adj* extremo/ma, sumo/ma; último/ma.

**utter** *adj* total; todo; entero/ra; * *vt* proferir; expresar; publicar.
**utterance** *n* expresion *f*.
**utterly** *adv* enteramente, del todo.

# V

vacancy *n* cuarto libre *m*, vacante *f*.
vacant *adj* vacío/cía; desocupado/da; vacante.
vacant lot *n* solar *m*.
vacate *vt* desocupar; dejar.
vacation *n* vacaciones *fpl*.
vaccinate *vt* vacunar.
vaccination *n* vacunación *f*.
vaccine *n* vacuna *f*.
vacuous *adj* vacío/cía, vacuo/cua.
vacuum *n* vacío *m*.
vacuum flask *n* termo *m*.
vagina *n* vagina *f*.
vagrant *n* vagabundo/da *m/f*.
vague *adj* vago/ga; ~ly *adv* vagamente.
vain *adj* vano/na, inútil; vanidoso/sa.
valet *n* criado *m*.
valiant *adj* valiente, valeroso/sa.
valid *adj* válido/da.
valley *n* valle *m*.
valour *n* valor, aliento, brío, esfuerzo *m*.
valuable *adj* valioso/sa; ~s *npl* objetos de valor *mpl*.
valuation *n* tasa, valuación *f*.
value *n* valor, precio *m*; * *vt* valuar; estimar, apreciar.
valued *adj* apreciado/da.
valve *n* válvula *f*.
vampire *n* vampiro *m*.
van *n* camioneta *f*.
vandal *n* gamberro/rra *m/f*.
vandalism *n* vandalismo *m*.
vandalize *vt* dañar.
vanguard *n* vanguardia *f*.
vanilla *n* vainilla *f*.
vanish *vi* desvanecerse, desaparecer.
vanity *n* vanidad *f*.
vanity case *n* neceser *m*.
vanquish *vt* vencer, conquistar.
vantage point *n* punto panorámico *m*.
vapour *n* vapor *m*; exhalación *f*.
variable *adj* variable; voluble.
variance *n* discordia, desavenencia *f*.
variation *n* variación *f*.
varicose vein *n* variz *f*.
varied *adj* variado/da.
variety *n* variedad *f*.
variety show *n* espectáculo de variedades *m*.
various *adj* vario/ria, diverso/sa, diferente.
varnish *n* barniz *m*; * *vt* barnizar.
vary *vt*, *vi* variar; cambiar.

vase *n* florero, jarrón *m*.
vast *adj* vasto/ta; inmenso/sa.
vat *n* tina *f*.
vault *n* bóveda *f*; cueva *f*; caverna *f*; * *vt* saltar.
veal *n* ternera *f*.
veer *vi* (*mar*) virar.
vegetable *adj* vegetal; * *n* vegetal *m*; ~s *pl* verduras *fpl*.
vegetable garden *n* huerta *f*.
vegetarian *n* vegetariano/na *m/f*.
vegetate *vi* vegetar.
vegetation *n* vegetación *f*.
vehemence *n* vehemencia, violencia *f*.
vehement *adj* vehemente, violento/ta; ~ly *adv* vehementemente.
vehicle *n* vehículo *m*; all-terrain ~ todoterreno *m*.
veil *n* velo *m*; * *vt* encubrir, ocultar.
vein *n* vena *f*; cavidad *f*; inclinación del ingenio *f*.
velocity *n* velocidad *f*.
velvet *n* terciopelo *m*.
vending machine *n* máquina expendedora *f*.
vendor *n* vendedor/a *m/f*.
veneer *n* chapa *f*; barniz *m*.
venerable *adj* venerable.
venerate *vt* venerar, honrar.
veneration *n* veneración *f*.
venereal *adj* venéreo.
vengeance *n* venganza *f*.
venial *adj* venial.
venison *n* (carne de) venado *f*.
venom *n* veneno *m*.
venomous *adj* venenoso/sa; ~ly *adv* venenosamente.
vent *n* respiradero *m*; salida *f*; * *vt* desahogar.
ventilate *vt* ventilar.
ventilation *n* ventilación *f*.
ventilator *n* ventilador *m*.
ventriloquist *n* ventrílocuo/cua *m/f*.
venture *n* empresa *f*; * *vi* aventurarse; * *vt* aventurar, arriesgar.
venue *n* lugar de reunión, local *m*.
veranda(h) *n* terraza *f*, porche *m*.
verb *n* (*gr*) verbo *m*.
verbal *adj* verbal, literal; ~ly *adv* verbalmente.
verbatim *adv* literalmente.
verbose *adj* verboso/sa.

**verdant** *adj* verde.
**verdict** *n* (*law*) veredicto *m*; opinión *f*.
**verification** *n* verificación *f*.
**verify** *vt* verificar.
**veritable** *adj* verdadero/ra.
**vermicelli** *npl* fideos *mpl*.
**vermin** *n* bichos *mpl*.
**vermouth** *n* vermut *m*.
**versatile** *adj* versátil; polifacético/ca.
**verse** *n* verso *m*; versículo *m*.
**versed** *adj* versado/da.
**version** *n* versión *f*.
**versus** *prep* contra.
**vertebra** *n* vértebra *f*.
**vertebral**, **vertebrate** *adj* vertebral.
**vertex** *n* cenit, vértice *m*.
**vertical** *adj* vertical; **~ly** *adv* verticalmente.
**vertigo** *n* vértigo *m*.
**verve** *n* brío *m*.
**very** *adj* idéntico/ca, mismo/ma; * *adv* muy, mucho, sumamente.
**vessel** *n* vasija *f*; vaso *m*; barco *m*.
**vest** *n* camiseta *f*.
**vestibule** *n* vestíbulo *m*.
**vestige** *n* vestigio *m*.
**vestment** *n* vestido *m*; vestidura *f*.
**vestry** *n* sacristía *f*.
**veteran** *adj*, *n* veterano/na *m/f*.
**veterinary** *adj* veterinario/ria.
**veterinary science** *n* veterinaria *f*.
**veterinary surgeon**, **vet** *n* veterinario/ria *m/f*.
**veto** *n* veto *m*; * *vt* vetar.
**vex** *vt* molestar.
**vexed** *adj* molesto/ta; controvertido/da.
**via** *prep* por.
**viaduct** *n* viaducto *m*.
**vial** *n* ampolla *f*, vial *m*.
**vibrate** *vi* vibrar.
**vibration** *n* vibración *f*.
**vicarious** *adj* sustituto/ta.
**vice** *n* vicio *m*; culpa *f*; tornillo *m*.
**vice-chairman** *n* vice-presidente *m*.
**vice-chancellor** (**of a university**) *n* rector/ra *m/f*.
**vice-chancellorship** *n* rectorado *m*.
**vice versa** *adv* viceversa.
**vicinity** *n* vecindad, proximidad *f*; **immediate ~** inmediaciones *fpl*.
**vicious** *adj* vicioso/sa; **~ly** *adv* de manera viciosa.
**victim** *n* víctima *f*.
**victimize** *vt* victimizar.
**victor** *n* vencedor/a *m/f*.
**victorious** *adj* victorioso/sa.

**victory** *n* victoria *f*.
**video** *n* vídeo *m*.
**video camera** *n* videocámara *f*.
**video cassette** *n* videocasete *m*.
**video game** *n* videojuego *m*.
**video tape** *n* cinta de vídeo *f*.
**vie** *vi* competir.
**view** *n* vista *f*; perspectiva *f*; aspecto *m*; opinión *f*; paisaje *m*; * *vt* mirar, ver; examinar.
**viewer** *n* televidente *m/f*.
**viewfinder** *n* visor *m*.
**viewpoint** *n* punto de vista *m*.
**vigil** *n* vela *f*; vigilia *f*.
**vigilance** *n* vigilancia *f*.
**vigilant** *adj* vigilante, atento/ta.
**vigorous** *adj* vigoroso/sa; **~ly** *adv* vigorosamente.
**vigour** *n* vigor *m*; energía *f*.
**vile** *adj* vil, bajo/ja; asqueroso/sa.
**vilify** *vt* envilecer.
**villa** *n* chalet *m*; casa de campo *f*.
**village** *n* aldea *f*.
**villager** *n* aldeano/na *m/f*.
**villain** *n* malvado/da *m/f*.
**vindicate** *vt* vindicar, defender.
**vindication** *n* vindicación *f*; justificación *f*.
**vindictive** *adj* vengativo/va.
**vine** *n* vid *f*.
**vinegar** *n* vinagre *m*.
**vineyard** *n* viña *f*.
**vintage** *n* vendimia *f*.
**vinyl** *n* vinilo *m*.
**viola** *n* (*mus*) viola *f*.
**violate** *vt* violar.
**violation** *n* violación *f*.
**violence** *n* violencia *f*.
**violent** *adj* violento/ta; **~ly** *adv* violentamente.
**violet** *n* (*bot*) violeta *f*.
**violin** *n* (*mus*) violín *m*.
**violinist** *n* violinista *m/f*.
**violoncello**, **cello** *n* (*mus*) violoncelo, violonchelo *m*.
**VIP** *n* vip *m/f*.
**viper** *n* víbora *f*.
**virgin** *n* virgen *f*; * *adj* virgen.
**virginity** *n* virginidad *f*.
**Virgo** *n* Virgo *f* (signo del zodiaco).
**virile** *adj* viril.
**virility** *n* virilidad *f*.
**virtual** *adj* virtual; **~ly** *adv* virtualmente.
**virtue** *n* virtud *f*.
**virtuous** *adj* virtuoso/sa.
**virulent** *adj* virulento/ta.

**virus** n virus m invar.
**visa** n visado m, visa f.
**vis-à-vis** prep con respecto a.
**viscous** adj viscoso/sa, glutinoso/sa.
**visibility** n visibilidad f.
**visible** adj visible.
**visibly** adv visiblemente.
**vision** n vista f; visión f.
**visit** vt visitar; * n visita f.
**visitation** n visitación, visita f.
**visiting hours** npl horas de visita fpl.
**visitor** n visitante m/f; turista m/f.
**visor** n visera f.
**vista** n vista, perspectiva f.
**visual** adj visual.
**visual aid** n medio visual m.
**visualize** vt imaginarse.
**vital** adj vital; esencial; imprescindible; ~ly
    adv vitalmente; ~s npl partes vitales fpl.
**vitality** n vitalidad f.
**vital statistics** npl medidas vitales fpl.
**vitamin** n vitamina f.
**vitiate** vt viciar, corromper.
**vivacious** adj vivaz.
**vivid** adj vivo/va; gráfico/ca; intenso/sa; ~ly
    adv vivamente; gráficamente.
**vivisection** n vivisección f.
**vixen** n zorra f.
**vocabulary** n vocabulario m.
**vocal** adj vocal.
**vocation** n vocación f; oficio m; carrera,
    profesión f; ~al adj profesional.
**vocative** n vocativo m.
**vociferous** adj vocinglero/ra, clamoroso/sa.
**vodka** n vodka m.

**vogue** n moda f; boga f.
**voice** n voz f; * vt expresar.
**void** adj nulo* n vacio m.
**volatile** adj volátil; voluble.
**volcanic** adj volcánico/ca.
**volcano** n volcán m.
**volition** n voluntad f.
**volley** n descarga f; salva f; rociada f;
    volea f.
**volleyball** n voleibol m.
**volt** n voltio m.
**voltage** n voltaje m.
**voluble** adj locuaz.
**volume** n volumen m; libro m.
**voluntarily** adv voluntariamente.
**voluntary** adj voluntario/ria.
**volunteer** n voluntario/ria m/f; * vi
    ofrecerse voluntariamente.
**voluptuous** adj voluptuoso/sa.
**vomit** vt, vi vomitar; * n vómito m.
**voracious** adj voraz; ~ly adv vorazmente.
**vortex** n remolino, torbellino m.
**vote** n voto, sufragio m; votación f; * vt
    votar.
**voter** n votante m/f.
**voting** n votación f.
**voucher** n vale m.
**vow** n voto m; * vi jurar.
**vowel** n vocal f.
**voyage** n viaje m; travesía f.
**vulgar** adj vulgar, ordinario/ria; de mal gusto.
**vulgarity** n vulgaridad f, grosería f; mal
    gusto m.
**vulnerable** adj vulnerable.
**vulture** n buitre m.

# W

**wad** *n* fajo *m*; bolita *f*.
**waddle** *vi* anadear.
**wade** *vi* vadear.
**wafer** *n* galleta *f*; oblea *f*.
**waffle** *n* gofre *m*.
**waft** *vt* hacer flotar; * *vi* flotar.
**wag** *vt* menear; * *vi* menearse.
**wage** *n* salario *m*.
**wage earner** *n* asalariado/da *m/f*.
**wager** *n* apuesta *f*; * *vt* apostar.
**wages** *npl* salario *m*.
**waggish** *adj* zumbón/ona.
**waggle** *vt* menear.
**wagon** *n* carro *m*; (*rail*) vagón *m*.
**wail** *n* lamento, gemido *m*; * *vi* gemir.
**waist** *n* cintura *f*.
**waistline** *n* talle *m*.
**wait** *vi* esperar; * *n* espera *f*; pausa *f*.
**waiter** *n* camarero *m*.
**waiting list** *n* lista de espera *f*.
**waiting room** *n* sala de espera *f*.
**waive** *vt* suspender.
**wake**[1] *vi* despertarse; * *vt* despertar; * *n* vela *f*.
**wake**[2] *n* (*mar*) estela *f*.
**wakefulness** *n* vela *f*.
**waken** *vt*, (*vi*) despertar(se).
**walk** *vt*, *vi* pasear, ir; andar, caminar; * *n* paseo *m*; caminata *f*.
**walker** *n* paseante *m/f*.
**walkie-talkie** *n* walkie-talkie *m*.
**walking** *n* paseos *mpl*.
**walking stick** *n* bastón *m*.
**walkout** *n* huelga *f*.
**walkover** *n* (*col*) pan comido *m*.
**walkway** *n* paseo *m*.
**wall** *n* pared *f*; muralla *f*; muro *m*.
**walled** *adj* amurallado/da.
**wallet** *n* cartera, billetera *f*.
**wallflower** *n* (*bot*) alhelí *m*.
**wallow** *vi* revolcarse.
**wallpaper** *n* papel pintado *m*.
**walnut** *n* nogal *m*; nuez *f*.
**walrus** *n* morsa *f*.
**waltz** *n* vals *m invar*.
**wan** *adj* pálido/da.
**wand** *n* varita mágica *f*.
**wander** *vt*, *vi* errar; vagar.
**wane** *vi* menguar.
**want** *vt* querer; necesitar; faltar; * *n* necesidad *f*; falta *f*.

**wanting** *adj* falto/ta, defectuoso/sa.
**wanton** *adj* lascivo/va; juguetón/ona.
**war** *n* guerra *f*.
**ward** *n* sala *f*; pupilo/la *m/f*.
**warden** (**game**) *n* guardabosques *m invar*.
**wardrobe** *n* guardarropa *f*, ropero *m*.
**warehouse** *n* almacén *m*.
**warfare** *n* guerra *f*.
**warhead** *n* ojiva *f*.
**warily** *adv* prudentemente.
**wariness** *n* cautela, prudencia *f*.
**warm** *adj* cálido/da; caliente; efusivo/va; * *vt* calentar; **to ~ up** *vi* calentarse; entrar en calor; acalorarse; *vt* calentar.
**warm-hearted** *adj* afectuoso/sa.
**warmly** *adv* con calor, ardientemente.
**warmth** *n* calor *m*.
**warn** *vt* avisar; advertir.
**warning** *n* aviso *m*.
**warning light** *n* luz de advertencia *f*.
**warp** *vi* torcerse; * *vt* torcer; pervertir.
**warrant** *n* orden judicial *f*; mandamiento judicial *m*.
**warranty** *n* garantía *f*.
**warren** *n* conejero *m*.
**warrior** *n* guerrero/ra, soldado/da *m/f*.
**warship** *n* barco de guerra *m*.
**wart** *n* verruga *f*.
**wary** *adj* cauto/ta, prudente.
**wash** *vt* lavar; bañar; * *vi* lavarse; * *n* lavado *m*; baño *m*.
**washable** *adj* lavable.
**washbowl, washbasin** *n* lavabo *m*.
**washer** *n* arandela *f*.
**washing** *n* ropa sucia *f*; colada *f*.
**washing machine** *n* lavadora *f*.
**washing-up** *n* fregado *m*.
**wash out** *n* (*col*) fracaso *m*.
**wasp** *n* avispa *f*.
**wastage** *n* desgaste *m*; pérdida *f*.
**waste** *vt* malgastar; destruir, arruinar; perder; * *vi* gastarse; * *n* desperdicio *m*; destrucción *f*; despilfarro *m*; basura *f*; yermo *m*.
**wasteful** *adj* destructivo/va; pródigo/ga; **~ly** *adv* pródigamente.
**wasteland** *n* yermo *m*.
**waste paper** *n* papel usado *m*.
**waste pipe** *n* tubo de desagüe *m*.
**watch** *n* reloj *m*; centinela *f*; guardia *f*; * *vt* mirar; ver; vigilar; tener cuidado; * *vi* ver; montar guardia.

**watchdog** *n* perro guardián *m*.
**watchful** *adj* vigilante; **~ly** *adv* vigilante-
mente.
**watchmaker** *n* relojero/ra *m/f*.
**watchman** *n* sereno *m*; vigilante *m*.
**watchtower** *n* atalaya, garita *f*.
**watchword** *n* santo *y* seña *m*.
**water** *n* agua *f*, * *vt* regar, humedecer, mojar;
* *vi* hacerse agua.
**water closet** *n* váter *m*.
**watercolour** *n* acuarela *f*.
**waterfall** *n* cascada *f*.
**water heater** *n* calentador de agua *m*.
**watering-can** *n* regadera *f*.
**water level** *n* nivel del agua *m*.
**water lily** *n* ninfea *f*.
**water line** *n* línea de flotación *f*.
**waterlogged** *adj* anegado/da.
**water main** *n* cañería del agua *f*.
**watermark** *n* filigrana *f*.
**water melon** *n* sandía *f*.
**watershed** *n* momento crítico *m*.
**watertight** *adj* impermeable.
**waterworks** *npl* depuradora de agua *f*.
**watery** *adj* aguado/da; desvaído/da; lloroso/
sa.
**watt** *n* vatio *m*.
**wave** *n* ola, onda *f*; oleada *f*; senal *f*; * *vi*
agitar la mano; ondear; * *vt* agitar.
**wavelength** *n* longitud de onda *f*.
**waver** *vi* vacilar, balancear.
**wavering** *adj* inconstante.
**wavy** *adj* ondulado/da.
**wax** *n* cera *f*; * *vt* encerar; * *vi* crecer.
**wax paper** *n* papel de cera *m*.
**waxworks** *n* museo de cera *m*.
**way** *n* camino *m*; vía *f*; ruta *f*; modo *m*;
recorrido *m*; **to give ~** ceder.
**waylay** *vt* salir al paso.
**wayward** *adj* caprichoso/sa.
**we** *pn* nosotros, nosotras.
**weak** *adj* débil; **~ly** *adv* débilmente.
**weaken** *vt* debilitar.
**weakling** *n* enclenque *m/f*.
**weakness** *n* debilidad *f*; punto débil *m*.
**weal**, **wheal** *n* roncha *f*.
**wealth** *n* riqueza *f*; bienes *mpl*.
**wealthy** *adj* rico/ca.
**wean** *vt* destetar.
**weapon** *n* arma *f*.
**wear** *vt* gastar, consumir; usar, llevar; * *vi*
consumirse; **to ~ away** *vt* gastar; *vi*
desgastarse; **to ~ down** gastar; agotar; **to ~
off** pasar; **to ~ out** desgastar; agotar; * *n*
uso *m*; desgaste *m*.

**weariness** *n* cansancio *m*; fatiga *f*;
enfado *m*.
**wearisome** *adj* tedioso/sa.
**weary** *adj* cansado/da, fatigado/da; tedioso/sa.
**weasel** *n* comadreja *f*.
**weather** *n* tiempo *m*; * *vt* (out) sufrir,
superar.
**weather-beaten** *adj* curtido/da.
**weather cock** *n* gallo de campanario *m*;
veleta *f*.
**weather forecast** *n* boletín meteoro-
lógico *m*.
**weave** *vt* tejer; trenzar; (*fig*) zurcir.
**weaving** *n* tejido *m*.
**web** *n* telarana *f*; membrana *f*; red *f*.
**wed** *vt* (*vi*) casar(se).
**wedding** *n* boda *f*; nupcias *fpl*; casamiento *m*.
**wedding day** *n* día de la boda *m*.
**wedding dress** *n* traje de novia *m*.
**wedding present** *n* regalo de boda *m*.
**wedding ring** *n* alianza *f*.
**wedge** *n* cuña *f*; * *vt* acuñar; apretar.
**wedlock** *n* matrimonio *m*.
**Wednesday** *n* miércoles *m invar*.
**wee** *adj* pequeñito/ta.
**weed** *n* mala hierba *f*, * *vt* escardar.
**weedkiller** *n* herbicida *m*.
**weedy** *adj* lleno/na de malas hierbas.
**week** *n* semana *f*; **tomorrow ~** mañana en
una semana; **yesterday ~** ayer hace ocho
dias.
**weekday** *n* día laborable *m*.
**weekend** *n* fin de semana *m*.
**weekly** *adj* semanal; * *adv* semanalmente,
por semana.
**weep** *vt*, *vi* llorar; lamentar.
**weeping willow** *n* sauce llorón *m*.
**weigh** *vt*, *vi* pesar.
**weight** *n* peso *m*.
**weightily** *adv* pesadamente.
**weightlifter** *n* levantador/a de pesas *m/f*.
**weighty** *adj* ponderoso/sa; importante.
**welcome** *adj* bienvenido/da; **~!** ¡bien-
venido!; * *n* bienvenida *f*; * *vt* dar la
bienvenida a.
**weld** *vt* soldar; * *n* soldadura *f*.
**welfare** *n* prosperidad *f*; bienestar *m*; subsidio
de paro *m*.
**welfare state** *n* estado del bienestar *m*.
**well** *n* fuente *f*; manantial *m*; pozo *m*; * *adj*
bueno/na, sano/na; * *adv* bien, felizmente;
favorablemente; suficientemente; convenientemente; **as ~ as** así como, además
de, lo mismo que.

**well-behaved** *adj* bien educado/da.
**wellbeing** *n* felicidad, prosperidad *f*.
**well-bred** *adj* bien criado/da, bien educado/da.
**well-built** *adj* fornido/da.
**well-deserved** *adj* merecido/da.
**well-dressed** *adj* bien vestido/da.
**well-known** *adj* conocido/da.
**well-mannered** *adj* educado/da.
**well-meaning** *adj* bien intencionado/da.
**well-off** *adj* acomodado/da.
**well-to-do** *adj* acomodado/da.
**well-wisher** *n* partidario/ria *m/f*.
**wench** *n* mozuela, cantonera *f*.
**west** *n* oeste, occidente *m*; * *adj* occidental; * *adv* hacia el oeste.
**westerly**, **western** *adj* occidental.
**westward** *adv* hacia el oeste.
**wet** *adj* húmedo/da, mojado/da; * *n* humedad *f*; * *vt* mojar, hume decer.
**wet-nurse** *n* ama de leche *f*.
**wet suit** *n* traje de buzo *m*.
**whack** *vt* aporrear; * *n* golpe *m*.
**whale** *n* ballena *f*.
**wharf** *n* muelle *m*.
**what** *pn* que, ¿qué?, el que, la que, lo que; * *adj* ¿qué?; * *excl* ¡cómo!
**whatever** *pn* cualquier, cualquiera cosa que, lo que sea.
**wheat** *n* trigo *m*.
**wheedle** *vt* halagar, engañar con lisonjas, sonsacar.
**wheedler** *n* zalamero/ra *m/f*.
**wheel** *n* rueda *f*; volante *m*; timón *m*; * *vt* (hacer) rodar; volver, girar; * *vi* rodar.
**wheelbarrow** *n* carretilla *f*.
**wheelchair** *n* silla de ruedas *f*.
**wheel clamp** *n* cepo *m*.
**wheeze** *vi* jadear.
**when** *adv* ¿cuándo?; mientras que; * *conj* cuando.
**whenever** *adv* cuando; cada vez que.
**where** *adv* ¿dónde?; * *conj* donde; **any~** en cualquier parte; **every~** en todas partes.
**whereabout(s)** *adv* ¿dónde?
**whereas** *conj* mientras que; pues que, ya que.
**whereby** *pn* por lo cual, con lo cual.
**whereupon** *conj* con lo cual.
**wherever** *adv* dondequiera que.
**wherewithal** *npl* recursos *mpl*.
**whet** *vt* excitar.
**whether** *conj* si.
**which** *pn* qué; lo que; el que, el cual; cuál; * *adj* ¿qué?; cuyo.

**whiff** *n* bocanada de humo *f*.
**while** *n* rato *m*; vez *f*; * *conj* durante; mientras; aunque.
**whim** *n* antojo, capricho *m*.
**whimper** *vi* sollozar, gemir.
**whimsical** *adj* caprichoso/sa, fantástico/ca.
**whine** *vi* llorar, lamentar; * *n* quejido, lamento *m*.
**whinny** *vi* relinchar.
**whip** *n* azote *m*; látigo *m*; * *vt* azotar; batir.
**whipped cream** *n* nata montada *f*.
**whirl** *vt*, *vi* girar; hacer girar; mover(se) rápidamente.
**whirlpool** *n* remolino *m*.
**whirlpool bath** *n* hidromasaje *m*.
**whirlwind** *n* torbellino *m*.
**whisky** *n* whisky *m*.
**whisper** *vi* cuchichear; susurrar.
**whispering** *n* cuchicheo *m*; susurro *m*.
**whistle** *vi* silbar; * *n* silbido *m*.
**white** *adj* blanco/ca, pálido/da; cano/na; puro/ra; * *n* color blanco *m*; clara del huevo *f*.
**white elephant** *n* maula *f*.
**white-hot** *adj* incandescente.
**white lie** *n* mentirijilla *f*.
**whiten** *vt*, *vi* blanquear; emblanquecerse.
**whiteness** *n* blancura *f*; palidez *f*.
**whitewash** *n* enlucimiento *m*; * *vt* encalar; jalbegar.
**whiting** *n* pescadilla *f*.
**whitish** *adj* blanquecino/na.
**who** *pn* ¿quién?; que.
**whoever** *pn* quienquiera, cualquiera.
**whole** *adj* todo/da, total; sano/na, entero/ra; * *n* total *m*; conjunto *m*.
**wholehearted** *adj* sincero/ra.
**wholemeal** *adj* integral.
**wholesale** *n* venta al por mayor *f*.
**wholesome** *adj* sano/na, saludable.
**wholly** *adv* enteramente.
**whom** *pn* ¿quién?; que.
**whooping cough** *n* tos ferina *f*.
**whore** *n* puta *f*; (*col*) zorra *f*.
**why** *n* ¿por qué?; * *conj* por qué; * *excl* ¡hombre!
**wick** *n* mecha *f*.
**wicked** *adj* malvado/da, perverso/sa; **~ly** *adv* malamente.
**wickedness** *n* perversidad, malignidad *f*.
**wicker** *n* mimbre *m*; * *adj* tejido/da de mimbre.
**wide** *adj* ancho/cha, vasto/ta; grande; **~ly** *adv* muy; **far and ~** por todos lados.
**wide-awake** *adj* despierto/ta.

**widen** *vt* ensanchar, extender.
**wide open** *adj* de par en par.
**widespread** *adj* extendido/da.
**widow** *n* viuda *f*.
**widower** *n* viudo *m*.
**width** *n* anchura *f*.
**wield** *vt* manejar, empuñar.
**wife** *n* esposa *f*; mujer *f*.
**wig** *n* peluca *f*; tupé *m*.
**wiggle** *vt* menear; * *vi* menearse.
**wild** *adj* silvestre, feroz; desierto/ta; descabellado/da; salvaje.
**wilderness** *n* desierto *m*; yermo *m*.
**wild life** *n* fauna *f*.
**wildly** *adv* violentamente; locamente; desatinadamente.
**wilful** *adj* deliberado/da; testarudo/da.
**wilfulness** *n* obstinación *f*.
**wiliness** *n* fraude, engaño *m*.
**will** *n* voluntad *f*; testamento *m*; * *vt* querer, desear.
**willing** *adj* inclinado/da, dispuesto/ta; **~ly** *adv* de buena gana.
**willingness** *n* buena voluntad, buena gana *f*.
**willow** *n* sauce *m* (árbol).
**willpower** *n* fuerza de voluntad *f*.
**wilt** *vi* marchitarse.
**wily** *adj* astuto/ta.
**win** *vt* ganar, conquistar; alcanzar; lograr.
**wince** *vi* encogerse, estremecerse.
**winch** *n* torno *m*.
**wind** *n* viento *m*; aliento *m*; flatulencia *f*.
**wind** *vt* enrollar; envolver; dar cuerda a; * *vi* serpentear.
**windfall** *n* golpe de suerte *m*.
**wind farm** *n* parque eólico *m*.
**winding** *adj* tortuoso/sa.
**windmill** *n* molino de viento *m*.
**window** *n* ventana *f*.
**window box** *n* jardinera de ventana *f*.
**window cleaner** *n* limpiacristales *m invar*.
**window ledge** *n* repisa *f*.
**windowpane** *n* cristal *m*.
**windowsill** *n* repisa *f*.
**windpipe** *n* tráquea *f*.
**windscreen** *n* parabrisas *m invar*.
**windscreen washer** *n* lavaparabrisas *m invar*.
**windscreen wiper** *n* limpiaparabrisas *m invar*.
**windsurfer** *n* windsurfista *m/f*.
**windsurfing** *n* windsurf *m*.
**wind turbine** *n* aerogenerador *m*.
**windy** *adj* de mucho viento.
**wine** *n* vino *m*.

**wine cellar** *n* bodega *f*.
**wine glass** *n* copa de vino *f*.
**wine list** *n* carta de vinos *f*.
**wine merchant** *n* vinatero/ra *m/f*.
**wine-tasting** *n* degustación de vinos *f*.
**wing** *n* ala *f*.
**winged** *adj* alado/da.
**winger** *n* extremo *m*.
**wink** *vi* guiñar; * *n* pestañeo *m*; guino *m*.
**winner** *n* ganador/a *m/f*; vencedor/a *m/f*.
**winning post** *n* meta *f*.
**winter** *n* invierno *m*; * *vi* invernar.
**winter sports** *npl* deportes de invierno *mpl*.
**wintry** *adj* invernal.
**wipe** *vt* limpiar; borrar.
**wire** *n* alambre *m*; telegrama *m*; * *vt* instalar el alambrado en; conectar.
**wiring** *n* alambrado *m*.
**wiry** *adj* delgado/da y fuerte.
**wisdom** *n* sabiduría, prudencia *f*.
**wisdom teeth** *npl* muelas del juicio *fpl*.
**wise** *adj* sabio/bia, docto/ta, juicioso/sa, prudente.
**wisecrack** *n* broma *f*.
**wish** *vt* querer, desear, anhelar; * *n* anhelo, deseo *m*.
**wishful** *adj* deseoso/sa.
**wisp** *n* mechón *m*; voluta *f*.
**wistful** *adj* pensativo/va, atento/ta.
**wit** *n* entendimiento, ingenio *m*.
**witch** *n* bruja, hechicera *f*.
**witchcraft** *n* brujería *f*; sortilegio *m*.
**with** *prep* con; por, de, a.
**withdraw** *vt* quitar; privar; retirar; * *vi* retirarse, apartarse.
**withdrawal** *n* retirada *f*.
**withdrawn** *adj* reservado/da.
**wither** *vi* marchitarse, secarse.
**withhold** *vt* detener, impedir, retener.
**within** *prep* dentro de, adentro; * *adv* interiormente; en casa.
**without** *prep* sin.
**withstand** *vt* resistir.
**witless** *adj* necio/cia, tonto/ta, falto/ta de ingenio.
**witness** *n* testimonio *m*; testgo *m/f*; * *vt* atestiguar, testificar.
**witness box** *n* estrado de los testigos *m*.
**witticism** *n* ocurrencia *f*.
**wittily** *adv* ingeniosamente.
**wittingly** *adv* adrede, de propósito.
**witty** *adj* ingenioso/sa, agudo/da, chistoso/sa.
**wizard** *n* brujo, hechicero *m*.
**wobble** *vi* tambalearse.

**woe** *n* dolor *m*; miseria *f*.
**woeful** *adj* triste, funesto/ta; **~ly** *adv* tristemente.
**wolf** *n* lobo *m*; **she ~** loba *f*.
**woman** *n* mujer *f*.
**womanish** *adj* mujeril.
**womanly** *adj* mujeril, mujeriego/ga.
**womb** *n* útero *m*.
**women's lib** *n* la líberación de la mujer *f*.
**wonder** *n* milagro *m*; maravilla *f*; asombro *m*; * *vi* maravil larse de; preguntarse si.
**wonderful** *adj* maravilloso/sa; **~ly** *adv* maravillosamente.
**wondrous** *adj* maravilloso/sa.
**won't** *abbrev* **will not**.
**wont** *n* uso *m*; costumbre *f*.
**woo** *vt* cortejar.
**wood** *n* bosque *m*; selva *f*; madera *f*; leña *f*.
**wood alcohol** *n* alcohol metílico *m*.
**wood carving** *n* tallado en madera *m*.
**woodcut** *n* estampa de madera *f*.
**woodcutter** *n* leñador/a *m/f*; grabador en láminas de madera, xilógrafo *m/f*.
**wooded** *adj* arbolado/da.
**wooden** *adj* de madera.
**wood engraver** *n* xilógrafo *m*.
**wooden shoe** *n* zueco *m*.
**woodland** *n* arbolado *m*.
**woodlouse** *n* cochinilla *f*.
**woodman** *n* cazador *m*; guardabosque *m*.
**woodpecker** *n* pájaro carpintero *m*.
**woodwind** *n* intrumento de viento de madera *m*.
**woodwork** *n* carpintería *f*.
**woodworm** *n* carcoma *f*.
**wool** *n* lana *f*.
**woollen** *adj* de lana.
**woollens** *npl* géneros de lana *mpl*.
**woolly** *adj* lanudo/da, lanoso/sa.
**word** *n* palabra *f*; noticia *f*; * *vt* expresar; componer en escri tura.
**wordiness** *n* verbosidad *f*.
**wording** *n* redacción *f*.
**word processing** *n* tratamiento de textos *m*.
**word processor** *n* procesador de textos *m*.
**wordy** *adj* verboso/sa.
**work** *vi* trabajar; obrar; estar en movimiento/en acción; fermentar; * *vt* trabajar, labrar; fabricar, manufacturar; **to ~ out** *vi* salir bien; * *vt* resolver; * *n* trabajo *m*; fábrica *f*; obra *f*; empleo *m*.
**workable** *adj* práctico/ca.
**workaholic** *n* trabajador obsesivo *m*, trabajadora obsesiva *f*.
**worker** *n* trabajador/a *m/f*; obrero/ra *m/f*.

**workforce** *n* mano de obra *f*.
**working-class** *adj* obrero/ra, de clase trabajadora.
**workman** *n* labrador *m*.
**workmanship** *n* manufactura *f*; destreza del artífice *f*.
**workmate** *n* compañero/ra de trabajo *m/f*.
**workshop** *n* taller, obrador *m*.
**world** *n* mundo *m*; * *adj* del mundo; mundial.
**worldliness** *n* mundanería *f*.
**worldly** *adj* mundano/na, terreno/na.
**worldwide** *adj* mundial.
**worm** *n* gusano *m*; (*tec*) rosca de tornillo *f*.
**worn-out** *adj* gastado/da; rendido/da.
**worried** *adj* preocupado/da.
**worry** *vt* preocupar; * *n* preocupación *f*; pensión *f*.
**worrying** *adj* inquietante.
**worse** *adj*, *adv* peor; **~ and ~** cada vez peor; * *n* lo peor.
**worship** *n* culto *m*; adoración *f*; **your ~** su señoría; * *vt* adorar, venerar.
**worst** *adj* el/la peor; * *adv* peor; * *n* lo peor *m*.
**worthily** *adv* dignamente, convenientemente.
**worthless** *adj* sin valor; inútil.
**worthwhile** *adj* que vale la pena; valioso/sa.
**worthy** *adj* digno/na; respetable; honesto/ta.
**would-be** *adj* aspirante.
**wound** *n* herida, llaga *f*; * *vt* herir, llagar.
**wrangle** *vi* reñir; * *n* riña *f*.
**wrap** *vt* envolver.
**wrath** *n* ira, rabia, cólera *f*.
**wreath** *n* corona, guirnalda *f*.
**wreck** *n* naufragio *m*; ruina *f*; destrucción *f*; navío naufragado *m*; * *vt* naufragar; arruinar.
**wreckage** *n* restos *mpl*; escombros *mpl*.
**wren** *n* chochín *m*.
**wrench** *vt* arrancar; dislocar; torcer; * *n* llave inglesa *f*; tirón *m*.
**wrest** *vt* arrancar, arrebatar.
**wrestle** *vi* luchar; disputar.
**wrestling** *n* lucha *f*.
**wretched** *adj* infeliz, miserable.
**wriggle** *vi* menearse, agitarse.
**wring** *vt* torcer; arrancar; estrujar.
**wrinkle** *n* arruga *f*; * *vt* arrugar; * *vi* arrugarse.
**wrist** *n* muñeca *f*.
**wristband** *n* puno de camisa *m*.

**wristwatch** n reloj de pulsera m.
**writ** n escrito m; escritura f; orden f.
**write** vt escribir; componer; **to ~ down** apuntar; **to ~ off** borrar; desechar; **to ~ up** redactar.
**write-off** n pérdida total f.
**writer** n escritor/a, m/f; autor/a m/f.
**writhe** vi retorcerse.
**writing** n escritura f; letra f; obras fpl; escrito m.

**writing desk** n escritorio m.
**writing paper** n papel para escribir m.
**wrong** n injuria f; injusticia f; perjuicio m; error m; * adj malo/la; injusto/ta; equivocado/da, inoportuno/na; falso/sa; * adv mal, equivocadamente; * vt· agraviar, injuriar.
**wrongful** adj injusto/ta.
**wrongly** adv injustamente.
**wry** adj irónico/ca.

# X Y Z

**xenophobia** n xenofobia f.
**Xmas** n Navidad f.
**X-ray** n radiografía f.
**xylographer** n xilógrafo m.
**xylophone** n xilófano m.

**yacht** n yate m.
**yachting** n vela f.
**Yankee** n yanqui m/f.
**yard** n corral m; yarda f.
**yardstick** n criterio m.
**yarn** n estambre m; hilo de lino m.
**yawn** vi bostezar; * n bostezo m.
**yawning** adj muy abierto/ta.
**yeah** adv sí.
**year** n año m.
**yearbook** n anuario m.
**yearling** n añal m.
**yearly** adj anual; * adv anualmente, todos los años.
**yearn** vi añorar.
**yearning** n añoranza f.
**yeast** n levadura f.
**yell** vi aullar; * n aullido m.
**yellow** adj amarillo/lla; * n amarillo m.
**yellowish** adj amarillento/ta.
**yelp** vi latir, gañir; * n aullido m.
**yes** adv sí; * n sí m.
**yesterday** adv ayer; * n ayer m.
**yet** conj sin embargo; pero; * adv todavía.
**yew** n tejo m.
**yield** vt dar, producir; rendir; * vi rendirse; ceder el paso; * n producción f; cosecha f; rendimiento m.
**yoga** n yoga m.
**yoghurt** n yogur m.
**yoke** n yugo m; yunta f.

**yolk** n yema (de huevo) f.
**yonder** adv allá.
**you** pn vosotros/tras, tú, usted, ustedes.
**young** adj joven, mozo/za; **~er** adj menor.
**youngster** n jovencito/ta m/f; joven m/f.
**your(s)** pn tuyo, tuya, vuestro, vuestra, suyo, suya.
**yourself** pn tú mismo, tú misma, usted mismo, usted misma.
**yourselves** pn pl vosotros mismos, vosotras mismas, ustedes mismos, ustedes mismas.
**youth** n juventud, adolescencia f; joven m/f.
**youthful** adj juvenil.
**youthfulness** n juventud f.
**yuppie** adj, n yupi m/f.

**zany** adj estrafalario/ria.
**zap** vt borrar.
**zeal** n celo m; ardor m.
**zealous** adj celoso/sa.
**zebra** n cebra f.
**zenith** n cénit m.
**zero** n zero, cero m.
**zest** n ánimo m.
**zigzag** n zigzag m; * adj zigzag; * vi zigzaguear.
**zinc** n zinc m.
**zip, zip fastener** n cremallera f; cierre de cremallera m.
**zodiac** n zodíaco m.
**zone** n banda, faja f; zona f.
**zoo** n zoo, zoológico m.
**zoological** adj zoológico/ca.
**zoologist** n zoólogo/ga m/f.
**zoology** n zoología f.
**zoom** vi zumbar.
**zoom lens** n zoom m.